Principles of Marketing

THE PRENTICE HALL SERIES IN MARKETING
Philip Kotler, Series Editor

SIXTH EDITION

Principles of Marketing

Philip Kotler

Northwestern University

Gary Armstrong

University of North Carolina

Prentice Hall, Englewood Cliffs, New Jersey 07632

Library of Congress Cataloging-in-Publication Data

Kotler, Philip.
    Principles of marketing/Philip Kotler, Gary Armstrong.—6th
ed.
      p.   cm.—(The Prentice Hall series in marketing)
    Includes bibliographical references and index.
    ISBN 0-13-030560-X
    1. Marketing. I. Armstrong, Gary. II. Title. III. Series:
Prentice Hall series in marketing.
    HF5415.K6314 1994
    658.8—dc20   93-28976
                                   CIP

To Nancy, Amy, Melissa, and Jessica Kotler
Kathy, K. C., and Mandy Armstrong

Acquisitions Editor: SANDRA STEINER
Development Editor: LESLYE GIVARZ
Production Editor: ANNE GRAYDON
Design Director: PATRICIA WOSCZYK
Interior Design: IRMGARD LOCHNER
Cover Design: DONNA WICKES and SUE BEHNKE
Photo Editor: LORI MORRIS-NANTZ
Photo Researchers: FRAN ANTMANN and TERI STRATFORD
Ad Researcher: MARY HELEN FITZGERALD
Manufacturing Buyers: PATRICE FRACCIO and TRUDY PISCIOTTI
Assistant Editor: WENDY GOLDNER
Editorial Assistant: CATHI PROFITKO
Production Assistant: RENEE PELLETIER
Marketing Manager: CAROL CARTER

Cover art: *Model "T"* by Perez Melero. Loaned by courtesy of the artist and Ambassador Galleries, Soho, NY.
Photo credits begin on page C1, after Glossary.

 © 1994, 1991, 1989, 1986, 1983, 1980 by Prentice-Hall, Inc.
A Paramount Communications Company
Englewood Cliffs, New Jersey 07632

All rights reserved. No part of this book may be reproduced, in any form or by any means, without permission in writing from the publisher.

Printed in the United States of America
10 9 8 7 6 5 4 3 2 1

0-13-030560-X

Prentice-Hall International (UK) Limited, *London*
Prentice-Hall of Australia Pty. Limited, *Sydney*
Prentice-Hall Canada Inc., *Toronto*
Prentice-Hall Hispanoamericana, S.A., *Mexico City*
Prentice-Hall of India Private Limited, *New Delhi*
Prentice-Hall of Japan, Inc., *Tokyo*
Simon & Schuster Asia Pte. Ltd., *Singapore*
Editora Prentice-Hall do Brasil, Ltda., *Rio de Janeiro*

About the Authors

As a team, Philip Kotler and Gary Armstrong provide a blend of skills uniquely suited to writing an introductory marketing text. Professor Kotler is one of the world's leading authorities on marketing. Professor Armstrong is an award-winning teacher of undergraduate business students. Together they make the complex world of marketing practical, approachable, and enjoyable.

Philip Kotler is S. C. Johnson & Son Distinguished Professor of International Marketing at the Kellogg Graduate School of Management, Northwestern University. He received his master's degree at the University of Chicago and his Ph.D. at M.I.T., both in economics. Dr. Kotler is author of *Marketing Management: Analysis, Planning, Implementation, and Control* (Prentice Hall), now in its eighth edition and the most widely used marketing textbook in graduate schools of business. He has authored several other successful books and he has written over 90 articles for leading journals. He is the only three-time winner of the coveted Alpha Kappa Psi award for the best annual article in the *Journal of Marketing*. Dr. Kotler's numerous major honors include the Paul D. Converse Award given by the American Marketing Association to honor "outstanding contributions to science in marketing" and the Stuart Henderson Britt Award as Marketer of the Year. In 1985, he was named the first recipient of two major awards: the Distinguished Marketing Educator of the Year Award given by the American Marketing Association and the Philip Kotler Award for Excellence in Health Care Marketing presented by the Academy for Health Care Services Marketing. In 1989, he received the Charles Coolidge Parlin Award, which each year honors an outstanding leader in the field of marketing. Dr. Kotler has served as chairman of the College on Marketing of the Institute of Management Sciences (TIMS) and a director of the American Marketing Association. He has consulted with many major U.S. and foreign companies on marketing strategy.

Gary Armstrong is Professor and Chair of Marketing in the Kenan-Flagler Business School at the University of North Carolina at Chapel Hill. He holds undergraduate and master's degrees in business from Wayne State University in Detroit, and he received his Ph.D. in marketing from Northwestern University. Dr. Armstrong has contributed numerous articles to leading business journals. As a consultant and researcher, he has worked with many companies on marketing research, sales management, and marketing strategy. But Professor Armstrong's first love is teaching. He has been very active in the teaching and administration of North Carolina's undergraduate business program. His recent administrative posts include Associate Director of the Undergraduate Business Program, Director of the Business Honors Program, and others. He works closely with business student groups and has received several campuswide and Business School teaching awards. He is the only repeat recipient of school's highly regarded Award for Excellence in Undergraduate Teaching, which he won for the third time in 1993.

ABC News/PH Video Library
for Principles of Marketing

Video is the most dynamic of all the supplements you can use to enhance your class. But the quality of the video material and how well it relates to your course can still make all the difference. For these reasons, Prentice Hall and ABC News have decided to work together to bring you the best and most comprehensive video ancillaries available in the college market.

Through its wide variety of award-winning programs—*Nightline, Business World, On Business, This Week with David Brinkley, World News Tonight,* and *The Health Show*—ABC offers a resource for feature and documentary-style videos related to text concepts and applications. The programs have extremely high production quality, present substantial content, and are hosted by well-versed, well-known anchors. Prentice Hall, its authors, and its editors provide the benefit of having selected videos on topics that will work well with this course and text and give the instructor teaching notes on how to use them in the classroom.

The ABC News/PH Video Library for *Principles of Marketing* offers video material for almost every chapter in the text. An excellent video guide that is included in the Instructor's Manual carefully and completely integrates the videos into your lecture.

The New York Times Program

The New York Times and Prentice Hall are sponsoring "Themes of the Times," a program designed to enhance student access to current information of relevance in the classroom.

Through this program, the core subject matter provided in the text is supplemented by a collection of time-sensitive articles from one of the world's most distinguished newspapers, *The New York Times.* These articles demonstrate the vital, ongoing connection between what is learned in the classroom and what is happening in the world around us.

To enjoy the wealth of information of *The New York Times* daily, a reduced subscription rate is available. For information, call toll-free: 1-800-631-1222.

Prentice Hall and *The New York Times* are proud to co-sponsor "Themes of the Times." We hope it will make the reading of both textbooks and newspapers a more dynamic, involving process.

Brief Contents

Contents

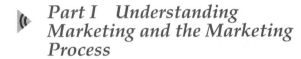

Part II Analyzing Marketing Opportunities

▶ *Part III Selecting Target Markets*

8 Measuring and Forecasting Demand 216

9 Market Segmentation, Targeting, and Positioning for Competitive Advantage 234

▶ *Part IV Developing The Marketing Mix*

10 Designing Products: Products, Brands, Packaging, and Services 274

Preface

Marketing is the business function that identifies an organization's customer needs and wants, determines which target markets it can serve best, and designs appropriate products, services, and programs to serve these markets. However, marketing is much more than just an isolated business function—it is a philosophy that guides the entire organization. The goal of marketing is to create customer satisfaction profitably by building value-laden relationships with important customers. The marketing department cannot accomplish this goal by itself. It must work closely with other departments in the company, and with other organizations throughout its entire value-delivery system, to provide superior value to customers. Thus, marketing calls upon everyone in the organization to "think customer" and to do all that they can to help create and deliver superior customer value and satisfaction. As Professor Stephen Burnett of Northwestern puts it, "In a truly great marketing organization, you can't tell who's in the marketing department. Everyone in the organization has to make decisions based on the impact on the consumer."

Many people see marketing only as advertising or selling. But real marketing does not involve the act of selling what you make so much as knowing *what* to make! Organizations gain market leadership by understanding consumer needs and finding solutions that delight customers through superior value, quality, and service. If customer value and satisfaction are absent, no amount of advertising or selling can compensate.

Marketing is all around us, and we all need to know something about it. Marketing is used not only by manufacturing companies, wholesalers, and retailers but by all kinds of individuals and organizations. Lawyers, accountants, and doctors use marketing to manage demand for their services. So do hospitals, museums, and performing arts groups. No politician can get the needed votes, and no resort the needed tourists, without developing and carrying out marketing plans. *Principles of Marketing* is designed to help students learn about and apply the basic concepts and practices of modern marketing as they are used in a wide variety of settings: in product and service firms, consumer and business markets, profit and nonprofit organizations, domestic and global companies, and small and large businesses.

People throughout these organizations need to know how to define and segment a market and how to position themselves strongly by developing need-satisfying products and services for chosen target segments. They must know how to price their offerings to make them attractive and affordable and how to choose and manage middlemen to make their products available to customers. And they need to know how to advertise and promote products so that customers will know about and want them. Clearly, marketers need a broad range of skills in order to sense, serve, and satisfy consumer needs.

Students also need to know marketing in their roles as consumers and citizens. Someone is always trying to sell us something, so we need to recognize the methods they use. And when students enter the job market, they must do "marketing research" to find the best opportunities and the best ways to "market themselves" to prospective employers. Many will start their careers with marketing jobs in salesforces, in retailing, in advertising, in research, or in one of a dozen other marketing areas.

Approach and Objectives

Principles of Marketing takes a *practical, managerial* approach to marketing. It provides a rich depth of practical examples and applications, showing the major decisions that marketing managers face in their efforts to balance the organization's objectives and resources against needs and opportunities in the global marketplace. Each chapter opens with a major example describing an actual company situation. Boxed Marketing Highlights, short examples, video cases, company cases, and color illustrations highlight high-interest ideas, stories, and marketing strategies.

Principles of Marketing tells the stories that reveal the drama of modern marketing: Kellogg's abrupt repositioning to meet changing baby-boomer lifestyles; Levi Strauss Co.'s startling success in finding new ways to grow, both in the United States and abroad; Church & Dwight's becoming "king of the (mole)hill" with Arm & Hammer baking soda products; Apple Computer's invasion of Japan; Motorola's quest for customer-driven, "six-sigma" quality; American Airline's struggle to bring sanity to air fares; 3M's legendary emphasis on new product development; Revlon's selling of not just products, but hopes and dreams; Rubbermaid's obsession with customer value and satisfaction; Disney's giving to consumers an America that still works the way it's supposed to; Gerber's difficult social-responsibility decisions following a product-tampering scare. These and dozens of other examples and illustrations throughout each chapter reinforce key concepts and bring marketing to life.

Thus, *Principles of Marketing* gives the marketing student a comprehensive and innovative, managerial and practical introduction to marketing. Its style and extensive use of examples and illustrations make the book straightforward, easy to read, and enjoyable.

Changes in the Sixth Edition

The sixth edition of *Principles of Marketing* offers important improvements in organization, content, and style. The former Chapters 2 and 20 have been combined to create a single, more streamlined Chapter 2, Strategic Planning and the Marketing Process, which provides an early framework for marketing thinking and sets the stage for the remainder of the text. A new Chapter 19, Building Customer Satisfaction Through Quality, Value, and Service, helps students to integrate what they've learned about marketing strategy and tactics around the key concepts of customer value and satisfaction.

The text's coverage of international marketing topics has been increased substantially. In addition to an already comprehensive chapter on international marketing, the sixth edition contains major new international coverage integrated into the text on a chapter-by-chapter basis. New chapter sections summarize the special challenges and opportunities that international marketers face in conducting international marketing research, attempting to understand global buyer behavior, segmenting international markets, and making decisions about global products, pricing, distribution, and promotion. New in-text examples and Marketing Highlights provide real examples of well-known companies—Levi Strauss Co., McDonald's, Apple Computer, Federal Express, Procter & Gamble, Pepsi Co, and dozens of others—competing in the global marketplace.

The sixth edition of *Principles of Marketing* also contains important new material on marketing ethics and social responsibility. New chapter sections outline general principles and explore specific examples of ethics and public policy issues in marketing research, target marketing, packaging and the environment, pricing, distribution, direct marketing, advertising and personal selling, and many other areas. These individual chapter discussions are brought together forcefully in the final chapter, Marketing and Society: Social Responsibility and Marketing Ethics.

The sixth edition includes substantial new or improved material on a wide range of other subjects: competitive advantage and differentiating the marketing offer, customer-driven marketing and developing a marketing culture, customer value and satisfaction, total quality management of marketing products and processes, relationship marketing, changing consumer values and lifestyles, changes in brand and category management, product design, direct marketing and single-source data systems, retailing strategy, services marketing strategy, global marketing strategy, marketing ethics and social responsibility, and the new environmentalism.

Finally, the sixth edition of *Principles of Marketing* contains dozens of new photographs and advertisements that illustrate key points and make the text more effective and appealing. Many new chapter-opening examples and Marketing Highlight exhibits illustrate important concepts with actual business applications. All tables, figures, examples, and references throughout the text have been thoroughly updated. Dozens of new examples have been added within the running text material. Most of the real-life company cases and video cases in the sixth edition are new or revised. These exciting new cases, and the quality videos that accompany them, help to bring the real world directly into the classroom.

Learning Aids

Many aids are provided within this book to help students learn about marketing. The main ones are:

- **Chapter Previews.** Each chapter begins with a preview that outlines the flow of concepts in the chapter.
- **Opening Examples.** Each chapter starts with a dramatic marketing story that introduces the chapter material and arouses student interest.
- **Full-Color Figures, Photographs, Advertisements, and Illustrations.** Throughout each chapter, key concepts and applications are illustrated with strong, full-color visual materials.
- **Marketing Highlights.** Additional examples and important information are highlighted in Marketing Highlight exhibits throughout the text.
- **Summaries.** Each chapter ends with a summary that wraps up the main points and concepts.
- **Review Questions.** Each chapter contains a set of "discussing the issues" questions covering the main chapter points, and "applying the concepts" exercises that build individual and group process and leadership skills.
- **Key Terms.** Key terms are highlighted within the text and listed at the end of each chapter with page references.
- **Building Case.** An evolving case, *Small World Communications, Inc.*, builds through new episodes at the end of each chapter. This case allows students to apply and integrate concepts from each chapter within a larger business context.
- **Company Cases.** Company cases for class or written discussion are provided at the end of each chapter, with integrative comprehensive cases following each major part of the text. These cases challenge students to apply marketing principles to real companies in real situations.
- **Video Cases.** Written video cases are provided at the end of each chapter, supported by the ABC News/PH Video Library for Marketing described in the next section. The videos and cases help to bring key marketing concepts and issues to life in the classroom.
- **Appendixes.** Two appendixes, "Marketing Arithmetic" and "Careers in Marketing," provide additional practical information for students.
- **Glossary.** At the end of the book, an extensive glossary provides quick reference to the key terms found in the book.
- **Indexes.** Subject, company, and author indexes reference all information and examples in the book.

Supplements

A successful marketing course requires more than a well-written book. Today's classroom requires a dedicated teacher and a fully-integrated teaching system. *Principles of Marketing* is supported by an extensive system of supplemental learning and teaching aids:

- **Annotated Instructor's Edition.** Prepared especially for the instructor by Richard G. Starr, Jr., this volume is an innovative teaching resource. It combines the student text with useful page-by-page annotations that provide teaching tips and real-world examples for use in class.
- **The Instructor's Resource Manual.** This helpful teaching resource, prepared by Lewis B. Hershey, contains chapter overviews, annotated outlines, class exercises, relevant stories and examples to help in class preparation, discussion notes for in-text company and video cases, and answers to end-of-chapter questions and exercises. A computerized version of this manual is also available.
- **Student Learning Guide.** Prepared by Thomas J. Paczkowski, this comprehensive study guide gives students an overview of the material, summarizes the major topics and concepts, and strengthens understanding through situational exercises, involving cases, chapter highlights, and quizzes. A new section of lecture notes reproduces the transparencies with the chapter outline for easy in-class note taking.
- **ATLAS (Academic Testing and Learning System) Test Item File.** The Test Item File, prepared by Lewis Hershey, has been extensively revised. It contains more than 3,700 items, including multiple-choice, true-false, and essay questions. The questions are available in the Test Item File booklet, on computer disk through the Prentice Hall TestManager testing system, or through the Prentice Hall Computerized Testing Service.

- **Full-Color Transparencies**. The transparencies package, also created by Lewis Hershey, includes more than 150 full-color transparencies of tables, figures, photographs, and advertisements painstakingly prepared to ensure clear classroom presentation. A full-page of teaching notes accompanies each transparency. Electronic color transparencies are also available on PowerPoint for IBM and Macintosh computers.

- **ABC News/Prentice Hall Video Library for Marketing.** Prentice Hall and ABC News have worked together to provide this video library, integrated throughout *Principles of Marketing* by specially written video cases for each chapter. The video Library pulls features and documentary-style footage from "World News Tonight," "American Agenda," "Nightline," "Business World," "On Business," and "This Week with David Brinkley." Hosted by well-known anchors, the programs are very well produced and contain high quality content that complements and enhances the text.

- **The New York Times *Prentice Hall Themes of the Times Program*.** Comprised of articles that have appeared in recent issues of *The New York Times*, this innovative program enhances student access to information relevant to the world of marketing.

- **Prentice Hall Images in Marketing Video Disk.** Images of Marketing presents images from both within the text and outside sources, including graphs, diagrams, ads, and other illustrations, as well as video segments taken from the acclaimed VideoArts video *Philip Kotler on Competitive Marketing*.

- **Personal Computer Applications Software.** BRANDS, a computer simulation by Randy Chapman, provides opportunities for students to apply their marketing knowledge and skills in realistic exercises and situations.

Acknowledgments

No book is the work only of its authors. We owe much to the pioneers of marketing who first identified its major issues and developed its concepts and techniques. Our thanks also go to our colleagues at the J. L. Kellogg Graduate School of Management, Northwestern University, and at the Kenan-Flagler Business School, University of North Carolina at Chapel Hill, for ideas and suggestions. We owe special thanks to Rick Starr, of UNC-Chapel Hill, who prepared the *Annotated Instructor's Edition* and the *Small World Communications, Inc.*, case. We also thank Lew Brown and Martha McEnally, both of the University of North Carolina, Greensboro, for their valuable work in preparing high-quality company cases and video cases, respectively. We also want to acknowledge Lewis Hershey, Tom Paczkowski, and Mike Fields for their work in preparing the *Test Item File, Color Transparencies Package*, and *Instructor's Resource Manual; Student Learning Guide*; and *Images in Marketing Video Disk*—respectively. Additional thanks go to Alan Shao for his help in preparing international examples, and to Leslye Givarz and Betsey Christian for their editing assistance.

Many reviewers at other colleges provided valuable comments and suggestions. We are indebted to the following colleagues:

Kerri Acheson
Moorhead State University

Gerald Albaum
University of Oregon

Sammy Amin
Frostburg State University

David Anderson
Wheaton College

Allen Appell
San Francisco State University

David L. Appel
University of Notre Dame

Boris W. Becker
Oregon State University

Robert L. Berl
Memphis State University

Paul N. Bloom
University of North Carolina

Robert Boris
Bryant and Stratton Business Institute

Arnold Bornfriend
Worcester State College

Jane Bradlee-Durfee
Mankato State University

Austin Byron
Northern Arizona University

Helen Caldwell
Providence College

Shelby Carter
University of Texas, Austin

Paul Cohen
CUNY of Staten Island, Sunnyside

Keith Cox
University of Houston

Robert Dalton
Russell Sage College

Ronald Decker
University of Wisconsin, Eau Claire

Rohit Deshpande
Dartmouth College

Michael Dotson
Appalachian State University

Lawrence Downs
Nichols College

Dale Duhan
Texas Tech

Thomas Falcone
Indiana University of Penna.

Michael Fowler
Brookdale Community College

David Georgoff
Florida Atlantic University

Robert Gwinner
Arizona State University

Thomas J. Hickey
SUNY, Oswego

Ralph Jackson
University of Tulsa

Raymond F. Keyes
Boston College

Irene Lange
California State University, Fullerton

Frederick Langrehr
University of Nebraska, Omaha

Ford Laumer
Auburn University

Ken Lord
SUNY, Buffalo

Charlotte Mason
University of North Carolina, Chapel Hill

H. Lee Meadow
Northern Illinois University

Douglas W. Mellott, Jr.
Radford University

Ronald Michaels
University of Kansas

Chip Miller
Pacific Lutheran University

Chem Narayana
University of Illinois at Chicago

Christopher P. Puto
University of Michigan

David R. Rink
Northern Illinois University

Dean Siewers
Rochester Institute of Technology

Clint B. Tankersley
Syracuse University

Robert E. Thompson
Indiana State University

We also owe a great deal to the people at Prentice Hall who helped develop this book. Marketing editor Sandra Steiner provided encouragement and sound advice. Anne Graydon, production editor, did a very fine job of guiding the book smoothly through production. Additional thanks go to Cathi Profitko, Carol Carter, Fran Russello, Lori Cowen, Robert Farrar-Wagner, and AnnMarie Dunn.

Finally, we owe many thanks to our families—Kathy, K.C., and Mandy Armstrong, and Nancy, Amy, Melissa, and Jessica Kotler—for their constant support and encouragement. To them, we dedicate this book.

Philip Kotler
Gary Armstrong

Principles of Marketing

*M*arketing in a Changing World: Satisfying Human Needs

*M*arketing touches all of us every day of our lives. We wake up to a Sears radio alarm clock playing an American Airlines commercial advertising a Bahamas vacation. Then we brush our teeth with Crest, shave with a Gillette Sensor razor, gargle with Scope, and use other toiletries and appliances produced by manufacturers around the world. We put on our Levi jeans and Nike shoes and head for the kitchen, where we drink Minute Maid orange juice and pour Borden milk over a bowl of Kellogg's Cracklin' Oat Bran. Later, we drink a cup of Maxwell House coffee with a teaspoon of Domino sugar while munching on a slice of Sara Lee coffee cake.

We consume oranges grown in California and coffee imported from Brazil, read a newspaper made of Canadian wood pulp, and tune in to radio news coming from as far away as Australia. We fetch our mail to find a Metropolitan Museum of Art catalog, a letter from a Prudential insurance agent, and coupons offering discounts on an array of our favorite brands. We step out the door and drive our car to the Northbrook Court Shopping Center with its Neiman Marcus, Lord & Taylor, Sears, and hundreds of other stores filled with goods from floor to ceiling. Later, we exercise at a Nautilus Fitness Center, have our hair trimmed at Super Cuts, grab a Big Mac at McDonald's, and plan a trip to Disney World at a Thomas Cook travel agency.

The *marketing system* has made all this possible with little effort on our part. It has given us a standard of living that our ancestors could not have imagined.

CHAPTER PREVIEW

Chapter 1 introduces the fundamental concepts of marketing. This chapter is divided into four key sections:

First, we ***define marketing*** as a social and managerial process dedicated to meeting human needs.

Next, we discuss ***five alternate marketing management philosophies***—the production, product, selling, marketing, and societal marketing concepts—which influence the way companies approach their customers.

Later we contrast the possible ***goals of the marketing system:*** maximizing consumption, consumer satisfaction, choice, or quality of life.

Finally, we expand on some of the ***challenges*** that marketers are facing in this last decade of the 20th century: globalization, a changing world economy, calls for stronger ethics and greater social responsibility, and the urgency of understanding a changing marketplace to provide real value and satisfaction to customers.

The marketing system that delivers our high standard of living consists of many large and small companies, all seeking success. Many factors contribute to making a business successful—great strategy, dedicated employees, good information systems, excellent implementation. However, today's successful companies at all levels have one thing in common—they are strongly customer focused and heavily committed to marketing. These companies share an absolute dedication to sensing, serving, and satisfying the needs of customers in well-understood markets. They motivate everyone in the organization to produce high quality and value for their customers.

Many people think that only large companies operating in highly developed economies use marketing, but marketing actually occurs both inside and outside the business sector, in small and large organizations, and in all kinds of countries. In the business sector, marketing first spread most rapidly in consumer packaged-goods companies, consumer durables companies, and industrial equipment companies. Within the past few decades, however, consumer service firms, especially airline, insurance, and financial services companies, also have adopted modern marketing practices. The latest business groups to take an interest in marketing are professionals such as lawyers, accountants, physicians, and architects, who now have begun to advertise and to price their services aggressively.

Marketing also has become a major component in the strategies of many *nonprofit* organizations such as colleges, hospitals, museums, symphonies, and even police departments. Consider the following developments:

As hospital costs and room rates soar, many hospitals face underutilization, especially in their maternity and pediatrics sections. Many have taken steps toward marketing. A Philadelphia hospital, competing for maternity patients, offered a steak and champagne dinner with candlelight for new parents. St. Mary's Medical Center in Evanston, Indiana, uses innovative billboards to promote its emergency care service. Other hospitals, in an effort to attract physicians, have installed services such as saunas, chauffeurs, and private tennis courts.[1]

Many private colleges, facing declining enrollments and rising costs, are using marketing to compete for students and funds. They are defining target markets, improving their communication and promotion, and responding better to student needs and wants. Many of America's 300,000 churches, having trouble keeping members and attracting financial support, are conducting marketing research to better understand member needs and are redesigning their "service offerings" accordingly. Many performing arts groups, even those like the Lyric Opera Company of Chicago that

Even the once-stodgy U.S. Postal Service now does innovative marketing. For example, it sponsored Olympic Spirit Week during which it invited customers to sign a piece of the world's largest postcard, a 348-foot by 523-foot giant that said "America Salutes Team USA," constructed behind the White House in Washington, D.C.

have seasonal sellouts, face huge operating deficits which they must cover by more aggressive donor marketing. Finally, many longstanding nonprofit organizations—the YMCA, the Salvation Army, the Girl Scouts—have lost members and are now modernizing their missions and "products" to attract more members and donors.[2]

Even government agencies have shown an increased interest in marketing. For example, the U.S. Army has a marketing plan to attract recruits, and various government agencies are now designing *social marketing campaigns* to encourage energy conservation and concern for the environment, or to discourage smoking, excessive drinking, and drug use.[3] The once-stodgy U.S. Postal Service has developed innovative marketing plans. For example, in one nationwide campaign, the postal service worked to gain support for the U.S. Olympic team:

> An official Olympic sponsor, the postal service launched a promotion designed to shower Olympic athletes with cards and to raise money for the team. It sponsored Olympic Spirit Week at 28,000 post offices around the nation, where it invited customers to sign a piece of the "world's largest postcard," a 348 foot by 523 foot giant that said "America Salutes Team USA." Customers who donated a dollar received two regular-size copies of the card. They were encouraged to send one copy to an Olympic athlete and keep the other as a souvenir. The postal service planned to spend about $100 million on Olympic sponsorship but expected a net profit of about $50 million through increased sales of postal products.[4]

Finally, marketing is practiced not only in the United States but also in the rest of the world. Most countries in North and South America, Western Europe, and the Far East have well-developed marketing systems. Even in Eastern Europe and the former Soviet republics, where marketing has long had a bad name, long-endured economic stagnation has caused nations to move toward market-oriented economies. Dramatic political and social changes have created new market opportunities and left business and government leaders in most of these nations eager to learn everything they can about modern marketing practices.

Sound marketing is critical to the success of every organization—whether large or small, for-profit or nonprofit, domestic or global. In this chapter, we define marketing and its core concepts, describe the major philosophies of marketing thinking and practice, explain the goals of the marketing system, and discuss some of the major new challenges that marketers now face.

WHAT IS MARKETING?

What does the term *marketing* mean? Marketing must be understood not in the old sense of making a sale—"selling"—but in the new sense of *satisfying customer needs*. Many people mistakenly think of marketing only as selling and promotion. And no wonder—every day we are bombarded with television commercials, newspaper ads, direct mail, and sales calls. Someone is always trying to sell us something. It seems that we cannot escape death, taxes, or selling.

Therefore, many students are surprised to learn that selling is only the tip of the marketing iceberg: It is but one of several marketing functions, and often not the most important one. If the marketer does a good job of identifying consumer needs, develops good products, and prices, distributes, and promotes them effectively, these goods will sell very easily.

Everyone knows something about "hot" products. When Sony designed its first Walkman cassette and disc players, when Nintendo first offered its improved video game console, and when Ford introduced its Taurus model, these manufacturers were swamped with orders. They had designed the "right" products: not "me-too" products, but ones offering new benefits. Peter Drucker, a leading management thinker, has put it this way: "The aim of marketing is to make selling superfluous. The aim is to know and understand the customer so well that the product or service fits ... and sells itself."[5]

This does not mean that selling and promotion are unimportant. Rather, it means that they are part of a larger "marketing mix"—a set of marketing tools that work together to affect the marketplace. We define **marketing** as a social and managerial process by which individuals and groups obtain what they need and want through creating and exchanging products and value with others.[6] To explain this definition, we examine the following important terms: *needs, wants, and demands; products; value and satisfaction; exchange, transactions, and relationships;* and *markets.* Figure 1-1 shows that these core marketing concepts are linked, with each concept building on the one before it.

Needs, Wants, and Demands

The most basic concept underlying marketing is that of human needs. A **human need** is a state of felt deprivation. Humans have many complex needs. These include basic *physical* needs for food, clothing, warmth, and safety; *social* needs for belonging and affection; and *individual* needs for knowledge and self-expression. These needs are not invented on Madison Avenue; they are a basic part of the human makeup.

When a need is not satisfied, a person will do one of two things—look for an object that will satisfy it or try to reduce the need. People in industrial societies may try to find or develop objects that will satisfy their desires. People in less-developed societies may try to reduce their desires and satisfy them with what is available.

Human wants are the form taken by human needs as they are shaped by

FIGURE 1–1
Core marketing concepts

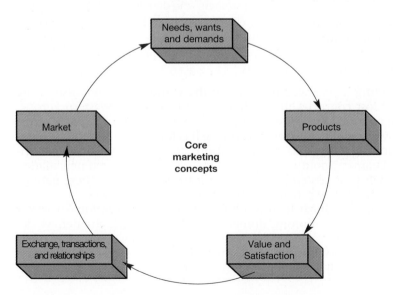

Kaiser Sand & Gravel Company's marketing mission is to "find a need and fill it."

culture and individual personality. A hungry person in Bali may want mangoes, suckling pig, and beans. A hungry person in the United States may want a hamburger, French fries, and a Coke. Wants are described in terms of objects that will satisfy needs. As a society evolves, the wants of its members expand. As people are exposed to more objects that arouse their interest and desire, producers try to provide more want-satisfying products and services.

People have almost unlimited wants but limited resources. Thus, they want to choose products that provide the most satisfaction for their money. When backed by buying power, wants become **demands.**

Listing the demands in a society at a given time is easy. In a single year, 254 million Americans might purchase 67 billion eggs, 6 billion chickens, 29 million telephones, 341 billion domestic air-passenger miles, and more than 20 million lectures by college English professors. These and other consumer goods and services lead, in turn, to a demand for more than 150 million tons of steel, 38 million tons of paper, 4 billion tons of cotton, and many other industrial goods. These are but a few of the demands in a $5.3 trillion economy.

Consumers view products as bundles of benefits and choose products that give them the best bundle for their money. Thus, a Ford Fiesta means basic transportation, low price, and fuel economy. A Mercedes means comfort, luxury, and status. Given their wants and resources, people choose the product with the benefits that add up to the most satisfaction.

Products

People satisfy their needs and wants with products. A **product** is anything that can be offered to a market to satisfy a need or want. Usually, the word *product* suggests a physical object, such as a car, a television set, or a bar of soap. However, the concept of *product* is not limited to physical objects—anything capable of satisfying a need can be called a product. The importance of physical goods lies not so much in owning them as in the benefits they provide. We don't buy food to look at, but because it satisfies our hunger. We don't buy a microwave to admire, but because it cooks our food.

Marketers often use the expressions *goods* and *services* to distinguish between physical products and intangible ones. Moreover, consumers obtain benefits through other vehicles, such as *persons, places, organizations, activities,* and *ideas.* Consumers decide which entertainers to watch on television, which places to visit on vacation, which organizations to support through contributions, and which ideas to adopt. Thus, the term *product* covers physical goods, services, and a variety of other vehicles that can satisfy consumers' needs and wants. If at times the term *product* does not seem to fit, we could substitute other terms such as *satisfier, resource,* or *offer.*

Many sellers make the mistake of paying more attention to the physical products they offer than to the benefits produced by these products. They see themselves as selling a product rather than providing a solution to a need. A manufacturer of drill bits may think that the customer needs a drill bit, but what the

Products do not have to be physical objects. In this classic ad campaign by the Advertising Council, which has been running for almost 50 years, the "product" is an idea—helping to prevent forest fires.

customer *really* needs is a hole. These sellers may suffer from "marketing myopia."[7] They are so taken with their products that they focus only on existing wants and lose sight of underlying customer needs. They forget that a physical product is only a tool to solve a consumer problem. These sellers have trouble if a new product comes along that serves the need better or less expensive. The customer with the same *need* will *want* the new product.

Value and Satisfaction

Consumers usually face a broad array of products that might satisfy a given need. How do they choose among these many products? Consumers make buying choices based on their perceptions of a product's value.

Suppose Paul Rosen needs to travel three miles each day to work. A variety of products could satisfy this need, ranging from roller skates, a bicycle, or motorcycle to a car, taxi, or bus. Besides simply getting to work, Paul also has several additional needs: He wants to get there easily, quickly, safely, and economically. Each product has a different capacity to satisfy these various needs. The bicycle would be slower, more effortful, and less safe than the car but more economical. Paul must decide which product delivers the most total satisfaction.

The guiding concept is **customer value.** Paul will estimate the capacity of each product to satisfy his total needs. He might rank the products from the most need-satisfying to the least need-satisfying. If we asked Paul to imagine the *ideal* product for this task, he might answer that it would get him to work in a split second with complete safety, no effort, and zero cost. Of course, no such product exists. Still, Paul will value each existing product according to how close it comes to his ideal product. Suppose Paul is mostly interested in the speed and ease of getting to work. If all of the products were free, we would predict that he would choose the automobile. But therein lies the rub. Because each product does involve a cost, and because the car costs much more than any of the other products, Paul will not necessarily buy the car. He will end up choosing the product that gives the most benefit for the dollar—the greatest value.

Today, consumer-behaviorists have gone far beyond narrow economic assumptions about how consumers form value judgments and make product choices. We will look at modern theories of consumer-choice behavior in chapters 5 and 6.

Exchange, Transactions, and Relationships

Marketing occurs when people decide to satisfy needs and wants through exchange. **Exchange** is the act of obtaining a desired object from someone by offering something in return. Exchange is only one of many ways people can obtain a desired object. For example, hungry people can find food by hunting, fishing, or gathering fruit. They could beg for food or take food from someone else. Finally, they could offer money, another good, or a service in return for food.

As a means of satisfying needs, exchange has much in its favor. People do not

GOING BACK TO BARTER

With today's high prices, many companies are returning to the primitive but time-honored practice of barter—trading goods and services that they make or provide for other goods and services that they need. Currently, companies barter more than $275 billion worth of goods and services a year worldwide, and the practice is growing rapidly.

Companies use barter to increase sales, unload extra goods, and save cash. For example, when Climaco Corporation was overstocked with bubble bath, it swapped the excess for $300,000 worth of advertising space for one of its other products. PepsiCo traded Pepsi-Cola and pizza parlors to the Russians for ships and Stolichnaya vodka, and Pierre Cardin served as a consultant to China in exchange for silks and cashmeres. The cash-poor U.S. Olympic Committee bartered the promotional use of its Olympic logo for products and services needed by its staff and athletes. It obtained free transportation from United Airlines, 500 cars from Buick, clothing from Levi Strauss, and shoes from Nike. The committee even traded the logo for a swimming pool built by McDonald's.

As a result of this increase in barter activity, many kinds of specialty companies have appeared to help other companies with their bartering. Retail-trade exchanges and trade clubs arrange barter for small retailers. Larger corporations use trade consultants and brokerage firms. Media brokerage houses provide advertising in exchange for products, and international barter often is handled by countertrade organizations.

Barter has become especially important in today's global markets, where it now accounts for as much as 40 percent of all world trade. The present world currency shortage means that more and more companies are being forced to trade for goods and services rather than cold, hard cash. International barter transactions can be very complex. For example, a trader for SGD International, a New York-based bartering company, arranged the following series of exchanges:

> [The trader] supplied a load of latex rubber to a Czech company in exchange for 10,000 yards of finished carpeting. He then traded the carpeting for hotel room credits. The rooms were traded to a Japanese company for electronic equipment, which [the trader] bartered away for convention space. The final [exchange] came when he swapped the convention space for ad space that his company used.

Sources: Quote from Cyndee Miller, "Worldwide Money Crunch Fuels More International Barter," Marketing News, March 2, 1992, p. 5. Also see Arthur Bragg, "Bartering Comes of Age," Sales & Marketing Management, January 1988, pp. 61-63; Gordon Platt, "Barter Tactic Makes Strides," Journal of Commerce and Commercial, May 6, 1990, p. 1A; Joe Mandese, "Marketers Swap Old Product for Ad Time, Space," Advertising Age, October 14, 1991, p. 3.

---

have to prey on others or depend on donations. Nor must they possess the skills to produce every necessity for themselves. They can concentrate on making things they are good at making and trade them for needed items made by others. Thus, exchange allows a society to produce much more than it would with any alternative system.

Exchange is the core concept of marketing. For an exchange to take place, several conditions must be satisfied. Of course, at least two parties must participate, and each must have something of value to the other. Each party also must want to deal with the other party and each must be free to accept or reject the other's offer. Finally, each party must be able to communicate and deliver.

These conditions simply make exchange *possible*. Whether exchange actually *takes place* depends on the parties' coming to an agreement. If they agree, we must conclude that the act of exchange has left both of them better off, or at least not worse off. After all, each was free to reject or accept the offer. In this sense, exchange creates value just as production creates value. It gives people more consumption possibilities.

Whereas exchange is the core concept of marketing, a transaction is marketing's unit of measurement. A **transaction** consists of a trade of values between two parties. In a transaction, we must be able to say that one party gives *X* to another party and gets *Y* in return. For example, you pay Sears $300 for a television set. This is a classic **monetary transaction**, but not all transactions involve money. In a **barter transaction**, you might trade your old refrigerator in return for a neighbor's secondhand television set. A barter transaction also can involve services as well as goods—for example, when a lawyer writes a will for a doctor in return for a medical exam (see Marketing Highlight 1-1). A transaction involves at least two things of value, conditions that are agreed upon, a time of agreement, and a place of agreement.

In the broadest sense, the marketer tries to bring about a response to some offer. The response may be more than simply "buying" or "trading" goods and services. A political candidate, for instance, wants a response called "votes," a church wants "membership," and a social-action group wants "idea acceptance." Marketing consists of actions taken to obtain a desired response from a target audience toward some product, service, idea, or other object.

Transaction marketing is part of the larger idea of **relationship marketing.** Smart marketers work at building long-term relationships with valued customers, distributors, dealers, and suppliers. They build strong economic and social ties by promising and consistently delivering high-quality products, good service, and fair prices. Increasingly, marketing is shifting from trying to maximize the profit on each individual transaction to maximizing mutually beneficial relationships with consumers and other parties. The operating assumption is: Build good relationships and profitable transactions will follow.

Markets

The concept of transactions leads to the concept of a market. A **market** is the set of actual and potential buyers of a product. To understand the nature of a market, imagine a primitive economy consisting of only four people: a fisherman, a hunter, a potter, and a farmer. Figure 1-2 shows the three different ways in which these traders could meet their needs. In the first case, *self-sufficiency,* they gather the needed goods for themselves. Thus, the hunter spends most of the time hunting, but also must take time to fish, make pottery, and farm to obtain the other goods. The hunter is thereby less efficient at hunting, and the same is true of the other traders.

In the second case, *decentralized exchange,* each person sees the other three as potential "buyers" who make up a market. Thus, the hunter may make separate trips to trade meat for the goods of the fisherman, the potter, and the farmer.

In the third case, *centralized exchange,* a new person called a *merchant* appears and locates in a central area called a *marketplace.* Each trader brings goods to the merchant and trades for other needed goods. Thus, rather than transacting with the other providers, the hunter transacts with one "market" to obtain all the needed goods. Merchants and central marketplaces greatly reduce the total number of transactions needed to accomplish a given volume of exchange.[8]

As the number of persons and transactions increases in a society, the number of merchants and marketplaces also increases. In advanced societies, markets need not be physical locations where buyers and sellers interact. With modern communications and transportation, a merchant easily can advertise a product on late evening television, take orders from thousands of customers over the phone, and mail the goods to the buyers on the following day without having had any physical contact with them.

A market can grow up around a product, a service, or anything else of value. For example, a *labor market* consists of people who are willing to offer their work in return for wages or products. In fact, various institutions, such as employment agencies and job-counseling firms, will grow up around a labor market to help it function better. The *money market* is another important market that emerges to meet the needs of people so that they can borrow, lend, save, and protect money. The *donor market* has emerged to meet the financial needs of nonprofit organizations.

FIGURE 1–2
Evolution toward centralized exchange

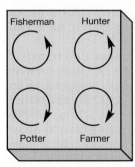

Self-sufficiency

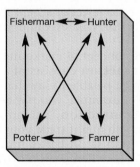

Decentralized exchange

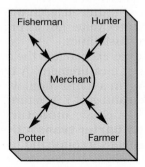

Centralized exchange

Marketing

The concept of markets finally brings us full circle to the concept of marketing. Marketing means working with markets to bring about exchanges for the purpose of satisfying human needs and wants. Thus, we return to our definition of marketing as a process by which individuals and groups obtain what they need and want by creating and exchanging products and value with others.

Exchange processes involve work. Sellers must search for buyers, identify their needs, design good products, promote them, store and deliver these products, and set prices for them. Activities such as product development, research, communication, distribution, pricing, and service are core marketing activities.

Although we normally think of marketing as being carried on by sellers, buyers also carry on marketing activities. Consumers do "marketing" when they search for the goods they need at prices they can afford. Company purchasing agents do "marketing" when they track down sellers and bargain for good terms. A *seller's market* is one in which sellers have more power and buyers must be the more active "marketers." In a *buyer's market,* buyers have more power and sellers have to be more active "marketers."

During the early 1950s, the supply of goods began to grow faster than the demand for them. Today, most markets have become buyer's markets, and marketing has become identified with sellers trying to find buyers. Therefore, this book examines the marketing problems of sellers in a buyer's market.

MARKETING MANAGEMENT

Most people think of marketing management as finding enough customers for the company's current output, but this is too limited a view. The organization has a desired level of demand for its products. At any point in time, there may be no demand, adequate demand, irregular demand, or too much demand, and marketing management must find ways to deal with these different demand states (see Marketing Highlight 1-2). Marketing management is concerned not only with finding and increasing demand, but also with changing or even reducing it. Thus, marketing management seeks to affect the level, timing, and nature of demand in a way that helps the organization achieve its objectives. Simply put, marketing management is *demand management.*

We define **marketing management** as the analysis, planning, implementation, and control of programs designed to create, build, and maintain beneficial exchanges with target buyers for the purpose of achieving organizational objectives. Marketing managers include sales managers and salespeople, advertising executives, sales-promotion people, marketing researchers, product managers, pricing specialists, and others. We will discuss these marketing jobs more in Chapter 2 and in Appendix 2, "Careers in Marketing."

MARKETING MANAGEMENT PHILOSOPHIES

We describe marketing management as carrying out tasks to achieve desired exchanges with target markets. What *philosophy* should guide these marketing efforts? What weight should be given to the interests of the organization, customers, and society? Very often these interests conflict.

There are five alternative concepts under which organizations conduct their marketing activities: the *production, product, selling, marketing,* and *societal marketing* concepts.

The Production Concept

The **production concept** holds that consumers will favor products that are available and highly affordable and that management therefore should focus on improving production and distribution efficiency. This concept is one of the oldest philosophies that guides sellers.

The production concept is a useful philosophy in two types of situations. The first occurs when the demand for a product exceeds the supply. Here, management should look for ways to increase production. The second situation occurs

MARKETING MANAGEMENT: MANAGING DEMAND EFFECTIVELY

Marketing managers in different organizations might face any of the following states of demand. The marketing task is to manage demand effectively.

Negative Demand. A major part of the market dislikes the product and may even pay to avoid it. Examples are vaccinations, dental work, and seat belts. Marketers must analyze why the market dislikes the product, and whether product redesign, lower prices, or more positive promotion can change the consumer attitudes.

No Demand. Target consumers may be uninterested in the product. Thus, farmers may not care about a new farming method, and college students may not be interested in taking foreign language courses. The marketer must find ways to connect the product's benefits with the market's needs and interests.

Latent Demand. Consumers have a want that is not satisfied by any existing product or service. There is strong latent demand for nonharmful cigarettes, safer neighborhoods, biodegradable packages, and more fuel-efficient cars. The marketing task is to measure the size of the potential market and develop effective goods and services that will satisfy the demand.

Falling Demand. Sooner or later, every organization faces falling demand for one of its products. Churches have seen their membership decline, and private colleges have seen fewer applications. The marketer must find the causes of market decline and restimulate demand by finding new markets, changing product features, or creating more effective communications.

Irregular Demand. Demand varies on a seasonal, daily, or even hourly basis, causing problems of idle or overworked capacity. In mass transit, much equipment is idle during slow travel hours and too little is available during peak hours. Museums are undervisited during weekdays and overcrowded during weekends. Marketers must find ways to change the time pattern of demand through flexible pricing, promotion, and other incentives.

Full Demand. The organization has just the amount of demand it wants and can handle. The marketer works to maintain the current level of demand in the face of changing consumer preferences and increasing competition. The organization maintains quality and continually measures consumer satisfaction to make sure it is doing a good job.

Overfull Demand. Demand is higher than the company can or wants to handle. Thus, the Golden Gate Bridge carries more traffic than is safe, and Yellowstone National Park is overcrowded in the summertime. Utilities, bus companies, restaurants, and other businesses often face overfull demand at peak times. The marketing task, called *demarketing*, is to find ways to reduce the demand temporarily or permanently. Demarketing involves actions such as raising prices and reducing promotion and service. Demarketing does not aim to destroy demand, but to selectively reduce it.

when the product's cost is too high and improved productivity is needed to bring it down. For example, Henry Ford's whole philosophy was to perfect the production of the Model T so that its cost could be reduced and more people could afford it. He joked about offering people a car of any color as long as it was black. Today, Texas Instruments (TI) follows this philosophy of increased production and lower costs in order to bring down prices. The company won a major share of the American hand-calculator market with this philosophy. But when it used the same strategy in the digital watch market, TI failed. Although TI's watches were priced low, customers did not find them very attractive. In its drive to bring down prices, TI lost sight of something else that its customers wanted—namely, *attractive,* affordable digital watches.

The Product Concept

Another major concept guiding sellers, the **product concept,** holds that consumers will favor products that offer the most quality, performance, and innovative features, and that an organization should thus devote energy to making continuous product improvements. Some manufacturers believe that if they can build a better mousetrap, the world will beat a path to their door.[9] But they are often rudely shocked. Buyers may well be looking for a better solution to a mouse problem, but not necessarily for a better mousetrap. The solution might be a chemical spray, an exterminating service, or something that works better than a

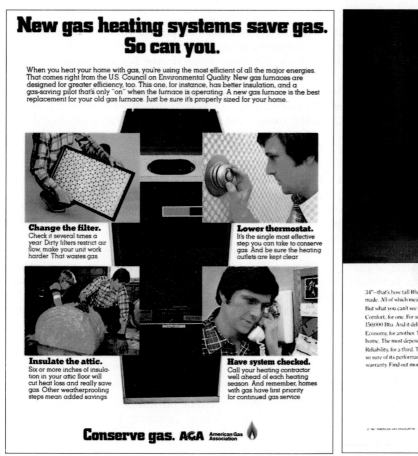

Managing demand: During the gas shortages of the 1970s, the American Gas Association demarketed natural gas by telling people how to conserve. Now that natural gas is readily available again, the AGA and gas appliance makers are running ads to stimulate sales.

mousetrap. Furthermore, a better mousetrap will not sell unless the manufacturer designs, packages, and prices it attractively; places it in convenient distribution channels; brings it to the attention of people who need it; and convinces them that it is a better product.

The product concept also can lead to "marketing myopia." For instance, railroad management once thought that users wanted *trains* rather than *transportation* and overlooked the growing challenge of airlines, buses, trucks, and automobiles. Many colleges have assumed that high school graduates want a liberal arts education and have thus overlooked the increasing challenge of vocational schools.

The Selling Concept

Many organizations follow the **selling concept,** which holds that consumers will not buy enough of the organization's products unless it undertakes a large-scale selling and promotion effort. The concept is typically practiced with *unsought goods*—those that buyers do not normally think of buying, such as encyclopedias and funeral plots. These industries must be good at tracking down prospects and selling them on product benefits.

The selling concept also is practiced in the nonprofit area. A political party, for example, will vigorously sell its candidate to voters as a fantastic person for the job. The candidate works in voting precincts from dawn to dusk—shaking hands, kissing babies, meeting donors, and making speeches. Much money is spent on radio and television advertising, posters, and mailings. Candidate flaws are hidden from the public because the aim is to get the sale, not to worry about consumer satisfaction afterward.

The Marketing Concept

The **marketing concept** holds that achieving organizational goals depends on determining the needs and wants of target markets and delivering the desired satisfactions more effectively and efficiently than competitors do. Surprisingly, this concept is a relatively recent business philosophy. The marketing concept has been stated in colorful ways such as "Find a need and fill it" (Kaiser Sand & Gravel); "To fly, to serve" (British Airways); and "We're not satisfied until you are" (GE). J. C. Penney's motto also summarizes the marketing concept: "To do all in our power to pack the customer's dollar full of value, quality, and satisfaction."

The selling concept and the marketing concept are frequently confused. Figure 1-3 compares the two concepts. The selling concept takes an *inside-out* perspective. It starts with the factory, focuses on the company's existing products, and calls for heavy selling and promotion to obtain profitable sales. In contrast, the marketing concept takes an *outside-in* perspective. It starts with a well-defined market, focuses on customer needs, coordinates all the marketing activities affecting customers, and makes profits by creating customer satisfaction. Under the marketing concept, companies produce what consumers want, thereby satisfying consumers and making profits.

Many successful and well-known companies have adopted the marketing concept. Procter & Gamble, Disney, Wal-Mart, Marriott, Nordstrom, and McDonald's follow it faithfully (see Marketing Highlight 1-3). L. L. Bean, the highly successful catalog retailer of clothing and outdoor sporting equipment, was founded on the marketing concept. In 1912, in his first circulars, L. L. Bean included the following notice:

> I do not consider a sale complete until goods are worn out and the customer still satisfied. We will thank anyone to return goods that are not perfectly satisfactory... Above all things we wish to avoid having a dissatisfied customer.

Today, L. L. Bean dedicates itself to giving "perfect satisfaction in every way." To inspire its employees to practice the marketing concept, L. L. Bean displays posters around its offices that proclaim the following:

> What is a customer? A customer is the most important person ever in this company—in person or by mail. A customer is not dependent on us, we are dependent on him. A customer is not an interruption of our work, he is the purpose of it. We are not doing a favor by serving him, he is doing us a favor by giving us the opportunity to do so. A customer is not someone to argue or match wits with—nobody ever won an argument with a customer. A customer is a person who brings us his wants—it is our job to handle them profitably to him and to ourselves.

In contrast, many companies claim to practice the marketing concept, but do not. They have the forms of marketing, such as a marketing vice-president, product managers, marketing plans, and marketing research, but this does not mean that they are market-focused and customer-driven companies. The question is whether they are finely tuned to changing customer needs and competitor strategies. Formerly great companies—General Motors, IBM, Singer, Zenith, Sears—all lost substantial market share because they failed to adjust their marketing strategies to the changing marketplace. Several years of hard work are needed to turn a sales-oriented company into a marketing-oriented company. The goal is to build customer satisfaction into the very fabric of the firm. Customer satisfac-

FIGURE 1–3
The selling and marketing concepts contrasted

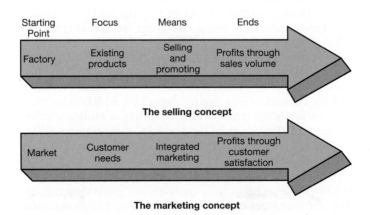

The selling concept

The marketing concept

tion is no longer a fad. As one marketing analyst notes: "It's becoming a way of life in corporate America…as embedded into corporate cultures as information technology and strategic planning."[10]

Why is it supremely important to satisfy customers? A company's sales come from two groups: new customers and repeat customers. It usually costs more to attract new customers than to retain current customers. Therefore, customer *retention* is often more critical than customer *attraction*. The key to customer retention is *customer satisfaction*. A satisfied customer buys more, stays "loyal" longer, talks favorably to others, pays less attention to competing brands and advertising, is less price sensitive, and costs less to serve than a first-time customer.

However, the marketing concept does not mean that a company should try to give *all* consumers *everything* they want. Marketers must balance creating more value for customers against making profits for the company.

> The purpose of marketing is not to *maximize* customer satisfaction. The shortest definition of marketing I know is "meeting needs profitably." The purpose of marketing is to generate customer value [at a profit]. The truth is [that the relationship with a customer] will break up if value evaporates. You've got to continue to generate more value for the consumer but not give away the house. It's a very delicate balance.[11]

The Societal Marketing Concept

The **societal marketing concept** holds that the organization should determine the needs, wants, and interests of target markets. It should then deliver the desired satisfactions more effectively and efficiently than competitors in a way that maintains or improves the consumer's *and the society's* well-being. The societal marketing concept is the newest of the five marketing management philosophies.

The societal marketing concept questions whether the pure marketing concept is adequate in an age of environmental problems, resource shortages, rapid population growth, worldwide economic problems, and neglected social services. It asks if the firm that senses, serves, and satisfies individual wants is always doing what's best for consumers and society in the long run. According to the societal marketing concept, the pure marketing concept overlooks possible conflicts between short-run consumer *wants* and long-run consumer *welfare*.

Consider the Coca-Cola Company. Most people see it as a highly responsible corporation producing fine soft drinks that satisfy consumer tastes. Yet certain consumer and environmental groups have voiced concerns that Coke has little nutritional value, can harm people's teeth, contains caffeine, and adds to the litter problem with disposable bottles and cans.

Such concerns and conflicts led to the societal marketing concept. As Figure 1-4 shows, the societal marketing concept calls upon marketers to balance three considerations in setting their marketing policies: company profits, consumer wants, and society's interests. Originally, most companies based their marketing decisions largely on short-run company profit. Eventually, they began to recognize the long-run importance of satisfying consumer wants, and the marketing concept emerged. Now many companies are beginning to think of society's interests when making their marketing decisions.

One such company is Johnson & Johnson, rated recently in a *Fortune* maga-

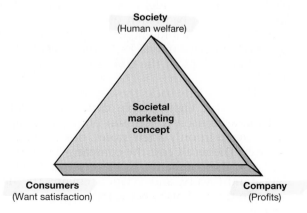

FIGURE 1–4
Three considerations underlying the societal marketing concept

MARKETING HIGHLIGHT 1-3

MCDONALD'S APPLIES THE MARKETING CONCEPT

McDonald's Corporation, the fast-food hamburger retailer, is a master marketer. With 11,000 outlets in 50 countries and more than $18.7 billion in annual systemwide sales, McDonald's doubles the sales of its nearest rival, Burger King, and triples those of third-place Wendy's. Nineteen million customers pass through the famous golden arches each day, and an astounding 96 percent of all Americans eat at McDonald's each year. McDonald's now serves 145 hamburgers per second. Credit for this performance belongs to a strong marketing orientation: McDonald's knows how to serve people and adapt to changing consumer wants.

Before McDonald's appeared, Americans could get hamburgers in restaurants or diners. But consumers often encountered poor-quality hamburgers, slow and unfriendly service, unattractive decor, unclean conditions, and a noisy atmosphere. In 1955, Ray Kroc, a 52-year-old salesman of milkshake-mixing machines, became excited about a string of seven restaurants owned by Richard and Maurice McDonald. Kroc liked their fast-food restaurant concept and bought the chain for $2.7 million. He decided to expand the chain by selling franchises, and the number of restaurants grew rapidly. As times changed, so did McDonald's. It expanded its sit-down sections, improved the decor, launched a breakfast menu, added new food items, and opened new outlets in high-traffic areas.

Kroc's marketing philosophy is captured in McDonald's motto of "Q.S.C. & V.," which stands for quality, service, cleanliness, and value. Customers enter a spotlessly clean restaurant, walk up to a friendly counterperson, quickly receive a good-tasting meal, and eat it there or take it out. There are no jukeboxes or telephones to create a teenage hangout. Nor are there any cigarette machines or newspaper racks—McDonald's is a family affair, appealing strongly to children.

McDonald's has mastered the art of serving consumers, and it carefully teaches the basics to its employees and franchisees. All franchisees take training courses at McDonald's "Hamburger University" in Elk Grove Village, Illinois. They emerge with a degree in "Hamburgerology" and a minor in French fries. McDonald's monitors product and service quality through continuous customer surveys and puts great energy into improving hamburger production methods in order to simplify operations, bring down costs, speed up service, and bring greater value to customers. Beyond these efforts, each McDonald's restaurant works to become a part of its neighborhood through community involvement and service projects.

In its 2,700 restaurants outside of the United States, McDonald's carefully customizes its menu and service to local tastes and customs. It serves corn soup and teriaki burgers in Japan, pasta salads in Rome, and wine and live piano music with its McNuggets in Paris. When McDonald's opened its first restaurant in Moscow, it quickly won the hearts of Russian consumers. However, the company had to overcome some monstrous hurdles in order to meet its high standards for consumer satisfaction in this new market. It had to educate suppliers, employees, and even consumers about the time-tested, McDonald's way of doing things. Technical experts with special strains of disease-resistant seed were brought in from Canada to teach Russian farmers how to grow russet Burbank potatoes for French fries, and the company built its own pasteurizing plant

zine poll as America's most admired company for community and environmental responsibility. J&J's concern for societal interests is summarized in a company document called "Our Credo," which stresses honesty, integrity, and putting people before profits. Under this credo, Johnson & Johnson would rather take a big loss than ship a bad batch of one of its products. And the company supports many community and employee programs that benefit its consumers and workers, and the environment. J&J's chief executive puts it this way: "If we keep trying to do what's right, at the end of the day we believe the marketplace will reward us."[12]

The company backs these words with actions. Consider the tragic tampering case in which eight people died from swallowing cyanide-laced capsules of Tylenol, a Johnson & Johnson brand. Although J&J believed that the pills had been altered in only a few stores, not in the factory, it quickly recalled all of its product. The recall cost the company $240 million in earnings. In the long run, however, the company's swift recall of Tylenol strengthened consumer confidence and loyalty, and Tylenol remains the nation's leading brand of pain reliever. In this and other cases, J&J management has found that doing what's right

McDonald's delivers "quality, service, cleanliness, and value" to consumers here in the United States and around the world.

train consumers—most Muscovites had never seen a fast-food restaurant. Customers waiting in line were shown videos telling them everything from how to order and pay at the counter to how to handle a Big Mac. And in its usual way, McDonald's began immediately to build community involvement. On opening day, it held a kick-off party for 700 Muscovite orphans, and it donated all opening-day proceeds to the Moscow Children's Fund. As a result, the new Moscow restaurant got off to a very successful start. About 50,000 customers swarmed through the restaurant during its first day of business.

Riding on its success in Moscow, McDonald's continues to pursue opportunities to serve new customers around the globe. It recently opened its largest restaurant anywhere, in Beijing, China. The 28,000-square-foot restaurant has 29 cash registers and seats 700 people. Through this huge Beijing outlet, McDonald's expects to treat more than ten thousand customers each day to its special brand of customer care.

Thus, McDonald's focus on consumers has made it the world's largest food-service organization. It now captures about 20 percent of America's fast-food business and is rapidly expanding its worldwide presence. The company's huge success has been reflected in the increased value of its stock over the years: 250 shares of McDonald's stock purchased for less that $6,000 in 1965 would be worth well over a million dollars today!

to ensure a plentiful supply of fresh milk. It trained Russian managers at Hamburger University and subjected each of 630 new employees (most of whom didn't know a Chicken McNugget from an Egg McMuffin) to 16 to 20 hours of training on such essentials as cooking meat patties, assembling Filet-O-Fish sandwiches, and giving service with a smile. McDonald's even had to

Sources: Penny Moser, "The McDonald's Mystique," *Fortune,* July 4, 1988; Scott Hume, "McDonald's Fred Turner: Making All the Right Moves," *Advertising Age,* January 1, 1990, pp. 6, 17; Gail McKnight, "Here Comes Bolshoi Mac," *USA Today Weekend,* January 26-28, 1990, pp. 4-5; Rosemarie Boyle, "McDonald's Gives Soviets Something Worth Waiting For," *Advertising Age,* March 19, 1990, p. 61; and "Food Draws Raves, Prices Don't at Beijing McDonald's Opening," *Durham Herald-Sun,* April 12, 1992, p. B12.

benefits both consumers and the company. Says the chief executive: "The Credo should not be viewed as some kind of social welfare program…it's just plain good business."[13] Thus, over the years, Johnson & Johnson's dedication to consumers and community service has made it one of America's most admired companies, *and* one of the most profitable.

THE GOALS OF THE MARKETING SYSTEM

Our marketing system consists of the collective marketing activities of tens of thousands of profit and nonprofit organizations at home and around the globe. This marketing system affects everyone—buyers, sellers, and many public groups with common characteristics. The goals of these groups may conflict. *Buyers* want good-quality products at reasonable prices in convenient locations. They want wide brand and feature assortments; helpful, pleasant, and honest salespeople; and strong warranties backed by good follow-up service. The marketing system can greatly affect buyer satisfaction.

Sellers face many challenging decisions when preparing an offer for the market. What consumer groups should be targeted? What do target consumers need, and how should products be designed and priced to give the greatest value? What wholesalers and retailers should be used? And what advertising, personal selling, and sales promotion would help sell the product? The market demands a lot. Sellers must apply modern marketing thinking in order to develop an offer that attracts and satisfies customers.

Legislators, public interest groups, and other *publics* have a strong interest in the marketing activities of business. Do manufacturers make safe and reliable products? Do they describe their products accurately in ads and packaging? Is competition working in the market to provide a reasonable range of quality and price choice? Are manufacturing and packaging activities hurting the environment? The marketing system has a major impact on the quality of life, and various groups of citizens want to make the system work as well as possible. They act as watchdogs of consumer interests and favor consumer education, information, and protection.

The marketing system affects so many people in so many ways that it inevitably stirs controversy. Some people intensely dislike modern marketing activity, charging it with ruining the environment, bombarding the public with senseless ads, creating unnecessary wants, teaching greed to youngsters, and committing several other sins. Consider the following:

> For the past 6,000 years the field of marketing has been thought of as made up of fast-buck artists, con-men, wheeler-dealers, and shoddy-goods distributors. Too many of us have been "taken" by the touts of con-men; and all of us at times have been prodded into buying all sorts of "things" we really did not need, and which we found later on we did not even want.[14]

Others vigorously defend marketing:

> Aggressive marketing policies and practices have been largely responsible for the high material standard of living in America. Today through mass, low-cost marketing we enjoy products which once were considered luxuries, and which still are so classified in many foreign countries.[15]

What should a society seek from its marketing system? Four goals have been suggested: maximize *consumption*, maximize *consumer satisfaction*, maximize *choice*, and maximize *quality of life*.

Maximize Consumption

Many business executives believe that marketing's job should be to stimulate maximum consumption, which in turn will create maximum production, employment, and wealth. This view has been promoted by slogans such as "Who says you can't have it all?" (Michelob); or "The costliest perfume in the world" (Joy); or "Greed is good" (from the movie *Wall Street*). The assumption is that the more people spend, buy, and consume, the happier they are. "More is better" is the war cry. Yet, some people doubt that increased material goods mean more happiness. They see too many affluent people leading unhappy lives. Their philosophy is "less is more" and "small is beautiful."

Maximize Consumer Satisfaction

Another view holds that the goal of the marketing system is to maximize consumer satisfaction, not simply the quantity of consumption. Buying a new car or owning more clothes counts only if this adds to the buyer's satisfaction.

Unfortunately, consumer satisfaction is difficult to measure. First, nobody has discovered how to measure the total satisfaction created by a particular product or marketing activity. Second, the satisfaction that some individual consumers get from the "goods" of a product or service must be offset by the "bads," such as pollution and environmental damage. Third, the satisfaction that some people get from consuming certain goods, such as status goods, depends on the fact that few other people have these goods. Thus, evaluating the marketing system in terms of how much satisfaction it delivers is difficult.

Maximize Choice

Some marketers believe that the goal of a marketing system should be to maximize product variety and consumer choice. This system would enable consumers to find goods that satisfy their tastes exactly. Consumers would be able to realize their lifestyles fully and, therefore, could maximize their overall satisfaction.

Unfortunately, maximizing consumer choice comes at a cost. First, the price of goods and services rises because producing great variety increases production and inventory costs. In turn, higher prices reduce consumers' real income and consumption. Second, the increase in product variety will require greater consumer search and effort: Consumers have to spend more time learning about and evaluating the different products. Third, the existence of more products will not necessarily increase the consumer's real choice. For example, hundreds of brands of beer are sold in the United States, but most of them taste about the same. Thus, when a product category contains many brands with few differences, consumers face a choice that is really no choice at all. Finally, not all consumers welcome great product variety. For some consumers, too much choice leads to confusion and frustration.

Maximize Life Quality

Many people believe that the goal of a marketing system should be to improve the *quality of life*. This includes not only the quality, quantity, availability, and cost of goods, but also the quality of the physical and cultural environments. Advocates of this view would judge marketing systems not only by the amount of direct consumer satisfaction, but also by the impact of marketing on the quality of the environment. Most people would agree that quality of life is a worthwhile goal for the marketing system. But they might also agree that "quality" is hard to measure and that it means different things to different people.

MARKETING CHALLENGES IN THE 1990s

Marketing operates within a dynamic global environment. Every decade calls upon marketing managers to think freshly about their marketing objectives and practices. Rapid changes can quickly make yesterday's winning strategies out of date. As management thought-leader Peter Drucker once observed, a company's winning formula for the last decade will probably be its undoing in the next decade.

What are the marketing challenges of the 1990s? With the end of the cold war, today's companies are wrestling with increased global competition, environmental decline, economic stagnation, and a host of other economic, political, and social problems. However, these problems also provide marketing opportunities. We now look more deeply into three key forces that are changing the marketing landscape and challenging marketing strategy: rapid globalization, the changing world economy, and the call for more socially responsible actions.

Rapid Globalization

The world economy has undergone radical change during the past two decades. Geographical and cultural distances have shrunk with the advent of jet planes, fax machines, global computer and telephone hookups, world television satellite broadcasts, and other technical advances. This has allowed companies to greatly expand their geographical market coverage, purchasing, and manufacturing. The result is a vastly more complex marketing environment, for both companies and consumers.

Today, almost every company, large or small, is touched in some way by global competition—from the neighborhood florist that buys its flowers from Mexican nurseries, to the small New York clothing retailer that sources its merchandise in Asia, to the U.S. electronics manufacturer competing in its home markets with giant Japanese rivals, to the large American consumer goods producer introducing new products into emerging markets abroad.

American firms have been challenged at home by the skillful marketing of European and Asian multinationals. Companies like Toyota, Siemens, Nestlé, Sony, and Samsung often have outperformed their U.S. competitors in American markets. Similarly, U.S. companies in a wide range of industries have found new opportunities abroad. General Motors, Exxon, IBM, General Electric, Du Pont, Coca-Cola, and dozens of other American companies have developed truly global operations, making and selling their products worldwide. The following are just a few of countless examples of U.S. companies taking advantage of international marketing opportunities:

Coca-Cola and Pepsi, fierce competitors in the United States, recently have watched the domestic soft-drink market go flat, growing at only about 1 percent per year. Thus, both now have created new marketing strategies to attack Western Europe, a market growing at an 8 percent clip. Coca-Cola has invested millions of dollars in marketing at the Barcelona Olympics and in the opening of EuroDisneyland. Coke makes about 80 percent of its profits outside of America, and it has always led Pepsi abroad. Still, Pepsi thinks that it can compete successfully with Coke in Europe. It plans to invest almost $500 million in European businesses during the next two years in what both companies view as their next big battleground.

Toys 'R' Us spent several years slogging through the swamps of Japanese bureaucracy before it was allowed to open the very first large U.S. discount store in Japan, the world's No. 2 toy market behind the United States. The entry of this foreign giant has Japanese toymakers and retailers edgy. The typical small Japanese toy store stocks only 1,000 to 2,000 items, whereas Toys 'R' Us stores carry as many as 15,000. And the discounter will likely offer toys at prices 10 percent to 15 percent below those of competitors. The opening of the first Japanese store was "astonishing," attracting more than 60,000 visitors in the first three days. Toys 'R' Us plans to open ten new Japanese stores each year from 1993 through the end of the decade. If the company's invasion of Japan succeeds as well as its recent entry into Europe, Japanese retailers will have their hands full. Toys 'R' Us began with just five European stores in 1985 but now has 76 and growing. European sales, now about $800 million, are growing at triple the rate of total sales.

After ten years of relentless growth in America, Music Television's (MTV) home market has become saturated. Now the company is looking abroad for growth. It recently set up MTV Europe, which reaches 27 countries and 25 million homes. It is "aggressively pan-European"—its programming and advertising are the same throughout Europe, and they are all in English. But MTV may find it difficult to repeat its phenomenal American success abroad. The challenge will be to convince advertisers that a true "Euroconsumer" exists. If successful in Europe, the company will soon follow with MTV Asia.[16]

Today, companies are not only trying to sell more of their locally produced goods in international markets, they also are buying more components and supplies abroad. Consider the following example:

In the past, most American clothing was made and sold in America. Much cutting and sewing were done in New York and New England "sweatshops" by immigrant laborers working long hours. The workers then joined unions and wages rose. Search-

Many U.S. companies are finding new global opportunities. Looking for growth, MTV tries to repeat its phenomenal American success abroad, here in Hungary.

ing for lower labor costs, many clothing manufacturers moved their manufacturing first to Southern states, and then to Asia. Today, Bill Blass, one of America's top fashion designers, will examine cloth woven from Australian wool with printed designs from Italy. He will design a dress and fax the drawing to a Hong Kong agent who will place the order with a mainland China factory. Finished dresses will be airfreighted to New York, where they will be redistributed to department and specialty stores around the country.

Many domestically purchased goods and services are "hybrids," with design, materials purchases, manufacturing, and marketing taking place in several countries. Americans who decide to "buy American" might reasonably decide to avoid Hondas and purchase Dodge Colts. Imagine their surprise when they learn that the Colt actually was made in Japan, whereas the Honda was primarily assembled in the United States from American-made parts.

Thus, managers in countries around the world are asking: Just what is global marketing? How does it differ from domestic marketing? How do global competitors and forces affect our business? To what extent should we "go global"? Many companies are forming strategic alliances with foreign companies, even competitors, who serve as suppliers or marketing partners. The past few years have produced some surprising alliances between competitors such as Ford and Mazda, General Electric and Matsushita, and AT&T and Olivetti. Winning companies in the 1990s may well be those that have built the best global networks.[17]

The Changing World Economy

A large part of the world has grown poorer during the past few decades. A sluggish world economy has resulted in more difficult times for both consumers and marketers. Around the world, people's needs are greater than ever, but in many areas, people lack the means to pay for needed goods. Markets, after all, consist of people with needs *and* purchasing power. In many cases, the latter currently is lacking. In the United States, although wages have risen, real buying power has declined, especially for the less skilled members of the work force. Many U.S. households have managed to maintain their buying power only because both spouses work. However, many workers have lost their jobs as manufacturers have "downsized" to cut costs.

Current economic conditions create both problems and opportunities for marketers. Some companies are facing declining demand and see few opportunities for growth. Others, however, are developing new solutions to changing consumer problems. Many are finding ways to offer consumers "more for less." America's largest retailer, Wal-Mart, rose to market leadership on two principles, emblazoned on every Wal-Mart store: "Satisfaction Guaranteed" and "We Sell for Less—Always." Consumers enter a Wal-Mart store, are welcomed by a friendly greeter, and find a huge assortment of good-quality merchandise at everyday low prices. The same principle explains the explosive growth of factory outlet malls and discount chains—these days, customers want value. This even applies to luxury products: Toyota introduced its successful Lexus luxury automobile with the headline "Perhaps the First Time in History that Trading a $72,000 Car for a $36,000 Car Could Be Considered Trading Up."

The Call for More Ethics and Social Responsibility

A third factor in today's marketing environment is the increased call for companies to take responsibility for the social and environmental impact of their actions. Corporate ethics has become a hot topic in almost every business arena, from the corporate boardroom to the business school classroom. And few companies can ignore the renewed and very demanding environmental movement.

The ethics and environmental movements will place even stricter demands on companies in the future. Consider recent environmental developments. The West was shocked after the fall of communism to find out about the massive environmental negligence of the former Eastern Bloc governments. In many Eastern European countries, the air is fouled, the water is polluted, and the soil is poisoned by chemical dumping. In June 1992, representatives from more than one hundred countries attended the Earth Summit in Rio de Janeiro to consider how to handle such problems as the destruction of rain forests, global warming, endangered species, and other environmental threats. Clearly, in the future, compa-

Today's forward-thinking companies are responding strongly to the ethics and environmental movements. Here, ITT states "All of our companies share a common goal: To improve the quality of life. Because it's not just how you make a living that's important, it's how you live."

nies will be held to an increasingly higher standard of environmental responsibility in their marketing and manufacturing activities.

The New Marketing Landscape

The past decade taught business firms everywhere a humbling lesson. Domestic companies learned that they can no longer ignore global markets and competitors. Successful firms in mature industries learned that they cannot overlook emerging markets, technologies, and management approaches. Companies of every sort learned that they cannot remain inwardly focused, ignoring the needs of their customers.

The most powerful U.S. companies of the 1970s included General Motors, Sears, and RCA. But all three of these giant companies failed at marketing, and today, all three are struggling. Each failed to understand its changing marketplace, its customers, and the need to provide value. Today, General Motors is still trying to figure out why so many consumers around the world have switched to Japanese and European cars. Mighty Sears has lost its way, losing share both to fashionable department and specialty stores on the one hand, and to discount mass merchandisers on the other. RCA, inventor of so many new products, never quite mastered the art of marketing and now puts its name on products largely imported from Asia.

In the 1990s, companies must become customer oriented and market driven in all that they do. It's not enough to be product or technology driven—too many companies still design their products without customer input, only to find them rejected in the marketplace. It is not enough to be good at winning new customers—too many companies forget about customers after the sale, only to lose their future business. Not surprisingly, we are now seeing a flood of books with titles such as *The Customer Driven Company, Keep the Customer, Customers for Life, Total Customer Service: The Ultimate Weapon,* and *The Only Thing that Matters: Bringing the Customer into the Center of Your Business.*[18] These books emphasize that for the 1990s and beyond, the key to success will be a strong focus on the marketplace and a total marketing commitment to providing value to customers.

SUMMARY

Marketing touches everyone's life. It is the means by which a standard of living is developed and delivered to a people. Many people confuse marketing with *selling*, but in fact, marketing occurs both before and after the selling event. Marketing actually combines many activities—marketing research, product development, distribution, pricing, advertising, personal selling, and others—designed to sense, serve, and satisfy consumer needs while meeting the organization's goals.

Marketing is human activity directed at satisfying needs and wants through *exchange processes*. The core concepts of marketing are *needs, wants, demands, products, exchange, transactions,* and *markets*.

Marketing management is the analysis, planning, implementation, and control of programs designed to create, build, and maintain beneficial exchanges with target markets in order to achieve organizational objectives. Marketers must be good at managing the level, timing, and composition of demand because actual demand can be different from what the organization wants.

Marketing management can be guided by five different philosophies. The *production concept* holds that consumers favor products that are available at low cost and that management's task is to improve production efficiency and bring down prices. The *product concept* holds that con-

sumers favor quality products and that little promotional effort is thus required. The *selling concept* holds that consumers will not buy enough of the company's products unless stimulated through heavy selling and promotion. The *marketing concept* holds that a company should research the needs and wants of a well-defined target market and deliver the desired satisfactions. The *societal marketing concept* holds that the company should generate customer satisfaction and long-run societal well-being as the key to achieving both its goals and its responsibilities.

Marketing practices have a major impact on people in our society. Different goals have been proposed for a marketing system, such as maximizing *consumption, consumer satisfaction, consumer choice,* or *quality of life*. Marketing operates within a dynamic global environment. Rapid changes can quickly make yesterday's winning strategies obsolete. Marketers are facing many new challenges and opportunities in the 1990s. With the end of the cold war, today's companies are wrestling with increased global competition, a sluggish world economy, a call for greater social responsibility, and a host of other economic, political, and social problems. However, these problems also offer marketing opportunities. To be successful in the 1990s, companies will have to be strongly market focused.

KEY TERMS

Barter transaction 9

Customer value 9

Demands 7

Exchange 9

Human need 7

Human want 7

Market 10

Marketing 6

Marketing concept 15

Marketing management 13

Monetary transaction 9

Product 7

Product concept 14

Production concept 14

Relationship marketing 10

Selling concept 14

Societal marketing concept 17

Transaction 9

DISCUSSING THE ISSUES

1. Why should *you* study marketing?

2. Historian Arnold Toynbee and economist John Kenneth Galbraith have argued that the desires stimulated by marketing efforts are not genuine: "A man who is hungry need never be told of his need for food." Is this a valid criticism of marketing? Why or why not?

3. Many people dislike or fear certain products and would not "demand" them at any price. How might a health-care marketer manage the *negative* demand for such products as colon-cancer screenings?

4. Changes in the world's political structure and balance of power are leading to smaller U.S. military budgets. Before these changes were made, defense contractors followed the product concept and focused on high

technology. Will military suppliers now need to change to the marketing concept? Who are their customers?

5. What is the single biggest difference between the marketing concept and the production, product, and selling concepts? Which concepts are easiest to apply in the short run? Which concept can offer the best long-term success?

6. According to economist Milton Friedman, "Few trends could so thoroughly undermine the very foundations of our free society as the acceptance by corporate officials of a social responsibility other than to make as much money for their stockholders as possible." Do you agree or disagree with Friedman's statement? What are some drawbacks of the societal marketing concept?

APPLYING THE CONCEPTS

1. Go to McDonald's and order a sandwich. Note the questions you are asked, and observe how special orders are handled. Next, go to Wendy's, Burger King, or a local pizza restaurant and order a sandwich or pizza. Note the questions you are asked here, and observe whether special orders are handled the same way as they are at McDonald's.

- Did you observe any significant differences in how orders are handled?

- Consider the differences you saw. Do you think the restaurants have different marketing management philosophies? Which is closest to the marketing concept? Is one closer to the selling or production concept?

- What are the advantages of closely following the marketing concept? Are there any disadvantages?

2. Take a trip to your local mall. Find the directory sign. Make a list of five major categories of stores, such as department stores, shoe stores, bookstores, women's clothing shops, and restaurants. List the competing stores in each category, and take a walk past them and quickly observe their merchandise and style. Take a look at the public spaces of the mall, and note how they are decorated. Watch the shoppers in the mall.

- Four basic goals for the marketing system have been suggested: maximizing consumption, consumer satisfaction, consumer choice, or quality of life. Do you think the mall serves some of these goals more, or better, than others?

- Are the competing stores really unique, or could one pretty much substitute for another? What does this say about the overall goals that the mall is fulfilling?

- Consider the attitudes of the shoppers you saw. Did some apparently find shopping a pleasure, while others found it a bother?

MAKING MARKETING DECISIONS:

SMALL WORLD COMMUNICATIONS, INC.

INTRODUCTION

Lynette Jones is currently a senior marketing manager for Fond du Lac Foods, a major marketer of grocery products, where she has worked for five years. Eighteen months ago, Lynette successfully launched a new line of low-fat ethnic foods (Mexican, Chinese, and Thai) which is doing very well. The line succeeded because of Lyn's innovative marketing plan. This plan was based on a thorough analysis of every key market, using detailed information gathered from several on-line computer databases. This success, and Lyn's reputation as an innovator, recently got her promoted to the number two position in the marketing department. Before joining Fond Du Lac Foods, Lynette had spent three years marketing antiperspirants and mouthwash for Rugby-Kelly, a multinational personal care firm. She had earned her MBA at the University of North Carolina after spending a year in the Dominican Republic with the Peace Corps. Before business school, Lyn had graduated from Spelman College in Atlanta.

Recently Lynette Jones attended her fifteenth high school reunion, and ran into an old acquaintance, Thomas Campbell. Tom had always been a whiz kid. In high school he was doing computer programming as a nearly full-time job, while attending just enough classes to avoid being expelled. After graduating, he went off to Rensselaer Polytechnic, and quickly became well-known to all his professors. Tom became rather impatient, however, and dropped out of the electrical engineering program at the end of his sophomore year. After stints at Sun Microsystems and Hewlett-Packard, Tom is now head electronics designer for San Andreas Products, makers of computer expansion boards for sophisticated users who are upgrading their current machines. Tom is an intuitive wonder. He specializes in designing circuits that get unique features and maximum performance from standard, "off the shelf" chips. Tom works 70- to 80-hour weeks, and every night-shift driver at the local Domino's Pizza knows his office location by heart. Tom's last date was nearly four months ago because, as he puts it, "I've been busy." He does, however, keep in touch with a number of people by electronic mail on the InterNet and CompuServe.

After they had talked for a while, Lyn remarked to Tom that she was amazed by the computer resources she had found while working on her new product launch. "It's incredible what's already out there. I just took my computer, put in a simple modem so I could hook up to a phone line, and started to play around. I'm working mostly with facts and figures that I found through on-line services like CompuServe. I could get U.S. Census data for my test markets, check the trademarks of our competitors, search *The Wall Street Journal* for related articles . . . it's phenomenal. But I'm really interested in the things that are coming down the pike—multimedia teleconferencing, pen-based computers, virtual reality—maybe even easier access to simple facts and figures, and a way to really run an office without boatloads of paper." Tom smiled, and Lyn could see his eyes brighten behind his thick glasses. "That's Bill Gates' vision of the future, Microsoft style—total information at your fingertips. I see big opportunities, I mean truly gigantic ones, that are coming out of this information revolution. The buzzword in the industry is 'connectivity.' All it means is connecting computers together so they can share data and communicate. Really big things can happen fast, because the basic technology already exists. I figure it will take some innovative new hardware, some advances in software—especially data compression—and a marketer to sell it to people when it's all done."

Now Lynette smiled. "You're probably right about the hardware and software, but dead wrong about the marketing. *Real* marketing—the kind that works—starts at the other end of the process. We find out what our potential customers need and want, and we design the product and the marketing to serve *them*."

"So?" replied Tom. "So *what*?" Lyn retorted, annoyed because she really loved marketing, and Tom obviously didn't have a clue. "So what do our customers need or want? You figure it out, I build it, and we both become rich and famous. I'm ready for a change anyway."

Lyn stared for a minute. This guy was really serious. Her mind reeled. Fond du Lac *was* awfully cold. Her husband, Bill, an accounting professor at Fond du Lac State, would be willing and able to move. Her boss, Scott Thompson, was only 42 and was at the top of the marketing ladder. He wasn't going anywhere—which meant that she wasn't either. She *could* afford to take a risk. She smiled. "So

we build a business to connect computers together. You're the technical guru, I'm the marketer. I could see it—'Small World Communications.' Let's hit the banquet now. I'll meet you for breakfast and we'll talk."

WHAT NOW?

Lynette and Thomas may start a company in the computer communications field. At this stage, they can approach the design of a new firm in any way they choose. To Lyn, management philosophy seems to be a logical starting point. Small World could operate under any one of the alternate philosophies—production, product, selling, marketing, or societal marketing concept.

1. Where would the company be likely to focus its people and capital resources under each of these five philosophies?

2. Does marketing management philosophy really affect how customers see a company? What might customers say about Small World if it were to operate under each of these philosophies?

3. What philosophy would you choose for this new company?

REFERENCES

1. For other examples, and for a good review of nonprofit marketing, see Philip Kotler and Alan R. Andreasen, *Strategic Marketing for Nonprofit Organizations* (Englewood Cliffs, NJ: Prentice Hall, 1991).

2. For more examples, see Philip Kotler and Karen Fox, *Strategic Marketing for Educational Institutions* (Englewood Cliffs, NJ: Prentice Hall, 1985); Bradley G. Morrison and Julie Gordon Dalgleish, *Waiting in the Wings: A Larger Audience for the Arts and How to Develop It* (New York: ACA Books, 1987); and Norman Shawchuck, Philip Kotler, Bruce Wren, and Gustave Rath, *Marketing for Congregations: Choosing to Serve People More Effectively* (Nashville, TN: Abingdon Press, 1993).

3. See Philip Kotler and Eduardo Roberto, *Social Marketing: Strategies for Changing Public Behavior* (New York: The Free Press, 1990).

4. Christy Fisher, "Postal Service Plans First-Class Promotion," *Advertising Age,* April 6, 1992, p. 26.

5. Peter F. Drucker, *Management: Tasks, Responsibilities, Practices* (New York: Harper & Row, 1973), pp. 64–65.

6. Here are some other definitions: "Marketing is the performance of business activities that direct the flow of goods and services from producer to consumer or user." "Marketing is getting the right goods and services to the right people at the right place at the right time at the right price with the right communication and promotion." "Marketing is the creation and delivery of a standard of living." In 1985, the American Marketing Association approved this definition: "Marketing is the process of planning and executing the conception, pricing, promotion, and distribution of ideas, goods, and services to create exchanges that satisfy individual and organizational objectives."

7. See Theodore Levitt's classic article, "Marketing Myopia," *Harvard Business Review,* July–August 1960, pp. 45–56.

8. The number of transactions in a decentralized exchange sys-

tem is given by $N(N-1)/2$. With four persons, this means $4(4-1)/2 = 6$ transactions. In a centralized exchange system, the number of transactions is given by N, here 4. Thus, a centralized exchange system reduces the number of transactions needed for exchange.

9. Ralph Waldo Emerson offered this advice: "If a man . . . makes a better mousetrap . . . the world will beat a path to his door." Several companies, however, have built better mousetraps yet failed. One was a laser mousetrap costing $1,500. Contrary to popular assumptions, people do not automatically learn about new products, believe product claims, or willingly pay higher prices.

10. Howard Schlossberg, "Customer Satisfaction: Not a Fad, but a Way of Life," *Marketing News,* June 10, 1991, p. 18.

11. Thomas E. Caruso, "Kotler: Future Marketers Will Focus on Customer Data Base to Compete Globally," *Marketing News,* June 8, 1992, pp. 21–22.

12. See "Leaders of the Most Admired," *Fortune,* January 29, 1990, pp. 40–54.

13. Ibid., p. 54.

14. Richard N. Farmer, "Would you Want Your Daughter to Marry a Marketing Man?" *Journal of Marketing,* January 1967, p. 1.

15. William J. Stanton and Charles Futrell, *Fundamentals of Marketing,* 8th ed. (New York: McGraw-Hill, 1987), p. 7.

16. For these and other examples, see "Soda-Pop Celebrity," *The Economist,* September 14, 1991, pp. 75–76; "MTV: Rock On," *The Economist,* August 3, 1991, p. 66; Robert Neff, "Guess Who's Selling Barbies in Japan Now?" *Business Week,* December 9, 1991, pp. 72–76; Patrick Oster, "Toys 'R' Us Making Europe Its Playpen," *Business Week,* January 20, 1992, pp. 88–91; Julie Skur Hill, "Toys 'R' Us Seeks Global Growth," *Advertising Age,* March 30, 1992, p. 33; and Kevin Cote, "Toys 'R' Us Grows in Europe," *Advertising Age,* April 27, 1992, p. I-16.

17. For more on strategic alliances, see Jordan D. Lewis, *Partnerships for Profit: Structuring and Managing Strategic Alliances* (New York: The Free Press, 1990); Peter Lorange and Johan Roos, *Strategic Alliances: Formation, Implementation, and Evolution* (Cambridge, MA: Blackwell Publishers, 1992); and Frederick E. Webster, Jr., "The Changing Role of Marketing in the Corporation," *Journal of Marketing,* October 1992, pp. 1–17.

18. Richard C. Whitely, *The Customer Driven Company* (Reading,

MA: Addison-Wesley, 1991); Robert L. Desanick, *Keep the Customer* (Boston: Houghton Mifflin Co., 1990); Charles Sewell; *Customers for Life: How to Turn the One-Time Buyer into a Lifetime Customer* (New York: Pocket Books, 1990); William H. Davidow and Bro Uttal, *Total Customer Service: The Ultimate Weapon* (New York: Harper & Row, 1989); and Karl Albrecht, *The Only Thing that Matters: Bringing the Customer into the Center of Your Business* (New York: Harper Business, 1992).

VIDEO CASE 1

ENVIRONMENTAL MARKETING: TRYING TO DO THE RIGHT THING

The "environmental marketing movement" is one result of Earth Day 1990. In response to studies indicating that consumers want environmentally friendly products, many firms have introduced "green" products, but the results have been disappointing. Why? To answer this question, we must examine the extent of "greenness" of the consumer market, current business actions, and the present regulatory and economic environments.

The consumer market consists of five groups, classified by their willingness to buy "green" products. The first group, the "true-blue greens" (11 percent of the population), are affluent individuals heavily involved in pro-environment practices. The second group, the "greenback greens" (11 percent), are younger and are the biggest environmental spenders. The third group, the "sprouts" (26 percent), are ambivalent about the environmental movement. Fourth, the "grousers" (24 percent) aren't involved in environmental activities because their friends aren't. Finally, the "basic browns" (28 percent) don't believe that individuals can make a difference in improving the environment. With the exception of the true-blue greens and the greenback greens, the market is uninterested in environmental efforts and unwilling to pay over 5 percent extra for green products. Because many of these products have higher prices, lack of consumer response should be expected.

Based on their environmental marketing efforts, businesses can be divided into two groups. First are the firms that readily label products as biodegradable or environmentally friendly, with only weak evidence to support the claim, in order to extract short-run returns. Publicity surrounding lawsuits based on these doubtful and often deceptive claims has further eroded consumer willingness to buy green products.

The second group of businesses have comprehensive, long-run environmental marketing plans. Even so, they find green marketing difficult. For example, Jack-in-the-Box replaced its foam clamshell packaging with a recyclable paper and foil wrapper. But the wrapper is recyclable only if you can find a recycle location that accepts it.

Because of questionable practices, states have enacted a number of regulations affecting environmental marketing. The sheer volume of regulations can often be overwhelming for a manufacturer. And because regulations vary from state to state, they may also be difficult to meet.

To deal with these problems, various industries have mounted environmental programs: the Responsible Care Program in the chemical industry, the Global Environmental Management Initiative in the petroleum industry, and the Business Charter for Sustainable Development by the International Chamber of Commerce. Although helpful, these programs lack strong enforcement and do not apply to firms outside selected industries.

In July 1992, the FTC issued a set of green guidelines. These guidelines are voluntary and do not offer precise definitions of environmental terms. Instead, they delineate broad parameters that, if followed, would probably render markets exempt from federal regulatory actions. Examples of the guidelines are:

- An ad touting a package as "50 percent more recycled content than before" could be misleading if the recycled content had increased from 2 percent to 3 percent.

- An ad calling a trash bag "recyclable" without qualification would be misleading because bags aren't ordinarily separated from other trash at landfills or incinerators.

- A shampoo advertised as "biodegradable" without qualification would not be deceptive if the marketer has competent and reliable scientific support showing it will decompose in a short time.

The FTC guidelines contain dozens of examples designed to identify allowable as well as deceptive marketing activities. Hence many firms may be encouraged to take advantage of two areas—recyclability and compostability—in making product claims.

Although laudable, the guidelines still fail to deal with several issues. First, they are voluntary and, therefore, not strictly enforceable. Second, they are not binding on states. Many states have already passed a number of environmental regulations that may be at odds with the FTC guidelines. In such cases, firms hope that the state would defer to the FTC. But, who knows?

With all the problems of green marketing, you might ask "Is it worth it?" The answer is yes. Companies that ignore environmental issues invite stiff fines, add to the current lack of confidence in business, and miss out on the substantial long-run rewards that can result for firms that build carefully crafted environmental marketing platforms now.

QUESTIONS

1. How does green marketing illustrate the societal marketing concept?

2. How will economic conditions and regulation affect each group of green consumers?

3. What goals of the marketing system does environmental marketing meet? With which ones does it conflict?

4. How can firms enhance the credibility of their environmental marketing efforts?

5. What impact do you think the FTC guidelines will have?

Sources: Howard Schlossberg, "Innovation Seems to Elude `Green Marketers,'" Marketing News, April 15, 1991, pp. 16, 20; Joseph M. Winski, "Green Marketing: Big Prizes, but No Easy Answers," Advertising Age, October 29, 1991, p. GR3; Carl Frankel, "Blueprint for Green Marketing," American Demographics, April 1992, pp. 34-8; Steven Colford, "FTC Green Guidelines May Spark Ad Efforts," Advertising Age, August 3, 1992, pp. 1, 29; Robert Gillespie, "Pitfalls and Opportunities for Environmental Marketers," Journal of Business Strategy, July-August 1992, pp. 14-17.

COMPANY CASE 1

DOORGUARD: TRYING TO MAKE A DENT IN THE MARKET

"Hey, Steven!"

Steven Harris looked up to see Todd Smith striding across the student parking lot at the University of South Carolina.

"Hello, Todd!" Steven responded as he finished locking his car door.

"Are you going over to the registrar's office to pick up your class schedule and register?" Todd asked as he neared the car.

"Yeah, guess I've got to do it. I'm not too excited about starting school again, even though we are seniors. I had a great summer."

"Wow! Is this your car?" asked Todd, admiring the new red Mustang convertible.

"You've got it. That's one reason my summer was so good. This was the third year that I've worked with my brother's yard maintenance service in Myrtle Beach. Not only did I have a good time, but with the money I saved from the three summers I was able to buy this car."

"I'm impressed. I notice you parked way out here away from any other cars."

"You bet. It didn't make much difference with my old Chevy, but I sure don't want thoughtless people denting the sides of my new car. People really dented the sides of my old car, especially in these student parking lots with their narrow spaces."

"I know what you mean," responded Todd. "I got here yesterday and stopped at student housing to pick up my dorm room key. I purposely parked diagonally across two spaces to protect my car. I was only in the office a few minutes, but when I came out a campus cop was writing me a $20 ticket! He wouldn't tear it up either."

"What a way to start a new year!"

"You know," added Todd, "there ought to be a law against banging doors into other people's cars. Or someone should come up with some way to protect car doors. Those rubber strips that manufacturers put on never seem to be in the right place."

"I agree," replied Steven, "or maybe cars should have a device that automatically dents the other car in return. Maybe that would make people more careful!"

Steven and Todd both laughed at the thought of such a device and began to dream up other wild ideas to solve the problem as they walked toward the registrar's office.

Over the next several days, Steven found himself thinking more and more about the problem of preventing side-panel damage. He had always been a tinkerer, and he had fairly well developed mechanical instincts. With the job outlook for college graduates in the doldrums, an entrepreneurial venture began to look attractive.

In his marketing class, Steven had learned how companies develop new products, and this semester he expected to learn about business start ups in his small-business management class. With this exposure and his knack for tinkering, perhaps he could develop and market a product for the automotive market.

Steven remembered one of his professors discussing the success of the people who had launched AutoShades, the cardboard panels used behind auto windshields to keep cars cool. AutoShades' inventors had succeeded because their product really worked. Further, because they could print on the panels, companies could use the product as a sales-promotion tool. Steven believed that if he could design a device to protect car doors that also served an advertising function, he too could be successful. He began to think more seriously about developing such a product.

The Product

Seeking practical new ideas for product concepts, Steven mentioned his project to a friend, a recent graduate with a degree in mechanical engineering. The engineer suggested a panel, perhaps made of rubber, that would attach to the outside of the car door. The panel would have to be lightweight, impact resistant, and waterproof. Steven bought a panel of natural rubber and began experimenting. However, after spending many hours on this prototype, he discovered that a section of rubber large enough to protect the doors would be very expensive and would weigh over 50 pounds.

Finally, after talking to numerous suppliers of resilient materials and visiting several trade shows, Steven found a unique foam that showed promise. Manufactured by a local firm, MiniCell 200 (M200) was lightweight, impact absorbent, and relatively thin (1/2 inch). The driver could roll it up for easy storage. M200 also had several drawbacks, however. It was expensive, could not be exposed to sunlight, and tore easily.

Steven thought he could resolve these problems by finding a fabric cover for the foam. He experimented with a material that had a sunlight blocker and high tear resistance, and came in a variety of colors. However, the material did not readily accept screen printing, an attribute that Steven believed to be necessary for the project's success. Steven discussed this problem with the manufacturer. Several weeks later, the manufacturer had developed a new way to treat the material so that it accepted printing. The material would cost 75 cents per square yard.

Having worked his way through the cover-material issue, Steven began experimenting with methods for attaching the panel to a car. He knew ease of use would be critical to his product's success, as it had been for AutoShades. Steven finally decided to use magnets, which could be easily attached to the foam, making the product easy to use. Equally important, the magnets cost only about 30 cents per foot.

Steven also spent an entire afternoon selecting a name for the product. He evaluated several names, such as DoorGuard, DDent, DentGuard, AbsorbaDoor, and DoorMate. On pure instinct, he chose DoorGuard.

Steven now had a name, but he realized that he still did not have a completed product. If he used only the magnets to attach the product to a door, what would prevent someone from stealing the panels? After trying several unsuccessful theft-prevention ideas, Steven settled on a cable that attached to the foam panel. After attaching the DoorGuard panel to the door, the user would toss the other end of the cable inside the car, then close and lock the door. Anyone who tried to steal the device would tear the panel, making it useless. The cable cost 15 cents per foot, and he would need 3 feet per panel. See Exhibit 1–1 for a DoorGuard schematic.

Steven believed he had now developed the perfect product. It absorbed impact from other car doors, resisted theft and water damage, stored easily in the trunk or back seat, and accepted screen printing. Exhibit 1–2

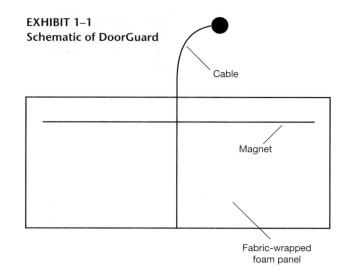

EXHIBIT 1–1
Schematic of DoorGuard

Cable

Magnet

Fabric-wrapped foam panel

illustrates a DoorGuard panel in use. DoorGuard would extend slightly beyond the door on a two-door car. On a four-door car, it would just cover both doors.

Steven next turned his attention to producing the new product. He knew that he did not have the time, experience, and money to make the product himself, but he was concerned that contract manufacturers might charge too much to produce DoorGuard. As a result, he approached organizations like Jobs for the Handicapped and Goodwill Industries that might assemble products less expensively. He eventually found an organization that could do everything needed to assemble and print one set of two panels for between $3 and $4.

Almost as an afterthought, Steven considered price. Remembering that his marketing professor had discussed cost-plus pricing in class last year, he developed a schedule of costs (see Exhibit 1-3). Based on a total cost of $14.74 per complete set of two panels, Steven used a 100 percent markup on cost (and a little psychological pricing) to arrive at a suggested retail price of $29.95 per set. Now that he had designed, named, and priced the product, Steven considered what market he would attack.

The Market

Steven knew that he should research the market potential, but believed that he had little basis for developing a reasonable estimate of DoorGuard's sales potential. Still, using secondary sources, he found that there were 122.8 million cars in use in the United States. nearly 80 percent of these cars were at least three years old; 50 percent were at least six years old. Because there were no products comparable to DoorGuard on the market, Steven

EXHIBIT 1–2   Illustration of DoorGuard in Use

DoorGuard
Clear Cola

EXHIBIT 1-3
Door Guard Cost/Price

Material Costs

M200 foam panel	$2.90 per panel
Fabric covering	.75 per sq. yd.
Magnets	.30 per ft.
Cable	.15 per ft.
Misc. (screen print, packaging)	.50 per panel
Assembly	1.50 per panel

Cost per panel

M200 ½" 1' x 4'	$2.90	
Material 1 ½ sq. yds.	1.12	
Magnets 3'	.90	
Cable 3'	.45	
Misc.	.50	
Assembly	1.50	
	Total	7.37
Cost per set of two panels		$14.74
*Retail price per set**		$29.95

100 percent markup on cost

wasn't certain what portion of the car owners would purchase the new product. AutoShades appeared to be about the only close comparison, but there was a huge cost difference: AutoShades cost from $1.49 to $6.00, whereas DoorGuard would cost nearly $30.00. Many companies gave away sun shades as advertising specialties; few companies would do the same with DoorGuard.

Still, Steven believed that DoorGuard targeted a wide-open market and that with the right marketing approach DoorGuard would be a winner. He knew that last year's new car sales in the United States totaled 9,853,000. Few new-car buyers purchased factory-installed body-protection packages, instead choosing fancy radios, air conditioners, cruise control, and other options. Steven felt that a person paying $15,000 or more for a car would pay a reasonable price to protect it. This helped to explain the success of AutoShades. Sales had started slowly for the initial sun shade—a piece of plain cardboard. But once the creators added graphics and messages to their products, AutoShades' sales heated up. In 1988, sales exceeded $20 million.

Steven dreamed about such spectacular sales results for DoorGuard. If he could capture just 5 percent of the new-car market, he would be selling nearly 500,000 sets. And sales to only 5 percent of the owners of the 122,800,000 cars on the road would generate sales of more than 6,100,000 DoorGuard sets. With such heady potential in mind, Steven began to think through the details of introducing DoorGuard.

The Marketing Approach

Proceeding cautiously, Steven consulted a local patent attorney who informed him that she would have to conduct a patent search before applying for the patent. The search would cost him $500 and the application process another $1,500 to $2,000.

Strapped for cash, Steven looked for a less expensive alternative. He found that anyone could perform a patent search. Every state has a depository for patents. All he had to do was visit a depository and conduct a computer search to see if any similar patents existed. Steven also learned that it took an average of two years for the patent office to approve a patent. During that period a competitor could copy and sell the product. Although inventors could sue the competitor after the patent office issued the patent, many inventors had insufficient funds to bring suit. Steven decided, however, to seek the patent on his own.

Steven next considered three different approaches for distributing the product. First, Steven thought that he might interest a national retail chain, such as Sears or K Mart, in carrying the product—both had large auto-supply departments. When he considered catalog sales, two catalog companies came to mind as potential distributors—Sharper Image and BrookStone. These catalogs reached people who could afford to purchase DoorGuard. Catalog companies had lower overhead and, therefore, lower markup. Finally, Steven considered selling direct to large companies such as R. J. Reynolds or Anheuser-Busch who could offer the product as an advertising specialty or premium item. If car owners accepted DoorGuard as readily as they had accepted AutoShades, these companies could tap a large market. Furthermore, because of their associations with auto racing, these companies might have a strong interest in the product. Steven wondered which of these distribution avenues would be best, or if he should consider others.

When Steven returned from class late one Thursday afternoon, he felt tired but excited. With the pressures and costs of his senior year, Steven's time and resources were scarce. Despite all of his development work, DoorGuard was still just an idea. He realized that he had no concrete notion about how to proceed. He knew that DoorGuard could be a great product but now realized how complicated it would be to take the idea to the market. He pulled out his yellow legal pad and started a new list of things he needed to do on the project. He glanced out the window at his new car, parked in the far corner of the parking lot. Steven smiled to himself. "Still no dents," he thought, "and I'm going to keep it that way."

QUESTIONS

1. What consumer needs and wants does DoorGuard satisfy?

2. Which of the marketing management philosophies discussed in the text is Steven Harris following?

3. If, as the text indicates, a market is "the set of actual and potential buyers of a product," what market does Steven wish to serve with DoorGuard?

4. What problems does Steven face? Has he forgotten to consider anything?

5. What recommendations would you make to Steven Harris? How can he adopt the marketing concept? What items should he put on his marketing "to-do" list?

Source: Adapted from "DoorMate: A New Product Venture" by Thomas H. Stevenson, University of North Carolina at Charlotte. Used with permission of the North American Case Research Association and Professor Stevenson.

Strategic Planning and the Marketing Process

2

Nobody does *Shirts* like Dockers

Dockers' Casual Pants & Chambray Shirts

For the Store nearest you call 1-800-Dockers

*I*nvented in 1850 by Levi Strauss, a Bavarian immigrant who sold canvas pants to California gold seekers, blue jeans have long been an institution in American life. And Levi Strauss & Co. has long dominated the jeans industry. From the 1950s through the 1970s, as the baby boom caused an explosion in the number of young people, Levi Strauss & Co. and other jeans makers experienced heady 10 percent to 15 percent annual sales growth, with little or no strategic or marketing planning effort. Selling jeans was easy—Levi concentrated on simply trying to make enough jeans to satisfy a seemingly insatiable market. However, by the early 1980s, demographics had caught up with the jeans industry. Its best customers, the baby boomers, were aging, and their tastes were changing with their waistlines—they bought fewer jeans and wore them longer. Meanwhile, the 18- to 24-year-old segment, the group traditionally most likely to buy jeans, was shrinking. Thus, Levi found itself fighting for share in a fading jeans market.

At first, despite the declining market, Levi Strauss & Co. stuck closely to its basic jeans business. It sought growth through mass-marketing strategies, substantially increasing its advertising and selling through mass retailers like Sears and J. C. Penney. When these tactics failed and profits continued to plummet, Levi tried diversification into faster-growing fashion and specialty apparel businesses. It hastily had added more than 75 new lines, including Ralph Lauren's Polo line (high fashion); the David Hunter line (classic men's sportswear); the Perry Ellis Collection (men's, women's, and children's casual sportswear); Tourage SSE (fashionable men's wear); Frank Shorter Sportswear (athletic wear); and many others. By 1984, Levi had diversified into a muddled array of businesses ranging from its true blue jeans to men's hats, skiwear, and even denim maternity wear.

As one analyst reported at the time in *Inc.* magazine:

> For years, Levi prospered with one strategy: chase the demand for blue jeans. Then came the designer jeans craze—and Levi became unstitched. The company diversified into fashion.... It slapped its famous name on everything from running suits to women's polyester pants. The results were disastrous: Profits collapsed by 79 percent last year, and the company slashed about 5,000 jobs.

In 1985, in an effort to turn around an ailing Levi Strauss & Co., new management implemented a bold new strategic plan, beginning with a drastic reorganization. It sold most of the ill-fated fashion and specialty apparel businesses and took the company back to what it had always done best—making and selling jeans. For starters, Levi rejuvenated its flagship product, the classic button-fly, shrink-to-fit 501 jeans. It invested $38 million in the now-classic "501 blues" advertising campaign, a series of hip, documentary-style "reality ads." Never before had a company spent so much on a single item of clothing. At the time, many analysts questioned this strategy. As one put it, "That's just too much to spend on one lousy pair of jeans." However, the 501 blues campaign spoke for all of the company's products. It reminded consumers of Levi's strong tradition and refocused the company on its basic, blue jeans heritage. During the next six years, the campaign would more than double the sales of 501s.

Building on this solid-blue base, Levi began to add new products. For example, it successfully added prewashed, stone washed, and brightly colored jeans to its basic line. In late 1986, Levi introduced Dockers, casual and comfortable cotton pants targeted toward the aging male baby boomers. A natural extension of the jeans business, the new line had even broader appeal than anticipated. Not only did adults buy Dockers, so did their children. It seems that every American adolescent needed at least one pair of casual cotton pants dressy enough to wear when meeting his girlfriend's parents. In the few years since its introduction, the Dockers line has become a one-billion-dollar-a-year success. Levi's has continued to develop new products for the aging boomers. In 1992, it introduced 550 and 560 loose-fitting jeans—"a loose interpretation of the original"—for men who've outgrown the company's slimmer-cut 501s.

In addition to introducing new products, Levi Strauss & Co. also stepped up its efforts to develop new markets. In 1991, for example, it developed jeans designed especially for women and launched an innovative five-month, $12 million "Jeans for Women" advertising campaign featuring renderings of the female form in blue jeans by four female artists. It also aired a national Spanish-language TV advertising campaign aimed at increasing its appeal to the young, fast-growing, and brand-loyal Hispanic market.

But Levi's most dramatic turnaround has been in its international markets. In 1985, Levi almost sold its then stumbling and unprofitable foreign operations. Since then, however, the company has turned what was a patchwork of foreign licensees into a well-coordinated team of worldwide subsidiaries. Levi now has become the only truly global U.S. apparel maker. Its strategy is to "think globally, act locally." It operates a closely coordinated worldwide marketing, manufacturing, and distribution system. Twice each year, Levi brings together managers from around the world to share product and advertising ideas and to search for those that have global appeal. For example, the Dockers line originated in Argentina, but has now become a worldwide bestseller. However, within its global strategy, Levi encourages local units to tailor products and programs to their home markets. For example, in Brazil, it developed the Feminina line of curvaceously cut jeans that provide the ultratight fit that Brazilian women favor.

In most markets abroad, Levi Strauss & Co. boldly plays up its deep American roots. For example, James Dean is a central figure in almost all Levi advertising in Japan. Indonesian ads show Levi-clad teenagers driving around Dubuque, Iowa, in 1960s convertibles. And almost all foreign ads feature English-language dialogue. However, whereas Americans usually think of their Levis as basic knock-around wear, most European and Asian consumers view them as upscale fashion statements. The prices match the snob appeal—a pair of Levi 501 jeans selling for $30 in the United States goes for $63 in Tokyo and $88 in Paris, creating lush profit margins.

Levi's aggressive and innovative global marketing efforts have produced stunning results. As the domestic market continues to shrink, foreign sales have accounted for most of Levi's growth. Overseas markets now yield 39 percent of the company's total revenues and 60 percent of its profits. Perhaps more impressive, its foreign business is growing at 32 percent per year, five times the growth rate of its domestic business. Levi continues to look for new international market opportunities. For example, the first Rumanian shop to officially sell Levi's jeans recently opened to large crowds, and Levi is now racing competitors to reach jeans-starved consumers in Eastern Europe and the former Soviet republics.

Dramatic strategic and marketing planning actions have transformed Levi Strauss into a vigorous and profitable company, one better matched to its changing market opportunities. Since its 1985 turnaround, Levi's sales have grown more than 31 percent and profits have increased fivefold. Thus, by building a strong base in its core jeans business, coupled with well-planned product and market development, Levi has found ways to grow profitably despite the decline in the domestic jeans market. As one company observer suggests, Levi has learned that "with the right mix of persistence and smarts, [planning new products and] cracking new markets can seem as effortless as breaking in a new pair of Levi's stone-washed jeans."[1]

CHAPTER PREVIEW

Chapter 2 presents the basics of strategic planning and the marketing process.

First, we discuss the four steps of company-wide strategic planning: defining the company ***mission,*** setting ***goals and objectives, designing a business portfolio*** to meet the mission, goals, and objectives; and ***planning functional strategies.***

Second, we outline the ***marketing process,*** including ***demand measurement*** and ***forecasting;*** market ***segmentation, targeting, and positioning;*** and setting ***competitive marketing strategies.***

Third, we set forth some of the ways companies translate their strategies into action through developing the ***marketing mix, managing the marketing effort,*** and marketplace ***analysis and planning.*** This section is a useful reference for the future, as it defines the ***sections of a marketing plan*** and their purposes.

Finally, we summarize the concepts of marketing ***implementation,*** departmental ***organization,*** and marketing ***control*** processes.

All companies must look ahead and develop long-term strategies to meet the changing conditions in their industries. No one strategy is best for all companies. Each company must find the game plan that makes the most sense given its specific situation, opportunities, objectives, and resources. The hard task of selecting an overall company strategy for long-run survival and growth is called *strategic planning.*

Marketing plays an important role in strategic planning. It provides information and other inputs to help prepare the strategic plan. In turn, strategic planning defines marketing's role in the organization. Guided by the strategic plan, marketing works with other departments in the organization to achieve overall strategic objectives.

In this chapter, we look first at the organization's overall strategic planning. Next, we discuss marketing's role in the organization as it is defined by the overall strategic plan. Finally, we explain the marketing management process—the process that marketers undertake to carry out their role in the organization.

STRATEGIC PLANNING

Overview of Planning

Many companies operate without formal plans. In new companies, managers are sometimes so busy they have no time for planning. In small companies, managers sometimes think that only large corporations need formal planning. In mature companies, many managers argue that they have done well without formal planning, and that therefore it cannot be too important. They may resist taking the time to prepare a written plan. They may argue that the marketplace changes too fast for a plan to be useful—that it would end up collecting dust.

Yet formal planning can yield many benefits for all types of companies, large and small, new and mature. It encourages management to think ahead systematically. It forces the company to sharpen its objectives and policies, leads to better coordination of company efforts, and provides clearer performance standards for control. The argument that planning is less useful in a fast-changing environment makes little sense. In fact, the opposite is true: Sound planning helps the company to anticipate and respond quickly to environmental changes, and to better prepare for sudden developments.

Companies usually prepare annual plans, long-range plans, and strategic plans. The *annual plan* is a short-term marketing plan that describes the current marketing situation, company objectives, the marketing strategy for the year, the action program, budgets, and controls. The *long-range plan* describes the major factors and forces affecting the organization during the next several years. It includes the long-term objectives, the major marketing strategies that will be used to attain them, and the resources required. This long-range plan is reviewed and updated each year so that the company always has a current long-range plan.

Whereas the company's annual and long-range plans deal with current businesses and how to keep them going, the strategic plan involves adapting the firm to take advantage of opportunities in its constantly changing environment. We define **strategic planning** as the process of developing and maintaining a strategic fit between the organization's goals and capabilities and its changing marketing opportunities.

Strategic planning sets the stage for the rest of the planning in the firm. It relies on developing a clear company mission, supporting objectives, a sound business portfolio, and coordinated functional strategies (see Figure 2-1). At the corporate level, the company first defines its overall purpose and mission. This mission then is turned into detailed supporting objectives that guide the whole company. Next, headquarters decides what portfolio of businesses and products is best for the company and how much support to give each one. In turn, each business and product unit must develop detailed marketing and other departmental plans that support the companywide plan. Thus, marketing planning occurs at the business-unit, product, and market levels. It supports company strategic planning with more detailed planning for specific marketing opportunities.[2]

Defining the Company Mission

An organization exists to accomplish something. At first, it has a clear purpose or mission, but over time its mission may become unclear as the organization grows and adds new products and markets. Or the mission may remain clear, but some managers may no longer be committed to it. Or the mission may remain clear but may no longer be the best choice given new conditions in the environment.

When management senses that the organization is drifting, it must renew its search for purpose. It is time to ask: What is our business? Who is the customer? What do consumers value? What will our business be? What should our business be? These simple-sounding questions are among the most difficult the company will ever have to answer. Successful companies continuously raise these questions and answer them carefully and completely.

Many organizations develop formal mission statements that answer these questions. A **mission statement** is a statement of the organization's purpose—what it wants to accomplish in the larger environment. A clear mission statement acts as an "invisible hand" that guides people in the organization so that they can work independently and yet collectively toward overall organizational goals.

Traditionally, companies have defined their business in product terms ("We manufacture furniture"), or in technological terms ("We are a chemical-processing firm"). But mission statements should be *market oriented*. Market definitions of a business are better than product or technological definitions. Products and technologies eventually become outdated, but basic market needs may last forever. A market-oriented mission statement defines the business in terms of satisfying basic customer needs. Thus, AT&T is in the communications business, not the telephone business. Visa defines its business not as credit cards, but as allowing customers to exchange value—to exchange assets such as cash on deposit or equity in a home for virtually anything, anywhere in the world. Wal-Mart's mission is not to run discount stores, but to provide a wide range of products and services that deliver value to middle-Americans. And 3M does more than simply make adhesives, scientific equipment, and health-care products; it solves people's problems by putting innovation to work for them.

FIGURE 2-1
Steps in strategic planning

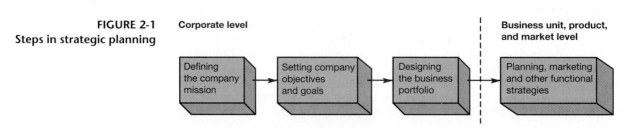

 To see why we made the sign on the right, look at the one on the left.

Anytime you're driving at night, what you can't see can hurt you.

That's why 3M invented Scotchlite™ reflective sheeting with up to ten times the reflective capability of other sign materials. So visibility and safety are dramatically improved, especially for older drivers and those with poor night vision.

But, this is just one innovative way 3M is making your world a little safer.

We also provide Safety-Walk™ anti-slip mats for business and industry. And, a wide range of health care products, including drapes, masks and dressings to help reduce the risk of infection during and after surgery.

3M is constantly solving problems with breakthrough ideas for home, office, industry and health care. So that every day, in 135 countries around the world, people benefit from 3M products and services.

Innovation working for you™

3M

Company mission: 3M sees its mission not as making adhesives, scientific equipment, and health-care products, but as "constantly solving [people's] problems with breakthrough ideas for home, office, industry, and health care. So that every day, in 135 countries around the world, people benefit from 3M products and services."

Management should avoid making its mission too narrow or too broad. A lead pencil manufacturer that says it is in the communication equipment business is stating its mission too broadly. Mission statements should be *realistic*—Singapore Airlines would be deluding itself if it adopted the mission to become the world's largest airline. They should also be *specific*. Many mission statements are written for public relations purposes and lack specific, workable guidelines. The statement "We want to become the leading company in this industry by producing the highest-quality products with the best service at the lowest prices" sounds good but is full of generalities and contradictions. It will not help the company make tough decisions. The organization should base its mission on its *distinctive competencies*. McDonald's could probably enter the solar energy business, but that would not take advantage of its core competence—providing low-cost food and fast service to large groups of customers. Finally, mission statements should be *motivating*. A company's mission should not be stated as making more sales or profits—profits are only a reward for undertaking a useful activity. A company's employees need to feel that their work is significant and that it contributes to people's lives. Contrast the missions of IBM and Apple Computer. When IBM sales were $50 billion, president John Akers said that IBM's goal was to become a $100 billion company by the end of the century. Meanwhile, Apple's long-term goal has been to put computer power into the hands of every person. Apple's mission is much more motivating than IBM's.

Missions are best when guided by a *vision,* an almost "impossible dream." Sony's president, Akio Morita, wanted everyone to have access to "personal portable sound," and his company created the Walkman. Fred Smith wanted to deliver mail anywhere in the United States before 10:30 A.M. the next day, and he created Federal Express. Thomas Monaghan wanted to deliver hot pizza to any home within 30 minutes, and he created Domino's Pizza.

The company's mission statement should provide a vision and direction for the company for the next ten to twenty years. Companies do not revise their missions every few years in response to each new turn in the environment. Still, a company must redefine its mission if that mission has lost credibility or no longer defines an optimal course for the company.[3]

Setting Company Objectives and Goals

The company's mission needs to be turned into detailed supporting objectives for each level of management. Each manager should have objectives and be responsible for reaching them. For example, International Minerals and Chemical Corporation is in many businesses, including the fertilizer business. The fertilizer division does not say that its mission is to produce fertilizer. Instead, it says that its mission is to "increase agricultural productivity." This mission leads to a hierarchy of objectives, including business objectives and marketing objectives. The mission of increasing agricultural productivity leads to the company's business objective of researching new fertilizers that promise higher yields. But research is expensive and requires improved profits to plow back into research programs. So improving profits becomes another major business objective. Profits can be improved by increasing sales or reducing costs. Sales can be increased by improving the company's share of the U.S. market, by entering new foreign markets, or both. These goals then become the company's current marketing objectives.

Marketing strategies must be developed to support these marketing objectives. To increase its U.S. market share, the company may increase its product's availability and promotion. To enter new foreign markets, the company may cut prices and target large farms abroad. These are its broad marketing strategies. Each broad marketing strategy must then be defined in greater detail. For example, increasing the product's promotion may require more salespeople and more advertising; if so, both requirements will have to be spelled out. In this way, the firm's mission is translated into a set of objectives for the current period. The objectives should be as specific as possible. The objective to "increase our market share" is not as useful as the objective to "increase our market share to 15 percent by the end of the second year."

Designing the Business Portfolio

Guided by the company's mission statement and objectives, management now must plan its **business portfolio**—the collection of businesses and products that make up the company. The best business portfolio is the one that best fits the company's strengths and weaknesses to opportunities in the environment. The company must (1) analyze its *current* business portfolio and decide which businesses should receive more, less, or no investment, and (2) develop growth strategies for adding *new* products or businesses to the portfolio.

Analyzing the Current Business Portfolio

The major tool in strategic planning is business **portfolio analysis,** whereby management evaluates the businesses making up the company. The company will want to put strong resources into its more profitable businesses and phase down or drop its weaker ones. For example, in recent years, Dial Corp has strengthened its portfolio by selling off its less attractive businesses: bus line (Greyhound), knitting supplies, meatpacking, and computer leasing businesses. At the same time, it invested more heavily in its consumer products (Dial soap, Armour Star meats, Purex laundry products, and others) and services (Premier Cruise Lines, Dobbs airport services).

Management's first step is to identify the key businesses making up the company. These can be called the strategic business units. A **strategic business unit (SBU)** is a unit of the company that has a separate mission and objectives and that can be planned independently from other company businesses. An SBU can be a company division, a product line within a division, or sometimes a single product or brand.

The next step in business portfolio analysis calls for management to assess the attractiveness of its various SBUs and decide how much support each deserves. In some companies, this is done informally. Management looks at the company's collection of businesses or products and uses judgment to decide how much each SBU should contribute and receive. Other companies use formal portfolio-planning methods.

The purpose of strategic planning is to find ways in which the company can best use its strengths to take advantage of attractive opportunities in the environment. So most standard portfolio-analysis methods evaluate SBUs on two important dimensions—the attractiveness of the SBU's market or industry and the strength of the SBU's position in that market or industry. The best known portfolio-planning methods were developed by the Boston Consulting Group, a leading management consulting firm, and by General Electric.

The Boston Consulting Group Approach. Using the Boston Consulting Group (BCG) approach, a company classifies all its SBUs according to the **growth-share matrix** shown in Figure 2-2. On the vertical axis, *market growth rate* provides a measure of market attractiveness. On the horizontal axis, *relative market share* serves as a measure of company strength in the market. By dividing the growth-share matrix as indicated, four types of SBUs can be distinguished;

Stars. Stars are high-growth, high-share businesses or products. They often need heavy investment to finance their rapid growth. Eventually their growth will slow down, and they will turn into cash cows.

Cash cows. Cash cows are low-growth, high-share businesses or products. These established and successful SBUs need less investment to hold their market share. Thus, they produce a lot of cash that the company uses to pay its bills and to support other SBUs that need investment.

Question marks. Question marks are low-share business units in high-growth markets. They require a lot of cash to hold their share, let alone increase it. Management has to think hard about which question marks it should try to build into stars and which should be phased out.

Dogs. Dogs are low-growth, low-share businesses and products. They may generate enough cash to maintain themselves, but do not promise to be large sources of cash.

The ten circles in the growth-share matrix in Figure 2-2 represent a company's ten current SBUs. The company has two stars, two cash cows, three question marks, and three dogs. The areas of the circles are proportional to the SBU's dollar sales. This company is in fair shape, although not in good shape. It wants to invest in the more promising question marks to make them stars, and to maintain the stars so that they will become cash cows as their markets mature. Fortunately, it has two goodsized cash cows whose income helps finance the company's question marks, stars, and dogs. The company should take some decisive action concerning its dogs and its question marks. The picture would be worse if the company had no stars, or had too many dogs, or had only one weak cash cow.

Once it has classified its SBUs, the company must determine what role each will play in the future. One of four strategies can be pursued for each SBU. The company can invest more in the business unit in order to *build* its share. Or it can invest just enough to *hold* the SBU's share at the current level. It can *harvest* the SBU, milking its short-term cash flow regardless of the long-term effect. Finally, the company can *divest* the SBU by selling it or phasing it out and using the resources elsewhere.

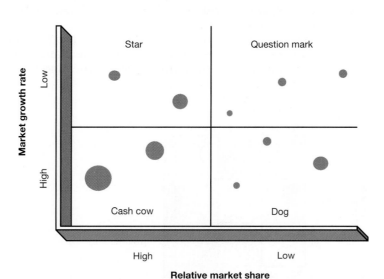

FIGURE 2-2
The BCG growth-share matrix

As time passes, SBUs change their positions in the growth-share matrix. Each SBU has a life cycle. Many SBUs start out as question marks and move into the star category if they succeed. They later become cash cows as market growth falls, then finally die off or turn into dogs toward the end of their life cycle. The company needs to add new products and units continuously so that some of them will become stars and, eventually, cash cows that will help finance other SBUs.

The General Electric Approach. General Electric introduced a comprehensive portfolio planning tool called a **strategic business-planning grid** (see Figure 2-3). Like the BCG approach, it uses a matrix with two dimensions—one representing industry attractiveness (the vertical axis) and one representing company strength in the industry (the horizontal axis). The best businesses are those located in highly attractive industries where the company has high business strength.

The GE approach considers many factors besides market growth rate as part of industry attractiveness. It uses an industry attractiveness index made up of market size, market growth rate, industry profit margin, amount of competition, seasonality and cyclicality of demand, and industry cost structure. Each of these factors is rated and combined in an index of industry attractiveness. For our purposes, an industry's attractiveness will be described as high, medium, or low. As an example, Kraft has identified numerous highly attractive industries—natural foods, specialty frozen foods, physical fitness products, and others. It has withdrawn from less attractive industries such as bulk oils and cardboard packaging.

For *business strength,* the GE approach again uses an index rather than a simple measure of relative market share. The business strength index includes factors such as the company's relative market share, price competitiveness, product quality, customer and market knowledge, sales effectiveness, and geographic advantages. These factors are rated and combined in an index of business strength, which can be described as strong, average, or weak. Thus, Kraft has substantial business strength in food and related industries, but is relatively weak in the home appliances industry.

The grid is divided into three zones. The green cells at the upper left include the strong SBUs in which the company should invest and grow. The yellow diagonal cells contain SBUs that are medium in overall attractiveness. The company should maintain its level of investment in these SBUs. The three magenta cells at the lower right indicate SBUs that are low in overall attractiveness. The company should give serious thought to harvesting or divesting these SBUs.

The circles represent four company SBUs; the areas of the circles are proportional to the relative sizes of the industries in which these SBUs compete. The pie slices within the circles represent each SBU's market share. Thus, circle A represents a company SBU with a 75 percent market share in a good-sized, highly attractive industry in which the company has strong business strength. Circle B represents an SBU that has a 50 percent market share, but the industry is not very attractive. Circles C and D represent two other company SBUs in industries where the company has small market shares and not much business strength. Altogether, the company should build A, maintain B, and make some hard decisions on what to do with C and D.

Management also would plot the projected positions of the SBUs with and without changes in strategies. By comparing current and projected business grids, management can identify the major strategic issues and opportunities it faces.

FIGURE 2-3
General Electric's strategic business-planning grid

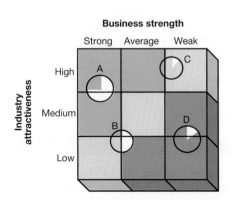

Problems with Matrix Approaches. The BCG, GE, and other formal methods revolutionized strategic planning. However, such approaches have limitations. They can be difficult, time-consuming, and costly to implement. Management may find it difficult to define SBUs and measure market share and growth. In addition, these approaches focus on classifying *current* businesses but provide little advice for *future* planning. Management must still rely on its own judgment to set the business objectives for each SBU, to determine what resources each will be given, and to figure out which new businesses should be added.

Formal planning approaches also can lead the company to place too much emphasis on market-share growth or growth through entry into attractive new markets. Using these approaches, many companies plunged into unrelated and new high-growth businesses that they did not know how to manage—with very bad results. At the same time, these companies often were too quick to abandon, sell, or milk to death their healthy mature businesses. As a result, many companies that diversified too broadly in the past now are narrowing their focus and getting back to the basics of serving one or a few industries that they know best (see Marketing Highlight 2-1).

Despite these and other problems, and although many companies have dropped formal matrix methods in favor of more customized approaches that are better suited to their situations, most companies remain firmly committed to strategic planning. Roughly 75 percent of the *Fortune* 500 companies practice some form of portfolio planning.[4]

Such analysis is no cure-all for finding the best strategy. But it can help management to understand the company's overall situation, to see how each business or product contributes, to assign resources to its businesses, and to orient the company for future success. When used properly, strategic planning is just one important aspect of overall strategic management, a way of thinking about how to manage a business.[5]

Developing Growth Strategies

Beyond evaluating current businesses, designing the business portfolio involves finding businesses and products the company should consider in the future. One useful device for identifying growth opportunities is the **product/market expansion grid**,[6] shown in Figure 2-4. We apply it here to Levi Strauss & Co.

Market Penetration. First, Levi Strauss management might consider whether the company's major brands can achieve deeper **market penetration**—making more sales to present customers without changing products in any way. For example, to increase its jeans sales, Levi might cut prices, increase advertising, get its products into more stores, or obtain better store displays and point-of-purchase merchandising from its retailers. Basically, Levi management would like to increase usage by current customers and attract customers of other clothing brands to Levis.

Market Development. Second, Levi Strauss management might consider possibilities for **market development**—identifying and developing new markets for its current products. For instance, managers could review new *demographic markets*—children, senior consumers, women, ethnic groups—to see if any new groups could be encouraged to buy Levi products for the first time or to buy more of them. For example, Levi recently launched new advertising campaigns to boost its jeans sales in female and Hispanic markets. Managers also could review new *geographical markets*. During the past few years, Levi has substantially increased its marketing efforts and sales to Western Europe, Asia, and Latin America. It now is targeting newly opened markets in Eastern Europe and the former Soviet republics.

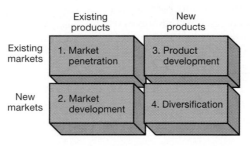

FIGURE 2-4
Market opportunity identification through the product/market expansion grid

AMERICAN BUSINESS GETS BACK TO THE BASICS

During the 1970s and early 1980s, strategic planners in many American companies got expansion fever. It seemed that everyone wanted to get bigger and grow faster by broadening their business portfolios. Companies milked their stodgy but profitable core businesses to get the cash needed to acquire glamorous, faster-growing businesses in more attractive industries. It didn't seem to matter that many of the acquired businesses fit poorly with old ones or that they operated in markets unfamiliar to company management.

Thus, many firms exploded into huge conglomerates, sometimes containing hundreds of unrelated products and businesses in a dozen diverse industries. Managing these "smorgasbord" portfolios often proved difficult. The conglomerate managers soon learned that it was tough to run businesses in industries they knew little about. Many newly acquired businesses bogged down under added layers of corporate management and increased administrative costs. Meanwhile, the profitable core businesses that had financed the acquisitions withered from lack of investment and management attention.

By the mid-1980s, as attempt after attempt at scatter-gun diversification foundered, acquisition fever gave way to a new philosophy—getting back to the basics. The new trend had many names—"narrowing the focus," "sticking to your knitting," "the contraction craze," "the urge to purge." They all mean narrowing the company's market focus and returning to the idea of serving one or a few core industries that the firm knows best. The company sheds businesses that don't fit its narrowed focus and rebuilds by concentrating resources on other businesses that do. The result is a smaller, but more focused company; a more muscular firm serving fewer markets, but serving them much better.

Since the mid-1980s, companies in all industries have worked at getting back in focus and shedding unrelated operations. Some companies have taken drastic steps. For example, during the 1970s, huge Gulf & Western acquired businesses in dozens of diverse industries ranging from auto parts and industrial equipment to apparel and furniture, from cement and cigars to racetracks and video games. But in 1983 and 1984, in order to regain focus and direction, the company purged itself of over 50 business units that made up nearly half of its $8 billion in sales. In 1989, the company changed its name to Paramount Communications, to better reflect its narrower focus on entertainment and communications. It now concentrates its energies and resources on a leaner, tighter portfolio of entertainment and publishing units including Paramount Pictures, Simon & Schuster/Prentice Hall publishers, USA Cable Network, Pocket Books, Cinamerica Theatres, and other related companies.

Several food companies also made strong moves back to the bread-and-butter basics. Quaker Oats sold its specialty retailing businesses—Jos. A. Bank (clothing), Brookstone (tools), and Eyelab (optical)—and probably will sell its profitable Fisher-Price toy operation. It used the proceeds to strengthen current food brands and to acquire the Golden Grain Macaroni Company (Rice-a-Roni and Noodle-Roni) and Gaines Foods (pet foods), whose products strongly complement Quaker's. General Mills ended 20 years of diversification by lopping off most of its nonfood businesses and moving back to the kitchen. It sold companies such as Izod (fashions), Monet (jewelry), Parker Brothers (games), Kenner (toys), and Eddie Bauer and Talbots (specialty retailers), while increasing investment in its basic consumer food brands (Wheaties and other cereals, Betty Crocker cake mixes, Gorton's seafoods, Gold Medal flour) and restaurants (Red Lobster, Darryl's).

Although the 1990s have seen a new wave of acquisitions and megamergers, the new expansion fever differs notably from that of the last decade. Today, fewer companies are seeking growth through broad diversification into attractive but unrelated new businesses. Instead, most are acquiring or merging with related companies, often competitors, in an attempt to build market power within their core businesses. Thus, Philip Morris acquired General Foods and Kraft to become the nation's number one food company, and Delta Airlines acquired Pan Am to strengthen its position in the airline industry.

These and other companies have concluded that fast-growing businesses in attractive industries are not good investments if they spread the company's resources too thin or if the company's managers cannot run them properly. They have learned that a company without market focus—one that tries to serve too many diverse markets—might end up serving few markets well.

Sources: See Thomas Moore, "Old-Line Industry Shapes Up," Fortune, April 27, 1987, pp. 23–32; Walter Kiechel III, "Corporate Strategy for the 1990s," Fortune, February 29, 1988, pp. 34–42; "G&W Plans to Expand in Entertainment and Publishing," press release, Paramount Communications, April 9, 1990; and Brian Bremner, "The Age of Consolidation," Business Week, October 14, 1991, pp. 86–94.

Market penetration: Arm & Hammer increases market penetration by suggesting new uses.

Product Development. Third, management could consider **product development**—offering modified or new products to current markets. Current Levi products could be offered in new styles, sizes, and colors. Or Levi could offer new lines and launch new brands of casual clothing to appeal to different users or to obtain more business from current customers. This occurred when Levi introduced its Dockers line, which now accounts for almost $600 million in annual sales.

Diversification. Fourth, Levi Strauss might consider **diversification.** It could start up or buy businesses outside of its current products and markets. For example, the company could move into industries such as men's fashions, recreational and exercise apparel, or other related businesses. Some companies try to identify the most attractive emerging industries. They feel that half the secret of success is to enter attractive industries instead of trying to be efficient in unattractive ones. However, a company that diversifies too broadly into unfamiliar products or industries can lose its market focus. For example, as discussed in the chapter-opening example, prior to 1984 Levi diversified hastily into a jumbled array of businesses, including skiwear, men's suits and hats, and other specialty apparel. In 1985, however, new management sold these unrelated businesses, refocused the company on its core business of denim jeans, and designed a solid growth strategy featuring closely related new products and bolder efforts to develop international markets. These actions resulted in a dramatic turnaround in the company's sales and profits.

Planning Functional Strategies

The company's strategic plan establishes what kinds of businesses the company will be in and its objectives for each. Then, within each business unit more detailed planning must take place. The major functional departments in each unit—marketing, finance, accounting, purchasing, manufacturing, human resources, and others—must work together to accomplish strategic objectives.

Each functional department deals with different publics to obtain inputs the business needs—inputs like cash, labor, raw materials, research ideas, and manufacturing processes. For example, marketing brings in revenues by negotiating exchanges with consumers. Finance arranges exchanges with lenders and stockholders to obtain cash. Thus, the marketing and finance departments must work together to obtain needed funds. Similarly, the human resources department supplies labor, and the purchasing department obtains materials needed for operations and manufacturing.

Marketing's Role in Strategic Planning

There is much overlap between overall company strategy and marketing strategy. Marketing looks at consumer needs and the company's ability to satisfy them; these same factors guide the company mission and objectives. Most company strategy planning deals with marketing variables—market share, market development, growth—and it is sometimes hard to separate strategic planning from marketing planning. In fact, some companies refer to their strategic planning as "strategic marketing planning."

Marketing plays a key role in the company's strategic planning in several ways. First, marketing provides a guiding *philosophy*—company strategy should revolve around serving the needs of important consumer groups. Second, marketing provides *inputs* to strategic planners by helping to identify attractive market opportunities and by assessing the firm's potential to take advantage of them. Finally, within individual business units, marketing designs *strategies* for reaching the unit's objectives.

Within each business unit, marketing management must determine the best way to help achieve strategic objectives. Some marketing managers will find that their objective is not necessarily to build sales. Rather, it may be to hold existing sales with a smaller marketing budget, or it actually may be to reduce demand. Thus, marketing management must manage demand to the level decided upon by the strategic planning prepared at headquarters. Marketing helps to assess each business unit's potential, but once the unit's objective is set, marketing's task is to carry it out profitably.

Marketing and the Other Business Functions

Confusion persists about marketing's importance in the firm. In some firms, it is just another function—all functions count in the company and none takes leadership. At the other extreme, some marketers claim that marketing is the *major* function of the firm. They quote Drucker's statement: "The aim of the business is to create customers." They say it is marketing's job to define the company's mission, products, and markets and to direct the other functions in the task of serving customers.

More enlightened marketers prefer to put the *customer* at the center of the company. These marketers argue that the firm cannot succeed without customers, so the crucial task is to attract and hold them. Customers are attracted by promises and held through satisfaction, and marketing defines the promise and ensures its delivery. However, because actual consumer satisfaction is affected by the performance of other departments, *all* functions should work together to sense, serve, and satisfy customer needs. Marketing plays an integrative role to help ensure that all departments work together toward consumer satisfaction.

Conflict Between Departments

Each business function has a different view of which publics and activities are most important. Manufacturing focuses on suppliers and production; finance is concerned with stockholders and sound investment; marketing emphasizes consumers and products, pricing, promotion, and distribution. Ideally, all the different functions should blend to achieve consumer satisfaction. But in practice, departmental relations are full of conflicts and misunderstandings. The marketing department takes the consumer's point of view. But when marketing tries to develop customer satisfaction, it often causes other departments to do a poorer job *in their terms*. Marketing department actions can increase purchasing costs, disrupt production schedules, increase inventories, and create budget headaches. Thus, the other departments may resist bending their efforts to the will of the marketing department.

Yet marketers must get all departments to "think consumer" and to put the consumer at the center of company activity. Customer satisfaction requires a total company effort to deliver superior value to target customers.

> Creating value for buyers is much more than a "marketing function;" rather, [it's] analogous to a symphony orchestra in which the contribution of each subgroup is tailored and integrated by a conductor—with a synergistic effect. A seller must draw upon and integrate effectively . . . its entire human and other capital resources. . . .

[Creating superior value for buyers] is the proper focus of the entire business and not merely of a single department in it.[7]

The Du Pont "Adopt a Customer" program recognizes the importance of having people in all of its functions who are "close to the customer." Through this program, Du Pont encourages people on the manufacturing line at many of its plants to develop and maintain a direct relationship with the customer. The manufacturing representatives meet with the assigned customer once a year and interact regularly by phone to learn about the company's needs and problems. Then, they represent the customer on the factory floor. If quality or delivery problems arise, the manufacturing representative is more likely to see the adopted customer's point of view and to make decisions that will keep this customer happy.[8]

Thus, marketing management can best gain support for its goal of consumer satisfaction by working to understand the company's other departments. Marketing managers must work closely with managers of other functions to develop a system of functional plans under which the different departments can work together to accomplish the company's overall strategic objectives.[9]

THE MARKETING PROCESS

The strategic plan defines the company's overall mission and objectives. Within each business unit, marketing plays a role in helping to accomplish the overall strategic objectives. Marketing's role and activities in the organization are shown in Figure 2-5, which summarizes the entire **marketing process** and the forces influencing company marketing strategy.

Target consumers stand in the center. The company identifies the total market, divides it into smaller segments, selects the most promising segments, and focuses on serving and satisfying these segments. It designs a marketing mix made up of factors under its control—product, price, place, and promotion. To find the best marketing mix and put it into action, the company engages in marketing analysis, planning, implementation, and control. Through these activities, the company watches and adapts to the marketing environment. We will now look briefly at each factor in the marketing process. In later chapters, we will discuss each factor in more depth.

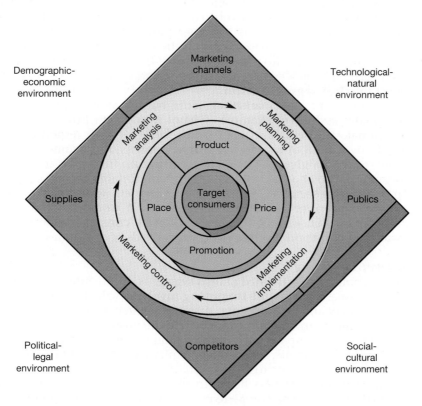

FIGURE 2-5
Factors influencing company marketing strategy

Target Consumers

To succeed in today's competitive marketplace, companies must be customer centered, winning customers from competitors by delivering greater value. But before it can satisfy consumers, a company must first understand their needs and wants. Thus, sound marketing requires a careful analysis of consumers. Companies know that they cannot satisfy all consumers in a given market—at least not all consumers in the same way. There are too many different kinds of consumers with too many different kinds of needs. And some companies are in a better position to serve certain segments of the market. Thus, each company must divide up the total market, choose the best segments, and design strategies for profitably serving chosen segments better than its competitors do. This process involves four steps: *demand measurement and forecasting, market segmentation, market targeting,* and *market positioning.*

Demand Measurement and Forecasting

Suppose a company is looking at possible markets for a potential new product. First, the company needs to make a careful estimate of the current and future size of the market and its various segments. To estimate current market size, the company would identify all competing products, estimate the current sales of these products, and determine whether the market is large enough to profitably support another product.

Equally important is future market growth. Companies want to enter markets that show strong growth prospects. Growth potential may depend on the growth rate of certain age, income, and nationality groups that use the product. Growth also may be related to larger developments in the environment, such as economic conditions, the crime rate, and lifestyle changes. For example, the future market for quality children's toys and clothing is strongly related to current birth rates, trends in consumer affluence, and projected family lifestyles. Forecasting the effect of these environmental forces is difficult, but it must be done in order to make decisions about the market. The company's marketing information specialists probably will use complex techniques to measure and forecast demand.

Market Segmentation

Suppose the demand forecast looks good. The company must now decide how to enter the market. The market consists of many types of customers, products, and needs, and the marketer has to determine which segments offer the best opportunity for achieving company objectives. Consumers can be grouped in various ways based on geographic factors (countries, regions, cities); demographic factors (sex, age, income, education); psychographic factors (social classes, lifestyles); and behavioral factors (purchase occasions, benefits sought, usage rates). The process of dividing a market into distinct groups of buyers with different needs, characteristics, or behavior who might require separate products or marketing mixes is called **market segmentation.**

Every market has market segments, but not all ways of segmenting a market are equally useful. For example, Tylenol would gain little by distinguishing between male and female users of pain relievers if both respond the same way to marketing stimuli. A **market segment** consists of consumers who respond in a similar way to a given set of marketing stimuli. In the car market, for example, consumers who choose the biggest, most comfortable car regardless of price make up one market segment. Another market segment would be customers who care mainly about price and operating economy. It would be difficult to make one model of car that was the first choice of every consumer. Companies are wise to focus their efforts on meeting the distinct needs of one or more market segments.

Market Targeting

After a company has defined market segments, it can enter one or many segments of a given market. **Market targeting** involves evaluating each market segment's attractiveness and selecting one or more segments to enter. A company should target segments in which it can generate the greatest customer value and sustain it over time. A company with limited resources might decide to serve only one or a few special segments. This strategy limits sales, but can be very profitable. Or a company might choose to serve several related segments—perhaps those with different kinds of customers but with the same basic wants. Or a large company might decide to offer a complete range of products to serve all market segments.

Most companies enter a new market by serving a single segment, and if this proves successful, they add segments. Large companies eventually seek full market coverage. They want to be the "General Motors" of their industry. GM says that it makes a car for every "person, purse, and personality." The leading company normally has different products designed to meet the special needs of each segment.

Market Positioning

After a company has decided which market segments to enter, it must decide what "positions" it wants to occupy in those segments. A product's *position* is the place the product occupies relative to competitors in consumers' minds. If a product is perceived to be exactly like another product on the market, consumers would have no reason to buy it.

Market positioning is arranging for a product to occupy a clear, distinctive, and desirable place, in the minds of target consumers, relative to competing products. Thus, marketers plan positions that distinguish their products from competing brands and give them the greatest strategic advantage in their target markets. For example, Chrysler compares its cars to those of various competitors and concludes "Advantage: Chrysler." Pontiac says "we build excitement," at Ford "quality is job one," and Mazda "just feels right." Jaguar is positioned as "a blending of art and machine," whereas Saab is "the most intelligent car ever built." Mercedes is "engineered like no other car in the world," the Lincoln Town Car is "what a luxury car should be," and the luxurious Bentley is "the closest a car can come to having wings." Such deceptively simple statements form the backbone of a product's marketing strategy.

In positioning its product, the company first identifies possible competitive advantages upon which to build the position. To gain competitive advantage, the company must offer greater value to chosen target segments, either by charging lower prices than competitors do or by offering more benefits to justify higher prices. But if the company positions the product as *offering* greater value, it must then *deliver* that greater value. Thus, effective positioning begins with actually *differentiating* the company's marketing offer so that it gives consumers more value than they are offered by the competition.

Market positioning: Red Roof Inns positions on value—It doesn't "add frills that only add to your bill." In contrast, Four Seasons Hotels positions on luxury. For those who can afford it, Four Seasons offers endless amenities—such as a seamstress, a valet, and a "tireless individual who collects your shoes each night and returns them at dawn, polished to perfection."

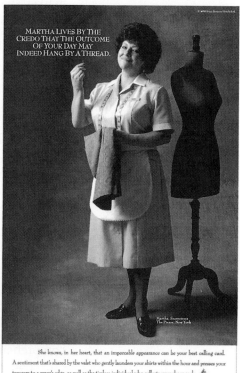

The company can position a product on only one major differentiating factor or on several. However, positioning on too many factors can result in consumer confusion or disbelief. Once the company has chosen a desired position, it must take strong steps to deliver and communicate that position to target consumers. The company's entire marketing program should support the chosen positioning strategy.

Marketing Strategies for Competitive Advantage

To be successful, the company must do a better job than its competitors of satisfying target consumers. Thus, marketing strategies must be geared to the needs of consumers and also to the strategies of competitors. Based on its size and industry position, the company must decide how it will position itself relative to competitors in order to gain the strongest possible competitive advantage.

Designing competitive marketing strategies begins with thorough competitor analysis. The company constantly compares the value and customer satisfaction delivered by its products, prices, channels, and promotion with that of its close competitors. In this way it can discern areas of potential advantage and disadvantage. The company must formally or informally monitor the competitive environment to answer these and other important questions: Who are our competitors? What are their objectives and strategies? What are their strengths and weaknesses? And how will they react to different competitive strategies we might use?

Which competitive marketing strategy a company adopts depends on its industry position. A firm that dominates a market can adopt one or more of several *market-leader* strategies. Well-known leaders include Coca-Cola (soft drinks), McDonald's (fast food), Caterpillar (large construction equipment), Kodak (photographic film), Wal-Mart (retailing), and Boeing (aircraft). *Market challengers* are runner-up companies that aggressively attack competitors to get more market share. For example, Pepsi challenges Coke and Apple Computer challenges IBM. The challenger might attack the market leader, other firms its own size, or smaller local and regional competitors. Some runner-up firms will choose to follow rather than challenge the market leader. Firms using *market-follower* strategies seek stable market shares and profits by following competitor's product offers, prices, and marketing programs.[10] Smaller firms in a market, or even larger firms that lack established positions, often adopt *market-nicher* strategies. They specialize in serving market niches that major competitors overlook or ignore (see Marketing Highlight 2-2). "Nichers" avoid direct confrontations with the majors by specializing along market, customer, product, or marketing-mix lines. Through smart niching, low-share firms in an industry can be as profitable as their larger competitors. We will discuss competitive marketing strategies more fully in Chapter 20.

Developing the Marketing Mix

Once the company has decided on its overall competitive marketing strategy, it is ready to begin planning the details of the marketing mix. The marketing mix is one of the major concepts in modern marketing. We define **marketing mix** as the set of controllable, tactical marketing tools that the firm blends to produce the response it wants in the target market. The marketing mix consists of everything the firm can do to influence the demand for its product. The many possibilities can be collected into four groups of variables known as the "four Ps": *product, price, place,* and *promotion.*[11] Figure 2-6 shows the particular marketing tools under each P.

Product means the "goods-and-service" combination the company offers to the target market. Thus, a Ford Taurus "product" consists of nuts and bolts, spark plugs, pistons, headlights, and thousands of other parts. Ford offers several Taurus styles and dozens of optional features. The car comes fully serviced and with a comprehensive warranty that is as much a part of the product as the tailpipe.

Price is the amount of money customers have to pay to obtain the product. Ford calculates suggested retail prices that its dealers might charge for each Taurus. But Ford dealers rarely charge the full sticker price. Instead, they negotiate the price with each customer, offering discounts, trade-in allowances, and credit terms to adjust for the current competitive situation and to bring the price into line with the buyer's perception of the car's value.

VERNOR'S THRIVES IN THE SHADOWS OF THE GIANTS

You've probably never heard of *Vernor's Ginger Ale*. And if you tried it, you might not even think it tastes like ginger ale. Vernor's is "aged in oak," the company boasts, and "deliciously different." The caramel-colored soft drink is sweeter and smoother than other ginger ales you've tasted. But to many people in Detroit who grew up with Vernor's, there's nothing quite like it. They drink it cold and hot; morning, noon, and night; summer and winter; from the bottle and at the soda fountain counter. They like the way the bubbles tickle their noses. And they'll say you haven't lived until you've tasted a Vernor's ice-cream float. To many, Vernor's even has some minor medicinal qualities—they use warm Vernor's to settle a child's upset stomach or to soothe a sore throat. To most Detroit adults, the familiar green and yellow packaging brings back many pleasant childhood memories.

The soft-drink industry is headed by two giants—Coca-Cola leads with a 41 percent market share and Pepsi challenges strongly with about 31 percent. Coke and Pepsi are the main combatants in the "soft-drink wars." They wage constant and pitched battles for retail shelf space. Their weapons include a steady stream of new products, heavy price discounts, an army of distributor salespeople, and huge advertising and promotion budgets.

A few "second-tier" brands—such brands as Dr Pepper, 7-Up, and Royal Crown—capture a combined 20 percent or so of the market. They challenge Coke and Pepsi in the smaller cola and noncola segments. When Coke and Pepsi battle for shelf space, these second-tier brands often get squeezed. Coke and Pepsi set the ground rules, and if the smaller brands don't follow along, they risk being pushed out or gobbled up.

At the same time, a group of specialty producers who concentrate on small but loyal market segments fights for what's left of the market. Although large in number, each of these small firms holds a tiny market share—usually less than one percent. Vernor's falls into this "all others" group, along with A&W root beer, Shasta sodas, Squirt, Faygo, Soho Natural Soda, Yoo-Hoo, Dr Brown's Cream Soda, A.J. Canfield's Diet Chocolate Fudge Soda, and a dozen others. Whereas Dr Pepper and 7-Up merely get squeezed in the soft-drink wars, these small fry risk being crushed.

When you compare Vernor's to Coca-Cola, for example, you wonder how Vernor's survives. Coca-Cola spends more than $375 million a year advertising its soft drinks; Vernor's spends less than $1 million. Coke offers a long list of brands and brand versions—Coke Classic, Coke II, Cherry Coke, Diet Coke, Caffeine-Free Coke, Diet Cherry Coke, Caffeine-Free Diet Coke, Sprite, Tab, Mellow Yellow, Minute Maid soda, and others; Vernor's sells only two versions—original and diet. Coke's large distributor salesforce sways retailers with huge dis-

counts and promotion allowances; Vernor's has only a small marketing budget and carries little clout with retailers. When you are lucky enough to find Vernor's at your local supermarket, it's usually tucked away on the bottom shelf with other specialty beverages. Even in Detroit, the company's stronghold, stores usually give Vernor's only a few shelf facings, compared with 50 or 100 facings for the many Coca-Cola brands.

Yet Vernor's does more than survive—it thrives! How? Instead of going head-to-head with the bigger companies in the major soft-drink segments, Vernor's "niches" in the market. It concentrates on serving the special needs of loyal Vernor's drinkers. Vernor's knows that it could never seriously challenge Coca-Cola for a large share of the soft-drink market. But it also knows that Coca-Cola could never create another Vernor's ginger ale—at least not in the minds of Vernor's drinkers. As long as Vernor's keeps these special customers happy, it can capture a small but profitable share of the market. And "small" in this market is nothing to sneeze at—a one-percent market share equals $440 million in retail sales! Thus, through smart market niching, Vernor's prospers in the shadows of the soft-drink giants.

Sources: See Betsy Bauer, "Giants Loom Larger Over Pint-Sized Soft-Drink Firms," USA Today, May 27, 1986, p. 5B; Ford S. Worthy, "Pop Goes Their Profit," Fortune, February 15, 1988, pp. 68–83; and Walecia Konrad, "The Cola Kings are Feeling a Bit Jumpy," Business Week, July 13, 1992, pp. 112–13.

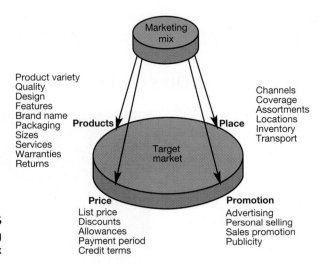

FIGURE 2-6
The four *P*s of the marketing mix

Place includes company activities that make the product available to target consumers. Ford maintains a large body of independently owned dealerships that sell the company's many different models. Ford selects its dealers carefully and supports them strongly. The dealers keep an inventory of Ford automobiles, demonstrate them to potential buyers, negotiate prices, close sales, and service the cars after the sale.

Promotion means activities that communicate the merits of the product and persuade target customers to buy it. Ford spends more than $600 million each year on advertising to tell consumers about the company and its products. Dealership salespeople assist potential buyers and persuade them that Ford is the best car for them. Ford and its dealers offer special promotions—sales, cash rebates, low financing rates—as added purchase incentives.

An effective marketing program blends all of the marketing mix elements into a coordinated program designed to achieve the company's marketing objectives. The marketing mix constitutes the company's tactical tool kit for establishing strong positioning in target markets. However, note that the four *P*s represent the sellers' view of the marketing tools available for influencing buyers. From a consumer viewpoint, each marketing tool is designed to deliver a customer benefit. One marketing expert[12] suggests that companies should view the four *P*s in terms of the customer's four *C*s:

Four *P*s	Four *C*s
Product	Customer needs and wants
Price	Cost to the customer
Place	Convenience
Promotion	Communication

Thus, winning companies will be those that can meet customer needs economically and conveniently and with effective communication.

Managing the Marketing Effort

The company wants to design and put into action the marketing mix that will best achieve its objectives in its target markets. This involves four marketing management functions—*analysis, planning, implementation,* and *control.* Figure 2-7 shows the relationship between these marketing activities. The company first develops overall strategic plans. These companywide strategic plans are then translated into marketing and other plans for each division, product, and brand.

Through implementation, the company turns the strategic and marketing plans into actions that will achieve the company's strategic objectives. Marketing plans are implemented by people in the marketing organization who work with others both inside and outside the company. Control consists of measuring and evaluating the results of marketing plans and activities and taking corrective ac-

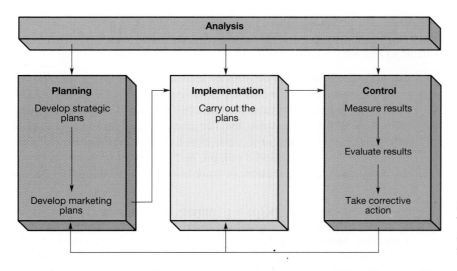

tion to make sure objectives are being reached. Marketing analysis provides information and evaluations needed for all of the other marketing activities.

Marketing Analysis

Managing the marketing function begins with a complete analysis of the company's situation. The company must analyze its markets and marketing environment to find attractive opportunities and to avoid environmental threats. It must analyze company strengths and weaknesses, as well as current and possible marketing actions, to determine which opportunities it can best pursue. Marketing analysis feeds information and other inputs to each of the other marketing management functions. Marketing analysis is discussed more fully in Chapter 4.

Marketing Planning

Through strategic planning, the company decides what it wants to do with each business unit. Marketing planning involves deciding on marketing strategies that will help the company attain its overall strategic objectives. A detailed marketing plan is needed for each business, product, or brand. What does a marketing plan look like? Our discussion focuses on product or brand plans. A product or brand plan should contain the following sections: *executive summary, current marketing situation, threats and opportunities, objectives and issues, marketing strategies, action programs, budgets,* and *controls* (see Table 2-1).

TABLE 2-1
Contents of a Marketing Plan

SECTION	PURPOSE
Executive summary	Presents a brief overview of the proposed plan for quick management review.
Current marketing situation	Presents relevant background data on the market, product, competition, and distribution.
Threats and opportunity analysis	Identifies the main threats and opportunities that might impact the product.
Objectives and issues	Defines the company's objectives for the product in the areas of sales, market share, and profit, and the issues that will affect these objectives.
Marketing strategy	Presents the broad marketing approach that will be used to achieve the plan's objectives.
Action programs	Specifies *what* will be done, *who* will do it, *when* it will be done, and *how much* it will cost.
Budgets	A projected profit and loss statement that forecasts the expected financial outcomes from the plan.
Controls	Indicates how the progress of the plan will be monitored.

Executive Summary. The marketing plan should open with a short summary of the main goals and recommendations to be presented in the plan. Here is a short example:

> The 1994 Marketing Plan outlines an approach to attaining a significant increase in company sales and profits over the preceding year. The sales target is $240 million, a planned 20 percent sales gain. We think this increase is attainable because of the improved economic, competitive, and distribution picture. The target operating margin is $25 million, a 25 percent increase over last year. To achieve these goals, the sales promotion budget will be $4.8 million, or 2 percent of projected sales. The advertising budget will be $7.2 million, or 3 percent of projected sales. . . . [More details follow.]

The **executive summary** helps top management to find the plan's major points quickly. A table of contents should follow the executive summary.

Current Marketing Situation. The first major section of the plan describes the target market and the company's position in it. In the **current marketing situation** section, the planner provides information about the market, product performance, competition, and distribution. It includes a *market description* that defines the market, including major market segments. The planner shows market size, in total and by segment, for several past years, then reviews customer needs and factors in the marketing environment that may affect customer purchasing. Next, the *product review* shows sales, prices, and gross margins of the major products in the product line. A section on *competition* identifies major competitors and by each of their strategies for product quality, pricing, distribution, and promotion. It also shows the market shares held by the company and each competitor. Finally, a section on *distribution* describes recent sales trends and developments in the major distribution channels.

Threats and Opportunities. This section requires the manager to look ahead for major threats and opportunities that the product might face. Its purpose is to make the manager anticipate important developments that can have an impact on the firm. Managers should list as many threats and opportunities as they can imagine. Suppose a major pet foods marketer comes up with the following list:

- A large competitor has just announced that it will introduce a new premium pet food line, backed by a huge advertising and sales promotion blitz.

- Industry analysts predict that supermarket chain buyers will face more than 10,000 new grocery product introductions next year. The buyers are expected to accept only 38 percent of these new products and give each one only five months to prove itself.

- Because of improved economic conditions during the past several years, pet ownership is increasing in almost all segments of the U.S. population.

- The company's researchers have found a way to make a new pet food that is low in fat and calories yet highly nutritious and tasty. This product will appeal strongly to many of today's pet food buyers, who are almost as concerned about their pets' health as they are about their own.

- Pet ownership and concern about proper pet care are increasing rapidly in foreign markets, especially in developing nations.

The first two items are *threats*. Not all threats call for the same attention or concern—the manager should assess the likelihood of each threat and the potential damage each could cause. The manager should then focus on the most probable and harmful threats and prepare plans in advance to meet them.

The last three items in the list are marketing opportunities. A *company marketing opportunity* is an attractive arena for marketing action in which the com-

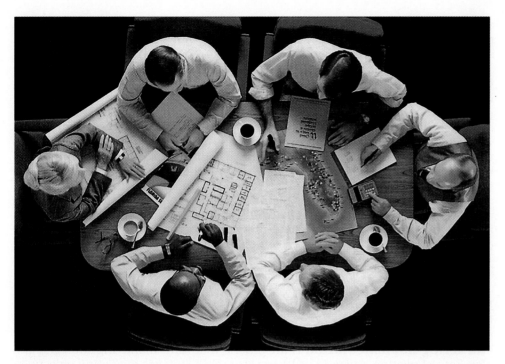

Marketers must continually plan their analysis, implementation, and control activities.

pany could enjoy a competitive advantage. The manager should assess each opportunity according to its potential attractiveness and the company's probability of success. Companies can rarely find ideal opportunities that exactly fit their objectives and resources. The development of opportunities involves risks. When evaluating opportunities, the manager must decide whether the expected returns justify these risks.

Objectives and Issues. Having studied the product's threats and opportunities, the manager can now set objectives and consider issues that will affect them. The objectives should be stated as goals the company would like to attain during the plan's term. For example, the manager might want to achieve a 15 percent market share, a 20 percent pretax profit on sales, and a 25 percent pretax profit on investment. Suppose the current market share is only 10 percent. This poses a key issue: How can market share be increased? The manager should consider the major issues involved in trying to increase market share.

Marketing Strategies. In this section of the marketing plan, the manager outlines the broad marketing strategy or "game plan" for attaining the objectives. **Marketing strategy** is the marketing logic by which the business unit hopes to achieve its marketing objectives. It consists of specific strategies for target markets, positioning, marketing mix, and marketing expenditure level. Marketing strategy should detail the market segments on which the company will focus. These segments differ in their needs and wants, responses to marketing, and profitability. The company would be smart to put its effort and energy into those market segments it can best serve from a competitive point of view. It should develop a marketing strategy for each targeted segment.

The manager should also outline specific strategies for such marketing mix elements as new products, field sales, advertising, sales promotion, prices, and distribution. The manager should explain how each strategy responds to the threats, opportunities, and critical issues spelled out earlier in the plan.

Action Programs. Marketing strategies should be turned into specific action programs that answer the following questions: *What* will be done? *When* will it be done? *Who* is responsible for doing it? And *how much* will it cost? For example, the manager may want to increase sales promotion as a key strategy for winning market share. A sales promotion action plan should be drawn up to outline

Marketing plans and strategies are of little value until they are properly implemented.

special offers and their dates, trade shows entered, new point-of-purchase displays, and other promotions. The action plan shows when activities will be started, reviewed, and completed.

Budgets. Action plans allow the manager to make a supporting **marketing budget** that is essentially a projected profit and loss statement. For revenues, it shows the forecasted number of units that would be sold and the average net price. On the expense side, it shows the cost of production, physical distribution, and marketing. The difference is the projected profit. Higher management will review the budget and either approve or modify it. Once approved, the budget is the basis for materials buying, production scheduling, personnel planning, and marketing operations. Budgeting can be very difficult, and budgeting methods range from simple "rules of thumb" to complex computer models.[13]

Controls. The last section of the plan outlines the controls that will be used to monitor progress. Typically, goals and budgets are spelled out for each month or quarter. This practice allows higher management to review the results each period and to spot businesses or products that are not meeting their goals. The managers of these businesses and products have to explain these problems and the corrective actions they will take.

Marketing Implementation

Planning good strategies is only a start toward successful marketing. A brilliant marketing strategy counts for little if the company fails to implement it properly. **Marketing implementation** is the process that turns marketing strategies and *plans* into marketing *actions* in order to accomplish strategic marketing objectives. Implementation involves day-to-day, month-to-month activities that effectively put the marketing plan to work. Whereas marketing planning addresses the *what* and *why* of marketing activities, implementation addresses the *who, where, when,* and *how.*

Many managers think that "doing things right" (implementation) is as important, or even more important, than "doing the right things" (strategy):

> A surprisingly large number of very successful large companies . . . don't have long-term strategic plans with an obsessive preoccupation on rivalry. They concentrate on operating details and doing things well. Hustle is their style and their strategy. They move fast and they get it right. . . . Countless companies in all industries, young or old, mature or booming, are finally learning the limits of strategy and concentrating on tactics and execution.[14]

Yet implementation is difficult—it is often easier to think up good marketing strategies than it is to carry them out.

People at all levels of the marketing system must work together to implement marketing plans and strategies. At Procter & Gamble, for example, marketing implementation requires day-to-day decisions and actions by thousands of people both inside and outside the organization. Marketing managers make decisions about target segments, branding, packaging, pricing, promoting, and distributing. They work with people elsewhere in the company to get support for their products and programs. They talk with engineering about product design, with manufacturing about production and inventory levels, and with finance about funding and cash flows. They also work with outside people. They meet with advertising agencies to plan ad campaigns and with the media to obtain publicity support. The salesforce urges retailers to advertise the P&G products, provide ample shelf space, and use company displays.

Successful implementation depends on several key elements. First, it requires an *action program* that pulls all of the people and activities together. The action program shows what must be done, who will do it, and how decisions and actions will be coordinated to reach the company's marketing objectives. Second, the company's formal *organization structure* plays an important role in implementing marketing strategy. In their study of successful companies, Peters and Waterman found that these firms tended to have simple, flexible structures that allowed them to adapt quickly to changing conditions.[15] Their structures also tended to be more informal—Hewlett-Packard's MBWA (management by walking around), 3M's "clubs" to create small-group interaction. However, the structures used by these companies may not be right for other types of firms, and many of the study's excellent companies have had to change their structures as their strategies and situations changed. For example, the same informal structure that made Hewlett-Packard so successful caused problems later. The company has since moved toward a more formal structure (see Marketing Highlight 2-3).

Another factor affecting successful implementation is the company's *decision and reward systems*—formal and informal operating procedures that guide planning, budgeting, compensation, and other activities. For example, if a company compensates managers for short-run results, they will have little incentive to work toward long-run objectives. Effective implementation also requires careful *human resources planning*. At all levels, the company must fill its structure and systems with people who have the needed skills, motivation, and personal characteristics. In recent years, more and more companies have recognized that long-run human resources planning can give the company a strong competitive advantage.

Finally, to be successfully implemented, the firm's marketing strategies must fit with its company culture. *Company culture* is a system of values and beliefs shared by people in an organization. It is the company's collective identity and meaning. The culture informally guides the behavior of people at all company levels. Marketing strategies that do not fit the company's style and culture will be difficult to implement. For example, a decision by Procter & Gamble to increase sales by reducing product quality and prices would not work well. It would be resisted by P&G people at all levels who identify strongly with the company's reputation for quality. Because managerial style and culture are so hard to change, companies usually design strategies that fit their current cultures rather than trying to change their styles and cultures to fit new strategies.[16]

Thus, successful marketing implementation depends on how well the company blends the five elements—action programs, organization structure, decision and reward systems, human resources, and company culture—into a cohesive program that supports its strategies.

Marketing Department Organization

The company must design a marketing department that can carry out marketing analysis, planning, implementation, and control. If the company is very small, one person might do all of the marketing work—research, selling, advertising, customer service, and other activities. As the company expands, a marketing department organization emerges to plan and carry out marketing activities. In large companies, this department contains many specialists. Thus, General Mills has product managers, salespeople and sales managers, market researchers, advertising experts, and other specialists.

Modern marketing departments can be arranged in several ways. The most common form of marketing organization is the *functional organization* in which different marketing activities are headed by a functional specialist—a sales manager, advertising manager, marketing research manager, customer service manager, new-product manager. A company that sells across the country or internationally often uses a *geographic organization* in which its sales and marketing people are assigned to specific countries, regions, and districts. Geographic organization allows salespeople to settle into a territory, get to know their customers, and work with a minimum of travel time and cost.

Companies with many, very different products or brands often create a *product management organization*. Using this approach, a product manager develops and implements a complete strategy and marketing program for a specific product or brand. Product management first appeared in the Procter & Gamble Company in 1929. A new company soap, Camay, was not doing well, and a young P&G executive was assigned to give his exclusive attention to developing and promoting this product. He was successful, and the company soon added other product managers.[17] Since then, many firms, especially in the food, soap, toiletries, and chemical industries, have set up product management organizations. Today, the product management system is firmly entrenched. However, recent dramatic changes in the marketing environment have caused many companies to rethink the role of the product manager (see Marketing Highlight 2-4).

For companies that sell one product line to many different types of markets which have different needs and preferences, a *market management organization* might be best. Many companies are organized along market lines. A market management organization is similar to the product management organization. Market

MARKETING HIGHLIGHT 2-3

HEWLETT-PACKARD'S STRUCTURE EVOLVES

In 1939, two engineers, Bill Hewlett and David Packard, started Hewlett-Packard in a Palo Alto garage to build test equipment. At the start, Bill and Dave did everything themselves, from designing and building their equipment to marketing it. As the firm grew out of the garage and began to offer more and different types of test equipment, Hewlett and Packard could no longer make all the necessary operating decisions themselves. They hired functional managers to run various company activities. These managers were relatively autonomous, but they were still closely tied to the owners.

By the mid-1970s, Hewlett-Packard's 42 divisions employed more than 30,000 people. The company's structure evolved to support its heavy emphasis on innovation and autonomy. Each division operated as an autonomous unit and was responsible for its own strategic planning, product development, marketing programs, and implementation.

In 1982, Peters and Waterman, in their book *In Search of Excellence,* cited HP's structure as a major reason for the company's continued excellence. They praised HP's unrestrictive structure and high degree of informal communication (its MBWA style—management by wandering around) that fostered autonomy by decentralizing decision-making responsibility and authority. The approach became known as the "HP Way," a structure that encouraged innovation by abolishing rigid chains of command and putting managers and employees on a first-name basis.

But by the mid-1980s, although still profitable, Hewlett-Packard had begun to encounter problems in the fast-changing microcomputer and minicomputer markets. According to *Business Week:*

> Hewlett-Packard's famed innovative culture and decentralization [had] spawned such enormously successful products as its 3000 minicomputer, the hand

held scientific calculator, and the ThinkJet nonimpact printer. But when a new climate required its fiercely autonomous divisions to cooperate in product development and marketing, HP's passionate devotion to "autonomy and entrepreneurship" that Peters and Waterman advocate became a hindrance.

Thus, Hewlett-Packard moved to change its structure and culture in order to bring them in line with its changing situation. It established a system of committees to foster communication within and across its many and varied divisions and to coordinate product development, marketing, and other activities.

The new structure seemed to work well—for a while. However, the move toward centralization soon got out of hand:

> The committees kept multiplying, like a virus. [Soon] everything was by committee . . . no one could make a decision. . . . By the late 1980s, an unwieldy bureaucracy had bogged down the HP Way. A web of committees, originally designed to foster communication . . . had pushed costs up and slowed down development.

Entering the 1990s, HP had no fewer than 38 inhouse committees that made decisions on everything from technical specifications for new products to the best cities for staging product launches. This suffocating structure dramatically increased HP's decision-making and market-reaction time. For example, in one case, it took almost 100 people over seven weeks just to come up with a name for the company's New Wave Computing software.

In the fast-paced workstation and personal computer markets, HP's sluggish decision making put it at a serious disadvantage against such nimble competitors as Compaq Computer Corporation and Sun Microsystems.

---

managers are responsible for developing long-range and annual plans for the sales and profits in their markets. This system's main advantage is that the company is organized around the needs of specific customer segments.

Large companies that produce many different products flowing into many different geographic and customer markets use some *combination* of the functional, geographic, product, and market organization forms. This assures that each function, product, and market receives its share of management attention. However, it can also add costly layers of management and reduce organizational flexibility. Still, the benefits of organizational specialization usually outweigh the drawbacks.[18]

Marketing Control

Because many surprises occur during the implementation of marketing plans, the marketing department must engage in constant marketing control. **Marketing**

Hewlett-Packard began in this garage in 1939; now it operates around the world from this headquarters complex. Structure and culture changed with growth.

When one of HP's most important projects, a series of high-speed workstations, slipped a year behind schedule as a result of seemingly endless committee meetings, top management finally took action. It removed the project's 200 engineers from the formal management structure so that they could continue work on the project free of the usual committee red tape. The workstation crisis convinced HP management that it must make similar changes throughout the company.

The cure was the company's most drastic reorganization in 10 years. [Top management] wiped out HP's committee structure and flattened the organization. "The results are incredible," says [HP executive Bob] Frankenberg, who now deals with three committees instead of 38. "We are doing more business and getting product out quicker with fewer people."

Thus, in less than a decade, Hewlett-Packard's structure has evolved from the highly decentralized and informal "HP Way" to a highly centralized committee system and back again to a point in between. HP is not likely to find a single best structure that will satisfy all of its future needs. Rather, it must continue adapting its structure to suit the requirements of its ever-changing environment.

Sources: See Donald F. Harvey, *Business Policy and Strategic Management* (Columbus, OH: Charles E. Merrill, 1982), pp. 269–70; and Thomas J. Peters and Robert H. Waterman, *In Search of Excellence: Lessons from America's Best-Run Companies* (New York: Harper & Row, 1982). Excerpts from "Who's Excellent Now?" *Business Week*, November 5, 1984, pp. 76–78; Barbara Buell, Robert D. Hof, and Gary McWilliams, "Hewlett-Packard Rethinks Itself," *Business Week*, April 1, 1991, pp. 76–79; and Robert D. Hof, "Suddenly, Hewlett-Packard Is Doing Everything Right," *Business Week*, March 23, 1992, pp. 88-89.

control is the process of measuring and evaluating the results of marketing strategies and plans and taking corrective action to ensure that marketing objectives are attained. It involves the four steps shown in Figure 2-8. Management first sets specific marketing goals. It then measures its performance in the marketplace

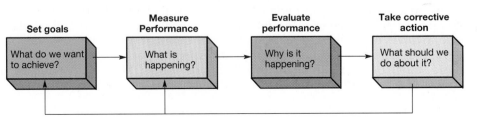

FIGURE 2-8
The control process

Set goals	Measure Performance	Evaluate performance	Take corrective action
What do we want to achieve?	What is happening?	Why is it happening?	What should we do about it?

RETHINKING BRAND MANAGEMENT

Brand management has become a fixture in most consumer packaged goods companies. Brand managers plan long-term brand strategy and watch over their brand's profits. Working closely with advertising agencies, they create national advertising campaigns to build market share and long-term consumer brand loyalty. The brand management system made sense in its earlier days, when the food companies were all-powerful, consumers were brand loyal, and national media could reach mass markets effectively. Recently, however, many companies have begun to question whether this system fits well with today's radically different marketing realities.

Two major environmental forces are causing companies to rethink brand management. First, consumers and markets have changed dramatically. For one thing, consumers are becoming less brand loyal. Today's consumers face an ever-growing set of acceptable brands, and they are exposed to so much price promotion that they are now more deal-prone than brand-prone. As a result, companies are shifting away from national advertising in favor of pricing and other point-of-sale promotions. Also, with the recent swing toward regionalized marketing, emphasis is shifting toward local markets and shorter-term strategies. Thus, whereas brand managers have traditionally focused on long-term, brand-building strategies targeting mass audiences, today's marketplace realities demand shorter-term, sales-building strategies designed for local markets.

A second major force affecting brand management is the growing power of retailers. Larger, more powerful, and better-informed retailers are now demanding and getting more trade promotions in exchange for their scarce shelf space. The increase in trade promotion spending leaves fewer dollars for national advertising, the brand manager's primary marketing tool. Retailers are also demanding more customized "multibrand" promotions that span many of the producer's brands and help retailers to compete better. Such promotions are beyond the scope of any single brand manager and must be designed at higher levels of the company. Yet each brand manager must chip in to support these deals. As a result, they are left with less control over their budgets and less money to invest in brand advertising.

Thus, changes in the marketplace have significantly altered the way companies market their products, causing marketers to rethink the brand management system that has served them so well for many years. Although it is unlikely that brand managers will soon be extinct, many companies are now groping for alternative ways to manage their brands.

One alternative is to change the nature of the brand manager's job. For example, some companies are asking their brand managers to spend more time in the field working with salespeople, learning what is happening in stores, and getting closer to the customer. Campbell Soup recently created "brand sales managers," combination product managers and salespeople charged with handling brands in the field, working with the trade, and designing more localized brand strategies.

As another alternative, Colgate-Palmolive, Procter & Gamble, Kraft, Nabisco, General Foods, and other companies have adopted *category management* systems. Under this system, brand managers report to a category manager who has total responsibility for an entire product line. For example, at Procter & Gamble, the brand manager for Dawn liquid dishwashing detergent reports to a manager who is responsible for Dawn, Ivory, Joy, and all other light-duty liquid detergents. The light-duty liquids manager, in turn, reports to a manager who is responsible for all of P&G's packaged soaps and detergents, including dishwashing detergents, and liquid and dry laundry detergents.

Category management offers many advantages. First, the category managers have broader planning perspectives than brand managers do. Rather than focusing

and evaluates the causes of any differences between expected and actual performance. Finally, management takes corrective action to close the gaps between its goals and its performance. This may require changing the action programs or even changing the goals.

Operating control involves checking ongoing performance against the annual plan and taking corrective action when necessary. Its purpose is to ensure that the company achieves the sales, profits, and other goals set out in its annual plan. It also involves determining the profitability of different products, territories, markets, and channels. *Strategic control* involves looking at whether the company's basic strategies are well matched to its opportunities. Marketing strategies and programs can quickly become outdated and each company should periodically re-

Rethinking the role of the product manager: Campbell set up "brand sales managers."

teams. For example, instead of having several cookie brand managers, Nabisco has three cookie category management teams—one each for adult rich cookies, nutritional cookies, and children's cookies. Headed by a category manager, each category team includes several marketing people—brand managers, a sales planning manager, and a marketing information specialist—who handle brand strategy, advertising, and sales promotion. Each team also includes specialists from other company departments: a finance manager, a research and development specialist, and representatives from manufacturing, engineering, and distribution. Thus, category managers act as small businesspeople, with complete responsibility for the performance of an entire category and with a full complement of people to help them plan and implement category marketing strategies.

Thus, although brand managers are far from extinct, their jobs are changing. And these changes are much needed. The brand management system is product driven, not customer driven. Brand managers focus on pushing their brands out to anyone and everyone, and they often concentrate so heavily on a single brand that they lose sight of the marketplace. Even category management focuses on products, for example, "cookies" as opposed to "Oreos." But today, more than ever, companies must start not with brands, but with the needs of the consumers and retailers that these brands serve. Colgate recently took a step in this direction. It moved from *brand management* (Colgate brand toothpaste) to *category management* (all Colgate-Palmolive toothpaste brands) to a new stage, *customer need management* (customers' oral health needs). This last stage finally gets the organization to focus on customer needs.

on specific brands, they shape the company's entire category offering. This results in a more complete and coordinated category offer. It also helps reduce internal brand conflicts—the category manager can allocate budgets, protect individual brand positions, and resolve disputes among brand managers. Perhaps the most important benefit of category management is that it better matches the buying processes of retailers. Recently, retailers have begun making their individual buyers responsible for working with all suppliers of a specific product category. A category management system links up better with these new retailer "category buying" systems.

Some companies are combining category management with another concept: *brand teams* or *category*

Sources: See Robert Dewar and Don Schultz, "The Product Manager: An Idea Whose Time Has Gone," *Marketing Communications,* May 1989, pp. 28–35; Kevin T. Higgins, "Category Management: New Tools Changing Life for Manufacturers, Retailers," *Marketing News,* September 25, 1989, pp. 2, 19; Ira Teinowitz, "Brand Managers: '90s Dinosaurs?" *Advertising Age,* December 19, 1988, p. 19; and Betsy Spethmann, "Category Management Multiplies," *Advertising Age,* May 11, 1992, p. 42.

assess its overall approach to the marketplace. A major tool for such strategic control is the **marketing audit,** a comprehensive, systematic, independent, and periodic examination of a company's environment, objectives, strategies, and activities to determine problem areas and opportunities and to recommend a plan of action to improve the company's marketing performance.[19]

The marketing audit covers *all* major marketing areas of a business, not just a few trouble spots. It is normally conducted by an objective and experienced outside party who is independent of the marketing department. Table 2-2 shows the kinds of questions the marketing auditor might ask. The findings may come as a surprise—and sometimes as a shock—to management. Management then decides which actions make sense and how and when to implement them.

TABLE 2-2
Marketing Audit Questions

MARKETING ENVIRONMENT AUDIT

The Macroenvironment

1. *Demographic.* What major demographic trends pose threats and opportunities for this company?
2. *Economic.* What developments in income, prices, savings, and credit will impact the company?
3. *Natural.* What is the outlook for costs and availability of natural resources and energy? Is the company environmentally responsible?
4. *Technology.* What technological changes are occurring? What is the company's position on technology?
5. *Political.* What current and proposed laws will affect company strategy?
6. *Cultural.* What is the public's attitude toward business and the company's products? What changes in consumer lifestyles might have an impact?

The Task Environment

1. *Markets.* What is happening to market size, growth, geographic distribution, and profits? What are the major market segments?
2. *Customers.* How do customers rate the company on product quality, service, and price? How do they make their buying decisions?
3. *Competitors.* Who are the major competitors? What are their strategies, market shares, and strengths and weaknesses?
4. *Channels.* What main channels does the company use to distribute products to customers? How are they performing?
5. *Suppliers.* What trends are affecting suppliers? What is the outlook for the availability of key production resources?
6. *Publics.* What key publics provide problems or opportunities? How should the company deal with these publics?

MARKETING STRATEGY AUDIT

1. *Business mission.* Is the mission clearly defined and market oriented?
2. *Marketing objectives.* Has the company set clear objectives to guide marketing planning and performance? Do these objectives fit with company opportunities and resources?
3. *Marketing strategy.* Does the company have a sound marketing strategy for achieving its objectives?
4. *Budgets.* Has the company budgeted sufficient resources to segments, products, territories, and marketing mix elements?

MARKETING ORGANIZATION AUDIT

1. *Formal structure.* Does the chief marketing officer have adequate authority over activities affecting customer satisfaction? Are marketing activities optimally structured along functional, product, market, and territory lines?

The Marketing Environment

Managing the marketing function would be hard enough if the marketer had to deal only with the controllable marketing-mix variables. But the company operates in a complex marketing environment, consisting of uncontrollable forces to which the company must adapt. The environment produces both threats and opportunities. The company must carefully analyze its environment so that it can avoid the threats and take advantage of the opportunities.

The company's marketing environment includes forces close to the company that affect its ability to serve its consumers, such as other company departments, channel members, suppliers, competitors, and publics. It also includes broader demographic and economic forces, political and legal forces, technological and ecological forces, and social and cultural forces. The company must consider all of these forces when developing and positioning its offer to the target market. The marketing environment is discussed more fully in Chapter 3.

2. *Functional efficiency.* Do marketing and sales communicate effectively? Is the marketing staff well trained, supervised, motivated, and evaluated?

4. *Interface efficiency.* Does the marketing staff work well with manufacturing, R&D, purchasing, human resources, and other nonmarketing areas?

MARKETING SYSTEMS AUDIT

1. *Marketing information system.* Is the marketing intelligence system providing accurate and timely information about marketplace developments? Are company decision makers using marketing research effectively?

2. *Marketing planning system.* Does the company prepare annual, long-term, and strategic plans? Are they used?

3. *Marketing control system.* Are annual plan objectives being achieved? Does management periodically analyze the sales and profitability of products, markets, territories, and channels?

4. *New-product development.* Is the company well organized to gather, generate, and screen new-product ideas? Does it carry out adequate product and market testing? Has the company succeeded with new products?

MARKETING PRODUCTIVITY AUDIT

1. *Profitability Analysis.* How profitable are the company's different products, markets, territories, and channels? Should the company enter, expand, or withdraw from any business segments? What would be the consequences?

2. *Cost-effectiveness analysis.* Do any marketing activities have excessive costs? How can costs be reduced?

MARKETING FUNCTION AUDIT

1. *Products.* Has the company developed sound product-line objectives? Should some products be phased out? Should some new products be added? Would some products benefit from quality, style, or feature changes?

2. *Price.* What are the company's pricing objectives, policies, strategies, and procedures? Are the company's prices in line with customers' perceived value? Are price promotions used properly?

3. *Distribution.* What are the distribution objectives and strategies? Does the company have adequate market coverage and service? Should existing channels be changed or new ones added?

4. *Advertising, sales promotion, and publicity.* What are the company's promotion objectives? How is the budget determined? Is it sufficient? Are advertising messages and media well developed and received? Does the company have well-developed sales promotion and public relations programs?

5. *Salesforce.* What are the company's salesforce objectives? Is the salesforce large enough? Is it properly organized? Is it well trained, supervised, and motivated? How is the salesforce rated relative to those of competitors?

SUMMARY

Strategic planning involves developing a strategy for long-run survival and growth. Marketing helps in strategic planning, and the overall strategic plan defines marketing's role in the company. Not all companies use formal planning or use it well, yet formal planning offers several benefits. Companies develop three kinds of plans: *annual plans, long-range plans,* and *strategic plans.*

Strategic planning sets the stage for the rest of company planning. The strategic planning process consists of developing the company's mission, objectives and goals,

business portfolio, and functional plans. Developing a sound *mission statement* is a challenging undertaking. The mission statement should be market oriented, feasible, motivating, and specific if it is to direct the firm to its best opportunities. The mission statement then leads to supporting objectives and goals.

From here, strategic planning calls for analyzing the company's *business portfolio* and deciding which businesses should receive more or fewer resources. The company might use a formal portfolio-planning method like the *BCG* growth-share matrix or the General Electric strategic business grid. But most companies are now designing more customized portfolio-planning approaches that better suit their unique situations. Beyond evaluating current strategic *business units,* management must plan for growth into new businesses and products. The *product/market expansion grid* shows four avenues for growth: market penetration, market development, product development, and diversification.

Each of the company's *functional departments* provides inputs for strategic planning. Once strategic objectives have been defined, management within each business must prepare a set of *functional plans* that coordinates the activities of the marketing, finance, manufacturing, and other departments. Each department has a different idea about which objectives and activities are most important. The marketing department stresses the consumer's point of view. Marketing managers must understand the points of view of the company's other functions and work with other functional managers to develop a system of plans that will best accomplish the firm's overall strategic objectives.

To fulfill their role in the organization, marketers engage in the *marketing process.* Consumers are at the center of the marketing process. The company divides the total market into smaller segments and selects the segments it can best serve. It then designs its *marketing mix* to differentiate its marketing offer and position this offer in selected target segments. To find the best mix and put it into action, the company engages in marketing analysis, marketing planning, marketing implementation, and marketing control.

Each business must prepare marketing plans for its products, brands, and markets. The main components of a *marketing plan* are the executive summary, current marketing situation, threats and opportunities, objectives and issues, marketing strategies, action programs, budgets, and controls. To plan good strategies is often easier than to carry them out. To be successful, companies must implement the strategies effectively. *Implementation* is the process that turns marketing strategies into marketing actions. The process consists of five key elements. The *action program* identifies crucial tasks and decisions needed to implement the marketing plan, assigns them to specific people, and es-

tablishes a timetable. The *organization structure* defines tasks and assignments and coordinates the efforts of the company's people and units. The company's *decision and reward systems* guide activities like planning, information, budgeting, training, control, and personnel evaluation and rewards. Well-designed action programs, organization structures, and decision and reward systems can encourage good implementation.

Successful implementation also requires careful *human resources planning.* The company must recruit, allocate, develop, and maintain good people. The firm's company culture can also make or break implementation. *Company culture* guides people in the company; good implementation relies on strong, clearly defined cultures that fit the chosen strategy.

Most of the responsibility for implementation goes to the company's marketing department. Modern marketing departments are organized in a number of ways. The most common form is the *functional marketing organization,* in which marketing functions are directed by separate managers who report to the marketing vice-president. The company might also use a *geographic organization* in which its salesforce or other functions specialize by geographic area. The company may also use the *product management organization,* in which products are assigned to product managers who work with functional specialists to develop and achieve their plans. Another form is the *market management organization,* in which major markets are assigned to market managers who work with functional specialists.

Marketing organizations carry out marketing control. *Operating control* involves monitoring current marketing results to make sure that the annual sales and profit goals will be achieved. It also calls for determining the profitability of the firm's products, territories, market segments, and channels. *Strategic control* makes sure that the company's marketing objectives, strategies, and systems fit with the current and forecasted marketing environment. It uses the *marketing audit* to determine marketing opportunities and problems and to recommend short-run and long-run actions to improve overall marketing performance. Through these activities, the company watches and adapts to the marketing environment.

····· **KEY TERMS**

DISCUSSING THE ISSUES

1. What are the benefits of a "rolling" five-year plan—that is, why should managers take time to write a five-year plan that will be changed every year?

2. In a series of job interviews, you ask three recruiters to describe the missions of their companies. One says, "To make profits." Another says, "To create customers." The third says, "To fight world hunger." What do these mission statements tell you about the companies?

3. An electronics manufacturer obtains the semiconductors it uses in production from a company-owned subsidiary that also sells to other manufacturers. The subsidiary is smaller and less profitable than are competing producers, and its growth rate has been below the industry average during the past five years. Into what cell of the BCG growth-share matrix does this strategic business unit fall? What should the parent company do with this SBU?

4. As companies become more customer and marketing oriented, many departments find that they must change their traditional way of doing things. How can a company's finance, accounting, and engineering departments help the company become more marketing oriented? Give examples.

5. The General Electric strategic business-planning grid provides a broad overview that can be very helpful in strategic decision making. For what types of decisions would this grid be helpful? Are there other types of strategic decisions where it is not useful?

6. Blockbuster Video is the market leader in home video rentals. It offers two-night rentals, large attractive stores, and wide variety at moderately high prices. Discuss how you would use market-challenger, market-follower, and market-nicher strategies to compete with Blockbuster.

APPLYING THE CONCEPTS

1. Sit down with a AM-FM radio and pencil and paper. Make a simple chart with four columns titled: *Frequency, Call Letters* (optional but helpful), *Format,* and *Notes.* Tune across the AM and FM bands from beginning to end, and make brief notes for each station with adequate reception. In the *Format* column, note the type of programming, such as student-run, public, classic rock, hip-hop, religious, and so forth. Under the *Notes* column, write down any station slogans you hear (such as "Your Concert Connection"), events that the station is sponsoring, and the types of advertising you hear.
   - Total the number of stations you received, and add up how many stations share each format. How many different market segments do these stations appear to target?

   - Are any of these stations positioned in an unusually clear and distinctive way? How?
   - Do advertisers choose different type of stations for different types of products? Does their market segmentation make sense? Give examples.

2. Think about the shopping area near your campus. Assume that you wish to start a business here, and are looking for a promising opportunity for a restaurant, a clothing store, or a music store.
   - Is there an opportunity to open a distinctive and promising business? Describe your target market, and how you would serve it differently than current businesses do.
   - What sort of marketing mix would you use for your business?

MAKING MARKETING DECISIONS:

SMALL WORLD COMMUNICATIONS, INC.

Lynette Jones was thinking during her morning run. She and Thomas Campbell had met for breakfast at the reunion and talked for three hours about the idea of starting Small World Communications. Each of them saw real potential in a possible partnership. They decided that each of them would remain in their current jobs for now, but make a serious effort to develop a viable concept for Small World Communications over the next six weeks. They were communicating daily by electronic mail (E-mail) on the CompuServe network. The ball was now in Lyn's court. Small World needed a corporate mission, and becoming "rich and fa-mous" (as Tom had put it) was just not going to cut it. "This is a real paradox," she mused. "The computer market moves incredibly fast. We've got to have a mission that is specific enough to guide us, but flexible enough to keep up with marketplace changes we can't predict. Maybe the Psychic Friends Network Hotline could help . . ." Lyn turned around at the 2.5 mile mark. "I'm running farther and faster than Bill Clinton," she thought, "but at least he's already decided on a mission. Maybe if *I* focus like a laser beam . . ."

WHAT NOW?

1. Define a mission for Small World Communications. This mission should (a) address a real need or want in the mar-ketplace; (b) fully use the skills that Thomas and Lynette each possess; (c) take into account their lack of facili-ties and capital; and (d) recognize that rapid change will probably continue in the computer marketplace.

2. How difficult was this question? What were the issues you encountered in developing a mission for the company?

 # REFERENCES

1. See "Levi's: The Jeans Giant Slipped as the Market Shifted," *Business Week,* November 5, 1984, pp. 79–80; Miriam Rozen, "The 501 Blues," *Madison Avenue,* November 1984, pp. 22–26; Marc Beauchamp, "Tight Fit," *Forbes,* August 11, 1986; Joshua Hyatt, "Levi Strauss Learns a Fitting Lesson," *Inc.,* August 1985, p. 17; Brenton R. Schlender, "How Levi Strauss Did an LBO Right," *Fortune,* May 7, 1990, pp. 105–7; Maria Shao, "For Levi's, A Flattering Fit Overseas," *Business Week,* November 5, 1990, pp. 76–77; "A Comfortable Fit," *The Economist,* June 22, 1991, pp. 67–68; Marcy Magiera and Pat Sloan, "Levi's, Lee Loosen Up for Baby Boomers," *Advertising Age,* August 3, 1992, p. 9; and Marcy Magiera, "Levi's Dockers Looks for Younger, Upscale Men with Authentics," *Advertising Age,* January 18, 1993, p. 4.

2. For a more detailed discussion of corporate and business-level strategic planning as they apply to marketing, see Philip Kotler, *Marketing Management: Analysis, Planning, Implementa-tion, and Control,* 8th ed. (Englewood Cliffs, NJ: Prentice Hall, 1994), Chap. 3.

3. For more on mission statements, see David A. Aaker, *Strategic Market Management,* 2nd ed. (New York: Wiley, 1988), Chap. 3; Laura Nash, "Mission Statements—Mirrors and Windows," *Harvard Business Review,* March–April 1988, pp. 155–56; and Fred R. David, "How Companies Define Their Mission State-ments," *Long Range Planning,* Vol. 22, No. 1, 1989, pp. 90–97.

4. Richard G. Hamermesh, "Making Planning Strategic," *Harvard Business Review,* July–August 1986, pp. 115–20.

5. See Daniel H. Gray, "Uses and Misuses of Strategic Planning," *Harvard Business Review,* January–February 1986, pp. 89–96; and Roger A. Kerin, Vijay Mahajan, and P. Rajan Varadarajan, *Contemporary Perspectives on Strategic Planning* (Boston: Allyn & Bacon, 1990).

6. H. Igor Ansoff, "Strategies for Diversification," *Harvard Busi-ness Review,* September–October 1957, pp. 113–24.

7. John C. Narver and Stanley F. Slater, "The Effect of a Market Orientation on Business Profitability," *Journal of Marketing,* October 1990, pp. 20–35.

8. See Brian Dumaine, "Creating a New Company Culture," *For-tune,* January 15, 1990, p. 128.

9. For more reading, see Yoram Wind, "Marketing and the Other Business Functions," in *Research in Marketing,* Vol. 5, Jagdish N. Sheth, ed. (Greenwich, CT: JAI Press, 1981), pp. 237–56; Robert W. Ruekert and Orville C. Walker, Jr., "Marketing's In-teraction with Other Functional Units: A Conceptual Frame-work and Empirical Evidence," *Journal of Marketing,* January 1987, pp. 1–19.

10. For more on follower strategies, see Daniel W. Haines, Rajan Chandran, and Arvind Parkhe, "Winning by Being First to Market . . . or Second?" *Journal of Consumer Marketing,* Winter 1989, pp. 63–69.

11. The four *P* classification was first suggested by E. Jerome Mc-Carthy, *Basic Marketing: A Managerial Approach,* (Homewood, IL: Irwin, 1960). For more discussion of this classification scheme, see Walter van Waterschoot and Christophe Van den Bulte, "The 4P Classification of the Marketing Mix Revisited," *Journal of Marketing,* October 1992, pp. 83–93.

12. Robert Lauterborn, "New Marketing Litany: Four P's Passé; C-Words Take Over," *Advertising Age,* October 1, 1990, p. 26.

13. For an interesting discussion of marketing budgeting methods and processes, see Nigel F. Piercy, "The Marketing Budgeting Process: Marketing Management Implications," *Journal of Mar-keting,* October 1987, pp. 45–59.

14. Amar Bhide, "Hustle as Strategy," *Harvard Business Review,* Sep-tember–October 1986, p. 59.

15. See Thomas J. Peters and Robert H. Waterman, *In Search of Ex-cellence: Lessons from America's Best-Run Companies* (New York: Harper & Row, 1982). For an excellent summary of the study's findings on structure, see Aaker, *Strategic Market Management,* pp. 154–57.

16. For more on company cultures, see Rohit Deshpande and Frederick E. Webster, Jr., "Organizational Culture and Market-ing: Defining the Research Agenda," *Journal of Marketing,* Jan-uary 1989, pp. 3–15; Brian Dumaine, "Creating a New Com-pany Culture," *Fortune,* January 15, 1990, pp.127–31; and John P. Kotter and James L. Heskett, *Corporate Culture and Per-formance* (New York: Free Press, 1992).

17. Joseph Winski, "One Brand, One Manager," *Advertising Age,* August 20, 1987, p. 86.

18. For more complete discussions of marketing organization ap-proaches and issues, see Robert W. Ruekert, Orville C. Walker, Jr., and Kenneth J. Roering, "The Organization of Marketing Activities: A Contingency Theory of Structure and Perfor-mance," *Journal of Marketing,* Winter 1985, pp. 13–25; and Ravi S. Achrol, "Evolution of the Marketing Organization: New Forms for Turbulent Environments," *Journal of Marketing,* October 1991, pp. 77–93.

19. For details, see Kotler, *Marketing Management: Analysis, Plan-ning, Implementation, and Control,* 8th ed. (Englewood Cliffs, NJ: Prentice Hall, 1994), Chap. 27.

VIDEO CASE 2

ABCNEWS

Restructuring IBM

Years ago, when the courts broke AT&T into eight pieces—AT&T and the "Baby Bells"—AT&T's market value stood at about $48 billion, compared to IBM's market value of $34 billion. Just ten years later, the combined market value of AT&T and the Baby Bells had soared to $180 billion, versus $56 billion for IBM. What happened? The breakup changed the lethargic, monolithic AT&T into eight smaller, more nimble and competitive companies. By contrast, IBM remained a sluggish giant. Worse, its highly centralized corporate culture remained devoted to selling and servicing mainframe computers, a slowly dying species. The company's successful personal computer, software, minicomputers, microcomputers, network servers, and other products played second fiddle to its mainframes. Managers of these products were forbidden to do anything that might infringe on mainframe sales.

IBM's heavy centralization stifled independent thinking and reduced the company's ability to respond quickly to competitor actions. A case in point: In 1991, when the personal computer division wanted to launch its new laptop at a competitive price of $4,995, headquarters insisted on a $5,995 price in order to meet traditional corporate profit margins. When sales lagged, IBM eventually cut the price to $3,645.

In 1991, IBM's revenues were down 5 percent and the company suffered its first-ever operating deficit. Something had to change. In a dramatic move, IBM "broke itself up" into 13 lines of business (or LOBs), quickly dubbed the "Baby Blues" by the media. Nine of these Baby Blues are manufacturing and development businesses, including Enterprise Systems (mainframe manufacturing, $22 billion in revenues); Adstar (storage devices and tape drives, $11.9 billion); Personal Systems (personal computers, $11.5 billion); Application Business Systems (minicomputers and processors, $11.4 billion); and five smaller LOBs that make products such as chips, software, and printers. The other four LOBs are marketing companies that are responsible for selling and servicing all IBM products in four global territories: Europe, Middle East, and Africa; North America; Asia Pacific; and Latin America.

The breakup sent a clear signal to the Baby Blue manufacturing units that mainframes are no longer sacred and that internal competition was not only allowed, but encouraged. Accordingly, in September 1992, IBM's Applications Business Systems unit introduced a new AS/400 minicomputer to compete with the small IBM ES/9000 mainframe. The Personal Systems unit also invaded the mainframe division's turf. It built PC-compatible network servers for use in connecting PC networks to a Parallan computer, thereby creating a system capable of tackling big commercial mainframe jobs for as little as one-tenth of the cost. Even the Enterprise

Systems mainframe unit got into the act. It created Genesis, a line of systems incorporating hundreds of powerful microprocessors that will compete with Enterprise's own mainframes!

The breakup not only increases competitiveness, it enables each LOB to respond more quickly. During the past decade, IBM has lagged far behind competitors in new product introductions. Although IBM's R&D division is the best in the computer industry for developing new products, IBM has had trouble getting its new products to market quickly. It trailed Digital in introducing minicomputers by 11 years, Apple in personal computers by 4 years, Toshiba in PC-compatible laptops by 5 years, and Sun Microsystems in RISC Workstations by 3 years. Unfortunately for Big Blue, being late to market usually means lower sales and profits.

Will Big Blue's new organization succeed? Some skeptics think that IBM's old and stodgy culture is too firmly entrenched to change. Moreover, already uneasy about IBM's recent downsizing and layoffs of 85,000 employees, IBM managers used to letting headquarters make the strategy and marketing decisions will be cautious about operating independently and being held accountable for the results.

Beyond changing its organization structure, IBM must also change its corporate culture, increasing its emphasis on customer service and satisfaction. Today, with computers and related technologies becoming more of a commodity, service is often the major factor that differentiates firms. But improving service can be difficult in a manufacturing-oriented firm like IBM, which sells such a complicated array of products and services that sales reps may not even know their own products in much depth.

In September 1992, IBM announced the formation of IBM-PC as a separate operating unit, but not as a division. Although the new unit gained control over its own costs and product development, it did not gain direct control of the marketing and selling of its products. It looks as though Big Blue still is having trouble completely severing the ties that bind it to the Baby Blues.

QUESTIONS

1. Describe IBM's mission and objectives in 1982. How will the recent breakup change the mission and objectives?

2. Describe IBM's portfolio of products in the mid-1980s in terms of the BCG growth-share matrix. How might the breakup affect the company's portfolio?

3. What kind of growth strategies, if any, will the breakup foster? Which growth strategies might it prevent?

4. What competitive marketing strategy did IBM appear to be pursuing in the late 1980s? What competitive market-

ing strategy should IBM pursue now? How should it go about implementing this new strategy?

Sources: Catherine Arnst, "Big Blue's New Baby," Business Week, September 14, 1992, pp. 32–34; David Kirkpatrick, "Breaking Up IBM," Fortune, July 27, 1992, pp. 44–58; John Verity and Catherine Arnst, "It's PCs vs. Mainframes—Even at IBM," Business Week, September 21, 1992, pp. 66–67; John Verity, "Out of One Big Blue, Many Little Blues," Business Week, December 9, 1991, p. 33; and John Verity, "The New IBM," Business Week, December 16, 1991, pp. 112–18.

COMPANY CASE 2

TRAP-EASE AMERICA: THE BIG CHEESE OF MOUSETRAPS

One April morning, Martha House, president of Trap-Ease America, entered her office in Costa Mesa, California. She paused for a moment to contemplate the Ralph Waldo Emerson quote which she had framed and hung near her desk.

> If a man [can] . . . make a better mousetrap than his neighbor . . . the world will make a beaten path to his door.

Perhaps, she mused, Emerson knew something that she didn't. She *had* the better mousetrap—Trap-Ease—but the world didn't seem all that excited about it.

Martha had just returned from the National Hardware Show in Chicago. Standing in the trade show display booth for long hours and answering the same questions hundreds of times had been tiring. Yet, this show had excited her. Each year, National Hardware Show officials hold a contest to select the best new product introduced at the show. Of the more than 300 new products introduced at that year's show, her mousetrap had won first place. Such notoriety was not new for the Trap-Ease mousetrap. It had been featured in *People* magazine and had been the subject of numerous talk shows and articles in various popular press and trade publications. Despite all of this attention, however, the expected demand for the trap had not materialized. Martha hoped that this award might stimulate increased interest and sales.

A group of investors who had obtained worldwide rights to market the innovative mousetrap had formed Trap-Ease America in January. In return for marketing rights, the group agreed to pay the inventor and patent holder, a retired rancher, a royalty fee for each trap sold. The group then hired Martha to serve as president and to develop and manage the Trap-Ease America organization.

The Trap-Ease, a simple yet clever device, is manufactured by a plastics firm under contract with Trap-Ease America. It consists of a square, plastic tube measuring about 6 inches long and 1½ inches square. The tube bends in the middle at a 30-degree angle, so that when the front part of the tube rests on a flat surface, the other end is elevated. The elevated end holds a removable cap into which the user places bait (cheese, dog food, or some other tidbit). A hinged door is attached to the front end of the tube. When the trap is "open," this door rests on two narrow "stilts" attached to the two bottom corners of the door.

The trap works with simple efficiency. A mouse, smelling the bait, enters the tube through the open end. As it walks up the angled bottom toward the bait, its weight makes the elevated end of the trap drop downward. This elevates the open end, allowing the hinged door to swing closed, trapping the mouse. Small teeth on the ends of the stilts catch in a groove on the bottom of the trap, locking the door closed. The mouse can be disposed of live, or it can be left alone for a few hours to suffocate in the trap.

Martha felt the trap had many advantages for the consumer when compared with traditional spring-loaded traps or poisons. Consumers can use it safely and easily with no risk of catching their fingers while loading it. It poses no injury or poisoning threat to children or pets. Furthermore, with Trap-Ease, consumers can avoid the unpleasant "mess" they encounter with the violent spring-loaded traps—it creates no "clean-up" problem. Finally, the trap can be reused or simply thrown away.

Martha's early research suggested that women are the best target market for the Trap-Ease. Men, it seems, are more willing to buy and use the traditional, spring-loaded trap. The targeted women, however, do not like the traditional trap. They often stay at home and take care of their children. Thus, they want a means of dealing with the mouse problem that avoids the unpleasantness and risks that the standard trap creates in the home.

To reach this target market, Martha decided to distribute Trap-Ease through national grocery, hardware, and drug chains such as Safeway, K Mart, Hechingers, and CB Drug. She sold the trap directly to these large retailers, avoiding any wholesalers or other middlemen.

The traps sold in packages of two, with a suggested retail price of $2.49. Although this price made the Trap-Ease about five to ten times more expensive than smaller, standard traps, consumers appeared to offer little initial price resistance. The manufacturing cost for the Trap-Ease, including freight and packaging costs, was about 31 cents per unit. The company paid an additional

8.2 cents per unit in royalty fees. Martha priced the traps to retailers at 99 cents per unit and estimated that, after sales and volume discounts, Trap-Ease would realize net revenues from retailers of 75 cents per unit.

To promote the product, Martha had budgeted approximately $60,000 for the first year. She planned to use $50,000 of this amount for travel costs to visit trade shows and to make sales calls on retailers. She would use the remaining $10,000 for advertising. So far, however, because the mousetrap had generated so much publicity, she had not felt that she needed to do much advertising. Still, she had placed advertising in *Good Housekeeping* and in other "home and shelter" magazines (Exhibit 2-1). Martha was the company's only "salesperson," but she intended to hire more salespeople soon.

Martha had initially forecasted Trap-Ease's first-year sales at five million units. Through April, however, the company had sold only several hundred thousand units. Martha wondered if most new products got off to such a slow start, or if she was dong something wrong. She had detected some problems, although none seemed overly serious. For one, there had not been enough repeat buying. For another, she had noted that many of the retailers upon whom she called kept their sample mousetraps on their desks as conversation pieces—she wanted the traps to be used and demonstrated. Martha wondered if consumers were also buying the traps as novelties rather than as solutions to their mouse problems.

Martha knew that the investor group believed that Trap-Ease America had a "once-in-a-lifetime chance" with its innovative mousetrap. She sensed the group's impatience. She had budgeted approximately $250,000 in administrative and fixed costs for the first year (not including marketing costs). To keep the investors happy, the company needed to sell enough traps to cover those costs and make a reasonable profit.

In these first few months, Martha had learned that marketing a new product is not an easy task. For example, one national retailer had placed a large order with instructions that the order was to be delivered to the loading dock at one of its warehouses between 1:00 and 3:00 P.M. on a specified day. When the truck delivering the order had arrived late, the retailer had refused to accept the shipment. The retailer had told Martha it would be a year before she got another chance. Perhaps, Martha thought, she should send the retailer and other customers a copy of Emerson's famous quote.

EXHIBIT 2–1

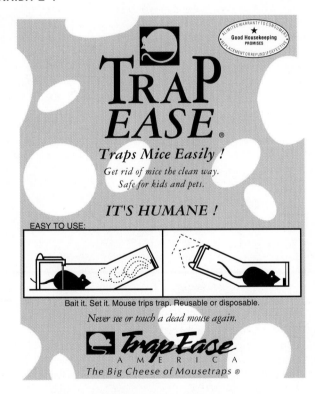

QUESTIONS

1. Martha and the Trap-Ease America investors feel they face a "once-in-a-lifetime" opportunity. What information do they need to evaluate this opportunity? How do you think the group would write its mission statement? How would *you* write it?

2. Has Martha identified the best target market for Trap-Ease? What other market segments might the firm target?

3. How has the company positioned the Trap-Ease relative to the chosen target market? Could it position the product in other ways?

4. Decribe the current marketing mix for Trap-Ease. Do you see any problems with this mix?

5. Who is Trap-Ease America's competition?

6. How would you change Trap-Ease's marketing strategy? What kinds of control procedures would you establish for this strategy?

*T*he Marketing Environment

3

*I*n 1894, vegetarian W. K. Kellogg of Battle Creek, Michigan, found a way to make nutritious wheat meal more appealing to patients in his brother's sanitarium. He invented a process to convert the unappetizing wheat meal into attractive, tasty little cereal flakes. The crunchy flakes quickly became popular. In 1906, W. K. founded the Kellogg Company to sell his cereal to the world at large, and the breakfast table would never again be the same. W. K. Kellogg's modest invention spawned the giant ready-to-eat cereal industry, in which half a dozen large competitors now battle for shares of $7.8 billion in yearly sales. Since its very beginning, the Kellogg Company has been atop the heap, leading the industry with innovative technology and marketing.

During the 1950s and 1960s, Kellogg and other cereal makers prospered. The post-World-War-II baby boom created lots of kids, and kids eat lots of cereal. As the baby-boom generation passed through its childhood and teen years, cereal sales grew naturally with increases in the child population. Kellogg and its competitors focused heavily on the glut of young munchers. They offered presweetened cereals in fetching shapes and colors, pitched by memorable animated characters. Remember Tony the Tiger, Toucan Sam, Dig 'Em, and Snap, Crackle, and Pop?

By 1980, however, the marketing environment had changed. The aging baby boomers, concerned about their spreading waistlines and declining fitness, launched a national obsession with clean living and good nutrition. They began giving up the cereals they'd loved as kids, and industry sales growth flattened. After decades of riding natural market growth, Kellogg and its competitors now had to fight for profitable shares of a stagnant market. But through the good years, Kellogg had grown complacent and sluggish. The company stumbled briefly in the early 1980s and its market share dropped off. Some analysts claimed that Kellogg was a company "past its prime."

To counter slow cereal industry growth, most of Kellogg's competitors—General Mills, General Foods, Quaker Oats, Ralston Purina—diversified broadly into faster-growing nonfood businesses. Kellogg chose a different course. It implemented an aggressive marketing strategy to revive industry sales by persuading the nation's 75 million baby boomers to eat cereal again.

Kellogg advertised heavily to reposition its old products and bring them more in line with changing adult lifestyles. New ad campaigns for the company's old brands stressed taste and nutrition. For example, a Kellogg's Corn Flakes ad shows adults discussing professional athletes who eat the cereal. In another spot, a young medical student tells his mom that Rice Krispies have more vitamins and minerals than her oatmeal does. In a Frosted Flakes ad, consumers sitting at a breakfast table, their features obscured by shadows, confess that they still eat the Frosted Flakes they loved as kids. "That's OK," they're told, "Frosted Flakes have the taste adults have grown to love."

Beyond repositioning the old standards, Kellogg invested heavily in new brands aimed at adult taste buds and lifestyles. Crispix, Raisin Squares, the Nutri-Grain line, Mueslix, Low-Fat Granola, and many other innovative adult Kellogg brands sprouted on grocers' shelves. In its push to capture the adult market, Kellogg also developed a growing line of high-fiber bran cereals—All-Bran, 40 Percent Bran Flakes, Bran Buds, Raisin Bran, Cracklin' Oat Bran, Common Sense Oat Bran, and Frosted Bran Flakes. Kellogg's advertising made some serious health pitches for these brands, tying them to high-fiber, low-fat diets, and to healthy living. One long-running ad campaign even linked Kellogg's All-Bran with reduced risks of cancer. The controversial campaign drew sharp criticism from competitors, strong praise from the National Cancer Institute, and increased sales from consumers. Kellogg did not make such strong claims, however, for all of its bran products. For example, one advertisement asked "Is your diet too fat for your own good?" and suggested that consumers eat Kellogg cereals to "get a taste for the healthy life." Another ad for Bran Flakes stated simply: "You take care of the outside; Kellogg's 40 Percent Bran Flakes will help you take care of the inside."

Kellogg's aggressive reaction to its changing marketing environment paid off handsomely. The company's high-powered marketing attack more than doubled the growth rate for the entire cereal in-dustry. Furthermore, while diversified competitors were spending time and money fixing or unloading their nonfood businesses, Kellogg remained sharply focused on cereals. In only four years, Kellogg's over-all market share grew from 35 percent to 42 percent, and the company's share of the fast-growing bran segment exceeded 50 percent.

Although General Mills and other competitors have regrouped to challenge Kellogg in the 1990s, the company's market share remains 30 percent higher than that of its nearest competitor. Four of the nation's five best-selling cereals are Kellogg brands. As Tony the Tiger would say, at Kellogg things are going G-r-r-reat![1]

 ## CHAPTER PREVIEW

Chapter 3 describes the environments in which companies operate, and shows the influence of external forces on marketing decisions.

Initially, we define a company's *microenvironment*, the forces close to the company that affect its ability to serve customers. The microenvironment includes the *company* itself, *suppliers, marketing channel firms, customers, competitors*, and *publics*.

Next, we put the microenvironment into a larger context: the *macroenvironment* of larger societal influences such as *demographic, economic, natural, technological, political*, and *cultural* environments. We discuss how these forces can affect marketing decisions.

Each of these environments is discussed, and the *major trends* in the macroenvironment of the United States are set forth.

We conclude with thoughts on *responding to the marketing environment.* Two alternate philosophies for dealing with these external forces are the typical passive response and adaptation, and the aggressive *environmental management perspective*.

A company's **marketing environment** consists of the actors and forces outside marketing that affect marketing management's ability to develop and maintain successful transactions with its target customers. The marketing environment offers both opportunities and threats. Companies must use their marketing research and intelligence systems to watch the changing environment and must adapt their marketing strategies to environmental trends and developments.

The marketing environment consists of a *microenvironment* and a *macroenvironment*. The **microenvironment** consists of the forces close to the company that affect its ability to serve its customers—the company, suppliers, marketing channel firms, customer markets, competitors, and publics. The **macroenvironment** consists of the larger societal forces that affect the whole microenvironment—demographic, economic, natural, technological, political, and cultural forces. We look first at the company's microenvironment and then at its macroenvironment.

THE COMPANY'S MICROENVIRONMENT

Marketing management's job is to create attractive offers for target markets. However, marketing managers cannot simply focus on the target market's needs. Their success also will be affected by actors in the company's microenvironment—other company departments, suppliers, marketing intermediaries, customers, competitors, and various publics (see Figure 3-1).

The Company

In designing marketing plans, marketing management takes other company groups into account—groups such as top management, finance, research and development (R&D), purchasing, manufacturing, and accounting. All these interrelated groups form the internal environment (see Figure 3-2). Top management sets the company's mission, objectives, broad strategies, and policies. Marketing managers must make decisions within the plans made by top management, and marketing plans must be approved by top management before they can be implemented.

Marketing managers also must work closely with other company departments. Finance is concerned with finding and using funds to carry out the marketing plan. The R&D department focuses on the problems of designing safe and attractive products. Purchasing worries about getting supplies and materials, whereas manufacturing is responsible for producing the desired quality and quantity of products. Accounting has to measure revenues and costs to help marketing know how well it is achieving its objectives. Therefore, all of these departments have an impact on the marketing department's plans and actions.

Suppliers

Suppliers are firms and individuals that provide the resources needed by the company to produce its goods and services. Supplier developments can seriously affect marketing. Marketing managers must watch supply availability. Supply shortages or delays, labor strikes, and other events can cost sales in the short run and damage customer goodwill in the long run. Marketing managers also monitor the price trends of their key inputs. Rising supply costs may force price increases that can harm the company's sales volume.

Marketing Intermediaries

Marketing intermediaries are firms that help the company to promote, sell, and distribute its goods to final buyers. They include *middlemen, physical distribution firms, marketing services agencies,* and *financial intermediaries.* **Middlemen** are distribution channel firms that help the company find customers or make sales to them. These include wholesalers and retailers who buy and resell merchandise (they are often called *resellers*). Selecting and working with middlemen is not easy. No longer do manufacturers have many small, independent middlemen from which to choose. They now face large and growing middlemen organizations. These organizations frequently have enough power to dictate terms or even shut the manufacturer out of large markets.

Physical distribution firms help the company to stock and move goods from their points of origin to their destinations. Warehouses are firms that store and protect goods before they move to the next destination. Transportation firms include railroads, trucking companies, airlines, barge companies, and others that specialize in moving goods from one location to another. A company must determine the best ways to store and ship goods, balancing such factors as cost, delivery, speed, and safety.

Marketing services agencies are the marketing research firms, advertising agencies, media firms, and marketing consulting firms that help the company

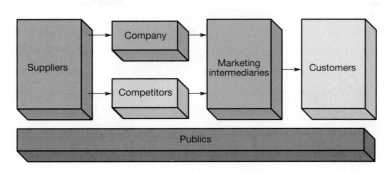

FIGURE 3-1
Major actors in the company's microenvironment

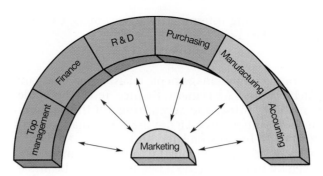

FIGURE 3-2
The company's internal environment

target and promote its products to the right markets. When the company decides to use one of these agencies, it must choose carefully because these firms vary in creativity, quality, service, and price. The company has to review the performance of these firms regularly and consider replacing those that no longer perform well.

Financial intermediaries include banks, credit companies, insurance companies, and other businesses that help finance transactions or insure against the risks associated with the buying and selling of goods. Most firms and customers depend on financial intermediaries to finance their transactions. The company's marketing performance can be seriously affected by rising credit costs and limited credit. For this reason, the company has to develop strong relationships with important financial institutions.

Customers

The company must study its customer markets closely. Figure 3-3 shows five types of customer markets. *Consumer markets* consist of individuals and households that buy goods and services for personal consumption. *Business markets* buy goods and services for further processing or for use in their production process, whereas *reseller markets* buy goods and services to resell at a profit. *Government markets* are made up of government agencies that buy goods and services in order to produce public services or transfer the goods and services to others who need them. Finally, *international markets* consist of buyers in other countries, including consumers, producers, resellers, and governments. Each market type has special characteristics that call for careful study by the seller.

Competitors

The marketing concept states that to be successful, a company must satisfy the needs and wants of consumers better than its competitors do. Thus, marketers must do more than simply adapt to the needs of target consumers. They also must gain strategic advantage by positioning their offerings strongly against competitors' offerings in the minds of consumers.

No single competitive marketing strategy is best for all companies. Each firm should consider its own size and industry position compared to those of its competitors. Large firms with dominant positions in an industry can use certain strategies that smaller firms cannot afford. But being large is not enough. There are winning strategies for large firms, but there are also losing ones. And small firms can develop strategies that give them better rates of return than large firms enjoy.

FIGURE 3-3
Types of customer markets

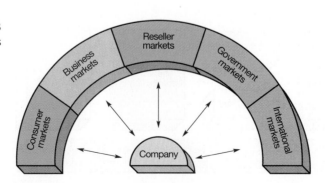

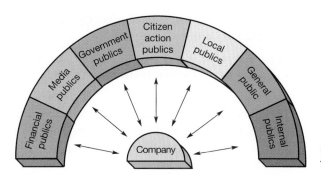

FIGURE 3-4
Types of publics

Publics

The company's marketing environment also includes various publics. A **public** is any group that has an actual or potential interest in or impact on an organization's ability to achieve its objectives. Figure 3-4 shows seven types of publics.

- *Financial publics*. Financial publics influence the company's ability to obtain funds. Banks, investment houses, and stockholders are the major financial publics.

- *Media publics*. Media publics are those that carry news, features, and editorial opinion. They include newspapers, magazines, and radio and television stations.

- *Government publics*. Management must take government developments into account. Marketers must often consult the company's lawyers on issues of product safety, truth-in-advertising, and other matters.

- *Citizen-action publics*. A company's marketing decisions may be questioned by consumer organizations, environmental groups, minority groups, and others. Its public relations department can help it stay in touch with consumer and citizen groups.

- *Local publics*. Every company has local publics, such as neighborhood residents and community organizations. Large companies usually appoint a community-relations

Companies market to internal publics as well as to customers: Wal-Mart includes employees as models in its advertising, making them feel good about working for the company.

officer to deal with the community, attend meetings, answer questions, and contribute to worthwhile causes.

- *General public.* A company needs to be concerned about the general public's attitude toward its products and activities. The public's image of the company affects its buying.

- *Internal publics.* A company's internal publics include its workers, managers, volunteers, and the board of directors. Large companies use newsletters and other means to inform and motivate their internal publics. When employees feel good about their company, this positive attitude spills over to external publics.

A company can prepare marketing plans for these major publics as well as for its customer markets. Suppose the company wants a specific response from a particular public, such as goodwill, favorable word of mouth, or donations of time or money. The company would have to design an offer to this public that is attractive enough to produce the desired response.

THE COMPANY'S MACROENVIRONMENT

The company and all of the other actors operate in a larger macroenvironment of forces that shape opportunities and pose threats to the company. Figure 3-5 shows the six major forces in the company's macroenvironment. The remaining sections of this chapter examine these forces and show how they affect marketing plans.

Demographic Environment

Demography is the study of human populations in terms of size, density, location, age, gender, race, occupation, and other statistics. The demographic environment is of major interest to marketers because it involves people, and people make up markets. Here, we discuss the most important demographic trends in the United States.

Changing Age Structure of the U.S. Population

The U.S. population stood at over about 250 million in 1993 and may reach 300 million by the year 2020. The single most important demographic trend in the United States is the changing age structure of the population. The U.S. population is getting *older* for two reasons. First, there is a long-term slowdown in the birthrate, so there are fewer young people to pull the population's average age down. Second, life expectancy is increasing, so there are more older people to pull the average age up.

During the **baby boom** that followed World War II and lasted until the early 1960s, the annual birthrate reached an all-time high. The baby boom created a huge "bulge" in the U.S. age distribution—the 75 million baby boomers now account for almost one-third of the nation's population. And as the baby-boom generation ages, the nation's average age climbs with it. Because of its sheer size, most major demographic and socioeconomic changes occurring during the next half decade will be tied to the baby-boom generation (see Marketing Highlight 3-1).

The baby boom was followed by a "birth dearth," and by the mid-1970s the birthrate had fallen sharply. This decrease was caused by smaller family sizes resulting from Americans' desire to improve their personal living standards, from the increasing desire of women to work outside the home, and from improved birth control. Although family sizes are expected to remain smaller, the birthrate is climbing again as the baby-boom generation moves through the childbearing years and creates a second but smaller baby boom (the "echo boom" or "baby boomlet"). However, through the remainder of the 1990s, the birthrate will again decline.[2]

The changing age structure of the population will result in different growth rates for various age groups over the decade, and these differences will strongly affect marketers' targeting strategies. For example, the echo boom has created an under-age-six market estimated at more than $6 billion per year. After years of

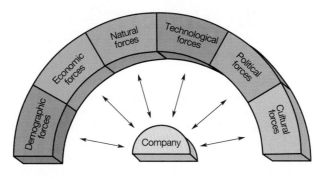

FIGURE 3-5
Major forces in the company's macroenvironment

"bust," markets for children's toys and games, clothes, furniture, and food are enjoying a short "boom." For example, Sony and other electronics firms are now offering products designed for children. Many retailers are opening separate children's clothing chains, such as GapKids and Kids 'R' Us. Such markets will continue to grow through most of this decade but will again decrease as the baby boomers move out of their childbearing years.[3]

At the other end of the spectrum, the 65-and-over group now makes up about 13 percent of all Americans. By 2030, however, it will make up almost 21 percent of the population—there will be about as many people 65 and older as there are people 18 and younger. As this group grows, so will the demand for retirement communities, quieter forms of recreation, single-portion food packaging, life-care and health-care services, and leisure travel.[4]

The Changing American Family

The American ideal of the two-children, two-car suburban family has lately been losing some of its luster. People are marrying later and having fewer children. Despite the recent "echo boom," the number of married couples with children will continue to decline through the 1990s. In fact, couples with no children under 18 now make up almost half of all families.

Also, the number of working mothers has increased. The percentage of mothers of children younger than age 18 who hold some kind of job has increased from 25 percent, in 1960, to more than 64 percent today. Marketers of tires, automobiles, insurance, travel, and financial services are increasingly directing their advertising to working women. As a result of the shift in the traditional roles and values of husbands and wives, with husbands assuming more domestic functions such as shopping and child care, more food and household appliance marketers are targeting husbands.

Folgers and other brands are targeting smaller households with single-serve portions.

THE BABY BOOMERS

The postwar baby boom, which began in 1946 and ran through 1964, produced 75 million babies. Since then, the baby boomers have become one of the biggest forces shaping the marketing environment. The boomers have presented a moving target, creating new markets as they grew through infancy to preadolescent, teenage, young-adult, and now middle-age years. They created markets for baby products and toys in the 1950s; jeans, records, and cosmetics in the 1960s; fun and informal fashions in the 1970s; premium foods and performance cars in the 1980s; and fitness, new homes, and child care in the 1990s.

Today, the baby boomers are starting to gray at the temples and spread at the waist. And they are reaching their peak earning and spending years—the boomers account for a third of the population but make up 40 percent of the work force and earn over half of all personal income. They are moving to the suburbs, settling into home ownership, raising families, and maturing into the most affluent generation in history. Thus, they constitute a lucrative market for housing, furniture and appliances, children's products, low-calorie foods and beverages, physical fitness products, high-priced cars, convenience products, and financial services.

Baby boomers cut across all walks of life. But marketers typically have paid the most attention to the small upper crust of the boomer generation—its more educated, mobile, and wealthy segments. These segments have gone by many names. In the early to mid-1980s, they were called "yuppies" (young urban professionals); "yumpies" (young upwardly mobile professionals); "bumpies" (black upwardly mobile professionals); and "yummies" (young upwardly mobile mommies). These groups were replaced by the "DINKs"—dual-income, no-kids couples.

In 1990s, however, yuppies and DINKs have given way to a new breed, with names such as DEWKs (dual earners with kids); MOBYs (mother older, baby younger); WOOFs (well-off older folks); or just plain GRUMPIES (just what the name suggests). The older boomers are now well into their forties; the youngest are in their thirties. Thus, the boomers are evolving from the "youthquake generation" to the "backache generation." They're slowing up, having children, and settling down. They're experiencing the pangs of midlife and rethinking the purpose and value of their work, responsibilities, and relationships.

The maturing boomers are approaching life with a new stability and reasonableness in the way they live, think, eat, and spend. Baby boomers now head up 44 percent of the nation's households, and 60 percent of all boomer households include children under 18 years old. Thus, they have shifted their focus from the outside world to the inside world. Staying home with the family is becoming their favorite way to spend an evening. Community and family values have become more important. The upscale boomers still exert their affluence, but they indulge themselves in more subtle and sensible ways. They spend heavily on convenience and high-quality products, but they have less of a taste for lavish or conspicuous buying.

Some marketers think that focusing on the boomers has caused companies to overlook other important segments. For example, one advertising executive suggests that marketers are in danger of losing touch with younger consumers, especially those now 18 to 29 years old, labeled by some as "Generation X":

> [Our fortunes] have been directly tied to the fortunes of the baby boomer generation for so long that we may have begun to lose our perspective. . . . Until now, Generation X has lived in the shadow of the baby boomers. But by the year 2000, Generation X will have grown to 62 million strong and, 10 years

Finally, the number of nonfamily households is increasing. Many young adults leave home and move into apartments. Other adults choose to remain single. Still others are divorced or widowed people living alone. By the year 2000, 47 percent of all households will be nonfamily or single-parent households—the fastest-growing categories of households. These groups have their own special needs. For example, they need smaller apartments; inexpensive and smaller appliances, furniture, and furnishings; and food that is packaged in smaller sizes.[5]

Geographic Shifts in Population
Americans are a mobile people with about 18 percent, or 43 million people, moving each year. Among the major trends are the following:[6]

■ *Movement to the Sunbelt states.* During the 1980s, the populations in the West and

The baby boomers have long been a prime target for marketers. However, the "Generation Xers," the generation following the boomers, will emerge as the major marketing opportunity of the next decade and beyond.

later, will have overtaken the boomers as the primary target for virtually every product category—for beauty, for fashion and fragrance, for package goods, travel and home furnishings. The Xers [have] open minds and still to be realized earning potential—not [like] the boomers [who will be] sitting on the edge of retirement, with established product preferences. The Xers will represent the market of opportunity for blue jeans and new cars and laundry soap from 1995 on into the next decade.

Still, for the present, the boomers continue to dominate the marketing scene. Some marketers think that upscale boomers are tiring of all the attention. They are using subtler approaches that avoid stereotyping

these consumers or tagging them as yuppies, or DEWKs, or something else. But whatever you call them, you can't ignore them. The baby boomers have been the most potent market force for the past 40 years, and they will continue to be for some time yet to come.

Sources: The quote is from Karen Ritchie, "Get Ready for 'Generation X,'" *Advertising Age,* November 9, 1992, p. 21. Also see Jon Berry, "It's Hip, It's Intense—The Midlife Crisis," *Adweek,* June 25, 1990, pp. 54-55; Cheryl Russell, "On the Babyboom Bandwagon," *American Demographics,* May 1991, pp. 25-31; Susan B. Garland, "Those Aging Boomers," *Business Week,* May 20, 1991, pp. 106-12; Margaret L. Usdansky, "Older, Younger Boomers Split by Time, Values," *USA Today,* February 11, 1992, p. 6A; and Scott Donaton, "The Media Wakes Up to Generation X," *Advertising Age,* February 1, 1993, pp. 16-17.

South grew. In contrast, many of the Midwest and Northeast states lost population. These shifts are continuing through the 1990s (see Figure 3-6). These population shifts interest marketers because people in different regions buy differently. For example, the movement to the Sunbelt states will lessen the demand for warm clothing and home heating equipment and increase the demand for air conditioning.

■ *Movement from rural to urban areas.* Except for a short period during the early 1970s, Americans have been moving from rural to metropolitan areas for over a century. The metropolitan areas show a faster pace of living, more commuting, higher incomes, and greater variety of goods and services than can be found in the small towns and rural areas that dot the United States.

■ *Movement from the city to the suburbs.* In the 1950s, Americans made a massive exit

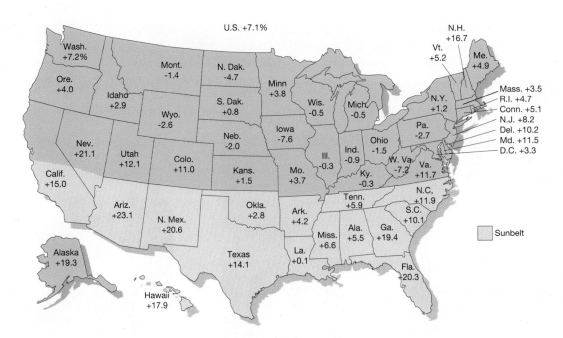

FIGURE 3-6 Projected population growth rates: 1990 to 2000
Source: U.S. Department of Commerce, Bureau of Census.

from the cities to the suburbs. Big cities became surrounded by even bigger suburbs. Today, the migration to the suburbs continues. The U.S. Census Bureau calls sprawling urban areas *MSAs* (Metropolitan Statistical Areas).[7] Companies use MSAs in researching the best geographical segments for their products and in deciding where to buy advertising time. MSA research shows, for example, that people in Seattle buy more toothbrushes per capita than any other U.S. city, people in Salt Lake City eat more candy bars, folks from New Orleans use more ketchup, and those in Miami drink more prune juice.[8]

A Better-Educated and More White-Collar Population

The population is becoming better educated. The rising number of educated people will increase the demand for quality products, books, magazines, and travel. It suggests a decline in television viewing because college-educated consumers watch less TV than does the population at large.

The work force also is becoming more white collar. Between 1950 and 1985, the proportion of white-collar workers rose from 41 percent to 54 percent, that of blue-collar workers declined from 47 percent to 33 percent, and that of service workers increased from 12 percent to 14 percent. These trends have continued into the 1990s. Through 1995, the most growth will come in the following occupational categories: computers, engineering, science, medicine, social service, buying, selling, secretarial, construction, refrigeration, health service, personal service, and protection.[9]

Increasing Ethnic and Racial Diversity

The United States has often been called a "melting pot" in which diverse groups from many nations and cultures have melted into a single, more homogeneous whole. But there are increasing signs that such melting did not occur. Rather, the United States seems to have become more of a "salad bowl" in which various groups have mixed together but have maintained their diversity by retaining and valuing important ethnic and cultural differences.

The U.S. population is 84 percent white, with blacks making up another 12 percent. The Hispanic population has grown rapidly and now stands at over 22 million people. The U.S. Asian population also has grown rapidly in recent years. During the 1980s, some 500,000 immigrants a year accounted for one-fifth of all U.S. population growth. Mexicans, Filipinos, Chinese, Koreans, and Vietnamese were the most common new arrivals. Each group has specific wants and buying habits.

Many marketers of food, clothing, furniture, and other products have targeted specially designed products and promotions to one or more of these groups.[10]

Economic Environment

Markets require buying power as well as people. The **economic environment** consists of factors that affect consumer purchasing power and spending patterns. Marketers should be aware of the following major economic trends.

Changes in Income

In the early 1980s, the economy entered the nation's longest peacetime boom. During the "roaring eighties," American consumers fell into a consumption frenzy, fueled by income growth, federal tax reductions, rapid increases in housing values, and a boom in borrowing. They bought and bought, seemingly without caution, amassing record levels of debt. "It was fashionable to describe yourself as `born to shop.' When the going gets tough, it was said, the tough go shopping. In the 1980s, many Americans became literally addicted to personal consumption."[11]

However, the free spending and high expectations were dashed by the recession in the early 1990s. Once again, consumers have sobered up, pulled back, and adjusted to leaner times. *Value marketing* has become the watchword for many marketers during this economic downturn. Rather than offering high quality at a high price, or lesser quality at very low prices, marketers are looking for ways to offer today's more financially cautious buyers greater value—just the right combination of product quality and good service at a fair price.[12]

Despite short-term economic swings, current projections suggest that real income will continue to rise modestly through the 1990s. This will result largely from rising income in certain important segments. The baby-boom generation is moving into its prime wage-earning years, and the number of small families headed by dual-career couples continues to increase. Thus, consumers will continue to demand quality products and better service, and they will be able to pay for it. They will spend more on time-saving products and services, travel and entertainment, physical fitness products, cultural activities, and continuing education. However, the 1990s will also be the decade of the "squeezed consumer." Along with rising incomes will come increased financial burdens—repaying debts acquired during the spending splurges of the 1980s, facing declining home values and increased taxes, and saving ahead for college tuition payments and retirement. Thus, despite their higher incomes, financially squeezed consumers will probably continue to spend more slowly and carefully than in the previous decade. And they will continue to seek greater value in the products and services they buy.

Marketers should pay attention to *income distribution* as well as average income. Income distribution in the United States is still very skewed. At the top are *upper-class* consumers, whose spending patterns are not affected by current economic events and who are a major market for luxury goods. There is a comfortable *middle class* that is somewhat careful about its spending but can still afford the good life some of the time. The *working class* must stick close to the basics of food, clothing, and shelter and must try hard to save. Finally, the *underclass* (persons on welfare and many retirees) must count their pennies when making even the most basic purchases.

Changing Consumer Spending Patterns

Table 3-1 shows the proportion of total expenditures made by households at different income levels for major categories of goods and services. Food, housing, and transportation use up most household income. However, consumers at different income levels have different spending patterns. Some of these differences were noted over a century ago by Ernst Engel, who studied how people shifted their spending as their income rose. He found that as family income rises, the percentage spent on food declines, the percentage spent on housing remains constant (except for such utilities as gas, electricity, and public services, which decrease), and both the percentage spent on other categories and that devoted to savings increase. **Engel's laws** generally have been supported by later studies.

Changes in major economic variables such as income, cost of living, interest

TABLE 3-1
Consumer Spending at Different Income Levels

| | INCOME LEVEL | | |
EXPENDITURE	$10,000-15,000	$20,000-30,000	$50,000 and Over
Food	17.7%	15.8%	12.6%
Housing	24.8	23.0	24.9
Utilities	8.6	7.1	4.7
Clothing	5.4	5.8	5.8
Transportation	17.4	19.1	17.6
Health Care	7.8	5.5	3.7
Entertainment	3.7	4.7	6.1
Tobacco	1.5	1.2	0.5
Contributions	2.2	2.9	4.3
Insurance and Pensions	4.5	8.2	13.2
Other	6.3	6.7	6.6

Source: Consumer Expenditure Survey, U.S. Department of Labor, Bureau of Labor Statistics, Bulletin 2383. August 1991, pp. 15-17.

rates, and savings and borrowing patterns have a large impact on the marketplace. Companies watch these variables by using economic forecasting. Businesses do not have to be wiped out by an economic downturn or caught short in a boom. With adequate warning, they can take advantage of changes in the economic environment.

Natural Environment

The **natural environment** involves the natural resources that are needed as inputs by marketers or that are affected by marketing activities. Environmental concerns have grown steadily during the past two decades. Some trend analysts believe that the 1990s will be the "Earth Decade," in which protection of the natural environment will be the major worldwide issue facing business and the public. In many cities around the world, air and water pollution have reached dangerous levels. Concern continues to mount about the depletion of the earth's ozone layer and the resulting "greenhouse effect," a dangerous warming of the earth. And many Americans fear that we soon will be buried in our own trash. Marketers should be aware of four trends in the natural environment.

Shortages of Raw Materials

Air and water may seem to be infinite resources, but some groups see long-run dangers. They warn of the potential dangers that propellants used in aerosol cans pose to the ozone layer. Water shortage is already a big problem in some parts of the United States and the world. Renewable resources, such as forests and food, also have to be used wisely. Companies in the forestry business are required to reforest timberlands in order to protect the soil and to ensure enough wood supplies to meet future demand. Food supply can be a major problem because more and more of our limited farmable land is being developed for urban areas.

Nonrenewable resources, such as oil, coal, and various minerals, pose a serious problem. Firms making products that require these increasingly scarce resources face large cost increases, even if the materials do remain available. They may not find it easy to pass these costs on to the consumer. However, firms engaged in research and development and in exploration can help by developing new sources and materials.

Increased Cost of Energy

One nonrenewable resource, oil, has created the most serious problem for future economic growth. The major industrial economies of the world depend heavily on oil, and until economical energy substitutes can be developed, oil will continue to dominate the world political and economic picture. Large increases in the price of oil during the 1970s, and dramatic events like the 1991 Persian Gulf War that af-

You're looking at 64 milk bottles and 2 shampoo containers.

Can you imagine chairs like this one made out of recycled plastic? We can. That and a whole lot more. If we do it together.

At Dow Plastics we're busy working with many companies—customers as well as competitors—to develop new recycling technologies. Like turning plastic bottles into durable products. Or manufacturing VCR cassettes and office equipment out of fast food packaging. Or making ski jacket insulation and shipping containers from recycled materials. The list goes on.

But it's only the beginning. We're looking for new projects and new partners. Maybe you? Call us. 1-800-441-4DOW.

DOW Dow Plastics
We don't succeed unless you do.
*Trademark of The Dow Chemical Company.

By developing new recycling technologies and products, Dow shows its concern for the environment while at the same time creating new marketing opportunities. Currently, however, the supply of many recycled products exceeds the demand. Thus, in this business-to-business ad, Dow seeks partners and new product ideas for recycled plastics.

fect oil availability, have spurred the search for alternative forms of energy. Coal is again popular; and many companies are searching for practical ways to harness solar, nuclear, wind, and other forms of energy. In fact, hundreds of firms already are offering products that use solar energy for heating homes and other uses.

Increased Pollution

Industry almost always will damage the quality of the natural environment. Consider the disposal of chemical and nuclear wastes; the dangerous mercury levels in the ocean; the quantity of chemical pollutants in the soil and food supply; and the littering of the environment with nonbiodegradable bottles, plastics, and other packaging materials.

In contrast, public concern creates a marketing opportunity for alert companies. Such concern creates a large market for pollution control solutions such as scrubbers, recycling centers, and landfill systems. It leads to a search for new ways to produce and package goods that do not cause environmental damage. Concern for the natural environment has recently spawned the so-called green movement. Increasing numbers of consumers have begun doing more business with ecologically responsible companies and avoiding those whose actions harm the environment. They buy "environmentally friendly" products, even if these products cost more. Many companies are responding to such consumer demands with ecologically safer products, recyclable or biodegradable packaging, better pollution controls, and more energy-efficient operations.[13]

Government Intervention in Natural Resource Management

Various government agencies play an active role in environmental protection. For example, the Environmental Protection Agency (EPA) was created in 1970 to set and enforce pollution standards and to conduct research on the causes and effects of pollution. In the future, business can expect strong controls from government and pressure groups. Instead of opposing regulation, marketers should help develop solutions to the material and energy problems facing the world.

Technological Environment

The **technological environment** is perhaps the most dramatic force now shaping our destiny. Technology has released such wonders as penicillin, organ transplants, and notebook computers. It also has released such horrors as the nuclear bomb, nerve gas, and the machine gun. It has released such mixed blessings as the automobile, television, and credit cards. Our attitude toward technology depends on whether we are more impressed with its wonders or its blunders.

Every new technology replaces an older technology. Transistors hurt the vacuum-tube industry, xerography hurt the carbon-paper business, the auto hurt the railroads, and television hurt the movies. When old industries fought or ignored new technologies, their businesses declined.

New technologies create new markets and opportunities. The marketer should watch the following trends in technology.

Fast Pace of Technological Change

Many of today's common products were not available even a hundred years ago. Abraham Lincoln did not know about automobiles, airplanes, phonographs, radios, or the electric light. Woodrow Wilson did not know about television, aerosol cans, home freezers, automatic dishwashers, room air conditioners, antibiotics, or electronic computers. Franklin Delano Roosevelt did not know about xerography, synthetic detergents, tape recorders, birth control pills, or earth satellites. And John F. Kennedy did not know about personal computers, compact disc players, digital watches, VCRs, or fax machines. Companies that do not keep up with technological change soon will find their products outdated. And they will miss new product and market opportunities.

Scientists today are working on a wide range of new technologies that will revolutionize our products and their manufacturing processes. Exciting work is being done in biotechnology, miniature electronics, robotics, and materials science. Scientists today are working on the following promising new products and services:

Practical solar energy	Commercial space shuttle	Effective superconductors
Cancer cures	Tiny but powerful supercomputers	Electric cars
Chemical control of mental health	Household robots that do cooking and cleaning	Electronic anesthetic for pain killing
Desalinization of seawater	Nonfattening, tasty, nutritious foods	Voice- and gesture-controlled computers

Scientists also speculate on fantasy products, such as flying cars, three-dimensional televisions, space colonies, and human clones. The challenge in each case is not only technical but also commercial—to make *practical, affordable* versions of these products.

High R&D Budgets

The United States leads the world in research and development spending. In 1991, R&D spending exceeded $156 billion, although it has been dropping slightly in recent years. The federal government supplied almost half of total R&D funds. Government research can be a rich source of new product and service ideas (see Marketing Highlight 3-2). Many companies also spend heavily on R&D. For example, companies such as General Motors, IBM, and AT&T spend billions on R&D each year.[14] Today's research usually is carried out by research teams rather than by lone inventors like Thomas Edison, Samuel Morse, or Alexander Graham Bell. Managing company scientists is a major challenge. They may resent too much cost control and are sometimes more interested in solving scientific problems than in creating marketable products. Companies are adding marketing people to R&D teams to try to obtain a stronger marketing orientation.

Concentration on Minor Improvements

As a result of the high cost of developing and introducing new technologies, many companies are making minor product improvements instead of gambling on major innovations. Even basic research companies like Du Pont, Bell Laboratories, and Pfizer are being cautious. Most companies are content to put their money into copying competitors' products, making minor feature and style improvements, or offering simple extensions of current brands. Thus, much research is defensive rather than offensive.

NASA: AN IMPORTANT SOURCE OF TECHNOLOGY FOR BUSINESS

Since 1958, the National Aeronautics and Space Administration (NASA) has sponsored billions of dollars' worth of aerospace research that has brought us thousands of new products. In 1962, NASA set up a program to help pass its aerospace technology along to other state and federal government agencies, public institutions, and private industry. Nine NASA applications centers across the country provide information about existing NASA technology and help in applying it.

NASA-backed aerospace research has had a great impact on industrial and consumer products. For example, NASA's need for small space systems resulted in startling advances in microcircuitry, which in turn revolutionized consumer and industrial electronics with new products ranging from home computers and video games to computerized appliances and medical systems. NASA was the first to develop communications satellites, which now carry over two-thirds of all overseas communications traffic. Here are just a few of countless other applications.

- NASA's need for lightweight and very thin reflective materials led to research that changed the previously small-scale plastics metalization business into a flourishing industry. Using such technology, the Metalized Products Division of King-Seeley Thermos Company now makes a large line of consumer and industrial products ranging from "insulated outdoor garments to packaging materials for frozen foods, from wall coverings to aircraft covers, from bed-warmers to window shades, labels to candy wrappings, reflective blankets to photographic reflectors."

- NASA's efforts to develop tasty, nutritional, lightweight, compactly packaged, nonperishable food for astronauts in outer space have found many applications in the food industry. Many commercial food firms are now producing astronaut-type meals for public distribution—freeze-dried foods and "retort-pouch" meals that can be used for a number of purposes.

- NASA's need for a superstrong safety net to protect people working high in the air on space shuttles led to a new fiber. A relatively small net made of this fiber's twine can support the average-size automobile. The twine is now used to make fishing nets more than a mile long and covering more than 86 acres. The twine is thinner and denser than nylon cord, so the new nets offer less water resistance, sink faster, go deeper, and offer 30 percent productivity gains.

- A portable X-ray machine developed by NASA uses less than 1 percent of the radiation required by conventional X-ray devices. About the size of a thermos, the unit gives instant images and is ideal for use in emergency field situations such as on-the-spot scanning for bone injuries to athletes. It can also be used for instant detection of product flaws or for security uses such as examining parcels in mailrooms and business entrances.

- Special high-intensity lights developed by NASA to stimulate the effect of sunlight on spacecraft resulted in several types of flashlights for professional and home use. One such hand-held light, which operates on a 12-volt auto or boat battery, is 50 times brighter than a car's high-beam headlights and projects a beam of light more than a mile. As a signal, it can be seen for over 30 miles.

- Bioengineering and physiological research to design cooling systems for astronaut space clothing has led to numerous commercial and consumer products—cooler athletic clothing, lightweight and heat-resistant clothing for firefighters, survival gear for hikers and campers, and dozens of others.

- While searching for a new material to be used in infrared tracking of heat-seeking missiles, Ceradyne developed a substance called translucent polycrystalline alumina (TPA). Ceradyne now uses TPA to make Transcend ceramic orthodontic braces, which are extremely strong yet virtually invisible during normal social interactions.

- Technology developed for the environmental control systems on the Apollo lunar landing spacecraft now is being used to reduce energy consumption in homes and commercial buildings. A company called Guaranteed Watt Savers now uses the technology in aluminized heat shields that keep heat, cold, and water vapor out or in as necessary. GWS calls its system "Smart House."

Source: Based on information found in *Spinoff* (Washington, DC: U.S. Government Printing Office), various issues between 1977 and 1989.

Increased Regulation

As products become more complex, the public needs to know that they are safe. Thus, government agencies investigate and ban potentially unsafe products. The Federal Food and Drug Administration has set up complex regulations for testing new drugs. The Consumer Product Safety Commission sets safety standards for consumer products and penalizes companies that fail to meet them. Such regulations have resulted in much higher research costs and in longer times between new-product ideas and their introductions. Marketers should be aware of these regulations when seeking and developing new products.

Marketers need to understand the changing technological environment and the ways that new technologies can serve human needs. They need to work closely with R&D people to encourage more market-oriented research. They also must be alert to the possible negative aspects of any innovation that might harm users or arouse opposition.

Political Environment

Marketing decisions are strongly affected by developments in the political environment. The **political environment** consists of laws, government agencies, and pressure groups that influence and limit various organizations and individuals in a given society.

Legislation Regulating Business

Even the most liberal advocates of free market economies agree that the system works best with at least some regulation. Well-conceived regulation can encourage competition and ensure fair markets for goods and services. Thus, governments develop *public policy* to guide commerce—sets of laws and regulations that limit business for the good of society as a whole. Almost every marketing activity is subject to a wide range of laws and regulations.

Understanding the public policy implications of a particular marketing activity is not a simple matter. First, there are many laws created at the federal, state, and local levels, and these regulations often overlap. For example, aspirins sold in Dallas are governed both by federal labeling laws and by Texas state advertising laws. Second, the regulations are constantly changing—what was allowed last year may now be prohibited. Marketers must work hard to keep up with these changes in the regulations and their interpretations.

Legislation affecting business has increased steadily over the years. This legislation has been enacted for a number of reasons. The first is to *protect companies* from each other. Although business executives may praise competition, they sometimes try to neutralize it when it threatens them. So laws are passed to define and prevent unfair competition. These laws are enforced by the Federal Trade Commission and the Antitrust Division of the Attorney General's office.

The second purpose of government regulation is to *protect consumers* from unfair business practices. Some firms, if left alone, would make poor products, tell lies in their advertising, and deceive consumers through their packaging and pricing. Unfair business practices have been defined and are enforced by various agencies.

The third purpose of government regulation is to *protect the interests of society* against unrestrained business behavior. Profitable business activity does not always create a better quality of life. Regulation arises to ensure that firms take responsibility for the social costs of their production or products.

New laws and their enforcement will continue or increase. Business executives must watch these developments when planning their products and marketing programs. Marketers need to know about the major laws protecting competition, consumers, and society. The main federal laws are listed in Table 3-2. Marketers also should be aware of state and local laws that affect their local marketing activity.[15]

Changing Government Agency Enforcement

To enforce the laws, Congress established federal regulatory agencies such as the Federal Trade Commission, the Food and Drug Administration, the Interstate Commerce Commission, the Federal Communications Commission, the Federal Power Commission, the Civil Aeronautics Board, the Consumer Products Safety Commission, the Environmental Protection Agency, and the Office of Consumer Affairs. Because such government agencies have some discretion in enforcing the laws, they can have a major impact on a company's marketing performance. At

TABLE 3-2
Milestone U.S. Legislation Affecting Marketing

Sherman Antitrust Act (1890)
Prohibits (a) "monopolies or attempts to monopolize"; and (b) "contracts, combinations, or conspiracies in restraint of trade" in interstate and foreign commerce.

Federal Food and Drug Act (1906)
Forbids the manufacture, sale, or transport of adulterated or fraudulently labeled foods and drugs in interstate commerce. Supplanted by the Food, Drug, and Cosmetic Act, 1938; amended by Food Additives Amendment in 1958 and the Kefauver-Harris Amendment in 1962. The 1962 amendment deals with pretesting of drugs for safety and effectiveness and labeling of drugs by generic name.

Meat Inspection Act (1906)
Provides for the enforcement of sanitary regulations in meat-packaging establishments and for federal inspection of all companies selling meats in interstate commerce.

Federal Trade Commission Act (1914)
Establishes the commission, a body of specialists with broad powers to investigate and to issue cease-and-desist orders to enforce Section 5, which declares that "unfair methods of competition in commerce are unlawful."

Clayton Act (1914)
Supplements the Sherman Act by prohibiting certain specific practices (certain types of price discrimination, tying clauses and exclusive dealing, intercorporate stockholdings, and interlocking directorates) "where the effect . . . may be to substantially lessen competition or tend to create a monopoly in any line of commerce." Provides that violating corporate officials can be held individually responsible; exempts labor and agricultural organizations from its provisions.

Robinson-Patman Act (1936)
Amends the Clayton Act. Adds the phrase "to injure, destroy, or prevent competition." Defines price discrimination as unlawful (subject to certain defenses) and provides the FTC with the right to establish limits on quantity discounts, to forbid brokerage allowances except to independent brokers, and to prohibit promotional allowances or the furnishing of services or facilities except where made available to all "on proportionately equal terms."

Miller-Tydings Act (1937)
Amends the Sherman Act to exempt interstate fair-trade (price fixing) agreements from antitrust prosecution. (The McGuire Act, 1952, reinstates the legality of the nonsigner clause.)

Wheeler-Lea Act (1938)
Prohibits unfair and deceptive acts and practices regardless of whether competition is injured; places advertising of foods and drugs under FTC jurisdiction.

Lanham Trademark Act (1946)
Requires that trademarks must be distinctive and makes it illegal to make any false representation of goods or services entering interstate commerce.

Antimerger Act (1950)
Amends Section 7 of the Clayton Act by broadening the power to prevent intercorporate acquisitions where the acquisition may have a substantially adverse effect on competition.

Automobile Information Disclosure Act (1958)
Prohibits car dealers from inflating the factory price of new cars.

National Traffic and Safety Act (1958)
Provides for the creation of compulsory safety standards for automobiles and tires.

Fair Packaging and Labeling Act (1966)
Provides for the regulation of the packaging and labeling of consumer goods. Requires manufacturers to state what the package contains, who made it, and how much it contains. Permits industries' voluntary adoption of uniform packaging standards.

Child Protection Act (1966)
Bans sale of hazardous toys and articles. Amended in 1969 to include articles that pose electrical, mechanical, or thermal hazards.

Federal Cigarette Labeling and Advertising Act (1967)
Requires that cigarette packages contain the following statement: "Warning: The Surgeon General Has Determined That Cigarette Smoking Is Dangerous to Your Health."

Truth-in-Lending Act (1968)
Requires lenders to state the true costs of a credit transaction, outlaws the use of actual or threatened violence in collecting loans, and restricts the amount of garnishments. Established a National Commission on Consumer Finance.

National Environmental Policy Act (1969)
Establishes a national policy on the environment and provides for the establishment of the Council on Environmental Quality. The Environmental Protection Agency was established by Reorganization Plan No. 3 of 1970.

Fair Credit Reporting Act (1970)
Ensures that a consumer's credit report will contain only accurate, relevant, and recent information and will be confidential unless requested for an appropriate reason by a proper party.

Consumer Product Safety Act (1972)
Establishes the Consumer Product Safety Commission and authorizes it to set safety standards for consumer products as well as exact penalties for failure to uphold the standards.

Consumer Goods Pricing Act (1975)
Prohibits the use of price maintenance agreements among manufacturers and resellers in interstate commerce.

Magnuson-Moss Warranty/FTC Improvement Act (1975)
Authorizes the FTC to determine rules concerning consumer warranties and provides for consumer access to means of redress, such as the "class action" suit. Also expands FTC regulatory powers over unfair or deceptive acts or practices.

Equal Credit Opportunity Act (1975)
Prohibits discrimination in a credit transaction because of sex, marital status, race, national origin, religion, age, or receipt of public assistance.

Fair Debt Collection Practice Act (1978)
Makes it illegal to abuse any person and make false statements or use unfair methods when collecting a debt.

FTC Improvement Act (1980)
Provides the House of Representatives and Senate jointly with veto power over FTC Trade Regulation Rules. Enacted to limit FTC's powers to regulate "unfairness" issues.

Toy Safety Act (1984)
Gives the government the power to recall dangerous toys quickly when they are found.

---

times, the staffs of these agencies have appeared to be overly eager and unpredictable. Some of the agencies sometimes have been dominated by lawyers and economists who lacked a practical sense of how business and marketing works. In recent years, the Federal Trade Commission has added staff marketing experts who can better understand complex business issues.

Growth of Public Interest Groups
The number and power of public interest groups have increased during the past two decades. The most successful is Ralph Nader's Public Citizen group, which acts as a watchdog on consumer interests. Nader lifted **consumerism,** an organized movement of citizens and government to strengthen the rights and power of buyers in relation to sellers, into a major social force. He did this first with his successful attack on unsafe automobiles (resulting in the passage of the National Traffic and Motor Vehicle Safety Act of 1962); and then through investigations into meat processing (resulting in the passage of the Wholesome Meat Act of 1967), truth-in-lending, auto repairs, insurance, and X-ray equipment. Hundreds of other consumer interest groups, private and governmental, operate at the national, state, and local levels. Other groups that marketers need to consider are those seeking to protect the environment and to advance the rights of various groups such as women, blacks, senior citizens, and others.

Increased Emphasis on Ethics and Socially Responsible Actions
Written regulations cannot possibly cover all potential marketing abuses, and existing laws are often difficult to enforce. However, beyond written laws and regulations, business is also governed by social codes and rules of professional ethics.

Enlightened companies encourage their managers to look beyond what the regulatory system allows and to simply "do the right thing." These socially responsible firms actively seek out ways to protect the long-run interests of their consumers and the environment.

The recent rash of business scandals and increased concerns about the environment have created fresh interest in the issues of ethics and social responsibility. Almost every aspect of marketing involves such issues. Unfortunately, because these issues usually involve conflicting interests, well-meaning people can disagree honestly about the right course of action in a particular situation. Thus, many industrial and professional trade associations have suggested codes of ethics, and many companies now are developing policies and guidelines to deal with complex social responsibility issues.

Throughout the text, we present Marketing Highlight exhibits that summarize the main public policy and social responsibility issues surrounding major marketing decisions. These exhibits discuss the legal issues that marketers should understand and the common ethical and societal concerns that marketers face. In Chapter 23, we discuss a broad range of societal marketing issues in greater depth.

Cultural Environment

The **cultural environment** is made up of institutions and other forces that affect society's basic values, perceptions, preferences, and behaviors. People grow up in a particular society that shapes their basic beliefs and values. They absorb a world view that defines their relationships to themselves and others. The following cultural characteristics can affect marketing decision making.

Persistence of Cultural Values

People in a given society hold many beliefs and values. Their core beliefs and values have a high degree of persistence. For example, most Americans believe in working, getting married, giving to charity, and being honest. These beliefs shape more specific attitudes and behaviors found in everyday life. *Core* beliefs and values are passed on from parents to children and are reinforced by schools, churches, business, and government.

Secondary beliefs and values are more open to change. Believing in marriage is a core belief; believing that people should get married early in life is a secondary belief. Marketers have some chance of changing secondary values, but little chance of changing core values. For example, family-planning marketers could argue more effectively that people should get married later than that they should not get married at all.

Shifts in Secondary Cultural Values

Although core values are fairly persistent, cultural swings do take place. Consider the impact of popular music groups, movie personalities, and other celebrities on young people's hair styling, clothing, and sexual norms. Marketers want to predict cultural shifts in order to spot new opportunities or threats. Several firms offer "futures" forecasts in this connection. For example, the Yankelovich marketing research firm tracks 41 cultural values, such as "anti-bigness,""mysticism," "living for today," "away from possessions," and "sensuousness." The firm describes the percentage of the population who share the attitude as well as the percentage who go against the trend. For instance, the percentage of people who value physical fitness and well-being has risen steadily over the years. Such information helps marketers cater to trends with appropriate products and communication appeals. (See Marketing Highlight 3-3 for a summary of today's cultural trends.)

The major cultural values of a society are expressed in people's views of themselves and others, as well as in their views of organizations, society, nature, and the universe.

People's Views of Themselves. People vary in their emphasis on serving themselves versus serving others. Some people seek personal pleasure, wanting fun, change, and escape. Others seek self-realization through religion, recreation, or the avid pursuit of careers or other life goals. People use products, brands, and services as a means of self-expression and buy products and services that match their views of themselves.

In the 1980s, personal ambition and materialism increased dramatically, with significant marketing implications. In a "me-society," people buy their

MARKETING HIGHLIGHT 3-3

POPCORN'S TEN CULTURAL TRENDS

Futurist Faith Popcorn runs BrainReserve, a marketing consulting firm that monitors cultural trends and advises companies such as AT&T, Citibank, Black & Decker, Hoffman-La Roche, Nissan, Rubbermaid, and many others on how these trends will affect their marketing and other business decisions. Using its trend predictions, BrainReserve offers several services: BrainJam generates new product ideas for clients, and Brand-Renewal attempts to breathe new life into fading brands. FutureFocus develops marketing strategies and concepts that create long-term competitive advantage. Another service, TrendBank, is a database containing culture monitoring and consumer interview information. Popcorn and her associates have identified ten major cultural trends affecting U.S. consumers:

Marketers follow cultural trends, such as "cocooning," in order to spot new marketing opportunities or threats.

1. *Cashing out:* the urge to change one's life to a slower but more rewarding pace. An executive suddenly quits his or her career, escapes the hassles of big city life, and turns up in Vermont or Montana running a small newspaper, managing a bed-and-breakfast establishment, or starting a band. People cash out because they don't think the stress is worth it. They nostalgically try to return to small town values, seeking clean air, safe schools, and plain-speaking neighbors.

2. *Cocooning:* the impulse to stay inside when the outside gets too tough and scary. More people are turning their homes into nests: redecorating their houses, becoming "couch potatoes," watching TV movies, ordering from catalogs, and using answering machines to filter out the outside world. In reaction to increases in crime and other social problems, cocooners are burrowing in and building bunkers. Self-preservation is the underlying theme. Another breed is Wandering Cocoons, people who

eat in their cars and communicate through their car phones. Socialized Cocooners form a small group of friends who frequently get together for conversation or for "salooning."

3. *Down-aging:* the tendency to act and feel younger than one's age. Today's sex symbols include Cher (over 45), Paul Newman (over 65), and Elizabeth Taylor (over 60). Older people spend more on youthful clothes, hair coloring, and facial plastic surgery. They engage in more playful behavior and act in ways previously thought not to be appropriate for their age group. They buy adult toys, attend adult camps, and sign up for adventure vacations.

4. *Egonomics:* the desire to develop individuality in order to be seen and treated as different from others. This is not an ego trip, but simply the wish to

"dream cars" and take their "dream vacations." They spend more time in outdoor health activities (jogging, tennis), in thought, and on arts and crafts. The leisure industry (camping, boating, arts and crafts, and sports) faces good growth prospects in a society where people seek self-fulfillment.

People's Views of Others. More recently, observers have noted a shift from a "me-society" to a "we-society" in which more people want to be with and serve others. Flashy spending and self-indulgence appear to be on the way out, whereas saving, family concerns, and helping others are on the rise. A recent survey showed that more people are becoming involved in charity, volunteer work, and social service activities.[16] This suggests a bright future for "social support" products and services that improve direct communication between people, such as health clubs, family vacations, and games. It also suggests a growing market for "social substitutes"—things like VCRs and computers that allow people who are alone to feel that they are not.

People's Views of Organizations. People vary in their attitudes toward individualize oneself through possessions and experiences. People increasingly subscribe to narrow-interest magazines; join small groups with narrow missions; and buy customized clothing, cars, and cosmetics. Egonomics gives marketers an opportunity to succeed by offering customized goods, services, and experiences.

5. *Fantasy adventure:* the need to find emotional escapes to offset one's daily routines. People might seek vacations, eat exotic foods, go to Disneyland and other fantasy parks, or redecorate their homes with a Sante Fe look. For marketers, this is an opportunity to create new fantasy products and services, or to add fantasy touches to their current products and services.

6. *99 lives:* the desperate state of people who must juggle many roles and responsibilities. An example is the "SuperMom" who must handle a full-time career while also managing her home and children. People today feel time-poor. They attempt to relieve time pressures by using fax machines and car phones, eating at fast food restaurants, and through other means. Marketers can meet this need by creating *cluster marketing* enterprises—all-in-one service stops, such as Video Town Launderette which, in addition to its laundry facilities, includes a tanning room, an exercise bike, copying and fax machines, and 6,000 video titles for rent.

7. *S.O.S. (Save Our Society):* the drive on the part of a growing number of people to make society more socially responsible with respect to education, ethics, and the environment. People join groups to promote more social responsibility on the part of companies and other citizens. The best response for marketers is to urge their own companies to practice more socially responsible marketing.

8. *Small indulgences:* the need on the part of stressed-out consumers for occasional emotional fixes. A consumer might not be able to afford a two-week trip to Europe but might spend a weekend in New Orleans instead. He or she might eat healthily all week, then splurge with a pint of superpremium Haagen-Dazs ice cream over the weekend. Marketers should be aware of the ways in which consumers feel deprived and look for opportunities to offer small indulgences that provide an emotional lift.

9. *Staying alive:* the drive to live longer and better lives. People now know that their lifestyles can kill them—eating the wrong foods, smoking, breathing bad air, abusing drugs. They are increasingly taking bad air, abusing drugs. They are increasingly taking responsibility for their own health and choosing better foods, exercising more regularly, and relaxing more often. Marketers can meet these needs by designing healthier products and services for consumers.

10. *The vigilante consumer:* Vigilante consumers are those who will no longer tolerate shoddy products and poor service. They want companies to be more aware and responsive. They want auto companies to take back "lemons" and fully refund their money. They subscribe to the *National Boycott News* and *Consumer Reports,* join MADD (Mothers Against Drunk Driving), buy "green products," and look for lists of good companies and bad companies. Marketers must serve as the consciences of their companies to bring these consumers better, more responsible products and services.

Source: From *The Popcorn Report* by Faith Popcorn. © 1991 by Faith Popcorn. Used by permission of Bantam Doubleday Dell Publishing Group.

corporations, government agencies, trade unions, universities, and other organizations. By and large, people are willing to work for major organizations and expect them, in turn, to carry out society's work. There has been, however, a decline in organizational loyalty. People are giving a little less to their organizations and are trusting them less.

This trend suggests that organizations need to find new ways to win consumer confidence. They need to review their advertising communications to make sure their messages are honest. Also, they need to review their various activities to make sure that they are coming across as "good corporate citizens." More companies are linking themselves to worthwhile causes, measuring their images with important publics, and using public relations to build more positive images (see Marketing Highlight 3-4).

People's Views of Society. People vary in their attitudes toward their society, from patriots who defend it, to reformers who want to change it, to malcontents who want to leave it. People's orientation to their society influences their

CAUSE-RELATED MARKETING: DOING WELL BY DOING GOOD

These days, every product seems to be tied to some cause. Buy Hellmann's mayonnaise or Skippy peanut butter and help "Keep America Beautiful." Drink Tang and earn money for Mothers Against Drunk Driving. Or, if you want to help the Leukemia Society of America, buy Helping Hand trash bags or toilet paper. Pay for these purchases with the right charge card and you can support a local cultural arts group or help fight cancer or heart disease.

Cause-related marketing has become one of the hottest forms of corporate giving. It lets companies "do well by doing good" by linking purchases of the company's products or services with fund raising for worthwhile causes or charitable organizations. Cause-related marketing has grown rapidly since the early 1980s, when American Express offered to donate 1 cent to the restoration of the Statue of Liberty for each use of its charge card. American Express ended up having to contribute $1.7 million, but the cause-related campaign produced a 28 percent increase in card usage.

Companies now sponsor dozens of cause-related marketing campaigns each year. Many are backed by large budgets and a full complement of marketing activities. Here are recent examples:

> Johnson & Johnson teamed with the Children's Hospital Medical Center and the National Safety Council to sponsor a five-year cause-related marketing campaign to reduce preventable children's injuries, the leading killer of children. Some 43 other nonprofit groups including the American Red Cross, National Parent Teachers Association, and the Boy and Girl Scouts of America helped to promote the campaign. The campaign offered consumers a free Safe Kids safety kit for children in exchange for proofs of purchase. Consumers could also buy a Child's Safety Video for $9.95. The video featured a game show format that made learning about safety entertaining as well as educational. To promote the campaign, J&J distributed almost 50 million advertising inserts in daily newspapers and developed a special information kit for retailers containing posters, floor displays, and other in-store promotion materials. Safe

Kids Safety Tip Sheets and emergency phone stickers were also available as free consumer handouts.

Procter & Gamble has sponsored many cause-related marketing campaigns. For example, during the past several years, P&G has mailed out billions of coupons on behalf of the Special Olympics for retarded children, helping make the event a household word. P&G supports its Special Olympics efforts with national advertising and public relations, and its salespeople work with local volunteers to encourage retailers to build point-of-purchase displays. In another recent cause-related marketing effort, Procter & Gamble has set up the Jif Children's Education Fund. For every pound of Jif peanut butter sold during the three-month promotion, P&G donates 10 cents to the fund, which will be distributed to parent-teacher groups at registered elementary schools in America. The program is designed to raise more than $4 million for U.S. elementary education.

Through focus group studies, Levi Strauss learned that young parents were greatly frustrated in their efforts to get their preschoolers dressed in the morning rush to work and daycare. The company also learned that only 40 percent of the parents knew of its Little Levi's line of clothing for young children. So Levi paid the Bank Street College of Education to create a booklet for preschoolers called "Let's Get Dressed!" The activity booklet uses fun games and puzzles to teach kids how to dress themselves. A companion booklet provides tips for parents on how to take the hassle out of dressing their children. Retailers offered the booklets as a gift with purchases of Little Levi's clothing and supported the campaign with in-store promotions and local ads. Readers were given an address from which they could order the booklets for 50 cents. The campaign also received substantial publicity coverage on TV talk shows and in national women's magazines. Sales of Little Levi's have tripled since the cause-related marketing campaign began.

Continental Airlines sponsored its FlyAmerica campaign as a companion to the annual March of Dimes WalkAmerica fundraiser. To participate in FlyAmer-

consumption patterns, levels of savings, and attitudes toward the marketplace.

The 1980s and early 1990s have seen an increase in consumer patriotism. Many U.S. companies have responded with "made in America" themes and flag-waving promotions. For example, Chevrolet is "the heartbeat of America." Black & Decker recently has added a flag-like symbol to its tools. And for the past several years, the American textile industry has blitzed consumers with its "Crafted with Pride in the USA" advertising campaign, insisting that "made in the USA" matters. In 1991, many companies used patriotic appeals and promotions to ex-

The more you buy, the more we'll give to America's schools.

Jif CREAMY

We at Jif know education takes money. Which is why we have created the Jif Children's Education Fund.

From February 1st through April 30th, every time you buy Jif® peanut butter, we'll make a donation to elementary schools across America. It's that simple. Our goal is to raise at least $4,000,000. And the more Jif you buy, the more we'll give. There's no limit!

Every elementary school has been invited to participate in this important program. Check with your parent-teacher group to see if your school has enrolled.

Remember, by choosing Jif, you'll be choosing to help America's kids.

Choose to help America's kids. Choose Jif.

Jif children's education fund

Cause marketing: Doing well by doing good—linking purchases of company products with fund raising for worthwhile projects.

ica, a sort of "fly-athon," consumers pledged to fly a certain number of miles on Continental and signed up sponsors who made donations based on the miles actually flown. Continental promoted the campaign with in-flight videos, brochures, and a $2-million advertising campaign that invited consumers to "Join us to help the March of Dimes work for healthier arrivals every day."

Cause-related marketing has stirred some controversy. Critics are concerned that cause-related marketing might eventually undercut traditional "no-strings" corporate giving, as more and more companies grow to expect marketing benefits from their contributions. Critics also worry that cause-related marketing will cause a shift in corporate charitable support toward more visible, popular, and low-risk charities—those with more certain and substantial marketing appeal. For example, MasterCard's Choose to Make a Difference campaign raises money for six charities, each selected in part because of its popularity in a consumer poll. Finally, critics worry that cause-related marketing is more a strategy for selling than a strategy for giving, that "cause-related" marketing is really "cause-exploitative" marketing. They fear that companies are simply trying to buy better images by trading on the good works and hard-won reputations of the charitable organizations. Thus, companies using cause-related marketing might find themselves walking a fine line between increased sales and an improved image, and charges of exploitation.

However, if handled well, cause-related marketing can greatly benefit both the company and the charitable organization. The company gains an effective marketing tool while building a more positive public image. And promoting a cause can make the company's offer stand out from the clutter of competing products and promotions. The charitable organization gains greater visibility and important new sources of funding. This additional funding can be substantial. For example, the American Red Cross plans to raise $10 million each year, or 10 percent of its annual national disaster relief budget, through cause-related marketing. In total, such campaigns now contribute some $100 million annually to the coffers of charitable organizations, and surveys show that these cause-related contributions usually add to, rather than undercut, direct company contributions. Thus, when cause marketing works, everyone wins.

Sources: See P. Rajan Varadarajan and Anil Menon, "Cause-Related Marketing: A Coalignment of Marketing Strategy and Corporate Philanthropy," *Journal of Marketing,* July 1988, pp. 58-74; Cyndee Miller, "Drug Company Begins Its Own Children's Crusade," *Marketing News,* June 6, 1988, pp. 1, 2; "School Kids Snack for Cash," *Advertising Age,* February 2, 1990, p. 36; Bill Kelley, "Cause-Related Marketing: Doing Well While Doing Good," *Sales & Marketing Management,* March 1991, pp. 60-65; Melanie Rigney and Julie Steenhuysen, "Conscience Raising," *Advertising Age,* August 26, 1991, p. 19; and Kim D. Shaver, "Cause Marketing: It Can Be a Win-Win-Win Strategy," *Furniture Today,* February 10, 1992, p. 12.

press their support of American troops in the Persian Gulf War and to ride the wave of national pride and patriotism that followed.[17]

People's Views of Nature. People vary in their attitudes toward the natural world. Some feel ruled by it, others feel in harmony with it, and still others seek to master it. A long-term trend has been people's growing mastery over nature through technology and the belief that nature is bountiful. More recently, however, people have recognized that nature is finite and fragile—that it can be destroyed or spoiled by human activities.

Many companies have responded to an increase in consumer patriotism with "flag-waving" ads and programs.

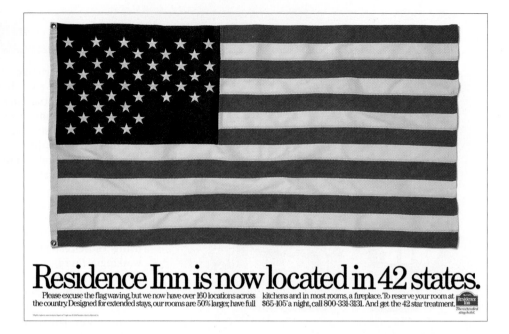

Residence Inn is now located in 42 states.

Please excuse the flag waving, but we now have over 160 locations across the country. Designed for extended stays, our rooms are 50% larger, have full kitchens and in most rooms, a fireplace. To reserve your room at $65-105 a night, call 800-331-3131. And get the 42 star treatment.

Love of nature is leading to more camping, hiking, boating, fishing, and other outdoor activities. Business has responded by offering more hiking gear, camping equipment, better insect repellents, and other products for nature enthusiasts. Tour operators are offering more tours to wilderness areas. Food producers have found growing markets for "natural" products like natural cereal, natural ice cream, and health foods. Marketing communicators are using appealing natural backgrounds in advertising their products.

People's Views of the Universe. Finally, people vary in their beliefs about the origin of the universe and their place in it. Although most Americans practice religion, religious conviction and practice have been dropping off through the years, and church attendance has fallen gradually. As people lose their religious orientation, they seek goods and experiences with more immediate satisfactions. During the 1980s, people increasingly measured success in terms of career achievement, wealth, and worldly possessions. Some futurists, however, have noted an emerging renewal of interest in religion, perhaps as a part of a broader search for a new inner purpose. In the 1990s, they believe, people are moving away from materialism and dog-eat-dog ambition to seek more permanent values and a more certain grasp of right and wrong.

> The Nineties will see a marked change in the way society defines success, with achievements such as a happy family life and service to one's community replacing money as the measure of one's worth.[18] The Nineties will be a far less cynical decade than the Eighties. Yes, we will still care what things cost. But we will seek to value only those things—family, community, earth, faith—that will endure.[19]

RESPONDING TO THE MARKETING ENVIRONMENT

Many companies view the marketing environment as an "uncontrollable" element to which they must adapt. They passively accept the marketing environment and do not try to change it. They analyze the environmental forces and design strategies that will help the company avoid the threats and take advantage of the opportunities the environment provides.

Other companies take an **environmental management perspective**.[20] Rather than simply watching and reacting, these firms take aggressive actions to affect the publics and forces in their marketing environment. Such companies hire lobbyists to influence legislation affecting their industries and stage media events to gain favorable press coverage. They run "advertorials" (ads expressing editorial points of view) to shape public opinion. They press law suits and file complaints with regulators to keep competitors in line, and they form contractual agreements to better control their distribution channels. The following example shows how one company overcame a seemingly uncontrollable environmental constraint:

> Citicorp, the U.S. banking giant, had been trying for years to start full-service banking in Maryland. It had only credit card and small service operations in the state. Under Maryland law, out-of-state banks could provide only certain services and were barred from advertising, setting up branches, and other types of marketing. In March 1985, Citicorp offered to build a major credit card center in Maryland that would create 1,000 white-collar jobs and further offered the state $1 million in cash for the property where it would locate. By imaginatively designing a proposal to benefit Maryland, Citicorp became the first out-of-state bank to provide full banking services there.[21]

Marketing management cannot always affect environmental forces. In many cases, it must settle for simply watching and reacting to the environment. For example, a company would have little success trying to influence geographic population shifts, the economic environment, or major cultural values. But whenever possible, smart marketing managers will take a *proactive* rather than *reactive* approach to the marketing environment.

 # SUMMARY

The company must start with the *marketing environment* in searching for opportunities and monitoring threats. The marketing environment consists of all the actors and forces that affect the company's ability to transact effectively with its target market. The company's marketing environment can be divided into the microenvironment and the macroenvironment.

The *microenvironment* consists of five components. The first is the company's *internal environment*—its several departments and management levels—as it affects marketing management's decision making. The second component includes the *marketing channel firms* that cooperate to create value: the suppliers and marketing intermediaries (middlemen, physical distribution firms, marketing services agencies, financial intermediaries). The third component consists of the five types of *markets* in which the company can sell: the consumer, producer, reseller, government, and international markets. The fourth component consists of the *competitors* facing the company. The fifth component consists of all the *publics* that have an actual or potential interest in or impact on the organization's ability to achieve its objectives. The seven types of publics include financial, media, government, citizen action, and local, general, and internal publics.

The company's *macroenvironment* consists of major forces that shape opportunities and pose threats to the company. These forces include demographic, economic, natural, technological, political, and cultural forces.

The *demographic environment* shows a changing age structure in the U.S. population, a changing American family, geographic population shifts, a better-educated and more white-collar population, and increasing ethnic and racial diversity. The *economic environment* shows changing real income and changing consumer spending patterns. The *natural environment* shows coming shortages of certain raw materials, increased energy costs, increased pollution levels, and increasing government intervention in natural resource management. The *technological environment* shows rapid technological change, unlimited innovational opportunities, high R&D budgets, concentration on minor improvements rather than major discoveries, and increased regulation of technological change. The *political environment* shows increasing business regulation, strong government agency enforcement, and the growth of public interest groups. The *cultural environment* shows long-run trends toward a "we-society," decreasing organizational loyalty, increasing patriotism, an increasing appreciation for nature, and a search for more meaningful and enduring values.

 # KEY TERMS

DISCUSSING THE ISSUES

1. In the 1930s, President Franklin Roosevelt used his cigarette holder as a personal "trademark." Would a president be seen smoking today? How has the cultural environment changed? How might a cigarette manufacturer market its products differently to meet this new environment?

2. What environmental trends will affect the success of Walt Disney Company throughout the 1990s? If you were in charge of marketing at Disney, what plans would you make to deal with these trends?

3. Immigration is an important component of U.S. population growth. Currently, there is one legal immigrant for every six or seven people born in the United States, twice the ratio of 20 years ago. How will this trend affect marketing over the next 5 years? Over the next 50 years?

4. Americans are becoming more concerned about the natural environment. How would this trend affect a company that markets plastic sandwich bags? Discuss some effective responses to this trend.

5. A major alcoholic beverage marketer is planning to introduce an "adult soft drink"—a socially acceptable substitute for stronger drinks that would be cheaper and lower in alcohol than wine coolers. What cultural and other factors might affect the success of this product?

6. Some marketing goals, such as improved quality, require strong support from an internal public—a company's own employees. But surveys show that employees increasingly distrust management, and company loyalty is eroding. How can a company market internally to help meet its goals?

 # APPLYING THE CONCEPTS

1. Changes in the marketing environment mean that marketers must meet new consumer needs that may be quite different—even directly opposite—from those in the past. Ben & Jerry's became successful by making great tasting ice cream with a huge butterfat content. They now offer low-fat frozen yogurt to appeal to soft-in-the-middle baby boomers. You can track changes in the marketing environment by looking at how companies modify their products.

   ■ Make a list of the products you encounter in one day that claim to be "low" or "high" in some ingredient, such as low-tar cigarettes, or high-fiber cereal.

   ■ Write down similar products that seem to offer the opposite characteristics.

   ■ In each case, which product do you think came first? Do you think that this is an effective response to a changing marketing environment?

2. The political environment can have a direct impact on marketers and their plans. In 1993, the inauguration of Bill Clinton as President of the United States signaled that the political environment was likely to change significantly through the mid-1990s.

   ■ Name three industries that will probably have their marketing plans and strategies affected by the political changes in Washington.

   ■ For each of the industries that you named, list three potential strategies to help adapt to the coming changes in the political environment.

   ■ Although environmental changes appear likely, are they *certain?* How should companies plan for unsettled conditions?

MAKING MARKETING DECISIONS:

SMALL WORLD COMMUNICATIONS, INC.

Lynette and Thomas have continued to talk and share information about starting a business. Lyn has drafted a mission statement that she likes. It reads: "Small World Communications will serve computer users by marketing innovative, high-value products which open doorways to people, information, and applications."

Tom was not completely sold on this mission. "It doesn't even say whether we're selling hardware or software," he protested. "I need to know my product." Lyn replied, "You need to know your *customers* first, then fill their needs. Look, Steve Jobs thought that Next Computers should sell computers. Turns out that users loved the NextStep software, but didn't need the machines. In 1993 he dropped computers and went into software full time. If Wang Labs had done the same thing, they could have been a major word processing company like WordPerfect, instead of a bankrupt dinosaur."

"I can't argue with that," said Tom, "so let's look at our potential users and the environment we're facing right now. This market changes fast, but some parts of it are pretty predictable over the next two years. I can tell you what's going to happen to hardware, and the major software projects that companies are working on for the future. You need to tell me what to look at, and how to make sense out of a mass of raw data." "What we need," said Lyn, "is a good analysis of our macro- and microenvironments. Let's start micro—you give me the industry status and opportunities in a nutshell."

"O.K., I'll start, but please interrupt me at 4 o'clock and remind me to go to my next meeting," said Tom. Lyn glanced at her watch. It was 10:45. Tom began, "Based on data from 1993, there were about 47 million PCs in the United States, 42 percent connected to local area networks. That should rise to 52 percent connected on LANs by 1996. Simple E-mail for messages is booming: 6 million users in 1991, 15 million in 1993, maybe 38 million by 1995. But two related trends are hitting big: a technical restructuring of E-mail, and collaborative computing. The new E-mail will allow multimedia mail. Two people in different places can look at the same spreadsheet at the same time, and have a picturephone conversation on their monitors to discuss it. People can also talk to virtual users—software processes, not people—to do stuff like check status on a special order in the factory, or route an incoming fax to the right person. And software can talk to software directly, without people, to share needed information. Overall it's a big market, huge growth, lots of little competitors, no standards set yet, and a lot of change coming."

"What about collaborative computing? Is that groupware?" asked Lynette. "Yep, but it's moving beyond what you may have seen so far. Groupware sales were about $1.9 billion in 1993. That includes software to do simple messaging, departmental appointment scheduling, group authoring of reports, that sort of thing. Now there are virtual team meetings going on by computer—same time but different places, or same place but different times, or different places and different times. The next step is adding artificial team members, artificial intelligence software that will search around for the data you need, sort it out, keep it up to date, and maybe give you advice." Tom paused. "I think there may be some opportunities here, Lyn. What do you think?" "Well, Toto, I think you're right—and I *know* we're not in Kansas anymore."

What Now?

1. A company's microenvironment can often be described simply as "rich" or "lean." Rich environments offer good growth and profit potential, and moderate levels of competition that allow many companies to thrive. Lean environments are much more difficult: low growth, low prices and profits, stiff competition, and few surviving companies. Would you describe Small World Communications as facing a rich or lean microenvironment? How might this affect their strategies for the future?

2. Consider the macroenvironment for Small World Communications. On a sheet of paper, make a simple chart listing the six major aspects of the macroenvironment—demographic, economic, natural, technological, political, and cultural. List your opinion about whether each environment is likely to be *positive, neutral, negative,* or *uncertain* for Small World. For each environment, write down one key issue you think Lyn and Tom will face. Could a creative strategy make new opportunities in a "negative" environment?

 # REFERENCES

1. For more information, see "Kellogg: Snap, Crackle, Profits," *Dun's Business Month*, December 1985, pp. 32-33; Russell Mitchell, "The Health Craze has Kellogg Feeling G-r-r-eat," *Business Week*, March 30, 1987, pp. 52-53; David Woodruff, "Winning the War of Battle Creek," *Business Week*, May 13, 1991, p. 80; John C. Maxwell, Jr., "Cold Cereals Growing; Kellogg Remains on Top," *Advertising Age*, May 11, 1992, p. 72; and Julie Liesse, "Kellogg, Alpo Top Hot New Product List," *Advertising Age*, January 4, 1993, pp. 14, 21.

2. See Thomas Exter, "And Baby Makes 20 Million," *American Demographics*, July 1991, p. 55; Christy Fisher, "Wooing Boomers' Babies," *Advertising Age*, July 22, 1991, pp. 3, 30; Joseph Spiers, "The Baby Boomlet Is for Real," *Fortune*, February 10, 1992, pp. 101-4; and Joe Schwartz, "Is the Baby Boomlet Ending?" *American Demographics*, May 1992, p. 9.

3. See Horst H. Stipp, "Boomlet Market," *American Demographics*, March 1989, pp. 14-15; Lynn G. Coleman, "Right Now, Kids Are Very Hot," *Marketing News*, June 25, 1990, pp. 1, 6; Christopher Power, "Getting 'Em While They're Young," *Busi*

ness Week, September 9, 1991, pp. 94-95; and James U. McNeal, "Growing Up in the Market," *American Demographics*, October 1992, pp. 46-50.

4. See Walecia Konrad and Gail DeGeorge, "U.S. Companies Go for the Gray," *Business Week*, April 3, 1989, pp. 64-67; and Melinda Beck, "The Geezer Boom," in "The 21st Century Family," a special issue of *Newsweek*, Winter/Spring 1990, pp. 62-67.

5. For an outstanding discussion of the changing nature of American Households, see *American Households*, American Demographic Desk Reference Series, No. 3, July 1992.

6. See Joe Schwartz, "On the Road Again," *American Demographics*, April 1987, pp. 39-42; "Americans Keep Going West—And South," *Business Week*, May 16, 1988, p. 30; Judith Waldrop, "2010," *American Demographics*, February 1989, pp. 18-21; and Judith Waldrop and Thomas Exter, "The Legacy of the 1980s," *American Demographics*, March 1991, pp. 33-38.

7. The MSA (Metropolitan Statistical Area) concept classified heavily populated areas as MSAs or PMSAs (Primary Metropol-

itan Statistical Areas). MSAs and PMSAs are defined in the same way, except that PMSAs are also components of larger "megalopolies" called CMSAs (Consolidated Metropolitan Statistical Areas). MSAs and PMSAs are areas consisting of (1) a city of at least 50,000 in population, or (2) an urbanized area of at least 50,000 with a total metropolitan area of at least 100,000. See Richard Kern, "You Say Potato and I Say ADIM-SADMAPMSA," *Sales & Marketing Management*, December 1988, p. 8.

8. See Thomas Moore, "Different Folks, Different Strokes," *Fortune*, September 16, 1985, pp. 65-68.

9. See Fabian Linden, "In the Rearview Mirror," *American Demographics*, April 1984, pp. 4-5. For more reading, see Bryant Robey and Cheryl Russell, "A Portrait of the American Worker," *American Demographics*, March 1984, pp. 17-21.

10. See Judith Waldrop and Thomas Exter, "What the 1990 Census Will Show," *American Demographics*, January 1990, p. 25; *American Diversity*, American Demographic Desk Reference Series, No. 1, July 1991; Brian Bremner, "A Spicier Stew in the Melting Pot," *Business Week*, December 21, 1992, pp. 29-30; and "New Projections Show Faster Growth, More Diversity," *American Demographics*, February 1993, pp. 9, 59.

11. James W. Hughes, "Understanding the Squeezed Consumer," *American Demographics*, July 1991, pp. 44-50. Also see Patricia Sellers, "Winning Over the New Consumer," *Fortune*, July 29, 1991, pp. 113-25; and Brian O'Reilly, "Preparing for Leaner Times," *Fortune*, January 27, 1992, pp. 40-47.

12. For more on value marketing, see Christopher Power, "Value Marketing," *Business Week*, November 11, 1991, pp. 132-40.

13. For more discussion, see the "Environmentalism" section in Chapter 23. Also see Joe Schwartz, "Earth Day Today," *American Demographics*, April 1990, pp. 40-41; Jennifer Lawrence, "Marketers Drop 'Recycled,'" *Advertising Age*, March 9, 1992, pp. 1, 48; and Carl Frankel, "Blueprint for Green Marketing," *American Demographics*, April 1992, pp. 34-38.

14. See Robert Buderi, "R&D Scoreboard: On a Clear Day You Can See Progress," *Business Week*, June 29, 1992, pp. 104-6; Cyndee Miller, "Report on R&D Spending Hints at Loss of U.S. Competitiveness," *Marketing News*, June 22, 1992, p. 1; and Lee Smith, "What the U.S. Can Do About R&D," *Fortune*, October 19, 1992, pp. 74-76.

15. For a summary of legal developments in marketing, see Louis W. Stern and Thomas L. Eovaldi, *Legal Aspects of Marketing Strategy: Antitrust and Consumer Protection Issues* (Englewood Cliffs, NJ: Prentice Hall, 1984); and Robert J. Posch, Jr., *The Complete Guide to Marketing and the Law* (Englewood Cliffs, NJ: Prentice Hall, 1988).

16. See Bill Barol, "The Eighties are Gone," *Newsweek*, January 14, 1988, p. 48; Natalie de Combray, "Volunteering in America," *American Demographics*, March 1987, pp. 50-52; Annetta Miller, "The New Volunteerism," *Newsweek*, February 8, 1988; pp. 42-43; and Ronald Henkoff, "Is Greed Dead?" *Fortune*, August 14, 1989, pp. 40-41.

17. See Kenneth Dreyfack, "Draping Old Glory Around Just About Everything," *Business Week*, October 27, 1986, pp. 66-67; Pat Sloan, "Ads Go All-American," *Advertising Age*, July 28, 1986, pp. 3, 52; "Retailers Rallying 'Round the Flag," *Advertising Age*, February 11, 1991, p. 4; and Gary Levin, "BASH, BASH, BASH: U.S. Marketers Turn Red, White, and Blue Against Japan," *Advertising Age*, February 3, 1992, pp. 1, 44.

18. Anne B. Fisher, "A Brewing Revolt Against the Rich," *Fortune*, December 17, 1990, pp. 89-94.

19. Anne B. Fisher, "What Consumers Want in the 1990s," *Fortune*, January 21, 1990, p. 112. Also see Joseph M. Winski, Who We Are, How We Live, What We Think," *Advertising Age*, January 20, 1992, pp. 16-18; and John Huey, "Finding New Heros for a New Era," *Fortune*, January 25, 1993, pp. 62-69.

20. See Carl P. Zeithaml and Valerie A. Zeithaml, "Environmental Management: Revising the Marketing Perspective," *Journal of Marketing*, Spring 1984, pp. 46-53.

21. Philip Kotler, "Megamarketing," *Harvard Business Review*, March-April 1986, p. 117.

VIDEO CASE 3

THE NEXT GENERATION: THE BUSTERS, YIFFIES, OR GENERATION XERS?

If "peace, love, groovy—let's get high" described the hippie-to-yuppie baby boomers, what describes the baby busters—people born between 1965 and 1976 during the birth dearth? While the more numerous and colorful boomers have captured more attention from marketers and the media, until recently, the baby busters have remained relatively obscure.

Author Douglas Coupland calls them "Generation X," because they lie in the shadow of the boomers and lack obvious distinguishing characteristics. Others call them Yiffies—young, individualistic, freedom-minded, few. Unlike the baby boomers, they did not share dramatic and wrenching experiences, such as the Vietnam War and Watergate, that might have drawn them together into a unified subculture and lifestyle. Instead,

the Generation Xers make up the nation's most diverse group—more of them are black, Hispanic, and Asian. They also are more geographically dispersed, more likely to be found in the South and West rather than in major cities.

Even so, the Generation Xers share some common influences. Increasing divorce rates and higher employment for mothers have made them the first generation of latchkey children. Having grown up during times of recession and corporate downsizing, they have less emotional stability. Whereas the boomers created a sexual revolution, the Xers live in the age of AIDS. Not surprisingly, the Xers have developed a pessimistic economic outlook. This outlook is aggravated by their problems in finding good jobs—the management ranks already are well stocked with boomers who won't retire for another 20 years or more.

As a result, the Xers are hostile. They frequently settle for "McJobs"—mundane and marginally challenging work that enables them to get by. Some are "boomerang kids"—living at home with Mom and Dad to get free room and board. Many are highly cynical of marketing pitches that are frivolous or that promise easy success. They know better.

The Xers' cynicism makes them more savvy shoppers. Because they often did much of the family shopping when growing, they are experienced shoppers. And their financial pressures make them value conscious and less susceptible to fancy packaging. They like lower prices and a more functional look. Fortunately for marketers, however, the Xers buy lots of products such as sweaters, boots, cosmetics, electronics, cars, fast food, beer, computers, mountain bikes, and rollerblades.

The Generation Xers have their own styles in music and clothes, such as grunge—the unkempt, lumberjack look popularized by such groups as Nirvana, Soundgarten, Mudhoney and, of course, the women—L7. Because of their ethnic diversity, minority styles such as hip hop and rap heavily influence Xer language, music, and dress. Those seeking fast action can attend raves: dance marathons (originating on the West Coast—where else?) in which dancers pumped up by smart drinks or supercaffeinated Jolt Cola gyrate to fast and wild music. The Xers respond to honesty in advertising, as exemplified by Nike ads that focus on fitness and a healthy lifestyle instead of hyping shoes. They like irreverence and sass and ads that mock the traditional advertising approach. They appreciate rebelliousness in ads as in the Isuzu commercial when an Xer leaves the straight and narrow highway, roaring off onto a dirt road. However, the Xers don't like sexism in advertising. When Anheuser Busch dropped the "bimbos" from its commercials, its market share increased by 1.3 percent.

Generation Xers have different cultural concerns.

They care about the environment and respond favorably to companies such as The Body Shop and Ben & Jerry's, which have proven records of environmental and socially responsible actions. Although they seek success, the Xers are less materialistic. They want better quality of life and are more interested in job satisfaction than in sacrificing personal happiness and growth for promotion. They prize experience, not acquisition. In addition, they are less likely to marry early—marriage rates among twenty-year-old Xers are down by roughly 20 percent. Finally, the Xers are less restricted by traditional sexual roles. They have many friends of both sexes and their notions of marriage more closely resemble "going out together" than the traditional matrimonial union.

The Generation Xers will have a big impact on the workplace and marketplace of the future. There are 40 million of them (not such a small group, after all) poised to displace the lifestyles, culture, and materialistic values of the baby boomers. The sixties legacy will soon fade. So get ready for a new wave in the nineties. Hey . . . you know!

QUESTIONS

1. Contrast the demographic, economic, and cultural characteristics of the baby boomers and the Generation Xers.

2. Contrast the baby boomers' and Xers' likely product and brand preferences for products such as the following: (a) vacations; (b) credit cards; (c) cosmetics; and (d) cars.

3. How might a marketer sell the same product to both baby boomers and Generation Xers?

Sources: "More Over, Boomers," *Business Week.* December 14, 1992, pp. 74–82; Alan Deutschman, What 25-Year-Olds Want." *Fortune*, August 27, 1990, pp. 42–50; William Dunn, "Hanging Out With American Youth," *American Demographics*, February 1992, pp. 24–35; Shlomo Maital, "Here Come the Twentysomethings," *Across the Board*, May 1991, pp. 5–7; Cyndee Miller, "Marketing to the Disillusioned," *Marketing News*, July 6, 1992, pp. 6–7; and Scott Donathon, "The Media Wakes Up to Generation X," *Advertising Age*, February 1, 1993, pp. 16–17.

COMPANY CASE 4

HEINZ WEIGHT WATCHERS: SEARCHING FOR A HEALTHIER MARKET SHARE

After a Hard Day

Jane Pennington grabbed the mail from her mailbox, unlocked the front door, and lugged her briefcase into the foyer. Letting out a deep sigh, she glared at the hall clock—6:30 p.m. After another long day at her Phoenix, Arizona law office, she still had to prepare for a court appearance the next day. Her husband Morris, a marketing executive for a local clock manufacturer, would not be home for at least another hour and a half.

Jane glanced through the mail and then dropped

it on the foyer table. She turned and walked into the kitchen to confront the nightly puzzle—what to have for dinner. With neither the time nor energy to cook, Jane headed for the freezer portion of her refrigerator and yanked the door open. An array of choices presented itself: Lean Cuisine, Weight Watchers, LeMenu, Budget Gourmet Light, and Healthy Choice. Jane smiled as she remembered that Morris had gone to the store over the weekend to stock up on frozen dinners.

A few years ago, Jane would never have thought

of eating a frozen dinner. She had seen them as cheap and tasteless—something that no real cook would use except in an emergency. But all that had changed. As Jane's law practice expanded, and with Morris's promotion, they found themselves with more money but less time. Moreover, they found that food producers were responding to people like them, offering an increasing variety of frozen dinners with higher prices but improved taste and quality. Morris had first tried Weight Watchers dinners, made by a wholly owned subsidiary of H.J. Heinz Co., when he had become concerned about his weight. Jane had never had a weight problem but worried about cholesterol and had tried ConAgra's Healthy Choice brand when it entered the market. Now the Penningtons were dedicated frozen-dinner addicts.

Jane selected a Healthy Choice sweet and sour chicken dinner, removed it from the package, and slid it into the microwave. In about 6 to 7 minutes, she would have a hot chicken entrée with brown rice, Oriental-style vegetables in butter sauce, and apples in plum sauce. As the microwave hummed, Jane glanced at the nutritional information printed on the package. The dinner contained only 280 calories, 2 grams of fat, 50 milligrams of cholesterol, and 260 milligrams of sodium. "Not bad," she thought.

The Frozen-Food Market

Jane's story is sweet music to frozen-dinner makers' ears. Stouffer Foods' Lean Cuisine brand successfully reinvigorated the frozen-dinner category several years ago. Then, in 1989, ConAgra introduced its Healthy Choice brand. ConAgra's president had heart trouble and found that he had a difficult time finding healthy food. He championed ConAgra's effort to offer heart-healthy dinners, resulting in the Healthy Choice line. Each Healthy Choice entrée contains an average of only 4 grams of fat as compared with Lean Cuisine's 7 grams and Weight Watchers' 5 grams. Healthy Choice attracts consumers who are worried about their health but who consider diet a nasty four-letter word. In addition to its low fat content, Healthy Choice is low in calories and claims to be low in sodium—claims that Weight Watchers and Lean Cuisine couldn't make until recently.

Healthy Choice has had a dramatic impact on the frozen-dinner market. One analyst notes that Healthy Choice appeals to a broader market. Weight Watchers' name and image suggest a target of overweight consumers, whereas Healthy Choice appeals to health-conscious men and women. A Heinz executive grudgingly admits that Healthy Choice has boosted the entire frozen-foods category. "They brought in people who'd never eaten frozen foods."

ConAgra made Healthy Choice successful without cannibalizing sales of its other frozen-food brands, Banquet and Armour. ConAgra currently controls 23.5 percent of the frozen-food market, followed by Stouffer (21 percent), Campbell Soup (15 percent), Philip Morris's Kraft division (13.5 percent), and Weight Watchers (7 percent). Weight Watchers has seen its market share fall to this level from a 10 percent share in just a few years. One analyst estimates that since Healthy Choice entered the market in 1989, Weight Watchers has lost $100 million in sales. Healthy Choice's market share has grown to 8.6 percent.

Increasing Competition

All this attention paid to the frozen-food market has caused competition to heat up. For consumers, the result has been an ever-increasing variety of low-salt, low-cholesterol, low-calorie dinners, desserts, and even breakfasts. For the companies operating in this market, however, all this competition has resulted in increased marketing headaches. Competing products are becoming increasingly alike in their salt, fat, and caloric levels. As a result, consumers are becoming more concerned about taste and companies are having to focus more on the price, place, and promotion elements of their marketing mixes.

For example, when Lean Cuisine fell behind ConAgra in the 1980s, Stouffer lowered the line's sodium and fat content, introduced eight new recipes, and increased its marketing budget. Its magazine ads boast that Lean Cuisine tastes better than Healthy Choice, and Stouffer offers consumers two Lean Cuisine coupons for every Healthy Choice coupon that they send into the company.

Weight Watchers Food Company has not taken the assault on its position lying down. The line's poor performance has hurt Heinz's overall corporate earnings. To fight back, Heinz recently introduced a new line of superlow-calorie frozen entrées called Weight Watchers Ultimate 200, positioned on both slimming and taste.

Weight Watchers hopes this new approach will attract consumers who as yet don't believe that health-oriented frozen meals taste as good as "regular" frozen meals. Many of these consumers are not concerned about their weight or their cholesterol. Weight Watchers' executives argue that these consumers will buy Weight Watchers' meals anyway if they can be convinced that the new dinners taste as good as regular frozen dinners.

Weight Watchers, however, is not retreating from the low-salt, low-fat, low-cholesterol battlefield. To continue to attack Healthy Choice, Weight Watchers has cooked up a new line of frozen main dishes that contain a miserly 1 gram of fat or less. The Smart Ones line represents another step in Heinz's move to introduce new products that have separate identities from the Weight Watchers' line. It hopes to attract health-conscious customers who are concerned about fat intake.

Weight Watchers has packaged Smart Ones in burgundy boxes with the Weight Watchers logo in small print. Traditional packaging for Weight Watchers consists of a pink-and-white box with the brand name prominently displayed. The fifteen Smart Ones main dishes average about 160 calories, contains less fat, and cost less than $2.00, slightly below Weight Watchers other frozen entrées.

Weight Watchers is counting on Smart Ones to attract men, young singles, and others who don't like the image associated with weight-loss products but who want to eat low-calorie, low-fat frozen foods. One investment analyst suggests that, "Heinz hopes to save Weight Watchers and make it into the growth vehicle it desperately needs by producing several products that

don't have the traditional pink box and indicate that the consumer is either healthy or smart."

But other analysts suggest that Weight Watchers faces two major problems in winning a place for Smart Ones. First, the frozen-food cases are crowded already. Many grocery stores now charge manufacturers slotting and stocking fees to introduce new items in their stores. As a result, competitors have resorted to aggressive couponing and promotional spending to pick up their sales and protect their places in the display cases. Second, there are so many products for sale that the variety may confuse consumers. One Pittsburgh woman notes that she had a frozen entrée for lunch recently, and it tasted awful. She adds, however, that "I can't remember which one it was. There are so many."

Taste may be Weight Watchers biggest problem. Although consumers may be concerned about fat, they still want good taste. Carolyn Wyman, a food columnist, observes that "Generally things suffer when you take fat out. Things are blander and the portions get smaller. These things [frozen meals] don't satisfy me. I literally have to buy two or three to feel like I had dinner." Brian Ruder, president of Weight Watchers Food Company admits that the company had to sacrifice some taste to develop low-fat, low-calorie foods. Weight Watchers introduced Smart Ones rather than just reducing the fat content of Weight Watchers' entrees because "the taste tradeoff would be too severe."

Consumers may be willing to give up some taste, however. Michelle Allen, a busy professional in Dallas, says she looks for the packages boasting the fewest calories and grams of fat. Ms. Allen points out that convenience, not taste, is her priority. "It all tastes sort of the same," she argues. "Since they don't taste that good, I have to have variety. So I never eat the same thing more than once every three weeks."

Meanwhile, ConAgra isn't taking its success for granted. It has introduced Healthy Choice frozen dairy desserts, muffins, breakfast sandwiches, French bread pizza, and pasta entrées. For dieters in its Ultra Slim Fast program, ConAgra launched a line of dinners that is slightly more expensive and features larger portions than Healthy Choice. It also served up a frozen-dinner line called Healthy Balance, which is less expensive than Healthy Choice.

Interestingly, however, ConAgra is not just focusing on frozen foods in its quest for the health-conscious consumer. It has also entered the soup market with Healthy Choice prepared soups. The soup product is a direct attack on Campbell Soup's dominant position—Campbell controls two-thirds of the $2.6 billion soup

market. Campbell also competes in the frozen-food category with its Swanson and LeMenu brands.

Despite Campbell's efforts to convince consumers that "soup is good food," increasing numbers of shoppers are avoiding soup because of concerns over high levels of sodium. Thus, Campbell is responding to ConAgra's challenge with its own line of soups called Healthy Request. The new line promises to be lower in fat, sodium, and cholesterol than regular soups.

Although Campbell holds a commanding position in the soup market, ConAgra is nearly three times larger in terms of total company revenues with $19.5 billion in sales. ConAgra believes it can invigorate the soup market just as it did the frozen food market. And ConAgra sent a strong message to Campbell when it tried to block Campbell's use of the word healthy on its label. Campbell won the right to keep the word on its new line of soups, but the court ruled that it can't use the Healthy Request brand on other food products without ConAgra's consent.

Whether with frozen dinners or soup, Weight Watchers will find that the increasing product similarity and cutthroat marketing competition will mean that it has to work hard to win each customer and then even harder to keep customers like Jane and Morris Pennington coming back again and again.

Back at the Pennington's

Morris Pennington finally struggled home about 8 P.M. and slumped into his favorite chair in the family room. Jane, now working on her court case for tomorrow, looked up.

"Have a hard day?" she asked.

"A real killer," Morris responded. "Preparing for these trade shows is going to finish me off."

"Can I fix you a frozen dinner?" Jane inquired.

"That would be really nice. I know you are busy, though." Morris replied.

"That's okay." Jane answered. "I need a break anyway and it won't take but a minute. Wht kind do you want?'

"It doesn't matter," Morris declared with a wave of his hand. "Just pick one."

QUESTIONS

1. How are the demographic, economic, technological, and political aspects of the macroenvironment affecting Heinz and its Weight Watchers brand?

2. What actors in the microenvironment affect the actions of the competitors in the frozen-food market and how?

3. How have Heinz, ConAgra, and Campbell tried to manage the environmental forces affecting them?

4. What marketing recommendations would you make to Weight Watchers?

Sources: Adapted from Garbiella Stern, "Makers of 'Healthy' Frozen Foods Watch Profits Melt as Competition Gets Hotter," *The Wall Street Journal,* February 6, 1992, p. B1; Stern, "Heinz to Introduce Line of Low-Fat Frozen Entrées," *The Wall Street Journal,* June 2, 1992, p. B9; Kathleen Deveny and Richard Gibson, "Campbell, ConAgra Hope 'Healthy' Soup Will Be Ingredient of Financial Success," *The Wall Street Journal,* September 4, 1991, p. B1. Used with permission.

PART I

COMPREHENSIVE CASE

MasterCard:
Charging the Competition

Fred Snook, owner of Fred's Bicycle Shop, finished adding the column of figures and looked up. "With the accessories, the total comes to $438.57, Mr. White. How would you like to pay for this?"

Lew White glanced over at his daughter Lauren who was supporting a new Cannondale mountain bike. In August, Lauren would be entering the University of Michigan. Lauren figured that she would need a bike to get around the huge campus. She had asked her dad to buy the bike as a graduation present so that she could get used to it during the summer.

"Well, Fred, I guess I'll just put it on one of these credit cards," Lew replied as he pulled out his tri-fold wallet and opened it to display nine different credit cards. "Which ones do you take?" he asked.

"I can take any major credit card you have, Mr. White. It doesn't make any difference to me," Fred responded.

Lew shuffled through his stack of cards. "Let's see. If I use American Express, I avoid any interest charges, but the company will expect me to pay in thirty days. That will be hard with Lauren's first tuition payment due soon. I could use my US Air Visa card and earn some more free air miles, but I have lots of frequent flier miles already. Or, I could use the MasterCard that's associated with my old fraternity. That way, I'd be making a contribution to the new scholarship fund. I could use my new General Motors MasterCard card and earn credit toward the purchase of a new car. I certainly couldn't afford a new car any other way during the next four years! Or, I could use my Citibank MasterCard so that the bank will extend the warranty on Lauren's bike."

"Dad!"

"Okay, okay. It's just getting so complicated to decide which credit card to use."

The Credit Card Industry
It hasn't always been this way. The bank credit card industry began in 1951 when Franklin National Bank of Long Island issued its customers a card with their account number on it. Customers could use this card to charge purchases at merchants who also banked at Franklin National. The bank charged the merchant a fee for processing the transaction. By 1959, approximately 150 banks offered credit cards, but they required the customer to pay off the balances in a month or two. Then they began to extend the repayment time period if the customer paid a monthly finance charge.

In the mid-1960s, banks began to form alliances so that they could offer cards with a common label. BankAmericard started the trend, becoming Visa in

1977. Master Charge evolved into MasterCard in 1979.

Until the mid-1980s, banks pretty much had their way in the credit card industry. Visa, MasterCard, and American Express, which had entered the business in 1958, dominated the industry. It was hard for banks not to make money on their credit cards.

The banks made money three ways. First, they charged credit card customers annual fees for the privilege of having the card. Then, they charged the customer interest on the unpaid balance each month, usually at a rate of 18 percent per year or higher. Finally, they charged the merchants who accepted their cards "discount" fees on each purchase.

With a system like this, bank credit cards produced gross margins in the 50 percent range and became banks' most profitable business. In 1989, Citibank received $3.6 billion in credit card interest alone and collected $500 million in card fees. Industry sources suggested that credit card operations generated 70 percent of Citibank's and Chase Manhattan's net profits.

While they were making all this money, the banks focused on getting their cards accepted at more establishments. Most stores that took either Visa or MasterCard seemed to accept the other card as well. Fewer stores accepted American Express because it charged a higher discount fee (3.5 percent on average, versus about 2 percent for Visa and MasterCard). American Express users had to pay their accounts in full each month and thus paid no interest on outstanding balances.

Gasoline companies, such as Texaco, British Petroleum, and Exxon, issued the only other widely accepted credit cards. Although some of these cards had tie-in programs with hotels, motels, or other travel-related services, most merchants did not accept them for normal consumer purchases.

At the other end of the scale were the retail charge cards issued by individual stores (often called proprietary cards) that customers could use only at a particular store. Retailers such as Sears, Macy's, Belk Stores, J. C. Penney, and Nordstrom's issued their own cards.

New Competition Enters
In the mid-1980s, however, competition jumped into the credit card arena from an unexpected source. Nonbanks examined the industry and saw the attractive profits. The opportunities were too good to pass up. In 1986, armed with the competitive advantage of a list of 70 million credit cardholders, Sears launched the Discover card. Although other banks had needed to spend from $25 to $80 to get each new cardholder, Sears had an acquisition cost of $6! Sears attracted cardholders by charging no annual fee and offering customers a rebate

of up to 1 percent of every dollar charged. Although a $1,000 balance produced only a $2.50 rebate, customers seemed to appreciate even that modest amount. By 1990, Sears had 34 million Discover cards in circulation, a 6 percent market share. More important, Discover produced $80 million in earnings for Sears at a time when the company needed the profits badly.

Suddenly, the credit card business became a battle for market share. The banks found three ways to fight back. First, they began buying customers by purchasing the credit card portfolios of savings and loans and other troubled financial institutions. Second, they differentiated their cards by adding services. For example, American Express introduced its Buyer's Assurance plan in 1986, which extended manufacturers' warranties by up to a year on goods purchased using American Express cards. Then, in 1987, it introduced collision insurance for rental cars; and in 1988, it added insurance on the occupants and contents of rental cars. In 1989, it offered medical monitoring and evacuation services. Visa responded in 1988 with its Visa Gold card, which offered enhanced services for a higher annual fee.

Finally, in some cases, the banks even lowered prices. Some banks began to offer no-fee Visa cards and MasterCards. Others offered "affinity" cards. Banks issued these cards in association with sports teams, service organizations, environmental groups, and universities. When a cardholder with an affinity card used it, the bank made a small contribution to the affiliated organization, thus lowering its gross margin.

These counterattacks, however, did not deter another nonbank entrant, AT&T. Like Sears, AT&T looked at the credit card industry and saw substantial profit potential. AT&T had the advantage of access to the credit histories of its 70 million long-distance customers. It could easily prequalify these customers, lowering its exposure to bad credit risks.

AT&T introduced its Universal card by offering it to customers at no fee for life and at an interest rate of prime plus 8.9 percent. In addition, the Universal card carried 90-day purchase insurance against loss, warranties doubled up to a year, $100,000 travel accident insurance, rental car insurance, and 10 percent off on AT&T long-distance calls billed to the card. AT&T also offered instant credit on disputed charges and said it would represent the customer in those disputes.

AT&T set up a customer service system using its phone network. Service representatives used custom computer workstations that gave them immediate access to customer information. Just days after the launch, 15,000 customers an hour were calling AT&T's offices.

Whereas Sear's Discover card had been a wake-up call for the banks, AT&T's Universal card caused them to sound "battle stations." With American Express adding services and AT&T cutting price and adding services, the banks saw a full frontal assault on their prized profit generator.

Maturity and Recession

With all the credit cards now in circulation, you might wonder how many people still need or want another card. The average U.S. adult has three of the approximately 260 million general purpose credit cards in circulation. Three out of four people have at least one card, and many people are canceling one or more cards that they have. The credit card market appears saturated.

Further, after years of astounding growth in charge volume, Americans are charging less. In 1990, dollar charge volume grew only 20 percent, slow growth by previous industry standards. In 1991, charges grew only 15 percent, and in 1992, only 5.9 percent. Moreover, the amount of credit card debt outstanding, a source of interest income, remained virtually flat in 1992 at $247 billion.

Despite all the price cutting, however, the average credit card interest rate remains at 17.5 percent, down only slightly in the last year, although rates range from 7 percent to 21 percent. The cost of delinquencies and fraud accounts for 4.5 percent of outstanding balances, up 50 percent in the last two years. Of course, the recession of the early 1990s contributed to the slowdown in the industry's growth. Consumers now are slower to use their credit cards, and their concerns about the future make them more prone to pay off or reduce their balances.

Visa and MasterCard felt these changes on their income statements. Combined profits for the two organizations declined 27 percent, from $3.32 billion to $2.4 billion, and after-tax return on assets declined from 2.3 percent to 1.5 percent. The percentage of cardholders carrying a no-fee card doubled to 41 percent in the last two years.

MasterCard Fights Back

MasterCard, however, was not going to take all this lying down. Working with General Electric, it developed a "co-branded" credit card. Co-branded cards feature both the name of the company sponsoring the card and the name of the associated credit card organization. In late 1992, GE Capital Corporation announced the GE Rewards MasterCard, featuring the GE and MasterCard logos. Although the GE card charges an annual $25 fee, it gives the customer $10 for every $500 charged. In addition, each quarter it offers $10 vouchers from two dozen well-known companies such as Hertz, Sprint, Macy's, K mart, or Toys "R" Us, which also joined as partners in the card.

Then, just a week later, General Motors announced its new GM MasterCard. The GM card requires

no annual fee and carries an adjustable rate of 10.4 percent above prime. The card allows customers to earn a 5 percent rebate on their annual charges—up to an annual total of $500—toward the purchase of a GM car or truck (excluding the Saturn). Customers can accumulate the rebates over seven years, meaning they could earn up to a $3,500 rebate, not counting additional dealer discounts. Further, GM, like GE, also has partners such as Avis, Marriott, and MCI. Customers earn an additional 5 percent rebate, with no cap on purchases, from these partners. GM said that it would mail packets describing its new card to 30 million households and spend $60 million advertising the card. Analysts predicted that GM would issue 3.5 million cards within two years.

Although the GE and GM cards generated lots of excitement, they were not the first co-branded cards. Eastern Airlines started the trend in 1986 when it issued MasterCards that earned the customer one frequent flier mile for each dollar charged on the card. Such cards have high annual fees and many restrictions, in contrast to the few restrictions GE and GM placed on their cards.

Visa Ponders

MasterCard has moved aggressively into co-branding. It sees co-branding as a way to catch up with Visa, which dominates the worldwide, general purpose credit card business with a 50.9 percent share as compared to MasterCard's 29.5 percent. MasterCard already has 26 percent of its 90 million U.S. cards as either affinity or co-branded cards, compared to 10 percent for the industry as a whole. MasterCard sees many more opportunities to build volume by converting department store or gasoline credit cards to co-branded MasterCards.

Co-branding seems to offer benefits for everyone involved. When merchants join a co-branding program, they gain the opportunity to offer a payment option tied to a nationally recognized payment system. Because the store's name remains on the card, the store builds loyalty. The sponsoring bank earns the transaction fees, adds value to its services, and may gain profitable customers in a cost-efficient manner. Also, the bank can cross-sell other products or services. MasterCard can claim more transactions, and both it and the member bank gain marketing information on a new set of cardholders.

MasterCard actively pursues co-branding opportunities as a part of its market segmentation program. Because it believes that the trend is toward the conversion of proprietary cards, such as store-based credit cards, into bank cards, MasterCard has divided the proprietary card market into three segments: telephone, retail, and gasoline company cards. The retail segment includes department stores, specialty stores, and regional chain stores which now issue proprietary cards.

Despite co-branding's appeal, however, Visa has moved cautiously into co-branding. Although Visa has specific policies and leaves the co-branding decision up to member banks, it has no market segmentation program like MasterCard's. Visa questions the wisdom of making co-branding a separate marketing program. First, Visa, MasterCard, believes that a merchant who uses the Visa logo on its credit card must honor all cards that carry the Visa logo, not just that store's cards. For example, if Macy's develops a Macy's Visa card, it must accept all Visa cards, even one from Bloomingdale's. Second, Visa believes it must process all transactions involving cards with the Visa logo. That way, each of its customers has a uniform set of rights associated with use of the Visa card. Otherwise, for example, customers could find themselves unsure if an extended warranty plan applied to a product in cases in which a store did not offer the plan but Visa did. Third, Visa wants to process the transactions using its sophisticated computer system. This system can, for example, spot criminal use of an account number, as when a thief gains access to a customer's account number and uses it to purchase many expensive items in a short time period.

Then, too, Visa understands the natural tension between a retailer and a bank card sponsor. Whereas the retailer may see its credit card as a cost of doing business rather than a profit-making product, the bank sees the credit card as a key profit producer that helps to shore up its business. The retailer uses its credit card as a way to encourage a customer to buy a product that the retailer has already marked up to include a profit. The retailer cares less about interest income from the card and about the customer's creditworthiness. In contrast, the bank issuing the credit card is very concerned about creditworthiness and about earning interest on the card's balances.

MasterCard and Visa are pursuing different strategic paths on this latest front in the credit card wars. Whether Visa will be more aggressive on co-branding is not clear, but MasterCard has sent clear signals that it wants to be more than just number two.

QUESTIONS

1. Do credit cards contribute to accomplishing the goals of the marketing system? Why or why not?

2. What forces in the macroenvironment have shaped the credit card industry's growth and development?

3. What competitive marketing strategies have the different firms followed?

4. How have the various competitors in the credit card industry used the marketing management process outlined in the text?

5. Using the product/market expansion grid, identify marketing opportunities that MasterCard should pursue. What other marketing recommendations would you make to MasterCard?

Sources: Bill Saporito, "Who's Winning the Credit Card War?" *Fortune,* July 2, 1990, pp. 66–71; "Credit Cards: Plastic Profits Go Pop," *The Economist,* September 12, 1992, p. 92; Gary Levin, "Co-Branding Trend Takes Credit Cards," *Advertising Age,* November 11, 1991, p. 69; Wanda Cantrell, "The Party's Over for Bank Cards," *Bank Management,* June 1992, pp. 44–48; Mark Arend, "Card Associations Weigh Co-Branding Merits," *ABA Banking Journal,* September 1992, pp. 84–86; Adam Bryant, "Raising the Stakes in a War of Plastic," *The New York Times,* September 13, 1992, sec. 3, p. 13; Adam Bryant, "G.M.'s Bold Move into Credit Cards," *The New York Times,* September 10, 1992, sec. D, p. 5.

Marketing Research and Information Systems

4

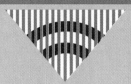

In 1985, the Coca-Cola Company made a spectacular marketing blunder. After 99 successful years, it set aside its long-standing rule—"don't mess with Mother Coke"—and dropped its original formula Coke! In its place came *New* Coke with a sweeter, smoother taste. The company boldly announced the new taste with a flurry of advertising and publicity.

At first, amid the introductory fanfare, New Coke sold well. But sales soon went flat, as a stunned public reacted. Coke began receiving sacks of mail and more than 1,500 phone calls each day from angry consumers. A group called "Old Cola Drinkers" staged protests, handed out T-shirts, and threatened a class-action suit unless Coca-Cola brought back the old formula. Most marketing experts predicted that New Coke would be the "Edsel of the Eighties."

After just three months, the Coca-Cola Company brought old Coke back. Now called "Coke Classic," it sold side-by-side with New Coke on supermarket shelves. The company said that New Coke would remain its "flagship" brand, but consumers had a different idea. By the end of 1985, Classic was outselling New Coke in supermarkets by two to one. By mid-1986, the company's two largest fountain accounts, McDonald's and Kentucky Fried Chicken, had returned to serving Coke Classic in their restaurants.

Quick reaction saved the company from potential disaster. It stepped up efforts for Coke Classic and slotted New Coke into a supporting role. By 1987, Coke Classic was again the company's main brand—and the country's leading soft drink. New Coke became the company's "attack brand"—its Pepsi stopper. With computer-enhanced star Max Headroom leading the charge, company ads boldly compared New Coke's taste with Pepsi's. Still, New Coke managed only a 2 percent market share. By 1989, Coke Classic was outselling New Coke ten to one. In the spring of 1990, the company repackaged New Coke and relaunched it as a brand extension with a new name—Coke II. In 1992, after two years of test marketing in Spokane, Washington, Coca-Cola expanded Coke II distribution to several major U.S. cities. New ads proclaimed "Real Cola Taste Plus the Sweetness of Pepsi." However, with a minuscule market share of .3 percent, Coke II appears destined to do little more than pester rival Pepsi.

Why was New Coke introduced in the first place? What went wrong? Many analysts blame the blunder on poor marketing research.

In the early 1980s, although Coke was still the leading soft drink, it was slowly losing market share to Pepsi. For years, Pepsi had successfully mounted the "Pepsi Challenge," a series of televised taste tests showing that consumers preferred the sweeter taste of Pepsi. By early 1985, although Coke led in the overall market, Pepsi led in share of supermarket sales by 2 percent. (That doesn't sound like much, but 2 percent of the huge soft-drink market amounts to $960 million in retail sales!) Coca-Cola had to do something to stop the loss of its market share, and the solution appeared to be a change in Coke's taste.

Coca-Cola began the largest new product research project in the company's history. It spent more than two years and $4 million on research before settling on a new formula. It conducted some 200,000 taste tests—30,000 on the final formula alone. In blind tests, 60 percent of consumers chose the new Coke over the old, and 52 percent chose it over Pepsi. Research showed that New Coke would be a winner and the company introduced it with confidence. So what happened?

Looking back, we can see that Coke's marketing research was focused too narrowly. The research looked only at taste; it did not explore consumers' feelings about dropping the old Coke and replacing it with a new version. It took no account of the *intangibles*—Coke's name, history, packaging, cultural heritage, and image. But to many people, Coke stands along side baseball, hot dogs, and apple pie as an American institution; it represents the very fabric of America. Coke's symbolic meaning turned out to be more important to many consumers than its taste. More complete marketing research would have detected these strong emotions.

Coke's managers also may have used poor judgment in interpreting the research and planning strategies around it. For example, they took the finding that 60 percent of consumers preferred New Coke's taste to mean that the new product would win in the marketplace, as when a political candidate wins with 60 percent of the vote. But it also meant that 40 percent still liked the old Coke. By dropping the old Coke, the company trampled the taste buds of the large core of loyal Coke drinkers who didn't want a change. The company might have been wiser to leave the old Coke alone and introduce New Coke as a brand extension, as it later did successfully with Cherry Coke.

The Coca-Cola Company has one of the largest, best managed, and most advanced marketing research operations in America. Good marketing research has kept the company atop the rough-and-tumble soft-drink market for decades. But marketing research is far from an exact science. Consumers are full of surprises and figuring them out can be awfully tough. If Coca-Cola can make a large marketing research mistake, any company can.[1]

 # CHAPTER PREVIEW

Chapter 4 explains the underlying concepts of marketing research, and details the importance of information to the company.

In the beginning of the chapter, we describe the *marketing information system*, an integrated collection of people, equipment, and procedures used to gather, evaluate, and distribute relevant information to marketing decision makers.

We continue with a discussion of the four key steps in the marketing research process: *defining the problem and objectives, developing a research plan, implementing the plan*, and *interpreting and reporting the findings*.

Next, we describe possible sources of information, including primary and secondary data, and approaches that can be used to collect such knowledge, including observational, survey, and experimental research.

We conclude with a discussion of ways to *distribute information* to the right managers at the right time.

In carrying out marketing analysis, planning, implementation, and control, marketing managers need information at almost every turn. They need information about customers, competitors, dealers, and other forces in the marketplace. One marketing executive put it this way: "To manage a business well is to manage its future; and to manage the future is to manage information."[2] Increasingly, marketers are viewing information not just as an input for making better decisions, but also as an important strategic asset and marketing tool.[3]

During the past century, most companies were small and knew their customers firsthand. Managers picked up marketing information by being around people, observing them, and asking questions. During this century, however, many factors have increased the need for more and better information. As companies become national or international in scope, they need more information on larger, more distant markets. As incomes increase and buyers become more selective, sellers need better information about how buyers respond to different products and appeals. As sellers use more complex marketing approaches and face more competition, they need information on the effectiveness of their marketing tools. Finally, in today's more rapidly changing environments, managers need more up-to-date information to make timely decisions.

The supply of information also has increased greatly. John Neisbitt suggests that the United States is undergoing a "megashift" from an industrial to an information-based economy.[4] He found that more than 65 percent of the U.S. work force now is employed in producing or processing information, compared to only 17 percent in 1950. Using improved computer systems and other technologies, companies now can provide information in great quantities. In fact, today's managers sometimes receive too much information. For example, one study found that with all the companies offering data, and with all the information now available through supermarket scanners, a packaged-goods brand manager is bombarded with one million to one *billion* new numbers each week.[5] As Neisbitt points out: "Running out of information is not a problem, but drowning in it is."[6]

Yet marketers frequently complain that they lack enough information of the *right* kind or have too much of the *wrong* kind. Or marketing information is so widely spread throughout the company that it takes great effort to locate even simple facts. Subordinates may withhold information they believe will reflect badly on their performance. Often, important information arrives too late to be useful, or on-time information is not accurate. So marketing managers need more and better information. Companies have greater capacity to provide managers with information, but often have not made good use of it. Many companies are now studying their managers' information needs and designing information systems to meet those needs.

THE MARKETING INFORMATION SYSTEM

A **marketing information system (MIS)** consists of people, equipment, and procedures to gather, sort, analyze, evaluate, and distribute needed, timely, and accurate information to marketing decision makers. Figure 4-1 illustrates the marketing information system concept. The MIS begins and ends with marketing managers. First, it interacts with these managers to assess their information needs. Next, it develops the needed information from internal company records, marketing intelligence activities, and the marketing research process. Information analysis processes the information to make it more useful. Finally, the MIS distributes information to managers in the right form at the right time to help them in marketing planning, implementation, and control.

ASSESSING INFORMATION NEEDS

A good marketing information system balances what the information managers would *like* to have against what they really *need* and what is *feasible* to offer. The company begins by interviewing managers to find out what information they would like (see Table 4-1 for a useful set of questions). But managers do not always need all the information they ask for, and they may not ask for all they really need. Moreover, the MIS cannot always supply all the information managers request.

Some managers will ask for whatever information they can get without thinking carefully about what they really need. With today's information technology, most companies can provide much more information than managers actually can use. Too much information can be as harmful as too little.

Other managers may omit things they ought to know. Or managers may not know to ask for some types of information they should have. For example, managers might need to know that a competitor plans to introduce a new product during the coming year. Because they do not know about the new product, they do not think to ask about it. The MIS must watch the marketing environment in order to provide decision makers with information they should have to make key marketing decisions.

Sometimes the company cannot provide the needed information, either because it is not available or because of MIS limitations. For example, a brand manager might want to know how competitors will change their advertising budgets next year and how these changes will affect industry market shares. The information on planned budgets probably is not available. Even if it is, the company's MIS may not be advanced enough to forecast resulting changes in market shares.

Finally, the costs of obtaining, processing, storing, and delivering information can mount quickly. The company must decide whether the benefits of hav-

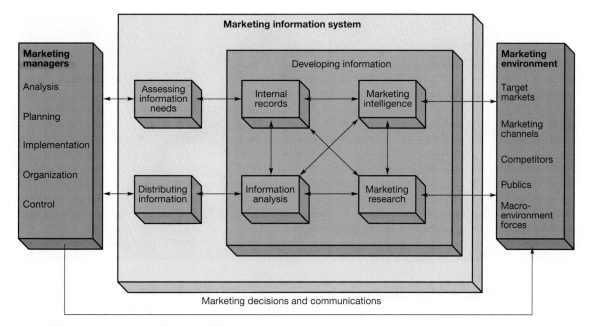

FIGURE 4-1   The marketing information system

ing an item of information are worth the costs of providing it—and both value and cost are often hard to assess. By itself, information has no worth; its value comes from its *use*. In many cases, additional information will do little to change or improve a manager's decision, or the costs of the information may exceed the returns from the improved decision. Marketers should not assume that additional information will always be worth obtaining. Rather, it should weigh carefully the costs of additional information against the benefits resulting from it.

DEVELOPING INFORMATION

The information needed by marketing managers can be obtained from *internal company records, marketing intelligence,* and *marketing research.* The information analysis system processes this information to make it more useful for managers.

Internal Records

Most marketing managers use internal records and reports regularly, especially for making day-to-day planning, implementation, and control decisions. **Internal**

TABLE 4-1
Questions for Assessing Marketing Information Needs

1. What types of decisions do you make regularly?

2. What types of information do you need in order to make these decisions?

3. What types of useful information do you get regularly?

4. What types of information would you like to get that you are not getting now?

5. What types of information do you get now that you don't really need?

6. What information would you want daily? Weekly? Monthly? Yearly?

7. What topics would you like to be kept informed about?

8. What databases would be useful to you?

9. What types of information analysis programs would you like to have?

10. What would be the four most helpful improvements that could be made in the present information system?

Information abounds—the problem is to give managers the *right information* at the *right time.*

records information consists of information gathered from sources within the company to evaluate marketing performance and to detect marketing problems and opportunities. The company's accounting department prepares financial statements and keeps detailed records of sales, orders, costs, and cash flows. Manufacturing reports on production schedules, shipments, and inventories. The salesforce reports on reseller reactions and competitor activities. The customer service department provides information on customer satisfaction or service problems. Research studies done for one department may provide useful information for several others. Managers can use information gathered from these and other sources within the company to evaluate performance and to detect problems and opportunities.

Here are examples of how companies use internal records information in making better marketing decisions:[7]

Sears. Sears uses internal records as a powerful marketing tool. Marketing managers use computerized information on Sears' 40 million customers to promote special product and service offers to diverse target segments such as gardeners, appliance buyers, and expectant mothers. For example, Sears keeps track of the appliance purchases of each customer and promotes special service-package deals to customers who have bought several appliances, but have not purchased maintenance contracts for them. Soon managers at other Sears subsidiaries—Allstate Insurance, Dean Witter Reynolds, and Coldwell Banker (real estate brokers)—will be able to develop sales leads using the same data.

Mead Paper. Mead salespeople can obtain on-the-spot answers to customers' questions about paper availability by dialing Mead Paper's computer center. The computer determines whether paper is available at the nearest warehouse and when it can be shipped. If it is not in stock, the computer checks the inventory at other nearby warehouses until a supply is located. If the paper is nowhere in stock, the computer determines where and when it can be produced. The salespeople get an answer in seconds and thus have an advantage over competitors.

Frito-Lay. Frito-Lay uses its sophisticated internal information system to analyze daily sales performance. Each day, Frito-Lay's salespeople report their day's efforts via hand-held computers into minicomputers at their local sales offices or into modems at home. These reports, in turn, are fed to Frito-Lay headquarters in Dallas. Twenty-four hours later, Frito-Lay's marketing managers have a complete report analyzing the previous day's sales performance of Fritos, Doritos, and the company's other brands—by total, brand, and location. The system helps Frito-Lay's marketing managers make better decisions and makes the salespeople more efficient and effective. It greatly reduces the number of hours spent filling out reports, giving salespeople extra time for selling. As a result, sales are going up 10 percent to 12 percent a year without the addition of a single salesperson.

Information from internal records usually can be obtained more quickly and cheaply than information from other sources, but it also presents some problems. Because internal information was collected for other purposes, it may be incomplete or in the wrong form for making marketing decisions. For example, accounting department sales and cost data used for preparing financial statements must be adapted for use in evaluating product, salesforce, or channel performance. In addition, the many different areas of a large company produce great amounts of information, and keeping track of it all is difficult. The marketing information system must gather, organize, process, and index this mountain of information so that managers can find it easily and get it quickly.

Marketing Intelligence

Marketing intelligence is everyday information about developments in the marketing environment that helps managers prepare and adjust marketing plans. The marketing intelligence system determines what intelligence is needed, collects it by searching the environment, and delivers it to marketing managers who need it.

Marketing intelligence can be gathered from many sources. Much intelligence can be collected from the company's own personnel—executives, engineers and scientists, purchasing agents, and the salesforce. But company people are often busy and fail to pass on important information. The company must "sell" its people on their importance as intelligence gatherers, train them to spot new developments, and urge them to report intelligence back to the company.

The company also must get suppliers, resellers, and customers to pass along important intelligence. Information on competitors can be obtained from what they say about themselves in annual reports, speeches and press releases, and advertisements. The company also can learn about competitors from what others say about them in business publications and at trade shows. Or the company can watch what competitors do—buying and analyzing competitors' products, monitoring their sales, and checking for new patents (see Marketing Highlight 4-1).

Companies also buy intelligence information from outside suppliers. The A. C. Nielsen Company sells data on brand shares, retail prices, and percentages of stores stocking different brands. Information Resources, Inc., sells supermarket scanner purchase data from a panel of 60,000 households nationally, with measures of trial and repeat purchasing, brand loyalty, and buyer demographics. For a fee, companies can subscribe to any of more than 3,000 online databases or information search services. For example, the *Adtrack* online database tracks all the advertisements of a quarter page or larger from 150 major consumer and business publications. Companies can use these data to assess their own and competitors' advertising strategies and styles, shares of advertising space, media usage, and ad budgets. The *Donnelly Demographics* database provides demographic data from the U.S. census plus Donnelly's own demographic projections by state, city, or zip code. Companies can use it to measure markets and develop segmentation strategies. The *Electronic Yellow Pages,* containing listings from nearly all the nation's 4,800 phone books, is the largest directory of American companies available. A firm such as Burger King might use this database to count McDonald's restaurants in different geographic locations. A readily available online database exists to fill almost any marketing information need. General database services such as CompuServe, Dialog, and Nexis put an incredible wealth of information at the fingertips of marketing decision makers.

> Doing business in Germany? Check out CompuServe's German Company Library of financial and product information on over 48,000 German-owned firms. Want biographical sketches of Ford Motor Co.'s key executives? Punch up Dun & Bradstreet Financial Profiles and Company Reports. Demographic data? Today's Associated Press news wire reports? A list of active trademarks in the United States? It's all available from online databases.[8]

Marketing intelligence can work not only for, but also against, a company. Therefore, companies must sometimes take steps to protect themselves from the snooping of competitors. For example, Kellogg had treated the public to tours of its Battle Creek plant since 1906, but recently closed its newly upgraded plant to outsiders to prevent competitors from getting intelligence on its high-tech equip-

MARKETING HIGHLIGHT 4-1

INTELLIGENCE GATHERING: SNOOPING ON COMPETITORS

Competitive intelligence gathering has grown dramatically as more and more companies need to know what their competitors are doing. Such well-known companies as Ford, Motorola, Westinghouse, General Electric, Gillette, Avon, Del Monte, Kraft, Marriott, and J. C. Penney are known to be busy snooping on their competitors.

Techniques that companies use to collect their own intelligence fall into four major groups.

Getting Information from Recruits and Competitors' Employees

Companies can obtain intelligence through job interviews or from conversations with competitors' employees. According to *Fortune*:

> When they interview students for jobs, some companies pay special attention to those who have worked for competitors, even temporarily. Job seekers are eager to impress and often have not been warned about divulging what is proprietary. They sometimes volunteer valuable information.
>
> Companies send engineers to conferences and trade shows to question competitors' technical people. Often conversations start innocently—just a few fellow technicians discussing processes and problems . . . [yet competitors'] engineers and scientists often brag about surmounting technical challenges, in the process divulging sensitive information.
>
> Companies sometimes advertise and hold interviews for jobs that don't exist in order to entice competitors' employees to spill the beans . . . Often applicants have toiled in obscurity or feel that their careers have stalled. They're dying to impress somebody.

Getting Information from People Who Do Business with Competitors

Key customers can keep the company informed about competitors and their products:

For example, a while back Gillette told a large Canadian account the date on which it planned to begin selling its new Good News disposable razor in the United States. The Canadian distributor promptly called Bic and told it about the impending product launch. Bic put on a crash program and was able to start selling its razor shortly after Gillette did.

Intelligence can also be gathered by infiltrating customers' business operations:

> Companies may provide their engineers free of charge to customers . . . The close, cooperative relationship that the engineers on loan cultivate with the customers' design staff often enables them to learn what new products competitors are pitching.

Getting Information from Published Materials and Public Documents

Keeping track of seemingly meaningless published information can provide competitor intelligence. For instance, the types of people sought in help-wanted ads can indicate something about a competitor's new strategies and products. Government agencies are another good source. For example:

> Although it is often illegal for a company to photograph a competitor's plant from the air, there are legitimate ways to get the photos . . . Aerial photos often are on file with the U.S. Geological Survey or Environmental Protection Agency. These are public documents, available for a nominal fee.
>
> Zoning and tax assessment offices often have tax information on local factories and even have blueprints of the facilities, showing square footage and types of machinery. It's all publicly available.

Getting Information by Observing Competitors or Analyzing Physical Evidence

Companies can get to know competitors better by buying their products or examining other physical evi-

ment. In its corporate offices, Du Pont displays a poster showing two people at a lunch table and warns, "Be careful in casual conversation. Keep security in mind."[9]

Some companies set up an office to collect and circulate marketing intelligence. The staff scans major publications, summarizes important news, and sends news bulletins to marketing managers. It develops a file of intelligence information and helps managers evaluate new information. These services greatly improve the quality of information available to marketing managers.[10]

Marketing Research

Managers cannot always wait for information to arrive in bits and pieces from the marketing intelligence system. They often require formal studies of specific situa-

Collecting intelligence: Xerox engineers tear apart a competitor's product to assess its design and to estimate cost.

dence. An increasingly important form of competitive intelligence is benchmarking, taking apart competitors' products and imitating or improving upon their best features. Popular since the early 1980s, benchmarking has helped Xerox turn around its copying business and Ford develop the successful Taurus.

> When Ford decided to build a better car back in the early Eighties, it compiled a list of some 400 features its customers said were the most important, then set about finding the car with the best of each. Then it tried to match or top the best of the competition. The result: the hot-selling Taurus. Updating the Taurus in 1992, Ford benchmarked all over again.

By 1993, thanks in large part to such benchmarking efforts, the Taurus had overtaken the Honda Accord as America's best-selling passenger car.

Beyond looking at competitors' products, companies can examine many other types of physical evidence:

In the absence of better information on market share and the volume of product competitors are shipping, companies have measured the rust on rails of railroad sidings to their competitors' plants or have counted the tractor-trailers leaving loading bays.

Some companies even rifle their competitors' garbage:

> Once it has left the competitors' premises, refuse is legally considered abandoned property. While some companies now shred the paper coming out of their design labs, they often neglect to do this for almost-as-revealing refuse from the marketing or public relations departments.

In a recent example of garbage snatching, Avon admitted that it had hired private detectives to paw through the dumpster of rival Mary Kay Cosmetics. Although an outraged Mary Kay sued to get its garbage back, Avon claimed that it had done nothing illegal. The dumpster had been located in a public parking lot, and Avon had videotapes to prove it.

Although most of these techniques are legal and some are considered to be shrewdly competitive, many involve questionable ethics. The company should take advantage of publicly available information, but avoid practices that might be considered illegal or unethical. A company does not have to break the law or accepted codes of ethics to get good intelligence.

Sources: Excerpts from Steven Flax, "How to Snoop on Your Competitors," *Fortune,* May 14, 1984, pp. 29–33; Brian Dumaine, "Corporate Spies Snoop to Conquer," *Fortune,* November 7, 1988, pp. 68–76; and Jeremy Main, "How to Steal the Best Ideas Around," *Fortune,* October 19, 1992, pp. 102–6. Copyright © 1984, 1988, and 1992, Time Inc. All rights reserved. Also see Wendy Zellner and Bruce Hager, "Dumpster Raids? That's Not Very Ladylike, Avon," *Business Week,* April 1, 1991, p. 32; Michele Galen, "These Guys Aren't Spooks, They're 'Competitive Analysts,'" *Business Week,* October 14, 1991, p. 97; and Richard S. Teitalbaum, "The New Race for Intelligence," *Fortune,* November 2, 1992, pp. 104–8.

tions. For example, Apple Computer wants to know how many and what kinds of people or companies will buy its new ultralight personal computer. Or Barat College in Lake Forest, Illinois needs to know what percentage of its target market has heard of Barat, what they know, how they heard about Barat, and how they feel about Barat. In such situations, the marketing intelligence system will not provide the detailed information needed. Because managers normally do not have the skills or time to obtain the information on their own, they need formal marketing research.

We define **marketing research** as the function that links the consumer, customer, and public to the marketer through information—information used to identify and define marketing opportunities and problems; to generate, refine, and evaluate marketing actions; to monitor marketing performance; and to improve understanding of the marketing process.[11] Marketing researchers specify the information needed to address marketing issues, design the method for collecting information, manage and implement the data collection process, analyze the results, and communicate the findings and their implications.

Table 4-2 shows that marketing researchers engage in a wide variety of activities, ranging from analyses of market potential and market shares to studies of customer satisfaction and purchase intentions. Every marketer needs research. A company can conduct marketing research in its own research department or have some or all of it done outside. Whether a company uses outside firms depends on the skills and resources within the company. Although most large companies have their own marketing research departments, they often use outside firms to do special research tasks or special studies. A company with no research department will have to buy the services of research firms.

Many people think of marketing research as a lengthy, formal process carried out by large marketing companies. But many small businesses and nonprofit organizations also use marketing research. Almost any organization can find informal, low-cost alternatives to the formal and complex marketing research techniques used by research experts in large firms (see Marketing Highlight 4-2).

The Marketing Research Process

The marketing research process (see Figure 4-2) consists of these four steps: *defining the problem and research objectives, developing the research plan, implementing the research plan,* and *interpreting and reporting the findings.*

Defining the Problem and Research Objectives

The marketing manager and the researcher must work closely together to define the problem carefully and must agree on the research objectives. The manager best understands the decision for which information is needed; the researcher best understands marketing research and how to obtain the information.

TABLE 4-2
Research Activities of 587 Companies

TYPE OF RESEARCH	% DOING	TYPE OF RESEARCH	% DOING
Business/Economic and Corporate Research		2. Channel performance studies	29
1. Industry and market characteristics and trends	83	3. Channel coverage studies	26
2. Acquisition and diversification studies	53	4. Export and international studies	19
3. Market share analyses	79	**Promotion**	
4. Internal employee studies (morale, communication, other)	54	1. Motivation research	37
		2. Media research	57
Pricing		3. Copy research	50
1. Cost analysis	60	4. Advertising effectiveness	65
2. Profit analysis	59	5. Competitive advertising studies	47
3. Price elasticity	45	6. Public image studies	60
4. Demand analysis:		7. Sales force compensation studies	30
a. Market potential	74	8. Sales force quota studies	26
b. Sales potential	69	9. Sales force territory structure	31
c. Sales forecasts	67	10. Studies of premiums, coupons, deals, other	36
5. Competitive pricing analysis	63	**Buying Behavior**	
Product		1. Brand preference	54
1. Concept development and testing	68	2. Brand attitudes	53
2. Brand name generation and testing	38	3. Product satisfaction	68
3. Test market	45	4. Purchase behavior	61
4. Product testing of existing products	47	5. Purchase intentions	60
5. Packaging design studies	31	6. Brand awareness	59
6. Competitive product studies	58	7. Segmentation studies	60
Distribution			
1. Plant and warehouse location studies	23		

Source: Thomas C. Kinnear and Ann R. Root, eds., *1988 Survey of Marketing Research: Organization, Functions, Budget, Compensation* (Chicago: American Marketing Association, 1989), p. 43.

MARKETING RESEARCH IN SMALL BUSINESS AND NONPROFIT ORGANIZATIONS

Managers of small businesses and nonprofit organizations often think that marketing research can be done only by experts in large companies with big research budgets. But many of the marketing research techniques discussed in this chapter also can be used by smaller organizations in a less formal manner and at little or no expense.

Managers of small businesses and nonprofit organizations can obtain good marketing information simply by *observing* things around them. For example, retailers can evaluate new locations by observing vehicle and pedestrian traffic. They can visit competing stores to check on facilities and prices. They can evaluate their customer mix by recording how many and what kinds of customers shop in the store at different times. Competitor advertising can be monitored by collecting advertisements from local media.

Managers can conduct informal *surveys* using small convenience samples. The director of an art museum can learn what patrons think about new exhibits by conducting informal "focus groups"—inviting small groups to lunch and having discussions on topics of interest. Retail salespeople can talk with customers visiting the store; hospital officials can interview patients. Restaurant managers might make random phone calls during slack hours to interview consumers about where they eat out and what they think of various restaurants in the area.

Managers also can conduct their own simple *experiments*. For example, by changing the themes in regular fund-raising mailings and watching the results, a nonprofit manager can find out much about which marketing strategies work best. By varying newspaper advertisements, a store manager can learn the effects of things such as ad size and position, price coupons, and media used.

Small organizations can obtain most of the secondary data available to large businesses. In addition, many associations, local media, chambers of commerce, and government agencies provide special help to small organizations. The U.S. Small Business Administration offers dozens of free publications giving advice on topics ranging from planning advertising to ordering business signs. Local newspapers often provide information on local shoppers and their buying patterns.

Sometimes volunteers and colleges are willing to help carry out research. Nonprofit organizations can often use volunteers from local service clubs and other sources. Many colleges are seeking small businesses and nonprofit organizations to serve as cases for projects in marketing research classes.

In summary, secondary data collection, observation, surveys, and experiments can all be used effectively by small organizations with small budgets. Although these informal research methods are less complex and less costly, they still must be conducted carefully. Managers must think carefully about the objectives of the research, formulate questions in advance, recognize the biases introduced by smaller samples and less-skilled researchers, and conduct the research systematically. If carefully planned and implemented, low-cost research can provide reliable information for improving marketing decision making.

Managers must know enough about marketing research to help in the planning and in the interpretation of research results. If they know little about marketing research, they may obtain the wrong information, accept wrong conclusions, or ask for information that costs too much. Experienced marketing researchers who understand the manager's problem also should be involved at this stage. The researcher must be able to help the manager define the problem and to suggest ways that research can help the manager make better decisions.

Defining the problem and research objectives is often the hardest step in the research process. The manager may know that something is wrong, without knowing the specific causes. For example, managers of a discount retail store chain hastily decided that falling sales were caused by poor advertising and ordered research to test the company's advertising. When this research showed that current advertising was reaching the right people with the right message, the managers were puzzled. It turned out that the chain's stores were not delivering what the advertising promised. Careful problem definition would have avoided the cost and delay of doing advertising research. It would have suggested research on the real problem of consumer reactions to the products, service, and prices offered in the chain's stores.

After the problem has been defined carefully, the manager and researcher

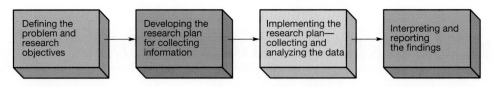

FIGURE 4-2
The marketing research
process

| Defining the problem and research objectives | → | Developing the research plan for collecting information | → | Implementing the research plan—collecting and analyzing the data | → | Interpreting and reporting the findings |

must set the research objectives. A marketing research project might have one of three types of objectives. The objective of **exploratory research** is to gather preliminary information that will help define the problem and suggest hypotheses. The objective of **descriptive research** is to describe things such as the market potential for a product or the demographics and attitudes of consumers who buy the product. The objective of **causal research** is to test hypotheses about cause-and-effect relationships. For example, would a 10 percent decrease in tuition at a private college result in an enrollment sufficient to offset the reduced tuition? Managers often start with exploratory research and later follow with descriptive or causal research.

The statement of the problem and research objectives guides the entire research process. The manager and researcher should put the statement in writing to be certain that they agree on the purpose and expected results of the research.

Developing the Research Plan

The second step of the marketing research process calls for determining the information needed, developing a plan for gathering it efficiently, and presenting the plan to marketing management. The plan outlines sources of existing data and spells out the specific research approaches, contact methods, sampling plans, and instruments that researchers will use to gather new data.

Determining Specific Information Needs. Research objectives must be translated into specific information needs. For example, suppose Campbell decides to conduct research to find out how consumers would react to the company replacing its familiar red and white can with new bowl-shaped plastic containers that it has used successfully for a number of its other products. The containers would cost more, but would allow consumers to heat the soup in a microwave oven and eat it without using dishes. This research might call for the following specific information:

- The demographic, economic, and lifestyle characteristics of current soup users. (Busy working couples might find the convenience of the new packaging worth the price; families with children might want to pay less and wash the pan and bowls.)

- Consumer-usage patterns for soup: how much soup they eat, where, and when. (The new packaging might be ideal for adults eating lunch on the go, but less convenient for parents feeding lunch to several children.)

- The number of microwave ovens in consumer and commercial markets. (The number of microwaves in homes and business lunchrooms will limit the demand for the new containers.)

- Retailer reactions to the new packaging. (Failure to get retailer support could hurt sales of the new package.)

- Consumer attitudes toward the new packaging. (The red and white Campbell can has become an American institution—will consumers accept the new packaging?)

- Forecasts of sales of both new and current packages. (Will the new packaging increase Campbell's profits?)

Campbell managers will need this and many other types of information to decide whether to introduce the new packaging.

Gathering Secondary Information. To meet the manager's information needs, the researcher can gather secondary data, primary data, or both. **Secondary data** consist of information that already exists somewhere, having been collected for another purpose. **Primary data** consist of information collected for the specific purpose at hand.

Researchers usually start by gathering secondary data. Table 4-3 shows the many secondary data sources, including *internal* and *external* sources.[12] Secondary data usually can be obtained more quickly and at a lower cost than primary data. For example, a visit to the library might provide all the information Campbell needs on microwave oven usage, at almost no cost. A study to collect primary in-

TABLE 4-3
Sources of Secondary Data

Internal sources

Internal sources include company profit and loss statements, balance sheets, sales figures, sales call reports, invoices, inventory records, and prior research reports.

Government publications

Statistical Abstract of the U.S., updated annually, provides summary data on demographic, economic, social, and other aspects of the American economy and society.

County and City Data Book, updated every three years, presents statistical information for counties, cities, and other geographical units on population, education, employment, aggregate and median income, housing, bank deposits, retail sales, etc.

U.S. Industrial Outlook provides projections of industrial activity by industry and includes data on production, sales, shipments, employment, etc.

Marketing Information Guide provides a monthly annotated bibliography of marketing information. Other government publications include the *Annual Survey of Manufacturers; Business Statistics; Census of Manufacturers; Census of Population; Census of Retail Trade, Wholesale Trade,* and *Selected Service Industries; Census of Transportation; Federal Reserve Bulletin; Monthly Labor Review; Survey of Current Business;* and *Vital Statistics Report.*

Periodicals and books

Business Periodicals Index, a monthly, lists business articles appearing in a wide variety of business publications.

Standard & Poor's Industry Surveys provide updated statistics and analyses of industries.

Moody's Manuals provide financial data and names of executives in major companies.

Encyclopedia of Associations provides information on every major trade and professional association in the United States.

Marketing journals include the *Journal of Marketing, Journal of Marketing Research,* and *Journal of Consumer Research.*

Useful trade magazines include *Advertising Age, Chain Store Age, Progressive Grocer, Sales & Marketing Management, Stores.*

Useful general business magazines include *Business Week, Fortune, Forbes,* and *Harvard Business Review.*

Commercial Data

Here are just a few of the dozens of commercial research houses selling data to subscribers:

A.C. Nielsen Company provides supermarket scanner data on sales, market share, and retail prices (Scantrack), data on household purchasing (Scantrack National Electronic Household Panel), data on television audiences (Nielsen National Television Index), and others.

IMS International provides reports on the movement of pharmaceuticals, hospital laboratory supplies, animal health products, and personal care products.

Information Resources, Inc. provides supermarket scanner data for tracking grocery product movement (InfoScan) and single-source data collection (BehaviorScan).

MRB Group (Simmons Market Research Bureau) provides annual reports covering television markets, sporting goods, and proprietary drugs. The reports give lifestyle and geodemographic data by sex, income, age, and brand preferences (selective markets and media reaching them).

NFO Research provides data for the beverage industry (SIPS), for mail order businesses (MOMS), and for carpet and rug industries (CARS). It also provides a mail panel for concept and product testing, attitude and usage studies, and tracking and segmentation (Analycor).

International Data

Here are only a few of the many sources providing international information:

United Nations publications include the *Statistical Yearbook,* a comprehensive source of international data for socioeconomic indicators; *Demographic Yearbook,* a collection of demographics data and vital statistics for 220 countries; and the *International Trade Statistics Yearbook,* which provides information on foreign trade for specific countries and commodities.

Europa Yearbook provides surveys on history, politics, population, economy, and natural resources for most countries of the world, along with information on major international organizations.

Political Risk Yearbook contains information on political situations in foreign countries, with reference to U.S. investment. It predicts the political climate in each country.

Foreign Economic Trends and Their Implications for the United States provides reports on recent business, economic, and political developments in specific countries.

International Marketing Data and Statistics provides marketing statistics by country, including data on consumer product markets for countries outside the United States and Europe.

Other sources include *Country Studies, OECD Economic Surveys, Economic Survey of Europe, Asian Economic Handbook*, and *International Financial Statistics.*

formation might take weeks or months and cost thousands of dollars. Also, secondary sources sometimes can provide data an individual company cannot collect on its own—information that either is not directly available or would be too expensive to collect. For example, it would be too expensive for Campbell to conduct a continuing retail store audit to find out about the market shares, prices, and displays of competitors' brands. But it can buy the Nielsen Scantrack service, which provides this information from 3,000 scanner-equipped supermarkets.

Secondary data can also present problems. The needed information may not exist—researchers can rarely obtain all the data they need from secondary sources. For example, Campbell will not find existing information about consumer reactions to new packaging that it has not yet placed on the market. Even when data can be found, they might not be very usable. The researcher must evaluate secondary information carefully to make certain it is *relevant* (fits research project needs), *accurate* (reliably collected and reported), *current* (up to date enough for current decisions), and *impartial* (objectively collected and reported).

Secondary data provide a good starting point for research and often help to define problems and research objectives. In most cases, however, secondary sources cannot provide all the needed information, and the company must collect primary data.

Planning Primary Data Collection. Good decisions require good data. Just as researchers must carefully evaluate the quality of secondary information they obtain, they also must take great care in collecting primary data to assure that they provide marketing decision makers with relevant, accurate, current, and unbiased information. Table 4-4 shows that designing a plan for primary data collection calls for a number of decisions on *research approaches, contact methods, sampling plan,* and *research instruments.*

Research Approaches. **Observational research** is the gathering of primary data by observing relevant people, actions, and situations. For example:

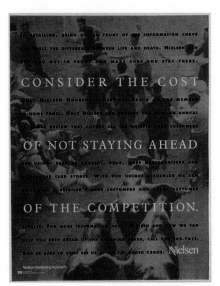

Secondary data sources: Here Nielsen Marketing Research suggests that information from its 40,000-member in-house consumer panel will give retailers a competitive edge by helping them to define their core customers and to gauge customer loyalty.

- A food-products manufacturer sends researchers into supermarkets to find out the prices of competing brands or how much shelf space and display support retailers give its brands.

- A bank evaluates possible new branch locations by checking traffic patterns, neighborhood conditions, and the locations of competing branches.

- A maker of personal care products pretests its ads by showing them to people and measuring eye movements, pulse rates, and other physical reactions.

- A department store chain sends observers who pose as customers into its stores to check on store conditions and customer service.

- A museum checks the popularity of various exhibits by noting the amount of floor wear around them.

Several companies sell information collected through *mechanical* observation. For example, the A. C. Nielsen Company attaches "people meters" to television sets in selected homes to record who watches which programs. Nielsen then provides summaries of the size and demographic makeup of audiences for different television programs. The television networks use these ratings to judge program popularity and to set charges for advertising time. Advertisers use the ratings when selecting programs for their commercials. *Checkout scanners* in retail stores also provide mechanical observation data. These laser scanners record consumer purchases in detail. Consumer products companies and retailers use scanner information to assess and improve product sales and store performance.[13] Some marketing research firms now offer **single-source data systems** that electronically monitor both consumers' purchases and consumers' exposure to various marketing activities in an effort to better evaluate the link between the two (see Marketing Highlight 4-3).

Observational research can be used to obtain information that people are unwilling or unable to provide. In some cases, observation may be the only way to obtain the needed information. In contrast, some things simply cannot be observed, such as feelings, attitudes and motives, or private behavior. Long-term or infrequent behavior is also difficult to observe. Because of these limitations, researchers often use observation along with other data collection methods.

Survey research is the approach best suited for gathering *descriptive* infor-

TABLE 4-4
Planning Primary Data Collection

RESEARCH APPROACHES	CONTACT METHODS	SAMPLING PLAN	RESEARCH INSTRUMENTS
Observation	Mail	Sampling unit	Questionnaire
Survey	Telephone	Sample size	Mechanical instruments
Experiment	Personal	Sampling procedure	

mation. A company that wants to know about people's knowledge, attitudes, preferences, or buying behavior often can find out by asking them directly. Survey research can be structured or unstructured. *Structured* surveys use formal lists of questions asked of all respondents in the same way. *Unstructured* surveys let the interviewer probe respondents and guide the interview according to their answers.

Survey research may be direct or indirect. In the *direct* approach, the researcher asks direct questions about behavior or thoughts—for example, "Why don't you buy clothes at Kmart?" In contrast, the researcher might use the *indirect* approach by asking, "What kinds of people buy clothes at Kmart?" From the response to this indirect question, the researcher may be able to discover why the consumer avoids Kmart clothing. In fact, it may suggest reasons the consumer is not consciously aware of.

Survey research is the most widely used method for primary data collection, and it is often the only method used in a research study. More than 72 million Americans are interviewed each year in surveys.[14] The major advantage of survey research is its flexibility. It can be used to obtain many different kinds of information in many different marketing situations. Depending on the survey design, it also may provide information more quickly and at lower cost than observational or experimental research.

However, survey research also presents some problems. Sometimes people are unable to answer survey questions because they cannot remember or never thought about what they do and why. Or people may be unwilling to respond to unknown interviewers or about things they consider private. Respondents may answer survey questions even when they do not know the answer in order to appear smarter or more informed than they are. Or they may try to help the interviewer by giving pleasing answers. Finally, busy people may not take the time, or they might resent the intrusion into their privacy. Careful survey design can help to minimize these problems.

Whereas observation is best suited for exploratory research and surveys for descriptive research, **experimental research** is best suited for gathering *causal* information. Experiments involve selecting matched groups of subjects, giving them different treatments, controlling unrelated factors, and checking for differences in group responses. Thus, experimental research tries to explain cause-and-effect relationships. Observation and surveys may be used to collect information in experimental research.

Researchers at McDonald's might use experiments, before adding a new sandwich to the menu, to answer questions such as the following:

- How much will the new sandwich increase McDonald's sales?

- How will the new sandwich affect the sales of other menu items?

- Which advertising approach would have the greatest effect on sales of the sandwich?

- How would different prices affect the sales of the product?

- Should the new item be targeted toward adults, children, or both?

For example, to test the effects of two different prices, McDonald's could set up the following simple experiment. It could introduce the new sandwich at one price in its restaurants in one city and at another price in restaurants in another city. If the cities are similar, and if all other marketing efforts for the sandwich are

SINGLE-SOURCE DATA SYSTEMS: A POWERFUL NEW WAY TO MEASURE MARKETING IMPACT

Information Resources, Inc., knows all there is to know about the members of its panel households—what they eat for lunch; what they put in their coffee; and what they use to wash their hair, quench their thirsts, or make up their faces. The research company electronically monitors the television programs these people watch and tracks the brands they buy, the coupons they use, where they shop, and what newspapers and magazines they read. These households are a part of IRI's BehaviorScan service, a *single-source data system* that links consumers' exposure to television advertising, sales promotion, and other marketing efforts with their store purchases. BehaviorScan and other single-source data systems have revolutionized the way consumer products companies measure the impact of their marketing activities.

The basics of single-source research are straightforward, and the IRI BehaviorScan system provides a good example. IRI maintains a panel of 60,000 households in 27 markets. The company meters each home's television set to track who watches what and when, and it quizzes family members to find out what they read. It carefully records important facts about each household, such as family income, age of children, lifestyle, and product and store buying history.

IRI also employs a panel of retail stores in each of its markets. For a fee, these stores agree to carry the new products that IRI wishes to test and they allow IRI to control such factors as shelf location, stocking, point-of-purchase displays, and pricing for these products.

Each BehaviorScan household receives an identification number. When household members shop for groceries in IRI panel stores, they give their identification number to the store checkout clerk. All the information about the family's purchases—brands bought, package sizes, prices paid—is recorded by the store's electronic scanner and immediately entered by computer into the family's purchase file. The system also records any other in-store factors that might affect purchase decisions, such as special competitor price promotions or shelf displays.

Thus, IRI builds a complete record of each household's demographic and psychographic makeup, purchasing behavior, media habits, and the conditions surrounding purchase. But IRI takes the process a step farther. Through cable television, IRI controls the advertisements being sent to each household. It can beam different ads and promotions to different panel households and then use the purchasing information obtained from scanners to assess which ads had more or less impact and how various promotions affected different kinds of

Single-source data systems: From a single source marketers can obtain information that links their marketing efforts directly with consumer buying behavior. Here a BehaviorScan card holder makes a purchase.

consumers. In short, from a single source, companies can obtain information that links their marketing efforts directly with consumer buying behavior.

BehaviorScan and other single-source systems have their drawbacks, and some researchers are skeptical. One hitch is that such systems produce truckloads of data, more than most companies can handle. Another problem is cost: Single-source data can cost marketers hundreds of thousands of dollars a year per brand. Also, because such systems are set up in only a few market areas, usually small cities, the marketer often finds it difficult to generalize from the measures and results. Finally, although single-source systems provide important information for assessing the impact of promotion and advertising, they shed little light on the effects of other key marketing actions.

Despite these drawbacks, more and more companies are relying on single-source data systems to test new products and new marketing strategies. When properly used, such systems can provide marketers with fast and detailed information about how their products are selling, who is buying them, and what factors affect purchase.

Sources: See Joanne Lipman, "Single-Source Ad Research Heralds Detailed Look at Household Habits," *The Wall Street Journal,* February 16, 1988, p. 39; Joe Schwartz, "Back to the Source," *American Demographics,* January 1989, pp. 22-26; Magid H. Abraham and Leonard M. Lodish, "Getting the Most Out of Advertising and Promotion," *Harvard Business Review,* May-June 1990, pp. 50-60; and Howard Schlossberg, "IRI, Nielsen Slug It Out in 'Scanning Wars,'" *Marketing News,* September 2, 1991, pp. 1, 47.

the same, then differences in sales in the two cities could be related to the price charged. More complex experiments could be designed to include other variables and other locations.

Contact Methods. Information can be collected by mail, telephone, or personal interview. Table 4-5 shows the strengths and weaknesses of each of these contact methods.

Mail questionnaires have many advantages. They can be used to collect large amounts of information at a low cost per respondent. Respondents may give more honest answers to more personal questions on a mail questionnaire than to an unknown interviewer in person or over the phone. No interviewer is involved to bias the respondent's answers.

However, mail questionnaires also have some disadvantages. They are not very flexible—they require simple and clearly worded questions; all respondents answer the same questions in a fixed order; and the researcher cannot adapt the questionnaire based on earlier answers. Mail surveys usually take longer to complete, and the response rate—the number of people returning completed questionnaires—is often very low. Finally, the researcher often has little control over the mail questionnaire sample. Even with a good mailing list, it is often hard to control *who* at the mailing address fills out the questionnaire.

Telephone interviewing is the best method for gathering information quickly, and it provides greater flexibility than mail questionnaires. Interviewers can explain questions that are not understood. Depending on the respondent's answers, they can skip some questions or probe further on others. Telephone interviewing also allows greater sample control. Interviewers can ask to speak to respondents with the desired characteristics, or even by name. Response rates tend to be higher than with mail questionnaires.

However, telephone interviewing also has drawbacks. The cost per respondent is higher than with mail questionnaires, and people may not want to discuss personal questions with an interviewer. Using an interviewer increases flexibility but also introduces interviewer bias. The way interviewers talk, small differences in how they ask questions, and other differences may affect respondents' answers. Finally, different interviewers may interpret and record responses differently, and under time pressures some interviewers might even cheat by recording answers without asking questions.

Personal interviewing takes two forms—individual and group interviewing. *Individual interviewing* involves talking with people in their homes or offices, on the street, or in shopping malls. The interviewer must gain their cooperation, and the time involved can range from a few minutes to several hours. Sometimes a small payment is given to people in return for their time.

Group interviewing consists of inviting six to ten people to gather for a few hours with a trained moderator to talk about a product, service, or organization. The moderator needs objectivity, knowledge of the subject and industry, and some understanding of group and consumer behavior. The participants normally are paid a small sum for attending. The meeting is held in a pleasant place and refreshments are served to foster an informal setting. The moderator starts with broad questions before moving to more specific issues and encourages free and

---

TABLE 4-5
Strengths and Weaknesses of the Three Contact Methods

	MAIL	TELEPHONE	PERSONAL
1. Flexibility	Poor	Good	Excellent
2. Quantity of data that can be collected	Good	Fair	Excellent
3. Control of interviewer effects	Excellent	Fair	Poor
4. Control of sample	Fair	Excellent	Fair
5. Speed of data collection	Poor	Excellent	Good
6. Response rate	Poor	Good	Good
7. Cost	Good	Fair	Poor

Source: Adapted with permission of Macmillan Publishing Company from *Marketing Research: Measurement and Method,* 6th ed., by Donald S. Tull and Del I. Hawkins. Copyright © 1993 by Macmillan Publishing Company.

Researchers watch a focus group session.

Computer-assisted telephone interviewing: The interviewer reads questions from the screen and types the respondent's answers directly into the computer, reducing errors and saving time.

easy discussion, hoping that group interactions will bring out actual feelings and thoughts. At the same time, the moderator "focuses" the discussion—hence the name **focus-group interviewing.** The comments are recorded through written notes or on videotapes that are studied later. Focus-group interviewing has become one of the major marketing research tools for gaining insight into consumer thoughts and feelings.[15]

Personal interviewing is quite flexible and can be used to collect large amounts of information. Trained interviewers can hold a respondent's attention for a long time and can explain difficult questions. They can guide interviews, explore issues, and probe as the situation requires. Personal interviews can be used with any type of questionnaire. Interviewers can show subjects actual products, advertisements, or packages and observe reactions and behavior. In most cases, personal interviews can be conducted fairly quickly.

The main drawbacks of personal interviewing are costs and sampling problems. Personal interviews may cost three to four times as much as telephone interviews. Group interview studies usually employ small sample sizes to keep time and costs down, and it may be hard to generalize from the results. Because interviewers have more freedom in personal interviews, the problem of interviewer bias is greater.

Which contact method is best depends on what information the researcher wants and on the number and types of respondents to be contacted. Advances in computers and communications have had an impact on methods of obtaining information. For example, most research firms now do Computer Assisted Telephone Interviewing (CATI). Professional interviewers call respondents around the country, often using phone numbers drawn at random. When the respondent answers, the interviewer reads a set of questions from a video screen and types the respondent's answers directly into the computer. Although this procedure requires a large investment in computer equipment and interviewer training, it eliminates data editing and coding, reduces errors, and saves time. Other research firms set up terminals in shopping centers—respondents sit down at a terminal, read questions from a screen, and type their own answers into the computer.[16]

Sampling Plans. Marketing researchers usually draw conclusions about large groups of consumers by studying a small sample of the total consumer population. A **sample** is a segment of the population selected to represent the population as a whole. Ideally, the sample should be representative so that the researcher can make accurate estimates of the thoughts and behaviors of the larger population.

Designing the sample calls for three decisions. First, *who* is to be surveyed (what *sampling unit*)? The answer to this question is not always obvious. For example, to study the decision-making process for a family automobile purchase, should the researcher interview the husband, wife, other family members, dealership salespeople, or all of these? The researcher must determine what information is needed and who is most likely to have it.

Second, *how many* people should be surveyed (what *sample size*)? Large samples give more reliable results than small samples. However, it is not necessary to sample the entire target market or even a large portion to get reliable results. If well chosen, samples of less than 1 percent of a population can often give good reliability.

TABLE 4-6
Types of Samples

Probability sample

Sample random sample	Every member of the population has a known and equal chance of selection.
Stratified random sample	The population is divided into mutually exclusive groups (such as age groups), and random samples are drawn from each group.
Cluster (area) sample	The population is divided into mutually exclusive groups (such as blocks), and the researcher draws a sample of the groups to interview.

Nonprobability sample

Convenience sample	The researcher selects the easiest population members from which to obtain information.
Judgment sample	The researcher uses his or her judgment to select population members who are good prospects for accurate information.
Quota sample	The researcher finds and interviews a prescribed number of people in each of several categories.

Third, *how* should the people in the sample be *chosen* (what *sampling procedure*)? Table 4-6 describes different kinds of samples. *Using probability samples,* each population member has a known chance of being included in the sample, and researchers can calculate confidence limits for sampling error. But when probability sampling costs too much or takes too much time, marketing researchers often take *nonprobability samples,* even though their sampling error cannot be measured. These varied ways of drawing samples have different costs and time limitations, as well as different accuracy and statistical properties. Which method is best depends on the needs of the research project.

Research Instruments. In collecting primary data, marketing researchers have a choice of two main research instruments—the *questionnaire* and *mechanical devices.*

The *questionnaire* is by far the most common instrument. Broadly speaking, a questionnaire consists of a set of questions presented to a respondent for his or her answers. The questionnaire is very flexible—there are many ways to ask questions. Questionnaires must be developed carefully and tested before they can be used on a large scale. A carelessly prepared questionnaire usually contains several errors (see Table 4-7).

In preparing a questionnaire, the marketing researcher must decide what questions to ask, the form of the questions, the wording of the questions, and the ordering of the questions. Questionnaires frequently leave out questions that should be answered and include questions that cannot be answered, will not be answered, or need not be answered. Each question should be checked to see that it contributes to the research objectives.

The *form* of the question can influence the response. Marketing researchers distinguish between closed-end and open-end questions. **Closed-end questions** include all the possible answers, and subjects make choices among them. Part A of Table 4-8 shows the most common forms of closed-end questions as they might appear in a Delta Airlines survey of airline users. **Open-end questions** allow respondents to answer in their own words. The most common forms are shown in Part B of Table 4-8. Open-end questions often reveal more than closed-end questions because respondents are not limited in their answers. Open-end questions are especially useful in exploratory research in which the researcher is trying to find out *what* people think but not measuring *how many* people think in a certain way. Closed-end questions, on the other hand, provide answers that are easier to interpret and tabulate.

Researchers should also use care in the *wording* of questions. They should use simple, direct, unbiased wording. The questions should be pretested before they are widely used. The *ordering* of questions is also important. The first question should create interest if possible. Difficult or personal questions should be asked last so that respondents do not become defensive. The questions should be arranged in a logical order.

| TABLE 4-7 |
| A "Questionable Questionnaire" |

Suppose that a summer camp director had prepared the following questionnaire to use in interviewing the parents of prospective campers. How would you assess each question?

1. What is your income to the nearest hundred dollars?

    People don't usually know their income to the nearest hundred dollars nor do they want to reveal their income that closely. Moreover, a researcher should never open a questionnaire with such a personal question.

2. Are you a strong or a weak supporter of overnight summer camping for your children?

    What do "strong" and "weak" mean?

3. Do your children behave themselves well at a summer camp?

    Yes ( )   No ( )

    "Behave" is a relative term. Furthermore, are "yes" and "no" the best response options for this question? Besides, will people want to answer this? Why ask the question in the first place?

4. How many camps mailed literature to you last April? This April?

    Who can remember this?

5. What are the most salient and determinant attributes in your evaluation of summer camps?

    What are "salient" and "determinant" attributes? Don't use big words on me!

6. Do you think it is right to deprive your child of the opportunity to grow into a mature person through the experience of summer camping?

    A loaded question. Given the bias, how can any parent answer "yes"?

Although questionnaires are the most common research instrument, *mechanical instruments* also are used. We discussed two mechanical instruments—people meters and supermarket scanners—earlier in the chapter. Another group of mechanical devices measures subjects' physical responses. For example, a galvanometer measures the strength of interest or emotions aroused by a subject's exposure to different stimuli: for instance, an ad or picture. The galvanometer detects the minute degree of sweating that accompanies emotional arousal. The tachistoscope flashes an ad to a subject at an exposure range from less than one-hundredth of a second to several seconds. After each exposure, the respondents describe everything they recall. Eye cameras are used to study respondents' eye movements to determine at what points their eyes focus first and how long they linger on a given item.[17]

Presenting the Research Plan. At this stage, the marketing researcher should summarize the plan in a *written proposal*. A written proposal is especially important when the research project is large and complex or when an outside firm carries it out. The proposal should cover the management problems addressed and the research objectives, the information to be obtained, the sources of secondary information or methods for collecting primary data, and the way the results will help management decision making. The proposal also should include research costs. A written research plan or proposal makes sure that the marketing manager and researchers have considered all the important aspects of the research and that they agree on why and how the research will be done.

Mechanical research instruments: Eye cameras determine where eyes land and how long they linger on a given item.

TABLE 4-8
Types of Questions

A. CLOSED-END QUESTIONS

Name	Description	Example
Dichotomous	A question offering two answer choices.	"In arranging this trip, did you personally phone Delta?" Yes ☐　No ☐
Multiple choice	A question offering three or more answer choices.	"With whom are you traveling on this flight?" No one ☐　Children only ☐　Spouse ☐　Business associates/friends/relatives ☐　Spouse and children ☐　An organized tour group ☐
Likert scale	A statement with which the respondent shows the amount of agreement or disagreement.	"Small airlines generally give better service than large ones." Strongly disagree 1 ☐　Disagree 2 ☐　Neither agree nor disagree 3 ☐　Agree 4 ☐　Strongly agree 5 ☐
Semantic differential	A scale is inscribed between two bipolar words, and the respondent selects the point that represents the direction and intensity of his or her feelings.	*Delta Airlines* Large ___X__:___:___:___:___:___ : Small　Experienced ___:___:___:___:__X_:___ : Inexperienced　Modern ___:___:___:__X_:___:___ : Old-fashioned
Importance scale	A scale that rates the importance of some attribute from "not at all important" to "extremely important."	"Airline food service to me is" Extremely Important 1 ___　Very important 2 ___　Somewhat important 3 ___　Not very important 4 ___　Not at all important 5 ___
Rating scale	A scale that rates some attribute from "poor" to "excellent."	"Delta's food service is" Excellent 1 ___　Very good 2 ___　Good 3 ___　Fair 4 ___　Poor 5 ___
Intention-to-buy scale	A scale that describes the respondent's intentions to buy	"If in-flight telephone service were available on a long flight, I would" Definitely buy 1 ___　Probably buy 2 ___　Not certain 3 ___　Probably not buy 4 ___　Definitely not buy 5 ___

B. OPEN-END QUESTIONS

Name	Description	Example
Completely unstructured	A question that respondents can answer in an almost unlimited number of ways.	"What is your opinion of Delta Airlines?"
Word association	Words are presented, one at a time, and respondents mention the first word that comes to mind.	"What is the first word that comes to your mind when you hear the following?" Airline_____ Delta_____ Travel_____
Sentence completion	Incomplete sentences are presented, one at a time, and respondents complete the sentence.	"When I choose an airline, the most important consideration in my decision is _____"
Story completion	An incomplete story is presented, and respondents are asked to complete it.	"I flew Delta a few days ago. I noticed that the exterior and interior of the plane had very bright colors. This aroused in me the following thoughts and feelings." *Now complete the story.*
Picture completion	A picture of two characters is presented, with one making a statement. Respondents are asked to identify with the other and fill in the empty balloon.	Fill in the empty balloon.
Thematic Apperception Tests (TAT)	A picture is presented, and respondents are asked to make up a story about what they think is happening or may happen in the picture.	Make up a story about what you see.

Implementing the Research Plan

The researcher next puts the marketing research plan into action. This involves collecting, processing, and analyzing the information. Data collection can be carried out by the company's marketing research staff or by outside firms. The company keeps more control over the collection process and data quality by using its own staff. However, outside firms that specialize in data collection often can do the job more quickly and at lower cost.

The data collection phase of the marketing research process is generally the most expensive and the most subject to error. The researcher should watch fieldwork closely to make sure that the plan is implemented correctly and to guard against problems with contacting respondents, with respondents who refuse to cooperate or who give biased or dishonest answers, and with interviewers who make mistakes or take shortcuts.

Researchers must process and analyze the collected data to isolate important information and findings. They need to check data from questionnaires for accuracy and completeness and code it for computer analysis. The researchers then tabulate the results and compute averages and other statistical measures.

Interpreting and Reporting the Findings

The researcher must now interpret the findings, draw conclusions, and report them to management. The researcher should not try to overwhelm managers with numbers and fancy statistical techniques. Rather, the researcher should present important findings that are useful in the major decisions faced by management.

However, interpretation should not be left only to the researchers. They are often experts in research design and statistics, but the marketing manager knows more about the problem and the decisions that must be made. In many cases, findings can be interpreted in different ways, and discussions between researchers and managers will help point to the best interpretations. The manager will also want to check that the research project was carried out properly and that all the necessary analysis was completed. Or, after seeing the findings, the manager may have additional questions that can be answered through further sifting of the data. Finally, the manager is the one who ultimately must decide what action the research suggests. The researchers may even make the data directly available to marketing managers so that they can perform new analyses and test new relationships on their own.

Interpretation is an important phase of the marketing process. The best research is meaningless if the manager blindly accepts wrong interpretations from the researcher. Similarly, managers may have biased interpretations—they tend to accept research results that show what they expected and to reject those that they did not expect or hope for. Thus, managers and researchers must work together closely when interpreting research results, and both share responsibility for the research process and resulting decisions.[18]

International Marketing Research

International marketing researchers follow the same steps as domestic researchers, from defining the research problem and developing a research plan to interpreting and reporting the results. However, these researchers often face more and different problems. Whereas domestic researchers deal with fairly homogeneous markets within a single country, international researchers deal with markets in many different countries. These different markets often vary dramatically in their levels of economic development, cultures and customs, and buying patterns.

In many foreign markets, the international researcher has a difficult time finding good *secondary data*. Whereas U.S. marketing researchers can obtain reliable secondary data from any of dozens of domestic research services, many countries have almost no research services at all. Even the largest international research services operate in only a relative handful of countries. For example, A. C. Nielsen, the world's largest marketing research company, has offices in only 28 countries outside the United States.[19] Thus, even when secondary information is available, it usually must be obtained from many different sources on a country-by-country basis, making the information difficult to combine or compare.

Because of the scarcity of good secondary data, international researchers often must collect their own primary data. Here, again, researchers face problems not encountered domestically. For example, they may find it difficult simply to develop appropriate samples. Whereas U.S. researchers can use current telephone directories, census tract data, and any of several sources of socioeconomic data to construct samples, such information is largely lacking in many countries. Once the sample is drawn, the U.S. researcher usually can reach most respondents easily by telephone, by mail, or in person. Reaching respondents is often not so easy in other parts of the world. In some countries, few people have phones—there are only four phones per thousand people in Egypt, six in Turkey, and thirty-two in Argentina. In other countries, the postal system is notoriously unreliable. In Brazil, for instance, an estimated 30 percent of the mail is never delivered. In many developing countries, poor roads and transportation systems make certain areas hard to reach, making personal interviews difficult and expensive.[20]

Differences in cultures from country to country cause additional problems for international researchers. Language is the most obvious culprit. For example, questionnaires must be prepared in one language and then translated into the languages of each country researched. Responses then must be translated back into the original language for analysis and interpretation. This adds to research costs and increases the risks of error:

> Translating a questionnaire from one language to another is far from easy. . . . Many points are [lost], because many idioms, phrases, and statements mean different things in different cultures. A Danish executive observed: "Check this out by having a different translator put back into English what you've translated from the English. You'll get the shock of your life. I remember [an example in which] 'out of sight, out of mind' had become 'invisible things are insane.'"[21]

Buying roles and consumer decision processes vary greatly from country to country, further complicating international marketing research. Consumers in different countries also vary in their attitudes toward marketing research. People in one country may be very willing to respond; in other countries, nonresponse can be a major problem. For example, customs in some Islamic countries prohibit people from talking with strangers—a researcher simply may not be allowed to speak by phone with women about brand attitudes or buying behavior. In certain cultures, research questions often are considered too personal. For example, in many Latin American countries, people may feel embarrassed to talk with researchers about their choices of shampoo, deodorant, or other personal care products. Even when respondents are *willing* to respond, they may not be *able* to because of high functional illiteracy rates. And middle-class people in developing countries often make false claims in order to appear well-off. For example, in a study of tea consumption in India, over 70 percent of middle-income respondents claimed that they used one of several national brands. However, the researchers had good reason to doubt these results—more than 60 percent of the tea sold in India is unbranded generic tea.

Despite these problems, the recent growth of international marketing has resulted in a rapid increase in the use of international marketing research. Global companies have little choice but to conduct such research. Although the costs and problems associated with international research may be high, the costs of not doing it—in terms of missed opportunities and mistakes—might be even higher. Once recognized, many of the problems associated with international marketing research can be overcome or avoided.

Public Policy and Ethics in Marketing Research

When properly used, marketing research benefits both the sponsoring company and its customers. It helps the company to make better marketing decisions, which in turn results in products and services that better meet the needs of consumers. However, when misused, marketing research also can abuse and annoy consumers. Marketing Highlight 4-4 summarizes the major public policy and ethics issues surrounding marketing research.

Information Analysis

Information gathered by the company's marketing intelligence and marketing research systems often requires more analysis, and sometimes managers may need more help to apply it to marketing problems and decisions. This help may include

....

MARKETING HIGHLIGHT 4-4

PUBLIC POLICY AND ETHICS IN MARKETING RESEARCH

Most marketing research benefits both the sponsoring company and its consumers. Through marketing research, companies learn more about consumers' needs, resulting in more satisfying products and services. However, the misuse of marketing research can also harm or annoy consumers. Two major public policy and ethics issues in marketing research are discussed here.

Intrusions on Consumer Privacy

Most consumers feel positively about marketing research and believe that it serves a useful purpose. Some actually enjoy being interviewed and giving their opinions. However, others strongly resent or even mistrust marketing research. A few consumers fear that researchers might use sophisticated techniques to probe our deepest feelings, and then use this knowledge to manipulate our buying. Others may have been taken in by previous "research surveys" that actually turned out to be attempts to sell them something. Still other consumers confuse legitimate marketing research studies with telemarketing or database development efforts and say "no" before the interviewer can even begin. Most, however, simply resent the intrusion. They dislike mail or telephone surveys that are too long or too personal, or that interrupt them at inconvenient times.

Increasing consumer resentment has become a major problem for the research industry. This resentment has led to lower survey response rates in recent years—one study found that 36 percent of Americans now refuse to be interviewed in an average survey, up dramatically from a decade ago. The research industry is considering several options for responding to this problem. One is to expand its "Your Opinion Counts" program to educate consumers about the benefits of legitimate marketing research and to distinguish it from telephone selling and database building. Another option is to provide a toll-free number that respondents can call to verify that a survey is legitimate. The industry also has considered adopting broad standards, perhaps based on Europe's International Code of Marketing and Social Research Practice. This code outlines researchers' responsibilities to respondents and to the general public. For example, it specifies that researchers should make their names and addresses available to participants, and it bans companies from representing activities like database compilation or sales and promotional pitches as research.

Misuse of Research Findings

Research studies can be powerful tools of persuasion—companies often use study results as claims in their advertising and promotion. Today, however, many research studies appear to be little more than vehicles for pitching the sponsor's products. In fact, in some cases,

advanced statistical analysis to learn more about both the relationships within a set of data and their statistical reliability. Such analysis allows managers to go beyond means and standard deviations in the data and to answer questions such as the following:

- What are the major variables affecting my sales and how important is each one?

- If I raised my price 10 percent and increased my advertising expenditures 20 percent, what would happen to sales?

- What are the best predictors of which consumers are likely to buy my brand versus my competitor's brand?

- What are the best variables for segmenting my market, and how many segments exist?

Information analysis might also involve a collection of mathematical models that will help marketers make better decisions. Each model represents some real system, process, or outcome. These models can help answer the questions of *what if* and *which is best*. During the past 20 years, marketing scientists have developed numerous models to help marketing managers make better marketing-mix decisions, design sales territories and sales-call plans, select sites for retail outlets, develop optimal advertising mixes, and forecast new-product sales.[22]

DISTRIBUTING INFORMATION

Marketing information has no value until managers use it to make better marketing decisions. The information gathered through marketing intelligence and mar-the research surveys appear to have been designed just to produce the intended effect. Few advertisers openly rig their research designs or blatantly misrepresent the findings—most abuses tend to be subtle "stretches." Consider the following examples:

A study by Chrysler contends that Americans overwhelmingly prefer Chrysler to Toyota after test driving both. However, the study included just 100 people in each of two tests. More importantly, none of the people surveyed owned a foreign car, so they appear to be favorably predisposed to U.S. cars.

Levi Strauss reports that when it asked college students which clothes would be most popular this year, 90 percent said Levi's 501 jeans. However, Levi's were the only jeans on the list.

A Black Flag survey asks: "A roach disk . . . poisons a roach slowly. The dying roach returns to the nest and after it dies is eaten by other roaches. In turn these roaches become poisoned and die. How effective do you think this type of product would be in killing roaches?" Not surprisingly, 79 percent said effective.

A poll sponsored by the disposable diaper industry asked: "It is estimated that disposable diapers account for less than 2 percent of the trash in today's landfills. In contrast, beverage containers, third-class mail, and yard waste are estimated to account for about 21 percent of the trash in landfills. Given this, in your opinion, would it be fair to ban disposable diapers?" Again, not surprisingly, 84 percent said no.

Thus, subtle manipulations of the study's sample, or the choice or wording of questions, can substantially affect the conclusions reached.

In others cases, so-called independent research studies actually are paid for by companies with an interest in the outcome. Small changes in study assumptions or in how results are interpreted can subtly affect the direction of the results. For example, at least four widely quoted studies compare the environmental effects of using disposable diapers to those of using cloth diapers. The two studies sponsored by the cloth-diaper industry conclude that cloth diapers are more environmentally friendly. Not surprisingly, the other two studies, sponsored by the paper-diaper industry, conclude just the opposite. Yet both appear to be correct *given* the underlying assumptions used.

Recognizing that surveys can be abused, several associations—including the American Marketing Association and the Council of American Survey Research Organizations—have developed codes of research ethics and standards of conduct. In the end, however, unethical or inappropriate actions cannot simply be regulated away. Each company must accept responsibility for policing the conduct and reporting of its own marketing research to protect consumers' best interests and its own.

Sources: Excerpts from Cynthia Crossen, "Studies Galore Support Products and Positions, but Are They Reliable?" *The Wall Street Journal,* November 14, 1991, pp. A1, A9. Also see Betsy Spethmann, "Cautious Consumers Have Surveyors Wary," *Advertising Age,* June 10, 1991, p. 34.

keting research must be distributed to the right marketing managers at the right time. Most companies have centralized marketing information systems that provide managers with regular performance reports, intelligence updates, and reports on the results of studies. Managers need these routine reports for making regular planning, implementation, and control decisions. But marketing managers also may need nonroutine information for special situations and on-the-spot decisions. For example, a sales manager having trouble with a large customer may want a summary of the account's sales and profitability over the past year. Or a retail store manager who has run out of a best-selling product may want to know the current inventory levels in the chain's other stores. In companies with only centralized information systems, these managers must request the information from the MIS staff and wait. Often, the information arrives too late to be useful.

Recent developments in information handling have caused a revolution in information distribution. With recent advances in computers, software, and communications, many companies are decentralizing their marketing information systems. They are giving managers direct access to information stored in the system. In some companies, marketing managers can use a personal computer to tie into the company's information network. From any location, they can obtain information from internal records or outside information services, analyze the information using statistical packages and models, prepare reports on a word processor, and communicate with others in the network through electronic communications.

Such systems offer exciting prospects. They allow the managers to get the information they need directly and quickly and to tailor it to their own needs. As more managers develop the skills needed to use such systems, and as improvements in the technology make them more economical, more and more marketing companies will use decentralized marketing information systems.

SUMMARY

In carrying out their marketing responsibilities, marketing managers need a great deal of information. Despite the growing supply of information, managers often lack enough information of the right kind or have too much of the wrong kind. To overcome these problems, many companies are taking steps to improve their marketing information systems.

A well-designed *marketing information system* (MIS) begins and ends with the user. The MIS first *assesses information needs* by interviewing marketing managers and surveying their decision environment to determine what information is desired, needed, and feasible to offer.

The MIS next *develops information* and helps managers to use it more effectively. *Internal records* provide information on sales, costs, inventories, cash flows, and accounts receivable and payable. Such data can be obtained quickly and cheaply, but must often be adapted for marketing decisions. The *marketing intelligence system* supplies marketing executives with everyday information about developments in the external marketing environment. Intelligence can be collected from company employees, customers, suppliers, and resellers; or by monitoring published reports, conferences, advertisements, competitor actions, and other activities in the environment.

Marketing research involves collecting information relevant to a specific marketing problem facing the company. Every marketer needs marketing research, and most large companies have their own marketing research departments. Marketing research involves a four-step process. The first step consists of the manager and researcher carefully *defining the problem and setting the research objectives.* The objective may be *exploratory, descriptive,* or *causal.* The second step consists of developing the *research plan* for collecting data from primary and secondary sources. *Primary data collection* calls for choosing a *research approach* (observation, survey, experiment); choosing a *contact method* (mail, telephone, personal); designing a *sampling plan* (whom to survey, how many to survey, and how to choose them); and developing *research instruments* (questionnaire, mechanical). The third step consists of *implementing the marketing research plan* by collecting, processing, and analyzing the information. The fourth step consists of *interpreting and reporting the findings.* Further information analysis helps marketing managers to apply the information and provides advanced statistical procedures and models to develop more rigorous findings from the information.

Finally, the marketing information system distributes information gathered from internal sources, marketing intelligence, and marketing research to the right managers at the right times. More and more companies are decentralizing their information systems through *networks* that allow managers to have direct access to information.

KEY TERMS

Causal research 112

Closed-end questions 119

Descriptive research 112

Experimental research 115

Exploratory research 112

Focus-group interviewing 118

Internal records information 105

Marketing information system (MIS) 104

Marketing intelligence 107

Marketing research 109

Observational research 114

Open-end questions 119

Primary data 112

Sample 118

Secondary data 112

Single-source data systems 114

Survey research 114

DISCUSSING THE ISSUES

1. You are a research supplier, designing and conducting studies for a variety of companies. What is the *most* important thing you can do to ensure that your clients will get their money's worth from your services?

2. Companies often test new products in plain white packages with no brand name or other marketing information. What does this "blind" testing really measure? Are there any issues in applying these results to the "real" world?

3. Companies often face quickly changing environments. Can market research information "go stale"? What issues does a manager face in using these research results?

4. What type of research would be appropriate in the following situations, and why?

   a. Kellogg's wants to investigate the impact of kids on their parents' decisions to buy breakfast foods.

   b. Your college bookstore wants to get some insights into how students feel about the store's merchandise, prices, and service.

c. McDonald's is considering where to locate a new outlet in a fast-growing suburb.

d. Gillette wants to determine whether a new line of deodorant for children will be profitable.

5. Focus group interviewing is both a widely used and widely criticized research technique in marketing. What are the advantages and disadvantages of focus groups? What are some kinds of questions focus groups can be used to investigate?

6. The IRI data system (see Marketing Highlight 4-3) gets its information from panels of volunteers who subscribe to cable television and live in small cities. Are these people typical? Does this make a difference in how a marketer should interpret these data?

APPLYING THE CONCEPTS

1. "Blind" taste tests often have surprising results. Demonstrate this by conducting a product test in your classroom.

- Purchase three comparable brands of soda such as Coca-Cola, Pepsi, and a regional favorite or store brand. Also buy three small paper cups for each student. Remove *all* identification from the bottles including labels and caps, and use paper to cover any differences in bottle design. Label the brands with neutral terms such as Brand G, Brand H, and Brand I. Pour a small sample of each into labeled cups and distribute them.

- Ask questions and tabulate the answers: (1) What brand do you normally prefer? (2) Which sample do you prefer? (3) What brand do you think each sample is?

- Write students' preferences on the board, then reveal which brand was which sample. Are the results what you had expected? Why or why not?

2. Run a small focus group in class to learn about the pros and cons of this technique.

- Pick one class member as a moderator, and select six to eight other volunteers. Try to include at least one strong personality and one shy member. Set them up in a circle at the front of class.

- Discuss a modestly controversial issue that is of current interest to the class. Avoid issues that are very controversial or emotional. Run the group for 10 to 15 minutes.

- Discuss the focus group "results" with the class. Were the conclusions fair or biased? What did class members find useful about the technique, and what problems did they see?

MAKING MARKETING DECISIONS:

SMALL WORLD COMMUNICATIONS, INC.

Tom called Lynette, clearly excited. "I've got a great new idea for our product. Advanced Micro Devices just announced a new data compression chipset. I won't bore you with the details, but the twist is that I can make it work on a network adapter card so we can . . . "Earth to Thomas—come in Major Tom!" Lyn said. "I agree that data compression on a network adapter is potentially neat, but we're not quite ready to commit to a product yet." "But we've done all the marketing background," he protested.

"I think," she said, "that we need to do a few more things before we're at that stage. I made my last products a success by doing thorough analysis up front, then designing the products to fit the needs I found. I'll fax you an outline of what we need to know before finalizing the product. In brief, we'll need some market research and competitive analysis, some ideas of what motivates consumers, and how they might make their buying decisions. Then . . . "Spare me," said Tom. "Just tell me what you want to know now, and I'll humor you."

They talked on for a bit, and agreed on a few strategic points. All Small World products would meet established industry hardware and software standards, not try to set new ones. All hardware should look like a finished product, not just a naked circuit board, and be installable by anyone, without tools. "Is that practical?" asked Lyn. Tom replied, "Technically, it's not ideal, but there are a lot of easy ways to plug into a PC—parallel and serial ports, keyboard connector, mouseport. For portables, there's a standard expansion bay—the PCMIA slot—that may get used on desktop machines later. For a lot of applications, that's enough." Finally, they agreed they had to find a major unmet consumer need, and develop whatever software and hardware it would take to fill that need.

WHAT NOW?

1. What are the key research problems that Small World needs to address?

2. Consider the situation of Small World Communications. They have no internal information or marketing information system, and no budget for market research. How might Lynette and Tom sidestep these problems, and gather the information they need in a way they can afford?

REFERENCES

1. See "Coke 'Family' Sales Fly as New Coke Stumbles," *Advertising Age*, January 17, 1986, p. 1; Jack Honomichl, "Missing Ingredients in 'New' Coke's Research," *Advertising Age*, July 22, 1985, p. 1; Patricia Winters, "For New Coke, 'What Price Success?'" *Advertising Age*, March 20, 1989, pp. S1-S2; Patricia Winters, "Coke II Enters Markets without Splashy Fanfare," *Advertising Age*, August 24, 1992, p. 2; and "Coke II Entry Quiet Across U.S.," *The Durham Herald-Sun*, January 13, 1993, p. D5.

2. Marion Harper, Jr., "A New Profession to Aid Management," *Journal of Marketing*, January 1961, p. 1.

3. Rashi Glazer, "Marketing in an Information-Intensive Environment: Strategic Implications of Knowledge as an Asset," *Journal of Marketing*, October 1991, pp. 1-19.

4. John Neisbitt, *Megatrends: Ten New Directions Transforming Our Lives* (New York: Warner Books, 1984).

5. "Harnessing the Data Explosion," *Sales & Marketing Management*, January 1987, p. 31; and Joseph M. Winski, "Gentle Rain Turns into Torrent," *Advertising Age*, June 3, 1991, p. 34.

6. Neisbitt, *Megatrends*, p. 16.

7. See "Business Is Turning Data into a Potent Strategic Weapon," *Business Week*, August 22, 1983, p. 92; and "Decision Systems for Marketers," *Marketing Communications*, March 1986, pp. 163-90; and Jeffrey Rotfeder and Jim Bartimo, "How Software Is Making Food Sales a Piece of Cake," *Business Week*, July 2, 1990, pp. 54-55.

8. See Christel Beard and Betsy Wiesendanger, "The Marketer's Guide to Online Databases," *Sales & Marketing Management*, January 1993, pp. 36-41.

9. Ibid., p. 46.; and Leonard M. Fuld, "Competitor Intelligence: Can You Plug the Leaks?" *Security Management*, August 1989, pp. 85-87.

10. See Howard Schlossberg, "Competitive Intelligence Pros Seek Formal Role in Marketing," *Marketing News*, March 5, 1990, pp. 2, 28; Gary B. Roush, "A Program for Sharing Corporate Intelligence," *Journal of Business Strategy*, January-February 1991, pp. 4-7; and Michele Galen, "These Guys Aren't Spooks. They're 'Competitive Analysts,'" *Business Week*, October 14, 1991, p. 97.

11. The American Marketing Association officially adopted this definition in 1987.

12. For more information on secondary sources of business and marketing data, see Gilbert A. Churchill, Jr., *Marketing Research: Methodological Foundations*, 5th ed. (Chicago: The Dryden Press, 1991), pp. 287-303; *The Best 100 Sources of Marketing Information*, a supplement to *American Demographics*, 1989; "Research Business Report," *Advertising Age*, June 3, 1991, pp. 31-35; and "The Honomichl 50: The 1992 Honomichl Business Report on the Marketing Research Industry," a special section in *Marketing News*, June 2, 1992.

13. See Scott Barrett, "The Power of the People," *Adweek*, April 2, 1990, p. 32; Zachary Schiller, "Thanks to the Checkout Scanner, Marketing Is Losing Some of Its Mystery," *Business Week*, August 28, 1989, p. 57; and Lynn G. Coleman, "IRI, Nielsen Slug It Out in the Scanning Wars," *The Marketing News*, September 2, 1991, pp. 1, 47.

14. Mark Landler, "The 'Bloodbath' in Market Research," *Business Week*, February 11, 1991, pp. 72-74.

15. See Thomas L. Greenbaum, "Focus Group Spurt Predicted for the '90s," *Marketing News*, January 8, 1990, pp. 21, 22; and *Marketing News*, special issue on focus groups, May 27, 1991.

16. Selwyn Feinstein, "Computers Replacing Interviewers for Personnel and Marketing Tasks," *The Wall Street Journal*, October 9, 1986, p. 35; and Diane Crispell, "People Talk, Computers Listen," *American Demographics*, October 1989, p. 8.

17. For more on mechanical measures, see Michael J. McCarthy, "Mind Probe," *The Wall Street Journal*, March 22, 1991, p. B3.

18. For an interesting discussion of the importance of the relationship between market researchers and research users, see Christine Moorman, Gerald Zaltman, and Rohit Deshpande, "Relationships Between Providers and Users of Market Research: The Dynamics of Trust Within and Between Organizations," *Journal of Marketing Research*, August 1992, pp. 314-28; and Christine Moorman, Rohit Deshpande, and Gerald Zaltman, "Factors Affecting Trust in Market Research Relationships," *Journal of Marketing*, January 1993, pp. 81-101.

19. Jack Honomichl, "Top Marketing/Ad/Opinion Research Firms Profiled," *Marketing News*, June 2, 1992, p. H2.

20. Many of the examples in this section, along with others, are found in Subhash C. Jain, *International Marketing Management*, 3rd ed. (Boston: PWS-Kent Publishing Company, 1990), pp. 334-39. Also see Vern Terpstra and Ravi Sarathy, *International Marketing* (Chicago: The Dryden Press, 1991), pp. 208-13.

21. Jain, *International Marketing Management*, p. 338.

22. For more on statistical analysis, consult a standard text, such as Tull and Hawkins, *Marketing Research*. For a review of marketing models, see Gary L. Lilien and Philip Kotler, *Marketing Decision Making: A Model Building Approach* (New York: Harper & Row, 1983).

VIDEO CASE 4

TREND TALKING AND TRACKING

We're now entering the "Decency Decade" in which corporations will use "Decency Positioning" to head off "Fight Back" by conscious consumers. Many of these consumers will be "Moby's" and "Doby's" who are "Streamlining" by "Cashing Out" during the "Folking of America." Their tastes may run to "Log Cabin Chic" while they satisfy themselves with "Mood Food" and "Foodaceuticals." But if they're "Puppies," they won't be able to afford "Couture for the Masses."

Did you understand the preceding paragraph? If not, you probably don't speak Trend Talk, developed by the BrainReserve, a small marketing consulting firm founded by Faith Popcorn in 1974 to track marketplace trends. The company uses three information sources: a panel of creative thinkers in a variety of occupations; consumer interviews (over 3,000 a year, nationwide); and scans of hundreds of journals in fields such as news, business, health, science, food/liquor, home, travel, literary/art, politics, environment, new age, and the offbeat (Utne Reader).

From the interviews and media scans, BrainReserve identifies the ten top trends. The trends provide insight into current consumer concerns, thinking, and lifestyles. BrainReserve can then test new product and service ideas against these trends to determine likely consumer response. If a product meshes with at least four trends, it is considered "on trend," or likely to succeed. If it does not mesh, it is "off trend," or likely to fail. Recently, the company tested a new idea by Bacardi—Bacardi Breezes, a new rum cooler—and found it right on trend. Within less than a year of its introduction, the new product jumped to third place in the liquor industry, even though sales of liquor and wine coolers as a whole were declining. Thus, trend tracking appears to work.

BrainReserve's current top ten trends are: (1) cocooning: a desire to retreat into one's shell as a safe place; (2) fantasy adventure: vicarious escape through consumption, which could be fantasy vacations or use of virtual reality machines; (3) small indulgences: buying the very best in a "small" product category—one piece of Godiva chocolate or one great hair cut; (4) egonomics: desire for custom-tailored products such as personalized issues of magazines or Prescriptives cosmetics blended for your skin; (5) cashing out: leaving careers to do "what we want," such as paint, renovate houses, or farm; (6) down-aging: discovering that old age is a state of mind that we haven't reached even if we're 40 . . . or older; (7) staying alive: the quest for health; (8) the vigilante consumer: strong consumer reaction to shabby merchandise and business practices; (9) 99 lives: we have multiple roles in family and career and need fewer, better designed products and services to help us perform; and (10) save our society: environmental concerns. Based on these trends, Popcorn and her colleagues predict a future of improvement based on consumer action and environmentalism.

Other trend trackers, however, are not so optimistic. They forecast a world of growing disparity between the haves and have nots that will lead to increased crime, reduced standards of living, and a decrease in environmental conditions. Patricia Aburdene, coauthor of *Megatrends for Women*, predicts increased demands that will overburden our health-care system, and Theodore J. Gordon of The Futures Group predicts that we will have to work harder.

On that low note, we're "cashing out." But first, here's a rough interpretation of the Trend Talk in the first paragraph.

- *Decency decade:* a decade of commitment to environment, education, and ethics.

- *Decency positioning:* a corporate policy to "be good, do good" and create a relationship with the consumer.

- *Fight back: Conscious consumers* attack to exert influence over the environment, government, and products.

- *MOBY:* Mother older, baby younger (life stage of older moms).

- *DOBY:* Daddy older, baby younger (life stage of older dads).

- *Streamlining:* consumers pare down to make lives easier.

- *Folking of America:* return to plans and simple values.

- *Log cabin chic:* style based on affection for the homespun look and feel of the American Frontier.

- *Mood food:* food to satisfy emotional needs, to calm you down or energize you.

- *Foodaceuticals:* food with medicinal qualities.

- *Puppies:* poor, urban professionals.

- *Couture for the masses:* high-quality, individually customized products, available on a large-scale basis.

QUESTIONS

1. Which macroenvironmental forces are affected by the BrainReserve's ten trends? Which microenvironmental forces? Which publics?

2. How could grocery stores, interior designers, or manufacturers of disposable razors or cosmetics test their products against BrainReserve's ten trends?

Sources: Mindy Drucker, "You Gotta Have Faith," *Target Marketing,* January 1992, pp. 10–11; Faith Popcorn, *The Popcorn Report* (New York: Doubleday Currency, 1991); Edith Weiner, "Six Principles for Revitalizing Your Planning," *Planning Review,* July–August 1990, pp. 16–19; Walter Wachel, "As They See It: Experts Forecast Trends and Challenges," *Healthcare Executive,* July–August 1992, pp. 16–20; and Edith Weiner, "Business and the Future: A Round-Table Discussion," *Futurist,* May–June 1992, pp. 23–27.

COMPANY CASE 4

ACT I: FEELING OUT THE APPLIANCE CONTROLS MARKET

Wallace C. Leyshon, president and CEO of Appliance Control Technology (ACT), looked up from the copy of *Appliance Manufacturer Magazine* he was reading as Gregory Pearl, ACT's director of marketing, entered his office.

Leyshon had recently founded ACT after leaving his position as business director of Motorola's electronic control appliance division. The Motorola division had achieved $30 million in sales and employed almost 600 people worldwide. But Leyshon felt that Motorola was pursuing conventional industry strategies such as manufacturing its products in foreign countries (offshore). Leyshon believed that the industry was ready for an unconventional strategy, and he had decided to leave Motorola to begin his own business, which would focus on designing, manufacturing, and selling touch-sensitive digital control panels for home appliances such as microwave ovens, ranges, and washing machines. These panels allow consumers to control appliances at the touch of a finger to set cooking time or to select the "cook" or "defrost" cycles on a microwave oven, for example. These controls replace the buttons and dials found on many appliances.

The home appliance industry is mature—shipments by U.S. manufacturers grew only 5 percent annually over the 1986 to 1990 period (see Exhibits 4-1 and 4-2). Furthermore, the Association of Home Appliance Manufacturers estimates that the number of home appliances per U.S. household rose from 3.3 in 1960 to 4.1 in 1970, to 5.4 in 1982, and to 6.1 in 1987. Industry an-

EXHIBIT 4-1   Household appliances: value of shipments 1972-1990

Source: U.S. Department of Commerce.

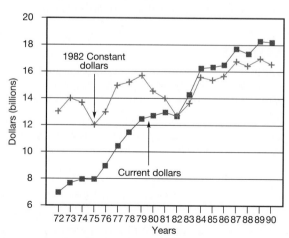

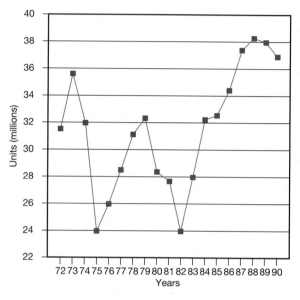

EXHIBIT 4-2   Shipments of major home appliances in units (excluding microwaves).

Source: Association of Home Appliance Manufacturers.

alysts question whether this level of penetration can increase further.

However, despite slow growth in the appliance industry as a whole, Leyshon's research predicts that sales of digital control panels for appliances could grow at a whopping 22 percent a year during the early 1990s. Only about 20 percent of American-made appliances now include digital controls. However, one industry analyst notes that, with the success of microwave ovens and videocassette recorders, consumers have become increasingly comfortable with digital touch-sensitive controls. Leyshon believes that increased consumer familiarity has opened the way for manufacturers to include digital control panels in other types of home appliances that users currently control with dials and buttons (electromechanical controls). With a digital control, for example, a standard electric range could offer users the wide range of special cooking programs that microwave ovens now provide.

After starting ACT, Leyshon landed a significant contract with a major microwave oven manufacturer. With this customer's business to support ACT, Leyshon realized he needed to conduct marketing research to help him develop a marketing strategy to attack the appliance controls market. Although there were only a limited number of digital controls suppliers and five major manufacturers in the industry, Leyshon could

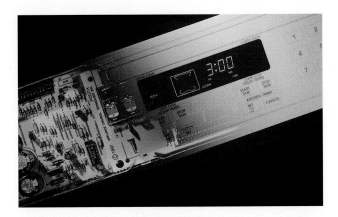

EXHIBIT 4-3   Steps in ACT marketing research process

1. Identify and articulate the problem.
2. Identify research goals.
3. Determine the information needed to achieve the research goals.
4. Determine research design.
5. Decide on research sample (i.e., whom to call).
6. Determine content of the individual questions.
7. Construct a questionnaire.
8. Test the questionnaire.
9. Adjust the questionnaire based on the test results.
10. Conduct the interviews.
11. Adjust the questionnaire and research questions as necessary.
12. Write up the results of each interview.
13. Write a report.

find very little readily available marketing research on the appliance controls industry, especially on digital controls.

"How's your morning going, Wallace?" Gregory Pearl asked as he entered Leyshon's office.

"Fine, Gregory. I was just looking through this magazine to see if I could find anything to help us in our marketing research. What have you got for me?"

"Well, during our last discussion, we outlined the market research process we want to follow" (see Exhibit 4-3). "Based on that outline, I've tried to write some research goals, develop a list of specific questions for our proposed telephone interviews, and figure out just whom we should call" (see Exhibit 4-4). "In fact, I've even drafted a preliminary version of the questionnaire" (see Exhibit 4-5).

EXHIBIT 4-4   ACT marketing research design issues

I. Survey goals	A. Gain insight into best strategy for approaching the electronic controls market.
	1. Types of appliances
	2. Features
	3. Cost issues
	4. Tactical selling techniques
	B. Determine how ACT can best serve original equipment manufacturers (OEMs).
	1. Research and development
	2. Partnering
	3. Product-development cycle
II. Specific questions to be addressed	A. What problems do equipment manufacturers and retailers face in making and selling home appliances? How can ACT help solve those problems?
	B. Who are the decision makers in the electronics buying process? Who has the power between the retailer and the equipment manufacturer?
	C. Are there any unidentified issues from ACT's, the manufacturers', or the retailers' perspectives?
	D. How rapidly will manufacturers adopt electronic controls for their appliances, by category of appliances?
	E. How sensitive are manufacturers to the price of electronic controls versus standard electromechanical controls?
	F. What are manufactuers' impressions of suppliers' strengths and weaknesses?
	G. What features and issues other than price drive the use of electronic controls?
	H. How can manufacturers use electronic controls to add value to mid-level appliances?
	I. How can a supplier be a better partner to manufacturers?
	J. What can a supplier do to help speed up manufacturers' product-development efforts?
III. Who should be interviewed?	A. Manufacturers
	1. Functional areas
	a. Purchasing
	b. Marketing
	c. Engineering
	2. Specific companies
	a. Whirlpool
	b. Frigidaire
	c. General Electric
	d. Maytag
	e. Raytheon
	B. Retailers
	1. Functional areas
	a. Buyers
	b. Store-level management
	c. Floor sales personnel
	2. Specific companies
	a. Sears
	b. Montgomery Ward
	c. Highland
	d. Wal-Mart
	C. Other
	1. Association of Home Appliance Manufacturers
	2. *Appliance Magazine* editor
	3. *Appliance Manufacturer Magazine* editor

Leyshon was pleased with his marketing director's progress. "Okay, let's take a look at what you've done. Then we can decide where we go from here."

EXHIBIT 4-5   Version 1—ACT marketing research questionnaire

Introduction	ACT is conducting a survey of decision makers and industry experts in the electronic appliance controls industry. We would appreciate your help in answering our questions. Your responses will be reported anonymously, if they are reported at all. Your responses will be used to help ACT determine how to serve the appliance industry better.

Questions

1. A. What are your opinions on the level of electronic controls usage, expressed in percentages, in the following appliance categories for 1991 and 1996?
   B. What are your opinions on the average cost per electronic control by appliance category in 1991 and 1996?

	Percent of units using electronic controls in:		Average cost per control unit in:	
Category	1991	1996	1991	1996
Dishwashers				
Dryers, electric				
Dryers, gas				
Microwaves				
Ranges, electric				
Ranges, gas				
Refrigerators				
Washers				
Room air conditioners				

2. For each of the following categories, what price must a supplier charge for an electronic control unit such that a manufacturer would be indifferent as to using electronic or electromechanical controls, taking into account the differences in functions and features?

Category	Price per electronic unit
Dishwashers	
Dryers, electric	
Dryers, gas	
Microwaves	
Ranges, electric	
Ranges, gas	
Refrigerators	
Washers	
Room air Conditioners	

3. What features, functions, and attributes do electronic controls need to have if they are to be used more often in appliances?
4. What impact will the upcoming Department of Energy regulations have on the appliance industry?
5. What can an electronic controls company do to be a better supplier?

Questions

1. Based on information in the case and in exhibits 4 and 5, just what *is* Leyshon trying to learn through marketing research? What additional trends and information might he want to monitor as a part of his ongoing marketing information system?

2. What sources of marketing intelligence can ACT use to gather information on the industry and its competition?

3. Based on the marketing research process discussed in the text, what is ACT's marketing research objective, and what problem is the company addressing? Evaluate ACT's marketing research process (Exhibit 4-3).

4. What sources of secondary data might ACT use?

5. What decisions has ACT made about its research approach, contact method, and sampling plan?

6. Evaluate ACT's proposed questionnaire (Exhibit 4-5). Does it address the issues raised in Exhibit 4-4? What changes would you recommend?

Source: Appliance Control Technology cooperated in the development of this case.

*C*onsumer Markets: Influences on Consumer Behavior

op managers at Porsche spend a great deal of time thinking about customers. They want to know who their customers are, what they think and how they feel, and why they buy a Porsche rather than a Jaguar, or a Ferrari, or a big Mercedes coupe. These are difficult questions—even Porsche owners themselves don't know exactly what motivates their buying. But management needs to put top priority on understanding customers and what makes them tick.

Porsche appeals to a very narrow segment of financially successful people—achievers who set very high goals for themselves and then work doggedly to meet them. They expect no less from "their hobbies, or the clothes they wear, or the restaurants they go to, or the cars they drive." These achievers see themselves not as a regular part of the larger world, but as exceptions. They buy Porsches because the car mirrors their self-image—it stands for the things owners like to see in themselves and in their lives.

Most of us buy what Porsche executives call utility vehicles—"cars to be used: to go to work, to deliver the kids, to go shopping." We base buying decisions on facts like price, size, function, fuel economy, and other practical considerations. But a Porsche is a more than a utility car—it is to be enjoyed, not just used. Most Porsche buyers are moved not by facts, but by feelings—they are trying to match their dreams. A Porsche is like a piece of clothing, "something the owner actually wears and is seen in. . . . It's a very personal relationship, one that has to do with the way the car sounds, the way it vibrates, the way it feels." People buy Porsches because they enjoy driving the car, just being in it. "Just to get there, they could do it a lot less expensively. The car is an expression of themselves." Surprisingly, many Porsche owners are not car enthusiasts—they are not interested in racing or learning how to drive a high-performance

car. They simply like the way a Porsche makes them feel or what the car tells others about their achievements, lifestyles, and stations in life.

A Porsche costs a lot of money, but price isn't much of an issue with such car buyers. The company deals often with people who can buy anything they want. To many Porsche owners, the car is a hobby. In fact, Porsche's competition comes not just from other cars, but from such things as sailboats, summer homes, and airplanes. But "most of those objects require a lot of one thing these folks don't have, and that's time. If you have a Porsche and make *it* your hobby, you can enjoy it every day on your way to work and on your way to the airport, something you can't do with a sailboat or summer home."

Porsche has traditionally worked hard to meet its buyers' expectations, but in the mid-1980s, the company made a serious marketing blunder when it shifted toward *mass* rather than *class* marketing. It increased its sales goal by nearly 50 percent, to 60,000 cars a year. To meet this volume goal, Porsche emphasized lower-priced models that sold for as little as $20,000. Moreover, after decades of priding itself on progressive engineering, high performance, and tasteful and timeless styling, the company allowed its models to grow out of date. These moves tarnished Porsche's exclusive image and confused its loyal but demanding customers. At the same time, Porsche was battered by a falling U.S. dollar and increasingly fierce competition from Nissan, Toyota, BMW, and other rivals pushing new luxury sports cars. As a result, Porsche's sales plunged by 51 percent in 1988.

Porsche then fought to rebuild its damaged image and to regain rapport with its customers. It revamped its model lines, once again targeting the high end of the market—the 1989 models started at $40,000 and ranged up to $75,000. It set sales goal at a modest 40,000 cars a year—less than a month's production at Chevrolet. The company now looks for only moderate but profitable growth; it wants to make one less Porsche than the demand. According to one executive, "we aren't looking for volume . . . we're searching for exclusivity." Porsche does all it can to make Porsche ownership very special. It has even hired a representative to sell its cars to celebrities, executives of large companies, top athletes, and other notables. Having high-profile individuals driving Porsches and talking to their friends about them is the best advertising the company could get.

Thus, understanding Porsche buyers is an essential but difficult task—the company must carefully craft the car and its image to match buyer needs and desires. But buyers are moved by a complex set of deep and subtle motivations. Buyer behavior springs from deeply held values and attitudes, from their views of the world and their place in it, from what they think of themselves and what they want others to think of them, from rationality and common sense, and from whimsy and impulse. The chief executive at Porsche summed it up this way: "If you really want to understand our customers, you have to understand the phrase, 'if I were going to be a car, I'd be a Porsche.'"[1]

 ## CHAPTER PREVIEW

Chapter 5 describes the general characteristics that influence consumers' behavior.

The chapter starts with a definition of the **consumer market,** and proposes a simple **model of consumer buying behavior.**

This model is then used to demonstrate the ways in which **culture, subculture,** and **social class** influence consumer buying behavior.

We continue with a discussion of the influence of **social factors,** show that a person's position within a reference group can be defined in terms of **role** and **status,** and suggest that people choose products and brands that reflect their role and status.

Next, we outline some of the **personal factors** that can influence consumer behavior, including **age, occupation, economic situation, lifestyle,** and **personality.**

The chapter ends with a look at four major **psychological factors** that influence consumer buying behavior—**motivation, perception, learning,** and **attitudes.**

The Porsche example shows that many different factors affect consumer buying behavior. Buying behavior is never simple, yet understanding it is the essential task of marketing management.

This chapter and the next explore the dynamics of consumer behavior and the consumer market. **Consumer buying behavior** refers to the buying behavior of final consumers—individuals and households who buy goods and services for personal consumption. All of these final consumers combined make up the **consumer market.** The American consumer market consists of about 254 million people who consume many trillions of dollars worth of goods and services each year, making it one of the most attractive consumer markets in the world.

American consumers vary tremendously in age, income, education level, and tastes. They also buy an incredible variety of goods and services. How these diverse consumers make their choices among various products embraces a fascinating array of factors.

MODEL OF CONSUMER BEHAVIOR

In earlier times, marketers could understand consumers well through the daily experience of selling to them. But as firms and markets have grown in size, many marketing decision makers have lost direct contact with their customers and now must turn to consumer research. They now spend more money than ever to study consumers, trying to learn more about consumer behavior. Who buys? How do they buy? When do they buy? Where do they buy? Why do they buy?

The central question for marketers is: How do consumers respond to various marketing stimuli the company might use? The company that really understands how consumers will respond to different product features, prices, and advertising appeals has a great advantage over its competitors. Therefore, companies and academics have researched heavily the relationship between marketing stimuli and consumer response. Their starting point is the stimulus-response model of buyer behavior shown in Figure 5-1. This figure shows that marketing and other stimuli enter the consumer's "black box" and produce certain responses. Marketers must figure out what is in the buyer's black box.[2]

Marketing stimuli consist of the four *P*s: product, price, place, and promotion. Other stimuli include major forces and events in the buyer's environment: economic, technological, political, and cultural. All these stimuli enter the buyer's black box, where they are turned into a set of observable buyer responses (shown on the right side of Figure 5-1): product choice, brand choice, dealer choice, purchase timing, and purchase amount.

The marketer wants to understand how the stimuli are changed into responses inside the consumer's black box, which has two parts. First, the buyer's characteristics influence how he or she perceives and reacts to the stimuli. Second, the buyer's decision process itself affects the buyer's behavior. This chapter looks first at buyer characteristics as they affect buying behavior. The next chapter examines the buyer decision process.

CHARACTERISTICS AFFECTING CONSUMER BEHAVIOR

Consumer purchases are influenced strongly by cultural, social, personal, and psychological characteristics, shown in Figure 5-2. For the most part, marketers cannot control such factors, but they must take them into account. We illustrate these characteristics for the case of a hypothetical consumer named Jennifer Flores. Jennifer is a married college graduate who works as a brand manager in a leading consumer packaged-goods company. She wants to find a new leisure-time activity that will provide some contrast to her working day. This need has led her to consider buying a camera and taking up photography. Many characteristics in her background will affect the way she evaluates cameras and chooses a brand.

Cultural Factors

Cultural factors exert the broadest and deepest influence on consumer behavior. The marketer needs to understand the role played by the buyer's *culture, subculture,* and *social class.*

Culture

Culture is the most basic cause of a person's wants and behavior. Human behavior is largely learned. Growing up in a society, a child learns basic values, perceptions, wants, and behaviors from the family and other important institutions. An American child normally learns or is exposed to the following values: achievement and success, activity and involvement, efficiency and practicality, progress, material comfort, individualism, freedom, humanitarianism, youthfulness, and fitness and health.[3]

Jennifer Flores's wanting a camera is a result of being raised in a modern society which has developed camera technology and a whole set of consumer learn-

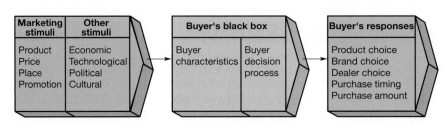

FIGURE 5–1
Model of buyer behavior

Marketing stimuli	Other stimuli	Buyer's black box	Buyer's responses
Product	Economic	Buyer characteristics / Buyer decision process	Product choice
Price	Technological		Brand choice
Place	Political		Dealer choice
Promotion	Cultural		Purchase timing
			Purchase amount

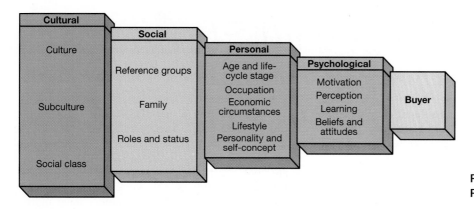

FIGURE 5–2
Factors influencing behavior

ings and values. Jennifer knows what cameras are. She knows how to read instructions, and her society has accepted the idea of women photographers. In another culture—say, a primitive tribe in central Australia—a camera may mean nothing. It may simply be a curiosity.

Marketers are always trying to spot *cultural shifts* in order to imagine new products that might be wanted. For example, the cultural shift toward greater concern about health and fitness has created a huge industry for exercise equipment and clothing, lower-calorie and more natural foods, and health and fitness services. The shift toward informality has resulted in more demand for casual clothing, simpler home furnishings, and lighter entertainment. And the increased desire for leisure time has resulted in more demand for convenience products and services, such as microwave ovens and fast food. It also has created a huge catalog-shopping industry. More than 6,500 catalog companies—ranging from giant retailers like Sears and Spiegel to specialty retailers like L. L. Bean, Sharper Image, Royal Silk, and Land's End—bombard American households with 8.5 billion catalogs each year.

Subculture

Each culture contains smaller **subcultures,** or groups of people with shared value systems based on common life experiences and situations. Subcultures include nationalities, religions, racial groups. and geographic regions. Many subcultures make up important market segments, and marketers often design products and marketing programs tailored to their needs (see Marketing Highlight 5-1).[4] Jennifer Flores's buying behavior will be influenced by her subculture identification. These factors will affect her food preferences, clothing choices, recreation activities, and career goals. Subcultures attach different meanings to picture taking, and this could affect both Jennifer's interest in cameras and the brand she buys.

Social Class

Almost every society has some form of social class structure. **Social classes** are society's relatively permanent and ordered divisions whose members share similar values, interests, and behaviors. Social scientists have identified the seven American social classes (see Table 5-1).

Social class is not determined by a single factor, such as income, but is measured as a combination of occupation, income, education, wealth, and other variables. In some social systems, members of different classes are reared for certain roles and cannot change their social positions. In the United States, however, the lines between social classes are not fixed and rigid; people can move to a higher social class or drop into a lower one. Marketers are interested in social class because people within a given social class tend to exhibit similar buying behavior.

Social classes show distinct product and brand preferences in areas such as clothing, home furnishings, leisure activity, and automobiles. Jennifer Flores's social class may affect her camera decision. If she comes from a higher social class background, her family probably owned an expensive camera and she may have dabbled in photography.

Social Factors

A consumer's behavior also is influenced by social factors, such as the consumer's *small groups, family,* and *social roles and status.* Because these social factors can

MARKETERS TARGET IMPORTANT SUBCULTURES

When subcultures grow large and affluent enough, companies often design special marketing programs to serve their needs. Here are examples of three such important subculture groups.

Hispanic Consumers. For years, marketers have viewed the Hispanic market—Americans of Mexican, Cuban, and Puerto Rican descent—as small and poverty stricken, but these perceptions are badly out of date. Expected to number almost 40 million by the year 2010, Hispanics are the second largest and the fastest-growing U.S. minority. Annual Hispanic purchasing power totals $171 billion. Over half of all Hispanics live in one of six metropolitan areas: Los Angeles, New York, Miami, San Antonio, San Francisco, and Chicago. They are easy to reach through the growing selection of Spanish-language broadcast and print media that cater to Hispanics. Hispanics have long been a target for marketers of food, beverages, and household care products. But as the segment's buying power increases, Hispanics are now emerging as an attractive market for pricier products such as computers, financial services, photography equipment, large appliances, life insurance, and automobiles. Hispanic consumers tend to be brand conscious and quality conscious—generics don't sell well to Hispanics. Perhaps more important, Hispanics are very brand loyal, and they favor companies who show special interest in them. Many companies are devoting larger ad budgets and preparing special appeals to woo Hispanics. Because of the segment's strong brand loyalty, companies that get the first foothold have an important head start in this fast-growing market.

Black Consumers. If the U.S. population of 31 million black Americans, with a total purchasing power of $218 billion annually, were a separate nation, their buying power would rank twelfth in the free world. The black population in the United States is growing in affluence and sophistication. Blacks spend relatively more than whites on clothing, personal care, home furnishings, and fragrances; and relatively less on food, transportation, and recreation. Although more price conscious, blacks are also strongly motivated by quality and selection. They place more importance than other groups on brand names, are more brand loyal, do less "shopping around," and shop more at neighborhood stores. In recent years, many large companies—Sears, McDonald's, Procter & Gamble, Coca-Cola—have stepped up their efforts to tap this lucrative market. They employ black-owned advertising agencies, use black models in their ads, and place ads in black consumer magazines. Some companies develop special products, packaging, and appeals for the black consumer market.

Mature Consumers. As the U.S. population ages, "mature" consumers—those 65 and older—are becoming a very attractive market. Now 32-million strong, the seniors market will grow to over 40 million consumers by the year 2000. Seniors are better off financially, spending about $200 billion each year, and they average twice the disposable income of consumers in the under-35 group. Mature consumers have long been the target of the makers of laxatives, tonics, and denture products. But many marketers know that not all seniors are poor and feeble. Most are healthy and active, and they have many of the same needs and wants as younger consumers. Because seniors have more time and money, they are an ideal market for exotic travel, restaurants, high-tech home entertainment products, leisure goods and services, designer furniture and fashions, financial services, and life- and health-care services. Their desire to look as young as they feel makes seniors good candidates for specially designed cosmetics and personal care products, health foods, home physical fitness products, and other items that combat aging. Several companies are hotly pursuing the seniors market. For example, Sears's 40,000-member "Mature Club" offers older consumers 25 percent discounts on everything from eyeglasses to lawnmowers. Southwestern Bell publishes the "Silver Pages," crammed full of ads offering discounts and coupons to 20 million seniors in 90 markets. To appeal more to mature consumers, McDonald's employs older folks as hosts and hostesses in its restaurants and casts them in its ads. And GrandTravel of Chevy Chase, Maryland, sponsors barge trips through Holland, safaris to Kenya, and other exotic vacations for grandparents and their grandchildren. As the seniors segment grows in size and buying power, and as the stereotypes of seniors as doddering, creaky, impoverished shut-ins fade, more and more marketers will develop special strategies for this important market.

Marketers target important sub-culture groups such as Hispanic, black, and senior consumers.

TABLE 5-1
Characteristics of Seven Major American Social Classes

Upper uppers (less than 1 percent)
Upper uppers are the social elite who live on inherited wealth and have well-known family backgrounds. They give large sums to charity, run debutante balls, own more than one home, and send their children to the finest schools. They are a market for jewelry, antiques, homes, and vacations. They often buy and dress conservatively rather than showing off their wealth. While small in number, upper uppers serve as a reference group for others to the extent that their consumption decisions trickle down and are imitated by the other social classes.

Lower uppers (about 2 percent)
Lower uppers have earned high income or wealth through exceptional ability in the professions or business. They usually begin in the middle class. They tend to be active in social and civic affairs and buy for themselves and their children the symbols of status, such as expensive homes, schools, yachts, swimming pools, and automobiles. They include the new rich who consume conspicuously to impress those below them. They want to be accepted in the upper-upper stratum, a status more likely to be achieved by their children than by themselves.

Upper middles (12 percent)
Upper middles possess neither family status nor unusual wealth. They are primarily concerned with "career." They have attained positions as professionals, independent businesspersons, and corporate managers. They believe in education and want their children to develop professional or administrative skills so that they will not drop into a lower stratum. Members of this class like to deal in ideas and "high culture." They are joiners and highly civic-minded. They are the quality market for good homes, clothes, furniture, and appliances. They seek to run a gracious home, entertaining friends and clients.

Middle class (32 percent)
The middle class is made up of average-pay white- and blue-collar workers who live on "the better side of town" and try to "do the proper things." To keep up with the trends, they often buy products that are popular. Twenty-five percent own imported cars, and most are concerned with fashion, seeking the better brand names. Better living means owning a nice home in a nice neighborhood with good schools. The middle class believes in spending more money on worthwhile experiences for their children and aiming them toward a college education.

Working class (38 percent)
The working class consists of average-pay blue-collar workers and those who lead a "working class lifestyle," whatever their income, school background, or job. The working class depends heavily on relatives for economic and emotional support, for tips on job opportunities, for advice on purchases, and for assistance in times of trouble. The working class maintains sharper sex role divisions and stereotyping. Car preferences include standard size and larger cars, rejecting domestic and foreign compacts.

Upper lowers (9 percent)
Upper lowers are working (are not on welfare), although their living standard is just above poverty. They perform unskilled work for very poor pay although they strive toward a high class. Often, upper lowers are educationally deficient. Although they fall near the poverty line financially, they manage to "present a picture of self-discipline" and "maintain some effort at cleanliness."

Lower lowers (7 percent)
Lower lowers are on welfare, visibly poverty stricken, and usually out of work or have "the dirtiest jobs." Often they are not interested in finding a job and are permanently dependent on public aid or charity for income. Their homes, clothes, and possessions are "dirty," "raggedy," and "broken-down."

Source: See Richard P. Coleman, "The Continuing Significance of Social Class to Marketing," *Journal of Consumer Research,* December 1983, pp. 265-80, © Journal of Consumer Research, Inc., 1983; and Richard P. Coleman and Lee P. Rainwater, *Social Standing in America: New Dimension of Class* (New York: Basic Books, 1978).

strongly affect consumer responses, companies must take them into account when designing their marketing strategies.

Groups

A person's behavior is influenced by many small groups. Groups which have a direct influence and to which a person belongs are called **membership groups.** Some are *primary groups* with whom there is regular but informal interaction—such as family, friends, neighbors, and co-workers. Some are *secondary groups,* which are more formal and have less regular interaction. These include organizations like religious groups, professional associations, and trade unions.

Reference groups are groups that serve as direct (face-to-face) or indirect points of comparison or reference in forming a person's attitudes or behavior. People often are influenced by reference groups to which they do not belong. For example, an **aspirational group** is one to which the individual wishes to belong, as when a teenage basketball player hopes to play someday for the Chicago

Bulls. He identifies with this group, although there is no face-to-face contact between him and the team.

Marketers try to identify the reference groups of their target markets. Reference groups influence a person in at least three ways. They expose the person to new behaviors and lifestyles. They influence the person's attitudes and self-concept because he or she wants to "fit in." They also create pressures to conform that may affect the person's product and brand choices. (See Marketing Highlight 5-2.)

The importance of group influence varies across products and brands, but it tends to be strongest for conspicuous purchases.[5] A product or brand can be conspicuous for one of two reasons. First, it may be noticeable because the buyer is one of few people who owns it—luxuries are more conspicuous than necessities because fewer people own the luxuries. Second, a product can be conspicuous because the buyer consumes it in public where others can see it. Figure 5-3 shows how group influence might affect product and brand choices for four types of products—public luxuries, private luxuries, public necessities, and private necessities.

A person considering the purchase of a public luxury, such as a sailboat, generally will be influenced strongly by others. Many people will notice the sailboat because few people own one. They will notice the brand because the boat is used in public. Thus, both the product and the brand will be conspicuous, and the opinions of others can strongly influence decisions about whether to own a boat and what brand to buy. At the other extreme, group influences do not much affect decisions for private necessities because other people will notice neither the product nor the brand.

Manufacturers of products and brands subject to strong group influence must figure out how to reach the opinion leaders in the relevant reference groups. **Opinion leaders** are people within a reference group who, because of special skills, knowledge, personality, or other characteristics, exert influence on others. Opinion leaders are found in all strata of society, and one person may be an opinion leader in certain product areas and an opinion follower in others. Marketers try to identify the personal characteristics of opinion leaders for their products, determine what media they use, and direct messages at them.

If Jennifer Flores buys a camera, both the product and the brand will be visible to others she respects, and her decision to buy the camera and her brand choice may be influenced strongly by some of her groups, such as friends who belong to a photography club.

Family

Family members can strongly influence buyer behavior. We can distinguish between two families in the buyer's life. The buyer's parents make up the *family of orientation.* Parents provide a person with an orientation toward religion, politics, and economics and a sense of personal ambition, self-worth, and love. Even if the buyer no longer interacts very much with parents, they can still significantly influence the buyer's behavior. In countries where parents continue to live with their children, their influence can be crucial.

The *family of procreation*—the buyer's spouse and children—have a more direct influence on everyday buying behavior. This family is the most important consumer buying organization in society, and it has been researched extensively. Marketers are interested in the roles and relative influence of the husband, wife, and children on the purchase of a large variety of products and services.

FIGURE 5–3
Extent of group influence on product and brand choice

Source: Adapted from William O. Bearden and Michael J. Etzel, "Reference Group Influence on Product and Brand Purchase Decisions," *The Journal of Consumer Research,* September 1982, p. 185. © Journal of Consumer Research, Inc., 1982. All rights reserved.

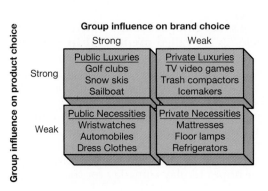

MARKETING HIGHLIGHT 5-2

USING REFERENCE GROUPS TO SELL: HOME-PARTY AND OFFICE-PARTY SELLING

Many companies capitalize on reference-group influence to sell their products. Home-party and office-party selling involves throwing sales parties in homes or work places and inviting friends and neighbors or co-workers to see products demonstrated. Companies such as Mary Kay Cosmetics, Avon, and Tupperware are masters at this form of selling.

Mary Kay Cosmetics provides a good example of home-party selling. A Mary Kay beauty consultant (of which there are 170,000) asks different women to host small beauty shows in their homes. Each hostess invites her friends and neighbors for a few hours of refreshments and informal socializing. Within this congenial atmosphere, the Mary Kay representative gives a two-hour beauty plan and free makeup lessons to the guests, hoping that many of them will buy some of the demonstrated cosmetics. The hostess receives a commission on sales plus a discount on personal purchases. Usually, about 60 percent of the guests buy something, partly because of the influence of the hostess and the other women attending the party.

In recent years, changing demographics have adversely affected home-party selling. An increasing proportion of women are working, which leaves fewer women with the time for shopping and fewer women at home to host or attend home sales parties. To overcome this problem, most party-plan sellers have followed their customers into the work place with office-party selling. For example, Avon now trains its 400,000 salespeople to sell through office parties during coffee and lunch breaks and after hours. The company once sold only door to door, but currently picks up a quarter of its sales from buyers at businesses. The well-known suburban Tupperware party has also invaded the worksite, in the form of Tupperware office parties. These events include a variety of formats, from the traditional party

Reference group selling: Tupperware office and home sales parties.

with a demonstrator to the Stop 'N' Shop at which employees talk one-on-one with the Tupperware consultant. Rush hour parties are held for employees after work at a home.

Home-party and office-party selling are now being used to market everything from cosmetics, kitchenware, and lingerie to exercise instruction and handmade suits. Such selling requires a sharp understanding of reference groups and how people influence each other in the buying process.

Sources: See Shannon Thurman, "Mary Kay Still in the Pink," *Advertising Age,* January 4, 1988, p. 32; Len Strazewski, "Tupperware Locks in a New Strategy," *Advertising Age,* February 8, 1988, p. 30; Kate Ballen, "Get Ready for Shopping at Work," *Fortune,* February 15, 1988, pp. 95–98; and Vic Sussman, "I Was the Only Virgin at the Party," *Sales & Marketing Management,* September 1989, pp.64–72.

Husband-wife involvement varies widely by product category and by stage in the buying process. Buying roles change with evolving consumer lifestyles. In the United States, the wife traditionally has been the main purchasing agent for the family, especially in the areas of food, household products, and clothing. But with 70 percent of women holding jobs outside the home and the willingness of husbands to do more of the family's purchasing, all this is changing. For example, women now buy about 45 percent of all cars and men account for about 40 percent of food-shopping dollars.[6] Such roles vary widely in different countries and social classes. As always, marketers must research specific patterns in their target markets.

In the case of expensive products and services, husbands and wives more often make joint decisions. Jennifer Flores's husband may play an *influencer role* in her camera-buying decision. He may have an opinion about her buying a camera and about the kind of camera to buy. At the same time, she will be the primary decider, purchaser, and user.[7]

Family buying decisions: Depending on the product and situation, individual family members exert different amounts of influence.

Roles and Status

A person belongs to many groups—family, clubs, organizations. The person's position in each group can be defined in terms of both *role* and *status*. With her parents, Jennifer Flores plays the role of daughter; in her family, she plays the role of wife; in her company, she plays the role of brand manager. A **role** consists of the activities people are expected to perform according to the persons around them. Each of Jennifer's roles will influence some of her buying behavior.

Each role carries a **status** reflecting the general esteem given to it by society. People often choose products that show their status in society. For example, the role of brand manager has more status in our society than the role of daughter. As a brand manager, Jennifer will buy the kind of clothing that reflects her role and status.

Personal Factors

A buyer's decisions also are influenced by personal characteristics such as the buyer's *age and life-cycle stage, occupation, economic situation, lifestyle,* and *personality and self-concept.*

Age and Life-Cycle Stage

People change the goods and services they buy over their lifetimes. Tastes in food, clothes, furniture, and recreation are often age related. Buying is also shaped by the stage of the **family life cycle**—the stages through which families might pass as they mature over time. Table 5-2 lists the stages of the family life cycle. Marketers often define their target markets in terms of life-cycle stage and develop appropriate products and marketing plans for each stage.

Psychological life-cycle stages have also been identified.[8] Adults experience certain passages or transformations as they go through life. Thus, Jennifer Flores may move from being a satisfied brand manager and wife to being an unsatisfied person searching for a new way to fulfill herself. In fact, such a change may have stimulated her strong interest in photography. Marketers should pay attention to the changing buying interests that might be associated with these adult passages.

Occupation

A person's occupation affects the goods and services bought. Blue-collar workers tend to buy more work clothes, whereas white-collar workers buy more suits and ties. Marketers try to identify the occupational groups that have an above-average interest in their products and services. A company can even specialize in making products needed by a given occupational group. Thus, computer software companies will design different products for brand managers, accountants, engineers, lawyers, and doctors.

Economic Situation

A person's economic situation will affect product choice. Jennifer Flores can consider buying an expensive Nikon if she has enough spendable income, savings, or borrowing power. Marketers of income-sensitive goods closely watch trends in personal income, savings, and interest rates. If economic indicators point to a recession, marketers can take steps to redesign, reposition, and reprice their products.

TABLE 5-2
Family Life-Cycle Stages

YOUNG	MIDDLE-AGED	OLDER
Single	Single	Older married
Married without children	Married without children	Older unmarried
Married with children	Married with children	
Infant children	Young children	
Young children	Adolescent children	
Adolescent children	Married without dependent children	
Divorced with children	Divorced without children	
	Divorced with children	
	Young children	
	Adolescent children	
	Divorced without dependent children	

Sources: Adapted from Patrick E. Murphy and William A. Staples, "A Modernized Family Life Cycle," *Journal of Consumer Research,* June 1979, p. 16; © Journal of Consumer Research, Inc., 1979. Also see Janet Wagner and Sherman Hanna, "The Effectiveness of Family Life Cycle Variables in Consumer Expenditure Research," *Journal of Consumer Research,* December 1983, pp. 281-91.

Lifestyle

People coming from the same subculture, social class, and occupation may have quite different lifestyles. **Lifestyle** is a person's pattern of living as expressed in his or her activities, interests, and opinions. Lifestyle captures something more than the person's social class or personality. It profiles a person's whole pattern of acting and interacting in the world.

The technique of measuring lifestyles is known as **psychographics.** It involves measuring the major dimensions shown in Table 5-3. The first three are known as the *AIO dimensions* (activities, interests, opinions). Several research firms have developed lifestyle classifications. The most widely used is the SRI *Values and Lifestyles (VALS)* typology. The original VALS typology, introduced in 1978, classified consumers into nine lifestyle groups according to whether they were inner directed (for example, "experientials"); outer directed ("achievers," "belongers"); or need driven ("survivors"). Using this VALS classification, Bank of America found that the businessmen they were targeting consisted mainly of "achievers" who were strongly competitive individualists. The bank designed highly successful ads showing men taking part in solo sports such as sailing, jogging, and water skiing.[9]

The more recent version, VALS 2, classifies people according to their consumption tendencies—by how they spend their time and money. It divides con-

TABLE 5-3
Lifestyle Dimensions

ACTIVITIES	INTERESTS	OPINIONS	DEMOGRAPHICS
Work	Family	Themselves	Age
Hobbies	Home	Social issues	Education
Social events	Job	Politics	Income
Vacation	Community	Business	Occupation
Entertainment	Recreation	Economics	Family size
Club membership	Fashion	Education	Dwelling
Community	Food	Products	Geography
Shopping	Media	Future	City size
Sports	Achievements	Culture	Stage in life cycle

Source: Joseph T. Plummer, "The Concept and Application of Life-Style Segmentation," *Journal of Marketing,* January 1974, p. 34.

Lifestyles: Lee Relaxed Riders fit the lifestyle of the modern woman on the go. "Nobody fits your body . . . or the way you live . . . better than Lee."

sumers into eight groups based on two major dimensions: self-orientation and resources (see Table 5-4). The *self-orientation* dimension captures three different buying approaches: Principle-oriented consumers buy based upon their views of how the world is or should be; status-oriented buyers base their purchases on the actions and opinions of others; and action-oriented buyers are driven by their desire for activity, variety, and risk-taking. Consumers within each orientation are further classified into one of two *resource* segments, depending on whether they have high or low levels of income, education, health, self-confidence, energy, and other factors. Consumers with either very high or very low levels of resources are classified into separate groups without regard to their self-orientations (actualizers, strugglers). The eight VALS 2 lifestyle groups are described in Table 5-4. A person may progress through several of these lifestyles over the course of a lifetime. People's lifestyles affect their buying behavior.[10]

Iron City beer used VALS 2 to update its image and improve sales. Iron City, a well-known brand in Pittsburgh, was losing sales. Its core users were growing older and drinking less beer, and younger men were bypassing the brand. VALS research showed that experiencers were the highest-volume beer drinkers, followed by strivers. To assess Iron City's image problems, the company's advertising agency interviewed men in these categories using a picture-sorting technique. They gave the men decks of cards showing different kinds of people and asked them to identify brand users and people most like themselves. The respondents pictured Iron City drinkers as blue-collar steelworkers stopping at the local bar, whereas they portrayed themselves as more modern, hard working, and fun loving. Like the city of Pittsburgh, they rejected the heavy-industry image. As a result of the research, Iron City designed ads that linked the brand to the changing self-image of target consumers. The ads mixed images of the old Pittsburgh with images of the new, vibrant city and shots of young experiencers and strivers working hard at having fun. The ads ran in media popular with strivers and experiencers. In the first month of the campaign, sales of Iron City beer increased by 26 percent.[11]

Lifestyle classifications are by no means universal—they can vary significantly from country to country. McCann-Erickson London, for example, found the following British lifestyles: Avant Guardians (interested in change); Pontificators (traditionalists, very British); Chameleons (follow the crowd); and Sleepwalkers (contented underachievers).

The lifestyle concept, when used carefully, can help the marketer understand changing consumer values and how they affect buying behavior.[12] Jennifer Flores, for example, can choose to live the role of a capable homemaker, a career

TABLE 5-4
VALS 2: Eight American Lifestyles

SELF-ORIENTATION

Principle Oriented

Fulfilleds

Mature, responsible, well-educated professionals. Their leisure activities center on their homes, but they are well informed about what goes on in the world, and they are open to new ideas and social change. They have high incomes, but they are practical, value-oriented consumers.

Believers

Principle-oriented consumers with more modest incomes. They are conservative and predictable consumers who favor American products and established brands. Their lives are centered on family, church, community, and nation.

Status Oriented

Achievers

Successful, work-oriented people who get their satisfaction from their jobs and their families. They are politically conservative and respect authority and the status quo. They favor established products and services that show off their success.

Strivers

People with values similar to those of achievers, but fewer economic, social, and psychological resources. Style is extremely important to them as they strive to emulate consumers in other, more resourceful groups.

Action Oriented

Experiencers

People who like to affect their environment in tangible ways. They are the youngest of all groups. They have a lot of energy, which they pour into physical exercise and social activities. They are avid consumers, spending heavily on clothing, fast food, music, and other youthful favorites. They especially like new things.

Makers

People who like to affect their environment, but in more practical ways. They value self-sufficiency. They are focused on the familiar—family, work, and physical recreation—and have little interest in the broader world. As consumers, they are unimpressed by material possessions other than those with a practical or functional purpose.

RESOURCES

Actualizers

People with the highest incomes and so many resources that they can indulge in any or all self-orientations. Image is important to them, not as evidence of status or power, but as an expression of their taste, independence, and character. Because of their wide range of interests and openness to change, they tend to buy "the finer things in life."

Strugglers

People with the lowest incomes and too few resources to be included in any consumer orientation. With their limited means, they tend to be brand-loyal consumers.

Source: See Martha Farnsworth Riche, "Psychographics for the 1990s," *American Demographics,* July 1989, pp. 25-31.

woman, or a free spirit—or all three. She plays several roles, and the way she blends them expresses her lifestyle. If she becomes a professional photographer, this would change her lifestyle, in turn changing what and how she buys.

Personality and Self-Concept

Each person's distinct personality influences his or her buying behavior. **Personality** refers to the unique psychological characteristics that lead to relatively consistent and lasting responses to one's own environment. Personality is usually described in terms of traits such as self-confidence, dominance, sociability, autonomy, defensiveness, adaptability, and aggressiveness.[13] Personality can be useful in analyzing consumer behavior for certain product or brand choices. For example, coffee makers have discovered that heavy coffee drinkers tend to be high on sociability. Thus, Maxwell House ads show people relaxing and socializing over a cup of steaming coffee.

Many marketers use a concept related to personality—a person's **self-concept** (also called *self-image*). The basic self-concept premise is that people's possessions contribute to and reflect their identities; that is, "we are what we have." Thus, in order to understand consumer behavior, the marketer must first understand the relationship between consumer self-concept and possessions. For example, Jennifer Flores may see herself as outgoing, creative, and active. Therefore, she will favor a camera that projects the same qualities. If the Nikon is promoted as a camera for outgoing, creative, and active people, then its brand image will match her self-image.[14]

The concept, admittedly, is not that simple. What if Jennifer's *actual self-concept* (how she views herself) differs from her *ideal self-concept* (how she would like to view herself) and from her *others self-concept* (how she thinks others see her). Which self will she try to satisfy when she buys a camera? Because this is unclear, self-concept theory has met with mixed success in predicting consumer responses to brand images.

Psychological Factors

A person's buying choices are further influenced by four major psychological factors: *motivation, perception, learning,* and *beliefs and attitudes.*

Motivation

We know that Jennifer Flores became interested in buying a camera. Why? What is she *really* seeking? What *needs* is she trying to satisfy?

A person has many needs at any given time. Some are *biological,* arising from states of tension such as hunger, thirst, or discomfort. Others are *psychological,* arising from the need for recognition, esteem, or belonging. Most of these needs will not be strong enough to motivate the person to act at a given point in time. A need becomes a *motive* when it is aroused to a sufficient level of intensity. A **motive** (or *drive*) is a need that is sufficiently pressing to direct the person to seek satisfaction. Psychologists have developed theories of human motivation. Two of the most popular—the theories of Sigmund Freud and Abraham Maslow—have quite different meanings for consumer analysis and marketing.

Freud's Theory of Motivation. Freud assumes that people are largely unconscious about the real psychological forces shaping their behavior. He sees the person as growing up and repressing many urges. These urges are never eliminated or under perfect control; they emerge in dreams, in slips of the tongue, in neurotic and obsessive behavior, or ultimately in psychoses.

Thus, Freud suggests that a person does not fully understand his or her motivation. If Jennifer Flores wants to purchase an expensive camera, she may describe her motive as wanting a hobby or career. At a deeper level, she may be purchasing the camera to impress others with her creative talent. At a still deeper level, she may be buying the camera to feel young and independent again.

Motivation researchers collect in-depth information from small samples of consumers to uncover the deeper motives for their product choices. They use nondirective depth interviews and various "projective techniques" to throw the ego off guard—techniques such as word association, sentence completion, picture interpretation, and role playing. Motivation researchers have reached some interesting and sometimes odd conclusions about what may be in the buyer's mind regarding certain purchases. For example, one classic study concluded that consumers resist prunes because they are wrinkled looking and remind people of sickness and old age. Despite its sometimes unusual conclusions, motivation research remains a useful tool for marketers seeking a deeper understanding of consumer behavior (see Marketing Highlight 5-3).[15]

Maslow's Theory of Motivation. Abraham Maslow sought to explain why people are driven by particular needs at particular times.[16] Why does one person spend much time and energy on personal safety and another on gaining the esteem of others? Maslow's answer is that human needs are arranged in a hierarchy, from the most pressing to the least pressing. Maslow's hierarchy of needs is shown in Figure 5-4. In order of importance, they are *physiological* needs, *safety* needs, *social* needs, *esteem* needs, and *self-actualization* needs. A person tries to sat-

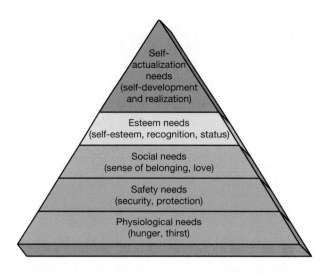

FIGURE 5–4
Maslow's hierarchy of needs

Source: Adapted from *Motivation and Personality,* 2nd ed., by Abraham H. Maslow. Copyright © 1970 by Abraham H. Maslow. Reprinted by permission of Harper & Row, Publishers, Inc.

isfy the most important need first. When that important need is satisfied, it will stop being a motivator and the person will then try to satisfy the next most important need. For example, a starving man (need 1) will not take an interest in the latest happenings in the art world (need 5), nor in how he is seen or esteemed by others (need 3 or 4), nor even in whether he is breathing clean air (need 2). But as each important need is satisfied, the next most important need will come into play.

What light does Maslow's theory throw on Jennifer Flores's interest in buying a camera? We can guess that Jennifer has satisfied her physiological, safety, and social needs; they do not motivate her interest in cameras. Her camera interest might come from a strong need for more esteem from others. Or it might come from a need for self-actualization—she might want to be a creative person and express herself through photography.

Perception

A motivated person is ready to act. How the person acts is influenced by his or her perception of the situation. Two people with the same motivation and in the same situation may act quite differently because they perceive the situation differently. Jennifer Flores might consider a fast-talking camera salesperson loud and phony. Another camera buyer might consider the same salesperson intelligent and helpful.

Why do people perceive the same situation differently? All of us learn by the flow of information through our five senses: sight, hearing, smell, touch, and taste. However, each of us receives, organizes, and interprets this sensory information in an individual way. **Perception** is the process by which people select, organize, and interpret information to form a meaningful picture of the world.

People can form different perceptions of the same stimulus because of three perceptual processes: *selective attention, selective distortion,* and *selective retention.*

Selective Attention. People are exposed to a great amount of stimuli every day. For example, the average person may be exposed to more than 1,500 ads a day. It is impossible for a person to pay attention to all these stimuli. **Selective attention**—the tendency for people to screen out most of the information to which they are exposed—means that marketers have to work especially hard to attract the consumer's attention. Their message will be lost on most people who are not in the market for the product. Moreover, even people who are in the market may not notice the message unless it stands out from the surrounding sea of other ads.

Selective Distortion. Even noted stimuli do not always come across in the intended way. Each person fits incoming information into an existing mind-set. **Selective distortion** describes the tendency of people to adapt information to personal meanings. Jennifer Flores may hear the salesperson mention some good and bad points about a competing camera brand. Because she already has a strong leaning toward Nikon, she is likely to distort those points in order to conclude that Nikon is the better camera. People tend to interpret information in a way that will support what they already believe. Selective distortion means that mar-

MARKETING HIGHLIGHT 5-3

"TOUCHY-FEELY" RESEARCH INTO CONSUMER MOTIVATIONS

The term *motivation research* refers to qualitative research designed to probe consumers' hidden, subconscious motivations. Because consumers often don't know or can't describe just why they act as they do, motivation researchers use a wide variety of nondirective and projective techniques to uncover underlying emotions and attitudes toward brands and buying situations. The techniques range from sentence completion, word association, and inkblot or cartoon interpretation tests, to having consumers describe typical brand users or form daydreams and fantasies about brands or buying situations. Some of these techniques verge on the bizarre. One writer offers the following tongue-in-cheek summary of a motivation research session:

> Good morning, ladies and gentlemen. We've called you here today for a little consumer research. Now, lie down on the couch, toss your inhibitions out the window, and let's try a little free association. First, think about brands as if they were your *friends*. Imagine you could talk to your TV dinner. What would he say? And what would you say to him? . . . Now, think of your shampoo as an animal. Go on, don't be shy. Would it be a panda or a lion? A snake or a wooly worm? For our final exercise, let's all sit up and pull out our magic markers. Draw a picture of a typical cake-mix user. Would she wear an apron or a negligee? A business suit or a can-can dress?

Such projective techniques seem pretty goofy. But more and more, marketers are turning to these touchy-feely, motivation research approaches to help them probe consumer psyches and develop better marketing strategies.

Many advertising agencies employ teams of psychologists, anthropologists, and other social scientists to carry out their motivation research. Says the research director of one large agency, "We believe people make choices on a basic primitive level . . . we use the probe to get down to the unconscious." This agency routinely conducts one-on-one, therapy-like interviews to delve into the inner workings of consumers. Another agency asks consumers to describe their favorite brands as animals or cars (say, Cadillacs versus Chevrolets) in order to assess the prestige associated with various brands. Still another agency has consumers draw figures of typical brand users:

> In one instance, the agency asked 50 interviewees to sketch likely buyers of two different brands of cake mixes. Consistently, the group portrayed Pillsbury customers as apron-clad, grandmotherly types, while they pictured Duncan Hines purchasers as svelte, contemporary women.

In a similar study, American Express had people sketch likely users of its gold card versus its green card. Respondents depicted gold card holders as active, broad-shoul-

keters must try to understand the mind-sets of consumers and how these will affect interpretations of advertising and sales information.

Selective Retention. People also will forget much that they learn. They tend to retain information that supports their attitudes and beliefs. Because of **selective retention,** Jennifer is likely to remember good points made about the

Selected perception: The average person is exposed to more than 1,500 ads per day—in magazines and newspapers, on radio and TV, and all around them on signs and billboards.

Motivation research: When asked to sketch figures of typical cake-mix users, subjects portrayed Pillsbury customers as grandmotherly types and Duncan Hines buyers as svelte and contemporary.

dered men; green card holders were perceived as "couch potatoes" lounging in front of television sets. Based on these results, the company positioned its gold card as a symbol of responsibility for people capable of controlling their lives and finances.

Some motivation research studies employ more basic techniques, such as simply mingling with consumers to find out what makes them tick:

Saatchi & Saatchi [an advertising agency] recently hired anthropologist Joe Lowe to spend a week in Texas sidling up to wearers of Wranglers blue jeans at rodeos and barbecues. His findings reinforced what

the jeans company suspected: Buyers associated Wranglers with cowboys. The company responded by running ads with plenty of Western touches. For a consumer-goods manufacturer, Lowe went to health clubs where he observed patrons applying deodorant. And for shampoo maker Helene Curtis, he spent three days in salons before coming to a somewhat predictable conclusion—going to the beauty shop makes women feel good.

Some marketers dismiss such motivation research as mumbo-jumbo. And these approaches do present some problems: They use small samples and researcher interpretations of results are often highly subjective, sometimes leading to rather exotic explanations of otherwise ordinary buying behavior. However, others believe strongly that these approaches can provide interesting nuggets of insight into the relationships between consumers and the brands they buy. To marketers who use them, motivation research techniques provide a flexible and varied means of gaining insights into deeply held and often mysterious motivations behind consumer buying behavior.

Sources: Excerpts from Annetta Miller and Dody Tsiantar, "Psyching Out Consumers," *Newsweek*, February 27, 1989, pp. 46–47 © 1989, Newsweek, Inc. All rights reserved. Reprinted by permission. Also see Sidney J. Levy, "Dreams, Fairy Tales, Animals, and Cars," *Psychology and Marketing*, Summer 1985, pp. 67–81; Ronald Alsop, "Advertisers Put Consumers on the Couch," *The Wall Street Journal*, May 13, 1988, p. 21; Rebecca Piirto, "Measuring Minds in the 1990s," *American Demographics*, December 1990, pp. 31–35; and Piirto, "Words that Sell," *American Demographics*, January 1992, p. 6.

Nikon and forget good points made about competing cameras. She may remember Nikon's good points because she "rehearses" them more whenever she thinks about choosing a camera.

Because of selective exposure, distortion, and retention, marketers have to work hard to get their messages through. This fact explains why marketers use so much drama and repetition in sending messages to their market. Interestingly, although most marketers worry about whether their offers will be perceived at all, some consumers are worried that they will be affected by marketing messages without even knowing it (see Marketing Highlight 5-4).

Learning

When people act, they learn. **Learning** describes changes in an individual's behavior arising from experience. Learning theorists say that most human behavior is learned. Learning occurs through the interplay of *drives, stimuli, cues, responses,* and *reinforcement.*

We saw that Jennifer Flores has a drive for self-actualization. A *drive* is a strong internal stimulus that calls for action. Her drive becomes a motive when it is directed toward a particular *stimulus object,* in this case a camera. Jennifer's response to the idea of buying a camera is conditioned by the surrounding cues. *Cues* are minor stimuli that determine when, where, and how the person responds. Seeing cameras in a shop window, hearing of a special sale price, and her husband's support are all cues that can influence Jennifer's *response* to her interest in buying a camera.

Suppose Jennifer buys the Nikon. If the experience is rewarding, she will probably use the camera more and more. Her response to cameras will be *rein-*

SUBLIMINAL PERCEPTION—CAN CONSUMERS BE AFFECTED WITHOUT KNOWING IT?

In 1957, the phrases "Eat popcorn" and "Drink Coca-Cola" were flashed on a screen in a New Jersey movie theater every five seconds for 1/300th of a second. The researchers reported that although the audience did not consciously recognize these messages, viewers absorbed them subconsciously and bought 58 percent more popcorn and 18 percent more Coke. Suddenly advertising agencies and consumer-protection groups became intensely interested in *subliminal perception*. People voiced fears of being brainwashed, and California and Canada declared the practice illegal. The controversy cooled when scientists failed to replicate the original results, but the issue did not die. In 1974, Wilson Bryan Key claimed in his book *Subliminal Seduction* that consumers were still being manipulated by advertisers in print ads and television commercials.

Subliminal perception has since been studied by many psychologists and consumer researchers. None of these experts have been able to show that subliminal messages have any effect on consumer behavior. It appears that subliminal advertising simply doesn't have the power attributed to it by its critics. Most advertisers scoff at the notion of an industry conspiracy to manipulate consumers through "invisible" messages. As one advertising agency executive put it, "We have enough trouble persuading consumers using a series of up-front thirty-second ads—how could we do it in 1/300th of a second?"

Although advertisers may avoid outright subliminal advertising, some critics claim that television advertising employs techniques approaching the subliminal. With more and more viewers reaching for their remote controls to avoid ads by switching channels or fast-forwarding through VCR tapes, advertisers are using new tricks to grab viewer attention and to affect consumers in ways they may not be aware of. Many ad agencies employ psychologists and neurophysiologists to help develop subtle psychological advertising strategies.

For example, some advertisers purposely try to confuse viewers, throw them off balance, or even make them uncomfortable:

[They use] film footage that wouldn't pass muster with a junior-high film club. You have to stare at the screen just to figure out what's going on—and that, of course, is the idea. Take the ads for Wang computers. In these hazy, washed-out spots, people walk partially in and out of the camera frame talking in computer jargon. But the confusion grabs attention. . . . Even people who don't understand a word are riveted to the screen.

Other advertisers use the rapid-fire technique. Images flash by so quickly you can barely register them. Pontiac used such "machine-gun editing" in recent ads—the longest shot flashed by in one and one-half seconds, the shortest in one-quarter of a second. The ads scored high in viewer recall.

Some advertisers go after our ears as well as our eyes, taking advantage of the powerful effects some sounds have on human brain waves:

Advertisers are using sounds to take advantage of the automatic systems built into the brain that force you to stop what you're doing and refocus on the screen. . . . You can't ignore these sounds. That's why commercials are starting off with noises ranging from a baby crying (Advil) to a car horn (Hertz) to a factory whistle (Almond Joy). In seeking the right sound . . . . advertisers can be downright merciless. . . . Ads for Nuprin pain reliever kick off by assaulting viewers with the whine of a dentist's drill . . . to help the viewer recall the type of pain we've all experienced. Hey, thanks.

A few experts are concerned that new high-tech advertising might even hypnotize consumers, whether knowingly or not. They suggest that several techniques—rapid scene changes, pulsating music and sounds, repetitive phrases, and flashing logos—might actually start to put some viewers under.

Some critics think that such subtle, hard-to-resist psychological techniques are unfair to consumers—that advertisers can use these techniques to bypass consumers' defenses and affect them without their being aware of it. The advertisers who use these techniques, however, view them as innovative, creative approaches to advertising.

Sources: See Wilson Bryan Key, *Subliminal Seduction* (New York: NAL, 1974); Timothy E. Moore, "Subliminal Advertising: What You See Is What You Get," *Journal of Marketing*, Spring 1982, pp. 38-47; Walter Weir, "Another Look at Subliminal 'Facts,'" *Advertising Age*, October 15, 1984, p. 46; and Michael J. McCarthy, "Mind Probe," *The Wall Street Journal*, March 22, 1991, p. B3. Excerpts from David H. Freedman, "Why You Watch Commercials—Whether You Mean to or Not," *TV Guide*, February 20, 1988, pp. 4–7.

forced. Then the next time she shops for a camera, binoculars, or some similar product, the probability is greater that she will buy a Nikon product. We say that she *generalizes* her response to similar stimuli.

The reverse of generalization is *discrimination*. When Jennifer examines binoculars made by Olympus, she sees that they are lighter and more compact than Nikon's binoculars. Discrimination means that she has learned to recognize differences in sets of products and can adjust her response accordingly.

The practical significance of learning theory for marketers is that they can build up demand for a product by associating it with strong drives, using motivating cues, and providing positive reinforcement. A new company can enter the market by appealing to the same drives that competitors appeal to, and by providing similar cues, because buyers are more likely to transfer loyalty to similar brands than to dissimilar ones (generalization). Or a new company may design its brand to appeal to a different set of drives and offer strong cue inducements to switch brands (discrimination).

Beliefs and Attitudes

Through doing and learning, people acquire their beliefs and attitudes. These, in turn, influence their buying behavior. A **belief** is a descriptive thought that a person has about something. Jennifer Flores may believe that a Nikon camera takes great pictures, stands up well under hard use, and costs $550. These beliefs may be based on real knowledge, opinion, or faith, and may or may not carry an emotional charge. For example, Jennifer Flores's belief that a Nikon camera is heavy may or may not matter to her decision.

Marketers are interested in the beliefs that people formulate about specific products and services, because these beliefs make up product and brand images that affect buying behavior. If some of the beliefs are wrong and prevent purchase, the marketer will want to launch a campaign to correct them.

People have attitudes regarding religion, politics, clothes, music, food, and almost everything else. An **attitude** describes a person's relatively consistent evaluations, feelings, and tendencies toward an object or idea. Attitudes put people into a frame of mind of liking or disliking things, of moving toward or away from them. Thus, Jennifer Flores may hold such attitudes as "Buy the best," "The Japanese make the best products in the world," and "Creativity and self-expression are among the most important things in life." If so, the Nikon camera would fit well into Jennifer's existing attitudes.

Attitudes are difficult to change. A person's attitudes fit into a pattern, and to change one attitude may require difficult adjustments in many others. Thus, a company should usually try to fit its products into existing attitudes rather than try to change attitudes. Of course, there are exceptions in which the great cost of trying to change attitudes may pay off. For example:

In the late 1950s, Honda entered the U.S. motorcycle market facing a major decision. It could either sell its motorcycles to the small but already established motorcycle market or try to increase the size of this market by attracting new types of consumers.

Attitudes are hard to change, but it can be done. Honda's "You meet the nicest people on a Honda" campaign changed people's attitudes about who rides motorcycles.

Increasing the size of the market would be more difficult and expensive because many people had negative attitudes toward motorcycles. They associated motorcycles with black leather jackets, switchblades, and outlaws. Despite these adverse attitudes, Honda took the second course of action. It launched a major campaign to position motorcycles as good clean fun. Its theme "You meet the nicest people on a Honda" worked well, and many people adopted a new attitude toward motorcycles. In the 1990s, however, Honda faces a similar problem. With the aging of the baby boomers, the market has once again shifted toward only hard-core motorcycling enthusiasts. So Honda has again set out to change consumer attitudes. It is spending $75 million on its new "Come Ride With Us" campaign to reestablish the wholesomeness of motorcycling and to position it as fun and exciting for everyone.[17]

We can now appreciate the many individual characteristics and forces acting on consumer behavior. The consumer's choice results from the complex interplay of cultural, social, personal, and psychological factors. Although many of these factors cannot be influenced by the marketer, they can be useful in identifying interested buyers and in shaping products and appeals to better serve their needs.

SUMMARY

Markets have to be understood before marketing strategies can be developed. The consumer market buys goods and services for personal consumption. Consumers vary tremendously in age, income, education, tastes, and other factors. Marketers must understand how consumers transform marketing and other inputs into buying responses. *Consumer behavior* is influenced by the buyer's characteristics and by the buyer's decision process. *Buyer characteristics* include four major factors: cultural, social, personal, and psychological.

Culture is the most basic determinant of a person's wants and behavior. It includes the basic values, perceptions, preferences, and behaviors that a person learns from family and other key institutions. Marketers try to track cultural shifts that might suggest new ways to serve consumers. *Subcultures* are "cultures within cultures" that have distinct values and lifestyles. *Social classes* are subcultures whose members have similar social prestige based on occupation, income, education, wealth, and other variables. People with different cultural, subcultural, and social class characteristics have different product and brand preferences. Marketers may want to focus their marketing programs on the special needs of certain groups.

Social factors also influence a buyer's behavior. A person's *reference groups*—family, friends, social organizations, professional associations—strongly affect product and brand choices. The person's position within each group can be defined in terms of *role and status*. A buyer chooses products and brands that reflect his or her role and status.

The buyer's age, life-cycle stage, occupation, economic circumstances, lifestyle, personality, and other *personal characteristics* influence his or her buying decisions. Young consumers have different needs and wants from older consumers; the needs of young married couples differ from those of retirees; consumers with higher incomes buy differently from those who have less to spend. Consumer *lifestyles*—the whole pattern of acting and interacting in the world—are also an important influence on buyers' choices.

Finally, consumer buying behavior is influenced by four major *psychological factors*—motivation, perception, learning, and attitudes. Each of these factors provides a different perspective for understanding the workings of the buyer's black box.

A person's buying behavior is the result of the complex interplay of all these cultural, social, personal, and psychological factors. Although many of these factors cannot be controlled by marketers, they are useful in identifying and understanding the consumers that marketers are trying to influence.

KEY TERMS

DISCUSSING THE ISSUES

1. What factors could you add to the model shown in Figure 5-1 to make it a more complete description of consumer behavior?

2. A new method of packaging wine in plastic-lined cardboard boxes offers more consumer convenience than traditional bottles. Instead of a cork, an airtight dispenser is used that allows servings of the desired amount while keeping the remaining wine fresh for weeks. How will the factors shown in Figure 5-2 work for or against the success of this packaging method?

3. What does each part of the following pairs tell you about a person's social class?
   a. Annual income of $30,000—annual income of $40,000
   b. Floors are covered with Oriental rugs—house has wall-to-wall carpeting
   c. Shops at Sears—shops at Neiman Marcus
   d. College graduate—high-school graduate

4. In designing the advertising for a soft drink, which would you find more helpful: information about consumer demographics or about consumer lifestyles? Give examples of how you would use each type of information.

5. Think about a very good or very bad experience you have had with a product. Did this shape your beliefs about this product? How long will these beliefs last?

6. One advertising agency president says, "Perception is reality." What does he mean by this? How is perception important to marketers?

APPLYING THE CONCEPTS

1. Different types of products can fulfill different functional and psychological needs.

   ■ List five public or private luxury products that are very interesting or important to you. Some possibilities might include cars, clothing, sports equipment, or cosmetics. List five other necessities that you use which have little interest to you, such as pencils, laundry detergent, or gasoline.

   ■ Make a list of words that describe how you feel about each of the products you listed. Are there differences between the types of words you used for luxuries and necessities? What does this tell you about the different psychological needs these products fulfill?

2. Different groups may have different types of effects on consumers.

   ■ Consider an item that you bought which is typical of what your peers (a key reference group) buy, such as a compact disc, a brand of athletic shoe, or a mountain bike. Were you conscious that your friends owned something similar when you made this purchase? Did this make you want the item more or less?

   ■ Now, think of brands that you currently use which your parents also use. Examples may include soap, shaving cream, or margarine. Did you think through these purchases as carefully as those influenced by your peers, or were these purchases simply the result of following old habits?

MAKING MARKETING DECISIONS:

SMALL WORLD COMMUNICATIONS, INC.

Tom and Lynette have decided that there is an unmet need for easy computer communications management. They now need to understand their potential customers in order to develop appealing products and effective marketing programs. "This stuff is so slippery," said Lyn. Tom waited, hoping that she would say more so he could understand what she was talking about. She continued, "I mean, marketing food was so straightforward. People get hungry, they

eat, they run out of food, go to the store, and buy more food 'cause they know they're going to be hungry again. People know what they need, and they know how to satisfy that need. Nothing is clear in the computer market—it's all changing." Tom replied, "Remember Maslow? Food marketers deal at the bottom of Maslow's hierarchy of needs, down at the hunger level. Computer users are a lot closer to the top of the pyramid. Electronic mail fills social needs, word processing and number crunching build esteem by helping their careers, and a few of us work on self-actualization by learning more and more about these little machines. I'm a musician, and this is my instrument."

"You've read *Maslow?*" asked Lyn, who was stunned enough to ignore the musician remark. "Well, *I* haven't, but I had a girlfriend who had, and I learned a little bit from her," answered Tom. Lynette almost said "You had a *girlfriend!?*" but she realized this sounded harsh, and she didn't mean to be. Instead she said, "Well, the Maslow ideas are helpful for looking at individual motivation, but I think we need to look at groups. I've got a feeling that there are important differences between the computer support staff and ordinary users. We need to learn as much as we can about these people. Maybe then we'll understand who will be making the purchase decisions, and what will influence them."

What Now?

1. Describe some of the computer users that you know and the different ways they use computers. (a) Do you think there is more than one group of users with different needs and interests? (b) If so, do you think that these groups could influence how their members buy computer products?

2. Question 1 asked you to identify one or more groups of computer users. (a) Make up a descriptive name for each group you identified. (b) List between three and five key beliefs and attitudes each group has about computers. (c) Discuss how different group beliefs and attitudes might affect how Lyn and Tom develop products to meet these groups' needs.

 ## REFERENCES

1. Quotes are from Peter Schutz and Jack Cook, "Porsche on Nichemanship," *Harvard Business Review,* March-April 1986, pp. 98–106. Copyright (c) 1986 by the President and Fellows of Harvard College; all rights reserved. Also see Cleveland Horton, "Porsche's Ads Get Racy in '88 with Tie to Indy," *Advertising Age,* November 2, 1987, p. 34; and Mark Maremont, "Europe's Long, Smooth Ride in Luxury Cars Is Over," *Business Week,* March 17, 1988, p. 57.

2. Several models of the consumer buying process have been developed by marketing scholars. The most prominent models are those of John A. Howard and Jagdish N. Sheth, *The Theory of Buyer Behavior* (New York: John Wiley, 1969); Francesco M. Nicosia, *Consumer Decision Processes* (Englewood Cliffs, NJ: Prentice Hall, 1966); James F. Engel, Roger D. Blackwell, and Paul W. Miniard, *Consumer Behavior,* 5th ed. (New York: Holt, Rinehart & Winston, 1986); and James R. Bettman, *An Information Processing Theory of Consumer Choice* (Reading, MA: Addison-Wesley, 1979). For a summary, see Leon G. Schiffman and Leslie Lazar Kanuk, *Consumer Behavior,* 4th ed. (Englewood Cliffs, NJ: Prentice Hall, 1991), Chap. 20.

3. See Schiffman and Kanuk, *Consumer Behavior,* Chap. 14.

4. For more on marketing to Hispanics, blacks, mature consumers, and Asians, see Thomas Exter, "One Million Hispanic Club," *American Demographics,* February 1991, p. 59; Gary L. Berman, "The Hispanic Market: Getting Down to Cases," *Sales & Marketing Management,* October 1991, pp. 65–74; Christy Fisher, "Poll: Hispanics Stick to Brands," *Advertising Age,* February 15, 1993, p. 6; Thomas G. Exter, "The Largest Minority," *American Demographics,* February 1993, p. 59; Judith Waldrop, "Shades of Black," *American Demographics,* September 1990, pp. 30–34; Melissa Campanelli, "The African-American Market: Community, Growth, and Change," *Sales & Marketing Management,* May 1991, pp. 75–81; Maria Mallory, "Waking Up to a Major Market," *Business Week,* March 23, 1992, pp. 70–73; Eugene Morris, "The Difference in Black and White," *American Demographics,* January 1993, pp. 44–49; Melissa Campanelli, "The Senior Market: Rewriting the Demographics and Definitions," *Sales & Marketing Management,* February 1991, pp. 63–70; Joseph M. Winski, "The Mature Market: Marketers Mature in Depicting Seniors," *Advertising Age,* November 16, 1992, p. S1; Tibbett L. Speer, "Older Consumers Follow Diferent Rules," *American Demographics,* February 1993, pp. 21–22; Maria Shao, "Suddenly, Asian-Americans Are

a Marketer's Dream," *Business Week,* June 17, 1991, pp. 54–55; and Carol J. Fouke, "Asian-American Market More Important than Ever," *Marketing News,* October 14, 1991, p. 10.

5. William O. Bearden and Michael J. Etzel, "Reference Group Influence on Product and Brand Purchase Decisions," *Journal of Consumer Research,* September 1982, p. 185.

6. Debra Goldman, "Spotlight Men," *Adweek,* August 13, 1990, pp. M1–M6; Dennis Rodkin, "A Manly Sport: Building Loyalty," *Advertising Age,* April 15, 1991, pp. S1, S12; Nancy Ten Kate, "Who Buys the Pants in the Family?" *American Demographics,* January 1992, p. 12; and Laura Zinn, "Real Men Buy Paper Towels, Too," *Business Week,* November 9, 1992, pp. 75-76.

7. For more on family decision making, see Schiffman and Kanuk, *Consumer Behavior,* Chap. 12; Rosann L. Spiro, "Persuasion in Family Decision Making," *Journal of Consumer Research,* March 1983, pp. 393–402; Michael B. Menasco and David J. Curry, "Utility and Choice: An Empirical Study of Husband/Wife Decision Making," *Journal of Consumer Research,* June 1989, pp. 87–97; and Eileen Fisher and Stephen J. Arnold, "More than a Labor of Love: Gender Roles and Christmas Gift Shopping," *Journal of Consumer Research,* December 1990, pp. 333–45.

8. See Lawrence Lepisto, "A Life Span Perspective of Consumer Behavior," in Elizabeth Hirshman and Morris Holbrook, *Advances in Consumer Research,* vol. 12 (Provo, UT: Association for Consumer Research, 1985), p. 47.

9. Kim Foltz, "Wizards of Marketing," *Newsweek,* July 22, 1985, p. 44.

10. For more on VALS and on psychographics in general, see William D. Wells, "Psychographics: A Critical Review," *Journal of Marketing Research,* May 1975, pp. 196–213; Arnold Mitchell, *The Nine American Lifestyles* (New York: Macmillan, 1983); Rebecca Piirto, "Measuring Minds in the 1990s," *American Demographics,* December 1990, pp. 35–39; and Piirto, "VALS the Second Time," *American Demographics,* July 1991, p. 6.

11. This and other examples of companies using VALS 2 can be found in Piirto, "VALS the Second Time."

12. For more reading on the pros and cons of using VALS and other lifestyle approaches, see Lynn R. Kahle, Sharon E. Beatty, and Pamela Homer, "Alternative Measurement Approaches to Consumer Values: The List of Values (LOV) and

Values and Life Styles (VALS)," *Journal of Consumer Research,* December 1986, pp. 405–9; and Mark Landler, "The Blood-bath in Market Research," *Business Week,* February 11, 1991, pp. 72–74.

13. See Harold H. Kassarjian and Mary Jane Sheffet, "Personality in Consumer Behavior: An Update," in *Perspectives in Consumer Behavior,* Harold H. Kassarjian and Thomas S. Robertson, eds. (Glenview, IL: Scott Foresman, 1981), pp. 160–80; and Joseph T. Plummer, "How Personality Can Make a Difference," *Marketing News,* March-April 1984, pp. 17–20.

14. See M. Joseph Sirgy, "Self-Concept in Consumer Behavior: A Critical Review," *Journal of Consumer Research,* December 1982,

pp. 287–300; and Russell W. Belk, "Possessions and the Extended Self," *Journal of Consumer Research,* September 1988, pp. 139–59.

15. See Annetta Miller and Dody Tsiantar, "Psyching Out Consumers," *Newsweek,* February 27, 1989, pp. 46–47; and Rebecca Piirto, "Words that Sell," *American Demographics,* January 1992, p. 6.

16. Abraham H. Maslow, *Motivation and Personality,* 2nd ed. (New York: Harper & Row, 1970), pp. 80–106.

17. See "Honda Hopes to Win New Riders by Emphasizing 'Fun' of Cycles," *Marketing News,* August 28, 1989, p. 6.

VIDEO CASE 5

MARKETING TO ASIAN AMERICANS

Let's go shopping at the Asian Garden, an ornate, two-story arcade with a tiled roof and lacquered pillars. A mammoth Buddha guards the entrance, flanked by the gods of prosperity, longevity, and happiness. Inside you'll find many typical suburban shopping mall businesses: CD and tape stores, travel agencies, restaurants, a supermarket, bookstores, and lots of jewelry shops. But some of the stores are different. For example, the pharmacy carries items such as ground antler, dried lizard, starfish flakes, and ginseng. The tailors and dressmakers prepare custom clothing and garments known as *ao dais* (flowing silk tunic-and-pants ensembles). Where are you? In Westminster, California—known locally as Little Saigon.

More than 2.7 million Asian Americans live in California, so it's not surprising to find oriental shopping malls there. By the year 2000, the state's Asian population will exceed 4.5 million, some 13 percent of its population. As compared to other U.S. households, Asian-American households have substantially higher income and education levels, and almost twice the proportion of Asian Americans are employed as managers or professionals.

Most Asian Americans cluster in large cities such as San Francisco, Los Angeles, or New York. They are strongly family oriented and often pool family efforts and resources to improve the lot of all. Extended families tend to live in the same household—a tradition carried over from their homelands. Further, members of the family often work in the family business. Marketers targeting Asian Americans must understand the importance of family. For example, when approaching this market, Metropolitan Life dropped the Peanuts characters used in its regular advertising. Instead it emphasized family security, especially financial benefits that would allow children to go to college. This strategy increased Met's sales to Asian Americans fivefold.

Asian-American consumption behavior differs from that of other segments. For example, Asian Americans are primarily interested in quality. They are brand loyal but not store loyal, and they prefer to do business with people they know. Asian Americans enjoy shopping as a leisure activity, love bargains, and often negotiate prices. They are at home with high technology, making them a good market for VCRs, home computers, CD players, cameras, camcorders, and telephone answering machines. And, of course, Asian Americans differ in their food preferences. They prefer such foods as sticky rice, pickled cabbage, and fish balls. Marketers may have to adapt their products for this market. For example, clothing must be made in smaller sizes with shorter sleeves and pant legs. Macy's, which has traditionally carried high-quality clothes in smaller sizes, has become a favorite of the Asian community.

Marketing to Asian-American immigrants has a big advantage: They do not have preconceived images of brands and companies. In a recent survey, 76 percent of these immigrants could not name the brand of frozen food they purchased last. Therefore, marketers often do not have to overcome well-entrenched images of competing brands when marketing their own brands to these consumers.

Selling to the Asian-American market is not easy. This highly diverse market consists of Japanese, Vietnamese, Koreans, Filipinos, Cambodians, Indians, Indonesians, Malaysians, and Chinese—all speaking multiple languages and dialects. Because of this linguistic diversity, television may not be an effective medium. Fortunately, Asian Americans like to read, making newspapers a more cost-effective medium. And many magazines cater specifically to the Asian-American market. In addition, numerous Asian-American consultants and ad agencies are available to help marketers design Asian-American marketing strategies.

Even so, many firms are shying away from the Asian-American market. During a recession, many advertisers eliminate ads aimed at specialty markets in order to concentrate on campaigns that target more general audiences. But this may be a doubtful way to save dollars. The Asian-American market appears to be recessionproof. Asian Americans have higher incomes, and because many are employed in a family business or in high-tech fields, fewer are unemployed. Even when unemployed, they still may have significant income because the other members of their extended family still work to support the household.

Thus, the Asian-American market may constitute a marketer's dream of a large, lucrative, and recession-proof market. AT&T is betting millions on the Asian-American market; it thinks that this market is ready to explode. In September 1992, AT&T sent nearly 100,000 postcards to Asian-American customers reminding them to call home during the upcoming "Moon Festival" celebration, a Chinese holiday similar to Thanksgiving.

Questions

1. What cultural, personal, social, and psychological charac-

teristics distinguish the Asian-American market?

2. How can Maslow's hierarchy of needs and reference group effects be used to explain Asian-American buying motives?

3. Why are Asian Americans more likely to buy high-tech products such as computers, CD players, and camcorders?

4. If Asian Americans are unfamiliar with American brands, how will this affect their perception and learning processes?

Sources: "Malls with Oriental Flair Fill Widening Niche," *Chain Store Age Executive,* May 1989, pp. 128-30; Dan Fost, "California's Asian Market," *American Demographics,* October 1990, pp. 34-37; Cyndee Miller, "Marketers Say Budgets Hinder Targeting of Asian-Americans," *Marketing News,* March 30, 1992, pp. 2, 15; Catherine A. Novak, "Profiting from Diversity," *Best's Review,* March 1992, pp. 18-22, 99-100; and Gerry Gropp, "Little Saigon: Where Vietnam Meets America," *Smithsonian,* August 1992, pp. 28-29.

COMPANY CASE 5

RJR's PREMIER: WHERE THERE IS NO SMOKE, ARE THERE CUSTOMERS?

How would the average smoker feel about buying a pack of cigarettes that came with a four-page instruction booklet? That's what happened when RJR/Nabisco launched its new smokeless cigarette, Premier, in St. Louis, Phoenix, and Tucson in late 1988. RJR used "The Cleaner Smoke" as Premier's advertising slogan. Instead of the glitzy, image-oriented advertising that typically accompanies a new cigarette, Premier featured a just-the-facts marketing message: a cigarette with no sidestream smoke, less nicotine than 97 percent of the brands on the market, and significant reductions in what RJR called "controversial compounds," such as tar.

RJR selected the initial markets with its targeted audience of older (over 25), urbanite smokers in mind. The Arizona cities in particular are skewed toward older smokers, many of whom are trying to quit and are looking for an alternative. And although Premier's ad campaign clearly lacked the pizzazz of the Marlboro man or Benson and Hedges's yuppies, it was tailor-made for the targeted consumers. RJR appealed on a rational basis to people hooked on smoking.

To attract these upscale smokers, RJR positioned the smokeless cigarette as a "technological breakthrough" and used ads that were less image oriented and more "copy oriented" than typical cigarette ads. It named the innovative new brand Premier because it represented "the beginning of a whole new era of smoking enjoyment—cleaner enjoyment than you may have thought possible. The essential theme [was to be] the totality of its attributes, so that the product [would] be

recognized as . . . a remarkable discovery."

But the company's marketing strategy was a risky one. For one thing, the firm priced Premier substantially higher than ordinary cigarettes. For another, by targeting older, better educated smokers, RJR ran the risk of hurting its own brands in the low-tar market. Furthermore, some saw the smokeless cigarette as hostile to smoking. Just as decaffeinated coffee helped accelerate the decline of coffee consumption, so might Premier speed the decline in cigarette smoking, which was already falling at 2 percent per year.

The marketing strategy, however, may have reflected the constraints imposed by the new product more than anything else. Premier needed lots of explanation, and hence, more ad copy. The higher costs of making the product forced a higher price tag—about 25 percent above ordinary cigarette brands—which also meant targeting more affluent customers. Beyond that, RJR had to walk a fine line in pitching the product as "cleaner" without representing it as "healthier."

Because of these problems, some skeptics questioned whether RJR's strategy would work. They noted, for instance, that cigarette ads usually try to push powerful images and simple themes: too many facts might only reinforce the negative impression people have of smoking. One advertising executive observed that cigarettes are a "very personal, image-driven product," and that RJR's approach would only work "if it's a terrific product."

According to RJR, consumers gave Premier generally high marks in taste tests—they found it to be roughly comparable to that of Winston Lights, one of the company's low-tar brands. However, to conduct an independent test of smokers' reactions to Premier, a reporter from The Wall Street Journal surveyed about two dozen smokers at Atlanta's Hartsfield International Airport. Although unscientific, the survey indicated what some smokers thought about the cigarette and also pointed up some marketing problems RJR would face.

Many smokers in the survey said they disliked Premier because of its taste and strangeness. Some who reacted favorably said they might buy Premier as a second brand for use where sidestream smoke isn't acceptable; others liked it as a step away from smoking. Overall, nearly twice as many smokers panned Premier as praised it. RJR officials cautioned against drawing conclusions from this sample, noting that for many of the 2,000-plus people who test-smoked Premier in their research, it "did take some getting used to." But, they claimed, once many of the first-time skeptics got used to it, they liked it.

So, RJR needed to get smokers to try lots of Premiers. To encourage extended trial in lead markets, the company gave away two packs when smokers bought two—four packs at a time in some outlets. The company believed that many smokers would be attracted enough by the reduced tar and decreased offensiveness that they would stick with Premier and learn to like it. Just how many people would stay with it that long? One smoker in the airport survey discarded his Premier after only two puffs. "That taste doesn't get it," he observed.

Premier's complexity presented a problem in the airport survey also. Nearly all the smokers had trouble lighting the cigarette, most needing two or three tries. The carbon tip, which heats air to pass through the cigarette rather than burning tobacco, also makes the nonfilter part of the cigarette hot—leaving some people suspicious about just what is going on in there.

Still, some smokers who were not enthusiastic about Premier said that they might try it to avoid offending nonsmokers. The chairman of an Atlanta bill-

board company noted that he didn't like the taste much but stated, "I'd smoke it to get rid of the nagging at home. You could use it as a substitute there, then use the high-octane stuff outside." An auditorium manager offered only faint praise for Premier but said he would consider switching because he was in a minority of smokers at work. He felt obliged to snuff out his cigarette when other people entered his office. But due to Premier's lack of sidestream smoke, "I wouldn't be embarrassed to keep this going."

RJR needed to make Premier successful. It had worked on the cigarette since 1981, and estimates are that it had invested several hundred million dollars in the product so far. Furthermore, RJR's share of the U.S. cigarette market had slid to 34 percent as compared with arch rival Philip Morris's 39 percent. RJR hoped that "no smoke" would attract customers and reverse this decline.

QUESTIONS

1. Make a list of the words and phrases used in the case to describe Premier's target market. Did RJR define Premier's target market well?

2. What cultural, social, personal, and psychological factors affect a consumer's decision to smoke? Did RJR effectively address these factors with Premier?

3. Did RJR properly shape its marketing mix to serve its targeted customers? What assumptions did RJR make about its customers?

4. What do the comments of the consumers surveyed in the Atlanta airport suggest about the consumer learning process?

5. In what alternative ways could RJR position Premier?

Source: Adapted from John Helyar, "RJR Plans to Market Smokeless Cigarette as Breakthrough with Hefty Price Tag," *The Wall Street Journal,* September 30, 1988; and "RJR Smokeless Cigarette Encounters Skeptical Public," *The Wall Street Journal,* September 8, 1988. Used with permission.

Consumer Markets: Buyer Decision Processes

6

*I*n the early 1980s, Nike won the opening battle in what many now call the "great sneaker wars." Based on the power of its running shoes, which were designed for fitness but used mostly for fun, Nike unseated Adidas and sprinted into the lead in the $6-billion U.S. athletic shoe market. But fashion is fickle, and Nike's lead was short-lived. In 1986, upstart Reebok caught Nike from behind with its new soft leather aerobics shoe. It turned sweaty sneakers into fashion statements and zoomed to the front. By 1987, Reebok had captured over 30 percent of the market, while Nike's share had slumped to 18 percent.

In 1988, however, Nike retaliated. It targeted the reemerging "performance" market with the hard-hitting $20-million "Just Do It" advertising campaign featuring sports stars. The company also introduced dozens of new products aimed at narrow segments in the rapidly fragmenting athletic shoe market. By 1990, Nike was selling footwear for almost every conceivable sport: hiking, walking, cycling, and even cheerleading and windsurfing. The numbers attest to the rejuvenated Nike: Its 1992 market share was 30 percent and growing; Reebok's share had fallen dramatically to less than 23 percent.

Today, the sneaker wars are far from over. Reebok is already counterattacking with new products and marketing programs. And in a volatile industry that has seen many leaders—from venerable Converse in the 1970s to Adidas and Nike in the 1980s—first soar to the top and then plunge abruptly, both Nike and Reebok are watching their flanks for new competitors. For example, the success story of 1989 was neither Nike nor Reebok, but number-three L.A. Gear, which came from nowhere to grab over $600 million in sales (triple its 1988 sales) and a 12 percent market share. By 1992, however, the once-hot L.A. Gear had cooled and was facing big

losses at the hands of a fickle teenage market to aggressive nichers like Asics Tiger, Keds, and Fila. In recent ad campaigns, large and small competitors alike have bashed market leader Nike with such themes as "Pump up and air out" (Reebok), "Everything else is just hot air" (L.A. Gear), and "Your mother wears Nike" (British Knights).

Winning the sneaker wars, or even just surviving, requires a keen understanding of consumer behavior. Because sneakers can be a major means of self-expression, people's choices are usually shaped by a rich mix of influences. Thus, understanding consumer behavior in this seesaw market can be extremely difficult; trying to predict behavior can be even more difficult. The shoe companies introduce scores of new styles and colors every year, chasing fads that often fade at blinding speed. One day salespeople will sell all they can get of a new style; the next day they can't discount it enough.

The fickle youth market is the biggest battleground in the sneaker wars, and the inner city is at the center of that. Consumers between 15 and 22 years old buy 30 percent of all sneakers and influence an additional 10 percent through word of mouth. Many trends start in the nation's inner cities and spread to suburbia and the rest of middle America. Urban kids represent authenticity to kids in the suburbs, so trends that catch on in the inner city often spread quickly to the rest of the country. It isn't surprising, then, that sneaker makers openly court inner-city shoe store owners and kids. Nike and the other shoe manufacturers often give free sneakers to trend-setting teens whom the masses copy. Reebok even rebuilds inner-city playgrounds and repaves basketball courts to woo this constituency. And companies often launch new sneakers first in the inner city to see how they catch on before going national.

Those in the know, of course, don't call them

sneakers. Instead, they're known as Alphas, Revolutions, 830s, Air Jordans, Blacktops—their model names and numbers. The shoes are the first and foremost fashion statement. Gone are the days when sneakers were mostly cheap, functional, and drab, when the choices were white or black canvas, low top or high top, with maybe a variation or two for avid runners. Now, sneakers are a status symbol, a subculture. Sneaker prices start at around $50 a pair and run to more than $180. You can get good sneakers for less, but nobody who is anybody would be caught dead in them.

Sneaker crazes are often hard to explain. For example, the fad of wearing sneakers with the laces untied apparently began because proud owners wanted to keep their shoes looking factory fresh. Pretty soon, everyone was doing it, and that was just the beginning. Next, some wearers untied the lace on one shoe only; then, they removed the laces completely. Soon after that, wearers switched back to tying their shoes, but with laces from a different shoe. Now many are wearing sneakers that don't match—say, a white Chuck Taylor Converse on one foot and a Black Cons Converse on the other—but brands can't be mixed. Another unwritten rule: When it comes to dates, Nikes don't mix with Reeboks, or Converse with Adidas. In some neighborhoods, teenage girls report that the first thing they look at when a boy asks them out is his choice of sneakers. Teenage romances have been thwarted by brand differences.

There are regional—and even local—preferences, too. Adidas is the "in" brand in Philadelphia, home of Temple University, whose basketball team wears Adidas shoes. Chicago is a Nike town because Chicago basketball star Michael Jordan endorses the shoes. (Celebrity endorsements are key: Nike paid Jordan more than $2.5 million over five years to wear the shoes.) In Boston, there are Nike streets and Adidas streets, and woe to anyone caught wearing the wrong brand on the wrong street.

When it comes to sneakers, some people get a little carried away. For example, Brian Washington has 150 pairs of sneakers scattered around his two-bedroom apartment in Harlem. For all-night dancing, he has the bright red and black Nike Airwalkers. For "impressing the ladies," there are the chartreuse and gold Adidas shoes with purple stripes. The black and sky-blue Evolvo low-tops are for Saturdays at the park. For just hanging out, he prefers ink-blue Nikes. "The fact is, in the inner city, you are what you wear—on your feet," he explains. Of course, owning too many pairs of shoes can be a problem. For one thing, it's hard to decide what is the moment's socially hip attire. Heading out for the playground one recent afternoon for a pickup basketball game, Mr. Washington stepped into a pair of white Nike Air Jordans. Under his arm he put a brown leather basketball, and over his shoulder he carried a white pair of Avia 830s—just in case he changed his mind on his walk to the playground. Says Mr. Washington, ever fashion conscious, "It's a jungle out there." Nike and the other sneaker wars combatants couldn't agree more.[1]

 ## CHAPTER PREVIEW

> *Chapter 6 develops the concepts of consumer behavior further and applies them to the actual buying decision.*
>
> At the beginning of the chapter, we summarize the **consumer buying roles** that people might play: **initiator**, **influencer**, **decider**, **buyer**, and **user**.
>
> We continue by classifying buying behavior into four types: **complex, dissonance reducing, habitual,** and **variety seeking.**
>
> The stages of the **buyer decision process** are defined as **need recognition, information search, evaluation of alternatives, purchase decision,** and **postpurchase behavior.**
>
> The decision process for new products is explained in terms of the **stages in the adoption process,** the individual **differences in innovativeness,** the role of **personal influence,** and the way product characteristics affect the **rate of adoption.**
>
> We conclude with a discussion of **international** differences in **consumer behavior.**

Marketers have to be extremely careful in analyzing consumer behavior. Consumers often turn down what appears to be a winning offer. Polaroid found this out when it lost $170 million on its Polarvision instant home movie system.

So did Ford when it launched the famous (or infamous) Edsel, losing a cool $350 million in the process. And so did RCA when it swallowed a huge $580 million loss on its SelectaVision videodisc player.

In the last chapter we looked at the cultural, social, personal, and psychological influences that affect buyers. In this chapter we look at how consumers make buying decisions. First, we examine consumer buying roles and the types of decisions consumers face. Then we look at the main steps in the buyer decision process. Finally we explore the process by which consumers learn about and buy new products.

CONSUMER BUYING ROLES

The marketer needs to know what people are involved in the buying decision and what role each person plays. For many products, it is fairly easy to identify the decision maker. For example, men normally choose their own shaving equipment and women choose their own pantyhose. Other products, however, involve a decision-making unit consisting of more than one person. Consider the selection of a family automobile. The suggestion to buy a new car might come from the oldest child. A friend might advise the family on the kind of car to buy. The husband might choose the make. The wife might have a definite opinion regarding the car's style. The husband and wife might then make the final decision jointly, and the wife might use the car more than her husband.

Figure 6-1 shows that people might play any of several roles in a buying decision:

- **Initiator:** the person who first suggests or thinks of the idea of buying a particular product or service
- **Influencer:** a person whose views or advice influences the buying decision
- **Decider:** the person who ultimately makes a buying decision or any part of it—whether to buy, what to buy, how to buy, or where to buy
- **Buyer:** the person who makes an actual purchase
- **User:** the person who consumes or uses a product or service

A company needs to identify who occupies these roles because they affect product design and advertising message decisions. If Chevrolet finds that husbands make buying decisions for the family minivan, it will direct most of its advertising for these models toward husbands. But Chevy ads will include wives, children, and others who might initiate or influence the buying decision. In addition, Chevrolet will design its minivans with features that meet the needs of all

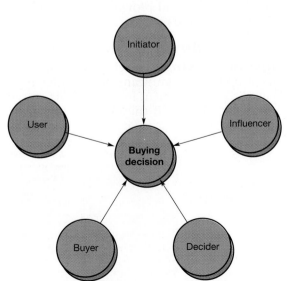

FIGURE 6-1
Consumer buying roles

buying decision participants. Knowing the main participants and the roles they play helps the marketer fine-tune the marketing program.

TYPES OF BUYING DECISION BEHAVIOR

Consumer decision making varies with the type of buying decision. Consumer buying behavior differs greatly for a tube of toothpaste, a tennis racket, an expensive camera, and a new car. More complex decisions usually involve more buying participants and more buyer deliberation. Figure 6-2 shows types of consumer buying behavior based on the degree of buyer involvement and the degree of differences among brands.[2]

Complex Buying Behavior

Consumers undertake **complex buying behavior** when they are highly involved in a purchase and perceive significant differences among brands. Consumers may be highly involved when the product is expensive, risky, purchased infrequently, and highly self-expressive. Typically, the consumer has much to learn about the product category. For example, a personal computer buyer may not know what attributes to consider. Many product features carry no real meaning: a "486 chip," "super VGA resolution," or "4 megs of RAM."

This buyer will pass through a learning process, first developing beliefs about the product, then attitudes, and then making a thoughtful purchase choice. Marketers of high-involvement products must understand the information-gathering and evaluation behavior of high-involvement consumers. They need to help buyers learn about product-class attributes and their relative importance, and about what the company's brand offers on the important attributes. Marketers need to differentiate their brand's features, perhaps by describing the brand's benefits using print media with long copy. They must motivate store salespeople and the buyer's acquaintances to influence the final brand choice.

Dissonance-Reducing Buying Behavior

Dissonance-reducing buying behavior occurs when consumers are highly involved with an expensive, infrequent, or risky purchase, but see little difference among brands. For example, consumers buying carpeting may face a high-involvement decision because carpeting is expensive and self-expressive. Yet buyers may consider most carpet brands in a given price range to be the same. In this case, because perceived brand differences are not large, buyers may shop around to learn what is available, but buy relatively quickly. They may respond primarily to a good price or to purchase convenience. After the purchase, consumers might experience postpurchase dissonance (after-sale discomfort) when they notice certain disadvantages of the purchased carpet brand or hear favorable things about brands not purchased. To counter such dissonance, the marketer's after-sale communications should provide evidence and support to help consumers feel good about their brand choices.

Habitual Buying Behavior

Habitual buying behavior occurs under conditions of low consumer involvement and little significant brand difference. For example, take salt. Consumers have little involvement in this product category—they simply go to the store and reach for a brand. If they keep reaching for the same brand, it is out of habit

FIGURE 6-2
Four Types of Buying Behavior
Source: Adapted from Henry Assael, *Consumer Behavior and Marketing Action* (Boston: Kent Publishing Company, 1987), p. 87. Copyright © 1987 by Wadsworth, Inc. Printed by permission of Kent Publishing Company, a division of Wadsworth, Inc.

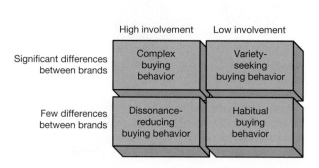

Complex buying behavior: Consumers are highly involved and see significant differences among brands.

rather than strong brand loyalty. Consumers appear to have low involvement with most low-cost, frequently purchased products.

In such cases, consumer behavior does not pass through the usual belief-attitude-behavior sequence. Consumers do not search extensively for information about the brands, evaluate brand characteristics, and make weighty decisions about which brands to buy. Instead, they passively receive information as they watch television or read magazines. Ad repetition creates *brand familiarity* rather than *brand conviction*. Consumers do not form strong attitudes toward a brand; they select the brand because it is familiar. Because they are not highly involved with the product, consumers may not evaluate the choice even after purchase. Thus, the buying process involves brand beliefs formed by passive learning, followed by purchase behavior, which may or may not be followed by evaluation.

Because buyers are not highly committed to any brands, marketers of low-involvement products with few brand differences often use price and sales promotions to stimulate product trial. In advertising for a low-involvement product, ad copy should stress only a few key points. Visual symbols and imagery are important because they can be remembered easily and associated with the brand. Ad campaigns should include high repetition of short-duration messages. Television is usually more effective than print media because it is a low-involvement medium suitable for passive learning. Advertising planning should be based on classical conditioning theory, in which buyers learn to identify a certain product by a symbol repeatedly attached to it.

Marketers can try to convert low-involvement products into higher involvement ones by linking them to some involving issue. Procter & Gamble does this when it links Crest toothpaste to avoiding cavities. Or the product can be linked to some involving personal situation. Nestlé did this in a recent series of ads for Taster's Choice coffee, each consisting of a new soap-opera-like episode featuring the evolving romantic relationship between two neighbors. Or an important product feature might be added to a low-involvement product, as when P&G added calcium to its Citrus Hill orange juice. At best, these strategies can raise consumer involvement from a low to a moderate level. However, they are not likely to propel the consumer into highly involved buying behavior.

Variety-Seeking Buying Behavior

Consumers undertake **variety-seeking buying behavior** in situations characterized by low consumer involvement, but significant perceived brand differences. In such cases, consumers often do a lot of brand switching. For example, when purchasing cookies, a consumer may hold some beliefs, choose a cookie brand without much evaluation, then evaluate that brand during consumption. But the next time, the consumer might pick another brand out of boredom or simply to try something different. Brand switching occurs for the sake of variety rather than because of dissatisfaction.

In such product categories, the marketing strategy may differ for the market leader and minor brands. The market leader will try to encourage habitual buying behavior by dominating shelf space, avoiding out-of-stock conditions, and running frequent reminder advertising. Challenger firms will encourage variety seek-

Marketers can convert low-involvement products into higher-involvement ones by linking them to involving situations. Here Nestle creates involvement with soap opera-like ads featuring the romantic relationship between two neighbors, Tony and Sharon.

ing by offering lower prices, deals, coupons, free samples, and advertising that presents reasons for trying something new.

THE BUYER DECISION PROCESS

Consumers make many buying decisions every day. Most large companies research consumer buying decisions in great detail to answer questions about what consumers buy, where they buy, how and how much they buy, when they buy, and why they buy (see Marketing Highlight 6-1). Marketers can study consumer purchases to find answers to questions about what they buy, where, and how much. But learning about the *whys* of consumer buying behavior and the buying decision process is not so easy—the answers are often locked deep within the consumer's head.

We are now ready to examine the stages buyers pass through to reach a buying decision. We will use the model in Figure 6-3, which shows the consumer as passing through five stages: *need recognition, information search, evaluation of alternatives, purchase decision,* and *postpurchase behavior.* Clearly, the buying process starts long before actual purchase and continues long after. This encourages the marketer to focus on the entire buying process rather than just the purchase decision.

This model implies that consumers pass through all five stages with every purchase. But in more routine purchases, consumers often skip or reverse some of these stages. A woman buying her regular brand of toothpaste would recognize the need and go right to the purchase decision, skipping information search and evaluation. However, we use the model in Figure 6-3 because it shows all the considerations that arise when a consumer faces a new and complex purchase situation.

To illustrate this model, we will again follow Jennifer Flores and try to understand how she became interested in buying an expensive camera and the stages she went through to make the final choice.

Need Recognition

The buying process starts with **need recognition**—with the buyer recognizing a problem or need. The buyer senses a difference between his or her *actual* state and some *desired* state. The need can be triggered by *internal stimuli* when one of the person's normal needs—hunger, thirst, sex—rises to a level high enough to become a drive. From previous experience, the person has learned how to cope with this drive and is motivated toward objects that he or she knows will satisfy it.

••••• ((((

MARKETING HIGHLIGHT 6-1

THE WHATS AND WHYS OF CONSUMER BUYING

No one knows better than Mom, right? But does she know how much underwear you own? Jockey International does. Or the number of ice cubes you put in a glass? Coca-Cola knows that one. Or how about which pretzels you usually eat first, the broken ones or the whole ones? Try asking Frito-Lay. Big companies know the whats, wheres, hows, and whens of their consumers. They figure out all sorts of things about us that we don't even know ourselves. To marketers, this isn't trivial pursuit—knowing all about the customer is the cornerstone of effective marketing. Most companies research us in detail and amass mountains of facts.

Coke knows that we put 3.2 ice cubes in a glass, see 69 of its commercials every year, and prefer cans to pop out of vending machines at a temperature of 35 degrees. One million of us drink Coke with breakfast every day. Kodak knows that amateur photographers muff more than two billion pictures every year. This fact led to the disc camera, which helped eliminate almost half of our out-of-focus and overexposed shots and became one of the most successful cameras in Kodak's history.

Each new day brings piles of fresh research reports detailing our buying habits and preferences. Did you know that 38 percent of Americans would rather have a tooth pulled than take their car to a dealership for repairs? We each spend $20 a year on flowers; Arkansas has the lowest consumption of peanut butter in the United States; 51 percent of all males put their left pants leg on first, whereas 65 percent of women start with the right leg; and if you send a husband and a wife to the store separately to buy beer, there is a 90 percent chance they will return with different brands.

Nothing about our behavior is sacred. Procter & Gamble once conducted a study to find out whether most of us fold or crumple our toilet paper; another study showed that 68 percent of consumers prefer their toilet paper to unwind over the spool rather than under. Abbott Laboratories figured out that one in four of us has "problem" dandruff, and Kimberly Clark, which makes Kleenex, has calculated that the average person blows his or her nose 256 times a year.

It's not that Americans are all that easy to figure

out. A few years ago, Campbell Soup gave up trying to learn our opinions about the ideal-sized meatball after a series of tests showed that we prefer one so big it wouldn't fit in the can.

Hoover hooked up timers and other equipment to vacuum cleaners in people's homes and learned that we spend about 35 minutes each week vacuuming, sucking up about 8 pounds of dust each year and using 6 bags to do so. Banks know that we write about 24 checks a month, and pharmaceutical companies know that all of us together take 52 million aspirins and 30 million sleeping pills a year. In fact, almost everything we swallow is closely monitored by someone. Each year, we consume 156 hamburgers, 95 hot dogs, 283 eggs, 5 pounds of yogurt, 9 pounds of cereal, 2 pounds of peanut butter, and 46 quarts of popcorn. We spend 90 minutes a day preparing our food and 40 minutes a day munching it. And as a nation, we down $650 million worth of antacid a year to help digest the food we eat.

Of all businesses, however, the prize for research thoroughness may go to toothpaste makers. Among other things, they know that our favorite toothbrush color is blue and that only 37 percent of us are using one that's more than six months old. About 47 percent of us put water on our brush before we apply the paste, 15 percent put water on after the paste, 24 percent do both, and 14 percent don't wet the brush at all.

Thus, most big marketing companies have answers to all the what, where, when, and how questions about their consumers' buying behavior. Seemingly trivial facts add up quickly and provide important input for designing marketing strategies. But to influence consumer behavior, marketers need the answer to one more question: Beyond knowing the whats and wherefores of behavior, they need to know the *whys*—what *causes* our buying behavior? That's a much harder question to answer.

Sources: John Koten, "You Aren't Paranoid If You Feel Someone Eyes You Constantly," *The Wall Street Journal*, March 29, 1985, pp. 1, 22; and "Offbeat Marketing," *Sales & Marketing Management*, January 1990, p. 35.

A need can also be triggered by *external stimuli*. Jennifer Flores passes a bakery and the sight of freshly baked bread stimulates her hunger; she admires a neighbor's new car; or she watches a television commercial for a Hawaiian vacation. These stimuli can lead her to recognize a problem or need. At this stage, the marketer needs to determine the factors and situations that usually trigger con-

FIGURE 6-3
Buyer decision process

sumer need recognition. The marketer should research consumers to find out what kinds of needs or problems arise, what brought them about, and how they led the consumer to this particular product.

Jennifer Flores might answer that she felt the need for a new hobby when her busy season at work slowed down, and she thought of cameras after talking to a friend about photography. By gathering such information, the marketer can identify the stimuli that most often trigger interest in the product and can develop marketing programs that involve these stimuli.

Information Search

An aroused consumer may or may not search for more information. If the consumer's drive is strong and a satisfying product is near at hand, the consumer is likely to buy it then. If not, the consumer may simply store the need in memory or undertake an **information search** related to the need.

At one level, the consumer may simply enter *heightened attention*. Here Jennifer Flores becomes more receptive to information about cameras. She pays attention to camera ads, cameras used by friends, and camera conversations. Or Jennifer may go into *active information search,* in which she looks for reading material, phones friends, and gathers information in other ways. The amount of searching she does will depend upon the strength of her drive, the amount of information she starts with, the ease of obtaining more information, the value she places on additional information, and the satisfaction she gets from searching. Normally the amount of consumer search activity increases as the consumer moves from decisions that involve limited problem solving to those that involve extensive problem solving.

The consumer can obtain information from any of several sources. These include

- *Personal sources:* family, friends, neighbors, acquaintances

- *Commercial sources:* advertising, salespeople, dealers, packaging, displays

- *Public sources:* mass media, consumer-rating organizations

- *Experiential sources:* handling, examining, using the product

The relative influence of these information sources varies with the product and the buyer. Generally, the consumer receives the most information about a product from commercial sources—those controlled by the marketer. The most effective sources, however, tend to be personal. Personal sources appear to be even more important in influencing the purchase of services.[3] Commercial sources normally *inform* the buyer, but personal sources *legitimize* or *evaluate* products for the buyer. For example, doctors normally learn of new drugs from commercial sources, but turn to other doctors for evaluative information.

As more information is obtained, the consumer's awareness and knowledge

Information sources: People usually receive the most information about a product from marketer-controlled sources.

of the available brands and features increases. In her information search, Jennifer Flores learned about the many camera brands available. The information also helped her drop certain brands from consideration. A company must design its marketing mix to make prospects aware of and knowledgeable about its brand. If it fails to do this, the company has lost its opportunity to sell to the customer. The company must also learn which other brands customers consider so that it knows its competition and can plan its own appeals.

The marketer should carefully identify consumers' sources of information and the importance of each source. Consumers should be asked how they first heard about the brand, what information they received, and the importance they place on different information sources. This information is critical in preparing effective communication to target markets.

Evaluation of Alternatives

We have seen how the consumer uses information to arrive at a set of final brand choices. How does the consumer choose among the alternative brands? The marketer needs to know about **alternative evaluation**—that is, how the consumer processes information to arrive at brand choices. Unfortunately, consumers do not use a simple and single evaluation process in all buying situations. Instead, several evaluation processes are at work.

Certain basic concepts help explain consumer evaluation processes. First, we assume that each consumer is trying to satisfy some need and is looking for certain *benefits* that can be acquired by buying a product or service. Further, each consumer sees a product as a bundle of *product attributes* with varying capacities for delivering these benefits and satisfying the need. For cameras, product attributes might include picture quality, ease of use, camera size, price, and other features. Consumers will vary as to which of these attributes they consider relevant and will pay the most attention to those attributes connected with their needs.

Second, the consumer will attach different *degrees of importance* to each attribute. A distinction can be drawn between the importance of an attribute and its salience. *Salient attributes* are those that come to a consumer's mind when he or she is asked to think of a product's characteristics. But these are not necessarily the most important attributes to the consumer. Some of them may be salient because the consumer has just seen an advertisement mentioning them or has had a problem with them, making these attributes "top-of-the-mind." There also may be other attributes that the consumer forgot, but whose importance would be recognized if they were mentioned. Marketers should be more concerned with attribute importance than attribute salience.

Third, the consumer is likely to develop a set of *brand beliefs* about where each brand stands on each attribute. The set of beliefs held about a particular brand is known as the **brand image.** The consumer's beliefs may vary from true attributes based on his or her experience and the effect of selective perception, selective distortion, and selective retention.

Fourth, the consumer is assumed to have a *utility function* for each attribute. The utility function shows how the consumer expects total product satisfaction to vary with different levels of different attributes. For example, Jennifer Flores may expect her satisfaction from a camera to increase with better picture quality; to peak with a medium-weight camera as opposed to a very light or very heavy one; to be higher for a 35-mm camera than for a 135-mm camera. If we combine the attribute levels at which her utilities are highest, they make up Jennifer's ideal camera. The camera would also be her preferred camera if it were available and affordable.

Fifth, the consumer arrives at attitudes toward the different brands through some *evaluation procedure*. Consumers have been found to use one or more of several evaluation procedures, depending on the consumer and the buying decision.

In Jennifer Flores's camera buying situation, suppose Jennifer has narrowed her choice set to four cameras: A, B, C, and D. Assume that she is interested primarily in four attributes—picture quality, ease of use, camera size, and price. Table 6-1 shows how she believes each brand rates on each attribute. Jennifer believes that brand A (say Nikon) will give her picture quality of 10 on a 10-point scale; is easy to use, 8; has medium size, 6; and is fairly expensive, 4. Similarly, she has beliefs about how the other cameras rate on these attributes. The marketer would like to be able to predict which camera Jennifer will buy.

TABLE 6-1
A Consumer's Brand Beliefs About Cameras

	ATTRIBUTE			
CAMERA	Picture Quality	Ease of Use	Camera Size	Price
A	10	8	6	4
B	8	9	8	3
C	6	8	10	5
D	4	3	7	8

Note: The number 10 represents the highest desirable score on that attribute. In the case of price, a high number means a low cost, which makes the camera more desirable.

Clearly, if one camera rated best on all the attributes, we could predict that Jennifer would choose it. But the brands vary in appeal. Some buyers will base their buying decision on only one attribute, and their choices are easy to predict. If Jennifer wants picture quality above everything, she should buy A; if she wants the camera that is easiest to use, she should buy B; if she wants the best camera size, she should buy C; if she wants the lowest-price camera, she should buy D.

Most buyers consider several attributes, but assign different importance to each. If we knew the importance weights that Jennifer assigns to the four attributes, we could predict her camera choice more reliably. Suppose Jennifer assigns 40 percent of the importance to the camera's picture quality, 30 percent to ease of use, 20 percent to its size, and 10 percent to its price. To find Jennifer's perceived value for each camera, we can multiply her importance weights by her beliefs about each camera. This gives us the following perceived values:

$$\text{Camera A} = .4(10) + .3(8) + .2(6) + .1(4) = 8.0$$

$$\text{Camera B} = .4(8) + .3(9) + .2(8) + .1(3) = 7.8$$

$$\text{Camera C} = .4(6) + .3(8) + .2(10) + .1(5) = 7.3$$

$$\text{Camera D} = .4(4) + .3(3) + .2(7) + .1(8) = 4.7$$

We would predict that Jennifer will favor camera A.

This model is called the *expectancy value model* of consumer choice.[4] It is one of several possible models describing how consumers go about evaluating alternatives. Consumers might evaluate a set of alternatives in other ways. For example, Jennifer might decide that she should consider only cameras that satisfy a set of minimum attribute levels. She might decide a camera would have to offer a picture quality greater than 7 *and* ease of use greater than 8. In this case, we would predict that she would choose camera B because only camera B satisfies the minimum requirements. This is called the *conjunctive model* of consumer choice. Or Jennifer might decide that she would settle for a camera that had a picture quality greater than 7 *or* ease of use greater than 8. In this case, A and B both meet the requirements. This is called the *disjunctive model* of consumer choice.

How consumers go about evaluating purchase alternatives depends on the individual consumer and the specific buying situation. In some cases, consumers use careful calculations and logical thinking. At other times, the same consumers do little or no evaluating; instead they buy on impulse and rely on intuition. Sometimes consumers make buying decisions on their own; sometimes they turn to friends, consumer guides, or salespeople for buying advice.

Marketers should study buyers to find out how they actually evaluate brand alternatives. If they know what evaluative processes go on, marketers can take steps to influence the buyer's decision. Suppose Jennifer is inclined to by a Nikon camera because she rates it high on picture quality and ease of use. What strategies might another camera maker, say Minolta, use to influence people like Jennifer? There are several. Minolta could modify its camera so that it delivers better pictures or other features that consumers like Jennifer want. It could try to change buyers' beliefs about how its camera rates on key attributes, especially if con-

Accept No Limitations.

A mountain climber caught forever halfway up the slope, frozen there by the Minolta Maxxum® 7000i. Because camera and athlete were equal to the challenge.

Here, Maxxum's multi-pattern metering captured the full contrast between climber and snow. While Maxxum's powerful telephoto zoom—one of over 30 autofocus lenses—spanned the distance between mountains.

Put simply, Maxxum technology can help you surmount any obstacle. With its unmatched autofocus system, the possibilities are as limitless as your imagination.

MAXXUM 7000i
ONLY FROM THE MIND OF MINOLTA

MINOLTA

To rate higher with consumers, Minolta added autofocus, motorized film control, and other features. It took major competitor Canon three years to catch up. Minolta continues to add new features in order to stay ahead of the competition.

sumers currently underestimate the camera's qualities. It could try to change buyers' beliefs about Nikon and other competitors. Finally, it could try to change the list of attributes that buyers consider, or the importance attached to these attributes. For example, it might advertise that all good cameras have about equal picture quality, and that its lighter-weight, lower-priced camera is a better buy for people like Jennifer.

Purchase Decision

In the evaluation stage, the consumer ranks brands and forms purchase intentions. Generally, the consumer's **purchase decision** will be to buy the most preferred brand, but two factors, shown in Figure 6-4, can come between the purchase *intention* and the purchase *decision*. The first factor is the *attitudes of others*. If Jennifer Flores's husband feels strongly that Jennifer should buy the lowest-priced camera, then the chances of Jennifer buying a more expensive camera will be reduced. How much another person's attitudes will affect Jennifer's choices depends both on the strength of the other person's attitudes toward her buying decision and on Jennifer's motivation to comply with that person's wishes.

Purchase intention is also influenced by *unexpected situational factors*. The consumer may form a purchase intention based on factors such as expected family income, expected price, and expected benefits from the product. When the consumer is about to act, unexpected situational factors may arise to change the purchase intention. Jennifer Flores may lose her job, some other purchase may be-

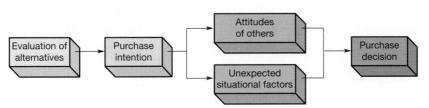

FIGURE 6-4
Steps between evaluation of alternatives and a purchase decision

come more urgent, or a friend may report being disappointed in her preferred camera.

Thus, preferences and even purchase intentions do not always result in actual purchase choice. They may direct purchase behavior, but may not fully determine the outcome. Figure 6-5 shows a fairly typical purchase outcome. In a study of 100 people who stated an intention to buy brand A of an appliance within the next 12 months, only 44 ended up buying the particular appliance, and only 30 purchased brand A.

A consumer's decision to change, postpone, or avoid a purchase decision is influenced heavily by *perceived risk*. Many purchases involve some risk taking.[5] Anxiety results when consumers cannot be certain about the purchase outcome. The amount of perceived risk varies with the amount of money at stake, the amount of purchase uncertainty, and the amount of consumer self-confidence. A consumer takes certain actions to reduce risk, such as avoiding purchase decisions, gathering more information, and looking for national brand names and products with warranties. The marketer must understand the factors that provoke feelings of risk in consumers and must provide information and support that will reduce the perceived risk.

Postpurchase Behavior

The marketer's job does not end when the product is bought. After purchasing the product, the consumer will be satisfied or dissatisfied and will engage in **postpurchase behavior** of interest to the marketer. What determines whether the buyer is satisfied or dissatisfied with a purchase? The answer lies in the relationship between the *consumer's expectations* and the product's *perceived performance*. If the product falls short of expectations, the consumer is disappointed; if it meets expectations, the consumer is satisfied; if it exceeds expectations, the consumer is delighted.

Consumers base their expectations on messages they receive from sellers, friends, and other information sources. If the seller exaggerates the product's performance, consumer expectations will not be met—a situation that leads to dissatisfaction. The larger the gap between expectations and performance, the greater the consumer's dissatisfaction. This fact suggests that the seller should make product claims that represent faithfully the product's performance so that buyers are satisfied.

Some sellers might even understate performance levels to boost consumer satisfaction with the product. For example, Boeing sells aircraft worth tens of millions of dollars each, and consumer satisfaction is important for repeat purchases and the company's reputation. Boeing's salespeople sell their products with facts and knowledge, not with inflated promises. In fact, these salespeople tend to be conservative when they estimate their product's potential benefits. They almost always underestimate fuel efficiency—they promise a 5 percent savings that turns out to be 8 percent. Customers are delighted with better-than-expected performance; they buy again and tell other potential customers that Boeing lives up to its promises.[6]

Almost all major purchases result in **cognitive dissonance,** or discomfort caused by postpurchase conflict. Consumers are satisfied with the benefits of the chosen brand and glad to avoid the drawbacks of the brands not purchased. On the other hand, every purchase involves compromise. Consumers feel uneasy about acquiring the drawbacks of the chosen brand and about losing the benefits of the brands not purchased. Thus, consumers feel at least some postpurchase dissonance for every purchase.[7]

FIGURE 6-5
Results of purchase intentions and purchase decisions

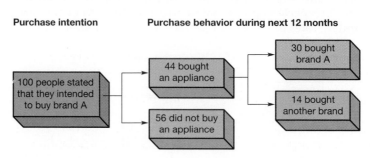

Why is it so important to satisfy the customer? Such satisfaction is important because a company's sales come from two basic groups—*new customers* and *repeat customers*. It usually costs more to attract new customers than to retain current ones. Thus, keeping current customers is often more critical than attracting new ones, and the best way to do this is to make current customers happy. A satisfied customer buys a product again, talks favorably to others about the product, pays less attention to competing brands and advertising, and buys other products from the company. Many marketers go beyond merely *meeting* the expectations of customers—they aim to *delight* the customer. A delighted customer is even more likely to purchase again and to talk favorably about the product and company.

A dissatisfied consumer responds differently. Whereas, on average, a satisfied customer tells 3 people about a good product experience, a dissatisfied customer gripes to 11 people. In fact, one study showed that 13 percent of the people who had a problem with an organization complained about the company to more than 20 people.[8] Clearly, bad word of mouth travels farther and faster than good word of mouth and can quickly damage consumer attitudes about a company and its products.

Therefore, a company would be wise to measure customer satisfaction regularly. It cannot simply rely on dissatisfied customers to volunteer their complaints when they are dissatisfied. In fact, 96 percent of unhappy customers never tell the company about their problem. Company's should set up suggestion systems to *encourage* customers to complain (see Marketing Highlight 6-2). In this way, the company can learn how well it is doing and how it can improve. The 3M Company claims that over two-thirds of its new-product ideas come from listening to customer complaints. But listening is not enough—the company also must respond constructively to the complaints it receives.

Thus, in general, dissatisfied consumers may try to reduce their dissonance by taking any of several actions. In the case of Jennifer Flores, Nikon purchaser, she may return the camera, or look at Nikon ads that tell of the camera's benefits, or talk with friends who will tell her how much they like her new camera.

Beyond seeking out and responding to complaints, marketers can take additional steps to reduce consumer postpurchase dissatisfaction and to help customers feel good about their purchases. For example, automobile companies can write or phone new car owners with congratulations on having selected a fine car. They can place ads showing satisfied owners driving their new cars. They can obtain customer suggestions for improvements and list the location of available services. Postpurchase communications to buyers have been shown to result in fewer product returns and order cancellations.

Understanding the consumer's needs and buying process is the foundation of successful marketing. By understanding how buyers go through need recognition, information search, evaluation of alternatives, the purchase decision, and postpurchase behavior, the marketer can pick up many clues as to how to meet the buyer's needs. By understanding the various participants in the buying process and the major influences on their buying behavior, the marketer can develop an effective program to support an attractive offer to the target market.

THE BUYER DECISION PROCESS FOR NEW PRODUCTS

We have looked at the stages buyers go through in trying to satisfy a need. Buyers may pass quickly or slowly through these stages, and some of the stages may even be reversed. Much depends on the nature of the buyer, the product, and the buying situation.

We now look at how buyers approach the purchase of new products. A **new product** is a good, service, or idea that is perceived by some potential customers as new.

It may have been around for a while, but our interest is in how consumers learn about products for the first time and make decisions on whether to adopt them. We define **adoption process** as "the mental process through which an individual passes from first learning about an innovation to final adoption,"[9]

POSTPURCHASE SATISFACTION: TURNING COMPANY CRITICS INTO LOYAL CUSTOMERS

What should companies do with dissatisfied customers? Everything they can! Studies show that customers tell four times as many other people about bad experiences as they do about good ones. Thus, unhappy customers not only stop buying but also can quickly damage the company's image. In contrast, dealing effectively with gripes can actually boost customer loyalty and the company's image. According to one study, 54 percent to 70 percent of consumers who register complaints will again do business with the company if their complaint is resolved. That figure jumps to a whopping 95 percent if the complaint was handled quickly. Moreover, customers whose complaints have been satisfactorily resolved tell an average of five other people about the good treatment they received. Thus, enlightened companies don't try to hide from dissatisfied customers or to dodge responsibility. To the contrary, they go out of their way to *encourage* customers to complain, then bend over backwards to make disgruntled buyers happy again.

The first opportunity to handle gripes often comes at the point of purchase. Thus, many retailers and other service firms teach their customer-contact people how to resolve problems and diffuse customer anger. They arm their customer service representatives with liberal return and refund policies and other damage-control tools. Some companies go to extremes to see things the customer's way and to reward complaining, seemingly without regard for profit impact. For example, Hechinger, the large hardware and garden products retailer, accepts returns of items even when customers have obviously abused them. In other cases, it sends a dozen roses to purchasers who are particularly upset.

Specialty retailer Neiman Marcus is equally gracious with complainers. "We're not just looking for today's sale. We want a long-term relationship with our customers," says Gwen Baum, the chain's director of customer satisfaction. "If that means taking back a piece of Baccarat crystal that isn't from one of our stores, we'll do it." This generosity appears to help profits more than harm them—both Hechinger and Neiman Marcus enjoy earnings well above industry averages. Such actions create tremendous buyer loyalty and goodwill, and for most retailers, customers who return items that they bought elsewhere or have already used account for less than 5 percent of all returns.

Many companies have also set up toll-free 800-number systems to better coax out and deal with consumer problems. Today, more than half of all companies with more than $10 million in sales use 800 numbers to handle complaints, inquiries, and orders. Last year, these companies spent some $4.5 billion on more than 8 billion 800-number calls. For example, Coca-Cola set up its 1-800-GET-COKE lines in late 1983 after studies showed that only 1 unhappy person in 50 bothers to complain. "The other 49 simply switch brands," explains the company's director of consumer affairs, "so it just makes good sense to seek them out." Consumers made good use of the 800 number some years ago when Coca-Cola tried to replace old Coke with new. Following the introduction of New Coke, the company received as many as 12,000 calls a day, most from unhappy Coke drinkers. However, on the day after it returned Coke Classic to the shelves, Coca-Cola received 18,000 calls saying thank you.

Since 1979, Procter & Gamble has put an 800

and **adoption** as the decision by an individual to become a regular user of the product.

Stages in the Adoption Process

Consumers go through five stages in the process of adopting a new product:

1. *Awareness.* The consumer becomes aware of the new product, but lacks information about it.

2. *Interest.* The consumer seeks information about the new product.

3. *Evaluation.* The consumer considers whether trying the new product makes sense.

4. *Trial.* The consumer tries the new product on a small scale to improve his or her estimate of its value.

5. *Adoption.* The consumer decides to make full and regular use of the new product.

Making buyers happy: GE's Answer Center handles customers' concerns 365 days a year, 24 hours a day.

number on every consumer product it sells in the United States. P&G now receives about 800,000 mail and phone contacts about its products each year—mostly complaints, requests for information, and testimonials. The 800-number system serves as an early warning signal for product and customer problems. So far, the system has resulted in hundreds of actions and improvements ranging from tracking down batches of defective packages to putting high-altitude baking instructions on Duncan Hines brownies packages.

General Electric's Answer Center may be the most extensive 800-number system in the nation. It handles 3 million calls a year, 15 percent of them complaints. At the heart of the system is a giant database that provides the center's service reps with instant access to 750,000 answers concerning 8,500 models in 120 product lines. The center receives some unusual calls, as when a submarine off the Connecticut coast requested help fixing a motor, or when technicians on a James Bond film

couldn't get their underwater lights working. Still, according to GE, its people resolve 90 percent of complaints or inquiries on the first call, and complainers often become even more loyal customers. Although the company may spend an average of $3.50 per call, it reaps two to three times that much in new sales and warranty savings.

In some companies, responsibility for assuring customer satisfaction goes all the way to the top. For example, J. W. Marriott, Jr., chairman of Marriott hotels, "reads about 10 percent of the 8,000 letters and 2 percent of the 750,000 guest comment cards the company receives each year. When Marriott was president in the late 1960s, some 30,000 hotel guests submitted comments each year. He read every one."

The best way to keep customers happy is to provide good products and services in the first place. Short of that, however, a company must develop a good system for ferreting out and handling consumer problems. Such a system can be much more than a necessary evil—customer happiness usually shows up on the company's bottom line. One recent study found that dollars invested in complaint-handling and inquiry systems yield an average return of between 100 percent and 200 percent. Maryanne Rasmussen, vice-president of worldwide quality at American Express, offers this formula: "Better complaint handling equals higher customer satisfaction equals higher brand loyalty equals higher performance."

Sources: Quotes from Patricia Sellers, "How to Handle Consumer Gripes," *Fortune,* October 24, 1988, pp. 88-100. Also see Mary C. Gilley and Richard W. Hansen, "Consumer Complaint Handling as a Strategic Marketing Tool," *Journal of Consumer Marketing,* Fall 1985, pp. 5-16; Joyce Wycoff, "Customer Service: Evolution and Revolution," *Sales & Marketing Management,* May 1991, pp. 44-51; Frank Rose, "Now Quality Means Service Too," *Fortune,* April 22, 1991, pp. 97-108; and Roland T. Rust, Bala Subramanian, and Mark Wells, "Making Complaints a Management Tool," *Marketing Management,* Vol. 1, No. 3, Fall 1992, pp. 41-45.

This model suggests that the new-product marketer should think about how to help consumers move through these stages. A manufacturer of large-screen televisions may discover that many consumers in the interest stage do not move to the trial stage because of uncertainty and the large investment. If these same consumers would be willing to use a large-screen television on a trial basis for a small fee, the manufacturer should consider offering a trial-use plan with an option to buy.

Individual Differences in Innovativeness

People differ greatly in their readiness to try new products. In each product area, there are "consumption pioneers" and early adopters. Other individuals adopt new products much later. This has led to a classification of people into the adopter categories shown in Figure 6-6.

After a slow start, an increasing number of people adopt the new product. The number of adopters reaches a peak and then drops off as fewer nonadopters remain. Innovators are defined as the first 2.5 percent of the buyers to adopt a new idea (those beyond 2 standard deviations from mean adoption time); the

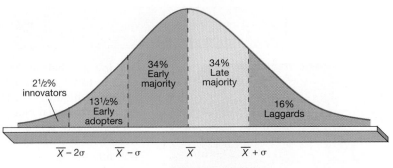

FIGURE 6-6
Adopter categorization on the basis of relative time of adoption of innovations
Source: Redrawn from Everett M. Rogers, *Diffusion of Innovations,* 3rd ed. (New York: 1983), p. 247. Adapted with permission of Macmillan Publishing Company, Inc. Copyright © 1962, 1971, 1983 by the Free Press.

early adopters are the next 13.5 percent (between one and two standard deviations); and so forth.

The five adopter groups have differing values. *Innovators* are venturesome—they try new ideas at some risk. *Early adopters* are guided by respect—they are opinion leaders in their community and adopt new ideas early but carefully. The *early majority* are deliberate—although they rarely are leaders, they adopt new ideas before the average person. The *late majority* are skeptical—they adopt an innovation only after a majority of people have tried it. Finally, *laggards* are tradition bound—they are suspicious of changes and adopt the innovation only when it has become something of a tradition itself.

This adopter classification suggests that an innovating firm should research the characteristics of innovators and early adopters and should direct marketing efforts to them. For example, home computer innovators have been found to be middle aged and higher in income and education than noninnovators, and they tend to be opinion leaders. They also tend to be more rational, more introverted, and less social. In general, innovators tend to be relatively younger, better educated, and higher in income than later adopters and nonadopters. They are more receptive to unfamiliar things, rely more on their own values and judgment, and are more willing to take risks. They are less brand loyal and more likely to take advantage of special promotions such as discounts, coupons, and samples.[10]

Role of Personal Influence

Personal influence plays a major role in the adoption of new products. **Personal influence** describes the effect of statements made by one person on another's attitude or probability of purchase. Consumers consult each other for opinions about new products and brands, and the advice of others can strongly influence buying behavior.

Personal influence is more important in some situations and for some individuals than for others. Personal influence is more important in the evaluation stage of the adoption process than in the other stages. It has more influence on later adopters than early adopters, and it is more important in risky buying situations than in safe situations.

Influence of Product Characteristics on Rate of Adoption

The characteristics of the new product affect its rate of adoption. Some products catch on almost overnight (frisbees), whereas others take a long time to gain acceptance (personal computers). Five characteristics are especially important in influencing an innovation's rate of adoption. For example, consider the characteristics of personal computers for home use in relation to the rate of adoption:

- *Relative advantage:* the degree to which the innovation appears superior to existing products. The greater the perceived relative advantage of using a personal computer—say, in preparing income taxes and keeping financial records—the sooner the personal computer will be adopted.

- *Compatibility:* the degree to which the innovation fits the values and experiences of potential consumers. Personal computers, for example, are highly compatible with the lifestyles found in upper-middle-class homes.

Product characteristics affect the rate of adoption—products like home computers take a long time to gain wide acceptance.

■ *Complexity:* the degree to which the innovation is difficult to understand or use. Personal computers are complex and will therefore take a longer time to penetrate U.S. homes.

■ *Divisibility:* the degree to which the innovation may be tried on a limited basis. To the extent that people can rent personal computers with an option to buy, the product's rate of adoption will increase.

■ *Communicability:* the degree to which the results of using the innovation can be observed or described to others. Because personal computers lend themselves to demonstration and description, their use will spread faster among consumers.

Other characteristics influence the rate of adoption, such as initial and ongoing costs, risk and uncertainty, and social approval. The new-product marketer has to research all these factors when developing the new product and its marketing program.

CONSUMER BEHAVIOR ACROSS INTERNATIONAL BORDERS

Understanding consumer behavior is difficult enough for companies marketing within the borders of a single country. For companies operating in many countries, however, understanding and serving the needs of consumers can be daunting. Although consumers in different countries may have some things in common, their values, attitudes, and behaviors often vary dramatically. International marketers must understand such differences and adjust their products and marketing programs accordingly.

Sometimes the differences are obvious. For example, in the United States, where most people eat cereal regularly for breakfast, Kellogg focuses its marketing on persuading consumers to select a Kellogg brand rather than a competitor's brand. In France, however, where most people prefer croissants and coffee or no breakfast at all, Kellogg advertising simply attempts to convince people that they should eat cereal for breakfast. Its packaging includes step-by-step instructions on how to prepare cereal.

Often, differences across international markets are more subtle. They may result from physical differences in consumers and their environments. For example, Remington makes smaller electric shavers to fit the smaller hands of Japanese consumers; and battery-powered shavers for the British market, where few bathrooms have electrical outlets. Other differences result from varying customs. Consider the following examples:

■ Shaking your head from side to side means "no" in most countries but "yes" in Bulgaria and Sri Lanka.

■ In South America, Southern Europe, and many Arab countries, touching another person is a sign of warmth and friendship. In the Orient, it is considered an invasion of privacy.

CONSUMER BEHAVIOR DIFFERENCES ACROSS BORDERS: GLOBAL STANDARDIZATION OR ADAPTATION?

The marketing concept holds that consumers vary in their needs and that marketing programs will be more effective if tailored to each customer target group. If this concept applies within a country, it should apply even more in foreign markets where economic, political, and cultural conditions vary widely. Consumers in different countries have varied geographic, demographic, economic, and cultural characteristics—a fact that results in different needs and wants, spending power, product preferences, and shopping patterns. Because most marketers believe that these differences are hard to change, they adapt their products, prices, distribution channels, and promotion approaches to fit unique consumer desires in each country.

However, some global marketers are bothered by what they see as too much adaptation. Consider Gillette:

> Gillette sells over eight hundred products in more than two hundred countries. It now finds itself in a situation where it uses different brand names and formulations for the same products in different countries. For example, Gillette's Silkience shampoo is called Soyance in France, Sientel in Italy, and Silience in Germany; it uses the same formula in some cases but varies it in others. It also varies the product's advertising messages because each Gillette country manager proposes several changes that he or she thinks will increase local sales. These and similar adaptations for its hundreds of other products raise Gillette's costs and dilute its global brand power.

As a result, many companies have imposed more standardization on their products and marketing efforts. They have created so-called world brands that are manufactured and marketed in much the same way worldwide. These marketers believe that advances in communication, transportation, and travel are turning the world into a common marketplace. They claim that people around the world want basically the same products and lifestyles. Everyone wants things that make life easier and that increase both free time and buying power. Common needs and wants thus create global markets for standardized products.

Whereas traditional marketers cater to differences between specific markets and respond with a proliferation of highly adapted products, marketers who standardize globally sell more or less the same product the same way to all consumers. They agree that differences exist in consumer wants and buying behavior and that these differences cannot be entirely ignored. But they argue that wants are changeable. Despite what consumers say they want, all consumers want good products at lower prices:

> If the price is low enough, they will take highly standardized world products, even if these aren't exactly what mother said was suitable, what immemorial custom decreed was right, or what market research . . . asserted was preferred.

Thus, proponents of global standardization claim, international marketers should adapt products and marketing programs only when local wants cannot be changed or avoided. Standardization results in lower production, distribution, marketing, and management costs, and thus lets the company offer consumers higher quality and more reliable products at lower prices. They would advise an auto company to make a world car, a shampoo company to make a world shampoo, and a farm-equipment company to make a world tractor. And, in fact, some companies have successfully marketed global products—for example, Coca-Cola, McDonald's hamburgers, A. T. Cross pens and pencils, Black & Decker tools, and Sony Walkmans. Some products are more global and require less adaptation. Yet, even in

- In Norway or Malaysia, it's rude to leave something on your plate when eating; in Egypt, it's rude *not* to leave something on your plate.
- A door-to-door salesperson might find it tough going in Italy, where it is improper for a man to call on a woman if she is home alone.[11]

Failing to understand such differences in customs and behaviors from one country to another can spell disaster for a marketer's international products and programs.

Coca-Cola sells highly standardized products world-wide, but even Coke adapts its product and packaging somewhat to local tastes and conditions.

these cases, companies make some adaptations. Coca-Cola is less sweet or less carbonated in certain countries; McDonald's uses chili sauce instead of ketchup on its hamburgers in Mexico; and Cross pens and pencils have different advertising messages in some countries.

Moreover, the assertion that global standardization will lead to lower costs and prices, causing more goods to be snapped up by price-sensitive consumers, is debatable:

Mattel Toys had sold its Barbie Doll successfully in dozens of countries without modification. But in Japan, it did not sell well. Takara, Mattel's Japanese licensee, surveyed eighth-grade Japanese girls and their parents and found that they thought the doll's breasts were too big and that its legs were too long. Mattell, however, was reluctant to modify the doll because this would require additional production, packaging, and advertising costs. Finally, Takara won out and Mattel made a special Japanese Barbie. Within two years, Takara had sold over two million of the modified dolls. Clearly, incremental revenues far exceeded the incremental costs.

Rather than assuming that their products can be introduced without change in other countries, companies should review all possible adaptation elements and determine which would add more revenues than costs. The adaptation elements include the following:

Product features	Colors	Advertising themes
Brand name	Materials	Advertising media
Labeling	Prices	Advertising execution
Packaging	Sales promotion	

One study showed that companies made adaptations in one or more of these areas on 80 percent of their foreign-directed products; the average product was adapted in 4 out of the 11 areas.

So which approach is best—global standardization or adaption? Clearly, global standardization is not an all-or-nothing proposition, but rather a matter of degree. Companies are justified in looking for more standardization to help keep down costs and prices and build greater global brand power. But they must remember that although standardization saves money, competitors are always ready to offer more of what consumers in each country want, and that they might pay dearly for replacing long-run marketing thinking with short-run financial thinking. Some international marketers suggest that companies should "think globally but act locally." The corporate level gives strategic direction; local units focus on the individual consumer differences. Global marketing, yes; global standardization, not necessarily.

Sources: See John A. Quelch and Edward J. Hoff, "Customizing Global Marketing," *Harvard Business Review,* May-June, 1986, pp. 59-68; Theodore Levitt, "The Globalization of Markets," *Harvard Business Review,* May-June 1983, pp. 92-102; George S. Yip, "Global Strategy . . . In a World of Nations?" *Sloan Management Review,* Fall 1989, pp. 29-41; Kamran Kashani, "Beware the Pitfalls of Global Marketing," *Harvard Business Review,* September-October 1989, pp. 91-98; and Saeed Saminee and Kendall Roth, "The Influence of Global Marketing Standardization on Performance," *Journal of Marketing,* April 1992, pp. 1-17.

Marketers must decide on the degree to which they will adapt their products and marketing programs to meet the unique needs of consumers in various markets. On the one hand, they want to standardize their offerings in order to simplify operations and take advantage of cost economies. On the other hand, adapting marketing efforts within each country results in products and programs that better satisfy the needs of local consumers. The question of whether to adapt or standardize the marketing mix across international markets has created a lively debate in recent years (see Marketing Highlight 6-3).

SUMMARY

Before planning its marketing strategy, a company needs to identify its target consumers and the types of decision processes they go through. Although many *buying decisions* involve only one decision maker, other decisions may involve several participants who play such roles as *initiator, influencer, decider, buyer,* and *user.* The marketer's job is to identify the other buying participants, their buying criteria, and their level of influence on the buyer. The marketing program should be designed to appeal to and reach the other key participants as well as the buyer.

The number of buying participants and the amount of buying effort increase with the complexity of the buying situation. There are three types of *buying decision behavior: routine response behavior, limited problem solving,* and *extensive problem solving.*

In buying something, the buyer goes through a decision process consisting of *need recognition, information search, evaluation of alternatives, purchase decision,* and *post-*

purchase behavior. The marketer's job is to understand the buyer's behavior at each stage and the influences that are operating. This allows the marketer to develop a significant and effective marketing program for the target market.

With regard to new products, consumers respond at different rates, depending on the consumer's characteristics and the product's characteristics. Manufacturers try to bring their new products to the attention of potential early adopters, particularly those with opinion leader characteristics.

Understanding consumer behavior is difficult enough for companies marketing within the borders of a single country. For companies operating internationally, however, understanding and serving the needs of consumers can be even more difficult. Consumers in different countries may vary dramatically in their values, attitudes, and behaviors. International marketers must understand such differences and adjust their products and marketing programs accordingly.

 # KEY TERMS

Adoption 174

Adoption process 173

Alternative evaluation 169

Brand image 169

Buyer 163

Cognitive dissonance 172

Complex buying behavior 164

Decider 163

Dissonance-reducing buying behavior 164

Habitual buying behavior 164

Influencer 163

Information search 168

Initiator 163

Need recognition 166

New product 173

Personal influence 176

Postpurchase behavior 172

Purchase decision 171

User 163

Variety-seeking buying behavior 165

 # DISCUSSING THE ISSUES

1. For many Americans, changing to a healthier lifestyle would be an innovation. This might require changes in diet, exercise, smoking, and drinking. Discuss this innovation in terms of its relative advantage, compatibility, complexity, divisibility, and communicability. Is a healthy lifestyle likely to be adopted quickly by most Americans?

2. What factors do you think would be very important to most consumers in deciding where to do their grocery shopping? Using these factors, discuss how the expectancy value, conjunctive, and disjunctive models of consumer choice could explain a shopper's choice of a supermarket.

3. Why is the postpurchase behavior stage included in the model of the buying process? What relevance does this stage have for marketers?

4. Describe how cents-off coupons, sweepstakes, bonus-

size packs, and other forms of sales promotion can help move consumers through the stages of the adoption process. Are there any drawbacks to using these techniques to promote product adoption?

5. Consumers play many different roles in the buying process: initiator, influencer, decider, buyer, and user. Who plays these roles when a mother is buying Teenage Mutant Ninja Turtles Breakfast Cereal? L'Eggs pantyhose? Purina Dog Chow? A new VCR?

6. Digital audiotape recorders (DATs) have been on the market for several years. They offer near-perfect fidelity in recording music and in playing prerecorded tapes. They are not compatible with existing cassette recorders; cost $500 to $1,000 or more; and the few available prerecorded tapes sell for more than $20. How common are DATs? How did this innovation's characteristics affect its rate of adoption in the consumer market?

APPLYING THE CONCEPTS

1. What people played the different buying decision roles that led to the choice of the school you are attending? List who was the initiator, the influencer, the decider, the buyer, and the user. Rank how strong the influence of each role was in the final choice.

2. Examining our own purchases can reveal ways in which buying decisions really occur.

- Describe the five stages of your own buyer decision process for a major purchase such as a camera, stereo, or car.
- Next, describe your decision process for a minor purchase such as a candy bar or a soda.
- Are the decision processes the same for major and minor purchases? Which steps differ, and why do they change?

MAKING MARKETING DECISIONS:

SMALL WORLD COMMUNICATIONS, INC.

Tom Campbell and Lyn Jones are developing the ideas for their company's product line. Their marketing research has told them that computer users have a need for products or services to help them manage their communications tasks more easily. It is also clear that there are segments of very different types of users. Each segment has a particular type of need, a certain level of computer expertise, and a general set of beliefs and attitudes. Tom was talking about the outlook: "It's an interesting situation from a marketing point of view. Some computer users—especially the really sophisticated business users—are really frustrated by trying to manage a whole array of communication functions. Take Susan Mahalanobis, a friend of mine who runs a small business research and consulting firm. She uses the InterNet network to reach academic centers and libraries, CompuServe for electronic mail and information services, Dow Jones for financial information, Lexis for legal references, MCI Mail for faxes, Prodigy for personal communications, and maybe more. She needs special software for most of those services, and she needs to input account numbers and passwords and special commands for each one. She also has the need to get visual information into her computer: sometimes scanning pictures, sometimes capturing little snapshots out of the training videos she produces. And she's got a Rolodex with a few hundred phone numbers to keep track of. Susan's a real innovator, and she'd buy almost anything to help her manage that stuff more efficiently. And at the other end of the spectrum, maybe half of computer users have barely heard about any of this." Lynette smiled. Tom was talking to her about consumer needs, and he hadn't mentioned a single technology or new chip design. He was learning.

"I think you've put the situation in a nutshell, Tom. Susan's a real expert, and she probably teaches herself almost everything she knows about computers. She recognizes her needs, but there isn't a product out there to help her—at least not yet. The other half of users might have a lot of use for computer communications, but they don't even have a clue about the possibilities that exist. A lot of those people probably have computer professionals at work

to train them and to help make decisions about what hardware and software to buy. The ones that don't have experts to help probably depend on magazine reviews and salespeople to help them along. We've got a real spectrum to deal with, and it will be changing fast. Today's beginner might be tomorrow's computer geek—no offense meant, old man."

WHAT NOW?

1. Small World Communications plans to sell hardware and software that offers unique solutions to users' communications problems. Consider the consumer buying roles illustrated in Figure 6-1. Different situations affect who plays the role of initiator, influencer, decider, buyer, and user. List who might play each of these roles in buying Small World products when the main user[s] is: (a) an independent businessperson, expert at computers, who operates with a staff of two part-time helpers; (b) a middle-management user at a large corporation with full computer services and purchasing departments; (c) several family members using a home computer for homework, amusement, and occasional business projects. Discuss how these different buyer decision processes might affect Small World's marketing programs.

2. Many factors affect how quickly products are adopted, including five key product characteristics: relative advantage, compatibility, complexity, divisibility, and communicability. (a) Small World is thinking of marketing a computer circuit board that would allow easy connections to a telephone line, a video camera or VCR, and a page scanner for inputting graphic images. Discuss how computer experts and novices might perceive this product in terms of its five characteristics. Do you think this product will be viewed differently by different groups? (b) Do you think individual users' perceptions might change with time? Discuss how this type of product might be viewed in 1998.

REFERENCES

1. Portions adapted from Joseph Pereira, "The Well-Healed: Pricey Sneakers Worn in Inner City Help Set Nation's Trend," *The Wall Street Journal,* December 1, 1988, pp. 1, 6. Also see Keith Hammonds, "The 'Blacktop' Is Paving Reebok's Road to Recovery," *Business Week,* August 12, 1991, p. 27; Marcy Magiera, "Small Rivals Leap as L.A. Gear Stumbles," *Advertising Age,* June 8, 1992, p. 12; and Geraldine E. Willigan, "High-Performance Marketing: An Interview with Nike's Phil Knight," *Harvard Business Review,* July-August 1992, pp. 90-101.

2. See Henry Assael, *Consumer Behavior and Marketing Action* (Boston: Kent Publishing, 1987), Chap. 4. An earlier classification of three types of consumer buying behavior—routine response behavior, limited problem solving, and extensive problem solving—can be found in John A. Howard and Jagdish Sheth, *The Theory of Consumer Behavior* (New York: John Wiley, 1969), pp. 27-28. Also see John A. Howard, *Consumer Behavior in Marketing Strategy* (Englewood Cliffs, NJ: Prentice Hall, 1989).

3. Keith B. Murray, "A Test of Services Marketing Theory: Consumer Information Acquisition Theory," *Journal of Marketing,* January 1991, pp. 10-25.

4. This model was developed by Martin Fishbein. See Martin Fishbein and Icek Ajzen, *Belief, Attitude, Intention, and Behavior* (Reading, MA: Addison-Wesley, 1975). For a critical review of this model, see Paul W. Miniard and Joel B. Cohen, "An Examination of the Fishbein-Ajzen Behavioral Intentions Model's Concepts and Measures," *Journal of Experimental Social Psychology,* May 1981, pp. 309-99.

5. See Raymond A. Bauer, "Consumer Behavior as Risk Taking," in *Risk Taking and Information Handling in Consumer Behavior,* Donald F. Cox, ed. (Boston: Division of Research, Harvard Business School, 1967); John W. Vann, "A Multi-Distributional Conceptual Framework for the Study of Perceived Risk," inThomas C. Kinnear, ed., *Advance in Consumer Research* (Association for Consumer Research, 1983), XI, pp. 442-46; and Robert B. Settle and Pamela L. Alreck, "Reducing Buyers' Sense of Risk," *Marketing Communications,* January 1989 pp. 19-24.

6. See Bill Kelley, "How to Sell Airplanes, Boeing-Style," *Sales and Marketing Management,* December 9, 1985, p. 34.

7. See Leon Festinger, *A Theory of Cognitive Dissonance* (Stanford, CA: Stanford University Press, 1957); and Leon G. Schiffman and Leslie Lazar Kanuk, *Consumer Behavior* (Englewood Cliffs, NJ: Prentice Hall, 1991), pp. 304-5.

8. See Karl Albrect and Ron Zemke, *Service America!* (Homewood, IL: Dow-Jones Irwin, 1985), pp. 6-7; and Frank Rose, "Now Quality Means Service Too," *Fortune,* April 22, 1991, pp. 97-108.

9. The following discussion draws heavily from Everett M. Rogers, *Diffusion of Innovations,* 3rd ed. (New York: Free Press, 1983). Also see Hubert Gatignon and Thomas S. Robertson, "A Propositional Inventory for New Diffusion Research," *Journal of Consumer Research,* March 1985, pp. 849-67.

10. See Schiffman and Kanuk, *Consumer Behavior,* Chap. 18.

11. For these and other examples, see William J. Stanton, Michael J. Etzel, and Bruce J. Walker, *Fundamentals of Marketing* (New York: McGraw-Hill, Inc., 1991), p. 536.

VIDEO CASE 6

SPENDING MONEY TO SAVE TIME

It's 6:15 P.M. and Charlotte Walker, a typical working parent, has just spent an hour on the freeway. Now she's home from work and it's "arsenic time"—the time of day when everyone wants a piece of her. Her children want her attention after they've been at school all day, and her spouse needs to talk with her about something important that's come up. The telephone is ringing, and even the dog is barking at her. If she had a cat, it would probably be scratching at her legs. How can an already stressed-out Charlotte accommodate all of these competing demands?

This could be time for Dial-a-Dinner. While Charlotte spends time with the family, this convenience service will cook her a gourmet dinner—not pizza or hamburgers—and deliver it to her door, complete with fresh flowers if she wants them. Relaxing and eating at home, she can avoid the hassle of doing the cooking herself or taking the kids out for another night of fast food. And after her Dial-a-Dinner meal, Charlotte can sit back with

her family and watch a video delivered by the mobile Video Van. The Dial-a-Dinner meal costs 20 percent more than a typical restaurant meal; the video rental costs an extra third. Are they worth it? It certainly seems so to Charlotte as she kicks off her shoes and slides into her comfy easy chair.

Imagine this scene repeated in thousands of American homes every evening. Millions of other adults like Charlotte must contend with a seemingly endless list of daily chores. They must get the car repaired, drop clothes at the dry cleaners, get their driver's license renewed, have the dishwasher repaired . . . the list goes on and on. How can they hold down a job and still tend to all these duties?

Smart marketers to the rescue! In recent years, a spate of organizations has appeared to provide services for over-extended consumers. Mobile auto services will change your oil, check out your carburetor, or even replace your windshield, all while you're at work, at home, or shopping. Other services will provide people to wait in line at the driver's license office, to buy theater tickets, or to wait in your home for repairmen. While there, they'll water your plants and walk your dog. And speaking of dogs, there are now mobile veterinarians who make house calls on sick animals. While the vet is tending to your dog, Doctor to Your Door will send a medical doctor to fix whatever ails you. If either you or Fido needs a prescription, many pharmacies will now deliver it to you. These days, food stores will shop for you and dry cleaners will pick up and return your laundry. Chances are, you can find a service somewhere that will tackle your entire list of odd jobs for you.

As the demand for convenience services jumps, service suppliers have begun to franchise their operations. For example, 20 Video Van franchises now produce over $1.2 million in revenues, delivering videos to customers' doors. Any of 109 Wash on Wheels (WOW) franchises will wash nearly anything in your home, or even your house. These franchises are relatively inexpensive and very lucrative. Doctor to Your Door franchises sell for just $25,000 to $75,000, and WOW franchises go for only $12,000 to $18,000 or so.

What makes these services viable? Computer technology is the answer. Computers can be used to process orders and route drivers, to build customer databases, and to target promotions to customers within a specific zip code who have spent a specified dollar amount in a particular month. They can help to manage raffles and operate special occasion promotions such as birthdays and anniversaries, to compute monthly statements, and to handle payroll and accounting. Without the low-cost data management provided by computers, the costs of most of these services would be exorbitant.

Even so, such convenience services do cost consumers more. Are they worth it? Consider the psychic costs that accrue to today's typical dual-income couple with children. These people suffer from strong time pressures. Today, Americans are working harder and

putting in more hours on the job. Add in time spent on required activities during nonwork hours, and they have precious little time left for leisure. To regain leisure time, consumers are buying convenience services and changing their shopping habits. Some "hire" others to shop for them. Others rely heavily on catalogs, or shop by computer: Computer systems such as CompuServe and Prodigy let consumers order from stores all across the nation. Buying is as easy as hitting the return key or clicking the mouse on "buy." Once their shopping is done, customers can turn off the computer and spend time "cocooning"—snuggling into the pleasures of home and hearth.

QUESTIONS

1. Contrast the buying processes of a typical buyer of a home-delivered meal with that of someone purchasing a new suit. How will the stages in the buying process differ in these two buying situations? What does this suggest to the marketer?

2. What major criteria will buyers use in purchasing a home-delivered meal as opposed to a suit?

3. How will consumers of home-delivered services differ in their postpurchase actions? How will this affect marketers' strategies?

4. How does computer technology affect the purchase process from the consumer's point of view?

5. How will the five product characteristics (relative advantage, compatibility, complexity, divisibility, and communicability) affect the adoption of home-delivered services?

Sources: Eugene H. Fram, "The Time-Compressed Shopper," *Marketing Insights,* Summer 1991, pp. 34-39; "Stressed-out Consumers Need Timesaving Innovations," *Marketing News,* March 2, 1992, p. 10; Paul B. Hertneky, "If They Won't Come to You . . . ," *Restaurant Hospitality,* June 1992, pp. 156-58.; Steve Ramos, "Kick the Tires on the Screen," *Forbes,* January 21, 1992, pp. 100-101; and Eric Weissenstein, "Papers Profit from Delivery," *Advertising Age,* June 17, 1991, p. 42.

COMPANY CASE 6

GILLETTE VERSUS BIC: DISPOSING OF DISPOSABLES

Half of all U.S. men get up each morning, confront their stubble in the bathroom mirror, and reach for a 30-cent disposable plastic razor. Schick, Bic, Gillette, or whatever—most men figure that one brand does about as well as the next. And the razor makers seem to always have them on sale, so you can scoop up a dozen of them for next to nothing.

Gillette Company doesn't like this sort of thinking. Of course, women also use Gillette's razors, but

Gillette is particularly concerned with the growing number of men who use disposables. The company makes about three times more money per unit on cartridge refills for its Atra and Trac II razor systems than it does on its Good News! disposables. However, since the first disposables appeared in 1975, their sales have grown faster than those of system razors. By 1988, disposables accounted for 40 percent of shaving-product dollar sales and more than 50 percent of unit sales.

Gillette and the Wet-Shave Market

Gillette dominates the wet-shave industry with a 62 percent share of the $700 million U.S. market and 60 percent worldwide. Schick (with a 16.2 percent share), Bic (9.3 percent), and others, including Wilkinson, account for most of the rest of the market. Gillette's blades and razors produced 32 percent of its $3.5 billion sales in 1988 and 61 percent of its $268 million net income.

Gillette earned its dominant position in the market, especially with men, through large investments in research and development and through careful consumer research. Every day, about 10,000 men carefully record the results of their shaves for Gillette. Five hundred of these men shave in special in-plant cubicles under carefully controlled and monitored conditions, including observation through two-way mirrors and video cameras. Shavers record the precise number of nicks and cuts. In certain cases, researchers even collect sheared whiskers to weigh and measure. As a result, Gillette scientists know that an average man's beard grows 15/1,000 of an inch a day (5.5 inches per year) and contains 15,500 hairs. During an average lifetime, a man will spend 3,350 hours scraping 27.5 feet of whiskers from his face. Gillette even uses electron microscopes to study blade surfaces and miniature cameras to analyze the actual shaving process.

Armed with its knowledge of shavers and shaving, Gillette prides itself in staying ahead of the competition. Just when competitors adjust to one shaving system, Gillette introduces yet another advance. In 1971, Gillette introduced the Trac II, the first razor system featuring two parallel blades mounted in a cartridge. In 1977, following $8 million in R&D expenditures the company introduced Atra, a twin-blade cartridge that swivels during shaving to follow the face's contours. In 1985, Gillette launched the Atra Plus, which added a lubricating strip to the Atra cartridge to make shaving even smoother.

Although the company's founder, King Gillette, was interested in developing a disposable product, one that would be used and then thrown away, Gillette's marketing strategy has focused on developing products that use refill blades on a permanent handle. Gillette works to give its blades, and especially its handles, an aura of class and superior performance. By promoting new captive systems, in which blade cartridges fit only a certain razor handle, Gillette raises price and profit margins with each new technological leap. Thus, because Atra cartridges do not fit the Trac II handle, men had to buy a new handle to allow them to use the Atra blades when Gillette introduced that system.

Gillette has never been concerned with the low end of the market—cheap, private-label blades. Status-seeking men, it believes, will always buy a classy product. Most men see shaving as a serious business and their appearance as a matter of some importance. Therefore, most men will not skimp and settle for an ordinary shave when, for a little more money, they can feel confident that Gillette's products give them the best shave.

Bic and the Rise of Disposables

The rapid rise of the disposable razor has challenged Gillette's view of men's shaving philosophy. Bic first introduced the disposable shaver in 1975 in Europe and then a year later in Canada. Realizing that the United States would be next, Gillette actually introduced the first disposable razor to the U.S. market in 1976—the blue plastic Good News! that used a Trac II blade. Despite its defensive reaction, however, Gillette predicted that men would use the disposable only for trips and locker rooms and when the real razor had been forgotten. Disposables would never capture more than 7 percent of the market, Gillette asserted.

Marcel Bich, Bic's founder and the force behind Bic's challenge to Gillette is, like King Gillette, devoted to disposability. Bich made his money by developing the familiar ballpoint pen. He pursues a strategy of turning status products into commodities. Often a product has status because it is difficult to make and must sell at a high price. But if a manufacturer develops ways to mass produce the product at low cost with little loss of functional quality, its status and allure will disappear. Consumers then will not feel embarrassed to buy and be seen using the new, cheaper version of the product. Thus, Bich brands his products, strips them of their glamour, distributes them widely, and sells them cheaply. His marketing strategy is simple: maximum service, minimum price.

Located in Milford, Connecticut, Bic attacks the shaving business in a very different manner than Gillette. It does not regularly assign anyone to explore the fringes of shaving technology—it does not even own an electron microscope and it does not know or care how many hairs the average man's beard contains. It maintains only a small shave-testing panel consisting of about 100 people. The Bic shaver (which sells for 25 cents or less) has only one blade mounted on a short, hollow handle. Still, the Bic disposable razor presents Gillette with its most serious challenge since the company's early days. In 1988, Bic's shaving products achieved $52 million in sales with a net income of $9.4 million and held a 22.4 percent share of the disposable market.

Gillette Versus Bic

In their separate pursuits of disposability, Gillette and Bic have clashed before on other product fronts. First, beginning in the 1950s, they fought for market share in the writing pen market. Gillette's Paper Mate products, however, were no match for Bic's mass-market advertising and promotion skills. The two firms met again in the 1970s in the disposable cigarette lighter arena, where they again made commodities of what had once been prestigious and sometimes expensive items. Although Gillette did better in disposable lighters than it had in pens, Bic's lighter captured the dominant market share.

In the most recent skirmish, however, Gillette's Good News! brand is winning with a 58 percent market share in the disposable razor market. But the victory is a bittersweet one. The problem? Good News! sells for a lot less than any of Gillette's older products. The key to commodity competition is price. To stay competitive with the 25-cent Bic razor and with other disposables, Gillette has to sell Good News! for much less than the retail price of an Atra or Trac II cartridge. As many Trac

II and Atra users have concluded, although a twin-blade refill cartridge from Gillette costs as much as 56 cents, you can get precisely the same blade mounted on a plastic handle for as little as 25 cents. Good News! not only produces less revenue per blade sold, it also costs more because Gillette has to supply the handle as well as the cartridge. Each time Good News! gains a market share point, Gillette loses millions of dollars in sales and profits from its Atra and Trac II products.

The Psychology of Shaving

The battle between Bic and Gillette represents more than a simple contest over what kinds of razors people want to use—it symbolizes a clash over one of the most enduring daily male rituals. Before King Gillette invented the safety razor, men found shaving a tedious, difficult, time-consuming, and often bloody task that they endured at most twice a week. Only the rich could afford to have a barber shave them daily.

Gillette patented the safety razor in 1904, but it was not until World War I that the product gained wide consumer acceptance. Gillette had the brilliant idea of having the military give a free Gillette razor to every soldier. In this manner, millions of men just entering the shaving age were introduced to the daily, self-shaving habit.

The morning shaving ritual continues to occupy a very special place in most men's lives—it affirms their masculinity. The first shave remains a rite of passage into manhood. A survey by New York psychologists reported that although men complain about the bother of shaving, 97 percent of the sample would not want to use a cream, were one to be developed, that would permanently rid them of all facial hair. Gillette once introduced a new razor that came in versions for heavy, medium, and light beards. Almost no one bought the light version, because few men wanted to publicly acknowledge their modest beard production.

Although shaving may require less skill and involve less danger than it once did, many men still want the razors they use to reflect their beliefs that shaving remains serious business. A typical man regards his razor as an important personal tool, a kind of extension of self, like an expensive pen, cigarette lighter, attaché case, or set of golf clubs.

Gillette's Challenge

For more than 80 years Gillette's perception of the men's shaving market and the psychology of shaving has been perfect. Its products hold a substantial 62 percent share, and its technology and marketing philosophy have held sway over the entire industry. Gillette has worked successfully to maintain the razor's masculine look, heft, and feel as well as its status as an item of personal identification. Now, however, millions of men are scraping their faces each day with small, nondescript, passionless pieces of plastic costing 25 cents—an act that seems to be the ultimate denial of the shaving ritual.

Thus, Good News! is really bad news for Gillette. Gillette must find a way to dispose of the disposables.

QUESTIONS

1. Who is involved in a man's decision to buy a disposable razor and what roles do various participants play? Do these participants and roles differ for the decision to buy a system razor?

2. What types of buying decision behavior do men exhibit when purchasing razors?

3. Examine a man's decision process for purchasing a wet-shave razor. How have Gillette and Bic pursued different strategies with respect to this process?

4. What marketing strategy should Gillette adopt in order to encourage men to switch from disposables to system razors? How would buyer decision processes toward new products affect your recommendations?

Source: Portions adapted "The Gillette Company," in Subhash C. Jain, Marketing Strategy & Policy, 3rd ed., Cincinnati, Ohio: Southwestern, 1990. Used with permission.

Business Markets and Business Buyer Behavior

Gulfstream Aerospace Corporation sells business jets with price tags as high as $20 million. Locating potential buyers isn't a problem—the organizations that can afford to own and operate multimillion dollar business aircraft are easily identified. Customers include Exxon, American Express, Seagram, Coca-Cola, and many others, including King Fahd of Saudi Arabia. Gulfstream's more difficult problems involve reaching key decision makers for jet purchases, understanding their motivations and decision processes, analyzing what factors are important in their decisions, and designing marketing approaches.

Gulfstream Aerospace recognizes the importance of *rational* motives and *objective* factors in buyers' decisions. A company buying a jet will evaluate Gulfstream aircraft on quality and performance, prices, operating costs, and service. At times, these may appear to be the only things that drive the buying decision. But having a superior product isn't enough to land the sale: Gulfstream Aerospace also must consider the more subtle *human factors* that affect the choice of a jet.

"The purchase process may be initiated by the chief executive officer (CEO), a board member wishing to increase efficiency or security, the company's chief pilot, or through vendor efforts like advertising or a sales visit. The CEO will be central in deciding whether to buy the jet, but he or she will be heavily influenced by the company's pilot, financial officer, and perhaps by the board itself.

"Each party in the buying process has subtle roles and needs. The salesperson who tries to impress, for example, both the CEO with depreciation schedules and the chief pilot with minimum runway statistics will almost certainly not sell a plane if he or she overlooks the psychological and emotional components of the buying decision. 'For the chief executive,' observes one salesperson, 'you need all the numbers for support, but if you can't find the kid inside the CEO and excite him or her with the raw beauty of the new plane, you'll never sell the equipment. If you sell the excitement, you sell the jet.'

"The chief pilot, as an equipment expert, often has veto power over purchase decisions and may be able to stop the purchase of a certain brand of jet by simply expressing a negative opinion about, say, the plane's bad weather capabilities. In this sense, the pilot not only influences the decision but also serves as an information 'gatekeeper' by advising management on the equipment to select. Though the corporate legal staff will handle the purchase agreement and the purchasing department will acquire the jet, these parties may have little to say about whether or how the plane will be obtained and which type will be selected. The users of the jet—middle and upper management of the buying company, important customers, and others—may have at least an indirect role in choosing the equipment.

"The involvement of many people in the purchase decision creates a group dynamic that the selling company must factor into its sales planning. Who makes up the buying group? How will the parties interact? Who will dominate and who submit? What priorities do the individuals have?"

In some ways, selling corporate jets to business buyers is like selling cars and kitchen appliances to families. Gulfstream Aerospace asks the same questions as consumer marketers: Who are the buyers and what are their needs? How do buyers make their buying decisions and what factors influence these decisions? What marketing program will be most effective? But the answers to these questions are usually different for the business buyer. Thus, Gulfstream Aerospace faces many of the same challenges as consumer marketers—and some additional ones.[1]

CHAPTER PREVIEW

Chapter 7 places the concepts of individual buyer behavior into a business market context.

We explain the **key differences** between business markets and consumer markets, including **market structure and demand,** the nature of the **buying unit,** and the **types of decisions** and the **decision process.**

Next, we look at **business buyer behavior** and the major types of buying situations: **straight rebuy, modified rebuy, new task,** and **systems buying.** This section also reviews major factors that influence business buyer behavior.

The steps of the business buying decision are covered: **problem recognition, need description, product specification, supplier search, proposal solicitation, supplier selection,** and **performance review.**

We finish the chapter with a discussion of **institutional and government markets** and the ways their buyers make decisions.

In one way or another, most large companies sell to other organizations. Many companies, such as Du Pont, Xerox, and countless other firms, sell *most* of their products to other businesses. Even large consumer-products companies, which make products used by final consumers, must first sell their products to other businesses. For example, General Mills makes many familiar consumer products— Cheerios, Betty Crocker cake mixes, Gold Medal flour, and others. But to sell these products to consumers, General Mills must first sell them to the wholesalers and retailers that serve the consumer market. General Mills also sells products such as specialty chemicals directly to other businesses.

The **business market** consists of all the organizations that buy goods and services to use in the production of other products and services that are sold, rented, or supplied to others. It also includes retailing and wholesaling firms that acquire goods for the purpose of reselling or renting them to others at a profit. The **business buying process** is the decision-making process by which business buyers establish the need for purchased products and services, and identify, evaluate, and choose among alternative brands and suppliers.[2] Companies that sell to other business organizations must do their best to understand business markets and business buyer behavior.

BUSINESS MARKETS

The business market is *huge:* In the U.S. alone, it consists of over 13 million organizations that buy trillions of dollars worth of goods and services each year. In fact, business markets involve many more dollars and items than do consumer markets. For example, Figure 7-1 shows the large number of business transactions needed to produce and sell a simple pair of shoes. Hide dealers sell to tanners, who sell leather to shoe manufacturers, who sell shoes to wholesalers, who in turn sell shoes to retailers, who finally sell the shoes to consumers. Each party in the chain also buys many other related goods and services. This example shows why there is more business buying than consumer buying—many sets of *business* purchases were made for only one set of *consumer* purchases.

Characteristics of Business Markets

In some ways, business markets are similar to consumer markets. Both involve people who assume buying roles and make purchase decisions to satisfy needs. However, business markets differ in many ways from consumer markets.[3] The main differences are in *market structure and demand,* the *nature of the buying unit,* and *the types of decisions and the decision process* involved.

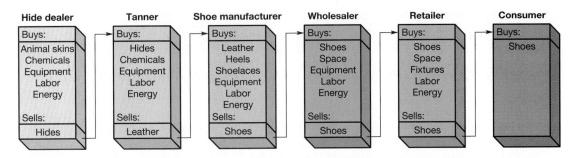

FIGURE 7-1 Business transactions involved in producing and distributing a pair of shoes

Market Structure and Demand

[handwritten: fewer but larger buyers, geographically concentrated, derived demand, inelastic demand]

[handwritten: fluctuating demand]

The business marketer normally deals with *far fewer but far larger buyers* than the consumer marketer does. For example, when Goodyear sells replacement tires to final consumers, its potential market includes the owners of the 112 million cars currently in use in the United States. But Goodyear's fate in the business market depends on getting orders from one of only a few large auto makers. Even in large business markets, a few buyers normally account for most of the purchasing.

Business markets are also more *geographically concentrated*. More than half the nation's business buyers are concentrated in seven states: California, New York, Ohio, Illinois, Michigan, Texas, Pennsylvania, and New Jersey. Further, business demand is **derived demand**—it ultimately derives from the demand for consumer goods. General Motors buys steel because consumers buy cars. If consumer demand for cars drops, so will the demand for steel and all the other products used to make cars. Therefore, business marketers sometimes promote their products directly to final consumers to increase business demand (see Marketing Highlight 7-1).[4]

Many business markets have **inelastic demand;** that is, total demand for many business products is not affected much by price changes, especially in the short run. A drop in the price of leather will not cause shoe manufacturers to buy much more leather unless it results in lower shoe prices that, in turn, will increase consumer demand for shoes.

Finally, business markets have more *fluctuating demand*. The demand for many business goods and services tends to change more—and more quickly—than the demand for consumer goods and services does. A small percentage increase in consumer demand can cause large increases in business demand. Sometimes a rise of only 10 percent in consumer demand can cause as much as a 200 percent rise in business demand during the next period.

Nature of the Buying Unit

[handwritten: more buyers, more professional purchasing agent]

Compared with consumer purchases, a business purchase usually involves *more buyers* and a *more professional purchasing effort*. Often, business buying is done by trained purchasing agents who spend their working lives learning how to buy better. The more complex the purchase, the more likely that several people will participate in the decision-making process. Buying committees made up of technical experts and top management are common in the buying of major goods. Therefore, business marketers must have well-trained salespeople to deal with well-trained buyers.

Types of Decisions and the Decision Process

[handwritten: more complex, more formalized, more dependent]

Business buyers usually face *more complex* buying decisions than do consumer buyers. Purchases often involve large sums of money, complex technical and economic considerations, and interactions among many people at many levels of the buyer's organization. Because the purchases are more complex, business buyers may take longer to make their decisions. For example, the purchase of a large computer system might take many months or more than a year to complete and could involve millions of dollars, thousands of technical details, and dozens of people ranging from top management to lower-level users.

The business buying process tends to be *more formalized* than the consumer buying process. Large business purchases usually call for detailed product specifications, written purchase orders, careful supplier searches, and formal approval. The buying firm might even prepare policy manuals that detail the purchase process.

INTEL: YOU CAN'T SEE IT, BUT YOU'RE GOING TO LOVE IT

In mid-1991, Intel launched its two-year, $100 million "Intel Inside" advertising campaign to sell personal computer buyers on the virtues of Intel microprocessors, the tiny chips that serve as the brains of microcomputers. So what, you say? Lots of companies run big consumer ad campaigns. However, although such a campaign might be business as usual for companies like Coca-Cola, Nike, or IBM that market products directly to final consumers, it is anything but usual for Intel.

Computer buyers can't purchase a microprocessor chip directly—in fact, most will never even see one. Demand for microprocessors is *derived demand*—it ultimately comes from demand for products that *contain* microprocessors. Consumers simply buy the computer and take whatever brand of chip the computer manufacturer chose to include as a component. Traditionally, chip companies like Intel market only to the manufacturers who buy chips directly. In contrast, the innovative "Intel Inside" campaign appeals directly to computer buyers—its customers' customers. If Intel can create brand preference among buyers for *its* chips, this in turn will make Intel chips more attractive to computer manufacturers.

Intel invented the first microprocessor in 1971 and for 20 years has held a near-monopoly, dominating the chip market for desktop computers. Its sales and profits have soared accordingly. In the decade since IBM introduced its first PCs based on Intel's 8088 microprocessor, Intel sales have jumped fivefold to more than $5 billion, and its earnings have grown even faster. Its popular 286, 386, and 486 chips power most of the microcomputers in use today.

Recently, however, a rush of imitators—Advanced Micro Devices (AMD), Chips & Technologies, Cyrix, and others—have begun to crack Intel's monopoly, flooding the market with new and improved clones of Intel chips. AMD alone now claims more than a third of the 386 chip market. The onslaught of 386 clones has escalated into a price war, denting Intel's bottom line. And although Intel has the next-generation 486 market to itself for now, AMD and other cloners will soon offer 486 chips as well.

Intel has responded fiercely to the cloners, slashing prices, spending heavily to develop new products, and advertising to differentiate its products. For example, it has cut prices on its 386s faster than for any new chip in its history. Moreover, in 1993, Intel invested a whopping $2.5 billion in R&D to get new products to the market more quickly. In 1992, the company marketed nearly 32 variants of its state-of-the-art 486 chip. And its next-generation Pentium microprocessor is a veritable one-chip mainframe. The Pentium contains 3 million transistors and will process 100 million instructions per second (MIPS), as compared to only one-half million transistors and five MIPS for the 386 chip. Intel plans to create a new chip family every two years. By the year 2000, it will offer a chip with an astounding 100 million transistors and 2 *billion* instructions per second—that's roughly equal to today's supercomputers.

Still, the clone makers are likely to continue nipping at Intel's heels, and advertising provides another means by which Intel can differentiate its "originals" from competitors' imitations. The "Intel Inside" campaign consists of two major efforts. First, in its brand-awareness ads, Intel attempts to convince microcomputer buyers that Intel microprocessors really are better. The first ad of the series contained the headline "How to spot the very best PC" nestled in a bed of colorful "Intel Inside" logos. The ad copy advised:

> Intel is the world's leader in microprocessor design and development. In fact, Intel introduced the very first microprocessor. So with Intel inside, you know you've got unquestioned compatibility and unparalleled quality. And you'll know you're getting the very best in PC technology.

As a second major element of the "Intel Inside" campaign, Intel also subsidizes ads by PC manufacturers that include the "Intel Inside" logo. So far, more than 100 companies have featured the logo in their ads, including IBM, NCR, Dell, Zenith Data Systems, and AST. Participating manufacturers claim that the campaign has increased their advertising effectiveness. "The 'Intel Inside' program

---

Finally, in the business buying process, buyer and seller are often much *more dependent* on each other. Consumer marketers are usually at a distance from their customers. In contrast, business marketers may roll up their sleeves and work closely with their customers during all stages of the buying process—from helping customers define problems, to finding solutions, to supporting after-sale operation. They often customize their offerings to individual customer needs. In the short run, sales go to suppliers who meet buyers' immediate product and service needs. However, business marketers also must build close *long-run* relationships with customers. In the long run, business marketers keep a customer's sales by meeting current needs *and* thinking ahead to meet the customer's future needs.[5]

How to spot the very best computers.

It's really quite easy. From notebooks to main-frames, just look for computers that have a genuine Intel microprocessor inside. Either the Intel386,™ Intel386 SX, Intel486™ or Intel486 SX microprocessor.

Intel is the world's leader in microprocessor design and development. And no other microprocessors have a larger installed base of software. Plus, every chip is literally put through millions of tests. So with Intel inside, you know you've got unquestioned com-

patibility and unparalleled quality. Or simply put, the very best computer technology.

So look for the Intel Inside symbol on ads for leading computers. Or call 800-548-4725. It'll show you've got an eye for spotting the best.

intel.
The Computer Inside.™

Intel launched its highly successful, $100-million "Intel Inside" advertising campaign to convince computer buyers that it really does matter what chip comes inside their computers.

has been a good program for us," says the advertising manager of a large computer manufacturing firm. "It has helped add some credibility and enhancements to our messages." In the first six months of the campaign, more than 1,500 pages of "Intel Inside" ads were run.

It remains to be seen whether the "Intel Inside" campaign can convince buyers to care about what chip comes in their computers. But as long as microprocessors remain anonymous little lumps hidden inside a user's computer, Intel remains at the mercy of the clone makers. In contrast, if Intel can convince buyers that its chips are superior, it will achieve a strong advantage in its dealings with computer makers.

History suggests that Intel's "branded-component" campaign might just work. The company learned the value of such advertising in 1988, when it spent $20 million to promote the low-cost, SX version of its 386

chip. That campaign, too, was unusual for an engineering company that sells few products directly to consumers, but it worked. Buyers began asking for PCs with Intel 386SX chips, and computer makers rushed to fill the demand. The 386SX became Intel's best-selling chip ever. Says one industry observer, "It's mind-boggling how successful they made the SX."

Sources: Quotes from Kate Bertrand, "Advertising a Chip You'll Never See," *Business Marketing,* February 1992, p. 19; and Richard Brandt, "Intel: Way Out in Front, but the Footsteps Are Getting Larger," *Business Week,* April 29, 1991, pp. 88-89. Also see Robert D. Hof, "Inside Intel," *Business Week,* June 1, 1992, pp. 86-94; Bertrand, "Chip Wars," *Business Marketing,* February 1992, pp. 16-18; Alan Deutschman, "If They're Gaining on You, Innovate," *Fortune,* November 2, 1992; Ani Hadjian, How Intel Makes Spending Pay Off," *Fortune,* February 22, 1993, pp. 56-61; and Richard Brandt, "Intel: What a Tease,—and What a Strategy," *Business Week,* February 22, 1993, p. 40.

Other Characteristics of Business Markets

Direct purchasing. Business buyers often buy directly from producers rather than through middlemen, especially for items that are technically complex or expensive. For example, Ryder buys thousands of trucks each year in all shapes and sizes. It rents some of these trucks to move-it-yourself customers (the familiar yellow Ryder trucks), leases some to other companies for their truck fleets, and uses the rest in its own freight-hauling businesses. When Ryder buys GMC trucks, it purchases them directly from General Motors rather than from independent GM truck dealers. Similarly, American Airlines buys airplanes directly from Boeing, Kroger buys package goods directly from Procter & Gamble, and the United States government buys personal computers directly from IBM.

Organizational marketers often work closely with customers during all stages of the buying process—from helping to define the problem, to finding solutions, to after-sale operation. Here, Olin Corporation identifies a difficult problem for fiber manufacturers and advises, "Don't be sheepish. Talk to Olin. We have the answers."

Reciprocity. Business buyers often practice *reciprocity*, selecting suppliers who also buy from them. For example, a paper company might buy needed chemicals from a chemical company that in turn buys the company's paper. The Federal Trade Commission and the Justice Department's antitrust division forbid reciprocity if it shuts out competition in an unfair manner. A buyer still can choose a supplier that it also sells something to, but the buyer should be able to show that it is getting competitive prices, quality, and service from that supplier.[6]

Leasing. Business buyers increasingly are leasing equipment instead of buying it outright. American companies lease over $108 billion of equipment each year—everything from printing presses to power plants, helicopters to hay balers, and office copiers to off-shore drilling rigs. The lessee can gain a number of advantages, such as having more available capital, getting the seller's latest products, receiving better servicing, and gaining some tax advantages. The lessor often ends up with a larger net income and the chance to sell to customers who might not have been able to afford outright purchase.

A Model of Business Buyer Behavior

At the most basic level, marketers want to know how business buyers will respond to various marketing stimuli. Figure 7-2 shows a model of business buyer behavior. In this model, marketing and other stimuli affect the buying organization and produce certain buyer responses. As with consumer buying, the marketing stimuli for business buying consist of the four *P*s: product, price, place, and promotion.

FIGURE 7-2 A model of business buyer behavior

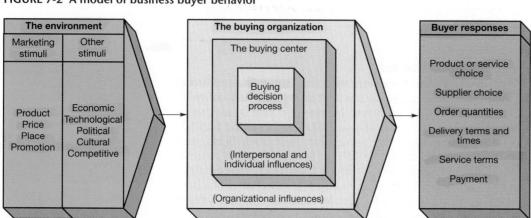

Other stimuli include major forces in the environment: economic, technological, political, cultural, and competitive. These stimuli enter the organization and are turned into buyer responses: product or service choice; supplier choice; order quantities; and delivery, service, and payment terms. In order to design good marketing-mix strategies, the marketer must understand what happens within the organization to turn stimuli into purchase responses.

Within the organization, buying activity consists of two major parts: the buying center, made up of all the people involved in the buying decision, and the buying decision process. Figure 7-2 shows that the buying center and the buying decision process are influenced by internal organizational, interpersonal, and individual factors as well as by external environmental factors.

BUSINESS BUYER BEHAVIOR

The model in Figure 7-2 suggests four questions about business buyer behavior: What buying decisions do business buyers make? Who participates in the buying process? What are the major influences on buyers? How do business buyers make their buying decisions?

What Buying Decisions Do Business Buyers Make?

The business buyer faces a whole set of decisions in making a purchase. The number of decisions depends on the type of buying situation.

Major Types of Buying Situations

There are three major types of buying situations.[7] At one extreme is the *straight rebuy,* which is a fairly routine decision. At the other extreme is the *new task,* which may call for thorough research. In the middle is the *modified rebuy,* which requires some research. (For examples, see Figure 7-3.)

Straight Rebuy. In a **straight rebuy,** the buyer reorders something without any modifications. It is usually handled on a routine basis by the purchasing department. Based on past buying satisfaction, the buyer simply chooses from the various suppliers on its list. "In" suppliers try to maintain product and service quality. They often propose automatic reordering systems so that the purchasing agent will save reordering time. The "out" suppliers try to offer something new or exploit dissatisfaction so that the buyer will consider them. "Out" suppliers try to get their foot in the door with a small order and then enlarge their purchase share over time.

Modified Rebuy. In a **modified rebuy,** the buyer wants to modify product specifications, prices, terms, or suppliers. The modified rebuy usually involves more decision participants than the straight rebuy. The "in" suppliers may become nervous and feel pressured to put their best foot forward to protect an account. "Out" suppliers may see the modified rebuy situation as an opportunity to make a better offer and gain new business.

New Task. A company buying a product or service for the first time faces a

FIGURE 7-3 Three types of business buying situations
Source: Marketing Principles, 3rd ed. by Ben M. Enis. Copyright © 1980 Scott, Foresman and Company. Reprinted by permission.

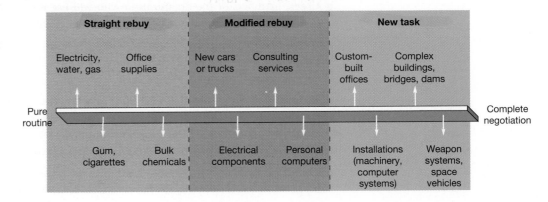

new task situation. In such cases, the greater the cost or risk, the larger the number of decision participants and the greater their efforts to collect information will be. The new-task situation is the marketer's greatest opportunity and challenge. The marketer not only tries to reach as many key buying influences as possible, but also provides help and information.

Specific Buying Decisions

The buyer makes the fewest decisions in the straight rebuy and the most in the new-task decision. In the new-task situation, the buyer must decide on product specifications, suppliers, price limits, payment terms, order quantities, delivery times, and service terms. The order of these decisions varies with each situation, and different decision participants influence each choice.

Systems Buying and Selling

Many business buyers prefer to buy a packaged solution to a problem from a single seller. Called **systems buying,** this practice began with government buying of major weapons and communication systems. Instead of buying and putting all the components together, the government asked for bids from suppliers who would supply the components *and* assemble the package or system.

Sellers increasingly have recognized that buyers like this method and have adopted systems selling as a marketing tool.[8] Systems selling is a two-step process. First, the supplier sells a group of interlocking products. For example, the supplier sells not only glue, but also applicators and dryers. Second, the supplier sells a system of production, inventory control, distribution, and other services to meet the buyer's need for a smooth-running operation.

Systems selling is a key business marketing strategy for winning and holding accounts. The contract often goes to the firm that provides the most complete system meeting the customer's needs. Consider the following:

> The Indonesian government requested bids to build a cement factory near Jakarta. An American firm's proposal included choosing the site, designing the cement factory, hiring the construction crews, assembling the materials and equipment, and turning the finished factory over to the Indonesian government. A Japanese firm's proposal included all of these services, plus hiring and training workers to run the factory, exporting the cement through their trading companies, and using the cement to build some needed roads and new office buildings in Jakarta. Although the Japanese firm's proposal cost more, it won the contract. Clearly the Japanese viewed the problem not as one of just building a cement factory (the narrow view of systems selling) but of running it in a way that would contribute to the country's economy. They took the broadest view of the customers' needs. This is true systems selling.

Who Participates in the Business Buying Process?

Who does the buying of the trillions of dollars worth of goods and services needed by business organizations? The decision-making unit of a buying organization is called its **buying center,** defined as all the individuals and units that participate in the business decision-making process.[9]

The buying center includes all members of the organization who play any of five roles in the purchase decision process.[10]

- **Users:** members of the organization who will use the product or service. In many cases, users initiate the buying proposal and help define product specifications.

- **Influencers:** people who affect the buying decision. They often help define specifications and also provide information for evaluating alternatives. Technical personnel are particularly important influencers.

- **Buyers:** people with formal authority to select the supplier and arrange terms of purchase. Buyers may help shape product specifications, but they play their major role in selecting vendors and in negotiating. In more complex purchases, buyers might include high-level officers participating in the negotiations.

- **Deciders:** people who have formal or informal power to select or approve the final suppliers. In routine buying, the buyers are often the deciders, or at least the approvers.

This ad recognizes the secretary as a key buying influence.

- **Gatekeepers:** people who control the flow of information to others. For example, purchasing agents often have authority to prevent salespersons from seeing users or deciders. Other gatekeepers include technical personnel and even personal secretaries.

The buying center is not a fixed and formally identified unit within the buying organization. It is a set of buying roles assumed by different people for different purchases. Within the organization, the size and makeup of the buying center will vary for different products and for different buying situations. For some routine purchases, one person—say a purchasing agent—may assume all the buying center roles and serve as the only person involved in the buying decision. For more complex purchases, the buying center may include 20 or 30 people from different levels and departments in the organization. One study of business buying showed that the typical business equipment purchase involved seven people from three management levels representing four different departments.[11]

The buying center concept presents a major marketing challenge. The business marketer must learn who participates in the decision, each participant's relative influence, and what evaluation criteria each decision participant uses. Consider the following example:

> Baxter sells disposable surgical gowns to hospitals. It tries to identify the hospital personnel involved in this buying decision. They turn out to be the vice-president of purchasing, the operating room administrator, and the surgeons. Each participant plays a different role. The vice-president of purchasing analyzes whether the hospital should buy disposable gowns or reusable gowns. If analysis favors disposable gowns, then the operating room administrator compares competing products and prices and makes a choice. This administrator considers the gown's absorbency, antiseptic quality, design, and cost and normally buys the brand that meets requirements at the lowest cost. Finally, surgeons affect the decision later by reporting their satisfaction or dissatisfaction with the brand.

The buying center usually includes some obvious participants who are involved formally in the buying decision. For example, the decision to buy a corporate jet will probably involve the company's chief pilot, a purchasing agent, some legal staff, a member of top management, and others formally charged with the buying decision. It may also involve less obvious, informal participants, some of whom may actually make or strongly affect the buying decision. Sometimes, even the people in the buying center are not aware of all the buying participants. For example, the decision about which corporate jet to buy may actually be made by a corporate board member who has an interest in flying and knows a lot about airplanes. This board member may work behind the scenes to sway the decision. Many business buying decisions result from the complex interactions of ever-changing buying center participants.

What Are the Major Influences on Business Buyers?

Business buyers are subject to many influences when they make their buying decisions. Some marketers assume that the major influences are economic. They think buyers will favor the supplier who offers the lowest price, or the best product, or the most service. They concentrate on offering strong economic benefits to buyers. However, business buyers actually respond to both economic and personal factors:

> It has not been fashionable lately to talk about relationships in business. We're told that it has to be devoid of emotion. We must be cold, calculating, and impersonal. Don't you believe it. Relationships make the world go round. Businesspeople are human and social as well as interested in economics and investments, and salespeople need to appeal to both sides. Purchasers may claim to be motivated by intellect alone, but the professional salesperson knows that they run on both reason and emotion.[12]

When suppliers' offers are very similar, business buyers have little basis for strictly rational choice. Because they can meet organizational goals with any supplier, buyers can allow personal factors to play a larger role in their decisions.

Industrial buyers respond to more than just economic factors. In this ad the words stress performance but the illustration suggests a smooth, comfortable ride.

Like nothing on earth

Peterbilt's new 4-point cab air suspension: remarkably smooth and stable.

That's because it's engineered like no other suspension system made. In fact, the only thing our Model 362 4-point cab air suspension has in common with competing designs, is its name.

Exclusive anti-roll bar cuts cab sway, even when cornering.

By combining a stout 1.25" anti-roll bar with our patented damper/snubber system, Peterbilt engineers have cut cab sway to virtually imperceptible levels. The result? No exaggerated side-to-side front-to-back cab motion so common to other 4-point suspensions. Cab stability and handling is excellent — even when cornering.

And since a suspended Model 362 cab sits only ⅝" higher than a standard 362 cab, we've also eliminated the need for special cab skirts, and expensive, unreliable modified linkages. In addition, the entire suspension weighs less than half of the nearest competing design.

500,000 mile cab warranty.

After putting a suspended Model 362 cab through 40 hours of brutal shake testing, not a single loose fastener was discovered. In fact, it does such a good job of protecting equipment against damage, we're able to offer a 500,000 mile cab warranty on all Model 362's with the 4-point suspension system.

Comfort, handling, reliability: it's all there. Call 800-447-4700.

Think of it. No unnerving cab sway. No expensive repairs on unfamiliar, modified linkages. An extended cab warranty. Increased resale value. And a ride that's remarkably smooth — but not at the expense of handling.

Peterbilt's Model 362 4-point cab air suspension: performance and value no other competing design can match. Just call 800-447-4700 for more information and the name of the Peterbilt dealer nearest you.

Peterbilt

A DIVISION OF PACCAR

Peterbilt Motors Company
38801 Cherry Street
Newark, CA 94560

However, when competing products differ greatly, business buyers are more accountable for their choice and tend to pay more attention to economic factors.

Figure 7-4 lists various groups of influences on business buyers—environmental, organizational, interpersonal, and individual.[13]

Environmental Factors

Business buyers are influenced heavily by factors in the current and expected *economic environment,* such as the level of primary demand, the economic outlook, and the cost of money. As economic uncertainty rises, business buyers cut back on new investments and attempt to reduce their inventories.

An increasingly important environmental factor is shortages in key materials. Many companies now are more willing to buy and hold larger inventories of scarce materials to ensure adequate supply. Business buyers also are affected by technological, political, and competitive developments in the environment. Culture and customs can strongly influence business buyer reactions to the marketer's behavior and strategies, especially in the international marketing environment (see Marketing Highlight 7-2). The business marketer must watch these factors, determine how they will affect the buyer, and try to turn these challenges into opportunities.

Organizational Factors

Each buying organization has its own objectives, policies, procedures, structure, and systems, which must be understood by the business marketer. Questions such as these arise: How many people are involved in the buying decision? Who are they? What are their evaluative criteria? What are the company's policies and limits on its buyers? In addition, the business marketer should be aware of the following organizational trends in the purchasing area.

Upgraded Purchasing. Purchasing departments have often occupied a low position in the management hierarchy, even though they often manage more than half of the company's costs. However, many companies recently have upgraded their purchasing departments. Several large corporations have elevated the heads of purchasing to vice-president. Some companies have combined several functions—such as purchasing, inventory control, production scheduling, and traffic—into a high-level function called *strategic materials management.* Purchasing departments in many multinational companies have responsibility for purchasing materials and service around the world. Many companies are offering higher compensation in order to attract top talent in the purchasing area. This means that business marketers also must upgrade their salespeople to match the quality of the today's business buyers.

Centralized Purchasing. In companies consisting of many divisions with differing needs, much of the purchasing is carried out at the division level. Recently, however, some large companies have tried to recentralize purchasing. Headquarters identifies materials purchased by several divisions and buys them centrally. Centralized purchasing gives the company more purchasing clout, which can produce substantial savings. For the business marketer, this development means dealing with fewer, higher-level buyers. Instead of using regional salesforces to sell to a large buyer's separate plants, the seller may use a *national account salesforce* to service the buyer. For example, at Xerox, over 250 national account managers each handle one to five large national accounts with many scat-

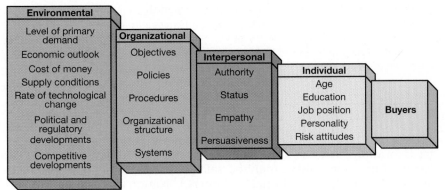

FIGURE 7-4
Major influences on business buying behavior

INTERNATIONAL MARKETING MANNERS: WHEN IN ROME, DO AS THE ROMANS DO

Picture this: Consolidated Amalgamation, Inc., thinks it's time that the rest of the world enjoyed the same fine products it has offered American consumers for two generations. It dispatches vice-president Harry E. Slicksmile to Europe to explore the territory. Mr. Slicksmile stops first in London, where he makes short work of some bankers—he rings them up on the phone. He handles Parisians with similar ease: After securing a table at La Tour d'Argent, he greets his luncheon guest, the director of an industrial engineering firm, with the words, "Just call me Harry, Jacques."

In Germany, Mr. Slicksmile is a powerhouse. Whisking through a lavish, state-of-the-art marketing presentation, complete with the flip charts and audiovisuals, he shows 'em that this Georgia boy *knows* how to make a buck. Heading on to Milan, Harry strikes up a conversation with the Japanese businessman sitting next to him on the plane. He flips his card onto the guy's tray and, when the two say good-bye, shakes hands warmly and clasps the man's right arm. Later, for his appointment with the owner of an Italian packaging-design firm, our hero wears his comfy corduroy sport coat, khaki pants, and Topsiders. Everybody knows Italians are zany and laid back, right?

Wrong. Six months later, Consolidated Amalgamation has nothing to show for the trip but a pile of bills. In Europe, they weren't wild about Harry.

This hypothetical case has been exaggerated for emphasis. Americans are seldom such dolts. But experts say success in international business has a lot to do with knowing the territory and its people. By learning English and extending themselves in other ways, the world's business leaders have met Americans more than halfway. In contrast, Americans too often do little except assume that others will march to their music. "We want things to be 'American' when we travel. Fast. Convenient. Easy. So we become 'ugly Americans' by demanding that others change," says one American world trade expert. "I think more business would be done if we tried harder."

Poor Harry tried, all right, but in all the wrong ways. The English do not, as a rule, make deals over the phone as much as Americans do. It's not so much a "cultural" difference as a difference in approach. A proper Frenchman neither likes instant familiarity—questions about family, church, or alma mater—nor refers to strangers by their first names. "That poor fellow,

Jacques, probably wouldn't show anything, but he'd recoil. He'd *not* be pleased," explains an expert on French business practices. "It's considered poor taste," he continues. "Even after months of business dealings, I'd wait for him or her to make the invitation [to use first names] . . . You are always right, in Europe, to say 'Mister.'"

Harry's flashy presentation would likely have been a flop with the Germans, who dislike overstatement and ostentatiousness. According to one German expert, however, German businessmen have become accustomed to dealing with Americans. Although differences in body language and customs remain, the past 20 years have softened them. "I hugged an American woman at a business meeting last night," he said. "That would be normal in France, but [older] Germans still have difficulty [with the custom]." He says that calling secretaries by their first names would still be considered rude: "They have a right to be called by the surname. You'd certainly ask—and get—permission first."

When Harry Slicksmile grabbed his new Japanese acquaintance by the arm, the executive probably considered him disrespectful and presumptuous. Harry made matters worse by tossing his business card. Japanese people revere the business card as an extension of self and as an indicator of rank. They do not *hand* it to people, they *present* it—with both hands. In addition, the Japanese are sticklers about rank. Unlike Americans, they don't heap praise on subordinates in a room; they will praise only the highest-ranking official present.

Hapless Harry's last gaffe was assuming that Italians are like Hollywood's stereotypes of them. The flair for design and style that has characterized Italian culture for centuries is embodied in the businesspeople of Milan and Rome. They dress beautifully and admire flair, but they blanch at garishness or impropriety in others' attire.

In order to compete successfully in global markets, or even to deal effectively with international firms in their home markets, American companies must help their managers to understand the needs, customs, and cultures of international business buyers. Here are additional examples of a few rules of social and business etiquette that American managers should understand when doing business abroad.

France   Dress conservatively, except in the south where more casual clothes are worn. Do

tered locations. The national account managers coordinate the efforts of an entire Xerox team—specialists, analysts, salespeople for individual products—to sell and service important national customers.[14] National account selling is challeng-

In order to succeed in global markets, American companies must help their managers to understand the needs, customs, and cultures of international business buyers.

	not refer to people by their first names— the French are formal with strangers.
Germany	Be especially punctual. An American businessman invited to someone's home should present flowers, preferably unwrapped, to the hostess. During introductions, greet women first and wait until, or if, they extend their hands before extending yours.
Italy	Whether you dress conservatively or go native in a Giorgio Armani suit, keep in mind that Italian businesspeople are style conscious. Make appointments well in advance. Prepare for and be patient with Italian bureaucracies.
United Kingdom	Toasts are often given at formal dinners. If the host honors you with a toast, be prepared to reciprocate. Business entertaining is done more often at lunch than at dinner.
Saudi Arabia	Although men will kiss each other in greeting, they will never kiss a woman in public. An American woman should wait for a man to extend his hand before offering hers. If a Saudi offers refreshment, accept—it is an insult to decline it.
Japan	Don't imitate Japanese bowing customs unless you understand them thoroughly—who bows to whom, how many times, and when. It's a complicated ritual. Presenting business cards is another ritual. Carry many cards, present them with both hands so your name can be easily read, and hand them to others in order of descending rank. Expect Japanese business executives to take time making decisions and to work through all of the details before making a commitment.

Sources: Adapted from Susan Harte, "When in Rome, You Should Learn to Do What the Romans Do," *The Atlanta Journal-Constitution,* January 22, 1990, pp. D1, D6; used with permission of The Atlanta Journal and The Atlanta Constitution. Also see Lufthansa's *Business Travel Guide/Europe;* and Sergey Frank, "Global Negotiating," *Sales & Marketing Management,* May 1992, pp. 64-69.

ing and demands both a high-level salesforce and sophisticated marketing effort.

Long-term Contracts. Business buyers are increasingly seeking long-term contracts with suppliers. For example, General Motors wants to buy from fewer

JUST-IN-TIME PRODUCTION CHANGES ORGANIZATIONAL SELLING

Over the past several years, as American business has studied the reasons for Japanese success in world markets, they have learned about and adopted several new manufacturing concepts such as just-in-time (JIT), early supplier involvement, value analysis, total quality management, and flexible manufacturing. These practices greatly affect how business marketers sell to and service their customers.

JIT, in particular, has produced major changes in business marketing. Just-in-time means that production materials arrive at the customer's factory exactly when needed for production, rather than being stored in the customer's inventory until used. The goal of JIT is zero inventory with 100 percent quality. It calls for coordination between the production schedules of supplier and customer so that neither has to carry much inventory. Effective use of JIT reduces inventory and lead times and increases quality, productivity, and adaptability to change.

Business marketers need to be aware of the changes that JIT has caused in business purchasing practices, and they must exploit the opportunities that JIT creates. Just-in-time has the following major features and effects.

- *Strict quality control.* Buyers can achieve maximum cost savings from JIT only if they receive consistently

high-quality goods. In fact, many analysts link JIT with the recent "total quality management" movement:

Most of the gains made in quality by American firms over the past decade can be credited to the JIT movement. JIT raised everyone's "quality consciousness"; indeed, it has made quality "job 1." . . . JIT brought the quality issue out in the open. You can't operate in a JIT mode without good quality.

Thus, JIT buyers expect suppliers to maintain strict quality. The business marketer needs to work closely with customers and meet their high quality standards.

- *Frequent and reliable delivery.* Daily delivery is often the only way to avoid inventory buildup. Increasingly, customers are setting delivery dates with penalties for not meeting them. Apple even penalizes for early delivery, and Kasle Steel makes around-the-clock deliveries to the General Motors plant in Buick City. Thus, JIT means that business marketers must develop reliable transportation arrangements.

- *Closer location.* Since JIT involves frequent delivery, many business marketers have set up locations closer to their large JIT customers. Closer locations enable them to deliver smaller shipments more efficiently and reliably. Kasle Steel set up a mill within Buick

suppliers who are willing to locate close to their plants and produce high-quality components. Business marketers also are beginning to offer *electronic order interchange* systems to their customers. When using such systems, the seller places terminals hooked to its own computers in customers' offices. Then, the customer can order needed items instantly by entering orders directly into the computer. The orders are transmitted automatically to the supplier. Many hospitals order directly from Baxter using order-taking terminals in their stockrooms. And many bookstores order from Follett's in this way.

Purchasing Performance Evaluation. Some companies are setting up incentive systems to reward purchasing managers for especially good purchasing performance, in much the same way that salespeople receive bonuses for especially good selling performance. These systems should lead purchasing managers to increase their pressure on sellers for the best terms.

Just-in-Time Production Systems. The emergence of *just-in-time production systems* has had a major impact on business purchasing policies. Marketing Highlight 7-3 describes the effects of just-in-time on business marketing.

Interpersonal Factors

The buying center usually includes many participants who influence each other. The business marketer often finds it difficult to determine what kinds of *interpersonal factors* and group dynamics enter into the buying process. As one writer notes: "Managers do not wear tags that say 'decision maker' or 'unimportant person.' The powerful are often invisible, at least to vendor representatives."[15] Nor does the buying center participant with the highest rank always have the most influence. Participants may have influence in the buying decision because they con-

City to serve the General Motors plant there. Thus, JIT means that a business marketer may have to make large commitments to major customers.

- *Telecommunication.* New communication technologies let suppliers set up computerized purchasing systems that are hooked up to their customers. One large customer even requires that suppliers put their inventory figures and prices in the system. This allows for on-line JIT ordering as the computer looks for the lowest prices for available inventory. Such systems reduce transaction costs, but put pressure on business marketers to keep prices very competitive.

- *Single sourcing.* JIT requires that the buyer and seller work closely together to reduce costs. Often the business customer awards a long-term contract to only one trusted supplier. Single sourcing is increasing rapidly under JIT. Thus, whereas General Motors still uses more than 3,500 suppliers, Toyota, which has totally adopted JIT, uses fewer than 250 suppliers.

- *Value analysis.* The major objectives of JIT are to reduce costs and improve quality, and value analysis is critical to that. To reduce costs of its product, a customer must not only reduce its own costs but also get its suppliers to reduce their costs. Suppliers with strong value analysis programs have a competitive edge because they can contribute to their customers' value analysis.

- *Early supplier involvement.* Business buyers are increasingly bringing business marketers into the design process. Thus, business marketers must employ qualified people who can work with customers' design teams.

- *Close relationship.* To make JIT successful, the business marketer and customer must work closely together to satisfy the customer's needs. If the company can customize offerings for the particular business customer, it will win the contract for a specific term. Both parties may invest lots of time and money to set up the JIT relationship. Because the costs of changing suppliers are high, business customers are very selective in choosing suppliers. Thus, business marketers must improve their skill in *relationship marketing* as compared to *transaction marketing.* The marketer must try to achieve maximum profits over the entire relationship rather than over each transaction.

Sources: See G. H. Manoochehri, "Suppliers and the Just-In-Time Concept," *Journal of Purchasing and Materials Management,* Winter 1984, pp. 16-21; Ernest Raia, "Just-in-time USA," *Purchasing,* February 13, 1986, pp. 48-62; Eric K. Clemons and F. Warren McFarlan, "Telecom: Hook Up or Lose Out," *Harvard Business Review,* July-August 1986, pp. 91-97; and Gary L. Frazier, Robert E. Spekman, and Charles R. O'Neal, "Just-In-Time Exchange Relationships in Industrial Markets," *Journal of Marketing,* October 1988, pp. 52-57. Quote from Ernest Raia, "JIT in the '90s: Zeroing in on Leadtimes," *Purchasing,* September 26, 1991, pp. 54-57.

trol rewards and punishments, are well liked, have special expertise, or have a special relationship with other important participants. Interpersonal factors are often very subtle. Whenever possible, business marketers must try to understand these factors and design strategies that take them into account.

Individual Factors

Each participant in the business buying decision process brings in personal motives, perceptions, and preferences. These individual factors are affected by personal characteristics such as age, income, education, professional identification, personality, and attitudes toward risk. Also, buyers have different buying styles. Some may be technical types who make in-depth analyses of competitive proposals before choosing a supplier. Other buyers may be intuitive negotiators who are adept at pitting the sellers against one another for the best deal.

How Do Business Buyers Make Their Buying Decisions?

Table 7-1 lists the eight stages of the business buying process.[16] Buyers who face a new-task buying situation usually go through all stages of the buying process. Buyers making modified or straight rebuys may skip some of the stages. We will examine these steps for the typical new-task buying situation.

Problem Recognition

The buying process begins when someone in the company recognizes a problem or need that can be met by acquiring a specific good or a service. **Problem recognition** can result from internal or external stimuli. Internally, the company may decide to launch a new product that requires new production equipment and materi-

	BUYING SITUATIONS		
STAGES OF THE BUYING PROCESS	New Task	Modified Rebuy	Straight Rebuy
1. Problem recognition	Yes	Maybe	No
2. General need description	Yes	Maybe	No
3. Product specification	Yes	Yes	Yes
4. Supplier search	Yes	Maybe	No
5. Proposal solicitation	Yes	Maybe	No
6. Supplier selection	Yes	Maybe	No
7. Order-routine specification	Yes	Maybe	No
8. Performance review	Yes	Yes	Yes

Source: Adapted from Patrick J. Robinson, Charles W. Faris, and Yoram Wind, *Industrial Buying and Creative Marketing* (Boston: Allyn & Bacon, 1967), p. 14.

als. Or a machine may break down and need new parts. Perhaps a purchasing manager is unhappy with a current supplier's product quality, service, or prices. Externally, the buyer may get some new ideas at a trade show, see an ad, or receive a call from a salesperson who offers a better product or a lower price.

General Need Description

Having recognized a need, the buyer next prepares a **general need description** that describes the characteristics and quantity of the needed item. For standard items, this process presents few problems. For complex items, however, the buyer may have to work with others—engineers, users, consultants—to define the item. The team may want to rank the importance of reliability, durability, price, and other attributes desired in the item. In this phase, the alert business marketer can help the buyers define their needs and provide information about the value of different product characteristics.

Product Specification

The buying organization next develops the item's technical **product specifications,** often with the help of a value analysis engineering team. **Value analysis** is an approach to cost reduction in which components are studied carefully to determine if they can be redesigned, standardized, or made by less costly methods of production. The team decides on the best product characteristics and specifies them accordingly. Sellers, too, can use value analysis as a tool to help secure a new account. By showing buyers a better way to make an object, outside sellers can turn straight rebuy situations into new-task situations which give them a chance to obtain new business.

Supplier Search

The buyer now conducts a **supplier search** to find the best vendors. The buyer can compile a small list of qualified suppliers by reviewing trade directories, doing a computer search, or phoning other companies for recommendations. The newer the buying task, and the more complex and costly the item, the greater the amount of time the buyer will spend searching for suppliers. The supplier's task is to get listed in major directories and build a good reputation in the marketplace. Salespeople should watch for companies in the process of searching for suppliers and make certain that their firm is considered.

Proposal Solicitation

In the **proposal solicitation** stage of the business buying process, the buyer invites qualified suppliers to submit proposals. In response, some suppliers will send only a catalog or a salesperson. However, when the item is complex or expensive, the buyer will usually require detailed written proposals or formal presentations from each potential supplier.

Business marketers must be skilled in researching, writing, and presenting proposals in response to buyer proposal solicitations. Proposals should be marketing documents, not just technical documents. Presentations should inspire confidence and should make the marketer's company stand out from the competition.

Supplier Selection

The members of the buying center now review the proposals and select a supplier or suppliers. During **supplier selection,** the buying center often will draw up a list of the desired supplier attributes and their relative importance. In one survey, purchasing executives listed the following attributes as most important in influencing the relationship between supplier and customer: quality products and services, on-time delivery, ethical corporate behavior, honest communication, and competitive prices.[17] Other important factors include repair and servicing capabilities, technical aid and advice, geographic location, performance history, and reputation. The members of the buying center will rate suppliers against these attributes and identify the best suppliers. They often use a supplier evaluation method similar to the one shown in Table 7-2.

The importance of various supplier attributes depends on the type of purchase situation the buyer faces.[18] One study of 220 purchasing managers showed that economic criteria were most important in situations involving routine purchases of standard products. Performance criteria became more important in purchases of nonstandard, more complex products. The supplier's ability to adapt to the buyer's changing needs was important for almost all types of purchases.

Buyers may attempt to negotiate with preferred suppliers for better prices and terms before making the final selections. In the end, they may select a single supplier or a few suppliers. Many buyers prefer multiple sources of supplies to avoid being totally dependent on one supplier and to allow comparisons of prices and performance of several suppliers over time.

Order-Routine Specification

The buyer now prepares an **order-routine specification.** It includes the final order with the chosen supplier or suppliers and lists items such as technical specifications, quantity needed, expected time of delivery, return policies, and warranties. In the case of maintenance, repair, and operating items, buyers are increasingly using *blanket contracts* rather than periodic purchase orders. A blanket contract creates a long-term relationship in which the supplier promises to resupply the buyer as needed at agreed prices for a set time period. The seller holds the stock and the buyer's computer automatically prints out an order to the seller when stock is needed. A blanket order eliminates the expensive process of renegotiating a purchase each time stock is required. It also allows buyers to write more, but smaller purchase orders, resulting in lower inventory levels and carrying costs.

Blanket contracting leads to more single-source buying and to buying more

---

TABLE 7-2
An Example of Vendor Analysis

	RATING SCALE				
ATTRIBUTES	Unacceptable (0)	Poor (1)	Fair (2)	Good (3)	Excellent (4)
Technical and production capabilities					x
Price competitiveness			x		
Product quality					x
Delivery reliability			x		
Service capability					x

4 + 2 + 4 + 2 + 4 = 16
Average score: 16/5 = 3.2

Note: This vendor shows up as strong except on two attributes. The purchasing agent has to decide how important the two weaknesses are. The analysis could be redone using importance weights for the five attributes.
Source: Adapted from Richard Hill, Ralph Alexander, and James Cross, *Industrial Marketing,* 4th ed. (Homewood, IL: Irwin, 1975), pp. 101-4.

items from that source. This practice locks the supplier in tighter with the buyer and makes it difficult for other suppliers to break in unless the buyer becomes dissatisfied with prices or service.

Performance Review

In this stage, the buyer reviews supplier performance. The buyer may contact users and ask them to rate their satisfaction. The **performance review** may lead the buyer to continue, modify, or drop the arrangement. The seller's job is to monitor the same factors used by the buyer to make sure that the seller is giving the expected satisfaction.

We have described the stages that typically would occur in a new-task buying situation. The eight-stage model provides a simple view of the actual business buying decision process. The actual process is usually much more complex. In the modified rebuy or straight rebuy situation, some of these stages would be compressed or bypassed. Each organization buys in its own way, and each buying situation has unique requirements. Different buying center participants may be involved at different stages of the process. Although certain buying-process steps usually do occur, buyers do not always follow them in the same order, and they may add other steps. Often, buyers will repeat certain stages of the process.

INSTITUTIONAL AND GOVERNMENT MARKETS

So far, our discussion of organizational buying has focused largely on the buying behavior of business buyers. Much of this discussion also applies to the buying practices of institutional and government organizations. However, these two non-business markets have additional characteristics and needs. Thus, in this final section, we will address the special features of institutional and government markets.

Institutional Markets

The **institutional market** consists of schools, hospitals, nursing homes, prisons, and other institutions that provide goods and services to people in their care. Institutions differ from one another in their sponsors and in their objectives. For example, Humana hospitals are operated for profit, whereas a nonprofit Sisters of Charity Hospital provides health care to the poor and a government-run hospital might provide special services to veterans.

Many institutional markets are characterized by low budgets and captive patrons. For example, hospital patients have little choice but to eat whatever food the hospital supplies. A hospital purchasing agent has to decide on the quality of food to buy for patients. Because the food is provided as a part of a total service package, the buying objective is not profit. Nor is strict cost minimization the goal—patients receiving poor-quality food will complain to others and damage the hospital's reputation. Thus, the hospital purchasing agent must search for institutional food vendors whose quality meets or exceeds a certain minimum standard and whose prices are low.

Many marketers set up separate divisions to meet the special characteristics and needs of institutional buyers. For example, Heinz produces, packages, and prices its ketchup and other products differently to better serve the requirements of hospitals, colleges, and other institutional markets.

Government Markets

The **government market** offers large opportunities for many companies. Federal, state, and local governments contain more than 82,000 buying units. Government buying and business buying are similar in many ways. But there are also differences that must be understood by companies that wish to sell products and services to governments. To succeed in the government market, sellers must locate key decision makers, identify the factors that affect buyer behavior, and understand the buying decision process.

Government buying organizations are found at the federal, state, and local levels. The federal level is the largest, and its buying units operate in both the civilian and military sectors. Various government departments, administrations, agencies, boards, commissions, executive offices, and other units carry out federal

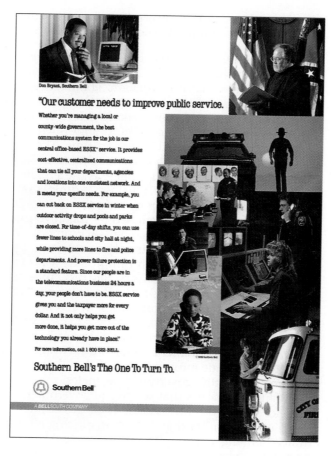

"Our customer needs to improve public service.

Whether you're managing a local or
county-wide government, the best
communications system for the job is our
central office-based ESSX® service. It provides
cost-effective, centralized communications
that can tie all your departments, agencies
and locations into one consistent network. And
it meets your specific needs. For example, you
can cut back on ESSX service in winter when
outdoor activity drops and pools and parks
are closed. For time-of-day shifts, you can use
fewer lines to schools and city hall at night,
while providing more lines to fire and police
departments. And power failure protection is
a standard feature. Since our people are in
the telecommunications business 24 hours a
day, your people don't have to be. ESSX service
gives you and the taxpayer more for every
dollar. And it not only helps you get
more done, it helps you get more out of the
technology you already have in place."
For more information, call 1 800 522-BELL.

Southern Bell's The One To Turn To.

Southern Bell
A BELLSOUTH COMPANY

The government market of-fers many opportunities for companies. Here Southern Bell markets its services to local and county govern-ments.

civilian buying. At the same time, the *General Services Administration* helps to centralize the buying of commonly used items in the civilian section (for example, office furniture and equipment, vehicles, fuels) and in standardizing buying procedures for the other agencies. Federal military buying is carried out by the Defense Department, largely through the *Defense Logistics Agency* and the Army, Navy, and Air Force. In an effort to reduce costly duplication, the Defense Logistics Agency buys and distributes supplies used by all military services. It operates six supply centers, which specialize in construction, electronics, fuel, personnel support, business products, and general supplies. State and local buying agencies include school districts, highway departments, hospitals, housing agencies, and many others. Each has its own buying process that sellers must master.

Major Influences on Government Buyers

Like consumer and business buyers, government buyers are affected by environmental, organizational, interpersonal, and individual factors. One unique thing about government buying is that it is carefully watched by outside publics, ranging from Congress to a variety of private groups interested in how the government spends taxpayers' money. Because their spending decisions are subject to public review, government organizations are buried in paper work. Elaborate forms must be filled out and signed before purchases are approved. The level of bureaucracy is high and marketers must cut through this red tape.

Noneconomic criteria also play a growing role in government buying. Government buyers are asked to favor depressed business firms and areas; small business firms; and business firms that avoid race, sex, or age discrimination. Sellers need to keep these factors in mind when deciding to seek government business.

Government organizations typically require suppliers to submit bids, and they normally award contracts to the lowest bidders. In some cases, however, government buyers make allowances for superior quality or for a firm's reputation for completing contracts on time. Governments also will buy on a negotiated contract basis for complex projects that involve major R&D costs and risks, or when there is little effective competition. Governments tend to favor domestic suppliers over foreign suppliers, which is a major complaint of multinational businesses. Each country tends to favor its own nationals, even when nondomestic firms make superior offers. The European Economic Commission is trying to reduce such biases.

How Do Government Buyers Make Their Buying Decisions?

Government buying practices often seem complex and frustrating to suppliers, who have voiced many complaints about government purchasing procedures. These include too much paper work and bureaucracy, needless regulations, emphasis on low bid prices, decision-making delays, frequent shifts in buying personnel, and too many policy changes. Yet, despite such obstacles, selling to the government often can be mastered in a short time. The government is generally helpful in providing information about its buying needs and procedures. Government is often as eager to attract new suppliers as the suppliers are to find customers.

For example, the Small Business Administration prints a booklet entitled *U.S. Government Purchasing, Specifications, and Sales Directory,* which lists thousands of items most frequently purchased by the government and the specific agencies most frequently buying them. The Government Printing Office issues the *Commerce Business Daily,* which lists major current and planned purchases and recent contract awards, both of which can provide leads to subcontracting markets. The Commerce Department publishes *Business America,* which provides interpretations of government policies and programs and gives concise information on potential worldwide trade opportunities. In several major cities, the General Services Administration operates *Business Service Centers* with staffs to provide a complete education on the way government agencies buy, the steps that suppliers should follow, and the procurement opportunities available. Various trade magazines and associations provide information on how to reach schools, hospitals, highway departments, and other government agencies.

Many companies that sell to the government have not been marketing oriented for a number of reasons. Total government spending is determined by elected officials rather than by any marketing effort to develop this market. Government buying has emphasized price, making suppliers invest their effort in technology to bring costs down. When the product's characteristics are specified carefully, product differentiation is not a marketing factor. Nor do advertising or personal selling matter much in winning bids on an open-bid basis.

More companies are now setting up separate marketing departments for government marketing efforts. Rockwell International, Eastman Kodak, and Goodyear are examples. These companies want to coordinate bids and prepare them more scientifically, to propose projects to meet government needs rather than just respond to government requests, to gather competitive intelligence, and to prepare stronger communications to describe the company's competence.[19]

 # SUMMARY

The business market is vast. In many ways, business markets are like consumer markets, but business markets usually have fewer, larger buyers who are more geographically concentrated. Business demand is *derived,* largely *inelastic,* and more *fluctuating.* More buyers usually are involved in the business buying decision, and business buyers are better trained and more professional than are consumer buyers. In general, business purchasing decisions are more complex, and the buying process is more formal than consumer buying.

The *business market* includes firms that buy goods and services in order to produce products and services to sell to others. It also includes retailing and wholesaling firms that buy goods in order to resell them at a profit. Business buyers make decisions that vary with the three types of buying situations: *straight rebuys, modified rebuys,* and *new tasks.* The decision-making unit of a buying organization—the *buying center*—may consist of many persons playing many roles. The business marketer needs to know the following: Who are the major participants? In what decisions do they exercise influence? What is their relative degree of influence? And what evaluation criteria does each decision participant use? The business marketer also needs to understand the major environmental, interpersonal, and individual influences on the buying process. The business buying decision process itself consists of eight stages: *problem recognition, general need description, product specification, supplier search, proposal solicitation, supplier selection, order-routine specification,* and *performance review.* As business buyers become more sophisticated, business marketers must keep in step by upgrading their marketing accordingly.

The *institutional market* consists of schools, hospitals, prisons, and other institutions that provide goods and services to people in their care. These markets are characterized by low budgets and captive patrons. The *government market* is also vast. Government buyers purchase products and services for defense, education, public welfare, and other public needs. Government buying practices are highly specialized and specified, with open bidding or negotiated contracts characterizing most of the buying. Government buyers operate under the watchful eye of Congress and many private watchdog groups. Hence, they tend to require more forms and signatures, and to respond more slowly in placing orders.

KEY TERMS

Business buying process 188
Business market 188
Buyers 194
Buying center 194
Deciders 194
Derived demand 189
Gatekeepers 195
General need description 202
Government market 204

Inelastic demand 189
Influencers 194
Institutional market 204
Modified rebuy 193
New task 194
Order-routine specification 203
Performance review 204
Problem recognition 201

Product specification 202
Proposal solicitation 202
Straight rebuy 193
Supplier search 202
Supplier selection 203
Systems buying 194
Users 194
Value analysis 202

DISCUSSING THE ISSUES

1. Apple Computer paid top prices for millions of computer memory chips during an industrywide shortage. Soon afterward, demand for memory dropped, and the chips became cheap and plentiful—leaving Apple with millions of dollars in losses. How would a long-term contract have helped in this situation?

2. Which of the major types of buying situations are represented by the following: (a) Chrysler's purchase of computers that go in cars and adjust engine performance to changing driving conditions; (b) Volkswagen's purchase of spark plugs for its line of Jettas; and (c) Honda's purchase of light bulbs for a new Acura model?

3. How could a marketer of office equipment identify the buying center for a law firm's purchase of dictation equipment for each of its partners?

4. Discuss the major environmental factors that would affect the purchase of radar speed detectors by state and local police forces.

5. NutraSweet and other companies have advertised products to the general public that consumers aren't able to buy. How does this strategy help a company sell products to resellers?

6. Assume you are selling a fleet of cars to be used by a company's salesforce. The salespeople need larger cars, which are more profitable for you, but the fleet buyer wants to buy smaller cars. Who might be in the buying center? How might you meet the varying needs of these participants?

APPLYING THE CONCEPTS

1. Many companies that were formerly vertically integrated, producing their own raw materials or parts, are now using outside suppliers to produce them instead. The extreme examples of this practice, such as Dell Computer, own no production facilities and have suppliers make everything to order. This type of company has been nicknamed a "virtual corporation."

   ■ Do you think that buyers and suppliers are likely to be closer or more adversarial in this type of corporate structure?

   ■ Name the advantages and disadvantages of this sort of supplier relationship for (a) the buyer; and (b) the supplier.

2. American corporations are working to improve quality, and many are using techniques such as Continuous Quality Improvement (CQI). A major element of CQI is feedback: When defects are discovered, the cause of the problem is tracked down and changes are made to prevent problems in the future.

   ■ List some of the ways using CQI might affect the relationship and information flow between buyers and suppliers.

   ■ Using CQI also means that purchasing agents become responsible for quality as well as costs. How does this change the role of the purchasing department within the firm?

MAKING MARKETING DECISIONS

SMALL WORLD COMMUNICATIONS, INC.

Lynette Jones wanted to develop a better feel for the customers that Small World Communications would need to attract. She had been calling her network of friends and business associates, talking with them about how they purchased, used, and felt about computer equipment. Lyn called Thomas Campbell, her partner, to talk about what she had learned. "I've been calling my old friends, pumping them for information. Two of them were really helpful. Ira Wolf was an MBA classmate—now he's at a big consumer products firm; and Amy Lightfoot is a branch manager for Computer Barn, the discount chain." "Let me guess," said Tom. "You found out there is a completely different set of needs to be served. The consumer goods company wants a solution to their communications problems, while Computer Barn wants a brand-name product to sell. So we treat Computer Barn like a reseller, and we treat the consumer products company like any other end user." "Tom, you amaze me. You have this uncanny knack for being able to cut right to the core issue, and then blowing it all by oversimplifying too much."

Thomas clicked his ball-point pen into the telephone mouthpiece and said, "I have a call waiting and . . . " "Tom, I'm sorry. Don't hang up. I think you're very astute for a person with your limited education, so tell me more. Ira Wolf's consumer company has everyday computer users, the information services department that sets up and runs their computer networks, the purchasing department, the financial staff, and general management. Who is the key player?" "Lyn, we've got to get to the information services people in a company like that. They like to standardize on a few types of hardware and software to make sure it all works together. They also want to stick with a handful of basic products so they can become real experts on them.

That lets them offer better user support. I've also dealt with the people at Computer Barn. They are completely different—they want products that get good reviews in *PC Magazine* and that offer them a nice profit margin when they sell for a moderately discounted price." "Well, it's obvious that we're going to be tailoring our approaches to different buyers. I'll make a list of what types of buyers we're going to be facing; then we can decide where to focus our strongest efforts, " said Lyn.

WHAT NOW?

1. Describe the buying center for Ira Wolf's consumer goods company that was discussed above. (a) Who would you consider to be the key members of the buying center? (b) What are the needs of each of these key members? (c) Chapter 7 lists a number of major influences on business buyers. Which of these do you think are most important for Ira Wolf's company?

2. Chapter 7 discusses eight stages of the business buying-decision process: problem recognition, general need description, product specification, supplier search, proposal solicitation, supplier selection, order routine specification, and performance review. Small World will offer a new communications software/hardware product that is unique: no existing product does what this product will do. (a) Do you think a product's uniqueness affects the buying-decision process? (b) If you feel uniqueness influences the buying decision, which stages are most likely to be affected? (c) Will the newness and uniqueness of Small World's product make business buyers more likely to purchase it, less likely, or a bit of each? Discuss.

REFERENCES

1. Excerpts from "Major Sales: Who Really Does the Buying," by Thomas V. Bonoma (May-June 1982). Copyright © 1982 by the President and Fellows of Harvard College; all rights reserved. Also see Scott Ticer, "Why Gulfstream's Rivals are Gazing Up in Envy," *Business Week*, February 16, 1987, pp. 66-67; and Sandra D. Atchison, "The Business Jet Pulls Out of Its Dive," *Business Week*, November 21, 1988, pp. 69-72.

2. This definition is adapted from Frederick E. Webster, Jr., and Yoram Wind, *Organizational Buying Behavior* (Englewood Cliffs, NJ: Prentice Hall, 1972), p. 2.

3. For discussions of similarities and differences in consumer and business marketing, see Edward F. Fern and James R. Brown, "The Industrial/Consumer Marketing Dichotomy: A Case of Insufficient Justification," *Journal of Marketing*, Fall 1984, pp. 68-77; and Ron J. Kornakovich, "Consumer Methods Work for Business Marketing: Yes; No," *Marketing News*, November 21, 1988, pp. 4, 13-14.

4. See William S. Bishop, John L. Graham, and Michael H. Jones,

"Volatility of Derived Demand in Industrial Markets and Its Management Implications," *Journal of Marketing*, Spring 1984, pp. 68-77.

5. See James C. Anderson and James A. Narus, "Value-Based Segmentation, Targeting, and Relationship-Building in Business Markets," ISBM Report #12—1989, The Institute for the Study of Business Markets, Pennsylvania State University, University Park, PA, 1989; Lawrence A. Crosby, Kenneth R. Evans, and Deborah Cowles, "Relationship Quality and Services Selling: An Interpersonal Influence Perspective," *Journal of Marketing*, July 1990, pp. 68-81; and Barry J. Farber and Joyce Wycoff, "Relationships: Six Steps to Success," *Sales & Marketing Management*, April 1992, pp. 50-58.

6. See Louis W. Stern and Thomas L. Eovaldi, *Legal Aspects of Marketing Strategy* (Englewood Cliffs, NJ: Prentice Hall, 1984), pp. 330-31; and Robert J. Posch, Jr., *The Complete Guide to Marketing and the Law* (Englewood Cliffs, NJ: Prentice Hall, 1988), pp. 339-40.

7. Patrick J. Robinson, Charles W. Faris, and Yoram Wind, *Industrial Buying Behavior and Creative Marketing* (Boston: Allyn & Bacon, 1967). Also see Erin Anderson, Weyien Chu, and Barton Weitz, "Industrial Purchasing: An Empirical Exploration of the Buyclass Framework," *Journal of Marketing*, July 1987, pp. 71-86.

8. For more on systems selling, see Robert R. Reeder, Edward G. Brierty, and Betty H. Reeder, *Industrial Marketing: Analysis, Planning, and Control* (Englewood Cliffs, NJ: Prentice Hall, 1991), pp. 264-67.

9. Webster and Wind, *Organizational Buying Behavior*, p. 6. For more reading on buying centers, see Bonoma, "Major Sales: Who Really Does the Buying"; and Donald W. Jackson, Jr., Janet E. Keith, and Richard K. Burdick, "Purchasing Agents' Perceptions of Industrial Buying Center Influence: A Situational Approach," *Journal of Marketing*, Fall 1984, pp. 75-83.

10. Webster and Wind, *Organizational Buying Behavior*, pp. 78-80.

11. Wesley J. Johnson and Thomas V. Bonoma, "Purchase Process for Capital Equipment and Services," *Industrial Marketing Management*, Vol. 10, 1981, pp. 258-59.

12. Clifton J. Reichard, "Industrial Selling: Beyond Price and Persistence," *Harvard Business Review*, March-April 1985, p. 128.

13. Webster and Wind, *Organizational Buyng Behavior*, pp. 33-37.

14. Thayer C. Taylor, "Xerox's Sales Force Learns a New Game," *Sales & Marketing Management*, July 1, 1985, pp. 48-51.

15. Bonoma, "Major Sales," p. 114. Also see Ajay Kohli, "Determinants of Influence in Organizational Buying: A Contingency Approach," *Journal of Marketing*, July 1989, pp. 50-65.

16. Robinson, Faris, and Wind, *Industrial Buying Behavior*, p. 14.

17. See "What Buyers Really Want," *Sales & Marketing Management*, October 1989, p. 30.

18. Donald R. Lehmann and John O'Shaughnessy "Decision Criteria Used in Buying Different Categories of Products," *Journal of Purchasing and Materials Management*, Spring 1982, pp. 9-14.

19. For more on U.S. government buying, see Warren H. Suss, "How to Sell to Uncle Sam," *Harvard Business Review*, November-December, 1984, pp. 136-44; Don Hill, "Who Says Uncle Sam's a Tough Sell?" *Sales & Marketing Management*, July 1988, pp. 56-60; John C. Franke, Marketing to the Government: Contracts There for Those Who Know Where to Look," *Marketing News*, October 9, 1989, pp. 1, 7; and Goldstein, "Customer No. 1," pp. M13-M14.

VIDEO CASE 7

CONVERTING GARBAGE TO GOLD

Paul Monroe has a problem. As assistant city manager of Elkton, USA, he is responsible for waste collection and disposal. Just five years ago, Elkton opened a new landfill and already that landfill is near capacity. "It's all these disposables," Paul said to Samantha Cox, his intern from the local university. "People buy disposable razors, pens, dishes, plastic bottles, and, above all, disposable diapers! If they'd outlaw disposables, we wouldn't need a new landfill for three years."

"So, just open a new landfill," Samantha concluded with a shrug. Paul shook his head. "It's not simple," he said. "It took three years just to find a site that Elkton citizens could agree on for the current landfill. It would be even more difficult for a new site now. Under new federal government requirements, landfills must have approved site-specific designs or composite liners. A liner system is very expensive. Furthermore, landfills can't be located on or adjacent to airports, flood plains, unstable areas, wetlands, fault areas, or seismic impact zones. That rules out most of the areas around Elkton."

Paul raised his eyebrows and turned to Samantha. "Say, I've got an idea. Why don't you go to the library and research how other towns are handling their waste problems." Samantha readily agreed. "My pleasure," she replied.

Two weeks later Samantha bounded into Paul's office. "I think I've found some solutions to our landfill problem," she proclaimed with a broad grin. She briefly outlined three basic possibilities: waste-to-energy conversion, recycling, and composting.

Waste-to-energy solutions turn money-draining landfills into money makers by using waste as a power source. Some towns simply burn waste materials to generate heat or electricity. However, that practice has become less common with the advent of stricter air pollution regulations. Now, towns such as Riverview, Michigan, vent methane gas from their landfills and burn it to power turbines which generate electricity. Other towns, such as Eden Prairie, Minnesota, combine waste-to-energy and recycling programs. They sort garbage into recyclable materials and process residues, both of which can be sold. The remaining material—mostly paper—is used to manufacture a "densified Refuse Derived Fuel" (dRDF), which they sell to industrial customers and utilities.

Recycling can also be combined with "landfilling in reverse"—opening a closed landfill and sorting reclaimable waste materials. The dirt from the landfill can be reused, the garbage can be converted to energy, and metals and other materials can be recycled. In Lancaster County, Pennsylvania, reverse landfilling generates revenues from the sale of electricity plus an additional $47,000 per week from the sale of recyclables.

Sevier County, Tennessee, handles its waste through simple composting. It combines garbage with sewage sludge to speed decomposition. The resulting composted product can be sold as a fertilizer/soil conditioner. Collier County, Florida, combines composting with recycling to handle almost all of its wastes. The county's philosophy is "bury, compost, mine, and refill." Burying the garbage accelerates its decomposition, so that the recyclable contents can be mined more easily. Besides selling the obvious recyclables, such as plastic bottles, it converts wood to mulch, turns concrete into aggregate, uses old tires for drainage material for the landfill, and sells the larger appliances to recyclers for their metal content. The county rotates its six landfills, closing the active landfill and reopening the oldest one each year.

"That's just the beginning," Samantha exclaimed. "To generate lots of electricity, you'll need lots of garbage. So, you can take in other cities' garbage and collect tipping fees. The more garbage you collect, the more electricity you can sell. Also, with a big landfill, you've got a small mountain of trash covered with dirt, which also can be a money maker. Riverview, Michigan, calls its mountain of trash Mt. Trashmore. It's become a popular ski slope in the winter, and the city has built a golf course next to it that makes money in the summer."

Samantha continued. "In Cambridge, Massachusetts, they turned a capped landfill into a multipurpose recreational park. Using free dirt from the Massachusetts Bay Tunnel excavation, the town constructed playing fields, parking areas, and jogging and biking paths. Next, they plan to add basketball and tennis courts and a running track. I know of one town that even put a cemetery on an old landfill. Who knows what you could think of for Elkton."

An excited Samantha was running out of breath.

"And, if you really want to sell Elkton on more garbage, point out that increased tipping fees, sales of electricity, and recreational receipts translate into *lower taxes*. As it turns out, garbage isn't a stinking problem, it's a regular gold mine!"

QUESTIONS

1. If Elkton implements Samantha's "solutions," it will become a manufacturer and a governmental buyer of various products. Which products are associated each role?

2. What environmental and organizational influences would affect Elkton's operation as a producer of electricity?

3. If Elkton buys composite liners for a landfill, what type of buying situation is this? Who might play the roles of user, influencer, buyer, decider, and gatekeeper for such a purchase?

4. When a utility buys electricity from a waste-to-energy landfill process, will it go though all eight stages of the industrial buying process? Which stages might be omitted?

5. If you were Paul Monroe, what would you do?

Sources: John A. Barnes, "Learning to Love the Dump Next Door," *The Wall Street Journal,* June 25, 1991, p. A22; Paul Beck, "Waste-to-Energy Plants Generate New Interest," *Consulting-Specifying Engineer,* June 1989, pp. 80-84; Jennifer Carlile, "Reclaiming Landfills," *American City and County,* July 1992, pp. 38, 42, 46; and John Guinan, "Winning Community Support for Waste to Energy," *World Wastes,* September 1992, pp. 39-40.

COMPANY CASE 7

ACT II: CONTROLLING AN INDUSTRIAL MARKET

Gregory Pearl, director of marketing for Appliance Control Technology (ACT), listened as Wallace Leyshon, ACT's president and CEO, conducted another meeting with a reporter from a national business magazine. ACT designs, manufactures, and markets touch-sensitive digital controls for home appliances such as microwave ovens, ranges, and washing machines. These controls allow users to direct the operations of appliances without using the traditional buttons and dials.

"My vision is that someday soon the consumer who owns a midpriced washer and dryer will be able to touch a digital keypad once and the washer or dryer will do everything else. All the consumer will have to do is touch the keypad to tell the unit what types of clothes are inside. For example, once the user tells the washer that the load contains delicate fabrics, it will automatically determine the size of the load, add water at the right temperature, and dispense the correct amount of detergent at the right time. As for the dryer, once the consumer indicates the types of clothes, it will dry the clothes at the correct temperature and cylinder speed, sense the moisture content, and shut off automatically

when the clothes are dry. That would save consumers a lot of time and worry, and it would save a lot of energy. Now consumers have to push lots of buttons and turn dials (electromechanical controls), and they have to be experts at knowing the right things to do to wash all kinds of clothes. In fact, significant progress has already been made in this direction in Europe."

"That sounds exciting," the reporter responded, "but is there a *market* for these electronic controls?"

"As you know," Leyshon continued, "the home appliance market is mature—the value of U.S. manufacturers' shipments totaled a little over $18 billion in 1990 and total units sold grew at an average rate of only 5.6 percent per year from 1980 to 1990 (see Exhibit 7.1). The growth rate is only 4.3 percent over that same period if you exclude microwave ovens. But the good news is that only an estimated 20 percent of home appliances offer the consumer touch-sensitive electronic controls, and most of these are high-end appliances. I think we can produce digital controls cheaply enough so that manufacturers can offer them in midrange appliances. There's huge growth potential in the elec-

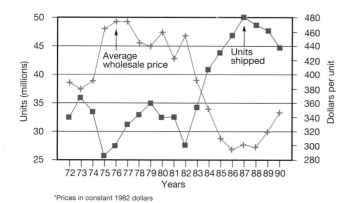

EXHIBIT 7-1
Household appliances: units shipped and average whole price*

Source: U.S. Department of Commerce. Association of Home Appliance Manufacturers.

*Prices in constant 1982 dollars

tronic controls market. And there are actually only five customers: General Electric, Whirlpool, Frigidaire, Maytag, and Raytheon. We know our customers. Furthermore, I think final consumers are ready for touch-sensitive controls on electric ranges and other appliances because they've gotten used to using such controls on microwave ovens."

"What's your marketing strategy to get these manufacturers to adopt electronic controls for their appliances?" asked the reporter.

"Gregory and I are continuously reviewing our marketing strategy. In fact, he has just completed some marketing research that we hope will help us make some additional marketing decisions."

"As you are aware," Leyshon continued, "a key part of our strategy is to manufacture our control units in the United States. Manufacturers are very sensitive about the prices of components in their appliances. Conventional wisdom in the controls industry is that you must manufacture in foreign countries, offshore, to keep your costs down. I just don't think this conventional strategy is necessary. Sure, you might save a little money on wages, but direct labor is only a small percentage of the product's cost. When you go offshore, you add the shipping costs, import-export fees and charges, and additional management personnel. When you look at the whole package, you don't save much money at all, and you make things much more complex. If I build my products in the United States, my research and development, engineering, and production staffs are just a few steps from each other. If a problem develops, we can solve it quickly. That's hard to do over the phone with an engineer who may be thousands of miles away."

The reporter interrupted. "You also mentioned that manufacturers are price sensitive and that they use electronic controls only on their more expensive appliances. How are you going to be price competitive with the standard electromechanical controls?"

Brian Althoff, ACT's vice-president of operations, who had joined the meeting, took up where Leyshon left off. "Another key part of our strategy is standardization. Many control manufacturers design and build controls specifically for one appliance manufacturer, or

even for one particular product that the manufacturer offers. This practice causes two problems. First, it increases costs because of all the different controls that are required. Second, it increases development time because the control maker has to design specific controls for each new product or product change. ACT's strategy will be to develop standard controls that a manufacturer can use across model lines. The touchpad will look different, and the products will have different features. But the control unit, microprocessor, components, and circuit boards will be basically the same for all units. We will use software to change the features and functions from unit to unit. This way we can make more controls of the same type, lowering our costs and passing the savings on to the customer."

The reporter was impressed. "That sounds good, but have you done it?"

"Yes," Leyshon answered enthusiastically. "For example, take our contract with a major company to supply controls for its microwave ovens. The company was using 12 different controls. We replaced those with just two controls, one for domestic models and one for export models. We priced our controls significantly lower than the competitive control it replaced. And we think the savings are even greater when you realize that the company and ACT can carry lower inventories because we don't have all these different models. Also, product-development lead times will be shorter."

"What do you mean by product-development lead times?" asked the reporter.

Gregory Pearl explained. "Remember that ACT sells to appliance manufacturers. These manufacturers either sell their own brand of appliances, such as Whirlpool, or they serve as original equipment manufacturers (OEMs) to retailers, such as Sears, selling them private-label brands like Kenmore. If Sears, for example, decides that it wants to offer a new dryer, it will give the OEM's marketing staff suggestions for the new product. The OEM's marketing staff will develop ideas for product features and give those ideas to the engineering staff so that it can develop a preliminary design and give the specifications for the new dryer to its purchasing department. The purchasing department will then send the specifications to suppliers, including control suppliers, who will submit bids to the OEM to supply the parts at certain prices. A series of negotiations then takes

Frigidaire Company digital keypad.

place between the suppliers and the OEM on prices and features. By the time all this has happened, it may have been a long time since Sears said it wanted a new dryer.

"If the appliance requires a new control, the maker must design it before it can know how to build and price the control. Or, the control maker may realize that Sears's or the OEM's ideas are outdated, because new technology or competitive products have made them obsolete," Pearl concluded.

"The process is too complicated and too slow," Leyshon interjected. "There's a good chance that by the time Sears's ideas have gone through all these groups, there may have been many communication problems."

"We want to change all this. We think that Sears's product-development staff, the appliance manufacturer's product-development staff, and ACT should all sit down together at the start of the process and jointly develop specifications to meet price and performance objectives. We will all have the same information and the process should go much faster with fewer changes along the way."

"Haven't I read that this is the way the Japanese carry out product development?" the reporter asked.

"That's exactly right, and the Koreans, too," Leyshon agreed. "And we'd better start doing it this way also if we are going to have a chance in what is rapidly becoming a global market."

"Who is your competition?"

"We have two groups of competitors: the electromechanical control makers and the electronic equipment makers. The electromechanical group is trying to convert to the new technology, but it will be a difficult process for them. They'll have to make their own products obsolete, and that's hard for companies to do.

"I'm more concerned about the firms now making electronic controls. We have some competition there, but they are following traditional industry strategies."

The reporter paused briefly, then asked, "You mentioned the size of the home appliance industry, but how big is the controls market?"

"We estimate that the controls market in the United States and Europe is about $2 billion a year with the market equally split between the two," Pearl answered. "In fact, the European market may be a little larger. Electronic controls account for a little less than 50 percent of the market."

"This all sounds very interesting," the reporter remarked as he arose from his chair. "I'd like to look over the material you gave me and set up another appointment for next week. I believe our editor will be very interested in what you are trying to accomplish and may want to make this a feature story. I want to make sure I've understood all you've told me so I can accurately capture your story in the article. Thanks for your time. I'll let you three get back to work."

After the reporter had left, Leyshon, Althoff, and Pearl returned to the conference table.

"Well, what do you think?" asked Pearl.

Leyshon reflected for a moment before responding. "Well, I guess some publicity won't hurt us. If they decide to do the article, I just hope they'll do a good job.

"While I've got you here, tell me what you've concluded from the market research project."

EXHIBIT 7-2
Profile of survey respondents

1. All Respondents

Function	Number	Percent
Manufacturers	67	65
Retailers	20	20
Other*	15	15
Total	102	100

2. Manufacturers

Function	Number	Percent
Purchasing and Engineering	36	53
Marketing	31	47

3. Retailers

Function	Number	Percent
Engineering/Service	4	22
Buyers	16	78

*"Other" consists of trade publishers and editors; consultants in the area of design, marketing, and engineering; employees of trade associations; U.S. government personnel, and so on.
Source: Appliance Control Technology.

Pearl had been conducting telephone interviews with manufacturers, retailers, and others in the home appliance industry over the last two months to gain insight into industry practices. He had used an open-ended questionnaire (see Company Case 4) as a script for the interviews and had recorded the information from each interview. He had prepared a set of exhibits summarizing the results.

"First, this exhibit tells you to whom we talked (see Exhibit 7-2). Next, we were interested in determining the respondents' best estimates of the percentage of appliances using electronic controls by type of appliance for 1991 and their projections for 1996. This exhibit summarizes their estimates (see Exhibit 7-3). I have also summarized the respondents' key comments on these pages (see Exhibit 7-4). Finally, I've developed two tables on market shares and price points that may help us (Exhibit 7-5 and 7-6). Let me give you two a few minutes to familiarize yourselves with these exhibits. Then we can discuss them and begin shaping our strategy."

EXHIBIT 7-3
Estimated electronic controls; penetration rates: 1991 and 1996

	1991 (%)	1996 (%)	5-Year Change Multiple
Dishwashers	5	10	2.0 times
Dryers, electric	5	15	3.0 times
Dryers, gas	5	15	3.0 times
Microwaves	90	90	1.0 times
Ranges, electric	20	50	2.5 times
Ranges, gas	15	40	2.7 times
Refrigerators	2	5–50	2.5–25.0 times
Washers	5	15	3.0 times
Room air conditioners	10	25	2.5 times

Source: Appliance Control Technology.

EXHIBIT 7-4
ACT market survey results; selected comments by functional area
Selected comments made by survey respondents, grouped by functional area.

I. Manufacturers: Engineers

- Most technology is closely held by the manufacturer. This is because a successful solution . . . can determine a company's future.
- New ways to save energy are of interest to the appliance industry.
- Suppliers need to tell the story of the electronic system better.
- I feel electronic controls costs are equal to those of electromechanical, or even cheaper if the entire control system is considered.
- Electronic controls are perceived as an unreliable technology by the customer, but the majority of electronics returned by service show "no defect found" (NDF).
- An important trend in supplier development . . . is to become involved up front with the manufacturer.
- I prefer an electronics firm doing controls rather than a controls firm doing electronics.
- The issue in electronic controls is not the technology, but the supplier; that is, the technology is reliable.

II. Manufacturers: Marketing

- There has been a traditional industry interest in electronic controls but the use of these controls in products has been poor.
- Two to three years in development is too long for any electronics program.
- Why aren't electronic controls in white goods [stoves, washers, dryers, and so on] as reliable as those in microwave ovens?
- Consumers are now beyond being intimidated by electronic controls.
- Manufacturers perceive that electronic controls costs are not in line with the benefits provided. There needs to be more parity between cost/benefit.
- If electronic controls were at cost parity, they would quickly replace electro-mechanical controls.
- The biggest problems with electronic controls are reliability and price.
- Electronic controls penetration is increasing.

III. Manufacturers: Purchasing

- One-button functionality is of interest.
- Electronics needs to offer some type of feature to encourage customers to pay a premium. Otherwise, electronic controls cost must be at parity with electromechanical.
- Some consumers have had a bad experience with electronics in the past. Consumers need to be convinced of the reliability.
- Suppliers must understand customer needs and the industry they are selling to.
- Suppliers need to be proactive and innovative.

IV. Trade Groups, Including Publishers and Editors

- Electronic controls are the wave of the future.
- Cost is probably the major issue holding back electronics at this time.
- Energy efficiency is now a big problem.
- A big complaint of the manufacturers was the long development time and the expense of the electronics.

V. Retailers

- Price is a major issue. The higher cost of electronic controls limits their use to only high-end appliances.
- Cost hurts the practicality of electronics.
- Consumers are frightened by the complexity of electronics. For electronics to gain greater acceptance, they need to be simpler.
- Electronic controls should do the thinking for the consumer.
- If possible, electronics should get down to just one button. Just load the machine, press the button, and let it run.

Source: Internal research, Appliance Control Technology.

EXHIBIT 7-5
Market shares for major appliances (%)—1990

	Electrolux	General Electric	Maytag	Raytheon	Whirlpool	Other
Dishwashers	19	35	11	N/A	34	1
Dryers, electric	8	19	15	4	52	2
Dryers, gas	9	13	15	3	55	4
Freezers	32	N/A	22	6	36	4
Rangers, electric	19	47	11	6	15	2
Ranges, gas	20	34	21	20	N/A	5
Refrigerators	19	36	7	9	27	2
Washers	9	15	17	4	52	3

Source: Appliance Magazine.

EXHIBIT 7-6
Home appliance industry: key brand names by price point

| | MANUFACTURER | | | | |
Price Point	Electrolux	General Electric	Maytag	Raytheon	Whirlpool
Premium-priced	Frigidaire	Monarch	Jenn-Air Maytag	Amana	KitchenAid Bauknecht
Midpriced	Frigidaire Westinghouse	General Electric	Maytag Magic Chef	Caloric Speed Queen	Kenmore Whirlpool
Lower priced —	Westinghouse Kelvinator Gibson	RCA Hotpoint	Admiral Norge Signature	Caloric	Roper Estate

Source: Merrill, Lynch.

QUESTIONS

1. Outline ACT's current marketing strategy. What decisions does ACT need to make?

2. What is the nature of demand in the home appliance industry? What factors shape that demand?

3. What is the nature of the buying decision process in the home appliance industry? How is ACT trying to change that process?

4. Who is involved in the buying center in a manufacturer's decisions concerning appliance controls?

5. What environmental and organizational factors should ACT consider in developing its strategy for dealing with buying centers?

6. What recommendations would you make to help ACT develop its marketing strategy?

Source: Based in part on Tom Richman, "Made in the U.S.A.," in *Anatomy of a Start-Up,* Boston: Goldhirsh Group, Inc., 1991, pp. 241-52. Used with permission. Appliance Control Technology also contributed information for this case.

PART II

COMPREHENSIVE CASE

MOTOROLA: GEEPERS, CREEPERS, WHERE'D YOU GET THOSE BEEPERS?

Dr. Niccolette Williamson leaned forward in her seat in University Medical Center's auditorium and studied the overhead being projected on the screen. Dr. Williamson, an ophthalmologist who specialized in cataract surgery, was interested in learning the latest developments in the use of lasers to remove the clouded lens from a patient's eye. Just as the presenter made an important point, Dr. Williamson felt the Motorola Bravo pager on her belt vibrate. Glancing at the display, she recognized her office number and realized that there must be an emergency. She had asked her assistant not to disturb her during this presentation otherwise.

As she stood and picked her way down the row to the aisle, Williamson leaned over and asked a friend to take notes for her, telling him that she had to call her office to check on a patient. Walking up the aisle, she wondered to herself, "How did we ever make it without pagers, and how will we ever get anything done with pagers!"

A few minutes later, Dr. Williamson's daughter Mary prepared to recite her lines from a scene in a play based on John Steinbeck's book, *The Grapes of Wrath,* which the Jefferson High Drama Club was rehearsing.

Just as she was about to speak, she heard a beeper emit a tone. The drama instructor looked up from his notes in disgust at this interruption and saw four members of the cast looking at their beepers to see whose beeper signaled. Mary glanced at the display on her neon green Motorola Bravo Express beeper and read, "942-7574 007." She didn't recognize the number, but the "007" was her mother's code.

Mary sheepishly apologized to the drama instructor for having forgotten to put the beeper in the vibrate mode. She asked to be excused to call her mother, suggesting that it must be important.

"Okay, okay. We'll take a short break while Mary makes her call. But you folks have to stop bringing these beepers to practice. We're never going to be ready if our practices keep getting interrupted by all your phone calls. If Shakespeare had encountered this problem, we would have fewer plays."

Mary called her mother, who informed her that she had an emergency operation and that she would be very late getting home.

"You'll have to pick up your brother after soccer practice. Tell your dad that I'll be late. You'll need to help with supper also. Sorry to bother you. Apologize to Mr. Miles for the interruption, but it surely is good to be able to find you at times like this."

Background

When Motorola Chairman Robert W. Galvin's father founded the Schaumburg, Illinois, company in 1928, neither he nor those working with him could have foreseen communication technology's rapid advance. Originally, the company manufactured and marketed car radios, taking its name from a combination of the words *motor* and *Victrola* (an early brand name for radios).

During the following years, Motorola entered the television, automotive electronics, semiconductor, pager, and cellular telephone businesses. Intense competition from Japanese electronics firms, however, forced Motorola from the television and even car radio markets. Then, in the mid-1980s, Japanese firms flooded the U.S. market with higher-quality pagers and cellular telephones, smashing Motorola's virtual monopoly of those two product markets.

Motorola, however, did not roll over and play dead. It learned from the very Japanese companies that were beating it in the marketplace. Under Galvin's leadership, the company dramatically improved product quality, reduced costs through improved manufacturing processes, and fought for market share. It supported these efforts by funneling billions into employee training, capital improvements, and research and development. Further, the company built on its strengths in marketing and software development, areas where its Japanese rivals were not as strong.

Motorola's efforts paid off. It reclaimed a leadership role in both U.S. and international semiconductor markets. The company also developed an especially strong position in the booming cellular phone market. The company separated its cellular phone business from its communications division, which made two-way radios and pagers, and cut development time for new phones in half. In 1989, Motorola introduced the MicroTac cellular phone. The phone was small enough to fit in a coat pocket and flipped open for use. Workers and robots assembled the MicroTac's 400 parts in 2 hours, down from the 40 hours required to assemble a similar phone in 1985. Motorola hoped that MicroTac and its other cellular phones would allow it to capture a significant portion of the estimated 10.5 million new cellular users who would sign up for cellular service between 1990 and 1995.

Also in 1989, Motorola scooped the competition by introducing the first wristwatch pager, a Dick-Tracy-like device developed in cooperation with Timex, which sold for $300. This was quite an achievement for the only remaining American producer of pagers as of 1985. Motorola realized that it had been taking too long to build pagers and that its products had erratic quality. As it did with cellular phones, Motorola revised the entire pager business process, from ordering to delivery. The company adopted the goal of delivering high-quality pagers that it customized to meet the customers' needs, but that also took advantage of economies of scale. Now, 20 minutes after a salesperson enters an order, the automated assembly line that includes 27 robots begins to produce the order. Motorola's efforts resulted in the wristwatch pager and the Bravo and Bravo Express pagers.

How Pagers Work

Motorola does not sell its pagers directly to end users. It sells to companies that the federal government licenses to serve as radio common carriers (RCCs). These firms have radio towers that serve designated geographic areas.

The RCCs sell their pagers in one of three ways. First, they may sell directly to business or nonbusiness end customers by establishing one or more offices in the geographic areas they serve. Customers come into these offices to buy or rent paging units. When they sign up for the service, the company provides each customer with a unique telephone number for his or her pager. The customer pays a monthly fee for use of the pager and usually a small monthly maintenance fee. Second, the RCC may sell through retailers. The company will package a pager and instructions and provide it to a retailer, such as Best Stores, Kmart, or electronics stores. Customers then purchase the pager at the retail store. The package contains usage instructions and an 800 telephone number for the customer to call to initiate service and billing. Third, some RCCs have authorized resellers who sell and initiate service for the customer. Customers may not even be aware of which RCC provides service for their units.

After customers obtain their pagers, they tell the pager's telephone number to people that they want to be able to call the pager. When someone dials the pager's telephone number from any touchtone telephone, the telephone system routes the call to the RCC's radio tower. The caller hears a beep tone and pushes the buttons on the telephone to enter the telephone number that the person with the pager should call. The caller can also enter additional numbers that serve as a code to identify the caller or to communicate other information. Equipment at the tower converts all this information to a radio signal that only the pager with that particular telephone number can receive. If that pager owner has the pager turned on and is in the RCC's service area, he or she will receive the message.

The pager owner will hear one to three beeps, indicating an incoming message, and will see the telephone number and other codes appear on the pager's LCD display. Some pagers offer the option of having the pager vibrate instead of emitting a beep tone. Other pagers can receive and display written messages. These systems require a special terminal to enter the message. Other pagers actually receive the caller's spoken message and broadcast it to the pager wearer. Pagers can store messages for later viewing and can "stamp" them with the time and date received.

Bravo Starts a Trend

Motorola launched the Bravo model in 1987. This pager was no larger than a box of kitchen matches, and each pager worked on a unique combination of an access code and radio frequency. The Bravo's smaller size made it more appealing to users.

When Motorola introduced the Bravo, it expected that, as for its other pagers, the target markets would be construction workers and doctors and other medical personnel. These business customers are often in remote locations away from a telephone or must respond to emergencies. Motorola also knew that there would be one unwanted business customer, the illegal drug dealer. Media reports had shown that many drug dealers were using pagers to keep in contact with suppliers or customers. As a result, some school systems banned pagers from their schools. Some sources estimated that, despite the popular culture's association of pagers with drug dealing, only one percent of customers used pagers in this manner.

However, Motorola didn't anticipate nonbusiness customers' interest in pagers. The new pagers attracted nonbusiness customers for several reasons. First, Motorola and the other manufacturers had steadily reduced the pager's size. The user could easily conceal the pager, which could fit in the palm of a hand. It was no longer a bulky box hanging on one's belt; in fact, pagers weighed as little as 4 ounces. Further, the pager could vibrate to inform the customer of a call as opposed to making a loud beep that disturbed others. Second, with increased production volume, manufacturers could reduce prices. Pagers ranged in price from $60 to $120, down from $400 just ten years ago. Third, besides the reduced purchase price, monthly service ranged from $9 to $15 for a basic package that included up to 300 calls per month.

With the lower prices, smaller sizes, and improved features, consumers began to find all sorts of uses for the pager, which they usually called the beeper. Adults realized that they did not have to be doctors or construction workers to afford or need a beeper. Adults with elderly parents, for example, may want a beeper to allow them to stay in contact. Or, they may just need to be available to family, friends, the baby sitter, or child-care centers or schools.

However, teenagers surprised Motorola and the other pager manufacturers by becoming the "hot" market segment. Teenagers who liked to hang out at the local mall for long hours discovered that personal beepers allowed them to keep in touch with friends. Wealthy teenagers realized that they could use the beepers to screen their calls and keep their monthly cellular phone bills under control. Popular teenagers perceived that the beeper allowed their friends to find them no matter where they were. Others noted that their friends could call them directly using the beeper, without having to go through their parents as they would when using the home telephone. Further, although many teenagers bought their own pagers, parents often bought them for their kids so they could find them at mealtime. This allowed kids not to have to tell their parents where they were going to be all the time, because the parents could beep them. Many teenagers could not resist this combination of freedom and access.

No one knows the size of the teenage market, but one major dealer estimated that teenagers accounted for 20 percent of its sales. Industry sources estimated that the total U.S. pager market grew 11 percent, to 4.1 million units in 1992. Another source estimated that the *retail* market (sales to nonbusiness customers) grew 50 percent to 600,000 units in 1992 and that it would reach 3.2 million retail units annually by 1996.

Telocator Network of America, the paging industry's trade association, estimated that Motorola controlled 85 percent of the $500 million annual pager market. Considering rental and leasing fees and monthly service charges, Telocator estimated the pager market to account for $2 billion in annual sales with 12 million pagers in use. Some observers predicted that by the year 2000 there will be 50 million pagers nationwide with most of the growth coming from personal use.

Pager manufacturers and other firms have been quick to react to this trend. In 1991, Motorola introduced the Bravo Express, the first colored pagers. Teenagers found the clear and neon green models so popular that Motorola introduced neon shades of pink, yellow, and blue in 1992. Swatch produced a $250 watch with limited pager features, calling it the Piepser (German for beeper). A blue jeans manufacturer introduced jeans with beeper pockets. One firm tied the pager to satellite technology to allow a person to beep anyone who was near any city in the United States,

Motorola's colored pagers.

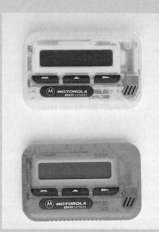

Canada, and Mexico. Some parents have found this service helpful for keeping in touch with out-of-town college students.

Despite the practical uses for pagers, however, no one could deny the product's image and status features. Having a beeper on one's belt has suddenly become the "in" thing in many high schools, especially in the Northeast. Some observers report that many teenagers continue to wear their beepers although the service agency had stopped service for them because of nonpayment. Other observers report an increase in the theft of garage door openers because they look like pagers when worn! The colored pagers even allow teenagers to make fashion statements.

Back at Play Practice

Mary Williamson returned to the rehearsal and apologized again to Mr. Miles. Following practice, she realized that she and her friend Susan had been planning to get together early that evening to study for a biology test. Mary thought that she should call Susan to postpone the session until later because of her change in plans. However, Mary didn't know where Susan was and would just have to hope that she was at home.

"Guess I'd better encourage Susan to get a beeper," she thought.

QUESTIONS

1. Motorola and other firms are interested in catering to the teenagers who want to use pagers. How would you conduct market research to learn more about this market?

2. How do teenagers' cultural, social, personal, and psychological characteristics affect their consumer behavior with respect to pagers?

3. How will pagers' product characteristics affect their rate of adoption? Would you predict a fast or slow rate of adoption for pagers in the teenage market?

4. Pagers represent a product originally targeted for organizational or business markets that has made the transition to the consumer market. What factors caused this transition? How are the marketing mixes for pagers different between organizational and consumer markets?

5. If an RCC's salesperson knows that local school systems have banned pagers or suspects that a potential teenage customer may be involved in drugs, should the salesperson sell or rent a pager to teenagers?

6. What marketing recommendations would you make to Motorola to help it address the teenage market?

Sources: William J. Hampton, "What Is Motorola Making at This Factory? History," *Business Week*, December 5, 1988, pp. 168D-H; Lois Therrien, "The Rival Japan Respects," *Business Week*, November 13, 1989, pp. 108-18; Jagannath Dubashi, "The Bandit Standoff," *Financial World*, September 17, 1991, pp. 48-50; Jonathan Rabinovitz, "Teen-Agers' Beepers: Communications as Fashion," *The New York Times*, March 18, 1991, p. 1A; Cathy Singer, "Now Hear This: The Beeper Has Become a Status Symbol," *The New York Times*, June 28, 1992, p. 1LI; William M. Bulkeley, "More and More Teens Can't Live Without Beepers on Their Belts," *The Wall Street Journal*, December 7, 1992, p. B5. Motorola also contributed information for this case.

*M*easuring and Forecasting Demand

8

Qantas, Australia's international airline, is experiencing a demand bonanza. Its market area in the Pacific Basin contains some of the fastest-growing economies in the world—including Japan; Australia; and the four newly industrialized countries of Hong Kong, Singapore, South Korea, and Taiwan. Thus, the area's growth rate for air travel far exceeds world averages. Industry forecasts suggest that Pacific Basin air travel will grow at 10 percent to 14 percent per year through 1995, and that the area will capture a 40-percent share of all international air passenger traffic by the year 2000.

Such explosive growth presents a huge opportunity for Qantas and the other airlines serving the Pacific Basin. However, it also presents some serious headaches. To take *advantage* of the growing demand, Qantas must first *forecast* it accurately and prepare to *meet* it. Air-travel demand has many dimensions. Qantas must forecast how many and what kinds of people will be traveling, where they will want to go, and when. It must project total demand as well as demand in each specific market it intends to serve. And Qantas must estimate what share of this total demand it can capture under alternative marketing strategies and in various competitive circumstances. Moreover, it must forecast demand not just for next year, but also for the next two years, five years, and even further into the future.

Forecasting air-travel demand is no easy task. A host of factors affect how often people will travel and where they will go. In order to make accurate demand forecasts, Qantas must first anticipate changes in the factors that influence demand—worldwide and country-by-country economic conditions, demographic characteristics, population growth, political developments, technological advances, competitive activity, and many other factors. Qantas has little control over many of these factors.

Demand can shift quickly and dramatically. For example, relative economic growth and political stability in Japan, Australia, and the other Pacific Basin countries have caused a virtual explosion of demand for air travel there. Ever-increasing numbers of tourists from around the world are visiting these areas. In Australia, for instance, foreign tourism more than doubled between 1984 and 1988, and it is expected to triple between 1988 and the year 2000. Also, people from the Pacific Basin countries are themselves traveling more. For example, almost 12 million Japanese took holidays abroad last year, a 10 percent increase over the previous year. Forecasting demand in the face of such drastic shifts can be difficult.

To make things even more complicated, Qantas must forecast more than just demand. The airline must also anticipate the many factors that can affect its ability to meet that demand. For example, what airport facilities will be available and how will this affect Qantas? Will there be enough skilled labor to staff and maintain its aircraft? In the Pacific Basin, as demand has skyrocketed, the support system has not. A shortage of runways and terminal space already limits the number of flights Qantas can schedule. As a result, Qantas may decide to purchase fewer but larger planes. Fewer planes would require fewer crews, and larger planes can hold more passengers at one time, making flights more profitable.

Qantas bases many important decisions on its forecasts. Perhaps the most important decision involves aircraft purchases. To meet burgeoning demand, Qantas knows that it will need more planes. But how many more planes? At about $150 million for each new Boeing 747-400, ordering even a few too many planes can be very costly. On the other hand, if Qantas buys too few planes, it has few short-run solutions. It usually takes about two years to get delivery of a new plane.

If Qantas overestimates demand by even a few percentage points, it will be burdened with costly overcapacity. If it underestimates demand, it could miss out on profit opportunities and disappoint customers who prefer to fly Qantas.

Ultimately, for Qantas, the forecasting problem is more than a matter of temporary gains or losses of customer satisfaction and sales—it's a matter of survival. Thus, Qantas has a lot flying on the accuracy of its forecasts.[1]

 ## CHAPTER PREVIEW

Chapter 8 presents the essentials of measuring and forecasting demand, information which marketers must have in order to manage effectively.

First, we define a market as the set of *actual* and *potential consumers.* Marketers must distinguish among the *potential, available, qualified available, served,* and *penetrated markets.*

Next, we explain methods for determining *current market demand,* including ways to estimate *total demand, area market demand, actual industry sales,* and *market shares* of competitors.

We conclude with techniques that companies use to *forecast future demand.* These include methods based on what *buyers, salesforce,* and *experts* say; what consumers do in *market tests;* and what consumers have done as seen in *time-series analysis, leading indicators,* and *statistical demand analysis.*

When a company finds an attractive market, it must estimate that market's current size and future potential carefully. The company can lose a lot of profit by overestimating or underestimating the market. This chapter presents the principles and tools for measuring and forecasting market demand. The next chapter will look at the more qualitative aspects of markets, and at how companies segment their markets and select the most attractive segments.

Demand can be measured and forecasted on many levels. Figure 8-1 shows *ninety* different types of demand measurement! Demand might be measured for six different *product levels* (product item, product form, product line, company sales, industry sales, and total sales); five different *space levels* (customer, territory, region, U.S.A., world); and three different *time levels* (short range, medium range, and long range).

Each demand measure serves a specific purpose. A company might forecast short-run total demand for a product as a basis for ordering raw materials, planning production, and borrowing cash. Or it might forecast long-run regional demand for a major product line as a basis for designing a market expansion strategy.

DEFINING THE MARKET

Market demand measurement calls for a clear understanding of the market involved. The term *market* has acquired many meanings over the years. In its original meaning, a market is a physical place where buyers and sellers gather to exchange goods and services. Medieval towns had market squares where sellers brought their goods and buyers shopped for goods. In today's cities, buying and selling occurs in what are called shopping areas rather than markets.

To an economist, a market describes all the buyers and sellers who transact over some good or service. Thus, the soft-drink market consists of sellers such as Coca-Cola, Pepsi-Cola, and 7-Up and all the consumers who buy soft drinks. The economist is interested in the structure, conduct, and performance of each market.

To a marketer, a **market** is the set of all actual and potential buyers of a product or service. A market is the set of buyers, and an **industry** is the set of sellers. The size of a market hinges on the number of buyers who might exist for a

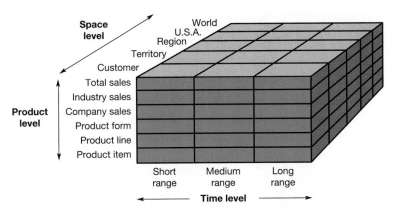

FIGURE 8-1
Ninety types of demand measurement (6 × 5 × 3)

particular market offer. Potential buyers for something have three characteristics: *interest, income,* and *access.*

Consider the consumer market for Honda motorcycles. To assess its market, Honda first must estimate the number of consumers who have a potential interest in owning a motorcycle. To do this, the company could contact a random sample of consumers and ask the following question: "Do you have an interest in buying and owning a motorcycle?" If one person out of ten says yes, Honda can assume that 10 percent of the total number of consumers would constitute the potential market for motorcycles. The **potential market** is the set of consumers who profess some level of interest in a particular product or service.

Consumer interest alone is not enough to define the motorcycle market. Potential consumers must have enough income to afford the product. They must be able to answer yes to the following question: "Can you afford to buy a motorcycle?" The higher the price, the fewer the number of people who can answer yes to this question. Thus, market size depends on both interest and income.

Access barriers further reduce motorcycle market size. If Honda does not distribute its products in certain remote areas, potential consumers in those areas are not available as customers. The **available market** is the set of consumers who have interest, income, and access to a particular product or service.

For some market offers, Honda might restrict sales to certain groups. A particular state might ban the sale of motorcycles to anyone under 18 years of age. The remaining adults make up the **qualified available market**—the set of consumers who have interest, income, access, and qualifications for the product or service.

Honda now has the choice of going after the whole qualified available market or concentrating on selected segments. Honda's **served market** is the part of the qualified available market it decides to pursue. For example, Honda may decide to concentrate its marketing and distribution efforts on the east and west coasts, which then become its served market.

Honda and its competitors will end up selling a certain number of motorcycles in their served market. The **penetrated market** is the set of consumers who already have bought motorcycles.

Figure 8-2 brings all these market concepts together with some hypothetical numbers. The bar on the left of the figure shows the ratio of the potential market—all interested persons—to the total population. Here the potential market is 10 percent. The bar on the right shows several possible breakdowns of the potential market. The available market—those who have interest, income, and access—is 40 percent of the potential market. The qualified available market—those who can meet the legal requirements—is 50 percent of the available market (or 20 percent of the potential market). Honda concentrates its efforts on 50 percent of the qualified available market—the served market, which is 10 percent of the potential market. Finally, Honda and its competitors already have penetrated 50 percent of the served market (or 5 percent of the potential market).

These market definitions are a useful tool for marketing planning. If Honda is not satisfied with current sales, it can take a number of actions. It can lobby for lower qualifications of potential buyers. It can expand to other available markets in the United States or in other countries. It can lower its price to expand the size of the potential market. It can try to attract a larger percentage of buyers from its served mar-

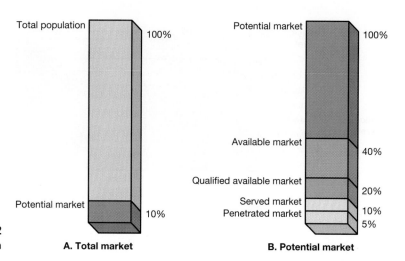

FIGURE 8-2
Levels of market definition

A. Total market

Total population — 100%

Potential market — 10%

B. Potential market

Potential market — 100%

Available market — 40%

Qualified available market — 20%

Served market — 10%

Penetrated market — 5%

ket through stronger promotion or distribution efforts to current target consumers. Or it can try to expand the potential market by increasing its advertising to convert noninterested consumers into interested consumers. This is what Honda did when it ran its successful campaign on the theme "You meet the nicest people on a Honda."

MEASURING CURRENT MARKET DEMAND

We now turn to some practical methods for estimating current market demand. Marketers will want to estimate three different aspects of current market demand—*total market demand, area market demand,* and *actual sales and market shares.*

Estimating Total Market Demand

The **total market demand** for a product or service is the total volume that would be bought by a defined consumer group in a defined geographic area in a defined time period in a defined marketing environment under a defined level and mix of industry marketing effort.

Total market demand is not a fixed number, but a function of the stated conditions. One of these conditions, for example, is the level and mix of industry marketing effort. Another is the state of the environment. Part A of Figure 8-3 shows the relationship between total market demand and these conditions. The horizontal axis shows different possible levels of industry marketing expenditure in a given time period. The vertical axis shows the resulting demand level. The curve represents the estimated level of market demand for varying levels of industry marketing expenditure. Some base sales (called the *market minimum*) would take place without any marketing expenditures. Greater marketing expenditures would yield higher levels of demand, first at an increasing rate, and then at a decreasing rate. Marketing expenditures above a certain level would not cause much more demand, suggesting an upper limit to market demand called the *market potential.* The industry market forecast shows the level of market demand corresponding to the planned level of industry marketing expenditure in the given environment.[2]

The distance between the market minimum and the market potential shows the overall sensitivity of demand to marketing efforts. We can think of two extreme types of markets, the *expandable* and the *nonexpandable.* An expandable market, such as the market for compact disc players, is one whose size is strongly affected by the level of industry marketing expenditures. In terms of Figure 8-3A, in an expandable market, the distance between Q_0 and Q_1 would be fairly large. A nonexpandable market, such as the market for opera, is one whose size is not much affected by the level of marketing expenditures; the distance between Q_0 and Q_1 would be fairly small. Organizations selling in a nonexpandable market can take **primary demand**—total demand for all brands of a given product or service—as a given. They concentrate their marketing resources on building **selective demand**—demand for *their* brand of the product or service.

Given a different marketing environment, we must estimate a new market demand curve. For example, the market for motorcycles is stronger during pros-

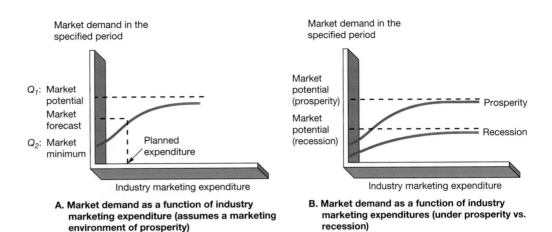

FIGURE 8-3 Market demand

perity than during recession. Figure 8-3B shows the relationship of market demand to the environment. A given level of marketing expenditure always will result in more demand during prosperity than it would during a recession. The main point is that marketers should carefully define the situation for which they are estimating market demand.

Companies have developed various practical methods for estimating total market demand. We will illustrate two here. Suppose Warner Communications Company wants to estimate the total annual sales of recorded compact discs. A common way to estimate total market demand is as follows:

Operating in a mature, non-expandable market, Quaker Oats works to increase selective demand for its Kibbles 'n Bits dog food products. Here, the coupons add urgency to buying the brand.

$$Q = n \times q \times p$$

where

Q = total market demand

n = number of buyers in the market

q = quantity purchased by an average buyer per year

p = price of an average unit

Thus, if there are 100 million buyers of compact discs each year, and the average buyer buys six discs a year, and the average price is $14, then the total market demand for cassette tapes is $8.4 billion (= 100,000,000 × 6 × $14).

A variation on the preceding equation is known as the *chain ratio method.* Using this method, the analyst multiplies a base number by a chain of adjusting percentages. For example, suppose the U.S. Navy wants to attract 112,000 new male recruits each year from American high schools. The marketing question is whether this is a reasonable target in relation to the market potential. The Navy estimates market potential using the following method:

Total number of male high school graduating students	10,000,000
Percentage who are militarily qualified (no physical, emotional, or mental handicaps)	×.50
Percentage of those qualified who are potentially interested in military service	×.15
Percentage of those qualified and interested in military service who consider the navy the preferred service	×.30

This chain of numbers shows a market potential of 225,000 recruits. Since this exceeds the target number of recruits sought, the U.S. Navy should have little trouble meeting its target if it does a reasonable job of marketing the navy.[3]

Estimating Area Market Demand

Companies face the problem of selecting the best sales territories and allocating their marketing budget optimally among these territories. Therefore they need to estimate the market potential of different cities, states, and even nations (see Marketing Highlight 8-1). Two major methods are available: the *market-buildup method,* which is used primarily by business goods firms, and the *market-factor index method,* which is used primarily by consumer goods firms.

Market-Buildup Method
The market-buildup method calls for identifying all the potential buyers in each market and estimating their potential purchases. Suppose a manufacturer of mining instruments developed an instrument for assessing the actual proportion of gold content in gold-bearing ores. The portable instrument can be used in the field to test gold ore. By using it, miners would not waste their time digging deposits of ore containing too little gold to be commercially profitable. The manufacturer wants to price the instrument at $1,000. It sees each mine as buying one or more instruments, depending on the mine's size. The company wants to determine the market potential for this instrument in each mining state and whether to hire a salesperson to cover that state. It would place a salesperson in each state that has a market potential of over $300,000. The company would like to start by finding the market potential in Colorado.

To estimate the market potential in Colorado, the manufacturer can consult the Standard Industrial Classification (SIC) developed by the U.S. Bureau of the Census. The SIC is the government's coding system that classifies industries, for purposes of data collection and reporting, according to the product produced or operation performed. All industries fall into the ten major divisions shown in column 1 of Table 8-1. Each major industrial group is assigned to a two-digit code.

KFC FINDS MORE POTENTIAL IN ASIA THAN IN THE UNITED STATES

Kentucky Fried Chicken's success in Asia dramatizes the case for becoming a global firm. Had PepsiCo's KFC Corporation remained only a domestic U.S. business, its overall fortunes would have fallen. In 1991, for example, its U.S. sales fell 5 percent as health-minded American consumers reduced their intake of fried foods and as other fast-food competitors moved up.

Not so in Asia. KFC, not McDonald's, is the fast-food leader in China, South Korea, Malaysia, Thailand, and Indonesia, and it is second to only McDonald's in Japan and Singapore. KFC's 1,470 outlets average $1.2 million per store, about 60 percent more than its average U.S. stores. In Tiananmen Square, KFC operates its busiest outlet, a 701-seat restaurant serving 2.5 million customers a year. No wonder KFC plans to double its number of Asian outlets during the next five years.

Why is KFC so successful in Asia? First, many of the large Asian cities have a growing concentration of young middle-class urban workers with rising incomes. Fast-food outlets represent a step up from buying food at hawkers' stalls, and Asians are willing to pay more for the quality and comfort of sitting in a well-decorated, American-style restaurant. Second, Asian women have been entering the labor force in large numbers, leaving them with less time for cooking meals at home. Third, chicken is more familiar to the Asian palate than pizza, and more available than beef. Further, chicken faces none of the religious strictures that beef faces in India or that pork faces in Muslim countries.

KFC serves its standard chicken, mashed potatoes, and cole slaw throughout Asia but has offered a few adaptations, such as Hot Wings, a spicier chicken, in Thailand, and fried fish and chicken curry in Japan.

Clearly, companies must increasingly view the world as their market. They must identify those areas that promise the greatest potential sales and profit growth, whether in their neighborhood, state, nation, or the world beyond.

Source: See Andrew Tanzer, "Hot Wings Take Off," *Forbes,* January 18, 1993, p. 74.

Mining bears the code numbers 10 to 14. Metal mining has the code number 10 (see column 2). Within metal mining are further breakdowns into three-digit SIC numbers (see column 3). The gold and silver ores category has the code number 104. Finally, gold and silver ores are subdivided into further groups, with four-digit code numbers (see column 4). Thus, lode gold has the code number 1042. Our manufacturer is interested in mines that mine lode deposits (those mined from underground) and placer deposits (those mined by dredging or washing).

Next the manufacturer can turn to the Census of Mining to determine the number of gold-mining operations in each state, their locations within the state, the number of employees, annual sales, and net worth. Using the data on Colorado, the company prepares the market potential estimate shown in Table 8-2. Column 1 classifies mines into three groups based on the number of employees. Column 2 shows the number of mines in each group. Column 3 shows the potential number of instruments that mines in each size class might buy. Column 4 shows the unit market potential (column 2 times column 3). Finally, column 5 shows the dollar market potential, given that each instrument sells for $1,000. Colorado has a dollar market potential of $370,000. Therefore, the mining instrument manufacturer should hire one salesperson for Colorado. In the same way, companies in other industries can use the market-buildup method to estimate market potential in specific market areas.

Market-Factor Index Method

Consumer goods companies also have to estimate area market potentials. Consider the following example: A manufacturer of men's dress shirts wishes to evaluate its

TABLE 8-1
The Standard Industrial Classification (SIC)

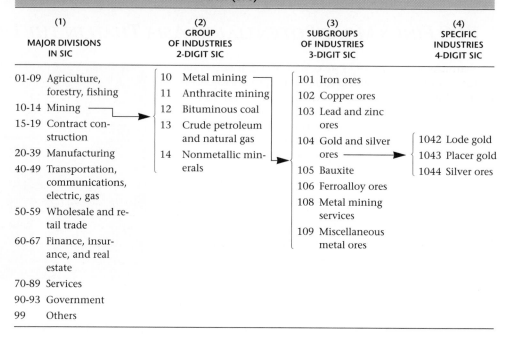

(1) MAJOR DIVISIONS IN SIC	(2) GROUP OF INDUSTRIES 2-DIGIT SIC	(3) SUBGROUPS OF INDUSTRIES 3-DIGIT SIC	(4) SPECIFIC INDUSTRIES 4-DIGIT SIC
01-09 Agriculture, forestry, fishing	10 Metal mining	101 Iron ores	
10-14 Mining	11 Anthracite mining	102 Copper ores	
15-19 Contract construction	12 Bituminous coal	103 Lead and zinc ores	
20-39 Manufacturing	13 Crude petroleum and natural gas	104 Gold and silver ores	1042 Lode gold
40-49 Transportation, communications, electric, gas	14 Nonmetallic minerals	105 Bauxite	1043 Placer gold
50-59 Wholesale and retail trade		106 Ferroalloy ores	1044 Silver ores
60-67 Finance, insurance, and real estate		108 Metal mining services	
70-89 Services		109 Miscellaneous metal ores	
90-93 Government			
99 Others			

sales performance relative to market potential in several major market areas, starting with Indianapolis. It estimates total national potential for dress shirts at about $2 billion per year. The company's current nationwide sales are $140 million, about a 7 percent share of the total potential market. Its sales in the Indianapolis metropolitan area are $1,100,000. It wants to know whether its share of the Indianapolis market is higher or lower than its national 7 percent market share. To find this out, the company first needs to calculate market potential in the Indianapolis area.

A common method for calculating area market potential is to identify market factors that correlate with market potential and combine them into a weighted index. An excellent example of this method is called the *buying power index,* which is published each year by *Sales & Marketing Management* magazine in its *Survey of Buying Power.*[4] This survey estimates the buying power for each region, state, and metropolitan area of the nation. The buying power index is based on three factors: the area's share of the nation's *disposable personal income, retail sales,* and *population.* The buying power index for a specific area is given by

$$B_i = .5y_i + .3r_i + .2p_i$$

where

TABLE 8-2
Market-Buildup Method Using SIC: Instrument Market Potential in Colorado

SIC	(1) Number of employees	(2) Number of mines	(3) Potential Number of Instrument Sales per Employee size class	(4) Unit Market Potential (2 × 3)	(5) Dollar Market Potential (at $1,000 per instrument)
1042	Under 10	80	1	80	
(lode deposits)	10 to 50	50	2	100	
	Over 50	20	4	80	
		150		260	$260,000
1043	Under 10	40	1	40	
(placer	10 to 50	20	2	40	
deposits)	Over 50	10	3	30	
		70		110	110,000
					$370,000

B_i = percentage of total national buying power in area i

y_i = percentage of national disposable personal income in area i

r_i = percentage of national retail sales in area i

p_i = percentage of national population in area i

The three coefficients in the formula reflect the relative weights of the three factors.

Using this index, the shirt manufacturer looks up Indianapolis, Indiana, and finds that this market has .4936 percent of the nation's disposable personal income, .5527 percent of the nation's retail sales, and .5016 percent of the nation's population. Thus, it calculates the buying power index for Indianapolis as follows:

$$B = .5(.4936) + .3(.5527) + .2(.5016) = .5129$$

That is, Indianapolis should account for .5129 percent of the nation's total potential demand for dress shirts. Since the total national potential is $2 billion nationally each year, total potential in Indianapolis equals $10,258,000 (= $2 billion $\times$ .005129). Thus, the company's sales in Indianapolis of $1,100,000 amount to a 10.7 percent share (=$1,100,000/$10,258,000) of area market potential. Comparing this with the 7 percent national share, the company appears to be doing better in Indianapolis than in other parts of the country.

The weights used in the buying power index are somewhat arbitrary. They apply mainly to consumer goods that are neither low-priced staples nor high-priced luxury goods. Other weights can be used. And the manufacturer would want to adjust the market potential for additional factors, such as level of competition in the market, local promotion costs, seasonal changes in demand, and unique local market characteristics.

Many companies compute additional area demand measures. Marketers now can refine state-by-state and city-by-city measures down to census tracts or ZIP code centers. Census tracts are small areas about the size of a neighborhood, and ZIP code centers (designed by the U.S. Post Office) are larger areas, often the size of small towns. Information on population size, family income, and other characteristics is available for each type of unit. Marketers can use this data for estimating demand in neighborhoods or other smaller geographic units within large cities. Marketing Highlight 8-2 describes some marketing firms that provide ZIP code or census information useful for refining market demand estimates and for improved customer targeting.

Estimating Actual Sales and Market Shares

Besides estimating total and area demand, a company will want to know the actual industry sales in its market. Thus, it must identify its competitors and estimate their sales.

The industry's trade association often will collect and publish total industry sales, although not listing individual company sales separately. In this way, each company can evaluate its performance against the industry as a whole. Suppose the company's sales are increasing at a rate of 5 percent a year and industry sales are increasing at 10 percent. This company actually is losing its relative standing in the industry.

Another way to estimate sales is to buy reports from marketing research firms that audit total sales and brand sales. For example, Nielsen, IRI, and other marketing research firms use scanner data to audit the retail sales of various product categories in supermarkets and drugstores and sell this information to interested companies. A company can obtain data on total product category sales as well as brand sales. It can compare its performance with that of the total industry or any particular competitor to see whether it is gaining or losing in its relative standing.[5]

FORECASTING FUTURE DEMAND

Having looked at ways to estimate current demand, we now examine ways to forecast future market demand. **Forecasting** is the art of estimating future demand by anticipating what buyers are likely to do under a given set of conditions.

A NEW TOOL FOR REFINING MARKET DEMAND ESTIMATES AND CHOOSING THE BEST MARKET TARGETS

In recent years, several new business information services have arisen to help marketing planners link U.S. Census data with lifestyle patterns to better refine their estimates of market potential down to ZIP code levels, neighborhoods, even blocks. Among the leading services are *PRIZM* (by Claritas) and *ClusterPLUS* (by Donnelley Marketing Information Services). These data services can help marketing planners find the best ZIP code areas in which to concentrate their marketing efforts. We will look at the PRIZM system as an example.

Using a host of demographic and socioeconomic factors drawn from the U.S. Census data, the PRIZM system has classified every one of the over 20 million U.S. neighborhood markets into one of forty clusters, such as Blue Blood Estates, Money & Brains, Furs & Station Wagons, Shotguns & Pickups, Tobacco Roads, and Gray Power. The clusters were formed by manipulating characteristics such as education, income, occupation, family life cycle, housing, ethnicity, and urbanization. For example, Blue Blood Estates neighborhoods are suburban areas populated mostly by active, college-educated, successful managers and professionals. They include some of America's wealthiest neighborhoods, areas characterized by low household density, highly homogeneous residents, a heavy family orientation, and mostly single-unit housing. In contrast, the Shotgun & Pickups clusters include the hundreds of small villages and four-corners towns that dot America's rural areas. Each of the other 38 clusters has a unique combination of characteristics.

Companies can combine these geodemographic PRIZM clusters with other data on product and service usage, media usage, and lifestyles to get a better picture of specific market areas. For example, the Shotguns & Pickups cluster is populated by lower-middle-class, blue-collar consumers who use chain saws and snuff and buy more canning jars, dried soups, and powdered softdrinks. The Hispanic Mix cluster prefers high-quality dresses, nonfilter cigarettes, and lip gloss. People in this cluster are highly brand conscious, quality conscious, and brand loyal. They have a strong family and home orientation. Such information provides a powerful tool for refining demand estimates, selecting target markets, and shaping promotion messages.

One large packaged-goods company used Donnelley's ClusterPLUS system in combination with Nielsen television ratings and data from Simmons Market Research Bureau to more effectively market an ingredient used in baking cakes and cookies. The company first identified the geodemographic clusters most likely to contain consumers who regularly bake from scratch. According to Simmons data, the top-ranking cluster is Low-Mobility Rural Families—39 percent of this group bake heavily

from scratch, far greater than the 17 percent national average. Merging the ten highest-ranking clusters, the company identified the best prospects as older, rural, and blue-collar consumers in the South and Midwest.

Next, using Nielsen ratings, the company examined the television viewing habits of the ten best clusters. It turns out that the from-scratch bakers watch many highly rated programs, such as "America's Funniest Home Videos" and "Cheers." But some less popular programs—such as "Rescue: 911," "Major Dad," and "In the Heat of the Night"—are also popular with this group. The packaged-goods company improved its efficiency by running ads only on programs reaching large concentrations of from-scratch bakers, regardless of the size of the total audience. Thus, the ClusterPLUS-Simmons-Nielsen connection resulted in a basic shift in the company's television advertising, from a mass-media, "shotgun" approach to a better-targeted one.

Sources: Michael J. Weiss, *The Clustering of America* (New York: Harper & Row, 1988); Martha Farnsworth Riche, "New Frontiers for Geodemographics," *American Demographics,* June 1990, p. 20; Leon G. Schiffman and Leslie Lazar Kanuk, *Consumer Behavior,* 4th ed. (Englewood Cliffs, NJ: Prentice Hall, 1991), Chap. 13; and Jonathon Marks, "Clusters Plus Nielsen Equals Efficient Marketing," *American Demographics,* September 1991, p. 16.

Forecasting is the art of estimating future demand, generally no easy task.

Very few products or services lend themselves to easy forecasting. Those that do generally involve a product with steady sales, or sales growth in a stable competitive situation. But most markets do not have stable total and company demand, so good forecasting becomes a key factor in company success. Poor forecasting can lead to overly large inventories, costly price markdowns, or lost sales due to being out of stock. The more unstable the demand, the more the company needs accurate forecasts and elaborate forecasting procedures.

Companies commonly use a three-stage procedure to arrive at a sales forecast. First they make an *environmental forecast,* followed by an *industry forecast,* followed by a *company sales forecast.* The environmental forecast calls for projecting inflation, unemployment, interest rates, consumer spending and saving, business investment, government expenditures, net exports, and other environmental events important to the company. The result is a forecast of gross national product, which is used along with other indicators to forecast industry sales. Then the company prepares its sales forecast by assuming that it will win a certain share of industry sales.

Companies use several specific techniques to forecast their sales. Table 8-3 lists many of these techniques.[6] All forecasts are built on one of three information bases: what people say, what people do, or what people have done. The first basis—*what people say*—involves surveying the opinions of buyers or those close to them, such as salespeople or outside experts. It includes three methods: surveys of buyer intentions, composites of salesforce opinions, and expert opinion. Building a forecast on *what people do* involves another method, that of putting the product into a test market to assess buyer response. The final basis—*what people have done*—involves analyzing records of past buying behavior or using time-series analysis or statistical demand analysis.

TABLE 8-3
Common Sales Forecasting Techniques

BASED ON:	METHODS
What people say	Surveys of buyers' intentions
	Composite salesforce opinions
	Expert opinion
What people do	Test markets
What people have done	Time-series analysis
	Leading indicators
	Statistical demand analysis

Survey of Buyers' Intentions

One way to forecast what buyers will do is to ask them directly. This suggests that the forecaster should survey buyers. Surveys are especially valuable if the buyers have clearly formed intentions, will carry them out, and can describe them to interviewers.

Several research organizations conduct periodic surveys of consumer buying intentions. These organizations ask questions like the following:

Do you intend to buy an automobile within the next six months?

0	.1	.2	.3	.4	.5	.6	.7	.8	.9	1.0
No chance		Slight chance		Fair chance		Good chance		Strong chance		For certain

This is called a *purchase probability scale*. In addition, the various surveys ask about the consumer's present and future personal finances, and their expectations about the economy. The various bits of information are combined into a *consumer sentiment measure* (Survey Research Center of the University of Michigan) or a *consumer confidence measure* (Sindlinger and Company). Consumer durable goods companies subscribe to these indexes to help them anticipate major shifts in consumer buying intentions so that they can adjust their production and marketing plans accordingly.

For *business buying,* various agencies carry out intention surveys about plant, equipment, and materials purchases. The two best-known surveys are conducted by the U.S. Department of Commerce and by McGraw-Hill. Most of the estimates have been within 10 percent of the actual outcomes.

Composite of Salesforce Opinions

When buyer interviewing is impractical, the company may base its sales forecasts on information provided by the salesforce. The company typically asks its salespeople to estimate sales by product for their individual territories. It then adds up the individual estimates to arrive at an overall sales forecast.

Few companies use their salesforce's estimates without some adjustments. Salespeople are biased observers. They may be naturally pessimistic or optimistic, or they may go to one extreme or another because of recent sales setbacks or successes. Furthermore, they are often unaware of larger economic developments and do not always know how their company's marketing plans will affect future sales in their territories. They may understate demand so that the company will set a low sales quota. They may not have the time to prepare careful estimates or may not consider it worthwhile.

Assuming these biases can be countered, a number of benefits can be gained by involving the salesforce in forecasting. Salespeople may have better insights into developing trends than any other group. After participating in the forecasting process, the salespeople may have greater confidence in their quotas and more incentive to achieve them. Also, such "grassroots" forecasting provides estimates broken down by product, territory, customer, and salesperson.[7]

Expert Opinion

Companies can also obtain forecasts by turning to experts. Experts include dealers, distributors, suppliers, marketing consultants, and trade associations. Thus, auto companies survey their dealers periodically for their forecasts of short-term demand. Dealer estimates, however, are subject to the same strengths and weaknesses as salesforce estimates.

Many companies buy economic and industry forecasts from well-known firms such as Data Resources, Wharton Econometric, and Chase Econometric. These forecasting specialists are in a better position than the company to prepare economic forecasts because they have more data available and more forecasting expertise.

Occasionally companies will invite a special group of experts to prepare a forecast. The experts may be asked to exchange views and come up with a group estimate (group discussion method). Or they may be asked to supply their estimates individually, with the company analyst combining them into a single estimate (pooling of individual estimates). Or they may supply individual estimates

MARKETING HIGHLIGHT 8-3

SOMETIMES "EXPERT OPINION" ISN'T ALL IT SHOULD BE

Before you rely too heavily on expert opinion, you might be interested in learning how some past "experts" came out with their predictions:

- "I think there's a world market for about five computers." Thomas J. Watson, IBM Chairman, 1943.

- "With over 50 foreign cars already on sale here, the Japanese auto industry isn't likely to carve out a big slice of the U.S. market for itself." *Business Week,* 1958.

- "TV won't be able to hold on to any market it captures after the first six months. People will soon get tired of staring at a plywood box every night." Daryl F. Zanuck, head of 20th Century Fox, 1946.

- "By 1980, all power (electric, atomic, solar) is likely to be virtually costless," Henry Luce, founder and publisher of *Time, Life,* and *Fortune,* 1956.

- "1930 will be a splendid employment year." U.S. Department of Labor, 1929.

- "My imagination refuses to see any sort of submarine doing anything but suffocating its crew and foundering at sea." H. G. Wells, 1902.

- "Airplanes are interesting toys, but of no military value." France's Marshal Foch, 1911.

Source: Adapted from "Sometimes Expert Opinion Isn't All It Should Be," *Go,* September-October 1985, p. 2.

---

and assumptions that are reviewed by a company analyst, revised, and followed by further rounds of estimation (Delphi method).[8]

Experts can provide good insights upon which to base forecasts, but they can also be wrong (see Marketing Highlight 8-3). Where possible, the company should back up experts' opinions with estimates obtained using other methods.

Test-Market Method

Where buyers do not plan their purchases carefully or where experts are not available or reliable, the company may want to conduct a direct test market. A direct test market is especially useful in forecasting new-product sales or established-product sales in a new distribution channel or territory. Test marketing is discussed in Chapter 11.

Time-Series Analysis

Many firms base their forecasts on past sales. They assume that the causes of past sales can be uncovered through statistical analysis. Then, analysts can use the causal relations to predict future sales. **Time-series analysis** consists of breaking down the original sales into four components—trend, cycle, season, and erratic components—then recombining these components to produce the sales forecast.

Trend is the long-term, underlying pattern of growth or decline in sales resulting from basic changes in population, capital formation, and technology. It is found by fitting a straight or curved line through past sales. *Cycle* captures the medium-term, wavelike movement of sales resulting from changes in general economic and competitive activity. The cyclical component can be useful for medium-range forecasting. Cyclical swings, however, are difficult to predict because they do not occur on a regular basis. *Season* refers to a consistent pattern of sales movements within the year. The term *season* describes any recurrent hourly, weekly, monthly, or quarterly sales pattern. The seasonal component may be related to weather factors, holidays, and trade customs. The seasonal pattern provides a norm for forecasting short-range sales. Finally, *erratic events* include fads, strikes, snow storms, earthquakes, riots, fires, and other disturbances. These components, by definition, are unpredictable and should be removed from past data to see the more normal behavior of sales.

Suppose an insurance company sold 12,000 new life insurance policies this year and wants to predict next year's December sales. The long-term trend shows a 5 percent sales growth rate per year. This information alone suggests sales next year of 12,600 (= 12,000 × 1.05). However, a business recession is expected next year and probably will result in total sales achieving only 90 percent of the expected trend-adjusted sales. Sales next year will more likely be 11,340 (= 12,600 × .90). If sales were the same each month, monthly sales would be 945 (= 11,340/12). However, December is an above-average month for insurance policy sales, with a seasonal index standing at 1.30. Therefore December sales may be as high as 1,228.5 (= 945 × 1.3). The company expects no erratic events, such as strikes or new insurance regulations. Thus, it estimates new policy sales next December at 1,228.5 policies.

Leading Indicators

Many companies try to forecast their sales by finding one or more **leading indicators**—other time series that change in the same direction but in advance of company sales. For example, a plumbing supply company might find that its sales lag the housing starts index by about four months. The housing starts index would then be a useful leading indicator. The National Bureau of Economic Research has identified 12 of the best leading indicators, and their values are published monthly in the *Survey of Current Business.*

Statistical Demand Analysis

Time-series analysis treats past and future sales as a function of time, rather than as a function of any real demand factors. But many real factors affect the sales of any product. **Statistical demand analysis** is a set of statistical procedures used to discover the most important real factors affecting sales and their relative influence. The factors most commonly analyzed are prices, income, population, and promotion.

Statistical demand analysis consists of expressing sales (Q) as a dependent variable and trying to explain sales as a function of a number of independent demand variables $X_1, X_2, \ldots, X_n$. That is:

$$Q = f(X1, X2, \ldots, Xn)$$

Using a technique called multiple-regression analysis, various equation forms can be statistically fitted to the data in the search for the best predicting factors and equation.[9]

For example, a soft-drink company found that the per capita sales of soft drinks by state was well explained by[10]

$$Q = -145.5 + 6.46X1 - 2.37X2$$

where

$$X1 = \text{mean annual temperature of the state (Fahrenheit)}$$

$$X2 = \text{annual per capita income in the state (in hundreds)}$$

For example, New Jersey had a mean annual temperature of 54 and an annual per capita income of 24 (in hundreds). Using the equation, we would predict per capita soft-drink consumption in New Jersey to be

$$Q = -145.5 + 6.46(54) - 2.37(24) = 146.6$$

Actual per capita consumption was 143. If the equation predicted this well for other states, it would serve as a useful forecasting tool. Marketing management would predict next year's mean temperature and per capita income for each state and use the equation to predict next year's sales.

Statistical demand analysis can be very complex, and the marketer must take care in designing, conducting, and interpreting such analysis. Yet constantly improving computer technology has made statistical demand analysis an increasingly popular approach to forecasting.

SUMMARY

To carry out their responsibilities, marketing managers need measures of current and future market size. We define a *market* as the set of actual and potential consumers of a market offer. Consumers in the market have *interest*, *income*, and *access* to the market offer. The marketer has to distinguish various levels of the market, such as the *potential market*, *available market*, *qualified available market*, *served market*, and *penetrated market*.

One task is to *estimate current demand*. Marketers can estimate total demand through the chain ratio method, which involves multiplying a base number by successive percentages. *Area market demand* can be estimated by the market-buildup method or the market-factor index

method. Estimating actual industry sales requires identifying competitors and using some method of estimating the sales of each. Finally, companies estimate the market shares of competitors to judge their relative performance.

For *estimating future demand*, the company can use one or a combination of seven possible forecasting methods, based on what consumers say (*buyers' intentions surveys, composite of salesforce opinions, expert opinion*); what consumers do (*market tests*); or what consumers have done (*time-series analysis, leading indicators,* and *statistical demand analysis*). The best method to use depends on the purpose of the forecast, the type of product, and the availability and reliability of data.

KEY TERMS

DISCUSSING THE ISSUES

1. In market measurement and forecasting, what is the more serious problem: to *overestimate* demand, or to *underestimate* it?

2. Retailers depend upon the Christmas season for up to 40 percent of the total year's sales. Many analysts forecast the strength of the Christmas retailing season by projecting from the sales level on a *single day,* the Friday after Thanksgiving. What are the issues in using such a forecast? Is it more difficult to forecast such highly seasonal demand?

3. Many long-term trends occur because of changes in technology or the environment. What effect have automobile catalytic converters had on the market for leaded and unleaded gasoline? How have higher gasoline prices affected spark plug manufacturers? Were these changes predictable?

4. Hess's, a chain of department stores, is looking for desirable locations for new stores. Which aspect of market demand would Hess's be interested in measuring, and what measuring methods would they use, in choosing where to locate new stores? What census tract or ZIP code information would be relevant?

5. As marketing manager for Cat's Pride cat litter, you have seen sales jump 50 percent in the last year after years of relatively stable sales. How will you forecast sales for the coming year?

6. What leading indicators might help you predict sales of diapers? Cars? Hamburgers? Can you describe a general procedure for finding leading indicators of product sales?

APPLYING THE CONCEPTS

1. Look at your school's schedule of classes for the coming semester. Examine the course offerings in your major area and try to predict which courses will have low, medium, and high demand. What factors do you think affect demand for courses? If a new course were offered, what information would you want to know in order to predict the level of demand for it?

2. People often make their own judgments about the potential for new products. You may hear someone say a new product will "never sell," or, perhaps, that it will "sell like hotcakes." Try to recall some recent new product or service that you saw and made an informal prediction. What was the product? What attracted your attention enough to get you to comment on the product's future? What was your forecast? Were you correct?

MAKING MARKETING DECISIONS:

SMALL WORLD COMMUNICATIONS, INC.

Thomas Campbell and Lynette Jones need to develop some initial sales forecasts for their new company, Small World Communications. During a business trip, Lyn was sitting in the Minneapolis airport, thinking quietly: "We need to put together some basic profit and loss projections for Small World to see if the company can make it financially. So we need to forecast market size and make estimates of our sales *before* we invest to develop a product. But here's the *Catch 22:* We have to figure out what the product is before we can forecast demand, but until we forecast demand, we can't develop the product." Tom and Lyn decided that they had to trust their instincts and develop a basic product concept before going further. As Tom put it, "Just punt. We've gotta start somewhere."

The basic product, code named "Unity" for the moment, will be a computer expansion accessory, using both hardware and software, that will help users integrate communications from many sources. Tom was explaining his vision of the product to Lyn. "It's sort of like an assistant to the president," he said. "The user will train Unity by answering some simple questions—in English, not computerese—and then Unity will keep things straight and make complicated communications look easy. Unity will recognize the incoming signals—data, fax, audio, or video—and route them however the user has requested. A fax could be printed automatically, if the user wants that, or be saved and shown on-screen to save paper. Unity could route electronic mail automatically: if I ask a message to be sent to you, Unity knows your electronic address, including what computer to hook up to, and the right phone number to call. It will let me watch TV, like having the "Nightly Business Report" showing in a corner of my screen while I work on other tasks. It could do call and fax forwarding when I'm on the road." Lyn said, "It's pretty clear that some of these abilities are hardware based, and some are built into software. I'd suggest that we build one basic circuit board that will cover almost all hardware-based needs. That

means we need a design with all the basic input connectors for telephone, video, and audio. It's like getting a Swiss Army knife. Most users don't need all of those built-in tools, but they'll get a good feeling knowing that they bought flexibility. Then we can use software modules to let different users set up the hardware in different ways." Tom replied, "I think you've got a good strategy. The all-in-one idea has worked well for other computer products like *The Norton Utilities* software. The extra features might not cost us very much, anyway. We can cut a lot of our costs by producing one design in volume, and by keeping our inventory handling simple. I'll bet we can put in lots of extra features and still come out ahead financially. Now let's put together those projections—I've already set up a spreadsheet titled "World Unity."

WHAT NOW?

1. Tom and Lynette have outlined a new product that is innovative, but not a radical departure. It performs the functions of several existing products, but it allows a level of integration that is not possible with other products. (a) Given this product background, discuss how Small World might define and estimate the *potential market, available market,* and *qualified available market.* [Some of the facts in the Small World Communications episode from Chapter 3 may be helpful.] (b) How is this market likely to change over time? Are there computer users who are not part of the potential market now who may be good prospects in the future?

2. Many issues are affected by the forecasts that Tom and Lyn make. (a) Consider how a high forecast will affect Small World's financial strategy, manufacturing plans, and inventory management. (b) Would Tom and Lyn run their company differently if they used a low forecast instead? (c) How reliable are these initial forecasts likely to be?

REFERENCES

1. See Hamish McDonald, "Caught on the Hop," *Far Eastern Economic Review,* February 18, 1988, pp. 72-73; "Quantas Embarks on Major Fleet Expansion Plan," *Aviation Week & Space Technology,* June 20, 1988, pp. 39, 42-43; Michael Westlake, "Stand-By Room Only," *Far Eastern Economic Review*, June 2, 1988, pp. 72-75; and Paul Proctor, "Pacific Rim Carriers Struggle to Cope with Impending Traffic Boom," *Aviation Week & Space Technology,* November 20, 1989, pp. 110-111. Additional information provided by Qantas Airways, Ltd., April 1993.

2. For further discussion, see Gary L. Lilien, Philip Kotler, and K. Sridhar Moorthy, *Marketing Models* (Englewood Cliffs, NJ: Prentice Hall, 1992).

3. For more on forecasting total market demand, see F. William Barnett, "Four Steps to Forecast Total Market Demand," *Harvard Business Review,* July-August 1988, pp. 28-34.

4. For more on using this survey, see "A User's Guide to the Survey of Buying Power," *Sales & Marketing Management,* August 24, 1992, pp. A6-A20.

5. For a more comprehensive discussion of measuring market demand, see Philip Kotler, *Marketing Management: Analysis, Planning, Implementation, and Control,* 8th ed. (Englewood Cliffs, NJ: Prentice Hall, 1994), Chap. 10.

6. For a listing and analysis of these and other forecasting techniques, see David M. Georgoff and Robert G. Murdick, "Manager's Guide to Forecasting," *Harvard Business Review,* January-February 1986, pp. 110-120; and Donald S. Tull and Del I. Hawkins, *Marketing Research: Measurement and Method,* 6th ed. (New York: Macmillan, 1990), Chap. 21.

7. For more on the salesforce composite method, see Tull and Hawkins, *Marketing Research: Measurement and Method,* pp. 705-6.

8. See Kip D. Cassino, "Delphi Method: A Practical 'Crystal Ball' for Researchers," *Marketing News,* January 6, 1984, Sec. 2, pp. 10-11.

9. See Tull and Hawkins, *Marketing Research: Measurement and Method,* pp. 686-91.

10. See "The Du Pont Company," in *Marketing Research: Text and Cases* (3rd ed.), Harper W. Boyd, Jr., Ralph Westfall, and Stanley Stasch, eds. (Homewood, IL: Irwin, 1977), pp. 498-500.

VIDEO CASE 8

MEASURING AND FORECASTING DEMAND

The 1974 energy crisis, with long lines at the gas pumps and high gas prices, made more fuel-efficient, lower-priced Japanese cars more attractive to U.S. car buyers. At the same time, the federal government, concerned over U.S. dependence on foreign oil, passed the corporate average fuel economy (CAFE) law in 1975. This law set average miles-per-gallonstandards for the U.S. fleet sales of auto manufacturers.

Ford, GM, and Chrysler reacted to both events by revving up their research on fuel efficiency. As a result, average domestic car fuel efficiency improved dramatically by the mid-1980s. As large cars became more economical to run, and Americans forgot about the long gas lines and adjusted to higher gas prices, automobile demand shifted back to larger, more luxurious and expensive cars. In spite of improvements in fuel efficiency, as the demand for larger cars increased, domestic car producers once again found it difficult to meet the CAFE fleet standards. To increase sales of small cars and reduce their fleet miles per gallon, the auto makers cut small car prices—in some cases, below cost. Ironically, in a reverse of their 1970s practice, they now found themselves pushing small cars in a large car market.

The energy crisis and its aftermath illustrate the problems of forecasting demand when sudden shifts in consumer buying cause product offerings to be off-cycle with demand. Forecasters must correctly anticipate future trends in consumer demand, competitors' actions, and changes in the market environment.

What trends will affect future automobile demand? Facing diminishing oil reserves, governments have pushed for greater fuel efficiency, and pollution concerns such as the greenhouse effect have resulted in more stringent clean-air standards. To gain greater fuel efficiency, the auto companies are researching alternative engines, such as the two-stroke and gas-turbine engines. To meet stricter clean-air standards, they are experimenting with cleaner fuels such as methanol and ethanol.

Although such research has improved fuel efficiency, increases in average car size have offset these gains, resulting in reduced average fuel-efficiency ratings. In order to produce larger and more fuel-efficient cars, auto makers are experimenting with new, lighter body materials, such as polymer-based composites. For example, Ford and General Electric have embarked on a five-year, $11 million joint venture to demonstrate the feasibility of making structural parts from GE's cyclic thermoplastic polymers, which are known for their strength. The 1992 Automotive Engineers International Congress & Exposition in Detroit showcased an impressive array of new space-age synthetics that will soon find their way into the frames and fabrics of tomorrow's new cars.

Other factors are also shaping the automobile market. Since the 1970s, congestion on America's urban freeways has increased dramatically. The solution? Intelligent Vehicle Highway Systems, known as IVHSs. These systems include radar (electronic eyes) that keep vehicles from colliding, transponders that allow tracking of commercial vehicles, and satellite-linked electronic navigation systems that can move columns of cars along highways—without the driver's control!

But developments don't stop there—cars will also become smarter. For example, imagine a "Smart" Oldsmobile Toronado, equipped with two computers, multiple antennas, a cellular phone, and a white cone-shaped transponder that communicates with Global Positioning Satellites. Want to know where traffic trouble spots are? Press the "Traffic Report" button. Want to see your car move through traffic or check its routing? Watch the triangle on the dashboard display. Press "Things to See and Do" and the computerized voice will guide you to Disney World, the Elvis Presley Museum, or the Gatorland Zoo. Of course, this feature is available only from Avis in Orlando.

When will IVHS systems be available? Not for some time yet. James Constantino, executive director of IVHS America, estimates that $35 billion to $40 billion will be needed to develop and test IVHS technologies, and another $225 billion will be needed to build a national system. So far, federally funded transportation research has grown only from $2 million in 1989 to $234 million in 1992. Smart cars, however, may soon be on the market. Most of the technology for these cars already exists.

Who will buy smart cars? The first models will be expensive. Initial buyers will probably be drivers aged 25 to 49 with household incomes in excess of $60,000. However, experts expect that these cars will not remain expensive for long. The typical car buyer already buys luxury and high-performance cars loaded with options. In addition, all drivers have strong needs to save time and increase safety, and society needs to reduce air pollution. Thus, by the year 2000, we might expect that many drivers will be cruising the highways in lightweight plastic smart cars.

QUESTIONS

1. Suppose that you work for an auto dealer in a city of 150,000 people. You want to forecast demand for all makes of automobiles in your town for the next five years. What forecasting techniques would you use?

2. Now, suppose you want to forecast five-year sales of your dealership's *brand*. What forecasting techniques would you use?

3. How would you forecast demand for Intelligent Vehicle Highway Systems? From where would the demand come?

4. How would you predict the rate of adoption of "smart cars"?

Sources: "Eye on the Road," *Car and Driver,* January 1990, p. 7; "Return of the Gas Guzzler," *Forbes,* October 1986, p. 10; "Japan Will Feast at the CAFE," *U.S. News & World Report,* May 29, 1989, p. 11; Karen Wright, "The Shape of Things to Go," *Scientific American,* May 1990, pp. 92-101; Samia El-Badry and Joseph Innace, "Ford and GE Join in Car Composites," *Modern Plastics,* June 1992, pp. 21-22; and Peter K. Nance, "Driving into the 21st Century," *American Demographics,* September 1992, pp. 46-53.

COMPANY CASE 8

GENENTECH: FORECASTING EUPHORIA

A year ago, Genentech toasted the regulatory approval of its heart drug TPA with champagne under circus tents, fireworks that closed the local airport, and roc 'n' roll by its biotech band, the Rolling Clones. Today, however, the company's supporters have lost their euphoria. Genentech is a victim of its own success—real success, that is—but success that paled when measured against the fantasy of success that had earlier excited investors, Wall Street, and Genentech itself.

In 1976 a biologist and an MBA who had only $500 between them founded Genentech. They dreamed of becoming the first company to prove the potential of reproducing human proteins through biotechnology. Biotechnology companies develop biologically based drugs, as opposed to chemically based drugs, because they believe that these drugs are as effective as chemically based drugs but without the side effects. Genentech had become the first company to commercialize such drugs, and sales grew rapidly (see Exhibit 8-1 for a sales history). By 1987, it had three products on the market: Humulin, a human insulin; Roferon, an alpha interferon used to treat a variety of leukemia; and Protropin, a human growth hormone.

Genentech markets its latest drug, a new thrombolytic drug called TPA, under the name Activase. Heart specialists administer single doses of thrombolytic drugs to patients as soon as possible after a heart attack. These drugs dissolve potentially deadly blood clots often associated with heart attacks. The body produces TPA naturally, but in very small amounts. Before recent advances, scientists had not developed a method to copy the natural TPA substance genetically and produce enough of it to meet the needs of heart-attack patients.

After spending $200 million over five years to develop TPA, Genentech launched the product in the atmosphere of a crusade against unbelievers in the Food and Drug Administration (FDA) and the medical community. Because a major study, announced in March 1985, indicated that TPA significantly outperformed its predecessor in dissolving deadly blood clots, Genentech management adopted the view that it would be "unethical" for a doctor *not* to use the drug to treat heart attacks. Enthusiastic Wall Street analysts uncritically embraced this view—some even went so far as to predict malpractice suits against doctors who failed to use TPA. Despite this enthusiasm, the FDA refused to approve the drug in May 1987, citing a lack of evidence supporting TPA's effectiveness. However, Genentech submitted further studies confirming that TPA dissolved clots, im-

---

EXHIBIT 8-1
Genentech, Inc., Sales and Income

YEAR	SALES (millions)	NET INCOME (millions)	EARNINGS (per share)
1983	$ 42.4	$ 1.1	$.03
1984	65.6	2.7	.05
1985	81.6	5.6	.09
1986	127.3	12.8	.18
1987	218.7	42.2	.50
1988 (est.)	380.0	90.0	.50

Source: Copyright © 1990, Value Line Publishing, Inc.; used by permission.

proved overall heart pumping action, and extended lives. Thus, in November 1987, the FDA approved TPA for sale in the United States. Within 15 days, Genentech held a nationwide teleconference to inform 12,000 physicians, hospital pharmacists, and nurses about TPA.

Genentech forecast that it would sell $180 million worth of TPA in 1988 at $2,200 per dose, a price more than ten times that of rival streptokinase made by Hoechst AG. Analysts, however, began forecasting 1988 sales at $400 million. The firm's stock price soared, rising 47 percent in only two weeks. Despite their own more modest forecasts, the people at Genentech did not argue with the analysts' highly optimistic projections. In fact, Genentech employees *joined* the excitement and invested heavily in the dream. One Genentech chemist recalls, "When the stock was leaping up, it was distracting. People were infatuated. People would ask, 'What's the price this hour?'"

At the end of TPA's first year, Genentech held a 65 percent share of the market for thrombolytic drugs, compared with competitor's streptokinase at 30 percent and urokinase at 5 percent. However, Genentech has captured a large part of a disappointingly small market. Several factors have contributed to this unexpectedly low market growth. Distributors sell 90 percent of TPA to hospitals, which hold it in their pharmacies for use by physicians. Although most hospitals stock TPA, doctors prescribe clot-dissolving drugs for only 120,000 out of the 400,000 patients medically eligible to receive them. Genentech feels that this reluctance is costing lives. Further, hospital pharmacies, under rigid cost controls from Medicare and insurance companies, cannot afford to give up streptokinase, which sells for about $200 per dose. Kirk Raab, president of Genentech, insists that TPA's high price is not to blame, but the market seems to indicate otherwise. Finally, doctors hesitate to use any new product, especially one carrying a small but measurable risk of undesirable side effects. Thus, Genentech appears to have underestimated the complexity of the medical marketplace, its cost regulations, and its innate conservatism. As the president of another biotech firm notes, "It was much too complex [a medical issue] to assume it was going to be zip-dee-do."

If these problems weren't enough, the results emerging from several recent studies show only a modest advantage for TPA—not the huge advantage predicted earlier. For example, in one major study, TPA reduced deaths 27 percent compared with a control group; in another test, streptokinase reduced deaths 21 percent. Another study found that TPA reduced deaths 51 percent in the first two weeks after a heart attack, against 47 percent for Eminase (a streptokinase product made by Beecham) after 30 days. Thus, doctors have been seeing confusing data, and Genentech's marketing team and 194-person salesforce have had a hard sell.

Market confusion will remain until researchers publish the first true head-to-head comparisons of the life-saving abilities of TPA and streptokinase. By the time such comparisons become available, Beecham's Eminase, the next serious contender for TPA's market share, may be on the U.S. market. Still, Mr. Raab remains confident. "Eminase is the only product we see on the horizon. And it's a form of streptokinase," he says. "We don't want to underestimate it, but we think TPA is superior." However, some observers believe that Eminase is easier to administer and has fewer side effects. Further, Beecham may price Eminase as much as $500 less than TPA.

Thus, although TPA's first-year sales reached an estimated $180 million, making it the top-selling first-year drug product in history, many analysts saw its performance as disappointing. Genentech's stock fell to one-third its previous levels, leaving many stockholders and employees disgruntled. "To say we oversold is unfair," says Mr. Raab. But he concedes, "We were optimistic as to how fast it would happen. And we undercalled the reluctance of physicians to use a revolutionary therapy."

Genentech now faces the challenge of shifting its marketing strategy and tightening its belt. Some analysts wonder how much profit Genentech can squeeze from TPA before a new generation of drugs enters the fray. Adds a Genentech scientist who saw the value of his stock options plunge, "The transition from dreams to reality is a hard one. The TPA launch was badly handled in that it has made a big success look like something between a disappointment and a failure."

QUESTIONS

1. In what market does Genentech sell TPA? How big are the *potential* market and the *penetrated* market for TPA? Why are the sizes of these two markets so different?

2. Given that a patient receives only one dose of TPA, immediately after a heart attack, what market share would Genentech have needed in order to reach the forecasted $400 million in sales?

3. Given that TPA was a new product in a relatively new market, how might management have attacked the problem of forecasting first-year sales?

4. What marketing mistakes do you think Genentech made?

5. Given Genentech's current position, what marketing strategy changes would you make?

6. In November 1991, a special task force of the American Heart Association reported that one obstacle to the control of heart disease is the inability of some heart patients to pay for drugs that treat heart problems. The task force announced plans to publicize government and drug company programs to provide patients heart drugs free, or at a reduced cost. Do you feel companies like Genentech have a responsibility to provide free or reduced-price drugs to low-income patients?

Source: Adapted from M. Chase, "Genentech, Battered by Great Expectations, Is Tightening Its Belt," *The Wall Street Journal,* October 11, 1988, and "Heart Association Targets Uninsured, Poor Patients," *The Wall Street Journal,* November 13, 1991. Used with permission.

9

*M*arket Segmentation, Targeting, and Positioning for Competitive Advantage

rocter & Gamble makes nine brands of laundry detergent (Tide, Cheer, Gain, Dash, Bold 3, Dreft, Ivory Snow, Oxydol, and Era). It also sells eight brands of hand soap (Zest, Coast, Ivory, Safeguard, Camay, Oil of Olay, Kirk's, and Lava); six shampoos (Prell, Head & Shoulders, Ivory, Pert, Pantene, and Vidal Sassoon); four brands each of liquid dishwashing detergents (Joy, Ivory, Dawn, and Liquid Cascade), toothpaste (Crest, Gleam, Complete, and Denquel), coffee (Folger's, High Point, Butternut, and Maryland Club), and toilet tissue (Charmin, White Cloud, Banner, and Summit); three brands of floor cleaner (Spic & Span, Top Job, and Mr. Clean); and two brands each of deodorant (Secret and Sure), cooking oil (Crisco and Puritan), fabric softener (Downy and Bounce), and disposable diapers (Pampers and Luvs). Moreover, many of the brands are offered in several sizes and formulations (for example, you can buy large or small packages of powdered or liquid Tide in any of three forms—regular, unscented, or with bleach).

These P&G brands compete with one another on the same supermarket shelves. But why would P&G introduce several brands in one category instead of concentrating its resources on a single leading brand? The answer lies in the fact that different people want different *mixes of benefits* from the products they buy. Take laundry detergents as an example. People use laundry detergents to get their clothes clean. But they also want other things from their detergents—such as economy, bleaching power, fabric softening, fresh smell, strength or mildness, and lots of suds. We all want *some* of every one of these benefits from our detergent, but we may have different *priorities* for each benefit. To some people, cleaning and bleaching power are most important; to others, fabric softening matters most; still others want a mild, fresh-scented detergent. Thus,

there are groups—or segments—of laundry detergent buyers, and each segment seeks a special combination of benefits.

Procter & Gamble has identified at least nine important laundry detergent segments, along with numerous subsegments, and has developed a different brand designed to meet the special needs of each. The nine P&G brands are positioned for different segments as follows:

- *Tide* is "so powerful, it cleans down to the fiber." It's the all-purpose family detergent for extra-tough laundry jobs. "Tide's in, dirt's out." *Tide with Bleach* is "so powerful, it whitens down to the fiber."

- *Cheer* with Color Guard gives "outstanding cleaning *and* color protection. So your family's clothes look clean, bright, and more like new." Cheer is also specially formulated for use in hot, warm, or cold water—it's "all tempera-Cheer." *Cheer Free* is "dermatologist tested . . . contains no irritating perfume or dye."

- *Oxydol* contains bleach. It "makes your white clothes really white and your colored clothes really bright. So don't reach for the bleach—grab a box of Ox!"

- *Gain,* originally P&G's "enzyme" detergent, was repositioned as the detergent that gives you clean, fresh-smelling clothes—it "freshens like sunshine."

- *Bold* is the detergent with fabric softener. It "cleans, softens, and controls static." Bold liquid adds "the fresh fabric softener scent."

- *Ivory Snow* is "Ninety-nine and forty-four one hundredths percent pure." It's the "mild, gentle soap for diapers and baby clothes."

- *Dreft* is also formulated for baby's diapers and

clothes. It contains borax, "nature's natural sweet-ener" for "a clean you can trust."

■ *Dash* is P&G's value entry. It "attacks tough dirt," but "Dash does it for a great low price."

■ *Era Plus* has "built-in stain removers." It "gets tough stains out and does a great job on your whole wash too."

By segmenting the market and having several detergent brands, P&G has an attractive offering for consumers in all important preference groups. All its brands combined hold more than a 55 percent share of the laundry detergent market—much more than any single brand could obtain by itself.

 # CHAPTER PREVIEW

Chapter 9 shows different approaches that companies can take to a market in order to best serve consumers', and the companies', needs.

We begin with an overview of three approaches that companies can take toward a market: ***mass marketing, product variety marketing,*** and ***target marketing.***

A fuller discussion of target marketing details ***market segmentation:*** dividing a market into groups that are ***measurable, accessible, substantial,*** and ***actionable.*** This can be done in different ways by using ***geographic, demographic, psychographic, behavioral,*** or other variables.

Next, we explain the process of ***market targeting*** and different approaches a company can take, including ***undifferentiated, differentiated,*** and ***concentrated marketing.***

We finish the chapter with a discussion of ***market positioning strategy*** and how companies can position their products for the best competitive advantage.

MARKETS

Organizations that sell to consumer and business markets recognize that they cannot appeal to all buyers in those markets, or at least not to all buyers in the same way. Buyers are too numerous, too widely scattered, and too varied in their needs and buying practices. And different companies vary widely in their abilities to serve different segments of the market. Rather than trying to compete in an entire market, sometimes against superior competitors, each company must identify the parts of the market that it can serve best.

Sellers have not always practiced this philosophy. Their thinking has passed through three stages:

■ *Mass marketing.* In mass marketing, the seller mass produces, mass distributes, and mass promotes one product to all buyers. At one time, Coca-Cola produced only one drink for the whole market, hoping it would appeal to everyone. The argument for mass marketing is that it should lead to the lowest costs and prices and create the largest potential market.

■ *Product-variety marketing.* Here, the seller produces two or more products that have different features, styles, quality, sizes, and so on. Later, Coca-Cola produced several soft drinks packaged in different sizes and containers. They were designed to offer variety to buyers rather than to appeal to different market segments. The argument for product-variety marketing is that consumers have different tastes that change over time. Consumers seek variety and change.

■ *Target marketing.* Here, the seller identifies market segments, selects one or more of them, and develops products and marketing mixes tailored to each. For example, Coca-Cola now produces soft drinks for the sugared-cola segment (Coca-Cola Classic and Cherry Coke), the diet segment (Diet Coke and Tab), the no-caffeine segment (Caffeine Free Coke), and the noncola segment (Minute Maid sodas).

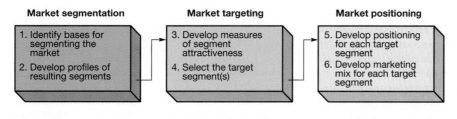

Market segmentation	Market targeting	Market positioning
1. Identify bases for segmenting the market 2. Develop profiles of resulting segments	3. Develop measures of segment attractiveness 4. Select the target segment(s)	5. Develop positioning for each target segment 6. Develop marketing mix for each target segment

FIGURE 9-1
Steps in market segmentation, targeting, and positioning

Today's companies are moving away from mass marketing and product-variety marketing and toward target marketing. Target marketing can better help sellers find their marketing opportunities. Sellers can develop the right product for each target market and adjust their prices, distribution channels, and advertising to reach the target market efficiently. Instead of scattering their marketing efforts (the "shotgun" approach), they can focus on the buyers who have greater purchase interest (the "rifle" approach).

As a result of the increasing fragmentation of American mass markets into hundreds of micromarkets, each with different needs and lifestyles, target marketing is increasingly taking the form of **micromarketing.** Using micromarketing, companies tailor their marketing programs to the needs and wants of narrowly defined geographic, demographic, psychographic, or behavior segments. The ultimate form of target marketing is *customized marketing* in which the company adapts its product and marketing program to the needs of a specific customer or buying organization (see Marketing Highlight 9-1).

Figure 9-1 shows the three major steps in target marketing. The first is **market segmentation**—dividing a market into distinct groups of buyers with different needs, characteristics, or behavior who might require separate products or

MARKETING HIGHLIGHT 9-1

MICROMARKETING: A NEW MARKETING ERA?

For most of this century, major consumer-products companies have held fast to two mass marketing principles—product standardization and national brand identification. They have marketed the same set of products in about the same way to masses of consumers all across the country. But recently, many companies have tried a new approach—*micromarketing.* Instead of marketing in the same way nationally to all customers, they are tailoring their products, advertising, sales promotions, and personal selling efforts to suit the tastes of specific geographic, demographic, psychographic, and behavioral segments.

Several factors have fueled the move toward micromarketing. First, the American mass market has slowly broken down into a profusion of smaller micromarkets—the baby boomer segment here, the mature segment there; here the Hispanic market, there the black market; here working women, there single parents; here the Sun Belt, there the Rust Belt. Today, marketers find it very hard to create a single product or program that appeals to all of these diverse groups. Second, improved information and marketing research technologies have also spurred micromarketing. For example, retail store scanners now allow instant tracking of product sales from store to store, helping companies pinpoint exactly which specific segments are buying

what. Third, scanners give retailers mountains of market information, and this information gives them more power over manufacturers. Retailers are often lukewarm about large, national marketing campaigns. Instead, they prefer localized promotions targeted toward the characteristics of consumers in their own cities and neighborhoods. Thus, to keep retailers happy, and to get precious retail shelf space for their products, manufacturers must now do more micromarketing.

One of the most common forms of micromarketing is *regionalization*—tailoring brands and promotions to suit individual geographic regions, cities, and even neighborhoods or specific stores. Campbell Soup, a pioneer in regionalization, has created many successful regional brands. For example, it sells spicy Ranchero beans, Brunswick stew, and spicy hot chili in the Southwest, Cajun gumbo soup in the South, and red bean soup in Hispanic areas. In fact, Campbell has reorganized its entire marketing operation to suit its regional strategy. It has divided its market into 22 regions. Within each region, sales managers and salespeople now have the authority to work closely with local retailers on displays, coupon offers, price specials, and promotional events geared to local market needs and conditions. For example, one sales manager recently offered Campbell's Pork & Beans at a 50-year-old price (5 cents) to help a local retailer celebrate its fiftieth anniversary. Campbell has allocated 15 percent to 20 percent of its total marketing budget to support local marketing, and this allocation may eventually rise to 50 percent.

Beyond regionalization, companies are also targeting specific demographic, psychographic, and behavioral micromarkets. For example, for its Crest toothpaste, Procter & Gamble uses six separate advertising campaigns targeting different age and ethnic segments including kids, blacks, and Hispanics. To reach these and other micromarkets, Procter & Gamble has greatly increased its use of highly focused media, such as cable television, direct mail, event sponsorships, electronic point-of-purchase media, and advertising display boards in locations such as doctors' and dentists' waiting rooms or elementary and high school cafeterias. And to satisfy the growing diversity of consumer tastes, P&G has created a shopping basket full of new products and brand extensions in all of its categories. For example, where once there was just Tide, now there are Regular Tide, Liquid Tide, Unscented Tide, and Tide with Bleach.

In the extreme, micromarketing becomes customization. Today, customized marketing is coming back in the form of *mass customization*—producing large quantities of custom-designed products to meet individual customer's needs. For example, home buyers in Japan can sit down at a computer with a salesperson and design their own future homes. They create an overall layout, making rooms as large or as small as they want, and then choose their own combinations of specific features from a list of 20,000 standardized parts. Their designs are sent electronically to the factory where the walls, ceilings, and floors are prepared on an assembly line that stretches out to one-third of a mile. Prefabricated modules are then delivered to the buyer's property and assembled. Within only 30 days, the family can move into its customized home.

Other marketers now are experimenting with new systems for providing custom-made products ranging from cars and bicycles to furniture and clothing. One such system, already installed in 18 stores across the country, consists of a camera linked to a computer that calculates customers' measurements and prints out a custom-fitted pattern for a bathing suit. The video screen shows the bedazzled and delighted buyer how the new suit will look from the front, side, and rear. The buyer chooses the fabric from about 150 samples, the custom-made design is sent to the producer's tailors, and the suit is stitched up.

Another example is a Japanese bicycle manufacturer that uses flexible manufacturing to turn out large numbers of bikes specially fitted to the needs of individual buyers. Customers visit their local bike shop where the shopkeeper measures them on a special frame and faxes the specifications to the factory. At the factory, the measurements are punched into a computer, which creates blueprints in three minutes that would take a draftsman 60 times that long. The computer then guides robots and workers through the production process. The factory is ready to produce any of 11,231,862 variations on 18 bicycle models in 199 color patterns and about as many sizes as there are people. The price is steep—between $545 and $3,200—but within two weeks the buyer is riding a custom-made, one-of-a-kind machine.

Business-to-business marketers are also finding new ways to customize their offerings. For example, Motorola salespeople now use a hand-held computer to custom design pagers following customer wishes. The design data are transmitted to the Motorola factory and production starts within 17 minutes. The customized pagers are ready for shipment within two hours.

Although micromarketing offers much promise, it also presents some problems. Trying to serve dozens or even hundreds of diverse micromarkets is vastly more complex than mass marketing. And offering many different products and promotion programs results in higher manufacturing and marketing costs. Thus, some marketers view micromarketing as just a fad—they think companies will quickly find that the extra sales gained will not cover the additional costs. But others think that micromarketing will revolutionize the way consumer products are marketed. Gone are the days, they say, when a company can effectively market one product to masses of consumers using a single promotion program. To these marketers, micromarketing signals the start of a whole new marketing era.

Sources: See Regis McKenna, "Marketing in an Age of Diversity," *Harvard Business Review,* September-October 1988, pp. 88-95; Zachary Schiller, "Stalking the New Consumer," *Business Week,* August 18, 1989, pp. 54-62; Susan Moffat, "Japan's New Personalized Production," *Fortune,* October 22, 1990, pp. 132-35; Shawn McKenna, *The Complete Guide to Regional Marketing* (Homewood, IL: Business One Irwin, 1992); Howard Schlossberg, "Packaged-Goods Experts: Micromarketing the Only Way to Go," *Marketing News,* July 6, 1992, p. 8; and B. Joseph Pine, *Mass Customization* (Boston: Harvard Business School Press, 1993).

marketing mixes. The company identifies different ways to segment the market and develops profiles of the resulting market segments. The second step is **market targeting**—evaluating each market segment's attractiveness and selecting one or more of the market segments to enter. The third step is **market positioning**—setting the competitive positioning for the product and creating a detailed marketing mix.

MARKET SEGMENTATION

Markets consist of buyers, and buyers differ in one or more ways. They may differ in their wants, resources, locations, buying attitudes, and buying practices. Any of these variables can be used to segment a market.

Segmenting a Market

Because buyers have unique needs and wants, each buyer is potentially a separate market. Ideally, then, a seller might design a separate marketing program for each buyer. For example, Boeing manufactures airplanes for only a few buyers and customizes its products and marketing program to satisfy each specific customer.

However, most sellers face larger numbers of smaller buyers and do not find complete segmentation worthwhile. Instead, they look for broad *classes* of buyers who differ in their product needs or buying responses. For example, General Motors has found that high- and low-income groups differ in their car-buying needs and wants. It also knows that young consumers' needs and wants differ from those of older consumers. Thus, GM has designed specific models for different income and age groups. In fact, it sells models for segments with varied *combinations* of age and income. For instance, GM designed its Buick Park Avenue for older, higher-income consumers. Age and income are only two of many bases that companies use for segmenting their markets.

Bases for Segmenting Consumer Markets

There is no single way to segment a market. A marketer has to try different segmentation variables, alone and in combination, to find the best way to view the market structure. Table 9-1 outlines the major variables that might be used in segmenting consumer markets. Here we look at the major *geographic, demographic, psychographic,* and *behavioral variables.*

Geographic Segmentation

Geographic segmentation calls for dividing the market into different geographical units such as nations, states, regions, counties, cities, or neighborhoods. A company may decide to operate in one or a few geographical areas, or to operate in all areas but pay attention to geographical differences in needs and wants. For example, General Foods' Maxwell House ground coffee is sold nationally but is flavored regionally: People in the West want stronger coffee than do people in the East. Campbell sells Cajun gumbo soup in Louisiana and Mississippi, makes its nacho cheese soup spicier in Texas and California, and sells its spicy Ranchero Beans only in the South and Southwest.

S. C. Johnson & Son practices geographic segmentation for its arsenal of Raid bug killers by emphasizing the right products in the right geographic areas at the right times:

> Concerned that its dominant share of the household insecticide market had plateaued just above 40 percent, Johnson figured out where and when different bugs were about to start biting, stinging, and otherwise making people's lives miserable. The company promoted cockroach zappers in roach capitals such as Houston and New York and flea sprays in flea-bitten cities like Tampa and Birmingham. Since the program began last year, Raid has increased its market share in 16 of 18 regions and its overall piece of the $450-million-a-year U.S. insecticide market by five percentage points.[1]

Many companies today are "regionalizing" their marketing programs—localizing their products, advertising, promotion, and sales efforts to fit the needs of individual regions, cities, and even neighborhoods. Others are seeking to cultivate as yet untapped territory. For example, many large companies are fleeing the fiercely competitive major cities and suburbs to set up shop in small-town America. McDonald's, for instance, recently began opening a chain of smaller-format Golden Arches Cafes in towns too small for its standard-sized restaurants. Hampton Inns is pursuing a similar strategy:

> Townsend, Tennessee, for example, is small even by small-town standards: Its population is 329. But looks are deceiving. Situated on a well-traveled and picturesque route between Knoxville and the Smokey Mountains, the village [serves both business and vacation travelers. Hampton Inns,] the 290-motel chain, opened [a unit] in

TABLE 9-1
Major Segmentation Variables for Consumer Markets

VARIABLE	TYPICAL BREAKDOWNS
Geographic	
Region	Pacific, Mountain, West North Central, West South Central, East North Central, East South Central, South Atlantic, Middle Atlantic, New England
County size	A, B, C, D
City size	Under 5,000; 5,000-20,000; 20,000-50,000; 50,000-100,000; 100,000-250,000; 250,000-500,000; 500,000-1,000,000; 1,000,000-4,000,000; 4,000,000 and over
Density	Urban, suburban, rural
Climate	Northern, Southern
Demographic	
Age	Under 6, 6-11, 12-19, 20-34, 35-49, 50-64, 65 +
Gender	Male, female
Family size	1-2, 3-4, 5 +
Family life cycle	Young, single; young, married, no children; young, married, youngest child under 6; young married, youngest child 6 or over; older, married, with children; older, married, no children under 18; older, single; other
Income	Under $10,000; $10,000-$15,000; $15,000-$20,000; $20,000-$30,000; $30,000-$50,000; $50,000-$75,000; $75,000 and over
Occupation	Professional and technical; managers, officials, and proprietors; clerical, sales; craftsmen, foremen; operatives; farmers; retired; students; homemakers; unemployed
Education	Grade school or less; some high school; high school graduate; some college; college graduate
Religion	Catholic, Protestant, Jewish, other
Race	White, black, Asian, Hispanic
Nationality	American, British, French, German, Scandinavian, Italian, Latin American, Middle Eastern, Japanese
Psychographic	
Social class	Lower lowers, upper lowers, working class, middle class, upper middles, lower uppers, upper uppers
Lifestyle	Achievers, believers, strivers
Personality	Compulsive, gregarious, authoritarian, ambitious
Behavioral	
Purchase occasion	Regular occasion, special occasion
Benefits sought	Quality, service, economy
User status	Nonuser, ex-user, potential user, first-time user, regular user
Usage rate	Light user, medium user, heavy user
Loyalty status	None, medium, strong, absolute
Readiness state	Unaware, aware, informed, interested, desirous, intending to buy
Attitude toward product	Enthusiastic, positive, indifferent, negative, hostile

Townsend and . . . plans to open 100 more in tiny towns by 1996. . . . Lower costs are an asset in this sort of micromarketing. But volume is usually smaller, too, so businesses must often rachet down. The Townsend Hampton Inn, for example, has 54 rooms instead of the usual 135.[2]

Demographic Segmentation
Demographic segmentation consists of dividing the market into groups based on variables such as age, gender, family size, family life cycle, income, occupation, education, religion, race, and nationality. Demographic factors are the most popular bases for segmenting customer groups. One reason is that consumer needs, wants, and usage rates often vary closely with demographic variables. Another is that demographic variables are easier to measure than most other types of

Geographic segmentation: Fleeing the fiercely competitive major cities, Hampton Inn is setting up smaller units in small-town America. This Hampton Inn has 54 rooms instead of the usual 135.

variables. Even when market segments are first defined using other bases, such as personality or behavior, their demographic characteristics must be known in order to assess the size of the target market and to reach it efficiently.

Age and Life-Cycle Stage. Consumer needs and wants change with age. Some companies use **age and life-cycle segmentation,** offering different products or using different marketing approaches for different age and life-cycle groups. For example, Life Stage vitamins come in four versions, each designed for the special needs of specific age segments: chewable Children's Formula for children from 4 to 12 years old; Teen's Formula for teenagers; and two adult versions (Men's Formula and Women's Formula). Johnson & Johnson developed Affinity Shampoo to help women over 40 overcome age-related hair changes. McDonald's targets children, teens, adults, and seniors with different ads and media. Its ads to teens feature dance-beat music, adventure, and fast-paced cutting from scene to scene; ads to seniors are softer and more sentimental.

However, marketers must be careful to guard against stereotypes when using age and life-cycle segmentation. Although you might find some 70-year-olds in wheelchairs, you will find others on tennis courts. Similarly, whereas some 40-year-old couples are sending their children off to college, others are just beginning new families. Thus, age is often a poor predictor of a person's life cycle, health, work or family status, needs, and buying power.

Demographic segmentation: Johnson & Johnson targets children with Band-Aid Sesame Street Bandages; Big Bird and Cookie Monster "help turn little people's tears into great big smiles." Toyota seeks "a beautiful new relationship" with women.

243

Gender. **Gender segmentation** has long been used in clothing, hairdressing, cosmetics, and magazines. Recently, other marketers have noticed opportunities for gender segmentation. For example, both men and women use most deodorant brands. Procter & Gamble, however, developed Secret as the brand specially formulated for a woman's chemistry and then packaged and advertised the product to reinforce the female image. The automobile industry also has begun to use gender segmentation extensively:

> Last year, women bought 49 percent of all new cars sold in the United States and influenced 80 percent of all new-car purchases. Thus, women have evolved as a valued target market. Selling to women should be no different than selling to men, but there are subtle differences. Women have different frames, less upper-body strength, and greater safety concerns. To address issues, automakers are redesigning their cars with hoods and trunks that are easier to open, seats that are easier to adjust, and seat belts that fit women better. In their advertising, some manufacturers target women directly. For example, Chevrolet devotes 30 percent of its television advertising budget to advertisements for women. Other companies avoid direct appeals. Instead, companies such as Toyota, Ford, and Pontiac try to include a realistic balance of men and women in their ads without specific reference to gender.[3]

Income. **Income segmentation** has long been used by the marketers of products and services such as automobiles, boats, clothing, cosmetics, and travel. Many companies target affluent consumers with luxury goods and convenience services. Stores like Neiman-Marcus pitch everything from expensive jewelry, fine fashions, and exotic furs to $4 jars of peanut butter and chocolate priced at $20 a pound.[4]

However, not all companies that use income segmentation target the affluent. Almost one-half of U.S. households have incomes of $25,000 or less. Despite their lower spending power, the nation's 40 million lower-income households offer an attractive market to many companies.

> It isn't sexy or glamorous, but selling to low-income Americans can still spell big profits. Reaching pinched Americans is not simply a matter of hauling out the sales signs and dressing down store displays, however. Getting their attention means understanding who they are and what they want. It means offering quality products at fair prices, with good-old-fashioned customer service.[5]

Many companies, such as Family Dollar stores, profitably target lower-income consumers. When Family Dollar real estate experts scout locations for new stores, they look for lower-middle-class neighborhoods where people wear less expensive shoes and drive old cars that drip a lot of oil. The income of a typical Family Dollar customer rarely exceeds $17,000 a year, and the average customer spends only about $6 per trip to the store. Yet the store's low-income strategy has made it one of the most profitable discount chains in the country.[6]

Multivariate Demographic Segmentation. Most companies will segment a market by combining two or more demographic variables. Consider the market for deodorant soaps. The top-selling deodorant soap brands are used by many different kinds of consumers, but two demographic variables—gender and age—coupled with geographic region, are the most useful in distinguishing the users of one brand from those of another.[7]

Men and women differ in their deodorant soap preferences. Top men's brands include Dial, Safeguard, and Irish Spring—these brands account for over 30 percent of the men's soap market. Women, in contrast, prefer Dial, Zest, and Coast, which account for 23 percent of the women's soap market. The leading deodorant soaps also appeal differently to different age segments. For example, Dial appeals more to men aged 45 to 68 than to younger men; women aged 35 to 44, however, are more likely than the average woman to use Dial. Coast appeals much more to younger men and women than to older people—men and women aged 18 to 24 are about a third more likely than the average to use Coast. Finally, deodorant soap preferences differ by region of the country. Although men in all geographic regions use deodorant soap, New Englanders use more Dial, southerners favor Safeguard, and westerners prefer Irish Spring. Thus, no single demographic variable captures all of the difference among the needs and preferences of deodorant soap buyers. To better define important market segments, soap marketers must use multivariate demographic segmentation.

Psychographic Segmentation

Psychographic segmentation divides buyers into different groups based on social class, lifestyle, or personality characteristics. People in the same demographic group can have very different psychographic makeups.

Social Class. In Chapter 5, we described American social classes and showed that social class has a strong effect on preferences in cars, clothes, home furnishings, leisure activities, reading habits, and retailers. Many companies design products or services for specific social classes, building in features that appeal to these classes.

Lifestyle. As discussed in Chapter 5, people's interest in various goods is affected by their lifestyles and the goods they buy express those lifestyles. Marketers are increasingly segmenting their markets by consumer lifestyles. For example, General Foods used lifestyle analysis in its successful repositioning of Sanka decaffeinated coffee. For years, Sanka's market was limited by the product's staid, older image. To turn this situation around, General Foods launched an advertising campaign that positioned Sanka as an ideal beverage for today's healthy, active lifestyles. The campaign targeted achievers of all ages, using a classic achiever appeal that Sanka "Lets you be your best." Advertising showed people in adventurous lifestyles, such as kayaking through rapids.[8]

Redbook magazine also targets a specific lifestyle segment—women it calls "*Redbook* Jugglers." The magazine defines the juggler as a 25- to 44-year-old woman who must juggle husband, family, home, and job. According to a recent *Redbook* ad, "She's a product of the 'me generation,' the thirty-something woman who balances home, family, and career—more than any generation before her, she refuses to put her own pleasures aside. She's old enough to know what she wants. And young enough to go after it." According to *Redbook,* this consumer makes an ideal target for marketers of health food and fitness products. She wears out more exercise shoes, swallows more vitamins, drinks more diet soda, and works out more often than do other consumer groups.

Personality. Marketers also have used personality variables to segment markets, giving their products personalities that correspond to consumer personalities. Successful market segmentation strategies based on personality have been used for products such as cosmetics, cigarettes, insurance, and liquor.[9] Honda's marketing campaign for its motor scooters provides another good example of personality segmentation:

> Honda *appears* to target its Spree, Elite, and Aero motor scooters at the hip and trendy 14- to 22-year-old age group. But the company *actually* designs ads that appeal to a much broader personality group. One ad, for example, shows a delighted child bouncing up and down on his bed while the announcer says, "You've been trying to get there all your life." The ad reminds viewers of the euphoric feelings they got when they broke away from authority and did things their parents told them not to do. And it suggests that they can feel that way again by riding a Honda scooter. So even though Honda seems to be targeting young consumers, the ads appeal to trend setters and independent personalities in all age groups. In fact, over half of Honda's scooter sales are to young professionals and older buyers—15 percent are purchased by the over-50 group. Thus, Honda is appealing to the rebellious, independent kid in all of us.[10]

Behavioral Segmentation

Behavioral segmentation divides buyers into groups based on their knowledge, attitudes, uses, or responses to a product. Many marketers believe that behavior variables are the best starting point for building market segments.

Occasions. Buyers can be grouped according to occasions when they get the idea to buy, actually make their purchase, or use the purchased item. **Occasion segmentation** can help firms build up product usage. For example, orange juice most often is consumed at breakfast, but orange growers have promoted drinking orange juice as a cool and refreshing drink at other times of the day. In contrast, Coca-Cola's "Coke in the Morning" advertising campaign attempts to increase Coke consumption by promoting the beverage as an early morning pick-

Occasion segmentation: Kodak has developed special versions of its single-use camera for about any picture-taking occasion, from underwater photography to taking baby pictures.

me-up. Some holidays, such as Mother's Day and Father's Day, were originally promoted partly to increase the sale of candy, flowers, cards, and other gifts. The Curtis Candy Company promoted the "trick-or-treat" custom at Halloween to encourage every home to have candy ready for eager little callers knocking at the door.

Kodak uses occasion segmentation in designing and marketing its single-use cameras, consisting of a roll of film with an inexpensive case and lens sold in a single, sealed unit. The customer simply snaps off the roll of pictures and returns the film, camera and all, to be processed. By mixing lenses, film speeds, and accessories, Kodak has developed special versions of the camera for about any picture-taking occasion, from underwater photography to taking baby pictures:

> Standing on the edge of the Grand Canyon? Single-use cameras can take panoramic, wide-angle shots. Snorkeling? Focus on that flounder with a different single-use camera. Sports fans are another target: Kodak now markets a telephoto version with ultrafast . . . film for the stadium set. . . . Planners are looking at a model equipped with a short focal-length lens and fast film requiring less light . . . they figure parents would like . . . to take snapshots of their babies without the disturbing flash. . . . In one Japanese catalog aimed at young women, Kodak sells a package of five pastel-colored cameras . . . including a version with a fish-eye lens to create a rosy, romantic glow.[11]

Benefits Sought. A powerful form of segmentation is to group buyers according to the different *benefits* that they seek from the product. **Benefit segmentation** requires finding the major benefits people look for in the product class, the kinds of people who look for each benefit, and the major brands that deliver each benefit. One of the best examples of benefit segmentation was conducted in the toothpaste market (see Table 9-2). Research found four benefit segments: economic, medicinal, cosmetic, and taste. Each benefit group had special demographic, behavioral, and psychographic characteristics. For example, the people seeking to prevent decay tended to have large families, were heavy toothpaste users, and were conservative. Each segment also favored certain brands. Most current brands appeal to one of these segments. For example, Crest tartar control toothpaste stresses protection and appeals to the family segment; Aim looks and tastes good and appeals to children.

Colgate-Palmolive used benefit segmentation to reposition its Irish Spring soap. Research showed three deodorant soap benefit segments: men who prefer lightly scented deodorant soap; women who want a mildly scented, gentle soap; and a mixed, mostly male segment that wanted a strongly scented, refreshing soap. The original Irish Spring did well with the last segment, but Colgate wanted to target the larger middle segment. Thus, it reformulated the soap and changed its advertising to give the product more of a family appeal.[12]

In short, companies can use benefit segmentation to clarify the benefit segment to which they are appealing, its characteristics, and the major competing

TABLE 9-2
Benefit Segmentation of the Toothpaste Market

BENEFIT SEGMENTS	DEMO-GRAPHICS	BEHAVIOR	PSYCHO-GRAPHICS	FAVORED BRANDS
Economy (low price)	Men	Heavy users	High autonomy, value oriented	Brands on sale
Medicinal (decay prevention)	Large families	Heavy users	Hypochondriacal, conservative	Crest
Cosmetic (bright teeth)	Teens, young adults	Smokers	High sociability, active	Aqua-Fresh, Ultra Brite
Taste (good tasting)	Children	Spearmint lovers	High self-involvement, hedonistic	Colgate, Aim

Source: Adapted from Russell J. Haley, "Benefit Segmentation: A Decision-Oriented Research Tool," *Journal of Marketing*, July 1968, pp. 30-35. Also see Haley, "Benefit Segmentation: Backwards and Forwards," *Journal of Advertising Research*, February-March 1984, pp. 19-25; and Haley, "Benefit Segmentation—20 Years Later," *Journal of Consumer Marketing*, Vol. 1, 1984, pp. 5-14.

brands. They also can search for new benefits and launch brands that deliver them.

User Status. Markets can be segmented into groups of nonusers, ex-users, potential users, first-time users, and regular users of a product. Potential users and regular users may require different kinds of marketing appeals. For example, one study found that blood donors are low in self-esteem, low risk takers, and more highly concerned about their health; nondonors tend to be the opposite on all three dimensions. This suggests that social agencies should use different marketing approaches for keeping current donors and attracting new ones. A company's market position will also influence its focus. Market share leaders will focus on attracting potential users, whereas smaller firms will focus on attracting current users away from the market leader.

Usage Rate. Markets also can be segmented into light-, medium-, and heavy-user groups. Heavy users are often a small percentage of the market, but account for a high percentage of total buying. Figure 9-2 shows usage rates for some popular consumer products. Product users were divided into two halves, a light-user half and a heavy-user half, according to their buying rates for the specific products. Using beer as an example, the figure shows that 41 percent of the

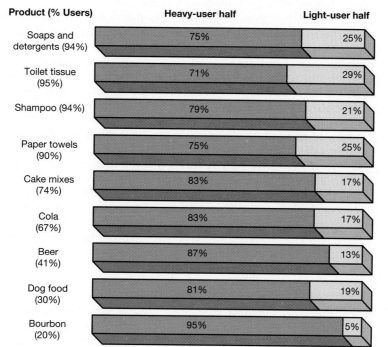

FIGURE 9-2
Heavy and light users of common consumer products
Source: See Victor J. Cook and William A. Mindak, "A Search for Constants: The 'Heavy User' Revisited!" *Journal of Consumer Marketing*, Vol. 1, No. 4 (Spring 1984), p. 80.

Product (% Users)	Heavy-user half	Light-user half
Soaps and detergents (94%)	75%	25%
Toilet tissue (95%)	71%	29%
Shampoo (94%)	79%	21%
Paper towels (90%)	75%	25%
Cake mixes (74%)	83%	17%
Cola (67%)	83%	17%
Beer (41%)	87%	13%
Dog food (30%)	81%	19%
Bourbon (20%)	95%	5%

households studied buy beer. However, the heavy-user half accounted for 87 percent of the beer consumed—almost seven times as much as the light-user half. Clearly, a beer company would prefer to attract one heavy user to its brand rather than several light users. Thus, most beer companies target the heavy beer drinker, using appeals such as Schaefer's "one beer to have when you're having more than one" or Miller Lite's "tastes great, less filling."

Loyalty Status. A market can also be segmented by consumer loyalty. Consumers can be loyal to brands (Tide), stores (Wal-Mart), and companies (Ford). Buyers can be divided into groups according to their degree of loyalty. Some consumers are completely loyal—they buy one brand all the time. Others are somewhat loyal—they are loyal to two or three brands of a given product or favor one brand while sometimes buying others. Still other buyers show no loyalty to any brand. They either want something different each time they buy or always buy a brand on sale.

Each market is made up of different numbers of each type of buyer. A brand-loyal market has a high percentage of buyers showing strong brand loyalty—for example, the toothpaste market and the beer market. Companies selling in a brand-loyal market have a hard time gaining more market share, and new companies have a hard time trying to enter.

A company can learn a lot by analyzing loyalty patterns in its market. It should start by studying its own loyal customers. Colgate finds that its loyal buyers are more middle class, have larger families, and are more health conscious. These characteristics pinpoint the target market for Colgate. By studying its less loyal buyers, the company can detect which brands are most competitive with its own. If many Colgate buyers also buy Crest, Colgate can attempt to improve its positioning against Crest, possibly by using direct-comparison advertising. By looking at customers who are shifting away from its brand, the company can learn about its marketing weaknesses. As for nonloyals, the company may attract them by putting its brand on sale.

Companies need to be careful when using brand loyalty in their segmentation strategies. What appear to be brand-loyal purchase patterns might reflect little more than *habit, indifference,* a *low price,* or *unavailability* of other brands. Thus, frequent or regular purchasing may not be the same as brand loyalty—marketers must examine the motivations behind observed purchase patterns.

Buyer-Readiness Stage. A market consists of people in different stages of readiness to buy a product. Some people are unaware of the product; some are aware; some are informed; some are interested; some want the product; and some intend to buy. The relative numbers at each stage make a big difference in designing the marketing program. For example, New York Institute of Technology recently began offering self-paced college courses via personal computer. Students can log onto their personal computers at any time and from any location to complete their lessons or "talk" to their teachers.[13] At first, potential students will be unaware of the new program. The initial marketing effort should thus employ high-awareness-building advertising and publicity that uses a simple message. If it is successful in building awareness, the marketing program should shift in order to move more people into the next readiness stage—say, interest in the program— by stressing the benefits of the "electronic university." Facilities should be readied for handling the large number of people who may be moved to enroll in the courses. In general, the marketing program must be adjusted to the changing distribution of buyer readiness.

Attitude toward Product. People in a market can be enthusiastic, positive, indifferent, negative, or hostile about a product. Door-to-door workers in a political campaign use a given voter's attitude to determine how much time to spend with that voter. They thank enthusiastic voters and remind them to vote; they spend little or no time trying to change the attitudes of negative and hostile voters. They reinforce those who are positive and try to win the votes of those who are indifferent. In such marketing situations, attitudes can be effective segmentation variables.

Segmenting Business Markets

Consumer and business marketers use many of the same variables to segment their markets. Business buyers can be segmented geographically or by benefits sought, user status, usage rate, loyalty status, readiness state, and attitudes. Yet,

TABLE 9-3
Major Segmentation Variables for Business Markets

Demographics

Industry: Which industries that buy this product should we focus on?

Company size: What size companies should we focus on?

Location: What geographical areas should we focus on?

Operating variables

Technology: What customer technologies should we focus on?

User/nonuser status: Should we focus on heavy, medium, or light users or nonusers?

Customer capabilities: Should we focus on customers needing many services or few services?

Purchasing approaches

Purchasing function organization: Should we focus on companies with highly centralized or decentralized purchasing organizations?

Power structure: Should we focus on companies that are engineering dominated, financially dominated, or marketing dominated?

Nature of existing relationships: Should we focus on companies with which we already have strong relationships or simply go after the most desirable companies?

General purchase policies: Should we focus on companies that prefer leasing? Service contracts? Systems purchases? Sealed bidding?

Purchasing criteria: Should we focus on companies that are seeking quality? Service? Price?

Situational factors

Urgency: Should we focus on companies that need quick delivery or service?

Specific application: Should we focus on certain applications of our product rather than all applications?

Size of order: Should we focus on large or small orders?

Personal characteristics

Buyer-seller similarity: Should we focus on companies whose people and values are similar to ours?

Attitudes toward risk: Should we focus on risk-taking or risk-avoiding customers?

Loyalty: Should we focus on companies that show high loyalty to their suppliers?

Source: Adapted from Thomas V. Bonoma and Benson P. Shapiro, *Segmenting the Industrial Market* (Lexington, MA: Lexington Books, 1983). Also see John Berrigan and Carl Finkbeiner, *Segmentation Marketing: New Methods for Capturing Business* (New York: Harper-Business, 1992).

business marketers also use also some additional variables. As Table 9-3 shows, these include business customer *demographics* (industry, company size); *operating characteristics; purchasing approaches; situational factors;* and *personal characteristics*.[14]

The table lists major questions that business marketers should ask in determining which customers they want to serve. By going after segments instead of the whole market, companies have a much better chance to deliver value to consumers and to receive maximum rewards for close attention to consumer needs. Thus, Goodyear and other tire companies should decide which *industries* they want to serve. Manufacturers buying tires vary in their needs. Makers of luxury and high-performance cars want higher-grade tires than makers of economy models. And the tires needed by aircraft manufacturers must meet much higher safety standards than tires needed by farm tractor manufacturers.

Within the chosen industry, a company can further segment by *customer size* or *geographic location.* The company might set up separate systems for dealing with larger or multiple-location customers. For example, Steelcase, a major producer of office furniture, first segments customers into ten industries, including banking, insurance, and electronics. Next, company salespeople work with independent Steelcase dealers to handle smaller, local, or regional Steelcase customers in each segment. But many national, multiple-location customers, such as Exxon or IBM, have special needs that may reach beyond the scope of individual dealers. So Steelcase uses national accounts managers to help its dealer networks handle its national accounts.

Within a given target industry and customer size, the company can segment by *purchase approaches and criteria*. For example, government, university, and industrial laboratories typically differ in their purchase criteria for scientific instruments. Government labs need low prices (because they have difficulty in getting funds to buy instruments) and service contracts (because they can easily get money to maintain instruments). University labs want equipment that needs little regular service because they don't have service people on their payrolls. Industrial labs need highly reliable equipment because they cannot afford downtime.

Table 9-3 focuses on business buyer *characteristics*. However, as in consumer segmentation, many marketers believe that *buying behavior* and *benefits* provide the best basis for segmenting business markets. For example, a recent study of the customers of Signode Corporation's industrial packaging division revealed four segments, each seeking a different mix of price and service benefits:

- *Programmed buyers*. These buyers view Signode's products as not very important to their operations. They buy the products as a routine purchase, usually pay full price, and accept below-average service. Clearly, this is a highly profitable segment for Signode.

- *Relationship buyers*. These buyers regard Signode's packaging products as moderately important and are knowledgeable about competitors' offerings. They prefer to buy from Signode as long as its price is reasonably competitive. They receive a small discount and a modest amount of service. This segment is Signode's second most profitable.

- *Transaction buyers*. These buyers see Signode's products as very important to their operations. They are price and service sensitive. They receive about a 10 percent discount and above-average service. They are knowledgeable about competitors' offerings and are ready to switch for a better price, even if it means losing some service.

- *Bargain hunters*. These buyers see Signode's products as very important and demand the deepest discount and the highest service. They know the alternative suppliers, bargain hard, and are ready to switch at the slightest dissatisfaction. Signode needs these buyers for volume purposes, but they are not very profitable.[15]

This segmentation scheme has helped Signode to do a better job of designing marketing strategies that take into account each segment's unique reactions to varying levels of price and service.[16]

Segmenting International Markets

Few companies have either the resources or the will to operate in all, or even most, of the more than 170 countries that dot the globe. Although some large companies, such as Coca-Cola or Sony, sell products in more than 100 countries, most international firms focus on a smaller set. Operating in many countries presents new challenges. The different countries of the world, even those that are close together, can vary dramatically in their economic, cultural, and political makeup. Thus, just as they do within their domestic markets, international firms need to group their world markets into segments with distinct buying needs and behaviors.

Companies can segment international markets using one or a combination of several variables. They can segment by *geographic location,* grouping countries by regions such as Western Europe, the Pacific Rim, the Middle East, or Africa. In fact, countries in many regions already have organized geographically into market groups or "free trade zones," such as the European Community, the European Free Trade Association, and the North American Free Trade Association. These associations reduce trade barriers between member countries, creating larger and more homogeneous markets.

Geographic segmentation assumes that nations close to one another will have many common traits and behaviors. Although this is often the case, there are many exceptions. For example, although the United States and Canada have much in common, both differ culturally and economically from neighboring Mexico. Even within a region, consumers can differ widely:

Many U.S. marketers think everything between the Rio Grande and Tierra del Fuego at the southern tip of South America is the same, including the 400 million inhabitants. In fact, [however,] the Dominican Republic is no more like Argentina than

Sicily is like Sweden. Many Latin Americans don't speak Spanish, including 140 million Portuguese-speaking Brazilians and the millions in other countries who speak a variety of Indian dialects.[17]

World markets can be segmented on the basis of *economic factors*. For example, countries might be grouped by population income levels or by their overall level of economic development. Some countries, such as the so-called Group of Seven—the United States, Britain, France, Germany, Japan, Canada, and Italy—have established, highly industrialized economies. Other countries have newly industrialized or developing economies (Singapore, Taiwan, Korea, Brazil, Mexico). Still others are less developed (China, India). A company's economic structure shapes its population's product and service needs and, therefore, the marketing opportunities it offers.

Countries can be segmented by *political and legal factors* such as the type and stability of government, receptivity toward foreign firms, monetary regulations, and the amount of bureaucracy. Such factors can play a crucial role in a company's choice of which countries to enter and how. *Cultural factors* also can be used to segment markets. International markets can be grouped according to common languages, religions, values and attitudes, customs, and behavioral patterns.

Segmenting international markets on the basis of geographic, economic, political, cultural, and other factors assumes that segments should consist of clusters of countries. However, many companies use a different approach, called *intermarket segmentation*. Using this approach, they form segments of consumers who have similar needs and buying behavior even though they are located in different countries.[18] For example, Mercedes-Benz targets the world's well-to-do, regardless of their country. Similarly, an agricultural chemicals manufacturer might focus on small farmers in a variety of developing countries:

> These [small farmers], whether from Pakistan or Indonesia or Kenya or Mexico, appear to represent common needs and behavior patterns. Most of them till the land using bullock carts and have very little cash to buy agricultural inputs. They lack the education . . . to appreciate fully the value of using fertilizer and depend on government help for such things as seeds, pesticides, and fertilizer. They acquire farming needs from local suppliers and count on word-of-mouth to learn and accept new things and ideas. Thus, even though these farmers are in different countries continents apart, and even though they speak different languages and have different cultural backgrounds, they may represent a homogeneous market segment.[19]

Requirements for Effective Segmentation

Clearly, there are many ways to segment a market, but not all segmentations are effective. For example, buyers of table salt could be divided into blond and brunette customers. But hair color obviously does not affect the purchase of salt. Furthermore, if all salt buyers bought the same amount of salt each month, believed all salt is the same, and wanted to pay the same price, the company would not benefit from segmenting this market.

To be useful, market segments must have the following characteristics:

Intermarket segmentation: Mercedes targets the world's well-to-do, regardless of their country.

- **Measurability.** The size, purchasing power, and profiles of the segments can be measured. Certain segmentation variables are difficult to measure. For example, there are 24 million left-handed people in the United States—almost equaling the entire population of Canada. Yet few products are targeted toward this left-handed segment. The major problem may be that the segment is hard to identify and measure. There are no data on the demographics of lefties, and the Census Bureau does not keep track of left-handedness in its surveys. Private data companies keep reams of statistics on other demographic segments, but not on left-handers.[20]

- **Accessibility.** The market segments can be effectively reached and served. Suppose a perfume company finds that heavy users of its brand are single women who stay out late and socialize a lot. Unless this group lives or shops at certain places and is exposed to certain media, its members will be difficult to reach.

- **Substantiality.** The market segments are large or profitable enough to serve. A segment should be the largest possible homogeneous group worth pursuing with a tailored marketing program. It would not pay, for example, for an automobile manufacturer to develop cars for persons whose height is less than four feet.

- **Actionability.** Effective programs can be designed for attracting and serving the segments. For example, although one small airline identified seven market segments, its staff was too small to develop separate marketing programs for each segment.

MARKET TARGETING

Marketing segmentation reveals the firm's market-segment opportunities. The firm now has to evaluate the various segments and decide how many and which ones to target. We now look at how companies evaluate and select target segments.

Evaluating Market Segments

In evaluating different market segments, a firm must look at three factors: segment size and growth, segment structural attractiveness, and company objectives and resources.

Segment Size and Growth

The company must first collect and analyze data on current dollar sales, projected sales-growth rates, and expected profit margins for the various segments. It will be interested in segments that have the right size and growth characteristics. But "right size and growth" is a relative matter. Some companies will want to target segments with large current sales, a high growth rate, and a high profit margin. However, the largest, fastest-growing segments are not always the most attractive ones for every company. Smaller companies may find that they lack the skills and resources needed to serve the larger segments or that these segments are too competitive. Such companies may select segments that are smaller and less attractive, in an absolute sense, but that are potentially more profitable for them.

Segment Structural Attractiveness

A segment might have desirable size and growth and still not be attractive from a profitability point of view. The company must examine several major structural factors that affect long-run segment attractiveness.[21] For example, the company should assess current and potential *competitors*. A segment is less attractive if it already contains many strong and aggressive competitors. Marketers also should consider the threat of *substitute products*. A segment is less attractive if actual or potential substitutes for the product already exist. Substitutes limit the potential prices and profits that can be earned in a segment. The relative *power of buyers* also affects segment attractiveness. If the buyers in a segment possess strong or increasing bargaining power relative to sellers, they will try to force prices down, demand more quality or services, and set competitors against one another, all at the expense of seller profitability. Finally, segment attractiveness depends on the relative *power of suppliers*. A segment is less attractive if the suppliers of raw materials, equipment, labor, and services in the segment are powerful enough to raise prices or reduce the quality or quantity of ordered goods and services. Suppliers tend to be powerful when they are large and concentrated, when few substitutes exist, or when the supplied product is an important input.

Company Objectives and Resources

Even if a segment has the right size and growth and is structurally attractive, the company must consider its own objectives and resources in relation to that segment. Some attractive segments could be dismissed quickly because they do not mesh with the company's long-run objectives. Although such segments might be tempting in themselves, they might divert the company's attention and energies away from its main goals. Or they might be a poor choice from an environmental, political, or social-responsibility viewpoint. For example, in recent years, several companies and industries have been criticized for unfairly targeting vulnerable segments—children, the aged, low-income minorities, and others—with questionable products or tactics (see Marketing Highlight 9-2).

If a segment fits the company's objectives, the company then must decide whether it possesses the skills and resources needed to succeed in that segment. Each segment has certain success requirements. If the company lacks and cannot readily obtain the strengths needed to compete successfully in a segment, it should not enter the segment. Even if the company possesses the *required* strengths, it needs to employ skills and resources *superior* to those of the competition in order to really win in a market segment. The company should enter segments only where it can offer superior value and gain advantages over competitors.

Selecting Market Segments

After evaluating different segments, the company must now decide which and how many segments to serve. This is the problem of *target-market selection*. A **target market** consists of a set of buyers who share common needs or characteristics that the company decides to serve. Figure 9-3 shows that the firm can adopt one of three market-coverage strategies: *undifferentiated marketing, differentiated marketing,* and *concentrated marketing.*

Undifferentiated Marketing

Using an **undifferentiated marketing** strategy, a firm might decide to ignore market segment differences and go after the whole market with one offer. The offer will focus on what is *common* in the needs of consumers rather than on what is *different.* The company designs a product and a marketing program that appeal

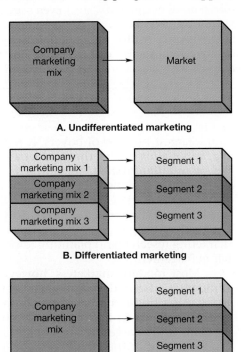

FIGURE 9-3
Three alternative market-coverage strategies

A. Undifferentiated marketing

B. Differentiated marketing

C. Concentrated marketing

SOCIALLY RESPONSIBLE MARKET TARGETING

Market segmentation and targeting form the core of modern marketing strategy. Smart targeting helps companies to be more efficient and effective by focusing on the segments that they can satisfy best. Targeting also benefits consumers—companies reach specific groups of consumers with offers carefully tailored to satisfy their needs. However, market targeting sometimes generates controversy and concern. Issues usually involve the targeting of vulnerable or disadvantaged consumers with controversial or potentially harmful products.

For example, over the years, the cereal industry has been heavily criticized for its marketing efforts directed toward children. Critics worry that sophisticated advertising, in which high-powered appeals are presented through the mouths of lovable animated characters, will overwhelm children's defenses. They claim that toys and other premiums offered with cereals will distract children and make them want a particular cereal for the wrong reasons. All of this, critics fear, will entice children to gobble too much sugared cereal or to eat poorly balanced breakfasts. The marketers of toys and other children's products have been similarly battered, often with good justification. Some critics have even called for a complete ban on advertising to children. Children cannot understand the selling intent of the advertiser, critics reason, so any advertising targeted toward children is inherently unfair. To encourage responsible advertising to children, the Children's Advertising Review Unit, the advertising industry's self-regulatory agency, has published extensive children's advertising guidelines that recognize the special needs of children.

Cigarette, beer, and fast-food marketers also have generated much controversy in recent years by their attempts to target inner-city minority consumers. For example, McDonald's and other chains have drawn criticism for pitching their high-fat, salt-laden fare to low-income, inner-city residents who are much more likely than suburbanites to be heavy consumers. R. J. Reynolds took heavy flak in 1990 when it announced plans to market Uptown, a menthol cigarette targeted toward low-income blacks. It quickly dropped the brand in the face of a loud public outcry and heavy pressure from black leaders. G. Heileman Brewing made a similar mistake with PowerMaster, a potent malt liquor targeted toward the black community. Although the brand seemed to make sense it was ill-fated from the start:

> Sales of ordinary beer (3.5 percent alcohol) have slowly been going pffffft for years now, while sales of some higher-proof beers have risen 25 to 30 percent annually. So the decision by G. Heileman Brewing to extend its Colt 45 malt liquor line with PowerMaster, a new high-test malt (5.9 percent alcohol), wasn't [at first glance] dumb. But malt liquor is consumed primarily by blacks. And targeting blacks with anything less wholesome than farina has become risky. . . . Heileman nonetheless rushed in where a smarter company might reasonably have hesitated. . . . PowerMaster became "a magnet of controversy from the moment it raised its alcohol-enhanced head. Federal officials, industry leaders, black activists, and media types weighed in with protests that PowerMaster . . . was an example of a bad product, bad marketing, and, essentially, a bad idea." . . . [Only] weeks after its planned debut, [it] was just a malty memory.

Even some industry insiders objected to the Heileman's targeting tactics. For example, when the PowerMaster controversy erupted, the president of Anheuser-Busch wrote to Heileman's chairman, suggesting that the planned product might indicate "that we put profits be-

to the largest number of buyers. It relies on mass distribution and mass advertising, and it aims to give the product a superior image in people's minds. An example of undifferentiated marketing is the Hershey Company's marketing some years ago of only one chocolate candy bar for everyone.

Undifferentiated marketing provides cost economies. The narrow product line keeps down production, inventory, and transportation costs. The undifferentiated advertising program keeps down advertising costs. The absence of segment marketing research and planning lowers the costs of marketing research and product management.

Most modern marketers, however, have strong doubts about this strategy. Difficulties arise in developing a product or brand that will satisfy all consumers. Firms using undifferentiated marketing typically develop an offer aimed at the largest segments in the market. When several firms do this, heavy competition develops in the largest segments, and less satisfaction results in the smaller ones. The result is that the larger segments may be less profitable because they attract heavy competition. Recognition of this problem has led firms to be more interested in smaller market segments.

Some women can't be fooled. they know **color** has to do **more** than just look **pretty.**

A natural born wiz? Get real.

Shades of **YOU** **Lipstick & NailColor**

Coordinated shades created expressly to flatter your looks.

Moisture-enriched formula conditions lips.

Keratin-A formula helps strengthen nails.

MAYBE SHE'S BORN WITH IT. MAYBE IT'S **MAYBELLINE.**

Most attempts to target minorities and other special segments benefit targeted consumers. For example, Maybelline developed Shades of You cosmetics to meet the special needs of black women.

fore the consideration of the communities we serve."

Not all attempts to target children, minorities, or other special segments draw such criticism. In fact, most provide benefits to targeted consumers. For example, Colgate-Palmolive's Colgate Junior toothpaste has special features designed to get children to brush longer and more often—it's less foamy, has a milder taste, and contains sparkles, and it exits the tube in a star-shaped column. Golden Ribbon Playthings has developed a highly acclaimed and very successful black character doll named "Huggy Bean" targeted toward minority consumers. Huggy comes with books and toys that connect her with her African heritage. Many cosmetics companies have responded to the special needs of minority segments by adding products specifically designed for black, Hispanic, or Asian women. For example, Maybelline introduced a highly successful line called Shades of You targeted to black women, and other companies have followed with their own lines of multicultural products.

Thus, in market targeting, the issue is not really *who* is targeted but rather *how* and for *what*. Controversies arise when marketers attempt to profit at the expense of targeted segments—when they unfairly target vulnerable segments or target them with questionable products or tactics. Socially responsible marketing calls for segmentation and targeting that serve not just the interests of the company, but also the interests of those targeted.

Sources: Excerpts from "PowerMaster," *Fortune,* January 13, 1992, p. 82. Also see "Selling Sin to Blacks," *Fortune,* October 21, 1991, p. 100; Martha T. Moore, "Putting on a Fresh Face," *USA Today,* January 3, 1992, pp. B1, B2; Dorothy J. Gaiter, "Black-Owned Firms Are Catching an Afrocentric Wave," *The Wall Street Journal,* January 8, 1992, p. B2; and Maria Mallory, "Waking Up to a Major Market," *Business Week,* March 23, 1992, pp. 70-73.

Differentiated Marketing

Using a **differentiated marketing** strategy, a firm decides to target several market segments and designs separate offers for each. General Motors tries to produce a car for every "purse, purpose, and personality." By offering product and marketing variations, it hopes for higher sales and a stronger position within each market segment. GM hopes that a stronger position in several segments will strengthen consumers' overall identification of the company with the product category. It also hopes for greater repeat purchasing because the firm's offer better matches the customer's desire.

A growing number of firms have adopted differentiated marketing. For example, A&P uses different food store formats to meet the needs of different customer segments:

A&P's merchandising strategy attempts to provide a supermarket for every kind of shopper: stark black-and-white Futurestores, with the latest in gourmet departments and electronic services, for exclusive neighborhoods; conventional A&P's . . . for middle-class markets; and full-service, warehouse-style Sav-A-Centers, where shoppers have come to expect them.[22]

MARKET NICHING: KING OF THE (MOLE)HILL

Ask almost anyone you know to name a brand of baking soda and they'll answer without hesitating: ARM & HAMMER. In fact, they'll find it hard to name any other brand. ARM & HAMMER baking soda, in its familiar little yellow box, has dominated the U.S. market for more than 115 years. But ask that same person to name the company that *makes* ARM & HAMMER baking soda and they'll probably draw a blank. The company is Church & Dwight. And although you won't find the firm listed among the Fortune 500, Church & Dwight is a giant in its baking soda niche. Founded in 1846, Church & Dwight is the world's leading producer of sodium bicarbonate—good ol' $NaHCO_3$.

Until the late 1960s, Church & Dwight was pretty much a one-product company, marketing sodium bicarbonate to consumers as ARM & HAMMER baking soda, or selling it in bulk to other companies for a variety of uses, from cake mixes to fire extinguishers. During the past two decades, however, as the consumer market for pure baking soda has matured, Church & Dwight has expanded its niche dramatically by finding ever more uses for its versatile white powder. In 1970, the company began its push into new consumer markets with a line of laundry products that capitalized both on the powerful ARM & HAMMER brand name and on consumer concerns about the environment. It introduced phosphate-free—but sodium-carbonate-rich—ARM & HAMMER detergent, which has since become the company's best-selling product, accounting for about a third of total sales. During the 1980s, Church & Dwight followed with a number of well-known consumer products, ranging from baking soda toothpaste to carpet deodorizers and air fresheners.

Although baking soda-based consumer products make up the bulk of Church & Dwight's current sales, the usefulness of sodium bicarbonate extends well beyond household cooking and cleaning. Church & Dwight also does a brisk and growing industrial business, which now contributes about 25 percent of annual sales. Business applications range from baking soda as a leavening agent in bakery products to treating municipal waste water. It's even used in animal nutrition products. For example, Church & Dwight markets an ARM & HAMMER product called MEGALAC, a high-energy feed supplement. It also markets ARM & HAMMER feed-grade sodium bicarbonate that helps dairy cows neutralize digestive acids and supplements the sodium bicarbonate produced naturally, allowing better feed efficiency and increased milk production.

Business markets may provide some of Church & Dwight's best opportunities for growth. As the world looks for new, more environmentally responsible solutions to nagging problems, the company has responded with a smorgasbord of new uses and products. For example, it recently introduced ARMEX, a blasting material made of baking soda and other ingredients. ARMEX has many advantages over current silicon-based sandblasting media, which can contribute to silicosis, a lung disease. ARMEX not only eliminates health and environmental hazards, it also has a more delicate touch—the sharp edges of its baking soda crystals wear down faster, stripping paint and grime without damaging underlying surfaces. ARMEX was originally developed to help strip tar and paint from the inside of the Statue of Liberty. Among the company's other new products is Armakleen, an industrial cleanser for printed circuit boards. It provides an environmentally safe alternative to current cleaners that contain chlorofluorocarbons (CFCs), thought to damage the earth's ozone layer. In addition to developing new baking soda-based products for its business markets, Church & Dwight has created a torrent of new commercial uses for plain old baking soda. For example, it has recently begun selling the stuff as an additive to municipal drinking water. Experiments have shown that baking soda neutralizes acids in the water supply, helping to inhibit corrosion and preventing lead and other toxic metals from leaching out of the plumbing. Church & Dwight is even rumored to be experi-

---

Differentiated marketing typically creates more total sales than does undifferentiated marketing. Procter & Gamble gets a higher total market share with ten brands of laundry detergent than it could with only one. But differentiated marketing also increases the costs of doing business. Modifying a product to meet different market-segment requirements usually involves some research and development, engineering, or special tooling costs. A firm usually finds it more expensive to produce, say, ten units of ten different products than one hundred units of one product. Developing separate marketing plans for the separate segments requires extra marketing research, forecasting, sales analysis, promotion planning, and channel management. And trying to reach different market segments with different advertising increases promotion costs. Thus, the company must weigh increased sales against increased costs when deciding on a differentiated marketing strategy.

Concentrated Marketing

A third market-coverage strategy, **concentrated marketing,** is especially ap-

Well-focused Church & Dwight has built a commanding position by concentrating on small, highly specialized niches.

menting with the ability of baking soda as an ingredient in a fungicide for plants.

Church & Dwight battles daily with much larger competitors—consumer companies like Procter & Gamble, Lever, and Colgate, and such international heavyweights as Rhône Poulenc and Solvay. At first glance, the company may appear to be fighting a losing battle. For example, in the $3.6 billion U.S. detergent market, ARM & HAMMER commands only a 4 percent market share, compared to P&G's 55 percent and Colgate's 24 percent. However, in the baking soda segment of the detergent market, ARM & HAMMER is among the leaders. In fact, when it comes to *anything* that has to do with baking soda, Church & Dwight is "king of the hill"— capturing 60 percent of the North American market for sodium bicarbonate. And even if the hill is more of a

molehill than a mountain, Church & Dwight outperforms many of its much larger competitors. The well-focused company has built a commanding position by concentrating on small, highly specialized market niches. During the past ten years, its annual sales have more than tripled, to $516 million, and profits have increased fourfold. Thus, Church & Dwight has proven once again what many concentrated marketers have learned—small can be beautiful.

Sources: James P. Meagher, "Church & Dwight: It Scores Big with the Brand-Name Pull of Arm & Hammer," *Barron's,* December 10, 1990, pp. 49-50; Peter Coombes, "Church & Dwight: On the Rise," *Chemical Week,* September 20, 1989, pp. 16-18; Peter Nulty, "Church & Dwight: No Product Is Too Dull to Shine," *Fortune,* July 27, 1992, pp. 95-96; and Riccardo A. Davis, "Arm & Hammer Seeks Growth Abroad," *Advertising Age,* August 17, 1992, pp. 3, 42.

pealing when company resources are limited. Instead of going after a small share of a large market, the firm goes after a large share of one or a few submarkets. For example, Oshkosh Truck is the world's largest producer of airport rescue trucks and front-loading concrete mixers. Recycled Paper Products concentrates on the market for alternative greeting cards. And Soho Natural Sodas concentrates on a narrow segment of the soft-drink market. Concentrated marketing provides an excellent way for small new businesses to get a foothold against larger, more resourceful competitors.

Through concentrated marketing, the firm achieves a strong market position in the segments (or niches) it serves because of its greater knowledge of the segments' needs and the special reputation it acquires (see Marketing Highlight 9-3). It also enjoys many operating economies because of specialization in production, distribution, and promotion. If the segment is well chosen, the firm can earn a high rate of return on its investment.

At the same time, concentrated marketing involves higher than normal risks. The particular market segment can turn sour. For example, when young women suddenly stopped buying sportswear, Bobbie Brooks's earnings went deeply into the red. Or larger competitors may decide to enter the same segment. California Cooler's success in the wine cooler segment attracted many large competitors, causing the original owners to sell to a larger company that had more marketing resources. For these reasons, many companies prefer to diversify in several market segments.

Choosing a Market-Coverage Strategy

Many factors need to be considered when choosing a market-coverage strategy. Which strategy is best depends on *company resources*. When the firm's resources are limited, concentrated marketing makes the most sense. The best strategy also depends on the degree of *product variability*. Undifferentiated marketing is more suited for uniform products such as grapefruit or steel. Products that can vary in design, such as cameras and automobiles, are more suited to differentiation or concentration. The *product's stage in the life cycle* also must be considered. When a firm introduces a new product, it is practical to launch only one version, and undifferentiated marketing or concentrated marketing makes the most sense. In the mature stage of the product life cycle, however, differentiated marketing begins to make more sense. Another factor is *market variability*. If most buyers have the same tastes, buy the same amounts, and react the same way to marketing efforts, undifferentiated marketing is appropriate. Finally, *competitors' marketing strategies* are important. When competitors use segmentation, undifferentiated marketing can be suicidal. Conversely, when competitors use undifferentiated marketing, a firm can gain by using differentiated or concentrated marketing.

POSITIONING FOR COMPETITIVE ADVANTAGE

Once a company has decided which segments of the market it will enter, it must decide what "positions" it wants to occupy in those segments.

What Is Market Positioning?

A **product's position** is the way the product is *defined by consumers* on important attributes—the place the product occupies in consumers' minds relative to competing products. Thus, Tide is positioned as a powerful, all-purpose family detergent; Era is positioned as a concentrated liquid stain remover; Cheer is positioned as the detergent for all temperatures. Toyota Tercel and Suburu are positioned on economy, Mercedes and Cadillac on luxury, and Porsche and BMW on performance.

Consumers are overloaded with information about products and services. They cannot reevaluate products every time they make a buying decision. To simplify buying decision making, consumers organize products into categories—they "position" products, services, and companies in their minds. A product's position is the complex set of perceptions, impressions, and feelings that consumers hold for the product compared with competing products. Consumers position products with or without the help of marketers. But marketers do not want to leave their products' positions to chance. They *plan* positions that will give their products the greatest advantage in selected target markets, and they *design* marketing mixes to create these planned positions.

Positioning Strategies

Marketers can follow several positioning strategies. They can position their products on specific *product attributes*—Ford Festiva advertises its low price; Saab promotes performance. Products can be positioned on the needs they fill or the *benefits* they offer—Crest reduces cavities; Aim tastes good. Or products can be positioned according to *usage occasions*—in the summer, Gatorade can be positioned as a beverage for replacing athletes' body fluids; in the winter, it can be positioned as the drink to use when the doctor recommends plenty of liquids. Another approach is to position the product for certain classes of *users*—Johnson & Johnson improved the market share for its baby shampoo from 3 percent to 14 percent by repositioning the product as one for adults who wash their hair frequently and need a gentle shampoo.

A product can also be positioned directly *against a competitor.* For example, in ads for their personal computers, Compaq and Tandy have directly compared their products with IBM personal computers. In its famous "We're number two, so we try harder" campaign, Avis successfully positioned itself against the larger Hertz. A product may also be positioned *away from competitors*—7-Up became the number-three soft drink when it was positioned as the "un-cola," the fresh and thirst-quenching alternative to Coke and Pepsi. Barbasol television ads position the company's shaving cream and other products as "great toiletries for a lot less money."

Finally, the product can be positioned for different *product classes.* For example, some margarines are positioned against butter, others against cooking oils. Camay hand soap is positioned with bath oils rather than with soap. Marketers often use a *combination* of these positioning strategies. Johnson & Johnson's Affinity shampoo is positioned as a hair conditioner for women over 40 (product class *and* user). And Arm & Hammer baking soda has been positioned as a deodorizer for refrigerators and garbage disposals (product class *and* usage situation).

Choosing and Implementing a Positioning Strategy

Some firms find it easy to choose their positioning strategy. For example, a firm well known for quality in certain segments will go for this position in a new segment if there are enough buyers seeking quality. But in many cases, two or more firms will go after the same position. Then, each will have to find other ways to set itself apart, such as promising "high quality for a lower cost" or "high quality with more technical service." Each firm must differentiate its offer by building a unique bundle of competitive advantages that appeal to a substantial group within the segment.

The positioning task consists of three steps: identifying a set of possible competitive advantages upon which to build a position, selecting the right competitive advantages, and effectively communicating and delivering the chosen position to the market.

Identifying Possible Competitive Advantages

Consumers typically choose products and services that give them the greatest value. Thus, the key to winning and keeping customers is to understand their needs and buying processes better than competitors do and to deliver more value. To the extent that a company can position itself as providing superior value to selected target markets, either by offering lower prices than competitors do or by providing more benefits to justify higher prices, it gains **competitive advantage.**[23] But solid positions cannot be built upon empty promises. If a company positions its product as *offering* the best quality and service, it must then *deliver* the promised quality and service. Thus, positioning begins with actually *differentiating* the company's marketing offer so that it will give consumers more value than competitors' offers do (see Marketing Highlight 9-4).

Not every company will find many opportunities for differentiating its offer and gaining competitive advantage. Some companies find many minor advantages that are easily copied by competitors and are, therefore, highly perishable. The solution for these companies is to keep identifying new potential advantages and to introduce them one by one to keep competitors off balance. These companies do not expect to gain a single major permanent advantage. Instead, they hope to gain many minor ones that can be introduced to win market share over a period of time.

In what specific ways can a company differentiate its offer from those of competitors? A company or market offer can be differentiated along the lines of *product, services, personnel,* or *image.*

Product Differentiation. A company can differentiate its physical product. At one extreme, some companies offer highly standardized products that allow little variation: chicken, steel, aspirin. Yet even here, some meaningful differentiation is possible. For example, Perdue claims that its branded chickens are better—fresher and more tender—and gets a 10 percent price premium based on this differentiation.

Other companies offer products that can be highly differentiated, such as automobiles, commercial buildings, and furniture. Here the company faces an

NINTENDO: MORE THAN JUST FUN AND GAMES

In the early 1980s, no home could be without a video game console and a dozen or so cartridges. By 1983, Atari, Coleco, Mattel, and a dozen other companies offered some version of a video game system and industry sales topped $3.2 billion. But by 1985, in just two short years, home video game sales had plummeted to a meager $100 million. Game consoles gathered dust in closets, and cartridges, originally priced as high as $35 each, sold from cardboard cartons in the backs of stores for as low as $5. Industry leader Atari, a subsidiary of Warner Communications, was hardest hit when the bottom fell out. Amid soaring losses, Warner fired Atari's president, sacked 4,500 employees, and sold the subsidiary at a fraction of its 1983 worth. Most industry experts simply shrugged their shoulders and blamed the death of the video game industry on fickle consumer tastes. Video games, they asserted, were just another fad.

But one company, Nintendo, a 100-year-old toy company from Kyoto, Japan, didn't think so. In late 1985, atop the still smoldering ruins of the U.S. video game business, the company introduced its Nintendo Entertainment System (NES) in the United States. By the end of 1986, just one year later, Nintendo had sold over 1 million NES units. And by 1992, Nintendo and its licensees were reaping annual sales of more than $4 billion in a now revitalized $5.6 billion U.S. video game industry. Nintendo had captured an astounding 80 percent share of the market, and more than one out of every two American households had a Nintendo system hooked up to one of its television sets.

How did Nintendo manage to single-handedly revive a dying industry? First, it recognized that video game customers weren't so much fickle as bored. The company sent researchers to visit popular video arcades to find out why alienated home video game fans still spent hours happily pumping quarters into arcade machines. The researchers found that Nintendo's own Donkey Kong and similar games were still mainstays of the arcades even though home versions were failing. The reason? The arcade games offered better quality, full animation, and challenging plots. Home video games, on the other hand, offered only crude quality and simple plots. Despite their exotic names and introductory hype, each new home game was boringly identical to all the others, featuring slow characters who moved through ugly animated scenes to the beat of monotonous, synthesized tones. The video kids of the early 1980s had quickly outgrown the elementary challenges of these first-generation home video games.

Nintendo saw the fall of the U.S. video game industry not as a catastrophe, but as a golden opportunity. It set out to differentiate itself from the ailing competition by offering superior quality—by giving home video game customers a full measure of quality entertainment value for their money. Nintendo designed a basic game system that sold for under $100 yet boasted near arcade-quality graphics. Equally important, it also developed innovative and high-quality software, or "Game Paks" as Nintendo calls them, to accompany the system. Today, the company's Game-Pak library features more than 1,000 titles. New games are constantly added and mature titles weeded out to keep the selection fresh and interesting. The games contain consistently high quality graphics, and game plots are varied and challenging. Colorful, cartoon-like characters move fluidly about cleverly animated screens. Amidst a chorus of boings, whistles, and bleeps, players can punch out the current heavyweight boxing champ or wrestle Hulk Hogan, play

---

abundance of design parameters.[24] It can offer a variety of standard or optional *features* not provided by competitors. Thus, Volvo provides new and better safety features; Delta Airlines offers wider seating and free in-flight telephone use. Companies also can differentiate their products on *performance*. Whirlpool designs its dishwasher to run more quietly; Procter & Gamble formulates Liquid Tide to get clothes cleaner. *Style* and *design* also can be important differentiating factors. Thus, many car buyers pay a premium for Jaguar automobiles because of their extraordinary look, even though Jaguar has sometimes had a poor reliability record. Similarly, companies can differentiate their products on such attributes as *consistency, durability, reliability,* or *repairability*.

Services Differentiation. In addition to differentiating its physical product, the firm also can differentiate the services that accompany the product. Some companies gain competitive advantage through speedy, reliable, or careful *delivery*. Deluxe, the check supply company, has built an impressive reputation for shipping out replacement checks one day after receiving an order—without being late once in 12 years. Domino's Pizza promises delivery in less than 30 minutes or takes $3 off the price.

Installation also can differentiate one company from another. IBM, for exam-

ice hockey or golf, or solve word and board games. The most popular games, however, involve complex sword-and-sorcery conflicts, or the series of Super Mario Brothers fantasy worlds, where young heroes battle to save endangered princesses or to fight the evil ruler, Wart, for peace in the World of Dreams.

Nintendo's quest to deliver superior quality and value, however, goes far beyond selling its home video game system. The company also worked to build lasting relationships with its ever-growing customer base. For example, to help young customers who are having trouble navigating a passage in one of its games, Nintendo set up one of the most extensive telephone hotline systems in the country. Some 100,000 game players telephone each week, seeking tips on game strategy from one of 250 Nintendo game counselors. The calls not only help create happy customers, they also provide Nintendo with valuable game-development and marketing information—the company learns firsthand what's hot and what's not. Nintendo has also introduced *Nintendo Power,* a monthly magazine that discusses the lat-

est developments in home video entertainment systems. The magazine became the fastest-growing paid-subscription magazine ever—in a little over one year, the magazine's circulation rocketed to more than 1.8 million subscribers. Nintendo further cements its customer relationships by licensing its most popular characters for a variety of uses, not just T-shirts and posters, but also movies, a syndicated TV show, cartoons, and magazines.

Thus, by differentiating itself through superior products and service, and by building strong relationships with its customers, Nintendo had built a seemingly invincible quality position in the video game market. Still, the company knows that it cannot simply rest on past success. New competitors such as Sega and NEC have already exploited opportunities created as Nintendo junkies became bored and sought the next new video thrill. Sega beat Nintendo at its own game—product superiority—when it hit the market first with its Genesis machine, an advanced new system that offered even richer graphics, more lifelike sound, and more complex plots. Nintendo countered with the Nintendo Super NES and a fresh blast of promotion. Within two months of the release of its Super NES, Nintendo had sold as many of these advanced units as Sega had in one year. Still, the competition has intensified. Nintendo must continue to find new ways to differentiate itself from aggressive competitors. The company's success in the home video game market involves more than just fun and games—it involves keeping the fun *in* the games.

Sources: See Rebecca Fannin, "Zap?," *Marketing and Media Decisions,* November 1989, pp. 35-40; Raymond Roel, "The Power of Nintendo," *Direct Marketing,* September 1989, pp. 24-29; Stewart Wolpin, "How Nintendo Revived a Dying Industry," *Marketing Communications,* May 1989, pp. 36-40; Kate Fitzgerald, "Nintendo, Sega Slash Price of Videogames," *Advertising Age,* June 8, 1992, p. 44; Richard Brandt, "Clash of the Titans," *Business Week,* September 7, 1992, p. 34; and Cleveland Horton, "Nintendo, Sega Boost Ad Pace," *Advertising Age,* January 25, 1993, p. 16.

ple, is known for its quality installation service. It delivers all pieces of purchased equipment to the site at one time rather than sending individual components to sit and wait for others to arrive. And when asked to move IBM equipment and install it in another location, IBM often moves competitors' equipment as well. Companies can further distinguish themselves through their *repair* services. Many an automobile buyer would gladly pay a little more and travel a little farther to buy a car from a dealer that provides top-notch repair service.

Some companies differentiate their offers by providing *customer training* service. Thus, General Electric not only sells and installs expensive X-ray equipment in hospitals, but also trains the hospital employees who will use this equipment. Other companies offer free or paid *consulting services*—data, information systems, and advising services that buyers need. For example, McKesson Corporation, a major drug wholesaler, consults with its 12,000 independent pharmacists to help them set up accounting, inventory, and computer ordering systems. By helping its customers compete better, McKesson gains greater customer loyalty and sales.

Companies can find many other ways to add value through differentiated services. In fact, they can choose from a virtually unlimited number of specific services and benefits through which to differentiate themselves from the competition. Milliken & Company provides one of the best examples of a company that has gained competitive advantage through superior service:

> Milliken sells shop towels to industrial launderers who rent them to factories. These towels are physically similar to competitors' towels. Yet Milliken charges a higher price for its towels and enjoys the leading market share. How can it charge more for essentially a commodity? The answer is that Milliken continuously "decommoditizes" this product through continuous service enhancement for its launderer customers. Milliken trains its customers' salespeople; supplies prospect leads and sales promotional material to them; supplies on-line computer order entry and freight optimization systems; carries on marketing research for customers; sponsors quality improvement workshops; and lends its salespeople to work with customers on Customer Action Teams. Launderers are more than willing to buy Milliken shop towels and pay a price premium because the extra services improve their profitability.[25]

Personnel Differentiation. Companies can gain a strong competitive advantage through hiring and training better people than their competitors do. Thus, Singapore Airlines enjoys an excellent reputation largely because of the grace of its flight attendants. McDonald's people are courteous, IBM people are professional and knowledgeable, and Disney people are friendly and upbeat. The salesforces of such companies as Connecticut General Life and Merck enjoy excellent reputations, which set their companies apart from competitors. Wal-Mart has differentiated its superstores by employing "people greeters" who welcome shoppers, give advice on where to find items, mark merchandise brought back for returns or exchanges, and give gifts to children.

Personnel differentiation requires that a company select its customer-contact people carefully and train them well. These personnel must be competent—they must possess the required skills and knowledge. They need to be courteous, friendly, and respectful. They must serve customers with consistency and accuracy. And they must make an effort to understand customers, to communicate clearly with them, and to respond quickly to customer requests and problems.

Image Differentiation. Even when competing offers look the same, buyers may perceive a difference based on company or brand images. Thus, companies work to establish *images* that differentiate them from competitors. A company or brand image should convey a singular and distinctive message that communicates the product's major benefits and positioning. Developing a strong and distinctive image calls for creativity and hard work. A company cannot implant an image in the public's mind overnight using only a few advertisements. If "IBM means service," this image must be supported by everything the company says and does.

Symbols can provide strong company or brand recognition and image differentiation. Companies design signs and logos that provide instant recognition. They associate themselves with objects or characters that symbolize quality or other attributes, such as the Harris Bank lion, the Apple Computer apple, the Prudential rock, or the Pillsbury doughboy. The company might build a brand around some famous person, as with perfumes such as Passion (Elizabeth Taylor) and Uninhibited (Cher). Some companies even become associated with colors, such as IBM (blue) or Campbell (red and white).

The chosen symbols must be communicated through advertising that conveys the company or brand's personality. The ads attempt to establish a storyline, a mood, a performance level—something distinctive about the company or brand. The atmosphere of the physical space in which the organization produces or delivers its products and services can be another powerful image generator. Hyatt hotels have become known for their atrium lobbies and Victoria Station restaurants for their boxcars. Thus, a bank that wants to distinguish itself as the "friendly bank" must choose the right building and interior design, layout, colors, materials, and furnishings to reflect these qualities.

A company also can create an image through the types of events it sponsors. Perrier, the bottled water company, became known by laying out exercise tracks and sponsoring health sports events. Other organizations, such as AT&T and IBM, have identified themselves closely with cultural events, such as symphony performances and art exhibits. Still other organizations support popular causes. For example, Heinz gives money to hospitals and Quaker gives food to the homeless.

Selecting the Right Competitive Advantages

Suppose a company is fortunate enough to discover several potential competitive advantages. It now must choose the ones upon which it will build its positioning strategy. It must decide *how many* differences to promote and *which ones*.

How Many Differences to Promote? Many marketers think that companies should aggressively promote only one benefit to the target market. Ad man Rosser Reeves, for example, said a company should develop a *unique selling proposition* (USP) for each brand and stick to it. Each brand should pick an attribute and tout itself as "number one" on that attribute. Buyers tend to remember "number one" better, especially in an overcommunicated society. Thus, Crest toothpaste consistently promotes its anticavity protection, and Mercedes promotes its great automotive engineering. What are some of the "number one" positions to promote? The major ones are "best quality," "best service," "lowest price," "best value," and "most advanced technology." A company that hammers away at one of these positions and consistently delivers on it probably will become best known and remembered for it.

Other marketers think that companies should position themselves on more than one differentiating factor. This may be necessary if two or more firms are claiming to be best on the same attribute. Steelcase, an office furniture systems company, differentiates itself from competitors on two benefits: best on-time delivery and best installation support. Volvo positions its automobiles as "safest" and "most durable." Fortunately, these two benefits are compatible—a very safe car would also be very durable.

Today, in a time when the mass market is fragmenting into many small segments, companies are trying to broaden their positioning strategies to appeal to more segments. For example, Beecham promotes its Aquafresh toothpaste as offering three benefits: "anti-cavity protection," "better breath," and "whiter teeth." Clearly, many people want all three benefits, and the challenge is to convince them that the brand delivers all three. Beecham's solution was to create a toothpaste that squeezed out of the tube in three colors, thus visually confirming the three benefits. In doing this, Beecham attracted three segments instead of one.

However, as companies increase the number of claims for their brands, they risk disbelief and a loss of clear positioning. In general, a company needs to avoid three major positioning errors. The first is *underpositioning*—failing to ever really position the company at all. Some companies discover that buyers have only a vague idea of the company or that they do not really know anything special about it. The second positioning error is *overpositioning*—giving buyers too narrow a picture of the company. Thus, a consumer might think that the Steuben glass company makes only fine art glass costing $1,000 and up, when in fact it makes affordable fine glass starting at around $50. Finally, companies must avoid *confused positioning*—leaving buyers with a confused image of a company. For example, Burger King has struggled without success for years to establish a profitable and consistent position. Since 1986, it has fielded five separate advertising campaigns, with themes ranging from "Herb the nerd doesn't eat here," and "This is a Burger King town," to "The right food for the right times," and "Sometimes you've got to break the rules." This barrage of positioning statements has left consumers confused and Burger King with poor sales and profits.[26]

Which Differences to Promote? Not all brand differences are meaningful or worthwhile. Not every difference makes a good differentiator. Each difference has the potential to create company costs as well as customer benefits. Therefore, the company must carefully select the ways in which it will distinguish itself from competitors. A difference is worth establishing to the extent that it satisfies the following criteria:

- *Important:* The difference delivers a highly valued benefit to target buyers.

- *Distinctive:* Competitors do not offer the difference, or the company can offer it in a more distinctive way.

- *Superior:* The difference is superior to other ways that customers might obtain the same benefit.

- *Communicable:* The difference is communicable and visible to buyers.

- *Preemptive:* Competitors cannot easily copy the difference.

- *Affordable:* Buyers can afford to pay for the difference.

- *Profitable:* The company can introduce the difference profitably.

Many companies have introduced differentiations that failed one or more of these tests. The Westin Stamford hotel in Singapore advertises that it is the world's tallest hotel, a distinction that is not important to many tourists—in fact, it turns many off. AT&T's original picturevision phones bombed, partly because the public did not think that seeing the other person was worth the phone's high cost. Polaroid's Polarvision, which produced instantly developed home movies, bombed too. Although Polarvision was distinctive and even preemptive, it was inferior to another way of capturing motion, namely, videocameras.

Some competitive advantages may be quickly ruled out because they are too slight, too costly to develop, or too inconsistent with the company's profile. Suppose that a company is designing its positioning strategy and has narrowed its list of possible competitive advantages to four. The company needs a framework for selecting the one advantage that makes the most sense to develop. Table 9-4 shows a systematic way to evaluate several potential competitive advantages and choose the right one.

In the table, the company compares its standing on four attributes—technology, cost, quality, and service—to the standing of its major competitor. Let's assume that both companies stand at 8 on technology (1 = low score, 10 = high score), which means they both have good technology. The company questions whether it can gain much by improving its technology further, especially given the high cost of new technology. The competitor has a better standing on cost (8 instead of 6), and this can hurt the company if the market gets more price sensitive. The company offers higher quality than its competitor (8 instead of 6). Finally, both companies offer below-average service (4 and 3).

At first glance, it appears that the company should go after cost or service to improve its market appeal relative to the competitor. However, it must consider other factors. First, how important are improvements in each of these attributes to the target customers? The fourth column shows that cost and service improvements would both be highly important to customers. Next, can the company afford to make the improvements? If so, how fast can it complete them? The fifth column shows that the company could improve service quickly and affordably. But if the firm decided to do this, would the competitor be able to improve its service also? The sixth column shows that the competitor's ability to improve service is low, perhaps because the competitor doesn't believe in service or is strapped for funds. The final column then shows the appropriate actions to take on each attribute. It makes the most sense for the company to invest in improving its service. Service is important to customers; the company can afford to improve its service and can do it fast, and the competitor probably will not be able to catch up.

Communicating and Delivering the Chosen Position

Once it has chosen a position, the company must take strong steps to deliver and communicate the desired position to target consumers. All the company's marketing-mix efforts must support the positioning strategy. Positioning the company calls for concrete action, not just talk. If the company decides to build a position on better quality and service, it must first *deliver* that position. Designing the marketing mix—product, price, place, and promotion—essentially involves working

TABLE 9-4
Finding Competitive Advantage

Competitive Advantage	Company Standing (1-10)	Competitor Standing (1-10)	Importance of Improving Standing (H-M-L)	Affordability and Speed (H-M-L)	Competitor's Ability to Improve Standing (H-M-L)	Recommended Action
Technology	8	8	L	L	M	Hold
Cost	6	8	H	M	M	Watch
Quality	8	6	L	L	H	Watch
Service	4	3	H	H	L	Invest

out the tactical details of the positioning strategy. Thus, a firm that seizes upon a "high-quality position" knows that it must produce high-quality products, charge a high price, distribute through high-quality dealers, and advertise in high-quality media. It must hire and train more service people, find retailers who have a good reputation for service, and develop sales and advertising messages that broadcast its superior service. This is the only way to build a consistent and believable high-quality, high-service position.

Companies often find it easier to come up with a good positioning strategy than to implement it. Establishing a position or changing one usually takes a long time. In contrast, positions that have taken years to build can quickly be lost. Once a company has built the desired position, it must take care to maintain the position through consistent performance and communication. It must closely monitor and adapt the position over time to match changes in consumer needs and competitors' strategies. However, the company should avoid abrupt changes that might confuse consumers. Instead, a product's position should evolve gradually as it adapts to the ever-changing marketing environment.

 # SUMMARY

Sellers can take three approaches to a market. *Mass marketing* is the decision to mass-produce and mass-distribute one product and attempt to attract all kinds of buyers. *Product variety marketing* is the decision to produce two or more market offers differentiated in style, features, quality, or sizes, designed to offer variety to the market and to set the seller's products apart from competitor's products. *Target marketing* is the decision to identify the different groups that make up a market and to develop products and marketing mixes for selected target markets. Sellers today are moving away from mass marketing and product differentiation toward target marketing because this approach is more helpful in spotting market opportunities and developing more effective products and marketing mixes.

The key steps in target marketing are market segmentation, market targeting, and market positioning. *Market segmentation* is the act of dividing a market into distinct groups of buyers who might merit separate products or marketing mixes. The marketer tries different variables to see which give the best segmentation opportunities. For consumer marketing, the major segmentation variables are geographic, demographic, psychographic, and behavioral. Business markets can be segmented by business consumer demographics, operating characteristics, purchasing approaches, and personal characteristics. The effectiveness of segmentation analysis depends on finding segments that are *measurable, accessible, substantial,* and *actionable.*

Next, the seller has to target the best market segments. The company first evaluates each segment's size and growth characteristics, structural attractiveness, and compatibility with company resources and objectives. It then chooses one of three market-coverage strategies. The seller can ignore segment differences (*undifferentiated marketing*), develop different market offers for several segments (*differentiated marketing*), or go after one or a few market segments (*concentrated marketing*). Much depends on company resources, product variability, product life-cycle stage, and competitive marketing strategies.

Once a company has decided what segments to enter, it must decide on its *market positioning* strategy—on which positions to occupy in its chosen segments. It can position its products on specific product attributes, according to usage occasion, for certain classes of users, or by product class. It can position either against or away from competitors. The positioning task consists of three steps: identifying a set of possible competitive advantages upon which to build a position, selecting the right competitive advantages, and effectively communicating and delivering the chosen position to the market.

 # KEY TERMS

DISCUSSING THE ISSUES

1. Describe how the Ford Motor Company has moved from mass marketing to product-variety marketing to target marketing. Can you think of other examples of companies whose marketing approaches have evolved over time?

2. What variables are used in segmenting the market for beer? Give examples.

3. Hispanics are now viewed as an attractive, distinct market segment. Can you market in the same way to a Puerto Rican seamstress in New York, a Cuban doctor in Miami, and a Mexican laborer in Houston? Discuss the similarities and differences that you see. What does this imply about market segments?

4. Some industrial suppliers make above-average profits by offering service, selection, and reliability—at a premium price. How can these suppliers segment the market to find customers who are willing to pay more for these benefits?

5. Think about your classmates in this course. Can you segment them into different groups with specific nicknames? What is your major segmentation variable? Could you effectively market products to these segments?

6. What roles do product attributes and perceptions of attributes play in positioning a product? Can an attribute held by several competing brands be used in a successful positioning strategy?

APPLYING THE CONCEPTS

1. By looking at advertising, and at products themselves, we can often see how marketers are attempting to position their products, and what target market they hope to reach. (a) Define the positionings of and the target markets for Coca-Cola, Pepsi Cola, Mountain Dew, Dr Pepper, and 7-Up. (b) Define the positionings of and target markets for McDonald's, Burger King, Wendy's, and a regional restaurant chain in your area such as Jack-in-the-Box, Bojangle's, or Friendly's. (c) Do you think the soft drinks and restaurants have distinctive positionings and target markets? Are some more clearly defined than others?

2. It is possible to market people as well as products or services [see Chapter 22 for more details]. When marketing a person, we can *position* that individual for a particular target market. Describe briefly how you would position yourself for the following target markets: (a) for a potential employer; (b) for a potential boyfriend or girlfriend; (c) for your mother or father. Would you position yourself in different ways for these different target markets? How do the positionings differ? *Why* do the positionings differ?

MAKING MARKETING DECISIONS:

SMALL WORLD COMMUNICATIONS, INC.

Tom Campbell and Lyn Jones are making good progress with their ideas for Small World Communications. They are now trying to refine their basic concept for an all-in-one communications hookup that can be customized with software. Each of them has been getting feedback and suggestions by showing the basic idea to a few trusted friends who are knowledgeable about computers.

"Lyn, I'm finding that the reactions to this product idea are more complicated than we thought. Remember our original idea that we wanted to sell a finished-looking product that would install without tools? That meant an extra box that would plug into the main computer somehow. That concept always seemed to me like an item for less sophisticated users. But here's what I'm seeing: your less geeky user likes the external box, but so does a group of really technical laptop users. They are seeing the external Unity as a product that can let them do more communica-

tions than they could ever do with their little machines. They also see it as an easy way to hook up their portable computer to their desktop machine to share files and software." Lyn said, "Yeah, I've heard the same thing, and that's interesting because portables are where the growth really is. But I also got one other surprise: There are a lot of average desktop computer users who want a naked circuit board that installs inside their main computer." "Let me guess," said Tom. "They want an internal board so they can keep their tangle of cables to a minimum.""That's one part," said Lyn, "but the other one is pretty obvious, too—most of them would have to put the Unity box right on top of their desks, and they don't want to give up that space. We may need to change our product to meet the needs of different segments of users."

WHAT NOW?

1. Tom and Lyn are segmenting their markets in a complex way that combines benefit segmentation with some psychographic insights into computer users. (a) Do you think this approach makes sense? (b) Are these segments *measurable, accessible, substantial,* and *actionable*? (c) Suggest some other ways Tom and Lyn might segment their markets.

2. Lyn and Tom have not yet discussed how they will position the Unity product. Chapter 9 mentions a number of possibilities for positioning, including *product attributes, benefits, usage occasions,* by *user type, against* or *away from competitors,* or for *different product classes.* (a) What positioning approach would you recommend to Lyn and Tom? (b) Is there only one way to position this product, or could a different approach or combination of approaches also work?

REFERENCES

1. Thomas Moore, "Different Folks, Different Strokes," *Fortune,* September 16, 1985, p. 65. Also see Michael Oneal, "Attack of the Bug Killers," *Business Week,* May 16, 1988, p. 81.

2. Bruce Hager, "Podunk Is Beckoning," *Business Week,* December 2, 1991, p. 76.

3. See Frieda Curtindale, "Marketing Cars to Women," *American Demographics,* November 1988, pp. 29-31; and Betsy Sharkey, "The Many Faces of Eve," *Adweek,* June 25, 1990, pp. 44-49. The quote is from "Automakers Learn Better Roads to Women's Market," *Marketing News,* October 12, 1992, p. 2.

4. See Pat Grey Thomas, "Marketing to the Affluent," *Advertising Age,* March 16, 1987, p. S-1.

5. Jan Larsen, "Reaching Downscale Markets," *American Demographics,* November 1991, pp. 38-40.

6. Steve Lawrence, "The Green in Blue-Collar Retailing," *Fortune,* May 27, 1985, pp. 74-77; and Dean Foust, "The Family Feud at Family Dollar Stores," *Business Week,* September 21, 1987, pp. 32-33. For other examples of companies targeting less affluent consumers, see Brian Bremmer, "Looking Downscale without Looking Down," *Business Week,* October 8, 1990, pp. 62-67; and Larsen, "Reaching Downscale Markets," *American Demographics.*

7. Thomas Exter, "Deodorant Demographics," *American Demographics,* December 1987, p. 39.

8. Bickley Townsend, "Psychographic Glitter and Gold," *American Demographics,* November 1985, p. 22.

9. For a detailed discussion of personality and buyer behavior, see Leon G. Schiffman and Leslie Lazar Kanuk, *Consumer Behavior,* 4th ed. (Englewood Cliffs, NJ: Prentice Hall, 1991), Chap. 4.

10. See Laurie Freeman and Cleveland Horton, "Spree: Honda's Scooters Ride the Cutting Edge," *Advertising Age,* September 5, 1985, pp. 3, 35.

11. Mark Maremont, "The Hottest Thing Since the Flashbulb," *Business Week,* September 7, 1992.

12. See Schiffman and Kanuk, *Consumer Behavior,* p. 48.

13. See Mark Ivey, "Long-Distance Learning Gets an 'A' at Last," *Business Week,* May 9, 1988, pp. 108-10.

14. See Thomas V. Bonoma and Benson P. Shapiro, *Segmenting the Industrial Market* (Lexington, MA.: Lexington Books, 1983).

For examples of segmenting business markets, see Kate Bertrand, "Market Segmentation: Divide and Conquer," *Business Marketing,* October 1989, pp. 48-54.

15. V. Kasturi Rangan, Rowland T. Moriarty, and Gordon S. Swartz, "Segmenting Customers in Mature Industrial Markets," *Journal of Marketing,* October 1992, pp. 72-82.

16. For another interesting approach to segmenting the business market, see John Berrigan and Carl Finkbeiner, *Segmentation Marketing: New Methods for Capturing Business* (New York: Harper-Business, 1992).

17. Marlene L. Rossman, "Understanding Five Nations of Latin America," *Marketing News,* October 11, 1985, p. 10; as quoted in Subhash C. Jain, *International Marketing Management,* 3rd ed. (Boston: PWS-Kent Publishing Company, 1990), p. 366.

18. For more on intermarket segmentation, see Jain, *International Marketing Management,* pp. 369-70.

19. Ibid., pp. 370-71.

20. See Joe Schwartz, "Southpaw Strategy," *American Demographics,* June 1988, p. 61; and "Few Companies Tailor Products for Lefties," *The Wall Street Journal,* August 2, 1989, p. 2.

21. See Michael Porter, *Competitive Advantage* (New York: Free Press, 1985), pp. 4-8 and pp. 234-36.

22. Bill Saporito, "Just How Good is the Great A&P?" *Fortune,* March 16, 1987, pp. 92-93.

23. For good discussions of the concepts of differentiation and competitive advantage and methods for assessing them, see Michael Porter, *Competitive Advantage,* Chap. 2; George S. Day and Robin Wensley, "Assessing Advantage: A Framework for Diagnosing Competitive Superiority," *Journal of Marketing,* April 1988, pp. 1-20; and Philip Kotler, *Marketing Management,* 7th ed. (Englewood Cliffs, NJ: Prentice Hall, 1991), Chap. 11.

24. See David A. Garvin, "Competing on the Eight Dimensions of Quality," *Harvard Business Review,* November-December 1987, pp. 101-9.

25. See Tom Peters, *Thriving on Chaos* (New York: Alfred A. Knopf, Inc., 1987), pp. 56-57.

26. Mark Landler and Gail DeGeorge, "Tempers Are Sizzling Over Burger King's New Ads," *Business Week,* February 12, 1990, p. 33; and Philip Stelly, Jr., "Burger King Rule Breaker," *Adweek,* November 9, 1990, pp. 24, 26.

VIDEO CASE 9

ABCNEWS

SPECIAL SIZE CLOTHING

The average American woman is a little over five feet tall, weighs 146 pounds, and wears a size 12 or 14. There are as many women who wear a size 18 as a size 8. Fifteen percent of American men are classified as big or tall, and fifty million American women are petite. These groups whether big, tall, large, or petite constitute the special size clothing market.

Until the late 1980s, most designers, manufacturers, and retailers neglected these segments, despite their large potential sales and greater spending power. Because larger consumers are frequently older, they tend to be more affluent.

The retailers who applied pressure backwards through the channel of distribution to their suppliers are responsible for opening this market. An example is Nancye Radmin, founder of The Forgotten Woman. When Ms. Radmin gained weight, she found only polyester muumuus available in her size. Her response? She started her own store. When it first opened, she had plenty of customers but little merchandise, so she resorted to developing her own private label designs, made by a Brazilian manufacturer. In addition, she continued to bang on doors in New York's garment district and to pop up in designers' showrooms. Although she eventually persuaded some manufacturers to produce larger sizes, the designers were not responsive.

Ms. Radmin finally realized that she couldn't speak the designers' language, so she hired Beau James, formerly of Bonwit Teller, to act as her go-between. He found that designers were worried that stores would not be able to merchandise large clothes in a way that would make them look truly elegant. To alleviate these concerns, Ms. Radmin spent $2 million to open just two salons, where the merchandise is showcased behind whitewashed wood doors with beveled glass and bronze knobs. The salons feature chandeliers, French writing desks, and a "Sugar Daddy Bar" where patrons can obtain coffee, champagne, and chocolates. As Ms. Radmin says, calories don't matter because this market is not dieting. The result? Her 20 stores generate more than $40 million in annual revenue and sell designer items such as $8,000 bejeweled suits by Oscar de la Renta, and Bob Mackie dresses at $10,000 apiece.

Many large customers, however, want lower prices. In 1970, The Casual Male Big & Tall Shop opened in Shrewsbury, Maine, to sell off-price, brand name, "plus size" casual and tailored menswear. Today, the chain has over 250 outlets nationwide. Department stores such as Hill's are also expanding their men's departments, and even the discounters have gotten into the act. Kmart does a booming business selling to big and tall men. Their sales of large sizes have grown annually at 5 percent to 7 percent, and now account for 10 percent of all menswear sales. Consequently, Kmart has increased the size of its big and tall departments from 100 square feet to more than 600 square feet.

Big and tall men require different styles. This group has created the market for the "oversized look"—oversized tops and fleece wear. Perhaps the baggier clothes make them feel smaller. Their favorite sweaters are all-cotton Shaker styles and cardigans, and they tend to prefer darker colors such as black, gray, or navy blue, which they wear with stretch jeans. Today they are more willing to wear shorts and actively seek other sportswear. Also, they want labels such as Pierre Cardin, Givenchy, and Arrow.

Catalogers have also entered the market. Spiegel produces a special catalog for larger-size women called For You. It includes everything from evening wear to work attire and lingerie. It emphasizes "fashion that flatters"—a major concern of larger women. Land's End carries lines in talls and petites and offers some larger sizes in its regular catalog.

From where did this market come? According to some observers, the baby boomers have gotten older, and as we age, we become larger. Increased nutritional levels may account for taller people. Others contend that the market has always been there but was just overlooked. Manufacturers and designers were so busy catering to the "ideal self" that they failed to provide nice clothes for the "actual self."

As designers such as Evan Picone, Liz Claiborne, Pierre Cardin, and Bill Blass enter the market, they are challenged to produce flattering clothing. But it's worth it. After only a year and a half on the market, Liz Claiborne's Elisabeth line topped $100 million in 1991 sales, and accounted for 6 percent of Claiborne's volume. And it's still growing. The opportunities are not exhausted. As Nancye Radmin says, the swimsuits still are just awful.

QUESTIONS

1. What criteria are most relevant for segmenting the special size market?

2. Why would designers and manufacturers resist entering the large size market?

3. What problems will retailers have in merchandising such clothing?

4. What targeting choices do designers and manufacturers have in regard to special size clothing?

5. Evaluate retailers' and manufacturers' positioning of large sizes.

Sources: "Spiegel Fills a Real Market Need," *Catalog Age,* September 1990, pp. 143, 147; Mary Beth Colacecchi, "Making It Big," *Catalog Age,* April 1992, pp. 5, 49; Pat Corwin, "Sales Surge in Big-and-Tall," *Discount Merchandiser,* February 1989, pp. 32-37; Amy Feldman, "Hello, Oprah, Good-Bye Iman," *Forbes,* March 16, 1992, pp. 116-17; Nancye Radmin, "Winning Over the Heavy Hitters," *Working Woman,* August 1991, pp. 28-30; and Susan L. Smarr, "Retail Now: Remembering the Forgotten Woman," February 1990, pp. 24, 26.

COMPANY CASE 9

QUAKER OATS: DOUSING THE COMPETITION

Every college of NFL football fan has watched the following scene often: As the end of an important game approaches, two burly linemen quietly remove the white top from a large orange cooler of iced sports drink. Then, when victory seems assured, they creep toward the sideline and dump the cooler's contents on their unsuspecting coach. If a television network carries the game, viewers cringe in their chairs as they imagine how it would feel to have all that icy liquid poured on them. Such dousings have replaced the traditional ride on the players' shoulders as the ultimate moment following victory in an important football game.

As you read the previous paragraph, you probably guessed the contents of the large orange cooler. You no doubt developed a mental picture of the linemen opening the cooler and dumping the familiar drink on the coach. Although some 40 national and regional brands compete in this market, Gatorade has achieved such a dominant position that the brand name has become almost a generic term for the sports-drink category.

However, perhaps you did not know that Quaker Oats Company owns Gatorade. Although most people associate Quaker Oats with oatmeal, cold breakfast cereals, snacks, and Wilford Brimley ("It's the right thing to do"), they are usually surprised to learn that Gatorade is Quaker Oats's single most important product. In 1992, Gatorade produced about $900 million in sales, 15 percent of Quaker Oats's total revenues, and about $90 million in operating profits, 17 percent of the company's total.

Analysts estimate that Gatorade controls up to 90 percent of the $1 billion sports-drink market. Moreover, the sports-drink market is the most rapidly growing beverage segment. Whereas the traditional soft-drink category is mature and growing at a sluggish 2 percent annual rate, down from almost 5 percent previously, analysts predict that sports-drink category volume will grow at double-digit rates during the 1990s.

It is not surprising, therefore, that many companies are entering the sports-drink market. It also is not surprising that Gatorade has sent clear signals that it will fight fiercely to defend its dominant market share.

Quaker Oats and Gatorade
The Quaker Mill Company began in 1877 in Ravenna, Ohio. In 1881, Henry Parson Crowell purchased the company and used new advertising and marketing techniques to lay the groundwork for the company's growth. Quaker was the first company to package a food product, oatmeal, in a cardboard container and the first to print recipes on the package. It was also the first company to advertise nationally and then globally. Quaker developed the strategy of acquiring products and using its marketing skills to build the products' market shares.

Today, Quaker's stable of products includes such familiar brands as Quaker, Aunt Jemima, Kibbles 'n Bits, Cycle, Gravy Train, Ken-L Ration, Gaines, Puss'n Boots, Van Camp's, Ardmore Farms, Rice-A-Roni, Noodle Roni, and Ghirardelli.

Dr. Robert Cade, a kidney expert at the University of Florida, along with a team of researchers who were studying heat exhaustion among the university's football players, developed Gatorade in the 1960s. The researchers analyzed the players' perspiration and devised a drink that prevented severe dehydration caused by fluid and mineral loss during physical exertion in high temperatures.

They tested the drink on the players, and the Florida Gators team used the drink on the sideline during all the games in the 1966 season. That year, observers designated the Gators as the "second-half team" because it consistently outplayed its opponents during the second half. The team also won the Orange Bowl that year, and Bobby Dodd, the losing Georgia Tech coach, noted that "We didn't have Gatorade. That made the difference." Sports Illustrated reported the remark, and Gatorade was on its way to creating and dominating a new product category—isotonic beverages.

Stokely-Van Camp, a processor and marketer of fruits and vegetables, acquired Gatorade in May 1967 and began marketing it during the summer of 1968. Stokely intended to promote Gatorade not only as a sports drink but also as a health food product because of its value in replacing electrolytes lost because of colds, flu, diarrhea, and vomiting. By September 1969, Stokely had established distribution in every state except Alaska. During the 1970s, Gatorade realized rapid growth as an increasingly fitness-minded public latched on to the product and its perceived benefits. Stokely also developed a strong position for Gatorade in the institutional team sales market. Because of Stokely's lock on this market and strong consumer loyalty at the retail level, few competitors who entered the market were successful.

Quaker Oats purchased Stokely-Van Camp in 1983. Quaker saw the opportunity to grow Gatorade's sales by increasing both its distribution and promotion, and it doubled Gatorade's marketing expenditures. Between 1983 and 1990, Gatorade's sales grew at a 28 percent compound annual growth rate.

The Product and the Market
Isotonic beverages, or sports drinks, replace fluids and minerals lost during physical activity. Research shows that an isotonic drink's effectiveness depends on several factors. The drink should provide enough carbohydrates (glucose and sucrose working in combination) to supply working muscles, yet not too much to slow fluid absorp-

tion. The drink should contain the proper level of electrolytes, particularly sodium, to enhance fluid absorption. FInally, research suggests that most people prefer a noncarbonated, slightly sweet drink when they are hot and sweaty. The taste is important to encourage the person to consume enough liquid to be effective in rehydration.

An 8-ounce serving of Gatorade contains few vitamins, no fat or proteins, 60 calories, 15 grams of carbohydrate, 110 milligrams of sodium, and 25 milligrams of potassium. Gatorade's calories are about one-half the level contained in fruit drinks and nondiet soft drinks.

The sports-drink market is highly seasonal and regional, with most sales occurring during the summer months in the southern, southeastern, and southwestern regions. Consumers in Florida, Texas, and California account for 38 percent of Gatorade's sales.

When Quaker Oats acquired Gatorade, it found that Stokely had targeted competitive athletes, and men and teenagers who were involved in competitive athletics. However, Quaker found that Stokely had neither positioned the brand well nor given it a consistent focus. No clear message specified the product's uses or the occasions when consumers should use it. Quaker's market research revealed that the main users were men ages 19 to 44. These men understood the product and knew when and how to use it.

Quaker decided to market the product in the northern United States under a narrow, solid positioning based on how southern consumers used it. Quaker also decided to portray Gatorade's users as accomplished but not necessarily professional athletes. Advertisements depicted serious athletes who enjoyed their sports and enjoyed Gatorade. These were athletes that the target customer could aspire to be like.

Despite its narrow focus for Gatorade, Quaker responded to market changes by introducing Gatorade Light in 1990. This line extension targeted calorie-conscious athletes, such as men and women engaged in aerobics or jogging. These customers exercised for short or moderate periods at low or moderate intensity. Gatorade Light came in three flavors and had less sodium and about half the calories of regular Gatorade. Quaker also introduced Freestyle, a more flavorful drink made with fruit juice. Freestyle targeted people who had more interest in the product's taste than in its rehydration aspects. By 1992, Quaker also offered original Gatorade in six flavors selected to appeal to different target groups.

Competition Tries to Make Gatorade Sweat

Competitors took note of Gatorade's success and the rapid growth of the sports-drink market. Suntory, a subsidiary of the Japanese beverage giant Suntory, introduced 10-K sports drink in the United States in 1985. Suntory made 10-K Gatorade's strongest competitor by promoting the fact that it produced the 10-K using salt-free spring water. 10-K contained 100 percent of the recommended daily allowance of vitamin C. It also had all-natural flavors, fructose, 60 calories per serving, no caffeine, and one-half the sodium of other products. Like Gatorade, 10-K focused on grocery store distribution and targeted sports teams. Suntory claimed that 10-K

beat Gatorade in taste tests and in repeat purchases.

Coca-Cola and Pepsi Cola also dabbled in the market. Coca-Cola introduced a powdered sports drink, Maxx, in 1987. Maxx never made it out of test markets, however. In 1989, Pepsi-Cola joined the party by introducing Mountain Dew Sport (MDS). MDS was lightly carbonated, caffeine-free, and came in regular and two-calorie formulas. Pepsi claimed that MDS tasted better than Gatorade. However, consumers felt that it had too much carbonation, and Pepsi pulled the product. Pepsi subsequently introduced AllSport, a more lightly carbonated drink that came in four flavors. Pepsi distributed AllSport through grocery and convenience stores, and it had a global distribution network in place should it decide to go international with the product.

In 1989, three rookie sports-drink makers tried to muscle in on the thirst-quenching business. PowerBurst Corp. introduced PowerBurst, a drink sweetened with fructose, which it claimed provided sustained energy rather than the short-term energy spike provided by Gatorade's sweeteners. PowerBurst targeted younger consumers, especially sports-minded females, claiming that its drink not only tasted better than Gatorade but that it surpassed it on seven product attributes. PowerBurst gained distribution in 17 states through large supermarket chains, convenience stores, and athletic and sports clubs.

White Rock Products introduced Workout and Workout Light as all-natural, complex carbohydrate, low-sodium, and no-caffeine thirst relievers. White Rock distributed Workout in 30 states through convenience and small independent stores.

Sports Beverage launched Pro Motion with the claim that it had less sodium and more potassium than Gatorade. It also claimed that Pro Motion contained 100 percent of the recommended daily allowance of vitamin C and satisfied thirst with no salty or sweet aftertaste.

In 1990, Coca-Cola reentered the market with PowerAde. Coca-Cola's second entry was noncarbonated and caffeine free and came in three flavors. Coca-Cola planned to distribute PowerAde only through soda fountains.

By early 1992, Quaker realized that despite Gatorade's rapid growth, new sales were becoming harder to find. Quaker approached Coca-Cola with the idea that the two companies could team up to distribute Gatorade through Coca-Cola's wide network of vending machines and fountains in restaurants and convenience stores. In mid-1992, however, the two companies halted their discussions, reportedly because they could not agree on who would take the lead in making marketing decisions.

Following that development, Coca-Cola announced that it would continue to challenge Gatorade with its PowerAde product. Coca-Cola argued that PowerAde had 33 percent more carbohydrates for energy than Gatorade, that it was lighter, and that it "went down" easier. PowerAde quenched thirst without the heavy salt flavor, Coca-Cola suggested. Coca-Cola would focus on distributing PowerAde in vending machines, in health and fitness clubs, and in industrial plant sites—"points of sweat," as Coca-Cola called them. To help in this effort, the firm introduced canned and bottled versions of PowerAde. Coca-Cola hoped that this emphasis would also help PowerAde's debut on Gatorade's turf, grocery stores. Coca-Cola had 1.5 million points of sale, including one million vending machines, as compared with Gatorade's 200,000 points of sale. Coca-Cola also started television and radio advertising and paid to make PowerAde the official drink of the 1992 Summer Olympic Games in Spain. Officials claimed that PowerAde would be the official drink of the 1996 Olympic Games in Atlanta, Coke's hometown.

Pepsi did not stand idly by with its AllSport drink during all this. Officials claimed that although Gatorade dominated the category, it lacked both taste and the strong distribution system that Pepsi could provide for AllSport. Pepsi had approximately one million points of sale and daily contact with 250,000 retailers that it could use to push AllSport. Like Coca-Cola, Pepsi had decided to confront Gatorade in supermarkets, construction sites, and health clubs. As it did with Coke, Pepsi challenged Gatorade with taste tests in stores. It also claimed that carbonated AllSport was more drinkable than Gatorade and that AllSport had one-half the sodium. Pepsi argued that consumers who ate a balanced diet did not need the extra sodium that Gatorade provided.

In response to the break off of negotiations with Coca-Cola, Quaker reorganized its operations. Previously, Quaker had relied on regional offices in North America, Europe, Asia, and Latin America to manage the brand in the 15 countries in which it sold Gatorade. Quaker announced that it now would form a separate division to market Gatorade worldwide. Gatorade officials also noted that they were still pursuing partnerships with other companies to expand distribution to "wherever there's thirst."

If Gatorade continues to expand internationally, however, it will find competition waiting. In Japan, Coca-Cola already offers a sports drink under the name Aquarius, and Gatorade has had problems with a locally produced sports beverage. In Italy, H. J. Heinz markets a beverage called Fitgar that it claims has 10 percent of the sports-drink market. In France, consumers seem to view bottled water as the product of choice for quenching their thirsts.

What Will the Future Bring?

Quaker Oats realizes just how important this battle is to its corporate health. Gatorade has said that it will continue to cultivate its sports image by using Michael Jordan as its spokesperson. It will also continue its multi-

year contracts with pro leagues ranging from the National Football League to the Ladies Professional Golf Association. Finally, Gatorade will continue to rely on its time-honored scientific studies to prove that the body absorbs Gatorade faster than water or any other soft drink. However, Quaker understands that to maintain its dominant position it must be willing to pursue innovative marketing strategies.

Coca-Cola and Pepsi represent strong competitors with deep pockets and strong determination. Although each has failed in previous attacks on Gatorade, no one should assume that they will fail in their current efforts.

Still, Quaker Oats has shown that it will be aggressively working and waiting for the opportunity to douse the competition with an orange container of icy liquid.

QUESTIONS

1. What major variables have Quaker Oats and its competitors used to segment the sports-drink market?

2. What type of market-coverage strategy did Quaker use for Gatorade during the early stages of the sports-drink market's life cycle? What coverage strategies are Quaker and its competitors using now?

3. How have Quaker and its competitors positioned their sports-drink products?

4. What competitive advantages do Gatorade and its competitors have?

5. Identify new marketing opportunities that Quaker should pursue for Gatorade, including new market segments that it should address. Develop a marketing strategy for exploiting one of these opportunities.

6. Quaker Oats's reorganization—forming one division to manage Gatorade worldwide—suggests that the company wants to make Gatorade a global brand, like Coke. *Is* Gatorade a global brand? What changes should Quaker consider as it markets Gatorade globally?

Sources: Michael J. McCarthy and Christina Duff, "Quaker Oats Weighs Linkup with Coke for Distribution of Gatorade Beverage," *The Wall Street Journal*, January 24, 1992, p. A8; Michael J. McCarthy, "Coke Hopes to Make Gatorade Sweat in Battle for U.S. Sports-Drink Market," *The Wall Street Journal*, April 27, 1992; Richard Gibson, "Gatorade Unit to Pour It on as Rivalry Rises," *The Wall Street Journal*, April 28, 1992, p. B1; "Gatorade Is Cornerstone to Quaker's Growth," *Advertising Age*, May 18, 1992, p. 12; "Soft Drinks: The Thirst of Champions," *The Economist*, June 6, 1992, p. 83; Richard Gibson, "Coca-Cola and PepsiCo Are Preparing to Give Gatorade a Run for Its Money," *The Wall Street Journal*, September 29, 1992, p. B1. This case also draws from Linda E. Swayne and Peter M. Ginter, "Gatorade Defends Its No. 1 Position," in L. E. Swayne and P. M. Ginter, *Cases in Strategic Marketing* (Englewood Cliffs, NJ: Prentice Hall, 1993), 2nd edition, pp. 1-21. Used with permission.

PART III

COMPREHENSIVE CASE

COCA-COLA: TARGETING A NEW COKE MACHINE

The world's largest soft-drink marketer has a new dream—to put a Coke within easy reach of every office worker. Coca-Cola hopes to realize this dream with BreakMate, a compact fountain dispensing system that may someday make Coke machines as common in the workplace as coffee machines.

Coca-Cola has been developing the BreakMate for more than 20 years and has tested it in 30 foreign and U.S. cities. Industry observers believe it represents the most expensive soft-drink development project in history.

Beyond its potential impact on Coca-Cola's $8 billion annual soft-drink sales, BreakMate promises to put some fizz in the entire industry. Per capita soft-drink consumption, which now stands at 45 gallons annually, surpassed water consumption in the United States in 1986. However, during the past decade, major beverage marketers have assumed that there are few new avenues of distribution to explore. Instead, they have sought growth only through new products, flooding the market with new brands and brand extensions. Retailers have often responded by charging companies fees to put their new brands on store shelves. As a result, the soft-drink manufacturers have seen the market shares of their major brands erode and their costs of doing business rise dramatically.

Coca-Cola's BreakMate signals a new emphasis on distribution and a new battle for the largely untapped office market. Beverage companies consider the office market especially important because of declining coffee consumption and the increasing popularity of carbonated soft drinks. As one industry analyst notes, "Brands have been segmented to death in the soft-drink business. The major channels of distribution are full and to get just a small percentage of growth takes tremendous sums of money. The workplace would represent a tremendous uncharted market for Coke syrup sales."

Coca-Cola doesn't have the office market all to itself, however. Pepsi previously introduced a 24-can mini-vending machine. These small machines, Pepsi claims, have increased its overall vending business by 10 percent. Although Coca-Cola is not positioning the BreakMate against canned drinks, it appears to have some advantages. Distributors point out that fountain drinks, at about eight cents per serving, are more economical than cans. The can by itself can cost a dime, and to deliver ten cases of cans or bottles requires bigger equipment and more storage space. Research also shows that women prefer the 61/2-ounce BreakMate fountain drink to a standard 12-ounce can.

Companies have tried to market office fountain systems before. In the early 1970s, Coca-Cola introduced the "Refresh" program for the office, but the program failed because the system consumed too much space and required the use of a bulky carbon-dioxide canister for carbonation. Attempts by other companies to break into the office market have also failed because they required office workers to mix their own syrup and water. Through its competitors' earlier attempts, Coca-Cola learned that a successful fountain system would have to be reliable, easy to use, and small enough to fit almost anywhere.

Bosch-Siemens, the West German appliance maker, has joined forces with Coca-Cola to produce the patented BreakMate. The machine is about the same size as a large microwave oven and weighs only 78 pounds when fully loaded. The customer connects the self-refrigerated BreakMate to a water source or, if no water source is available, uses an optional water reservoir attachment. The machine holds three one-liter syrup cartridges, each of which can produce approximately 30 61/2-ounce drinks. Only Coke syrup cartridges work with the Breakmate. The customer also installs a carbon-dioxide cylinder which is good for about 250 drinks. When a user presses one of the three flavor selection buttons, water passes from the refrigerated area into the mixing channel and carbon dioxide is injected to produce carbonated water. Then, a "doser" attached to each syrup cartridge measures the amount of syrup needed to make a perfect soda. Bosch-Siemens has added a light that indicates when the carbon-dioxide container is empty. It has also developed an optional coin acceptor that accepts nickels, dimes, and quarters for use in offices where users will have to pay. Coca-Cola may also add an ice-crushing mechanism. Ice is not necessary because the machine delivers the drink at 32°F.

Market tests have convinced Coca-Cola that BreakMate produces soft drinks of consistent quality. Coca-Cola claims that users find the system as easy to use as a coffee machine.

Coca-Cola has also worked to develop BreakMate's distribution system. Coca-Cola could ship the syrup and carbon-dioxide cylinders needed to replenish

the BreakMate directly to customers by UPS. However, the company wants to develop a distributor system to work directly with customers. In Europe, bottler networks service BreakMate accounts. In the United States, however, most large bottlers aren't providing the required level of service, so coffee distributors, bottled water firms, vending companies, and small independent bottlers will be the primary service providers.

These service companies in the United States will purchase the machines from Coca-Cola, install them in their customers' workplaces, and supply the syrup cannisters in much the same way they service coffee and vending machines. Depending on the options selected, the distributors will be able to buy the machines for $800 to $1,000. Coca-Cola promotes BreakMate to coffee distributors who service offices as a system that can help them increase their gross profits. BreakMate allows these distributors to offer a daylong "total refreshment system" that picks up with soft-drink sales where coffee consumption leaves off.

Using its experience from three years of market testing, Coca-Cola appears to have refined the BreakMate machines and is well along in developing its distribution strategy. However, the company has yet to clarify its end-customer target markets. Coca-Cola's previous research has shown that a standard soft-drink vending machine can be profitable in business locations with 20 or more employees. This means, however, that employees in the more than one million offices in the United States employing fewer than 20 people have limited access to soft drinks. Further, observers estimate that the number of these smaller offices will grow rapidly as the nation moves toward a more service-oriented economy. Therefore, Coca-Cola originally intended to focus on these small-to-medium-sized work locations—offices with less than 20 employees. However, Coca-Cola figures that BreakMate can be profitable in offices with as few as five employees if the office has substantial foot traffic. In addition, distributors could locate the machines in areas of larger offices where employees may have to take a long walk or an elevator ride to get to a larger drink machine.

Given this expanded view of potential BreakMate locations, Coca-Cola faces a real challenge. Coca-Cola and its distributors will not be able to develop and serve the millions of possible locations all at once. Can it segment the market in better ways than just by the number of employees? Will certain types of business be more receptive to the BreakMate than others? Will different types of businesses have different buying decision processes?

Coca-Cola believes it has an 18-month lead on rival Pepsi in this new front in the great Cola Wars. But to take advantage of this lead, it must move quickly and effectively to refine its marketing strategy. Moreover, if it succeeds in the office market, Coca-Cola might be able to open still another front—BreakMate might just lead the way to a dispenser that will one day make fountain Coke available in the home.

QUESTIONS

1. What bases can be used to segment the small office market? What market segments can you identify?

2. How would you go about forecasting demand for the BreakMate in each segment? What other criteria would you use to evaluate the segments?

3. Which type of market coverage strategy should Coca-Cola adopt and which specific segment(s) should the company target. Why?

4. How should Coca-Cola position BreakMate to appeal to customers in the target segments(s).

Source: Adapted from Laurie Petersen, "The New Coke Machine," *Adweek's Marketing Week,* September 26, 1988. Used with permission.

*D*esigning Products: Products, Brands, Packaging, and Services

10

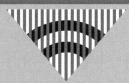

*E*ach year, Revlon sells more than $1 billion worth of cosmetics, toiletries, and fragrances to consumers around the world. Its many successful perfume products make Revlon number one in the popular-price segment of the $4 billion fragrance market. In one sense, Revlon's perfumes are no more than careful mixtures of oils and chemicals that have nice scents. But Revlon knows that when it sells perfume, it sells much more than fragrant fluids—it sells what the fragrances can do for the women who use them.

Of course, a perfume's scent contributes to its success or failure. Fragrance marketers agree: "No smell; no sell." Most new aromas are developed by elite "perfumers" at one of many select "fragrance houses." Perfume is shipped from the fragrance houses in big, ugly drums—hardly the stuff of which dreams are made! Although a $180-an-ounce perfume may cost no more than $10 to produce, to perfume consumers the product is much more than a few dollars worth of ingredients and a pleasing smell.

Many things beyond the ingredients and scent add to a perfume's allure. In fact, when Revlon designs a new perfume, the scent may be the *last* element developed. Revlon first researches women's feelings about themselves and their relationships with others. It then develops and tests new perfume concepts that match women's changing values, desires, and lifestyles. When Revlon finds a promising new concept, it creates and names a scent to fit the idea. Revlon's research in the early 1970s showed that women were feeling more competitive with men and that they were striving to find individual identities. For this new woman of the 1970s, Revlon created Charlie, the first of the "lifestyle" perfumes. Thousands of women adopted Charlie as a bold statement of independence, and it quickly became the world's best-selling perfume.

In the late 1970s, Revlon research showed a shift in women's attitudes—"women had made the equality point, which Charlie addressed. Now women were hungering for an expression of femininity." The Charlie girls had grown up; they now wanted perfumes that were subtle rather than shocking. Thus, Revlon subtly shifted Charlie's position: The perfume still made its "independent lifestyle" statement, but with an added tinge of "femininity and romance." Revlon also launched a perfume for the woman of the 1980s, Jontue, which was positioned on a theme of romance.

Revlon continues to refine Charlie's position, now targeting the woman of the 1990s who is "able to do it all, but smart enough to know what she wants to do." After almost 20 years, aided by continuous but subtle repositioning, Charlie remains the best-selling mass market perfume.

A perfume's *name* is an important product attribute. Revlon uses such names as Charlie, Fleurs de Jontue, Ciara, Scoundrel, Guess, and Unforgettable to create images that support each perfume's positioning. Competitors offer perfumes with such names as Obsession, Passion, Uninhibited, Opium, Joy, Exclamation!, White Linen, Youth Dew, and Eternity. These names suggest that the perfumes will do something more than just make you smell better. Oscar de la Renta's Ruffles perfume *began* as a name, one chosen because it created images of whimsy, youth, glamour, and femininity—all well suited to the target market of young, stylish women. Only later was a scent selected to go with the product's name and positioning.

Revlon must also carefully *package* its perfumes. To consumers, the bottle and package are the most real symbol of the perfume and its image. Bottles must feel comfortable and be easy to handle, and they must look impressive when displayed in stores. Most important, they must support the perfume's concept and image.

So when a woman buys perfume, she buys much, much more than simply fragrant fluids. The perfume's image, its promises, its scent, its name and package, the company that makes it, the stores that sell it—all become a part of the total perfume product. When Revlon sells perfume, it sells more than just the tangible product. It sells lifestyle, self-expression, and exclusivity; achievement, success, and status; femininity, romance, passion, and fantasy; memories, hopes, and dreams.[1]

 ## CHAPTER PREVIEW

Chapter 10 addresses some of the most visible aspects of marketing: how products are designed, named, packaged, and formed into product lines.

The product itself is defined in the first section of the chapter. This complex concept includes the *core product*, *actual product*, and *augmented product*. Products may be *durable goods*, *nondurable goods*, or *services*, and may be aimed at *consumer* or *industrial* markets.

Later, we discuss the broad range of decisions that marketers make for each product. *Product attribute* decisions include *quality*, *features*, and *design*. Marketers must decide on whether or not to *brand;* and on *brand sponsorship*, *strategy*, and *repositioning.*

Next, we review the issues that marketers must address in *packaging* and *labeling* the product. *Product-support* decisions, including the *service mix* and *service delivery*, are also covered.

Product line decisions are introduced, including *line length, line stretching, line filling, line modernization,* and *line featuring.* The related concept of *product mix decisions,* and adapting them to *international markets*, concludes the chapter.

Clearly, perfume is more than just perfume when Revlon sells it. Revlon's great success in the rough-and-tumble fragrance world comes from developing an innovative product concept. An effective product concept is the first step in marketing-mix planning.

This chapter begins with a deceptively simple question: *What is a product?* After answering this question, we look at ways to classify products in consumer and business markets, and look for links between types of products and types of marketing strategies. Next, we see that each product requires several decisions that go beyond basic product design. These decisions involve *branding, packaging* and *labeling,* and *product-support services.* Finally, we move from decisions about individual products to decisions about building product lines and product mixes.

WHAT IS A PRODUCT?

A Kennex tennis racquet, a Supercuts haircut, a Billy Joel concert, a Hawaiian vacation, advice from an attorney, a GMC truck, and tax preparation services are all products. We define *product* as follows: A **product** is anything that can be offered to a market for attention, acquisition, use, or consumption and that might satisfy a want or need; it includes physical objects, services, persons, places, organizations, and ideas.

Product planners need to think about the product on three levels. The most basic level is the **core product,** which addresses the question: *What is the buyer really buying?* As Figure 10-1 illustrates, the core product stands at the center of the total product. It consists of the problem-solving services or core benefits that consumers seek when they buy a product. A woman buying lipstick buys more than

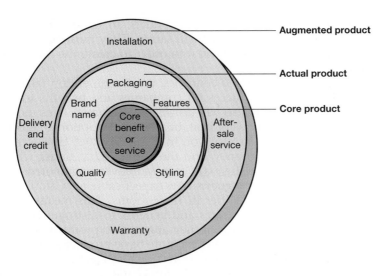

Installation

Augmented product

Packaging

Actual product

Brand name   Features

Core product

Core benefit or service

Delivery and credit

After-sale service

Quality   Styling

Warranty

FIGURE 10–1
Three levels of product

lip color. Charles Revson of Revlon saw this early: "In the factory, we make cosmetics; in the store, we sell hope." Theodore Levitt has pointed out that buyers "do not buy quarter-inch drills; they buy quarter-inch holes." Thus, when designing products, marketers must first define the core of *benefits* the product will provide to consumers.

The product planner must next build an **actual product** around the core product. Actual products may have as many as five characteristics: a *quality level, features, design,* a *brand name,* and *packaging.* For example, Sony's Handycam Camcorder is an actual product. Its name, parts, styling, features, packaging, and other attributes have all been combined carefully to deliver the core benefit—a convenient, high-quality way to capture important moments.

Finally, the product planner must build an **augmented product** around the core and actual products by offering additional consumer services and benefits. Sony must offer more than a camcorder. It must provide consumers with a complete solution to their picture-taking problems. Thus, when consumers buy a Sony Handycam, they receive more than just the camcorder itself. Sony and its dealers also might give buyers a warranty on parts and workmanship, free lessons on how to use the camcorder, quick repair services when needed, and a toll-free telephone number to call if they have problems or questions. To the consumer, all of these augmentations become an important part of the total product.

Therefore, a product is more than a simple set of tangible features. In fact, some products, such as a haircut or a doctor's exam, have no tangible features at all. Consumers tend to see products as complex bundles of benefits that satisfy

CAPTURE THE ONES YOU LOVE

SONY

Core, actual, and augmented product: Consumers perceive this Sony Camcorder as a complex bundle of tangible and intangible features and services that deliver a core benefit—a convenient, high-quality way to capture important moments.

their needs. When developing products, marketers first must identify the *core* consumer needs the product will satisfy. They must then design the *actual* product and find ways to *augment* it in order to create the bundle of benefits that will best satisfy consumers.

Today, in developed countries, most competition takes place at the product augmentation level. Successful companies add benefits to their offers that not only will *satisfy*, but also will *delight* the customer. Thus, hotel guests find candy on the pillow, or a bowl of fruit, or a VCR with optional videotapes. The company is saying "we want to treat you in a special way." However, each augmentation costs the company money, and the marketer has to ask whether customers will pay enough to cover the extra cost. Moreover, augmented benefits soon become *expected* benefits: Hotel guests now expect cable television sets, small trays of toiletries, and other amenities in their rooms. This means that competitors must search for still more features and benefits to distinguish their offers. Finally, as companies raise the prices of their augmented products, some competitors can go back to the strategy of offering a more basic product at a much lower price. Thus, along with the growth of fine hotels such as Four Seasons, Westin, and Hyatt, we see the emergence of lower-cost hotels and motels like Red Roof Inns, Fairfield Inns, and Motel 6 for clients who want only basic room accommodations.

PRODUCT CLASSIFICATIONS

In seeking marketing strategies for individual products and services, marketers have developed several product-classification schemes based on product characteristics. We now examine these schemes and characteristics.

Durable Goods, Nondurable Goods, and Services

Products can be classified into three groups according to their *durability* or *tangibility*.[2] **Nondurable goods** are consumer goods that normally are consumed in one or a few uses, such as beer, soap, and salt. **Durable goods** are consumer goods that are used over an extended period of time and that normally survive many uses. Examples include refrigerators, automobiles, and furniture. **Services** are activities, benefits, or satisfactions that are offered for sale, such as haircuts and home repairs. Services are essentially intangible and do not result in the ownership of anything. (Because of the growing importance of services in our society, we will look at them more closely in Chapter 22.)

Consumer Goods

Consumer goods are those bought by final consumers for personal consumption. Marketers usually classify these goods based on *consumer shopping habits*. Consumer goods include *convenience goods, shopping goods, specialty goods,* and *unsought goods* (see Figure 10-2).[3]

Convenience goods are consumer goods and services that the customer usually buys frequently, immediately, and with a minimum of comparison and buying effort. They are usually low priced and widely available. Examples include tobacco products, soap, and newspapers. Convenience goods can be divided further into *staples, impulse goods,* and *emergency goods. Staples* are goods that consumers buy on a regular basis, such as ketchup, toothpaste, or crackers. *Impulse*

FIGURE 10–2
Classification of consumer goods

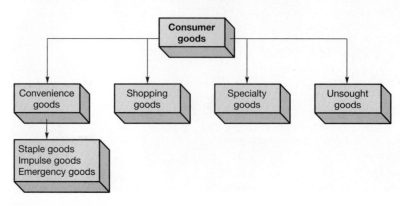

goods are purchased with little planning or search effort. These goods are normally available in many places because consumers seldom seek them out. Thus, candy bars and magazines are placed next to checkout counters because shoppers may not otherwise think of buying them. *Emergency goods* are purchased when a need is urgent—umbrellas during a rainstorm, or boots and shovels during the year's first snowstorm. Manufacturers of emergency goods will place them in many outlets to make them readily available when the customer needs them.

Shopping goods are consumer goods that the customer, in the process of selection and purchase, usually compares on such bases as suitability, quality, price, and style. When purchasing shopping goods, consumers spend considerable time and effort in gathering information and making comparisons. Examples include furniture, clothing, used cars, and major appliances. Shopping goods can be divided into *uniform* and *nonuniform* goods. The buyer sees uniform shopping goods, such as major appliances, as similar in quality but different enough in price to justify shopping comparisons. The seller has to "talk price" to the buyer. However, when a consumer is shopping for clothing, furniture, and other nonuniform goods, product features are often more important than price. If the buyer wants a new suit, the cut, fit, and look are likely to be more important than small price differences. The seller of nonuniform shopping goods therefore must carry a wide assortment to satisfy individual tastes and must have well-trained salespeople to give information and advice to customers.

Specialty goods are consumer goods with unique characteristics or brand identification for which a significant group of buyers is willing to make a special purchase effort. Examples include specific brands and types of cars, high-priced photographic equipment, and custom-made men's suits. A Jaguar, for example, is a specialty good because buyers are usually willing to travel great distances to buy one. Buyers normally do not compare specialty goods. They invest only the time needed to reach dealers carrying the wanted products. Although these dealers do not need convenient locations, they still must let buyers know where to find them.

Unsought goods are consumer goods that the consumer either does not know about or knows about but does not normally think of buying. A new product like the digital audio tape player is unsought until the consumer becomes aware of it through advertising. Classic examples of known but unsought goods are life insurance and encyclopedias. By their very nature, unsought goods require a lot of advertising, personal selling, and other marketing efforts. Some of the most advanced personal selling methods have developed out of the challenge of selling unsought goods.

Industrial Goods

Industrial goods are those bought by individuals and organizations for further processing or for use in conducting a business. Thus, the distinction between a consumer good and an industrial good is based on the *purpose* for which the product is purchased. If a consumer buys a lawn mower for use around the home, the lawn mower is a consumer good. If the same consumer buys the same lawn mower for use in a landscaping business, the lawn mower is an industrial good.

Industrial goods can be classified according to how they enter the production process and according to what they cost. There are three groups: *materials and parts, capital items,* and *supplies and services* (see Figure 10-3).

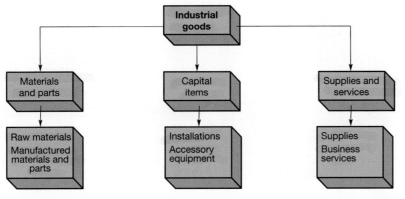

FIGURE 10–3
Classification of industrial goods

Materials and parts are industrial goods that enter the manufacturer's product completely, either through further processing or as components. They fall into two classes: raw materials and manufactured materials and parts.

Raw materials include farm products (wheat, cotton, livestock, fruits, vegetables) and natural products (fish, lumber, crude petroleum, iron ore). Farm products are supplied by many small producers who turn them over to marketing intermediaries that process and sell them. Natural products usually have great bulk and low unit value and require a lot of transportation to move them from producer to user. They are supplied by fewer and larger producers, who tend to market them directly to industrial users.

Manufactured materials and parts include component materials (iron, yarn, cement, wires) and component parts (small motors, tires, castings). Component materials usually are processed further—for example, pig iron is made into steel and yarn is woven into cloth. Component parts enter the finished product completely with no further change in form, as when small motors are put into vacuum cleaners and tires are added to automobiles. Most manufactured materials and parts are sold directly to industrial users. Price and service are the major marketing factors, and branding and advertising tend to be less important.

Capital items are industrial goods that partly enter the finished product. They include two groups: installations and accessory equipment. *Installations* consist of buildings (factories, offices) and fixed equipment (generators, drill presses, large computers, elevators). Because installations are major purchases, they usually are bought directly from the producer after a long decision period.

Accessory equipment includes portable factory equipment and tools (hand tools, lift trucks) and office equipment (fax machines, desks). These products do not become part of the finished product. They have a shorter life than installations and simply aid in the production process. Most sellers of accessory equipment use middlemen because the market is spread out geographically, the buyers are numerous, and the orders are small.

Supplies and services are industrial goods that do not enter the finished product at all. *Supplies* include operating supplies (lubricants, coal, computer paper, pencils) and repair and maintenance items (paint, nails, brooms). Supplies are the convenience goods of the industrial field because they usually are purchased with a minimum of effort or comparison. *Business services* include maintenance and repair services (window cleaning, computer repair) and business advisory services (legal, management consulting, advertising). These services are usually supplied under contract. Maintenance services often are provided by small producers, and repair services are often available from the manufacturers of the original equipment.

Component parts: Texas Instruments markets integrated circuit chips to manufacturers. This ad stresses service: "Total integration combines our best technologies, tools, information, and talent . . . all to give you a competitive edge."

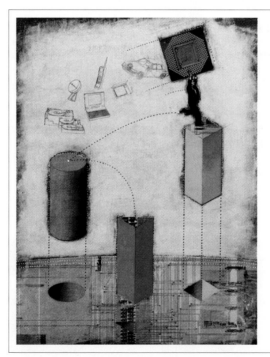

Thus, we see that a product's characteristics have a major effect on marketing strategy. At the same time, marketing strategy also depends on factors such as the product's stage in its life cycle, the number of competitors, the degree of market segmentation, and the condition of the economy.

INDIVIDUAL PRODUCT DECISIONS

We now look at decisions relating to the development and marketing of individual products. We will focus on decisions about *product attributes, branding, packaging, labeling,* and product-support services.

Product Attribute Decisions

Developing a product involves defining the benefits that the product will offer. These benefits are communicated and delivered by tangible product attributes, such as *quality, features,* and *design.* Decisions about these attributes greatly affect consumer reactions to a product. We now discuss the issues involved in each decision.

Product Quality

Quality has two dimensions—level and consistency. In developing a product, the marketer must first choose a *quality level* that will support the product's position in the target market. Quality is one of the marketer's major positioning tools. Here, **product quality** stands for the ability of a product to perform its functions. It includes the product's overall durability, reliability, precision, ease of operation and repair, and other valued attributes. Although some of these attributes can be measured objectively, from a marketing point of view, quality should be measured in terms of buyers' perceptions. Companies rarely try to offer the highest possible quality level—few customers want or can afford the high levels of quality offered in products such as a Rolls Royce, a Sub Zero refrigerator, or a Rolex watch. Instead, companies choose a quality level that matches target market needs and the quality levels of competing products.

No matter what the targeted quality level, all companies should strive for high levels of *quality consistency.* That is, beyond quality level, high quality also can mean consistently delivering the targeted level of quality to consumers. In this sense, quality means "absence of defects or variation."

> Thus, a Chevrolet can have just as much quality as a Rolls-Royce, and the service at a discount store can be equally "good"—free of variations—as at Bergdorf-Goodman. Even a perfect product can't do more than it was designed to do: Don't count on a Chevy to perform like a Rolls. Still, reducing the variations that cause defects [ensures] that customers get what they pay for.[4]

During the past decade, a renewed emphasis on quality has spawned a global quality movement. Japanese firms have long practiced "Total Quality Management" (TQM), an effort to constantly improve product and process quality in every phase of their operations. "In 40 years, a focus on quality has turned Japan from a maker of knick-knacks into an economic powerhouse—and U.S. and European companies are being forced to respond. The result: a global revolution affecting every facet of business."[5] For more than 40 years, the Japanese have awarded the Demming prize (named after quality pioneer W. Edwards Demming) to companies that have achieved outstanding quality. Recently, the U.S. Department of Commerce began granting similar awards—the annual Malcolm Baldridge National Quality Awards—to U.S. companies demonstrating outstanding quality leadership.

To some companies, improving quality means using better quality control to reduce defects that annoy consumers. To others, it means making lofty speeches about the importance of quality and passing out lapel pins with quality slogans on them. But total quality management means much more than this. It requires a total-company dedication to continuous quality improvement. Quality starts with a strong commitment by top management—many companies have now created "total quality programs" headed by vice-presidents or directors of quality. Then, employees at all levels of the organization must be educated and motivated to put quality first.

MOTOROLA'S CUSTOMER-DEFINED, "SIX-SIGMA" QUALITY

Founded in 1928, Motorola introduced the first car radio—hence the name Motorola, suggesting "sound in motion." During World War II, it developed the first two-way radios ("walkie-talkies"), and by the 1950s, Motorola had become a household name in consumer electronics products. In the 1970s, however, facing intense competition, much of it from Japanese firms, Motorola abandoned the radios and televisions that had made it famous. Instead, it focused on advanced telecommunications and electronics products—semiconductors, two-way radios, pagers, cellular telephones, and related gear. But by the early 1980s, Motorola still faced a challenge. Japanese competitors were threatening Motorola with higher-quality products at lower prices.

Then things changed. During the past decade, Motorola has come roaring back. It is now one of the leaders in the U.S. semiconductor market and ranks number one worldwide in the fast-growing cellular telephone industry. It dominates the world's two-way mobile radio market and leads all competitors in pagers. Rather than suffering at the hands of Japanese competitors, Motorola now has them on the run, even on their home turf. It ranks third in the fiercely competitive Asian chip market and is threatening to overtake number-two Toshiba. Once in danger of being forced out of the pager market altogether, Motorola now holds the number 1 position in the world. And the company has become Asia's leading supplier of two-way radios and digital cordless phones. Motorola's sales in Japan now exceed $1 billion, accounting for almost 7 percent of total company sales.

How has Motorola achieved such remarkable leadership? The answer is deceptively simple: an obsessive dedication to *quality*. In the early 1980s, Motorola launched an aggressive crusade to improve product quality, first by tenfold, then by a hundredfold. Ulti-

mately, it set the unheard-of goal of "six-sigma" quality by 1992. Six sigma is a statistical term that means "six standard deviations from a statistical performance average." In plain English, the six-sigma standard means that Motorola set out to slash product defects to fewer than 3.4 per million components manufactured—99.9997 percent defect-free. "Six sigma" became Motorola's rallying cry, and the company is now an acknowledged pioneer in quality—achieving constant quality improvement by applying quality principles to every phase of company operations. In 1988, Motorola received one of the first annual Malcolm Baldrige National Quality Awards recognizing "preeminent quality leadership."

Motorola's initial efforts were focused on improving product quality through manufacturing improvements. This involved much more than simply increasing the number of quality control inspectors. The goal was to prevent defects from occurring in the first place. This meant *designing* products from the onset for quality and making things right the *first* time and *every* time. For example, Motorola's highly successful MicroTAC foldable, hand-held cellular phone has only one-eighth the number of parts contained in its original 1978 portable telephone; components snap together instead of being joined by screws or fasteners. This simpler design results in fewer component defects and production errors.

Meeting the six-sigma standard means that everyone in the organization must be dedicated to quality. Motorola spends $120 million annually to educate employees about quality—to teach them to inspect their own work and improve their own performance. Then, it rewards people when they make things right. Finally, because Motorola's products can be only as good as the components that go into them, the company forces its suppliers to meet the same exacting quality standards.

Rather than catching and correcting defects after the fact, total quality management involves preventing defects before they occur, through better product design and improved manufacturing processes. Beyond simply reducing product defects, the ultimate goal of total quality is to improve customer value. For example, when Motorola first began its total quality program in the early 1980s, its goal was to drastically reduce manufacturing defects. In recent years, however, Motorola has adapted its quality concept to one of "customer-defined quality." It now states its quality goal as "total customer satisfaction" and it defines defects in terms of customer needs and expectations: "Our definition of a defect is 'if the customer doesn't like it, it's a defect.'"[6] (See Marketing Highlight 10-1.) Customer satisfaction is the most important consideration used in evaluating Baldridge Quality Award contestants.

Many companies have turned quality into a potent strategic weapon. *Strategic* quality involves gaining an edge over competitors by consistently offering products and services that better serve customers' needs and preferences for quality. As one expert proclaims, "Quality is not simply a problem to be solved; it is a

Some suppliers grumble, but those that survive benefit greatly from their own quality improvements. As an executive from one of Motorola's suppliers puts it, "If we can supply Motorola, we can supply God." Thus, total quality has become an important part of Motorola's basic corporate culture, and everyone associated with Motorola strives for quality improvement.

More recently, as Motorola has developed a broader and deeper understanding of the meaning of quality, its initial focus on preventing manufacturing defects has evolved into an emphasis on improving customer value. "Quality," notes Motorola's vice-president of quality, "has to do something for the customer." Thus, the fundamental aim of the company's quality movement is "total customer satisfaction":

[The focus of the first quality-improvement efforts] was very internal, looking at things like defects on printed circuit boards manufactured in the factory. . . . Now we're taking the customer's values and establishing quality criteria directly [from those]. . . . Beauty is in the eye of the user. If [a product] does not work the way that the user needs it to work, the defect is as big to the user as if it doesn't work the way the designer planned it. Our definition of a defect is "if the customer doesn't like it, it's a defect."

This concept of *customer-defined quality* has put more pressure on the company to understand the customer better. Instead of focusing just on manufacturing defects, Motorola now surveys customers about their quality needs, analyzes customer complaints, and studies service records in a constant quest to improve value to the customer. Motorola's executives routinely visit customer offices to gain more detailed, deeper insights into customer needs. As a result, Motorola's total quality management program has done more than reduce product defects; it has helped the company to shift from an inwardly focused engineering orientation to a market-driven, customer-focused one.

Although Motorola missed its target of 3.4 defects per million in 1992, it did improve manufacturing quality 170-fold, to a current 30 defects per million compared to 6,000 per million just five years ago. Building on this success, Motorola has set a new quality goal: to cut defects by 90 percent every two years throughout the 1990s. And it has now expanded the quality goal to all of its departments and processes, from manufacturing and product development to market research, finance, and even advertising. Each department now has its own six-sigma quality goal.

Some skeptics are concerned that Motorola's obsession with quality might result in problems. For example, the company's products sometimes have been late to the market. Others worry that building so much quality into a product might be too expensive. Not so, claims Motorola. In fact, the reverse is true—superior quality is the lowest-cost way to do things. The costs of monitoring and fixing mistakes can far exceed the costs of getting things right in the first place. Motorola estimates that its quality efforts have resulted in savings of more than $3 billion during the past six years. Finally, the skeptics fear that the quality crusade might stifle innovation by forcing research, design, and production staffs to stick with safe, proven methods and technologies. But the results suggest otherwise. "We're doing a lot more now than we've ever done," says Motorola's chairman, "and doing most of it better."

And so Motorola's quest for quality continues. By the year 2001, Motorola is shooting for near perfection—a mind-boggling rate of just *one* defect per *billion*.

Sources: Quotes from "Future Perfect," *The Economist,* January 4, 1992, p. 61; Lois Therrien, "Motorola and NEC: Going for Glory," *Business Week,* Special issue on quality, 1991, pp. 60-61; and B. G. Yovovich, "Motorola's Quest for Quality," *Business Marketing,* September 1991, pp. 14-16. Also see William Wiggenhorn, "Motorola U: When Training Becomes an Education," *Harvard Business Review,* July-August 1990, pp. 71-83; and Ernest Raia, "1991 Medal of Professional Excellence," *Purchasing,* September 26, 1991, pp. 38-57.

competitive opportunity."[7] Others suggest, however, that quality has now become a competitive *necessity*—that in the 1990s and beyond, only companies with the best quality will thrive.

Product Features

A product can be offered with varying features. A "stripped-down" model, one without any extras, is the starting point. The company can create higher-level models by adding more features. Features are a competitive tool for differentiating the company's product from competitors' products. Being the first producer to introduce a needed and valued new feature is one of the most effective ways to compete. Some companies are very innovative in adding new features.

How can a company identify new features and decide which ones to add to its product? The company should periodically survey buyers who have used the product and ask these questions: How do you like the product? Which specific features of the product do you like most? Which features could we add to improve the product? How much would you pay for each feature? The answers provide the company with a rich list of feature ideas. The company then can assess each feature's *customer value* versus its *company cost*. Features that customers value little in relation to costs should be dropped; those that customers value highly in relation to costs should be added.

Product Design

Another way to add product distinctiveness is through **product design.** Some companies have reputations for outstanding design, such as Black & Decker in cordless appliances and tools, Steelcase in office furniture and systems, Bose in audio equipment, and Ciba Corning in medical equipment. Many companies, however, lack a "design touch." Their product designs function poorly or are dull or common looking. Yet design can be one of the most powerful competitive weapons in a company's marketing arsenal.

Design is a larger concept than style. *Style* simply describes the appearance of a product. Styles can be eye-catching or yawn-inspiring. A sensational style may grab attention, but it does not necessarily make the product *perform* better. In some cases, it might even result in worse performance. For example, a chair may look great yet be extremely uncomfortable. Unlike style, *design* is more than skin deep—it goes to the very heart of a product. Good design contributes to a product's usefulness as well as to its looks. A good designer considers appearance but also creates products that are easy, safe, inexpensive to use and service, and simple and economical to produce and distribute.

As competition intensifies, design will offer one of the most potent tools for differentiating and positioning a company's products and services. Design investment pays off. For example, the radical design of the Ford Taurus, with its sleek styling, passenger comforts, engineering advances, and efficient manufacturing, made the car a huge success. Herman Miller, the American office furniture company, has won admiration and sales with the distinctive comfort and looks of its furniture. And Braun, a German division of Gillette which has elevated design to a high art, has had outstanding success with its coffee makers, food processors, hair dryers, electric razors, and other small appliances. Good design can attract attention, improve product performance, cut production costs, and give the product a strong competitive advantage in the target market.[8]

Brand Decisions

Consumers view a brand as an important part of a product, and branding can add value to a product. For example, most consumers would perceive a bottle of White Linen perfume as a high-quality, expensive product. But the same perfume in an unmarked bottle would likely be viewed as lower in quality, even if the fragrance were identical.

Branding has become a major issue in product strategy. On the one hand, developing a branded product requires a great deal of long-term marketing investment, especially for advertising, promotion, and packaging. Manufacturers often find it easier and less expensive simply to make the product and let others do the brand building. Taiwanese manufacturers have taken this course. They make a large amount of the world's clothing, consumer electronics, and computers, but these products are sold under non-Taiwanese brand names.

On the other hand, most manufacturers eventually learn that the power lies with the companies that control the brand names. For example, brand name clothing, electronics, and computer companies can replace their Taiwanese manufacturing sources with cheaper sources in Malaysia and elsewhere. The Taiwanese producers can do little to prevent the loss of sales to less expensive suppliers—consumers are loyal to the brands, not to the producers. Japanese and South Korean companies, however, have not made this mistake. They have spent heavily to build up brand names such as Sony, Panasonic, JVC, Goldstar, and Samsung for their products. Even when these companies no longer can afford to manufacture their products in their homelands, their brand names continue to command customer loyalty.[9]

Powerful brand names have *consumer franchise*—they command strong consumer loyalty. A sufficient number of customers demand these brands and refuse substitutes, even if the substitutes are offered at somewhat lower prices. Companies that develop brands with a strong consumer franchise are insulated from competitors' promotional strategies. Thus, companies around the world invest heavily to create strong national or even global recognition and preference for their brand names.

What Is a Brand?

Perhaps the most distinctive skill of professional marketers is their ability to create, maintain, protect, and enhance brands. A **brand** is a name, term, sign, symbol, or design, or a combination of these intended to identify the goods or services of one seller or group of sellers and to differentiate them from those of competitors.[10] Thus, a brand identifies the maker or seller of a product. Brands differ from other assets such as patents and copyrights, which have expiration dates. Under trademark law, the seller receives exclusive rights to use a brand name for an unlimited period of time.

A brand is a seller's promise to consistently deliver a specific set of features, benefits, and services to buyers. The best brands convey a warranty of quality. According to one marketing executive, a brand can deliver up to four levels of meaning:

- *Attributes*. A brand first brings to mind certain product attributes. For example, Mercedes suggests such attributes as "well engineered," "well built," "durable," "high prestige," "fast," "expensive," and "high resale value." The company may use one or more of these attributes in its advertising for the car. For years, Mercedes advertised "Engineered like no other car in the world." This provided a positioning platform for other attributes of the car.

- *Benefits*. Customers do not buy attributes, they buy benefits. Therefore, attributes must be translated into functional and emotional benefits. For example, the attribute "durable" could translate into the functional benefit, "I won't have to buy a new car every few years." The attribute "expensive" might translate into the emotional benefit, "The car makes me feel important and admired." The attribute "well built" might translate into the functional and emotional benefit, "I am safe in the event of an accident."

- *Values*. A brand also says something about the buyers' values. Thus, Mercedes buyers value high performance, safety, and prestige. A brand marketer must identify the specific groups of car buyers whose values coincide with the delivered benefit package.

- *Personality*. A brand also projects a personality. Motivation researchers sometimes ask, "If this brand were a person, what kind of person would it be?" Consumers might visualize a Mercedes automobile as being a wealthy, middle-aged business executive. The brand will attract people whose actual or desired self-images match the brand's image.[11]

Familiar brands provide consumer information, recognition, and confidence.

All this suggests that a brand is a complex symbol. If a company treats a brand only as a name, it misses the point of branding. The challenge of branding is to develop a deep set of meanings for the brand.

Given the four levels of a brand's meaning, marketers must decide the levels at which they will build the brand's identity. It would be a mistake to promote only the brand's attributes. Buyers are not so much interested in brand attributes as in brand benefits. Moreover, competitors can easily copy attributes. Or, the current attributes may later become less valuable to consumers, hurting a brand that is tied too strongly to specific attributes.

Even promoting the brand on one or more of its benefits can be risky. Suppose Mercedes touts its main benefit as "high performance." If several competing brands emerge with as high or higher performance, or if car buyers begin placing less importance on performance as compared to other benefits, Mercedes will need the freedom to move into a new benefit positioning.

The most lasting meanings of a brand are its values and personality. They define the brand's essence. Thus, Mercedes stands for "high achievers and success." The company must build its brand strategy around creating and protecting this brand personality. Although Mercedes has recently yielded to market pressures by introducing lower-price models, this might prove risky. Marketing less expensive models might dilute the value and personality that Mercedes has built up over the decades.

Brand Equity

Brands vary in the amount of power and value they have in the marketplace. At one extreme are brands that are largely unknown to most buyers in the marketplace. Next are brands with a fairly high degree of consumer *brand awareness*. Still other brands enjoy *brand preference*—buyers select them over the others. Finally, some brands command a high degree of *brand loyalty*. A top executive at H. J. Heinz proposes this test of brand loyalty: "My acid test . . . is whether a [consumer], intending to buy Heinz Ketchup in a store but finding it out of stock, will walk out of the store to buy it elsewhere or switch to an alternative product."

A powerful brand has high **brand equity.** Brands have higher brand equity to the extent that they have higher brand loyalty, name awareness, perceived quality, strong brand associations, and other assets such as patents, trademarks, and channel relationships.[12] A brand with strong brand equity is a valuable asset. In fact, it can even be bought or sold for a price. Many companies base their growth strategies on acquiring and building rich *brand portfolios*. For example, Grand Metropolitan acquired various Pillsbury brands, including Green Giant vegetables, Haagen-Dazs ice cream, and Burger King restaurants. Nestlé bought Rowntree (UK), Carnation (US), Stouffer (US), Buitoni-Perugina (Italy), and Perrier (France), making it the world's largest food company.

Measuring the actual equity of a brand name is difficult.[13] Because it is so hard to measure, companies usually do not list brand equity on their balance sheets. Still, they pay handsomely for it. For example, Nestlé paid $4.5 billion to buy Rowntree, five times its book value. And when Grand Metropolitan bought Heublein, it added $800 million to its assets to reflect the value of Smirnoff and other names. According to one estimate, the brand equity of Marlboro is $31 billion, Coca-Cola $24 billion, and Kodak $13 billion.

The world's top brands include such superpowers as Coca-Cola, Campbell, Disney, Kodak, Sony, Mercedes-Benz, and McDonald's (see Marketing Highlight 10-2). High brand equity provides a company with many competitive advantages. Because a powerful brand enjoys a high level of consumer brand awareness and loyalty, the company will incur lower marketing costs relative to revenues. Because consumers expect stores to carry the brand, the company has more leverage in bargaining with resellers. And because the brand name carries high credibility, the company can more easily launch brand extensions. Above all, a powerful brand offers the company some defense against fierce price competition.

Marketers need to manage their brands carefully in order to preserve brand equity. They must develop strategies that effectively maintain or improve brand awareness, perceived brand quality and usefulness, and positive brand associations over time. This requires continuous R&D investment, skillful advertising, and excellent trade and consumer service. Some companies, such as Canada Dry and Colgate-Palmolive, have appointed "brand equity managers" to guard their

MARKETING HIGHLIGHT 10-2

THE WORLD'S MOST POWERFUL BRAND NAMES

Coca-Cola, McDonald's, AT&T, Campbell, Disney, Kodak, Kellogg, Hershey—such familiar brand names are daily household words to most Americans. Companies around the world invest billions of dollars each year to create awareness and preference for these and hundreds of other major brands. For example, AT&T, the nation's most heavily advertised brand name, is backed by more than $400 million in advertising each year, with other familiar brands like Ford and McDonald's close behind. The average top-20 U.S. brand receives almost $230 million annually in ad spending; the average top-50 brand receives $158 million. Powerful brand names command strong consumer loyalty and provide competitive advantage in the marketplace.

What are the world's most powerful brands? In a recent study, Landor Associates, an image consulting firm, surveyed 9,000 consumers in the United States, Western Europe, and Japan about their familiarity with and esteem for more than 6,000 brands. It then combined the familiarity and esteem scores to develop brand "image-power" rankings. Listed next are the top brands for each part of the world.

The World's Most Powerful Brand Names

United States	Europe	Japan
Coca-Cola	Coca-Cola	Sony
Campbell	Sony	National
Disney	Mercedes-Benz	Mercedes-Benz
Pepsi-Cola	BMW	Toyota
Kodak	Philips	Rolls Royce
NBC	Volkswagen	Seiko
Black & Decker	Adidas	Suntory
Kellogg	Kodak	Matsushita
McDonald's	Nivea	Hitachi
Hershey	Porsche	

The Landor study suggests some interesting conclusions. Perhaps most notably, the top brands varied greatly across regions. In recent years, many companies have worked to build global brands that are recognized and preferred not only in their home countries, but by consumers around the world. However, the Landor study suggests that few brands have yet achieved true global status. Although some 20 brands were internationally known, and another 45 were poised for global prominence, only two brands—Coca-Cola and Sony—appeared in the top-40 image-power rankings in all three markets. And only six other brands made the top 100 in each market: Disney, Nestlé, Toyota, McDonald's, Panasonic, and Kleenex. No product made it onto the top-ten lists of all three countries.

Further, the study appears to counter the recent contention, summarized by Chrysler chairman Lee Iacocca, that U.S. consumers believe "Everything from Japan is perfect. Everything from America is lousy." The study reveals that Americans do like American products. According to Don Casey, Landor's president, "What's playing in America today is warm and fuzzy and family and traditional." The list of top-ten American brands bears this out—it reads like a page out of the corporate American history book. And of the top-100 ranked brands in the United States, 97 claim American roots. Brand consultants see the high recognition of American brands as proof that it takes decades to construct an image powerhouse such as Coca-Cola or Kodak. For instance, "The Great American Chocolate Bar" Hershey, which ranks highest among candies in America, was also the nation's top-ranked candy in 1925.

The rankings also suggest strong cultural differences among consumers in the United States, Europe, and Japan. For example, Americans appear food oriented—six of the top ten brands are food related. In the other regions, cars and high-tech brands are more revered. Based on the top-ten list, American consumers appear satisfied with simple pleasures like a Big Mac, chocolates, and as a really self-indulgent treat, luxury ice creams. European and Japanese consumers seem to have more expensive tastes, at least as reflected by the brands they hold in high regard. Casey believes that these differences are tied not just to differing appetites, but to varying aspirations. "I think that there is a sense of realism in this country of what you can expect from your life," he says. " . . . The mindset of Americans is more practical than it is aspirational." Thus, the Landor study suggests that a global marketer may face many cultural hurdles in its attempts to create worldwide brands.

The power of a brand is very difficult to measure. Some critics question the value of asking consumers to rate brands on such subjective factors as "esteem." People will probably hold a Mercedes in higher esteem than a brand of laundry detergent. Thus, noticeably absent from the list are top brands from some of the world's most powerful marketers, including such giant consumer goods companies as Procter & Gamble, Unilever, and Philip Morris. Further, people often don't buy the brands they regard most highly—many people who hold a Mercedes in high esteem can't afford one. But no matter how you measure brand power, few marketers doubt the value of a powerful brand, as both a verbal and visual entity. As one brand consultant states, almost anywhere in the world, "When you mention Kodak, I'm pretty sure everyone sees that yellow box."

Sources: Portions adapted from Cathy Taylor, "Consumers Know Native Brands Best," *Adweek*, September 17, 1990, p. 31. Also see Kathleen Deveny, "More Brand Names Gain Recognition Around the World," *The Wall Street Journal*, September 13, 1990, p. B7; "Hard Sellers: The Leading Advertisers," *The Wall Street Journal*, March 21, 1991, p. B4; R. Craig Endicott, "The Top 200 Brands," *Advertising Age*, November 9, 1992, p. 16; and Interbrand, *World's Greatest Brands* (New York: John Wiley & Son, 1992).

brands' images, associations, and quality. They work to prevent brand managers from overpromoting brands in order to produce short-term profits at the expense of long-term brand equity.

Such companies as Procter & Gamble, Caterpillar, IBM, and Sony have achieved outstanding *company brand strength,* measured by the proportion of product/markets in which the company markets the leading brand. For example, P&G's impressive marketing reputation in the United States rests on the fact that it markets the leading brand in 19 of the 39 categories in which it competes and has one of the top three brands in 34 of its categories. Its average brand's market share is an astounding 25 percent.

Some analysts see brands as *the* major enduring asset of a company, outlasting the company's specific products and facilities. Yet, behind every powerful brand stands a set of loyal customers. Therefore, the basic asset underlying brand equity is *customer equity.* This suggests that marketing strategy should focus on extending *loyal customer lifetime value,* with brand management serving as a major marketing tool.

Branding poses challenging decisions to the marketer. Figure 10-4 shows the key branding decisions.

To Brand or Not to Brand

The company first must decide whether it should put a brand name on its product. Branding has become so strong that today hardly anything goes unbranded. Salt is packaged in branded containers, common nuts and bolts are packaged with a distributor's label, and automobile parts—spark plugs, tires, filters—bear brand names that differ from those of the auto makers. Even fruits and vegetables are branded—Sunkist oranges, Dole pineapples, and Chiquita bananas.

Recently, however, there has also been a return to "nonbranding" certain consumer goods. In the late 1970s, "generic" products took brand name manufacturers by surprise. Generics are unbranded, plainly packaged, less expensive versions of common products such as spaghetti, paper towels, and canned peaches. They often bear only black-stenciled labels—TOWELS, SUGAR, CAT FOOD—and offer prices as much as 40 percent lower than those of national brands. The lower price is made possible by lower-quality ingredients, lower-cost packaging, and lower advertising costs.

Although generics are probably here to stay, it appears that their popularity peaked in the early 1980s. Since then, the market share for generics has dropped, largely as a result of better marketing strategies by brand name manufacturers. These marketers responded by emphasizing brand image and quality. For example, when threatened by generic pet foods, Ralston Purina increased its quality rather than reducing its price, and targeted pet owners who identified strongly with their pets and cared most about quality.

Despite the decline in the popularity of generics, the issue of whether or not to brand is very much alive today. This situation highlights some key questions: Why have branding in the first place? Who benefits? How do they benefit? At what cost? Branding helps buyers in many ways. Brand names tell the buyer something about product quality. Buyers who always buy the same brand know that they will get the same quality each time they buy. Brand names also increase the shopper's efficiency. Imagine a buyer going into a supermarket and finding thousands of generic products. Finally, brand names help call consumers' attention to new products that might benefit them. The brand name becomes the basis upon which a whole story can be built about the new product's special qualities.

Branding also gives the seller several advantages. The brand name makes it easier for the seller to process orders and track down problems. Thus, Anheuser-Busch receives an order for a hundred cases of Michelob beer instead of an order for "some of your better beer." The seller's brand name and trademark provide

FIGURE 10–4 Major branding decisions

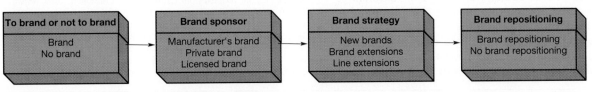

legal protection for unique product features that otherwise might be copied by competitors. Branding lets the seller attract a loyal and profitable set of customers. Branding helps the seller to segment markets. For example, General Mills can offer Cheerios, Wheaties, Total, Lucky Charms, and many other cereal brands, not just one general product for all consumers.

Branding also adds value to consumers and society. Those who favor branding suggest that it leads to higher and more consistent product quality. Branding also increases innovation by giving producers an incentive to look for new features that can be protected against imitating competitors. Thus, branding results in more product variety and choice for consumers. Finally, branding increases shopper efficiency because it provides much more information about products and where to find them.

Brand Sponsor

A manufacturer has three sponsorship options. The product may be launched as a **manufacturer's brand** (or national brand), as when Kellogg and IBM sell their output under their own manufacturer's brand names. Or the manufacturer may sell to resellers who give it a **private brand** (also called *retailer brand, distributor brand,* or *store brand*). For example, BASF Wyandotte, the world's second-largest antifreeze maker, sells its Alugard antifreeze through middlemen who market the product under about 80 private brands, including Kmart, True Value, Pathmark, and Rite Aid. Finally, although most manufacturers create their own brand names, others market *licensed brands.* For example, Rose Art Industries sells its children's art sets under the Kodak brand name licensed from Eastman Kodak Company.

Manufacturers' brands have long dominated the retail scene. Most manufacturers take years and spend millions to create their own brand names. However, some companies license names or symbols previously created by other manufacturers, names of well-known celebrities, characters from popular movies and books—for a fee, any of these can provide an instant and proven brand name. Apparel and accessories sellers pay large royalties to adorn their products—from blouses to ties, and linens to luggage—with the names or initials of such fashion innovators as Bill Blass, Calvin Klein, Pierre Cardin, Gucci, and Halston. Sellers of children's products attach an almost endless list of character names to clothing, toys, school supplies, linens, dolls, lunch boxes, cereals, and other items. The character names range from such classics as Disney, Peanuts, Barbie, and Flintstones characters, to the Muppets, Garfield, Batman, and the Simpsons. The newest form of licensing is corporate licensing—renting a corporate trademark or logo made famous in one category and using it in a related category. Some exam-

A licensed name can give a new product immediate familiarity and distinction. Here, Rose Art Industries licenses the familiar Kodak name and brandmark for its new Kodak art sets.

ples include Singer sewing supplies, Caterpillar work clothes, Old Spice shaving mugs and razors, Faberge costume jewelry, Winnebago camping equipment, and Coppertone swimwear and sunglasses.

In recent times, most large retailers and wholesalers have developed their own brands. The private-label tires of Sears and J. C. Penney are as well known today as the manufacturers' brands of Goodyear and Bridgestone. Sears has created several names—Diehard batteries, Craftsman tools, Weatherbeater paints—that buyers look for and demand. An increasing number of department and discount stores, supermarkets, service stations, clothiers, drugstores, and appliance dealers are launching private labels. For instance, Wal-Mart recently introduced its price-driven Great Value brand, which may eventually include more than 1,000 items across most major food categories. This new line joins Wal-Mart's higher-priced "Sam's American Choice" brand of colas and fruit juices to compete against major national brands. Wal-Mart claims that its own brand offers better value—"great taste at Wal-Mart's always low prices." Analysts expect that the retailer will quickly expand its Sam's Choice line to include chocolate-chip cookies, snack foods, and a slew of other products.[14]

Despite the fact that private brands are often hard to establish and costly to stock and promote, middlemen develop private brands because they can be profitable. Middlemen often can locate manufacturers with excess capacity who will produce the private label at a low cost, resulting in a higher profit margin for the middleman. Private brands also give middlemen exclusive products that cannot be bought from competitors, resulting in greater store traffic and loyalty. For example, if Sears promotes General Electric appliances, other stores that sell GE products will also benefit. Further, if Sears drops the GE brand, it loses the benefit of its previous promotion for GE. But when Sears promotes its private brand of Kenmore appliances, Sears alone benefits from the promotion, and consumer loyalty to the Kenmore brand becomes loyalty to Sears.

The competition between manufacturers' and middlemen's brands is called the *battle of the brands*. In this battle, middlemen have many advantages. Retailers control scarce shelf space. Many supermarkets now charge **slotting fees**—payments demanded by retailers from producers before they will accept new products and find "slots" for them on the shelves. For example, Safeway required a payment of $25,000 from a small pizza roll manufacturer to stock its new product. Middlemen give their own brands better display space and make certain they are better stocked. They price their store brands lower than comparable manufacturers' brands, thereby appealing to budget-conscious shoppers, especially in difficult economic times. And most shoppers know that store brands are often made by one of the larger manufacturers anyway.

As a result, the dominance of manufacturers' brands is weakening. Today's more financially squeezed consumers, hard pressed to spend wisely, are increasingly sensitive to quality, price, and value. The barrage of coupons and price specials has trained a generation of consumers to buy on price. Product proliferation and the seemingly endless stream of brand extensions and line extensions have blurred brand identity. Consumers see ever-greater similarities across brands, as competing manufacturers and retailers copy the qualities of the best brands. As store brands improve in quality, and as consumers gain confidence in their store chains, store brands are posing a strong challenge to manufacturers' brands. Consider the following case:

> Loblaw, the Canadian supermarket chain, is increasing the number of its house brands. Loblaw now sells the leading cookie brand in Canada, its President's Choice Decadent Chocolate Chip Cookie, which tastes better and costs less than Nabisco's Chips Ahoy brand. It has captured 14 percent of the market, mostly from Nabisco. Loblaw also introduced its private label cola, called President's Choice cola, which racked up 50 percent of Loblaw's canned cola sales.

In America's supermarkets, store brands now capture $22 billion in sales and a 13 percent share of dollar purchases, and this share is growing. Taken as a single brand, private-label products are the number one, two, or three brand in over 40 percent of all grocery product categories. For example, store brands account for 44 percent of natural cheese sales, 36 percent of frozen orange juice sales, and 14 percent of disposable diaper sales.[15] A recent study found that the percentage of packaged-goods consumers saying that they bought only well-known brands fell from 77 percent in 1975 to 62 percent in 1990. Another study reported that 66 percent of consumers said they were trading down to lower-priced brands, particularly to store brands.

Manufacturers of national brands are very frustrated by the growing power of retailers. As one executive remarks:

> A decade ago, the retailer was a chihuahua nipping at the manufacturer's heels—a nuisance, yes, but only a minor irritant. You fed it and it went away. Today it's a pit bull and it wants to rip your arms and legs off. You'd like to see it roll over, but you're too busy defending yourself to even try.[16]

Some marketing analysts predict that middlemen's brands eventually will knock out all but the strongest manufacturers' brands.

Manufacturers react by spending large amounts of money on consumer advertising and promotion to build strong brand preference. In turn, they must charge somewhat higher prices to cover this promotion. At the same time, the large retailers pressure them to spend more of their promotional money on trade allowances and deals if they want adequate shelf space. Once manufacturers start giving in to the trade, they have less to spend on consumer promotion and advertising, and their brand leadership starts slipping. This is the national brand manufacturers' dilemma.

To retain their power relative to the trade, leading brand marketers must invest in R&D to bring out new brands, new features, and continuous quality improvements. They must design strong advertising programs to maintain high brand awareness and preference. They must find ways to "partner" with major distributors in a search for distribution economies and competitive strategies that improve their joint performance. For example, P&G has assigned 20 of its managers to Wal-Mart headquarters in Bentonville, Arkansas, to work alongside Wal-Mart managers in a search for ways to improve their joint cost and competitive performance.

Brand Strategy

A company's new product activity consists of introducing *new brands, brand extensions* (brand names extended to new categories), or *line extensions* (brand names extended to new forms, sizes, and flavors of an existing brand).

New Brands. A company may create a new brand name when it enters a new product category for which none of the company's current brand names are appropriate. For example, Sears establishes separate family names for different product categories (Kenmore for appliances, Craftsman for tools, and Homart for major home installations). Alternatively, the company may enter an existing category, but seek to differentiate its new product for some reason. For example, the product may have higher or lower quality than the current brand. Seiko produces a line of lower-priced watches under the Pulsar brand name. Pulsar is used as a *flanker* or *fighter brand* targeted at customers who want a less expensive watch. Still another reason for introducing a new brand name is that the company wants to manage a stable of brand names within the category to suggest different functions or benefits (often called a **multibrand strategy**). Thus, Procter & Gamble produces nine brands of laundry detergents, each positioned on a different benefit.

Introducing multiple brands within a category can be risky—each brand might obtain only a small market share and none may be very profitable. The company will have spread its resources over several brands instead of building one or a few brands to a highly profitable level. Companies should weed out weaker brands and set high standards for choosing new brands. Ideally, a company's brands should take sales away from competitors' brands, not from each other.

Brand Extensions. A **brand-extension** strategy is any effort to use a successful brand name to launch new or modified products in a new category. Procter & Gamble put its Ivory name on dishwashing detergent, liquid hand soap, and shampoo with excellent results. Fruit of the Loom took advantage of its very high name recognition to launch new lines of socks, men's fashion underwear, and women's underwear. Honda uses its company name to cover such different products as its automobiles, motorcycles, snowblowers, lawn mowers, marine engines, and snowmobiles. This allows Honda to advertise that it can fit "six Hondas in a two-car garage."

Brands extensions: Companies increasingly are using established, successful brand names to launch products in new categories.

A brand extension strategy offers many advantages. A recent study found that brand extensions capture greater market share and realize greater advertising efficiency than individual brands.[17] A well-regarded brand name helps the company enter new product categories more easily and gives a new product instant recognition and faster acceptance. Sony puts its name on most of its new electronic products, creating an instant perception of high quality for each new product. Brand extensions also save the high advertising cost usually required to familiarize consumers with a new brand name.

At the same time, a brand extension strategy involves some risk. Brand extensions such as Bic pantyhose, Life Savers gum, and Clorox laundry detergent met early deaths. If an extension brand fails, it may harm consumer attitudes toward the other products carrying the same brand name. Further, a brand name may not be appropriate to a particular new product, even if it is well made and satisfying—would you consider buying Texaco milk or Alpo chile? And a brand name may lose its special positioning in the consumer's mind through overuse. *Brand dilution* occurs when consumers no longer associate a brand with a specific product or even highly similar products. Consider the contrast between how Hyatt and Marriott hotels are named:

> Hyatt practices a brand extension strategy. Its name appears in every hotel variation—Hyatt Resorts, Hyatt Regency, Hyatt Suites, and Park Hyatt. Marriott, in contrast, practices multibranding. Its various types of hotels are called Marriott Marquis, Marriott, Residence Inn, Courtyard, and Fairfield Inns. It is harder for Hyatt guests to know the differences between Hyatt hotel types, whereas Marriott more clearly aims its hotels at different segments and builds distinct brand names and images for each.

Transferring an existing brand name to a new category requires great care. For example, S. C. Johnson's popular shaving cream is called Edge. This name was successfully extended to its after-shave lotion. The name Edge probably could also be used to introduce a brand of razor blades if S. C. Johnson Company wanted to do this. However, the risk would increase if the company tried to use the Edge brand name to launch a new shampoo or toothpaste. Then Edge would lose its meaning as a name for shaving products. Companies that are tempted to transfer a brand name must research how well the brand's associations fit the new product. The best result would occur when a brand extension builds the sales of both the new product and existing products. An acceptable result would be when the new product sells well without affecting the sales of existing products. The worst result would be when the new product fails, or when it hurts the sales of the existing products.[18]

Line Extensions. **Line extensions** occur when a company introduces additional items in a given product category under the same brand name, such as new flavors, forms, colors, ingredients, or package sizes. Thus, Danon Company recently introduced several line extensions, including seven new yogurt flavors, a fat-free yogurt, and a large economy size yogurt.

The vast majority of new product activity consists of line extensions. For example, according to *Gorman's New Product News,* of the 6,125 new products accepted by grocery stores in the first five months of 1991, only 5 percent bore new brand names, 6 percent were brand extensions, and 89 percent were line extensions. A company might introduce line extensions for any of several reasons. It might want to meet the consumer desires for variety or it might recognize a latent consumer want and try to capitalize on it. Excess manufacturing capacity might drive the company to introduce additional items, or the company might want to match a competitor's successful line extension. Some companies introduce line extensions simply to command more shelf space from resellers.

Line extensions, like brand extensions, involve some risks. The brand name might lose its specific meaning—some marketing strategists call this the "line-extension trap."[19] In the past, when consumers asked for a Coke, they received a 6-ounce bottle of the classic beverage. Today the vendor has to ask: New, Classic, or Cherry Coke? Regular or diet? Caffeine or caffeine free? Bottle or can? Another risk is that many line extensions will not sell enough to cover their development and promotion costs. Or, even when they sell enough, the sales may come at the expense of other items in the line. A line extension works best when it takes sales away from competing brands, not when it "cannibalizes" the company's other items.

Brand Repositioning

However well a brand is initially positioned in a market, the company may have to reposition it later. A competitor may launch a brand positioned next to the company's brand and cut into its market share. Or customer wants may shift, leaving the company's brand with less demand. Marketers should consider repositioning existing brands before introducing new ones. In this way, they can build on existing brand recognition and consumer loyalty.

Repositioning may require changing both the product and its image. For example, Arrow added a new line of casual shirts before trying to change its image. Kentucky Fried Chicken changed its menu, adding lower-fat skinless chicken, and nonfried items such as broiled chicken and chicken salad sandwiches to reposition itself toward more health-conscious fast-food consumers. It even appears to be changing its name—to KFC. A brand also can be repositioned by changing only the product's image. Ivory Soap was repositioned without a physical change from a "baby soap" to an "all-natural soap" for adults who want healthy-looking skin. Similarly, Kraft repositioned Velveeta from a "cooking cheese" to a "good tasting, natural, and nutritious" snack cheese. Although the product remained unchanged, Kraft used new advertising appeals to change consumer perceptions of Velveeta. When repositioning a brand, the marketer must be careful not to lose or confuse current loyal users. When shifting Velveeta's position, Kraft made certain that the product's new position was compatible with its old one. Thus, Kraft kept loyal customers while attracting new users.[20]

Brand Name Selection

The brand name should be carefully chosen. A good name can add greatly to a product's success. Most large marketing companies have developed a formal, brand name selection process. Finding the best brand name is a difficult task. It begins with a careful review of the product and its benefits, the target market, and proposed marketing strategies.

Desirable qualities for a brand name include these: (1) It should suggest something about the product's benefits and qualities. Examples: Beautyrest, Craftsman, Sunkist, Spic and Span, Snuggles. (2) It should be easy to pronounce, recognize, and remember. Short names help. Examples: Tide, Aim, Puffs. But longer ones are sometimes effective. Examples: "Love My Carpet" carpet cleaner, "I Can't Believe It's Not Butter" margarine, Better Business Bureau. (3) The brand name should be distinctive. Examples: Taurus, Kodak, Exxon. (4) The name should translate easily into foreign languages. Before spending $100 million to change its name to Exxon, Standard Oil of New Jersey tested the name in 54 languages in more than 150 foreign markets. It found that the name Enco referred to a stalled engine when pronounced in Japanese. (5) It should be capable of registration and legal protection. A brand name cannot be registered if it infringes on existing brand names. Also, brand names that are merely descriptive or suggestive may be unprotectable. For example, the Miller Brewing Company registered the name Lite for its low-calorie beer and invested millions in establishing the name with consumers. But the courts later ruled that the terms *lite* and *light* are generic or common descriptive terms applied to beer and that Miller could not use the Lite name exclusively.[21]

Once chosen, the brand name must be protected. Many firms try to build a brand name that will eventually become identified with the product category. Brand names such as Frigidaire, Kleenex, Levi's, Jell-O, Scotch Tape, Formica, and Fiberglas have succeeded in this way. However, their very success may threaten the company's rights to the name. Many originally protected brand names, such as cellophane, aspirin, nylon, kerosene, linoleum, yo-yo, trampoline, escalator, thermos, and shredded wheat, are now names that any seller can use.[22]

Packaging Decisions

Many products offered to the market have to be packaged. Some marketers have called packaging a fifth *P*, along with price, product, place, and promotion. Most marketers, however, treat packaging as an element of product strategy.

Packaging includes the activities of designing and producing the container or wrapper for a product. The package may include the product's immediate container (the bottle holding Old Spice After-Shave Lotion); a secondary package that is thrown away when the product is about to be used (the cardboard box containing the bottle of Old Spice); and the shipping package necessary to store, identify, and ship the product (a corrugated box carrying six dozen bottles of Old Spice). Labeling is also part of packaging and consists of printed information appearing on or with the package.

Traditionally, packaging decisions were based primarily on cost and production factors; the primary function of the package was to contain and protect the product. In recent times, however, numerous factors have made packaging an important marketing tool. An increase in self-service means that packages now must perform many sales tasks—from attracting attention, to describing the product, to making the sale. Rising consumer affluence means that consumers are willing to pay a little more for the convenience, appearance, dependability, and prestige of better packages.

Companies are also realizing the power of good packaging to create instant consumer recognition of the company or brand. For example, in an average supermarket, which stocks 15,000 to 17,000 items, the typical shopper passes by some 300 items per minute, and 53 percent of all purchases are made on impulse. In this highly competitive environment, the package may be the seller's last chance to influence buyers. It becomes a "five-second commercial." The Campbell Soup Company estimates that the average shopper sees its familiar red and white can 76 times a year, creating the equivalent of $26 million worth of advertising.[23]

Innovative packaging can give a company an advantage over competitors. Liquid Tide quickly attained a 10 percent share of the heavy-duty detergent market, partly because of the popularity of its container's innovative drip-proof spout and cap. The first companies to put their fruit drinks in airtight foil and paper cartons (aseptic packages), and toothpastes in pump dispensers, attracted many new customers. In contrast, poorly designed packages can cause headaches for consumers and lost sales for the company (see Marketing Highlight 10-3).

In recent years, product safety has also become a major packaging concern. We have all learned to deal with hard-to-open "childproof" packages. And after the rash of product tampering scares during the 1980s, most drug producers and food makers are now putting their products in tamper-resistant packages.[24]

Developing a good package for a new product requires making many decisions. The first task is to establish the packaging concept. The **packaging concept** states what the package should *be* or *do* for the product. Should the main functions of the package be to offer product protection, introduce a new dispensing method, suggest certain qualities about the product or the company, or something else? Decisions then must be made on specific elements of the package, such as size, shape, materials, color, text, and brand mark. These various elements must work together to support the product's position and marketing strategy. The package must be consistent with the product's advertising, pricing, and distribution.

Companies usually consider several different package designs for a new product. To select the best package, they usually test the various designs to find the one that stands up best under normal use, is easiest for dealers to handle, and receives the most favorable consumer response. After selecting and introducing the package, the company should check it regularly in the face of changing consumer preferences and advances in technology. In the past, a package design

THOSE FRUSTRATING, NOT-SO-EASY-TO-OPEN PACKAGES

The following letter from an angry consumer to Robert D. Stuart, then chairman of Quaker Oats, beautifully expresses the utter frustration all of us have experienced in dealing with so-called easy-opening packages.

Dear Mr. Stuart:

I am an 86-year-old widow in fairly good health. (You may think of this as advanced age, but for me that description pertains to the years ahead. Nevertheless, if you decide to reply to this letter I wouldn't dawdle, actuarial tables being what they are.)

As I said, my health is fairly good. Feeble and elderly, as one understands these terms, I am not. My two Doberman Pinschers and I take a brisk 3-mile walk every day. They are two strong and energetic animals and it takes a bit of doing to keep "brisk" closer to a stroll than a mad dash. But I manage because as yet I don't lack the strength. You will shortly see why this fact is relevant.

I am writing to call your attention to the cruel, deceptive and utterly [false] copy on your Aunt Jemima buttermilk complete pancake and waffle mix. The words on your package read, "to open—press here and pull back."

Mr. Stuart, though I push and press and groan and strive and writhe and curse and sweat and jab and push, poke and ram . . . whew!—I have never once been able to do what the package instructs—to "press here and pull back" the [blankety-blank].

It can't be done! Talk about failing strength! Have you ever tried and succeeded?

My late husband was a gun collector who among other lethal weapons kept a Thompson machine gun in a locked cabinet. It was a good thing that the cabinet was locked. Oh, the number of times I was tempted to give your package a few short bursts.

That lock and a sense of ladylike delicacy kept me from pursuing that vengeful fantasy. Instead, I keep a small cleaver in my pantry for those occasions when I need to open a package of your delicious Aunt Jemima pancakes.

For many years that whacking away with my cleaver served a dual purpose. Not only to open the [blankety-blank] package but also to vent my fury at your sadists who willfully and maliciously did design that torture apparatus that passes for a package.

Sometimes just for the [blank] of it I let myself get carried away. I don't stop after I've lopped off the

An easy-to-open package?

top. I whack away until the package is utterly destroyed in an outburst of rage, frustration, and vindictiveness. I wind up with a floorful of your delicious Aunt Jemima pancake mix. But that's a small price to pay for blessed release. (Anyway, the Pinschers lap up the mess.)

So many ingenious, considerate (even compassionate) innovations in package closures have been designed since Aunt Jemima first donned her red bandana. Wouldn't you consider the introduction of a more humane package to replace the example of marketing malevolence to which you resolutely cling? Don't you care, Mr. Stuart?

I'm really writing this to be helpful and in that spirit I am sending a copy to Mr. Tucker, president of Container Corp. I'm sure their clever young designers could be of immeasurable help to you in this matter. At least I feel it's worth a try.

Really, Mr. Stuart, I hope you will not regard me as just another cranky old biddy. I am The Public, the source of your fortunes.

Ms. Roberta Pavloff
Malvern, Pa.

Source: This letter was reprinted in "Some Designs Should Just Be Torn Asunder," *Advertising Age,* January 17, 1983, p. M54.

might last for 15 years before it needed changes. However, in today's rapidly changing environment, most companies must recheck their packaging every two or three years.[25]

Keeping a package up to date usually requires only minor but regular changes—changes so subtle that they may go unnoticed by most consumers. But some packaging changes involve complex decisions, drastic action, high cost, and risk. For example, Campbell has for years been searching for a new container to replace its venerable old soup can. It has experimented with a variety of containers, such as a sealed plastic bowl that can be popped into a microwave oven to produce hot soup in a hurry with no can to open and no dishes to wash. Given Campbell's 80 percent share of the canned-soup market, the potential risks and benefits of changing the package are huge. Although eliminating the can could cut Campbell's packaging costs by as much as 15 percent, revamping production facilities would cost $100 million or more. And Campbell management estimates that the change would take at least five more years to implement. Finally, and perhaps most importantly, Campbell risks alienating loyal consumers who think of the familiar red and white can as an American tradition.

Cost remains an important packaging consideration. Developing the packaging for a new product may cost a few hundred thousand dollars and take from a few months to a year. Or, as in the Campbell example, converting to a new package may cost millions, and implementing a new package design may take several years. Marketers must weigh packaging costs against both consumer perceptions of value added by the packaging and the role of packaging in helping to attain marketing objectives. In making packaging decisions, the company also must heed growing environmental concerns about packaging and make decisions that serve society's interests as well as immediate customer and company objectives. However, determining just what serves the best interests of consumers can sometimes be tricky (see Marketing Highlight 10-4).

Labeling Decisions

Labels may range from simple tags attached to products to complex graphics that are part of the package. They perform several functions, and the seller has to decide which ones to use. At the very least, the label *identifies* the product or brand, such as the name Sunkist stamped on oranges. The label might also *grade* the product—canned peaches are grade-labeled A, B, and C. The label might *describe* several things about the product—who made it, where it was made, when it was made, its contents, how it is to be used, and how to use it safely. Finally, the label might *promote* the product through attractive graphics.

Labels of well-known brands may seem old-fashioned after a while and may need freshening up. For example, the label on Ivory Soap has been redone 18 times since the 1890s, but simply with gradual changes in the lettering. In contrast, the label on Orange Crush soft drink was changed substantially when its competitors' labels began to picture fresh fruits and pull in more sales. Orange Crush developed a label with new symbols and much stronger, deeper colors to suggest freshness and more orange flavor.

There has been a long history of legal concerns about labels. Labels can mislead customers, fail to describe important ingredients, or fail to include needed safety warnings. As a result, several federal and state laws regulate labeling, the most prominent being the Fair Packaging and Labeling Act of 1966. Labeling has been affected in recent times by *unit pricing* (stating the price per unit of standard measure), *open dating* (stating the expected shelf life of the product), and *nutritional labeling* (stating the nutritional values in the product). Sellers must ensure that their labels contain all the required information.

Product-Support Services Decisions

Customer service is another element of product strategy. A company's offer to the marketplace usually includes some services, which can be a minor or a major part of the total offer. In fact, the offer can range from a pure good on the one hand to a pure service on the other. In Chapter 22, we will discuss services as products in themselves. Here, we discuss **product-support services**—services that augment actual products. More and more companies are using product-support services as a major tool in gaining competitive advantage.

Good customer service is good for business. It costs less to keep the goodwill of existing customers than it does to attract new customers or woo back lost customers. Firms that provide high-quality service usually outperform their less service-oriented competitors. A study by the Strategic Planning Institute compared

MARKETING HIGHLIGHT 10-4

ASEPTIC PACKAGES: A FOOD-SCIENCE BREAKTHROUGH OR ENVIRONMENTAL THREAT?

Aseptic packages, those airtight foil and paper cartons containing individual servings of juice and other non-carbonated drinks, have been hailed by many as a food-science breakthrough. They are unbreakable, convenient to use, and easy to store, and they keep their contents fresh for several months without refrigeration. As a result, they have become very popular with consumers—more than $600 million worth of aseptic packages are sold in the United States each year.

However, their very popularity in school lunch pails and picnic baskets has made them *un*popular with environmentalists. In fact, just one year after aseptic packages appeared on supermarket shelves, the State of Maine moved to ban them. The packages are made of a six-layer sandwich of plastic, paper, and aluminum foil. This construction provides important benefits such as long shelf life, strength, and purity. But when empty, these packaging marvels become "mixed waste," the bane of recycling. They can't be easily recycled through most collection programs. Where should the empty drink cartons go? Do they belong in the plastics bin, with waste paper, or in the aluminum recycling pile? Even when collected, the tough little juice boxes pose a very difficult recycling challenge. And critics have some additional concerns. The arrival of the drink boxes on grocery store shelves has undermined recent state bottle deposit laws, which encourage recycling. Moreover, critics claim, teaching children to throw cartons away after just one use sends a bad message to tomorrow's consumers.

The industry counters that aseptic packages are actually environmentally sound. They can be compacted to take up much less landfill space than other packaging, and because they are lighter than glass bottles, they use less energy for transportation. Concerned with the possibility of further bans, aseptic packaging manufacturers began a pilot recycling program. They took out large newspaper advertisements claiming that "Drink boxes are as easy to recycle as this page." These claims landed them in court. The attorneys general of several states filed suit, pointing out that the drink-box recycling process is not economically viable. Recovering the wood pulp from aseptic packages requires an extensive soaking process. And although the boxes can be ground and mixed in with other plastics to make synthetic wood, such programs are not as widely available as are those that recycle plastic bottles into new plastic.

The debate continues with strong emotions on both sides. Is a small addition to the nation's landfills a reasonable price to pay for the safety and convenience of aseptic drink boxes? As is often the case in matters of public policy, there are many sides to the issue.

Sources: Gary McWilliams, "The Big Brouhaha Over the Little Juice Box," *Business Week,* September 17, 1990, p. 36; John Holusha, "Drink-Box Makers Fighting Back," *The New York Times,* December 15, 1990, pp. A33, A35; David Stipp, "Lunch-Box Staple Runs Afoul of Activists," *The Wall Street Journal,* March 14, 1991, pp. B1, B8; and Edward J. Stana, "Letter: Drink Box Can Help Reduce Landfill Need," *The Wall Street Journal,* April 8, 1991, p. A19.

---

the performance of businesses that had high customer ratings of service quality with those that had lower ratings. It found that the high-service businesses managed to charge more, grow faster, and make more profits.[26] Clearly, marketers need to think carefully about their service strategies.

Deciding on the Service Mix

A company should design its product and support services to meet the needs of target customers. Thus, the first step in deciding which product-support services to offer is to determine both the services that target consumers value and the relative importance of these services. Customers vary in the value they assign to different services. Some consumers want credit and financing services, fast and reliable delivery, or quick installation. Others put more weight on technical information and advice, training in product use, or after-sale service and repair.

Determining customers' service needs involves more than simply monitoring complaints that come in over toll-free telephone lines or on comment cards. The company should periodically survey its customers to get ratings of current services as well as ideas for new ones. For example, Cadillac holds regular focus-group interviews with owners and carefully watches complaints that come into its dealerships. From this careful monitoring, Cadillac has learned that buyers are very upset by repairs that are not done correctly the first time. As a result, the company has set up a system directly linking each dealership with a group of ten engineers who can help walk mechanics through difficult repairs. Such actions have helped Cadillac jump, in one year, from fourteenth to seventh in independent rankings of service.[27]

Products often can be designed to reduce the amount of required servicing. Thus, companies need to coordinate their product-design and service-mix decisions. For example, the Canon home copier uses a disposable toner cartridge that greatly reduces the need for service calls. Kodak and 3M are designing products that can be "plugged in" to a central diagnostic facility that performs tests, locates troubles, and fixes equipment over telephone lines. Thus, a key to successful service strategy is to design products that rarely break down and are easily fixable with little service expense.

Delivering Product-Support Services

Finally, companies must decide how they want to deliver product-support services to customers. For example, consider the many ways Maytag might offer repair services on its major appliances. It could hire and train its own service people and locate them across the country. It could arrange with distributors and dealers to provide the repair services, or it could leave it to independent companies to provide these services.

Most equipment companies start out adopting the first alternative, providing their own service. They want to stay close to the equipment and know its problems. They also find that they can make good money running the "parts and service business." As long as they are the only supplier of the needed parts, they can charge a premium price. Indeed, some equipment manufacturers make more than half of their profits in after-sale service.

Over time, producers shift more of the maintenance and repair service to authorized distributors and dealers. These middlemen are closer to customers, have more locations, and can offer quicker if not better service. The producer still makes a profit on selling the parts but leaves the servicing cost to middlemen.

Still later, independent service firms emerge. For example, more than 40 percent of all auto service work now is done outside of franchised automobile dealerships, by independent garages and by chains such as Midas Muffler, Sears, and Kmart. Such independent service firms have emerged in most industries. They typically offer lower cost or faster service than the manufacturer or authorized middlemen do.

Ultimately, some large customers start to handle their own maintenance and repair services. Thus, a company with several hundred personal computers, printers, and related equipment might find it cheaper to have its own service people on site.

The Customer Service Department

Given the importance of customer service as a marketing tool, many companies have set up strong customer service departments to handle complaints and adjustments, credit service, maintenance service, technical service, and consumer information. For example, Whirlpool, Procter & Gamble, and many other companies have set up hotlines to handle consumer complaints and requests for information. By keeping records on the types of requests and complaints, the customer service department can press for needed changes in product design, quality control, high-pressure selling, and so on. An active customer service department coordinates all the company's services, creates consumer satisfaction and loyalty, and helps the company to further set itself apart from competitors.

PRODUCT LINE DECISIONS

We have looked at product strategy decisions such as branding, packaging, labeling, and services for individual products. But product strategy also calls for building a product line. A **product line** is a group of products that are closely related because they function in a similar manner, are sold to the same customer groups, are marketed through the same types of outlets, or fall within given price ranges. For example, General Motors produces several lines of cars, Revlon produces several lines of cosmetics, and IBM produces several lines of computers. In developing product line strategies, marketers face a number of tough decisions on product line length and product line featuring.

Product Line-Length Decision

Product line managers have to decide on product line length. The line is too short if the manager can increase profits by adding items; the line is too long if the manager can increase profits by dropping items. Product line length is influenced by company objectives. Companies that want to be positioned as full-line companies or that are seeking high market share and market growth usually carry longer lines. They are less concerned when some items do not add to profits. Companies that are keen on high short-term profitability generally carry shorter lines consisting of selected items.

Product lines tend to lengthen over time. The product line manager will feel pressure to add new products to use up excess manufacturing capacity. The salesforce and distributors will be pressured by the manager for a more complete product line to satisfy their customers. The product line manager will want to add items to the product line to increase sales and profits.

However, as the manager adds items, several costs rise: design and engineering costs, inventory carrying costs, manufacturing changeover costs, order processing costs, transportation costs, and promotional costs to introduce new items. Eventually someone calls a halt to the mushrooming product line. Top management may freeze things because of insufficient funds or manufacturing capacity. Or the controller may question the line's profitability and call for a study. The study will probably show a number of money-losing items, and they will be pruned from the line in a major effort to increase profitability. A pattern of uncontrolled product line growth followed by heavy pruning is typical and may repeat itself many times.

The company must plan product line growth carefully. It can systematically increase the length of its product line in two ways: by *stretching* its line and by *filling* its line.

Product Line-Stretching Decision

Every company's product line covers a certain range of the products offered by the industry as a whole. For example, BMW automobiles are located in the medium-high price range of the automobile market. Toyota focuses on the low-to-medium price range. **Product line stretching** occurs when a company lengthens its product line beyond its current range. Figure 10-5 shows that the company can stretch its line downward, upward, or both ways.

Downward Stretch

Many companies initially locate at the upper end of the market and later stretch their lines downward. A company may stretch downward for any number of reasons. It may have first entered the upper end to establish a quality image and intended to roll downward later. It may respond to an attack on the upper end by invading the low end. Or a company may add a low-end product to plug a market hole that otherwise would attract a new competitor. It may find faster growth tak-

FIGURE 10–5 Product line-stretching decision

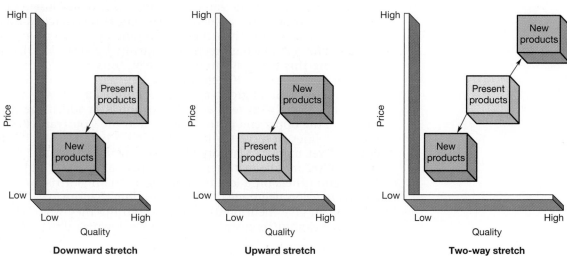

ing place at the low end. Thus, Compaq and IBM both added inexpensive personal computer lines to fend off competition from low-priced "clones" and to take advantage of faster market growth at the lower end of the market.

In making a downward stretch, the company faces some risks. The low-end item might provoke competitors to counteract by moving into the higher end. The company's dealers may not be willing or able to handle the lower-end products. Or the new low-end item might eat away at the sales of—*cannibalize*—the company's higher-end items, leaving the company worse off. Consider the following:

> General Electric's Medical Systems Division is the market leader in CAT scanners, expensive diagnostic machines used in hospitals. GE learned that a Japanese competitor was planning to attack its market. GE executives guessed that the new Japanese model would be smaller, more electronically advanced, and less expensive. GE's best defense would be to introduce a similar lower-priced machine before the Japanese model entered the market. But some GE executives expressed concerned that this lower-priced version would hurt the sales and higher profit margins on their large CAT scanner. One manager finally settled the issue by saying: "Aren't we better off to cannibalize ourselves than to let the Japanese do it?"

A major miscalculation of several American companies has been their failure to plug holes in the lower end of their markets. General Motors resisted building smaller cars, and Xerox resisted building smaller copying machines. Japanese companies found a major opening at the lower end and moved in quickly and successfully.

Upward Stretch

Companies at the lower end of the market may want to enter the higher end. They may be attracted by a faster growth rate or higher margins at the higher end, or they may simply want to position themselves as full-line manufacturers. For example, General Electric added its Monogram line of high-quality built-in kitchen appliances targeted at the select few households earning more than $100,000 a year and living in homes valued at over $400,000. Sometimes, companies stretch upward in order to add prestige to their current products, as when Chrysler purchased Lamborghini, the maker of exotic, handcrafted sports cars.

An upward stretch decision can be risky. The higher-end competitors not only are well entrenched, but also may strike back by entering the lower end of the market. Prospective customers may not believe that the newcomer can produce quality products. Finally, the company's salespeople and distributors may lack the talent and training to serve the higher end of the market.

Two-Way Stretch

Companies in the middle range of the market may decide to stretch their lines in both directions. Sony did this to hold off copycat competitors of its Walkman line of personal tape players. Sony introduced its first Walkman in the middle of the market. As imitative competitors moved in with lower-priced models, Sony stretched downward. At the same time, in order to add luster to its lower-price models and to attract more affluent consumers, Sony stretched the Walkman line upward. It now sells more than 100 models ranging from a plain-vanilla playback-only version for $32 to a high-tech, high-quality $450 version that both plays and records. Using this two-way stretch strategy, Sony now dominates the personal tape player market with a 30 percent share.

The Marriott Hotel group also has performed a two-way stretch of its hotel product line. Along with regular Marriott hotels, it added the Marriott Marquis line to serve the upper end of the market, and the Courtyard, Residence Inn, and Fairfield Inn lines to serve the lower end. Each branded hotel line is aimed at a different target market. Marriott Marquis aims to attract and please top executives; Marriotts, middle managers; Courtyards, salespeople; and Fairfield Inns, vacationers and others on a low travel budget. The major risk with this strategy is that some travelers will trade down after finding that the lower-price hotels in the Marriott chain give them pretty much everything they want. However, Marriott would rather capture its customers who move downward than lose them competitors.

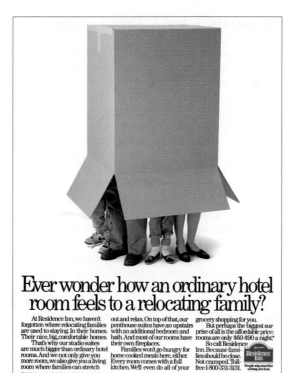

Ever wonder how an ordinary hotel room feels to a relocating family?

At Residence Inn, we haven't forgotten where relocating families are used to staying. In their homes. Their nice, big, comfortable homes.

That's why our studio suites are much bigger than ordinary hotel rooms. And we not only give you more room, we also give you a living room where families can stretch out and relax. On top of that, our penthouse suites have an upstairs with an additional bedroom and bath. And most of our rooms have their own fireplaces.

Families won't go hungry for home cooked meals here, either. Every room comes with a full kitchen. We'll even do all of your grocery shopping for you.

But perhaps the biggest surprise of all is the affordable price: rooms are only $60-$90 a night.*

So call Residence Inn. Because families should be close. Not cramped. Toll-free 1-800-331-3131.

Product line stretching: Marriott stretched its hotel product line to include several branded hotels aimed at a different target market. Residence Inn, for example, provides a "home away from home" for people who travel for a living, who are relocating, or who are on temporary assignment and need inexpensive, temporary lodging.

Product Line-Filling Decision

A product line can be lengthened by adding more items within the present range of the line. There are several reasons for **product line filling:** reaching for extra profits, trying to satisfy dealers, trying to use excess capacity, trying to be the leading full-line company, and trying to plug holes to keep out competitors. Thus, Sony filled its line by adding solar-powered and waterproof Walkmans and an ultralight model that attaches to a sweatband for joggers, bicyclers, tennis players, and other exercisers.

However, line filling is overdone if it results in cannibalization and customer confusion. The company should ensure that new items are noticeably different from existing ones.

Product Line-Modernization Decision

In some cases, product line length is adequate, but the line needs to be modernized. For example, a company's machine tools may have a 1950s look and lose out to better-styled competitors' lines.

The central issue in product line modernization is whether to overhaul the line piecemeal or all at once. A piecemeal approach allows the company to see how customers and dealers like the new styles before changing the whole line. Piecemeal modernization also causes less drain on the company's cash flow. A major disadvantage of piecemeal modernization is that it allows competitors to see changes and start redesigning their own lines.

Product Line-Featuring Decision

The product line manager typically selects one or a few items in the line to feature. This is **product line featuring.** Sometimes, managers feature promotional models at the low end of the line to serve as "traffic builders." For example, Sears might advertise a special low-priced sewing machine to attract shoppers. And Rolls Royce announced an "economy model" selling for only $125,000, in contrast to its high-end model selling for over $200,000, to bring people into its showrooms.

At other times, managers feature a high-end item to give the product line "class." For example, Audimar Piguet advertises a $25,000 watch which few people buy, but which acts as a "flagship" to enhance the whole line.

PRODUCT MIX DECISIONS

An organization with several product lines has a product mix. A **product mix** (or **product assortment**) is the set of all product lines and items that a particular seller offers for sale. Avon's product mix consists of four major product lines: cosmetics, jewelry, fashions, and household items. Each product line consists of several sublines. For example, cosmetics breaks down into lipstick, rouge, powder, and so on. Each line and subline has many individual items. Altogether, Avon's product mix includes 1,300 items. In contrast, a large supermarket handles as many as 17,000 items; a typical Kmart stocks 15,000 items; and General Electric manufactures as many as 250,000 items.

A company's product mix has four important dimensions: width, length, depth, and consistency. Table 10-1 illustrates these concepts with selected Procter & Gamble consumer products.

The *width* of P&G's product mix refers to the number of different product lines the company carries. Table 10-1 shows a product mix width of six lines. (In fact, P&G produces many more lines, including mouthwashes, paper towels, disposable diapers, pain relievers, and cosmetics.)

The *length* of P&G's product mix refers to the total number of items the company carries. In Table 10-1, the total number of items is 42. We can also compute the average length of a line at P&G by dividing the total length (here 42) by the number of lines (here 6). In Table 10-1, the average P&G product line consists of 7 brands.

The *depth* of P&G's product mix refers to the number of versions offered of each product in the line. Thus, if Crest comes in three sizes and two formulations (paste and gel), Crest has a depth of six. By counting the number of versions within each brand, we can calculate the average depth of P&G's product mix.

The *consistency* of the product mix refers to how closely related the various product lines are in end use, production requirements, distribution channels, or in some other way. P&G's product lines are consistent insofar as they are consumer goods that go through the same distribution channels. The lines are less consistent insofar as they perform different functions for buyers.

These product mix dimensions provide the handles for defining the company's product strategy. The company can increase its business in four ways. It can add new product lines, thus widening its product mix. In this way, its new

---

TABLE 10-1
Product Mix Width and Product Line Length Shown for Selected Procter & Gamble Products

◄——————————————— PRODUCT MIX WIDTH ———————————————►

	Detergents	Toothpaste	Bar Soap	Deodorants	Fruit Juices	Lotions
PRODUCT LINE LENGTH	Ivory Snow	Gleem	Ivory	Secret	Citrus Hill	Wondra
	Dreft	Crest	Camay	Sure	Sunny Delight	Noxema
	Tide	Complete	Lava		Winter Hill	Oil of Olay
	Joy	Denquel	Kirk's		Texsun	Camay
	Cheer		Zest		Lincoln	Raintree
	Oxydol		Safeguard		Speas Farm	Tropic Tan
	Dash		Coast			Bain de Soleil
	Cascade		Oil of Olay			
	Ivory Liquid					
	Gain					
	Dawn					
	Era					
	Bold 3					
	Liquid Tide					
	Solo					

lines build on the company's reputation in its other lines. The company can lengthen its existing product lines to become a more full-line company. Or it can add more product versions of each product and thus deepen its product mix. Finally, the company can pursue more product line consistency—or less—depending on whether it wants to have a strong reputation in a single field or in several fields.

INTERNATIONAL PRODUCT DECISIONS

International marketers face special product and packaging challenges. First, they must figure out what products to introduce in which countries. Then, they must decide how much to standardize or adapt their products for world markets. On the one hand, companies would like to standardize their offerings. Standardization helps a company to develop a consistent worldwide image. It also results in lower manufacturing costs and eliminates duplication of research and development, advertising, and product design efforts. On the other hand, consumers around the world differ in their cultures, attitudes, and buying behaviors. And markets vary in their economic conditions, competition, legal requirements, and physical environments. Companies usually must respond to these differences by adapting their product offerings. Something as simple as an electrical outlet can create big product problems:

> Those who have traveled to Europe know the frustration of electrical plugs, different voltages, and other annoyances of international travel. . . . Philips, the electrical appliance manufacturer, has to produce 12 kinds of irons to serve just its European market. The problem is that Europe does not have a universal [electrical] standard. The ends of irons bristle with different plugs for different countries. Some have three prongs, others two; prongs protrude straight or angled, round or rectangular, fat, thin, and sometimes sheathed. There are circular plug faces, squares, pentagons, and hexagons. Some are perforated and some are notched. One French plug has a niche like a keyhole; British plugs carry fuses.[28]

Packaging also presents new challenges for international marketers. Penn Racquet Sports found this out when it attempted to launch its line of tennis balls in Japan in a "traditional" three-ball can. After netting an initial 8 percent market share, Penn's Japanese sales quickly plummeted to less than 1 percent. The problem: poor packaging. Whereas Americans play with three balls, the Japanese use only two. Explains one Penn manager, "The Japanese thought a three-ball can was a discount, and they passed us over. Our big mistake was that we didn't know the market." Penn redesigned its package and sales recovered. It now designs its containers to fit the needs of each market: Japan gets a two-ball can, whereas Australia and Europe receive four-ball plastic tubes.[29]

Packaging issues can be subtle. For example, names, labels, and colors may not translate easily from one country to another. A firm using yellow flowers in its logo might fare well in the United States, but meet with disaster in Mexico, where a yellow flower symbolizes death or disrespect. Similarly, although "Nature's Gift" might be an appealing name for gourmet mushrooms in America, it would be deadly in Germany, where "gift" means "poison." Consumers in different countries vary in their packaging preferences. Europeans like efficient, functional, recyclable boxes with understated designs. In contrast, the Japanese often use packages as gifts. Thus, in Japan, Lever Brothers packages its Lux soap in stylish gift boxes. Packaging even may have to be tailored to meet the physical characteristics of consumers in various parts of the world. For instance, soft drinks are sold in smaller cans in Japan to better fit the smaller Japanese hand.

Companies may have to adapt their packaging to meet specific regulations regarding package design or label contents. For instance, some countries ban the use of any foreign language on labels; other countries require that labels be printed in two or more languages. Labeling laws vary change greatly from country to country:

> In Saudi Arabia . . . product names must be specific. "Hot Chili" will not do, it must be "Spiced Hot Chili." Prices are required to be printed on the labels in Venezuela, but

SOCIALLY RESPONSIBLE PRODUCT AND PACKAGING DECISIONS

Product and packaging decisions are attracting increasing public attention. When making such decisions, marketers should consider carefully the following issues and regulations.

Product Decisions and Public Policy

Product Additions and Deletions. Under the Antimerger Act, the government may prevent companies from adding products through acquisitions if the effect threatens to lessen competition. Companies dropping products must be aware that they have legal obligations, written or implied, to their suppliers, dealers, and customers who have a stake in the discontinued product.

Patent Protection. A firm must obey the U.S. patent laws when developing new products. A company cannot make its product "illegally similar" to another company's established product. An example is Polaroid's successful suit to prevent Kodak from selling its new instant-picture camera on the grounds that it infringed on Polaroid's instant-camera patents.

Product Quality and Safety. Manufacturers must comply with specific laws regarding product quality and safety. The Federal Food, Drug, and Cosmetic Act protects consumers from unsafe and adulterated food, drugs, and cosmetics. Various acts provide for the inspection of sanitary conditions in the meat- and poultry-processing industries. Safety legislation has been passed to regulate fabrics, chemical substances, automobiles, toys, and drugs and poisons. The Consumer Product Safety Act of 1972 established a Consumer Product Safety Commission, which has the authority to ban or seize potentially harmful products and set severe penalties for violation of the law. If consumers have been injured by a product that has been designed defectively, they can sue manufacturers or dealers. Product liability suits now are occurring at the rate of over one million per year, with individual awards often running in the millions of dollars. This phenomenon has resulted in huge increases in product-liability insurance premiums, causing big problems in some industries. Some companies pass these higher rates along to consumers by raising prices. Others are forced to discontinue high-risk product lines. For example, the U.S. small-airplane industry has been virtually wiped out. Cessna Aircraft, once the dominant worldwide leader, stopped making small planes in 1986. Piper Aircraft entered bankruptcy in mid-1991. Under the onslaught of product-liability lawsuits and high insurance premiums, these companies simply could not produce an airplane at prices that customers would be willing to pay. The cost of liability insurance for producers of children's car seats rose from $50,000 in 1984 to over $750,000 in 1986.

Product Warranties. Many manufacturers offer written product warranties to convince customers of their products' quality. But these warranties are often limited and written in a language the average consumer does not understand. Too often, consumers learn that they are not entitled to services, repairs, and replacements that seem to be implied. To protect consumers, Congress passed the Magnuson-Moss Warranty Act in 1975. The act requires that full warranties meet certain minimum standards, including repair "within a reasonable time and without charge" or a replacement or full refund if the product does not work "after a reasonable number of attempts" at repair. Otherwise, the company

---

in Chile, it is illegal to put prices on labels or in any way suggest retail prices. Coca-Cola ran into a legal problem in Brazil with its Diet Coke. Brazilian law interprets "diet" to have medicinal qualities. Under the law, producers must give daily recommended consumption on the label of all medicines. Coke had to get special approval to get around this restriction.[30]

Thus, although product and package standardization can produce benefits, companies usually must adapt their offerings to serve the unique needs and requirements of specific international markets.

In summary, whether domestic or international, product strategy calls for complex decisions on product mix, product line, branding, packaging, and service strategy. These decisions must be made not only with a full understanding of consumer wants and competitors' strategies but also with increasing attention to the growing public policy affecting product and packaging decisions (see Marketing Highlight 10-5).

must make it clear that it is offering only a limited warranty. The law has led several manufacturers to switch from full to limited warranties and others to drop warranties altogether as a marketing tool.

Packaging Decisions and Public Policy

Fair Packaging and Labeling. The public is concerned about false and potentially misleading packaging and labeling. The Federal Trade Commission Act of 1914 held that false, misleading, or deceptive labels or packages constitute unfair competition. Consumers also are concerned about confusing package sizes and shapes that make price comparisons difficult. The Fair Packaging and Labeling Act, passed by Congress in 1967, set mandatory labeling requirements, encouraged voluntary industry packaging standards, and allowed federal agencies to set packaging regulations in specific industries. The Food and Drug Administration has required processed-food producers to include nutritional labeling that clearly states the amounts of protein, fat, carbohydrates, and calories contained in products, as well as their vitamin and mineral content as a percentage of the recommended daily allowance. The FDA recently has launched a drive to control health claims in food labeling by taking action against the potentially misleading use of such descriptions as "light," "high fiber," "no cholesterol," and others. Consumerists have lobbied for additional labeling laws to require *open dating* (to describe product freshness), *unit pricing* (to state the product cost in some standard measurement unit), *grade labeling* (to rate the quality level of certain consumer goods), and *percentage labeling* (to show the percentage of each important ingredient).

Excessive Cost. Critics have claimed that excessive packaging on some products raises prices. They point to secondary "throwaway" packaging and question its value to the consumer. They note that the package sometimes costs more than the contents; for example, Evian moisturizer consists of five ounces of natural spring water packaged as an aerosol spray selling for $5.50. Marketers respond that they also want to keep packaging costs down, but that the critics do not understand all the functions of the package.

Scarce Resources. The growing concern over shortages of paper, aluminum, and other materials suggests that marketers should try harder to reduce their packaging. For example, the growth of nonreturnable glass containers has resulted in using up to 17 times as much glass as with returnable containers. Glass and other throwaway bottles also waste energy. Some states have passed laws prohibiting or taxing nonreturnable containers.

Pollution. As much as 40 percent of the total solid waste in this country is made up of package material. Many packages end up as broken bottles and crumpled cans littering the streets and countryside. All of this packaging creates a major problem in solid waste disposal, requiring huge amounts of labor and energy.

These packaging questions have mobilized public interest in new packaging laws. Marketers must be equally concerned. They must try to design fair, economical, and ecological packages for their products.

Sources: See Louis W. Stern and Thomas L. Eovaldi, *Legal Aspects of Marketing Strategy* (Englewood Cliffs, NJ: Prentice Hall, 1984), pp. 76-116; Marisa Manley, "Product Liability: You're More Exposed Than You Think," *Harvard Business Review,* September-October 1987, pp. 28-40; Timothy K. Smith, "Liability Costs Drive Small-Plane Business Back into Pilot's Barns," *The Wall Street Journal,* December 11, 1991, pp. A1, A10; and John Carey, "Food Labeling: The FDA Has the Right Ingredients," *Business Week,* November 23, 1992, p. 42.

SUMMARY

Product is a complex concept that must be defined carefully. Product strategy calls for making coordinated decisions on product items, product lines, and the product mix.

Each product item offered to customers can be viewed on three levels. The *core product* is the essential benefit the customer is really buying. The *actual product* includes the features, styling, quality, brand name, and packaging of the product offered for sale. The *augmented product* is the actual product plus the various services offered with it, such as warranty, installation, maintenance, and free delivery.

All products can be classified into three groups according to their durability or tangibility (nondurable goods, durable goods, and services). *Consumer goods* are usually classified according to consumer shopping habits (convenience goods, shopping goods, specialty goods, and unsought goods). *Industrial goods* are classified according to their cost and the way they enter the production process (materials and parts, capital items, and supplies and services).

Companies have to develop strategies for the items in their product lines. They must decide on product attributes, branding, packaging, labeling, and product-support services. *Product attribute decisions* involve the product quality, features, and design the company will offer. Regarding *brands,* the company must decide on branding versus no branding, brand sponsorship, brand strategy, and brand repositioning.

Products also require *packaging decisions* to create benefits such as protection, economy, convenience, and promotion. Marketers have to develop a packaging concept and test it to be sure that it both achieves desired objectives and is compatible with public policy.

Products also require *labeling* for identification and

possible grading, description, and promotion of the product. Laws in the United States require sellers to present certain minimum information on the label to inform and protect consumers.

Companies have to develop *product-support services* that are desired by customers and effective against competitors. The company must determine the most important services to offer and the best ways to deliver these services. The *service mix* can be coordinated by a customer service department that handles complaints and adjustments, credit, maintenance, technical service, and customer information. *Customer service* should be used as a marketing tool to create customer satisfaction and competitive advantage.

Most companies produce a product line instead of a single product. A *product line* is a group of products that are related in function, customer-purchase needs, or distribution channels. Each product line requires a product strategy. *Line stretching* raises the question of whether a line should be extended downward, upward, or in both directions. *Line filling* raises the question of whether additional items should be added within the present range of the line. *Line featuring* raises the question of which items to feature in promoting the line.

Product mix describes the set of product lines and items offered to customers by a particular seller. The product mix can be described by four dimensions: width, length, depth, and consistency. These dimensions are the tools for developing the company's product strategy.

KEY TERMS

Actual product 277

Augmented product 277

Brand 285

Brand equity 286

Brand extension 291

Capital items 280

Consumer goods 278

Convenience goods 278

Core product 276

Durable goods 278

Industrial goods 279

Line extension 292

Manufacturer's brand (or national brand) 289

Materials and parts 280

Multibrand strategy 291

Nondurable goods 278

Packaging 294

Packaging concept 294

Private brand 289

Product 276

Product design 284

Product line 298

Product line featuring 301

Product line filling 301

Product line stretching 299

Product mix (or product assortment) 302

Product quality 281

Product-support services 296

Services 278

Shopping goods 279

Slotting fees 290

Specialty goods 279

Supplies and services 280

Unsought goods 279

DISCUSSING THE ISSUES

1. What are the core, tangible, and augmented products of the educational experience that universities offer?

2. How would you classify the product offered by restaurants: as nondurable goods or as services? Why?

3. In recent years, U.S. auto makers have tried to reposition many of their brands to the high-quality end of the market. How well have they succeeded? What else could they do to change consumers' perceptions of their cars?

4. Why are many people willing to pay more for branded products than for unbranded products? What does this tell you about the value of branding?

5. For many years there was one type of Coca-Cola, one type of Tide, and one type of Crest (in mint and regular). Now we find Coke in six or more varieties; Ultra, Liquid, and Unscented Tide; and Crest Gel with sparkles for kids. What issues do these brand extensions raise for manufacturers, retailers, and consumers?

6. Compare brand extension by the brand owner with licensing a brand name for use by another company. What are the opportunities and risks of each approach?

APPLYING THE CONCEPTS

1. Different areas of a town may attract different sorts of businesses. (a) Go to your local mall and find the direc-

tions kiosk. Look at the map and count the number of retail outlets for each type of consumer good: convenience, shopping, specialty, or unsought goods. (Often the map index is organized into categories that are helpful for this task.) (b) Drive down the road that serves as your local commercial "strip" and do a quick count in the same categories. (c) Calculate what percentage of businesses fall into each category for the two areas. Do you see any differences? If so, why do you think these differences exist?

2. Go to the area of your town that has a number of fast-food outlets. Compare the product mix of McDonald's to Kentucky Fried Chicken. Are there differences in width or depth? How could they stretch their lines upward or downward?

MAKING MARKETING DECISIONS:

SMALL WORLD COMMUNICATIONS, INC.

Lynette Jones and Thomas Campbell are very encouraged about the prospects for Small World Communications. They made a range of sales forecasts for the company: a conservative forecast, their "best guess," and a "wildly optimistic" projection. Then Lyn made financial estimates, and she found that Small World could be profitable at any of these sales levels *if* they did a careful job of management and budgeting. ("But that's a 'big if,' as we say in Fond du Lac," Lyn told Tom. "You guys can really turn a phrase up there," Tom replied. "Well," said Lyn, "my classic American vernacular may not be elegant, but at least I don't keep quoting Jerry Garcia and various grunge bands nobody's heard of." "Please don't murder me," he said. "Let's pack it up and see what tomorrow brings. I'll talk to you in the morning.")

Computer users are very positive towards their basic concept of an all-in-one communications hookup, and they now need to make a branding decision. Tom was talking to Lyn, "I've been thinking about our product, and the benefits it offers. We need a brand name that tells users what we do, but it shouldn't be boring. I got an idea: We're carrying information just like planes and trains and trucks carry people and freight. We call the basic product something like 'Airport.' O.K., that sounds a little lame, but the add-on names for our other features and software could be great. Our diagnostic program, telling users how to set it all up, could be 'Port Authority.' We could use terms like *terminal, concourse, hub, control tower, arrival, departure . . .*" Lyn was impressed that he was thinking in marketing terms. "And to bring it into the real world," she said, "we could use realistic words like *delay, cancellation, layover,* and *rerout-*

ing. It really could work. I'll play with the idea for a while, and get back to you."

WHAT NOW?

1. Put yourself in Lyn's place. You are the chief marketer for Small World, and you want to successfully launch your first product. (a) Would you create a new brand name, license a existing brand name, seek an endorsement (such as certification that the product is approved by Novell for use on their networks), or set up a joint venture with an existing well-known company (such as Microsoft, CompuServe, or Peter Norton)? (b) What are the trade-offs in each of these options?

2. Tom has suggested a range of words as possible brand names. You may like his suggestions, or you may not. Can you pick a better name? (a) Draw three columns on a sheet of paper. In the first column, make a list of at least ten possible brand names for the Small World product. Try to include some names that are very technical sounding, some that are very fanciful, and some that are in between. (b) Take the list you just made and label the second and third columns *technically-oriented users* and *nontechnical users*. Think about how much these groups of users might like each brand name. Fill in the columns by rating each brand name on a 1 to 10 scale for both sets of users. Do you see anything interesting about your results?

REFERENCES

1. See "What Lies Behind the Sweet Smell of Success," *Business Week,* February 27, 1984, pp. 139-43; S. J. Diamond, "Perfume Equals Part Mystery, Part Marketing," *Los Angeles Times,* April 22, 1988, Sec. 4, p. 1; Pat Sloan, "Revlon Leads New Fragrance Charge," *Advertising Age,* July 16, 1990, p. 14; and Joanne Lip man, "Big 'Outsert' Really Puts Revlon in Vogue," *The Wall Street Journal,* September 17, 1992, p. B6.

2. See Peter D. Bennett, *Dictionary of Marketing Terms* (Chicago: American Marketing Association, 1988).

3. See Bennett, *Dictionary of Marketing Terms.* For more information on product classifications, see Patrick E. Murphy and Ben

M. Enis, "Classifying Products Strategically," *Journal of Marketing,* July 1986, pp. 24-42.

4. Otis Port, "The Quality Imperative: Questing for the Best," *Business Week,* special issue on quality, 1991, pp. 7-16.

5. Ibid., p. 7.

6. B. G. Yovovich, "Motorola's Quest for Quality," *Business Marketing,* September 1991, p. 15.

7. David A. Garvin, "Competing on Eight Dimensions of Quality," *Harvard Business Review,* November-December 1987, p. 109. Also see Robert Jacobson and David A. Aaker, "The Strate-

gic Role of Product Equality," *Journal of Marketing,* October 1987, pp. 31-44; and Frank Rose, "Now Quality Means Service Too," *Fortune,* April 22, 1992, pp. 97-108.

8. For more on design, see Philip Kotler, "Design: A Powerful but Neglected Strategic Tool," *Journal of Business Strategy,* Fall 1984, pp. 16-21; "Competing by Design," *Business Week,* March 25, 1991, pp. 51-63; Brian Dumaine, "Design that Sells and Sells and . . . ," *Fortune,* March 11, 1991, pp. 86-94; and Stephen Potter, et. al, *The Benefits and Costs of Investment in Design: Using Professional Design Expertise in Product, Engineering and Graphics Projects,* (Manchester, UK: The Open University/UMIST, September 1991).

9. Pete Engardio, "Quick, Name Five Taiwanese PC Makers," *Business Week,* May 18, 1992, pp. 128-29.

10. See Bennett, *Dictionary of Marketing Terms.*

11. From a presentation delivered at Northwestern University by Larry Light, former international division chairman of Ted Bates Advertising, October 27, 1992.

12. David A. Aaker, *Managing Brand Equity* (New York: The Free Press, 1991).

13. See Patrick Barwise, et al., *Accounting for Brands* (London: Institute of Chartered Accountants in England and Wales, 1990); Peter H. Farquhar, Julia Y. Han, and Yuji Ijiri, "Brands on the Balance Sheet," *Marketing Management,* Winter 1992, pp. 16-22; and Kevin Lane Keller, "Conceptualizing, Measuring, and Managing Customer-Based Brand Equity," *Journal of Marketing,* January 1993, pp. 1-22.

14. Wendy Zellner, "The Sam's Generation?" *Business Week,* November 25, 1991, pp. 36-38; and Jennifer Lawrence, "Wal-Mart Expands Sam's Choice Line," *Advertising Age,* April 27, 1992, p. 4.

15. See Chip Walker, "What's in a Brand?" *American Demographics,* February 1991, pp. 54-56; Julie Liesse, "Making a Name for Selves," *Advertising Age,* May 6, 1991, p. 36; Jennifer Lawrence, "P&G Battles Private Labels with New Products," *Advertising Age,* March 16, 1992, pp. 3, 49 and "Retailers Hungry for Store Brands," *Advertising Age,* Jan. 11, 1993, p. 20.

16. Kevin Price, quoted in "Trade Promotion: Much Ado About Nothing," *Promo,* October 1991, p. 37.

17. Daniel C. Smith and C. Whan Park, "The Effects of Brand Extensions on Market Share and Advertising Efficiency," *Journal*

of Marketing Research, August 1992, pp. 296-313.

18. For more on consumer attitudes toward brand extensions, see David A. Aaker and Kevin L. Keller, "Consumer Evaluations of Brand Extensions," *Journal of Marketing,* January 1990, pp. 27-41.

19. Al Ries and Jack Trout, *Positioning: The Battle for Your Mind* (New York: McGraw-Hill, 1981).

20. See Christopher Power, "And Now, Finger-Lickin' Good for Ya?" *Business Week,* February 18, 1991, p. 60; and Gary Strauss, "Building on Brand Names: Companies Freshen Old Product Lines," *USA Today,* March 20, 1992, pp. 1, 2.

21. Thomas M. S. Hemnes, "How Can You Find a Safe Trademark?" *Harvard Business Review,* March-April 1985, p. 44.

22. For a discussion of legal issues surrounding the use of brand names, see Dorothy Cohen, "Trademark Strategy," *Journal of Marketing,* January 1986, pp. 61-74; "Trademark Woes: Help Is Coming," *Sales & Marketing Management,* January 1988, p. 84; and Jack Alexander, "What's in a Name? Too Much, Said the FCC," *Sales & Marketing Management,* January 1989, pp. 75-78.

23. See Bill Abrams, "Marketing," *The Wall Street Journal,* May 20, 1982, p. 33; and Bernice Kanner, "Package Deals," *New York,* August 22, 1988, pp. 267-68.

24. See Fred W. Morgan, "Tampered Goods: Legal Developments and Marketing Guidelines," *Journal of Marketing,* April 1988, pp. 86-96.

25. See Alicia Swasy, "Sales Lost Their Vim? Try Repackaging," *The Wall Street Journal,* October 11, 1989, p. B1.

26. Bro Uttal, "Companies That Serve You Best," *Fortune,* December 7, 1987, pp. 98-116. Also see William H. Davidow, "Customer Service: The Ultimate Marketing Weapon," *Business Marketing,* October 1989, pp. 56-64; and Barry Farber and Joyce Wycoff, "Customer Service: Evolution and Revolution," *Sales & Marketing Management,* May 1991, pp. 44-51.

27. Bro Uttal, "Companies That Serve You Best," p. 116.

28. Philip Cateora, *International Marketing,* 7th ed. (Homewood, IL: Irwin, 1990), p. 260.

29. David J. Morrow, "Sitting Pretty: How to Make Your Package Stand Out in a Crowd," *International Business,* November 1991, pp. 30-32.

30. Cateora, *International Marketing,* p. 426.

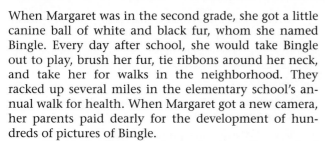

VIDEO CASE 10

A LONG AND HAPPY LIFE FOR BINGLE

When Margaret was in the second grade, she got a little canine ball of white and black fur, whom she named Bingle. Every day after school, she would take Bingle out to play, brush her fur, tie ribbons around her neck, and take her for walks in the neighborhood. They racked up several miles in the elementary school's annual walk for health. When Margaret got a new camera, her parents paid dearly for the development of hundreds of pictures of Bingle.

All of her life, Bingle received quality medical care. She had regular checkups and got shots (which she

hated) on time. When she was six, the vet discovered she had kidney stones and surgically removed them. By the time she was ten, one of her spinal disks had partially degenerated, and she sometimes needed shots to ease the pain. At twelve, she developed cancer, which required fairly expensive treatment. Bingle was fortunate that Margaret's parents were able to pay for her health care. As a result, Bingle lived a long and happy thirteen years.

However, many pet owners can't afford the cost of animal medical care. A regular visit to the vet can cost from $40 to $80. If there's a problem, hospitalization and workup charges can be quite high. For example, removing a brain tumor costs about $4,000 for treatment that includes magnetic resonance imaging and surgery. Accidents can also be expensive. Consider the recent treatment of a dog that swallowed a live frog. The dog and frog (still alive) turned out fine, but the owner had to swallow a $1,150 bill for the surgery.

Because of high health-care costs, many beloved pets fall victim to euthanasia. Knowing that modern medical treatments such as magnetic resonance imaging, CAT scans, radiation treatments, chemotherapy, and sophisticated laboratory tests are readily available to extend and ease their pets' lives only adds to the owner's heartbreak over the loss.

Some insurance companies have traditionally offered coverage for income-producing animals such as racehorses and livestock. Only recently, however, have they realized the potential of insuring household pets. The market is huge—nearly 110 million household pets (over 52 million dogs and 55 million cats). Most have no medical or health protection except what their owners can afford. Moreover, members of this potential market present a good risk—they don't smoke, drink, or drive. Whereas many of them are children's pets, others are a primary source of companionship, protection, and joy to elderly or single people. These owners have a strong and compelling need to provide health care for their furry companions.

Although companies such as Veterinary Pet Insurance (VPI) of Anaheim, California, have offered coverage of household pets for years, such insurance was considered an oddity. But that seems to be changing. Major insurer Fireman's Fund now has entered the market with Medipet. Medipet Plan A, with a $99 annual premium and a modest $50 deductible, pays 70 percent of pet care bills up to $1,000. Medipet Plan B, with its $42 annual premium and $250 deductible, pays 70 percent up to $2,500. How much do these plans benefit owners? For treatment costing $1,031, the owner's outlay would be only $344 under Medipet Plan A, and $484 under Plan B. In 1992, Medipet was available for pets ten years old and older in all states except Tennessee. VPI was available in 34 states.

To launch Medipet, Fireman's Fund used a series of direct mail campaigns targeted to 600,000 households. It reached an additional 20 million viewers with half-hour infomercials on cable television. Veterinary Pet Insurance (VPI) has also stepped up its sales efforts, with stunning results. VPI's sales surged to 90,000 policies in 1991—up 20 percent.

Many experts think that the future looks very bright for pet insurance sales. Others aren't so certain. Critics such as Robert Hunter of the National Insurance Consumer Organization and economist Orin Kramer of Princeton claim that insurance coverage will encourage an escalating spiral of higher costs. Insurance coverage, they claim, will motivate owners to agree to expensive treatments that they would not otherwise accept. As a result, everyone's animal care costs will increase and so will insurance premiums. Veterinarians would make more money and applications to veterinary school would rise.

Even if their forecasts prove accurate, pet owners may not see an alternative. Just ask Margaret. She won't hesitate to tell you that Bingle's well-being was worth every penny that it cost.

QUESTIONS

1. Describe the core, actual, and augmented product characteristics of pet insurance.

2. What type of consumer good is pet insurance? Is this changing?

3. What product quality, features, packaging, and labeling issues surround pet insurance? How will these change as more insurance companies offer such insurance?

4. What brand strategy did Fireman's Fund use? What brand strategy might a firm such as Prudential use? How might this strategy affect brand equity?

Sources: William A. Carl, "Finishing in the Money with Horse Mortality Insurance," *American Agent & Broker,* March 1991, pp. 45-48; Peter Kerr, "A New Health-Care Crisis Underfoot," *The New York Times,* February 15, 1992, pp. A1, A50; Barbara Morris, "Uncommon Perils," *Insurance Review,* March 1989, pp. 37-41; and Candyce H. Stapen, "Insuring Your Pet's Health," *Better Homes and Gardens,* November 1992, p. 204.

COMPANY CASE 10

COLGATE: SQUEEZING MORE FROM A BRAND NAME

You probably know about Colgate toothpaste—perhaps you've even used it. But what would you think of Colgate aspirin or Colgate antacid? How about Colgate laxative or Colgate dandruff shampoo?

That is exactly what Colgate-Palmolive would like

to find out. Colgate wants to investigate the possibility of entering the over-the-counter (OTC) drug market. Can it use its Colgate brand name, developed in the oral-care products market, in the OTC health-care market?

Why is Colgate interested in the OTC market? The

first reason is market size. The worldwide OTC market annually accounts for $27.3 billion in sales—the largest nonfood consumer products industry. Of this total, the United States accounts for $11.9 billion and international markets generate $15.4 billion. Further, the U.S. market is growing at a 4.4 percent annual rate and international markets are growing at 25 percent annually! Analysts predict that the U.S. market will reach $30 billion by 2010.

Several trends are fueling this rapid growth. Consumers are becoming more sophisticated and increasingly are interested in self-medication as opposed to seeing a doctor. Companies are also switching many previously prescription-only drugs to OTC drugs. The companies can do this when they can show, based on extensive clinical tests, that the drug is safe for consumers to use without monitoring by a doctor. Moreover, OTC drugs tend to have very long product life cycles. Medical researchers are also discovering new drugs or new uses or benefits of existing drugs. For example, researchers have found that the psyllium fiber used in some OTC natural laxatives is effective in controlling cholesterol.

Beyond the size and growth of the market, Colgate also knows that the OTC market can be extremely profitable. Analysts estimate that the average cost of goods sold for an OTC drug is only 29 percent, leaving a gross margin of 71 percent. Advertising and sales promotions are actually the largest expenditure categories for these products, accounting for an average of 42 percent of sales. OTC drugs produce an average 11 percent after-tax profit.

Because of the OTC market's attractiveness, Colgate conducted studies to learn the strength of its brand name with consumers. Colgate believes in the following equation: brand awareness + brand image = brand equity. Its studies found that Colgate was number one in brand awareness, number two in brand image, and number two in brand equity among OTC consumers, even though it did not sell OTC products. The Tylenol brand name earned the number-one spot in both brand image and brand equity.

Thus, Colgate's research shows that the OTC market is very large, is growing rapidly, and is very profitable, and that Colgate has a strong brand equity position with OTC consumers. Most companies would find such a situation very attractive.

Colgate realizes that entering the OTC market will not be easy. First, its research suggests that the typical OTC product does not reach the breakeven point for four years and does not recover development costs until the seventh year. Thus, OTC firms must be correct in their product development decisions or they risk losing a great deal of money.

Second, OTC drugs require a high level of advertising and promotion expenditures, 25 percent of sales on year-round media alone. A firm must have substantial financial resources to enter this market.

Third, because of the market's attractiveness, entering firms face stiff competition. Established companies like Procter & Gamble, Johnson & Johnson, and Warner-Lambert have strong salesforces and marketing organizations. They are strong financially and are willing to take competitors to court if they perceive any violations of laws or regulations. These firms also have strong research and development organizations that spin out new products.

Fourth, because of the high and rising level of fixed costs, such as the costs of advertising and R&D, many smaller firms are leaving the industry or being acquired by larger firms. Industry observers estimate that an OTC firm must have at least several hundred million dollars in sales to be large enough to afford the fixed costs and to have power versus the major retailers like Wal-Mart. So, the OTC firms are growing larger and larger, and they are willing to fight aggressively for market share.

Given all these barriers to entry, you might wonder why Colgate would want to pursue OTC products, even if the industry is growing and profitable. Colgate has adopted a strategy that aims to make it the best global consumer products company. It believes that oral-care and OTC products are very similar. Both rely on their ingredients for effectiveness; both are strictly regulated; and both have virtually identical marketing elements, including common distribution channels.

Colgate set up its Colgate Health Care Laboratories to explore product and market development opportunities in the OTC market. In 1987 and 1988 Colgate carried out a test market for a line of OTC products developed by its Health Care Laboratories. In cities like San Antonio, Texas, and Richmond, Virginia, it marketed a wide line of OTC products, from a nasal decongestant to a natural fiber laxative, under the brand name Ektra. The predominantly white packages featured the Ektra name with the Colgate name in smaller letters below it.

Based on the results of that test market, Colgate quietly established a test market in Peoria, Illinois, to test a line of ten OTC health-care products, all using the Colgate name as the brand name. The line includes Colgate aspirin-free pain reliever to compete with Tylenol, Colgate ibuprofen to compete with Advil, Colgate cold tablets to compete with Contact, Colgate night-time cold medicine to compete with Nyquil, Colgate antacid to compete with Rolaids, Colgate natural laxative to compete with Metamucil, and Colgate dandruff shampoo to compete with Head and Shoulders.

Industry observers realize that the new line represents a significant departure from Colgate's traditional, high-visibility household goods and oral-care products. Responding to inquiries, Colgate Chairman Reuben Marks suggests that "The Colgate name is already strong in oral hygiene, now we want to learn whether it can represent health care across the board. We need to expand into more profitable categories."

Colgate won't talk specifically about its new line. Peoria drugstore operators say, however, that Colgate has blitzed the town with coupons and ads. Representatives have given away free tubes of toothpaste with purchases of the new Colgate products and have handed out coupons worth virtually the full price of the new products. One store owner notes, "They're spending major money out here."

If all that promotion weren't enough, the manager of one Walgreen store points out that Colgate has priced its line well below competing brands, as much as 20 percent below in some cases. The same manager reports that the new products' sales are strong but also adds, "With all the promotion they've done, they should be. They're cheaper, and they've got Colgate's name on them."

Yet, even if Colgate's test proves a resounding success, marketing consultants say expanding the new line could prove dangerous and, ultimately, more expensive than Colgate can imagine. "If you put the Colgate brand name on a bunch of different products, if you do it willy-nilly at the lowest end, you're going to dilute what it stands for—and if you stand for nothing, you're worthless," observes Clive Chajet, chairman of Lipincott and Margulies, a firm that handles corporate identity projects.

Mr. Chajet suggests that Colgate also might end up alienating customers by slapping its name on so many products. If consumers are "dissatisfied with one product, they might be dissatisfied with everything across the board. I wouldn't risk it," he says. What would have happened to Johnson & Johnson during the Tylenol poison scare, he asks, if the Tylenol name were plastered across everything from baby shampoo to birth control pills?

Colgate's test is one of the bolder forays into line extensions by consumer products companies. Companies saddled with "mature" brands—brands that can't grow much more—often try to use those brands' solid gold names to make a new fortune, generally with a related product. Thus, Procter & Gamble's Ivory soap came up with a shampoo and conditioner. Coca-Cola concocted Diet Coke. Arm & Hammer baking soda expanded into carpet deodorizer.

Unlike those products, however, Colgate's new line moves far afield from its familiar turf. And although its new line is selling well, sales might not stay so strong without budget prices and a barrage of advertising and promotion. "People are looking at it right now as a generic-style product," observes one store manager. "People are really price conscious, and as long as the price is cheaper, along with a name that you can trust, people are going to buy that over others."

Al Ries, chairman of Trout & Ries, a Greenwich, Connecticut, marketing consultant, questions whether any line extensions make sense—not only for Colgate, but other strong brand names. He says the reason Colgate has been able to break into the over-the-counter drug market in the first place is because other drugs have expanded and lost their niches; Tylenol and Alka-Seltzer both now make cold medicines, for example, and "that allows an opportunity for the outsiders, the Colgates, to come in and say there's no perception that anybody is any different. The consumer will look for any acceptable brand name."

Mr. Ries argues that Colgate and the traditional over-the-counter medicine companies are basically turning their products into generic drugs instead of brands. They're losing "the power of a narrow focus," he says, adding, "It reflects stupidity on the part of the traditional over-the-counter marketers. . . . If the traditional medicines maintained their narrow focus, they wouldn't leave room for an outsider such as Colgate."

If Colgate is too successful, meanwhile, it also risks cannibalizing its flagship product. Consultants note that almost all successful line extensions, and a lot of not-so-successful ones, hurt the product from which they took their name. They cite Miller High Life, whose share of the beer market has dwindled since the introduction of Miller Lite. "If Colgate made themselves to mean over-the-counter medicine, nobody would want to buy Colgate toothpaste," contends Mr. Ries.

Mr. Chajet agrees. Colgate could "save tens of millions of dollars by not having to introduce a new brand name" for its new products, he says. But in doing so, it might also "kill the goose that laid the golden egg." Other marketing consultants believe that Colgate may be able to break into the market but that it will take a lot of time and money. "They just don't bring a lot to the OTC party," one consultant indicates.

Although chairman Marks admits that Colgate will continue to try to build share in its traditional cleanser and detergent markets, the company seems to consider personal care as a stronger area. But leveraging a name into new categories can be tricky, requiring patience from skeptical retailers and fickle consumers. "It isn't so much a question of where you can put the brand name" says one marketing consultant. "It's what products the consumer will let you put the brand name on."

QUESTIONS

1. What core product is Colgate selling when it sells toothpaste or the other products in its new line?

2. How would you classify these new products? What implications does this classification have for marketing the new line?

3. What brand decisions has Colgate made? What kinds of product line decisions? Are these decisions consistent?

4. If you were the marketing manager for the extended Colgate line, how would you package the new products? What risks do you see in these packaging decisions?

Source: Adapted from Joanne Lipman, "Colgate Tests Putting Its Name on Over-the-Counter Drug Line," *The Wall Street Journal*, July 19, 1989. Used with permission. Also see Dan Koeppel. "Now Playing in Peoria: Colgate Generics," *Adweek's Marketing Week*, September 18, 1989, p. 5. Colgate Health Care Laboratories also cooperated in the development of this case.

Designing Products: New-Product Development and Product Life-Cycle Strategies

11

The 3M Company markets more than 60,000 products. These products range from sandpaper, adhesives, and floppy disks to contact lenses, laser optical disks, heart-lung machines, translucent braces, and futuristic synthetic ligaments; from coatings that sleeken boat hulls to hundreds of sticky tapes—Scotch Tape, masking tape, superbonding tape, and even refastening disposable diaper tape. 3M views *innovation* as its path to growth, and new products as its lifeblood. The company's longstanding goal is to derive an astonishing 25 percent of each year's sales from products introduced within the previous five years. More astonishing, it usually succeeds! Each year 3M launches more than 200 new products. And last year, 30 percent of its almost $13 billion in sales came from products introduced within the past five years. Its legendary emphasis on innovation has consistently made 3M one of America's most admired companies.

New products don't just happen. 3M works hard to create an environment that supports innovation. It invests 6.5 percent of its annual sales in research and development—twice as much as the average company. Its Innovation Task Force seeks out and destroys corporate bureaucracy that might interfere with new-product progress. Hired consultants help 3M find ways to make employees more inventive.

3M encourages everyone to look for new products. The company's renowned "15 percent rule" allows all employees to spend up to 15 percent of their time "bootlegging"—working on projects of personal interest whether those projects directly benefit the company or not. When a promising idea comes along, 3M forms a venture team made up of the researcher who developed the idea and volunteers from manufacturing, sales, marketing, and legal. The team nurtures the product and protects it from company bureaucracy. Team members stay with the product until it succeeds or fails and then return to their previous jobs. Some teams have tried three or four times before finally making a success of an idea. Each year, 3M hands out Golden Step Awards to venture teams whose new products earned more than $2 million in U.S. sales, or $4 million in worldwide sales, within three years of introduction.

3M knows that it must try thousands of new-product ideas to hit one big jackpot. One well-worn slogan at 3M is, "You have to kiss a lot of frogs to find a prince." "Kissing frogs" often means making mistakes, but 3M accepts blunders and dead ends as a normal part of creativity and innovation. In fact, its philosophy seems to be "if you aren't making mistakes, you probably aren't doing anything." But as it turns out, "blunders" have turned into some of 3M's most successful products. Old-timers at 3M love to tell the story about the chemist who accidentally spilled a new chemical on her tennis shoes. Some days later, she noticed that the spots hit by the chemical had not gotten dirty. Eureka! The chemical eventually became Scotchgard fabric protector.

And then there's the one about 3M scientist Spencer Silver. Silver started out to develop a super-strong adhesive; instead he came up with one that didn't stick very well at all. He sent the apparently useless substance on to other 3M researchers to see whether they could find something to do with it. Nothing happened for several years. Then Arthur Fry, another 3M scientist, had a problem—and an idea. As a choir member in a local church, Mr. Fry was having trouble marking places in his hymnal—the little scraps of paper he used kept falling out. He tried dabbing some of Mr. Silver's weak glue on one of the scraps. It stuck nicely and later peeled off without damaging the hymnal. Thus, were born 3M's Post-It Notes, a product that now has sales of almost $100 million a year![1]

Chapter 11 outlines the process of new-product development and discusses the strategies for managing different stages of the product life cycle.

We begin with a discussion of the early stages of the new-product development process: **idea generation, idea screening,** and **concept development** and **testing.**

Next, we follow an idea as it progresses from a concept to an actual product through **marketing strategy** development, **business analysis,** and **product development.**

We continue with an explanation of the final stages of the development process, **test marketing** and **commercialization.**

The chapter concludes with a discussion of the stages of the **product life cycle—product development, introduction, growth, maturity,** and **decline**—and the need to match marketing strategies to help manage a product's life cycle.

A company has to be good at developing new products. It also must manage them in the face of changing tastes, technologies, and competition. Every product seems to go through a life cycle—it is born, goes through several phases, and eventually dies as newer products come along that better serve consumer needs.

This product life cycle presents two major challenges. First, because all products eventually decline, the firm must find new products to replace aging ones (the problem of *new-product development*). Second, the firm must understand how its products age and adapt its marketing strategies as products pass through life-cycle stages (the problem of *product life-cycle strategies*). We first look at the problem of finding and developing new products and then at the problem of managing them successfully over their life cycles.

NEW-PRODUCT DEVELOPMENT STRATEGY

Given the rapid changes in tastes, technology, and competition, a company cannot rely solely on its existing products. Customers want the new and improved products that come about because of competition. Every company needs a new-product development program. One expert estimates that half of the profits of all U.S. companies come from products that didn't exist ten years ago.[2]

A company can obtain new products in two ways. One is through *acquisition*—by buying a whole company, a patent, or a license to produce someone else's product. The other is through **new-product development** in the company's own research and development department. As the costs of developing and introducing major new products have climbed, many large companies have decided to acquire existing brands rather than to create new ones. Other firms have saved money by copying competitors' brands or by reviving old brands (see Marketing Highlight 11-1).

By *new products* we mean original products, product improvements, product modifications, and new brands that the firm develops through its own research and development efforts. In this chapter, we concentrate on new-product development.

Innovation can be very risky. Ford lost $350 million on its Edsel automobile; RCA lost $580 million on its SelectaVision videodisc player; Texas Instruments lost a staggering $660 million before withdrawing from the home computer business; and the Concorde aircraft will never pay back its investment. Following are other consumer products, each launched by sophisticated companies, that failed:

- Juice Works fruit juice for children (Campbell)

- Fab 1 Shot detergent (Colgate-Palmolive)

- LA low-alcohol beer (Anheuser-Busch)

- PCjr personal computer (IBM)

- Zap Mail electronic mail (Federal Express)

- Polarvision instant movies (Polaroid)

- Premier "smokeless" cigarettes (R. J. Reynolds)

- Clorox Detergent (Clorox Company)

New products continue to fail at a disturbing rate. One recent study estimated that new consumer packaged goods (consisting mostly of line extensions) fail at a rate of 80 percent. The same high failure rate appears to befall new financial products and services, such as credit cards, insurance plans, and brokerage services. Another study found that about 33 percent of new industrial products fail at launch.[3]

Why do so many new products fail? There are several reasons. Although an idea may be good, the market size may have been overestimated. Perhaps the actual product was not designed as well as it should have been. Or maybe it was incorrectly positioned in the market, priced too high, or advertised poorly. A high-level executive might push a favorite idea despite poor marketing research findings. Sometimes the costs of product development are higher than expected and sometimes competitors fight back harder than expected.

Because so many new products fail, companies are anxious to learn how to improve their odds of new-product success. One way is to identify successful new products and find out what they have in common. A recent study of 200 moderate- to high-technology new-product launches, which looked for factors shared by successful products but not by product failures, found that the number one success factor is a *unique superior product*, one with higher quality, new features, higher value in use, and other such attributes. Specifically, products with a high product advantage succeed 98 percent of the time, compared to products with a moderate advantage (58 percent success) or minimal advantage (18 percent success). Another key success factor is a *well-defined product concept* prior to development, in which the company carefully defines and assesses the target market, the product requirements, and the benefits before proceeding. Other success factors included *technological and marketing synergy*, *quality of execution in all stages*, and *market attractiveness*.[4] In all, to create successful new products, a company must understand its consumers, markets, and competitors and develop products that deliver superior value to customers.

Successful new-product development may be even more difficult in the future. Keen competition has lead to increasing market fragmentation—companies now must aim at smaller market segments rather than the mass market, and this means smaller sales and profits for each product. New products must meet growing social and government constraints such as consumer safety and ecological standards. The costs of finding, developing, and launching new products will rise steadily due to rising manufacturing, media, and distribution costs. Many companies cannot afford or cannot raise the funds needed for new-product development. Instead, they emphasize product modification and imitation rather than true innovation. Even when a new product is successful, rivals are so quick to follow suit that the new product typically is fated for only a short happy life.

So companies face a problem—they must develop new products, but the odds weigh heavily against success. The solution lies in strong new-product planning. Top management is ultimately accountable for the new-product success record. It cannot simply ask the new-product manager to come up with great ideas. Rather, top management must define the business domains and product categories that the company wants to emphasize. In one food company, the new-product manager spent thousands of dollars researching a new snack idea only to hear the president say, "Drop it. We don't want to be in the snack business."

Top management must establish specific criteria for new-product idea acceptance, especially in large multidivisional companies where all kinds of projects bubble up as favorites of various managers. These criteria will vary with the specific *strategic role* the product is expected to play. The product's role might be to help the company maintain its industry position as an innovator, to defend a market-share position, or to get a foothold in a future new market. Or the new product might help the company to take advantage of its special strengths or exploit technology in a new way. For example, the Gould Corporation set the following acceptance criteria for new products aimed at exploiting a technology in a

MARKETING HIGHLIGHT 11-1

GETTING AROUND THE HIGH COSTS AND RISKS OF NEW-PRODUCT DEVELOPMENT

The average cost of developing and introducing a major new product from scratch has jumped to well over $100 million. What's worse, many of these costly new products fail. Because of this, companies are now pursuing new-product strategies that are less costly and risky than developing completely new brands. We discussed two of these strategies—*licensing* and *brand extensions*—in Chapter 10. Here we describe three other new product strategies—*acquiring new brands, developing "me-too" products,* and *reviving old brands.*

Acquiring New Products

Instead of building its own new products, a company can buy another company and its established brands. During the 1980s and early 1990s, big consumer companies devoured one another in a dramatic flurry. Procter & Gamble acquired Richardson-Vicks, Noxell, and several Revlon brands; R. J. Reynolds bought Nabisco; Philip Morris obtained General Foods and Kraft; Nestlé absorbed Carnation; General Electric bought RCA; Bristol-Myers merged with Squibb; and Unilever picked up Chesebrough-Ponds.

Such acquisitions can be tricky—the company must be certain that the acquired products blend well with its own current products and that the firm has the skills and resources needed to continue to run the acquired products profitably. Acquisitions also can run into snags with government regulators. For example, even under the Reagan administration's loose antitrust policy, regulators did not allow Pepsi to acquire 7-Up or Coke to buy Dr Pepper. Finally, such acquisitions have high price tags. Nestlé paid $3 billion for Carnation, RJR paid $4.9 billion for Nabisco, GE forked over $6.1 billion for RCA, and Philip Morris coughed up $12.6 billion for Kraft. Not many companies can afford to buy up market-winning brands.

Despite high initial outlays, however, buying established brands may be cheaper in the long run than paying the enormous costs of trying to create well-know brands from scratch. And acquiring proven winners eliminates almost all the risks of new-product failure. Acquisition also provides a quick and easy way to gain access to new markets or strengthen positions in current markets. For example, by acquiring Richardson-Vicks, P&G moved immediately into the health and beauty aids market. It also strengthened its hold in the home remedies segment by getting a medicine cabinet full of top brands such as Vicks VapoRub, Formula 44D Cough Syrup, Sinex, NyQuil, and Clearasil to add to its own Pepto-Bismol and Chloraseptic brands.

Developing "Me-Too" Products

In recent years, many companies have used "me-too" product strategies—introducing imitations of successful competitors' products. Thus, Tandy, AT&T, Compaq, and many others produce IBM-compatible personal computers. Moreover, these "clones" sometimes sell for less than half the price of the IBM models they emulate.

new way: (1) the product can be introduced within five years; (2) the product has a market potential of at least $50 million and a 15 percent growth rate; (3) the product will provide at least 30 percent return on sales and 40 percent on investment; and (4) the product will achieve technical or market leadership.

Another major decision facing top management is how much to budget for new-product development. New-product outcomes are so uncertain that it is difficult to use normal investment criteria for budgeting. Some companies solve this problem by encouraging and financing as many projects as possible, hoping to achieve a few winners. Other companies set their R&D budgets by applying a conventional percentage-to-sales figure or by spending what the competition spends. Still other companies decide how many successful new products they need and work backwards to estimate the required R&D investment.

Another important factor in new-product development work is to set up effective organizational structures for nurturing and handling new products. Table 11-1 (see page 318) presents the most common organizational arrangements for new-product development—product managers; new-product managers; new-product committees, departments, and venture teams.

Thus, successful new-product development requires a total-company effort. The most successful innovating companies make a consistent commitment of resources to new-product development, design a new-product strategy that is linked to their strategic planning process, and set up formal and sophisticated organizational arrangements for managing the new-product development process.

Me-too products also have hit the fragrance industry. Several companies now offer smell-alike knockoffs of popular, high-priced perfumes like Obsession, Opium, and Giorgio at 20 percent of the originals' prices. The success of knockoff fragrances has also inspired a wave of look-alike designer fashions and imitative versions of prestige cosmetics and hair-care brands. Imitation is now fair play for products ranging from soft drinks and food to mousses and minivans.

Me-too products are often quicker and less expensive to develop—the market leader pioneers the technology and bears most of the product-development costs. The imitative products sometimes give consumers even more value than the market-leading originals. The copycat company can build on the leader's design and technology to create an equivalent product at a lower price, or an even better product at the same or a higher price. Me-too products are also less costly and less risky to introduce—they enter a proven market already developed by the market leader. Thus, IBM invested millions to develop its personal computers and cultivate a market, and the clone makers simply rode IBM's generous coattails.

However, a me-too strategy also has some drawbacks. The imitating company enters the market late and must battle a successful, firmly entrenched competitor. Some me-too products never take much business from the leader. Others succeed broadly and end up challenging for market leadership. Still others settle into small but profitable niches in the market created by the leader.

Reviving Old Products

Many companies have found "new gold in the old" by reviving once-successful brands that are now dead or dying. Many old and tarnished brand names still hold magic for consumers. Often, simply reviving, reformulating, and repositioning an old brand can give the company a successful "new" product at a fraction of the cost of building new brands.

There are some classic examples of brand revivals—Arm & Hammer Baking Soda sales spurted after it was promoted as deodorizer for refrigerators, garbage disposals, cars, and kitty litter boxes. Ivory Soap reversed its sales decline in the early 1970s when it was promoted for adult use rather than just for babies. Dannon Yogurt sales rocketed when it was linked to healthy living. In recent years, Warner-Lambert revived Black Jack gum, playing on the nostalgia of its 110-year-old name; Buick dusted off its venerable Roadmaster name, last used in 1958; Coca-Cola rejuvenated Fresca by adding NutraSweet and real fruit juice; and Campbell expanded the appeal of V8 Juice by tying it to today's fitness craze.

Sometimes, a dead product rises again with a new name, as happened with Nestlé's New Cookery brand of low-fat, low-sugar, low-salt entrées. Some years ago, Nestlé withdrew the product when it failed in test markets—the company blamed the times, the product's name, and the ordinary packaging. But New Cookery was well suited to today's health-conscious consumers, and Stouffer, a Nestlé company, revived the line under the Lean Cuisine brand. Lean Cuisine proved a resounding success.

Sources: See Arthur Bragg, "Back to the Future," *Sales & Marketing Management,* November 1986, pp. 61-62; and Gary Strauss, "Building on Brand Names: Companies Freshen Old Product Lines," *USA Today,* March 20, 1992, pp. B1, B2.

The *new-product development process* for finding and growing new products consists of eight major steps (see Figure 11-1).

Idea Generation

New-product development starts with **idea generation**—the systematic search for new-product ideas. A company typically has to generate many ideas in order to find a few good ones. The search for new-product ideas should be systematic rather than haphazard. Otherwise, although the company will find many ideas, most will not be good ones for its type of business. Top management can avoid this error by carefully defining its new-product development strategy. It should state what products and markets to emphasize. It should state what the company wants from its new products, whether it be high cash flow, market share, or some

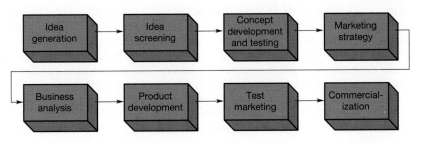

FIGURE 11-1
Major stages in new-product development

TABLE 11-1
Ways Companies Organize for New-Product Development

Product managers

Many companies assign responsibility for new-product ideas to their product managers. Because these managers are close to the market and competition, they are ideally situated to find and develop new-product opportunities. In practice, however, this system has several faults. Product managers are usually so busy managing their product lines that they give little thought to new products other than brand modifications or extensions. They also lack the specific skills and knowledge needed to critique and develop new products.

New-product managers

General Foods and Johnson & Johnson have new-product managers who report to group product managers. This position "professionalizes" the new-product function. On the other hand, new-product managers tend to think in terms of product modifications and line extensions limited to their current product and markets.

New-product committees

Most companies have a high-level management committee charged with reviewing and approving new-product proposals. It usually consists of representatives from marketing, manufacturing, finance, engineering, and other departments. Its function is not developing or coordinating new products so much as reviewing and approving new-product plans.

New-product departments

Large companies often establish a new-product department headed by a manager who has substantial authority and access to top management. The department's major responsibilities include generating and screening new ideas, working with the R&D department, and carrying out field testing and commercialization.

New-product venture teams

The 3M Company, Dow, Westinghouse, and General Mills often assign major new-product development work to venture teams. A venture team is a group brought together from various operating departments and charged with developing a specific product or business. Team members are relieved of their other duties, and given a budget and a time frame. In some cases, this team stays with the product long after it is successfully introduced.

other objective. It should state the effort to be devoted to developing breakthrough products, changing existing ones, and imitating those of competitors.

To obtain a flow of new-product ideas, the company can tap many sources. Major sources of new-product ideas include internal sources, customers, competitors, distributors and suppliers, and others.

Internal Sources

One study found that more than 55 percent of all new-product ideas come from within the company.[5] The company can find new ideas through formal research and development. It can pick the brains of its scientists, engineers, and manufacturing people. Or company executives can brainstorm new-product ideas. The company's salespeople are another good source of ideas because they are in daily contact with customers. Toyota claims that employees submit two million ideas annually—about 35 suggestions per employee—and that more than 85 percent of these ideas are implemented.

Customers

Almost 28 percent of all new-product ideas come from watching and listening to customers. The company can conduct surveys to learn about consumer needs and wants. It can analyze customer questions and complaints to find new products that better solve consumer problems. Company engineers or salespeople can meet with customers to get suggestions. General Electric's Video Products Division has its design engineers talk with final consumers to get ideas for new home electronics products. National Steel has a product application center where company engineers work with automotive customers to discover customer needs that might require new products. Many new ideas come from simply observing consumers:[6]

- Honda's highly acclaimed City model was conceived in this manner. Honda sent designers and engineers from the City project team to Europe to "look around" for the best product concept for City. Based on the British Mini-Cooper, developed decades earlier, the Honda team designed a "short and tall" car which countered the prevailing wisdom that cars should be long and low.

- Observing the growing market potential in Third World countries, Boeing sent a team of engineers to those countries to study the idiosyncrasies of Third World aviation. The engineers found that many runways were too short for jet planes. Boeing redesigned the wings on its 737, added lower pressure tires to prevent bouncing on short landings, and redesigned the engines for quicker takeoff. As a result, the Boeing 737 became the best-selling commercial jet in history.

- In any ten-day period, United States Surgical salespeople visit every one of the 5,000 U.S. hospitals where surgery is performed. They gown up and march right into operating rooms to coach surgeons in the use of the complex instruments their company makes. They listen to what the doctors like and don't like, need and don't need. Its close connection to customers made U.S. Surgical quick to pick up on early experiments in laparoscopy—surgery by inserting a tiny TV camera into the body along with slim, long-handled instruments. The company now captures about 85 percent of the laparoscopy market.

Finally, consumers often create new products on their own, and companies can benefit by finding these products and putting them on the market. Pillsbury gets promising new recipes through its annual Bake-Off. One of Pillsbury's four cake-mix lines and several variations of another came directly from Bake-Off winners' recipes. About one-third of all the software IBM leases for its computers is developed by outside users.[7]

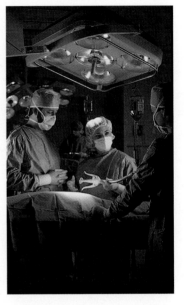

New product ideas from customers: In any ten-day period, United States Surgical salespeople visit every one of the 5,000 U.S. hospitals where surgery is performed. They gown up and accompany surgeons in operating rooms to provide technical assistance in the use of U.S. Surgical's products. Importantly, they also listen to what doctors like and don't like, need and don't need. The company's close connections to customers has resulted in many innovative new products.

Competitors
About 30 percent of new-product ideas come from analyzing competitors' products. The company can watch competitors' ads and other communications to get clues about their new products. Companies buy competing new products, take them apart to see how they work, analyze their sales, and decide whether the company should bring out a new product of its own. For example, when designing its highly successful Taurus, Ford tore down more than 50 competing models, layer by layer, looking for things to copy or improve upon. It copied the Audi's accelerator-pedal "feel," the Toyota Supra fuel gauge, the BMW 528e tire and jack storage system, and 400 other such outstanding features. Ford did this again when it redesigned the Taurus in 1992.[8]

Distributors, Suppliers, and Others
Resellers are close to the market and can pass along information about consumer problems and new-product possibilities. Suppliers can tell the company about new concepts, techniques, and materials that can be used to develop new products. Other idea sources include trade magazines, shows, and seminars; government agencies; new-product consultants; advertising agencies; marketing research firms; university and commercial laboratories; and inventors.

Idea Screening

The purpose of idea generation is to create a large number of ideas. The purpose of the succeeding stages is to *reduce* that number. The first idea-reducing stage is **idea screening.** The purpose of screening is to spot good ideas and drop poor ones as soon as possible. Product-development costs rise greatly in later stages. The company wants to go ahead only with the product ideas that will turn into profitable products.

Most companies require their executives to write up new-product ideas on a standard form that can be reviewed by a new-product committee. The writeup describes the product, the target market, and the competition, and makes some rough estimates of market size, product price, development time and costs, manufacturing costs, and rate of return. The committee then evaluates the idea against a set of general criteria. At Kao Company of Japan, for example, the committee asks questions such as these: Is the product truly useful to consumers and society? Is this product good for our particular company? Does it mesh well with the company's objectives and strategies? Do we have the people, skills, and resources to make it succeed? Is its cost performance superior to competitive products? Is it easy to advertise and distribute?

Surviving ideas can be screened further using a simple rating process such as the one shown in Table 11-2. The first column lists factors required for the successful launching of the product in the marketplace. In the next column, management rates these factors on their relative importance. Thus, management believes that marketing skills and experience are very important (.20) and purchasing and supplies competence is of minor importance (.05).

Next, on a scale of .0 to 1.0, management rates how well the new-product idea fits the company's profile on each factor. Here management feels that the product idea fits very well with the company's marketing skills and experience (.9), but not too well with its purchasing and supplies capabilities (.5). Finally, management multiplies the importance of each success factor by the rating of fit to obtain an overall rating of the company's ability to launch the product successfully. Thus, if marketing is an important success factor and if this product fits the company's marketing skills, this will increase the overall rating of the product idea. In the example, the product idea scored .74, which places it at the high end of the "fair idea" level.

The checklist promotes a more systematic product idea evaluation and basis for discussion—however, it is not designed to make the decision for management.

Concept Development and Testing

Attractive ideas now must be developed into product concepts. It is important to distinguish between a *product idea,* a *product concept,* and a *product image.* A **product idea** is an idea for a possible product that the company can see itself offering to the market. A **product concept** is a detailed version of the idea stated in meaningful consumer terms. A **product image** is the way consumers perceive an actual or potential product.

Concept Development

Suppose a car manufacturer figures out how to design an electric car that can go as fast as 60 miles per hour and as far as 120 miles before needing to be recharged. The manufacturer estimates that the electric car's operating costs will be about half those of a regular car.

This is a product idea. Customers, however, do not buy a product idea; they buy a product *concept.* The marketer's task is to develop this idea into some alternative product concepts, find out how attractive each concept is to customers, and choose the best one.

TABLE 11-2
Product Idea Rating Process

NEW-PRODUCT SUCCESS FACTORS	(A) RELATIVE IMPORTANCE	(B) FIT BETWEEN PRODUCT IDEA AND COMPANY CAPABILITIES .0 .1 .2 .3 .4 .5 .6 .7 .8 .9 1.0	IDEA RATING (A × B)
Company strategy and objectives	.20	x (at .8)	.160
Marketing skills and experience	.20	x (at .9)	.180
Financial resources	.15	x (at .7)	.105
Channels of distribution	.15	x' (at .8)	.120
Production capabilities	.10	x (at .8)	.080
Research and development	.10	x (at .7)	.070
Purchasing and supplies	.05	x (at .5)	.025
Total	1.00		.740*

*Rating scale: .00-.40, poor; .50-.75, fair; .76-1.00 good. Minimum acceptance level: .70

GM's Impact electric car, scheduled for introduction later this decade: This proto-type goes from 0 to 60 MPH in eight seconds and travels over 120 miles at 55 MPH on a single charge.

The marketer might create the following product concepts for the electric car:

- *Concept 1.* An inexpensive subcompact designed as a second family car to be used around town. The car is ideal for loading groceries and hauling children, and it is easy to enter.

- *Concept 2.* A medium-cost, medium-size car designed as an all-purpose family car.

- *Concept 3.* A medium-cost sporty compact appealing to young people.

- *Concept 4.* An inexpensive subcompact appealing to conscientious people who want basic transportation, low fuel cost, and low pollution.

Concept Testing

Concept testing calls for testing new-product concepts with a group of target consumers. The concepts may be presented to consumers symbolically or physically. Here, in words, is Concept 1:

> An efficient, fun-to-drive, electric-powered subcompact car that seats four. Great for shopping trips and visits to friends. Costs half as much to operate as similar gasoline-driven cars. Goes up to 60 miles per hour and does not need to be recharged for 120 miles. Priced at $9,000.

In this case, a word or picture description might be sufficient. However, a more concrete and physical presentation of the concept will increase the reliability of the concept test. Today, marketers are finding innovative ways to make product concepts more real to concept-test subjects (see Marketing Highlight 11-2).

After being exposed to the concept, consumers then may be asked to react to it by answering the questions in Table 11-3. The answers will help the company decide which concept has the strongest appeal. For example, the last question asks about the consumer's intention to buy. Suppose 10 percent of the consumers said they "definitely" would buy and another 5 percent said "probably." The com-

---

TABLE 11-3
Questions for Electric Car Concept Test

1. Do you understand the concept of an electric car?
2. Do you believe the claims about the electric car's performance?
3. What are the major benefits of the electric car compared with a conventional car?
4. What improvements in the car's features would you suggest?
5. For what uses would you prefer an electric car to a conventional car?
6. What would be a reasonable price to charge for the electric car?
7. Who would be involved in your decision to buy such a car? Who would drive it?
8. Would you buy such a car? (Definitely, probably, probably not, definitely not)

THE NEW WORLD OF CONCEPT TESTING: STEREOLITHOGRAPHY AND VIRTUAL REALITY

Product concept testing can be reliable only to the extent that the concept can be made real to consumers. The more the presentation of the concept resembles the final product or experience, the more dependable the concept testing. Today, many firms are developing interesting new methods for product concept testing.

For example, 3D Systems, Inc., uses a technique know as 3-D printing—or "stereolithography"—to create three-dimensional models of physical products, such as small appliances and toys. The process begins with a computer-generated, three-dimensional image of the prototype.

A three-dimensional design is first simulated on a computer, which then electronically "slices" the image into wafer thin segments. The digital information that designs each of these segments is then used to guide a robotically controlled laser beam, which focuses on a soup of liquid plastic formulated to turn solid when exposed to light. The laser builds the object as it creates layer upon microthin layer of hardened plastic.

Within a few hours, the process turns out plastic prototypes that would otherwise take weeks to create. Researchers can show these models to consumers to gather their comments and reactions.

Stereolithography has produced some amazing success stories. Logitech, a company that produces computer mice and other peripherals, used stereolithography to win a highly sought contract from a major computer maker. Logitech was delighted when the computer maker requested a bid to manufacture a specific mouse. The only hitch—the bid had to be submitted within two weeks. Using stereolithography, Logitech was able to design, build, and assemble a fully functional, superior-quality prototype within the allotted time. The disbelieving customer awarded the contract to Logitech on the spot. Logitech now ships more than one million of its snappy mice each year to the computer manufacturer.

Beyond making prototypes, 3-D printing (also called "desktop manufacturing") offers exciting prospects for manufacturing custom-made products at the push of a button:

In the future lie 3D "factories" churning out custom-designed parts, companies storing their entire inventory electronically in a computer's memory banks, and possibly even the ability to "fax" a solid object to distant locations.

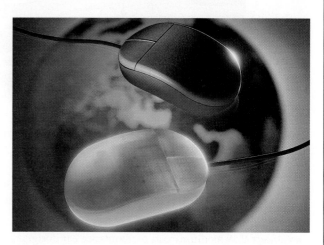

Using stereolithography, Logitech was able to design, build, and assemble a fully-functional prototype of this computer mouse in less than two weeks.

When a large physical product such as an automobile is involved, it can be tested using a radically new approach called "virtual reality." Researchers use a software package to design a car on a computer. Subjects can then manipulate the simulated car as if it were a real object. By operating certain controls, a respondent can approach the simulated car, open the door, sit in the car, start the engine, hear the sound, drive away, and experience the ride. The entire experience can be enriched by placing the simulated car in a simulated showroom and having a simulated salesperson approach the customer with a certain manner and words. After completing this experience, the respondent is asked a series of questions about what he or she liked and disliked, as well as the likelihood of buying such a car. Researchers can vary car features and salesroom encounters to see which have the greatest appeal. Although this approach may be expensive, researchers learn a great deal about designing the right car before investing millions of dollars to build the real product.

Sources: Quotes from "The Ultimate Widget: 3-D 'Printing' May Revolutionize Product Design and Manufacturing," *U.S. News & World Report,* July 20, 1992, p. 55. Also see Benjamin Wooley, *Virtual Worlds* (London: Blackwell, 1992); and "The World Leader in Senseware Orchestrates a Sales Tour de Force Using Solid Imaging," *The Edge,* 3D Systems, Inc., Spring 1993, pp. 4-5.

pany could project these figures to the population size of this target group to estimate sales volume. Even then, the estimate is uncertain because people do not always carry out their stated intentions.[9]

Marketing Strategy Development

Suppose Concept 1 for the electric car tests best. The next step is **marketing strategy development**, designing an initial marketing strategy for introducing this car to the market.

The **marketing strategy statement** consists of three parts. The first part describes the target market; the planned product positioning; and the sales, market share, and profit goals for the first few years. Thus:

> The target market is households that need a second car for going shopping, running errands, and visiting friends. The car will be positioned as more economical to buy and operate, and more fun to drive, than cars now available to this market. The company will aim to sell 200,000 cars in the first year, at a loss of not more than $3 million. In the second year, the company will aim for sales of 220,000 cars and a profit of $5 million.

The second part of the marketing strategy statement outlines the product's planned price, distribution, and marketing budget for the first year:

> The electric car will be offered in three colors and will have optional air-conditioning and power-drive features. It will sell at a retail price of $9,000—with 15 percent off the list price to dealers. Dealers who sell more than ten cars per month will get an additional discount of 5 percent on each car sold that month. An advertising budget of $10 million will be split fifty-fifty between national and local advertising. Advertising will emphasize the car's economy and fun. During the first year, $100,000 will be spent on marketing research to find out who is buying the car and to determine their satisfaction levels.

The third part of the marketing strategy statement describes the planned long-run sales, profit goals, and marketing mix strategy:

> The company intends to capture a 3 percent long-run share of the total auto market and realize an after-tax return on investment of 15 percent. To achieve this, product quality will start high and be improved over time. Price will be raised in the second and third years if competition permits. The total advertising budget will be raised each year by about 10 percent. Marketing research will be reduced to $60,000 per year after the first year.

Business Analysis

Once management has decided on its product concept and marketing strategy, it can evaluate the business attractiveness of the proposal. **Business analysis** involves a review of the sales, costs, and profit projections for a new product to find out whether they satisfy the company's objectives. If they do, the product can move to the product-development stage.

To estimate sales, the company should look at the sales history of similar products and should survey market opinion. The firm should estimate minimum and maximum sales to learn the range of risk. After preparing the sales forecast, management can estimate the expected costs and profits for the product, including marketing, R&D, manufacturing, accounting, and finance costs. The company then uses the sales and costs figures to analyze the new product's financial attractiveness.

Product Development

If the product concept passes the business test, it moves into **product development**. Here, R&D or engineering develops the product concept into a physical product. So far, the product has existed only as a word description, a drawing, or perhaps a crude mockup. The product-development step, however, now calls for a large jump in investment. It will show whether the product idea can be turned into a workable product.

The R&D department will develop one or more physical versions of the product concept. R&D hopes to design a prototype that will satisfy and excite consumers and that can be produced quickly and at budgeted costs.

Developing a successful prototype can take days, weeks, months, or even years. The prototype must have the required functional features and also convey the intended psychological characteristics. The electric car, for example, should strike consumers as being well built and safe. Management must learn what makes consumers decide that a car is well built. Some consumers slam the door to hear its "sound." If the car does not have "solid-sounding" doors, consumers may think it is poorly built.

When the prototypes are ready, they must be tested. Functional tests are then conducted under laboratory and field conditions to make sure that the product performs safely and effectively. The new car must start easily; it must be comfortable; it must be able to go around corners without overturning. Consumer tests are conducted, in which consumers test-drive the car and rate its attributes.

When designing products, the company should look beyond simply creating products that satisfy consumer needs and wants. Too often, companies design their new products without enough concern for how the designs will be produced—their main goal is to create customer-satisfying products. The designs are then passed along to manufacturing, where engineers must try to find the best ways to produce the product.

Recently, many companies have adopted a new approach toward product development called *design for manufacturability and assembly* (DFMA). Using this approach, companies work to fashion products that are *both* satisfying to consumers *and* easy to manufacture. This often results not only in lower costs but also in higher quality and more reliable products. For example, using DFMA analysis, Texas Instruments redesigned an infrared gun-sighting mechanism that it supplies to the Pentagon. The redesigned product required 75 fewer parts, 78 percent fewer assembly steps, and 85 percent less assembly time. The new design did more than reduce production time and costs, it also worked better than the previous, more complex version. Thus, DFMA can be a potent weapon in helping companies to get products to market sooner and to offer higher quality at lower prices.[10]

Test Marketing

If the product passes functional and consumer tests, the next step is **test marketing,** the stage at which the product and marketing program are introduced into more realistic market settings.

Test marketing lets the marketer get experience with marketing the product. It allows the marketer to find potential problems and learn where more information is needed before going to the great expense of full introduction. The basic purpose of test marketing is to test the product itself in real market situations. But test marketing also allows the company to test its entire marketing program for the product—its positioning strategy, advertising, distribution, pricing, branding and packaging, and budget levels. The company uses test marketing to learn how consumers and dealers will react to handling, using, and repurchasing the product. The results can be used to make better sales and profit forecasts. Thus, a good test market can provide a wealth of information about the potential success of the product and marketing program.

The amount of test marketing needed varies with each new product. Test marketing costs can be enormous, and test marketing takes time that may allow competitors to gain advantages. When the costs of developing and introducing the product are low or when management is already confident that the new product will succeed, the company may do little or no test marketing. Minor modifications of current products or copies of successful competitor products might not need testing. For example, Procter & Gamble introduced its Folger's decaffeinated coffee crystals without test marketing, and Pillsbury rolled out Chewy granola bars and chocolate-covered Granola Dipps with no standard test market. But when introducing the new product requires a large investment, or when management is not sure of the product or marketing program, the company may do a lot of test marketing. In fact, some products and marketing programs are tested, withdrawn, changed, and retested many times during a period of several years before they finally are introduced. The costs of such test markets are high, but they are often small compared with the costs of making a major mistake.

Thus, whether or not a company test markets, and the amount of testing it does, depend on the investment cost and risk of introducing the product on the one hand, and on the testing costs and time pressures on the other. Test marketing methods vary with the type of product and market situation, and each method has advantages and disadvantages.

When using test marketing, consumer-products companies usually choose one of three approaches—standard test markets, controlled test markets, or simulated test markets.

Standard Test Markets

Standard test markets test the new consumer product in situations similar to those it would face in a full-scale launch. The company finds a small number of representative test cities where the company's salesforce tries to persuade resellers to carry the product and give it good shelf space and promotional support. The company puts on a full advertising and promotion campaign in these markets and uses store audits, consumer and distributor surveys, and other measures to gauge product performance. It then uses the results to forecast national sales and profits, to discover potential product problems, and to fine-tune the marketing program (see Marketing Highlight 11-3).

Standard market tests have some drawbacks. First, they take a long time to complete, sometimes from one to three years. If the testing proves to be unnecessary, the company will have lost many months of sales and profits. Second, extensive standard test markets may be very costly—the average standard test market costs over $3 million, and costs can go much higher. Procter & Gamble spent $15 million developing Duncan Hines ready-to-eat cookies in test market.[11] Finally, standard test markets give competitors a look at the company's new product well before it is introduced nationally. Many competitors will analyze the product and monitor the company's test market results. If the testing goes on too long, competitors will have time to develop defensive strategies and may even beat the company's product to the market. For example, a few years ago, while Clorox was still test marketing its new detergent with bleach in selected markets, P&G launched Tide with Bleach nationally. Tide with Bleach quickly became the segment leader; Clorox later withdrew its detergent. Furthermore, competitors often try to distort test market results by cutting their prices in test cities, increasing their promotion, or even buying up the product being tested. Despite these disadvantages, standard test markets still are the most widely used approach for major market testing. But many companies today are shifting toward quicker and cheaper controlled and simulated test marketing methods.

Controlled Test Markets

Several research firms keep controlled panels of stores which have agreed to carry new products for a fee. The company with the new product specifies the number of stores and geographical locations it wants. The research firm delivers the product to the participating stores and controls shelf location, amount of shelf space, displays and point-of-purchase promotions, and pricing according to specified plans. Sales results are tracked to determine the impact of these factors on demand.

Controlled test marketing systems like Nielsen's Scantrack and Information Resources Inc.'s (IRI) BehaviorScan track individual behavior from the television set to the checkout counter. IRI, for example, keeps panels of shoppers in carefully selected cities. It uses microcomputers to measure TV viewing in each panel household and can send special commercials to panel member television sets. Panel consumers buy from cooperating stores and show identification cards when making purchases. Detailed electronic scanner information on each consumer's purchases is fed into a central computer, where it is combined with the consumer's demographic and TV viewing information and reported daily. Thus, BehaviorScan can provide store-by-store, week-by-week reports on the sales of new products being tested. And because the scanners record the specific purchases of individual consumers, the system also can provide information on repeat purchases and the ways that different types of consumers are reacting to the new product, its advertising, and various other elements of the marketing program.[12]

Controlled test markets take less time than standard test markets (six months to a year) and usually cost less (a year-long BehaviorScan test might cost from $200,000 to $2,000,000). However, some companies are concerned that the limited number of small cities and panel consumers used by the research services may not be representative of their products' markets or target consumers. And, as in standard test markets, controlled test markets allow competitors to get a look at the company's new product.

A TEST MARKET THAT REALLY MADE A DIFFERENCE

Some test markets do little more than confirm what management already knows. Others prune out the new-product losers—half of all test-marketed consumer products are killed before they reach national distribution. Still other test markets provide highly useful information that can save a promising product or turn an otherwise average product into a blockbuster. Here's a story about a test market that really made a difference.

After its stunning success several years ago with Dole Fruit 'n Juice Bars, Dole Foods worked feverishly to find a follow-up product with the same kind of consumer appeal. It soon came up with Fruit and Cream Bars. Before investing in a costly national rollout, Dole decided to run a test market. The company began the test market with high expectations—the Fruit and Cream brand manager predicted high sales and market share.

In the test market, Dole offered Fruit and Cream in three flavors—strawberry, blueberry, and peach—packed four to a box. Packaging modestly mentioned "100% natural" ingredients and showed a bowl of fruit and cream. Dole supported the test market with standard advertising and promotion, including television, newspaper, direct-mail, point-of-purchase, and coupon campaigns to stimulate trial and repeat purchasing. Fruit and Cream ads targeted upscale consumers aged 25 to 54 with kids, centering on the product and its taste and health appeal.

The test market quickly yielded some surprises. It showed that Fruit and Cream had much broader appeal than Dole had expected. By the end of the third month, it had become the number one brand in the test market area. Focus groups showed that Fruit and Cream buyers saw the product as a real treat and felt they could eat it without feeling too much caloric guilt. Consumers said that Fruit and Cream's natural ingredients and natural taste made it superior to the competition. Despite dazzling sales performance, however, Dole discovered that its television advertising performed poorly—sales didn't jump when the television campaign began.

Based on the test-market results, Dole made several changes in the Fruit and Cream marketing mix. It redesigned the packaging to make the size of the "100% natural" claim much larger. And a new package picture showed cream being poured over the fruit—a subtle dif-

ference that emphasized Fruit and Cream's appetite appeal. Dole developed a new advertising campaign that created a mellow feeling and focused more heavily on natural taste. The new ads used a golden oldie song, "You're Sweet 16, Peaches and Cream," and stressed the product's luxury. Dole also shortened the test market from one year to six months, increased its projection for Fruit and Cream sales, and rushed to get two more flavors (banana and raspberry) ready.

With all the marketing changes, Dole was convinced that Fruit and Cream would take off like a rocket when it went national. But test markets can't predict future market events. Four new competing fruit-based novelty ice cream products came out at the same time as Fruit and Cream—two from Chiquita, one from Jell-O, and one from Minute Maid. The result was a marketer's nightmare. Fruit and Cream missed all its sales projections. But so did all the competitors, and Fruit and Cream held on, achieving a 3 percent market share instead of the expected 4 percent. The dust finally settled, and Dole hit its original projections the following year.

No test market can predict future competitor actions and reactions, economic conditions, changing consumer tastes, or other factors that can affect a new product's success. It can only show how consumers in a selected market area react to a new product and its marketing program. But the people at Dole are still strong believers. According to the Fruit and Cream brand manager, "Without the changes we made as a result of the test market, we would have been hurt much more than we were."

Source: Adapted from Leslie Brennan, "Test Marketing Put to the Test," *Sales and Marketing Management,* March 1987, pp. 65-68.

Simulated Test Markets

Companies also can test new products in a simulated shopping environment. The company or research firm shows to a sample of consumers ads and promotions for a variety of products, including the new product being tested. It gives consumers a small amount of money and invites them to a real or laboratory store where they may keep the money or use it to buy items. The researchers note how many consumers buy the new product and competing brands. This simulation provides a measure of trial and the commercial's effectiveness against competing commercials. The researchers then ask consumers the reasons for their purchase or nonpurchase. Some weeks later, they interview the consumers by phone to determine product attitudes, usage, satisfaction, and repurchase intentions. Using sophisticated computer models, the researchers then project national sales from results of the simulated test market.

Simulated test markets overcome some of the disadvantages of standard and controlled test markets. They usually cost much less ($35,000 to $75,000), can be run in eight weeks, and keep the new product out of competitors' view. Yet, because of their small samples and simulated shopping environments, many marketers do not think that simulated test markets are as accurate or reliable as larger, real-world tests. Still, simulated test markets are used widely, often as "pretest" markets. Because they are fast and inexpensive, one or more simulated tests can be run to quickly assess a new product or its marketing program. If the pretest results are strongly positive, the product might be introduced without further testing. If the results are very poor, the product might be dropped or substantially redesigned and retested. If the results are promising but indefinite, the product and marketing program can be tested further in controlled or standard test markets.[13]

Test Marketing Industrial Goods

Business marketers use different methods for test marketing their new products. For example, they may conduct *product-use tests*. Here the business marketer selects a small group of potential customers who agree to use the new product for a limited time. The manufacturer's technical people watch how these customers use the product. From this test the manufacturer learns about customer training and servicing requirements. After the test, the marketer asks the customer about purchase intent and other reactions.

New industrial products also can be tested at *trade shows*. These shows draw a large number of buyers who view new products in a few concentrated days. The manufacturer sees how buyers react to various product features and terms, and can assess buyer interest and purchase intentions. The business marketer also can test new industrial products in *distributor and dealer display rooms,* where they may stand next to other company products and possibly competitors' products. This method yields preference and pricing information in the normal selling atmosphere of the product.

Finally, some business marketers use *standard or controlled test markets* to measure the potential of their new products. They produce a limited supply of the product and give it to the salesforce to sell in a limited number of geographical areas. The company gives the product full advertising, sales promotion, and other marketing support. Such test markets let the company test the product and its marketing program in real market situations.

Commercialization

Test marketing gives management the information needed to make a final decision about whether to launch the new product. If the company goes ahead with **commercialization**—introducing the new product into the market—it will face high costs. The company will have to build or rent a manufacturing facility. And it may have to spend, in the case of a new consumer packaged good, between $10 million and $100 million for advertising and sales promotion in the first year. For example, McDonald's spent more than $5 million *per week* on the introductory advertising campaign for its McDLT sandwich.

The company launching a new product must make four decisions.

When?

The first decision is whether the time is right to introduce the new product. If the electric car will eat into the sales of the company's other cars, its introduction may be delayed. If the electric car can be improved further, or if the economy is down, the company may wait until the following year to launch it.[14]

Where?

The company must decide whether to launch the new product in a single location, a region, several regions, the national market, or the international market. Few companies have the confidence, capital, and capacity to launch new products into full national or international distribution. They will develop a planned *market rollout* over time. In particular, small companies may select an attractive city and conduct a blitz campaign to enter the market. They then may enter other cities one at a time. Larger companies can introduce their products into a whole region and

SIMULTANEOUS PRODUCT DEVELOPMENT: SPEEDING NEW PRODUCTS TO MARKET

Philips, the giant Dutch consumer electronics company, marketed the first practical videocassette recorder in 1972, gaining a three-year lead on its Japanese competitors. But in the seven years that it took Philips to develop its second generation of VCR models, Japanese manufacturers had launched at least three generations of new products. A victim of its own creaky product-development process, Philips never recovered from the Japanese onslaught. Today, the company is an also-ran with only a 2 percent market share; it still loses money on VCRs. The Philips story is typical—during the past few decades, dozens of large companies have fallen victim to competitors with faster, more flexible new-product development programs. In today's fast-changing, fiercely competitive world, turning out new products too slowly can result in product failures, lost sales and profits, and crumbling market positions. "Speed to market" has become a pressing concern to companies in all industries.

Large companies traditionally have used a sequential product-development approach in which new products are developed in an orderly series of steps. In a kind of relay race, each company department completes its phase of the development process before passing the new product on. The sequential process has merits—it helps bring order to risky and complex new-product development projects. But the approach also can be fatally slow.

To speed up their product-development cycles, many companies are now adopting a faster, more agile, team-oriented approach called "simultaneous product development." Instead of passing the new product from department to department, the company assembles a team of people from various departments that stays with the new product from start to finish. Such teams usually include representatives from the marketing, finance, design, manufacturing, and legal departments, and even supplier companies. Simultaneous development is more like a rugby match than a relay race—team members pass the new product back and forth as they move downfield toward the common goal of a speedy and successful new-product launch.

Top management gives the product-development team general strategic direction but no clear-cut product idea or work plan. It challenges the team with stiff and seemingly contradictory goals—"turn out carefully planned and superior new products, but do it quickly"—and then gives the team whatever freedom and resources it needs to meet the challenge. The team becomes a driving force that pushes the product forward. In the sequential process, a bottleneck at one phase can seriously slow or even halt the entire project. In the simultaneous approach, if one functional area hits snags, it works to resolve them while the team moves on.

The Allen-Bradley Company, a maker of industrial controls, provides an example of the tremendous benefits gained by using simultaneous development. Under the old sequential approach, the company's marketing department handed off a new-product idea to designers. The designers, working in isolation, prepared concepts and passed them along to product engineers. The engineers, also working by themselves, developed expensive

then expand into the next region. Companies with national distribution networks, such as auto companies, often launch their new models in the national market.

Companies with international distribution systems are increasingly introducing their new products in swift global assaults. Procter & Gamble did this with its Pampers Phases line of disposable diapers. In the past, P&G typically introduced a new product in the U.S. market. If it was successful, overseas competitors would copy the product in their home markets before P&G could expand distribution globally. With Pampers Phases, however, the company introduced the new product into global markets within one month of introducing it in the United States. It planned to have the product on the shelf in 90 countries within just 12 months of introduction. Such rapid worldwide expansion solidified the brand's market position before foreign competitors could react. P&G has since mounted worldwide introductions of several other new products.[15]

To Whom?
Within the rollout markets, the company must target its distribution and promotion to the best prospect groups. The company already has profiled the prime prospects in earlier test marketing. It must now fine-tune its market identification, looking especially for early adopters, heavy users, and opinion leaders.

How?
The company also must develop an action plan for introducing the new product into

Ford's successful Taurus was the first American car developed using simultaneous product development.

prototypes and handed them off to manufacturing, which tried to find a way to build the new product. Finally, after many years and dozens of costly design compromises and delays, marketing was asked to sell the new product—which it often found to be too high priced or sadly out of date. Now, Allen-Bradley has adopted the simultaneous product-development approach. All of the company's departments work together—from beginning to end—to design and develop new products that meet customer needs and company capabilities. The results have been astonishing. For example, the company recently developed a new electrical control in just two years; under the old system, it would have taken six years.

The auto industry also has discovered the benefits of simultaneous product development. The approach is called "simultaneous engineering" at GM, the "team concept" at Ford, and "process-driven design" at

Chrysler. The first American cars built using this process, the Ford Taurus and Mercury Sable, have been major marketing successes. Using simultaneous product development, Ford slashed development time from 60 months to less than 40. It squeezed 14 weeks from its cycle by simply getting the engineering and finance departments to review designs at the same time instead of sequentially. It claims that such actions have helped cut average engineering costs for a project by 35 percent.

However, the simultaneous approach has some limitations. Superfast product development can be riskier and more costly than the slower, more orderly sequential approach. And it often creates increased organizational tension and confusion. But in rapidly changing industries facing increasingly shorter product life cycles, the rewards of fast and flexible product development far exceed the risks. Companies that get new and improved products to the market faster than competitors gain a dramatic competitive edge. They can respond more quickly to emerging consumer tastes and charge higher prices for more advanced designs. As one auto industry executive states, "What we want to do is get the new car approved, built, and in the consumer's hands in the shortest time possible. . . . Whoever gets there first gets all the marbles."

Sources: Hirotaka Takeuchi and Ikujiro Nonaka, "The New New Product Development Game," *Harvard Business Review,* January-February 1986, pp. 137-46; Bro Uttal, "Speeding New Ideas to Market," *Fortune,* March 2, 1987, pp. 62-65; John Bussey and Douglas R. Sease, "Speeding Up: Manufacturers Strive to Slice Time Needed to Develop New Products," *The Wall Street Journal,* February 23, 1988, pp. 1, 24; Paul Kunkel, "Competing by Design," *Business Week,* March 25, 1991, pp. 51-63; and Homer F. Hagedorn, "High Performance in Product Development: An Agenda for Senior Management," in Arthur D. Little Company, *PRISM,* First Quarter, 1992, pp. 47-58.

the selected markets. It must spend the marketing budget on the marketing mix and various other activities. Thus, the electric car's launch may be supported by a publicity campaign and then by offers of gifts to draw more people to the showrooms. The company needs to prepare a separate marketing plan for each new market.

Speeding Up New-Product Development

Many companies organize their new-product development process into an orderly sequence of steps, starting with idea generation and ending with commercialization. Under this **sequential product-development** approach, one company department works individually to complete its stage of the process before passing the new product along to the next department and stage. This orderly, step-by-step process can help bring control to complex and risky projects. But it also can be dangerously slow. In fast-changing, highly competitive markets, such slow-but-sure product development can cost the company potential sales and profits at the hands of more nimble competitors.

Today, in order to get their new products to market more quickly, many companies are dropping the *sequential product-development* method in favor of the faster, more flexible **simultaneous product-development** approach. Under the new approach, various company departments work closely together, overlapping the steps in the product-development process to save time and increase effectiveness (see Marketing Highlight 11-4).

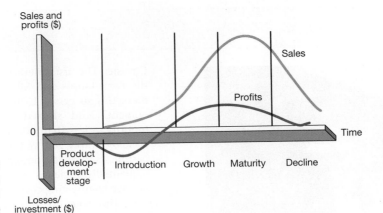

FIGURE 11-2
Sales and profits over the product's life from inception to demise

PRODUCT LIFE-CYCLE STRATEGIES

After launching the new product, management wants the product to enjoy a long and happy life. Although it does not expect the product to sell forever, management wants to earn a decent profit to cover all the effort and risk that went into launching it. Management is aware that each product will have a life cycle, although the exact shape and length is not known in advance.

Figure 11-2 shows a typical **product life cycle (PLC),** the course that a product's sales and profits take over its lifetime. The product life cycle has five distinct stages:

1. *Product development* begins when the company finds and develops a new-product idea. During product development, sales are zero and the company's investment costs mount.

2. *Introduction* is a period of slow sales growth as the product is being introduced in the market. Profits are nonexistent in this stage because of the heavy expenses of product introduction.

3. *Growth* is a period of rapid market acceptance and increasing profits.

4. *Maturity* is a period of slowdown in sales growth because the product has achieved acceptance by most potential buyers. Profits level off or decline because of increased marketing outlays to defend the product against competition.

5. *Decline* is the period when sales fall off and profits drop.

Not all products follow this S-shaped product life cycle. Some products are introduced and die quickly; Others stay in the mature stage for a long, long time. Some enter the decline stage and are then cycled back into the growth stage through strong promotion or repositioning.

The PLC concept can describe a *product class* (gasoline-powered automobiles), a p*roduct form* (station wagons), or a *brand* (the Ford Taurus). The PLC concept applies differently in each case. Product classes have the longest life cycles. The sales of many product classes stay in the mature stage for a long time. Product forms, in contrast, tend to have the standard PLC shape. Product forms such as "cream deodorants," the "dial telephone" and "phonograph records" passed through a regular history of introduction, rapid growth, maturity, and decline. A specific brand's life cycle can change quickly because of changing competitive attacks and responses. For example, although teeth-cleaning products (product class) and toothpastes (product form) have enjoyed fairly long life cycles, the life cycles of specific brands have tended to be much shorter.

The PLC concept also can be applied to what are known as styles, fashions, and fads. Their special life cycles are shown in Figure 11-3. A **style** is a basic and distinctive mode of expression. For example, styles appear in homes (colonial, ranch, Cape Cod); clothing (formal, casual); and art (realistic, surrealistic, abstract). Once a style is invented, it may last for generations, coming in and out of vogue. A style has a cycle showing several periods of renewed interest.

A **fashion** is a currently accepted or popular style in a given field. For ex-

Some products stay in the maturity stage of the product life cycle for a long, long time: Kikkoman is 358 years old!

ample, the "preppie look" in the clothing of the late 1970s gave way to the "loose and layered look" of the 1980s, which in turn yielded to the less conservative but more tailored look of the 1990s. Fashions pass through many stages. First, a small number of consumers typically take an interest in something new that sets them apart. Then, other consumers take an interest out of a desire to copy the fashion leaders. Next, the fashion becomes popular and is adopted by the mass market. Finally, the fashion fades away as consumers start moving toward other fashions that are beginning to catch their eye. Thus, fashions tend to grow slowly, remain popular for a while, then decline slowly.

Fads are fashions that enter quickly, are adopted with great zeal, peak early, and decline very fast. They last only a short time and tend to attract only a limited following. Fads often have a novel or quirky nature, as when people start buying Rubik's Cubes, "pet rocks," Cabbage Patch dolls, or yo-yos. Fads appeal to people who are looking for excitement, a way to set themselves apart, or something to talk about to others. Fads do not survive for long because they normally do not satisfy a strong need or satisfy it well.

The PLC concept can be applied by marketers as a useful framework for describing how products and markets work. But using the PLC concept for forecasting product performance or for developing marketing strategies presents some practical problems.[16] For example, managers may have trouble identifying which stage of the PLC the product is in, pinpointing when the product moves into the next stage, and determining the factors that affect the product's movement through the stages. In practice, it is difficult to forecast the sales level at each PLC stage, the length of each stage, and the shape of the PLC curve.

Using the PLC concept to develop marketing strategy also can be difficult because strategy is both a cause and a result of the product's life cycle. The product's current PLC position suggests the best marketing strategies, and the resulting

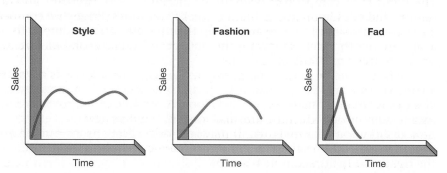

FIGURE 11-3
Marketers need to understand and predict style, fashion, and fad

marketing strategies affect product performance in later life-cycle stages. Yet, when used carefully, the PLC concept can help in developing good marketing strategies for different stages of the product life cycle.

We looked at the product-development stage of the product life cycle in the first part of the chapter. We now look at strategies for each of the other life-cycle stages.

Introduction Stage

The **introduction stage** starts when the new product is first launched. Introduction takes time, and sales growth is apt to be slow. Well-known products such as instant coffee, frozen orange juice, and powdered coffee creamers lingered for many years before they entered a stage of rapid growth.

In this stage, as compared to other stages, profits are negative or low because of the low sales and high distribution and promotion expenses. Much money is needed to attract distributors and build their inventories. Promotion spending is relatively high to inform consumers of the new product and get them to try it. Because the market is not generally ready for product refinements at this stage, the company and its few competitors produce basic versions of the product. These firms focus their selling on those buyers who are the readiest to buy—usually the higher-income groups.

A company might adopt one of several marketing strategies for introducing a new product. It can set a high or low level for each marketing variable, such as price, promotion, distribution, and product quality. Considering only price and promotion, for example, management might launch the new product with a high price and low promotion spending. The high price helps recover as much gross profit per unit as possible while the low promotion spending keeps marketing spending down. Such a strategy makes sense when the market is limited in size, when most consumers in the market know about the product and are willing to pay a high price, and when there is little immediate potential competition.

On the other hand, a company might introduce its new product with a low price and heavy promotion spending. This strategy promises to bring the fastest market penetration and the largest market share. It makes sense when the market is large, potential buyers are price sensitive and unaware of the product, there is strong potential competition, and the company's unit manufacturing costs fall with the scale of production and accumulated manufacturing experience.

A company, especially the *market pioneer,* must choose its launch strategy consistent with its intended product positioning. It should realize that the initial strategy is just the first step in a grander marketing plan for the product's entire life cycle. If the pioneer chooses its launch strategy to make a "killing," it will be sacrificing long-run revenue for the sake of short-run gain. As the pioneer moves through later stages of the life cycle, it will have to continuously formulate new pricing, promotion, and other marketing strategies. It has the best chance of building and retaining market leadership if it plays its cards correctly from the start.

Growth Stage

If the new product satisfies the market, it will enter a **growth stage,** in which sales will start climbing quickly. The early adopters will continue to buy, and later buyers will start following their lead, especially if they hear favorable word of mouth. Attracted by the opportunities for profit, new competitors will enter the market. They will introduce new product features, and the market will expand. The increase in competitors leads to an increase in the number of distribution outlets, and sales jump just to build reseller inventories. Prices remain where they are or fall only slightly. Companies keep their promotion spending at the same or a slightly higher level. Educating the market remains a goal, but now the company also must meet the competition.

Profits increase during the growth stage, as promotion costs are spread over a large volume and as unit-manufacturing costs fall. The firm uses several strategies to sustain rapid market growth as long as possible. It improves product quality and adds new product features and models. It enters new market segments and new distribution channels. It shifts some advertising from building product awareness to building product conviction and purchase, and it lowers prices at the right time to attract more buyers.

To sustain growth, Sony keeps adding new features to its Walkman line.

In the growth stage, the firm faces a trade-off between high market share and high current profit. By spending a lot of money on product improvement, promotion, and distribution, the company can capture a dominant position. In doing so, however, it gives up maximum current profit, which it hopes to make up in the next stage.

Maturity Stage

At some point, a product's sales growth will slow down, and the product will enter a **maturity stage.** This maturity stage normally lasts longer than the previous stages, and it poses strong challenges to marketing management. Most products are in the maturity stage of the life cycle, and therefore most of marketing management deals with the mature product.

The slowdown in sales growth results in many producers with many products to sell. In turn, this overcapacity leads to greater competition. Competitors begin marking down prices, increasing their advertising and sales promotions, and upping their R&D budgets to find better versions of the product. These steps lead to a drop in profit. Some of the weaker competitors start dropping out, and the industry eventually contains only well-established competitors.

Although many products in the mature stage appear to remain unchanged for long periods, most successful ones are actually evolving to meet changing consumer needs (see Marketing Highlight 11-5). Product managers should do more than simply ride along with or defend their mature products—a good offense is the best defense. They should consider modifying the market, product, and marketing mix.

Market Modification

During this stage, the company tries to increase the consumption of the current product. It looks for new users and market segments, as when Johnson & Johnson targeted the adult market with its baby powder and shampoo. The manager also looks for ways to increase usage among present customers. Campbell does this by offering recipes and convincing consumers that "soup is good food." Or the company may want to reposition the brand to appeal to a larger or faster-growing segment, as Arrow did when it introduced its new line of casual shirts and announced, "We're loosening our collars."

Product Modification

The product manager also can change product characteristics—such as quality, features, or style—to attract new users and to inspire more usage.

A strategy of *quality improvement* aims at increasing product performance—

CRAYOLA CRAYONS: A LONG AND COLORFUL LIFECYCLE

Binney & Smith Company began making crayons down by Bushkill Creek near Peekskill, New York, in 1903. Partner Edwin Binney's wife, Alice, named them Crayola crayons—after the French *craie,* meaning "stick of color," and *ola,* meaning "oil." In the 90-odd years since, Crayola crayons have become a household staple, not just in the United States, but in more than 60 countries around the world, in boxes printed in 11 languages. If you placed all the Crayola crayons made in a single year end to end, they would circle the earth four and a half times.

Few people can forget their first pack of "64s"—64 beauties neatly arranged in the familiar green and yellow flip-top box with a sharpener on the back. The aroma of a freshly opened Crayola box still drives kids into a frenzy and takes members of the older generation back to some of their fondest childhood memories. Binney & Smith, now a subsidiary of Hallmark, dominates the crayon market. Sixty-five percent of all American children between the ages of 2 and 7 pick up a crayon at least once a day and color for an average of 28 minutes—80 percent of the time, they pick up Crayolas.

In some ways, Crayola crayons haven't changed much since 1903, when they were sold in an eight-pack for a nickel. Crayola has always been the number one brand, and the crayons are still made by hand in much the same way as then. But a closer look reveals that Binney & Smith has made many adjustments in order to keep the Crayola brand in the mature stage and out of decline. Over the years, the company has added a steady stream of new colors, shapes, sizes, and packages. It increased the number of colors from the original 8 in 1903 (red, yellow, blue, green, orange, black, brown, and white) to 48 in 1949, to 64 in 1958. In 1972, it added 8 fluorescent colors—with hot names like Laser Lemon, Screamin' Green, and Atomic Tangerine; and in 1990, an additional 7 fluorescents, including Electric Lime and Razzle-Dazzle Rose. Most recently, it created a new line of Silver Swirls colors—Cerulean Frost, Cosmic Cobalt, Misty Moss, Rose Dust, and 20 others. In all, Crayola crayons now come in 103 colors and a variety of packages, including a 72-crayon attache-like case.

Over the years, the Crayola line has grown to include many new sizes and shapes. In addition to the standard 3 5/8-inch crayon, it now includes flat, jumbo, and "So Big" crayons. Crayola Washable Crayons were added in 1991. Binney & Smith also extended the Crayola brand to new markets when it developed Crayola Markers and related products. Finally, the company has added several programs and services to help strengthen its relationships with Crayola customers. For example, in 1984 it began its Dream Makers art education program, a national elementary-school art program design to help students capture their dreams on paper and to use the artistic process to make the dreams more tangible. In 1986, it set up a toll-free 1-800-CRAYOLA hotline to provide better customer service. And it recently implemented a national recycling effort. Each store now has a crayon collection bin—the collected bits and pieces of crayon are melted down and used to make the most-used hue—black.

Not all of Binney & Smith's life-cycle adjustments have been greeted with open arms by consumers. For example, facing flat sales throughout the 1980s, the company conducted market research that showed that children were ready to break with tradition in favor of some exciting new colors. They were seeing and wearing brighter colors and wanted to be able to color with them as well. So, in 1990, Binney & Smith retired eight colors from the time-honored box of 64—raw umber, lemon yellow, maize, blue grey, orange yellow, orange red, green blue, and violet blue—into the Crayola Hall of Fame. In their place, it introduced eight more-modern shades—Cerulean, Vivid Tangerine, Jungle Green, Fuchsia, Dandelion, Teal Blue, Royal Purple, and Wild Strawberry. The move unleashed a ground-swell of protest from loyal Crayola users, who formed such organizations as the Raw Umber and Maize Preservation Society and the National Committee to Save Lemon Yellow. Binney & Smith received an average of 334 calls a month from concerned customers. Company executives were flabbergasted—"We were aware of the loyalty and nostalgia surrounding Crayola crayons," a spokesperson says, "but we didn't know we [would] hit such a nerve." Still, fans of the new colors outnumbered the protestors, and the new colors are here to stay. However, the company did revive the old standards for one last hurrah in a special collectors tin—it sold all of the 2.5 million tins made. Thus, the Crayola brand continues through its long and colorful life cycle.

Sources: Quote from "Hue and Cry Over Crayola May Revive Old Colors," *The Wall Street Journal,* June 14, 1991, p. B1. Also see Margaret O. Kirk, "Coloring Our Children's World Since '03," *Chicago Tribune,* October 29, 1986, Sec. 5, p. 1; Catherine Foster, "Drawing Dreams," *Christian Science Monitor,* June 5, 1989, p. 13; Mike Christiansen, "Waxing Nostalgic: Crayola Retires a Colorful Octet," *Atlanta Constitution,* August 8, 1990, pp. B1, B4; and Ellen Neuborne, "Expansion Goes Outside Crayon Lines," *USA Today,* October 2, 1992, pp. B1, B2.

its durability, reliability, speed, taste. This strategy is effective when the quality can be improved, when buyers believe the claim of improved quality, and when enough buyers want higher quality.

A strategy of *feature improvement* adds new features that expand the product's usefulness, safety, or convenience. Feature improvement has been successfully by Japanese makers of watches, calculators, and copying machines. For example, Seiko keeps adding new styles and features to its line of watches.

A strategy of *style improvement* aims to increase the attractiveness of the product. Thus, car manufacturers restyle their cars to attract buyers who want a new look. The makers of consumer food and household products introduce new flavors, colors, ingredients, or packages to revitalize consumer buying.

Marketing-Mix Modification

Marketers also can try to improve sales by changing one or more marketing-mix elements. They can cut prices to attract new users and competitors' customers. They can launch a better advertising campaign or use aggressive sales promotions—trade deals, cents-off, premiums, and contests. The company can also move into larger market channels, using mass merchandisers, if these channels are growing. Finally, the company can offer new or improved services to buyers.

Decline Stage

The sales of most product forms and brands eventually dip. The decline may be slow, as in the case of oatmeal cereal; or rapid, as in the case of phonograph records. Sales may plunge to zero, or they may drop to a low level where they continue for many years. This is the **decline stage.**

Sales decline for many reasons, including technological advances, shifts in consumer tastes, and increased competition. As sales and profits decline, some firms withdraw from the market. Those remaining may reduce the number of their product offerings. They may drop smaller market segments and marginal trade channels, or they may cut the promotion budget and reduce their prices further.

Carrying a weak product can be very costly to a firm, and not just in profit terms. There are many hidden costs. A weak product may take up too much of management's time. It often requires frequent price and inventory adjustments. It requires advertising and salesforce attention that might be better used to make "healthy" products more profitable. A product's failing reputation can cause customer concerns about the company and its other products. The biggest cost may well lie in the future. Keeping weak products delays the search for replacements, creates a lopsided product mix, hurts current profits, and weakens the company's foothold on the future.

For these reasons, companies need to pay more attention to their aging products. The firm's first task is to identify those products in the decline stage by regularly reviewing sales, market shares, costs, and profit trends. Then, management must decide whether to maintain, harvest, or drop each of these declining products.

Management may decide to *maintain* its brand without change in the hope that competitors will leave the industry. For example, Procter & Gamble made good profits by remaining in the declining liquid-soap business as others withdrew. Or management may decide to reposition the brand in hopes of moving it back into the growth stage of the product life cycle. For instance, after watching sales of its Tostitos tortilla chips plunge 50 percent from their mid-1980s high, Frito-Lay reformulated the chips by doubling their size, changing their shape from round to triangular, and using white corn flour instead of yellow. The new Tostitos Restaurant Style Tortilla Chips have ridden the crest of the recent Tex-Mex food craze's record revenues.

Management may decide to *harvest* the product, which means reducing various costs (plant and equipment, maintenance, R&D, advertising, salesforce) and hoping that sales hold up. If successful, harvesting will increase the company's profits in the short run. Or management may decide to *drop* the product from the line. It can sell it to another firm or simply liquidate it at salvage value. If the company plans to find a buyer, it will not want to run down the product through harvesting.[17]

Table 11-4 summarizes the key characteristics of each stage of the product life cycle. The table also lists the marketing objectives and strategies for each stage.[18]

	INTRODUCTION	GROWTH	MATURITY	DECLINE
Characteristics				
Sales	Low sales	Rapidly rising sales	Peak sales	Declining sales
Costs	High cost per customer	Average cost per customer	Low cost per customer	Low cost per customer
Profits	Negative	Rising profits	High profits	Declining profits
Customers	Innovators	Early adopters	Middle majority	Laggards
Competitors	Few	Growing number	Stable number beginning to decline	Declining number
Marketing Objectives	Create product awareness and trial	Maximize market share	Maximize profit while defending market share	Reduce expenditure and milk the brand
Strategies				
Product	Offer a basic product	Offer product extensions, service, warranty	Diversify brand and models	Phase out weak items
Price	Use cost-plus	Price to penetrate market	Price to match or best competitors	Cut price
Distribution	Build selective distribution	Build intensive distribution	Build more intensive distribution	Go selective: phase out unprofitable outlets
Advertising	Build product awareness among early adopters and dealers	Build awareness and interest in the mass market	Stress brand differences and benefits	Reduce to level needed to retain hard-core loyals
Sales Promotion	Use heavy sales promotion to entice trial	Reduce to take advantage of heavy consumer demand	Increase to encourage brand switching	Reduce to minimal level

Source: Philip Kotler, *Marketing Management: Analysis, Planning, Implementation, and Control,* 8th ed. (Englewood Cliffs, NJ: Prentice Hall, 1994), p. 365.

SUMMARY

Organizations must develop new products and services. Their current products face limited life spans and must be replaced by newer products. But new products can fail—the risks of innovation are as great as the rewards. The key to successful innovation lies in a total-company effort, strong planning, and a systematic *new-product development process.*

The new-product development process consists of eight stages: *idea generation, idea screening, concept development and testing, marketing strategy development, business analysis, product development, test marketing,* and *commercialization.* The purpose of each stage is to decide whether the idea should be further developed or dropped. The company wants to minimize the chances of poor ideas moving forward and good ideas being rejected.

Each product has a *life cycle* marked by a changing set of problems and opportunities. The sales of the typical product follow an S-shaped curve made up of five stages.

The cycle begins with the *product-development* stage when the company finds and develops a new-product idea. The *introduction stage* is marked by slow growth and low profits as the product is being pushed into distribution. If successful, the product enters a *growth stage* marked by rapid sales growth and increasing profits. During this stage, the company tries to improve the product, enter new market segments and distribution channels, and reduce its prices slightly. Then comes a *maturity stage* in which sales growth slows down and profits stabilize. The company seeks strategies to renew sales growth, including market, product, and marketing-mix modification. Finally, the product enters a *decline stage* in which sales and profits dwindle. The company's task during this stage is to identify the declining product and decide whether it should be maintained, harvested, or dropped. If dropped, the product can be sold to another firm or liquidated for salvage value.

KEY TERMS

DISCUSSING THE ISSUES

1. Before videotape cameras were available for home use, Polaroid introduced Polavision, a system for making home movies that did not require laboratory processing. Like most other home-movie systems, Polavision film cassettes lasted only a few minutes and did not record sound. Despite the advantage of "instant developing" and heavy promotional expenditures by Polaroid, Polavision never gained wide acceptance. Why do you think Polavision flopped, given Polaroid's previous record of new-product successes?

2. Less than one-third of new-product ideas come from the customer. Does this low percentage conflict with the marketing concept's philosophy of "find a need and fill it"? Why or why not?

3. Many companies have formal new-product development systems and committees. Yet one recent study found that most successful new products were those that had been kept away from the formal system. Why might this be true?

4. What factors would you consider in choosing cities for test marketing a new snack? Would the place where you live be a good test market? Why or why not?

5. Test market results for a new product are usually better than the business results the same brand achieves after it is launched. Name some reasons for this.

6. Recent evidence suggests that consuming oatmeal, and especially oat bran, may be helpful in reducing cholesterol levels. What impact could this health benefit have on the life cycle of oatmeal and oat-based products?

 ## APPLYING THE CONCEPTS

1. List at least 10 new product ideas for your favorite fast-food chain. Out of all these ideas, which ones (if any) do you think would have a good chance of succeeding? What percentage of your ideas did you rate as having a good chance of success? [Divide the number of potentially successful ideas by the total number of ideas you listed, and multiply the result by 100 to get a percentage.] Can you explain why the potentially successful ideas seem stronger?

2. Go to the grocery store and make a list of 15 items that appear to be new products. Rate each product for its level of innovation: Give a "10" for extremely novel and highly innovative products, and "1" for a very minor change such as an improved package or fragrance. How truly new and innovative are these products overall? Do you think companies are being risk averse because "pioneers are the ones who get shot?"

MAKING MARKETING DECISIONS:

SMALL WORLD COMMUNICATIONS, INC.

Lynette Jones and Thomas Campbell are deciding how to test the marketplace potential of their new product. "If you're thinking about a test market for this product, you can forget it," said Tom. "There aren't any self-contained geographical areas in computer sales. Lots of computer gear is sold by mail-order dealers, and quite a bit is sold directly by mail from the manufacturers the way Dell Computers does it. Even if we ran a test market, those factors would make it impossible to interpret the results anyway. But the biggest issue is just the speed of this market. By the time we got test market results, the product would be out of date and need to be upgraded—so the results wouldn't be valid for the future. But we wouldn't need to worry about that anyway, because if we really waited for test market results someone else would steal our idea, clone our product, and launch it nationally before we did. And we could move our home office to the Dinosaur National Monument." "I love your boundless optimism," said Lyn, "but I do happen to agree with you. I think we need to do a beta test the way the software companies do. We'll do the best development we can in your basement, then get initial prototypes shipped out to a dozen users or so. We can let them use the product, tell us what's good, what's bad, and what we might want to add or take off. Then we'll modify the design, get our contract manufacturer to assemble it for us, and launch it. Is that feasible?" "I can do that," said Tom. "I know a small circuit board manufacturer that specializes in prototypes and fast turnarounds. Based on our interviews so far, I know what to design, so I'll get on it. But please—when talking to bankers, or potential customers, please refer to the facility as our 'Development Labs.' It inspires more confidence than telling people the product came from 'Tom's Basement.'"

WHAT NOW?

1. There are many different ways to test a new product. (a) What are the advantages of the testing approach that Tom and Lyn are using? (b) What are the disadvantages and risks of Tom and Lyn's plan? (c) What would you do in this situation?

2. Consider the product life cycles in the computer industry. Tom feels that the life cycle for a particular model of their product will be very short, and that one product will need to replace the next very quickly. (a) If you were putting together a plan for new model development and launches over the next five years, what would it look like? (b) How could you manage the life cycle to extend the life of last year's model? What are the pluses and minuses of extending the life cycle in the ways you suggested?

REFERENCES

1. See Russell Mitchell, "Masters of Innovation: How 3M Keeps Its New Products Coming," *Business Week*, April 10, 1989, pp. 58-64; Joyce Anne Oliver, "3M Vet Enjoys Taking Risks, Knocking Down Barriers," *Marketing News*, April 15, 1991, p. 13; and Kevin Kelly, "3M Running Scared? Forget About It," *Business Week*, September 16, 1991, pp. 59-62.

2. See "Products of the Year," *Fortune*, December 9, 1985, pp. 106-12.

3. Kevin J. Clancy and Robert S. Shulman, *The Marketing Revolution: A Radical Manifesto for Dominating the Marketplace* (New York: Harper Business, 1991), p. 6; and Robert G. Cooper, "New Product Success in Industrial Firms," *Industrial Marketing Management*, 1992, pp. 215-23. Also see Brian Dumaine, "Closing the Innovation Gap," *Fortune*, December 2, 1991, pp. 56-62; and Gary Strauss, "Building on Brand Names: Companies Freshen Old Product Lines," *USA Today*, March 20, 1992, pp. B1, B2.

4. Robert G. Cooper and Elko J. Kleinschmidt, *New Product: The Key Factors in Success* (Chicago: American Marketing Association, 1990).

5. See Leigh Lawton and A. Parasuraman, "So You Want Your New Product Planning to Be Productive," *Business Horizons*, December 1980, pp. 29-34. The percentages in this section add to more than 100 because more than one source was named for some products in the study.

6. For these and other examples, see Michael Czinkota and Masaaki Kotabe, "Product Development the Japanese Way," *The Journal of Business Strategy*, November/December 1990, pp. 31-36; and Jennifer Reese, "Getting Hot Ideas from Customers," *Fortune*, May 18, 1992, pp. 86-87.

7. See "Listening to the Voice of the Marketplace," *Business Week*, February 21, 1983, p. 90; and Eric vonHipple, "Get New Products from Consumers," *Harvard Business Review*, March–April 1982, pp. 117-22.

8. Russell Mitchell, "How Ford Hit the Bullseye with Taurus," *Business Week*, June 30, 1986, pp. 69-70; "Copycat Stuff? Hardly!" *Business Week*, September 14, 1987, p. 112; and Jeremy Main, "How to Steal the Best Ideas Around," *Fortune*, October 19, 1992, pp. 102-6.

9. For more on product concept testing, see William L. Moore, "Concept Testing," *Journal of Business Research*, Vol. 10, 1982, pp. 279-94; and David A. Schwartz, "Concept Testing Can Be Improved–and Here's How," *Market News*, January 6, 1984, pp. 22-23.

10. See Otis Port, "Pssst! Want a Secret for Making Superproducts?" *Business Week*, October 2, 1989, pp. 106-10.

11. Julie Franz, "Test Marketing: Traveling Through a Maze of Choices," *Advertising Age*, February 13, 1986, p. 11.

12. See Howard Schlossberg, "IRI, Nielsen Slug It Out in "Scanning Wars,'" *Marketing News*, September 2, 1991, pp. 1, 47.

13. For more on simulated test markets, see Kevin Higgins, "Simulated Test Marketing Winning Acceptance," *Marketing News*, March 1, 1985, pp. 15, 19; and Howard Schlossberg, "Simulated vs. Traditional Test Marketing," *Marketing News*, October 23, 1989, pp. 1-2.

14. See Robert J. Thomas, "Timing–The Key to Market Entry," *The Journal of Consumer Marketing*," Summer 1985, pp. 77-87.

15. Jennifer Lawrence, "P&G Rushes on Global Diaper Rollout," *Advertising Age*, October 14, 1991, p. 6; and Zachary Schiller, "No More Mr. Nice Guy at P&G–Not by a Long Shot," *Business Week*, February 3, 1992, pp. 54-56.

16. See George S. Day, "The Product Life Cycle: Analysis and Applications Issues," *Journal of Marketing*, Fall 1981, pp. 60-67; John E. Swan and David R. Rink, "Fitting Marketing Strategy to Varying Life Cycles," *Business Horizons*, January-February 1982, pp. 72-76; and Sak Onkvisit and John J. Shaw, "Competition and Product Management: Can the Product Life Cycle Help?" *Business Horizons*, July-August 1986, pp. 51-62.

17. See Laurence P. Feldman and Albert L. Page, "Harvesting: The Misunderstood Market Exit Strategy," *Journal of Business Strategy*, Spring 1985, pp. 79-85.

18. For a more comprehensive discussion of marketing strategies over the course of the product life cycle, see Philip Kotler, *Marketing Management*, 8th ed. (Englewood Cliffs, NJ: Prentice Hall, 1994), Chap. 14.

VIDEO CASE 11

ABCNEWS

NEW PRODUCTS, NEW REALITIES

. . . It's dark here, but gradually I can see a room filled with kitchen appliances. With my magic glove, I select appliances and arrange them in a layout of my kitchen. Soon bored, I turn left and find myself in a Persian Gulf battlefield, shells bursting around my tank. In horror, I flee to the right and find myself in a room of bright squares. But what is this? One of the red squares is pulsing. I pull it closer to find that stock prices of small computer firms are declining. Thinking "I must invest... I must invest...," I try to leave but can't. Oh! I forgot to remove the glove. If only I can get it off in time....

Alice in a weird rabbit hole? Something from a new Stephen King novel? No, it's virtual reality (also called cyberspace) and it's already here. Universities such as MIT, and avant garde computer companies such as Fake Space Labs, Telepresence Research, and VPL Research, are developing and building virtual reality systems for use in the military, medicine, architecture, education, and business.

Take the room with kitchen appliances. In Japan, the Matsushita Electric Works store contains a "virtual kitchen." Customers bring their kitchen layouts to the store, where store personnel input a copy into the computer system. Then, in the computerized simulation of their kitchen, customers add cabinets, place appliances, and change colors and sizes until they have a kitchen that they like. Customers don't have to install items to know whether they will like them, and Matsushita makes on-the-spot sales.

The Institute for Defense Analyses in Arlington, Virginia, created the Persian Gulf Battlefield for training soldiers. At the touch of a button, this virtual reality system puts soldiers inside tanks rolling across the Iraqi desert, performing the same maneuvers as a unit of the 2nd Armored Cavalry during "73 Easting," an actual Persian Gulf battle. Soldiers learn very quickly—if they fail, they can be blown up in cyberspace.

What about the room with the bright squares? Unlike the kitchen and battlefield rooms, which recreate the real world, this room simulated a computer data storage area in which each square represents a set of data. Standing in the midst of the computer data, users can spot and correct data problems, "see" data relationships, and experiment by moving data sets to find better relationships.

How does virtual reality work? First, designers feed data about a specific "world," such as a battlefield or the stock market, into powerful computers that are connected by fiber-optic cables to a special glove and to a helmet containing 3-D screens. When users don the helmet, images appear in front of their eyes. The glove lets the user interact with the images on the screen. The virtual world also incorporates audio effects; and when

weight, resistance, and attraction are built into the glove, virtual reality can even provide a sense of touch.

Virtual reality is now being used to design products. Aeronautical and automotive engineers find that using virtual reality lets them determine how well the parts will work without building expensive prototypes. Architects can "walk through" new building designs to find design glitches, again without expensive prototypes. And consumers could shop for almost anything in computerized "virtual catalogs."

Virtual reality presents some problems, however. Image, sound, and feel capabilities are still rather crude. Current systems sometimes produce a "barfogenic zone"—viewers may become disoriented and nauseous in virtual space. Also, the costs of virtual reality systems can be staggering. A set for home use would cost at least $55,000; commercial systems may cost $250,000 or more. Finally, critics fear that strange new worlds might not only change reality, but also distort it. After a while, critics contend, who can tell what is real?

Virtual entertainment may offer the key to growing the consumer market. To some extent, virtual entertainment is already here in the form of 3-D video games and Nintendo—the Nintendo gloves are copies of VPL's $15,000 data glove. In virtual television or video, you would see musicians and actors in 3-D *and* be able to interact with them. Forget laser karaoke—bring on those virtual videos!

QUESTIONS

1. In what stage of the new-product development process is virtual video? What development stages might occur before it reaches commercialization?

2. Only a few architects now use virtual reality to design buildings. In what stage of the product life cycle is architectural use? If almost all automotive companies now use virtual reality to design parts, in what stage of the product life cycle is automotive use? How would product life-cycle stage affect the marketing of each of these uses?

3. What pricing strategy would a producer of virtual systems use to introduce (a) a computerized simulation of the stock market, and (b) Nintendo gloves?

4. Why might a typical consumer resist using virtual systems to go shopping? How might marketers overcome such resistance?

5. What other marketing uses can you suggest for virtual reality?

Sources: David C. Churbuck, "Applied Reality," *Forbes,* September 14, 1992, pp. 486-90; Joan Hamilton, "Virtual Reality," *Business Week,* October 5, 1992, pp. 96-105; Harvey P. Newquist, "Virtual Reality's Commercial Reality," *Computerworld,* March 30, 1992, pp. 93-95; Clinton Wilder, "Virtual Reality Seeks Practicality," *Computerworld,* April 27, 1992, p. 26.

COMPANY CASE 11

POLAROID: TAKING VISION TO THE MARKETPLACE

Edwin Land, Polaroid's founder, had a personal motto: "Don't do anything that someone else can do. Don't undertake a project unless it is manifestly important and nearly impossible."

Land lived by this motto. In 1937, he started Polaroid Corporation in a Cambridge, Massachusetts, garage and developed the polarization process. In 1943, as he vacationed with his family in Santa Fe, New Mexico, his three-year-old daughter asked why she could not see right away the picture he had just taken of her. Within an hour, Land had developed a mental picture of the camera, the film, and the chemistry that would allow him to solve the puzzle his daughter had presented. In 1948, Land introduced the first Polaroid instant camera. By the time he stepped down as the company's chief executive officer in 1980, at age 70, he had built Polaroid into a $1.4 billion company. When he died in 1991, he left behind 537 patents, second only to Thomas A. Edison.

Land's single-minded pursuit of technology led to many successes, but also to his career's major failure. Convinced that he needed to take his instant photography concept from the portrait camera to the movie camera, Land and his engineers developed the Polavision instant movie system, launched in 1977. Although Polavision met Land's criteria of being "nearly impossible," it was not quite "manifestly important." Polavision was too late—other companies had already invented videotape recording. Within two years, Polaroid had to write off the project at a cost of $68.5 million.

William McCune, Jr., Polaroid's president, felt that the company needed to move away from its dependence on amateur instant photography. Rather than stand in the way, Land resigned in 1980, and McCune became chairman.

McCune led Polaroid's diversification effort, moving into disk drives, fiber optics, video recorders, inkjet printers, and floppy disks. But by the mid-1980s, some observers argued that the diversification effort was not paying off.

However, sales to amateur photographers and sales of instant cameras for business use were going strong. By 1986, these sales accounted for 55 percent of Polaroid's revenues. Consumers were still interested in instant cameras. To stimulate that demand, Polaroid introduced the Spectra camera in 1986, its first major new camera since the SX-70 in 1972. Some observers predicted that the new camera, priced at $150 to $225, was too expensive and would not sell. It sold anyway.

Edwin Land probably felt somewhat vindicated that his former company was refocusing on its core business, amateur instant photography. But Land and Polaroid knew that the company faced severe competition in this market. Video camcorders, easy-to-use 35mm single-lens-reflex (SLR) cameras, and one-hour film developing were cutting deeply into Polaroid's market. Sales of instant cameras had fallen from a peak of 13 million units in 1978 to 4.5 million in 1990. The new 35mm cameras were outselling instant cameras five to one. Polaroid realized that it had to do something to reinvigorate the amateur photography market and to expand its base.

New Product Development at Polaroid

In the 1940s and 1950s, Edwin Land gave implied approval to a product development process called "skunkworks." This process allowed maverick individuals or groups to pursue new product design ideas unofficially and often in secret. These individuals or groups frequently generated technology-driven new product designs. However, they developed these designs with little consideration for marketing or business strategy. Further, operating managers often had only limited influence over the design of machinery. Film and camera development followed parallel paths. Development of the film pack occurred after development of the film components. This development process invariably resulted in major problems when managers tried to get all the parts to work together.

In 1984, a skunkworks team from camera engineering began discussing Polaroid's next camera, and a team from film research began to work on possibilities for a new film. The two groups met unofficially to share ideas. These "blue sky" meetings focused on the big problems of picture quality, film cost, and camera size. The groups soon narrowed their discussions to a film that would fit a smaller camera. They also decided that the camera should store pictures internally rather than automatically ejecting them as did other Polaroid cameras.

Unlike some skunkworks groups, these two groups sought marketing's input. In 1984 and 1985, Polaroid's internal market research group conducted focus groups to get consumer reactions to small, medium, and standard-sized instant cameras with picture storage features. The focus groups suggested that some consumers would be interested in the smaller camera and its smaller pictures.

Although there was not enough market evidence to gain full corporate support for the new camera concept, Polaroid president MacAllister Booth asked his assistant, Roger Clapp, to investigate the idea.

The Joshua Story

Enter Joshua. Even as Polaroid introduced the Spectra camera in 1986, Booth, who had just assumed the

CEO's position, realized that the company had to continue work on its next new camera. He appointed Peter Kliem as director of research and engineering, combining two departments that had traditionally had separate responsibilities for new-product development. Booth also asked Hal Page, Polaroid's vice-president for quality, to become program manager for the next consumer camera. For the first time, Polaroid had a single, high-level program manager responsible for all aspects of new-product development—for film as well as camera, for manufacturing as well as marketing.

Page began a year-long process of reexamination to generate ideas for a new camera. He started brainstorming sessions by showing a training film that featured a cartoon character named Joshua. In the film, Joshua finds himself trapped in a box and tries all the obvious ways to escape. Finally, in frustration, Joshua gently taps his finger against the box's wall and unexpectedly finds that his finger has poked a hole in the wall. He struggles to make the hole bigger and escapes.

Joshua sent a message to the hundreds of people from many functional groups who attended Page's brainstorming sessions. To generate truly innovative ideas for a new camera, the employees would have to attack new problems with new ways of thinking—"out-of-the-box" approaches. To create something other than an extension of Polaroid's existing cameras, people would have to think creatively and give up old prejudices, including, perhaps, their prejudice against small cameras. The brainstorming sessions also helped participants face the tension-filled question of whether new products should be technology driven or marketing driven. Participants soon learned the answer: They had to be both.

Hal Page also showed the groups a film that dramatically illustrated the value of internal picture storage for the new camera. The film showed people at Disney World using 35mm automatic cameras to take picture after picture, while others stood around watching their one Polaroid picture develop and struggled to find a place to put it. Page and others thought consumers would take more pictures if they did not have to stop after each one to find a place to put it while it developed. Further, consumers would damage and lose fewer pictures.

This storage feature, however, required that the camera's film bend around a chute after exposure in order to enter the storage compartment. Larry Swensen, a member of the marketing department, was told that Polaroid's standard film would not bend without breaking or coming apart. Swensen, however, refused to accept this conventional wisdom. He made a working model of a camera that allowed standard film to make a 180-degree U-turn during processing. Instead of ejecting out of the camera, pocket-sized photographs were released into a built-in storage chamber where the user could view them as they developed. No longer would the user need to interrupt picture taking to find a safe place for each picture. Out-of-the-box thinking had begun to work.

Page also used outside marketing consultants. Based on studies of small cameras that Polaroid had conducted during 1984 to 1986, the consultants con-cluded that there would be a market for a small camera and that the camera would not cannibalize Polaroid's existing lines. Additional outside studies in 1987 and 1988 examined consumer preferences regarding camera size, camera price, and film price. Another study estimated the sales volume that Polaroid could expect from various feature combinations.

Polaroid had based these studies on the assumption that it would price the new camera at $150. As the studies progressed, however, management concluded that the market at the $150 price would be too small and that it should price the camera around $100. This change required more market studies.

In 1988, Hal Page left Polaroid, and Roger Clapp took over what employees had dubbed the "Joshua Program." Although Page and his groups had made much progress, many technical and marketing hurdles remained. Design engineers faced many trade-offs between size and other features, such as performance and cost. Roger Clapp stopped the design process and ordered the developers to reconsider all trade-offs. This planned four-week pause, however, turned into an eight-month interruption, as it opened the door for reconsideration of all the lingering issues.

As Clapp's managers reviewed the Joshua project, it became clear that they needed to clarify the lower-priced camera's market potential and to conduct new research to get marketing fully behind the program. Finally, the managers agreed that the last market research hurdle would be an "Assessor Test" conducted by Professor Glenn Urban of MIT's Sloan School of Management.

The Assessor Test involved setting up mock stores at five geographically diverse sites across the country. These stores offered 25 different cameras (both Polaroid and competing models), with prices ranging from inexpensive to expensive. Each store had a real counter, a film rack, feature cards, and sales clerks to answer questions. As a part of the interview process, the researchers created full-color sheets of print advertising for the new camera. Polaroid also developed a realistic Joshua camera model. Over a one-month period, 2,400 people participated in market interviews and testing at the five stores. Researchers carefully screened participants on factors such as age, sex, race, and economic status to make sure the group represented demographics of the U.S. population as a whole.

During this time, another camera design emerged from a one-man skunkworks. Although the Joshua project was well underway, Larry Douglas had continued to work on his idea. Douglas's camera offered an ingenious design for a camera that popped open to take a picture, then closed automatically. Because Joshua still had tenuous corporate support, Polaroid also ordered market research for Douglas's camera.

The two studies provided convincing evidence that there was a market for a small instant camera and that Joshua would be the preferred product. Polaroid gave Joshua the go-ahead in late 1989.

Vision to Reality

Although Polaroid had devoted an extraordinary amount of time and energy to the Joshua project before its approval in late 1989, the camera and the film were still in

Back and front views of Polaroid's new Vision/Captiva camera.

the development stage. Polaroid employees throughout the company still had to solve many problems.

Manufacturing had to install a new computer-aided-design system (CAD) and to select a new material and design for the camera's mainframe. The camera would employ through-the-lens viewing, the same viewing system found on millions of 35mm cameras. The picture storage compartment would have to hold up to all ten pictures in a film package. And the camera would have to pass Polaroid's four-foot drop test.

Polaroid created a cross-functional steering committee to manage the film-manufacturing process. This team addressed problems such as how toinclude the battery in the film pack and how to design the film-manufacturing process itself. Like Polaroid's other instant film, Joshua's film would come in a package of ten exposures and would cost the consumer about $1.00 per picture, as compared to about $.40 for a conventional 35mm picture. The picture would be about 2 1/8" by 2 7/8", smaller than conventional 35mm prints.

Electronics engineers designed a new microcontroller to be the heart of the Joshua camera. The new controller solved many longstanding technical and manufacturing problems. Using software, it provided "track and hold," "trim and speed," and "wink" features to measure the light available for the picture, set the exposure, and find the distance from the camera to the subject. In other words, like many of the 35mm cameras on the market, Joshua would have "automatic every-

Actual-size photograph from Vision/Captiva.

thing." In all of these processes, managers insisted on meeting the highest quality and reliability standards.

By Labor Day, 1991, the Joshua team had produced 24 Joshua prototype cameras for testing by Polaroid employees over the holiday weekend. Twenty-three cameras worked. The team continued to produce cameras for weekend tests and made a concentrated assault on any problems the tests identified. For Christmas, 1991, the team produced 300 Joshua cameras for non-Polaroid employees from coast to coast to test. This test represented the earliest time in a product's development that Polaroid had ever placed cameras with outside users. Managers believed that they were making a new camera that met real customer needs, but they wanted to base their decisions on market research, not on instincts.

These field tests suggested that Joshua users took more vertical pictures and more close-ups than did users of other Polaroid cameras. Based on these reactions, engineers adjusted the camera's exposure systems to perform optimally in vertical format or close-up situations. Polaroid also conducted market tests in foreign countries. Polaroid calculated that, by the time it announced the camera, more than 2,000 Polaroid and non-Polaroid consumers would have made more than 55,000 images for picture analysis.

Launching the Vision

The company decided to introduce the new camera at the September 1992 Photokina trade show. Photokina, the world's largest photographic trade show, is held every two years in Cologne, Germany. Approximately 200,000 visitors from 150 companies attend the show. Because Polaroid had decided to market the camera first in Germany, Photokina represented the perfect place to introduce the camera. This decision itself represented a significant departure from Polaroid's previous practice of going for the big splash by selling in the United States first. After Germany, Polaroid would introduce the camera in other European countries and then in Japan in early 1993. It would not bring the camera to the U.S. market until the late summer of 1993.

This sequential introduction would allow the product team to accelerate production gradually through successive launches in discrete international markets. By the time the company takes Joshua to the U.S. market, it will have had a chance to work out any production problems and to build up production quantities to the much higher volume that the U.S. market requires.

Still, before introduction, the camera needed a name for the marketplace. The name had to make sense in at least 11 languages. Polaroid selected the name Vision, a name that conveyed the essence of Polaroid's spirit and mission. The company would use this name for the camera in the European market.

Reflecting on the Vision's development, Roger Clapp noted that the team approach Polaroid used in developing Vision ". . . is part of a larger corporate initiative in which manufacturing and development has been aligned with marketing early on in the process to allow us to get high-quality products to market much quicker and with much less effort."

Clapp knows, however, that as Vision rolls across Europe and Japan toward the U.S. market, his team must continue to learn and to revise its marketing plans. Already, the team has decided to use the name, Captiva, for the camera in the U.S. market. Given that Polaroid has established distribution in the U.S. market and that it has made its other product and pricing decisions, Polaroid must still decide how to promote the Captiva so that it will spur the continued growth of the amateur instant photography market.

QUESTIONS

1. Compare Polaroid's traditional new-product development process with the process it followed for Joshua. Would you predict that Joshua (Vision) will be more successful than a product like Polavision, developed under the traditional system? Why or why not?

2. As it worked on the Joshua project, did Polaroid do a good job of following the text's eight-step product development process? How could Polaroid improve this process for future products?

3. Whom should Polaroid target with its U.S. promotion campaign for the Captiva, and what promotional ideas would you recommend to Polaroid for developing interest in its new product?

Sources Subrata N. Chakravarty, "The Vindication of Edwin Land," *Forbes,* May 4, 1987, pp. 83-84; Frances Westley and Henry Mintzberg, "Visionary Leadership and Strategic Management," *Strategic Management Journal,* Vol. 10, 1989, pp. 17-32; Jane Poss, "Edwin Land Dead at 81," *Boston Globe,* March 2, 1991, p. 1; Joseph Pereira, "Polaroid Points a Smaller Instant Camera at 35mm Users," *The Wall Street Journal,* September 11, 1992, p. B1. The majority of this case is adapted from articles in *Viewpoint,* a publication of Polaroid's Internal Communications department, October 1992 issue, especially "The Joshua Story: Polaroid Takes its Vision to the Marketplace." Used with permission of Polaroid Corporation.

*P*ricing Products: Pricing Considerations and Approaches

12

A consumer buying a videocassette recorder from Sears faces a bewildering array of models and prices: The recent Sears catalog features 14 different VCR models at 12 different prices, ranging from $294.97 to $629.99. However, although consumers may have trouble choosing among the different prices, Sears probably has more trouble *setting* them. Sears must consider numerous factors in its complex price-setting process.

In setting prices, Sears first must consider its overall *marketing objectives* and the role of price in the marketing mix. Should Sears price to maximize current profits on VCRs or to maximize long-run market share? Should it use a high-price, low-volume strategy or a low-price, high-volume strategy? The giant retailer also must consider its *costs*—the costs of making VCRs or buying them from suppliers; the costs of shipping, storing, stocking, and selling inventory; and the costs of providing customer services. Sears must price its VCRs to cover these costs plus a target profit.

However, if Sears considered only costs when setting prices it would ignore other important factors. Beyond costs, Sears also must understand the relationship between price and *demand* for its VCRs and must set prices that match consumer value perceptions. If Sears charges more than buyers' perceived value, its VCRs will sell poorly. If it charges less, its VCRs may sell very well but will provide less overall revenue. Finally, Sears must consider *competitors'* VCR quality and prices. If Sears charges more for VCRs that are similar to those of its major competitors, it risks losing sales. If it sets prices much lower than those of comparable products, it will lose profit opportunities even if it wins sales from competitors.

Thus, Sears sets its VCR prices on the basis of numerous factors—overall marketing objectives, costs, competitors' prices, and consumer value perceptions and demand. But setting basic prices is just

the beginning. Sears now must adjust these prices to account for different buyers and different market situations. For example, because consumers vary in how they value different VCR features, Sears offers many models for different price segments. The basic VHS 117-channel, two-head model with no extras sells for $294.97. At the other extreme, Sears's best model—a 120-channel, four-head, stereo VCR with 35-function remote control, on-screen programming, picture-in-picture capability, and multichannel scan and freeze features—goes for $629.99. Thus, Sears offers a model to fit any consumer preference and pocketbook.

Sears also adjusts its prices for psychological impact. For example, instead of charging $300 for its basic model, Sears charges $294.97. This price suggests a bargain, and consumers will perceive the model as belonging to the under-$300 rather than the $300-and-over price range. Sears also adjusts prices to meet market conditions and competitor actions. After Christmas, for example, Sears might knock $100 off the price of its best model, both to clear inventories and to boost demand. Thus, Sears must adjust prices constantly to account for buyer differences and changing market conditions. And it must do this for each of the thousands of products that it sells.

Sears's pricing strategies have played a major role in the company's ups and downs over the course of ten decades. Sears originally became America's largest retailer by offering quality merchandise at affordable prices. In the late 1960s, however, the company decided to upgrade its merchandise and raise prices. When higher prices caused many loyal shoppers to switch to lower-priced competitors, Sears began using weekly price-off sales to make its prices more competitive. Despite this strategy of continuous sales, however, Sears continued to lose customers to K mart, Wal-Mart, and other discounters. Its market share slid 33 percent during the 1980s, and America's largest retailer found itself in big trouble.

In the spring of 1989, in what it called the biggest change in its 102-year history, Sears launched a bold new pricing strategy. Scrapping its decades-old weekly sales approach, it adopted a no-sales, *everyday low-price* strategy. Sears closed all of its 824 stores for 42 hours and retagged every piece of merchandise, slashing prices by as much as 50 percent. In its biggest-ever advertising campaign, the huge retailer proclaimed, "We've lowered our prices on over 50,000 items! Sears: your money's worth and a whole lot more."

Sears bet that its new everyday low-price strategy would pull consumers back into its stores and revive sagging profits. And at first, sales did surge under the new pricing policy. But the ploy involved many risks, and after the initial fanfare died down, Sears's sales and profits began to decline once more. To be successful with everyday low *prices,* Sears first had to achieve everyday low *costs.* However, its costs traditionally had run much higher than those of its competitors. With its bloated cost structure, the price slashing left Sears with paper-thin margins, causing profits to fall. Beyond cost problems, Sears faced the even tougher problem of trying to change consumer perceptions of its prices and practices. For decades,

Sears had conditioned customers to "hold out" for its traditional price-off sales. The rapid switch to a one-price policy and everyday low-price position confused consumers. Moreover, consumers who were being assaulted by everyday low-price claims from many retailers were no longer paying much attention to such claims. Worse yet, surveys showed that consumers simply did not believe Sears's new prices *were* the lowest in the marketplace.

By early 1990, after only ten months, Sears' everyday low-price strategy appeared to be on the way out. The company began to phase in a new strategy that put less emphasis on price and more on "value," returning to its traditional strengths—reliability, merchandise return, and "satisfaction guaranteed" policies. And it began again to feature major sales events in an attempt to rekindle consumer excitement and buying. In 1991, after decades as industry sales leader, Sears slid to number three behind new market leader Wal-Mart and number two K mart. By 1993, despite deep cost cutting that resulted in improved profits, Sears's price positioning remained clouded for most consumers, and sales continued to slide relative to more strongly positioned competitors.

Thus, Sears continues to search for the right pricing strategy. How well the huge retailer handles its pricing and related problems will dramatically affect its sales and profits—perhaps even its survival.[1]

 ## Chapter Preview

Chapter 12 provides an overview of factors that affect pricing and compares general pricing approaches.

To start, we consider pricing as one element of the marketing mix and show how it can be used to support broader marketing objectives.

We follow with a discussion of costs, including **variable costs, fixed costs,** and **total costs** and demonstrate that costs set the floor for the company's pricing.

The chapter continues with a discussion of the external factors affecting pricing, including pricing in different **types of markets,** consumer perceptions of price and **value,** the **price elasticity of demand,** and an overview of competitive factors.

We conclude the chapter with a discussion of general pricing approaches, including **cost-plus pricing** and the related concept of **target profit pricing, buyer-based pricing,** and **competition-based pricing.**

All profit organizations and many nonprofit organizations must set prices on their products or services. *Price* goes by many names:

Price is all around us. You pay *rent* for your apartment, *tuition* for your education, and a *fee* to your physician or dentist. The airline, railway, taxi, and bus companies charge you a *fare;* the local utilities call their price a *rate;* and the local bank charges you *inter-*

est for the money you borrow. The price for driving your car on Florida's Sunshine Parkway is a *toll,* and the company that insures your car charges you a *premium.* The guest lecturer charges an *honorarium* to tell you about a government official who took a *bribe* to help a shady character steal *dues* collected by a trade association. Clubs or societies to which you belong may make a special *assessment* to pay unusual expenses. Your regular lawyer may ask for a *retainer* to cover her services. The "price" of an executive is a *salary,* the price of a salesperson may be a *commission,* and the price of a worker is a *wage.* Finally, although economists would disagree, many of us feel that *income taxes* are the price we pay for the privilege of making money.[2]

Simply defined, **price** is the amount of money charged for a product or service. More broadly, price is the sum of the values that consumers exchange for the benefits of having or using the product or service.

How are prices set? Historically, prices usually were set by buyers and sellers bargaining with each other. Sellers would ask for a higher price than they expected to get, and buyers would offer less than they expected to pay. Through bargaining, they would arrive at an acceptable price. Individual buyers paid different prices for the same products, depending on their needs and bargaining skills.

Today, most sellers set *one* price for *all* buyers. This idea was helped along by the development of large-scale retailing at the end of the nineteenth century. F.W. Woolworth, Tiffany and Co., John Wanamaker, J.L. Hudson, and others advertised a "strictly one-price policy" because they carried so many items and had so many employees.

Historically, price has been the major factor affecting buyer choice. This is still true in poorer nations, among poorer groups, and with commodity products. However, nonprice factors have become more important in buyer-choice behavior in recent decades.

Price is the only element in the marketing mix that produces revenue; all other elements represent costs. Price is also one of the most flexible elements of the marketing mix. Unlike product features and channel commitments, price can be changed quickly. At the same time, pricing and price competition is the number-one problem facing many marketing executives. Yet, many companies do not handle pricing well. The most common mistakes are: pricing that is too cost oriented; prices that are not revised often enough to reflect market changes; pricing that does not take the rest of the marketing mix into account; and prices that are not varied enough for different products, market segments, and purchase occasions.

In this and the next chapter, we focus on the problem of setting prices. This chapter looks at the factors marketers must consider when setting prices and at general pricing approaches. In the next chapter, we examine pricing strategies for new-product pricing, product mix pricing, price changes, and price adjustments for buyer and situational factors.

FACTORS TO CONSIDER WHEN SETTING PRICES

A company's pricing decisions are affected both by internal company factors and external environmental factors (see Figure 12-1). *Internal factors* include the company's marketing objectives, marketing-mix strategy, costs, and organization. *External factors* include the nature of the market and demand, competition, and other environmental elements.

Internal Factors Affecting Pricing Decisions

Marketing Objectives

Before setting price, the company must decide on its strategy for the product. If the company has selected its target market and positioning carefully, then its mar-

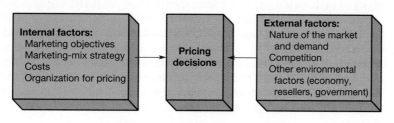

FIGURE 12-1
Factors affecting price decisions

Internal factors:
Marketing objectives
Marketing-mix strategy
Costs
Organization for pricing

Pricing decisions

External factors:
Nature of the market and demand
Competition
Other environmental factors (economy, resellers, government)

keting-mix strategy, including price, will be fairly straightforward. For example, if General Motors decides to produce a new sports car to compete with European sports cars in the high-income segment, this suggests charging a high price. Motel 6, Econo Lodge, and Red Roof Inn have positioned themselves as motels that provide economical rooms for budget-minded travelers; this position requires charging a low price. Thus, pricing strategy is largely determined by past decisions on market positioning.

At the same time, the company may seek additional objectives. The clearer a firm is about its objectives, the easier it is to set price. Examples of common objectives are *survival, current profit maximization, market-share maximization,* and *product-quality leadership.*

Survival. Companies set *survival* as their major objective if they are troubled by too much capacity, heavy competition, or changing consumer wants. To keep a plant going, a company may set a low price, hoping to increase demand. In this case, profits are less important than survival. In recent years, many automobile dealers have resorted to pricing below cost or offering large price rebate programs in order to survive. As long as their prices cover variable costs and some fixed costs, they can stay in business until conditions change or other problems are corrected.

Current Profit Maximization. Many companies want to set a price that will maximize current profits. They estimate what demand and costs will be at different prices and choose the price that will produce the maximum current profit, cash flow, or return on investment. In all cases, the company wants current financial results rather than long-run performance.

Market-Share Leadership. Other companies want to obtain the dominant market share. They believe that the company with the largest market share will enjoy the lowest costs and highest long-run profit. To become the market-share leader, these firms set prices as low as possible. A variation of this objective is to pursue a specific market-share gain. Say the company wants to increase its market share from 10 percent to 15 percent in one year. It will search for the price and marketing program that will achieve this goal.

Product-Quality Leadership. A company might decide it wants to have the highest-quality product on the market. This normally calls for charging a high price to cover such quality and the high cost of R&D. For example, the Sub-Zero Freezer Company seeks product-quality leadership. Sub-Zero makes the Rolls-Royce of refrigerators—custom-made, built-in units that look more like hardwood cabinets or pieces of furniture than refrigerators. By offering the highest quality, Sub-Zero sells more than $50 million worth of fancy refrigerators a year, priced at up to $3,000 each.

Other Objectives. A company also might use price to attain other more specific objectives. It can set prices low to prevent competition from entering the market or set prices at competitors' levels to stabilize the market. Prices can be set to keep the loyalty and support of resellers or to avoid government intervention. Prices can be reduced temporarily to create excitement for a product or to draw more customers into a retail store. One product may be priced to help the sales of other products in the company's line. Thus, pricing may play an important role in helping to accomplish the company's objectives at many levels.

Nonprofit and public organizations may adopt a number of other pricing objectives. A university aims for *partial cost recovery,* knowing that it must rely on private gifts and public grants to cover the remaining costs. A nonprofit hospital may aim for *full cost recovery* in its pricing. A nonprofit theatre company may price its productions to fill the maximum number of theatre seats. A social service agency may set a *social price* geared to the varying income situations of different clients.

Marketing-Mix Strategy

Price is only one of the marketing-mix tools that the company uses to achieve its marketing objectives. Price decisions must be coordinated with product design, distribution, and promotion decisions to form a consistent and effective marketing program. Decisions made for other marketing-mix variables may affect pricing decisions. For example, producers using many resellers who are expected to support and promote their products may have to build larger reseller margins into their prices. The decision to position the product on high quality will mean that the seller must charge a higher price to cover higher costs.

Sub-Zero charges a premium price for its custom-made refrigerators to attain product-quality leadership.

Companies often make their pricing decisions first and then base other marketing-mix decisions on the prices they want to charge. Here, price is a crucial product positioning factor that defines the product's market, competition, and design. The intended price determines what product features can be offered and what production costs can be incurred.

Japanese firms like NEC, Sharp, Nissan, and Toyota support such price-positioning strategies with a technique called *target costing,* a potent strategic weapon. Companies typically will design a new product, determine its cost, and then ask "Can we sell it for that?" This approach slights the notion of what the product *should* cost. Target costing reverses this process:

> The team in charge of bringing a new product to market determines the price at which the product is most likely to appeal to potential buyers. From this crucial judgment all else follows. After deducting the desired profit margin from the forecasted sales price, the planners develop estimates for each of the elements that make up a product's costs. . . . Every part or function is treated as a component—not only windshields but also spaces such as the trunk—and each is assigned a target cost. This is where the battle begins . . . [now starts] an intense negotiating process between the company and outside suppliers, and among departments that are responsible for different aspects of the product. . . . By the time the battle is over, . . . compromises and trade-offs . . . generally produce a projected cost that is within close range of the original target.[3]

By meeting its target *costs,* the company can set its target *price* and establish the desired price position.

Other companies deemphasize price and use other marketing-mix tools to create *nonprice* positions. For example, for years Johnson Controls, a producer of climate control systems for office buildings, used price as its primary competitive tool. However, when research showed that customers were more concerned about the total cost of installing and maintaining a system than with its initial price, the company decided to change its strategy:

> When an old system broke, it was hard and expensive to fix. You had to shut down the heat or air conditioning in the whole building and then disconnect a lot of wires, facing the danger of electrocution. To change that, . . . [Johnson] designed an entirely new system called Metasys. Now, to fix a problem, a building owner need only pull out a gray plastic module and slip in a new one—no screwdrivers or tools necessary. Although Metasys costs more to make than the old system [and customers must pay a higher initial price], it costs less to install and maintain. Introduced in 1990, [Johnson's new system] brought in $500 million in revenues in its first year.[4]

Non-price competition: When research showed that customers were more concerned about the total cost of installing and maintaining a system than with its initial price, Johnson Controls changed its strategy. Customers gladly pay a higher initial price for its Metasys system in return for lower installation and maintenance costs.

Thus, the marketer must consider the total marketing mix when setting prices. If the product is positioned on nonprice factors, then decisions about quality, promotion, and distribution will strongly affect price. If price is a crucial positioning factor, then price will strongly affect decisions made about the other marketing-mix elements. In most cases, the company will consider all of the marketing-mix decisions together when developing the marketing program.

Costs

Costs set the floor for the price that the company can charge for its product. The company wants to charge a price that both covers all its costs for producing, distributing, and selling the product and delivers a fair rate of return for its effort and risk. A company's costs may be an important element in its pricing strategy. Many companies work to become the "low-cost producers" in their industries. Companies with lower costs can set lower prices that result in greater sales and profits (see Marketing Highlight 12-1).

Types of Costs. A company's costs take two forms, fixed and variable. **Fixed costs** (also known as overhead) are costs that do not vary with production or sales level. For example, a company must pay each month's bills for rent, heat, interest, and executive salaries, whatever the company's output.

Variable costs vary directly with the level of production. Each hand-held calculator produced by Texas Instruments involves a cost of plastic, wires, packaging, and other inputs. These costs tend to be the same for each unit produced. They are called variable because their total varies with the number of units produced.

Total costs are the sum of the fixed and variable costs for any given level of production. Management wants to charge a price that will at least cover the total production costs at a given level of production. The company must watch its costs carefully. If it costs the company more than competitors to produce and sell its product, the company will have to charge a higher price or make less profit, putting it at a competitive disadvantage.

Costs at Different Levels of Production. To price wisely, management needs to know how its costs vary with different levels of production. For example, suppose Texas Instruments (TI) has built a plant to produce 1,000 hand-held calculators per day. Figure 12-2A shows the typical short-run average cost curve (SRAC). It shows that the cost per calculator is high if TI's factory produces only a few per day. But as production moves up to 1,000 calculators per day, average cost falls. This is because fixed costs are spread over more units, with each one bearing a smaller fixed cost. TI can try to produce more than 1,000 calculators per day, but average costs will increase because the plant becomes inefficient. Workers have to wait for machines, the machines break down more often, and workers get in each other's way.

If TI believed it could sell 2,000 calculators a day, it should consider building a larger plant. The plant would use more efficient machinery and work arrangements. Also, the unit cost of producing 2,000 units per day would be lower than the unit cost of producing 1,000 units per day, as shown in the long-run average cost (LRAC) curve (Figure 12-2B). In fact, a 3,000-capacity plant would even be more efficient, according to Figure 12-2B. But a 4,000 daily production plant would be less efficient because of increasing diseconomies of scale—too many workers to manage, paperwork slows things down, and so on. Figure 12-2B shows

FIGURE 12-2
Cost per unit at different levels of production per period

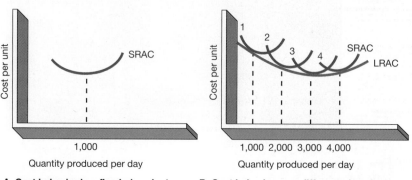

A. Cost behavior in a fixed-size plant

B. Cost behavior over different-size plants

FOOD LION'S WINNING LOW-COST, LOW-PRICE STRATEGY

The Food Lion grocery chain began operations in 1957 in a small North Carolina town. At first, despite its heavy use of trading stamps, giveaways, and other marketing gimmicks, Food Lion had trouble drawing shoppers away from more established competitors. Ten years later, the company closed nine of its first sixteen stores. In 1967, out of desperation, Food Lion slashed storewide prices by 10 percent in its remaining units. The results were startling—sales shot up 54 percent and profits increased 165 percent by year's end. The chain had found its niche and a potent competitive weapon—low prices.

Food Lion aggressively pursued this low-price, low-frills strategy and grew quickly in North Carolina. Its new slogan, LFPINC ("Lowest Food Prices in North Carolina") was featured in advertising, printed on shopping bags, and plastered to the bumpers of thousands of shoppers' cars and became a welcome and familiar sight in cities and towns around the state. In recent years, Food Lion has prospered even more. Positioned strongly as the low-price leader in most of its markets, the chain now operates more than 900 stores across the Southeast. Food Lion ads confidently claim "extra low everyday prices." And when Food Lion moves into a new town, competitors generally must drop their prices substantially to compete—a fact Food Lion points out in its advertising. When the chain entered Florida, its ads boldly asserted, "Food Lion is coming to town, and prices will be coming down!" Sure enough, by the time Food Lion opened its stores, prices in the market were down almost 15 percent.

Food Lion's price claims are more than empty boasts. In most cases, it really does offer lower prices. Yet the chain remains highly profitable—Food Lion earns an overall net profit margin of 3 percent, triple the industry average. The reason: a total dedication to cost control. The company doggedly pursues even remote opportunities to reduce costs, and its cost-cutting efforts bring big returns. For example, Food Lion pays just $650,000 for each new, no-frills store it builds—much lower than the $1.5 million competitors typically spend for their outlets. It saves on distribution costs by locating stores within 200 miles of one of its three modern distribution warehouses. To streamline and simplify operations, Food Lion stocks 25 percent fewer brands and sizes than other grocery stores and shuns costly extras such as fresh seafood counters, from-scratch bakeries, and flower shops. And Food Lion is itself a thrifty shopper—it ferrets out wholesaler specials and squeezes suppliers for extra savings.

Food Lion rarely overlooks a chance to economize. It recycles waste heat from refrigeration units to warm its stores and reuses banana crates as bins for cosmetics. It makes $1 million a year selling ground-up bones and fat for fertilizer. Food Lion even economizes on its advertising. The company produces its own ads, using few paid actors and relying on Chief Executive Tom E. Smith as advertising spokesman. Its average television spot costs only $6,000. And Food Lion saves about $8 million each year by keeping its newspaper ads smaller than those of competitors. As a result, Food Lion's advertising costs amount to one-fourth the industry average. Overall, major competitors spend an average of 19 percent of sales on their total expenses. Food Lion has kept these expenses under 13 percent of sales.

Food Lion's low-cost, low-price strategy has made it the fastest growing and most profitable grocery chain in the nation. During the past five years, sales have tripled—so have profits. Food Lion's 900 stores now reap over $6.4 billion in annual revenues and management confidently predicts that sales will double by 1997. The chain's five-year average return on equity of 32 percent almost doubles the average return of its major competitors. Food Lion's success hinges on a simple strategy—lower costs mean lower prices, and lower prices mean greater sales and greater profits.

Food Lion overlooks few opportunities to economize. For example, it produces its own ads, keeps them smaller, and uses few paid actors. As a result, Food Lion's advertising costs amount to one-fourth the industry average.

Sources: Richard W. Anderson, "That Roar You Hear Is Food Lion," *Business Week*, August 24, 1987, pp. 65-66; William E. Sheeline, "Making Them Rich Down Home," *Fortune*, August 15, 1988, pp. 51-55; Claire Poole, "Stalking Bigger Game," *Forbes*, April 1, 1991, pp. 73-74; and Walecia Konrad, "Food Lion: Still Stalking in Tough Times," June 22, 1992, p. 70.

that a 3,000 daily production plant is the best size to build if demand is strong enough to support this level of production.

Costs as a Function of Production Experience. Suppose TI runs a plant that produces 3,000 calculators per day. As TI gains experience in producing hand-held calculators, it learns how to do it better. Workers learn shortcuts and become more familiar with their equipment. With practice, the work becomes better organized, and TI finds better equipment and production processes. With higher volume, TI becomes more efficient and gains economies of scale. As a result, average cost tends to fall with accumulated production experience. This is shown in Figure 12-3.[5] Thus the average cost of producing the first 100,000 calculators is $10 per calculator. When the company has produced the first 200,000 calculators, the average cost has fallen to $9. After its accumulated production experience doubles again to 400,000, the average cost is $7. This drop in the average cost with accumulated production experience is called the **experience curve** (or the **learning curve**).

If a downward-sloping experience curve exists, this is highly significant for the company. Not only will the company's unit production cost fall, it will fall faster if the company makes and sells more during a given time period. But the market has to stand ready to buy the higher output. And to take advantage of the experience curve, TI must get a large market share early in the product's life cycle. This suggests the following pricing strategy. TI should price its calculators low; its sales will then increase, and its costs will decrease through gaining more experience, and then it can lower its prices further.

Some companies have built successful strategies around the experience curve. For example, during the 1980s, Bausch & Lomb solidified its position in the soft contact lens market by using computerized lens design and steadily expanding its one Soflens plant. As a result, its market share climbed steadily to 65 percent. Yet, a single-minded focus on reducing costs and exploiting the experience curve will not always work. Experience curves became somewhat of a fad during the 1970s, and like many fads, the strategy was sometimes misused. Experience curve pricing carries some major risks. The aggressive pricing might give the product a cheap image, as happened when Texas Instruments ran the price of its personal computers down to just $99, compared to competitors' machines selling for over $300. The strategy also assumes that competitors are weak and not willing to fight it out by meeting the company's price cuts. Finally, while the company is building volume under one technology, a competitor may find a lower-cost technology which lets it start at lower prices than the market leader, who still operates on the old experience curve.[6]

Organizational Considerations

Management must decide who within the organization should set prices. Companies handle pricing in a variety of ways. In small companies, prices often are set by top management rather than by the marketing or sales departments. In large companies, pricing typically is handled by divisional or product line managers. In industrial markets, salespeople may be allowed to negotiate with customers within certain price ranges. Even so, top management sets the pricing objectives and policies, and it often approves the prices proposed by lower-level management or salespeople. In industries in which pricing is a key factor (aerospace, railroads, oil companies), companies often will have a pricing department to set the best prices or help others in setting them. This department reports to the market-

FIGURE 12-3
Cost per unit as a function of accumulated production: the experience curve

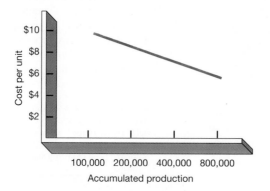

ing department or top management. Others who have an influence on pricing include sales managers, production managers, finance managers, and accountants.

External Factors Affecting Pricing Decisions

The Market and Demand

Whereas costs set the lower limit of prices, the market and demand set the upper limit. Both consumer and industrial buyers balance the price of a product or service against the benefits of owning it. Thus, before setting prices, the marketer must understand the relationship between price and demand for its product.

In this section, we explain how the price-demand relationship varies for different types of markets and how buyer perceptions of price affect the pricing decision. We then discuss methods for measuring the price-demand relationship.

Pricing in Different Types of Markets. The seller's pricing freedom varies with different types of markets. Economists recognize four types of markets, each presenting a different pricing challenge.

Under **pure competition,** the market consists of many buyers and sellers trading in a uniform commodity such as wheat, copper, or financial securities. No single buyer or seller has much effect on the going market price. A seller cannot charge more than the going price because buyers can obtain as much as they need at the going price. Nor would sellers charge less than the market price because they can sell all they want at this price. If price and profits rise, new sellers can easily enter the market. In a purely competitive market, marketing research, product development, pricing, advertising, and sales promotion play little or no role. Thus, sellers in these markets do not spend much time on marketing strategy.

Under **monopolistic competition,** the market consists of many buyers and sellers who trade over a range of prices rather than a single market price. A range of prices occurs because sellers can differentiate their offers to buyers. Either the physical product can be varied in quality, features, or style, or the accompanying services can be varied. Buyers see differences in sellers' products and will pay different prices for them. Sellers try to develop differentiated offers for different customer segments and, in addition to price, freely use branding, advertising, and personal selling to set their offers apart. For example, H.J. Heinz, Vlasic, and several other national brands of pickles compete with dozens of regional and local brands, all differentiated by price and nonprice factors. Because there are many competitors, each firm is less affected by competitors' marketing strategies than in oligopolistic markets.

Monopolistic competition: In the industrial market, Stanley sets its hinges apart from dozens of other brands using both price and nonprice factors.

Under **oligopolistic competition,** the market consists of a few sellers who are highly sensitive to each other's pricing and marketing strategies. The product can be uniform (steel, aluminum) or nonuniform (cars, computers). There are few sellers because it is difficult for new sellers to enter the market. Each seller is alert to competitors' strategies and moves. If a steel company slashes its price by 10 percent, buyers will quickly switch to this supplier. The other steel-makers must respond by lowering their prices or increasing their services. An oligopolist is never sure that it will gain anything permanent through a price cut. In contrast, if an oligopolist raises its price, its competitors might not follow this lead. The oligopolist then would have to retract its price increase or risk losing customers to competitors.

In a **pure monopoly,** the market consists of one seller. The seller may be a government monopoly (the U.S. Postal Service), a private regulated monopoly (a power company), or a private nonregulated monopoly (Du Pont when it introduced nylon). Pricing is handled differently in each case. A government monopoly can pursue a variety of pricing objectives. It might set a price below cost because the product is important to buyers who cannot afford to pay full cost. Or the price might be set either to cover costs or to produce good revenue. It can even be set quite high to slow down consumption. In a regulated monopoly, the government permits the company to set rates that will yield a "fair return," one that will let the company maintain and expand its operations as needed. Nonregulated monopolies are free to price at what the market will bear. However, they do not always charge the full price for a number of reasons: a desire not to attract competition, a desire to penetrate the market faster with a low price, a fear of government regulation.

Consumer Perceptions of Price and Value. In the end, the consumer will decide whether a product's price is right. When setting prices, the company must consider consumer perceptions of price and how these perceptions affect consumers' buying decisions. Pricing decisions, like other marketing-mix decisions, must be buyer oriented:

> Pricing requires more than technical expertise. It requires creative judgment and an awareness of buyers' motivations. . . . The key to effective pricing is the same one that opens doors . . . in other marketing functions: a creative awareness of who buyers are, why they buy, and how they make their buying decisions. The recognition that buyers differ in these dimensions is as important for effective pricing as it is for effective promotion, distribution, or product development.[7]

When consumers buy a product, they exchange something of value (the price) to get something of value (the benefits of having or using the product). Effective, buyer-oriented pricing involves understanding how much value consumers place on the benefits they receive from the product and setting a price that fits this value. These benefits can be actual or perceived. For example, calculating the cost of ingredients in a meal at a fancy restaurant is relatively easy. But assigning a value to other satisfactions such as taste, environment, relaxation, conversation, and status is very hard. And these values will vary both for different consumers and different situations. Thus, the company often will find it hard to measure the values customers will attach to its product. But the consumer does use these values to evaluate a product's price. If the consumer perceives that the price is greater than the product's value, the consumer will not buy the product. If consumers perceive that the price is below the product's value, they will buy it, but the seller loses profit opportunities (see Marketing Highlight 12-2).

Marketers therefore must try to understand the consumer's reasons for buying the product and set price according to consumer perceptions of the product's value. Because consumers vary in the values they assign to different product features, marketers often vary their pricing strategies for different segments. They offer different sets of product features at different prices. For example, television manufacturers offer small, inexpensive models for consumers who want basic sets and larger, higher-priced models loaded with features for consumers who want the extras.

Buyer-oriented pricing means that the marketer cannot design a product and marketing program and then set the price. Good pricing begins with analyzing consumer needs and price perceptions. Price must be considered along with the other marketing-mix variables *before* the marketing program is set.[8]

Miata's Popularity Drives Its Prices

How much would you pay for a curvaceous new two-seat convertible that has the reliability of modern engineering yet the look, feel, and sound of such classic roadsters as the 1959 Triumph TR3, the 1958 MGA, the 1962 Lotus Elan, or the Austin-Healy Sprite? The car was the Mazda MX-5 Miata, *the* hot new car of 1990. Not only did consumers rave about its looks, car critics passionately praised its performance. According to *Car and Driver*, if the Miata "were any more talented or tempting, driving one would be illegal." And judging on design, performance, durability and reliability, entertainment, and value, *Road & Track* named it one of the five best cars in the world. Others included in the rankings along with the Miata included the Porsche 911 Carrera, the Corvette ZR-1, the Mercedes-Benz 300 E, and the $140,000 Ferrari Testarossa. Not bad company for a car with a base sticker price of just $13,800 that was designed "just to be fun." Aside from its good looks, performance, and price, the Miata rocketed to success because it had no substitutes. Its closest competitors were the Honda CRX Si and the Toyota MR2, but they lacked its singular looks and neither came as a convertible. Thus, the Miata drove rivals to despair and customers into a covetous swoon.

Mazda had a hard time with the question of how to price its classy little car. The Japanese importer carefully controlled costs to keep the Miata's base price below $15,000. But it seems that consumers cared little about Mazda's costs, or about its intended price. When the Miata debuted, sales soared—and so did its prices. The first few thousand Miatas to arrive at Mazda dealerships sold out instantly. To make things even more interesting, Mazda planned to ship only 20,000 Miatas (in three colors—red, white, and blue) to its 844 dealers in 1989, and only 40,000 more in 1990. Thus, demand exceeded the limited supply by a reported ratio of ten to one.

The Miata was in such demand that dealers jacked up the price way beyond the sticker and still had barely enough cars to sell. Because of the car's popularity, customers were more than willing to pay the higher price. As one dealer noted, "People are offering more than what we're asking just to get [the car]." On average, dealers across the United States marked up prices $4,000; in California, they added as much as $8,000. Some enterprising owners even offered to sell their Miatas for prices ranging up to $45,000. Ads appeared daily in the *Los Angeles Times* from owners in Kansas, Nebraska, or Michigan proffering their Miatas for $32,000 plus delivery fees.

Thus, although many companies focus on costs as a key to setting prices, consumers rarely know of or care about the seller's costs. What really counts is what consumers are willing to pay for the benefits of owning the product. To some consumers, the sharp little Miata added up to much more than the sum of its mechanical parts. To them, it delivered the same pleasures and prestige as cars selling at much higher prices. Therefore, even at above-sticker prices, most buyers got a good deal. Mazda, on the other hand, may have left some money on the table.

Sources: Rebecca Fannin, "Mazda's Sporting Chance," *Marketing & Media Decisions*, October 1989, pp. 24-30; S. C. Gwynne, "Romancing the Roadster," *Time*, July 24, 1989, p. 39; "The Roadster Returns," *Consumer Reports*, April 1990, pp. 232-34; and Larry Armstrong, "After the Miata, Mazda Isn't Just Idling," *Business Week*, September 2, 1991, p. 35.

Aside from its good looks, performance, and price, the Miata rocketed to success because it had no substitutes.

Analyzing the Price-Demand Relationship. Each price the company might charge will lead to a different level of demand. The relation between the price charged and the resulting demand level is shown in the **demand curve** in Figure 12-4A. The demand curve shows the number of units the market will buy in a given time period at different prices that might be charged. In the normal case, demand and price are inversely related: That is, the higher the price, the lower the demand. Thus, the company would sell less if it raised its price from P_1 to P_2. In short, consumers with limited budgets probably will buy less of something if its price is too high.

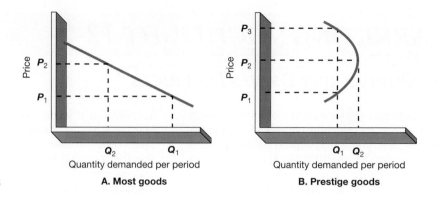

FIGURE 12-4
Hypothetical demand curves

A. Most goods

B. Prestige goods

Most demand curves slope downward in either a straight or a curved line, as in Figure 12-4A. But for prestige goods, the demand curve sometimes slopes upward, as in Figure 12-4B. For example, one perfume company found that by raising its price from P_1 to P_2, it sold more perfume rather than less. Consumers thought the higher price meant a better or more desirable perfume. However, if the company charges too high a price (P_3), the level of demand will be lower than at P_2.

Most companies try to measure their demand curves. The type of market makes a difference. In a monopoly, the demand curve shows the total market demand resulting from different prices. If the company faces competition, its demand at different prices will depend on whether competitors' prices stay constant or change with the company's own prices. Here, we will assume that competitors' prices remain constant. Later in this chapter, we will discuss what happens when competitors' prices change. To measure a demand curve requires estimating demand at different prices.

In measuring the price-demand relationship, the market researcher must not allow other factors affecting demand to vary. For example, if Quaker State raised its advertising budget at the same time that it lowered its price, we would not know how much of the increased demand was due to the lower price and how much was due to the increased advertising. The same problem arises if a holiday weekend occurs when the lower price is set—more travel over the holidays causes people to buy more oil.

Economists show the impact of nonprice factors on demand through shifts in the demand curve rather than movements along it. Suppose the initial demand curve is D_1 in Figure 12-5. The seller is charging P and selling Q_1 units. Now suppose the economy suddenly improves or the seller doubles its advertising budget. The higher demand is reflected through an upward shift of the demand curve from D_1 to D_2. Without changing the price, P, the seller's demand is now Q_2.

Price Elasticity of Demand. Marketers also need to know **price elasticity**—how responsive demand will be to a change in price. Consider the two demand curves in Figure 12-6. In Figure 12-6A, a price increase from P_1 to P_2 leads to a relatively small drop in demand from Q_1 to Q_2. In Figure 12-6B, however, the same price increase leads to a large drop in demand from Q_1 to Q_2. If demand hardly changes with a small change in price, we say the demand is *inelastic*. If de-

FIGURE 12–5
Effects of promotion and other nonprice variables on demand shown through shifts of the demand curve

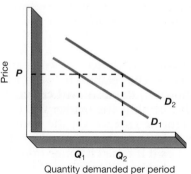

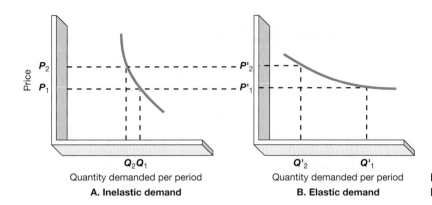

Quantity demanded per period
A. Inelastic demand

Quantity demanded per period
B. Elastic demand

FIGURE 12-6
Inelastic and elastic demand

mand changes greatly, we say the demand is *elastic*. The price elasticity of demand is given by the following formula:

$$\text{Price elasticity of demand} = \frac{\%\ \text{change in quantity demanded}}{\%\ \text{change in price}}$$

Suppose demand falls by 10 percent when a seller raises its price by 2 percent. Price elasticity of demand is therefore –5 (the minus sign confirms the inverse relation between price and demand) and demand is elastic. If demand falls by 2 percent with a 2 percent increase in price, then elasticity is –1. In this case, the seller's total revenue stays the same: The seller sells fewer items but at a higher price that preserves the same total revenue. If demand falls by 1 percent when price is increased by 2 percent, then elasticity is –1/2 and demand is inelastic. The less elastic the demand, the more it pays for the seller to raise the price.

What determines the price elasticity of demand? Buyers are less price sensitive when the product they are buying is unique or when it is high in quality, prestige, or exclusiveness. They are also less price sensitive when substitute products are hard to find or when they cannot easily compare the quality of substitutes. Finally, buyers are less price sensitive when the total expenditure for a product is low relative to their income or when the cost is shared by another party.[9]

If demand is elastic rather than inelastic, sellers will consider lowering their price. A lower price will produce more total revenue. This practice makes sense as long as the extra costs of producing and selling more do not exceed the extra revenue.

Competitors' Costs, Prices, and Offers

Another external factor affecting the company's pricing decisions is competitors' costs and prices and possible competitor reactions to the company's own pricing moves. A consumer who is considering the purchase of a Canon camera will evaluate Canon's price and value against the prices and values of comparable products made by Nikon, Minolta, Pentax, and others. In addition, the company's pricing strategy may affect the nature of the competition it faces. If Canon follows a high-price, high-margin strategy, it may attract competition. A low-price, low-margin strategy, however, may stop competitors or drive them out of the market.

Canon needs to benchmark its costs against its competitors' costs to learn whether it is operating at a cost advantage or disadvantage. It also needs to learn the price and quality of each competitor's offer. Canon might do this in several ways. It can send out comparison shoppers to price and compare the products of Nikon, Minolta, and other competitors. It can get competitors' price lists and buy competitors' equipment and take it apart. It can ask buyers how they view the price and quality of each competitor's camera.

Once Canon is aware of competitors' prices and offers, it can use them as a starting point for its own pricing. If Canon's cameras are similar to Nikon's, it will have to price close to Nikon or lose sales. If Canon's cameras are not as good as Nikon's, the firm will not be able to charge as much. If Canon's products are better than Nikon's, it can charge more. Basically, Canon will use price to position its offer relative to the competition.

MARKETING HIGHLIGHT 12-3

PRICING PHARMACEUTICAL PRODUCTS: MORE THAN SALES AND PROFITS

The U.S. pharmaceutical industry has been the nation's most profitable industry. On average, as a result of the hefty margins they attach to the medicines they sell, U.S. drug makers earn a 50 percent greater return on investment than large companies in other industries do. And while many American industries have suffered in the global marketplace, the U.S. pharmaceutical industry, with annual revenues of more than $50 billion, claims more than 40 percent of the world's pharmaceutical business.

However, critics of the industry claim that this success has come at the expense of consumers—that such success is possible only because competitive forces do not operate well in the pharmaceutical market. Consumers don't usually shop around for the best deal on medicines—they simply take what the doctor orders. Because physicians who write the prescriptions don't pay for the medicines they recommend, they have little incentive to be price conscious. Moreover, third-party payers—insurance companies, health plans, and government programs—often pay all or part of the bill. Finally, competition is less of a factor. In other industries, a highly profitable market leader attracts imitators that compete by offering additional features or lower prices. In the pharmaceutical industry, however, the huge investment and time needed to develop and test a new drug discourages competitors from challenging the market leader.

These market factors sometimes leave pharmaceutical companies free to practice monopoly pricing. As a result, during the past decade, pharmaceutical prices have risen at more than twice the rate of inflation. New drugs commonly sell at wholesale prices that are three to six times what the drugs cost to make. In some cases, the seemingly outlandish pricing of specific drugs has led to accusations of price gouging and profiteering by outraged consumers, advocacy groups, and public policy makers. For example, Burroughs Wellcome initially priced AZT, its patented medicine for treating AIDS, at $10,000 per yearly dosage, far in excess of the manufacturing costs and much more than many AIDS sufferers could afford. Another controversial case involved Sandoz, maker of Clozaril, a breakthrough medicine for treating schizophrenia. Sandoz initially required that Clozaril users take weekly blood tests and insisted that the drug and tests be purchased from a specified California supplier. The cost per year to buyers: $9,000. Although Burroughs Wellcome later reduced its prices and Sandoz dropped its testing requirement, the industry remains under assault for its pricing practices.

Pharmaceutical firms counter charges of unfair pricing by pointing to the enormous costs of developing new medicines. The Food and Drug Administration has developed strict rules for the introduction of new drugs—FDA testing and evaluation can take more than ten years. Drug makers estimate that it costs more than $230 million to develop a new medicine, including costs of compounds that never make it through the approval process. And after a decade of testing, they have only a few years left in which to recoup development costs before their 17-year patent protection runs out. Once a patent expires, the drug becomes "generic"—any

Other External Factors

When setting prices, the company also must consider other factors in its external environment. *Economic conditions* can have a strong impact on the firm's pricing strategies. Economic factors such as inflation, boom or recession, and interest rates affect pricing decisions because they affect both the costs of producing a product and consumer perceptions of the product's price and value. The company also must consider what impact its prices will have on other parties in its environment. How will *resellers* react to various prices? The company should set prices that give resellers a fair profit, encourage their support, and help them to sell the product effectively. The *government* is another important external influence on pricing decisions. Finally, *social concerns* may have to be taken into account. In setting prices, a company's short-term sales, market share, and profit goals may have to be tempered by broader societal considerations (see Marketing Highlight 12-3).

GENERAL PRICING APPROACHES

The price the company charges will be somewhere between one that is too low to produce a profit and one that is too high to produce any demand. Figure 12-7 summarizes the major considerations in setting price. Product costs set a floor to pharmaceutical manufacturer can make it. Competition from generic medicines lowers prices dramatically. Thus, the industry argues that high prices and margins on patented medicines are essential to fund future research and the development of new drugs.

Advocates also point out that although drugs are expensive, they are a bargain. For example, drugs and supplies as a percent of all U.S. medical spending have declined from 16 percent in the 1960s to only 7 percent today. This is far less than in Japan, where drugs make up 17 percent of health spending. Advocates further argue that the industry's life-saving work *should* be well paid. True, they say, many pharmaceutical products are expensive, but this business saves lives. The benefits are incalculable, and treatment with medication is often much cheaper than alternatives such as surgery. Critics don't buy this argument. Says one U.S. senator, "It may be lifesaving . . . but that does not mean you can charge whatever you want for it. I can afford to buy my drugs. Too many other Americans simply cannot."

Most Americans appreciate the steady stream of beneficial drugs produced by the U.S. pharmaceutical industry. Although some may be concerned about delays in getting lifesaving medicines to the market, most are also grateful for the careful weighing of risks and benefits provided by the FDA review process. However, there is increasing concern that the industry may be taking advantage of its monopoly pricing power—the United States remains the only country in the world which has no governmental review of pharmaceutical prices. As a result, the industry is facing ever-greater pressure from the federal government, insurance companies, and consumer advocates to exercise restraint in setting prices. Legislation has been passed to curb drug pricing, and more is pending. For example, a new federal law requires pharmaceutical companies to give 12.5 percent discounts to state medicaid programs for the poor.

Rather than waiting for tougher legislation on drug prices, some forward-thinking drug companies are taking action on their own. For example, Merck and Glaxo have agreed to keep their average price hikes at or below inflation. Bristol-Meyers Squibb has voluntarily provided discounts to agencies such as the U.S. Public Health Service and to federally funded drug- and alcohol-treatment centers. Glaxo and other companies make free drugs available to people who cannot afford them. These companies recognize that in setting prices, their short-term sales, market share, and profit goals must be tempered by broader societal considerations. They know that in the long run, socially responsible pricing will benefit both the consumer and the company.

Sources: Quoted material from Brian O'Reilly, "Drugmakers Under Attack," *Fortune*, July 29, 1991, pp. 48-63. Also see Joseph Weber, "For Drugmakers, the Sky's no Longer the Limit," *Business Week*, January 27, 1992, p. 68; Ronald Kotulak, "Companies Attacked for Rising Drug Prices," *Durham Herald-Sun*, May 25, 1992, pp. A1-A2; Elyse Tanouye, "Price Rises for Drugs Cool, Manufacturer Profits Chill," *The Wall Street Journal*, April 9, 1992, p. B4; Patricia Winters, "Drugmakers Portrayed as Villains, Worry about Image," *Advertising Age*, February 22, 1993, pp. 1, 42; John Carey, "A Bitter Tonic for Drugmakers," *Business Week*, March 8, 1993, pp. 84-86; and Shawn Tully, "Why Drug Prices Will Go Lower," *Fortune*, May 3, 1993, pp. 56-66.

the price; consumer perceptions of the product's value set the ceiling. The company must consider competitors' prices and other external and internal factors to find the best price between these two extremes.

Companies set prices by selecting a general pricing approach that includes one or more of these three sets of factors. We will examine the following approaches: the *cost-based approach* (cost-plus pricing, breakeven analysis, and target profit pricing); the *buyer-based approach* (perceived-value pricing); and the *competition-based approach* (going-rate and sealed-bid pricing).

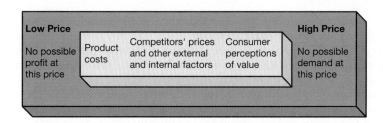

Cost-Based Pricing

Cost-Plus Pricing

The simplest pricing method is **cost-plus pricing**—adding a standard markup to the cost of the product. Construction companies, for example, submit job bids by estimating the total project cost and adding a standard markup for profit. Lawyers, accountants, and other professionals typically price by adding a standard markup to their costs. Some sellers tell their customers they will charge cost plus a specified markup; for example, aerospace companies price this way to the government.

To illustrate markup pricing, suppose a toaster manufacturer had the following costs and expected sales:

Variable cost	$10
Fixed cost	$300,000
Expected unit sales	50,000

Then the manufacturer's cost per toaster is given by:

$$\text{Unit cost} = \text{Variable cost} + \frac{\text{fixed costs}}{\text{unit sales}} = \$10 + \frac{\$300,000}{50,000} = \$16$$

Now suppose the manufacturer wants to earn a 20 percent markup on sales. The manufacturer's markup price is given by:[10]

$$\text{Markup price} = \frac{\text{unit cost}}{(1 - \text{desired return on sales})} = \frac{\$16}{1 - .2} = \$20$$

The manufacturer would charge dealers $20 a toaster and make a profit of $4 per unit. The dealers, in turn, will mark up the toaster. If dealers want to earn 50 percent on sales price, they will mark up the toaster to $40 ($20 + 50% of $40). This number is equivalent to a *markup on cost* of 100 percent ($20/$20).

Markups vary greatly among different goods. Some common markups (on price, not cost) in supermarkets are 9 percent on baby foods, 14 percent on tobacco products, 20 percent on bakery products, 27 percent on dried foods and vegetables, 37 percent on spices and extracts, and 50 percent on greeting cards.[11] But these markups vary greatly around the averages. In the spices and extracts category, for example, markups on retail price range from a low of 19 percent to a high of 56 percent. Markups are generally higher on seasonal items (to cover the risk of not selling), and on specialty items, slower moving items, items with high storage and handling costs, and items with inelastic demand.

Does using standard markups to set prices make logical sense? Generally, no. Any pricing method that ignores current demand and competition is not likely to lead to the best price. Suppose the toaster manufacturer charged $20 but only sold 30,000 toasters instead of 50,000. Then the unit cost would have been higher since the fixed costs are spread over fewer units, and the realized percentage markup on sales would have been lower. Markup pricing only works if that price actually brings in the expected level of sales.

Still, markup pricing remains popular for many reasons. First, sellers are more certain about costs than about demand. By tying the price to cost, sellers simplify pricing—they do not have to make frequent adjustments as demand changes. Second, when all firms in the industry use this pricing method, prices tend to be similar and price competition is thus minimized. Third, many people feel that cost-plus pricing is fairer to both buyers and sellers. Sellers earn a fair return on their investment but do not take advantage of buyers when buyers' demand becomes great.

Breakeven Analysis and Target Profit Pricing

Another cost-oriented pricing approach is **breakeven pricing,** or a variation called **target profit pricing.** The firm tries to determine the price at which it will break even or make the target profit it is seeking. Target pricing is used by General Motors, which prices its automobiles to achieve a 15 percent to 20 percent profit on its investment. This pricing method is also used by public utilities, which are constrained to make a fair return on their investment.

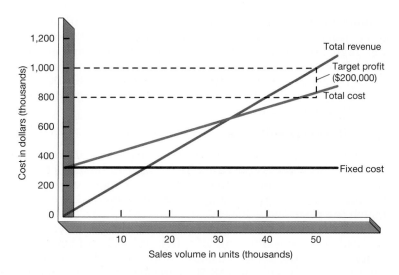

FIGURE 12-8
Breakeven chart for determining target price

Target pricing uses the concept of a *breakeven chart*. A breakeven chart shows the total cost and total revenue expected at different sales volume levels. Figure 12-8 shows a breakeven chart for the toaster manufacturer discussed here. Fixed costs are $300,000 regardless of sales volume. Variable costs are added to fixed costs to form total costs, which rise with volume. The total revenue curve starts at zero and rises with each unit sold. The slope of the total revenue curve reflects the price of $20 per unit.

The total revenue and total cost curves cross at 30,000 units. This is the *breakeven volume*. At $20, the company must sell at least 30,000 units to break even; that is, for total revenue to cover total cost. Breakeven volume can be calculated using the following formula:

$$\text{Breakeven volume} = \frac{\text{fixed cost}}{\text{price} - \text{variable cost}} = \frac{\$300,000}{\$20 - \$10} = 30,000$$

If the company wants to make a target profit, it must sell more than 30,000 units at $20 each. Suppose the toaster manufacturer has invested $1,000,000 in the business and wants to set a price to earn a 20 percent return, or $200,000. In that case, it must sell at least 50,000 units at $20 each. If the company charges a higher price, it will not need to sell as many toasters to achieve its target return. But the market may not buy even this lower volume at the higher price. Much depends on the price elasticity and competitors' prices.

The manufacturer should consider different prices and estimate breakeven volumes, probable demand, and profits for each. This is done in Table 12-1. The table shows that as price increases, breakeven volume drops (column 2). But as price increases, demand for the toasters also falls off (column 3). At the $14 price, because the manufacturer clears only $4 per toaster ($14 less $10 in variable costs), it must sell a very high volume to break even. Even though the low price attracts many buyers, demand still falls below the high breakeven point, and the

TABLE 12-1
Breakeven Volume and Profits at Different Prices

(1) PRICE	(2) UNIT DEMAND NEEDED TO BREAK EVEN	(3) EXPECTED UNIT DEMAND AT GIVEN PRICE	(4) TOTAL REVENUES (1) × (3)	(5) TOTAL COSTS*	(6) PROFIT (4) – (5)
$14	75,000	71,000	$ 994,000	$1,100,000	–$32,000
16	50,000	67,000	1,072,000	970,000	102,000
18	37,500	60,000	1,080,000	900,000	180,000
20	30,000	42,000	840,000	720,000	120,000
22	25,000	23,000	506,000	530,000	–24,000

*Assumes fixed costs of $300,000 and constant unit variable costs of $10.

manufacturer loses money. At the other extreme, with a $22 price the manufacturer clears $12 per toaster and must sell only 25,000 units to break even. But at this high price, consumers buy too few toasters, and profits are negative. The table shows that a price of $18 yields the highest profits. Note that none of the prices produce the manufacturer's target profit of $200,000. To achieve this target return, the manufacturer will have to search for ways to lower fixed or variable costs, thus lowering the breakeven volume.

Buyer-Based Pricing

An increasing number of companies are basing their prices on the product's perceived value. **Perceived-value pricing** uses buyers' perceptions of value, not the seller's cost, as the key to pricing. The company uses the nonprice variables in the marketing mix to build up perceived value in buyers' minds. Price is set to match the perceived value.

Consider the various prices different restaurants charge for the same items. A consumer who wants a cup of coffee and a slice of apple pie may pay $1.75 at a drugstore counter, $3.00 at a family restaurant, $4.50 at a hotel coffee shop, $6.00 for hotel room service, and $8.50 at an elegant restaurant. Each succeeding restaurant can charge more because of the value added by the atmosphere.

A company using perceived-value pricing must find out what value buyers assign to different competitive offers. In the preceding example, consumers could be asked how much they would pay for the same coffee and pie in the different surroundings. Sometimes consumers are asked how much they would pay for each benefit added to the offer. If the seller charges more than the buyers' perceived value, the company's sales will suffer. Many companies overprice their products, and their products sell poorly. Other companies underprice. Underpriced products sell very well, but they produce less revenue than they would if price were raised to the perceived-value level.

Competition-Based Pricing

Going-Rate Pricing

In **going-rate pricing**, the firm bases its price largely on *competitors'* prices, with less attention paid to its *own* costs or to demand. The firm might charge the same, more, or less than its major competitors. In oligopolistic industries that sell a commodity such as steel, paper, or fertilizer, firms normally charge the same price. The smaller firms follow the leader: They change their prices when the market leader's prices change, rather than when their own demand or costs change. Some firms may charge a bit more or less, but they hold the amount of difference constant. Thus, minor gasoline retailers usually charge a few cents less than the major oil companies, without letting the difference increase or decrease.

Going-rate pricing is quite popular. When demand elasticity is hard to measure, firms feel that the going price represents the collective wisdom of the industry concerning the price that will yield a fair return. They also feel that holding to the going price will prevent harmful price wars.

Sealed-Bid Pricing

Competition-based pricing is also used when firms *bid* for jobs. Using **sealed-bid pricing,** a firm bases its price on how it thinks competitors will price rather than on its own costs or on the demand. The firm wants to win a contract, and winning the contract requires pricing lower than other firms.

Yet the firm cannot set its price below a certain level. It cannot price below cost without harming its position. In contrast, the higher the company sets its price above its costs, the less its chance of getting the contract.

The net effect of the two opposite pulls can be described in terms of the *expected profit* of the particular bid (see Table 12-2). Suppose a bid of $9,500 would yield a high chance (say .81) of getting the contract, but only a low profit (say $100). The expected profit with this bid is therefore $81. If the firm bid $11,000, its profit would be $1,600, but its chance of getting the contract might be reduced to .01. The expected profit would be only $16. Thus the company might bid the price that would maximize the expected profit. According to Table 12-2, the best bid would be $10,000, for which the expected profit is $216.

Using expected profit as a basis for setting price makes sense for the large firm that makes many bids. In playing the odds, the firm will make maximum

Perceived value: A less expensive pen might write as well, but some consumers will pay much more for the intangibles. This Parker model runs $185. Others are priced as high as $3,500.

TABLE 12-2
Effect of Different Bids on Expected Profit

COMPANY'S BID	COMPANY'S PROFIT (1)	PROBABILITY OF WINNING WITH THIS BID (ASSUMED) (2)	EXPECTED PROFIT [(1) × (2)]
$ 9,500	$ 100	.81	$ 81
10,000	600	.36	216
10,500	1,100	.09	99
11,000	1,600	.01	16

profits in the long run. But a firm that bids only occasionally or needs a particular contract badly will not find the expected-profit approach useful. The approach, for example, does not distinguish between a $100,000 profit with a .10 probability and a $12,500 profit with an .80 probability. Yet the firm that wants to keep production going would prefer the second contract to the first.

 # SUMMARY

Despite the increased role of nonprice factors in the modern marketing process, *price* remains an important element in the marketing mix. Many internal and external factors influence the company's pricing decisions. *Internal factors* include the firm's *marketing objectives, marketing-mix strategy, costs*, and *organization for pricing*.

The pricing strategy is largely determined by the company's *target market and positioning objectives*. Common pricing objectives include survival, current profit maximization, market-share leadership, and product-quality leadership.

Price is only one of the marketing-mix tools the company uses to accomplish its objectives, and pricing decisions affect and are affected by product design, distribution, and promotion decisions. Price decisions must be carefully coordinated with the other marketing-mix decisions when designing the marketing program.

Costs set the floor for the company's price—the price must cover all the costs of making and selling the product, plus a fair rate of return. Management must decide who within the organization is responsible for setting price. In large companies, some pricing authority may be delegated to lower-level managers and salespeople, but top management usually sets pricing policies and approves proposed prices. Production, finance, and accounting managers also influence pricing.

External factors that influence pricing decisions include the nature of the market and demand;

competitors' prices and offers; and factors such as the economy, reseller needs, and government actions. The seller's pricing freedom varies with different types of markets. Pricing is especially challenging in markets characterized by monopolistic competition or oligopoly.

In the end, the consumer decides whether the company has set the right price. The consumer weighs the price against the perceived values of using the product—if the price exceeds the sum of the values, consumers will not buy the product. Consumers differ in the values they assign to different product features, and marketers often vary their pricing strategies for different price segments. When assessing the market and demand, the company estimates the demand schedule, which shows the probable quantity purchased per period at alternative price levels. The more *inelastic* the demand, the higher the company can set its price. *Demand* and *consumer value perceptions* set the ceiling for prices.

Consumers compare a product's price to the prices of *competitors'* products. A company must learn the price and quality of competitors' offers and use them as a starting point for its own pricing.

The company can select one or a combination of three general pricing approaches: the *cost-based approach* (cost-plus pricing, breakeven analysis, and target profit pricing); the *buyer-based approach* (perceived-value pricing); and the *competition-based approach* (going-rate or sealed-bid pricing).

KEY TERMS

Breakeven pricing (target profit pricing) 360

Cost-plus pricing 360

Demand curve 355

Experience curve (learning curve) 352

Fixed costs 350

Going-rate pricing 362

Monopolistic competition 353

Oligopolistic competition 354

Perceived-value pricing 362

Price 347

Price elasticity 356

Pure competition 353

Pure monopoly 354

Sealed-bid pricing 362

Total costs 350

Variable costs 350

DISCUSSING THE ISSUES

1. Certain "inexpensive" products that waste energy, provide few servings per container, or require frequent maintenance may *cost* much more to own and use than do products selling for a higher *price*. How can marketers use this information on "true cost" to gain a competitive edge in pricing and promoting their products?

2. Detergent A is priced at $2.19 for 32 ounces, and detergent B is priced at $1.99 for 26 ounces. Which appears most attractive? Which is the better value, assuming equal quality? Is there a psychological reason to price in this way?

3. Procter & Gamble replaced its 16-ounce packages of regular Folgers coffee with 13-ounce "fast-roast" packages. Fast roasting allows Procter & Gamble to use fewer coffee beans per pack with no impact on flavor or the number of servings per package. Which pricing approach was appropriate for setting the price for the fast-roast coffee—cost-based, buyer-based, or competition-based pricing?

4. Sales of Fleischmann's gin *increased* when prices were raised 22 percent over a two-year period. What does this tell you about the demand curve and the elasticity of demand for Fleischmann's gin? What does this suggest about using perceived-value pricing in marketing alcoholic beverages?

5. Genentech, a high-technology pharmaceutical company, has developed a clot-dissolving drug called TPA that will halt a heart attack in progress. TPA saves lives, minimizes hospital stays, and reduces damage to the heart itself. It was initially priced at $2,200 per dose. What pricing approach does Genentech appear to be using? Is demand for this drug likely to be elastic with price?

6. Columnist Dave Barry jokes that federal law requires this message under the sticker price of new cars: "Warning to stupid people: Do not pay this amount." Why is the sticker price generally higher than the actual selling price of a car? How do car dealers set the actual prices of the cars they sell?

APPLYING THE CONCEPTS

1. Do a pricing survey of several gasoline stations in your town in different locations. If possible, check prices at the following: stations at an exit ramp on a major highway, stations on your local strip, convenience stores, and a smaller station that is not near any other stations. Write down the brand of gasoline, prices of regular and premium grades, type of location, distance to the nearest competitor, and the competitor's prices. (a) Is there a pattern to the pricing of gasoline at various outlets? (b) Do you think that these stations are using cost-based, buyer-based, or going-rate pricing?

2. You have inherited an automatic car wash where annual fixed costs are $50,000 and variable costs are $0.50 per car washed. You think people would be willing to pay $1 to have their car washed. What would be the break-even volume at that price?

MAKING MARKETING DECISIONS:

SMALL WORLD COMMUNICATIONS, INC.

Lynette Jones and Thomas Campbell are moving ahead with plans to market a communications device for personal computers. Based on their research and conversations, they have tentatively named the product "Airport." This unique product combines the functions of a modem, fax, and voice mail with additional inputs for image scanners, video, and audio. Several modules of integrated software will allow users to interlink their current programs with database services and other hardware. Their positioning statement reads: "For computer users who are interested in communications, Airport is the communications integrator that connects your world."

"How on earth are we going to price this product?" wondered Tom as he spoke to Lyn on the phone. "It looks like pricing is the only part of the marketing mix that computer makers know how to use, and they use it to shoot themselves in the foot. In most product categories you can count on a bit of price inflation, or at least price stability. But in computer gear I'm seeing a lot of products that are selling for *half* the price they were a year ago." Lyn replied, "Well, you've seen this pricing frenzy all along at San Andreas Products, your former employer. What did you do there?" "I ignore it," Tom said. "San Andreas uses a mix of two approaches. The finance guys set target profit levels for new products, and then they set target cost levels for the product. My mission, should I choose to accept it, is to design a working product that meets their unworkable cost goals. Then comes the fun. The marketing department lowers the price to the going rate—the original target price is always out of date by this time—and the finance guys scream. Then management hammers purchasing and manufacturing into starting frantic cost savings programs, and . . . wait a minute. Lyn, did you say my *former* employer, San Andreas Products? I'm sitting at S.A.P. as we speak, and

I'm under the impression that I still work here." "Not for long, bucko," Lyn replied. "Our lawyer's drawn up the incorporation papers, I just got my annual bonus, and I'm ready to say goodbye to Fond du Lac Foods. I need you on board full time so that everything's ready when we go to the venture capitalists next month." "Lynette," he said, attempting to sound icy, "just what do you mean by *everything*?" Lyn knew that he wasn't really ready for the truth, so she stalled him. "I'm putting together a chart with all of our timelines on it, and I'll show it to you in the next day or two. In the meantime, give your employer notice and sell some of your stock to tide you over until the venture capital comes in."

WHAT NOW?

1. Small World's new product, the Airport, currently has no direct competitors that offer all of the same benefits. There are, however, many existing products that perform some of the same functions. (a) Do you think Tom and Lyn should price for high volume at a low price (market-share leadership), or lower volume at a higher price (product-quality leadership)? Why? (b) What effect, if any, might these different strategies have on brand image? On profitability?

2. Small World plans to use a contract manufacturer to assemble its products. The manufacturer has given them a price quotation of $67.50 per unit, but requires a minimum volume of 5,000 units. (a) What are the variable costs to Small World? (b) What are the minimum expenditures that Small World can make for manufacturing? Do you think these minimum costs are a type of fixed cost? Explain.

REFERENCES

1. See James E. Ellis and Brian Bremner, "Will the Big Markdown Get the Big Store Moving Again?" *Business Week*, March 13, 1989, pp. 110-114; Kate Fitzgerald, "Sears' Plan on the Ropes," January 8, 1990, pp. 1, 42; Susan Caminiti, "Sears' Need: More Speed," *Fortune*, July 15, 1991; and Julia Flynn, "Smaller but Wiser," *Business Week*, October 12, 1992, pp. 28-29.

2. See David J. Schwartz, *Marketing Today: A Basic Approach*, 3rd ed. (New York: Harcourt Brace Jovanovich, 1981), pp. 270-73.

3. Ford S. Worthy, "Japan's Smart Secret Weapon," *Fortune*, August 12, 1991, pp. 72-75.

4. Brian Dumaine, "Closing the Innovation Gap," *Fortune*, December 2, 1991, pp. 56-62.

5. Here accumulated production is drawn on a semi-log scale so that equal distances represent the same percentage increase in output.

6. For more on experience curve strategies, see Pankaj Ghemawat, "Building Strategy on the Experience Curve," *Harvard Business Review*, March-April 1985, pp. 143-149; and William W. Alberts, "The Experience Curve Doctrine Reconsidered," *Journal of Marketing*, July 1989, pp. 36-49.

7. Thomas T. Nagle, "Pricing as Creative Marketing," *Business Horizons*, July-August 1983, p. 19.

8. See Thomas T. Nagle, *The Strategy and Tactics of Pricing* (Englewood Cliffs, NJ: Prentice Hall, 1987), pp. 1-9.

9. Ibid., Chap 3.

10. The arithmetic of markups and margins is discussed in Appendix 1, "Marketing Arithmetic."

11. "Supermarket 1984 Sales Manual," *Progressive Grocer*, July 1984.

VIDEO CASE 12

AMERICAN AIRLINES: PRICING VICTIM OR VILLAIN?

In the 19 years since Bob Crandall, the CEO of American Airlines, joined the company, he converted American from an also-ran to the nation's number-one air carrier. He accomplished this by developing the SABRE reservation system used as a travel agency booking tool and a sophisticated forecasting device; by introducing a two-tier wage structure to lower costs; by buying routes from failing Eastern Airlines and TWA; by introducing the Super Saver Fare Program to lure leisure travelers; and by creating AAdvantage, the industry's first frequent-flier program. Through greater efficiencies, lower costs, and creative pricing structures, American surged to the top of the airline industry.

By 1992, all airlines offered an incredible array of discount fares, based on time of day and day of the week flown, date of advance booking, and length of stay. They all had introduced special discounts such as bereavement, senior citizen, military, and corporate meeting fares; and they all promoted regular special sales and vacation packages that included airfares, hotels, and car rentals for a single low price. These pricing practices eroded industry profits and created losses for many airlines. Only nine domestic air carriers remained in business and three of these—Continental, America West and TWA—were in bankruptcy. Using its bankruptcy status to lower costs, TWA had carved a price niche in the market by charging fares 20 percent below American's.

In 1992, as industry leader, Bob Crandall decided that the time had come to eliminate the industry's messy pricing structure and frequent price cutting. In April, he introduced the Value Pricing Plan with the hope of creating price stability in the industry. The Plan offered only four fares on any route. Coach fares were reduced by 38 percent, but corporate and deep discounts were discontinued so that the average fare would rise.

The other airlines liked the structure and followed American's lead. But consumers, schooled to expect discounted and promotional ticket prices, did not like the new fares. When consumers failed to respond, TWA resumed its discounting and began holding one-day sales that ended before competitors could react. Then, US Air and Continental cut fares on flights to Florida, and America West offered cheaper off-peak fares. American responded by cutting fares in markets where it competed with these renegade carriers, and the simplified pricing structure was no longer very simple. To cap things off, in late May, 1992, Northwest Airlines introduced an adults-fly-free promotion to encourage families to fly during the summer season. Although some other carriers matched the promotion, Northwest's lead in announcing the special enabled it to garner most of the benefits. Its reservations shot up 176 percent in 24 hours.

American responded with a vengeance—it slashed all summer advance-purchase fares a thundering 50 percent. Other carriers had to follow suit and a fierce price war ensued. Consumers, in turn, responded with equal force, swamping travel agents and ticket counters. As consumers exchanged previously higher-priced tickets for discounted ones, travel agents found themselves working harder but losing commissions. Consequently, American, Delta, and Continental agreed to reimburse ticket agents for their losses.

The fare war resulted in a flood of red ink as airline losses mounted. Instead of the modest $300 million profit forecasted for the industry in 1992, losses for the year were expected to reach $3.5 billion—$500 million for the summer alone. In addition, other airlines accused American of engaging in predatory pricing. Bob Crandall countered that American's price discounting was necessary to discipline other firms in the industry. According to him, American was "victims of our dumbest competitors"—those that charge low fares, which American and others are forced to match but that often make it impossible for any carrier to make money.

After the 1992 fare war, American's parent company, AMR, apparently agreed with Crandall. It decided to cut its airline losses and enhance its competitive advantage in managing large information bases. To accomplish this, it laid off more than 500 airline employees and eliminated short-hop competitive routes that were losing money. In the future, American will use the SABRE Network to build the most extensive information and transportation databases in the United States, to plan pricing and information systems for the French high-speed train system, and to train ticket processors to handle medical and insurance claims for clients such as Blue Cross and Blue Shield, and Travelers. If these moves do not restore profitability to American, the next move could be to drop American Airlines as an AMR subsidiary.

QUESTIONS

1. In economic terms, how would you describe the airline industry? What can you say about demand?

2. What types of pricing practices do the airlines use? Are these appropriate?

3. Was American's attempt to simplify pricing a good idea? Was its "disciplinary action" appropriate?

4. Is American a "villain" or a victim?

Sources: Christina Duff, "Airlines Expect Break in Marathon of Ticket Sales," *The Wall Street Journal*, June 8, 1992, p. B5; James S. Hirsch, "Delta and Northwest Announce Boosts in Prices of Some Discounted Tickets, *The Wall Street Journal*, June 3, 1992, p. A2; Bridget O'Brian, "Tired of Airline Losses, AMR Pushes its Bid to Diversify Business, *The Wall Street Journal*, February 18, 1993, pp. A1, A8; "Simplifying Their Fares Proves More Difficult than Airlines Expected," *The Wall Street Journal*, June 4, 1992, pp. A1, A5; "AMR Expects to Report Loss for 2nd Period," *The Wall Street Journal*, June 18, 1992, p. A4; and Wendy Zellner, "The Airline Mess," *Business Week*, July 6, 1992, pp. 50-55.

COMPANY CASE 12

SILVERADO JEWELRY: A PRICING PARADOX

Silverado Jewelry Store, located in downtown Tempe, Arizona, specializes in handcrafted jewelry made by local Native Americans. Sheila Becker, the owner of Silverado, has just returned from a buying trip and is discussing an interesting pricing phenomenon with assistant store manager Mary Meindl.

Several months ago, the store had received a selection of mother-of-pearl stone and silver bracelets, earrings, and necklaces. Unlike the blue-green tones in typical turquoise jewelry designs, mother-of-pearl stone is pink with white marbling. In terms of size and style, the selection included a wide range of items. While some were small, round, rather simple designs, others were larger, bolder designs that were quite intricate. In addition, the collection included an assortment of traditionally styled men's studded string ties.

Sheila had purchased the mother-of-pearl selection at a very reasonable cost and was quite pleased with the distinctive product assortment. She thought the jewelry would appeal particularly to the general buyer seeking an alternative to the turquoise jewelry usually offered in shops all around Tempe. She priced the new jewelry so that shoppers would receive a good value for their money but also included a markup sufficient to cover the costs of doing business plus an average profit margin.

After the items had been displayed in the store for about a month, Sheila was disappointed in their sales. She decided to try several merchandising tactics that she had learned as a student at the University of Nevada. For example, realizing that the location of an item in the store will often influence whether or not patrons will examine merchandise, she moved the mother-of-pearl jewelry to a glass display case just to the right of the store entrance.

When sales of the mother-of-pearl merchandise still remained sluggish after the relocation, she decided to talk to store clerks about the jewelry during their weekly meeting. Suggesting that they put more effort into "pushing" this particular line, she provided them with a detailed description of the mother-of-pearl stone and supplied a short, scripted talk that they could memorize and recite for customers.

Unfortunately, this approach also failed. At this point, Sheila was preparing to leave on a buying trip. Frustrated over the sagging sales of the mother-of-pearl jewelry and anxious to reduce current inventory in order to make room for the newer selections that she would be buying, she decided to take drastic action: She would cut the mother-of-pearl prices in half. On her way out of the store, she hastily left a note for Mary Meindl. The note read:

Upon her return, Sheila was pleasantly surprised to find that the entire selection of mother-of-pearl jewelry had been sold. "I really can't understand why," she commented to Mary Meindl, "but that mother-of-pearl stuff just didn't appeal to our customers. I'll have to be more careful the next time I try to increase our variety of stones." Mary responded that although she couldn't quite understand why Sheila wanted to raise the price of slow-moving merchandise, she was surprised at how quickly it had sold at the higher price. Sheila was puzzled. "What higher price?" she asked. "My note said to cut the prices in half." "In *half*?" replied a startled Mary. "I thought your note said, 'Everything in this case *times two*!'" As a result, Mary had *doubled* rather than halved the prices.

QUESTIONS

1. Explain what happened in this situation. Why did the jewelry sell so quickly at twice its normal price?

2. What assumption had Sheila Becker made about the demand curve for the mother-of-pearl jewelry? What did the demand curve for this particular product actually look like?

3. In what type of market is Silverado Jewelry operating (pure competition, monopolistic competition, oligopolistic competition, or pure monopoly)? What leads you to this conclusion?

4. How would the concept of psychological pricing be useful to Sheila Becker? How would you advise her about future pricing decisions?

The introduction of a highly simplified, cost-efficient fare structure by American Airlines represents a significant step in bringing value back to air travel. What's behind this effort? How will it impact you? How will it benefit your operation and your clients? The answers to these and other questions are outlined below.

2. HOW LONG WILL THIS PROGRAM LAST?
These new fares are and part of a short-term sale. And our simplified fare structure is not a one-some airline promotion. It is the way we intend to do business from now on. Because we believe that booking and purchasing an airline ticket should be an easy, painless process. For us. For you. And for all of our customers.

3. WHY IS AMERICAN DOING THIS?
The most successful companies are those that listen to their customers. And you and our customers have told us not only that many airline fares are too expensive, but that the whole fare structure is far too complicated. Our new plan is in direct response to that feedback. The result is a new pricing program that is a more sensible and more simplified way to book and purchase air travel on American.

4. HOW CAN AMERICAN REDUCE FARES IN TODAY'S ECONOMY?
It is no secret that most airlines are struggling to make a profit in today's weak economy. And on the surface, it would appear that reducing our fares will only mean additional losses and less commission income for you. However, we expect that these lower prices will stimulate demand for our product and substantially increase the number of passengers we carry.

5. HOW WILL THIS NEW PRICING PROGRAM BENEFIT YOU?
With the elimination of so many complex fares, your clients will have greater confidence that they will be getting the best value for their money from American. More importantly, you will no longer have to go through the time-consuming and complex process of sorting through hundreds of fares to work out the best one for your clients. In addition, the new flexibility in our PlanAAhead fares will reduce the hassle of

HOW AMERICAN IS BRINGING VALUE BACK TO AIR TRAVEL.

dealing with clients who want to change their plans that don't want to lose their money. Our new fare structure will also mean additional benefits for your agency, since you will now receive 15% of the administrative service charge every time you refund or reissue a ticket. So not only will your clients enjoy lower ticket prices and more travel flexibility, you will now be more directly compensated for the service you provide.

6. HOW WILL IT BENEFIT PEOPLE WHO TRAVEL ON BUSINESS?
We all know that business travelers often cannot plan their flights very far in advance. And with our new AAnytime fare, they won't have to. Our new First Class and AAnytime fares will greatly reduce the cost of flying on business and make travel more accessible to large and small businesses across the country. We believe that these savings will reduce overall company travel costs—which will result in a net increase in business travelers for us and for you.

7. HOW WILL IT BENEFIT LEISURE TRAVELERS?
Our two domestic PlanAAhead fares make flying more economical and simple for your clients to understand, and for you to sell. We'll offer only two basic advance-purchase fares, PlanAAhead 7 and PlanAAhead 21. While these tickets will still be nonrefundable, they can now be reissued for flights at a later date. And, if your leisure clients can't plan their trip in advance, our AAnytime fare at 38% off is still a great value.

8. WILL AMERICAN'S NEW REDUCED FARES MEAN REDUCED SERVICE?
Absolutely not. American has been, and always will be, committed to providing the highest level of customer service regardless of the price your clients pay for a ticket. And our new simplified fare structure is a commitment to making your job easier and your time more productive. In addition, you can assure your clients that they will continue to earn full mileage credit with our AAdvantage program, the airline industry's largest travel awards program.
For more information on American's new AAnytime, PlanAAhead and First Class fares, consult SABRE using the formats listed below. Together, we can make this business of ours more efficient. More sensible. And a lot simpler for everyone.

SABRE: F*SRS VALUE
APOLLO: S*AAB FARES
SYSTEM ONE: G/GHQ/AAFARES
WORLDSPAN: PARS: G/AIR/AAQ-FARES
WORLDSPAN: DATAS II: G AA-FARES

American Airlines
Bringing Value Back To Air Travel.

AAdvantage is a registered trademark and AAnytime and PlanAAhead are service marks of American Airlines, Inc. American Airlines reserves the right to change AAdvantage program rules, regulations, travel awards and special offers at any time without notice, and to end the AAdvantage program with six months notice.

AAANYTIME FARE
38% Off Today's Domestic Full Coach Fare.
No Advance Purchase Required.

PLANAAHEAD 7
A Further Reduced Coach Fare.
Purchase Your Ticket 7 Days In Advance.
Nonrefundable But Reusable.

PLANAAHEAD 21
Our Lowest Coach Fare. Purchase
Your Ticket 21 Days In Advance.
Nonrefundable But Reusable.

NEW FIRST CLASS
20%-50% Off Today's Full First Class Fare.

1. HOW IS AMERICAN'S NEW FARE STRUCTURE DIFFERENT?
Unlike the countless Coach fares that used to exist on every flight, American will now offer three new basic fares in our main cabin. Our new "AAnytime" fare is 38% less than today's full Coach fare and is good on any domestic flight any day, with no advance purchase requirements. Your clients can also choose from two new advance-purchase fares that have certain restrictions. These new Plan/Ahead fares represent substantial savings, based on how far in advance your clients book and purchase their tickets. Finally, we've introduced a new First Class fare, which is available on flights throughout the continental U.S.
All of these new fares are good any day of the week, with no charge to change reservations prior to ticketing. After ticketing, if your clients need to change their routing or cancel an AAnytime or First Class ticket for a refund, they can do so for a $25 administrative service charge. Your clients can also change PlanAAhead tickets for the same $25 service charge as long as they meet applicable advance-purchase and length-of-stay requirements.

Entering the 1992 summer season, American Airlines and its competitors were looking for ways to kick-start the stalled travel industry. Coming off two years of record billion-dollar-plus losses, the troubled U.S. airline industry faced many problems—an ailing economy, rising costs, industry overcapacity, and severe price competition. Several airlines recently had been forced out of business, and a number of others were operating under bankruptcy protection.

One major factor contributing to the industry's woes was its convoluted pricing structure. For years, American and the other airlines had offered a bewildering array of fares, including deep promotional discounts designed to stimulate air travel or to give one airline a temporary advantage over the others. But such promotional pricing often had erupted into costly price wars that sapped long-term industry profits. Perhaps worse, the complex fare structure and never-ending promotions resulted in customer confusion and frustration. Business travelers were especially frustrated. Because their schedules rarely allowed them to take advantage of lower advance-purchase rates, they often paid four to five times the price of the cheapest fares. But as the feeble economy dragged on, even people traveling at the lowest rates were complaining about the high cost of airline travel. Both business and leisure travelers were flying less, and both persisted in their long-held beliefs that the airlines were gouging them on price.

In mid-April 1992, American stepped forward with a bold new fare plan that it hoped would lead the way in simplifying the industry's fare structure, put an end to constant price squabbling, and restore its own and the industry's profitability. The leading U.S. carrier ran four-page ads in major newspapers across the country, announcing "The Next Page in the History of Air Fares." Gone were superlow promotional fares and special discounts for children, senior citizens, the military, bereaved families, and large corporate users. In their place was a slimmed-down structure with just four fares: *anytime coach fares* (now an average of 38 percent lower than previous full-coach fares); lower-price *first class fares* (20 percent to 50 percent lower than before); *21-day advance-purchase fares* (at about half the price of full-coach fares); and *7-day advance-purchase fares* (running $20 to $60 more than 21-day fares).

The new plan was good for everyone, American claimed. Although some of the cheapest fares rose slightly, consumers benefitted from the overall 38 percent cut in top fares. At the same time, it helped the airlines: eliminating deep discounts meant that average fares would rise. For the plan to work, however, American would need help from two key groups: customers and competitors. The plan wouldn't restore industry profits unless it stimulated increased travel. And American couldn't go it alone—competitors would have to set similar fare structures. Unfortunately, American got little help from either group.

The lower fares didn't cause the hoped for stampede to the ticket counter. During the high-flying 1980s, the airlines had schooled travelers to wait for special discounts and promotions. When American eliminated them in the recessionary 1990s, consumers balked. They waited to see if the new fares would stick. On the other side of the ticket counter, most major competing carriers followed American's lead—for a while. However, weaker airlines such as Trans World Airlines, America West, and Continental—all operating out of bankruptcy—began to undercut American's new prices as soon as they were announced. TWA, which had survived against its healthier rivals by carving out a low-price niche, responded immediately with fares 10 percent to 20 percent below American's. It also began to offer one-day sales in selected cities, sales that ended before competitors could react. America West undercut fares on transcontinental trips and promoted cheaper off-peak fares. No-frills Southwest Airlines announced a kids-fly-free program for the summer.

When the American plan failed to produce enough new business, the other carriers began to add their own twists. TWA replaced the original 21-day advance-purchase fares with less restrictive 14-day fares. US Air discounted fares from major Northeast cities to Florida, and Continental quickly followed. However, still hoping to succeed with its simplified fare plan, powerful American Airlines responded to these breeches with remarkable restraint. It cut its fares only as necessary in markets where it competed with TWA, America West, Southwest, US Air, and the other renegade airlines. But once the discounting started, it soon snowballed.

In late April, Northwest Airlines broke ranks. To attract family travelers for the summer season, it launched an "adults-fly free" promotion in which it gave a free ticket to any adult traveling with a child. Northwest ran its first ads announcing the promotion on Tuesday evening, May 26. Before the night had ended, the carrier's reservations had risen 53 percent; by mid-day Wednesday, they'd jumped an incredible 176 percent. American responded with a vengeance to Northwest's defection, slashing all of its advance-purchase fares in half. The other airlines jumped in, setting off a brutal 10-day price war.

The incredibly low fares created a tidal wave of demand. Consumers swamped travel agents and airline ticket counters, greedily buying up two, three, or more tickets for summer trips. On Sunday, May 31, at the height of the buying frenzy, reservations at Northwest were up 563 percent compared with a

week earlier. On Tuesday, June 2, Delta received a mind-boggling 2.5 million calls, compared with 300,000 on a typical day. The industry sold a summer's worth of travel in a little over a week.

Although those days in May and early June marked a happy time for air travelers, they spelled disaster for the airlines. As one analyst notes, "For most of the stronger airlines . . . it wiped out chances for a profitable summer. For the weaker ones, the low fares may have been the kiss of death." When the air had cleared, analysts predicted that the industry would lose $3.5 billion dollars in 1992. Travel agents also lost out, working harder for lower commissions. They had to reissue previously purchased tickets at the new lower prices. And although the major airlines eventually allowed the agents to keep the commissions they'd earned on the earlier purchases, prices of new tickets were often so low that the agents couldn't make enough in commissions to cover the costs of writing them. Many travel agents blamed American; some even vowed to steer future business to other carriers when possible. To make matters worse, Continental sued American, claiming that it had engaged in predatory pricing—setting fares that could not be profitable in order to drive out weaker competitors. American responded that it was only trying to establish an industry pricing discipline that would let it and other airlines earn a profit.

By fall, on many American Airlines routes, travelers were once again confronted with a complex array of fares. American's revolutionary fare plan never really had a chance to get off the ground. Instead, its attempts to bring sanity to the industry's pricing practices created even greater losses, in terms of both dollars and credibility with consumers. Laments one airline executive, "The damage done will be with us for a long, long time."[1]

 # CHAPTER PREVIEW

Chapter 13 builds on the last chapter by detailing specific pricing strategies which can be used in different situations.

Initially, we discuss strategies for pricing innovative new products, including **market-skimming** and **market-penetration** approaches, and the issues involved in pricing imitative new products.

Next, we survey **product-mix pricing strategies**, including **product line** pricing, **optional-product, captive-product, by-product,** and **product-bundle** pricing.

We continue with an overview of **price-adjustment** strategies, including several forms of **discounts**, and **discriminatory, psychological, promotional, value, geographical,** and **international** pricing.

Finally, we conclude with the topics of **initiating price changes** and **responding to price changes.**

In this chapter, we will look at pricing dynamics. A company sets not a single price, but rather a *pricing structure* that covers different items in its line. This pricing structure changes over time as products move through their life cycles. The company adjusts product prices to reflect changes in costs and demand and to account for variations in buyers and situations. As the competitive environment changes, the company considers when to initiate price changes and when to respond to them.

This chapter examines the major dynamic pricing strategies available to management. In turn, we look at *new-product pricing strategies* for products in the introductory stage of the product life cycle, *product-mix pricing strategies* for related products in the product mix, *price-adjustment strategies* that account for customer differences and changing situations, and *strategies for initiating and responding to price changes*.[2]

NEW-PRODUCT PRICING STRATEGIES

Pricing strategies usually change as the product passes through its life cycle. The introductory stage is especially challenging. We can distinguish between pricing an innovative product that is patent protected and pricing a product that imitates existing products.

Pricing an Innovative Product

Companies bringing out an innovative patent-protected product can choose between two strategies: *market-skimming pricing* and *market-penetration pricing*.

Market-Skimming Pricing

Many companies that invent new products initially set high prices to "skim" revenues layer by layer from the market. Polaroid is a prime user of this strategy, called **market-skimming pricing.** On its original instant camera, for example, Polaroid charged the highest price it could given the benefits of its new product over competing products. The company set a price that made it *just* worthwhile for some segments of the market to adopt the new camera. After an initial sales slowdown, it then lowered the price to draw in the next price sensitive layer of customers. Polaroid also used the same approach with its Spectra camera. The Spectra was introduced at about twice the price of Polaroid's previous entry in the field. After about a year, Polaroid began bringing out even simpler, lower-priced versions to draw in new segments. In this way, Polaroid skimmed a maximum amount of revenue from the various segments of the market.[3]

Market skimming: Polaroid introduced its Spectra at a high price, then brought out lower-priced versions to draw in new segments.

Market skimming makes sense only under certain conditions. First, the product's quality and image must support its higher price, and enough buyers must want the product at that price. Second, the costs of producing a small volume cannot be so high that they cancel the advantage of charging more. Finally, competitors should not be able to enter the market easily and undercut the high price.

Market-Penetration Pricing

Rather than setting a high initial price to *skim* off small but profitable market segments, some companies set a low initial price in order to *penetrate* the market quickly and deeply—to attract a large number of buyers quickly and win a large market share. Texas Instruments (TI) is a prime user of this strategy, called **market-penetration pricing.** The company will build a large plant, set its price as low as possible, win a large market share, realize falling costs, and then cut its price further as costs fall. Warehouse stores and discount retailers also use penetration pricing. They charge low prices to attract high volume; the high volume results in lower costs which, in turn, let the discounter keep prices low.

Several conditions favor setting a low price. First, the market must be highly price sensitive so that a low price produces more market growth. Second, production and distribution costs must fall as sales volume increases. Finally, the low price must help keep out the competition.

Pricing an Imitative New Product

A company that plans to develop an imitative new product faces a product-positioning problem. It must decide where to position the product in terms of quality and price. Figure 13-1 shows nine possible price-quality strategies. For example, if the existing market leader has used premium strategy (box 1) by producing a premium product and charging the highest price, then the newcomer might prefer to use one of the other strategies. It could design a high-quality product and charge a medium price (box 2), design a medium-quality product and charge a medium price (box 5), and so on. The newcomer must consider the size and growth rate of the market in each box as well as the competitors it would face.

PRODUCT-MIX PRICING STRATEGIES

The strategy for setting a product's price often has to be changed when the product is part of a product mix. In this case, the firm looks for a set of prices that maximizes the profits on the total product mix. Pricing is difficult because the various products have related demand and costs and face different degrees of competition. We now take a closer look at five *product-mix pricing* situations shown in Figure 13-2.

Product Line Pricing

Companies usually develop product lines rather than single products. For example, Snapper makes many different lawn mowers, ranging from simple walk-behind versions priced at $259.95, $299.95, and $399.95, to elaborate riding mowers priced at $1,000 or more. Each successive lawn mower in the line offers more

FIGURE 13-1
Nine price-quality strategies

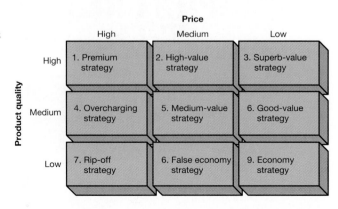

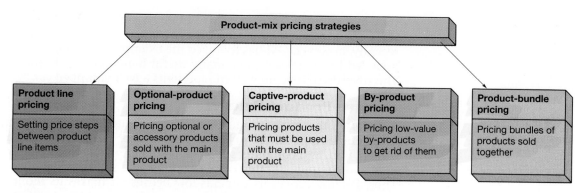

Product-mix pricing strategies				
Product line pricing Setting price steps between product line items	**Optional-product pricing** Pricing optional or accessory products sold with the main product	**Captive-product pricing** Pricing products that must be used with the main product	**By-product pricing** Pricing low-value by-products to get rid of them	**Product-bundle pricing** Pricing bundles of products sold together

FIGURE 13-2 Product mix pricing strategies

features. In **product line pricing,** management must decide on the price steps to set between the various mowers.

The price steps should take into account cost differences between the mowers, customer evaluations of their different features, and competitors' prices. If the price difference between two successive lawn mowers is small, buyers usually will buy the more advanced mower. This likelihood will increase company profits if the cost difference is smaller than the price difference. If the price difference is large, however, customers will generally buy the less-advanced mowers.

In many industries, sellers use well-established *price points* for the products in their line. Thus, men's clothing stores might carry men's suits at three price levels: $185, $285, and $385. The customer probably will associate low-, average-, and high-quality suits with the three price points. Even if the three prices are raised a little, men normally will buy suits at their own preferred price points. The seller's task is to establish perceived quality differences that support the price differences.

Optional-Product Pricing

Many companies use **optional-product pricing**—offering to sell optional or accessory products along with their main product. For example, a car buyer may choose to order electric windows, defoggers, and cruise control. Pricing these options is a sticky problem. Automobile companies have to decide which items to include in the base price and which to offer as options. General Motors' normal pricing strategy has been to advertise a stripped-down model for, say, $12,000 to pull people into showrooms and then devote to most of the showroom space to

Product-line pricing: Infinity offers a line of home stereo speakers at prices ranging from $275 to $50,000 per pair.

showing option-loaded cars at $14,000 or $15,000. The economy model is stripped of so many comforts and conveniences that most buyers reject it. More recently, however, GM has followed the example of the Japanese auto makers and included in the sticker price many useful items previously sold only as options. The advertised price now often represents a well-equipped car.

Captive-Product Pricing

Companies that make products that must be used along with a main product are using **captive-product pricing.** Examples of captive products are razor blades, camera film, and computer software. Producers of the main products (razors, cameras, and computers) often price them low and set high markups on the supplies. Thus, Polaroid prices its cameras low because it makes its money on the film it sells. Those camera makers who do not sell film have to price their cameras higher in order to make the same overall profit.

In the case of services, this strategy is called **two-part pricing.** The price of the service is broken into a *fixed fee* plus a *variable usage rate.* Thus, a telephone company charges a monthly rate—the fixed fee—plus charges for calls beyond some minimum number—the variable usage rate. Amusement parks charge admission plus fees for food, midway attractions, and rides over a minimum. The service firm must decide how much to charge for the basic service and how much for the variable usage. The fixed amount should be low enough to induce usage of the service and profit can be made on the variable usage fees.

By-Product Pricing

In producing processed meats, petroleum products, chemicals, and other products, there are often by-products. If the by-products have no value and if getting rid of them is costly, this will affect the pricing of the main product. Using **by-product pricing,** the manufacturer will seek a market for these by-products and should accept any price that covers more than the cost of storing and delivering them. This practice allows the seller to reduce the main product's price to make it more competitive.

Product-Bundle Pricing

Using **product-bundle pricing,** sellers often combine several of their products and offer the bundle at a reduced price. Thus, theaters and sports teams sell season tickets at less than the cost of single tickets; hotels sell specially priced packages that include room, meals, and entertainment; automobile companies sell attractively priced options packages. Price bundling can promote the sales of products consumers might not otherwise buy, but the combined price must be low enough to get them to buy the bundle.[4]

PRICE-ADJUSTMENT STRATEGIES

Companies usually adjust their basic prices to account for various customer differences and changing situations. Figure 13-3 summarizes six price-adjustment

FIGURE 13-3 Price adjustment strategies

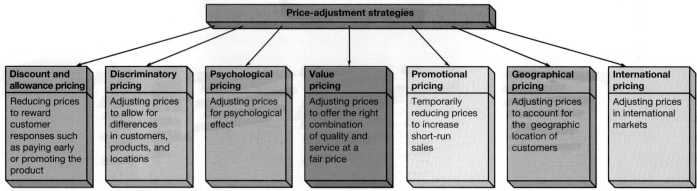

strategies: *discount pricing and allowances, discriminatory pricing, psychological pricing, promotional pricing, value pricing, geographical pricing,* and *international pricing.*

Discount Pricing and Allowances

Most companies adjust their basic price to reward customers for certain responses, such as early payment of bills, volume purchases, and off-season buying. These price adjustments—called *discounts* and *allowances*—are described next.

Cash Discounts

A **cash discount** is a price reduction to buyers who pay their bills promptly. A typical example is "2/10, net 30," which means that although payment is due within 30 days, the buyer can deduct 2 percent if the bill is paid within 10 days. The discount must be granted to all buyers meeting these terms. Such discounts are customary in many industries and help to improve the sellers' cash situation and reduce bad debts and credit-collection costs.

Quantity Discounts

A **quantity discount** is a price reduction to buyers who buy large volumes. A typical example might be "$10 per unit for less than 100 units, $9 per unit for 100 or more units." Quantity discounts must be offered to all customers and must not exceed the seller's cost savings associated with selling large quantities. These savings include lower selling, inventory, and transportation expenses. Discounts provide an incentive to the customer to buy more from one given seller, rather than from many different sources.

Functional Discounts

A **functional discount** (also called a *trade discount*) is offered by the seller to trade channel members who perform certain functions, such as selling, storing, and record keeping. Manufacturers may offer different functional discounts to different trade channels because of the varying services they perform, but manufacturers must offer the same functional discounts within each trade channel.

Seasonal Discounts

A **seasonal discount** is a price reduction to buyers who buy merchandise or services out of season. For example, ski manufacturers will offer seasonal discounts to retailers in the spring and summer to encourage early ordering. Hotels, motels, and airlines will offer seasonal discounts in their slower selling periods. Seasonal discounts allow the seller to keep production steady during an entire year.

Allowances

Allowances are another type of reductions from the list price. For example, **trade-in allowances** are price reductions given for turning in an old item when buying a new one. Trade-in allowances are most common in the automobile industry and are also given for some other durable goods. **Promotional allowances** are payments or price reductions to reward dealers for participating in advertising and sales-support programs.

Discriminatory Pricing

Companies often will adjust their basic prices to allow for differences in customers, products, and locations. In **discriminatory pricing,** the company sells a product or service at two or more prices, even though the difference in prices is not based on differences in costs. Discriminatory pricing takes several forms:

Customer-segment pricing. Different customers pay different prices for the same product or service. Museums, for example, will charge a lower admission for students and senior citizens.

Product-form pricing. Different versions of the product are priced differently, but not according to differences in their costs. For instance, Black & Decker prices its most expensive iron at $54.98, which is $12 more than the price of its next most expensive iron. The top model has a self-cleaning feature, yet this extra feature costs only a few more dollars to make.

Location pricing. Different locations are priced differently, even though the cost of offering each location is the same. For instance, theaters vary their seat prices because of audience preferences for certain locations, and state universities charge higher tuition for out-of-state students.

Time pricing. Prices vary by the season, the month, the day, and even the hour. Public utilities vary their prices to commercial users by time of day and weekend versus weekday. The telephone company offers lower "off-peak" charges, and resorts give seasonal discounts.

For discriminatory pricing to be an effective strategy, certain conditions must exist. The market must be segmentable, and the segments must show different degrees of demand. Members of the segment paying the lower price should not be able to turn around and resell the product to the segment paying the higher price. Competitors should not be able to undersell the firm in the segment being charged the higher price. Nor should the costs of segmenting and watching the market exceed the extra revenue obtained from the price difference. The practice should not lead to customer resentment and ill will. Finally, the discriminatory pricing must be legal.

Psychological Pricing

Price says something about the product. For example, many consumers use price to judge quality. A $100 bottle of perfume may contain only $3 worth of scent, but some people are willing to pay the $100 because this price indicates something special.

In using **psychological pricing,** sellers consider the psychology of prices and not simply the economics. For example, one study of the relationship between price and quality perceptions of cars found that consumers perceive higher-priced cars as having higher quality.[5] By the same token, higher-quality cars are perceived to be even higher priced than they actually are! When consumers can judge the quality of a product by examining it or by calling on past experience with it, they use price less to judge quality. When consumers cannot judge quality because they lack the information or skill, price becomes an important quality signal (see Marketing Highlight 13-1).[6]

Another aspect of psychological pricing is **reference prices**—prices that buyers carry in their minds and refer to when looking at a given product. The reference price might be formed by noting current prices, remembering past prices, or assessing the buying situation. Sellers can influence or use these consumers' reference prices when setting price. For example, a company could display its product next to more expensive ones in order to imply that it belongs in the same class. Department stores often sell women's clothing in separate departments differentiated by price: Clothing found in the more expensive department is assumed to be of better quality. Companies also can influence consumers' reference prices by stating high manufacturer's suggested prices, by indicating that the product was originally priced much higher, or by pointing to a competitor's higher price.

Even small differences in price can suggest product differences. Consider a stereo priced at $300 compared to one priced at $299.95. The actual price difference is only 5 cents, but the psychological difference can be much greater. For example, some consumers will see the $299.95 as a price in the $200 range rather than the $300 range. Whereas the $299.95 will more likely be seen as a bargain price, the $300 price suggests more quality. Some psychologists argue that each digit has symbolic and visual qualities that should be considered in pricing. Thus, 8 is round and even and creates a soothing effect, whereas 7 is angular and creates a jarring effect.

Promotional Pricing

With **promotional pricing,** companies will temporarily price their products below list price and sometimes even below cost. Promotional pricing takes several forms. Supermarkets and department stores will price a few products as *loss leaders* to attract customers to the store in the hope that they will buy other items at normal markups. Sellers will also use *special-event pricing* in certain seasons to draw in more customers. Thus, linens are promotionally priced every January to attract

Marketing Highlight 13-1

How Price Signals Product Quality

Heublein produces Smirnoff, America's leading brand of vodka. Some years ago, Smirnoff was attacked by another brand. Wolfschmidt, priced at one dollar less per bottle, claimed to have the same quality as Smirnoff. Concerned that customers might switch to Wolfschmidt, Heublein considered several possible counterstrategies. It could lower Smirnoff's price by one dollar to hold on to market share; it could hold Smirnoff's price but increase advertising and promotion expenditures; or it could hold Smirnoff's price and let its market share fall. All three strategies would lead to lower profits, and it seemed that Heublein faced a no-win situation.

At this point, however, Heublein's marketers thought of a fourth strategy—and it was brilliant. Heublein *raised* the price of Smirnoff by one dollar! The company then introduced a new brand, Relska, to compete with Wolfschmidt. Moreover, it introduced yet another brand, Popov, priced even *lower* than Wolfschmidt. This product line-pricing strategy positioned Smirnoff as the elite brand and Wolfschmidt as an ordinary brand. Heublein's clever strategy produced a large increase in its overall profits.

The irony is that Heublein's three brands are pretty much the same in taste and manufacturing costs. Heublein knew that a product's price signals its quality. Using price as a signal, Heublein sells roughly the same product at three different quality positions.

---

weary Christmas shoppers back into stores. Manufacturers will sometimes offer *cash rebates* to consumers who buy the product from dealers within a specified time; the manufacturer sends the rebate directly to the customer. Rebates have recently been popular with auto makers and producers of durable goods and small appliances. Some manufacturers offer *low-interest financing, longer warranties,* or *free maintenance* to reduce the consumer's "price." This practice has recently become a favorite of the auto industry. Or, the seller may simply offer *discounts* from normal prices to increase sales and reduce inventories.

Value Pricing

During the recessionary, slow-growth 1990s, many companies adjusted their prices to bring them into line with economic conditions and with the resulting fundamental shift in consumer attitudes toward quality and value. More and more, marketers have adopted **value pricing** strategies—offering just the right combination of quality and good service at a fair price. In many cases, this has involved the introduction of less expensive versions of established, brand name products. Thus, Campbell introduced its Great Starts Budget frozen-food line, Holiday Inn opened several Holiday Express budget hotels, Revlon's Charles of the Ritz offered the Express Bar collection of affordable cosmetics, and fast-food

Promotional pricing: Companies often reduce their prices temporarily to produce sales.

VALUE PRICING: OFFERING MORE FOR LESS

Marketers have a new buzzword for the 1990s, and its spelled V-A-L-U-E. Throughout the 1980s, marketers pitched luxury, prestige, extravagance—even expensiveness—for everything from ice cream to autos. But after the recession began, they started redesigning, repackaging, repositioning, and remarketing products to emphasize value. Now, value pricing—offering more for a lot less by underscoring a product's quality while at the same time featuring its price—has gone from a groundswell to a tidal wave.

Value pricing can mean many things to marketers. To some, it means price cutting. To others, its means special deals, such as providing more of a product at the same price. And to others, it means a new image—one that convinces consumers they're receiving a good deal. No matter how it's defined, however, value pricing has become a prime strategy for wooing consumers. The upscale tactics that dominated the 1980s have virtually disappeared. Now, 1980s pretentiousness is used as the antithesis. Take the magazine ad for Nissan's Maxima GXE: "Today, the idea of spending thousands more on a luxury sedan for the cachet of having a hood ornament appears hopelessly unjustified. No, these are the 1990s, an era of renewed sensibility."

Marketers are finding that the flat economy and changing consumer demographics have created a new class of sophisticated, bargain-hunting shoppers who are careful of what, where, and how they shop. Whereas it used to be fashionable to flaunt affluence and spend conspicuously, now it's fashionable to say you got a good deal. To convince consumers they're getting more for their money, companies from fast-food chains to stock brokerages and car makers have revamped their marketing pitches:

- Mobil's Hefty division slashed prices as much as 20 percent and added 20 percent more plastic bags per box. Hefty also trashed its two-decade-old marketing effort centering on bag strength. The new motto: "Our strength is value." Says one Mobil manager:

"People are looking for value in the 1990s, even in trash bags."

- PepsiCo's Taco Bell chain introduced an incredibly successful "value menu" offering 59-cent tacos and 15 other items for either 59 cents, 79 cents, or 99 cents. McDonald's followed suit with its Extra-Value meals, underscored by the ad theme, "Good food. Good value." Soon, Wendy's, Burger King, and other competitors entered the fray with their own value-pricing schemes.

- Stock brokerage Shearson-Lehman Hutton is searching for a new ad campaign to help it counter the low-price claims of discount stockbrokers. "People are asking, 'Am I getting what I paid for, and is there value in it?'" notes a Shearson marketing executive. "Companies are being challenged to [define] the value they offer versus the price they charge." The new campaign will focus on services such as investment advice and financial planning that make Shearson's full-service offering a better value, even at the higher prices it charges.

- In a recent world tour, General Electric Chairman Jack Welch noted that customers around the globe are now more interested in price than technology. "The value decade is upon us," he states. "If you can't sell a top-quality product at the world's lowest price, you're going to be out of the game." As a result, in products ranging from refrigerators to CAT scanners and jet engines, GE is working to offer basic, dependable units at unbeatable prices.

- Buick is pitching its top-of-the-line full-size Park Avenue as "America's best car value" at a suggested list price of $25,800. Buick's boast is backed by findings from IntelliChoice, an independent research firm that ranked the Park Avenue number one on factors such as maintenance costs, fuel economy, and depreciation. "We're saying that you don't have to buy [an economy car] to get value for your dollar," says

restaurants such as Taco Bell and McDonald's offered "value menus." In other cases, value pricing has involved redesigning existing brands in order to offer more quality for a given price or the same quality for less (see Marketing Highlight 13-2).

Geographical Pricing

A company also must decide how to price its products to customers located in different parts of the country or world. Should the company risk losing the business of more distant customers by charging them higher prices to cover the higher shipping costs? Or should the company charge all customers the same prices regardless of location? We will look at five geographical pricing strategies for the following hypothetical situation:

The Peerless Paper Company is located in Atlanta, Georgia, and sells paper products to customers all over the United States. The cost of freight is high and affects the

The Best American Car Value.

According to the experts at IntelliChoice, publisher of *The Complete Car Cost Guide*, the best American car value is the Buick Park Avenue.*

IntelliChoice came to this solid conclusion after considering not just purchase price, but the costs of

Just because you've earned it, doesn't mean you have to spend it.

BUICK
The New Standard For Quality In America

depreciation, financing, insurance, taxes, fuel, maintenance and repairs over a five-year period.

Reward your success with the quality, luxury, safety and lasting value of the Buick Park Avenue. You've earned it.

Call 1-800-4A-BUICK to find out more. Or see your Buick dealer for a test drive today.

Value pricing: Based on such factors as maintenance costs, fuel economy, and depreciation, Buick pitches its $25,800, top-of-the-line, full-size Park Avenue as "America's best car value."

Buick's national advertising manager. "You don't have to give up luxury, performance, or size to get great value."

Value pricing involves more than just cutting prices. It means finding the delicate balance between quality and price that gives target consumers the value they seek. To consumers, "value" is not the same as "cheap." Value pricing requires price cutting coupled with finding ways to maintain or even improve quality while still making a profit. Consumers who enjoyed high-quality brand name products during the 1980s now want the same high quality, but at much lower

prices. Thus, value pricing often involves redesigning products and production processes to lower costs and preserve profit margins at lower prices. For example, before launching its value menu, Taco Bell redesigned its restaurants to increase customer traffic and reduce costs. It shrank its kitchens, expanded seating space, and introduced new menu items specifically designed for easy preparation in the new, smaller kitchens. Similarly, when designing the Macintosh Classic computer, which would be value priced at less than $1,000, Apple engineers began with the old Macintosh SE and stripped away features that most users had ignored. The result was a simple, but high-quality machine that provided consumers with a bargain price and Apple with good profits margins.

Although the trend toward value pricing began with the recession, its roots run much deeper. The trend reflects marketers' reactions to a fundamental change in consumer attitudes, resulting from the aging of the baby boomers and their increased financial pressures. Today's "squeezed consumers"—saddled with debt acquired during the free-spending 1980s and facing increased expenses for child rearing, home buying, and pending retirement—will continue to demand more value long after the economy improves. Even before the economy soured, buyers were beginning to rethink the price-quality equation. Thus, value pricing will likely remain a crucial strategy throughout the 1990s and beyond. Winning over tomorrow's increasingly shrewd consumers will require finding ever-new ways to offer them more for less.

Sources: Portions adapted from Gary Strauss, "Marketers Plea: Let's Make a Deal," *USA Today*, September 29, 1992, pp. B1-B2. Copyright 1992, USA TODAY. Reprinted with permission. The Jack Welch quote is from Stratford Sherman, "How to Prosper in the Value Decade," *Fortune*, November 30, 1992, pp. 90-104. Also see Joseph B. White, "`Value Pricing' Is Hot as Shrewd Consumers Seek Low-Cost Quality," *The Wall Street Journal*, March 12, 1991, pp. A1, A9; Kathleen Madigan, "The Latest Mad Plunge of the Price Slashers," *Business Week*, May 11, 1992, p. 36; Faye Rice, "What Intelligent Consumers Want," *Fortune*, December 28, 1992, pp. 56-60; and Bill Kelley, "The New Consumer Revealed," *Sales & Marketing Management*, May 1993, pp. 46-52.

companies from whom customers buy their paper. Peerless wants to establish a geographical pricing policy. It is trying to determine how to price a $100 order to three specific customers: Customer A (Atlanta); Customer B (Bloomington; Indiana), and Customer C (Compton, California).

FOB-Origin Pricing

One option is for Peerless to ask each customer to pay the shipping cost from the Atlanta factory to the customer's location. All three customers would pay the same factory price of $100, with Customer A paying, say, $10 for shipping; Customer B, $15; and Customer C, $25. Called **FOB-origin pricing**, this practice means that the goods are placed *free on board* (hence, *FOB*) a carrier, at which point the title and responsibility pass to the customer, who pays the freight from the factory to the destination.

Because each customer picks up its own cost, supporters of FOB pricing feel that this is the fairest way to assess freight charges. The disadvantage, however, is that Peerless will be a high-cost firm to distant customers. If Peerless's main competitor happens to be in California, this competitor will no doubt outsell Peerless in California. In fact, the competitor would outsell Peerless in most of the West, whereas Peerless would dominate the East. A vertical line actually could be drawn on a map connecting the cities where the two companies' prices plus freight would roughly be equal. Peerless would have the price advantage east of this line, and its competitor would have the price advantage west of this line.

Uniform Delivered Pricing

Uniform delivered pricing is the exact opposite of FOB pricing. Here, the company charges the same price plus freight to all customers, regardless of their location. The freight charge is set at the average freight cost. Suppose this is $15. Uniform delivered pricing therefore results in a higher charge to the Atlanta customer (who pays $15 freight instead of $10) and a lower charge to the Compton customer (who pays $15 instead of $25). On the one hand, the Atlanta customer would prefer to buy paper from another local paper company that uses FOB-origin pricing. On the other hand, Peerless has a better chance of winning over the California customer. Other advantages of uniform delivered pricing are that it is fairly easy to administer and it lets the firm advertise its price nationally.

Zone Pricing

Zone pricing falls between FOB-origin pricing and uniform delivered pricing. The company sets up two or more zones. All customers within a given zone pay a single total price; the more distant the zone, the higher the price. For example, Peerless might set up an East Zone and charge $10 freight to all customers in this zone, a Midwest Zone in which it charges $15, and a West Zone in which it charges $25. In this way, the customers within a given price zone receive no price advantage from the company. For example, customers in Atlanta and Boston pay the same total price to Peerless. The complaint, however, is that the Atlanta customer is paying part of the Boston customer's freight cost. In addition, even though they may be within a few miles of each other, a customer just barely on the west side of the line dividing the East and Midwest pays much more than does one just barely on the east side of the line.

Basing-Point Pricing

Using **basing-point pricing,** the seller selects a given city as a "basing point" and charges all customers the freight cost from that city to the customer location, regardless of the city from which the goods actually are shipped. For example, Peerless might set Chicago as the basing point and charge all customers $100 plus the freight from Chicago to their locations. This means that an Atlanta customer pays the freight cost from Chicago to Atlanta even though the goods may be shipped from Atlanta. Using a basing-point location other than the factory raises the total price for customers near the factory and lowers the total price for customers far from the factory.

If all sellers used the same basing-point city, delivered prices would be the same for all customers and price competition would be eliminated. Industries such as sugar, cement, steel, and automobiles used basing-point pricing for years, but this method has become less popular today. Some companies set up multiple basing points to create more flexibility: They quote freight charges from the basing-point city nearest to the customer.

Freight-Absorption Pricing

Finally, the seller who is anxious to do business with a certain customer or geographical area might use **freight-absorption pricing.** This strategy involves absorbing all or part of the actual freight charges in order to get the desired business. The seller might reason that if it can get more business, its average costs will fall and more than compensate for its extra freight cost. Freight-absorption pricing is used for market penetration and to hold on to increasingly competitive markets.

International Pricing

Companies that market their products internationally must decide what prices to charge in the different countries in which they operate. In some cases, a company can set a uniform worldwide price. For example, Boeing sells its jetliners at about the same price everywhere, whether in the United States, Europe, or a Third World country. However, most companies adjust their prices to reflect local market conditions and cost considerations.

The price that a company should charge in a specific country depends on many factors, including economic conditions, competitive situations, laws and regulations, and development of the wholesaling and retailing system. Consumer perceptions and preferences also may vary from country to country, calling for different prices. Or the company may have different marketing objectives in various world markets, which require changes in pricing strategy. For example, Sony might introduce a new product into mature markets in highly developed countries with the goal of quickly gaining mass-market share—this would call for a penetration pricing strategy. In contrast, it might enter a less developed market by targeting smaller, less price-sensitive segments—in this case, market-skimming pricing makes sense.

Costs play an important role in setting international prices. Travelers abroad are often surprised to find that goods that are relatively inexpensive at home may carry outrageously higher price tags in other countries. A pair of Levis selling for $30 in the United States goes for about $63 in Tokyo and $88 in Paris. A McDonald's Big Mac selling for a modest $2.25 here costs $5.75 in Moscow. Conversely, a Gucci handbag going for only $60 in Milan, Italy, fetches $240 in the United States. In some cases, such *price escalation* may result from differences in selling strategies or market conditions. In most instances, however, it is simply a result of the higher costs of selling in foreign markets—the additional costs of modifying the product, higher shipping and insurance costs, import tariffs and taxes, costs associated with exchange-rate fluctuations, and higher channel and physical distribution costs. Consider Campbell's experience in the United Kingdom:

> [Campbell] found its . . . distribution costs in the United Kingdom were 30 percent higher than in the United States. Extra costs were incurred because soup was purchased in small quantities—English grocers typically purchase 24-can cases of *assorted* soups (each case being hand-packed for shipment). In the United States, typical purchase units are 48-can cases of one soup purchased by the dozens, hundreds, or carloads. The purchase habits in Europe forced the company to [add] an extra wholesale level in its channel to [handle] small orders. Purchase frequency patterns also [bumped] up billing and order costs: Wholesalers and retailers purchase two or three times as often as their U.S. counterparts. . . . These and other distribution cost factors not only caused [Campbell] to change its price . . . but also forced a complete restructuring of the channel system.[7]

Thus, international pricing presents some special problems and complexities. We discuss international pricing issues in more detail in Chapter 21.

PRICE CHANGES

Initiating Price Changes

After developing its price structures and strategies, a company may face occasions when it will want either to cut or to raise prices.

Initiating Price Cuts

Several situations may lead a firm to consider cutting its price. One such circumstance is excess capacity. In this case, the firm needs more business and cannot get it through increased sales effort, product improvement, or other measures. In the late 1970s, many companies dropped "follow-the-leader pricing"—charging about the same price as their leading competitor—and aggressively cut prices to boost their sales. But as the airline, construction equipment, and other industries have learned in recent years, cutting prices in an industry loaded with excess capacity may lead to price wars as competitors try to hold on to market share.

Another situation leading to price changes is falling market share in the face of strong price competition. Several American industries—automobiles, consumer electronics, cameras, watches, and steel, for example—have lost market share to Japanese competitors whose high-quality products carried lower prices than did their American counterparts. In response, American companies resorted to more aggressive pricing action. General Motors, for example, cut its subcompact car prices by 10 percent on the West Coast, where Japanese competition was strongest.[8]

A company also may cut prices in a drive to dominate the market through lower costs. Either the company starts with lower costs than its competitors, or it cuts prices in the hope of gaining market share that will further cut costs through larger volume. Bausch & Lomb used an aggressive low-cost, low-price strategy to become the leader in the competitive soft contact lens market.

Initiating Price Increases

In contrast, many companies have had to *raise* prices in recent years. They do this knowing that the price increases may be resented by customers, dealers, and even their own salesforce. Yet a successful price increase can greatly increase profits. For example, if the company's profit margin is 3 percent of sales, a 1 percent price increase will increase profits by 33 percent if sales volume is unaffected.

A major factor in price increases is cost inflation. Rising costs squeeze profit margins and lead companies to regular rounds of price increases. Companies often raise their prices by more than the cost increase in anticipation of further inflation. Companies do not want to make long-run price agreements with customers—they fear that cost inflation will eat up their profit margins. Another factor leading to price increases is overdemand: When a company cannot supply all its customers' needs, it can raise its prices, ration products to customers, or both.

Companies can increase their prices in a number of ways to keep up with rising costs. Prices can be raised almost invisibly by dropping discounts and adding higher-priced units to the line. Or prices can be pushed up openly. In passing price increases on to customers, the company should avoid the image of price gouging. The price increases should be supported with a company communication program telling customers why prices are being increased. The company salesforce should help customers find ways to economize.

Where possible, the company should consider ways to meet higher costs or demand without raising prices. For example, it can shrink the product instead of raising the price, as candy bar manufacturers often do. Or it can substitute less expensive ingredients, or remove certain product features, packaging, or services. Or it can "unbundle" its products and services, removing and separately pricing elements that were formerly part of the offer. IBM, for example, now offers training as a separately priced service. Many restaurants have shifted from dinner pricing to a la carte pricing.

Buyer Reactions to Price Changes

Whether the price is raised or lowered, the action will affect buyers, competitors, distributors, and suppliers and may interest government as well. Customers do not always interpret prices in a straightforward way. They may view a price *cut* in several ways. For example, what would you think if Sony were suddenly to cut its videocassette recorder prices in half? You might think that these VCRs are about to be replaced by newer models or that they have some fault and are not selling well. You might think that Sony is in financial trouble and may not stay in the business long enough to supply future parts. You might believe that quality has been reduced. Or you might think that the price will come down even further and that it will pay to wait and see.

Similarly, a price *increase*, which normally would lower sales, may have some positive meanings for buyers. What would you think if Sony *raised* the price of its latest VCR model? On the one hand, you might think that the item is very "hot" and may be unobtainable unless you buy it soon. Or you might think that the recorder is an unusually good value. On the other hand, you might think that Sony is greedy and charging what the traffic will bear.

Competitor Reactions to Price Changes

A firm considering a price change has to worry about the reactions of its competitors as well as its customers. Competitors are most likely to react when the number of firms involved is small, when the product is uniform, and when the buyers are well informed.

How can the firm figure out the likely reactions of its competitors? Assuming that the firm faces one large competitor, if the competitor tends to react in a set way to price changes, that reaction can be anticipated. But if the competitor

The costliest perfume in the world.

NEIMAN-MARCUS

Buyer reactions to price changes? What would you think if the price of Joy was suddenly cut in half?

treats each price change as a fresh challenge and reacts according to its self-interest, the company will have to figure out just what makes up the competitor's self-interest at the time.

The problem is complex because, like the customer, the competitor can interpret a company price cut in many ways. It might think the company is trying to grab a larger market share, that the company is doing poorly and trying to boost its sales, or that the company wants the whole industry to cut prices to increase total demand.

When there are several competitors, the company must guess each competitor's likely reaction. If all competitors behave alike, this amounts to analyzing only a typical competitor. In contrast, if the competitors do not behave alike—perhaps because of differences in size, market shares, or policies—then separate analyses are necessary. However, if some competitors will match the price change, there is good reason to expect that the rest also will match it.

Responding to Price Changes

Here we reverse the question and ask how a firm should respond to a price change by a competitor. The firm needs to consider several issues: Why did the competitor change the price? Was it to take more market share, to use excess capacity, to meet changing cost conditions, or to lead an industrywide price change? Is the price change temporary or permanent? What will happen to the company's market share and profits if it does not respond? Are other companies going to respond? And what are the competitor's and other firms' responses to each possible reaction likely to be?

Besides these issues, the company must make a broader analysis. It has to consider its own product's stage in the life cycle, its importance in the company's product mix, the intentions and resources of the competitor, and the possible consumer reactions to price changes. The company cannot always make an extended analysis of its alternatives at the time of a price change, however. The competitor may have spent much time preparing this decision, but the company may have to react within hours or days. About the only way to cut down reaction time is to plan ahead for both possible competitor's price changes and possible responses. Figure 13-4 shows one company's price reaction program for meeting a competitor's possible price cut. Reaction programs for meeting price changes most often are used in industries where price changes occur often and where it is important to react quickly. Examples can be found in the meatpacking, lumber, and oil industries.

Pricing strategies and tactics form an important element of a company's marketing mix. In setting prices, companies must carefully consider a great many

PUBLIC POLICY AND PRICING

When Russia lifted controls on bread prices as part of its dramatic move towards a free-market economy, Moscow bakers phoned around each morning to agree on regular rounds of price increases. This caused *The Wall Street Journal* to comment: "They still don't get it!" Those who have grown up under a well-regulated, free-market economy understand that such price fixing is clearly against the rules of fair competition. Setting prices is an important element of a competitive marketplace, and many federal and state laws govern the rules of fair play in pricing.

The most important pieces of legislation affecting pricing are the Sherman, Clayton, and Robinson-Patman Acts, initially adopted to curb the formation of monopolies and to regulate business practices that might unfairly restrain trade. Because these federal statutes can be applied only to interstate commerce, some states have adopted similar provisions for companies that operate locally. Public policy on pricing centers on three potentially damaging pricing practices: price fixing, price discrimination, and deceptive pricing.

Price Fixing. Federal legislation on price fixing states that sellers must set prices without talking to competitors. Otherwise, price collusion is suspected. Price fixing is illegal per se—that is, the government does not accept any excuses for price fixing. Even a simple conversation between competitors can have serious consequences:

During the early 1980s, American Airlines and Braniff were immersed in a price war in the Texas market. Each carrier undercut the other until both were offering absurdly low fares and each was losing money on many flights. In the heat of the battle, American's CEO, Robert Crandall, called the president of Braniff and said: "Raise your . . . fares 20 percent. I'll raise mine the next morning." Fortunately for Crandall, the Braniff president warned him off, saying, "We can't talk about pricing!" As it turns out, the phone conversation had been recorded, and the U.S. Justice Department began action against Crandall and American for price fixing. The charges were eventually dropped—the courts ruled that because Braniff had rejected Crandall's proposal, no actual collusion had occurred, and that a proposal to fix prices was not an actual violation of the law. This case and others like it have made most executives very reluctant to discuss prices in any way with competitors. In obtaining information on competitors' pricing, they rely only on openly published materials, such as trade association surveys and competitors' catalogs.

Price Discrimination. The Robinson-Patman Act seeks to ensure that sellers offer the same price terms to a given level of trade. For example, every retailer is entitled to the same price terms whether the retailer is Sears or

internal and external factors before choosing a price that will give them the greatest competitive advantage in selected target markets. However, companies are not usually free to charge whatever prices they wish. Several laws restrict pricing practices, and a number of ethical considerations affect pricing decisions. Marketing Highlight 13-3 discusses the many public policy issues surrounding pricing.

FIGURE 13-4
Price reaction program for meeting a competitor's price cut
Source: Redrawn with permission from a working paper by Raymond J. Trapp. Northwestern University, 1964.

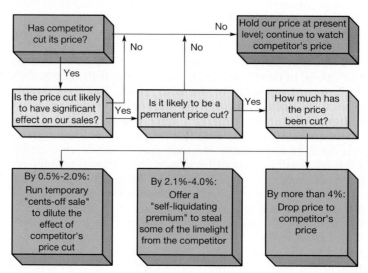

the local bicycle shop. However, price discrimination is allowed if the seller can prove that its costs are different when selling to different retailers—for example, that it costs less per unit to sell a large volume of bicycles to Sears than to sell a few bicycles to a local dealer. Or the seller can discriminate in its pricing if the seller manufactures different qualities of the same product for different retailers. The seller has to prove that these differences are proportional. Price differentials also may be used to "match competition" in "good faith," provided that the firm is trying to meet competitors at its own level of competition and that the price discrimination is temporary, localized, and defensive rather than offensive.

Deceptive Pricing. Deceptive pricing occurs when a seller states prices or price savings that are not actually available to consumers. Some such deceptions are difficult for consumers to discern, as when an airline advertises a low one-way fare that is available only with the purchase of a round-trip ticket, or when a retailer sets artificially high "regular" prices, then announces "sale" prices close to its previous everyday prices. Many federal and state statutes regulate against deceptive pricing practices. For example, the Automobile Information Disclosure Act requires auto makers to attach a statement to new-car windows stating the manufacturer's suggested retail price, the prices of optional equipment, and the dealer's transportation charges. The FTC issues its *Guides Against Deceptive Pricing,* warning sellers not to advertise a price reduction unless it is a saving from the usual retail price, not to advertise "factory" or "wholesale" prices unless such prices are what they are claimed to be, and not to advertise comparable value prices on imperfect goods. Many states have developed retail advertising guidelines to ensure that locally advertised prices are accurately stated and clearly understood by consumers.

Other Regulated Pricing Practices. Sellers also are prohibited from using *predatory pricing*—selling below cost with the intention of destroying competition. Wholesalers and retailers in over half the states face laws requiring a minimum percentage markup over their cost of merchandise plus transportation. These laws attempt to protect small sellers from larger ones who might sell items below cost to attract customers. *Resale price maintenance* is also prohibited—a manufacturer cannot require dealers to charge a specified retail price for its product. Although the seller can propose a manufacturer's *suggested* retail price to dealers, it cannot refuse to sell to a dealer who takes independent pricing action nor can it punish the dealer by shipping late or denying advertising allowances.

Sources: For more on public policy and pricing, see Louis W. Stern and Thomas L. Eovaldi, *Legal Aspects of Marketing Strategy* (Englewood Cliffs, NJ: Prentice Hall, 1984), Chap. 5; Thomas T. Nagle, *The Strategy and Tactics of Pricing* (Englewood Cliffs, NJ: Prentice Hall, 1987), pp. 321-37; and Robert J. Posch, *The Complete Guide to Marketing and the Law* (Englewood Cliffs, NJ: Prentice Hall, 1988), Chap. 28.

SUMMARY

Pricing is a dynamic process. Companies design a *pricing structure* that covers all their products. They change this structure over time and adjust it to account for different customers and situations.

Pricing strategies usually change as a product passes through its life cycle. In pricing innovative new products, the company can follow a *skimming policy* by initially setting high prices to "skim" the maximum amount of revenue from various segments of the market. Or it can use *penetration pricing* by setting a low initial price to win a large market share. The company can decide on one of nine price-quality strategies for introducing an imitative product.

When the product is part of a product mix, the firm searches for a set of prices that will maximize the profits from the total mix. The company decides on *price zones* for items in its product line and on the pricing of *optional products,* *captive products,* and *by-products.*

Companies apply a variety of *price-adjustment strategies* to account for differences in consumer segments and situations. One is *geographical pricing,* whereby the company decides how to price to distant customers, choosing from such alternatives as FOB pricing, uniform delivered pricing, zone pricing, basing-point pricing, and freight-ab-

sorption pricing. A second is *discount pricing and allowances,* whereby the company establishes cash discounts, quantity discounts, functional discounts, seasonal discounts, and allowances. A third is *discriminatory pricing,* whereby the company sets different prices for different customers, product forms, places, or times. A fourth is *psychological pricing,* whereby the company adjusts the price to better communicate a product's intended position. A fifth is *promotional pricing,* whereby the company decides on loss-leader pricing, special-event pricing, and psychological discounting. A sixth in *value pricing,* whereby the company offers just the right combination of quality and good service at a fair price. A seventh is *international pricing,* whereby the company adjusts its price to meet different conditions and expectations in different world markets.

When a firm considers initiating a *price change,* it must consider customers' and competitors' reactions. Customers' reactions are influenced by the meaning customers see in the price change. Competitors' reactions flow from a set reaction policy or a fresh analysis of each situation. The firm initiating the price change must also anticipate the probable reactions of suppliers, middlemen, and government.

The firm that faces a price change initiated by a competitor must try to understand the competitor's intent as well as the likely duration and impact of the change. If a swift reaction is desirable, the firm should preplan its reactions to different possible price actions by competitors.

KEY TERMS

Basing-point pricing 380

By-product pricing 374

Captive-product pricing 374

Cash discount 375

Discriminatory pricing 375

FOB-origin pricing 379

Freight-absorption pricing 380

Functional discount 375

Market-penetration pricing 372

Market-skimming pricing 371

Optional-product pricing 373

Product-bundle pricing 374

Product line pricing 373

Promotional allowance 375

Promotional pricing 376

Psychological pricing 376

Quantity discount 375

Reference prices 376

Seasonal discount 375

Trade-in allowance 375

Two-part pricing 374

Uniform delivered pricing 380

Value pricing 377

Zone pricing 380

DISCUSSING THE ISSUES

1. When the dollar is weak, import prices rise, and Mercedes and Porsche prices rise with them. Yet when the dollar strengthens, the prices for these cars are kept high, yielding unusually large profits. Discuss whether Mercedes and Porsche should drop prices when their costs drop. What effect would this have on used-car prices and trade-in values?

2. Describe which strategy—market skimming or market penetration—these companies use in pricing their products: (a) McDonald's; (b) Curtis Mathes (television and other home electronics); (c) Bic Corporation (pens, lighters, shavers, and related products); and (d) IBM. Are these the right strategies for these companies? Why or why not?

3. Carpet Fresh was the leading carpet deodorizer, priced at $2.49 for 13 ounces. Arm & Hammer launched a competitive product priced at $1.99 for 26 ounces and quickly became the number-one brand. Discuss the psychological aspects of this pricing. Does this superb-value strategy fit with Arm & Hammer's image?

4. The formula for chlorine bleach is virtually identical for all brands. Clorox charges a premium price for this same product, yet remains the unchallenged market leader. Discuss what this implies about the value of a brand name. Are there ethical issues involved in this type of pricing?

5. A by-product of manufacturing tennis balls is "dead" balls—ones that do not bounce high enough to meet standards (that is, they bounce less than 53 inches when dropped from 100 inches onto a concrete surface). What strategy should be used for pricing these balls?

6. A clothing store sells men's suits at three price levels—$180, $250, and $340. If shoppers use these price points as reference prices in comparing different suits, what would be the effect of adding a new line of suits at a cost of $280? Would you expect sales of the $250 suits to increase, decrease, or stay the same?

APPLYING THE CONCEPTS

1. List at least five examples of stores that use their pricing strategies as part of their marketing communications, such as a supermarket calling itself "the low-price leader" or even the name of Cost Plus Imports. Do any of your examples discuss offering average or high prices? Why not?

2. Go to your local supermarket and observe sizes and prices within product categories. Are the package sizes (the weight or number of units contained) comparable across brands? Find at least two instances where a manufacturer seems to have made a smaller package in order to achieve a lower retail price. Does this appear effective? If your market has unit pricing labels, see if the unit price is higher, lower, or the same as this brand's competitors. Does unit pricing information change your opinion about the effectiveness of this strategy?

MAKING MARKETING DECISIONS:

SMALL WORLD COMMUNICATIONS, INC.

Thomas Campbell and Lynette Jones have moved Small World Communications into a new phase: they have both quit their jobs and begun working full-time on the new company. Currently, they are working out of their homes while they decide on a final location for the company. Tom's prototypes of the Airport product have met with very favorable comments from computer users who have tried it. Tom is now refining the design into final form, adding a few new features that users asked for, and they have hired a programmer to complete the custom software modules.

Tom was flying to the East Coast to meet with a chip manufacturer, and he agreed to stop and meet Lyn in Chicago. "Do you have big plans while you's here?" Lyn asked. "Maybe," Tom said. "I'm going to stop off and see my cousin Wayne in Aurora, and possibly check out a little Chicago nightlife. He knows a club where Buddy Guy and Junior Wells play, and . . ." "Please don't listen to the blues while you're here, Lyn pleaded. "I hate it when you've been listening to the blues." "Why? You don't like my air guitar version of B.B. King?" he asked. "Tom, you need a therapist. But the biggest problem is that after you listen to the blues, you drag and mope—sometimes for days. I need you in peak form now, so listen to light, cheery music, and maybe some motivational tapes. In the meantime, we need to get our pricing strategy set."

"I've been thinking abut this," Tom said. "We've got the only solution to people's communication integration needs, at least for a few months. We need to build a quality image, and we need some cash flow. All of those things fit with a market-skimming pricing strategy. We price higher at first, and when a competitor launches, we drop our price immediately to a very slight premium over the other guys. There's a psychological edge to it—people will know we were the first, and a small premium will still help signal that we're the best." "It sounds good so far," Lyn said, "But what about the long term?" "Easy," he said, "When our next generation Airport II is ready, we go to a two-line strategy: market skimming for the high end, and market penetration for the low end by cutting the price way down on our original product." "That sounds really workable, assuming we can get enough marketing intelligence about what our competitors are doing. I need to check my voice mail right now, but remind me to ask you about how we can use pricing to get computer makers to bundle Airport with their machines."

WHAT NOW?

1. Early in the product life cycle, new, innovative, or improved computer products can use a market-skimming strategy to earn high profits. As the market matures, competitors bring out products with similar or better features, and the average prices and profits fall. Discuss how Small World plans to integrate its new product plans with its pricing strategy. (a) Does this plan sound reasonable? (b) What risks does this plan have?

2. Compaq computer uses brand-named elements from other manufacturers, including software (Microsoft Windows), hardware (a Logitech trackball), and even services (a trial membership to the Prodigy database). Lyn would love to have Compaq and other Original Equipment Manufacturers (OEMs) purchase Small World's product directly. (a) What factors should Small World consider in pricing its product for OEM's? (b) What marketing advantages—and/or disadvantages—would Small World gain from such an arrangement? (c) Should the potential advantages and disadvantages influence the pricing decision?

REFERENCES

1. Quotes from Andrea Rothman, "The Superlosers in the Supersaver War," *Business Week*, June 15, 1992, p. 44. Also see Bridget O'Brian, "Airlines Seek to Earn More from an Irritated Clientele," *The Wall Street Journal*, March 16, 1992, pp. B1, B6; James E. Ellis, "Sure They're Simpler, But . . ." *Business Week*, April 27, 1992, p. 40; Bridget O'Brian and James S. Hirsch, "Flying Low: Simplifying Their Fares Proves More Difficult than Airlines Expect," *The Wall Street Journal*, June 4, 1992, pp. A1, A5; Wendy Zellner, "The Airlines Are Killing Each Other Again," *Business Week*, June 8, 1992, p. 32; and Julie Schmit, "American Says Fare Structure Failed," *USA Today*, October 12, 1992, p. 1B.

2. For a comprehensive description and comparison of various pricing strategies, see Gerard J. Tellis, "Beyond the Many Faces of Price: An Integration of Pricing Strategies," *Journal of Marketing*, October 1986, pp. 146–60.

3. See James E. Ellis, "Spectra's Instant Success Gives Polaroid a Shot in the Arm," *Business Week*, November 3, 1986, pp. 32–34; and Thomas T. Nagle, *The Strategy and Tactics of Pricing* (Englewood Cliffs, NJ: Prentice Hall, 1987), pp. 116–17.

4. See Tellis, "Beyond the Many Faces of Price," p. 155; and Nagle, *The Strategy and Tactics of Pricing*, pp. 170–72.

5. Gary M. Erickson and Johny K. Johansson, "The Role of Price in Multi-Attribute Product Evaluations," *Journal of Consumer Research*, September 1985, pp. 195–99.

6. See Nagle, *The Strategy and Tactics of Pricing*, pp. 66–68; Tellis, "Beyond the Many Faces of Price," pp. 152–53; and Gerard J. Tellis and Gary J. Gaeth, "Best Value, Price-Seeking, and Price Aversion: The Impact of information and Learning on Consumer Choices," *Journal of Marketing*, April 1990, pp. 34–52.

7. Philip R. Cateora, *International Marketing*, 7th ed. (Homewood, IL: Irwin, 1990), p. 540.

8. For more on price cutting and its consequences, see Kathleen Madigan, "The Latest Mad Plunge of the Price Slashers," *Business Week*, May 11, 1992, p. 36; and Bill Saporito, "Why the Price Wars Never End," *Fortune*, March 23, 1992, pp. 68–78.

VIDEO CASE 13

SHEEP PILLS FOR HUMANS

Thirty years ago, Johnson & Johnson introduced levamisole, a drug used to deworm sheep. When farmers using the drug noticed that dewormed sheep also suffered fewer cases of shipping fever, researchers began investigating the drug for human use. Under the sponsorship of the National Cancer Institute, and with free pills provided by Johnson & Johnson, Dr. Charles Moertel of the Mayo Comprehensive Cancer Center tested levamisole in combination with a staple chemotherapy drug called 5-fluorouracil as a treatment for cancer. The combination proved effective in patients with advanced (Stage C) colon cancer. It reduced recurrence of the disease by 40 percent and cut deaths by a third.

This treatment was a major breakthrough. Colon cancer is the second largest cause of cancer deaths. About 22,000 patients are diagnosed each year with Stage C colon cancer, and many times that number are diagnosed with earlier stages of the disease. Based on Dr. Moertel's research, the FDA quickly approved levamisole for human use. In 1990, the Janssen division of Johnson & Johnson introduced the drug under the brand name Ergamisol.

Since then, sales of levamisole have reached $15 million annually—respectable, but not large by drug industry standards. Everything appeared to be sailing along for Janssen until an Illinois farmwoman noticed that her cancer pills contained the same active ingredient as the medicine that she used to deworm her sheep. It wasn't the fact that both humans and sheep were using the drug that disturbed her. What really rankled her was that the sheep medicine sells for pennies a pill, whereas the human medicine sells for $5 to $6 per tablet. In a year's time, humans may spend from $1,250 to $3,000 for Ergamisol; the cost for treating sheep may be as low as $14.95.

The price discrepancy has caused quite a stir. Doctors at the MacNeal Hospital Cancer Center in Chicago surveyed local pharmacies and found that patients paid an average of $1,200 per year for levamisole. At the annual meetings of the American Society for Clinical Oncology in May 1992, Dr. Moertel blasted Johnson & Johnson for its unconscionable pricing of the drug. His salvo marked the first time that marketplace issues had taken center stage at that scholarly forum, and it had great impact. With gratification, Dr. Moertel noted that his presentation drew "the loudest applause you've ever heard at an ASCO meeting, reflecting the outrage of the practicing physician."

As if publicity of Dr. Moertel's comments were not enough, in August 1992, Chicago consumer Frank Glickman filed suit against Janssen. He claimed that he was forced to pay "an outrageous, unconscionable, and extortionate price for a life-saving drug" that is sold at a fraction of the cost for treating sheep. Janssen replied that the cost of Ergamisol is reasonable when compared to other lifesaving drugs such as AZT, which can cost $6,000 to $8,000 a year. The company also claims that the price reflects decades of costly research conducted to determine if levamisole could be used to treat humans. The company says it conducted over 1,400 studies with 40,000 subjects.

Dr. Moertel disagrees. He claims that the Cancer Institute, funded by the American taxpayer, sponsored the studies proving levamisole useful for treating humans. Further, he proclaims, FDA approval was obtained on the basis of his research, which cost Janssen only pennies. Moertel sums it up this way: "The company got a present dumped in its lap. . . . We gave it to them on a silver platter." He goes on to point out that Janssen had 25 years to recoup its investment before it ever sold the drug to humans.

The levamisole example highlights several important drug pricing issues. First, drug prices have risen astronomically—about 158 percent during the 1980s alone. Although part of the increase is attributable to increasing material and production costs, a major part is accounted for by promotion and selling costs of drug products. Each year, pharmaceutical representatives give away thousands of free samples and other inducements to doctors.

Second, when attacked, the drug industry flexes heavy lobbying muscle in Congress. As a result, the pharmaceutical industry in this country—in contrast to its European counterpart—remains largely unregulated. Finally, increasing drug prices contribute greatly to escalating health-care costs, which are reflected in the insurance premiums that we all pay.

Perhaps the most serious charge against high drug prices is that they have life-and-death consequences. Without levamisole, some colon cancer patients would die. Unlike purchases of other consumer products, drug purchases cannot be postponed. Nor can consumers shop around to save money. Because of patents and FDA approvals, few competing brands exist, and they don't go on sale. All of this raises an important question: Should drug company profits come at the expense of human life?

QUESTIONS

1. Is Ergamisol a new product? How should it be priced?

2. How does the levamisole/Ergamisol case illustrate product line pricing?

3. Does levamisole/Ergamisol pricing constitute discriminatory pricing? Is it defensible? What does your answer suggest about perceived value pricing?

4. Is Janssen's argument that Ergamisol is relatively cheap compared to other lifesaving drugs such as AZT appropriate? If not, what does your answer suggest about perceived value pricing?

5. Some critics suggest that drug industry pricing should be regulated. What would be the consequences of such regulation? What would be the costs?

Sources: Quotes from Marilyn Chase, "Doctor Assails J&J Price Tag on Cancer Drug," *The Wall Street Journal*, May 20, 1992, p. B1. Also see "Cancer Patient Sues Johnson & Johnson over Drug Pricing," *The Wall Street Journal*, August 13, 1992, p. B6; and Mike King, "Colon Cancer Drug: 5 Cents for an Animal, $5 for Humans," *Atlanta Constitution*, March 11, 1991, p. E1.

COMPANY CASE 13

NISSAN: PRICING THE ALTIMA

Creating an Image

Beginning in the 1970s, through the 1980s, and into the 1990s, it seemed that Japanese auto makes could do no wrong. These same auto makers had gotten off to a rocky start in the 1950s and 1960s, when they entered the U.S. market with cars that consumers mocked as looking like "fat roller skates." Consumers saw the cars as cheap and suitable only for basic transportation.

The Japanese firms were patient, however. They studied U.S. consumers to determine what they wanted. They improved their manufacturing processes and their product quality and styling. They developed strong U.S. dealer networks and worked with dealers to stress customer satisfaction.

The hard work, patience, and customer focus paid off for the Japanese firms. During the oil crises of the 1970s, when gasoline prices skyrocketed overnight and supplies dwindled, American consumers rushed to buy the fuel-efficient, reasonably priced Japanese cars. These consumers discovered that Japanese cars offered high quality as well as economy and that they came fully equipped, with few options. Because Japanese models had few options and because dealers adhered to the cars' sticker prices, consumers faced less haggling over price. Moreover, Japanese cars held their value, whereas U.S. cars seemed to lose theirs rapidly. Consumers also found that Japanese cars had very few operational problems; when repairs *were* necessary, consumers encountered courteous dealers who worked hard to satisfy them.

The Japanese auto makers had learned their lessons well, and American consumers also learned quickly. Sales of Japanese cars soared. The Japanese car makers gobbled up market share that American companies had previously captured by default, until one in every four cars sold in the United States had a Japanese nameplate. During the 1980s, the Japanese firms always seemed to be one step ahead of the market and at least two steps ahead of their American competitors. Ford struggled, Chrysler nearly went bankrupt, and General Motors continues to look for the right formula.

An Exception to the Rule

In 1960, Nissan sent Yukata Katayama to the United States to set up dealerships for its Datsun cars. Like other Japanese cars at the time, the tiny, underpowered, ugly Datsuns did not fit well in the U.S. market. Katayama, however, worked with engineers in Japan and by the end of the 1960s, Nissan was selling over 150,000 cars a year in the United States. Success had come in 1968 with the introduction of the Datsun 510 models. These small, durable four-door sedans performed well and sold for $1,800, a price within almost everyone's reach.

In 1969, at Katayama's urging, Nissan introduced the Datsun 240Z, a sleek two-seat sports car priced at $3,500. The 240Z redefined the sports-car market and reshaped Datsun's sedan image. The 240Z's success convinced Nissan that it should focus on the sports-car market. As a result, during the 1970s, Nissan pursued speed and performance while its rival, Toyota, focused on four-door sedans. In 1975, Nissan sprinted past Volkswagen as the number one exporter to the United States.

Katayama retired in 1977, and Nissan's managers in Japan gradually began to take control of product decisions for the U.S. market. During the 1970s and 1980s, competitor Toyota was strong enough to build cars specifically designed for the United States, while at the same time designing cars for its home market. Honda, although smaller than either Nissan or Toyota in Japan, focused its resources on designing cars specifically for the U.S. market. Nissan did not have the resources to serve both the U.S. and Japanese markets, so it built cars for the Japanese market and expected Datsun's U.S. dealers to sell what it sent them.

By 1980, Nissan, Toyota, and Honda were virtually neck and neck in the United States. Then in 1981, Nissan's managers decided that they wanted to consolidate the company's brands worldwide. They decreed that the U.S. division would drop the Datsun name and begin to use the corporate name, Nissan, for the cars it sold in the United States. The name change dragged on for five years as frustrated dealers fought the conversion and confused customers wondered what a Nissan was.

During the 1980s, Nissan continued to focus on speed, performance, and sporty models. As a result, the quality and design of its sedans suffered. The Honda Accord and the Toyota Corolla stole market share from Nissan's Sentra and Stanza models. Nissan's U.S. executives became frustrated with their inability to win against their arch rivals. Nissan did not even start designing a minivan for the U.S. market until five years after Chrysler had introduced its highly successful minivan. Moreover, Nissan had been slow to begin producing cars in the United States. It did not begin manufacturing its first cars in the United States until 1985, a year in which Honda would produce over 117,000 cars here. Fifty-seven percent of Nissan's U.S. sales that year would consist of its two lowest-priced, lowest-margin vehicles, the Sentra and an entry-level pickup truck.

By 1992, Japanese auto makers' U.S. share had risen from 18.7 percent to 25 percent. During this same period, Nissan's U.S. market share had *fallen* to 4.5 percent from a high of 5.7 percent in 1983. Nissan sold fewer cars in 1991 then it had in any year since 1982. In early 1992, it even fell behind Mazda in U.S. sales. Perhaps more importantly, among all 34 brands that J. D. Power and Associates measures, Nissan ranked below average in two critical areas: initial quality and owner satisfaction with the car at delivery.

In a single decade, Nissan had squandered its competitive advantage. Although industry analysts ranked some of its cars among the best against their direct competition, Nissan lacked a strong car at the core of its product line—something between the entry level Sentra and the top-of-the-line Maxima. While Toyota and Honda had vigorously pursued the U.S. family-sedan market with their Camrys and Accords, Nissan had been left at the starting gate. It never realized that, as memories of the 1970s fuel crises faded, American consumers wanted to trade in their smaller Honda Civics and Toyota Corollas for larger, family-sized cars. In addition, Nissan had confused customers with its marketing shifts and had strained its relations with its dealers.

Prescription for a Turnaround

To fill the hole in its product line and to develop a car that would challenge the Toyota Camry, the Ford Taurus, and the Honda Accord, in 1988 Nissan officials authorized a competition between its design staffs located in Japan and in La Jolla, California. Each group was to design a new car that would compete for the broad middle market in the United States. This segment, after all, generated the real volume in the U.S. car market—and in a high-fixed-cost business, volume is critical to profitability.

The La Jolla design team, headed by Gerald P. Hirshberg, won the competition. Hirshberg, an Ohio State graduate with a degree in mechanical engineering, had left General Motors to join Nissan in 1979. Hirshberg wanted his team to design a car that would help Nissan make the change from a company known for fast, sporty cars to one known for dependable quality. He also wanted the design to break the "tyranny of the wedge" shape that he felt dominated sedan designs. Hir-

shberg realized that Nissan had painted itself into a make-or-break corner. The new car had to change Nissan's image.

Hirshberg and his team designed a new mid-sized car that Nissan dubbed the Altima (AHL-ti-ma), derived from the Latin word "altus" which suggested "a higher order." Research indicated that buyers increasingly decided among car models based on the emotional appeal of the car's styling and its image. The car's name served to trigger those emotions.

The new Altima faced stiff competition on features. It came with a 2.4 liter four-cylinder engine that delivered 150 horsepower. The Taurus came with a standard six-cylinder engine, and the V-6 was an option on the Camry. A redesigned Accord would debut soon with a V-6. Although the competitors often offered sedans, wagons, and coupes, Altima came only as a four-door sedan. The competitors' cars were also bigger by almost any method of measurement.

The Altima had front-wheel drive, and with an automatic transmission it accelerated from zero to 60 miles per hour in 9.5 seconds. It had an estimated top speed of 118 miles per hour and EPA fuel economy ratings of 21 miles per gallon in the city and 29 miles per gallon on the highway.

The standard Altima, the XE model, featured power steering, power mirrors, tilt steering wheel, remote releases for trunk and gas cap, tachometer, and driver's side air bag. Options included a power sunroof, automatic transmission, air conditioning, anti-lock brakes, a leather interior, and a CD player. The Altima came in four models, the XE, the GXE, the SE, and the GLE, each with different option packages.

One reviewer who tested the new car reported that the Altima, with its sloping lines, had a styling edge on the competition. He also suggested that it had a pleasant, familiar interior. However, the reviewer did not like the mechanical seat belts and the four-cylinder engine.

To manufacture the Altima and a new minivan, the Quest, Nissan invested $490 million to expand its plant in Smyrna, Tennessee. Altima's sales needed to top 100,000 units per year to make the plant operate profitably. However, Nissan's sales of its Stanza, the car that Altima replaced, had averaged only 50,000 units per year over the previous five years.

Marketing the Altima

Nissan gave Thomas D. Mignanelli, Nissan's U.S. sales and marketing director and a former sales executive at Ford, the task of marketing the Altima and reaching its lofty sales goals. Mignanelli predicted that Altima's sales would top 150,000 units, triple the Stanza's sales.

Mignanelli made two important changes. First, he replaced Nissan's advertising agency with Chiat/Day/Mojo, Inc., and ordered the new agency to move Nissan's image back into the mainstream by producing ads that emphasized durability, quality, and reliability. Second, Mignanelli brought in the Boston Consulting Group to help with dealer relations. The consultants helped Nissan create the position of dealer-operations manager (DOM). The DOMs work with dealers to help them reduce fixed costs, improve customer satisfaction, and develop their own local ads. Mignanelli also reorganized the headquarters staff along brand-manager lines, making one person responsible for the full marketing plan for each vehicle model.

Now Mignanelli has only one other major decision—how to price the Altima. Like every other decision, however, the pricing decision has generated lots of debate between the U.S. division and headquarters in Japan. One group argues that Nissan should set the Altima's base price in the $13,000 range, putting it about $2,000 below the base prices for the Accord and the Camry. This would mean that the prices for the higher-priced Altima models, like the SE or GLE, would also be $1,500 to $2,000 cheaper than comparably equipped competitive models. The higher-priced models could have sticker prices as high as $20,000 with a full range of options. This group argues that Nissan and its dealers can make acceptable profits at these prices.

Nissan's Sentra XE has a base price of $10,685. With air conditioning, AM/FM radio, and cruise control, it carries a sticker price of $12,610. A Sentra GXE has a base price of $15,020. With an air conditioner, sunroof, air bag, radio, cruise control, and power doors, it carries a sticker price of $16,195. A Nissan Maxima SE carries a sticker price of $24,435.

Another group argues that the company should price the Altima in the same price range as its direct competitors. It believes that if the Altima offers comparable features, Nissan should price it comparably. They wonder how customers will react if Nissan prices Altima significantly below comparably priced competitive models. This group also notes that the declining value of the U.S. dollar, relative to the Japanese yen during the early 1990s, is already putting pressure on all Japanese car companies to raise prices. The U.S. dollar's declining value means that the U.S. dollars that Japanese auto makers receive are worth less in Japan than they used to be. The declining value has the same effect as a price reduction—slimmer margins.

Mignanelli and the other Nissan officials realize the importance of the pricing decision. Nissan lost $178 million during the first six months of the fiscal year beginning April 1, 1992—its first loss in 40 years. Furthermore, the 1990s have not been good for many of the previously invincible Japanese companies. Honda, Toyota, Isuzu, and Mazda have all had troubles; Daihatsu quit the U.S. market altogether. Thus, Nissan hopes that it can ride the Altima to a new image and to revived profitability.

QUESTIONS

1. What product-mix pricing strategies do automobile companies typically use?

2. What price-adjustment strategies do automobile companies and dealers typically use?

3. How do these pricing strategies affect consumer feelings about the automobile purchasing process?

4. What specific pricing recommendations would you make for Nissan's Altima? Why? How would competitors, especially Toyota and Honda, react if Nissan implemented your recommendations?

5. What other marketing mix recommendations would you make for the Altima?

Sources: Karen Lowry Miller, Larry Armstrong, and James B. Treece, "Will Nissan Get It Right This Time?" *Business Week,* April 20, 1992, pp. 82–87; Amy Harmon, "Hopes Riding High on New Car," *The Los Angeles Times,* May 9, 1992, pp. D1–D2; Alex Taylor, III, "Driving for the Market's Heart," *Fortune,* June 15, 1992, pp. 120–21; "Ultimately, Nissan Calls Car 'Altima,'" *New York Times,* June 24, 1992, p. D17; Jacqueline Mitchell, "Nissan Has a Lot Riding on New Altima," *The Wall Street Journal,* August 24, 1992, p. B1; Paul Dean, "A New Contender for Mid-Size Title," *The Los Angeles Times,* November 6, 1992, pp. E1, E10; Patrick Boyle, "The Sun Also Sets," *Los Angeles Time Magazine,* January 10, 1993, pp. 15–19; Larry Armstrong, "Altima's Secret: The Right Kind of Sticker Shock," *Business Week,* January 18, 1993, p. 37; Marshall Schuon, "From Nissan, a New Name, a New Car," *New York Times,* January 31, 1993, Section 8, p. 14.

14

*P*lacing Products: Distribution Channels and Physical Distribution

For more than 60 years, Goodyear Tire & Rubber Company sold replacement tires exclusively through its powerful network of independent Goodyear dealers. Both Goodyear and its 2,500 dealers profited from this partnership. Goodyear received the undivided attention and loyalty of its single-brand dealers, and the dealers gained the exclusive right to sell the highly respected Goodyear tire line. In mid-1992, however, Goodyear shattered tradition and jolted its dealers by announcing that it would now sell Goodyear-brand tires through Sears auto centers, placing Goodyear dealers in direct competition with the giant retailer. This departure from the previously sacred dealer network left many dealers shaken and angry. Said one Goodyear dealer: "You feel like after 35 years of marriage, your [spouse] is stepping out on you."

Several factors forced the change in Goodyear's distribution system. During the late 1980s, massive international consolidation reshaped the tire industry, leaving only five competitors. Japan's Bridgestone acquired Firestone, Germany's Continental bought General Tire, Italy's Pirelli snapped up Armstrong, and France's Michelin acquired Uniroyal Goodrich. After six decades as the world's largest tire maker, Goodyear slipped to second behind Michelin. As the only remaining U.S.-owned tire company, instead of having its way with smaller domestic rivals, Goodyear now found itself battling for U.S. market share against large and newly strengthened international competitors.

To add to Goodyear's woes, consumers were changing how and where they bought tires. Value-minded tire buyers were increasingly buying from cheaper, multibrand discount outlets, department stores, and warehouse clubs. The market share of these outlets had grown 30 percent in the previous five years, while that of tire dealers had fallen 4

percent. By selling exclusively through its dealer network, Goodyear simply wasn't putting its tires where many consumers were buying them. The shifts in consumer buying were also causing problems for dealers. Although Goodyear offered an ample variety of premium lines, it provided its dealers with none of the lower-priced lines that many consumers were demanding.

Entering the 1990s, Goodyear was foundering. Although it remained number one in the United States, its share of the U.S. replacement-tire market had fallen 3 percent in only five years. Battling a prolonged recession and vicious price competition from Michelin and Bridgestone, Goodyear suffered its first money-losing year since the Great Depression. Drastic measures were needed.

Enter new management, headed by Stanley Gault, the miracle-working manager who had recently transformed Rubbermaid from a sleepy Ohio rubber company into one of America's most admired market leaders. Gault took the helm in mid-1991 and moved quickly to streamline Goodyear, reducing its heavy debt, cutting costs, and selling off noncore businesses. But the biggest changes came in marketing. Under Gault, Goodyear speeded up new-product development and boosted ad spending. For example, in late 1991, it introduced four new tires simultaneously—the innovative, nonhydroplaning Aquatred, the Wrangler line for pickup trucks and vans, a fuel-efficient "green" tire, and a new high-performance Eagle model. In 1992, Goodyear brought out 12 more new tires, three times the usual number.

Gault also wasted little time in shaking up Goodyear's stodgy distribution system. In addition to selling Goodyear tires through Sears, the company began drumming up new private-label business. Its Kelly-Springfield unit soon inked a deal to sell private label tires through Wal-Mart, and eventual agreements with Kmart, Montgomery Ward, and even the warehouse clubs seem likely. Goodyear has since begun exploring other new distribution options as well. For example, it is now testing a no-frills, quick-serve discount store concept—Just Tires—designed to fend off low-priced competitors. In another test, it recently began selling Goodyear brand tires to multi-brand retailers in selected U.S. cities.

The marketing, distribution, and other changes have Goodyear rolling again. In its first year under Gault, Goodyear's sales and earnings soared, its market share increased 1 percent, and its stock price quadrupled. The expanded distribution system appears to be a significant plus, at least in the short run. For example, by itself, Sears controls 10 percent of the U.S. replacement-tire market. Even a 20 percent share of Sears's business for Goodyear means three million additional tires a year, enough to erase more than half of the company's previous market-share losses.

In the long run, however, the plan could backfire. Developing new channels might well boost immediate market share and profits, but it also risks eroding the loyalty and effectiveness of Goodyear's prized exclusive dealer network, one of the company's major competitive assets. To be fully effective, Goodyear and its dealers must work together in harmony for their mutual benefit. But the Sears agreement has created hard feelings and conflict between them. Many disgruntled dealers are striking back by taking on and aggressively promoting cheaper, private label brands—brands that offer higher margins to dealers and more appeal to some value-conscious consumers. Such dealer actions may eventually weaken the Goodyear name and the premium price that it can command.

Goodyear has taken steps to bolster anxious dealers. For example, it is now supplying dealers with a much-needed line of lower-priced Goodyear-brand tires. Goodyear sincerely believes that expanded distribution will help its dealers more than harm them. In the end, selling through Sears means better visibility for the Goodyear name, Gault contends, and the resulting expansion of business will mean more money for dealer support. However, many dealers remain skeptical. In the long run, dealer defections could lessen Goodyear's market power and offset sales gains from new channels. For example, shortly after the Sears announcement, one large Goodyear dealership in Florida adopted several lower-priced private brands, reducing its sales of Goodyear tires by 20 percent, but increasing its profit margins. The defiant dealer notes: "We [now] sell what we think will give the customer the best value, and that's not necessarily Goodyear." Thus, although Goodyear may be rolling again, the ride's not over. There are still many bumps in the road ahead.[1]

 ## CHAPTER PREVIEW

Chapter 14 presents a general outline of the key concepts of distribution channels and physical distribution.

First, we look at the nature of **distribution channels:** why **middlemen** are used, the **functions** of the distribution channel, the **number of levels** in a channel, and how channels operate in the **service sector.**

The chapter continues with a look at **channel behavior and organization,** types of **vertical marketing systems,** and the growth of **horizontal** and **multichannel** marketing systems.

The chapter also covers the key issues of **channel design** including **analyzing customer service needs,** setting **channel objectives,** considering alternative **types and numbers of middlemen,** including **intensive, selective,** and **exclusive distribution. Channel management** decisions are reviewed, including **selecting, motivating,** and **evaluating** channel members.

We conclude with a summary of the issues firms face when setting up **physical distribution systems,** including **order processing, warehousing, inventory management,** and **transportation modes.**

Marketing channel decisions are among the most important decisions that management faces. A company's channel decisions directly affect every other marketing decision. The company's pricing depends on whether it uses mass merchandisers or high-quality specialty stores. The firm's salesforce and advertising decisions depend on how much persuasion, training, and motivation the dealers need. Whether a company develops or acquires certain new products may depend on how well those products fit the abilities of its channel members.

Companies often pay too little attention to their distribution channels, however, sometimes with damaging results. For example, automobile manufacturers have lost large shares of their parts and service business to companies like NAPA, Midas, Goodyear, and others because they have resisted making needed changes in their dealer franchise networks. In contrast, many companies have used imaginative distribution systems to *gain* a competitive advantage. Federal Express's creative and imposing distribution system made it the leader in the small-package delivery industry. And American Hospital Supply gained a strong advantage over its competition by linking its distribution system directly to hospitals through a sophisticated data-processing system.[2]

Distribution channel decisions often involve long-term commitments to other firms. For example, a furniture manufacturer can easily change its advertising, pricing, or promotion programs. It can scrap old product designs and introduce new ones as market tastes demand. But when it sets up a distribution channel through contracts with independent dealers, it cannot readily replace this channel with company-owned branches if conditions change. Therefore, management must design its channels carefully, with an eye on tomorrow's likely selling environment as well as today's.

This chapter examines four major questions concerning distribution channels: *What is the nature of distribution channels? How do channel firms interact and organize to do the work of the channel? What problems do companies face in designing and managing their channels? What role does physical distribution play in attracting and satisfying customers?* In Chapter 15, we will look at distribution channel issues from the viewpoint of retailers and wholesalers.

THE NATURE OF DISTRIBUTION CHANNELS

Most producers use middlemen to bring their products to market. They try to forge a **distribution channel**—a set of interdependent organizations involved in the process of making a product or service available for use or consumption by the consumer or industrial user.[3]

Why Are Middlemen Used?

Why do producers give some of the selling job to middlemen? After all, doing so means giving up some control over how and to whom the products are sold. The use of middlemen results from their greater efficiency in making goods available to target markets. Through their contacts, experience, specialization, and scale of operation, middlemen usually offer the firm more than it can achieve on its own.

Figure 14-1 shows how using middlemen can provide economies. Part A shows three manufacturers, each using direct marketing to reach three customers. This system requires nine different contacts. Part B shows the three manufacturers working through one distributor, who contacts the three customers. This system requires only six contacts. In this way, middlemen reduce the amount of work that must be done by both producers and consumers.

From the economic system's point of view, the role of middlemen is to transform the assortments of products made by producers into the assortments wanted by consumers. Producers make narrow assortments of products in large quantities, but consumers want broad assortments of products in small quantities. In the distribution channels, middlemen buy the large quantities of many producers and break them down into the smaller quantities and broader assortments wanted by consumers. Thus, middlemen play an important role in matching supply and demand.

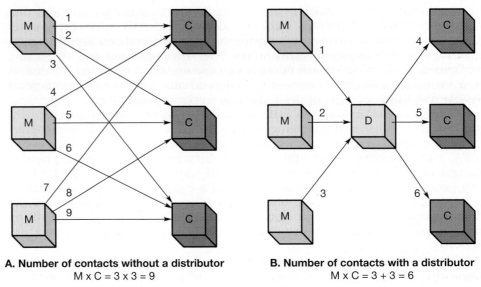

FIGURE 14-1
How a distributor reduces the number of channel transactions

A. Number of contacts without a distributor
M x C = 3 x 3 = 9

B. Number of contacts with a distributor
M x C = 3 + 3 = 6

M = Manufacturer   C = Customer   D = Distributor

Distribution Channel Functions

A distribution channel moves goods from producers to consumers. It overcomes the major time, place, and possession gaps that separate goods and services from those who would use them. Members of the marketing channel perform many key functions:

- *Information:* gathering and distributing marketing research and intelligence information about actors and forces in the marketing environment needed for planning and aiding exchange.

- *Promotion:* developing and spreading persuasive communications about an offer.

- *Contact:* finding and communicating with prospective buyers.

- *Matching:* shaping and fitting the offer to the buyer's needs, including such activities as manufacturing, grading, assembling, and packaging.

- *Negotiation:* reaching an agreement on price and other terms of the offer so that ownership or possession can be transferred.

- *Physical distribution:* transporting and storing goods.

- *Financing:* acquiring and using funds to cover the costs of the channel work.

- *Risk taking:* assuming the risks of carrying out the channel work.

The first five functions help to complete transactions; the last three help fulfill the completed transactions.

The question is not *whether* these functions need to be performed—they must be—but rather *who* is to perform them. All the functions have three things in common: They use up scarce resources, they often can be performed better through specialization, and they can be shifted among channel members. To the extent that the manufacturer performs these functions, its costs go up and its prices have to be higher. At the same time, when some of these functions are shifted to middlemen, the producer's costs and prices may be lower, but the middlemen must charge more to cover the costs of their work. In dividing the work of the channel, the various functions should be assigned to the channel members who can perform them most efficiently and effectively to provide satisfactory assortments of goods to target consumers.

Number of Channel Levels

Distribution channels can be described by the number of channel levels involved. Each layer of middlemen that performs some work in bringing the product and its ownership closer to the final buyer is a **channel level.** Because the producer and the final consumer both perform some work, they are part of every channel. We use the *number of intermediary levels* to indicate the *length* of a channel. Figure 14-2A shows several consumer distribution channels of different lengths.

Channel 1, called a **direct-marketing channel,** has no intermediary levels. It consists of a manufacturer selling directly to consumers. For example, both Avon and World Book Encyclopedia sell their products door to door; L. L. Bean sells clothing direct through mail order and by telephone; and Singer sells its sewing machines through its own stores. Channel 2 contains one middleman level. In consumer markets, this level is typically a retailer. For example, large retailers such as Wal-Mart and Sears sell televisions, cameras, tires, furniture, major appliances, and many other products they buy directly from manufacturers. Channel 3 contains two middleman levels. In consumer markets, these levels are typically a wholesaler and a retailer. This channel often is used by small manufacturers of food, drugs, hardware, and other products. Channel 4 contains three middleman levels. In the meatpacking industry, for example, jobbers usually come between wholesalers and retailers. The jobber buys from wholesalers and sells to smaller retailers who generally are not served by larger wholesalers. Distribution channels with even more levels are sometimes found, but less often. From the producer's point of view, a greater number of levels means less control and greater channel complexity.

Figure 14-2B shows some common industrial distribution channels. The industrial goods producer can use its own salesforce to sell directly to industrial customers. It also can sell to industrial distributors, who in turn sell to industrial customers. It can sell through manufacturer's representatives or its own sales branches to industrial customers, or it can use these representatives and branches to sell through industrial distributors. Thus, industrial goods markets commonly include zero-, one-, and two-level distribution channels.

All of the institutions in the channel are connected by several types of *flows.* These include the *physical flow* of products, the *flow of ownership,* the *payment flow,*

From the Coca-Cola Company, to the bottler, to the retailer, to the consumer—channel members must all work together to make Coke successful.

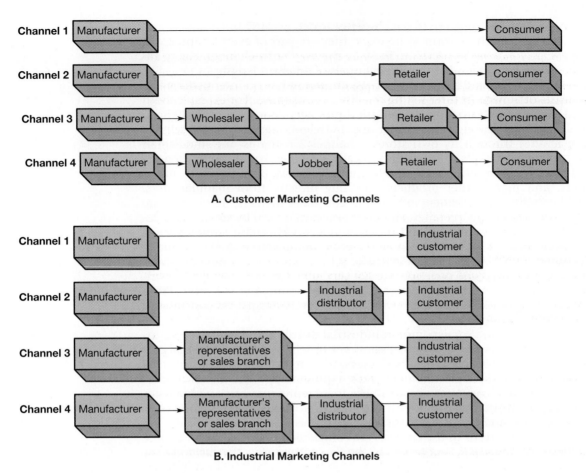

FIGURE 14-2
Consumer and industrial marketing channels

the *information flow,* and the *promotion flow.* These flows can even make channels with only one or a few levels very complex.

Channels in the Service Sector

The concept of distribution channels is not limited to the distribution of physical goods. Producers of services and ideas also face the problem of making their output *available* to target populations. They develop "educational distribution systems" and "health delivery systems." They must figure out agencies and locations for reaching a widely spread population:

> Hospitals must be located in geographic space to serve the people with complete medical care, and we must build schools close to the children who have to learn. Fire stations must be located to give rapid access to potential conflagrations, and voting booths must be placed so that people can cast their ballots without expending unreasonable amounts of time, effort, or money to reach the polling stations. Many of our states face the problem of locating branch campuses to serve a burgeoning and increasingly well educated population. In the cities we must create and locate playgrounds for the children. Many overpopulated countries must assign birth control clinics to reach the people with contraceptive and family planning information.[4]

Distribution channels also are used in "person" marketing. Before 1940, professional comedians could reach audiences through vaudeville houses, special events, nightclubs, radio, movies, carnivals, and theaters. In the 1950s, television became a strong channel and vaudeville disappeared. More recently, the comedian's channels have grown to include promotional events, product endorsements, cable television, and videotapes. Politicians must also find cost-effective channels—mass media, rallies, coffee hours—for distributing their messages to voters. We will discuss person marketing in more depth in Chapter 22.

CHANNEL BEHAVIOR AND ORGANIZATION

Distribution channels are more than simple collections of firms tied together by various flows. They are complex behavioral systems in which people and companies interact to accomplish individual, company, and channel goals. Some channel systems consist only of informal interactions among loosely organized firms; others consist of formal interactions guided by strong organizational structures. Moreover, channel systems do not stand still—new types of middlemen surface, and whole new channel systems evolve. Here we look at channel behavior and at how members organize to do the work of the channel.

Channel Behavior

A distribution channel consists of dissimilar firms that have banded together for their common good. Each channel member is dependent on the others. For example, a Ford dealer depends on the Ford Motor Company to design cars that meet consumer needs. In turn, Ford depends on the dealer to attract consumers, persuade them to buy Ford cars, and service cars after the sale. The Ford dealer also depends on other dealers to provide good sales and service that will uphold the reputation of Ford and its dealer body. In fact, the success of individual Ford dealers depends on how well the entire Ford distribution channel competes with the channels of other auto manufacturers.

Each channel member plays a role in the channel and specializes in performing one or more functions. For example, IBM's role is to produce personal computers that consumers will like and to create demand through national advertising. Computerland's role is to display these IBM computers in convenient locations, to answer buyers' questions, to close sales, and to provide service. The channel will be most effective when each member is assigned the tasks it can do best.

Ideally, because the success of individual channel members depends on overall channel success, all channel firms should work together smoothly. They should understand and accept their roles, coordinate their goals and activities, and cooperate to attain overall channel goals. By cooperating, they can more effectively sense, serve, and satisfy the target market.

However, individual channel members rarely take such a broad view. They are usually more concerned with their own short-run goals and their dealings with those firms closest to them in the channel. Cooperating to achieve overall channel goals sometimes means giving up individual company goals. Although channel members are dependent on one another, they often act alone in their own short-run best interests. They often disagree on the roles each should play—on who should do what and for what rewards. Such disagreements over goals and roles generate **channel conflict** (see Marketing Highlight 14-1).

Horizontal conflict is conflict among firms at the same level of the channel. For instance, some Ford dealers in Chicago complain about other dealers in the city who steal sales from them by being too aggressive in their pricing and advertising or by selling outside their assigned territories. Some Pizza Inn franchisees complain about other Pizza Inn franchisees cheating on ingredients, giving poor service, and hurting the overall Pizza Inn image.

Vertical conflict is even more common and refers to conflicts between different levels of the same channel. For example, General Motors came into conflict with its dealers some years ago by trying to enforce service, pricing, and advertising policies. Coca-Cola came into conflict with some of its bottlers who agreed to bottle competitor Dr Pepper. A large chain-saw company caused conflict when it decided to bypass its wholesale distributors and sell directly to large retailers such as J. C. Penney and Kmart, which then competed directly with its smaller retailers.

Some conflict in the channel takes the form of healthy competition. Such competition can be good for the channel—without it, the channel could become passive and noninnovative. But sometimes conflict can damage the channel. For the channel as a whole to perform well, each channel member's role must be specified and channel conflict must be managed. Cooperation, role assignment, and conflict management in the channel are attained through strong channel leadership. The channel will perform better if it includes a firm, agency, or mechanism that has the power to assign roles and manage conflict.

MARKETING HIGHLIGHT 14-1

CHANNEL CONFLICT: PROCTER & GAMBLE WRESTLES WITH RESELLERS

Procter & Gamble, the huge consumer packaged-goods producer, is part of a complex food-industry distribution channel consisting of producers, wholesale food distributors, and grocery retailers. Despite the immense popularity of its brands with consumers, P&G has never gotten along all that well with retailers and wholesalers. Instead, over the years, the company has acquired a reputation for wielding its market power in a somewhat high-handed fashion, without enough regard for reseller wishes. Recently, P&G's relations with many of these resellers took a decided turn for the worse. "We think that [P&G] will end up where most dictators end up—in trouble," fumes the chairman of Stop & Shop, a chain of 119 groceries in the Northeast. Hundreds of miles away, the assistant manager of Paulbeck's Super Valu in International Falls, Minnesota, shares these harsh feelings: "We should drop their top dogs—like half the sizes of Tide—and say 'Now see who put you on the shelf and who'll take you off of it.'"

The cause of the uproar is P&G's new "value pricing" policy. Under this sweeping new plan, the company is phasing out most of the large promotional discounts that it has offered resellers in the past. At the same time, it is lowering its everyday wholesale list prices for these products by 10 percent to 25 percent. P&G insists that price fluctuations and promotions have gotten out of hand. During the past decade, average trade discounts have more than tripled. Now, some 44 percent of all marketing dollars spent by manufacturers goes to trade promotions, up from 24 percent only a decade ago.

Manufacturers have come to rely on price-oriented trade promotions to differentiate their brands and boost short-term sales. In turn, wholesalers and retail chains have been conditioned to wait for manufacturers' "deals." Many have perfected "forward buying"—stocking up during manufacturers' price promotions on far more merchandise than they can sell, then reselling it to consumers at higher prices once the promotion is over. Such forward buying creates costly production and distribution inefficiencies. P&G's factories must gear up to meet the resulting huge demand swings. Meanwhile, supermarkets need more buyers to find the best prices and extra warehouses to store and handle merchandise bought "on deal." P&G claims that only 30 percent of trade promotion money actually reaches consumers in the form of lower prices, while 35 percent is lost to inefficiencies, and another 35 percent winds up in retailers' pockets. The industry's "promotion sickness" has also infected consumers. Wildly fluctuating retail prices have eroded brand loyalty by teaching consumers to shop for what's on sale, rather than by assessing the merits of each brand.

Through value pricing, P&G hopes to restore the price integrity of its brands and to begin weaning the industry and consumers from discount pricing. But the strategy has created substantial conflict in P&G's distribution channels. Discounts are the bread and butter of many retailers and wholesalers, who use products purchased from P&G at special low prices for weekly sales to lure value-minded consumers into supermarkets or stores. In other cases, retailers and wholesalers rely on the discounts to pad their profits through forward buying. And although the average costs of products to re-

Through value pricing, Procter & Gamble hopes to work with retailers to restore the price integrity of its brands.

In a large company, the formal organization structure assigns roles and provides needed leadership. But in a distribution channel made up of independent firms, leadership and power are not formally set. Traditionally, distribution channels have lacked the leadership needed to assign roles and manage conflict. In recent years, however, new types of channel organizations have appeared that provide stronger leadership and improved performance.[5]

Channel Organization

Historically, distribution channels have been loose collections of independent companies, each showing little concern for overall channel performance. These *conventional distribution channels* have lacked strong leadership and have been troubled by damaging conflict and poor performance.

sellers remain unchanged, resellers lose promotional dollars that they—not P&G—controlled. Thus, the new system gives P&G greater control over how its products are marketed, but reduces retailer and wholesaler pricing flexibility.

P&G's new strategy is risky. It alienates some of the very businesses that sell its wares to the public, and it gives competitors an opportunity to take advantage of the ban on promotions by highlighting their own specials. P&G is counting on its enormous market clout—retailers can ill afford, the company hopes, to eliminate heavily advertised powerhouse brands such as Tide detergent, Crest toothpaste, Folger's coffee, Pert shampoo, and Ivory soap. But even P&G's size and power may not be enough. Some large chains such as A&P, Safeway, and Rite-Aid drugstores are pruning out selected P&G sizes or dropping marginal brands such as Prell and Gleem. Certified Grocers, a Midwestern wholesaler, has dropped about 50 of the 300 P&G varieties it stocked. And numerous other chains are considering moving P&G brands from prime, eye-level space to less visible shelves, stocking more profitable private-label brands and competitors' products in P&G's place.

Super Valu, the nation's largest wholesaler, which also runs retail stores, is adding surcharges to some P&G products and paring back orders to make up for profits it says it's losing. One Super Valu buyer estimates that forward buying generates 70 percent of the profits for most wholesalers and 40 percent for supermarkets. But under the new system, they won't receive as much profit because they can't charge their customers much more than their own price. The buyer is not happy with P&G. "Any P&G items that are fringe, I'm gonna throw out," he says.

Despite these strong reactions, P&G plans to stay the course with its bold new pricing approach. Once in place, the company believes, value pricing will benefit all parties—manufacturers, resellers, and consumers—through lower and more stable costs and prices. Many resellers, and even competitors, are quietly cheering P&G's actions from the sidelines, hoping that order will

be restored to prices and promotions. P&G says that many of its largest retailers—especially mass merchandisers like Wal-Mart, which already employ everyday low pricing strategies—love the new system, and in fact inspired it. Moreover, most of P&G's largest competitors, while not jumping in with value pricing schemes of their own, have refrained from boosting their price promotions to take advantage of the situation.

P&G's struggle to reshape the industry's distorted pricing system demonstrates the dynamic forces of cooperation, power, and conflict found in distribution channels. Clearly, for the good of all parties, P&G and its resellers should work as partners to profitably market food products to consumers. But often, channels don't operate that smoothly; conflicts and power struggles sometimes flare up. In recent years, as more and more products have competed for limited supermarket shelf space, and as scanners have given retailers ever-greater leverage through market information, the balance of channel power has shifted—perhaps too far—toward grocery retailers. With its new pricing policy, P&G appears to be trying to wrestle back some of its lost marketplace control. The stakes are high: The new program stands to either empower P&G and overhaul the way most wholesalers and retailers do business—or to damage P&G's market share and force it to retreat. In the short run, the conflict will produce some bruises for all parties. In the long run, however, the struggle probably will be healthy for the channel, helping it to adapt and grow.

Sources: Portions adapted from Valerie Reitman, "Retail Resistance: Eliminated Discounts on P&G Goods Annoy Many Who Sell Them," *The Wall Street Journal,* August 11, 1992, pp. A1, A3. Used by permission. © Dow Jones & Company, Inc. All Rights Reserved Worldwide. Also see Jennifer Lawrence and Judann Dagnoli, "P&G's Low-Price Strategy Cuts Trade Fees, Irks Retailers," *Advertising Age,* December 23, 1991, p. 3; Zachary Schiller, "Not Everyone Loves a Supermarket Special," *Business Week,* February 17, 1992, pp. 64-68; "P&G Plays Pied Piper on Pricing," *Advertising Age,* March 9, 1992, p. 6; Patricia Sellers, "The Dumbest Marketing Ploy," *Fortune,* October 5, 1992, pp. 88-94; and Jennifer Lawrence, "Supermarket Tug of War," *Advertising Age,* April 19, 1993, pp. 1, 42.

Growth of Vertical Marketing Systems

One of the biggest recent channel developments has been the *vertical marketing systems* that have emerged to challenge conventional marketing channels. Figure 14-3 contrasts the two types of channel arrangements.

A **conventional distribution channel** consists of one or more independent producers, wholesalers, and retailers. Each is a separate business seeking to maximize its own profits, even at the expense of profits for the system as a whole. No channel member has much control over the other members, and no formal means exists for assigning roles and resolving channel conflict. In contrast, a **vertical marketing system (VMS)** consists of producers, wholesalers, and retailers acting as a unified system. One channel member owns the others, has contracts with them, or wields so much power that they all cooperate. The VMS can

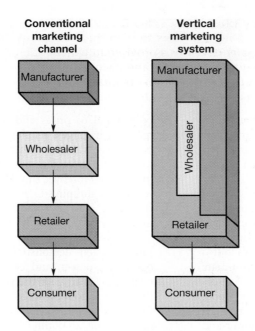

Conventional marketing channel

Manufacturer → Wholesaler → Retailer → Consumer

Vertical marketing system

Manufacturer / Wholesaler / Retailer → Consumer

FIGURE 14-3
A conventional marketing channel versus a vertical marketing system

be dominated by the producer, wholesaler, or retailer. Vertical marketing systems came into being to control channel behavior and manage channel conflict. They achieve economies through size, bargaining power, and elimination of duplicated services. Vertical marketing systems have become dominant in consumer marketing, serving as much as 64 percent of the total market.

We look now at the three major types of VMSs shown in Figure 14-4. Each type uses a different means for setting up leadership and power in the channel. In a *corporate VMS*, coordination and conflict management are attained through common ownership at different levels of the channel. In a *contractual VMS*, they are attained through contractual agreements among channel members. In an *administered VMS*, leadership is assumed by one or a few dominant channel members. We now take a closer look at each type of VMS.

Corporate VMS. A **corporate VMS** combines successive stages of production and distribution under single ownership. For example, Sears obtains more than 50 percent of its goods from companies that it partly or wholly owns. Sherwin-Williams makes paint but also owns and operates 2,000 retail outlets that sell its paints and other products. Giant Food Stores operates an ice-making facility, a soft-drink bottling operation, an ice-cream-making plant, and a bakery that supplies Giant stores with everything from bagels to birthday cakes. And Gallo, the world's largest wine maker, does much more than simply turn grapes into wine:

> The [Gallo] brothers own Fairbanks Trucking Company, one of the largest intrastate truckers in California. Its 200 semis and 500 trailers are constantly hauling wine out of Modesto and raw materials back in—including . . . lime from Gallo's quarry east of Sacramento. Alone among wine producers, Gallo makes bottles—two million a day—and its Midcal Aluminum Co. spews out screw tops as fast as the bottles are filled. Most of the country's 1,300 or so wineries concentrate on production to the neglect of marketing. Gallo, by contrast, participates in every aspect of selling short of whispering in the ear of each imbiber. The company owns its distributors in about a dozen markets and probably would buy many . . . more . . . if the laws in most states did not prohibit doing so.[6]

In such corporate systems, cooperation and conflict management are handled through regular organizational channels.

Contractual VMS. A **contractual VMS** consists of independent firms at different levels of production and distribution who join together through contracts to obtain more economies or sales impact than each could achieve alone. Contractual VMSs have expanded rapidly in recent years. There are three types of contractual VMSs: wholesaler-sponsored voluntary chains, retailer cooperatives, and franchise organizations.

Wholesaler-sponsored voluntary chains are systems in which wholesalers organize voluntary chains of independent retailers to help them compete with large chain organizations. The wholesaler develops a program in which independent retailers standardize their selling practices and achieve buying economies that let the group compete effectively with chain organizations. Examples include the Independent Grocers Alliance (IGA), Western Auto, and Sentry Hardwares.

Retailer cooperatives are systems in which retailers organize a new, jointly owned business to carry on wholesaling and possibly production. Members buy most of their goods through the retailer co-op and plan their advertising jointly. Profits are passed back to members in proportion to their purchases. Nonmember retailers also may buy through the co-op but do not share in the profits. Examples include Certified Grocers, Associated Grocers, and True Value Hardware.

In **franchise organizations**, a channel member called a *franchiser* links several stages in the production-distribution process. Franchising has been the fastest-growing retailing form in recent years. The more than 500,000 franchise operations in the United States now account for about one-third of all retail sales and may account for one-half by the year 2000.[7] Almost every kind of business has been franchised—from motels and fast-food restaurants to dentists and dating services, from wedding consultants and maid services to funeral homes and tub and tile refinishers. Although the basic idea is an old one, some forms of franchising are quite new.

There are three forms of franchises. The first form is the *manufacturer-sponsored retailer franchise system*, as found in the automobile industry. Ford, for example, licenses dealers to sell its cars; the dealers are independent businesspeople who agree to meet various conditions of sales and service. The second type of

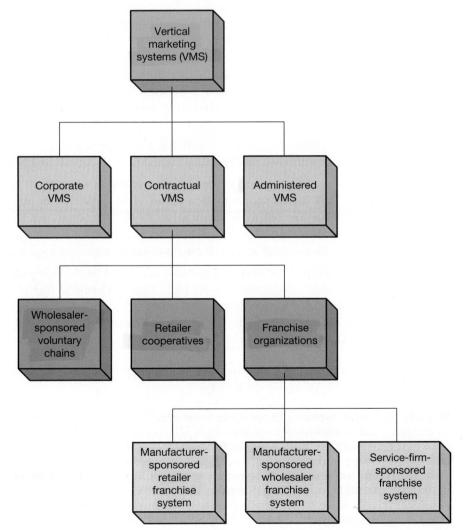

FIGURE 14-4
Major types of vertical marketing systems

franchise is the *manufacturer-sponsored wholesaler franchise system*, as found in the soft-drink industry. Coca-Cola, for example, licenses bottlers (wholesalers) in various markets, who buy Coca-Cola syrup concentrate and then carbonate, bottle, and sell the finished product to retailers in local markets. The third franchise form is the *service-firm-sponsored retailer franchise system*, in which a service firm licenses a system of retailers to bring its service to consumers. Examples are found in the auto-rental business (Hertz, Avis); the fast-food service business (McDonald's, Burger King); and the motel business (Holiday Inn, Ramada Inn).

The fact that most consumers cannot tell the difference between contractual and corporate VMSs shows how successfully the contractual organizations compete with corporate chains. Chapter 15 presents a fuller discussion of the various contractual VMSs.

Administered VMS. An **administered VMS** coordinates successive stages of production and distribution—not through common ownership or contractual ties but through the size and power of one of the parties. Manufacturers of a top brand can obtain strong trade cooperation and support from resellers. For example, General Electric, Procter & Gamble, Kraft, and Campbell Soup can command unusual cooperation from resellers regarding displays, shelf space, promotions, and price policies. And large retailers like Wal-Mart and Toys 'R' Us can exert strong influence on the manufacturers that supply the products they sell (see Marketing Highlight 14-2).

Growth of Horizontal Marketing Systems

Another channel development is the **horizontal marketing system**, in which two or more companies at one level join together to follow a new marketing opportunity. By working together, companies can combine their capital, production capabilities, or marketing resources to accomplish more than any one company could working alone. Companies might join forces with competitors or noncompetitors.[8] They might work with each other on a temporary or permanent basis, or they may create a separate company:

- The Lamar Savings Bank of Texas arranged to locate its savings offices and automated teller machines in Safeway stores. Lamar gained quicker market entry at a low cost, and Safeway was able to offer in-store banking convenience to its customers.

- Coca-Cola and Nestlé formed a joint venture to market ready-to-drink coffee and tea worldwide. Coke provided worldwide experience in marketing and distributing beverages and Nestlé contributed two established brand names—Nescafé and Nestea.

- H&R Block and Hyatt Legal Services formed a joint venture in which Hyatt houses its legal clinics in H&R Block's tax-preparation offices. Hyatt pays a fee for office space, secretarial assistance, and office equipment usage. By working out of H&R Block's nationwide office network, Hyatt gains quick market penetration. In turn, H&R Block benefits from renting its facilities, which otherwise have a highly seasonal pattern.

- Such channel arrangements work well globally. Because of its excellent coverage of international markets, Nestlé sells General Mills' Cheerios brand in markets outside North America. Seiko Watch's distribution partner in Japan, K. Hattori, markets Schick's razors and, as a result, Schick has the leading market share in Japan, despite Gillette's overall strength in many other markets.[9]

The number of such horizontal marketing systems has increased dramatically in recent years, and the end is nowhere in sight.

Growth of Multichannel Marketing Systems

In the past, many companies used a single channel to sell to a single market or market segment. Today, with the proliferation of customer segments and channel possibilities, more and more companies have adopted multichannel distribution. Such **multichannel marketing** occurs when a single firm sets up two or more marketing channels to reach one or more customer segments. For example, General Electric sells large home appliances both through independent retailers (department stores, discount houses, catalog houses) and through its direct salesforce

MARKETING HIGHLIGHT 14-2

TOYS 'R' US ADMINISTERS ITS CHANNEL

Toys 'R' Us operates 411 toy supermarkets that pull in $5.5 billion in annual sales and capture about 25 percent of the huge U.S. toy market. And the giant retailer is growing explosively—some experts predict that its market share will double during the 1990s. Because of its size and massive market power, Toys 'R' Us exerts strong influence on toy manufacturers—on their product, pricing, and promotion strategies—and on almost everything else they do.

Critics worry that Toys 'R' Us is *too* big and influential and that it takes unfair advantage of toy producers. The reactions of Toys 'R' Us buyers can make or break a new toy. For example, Hasbro invested some $20 million to develop Nemo—a home video game system to compete with the hugely successful Nintendo system—but then quickly canceled the project when Toys 'R' Us executives reacted negatively. Toys 'R' Us also sells its toys at everyday low prices. This sometimes frustrates toy manufacturers because Toys 'R' Us is selling toys at far below recommended retail prices, forcing producers to settle for lower margins and profits. And some analysts have accused Toys 'R' Us of placing an unfair burden on smaller toy makers by requiring all of its suppliers to pay a fee if they want their toys to be included in Toys 'R' Us newspaper advertisements.

But other industry experts think that Toys 'R' Us helps the toy industry more than it hurts it. For example, whereas other retailers feature toys during the Christmas season, Toys 'R' Us has created a year-round market for toys. Moreover, its low prices cause greater overall industry sales and force producers to operate more efficiently. Finally, Toys 'R' Us shares its extensive market data with toy producers, giving them immediate feedback on which products and marketing programs are working and which are not.

Clearly, Toys 'R' Us and the toy manufacturers need each other—the toy makers need Toys 'R' Us to market their products aggressively, and the giant retailer needs a corps of healthy producers to provide a constant stream of popular new products to fill its shelves. Through the years, both sides have recognized this interdependence. For example, in the mid-1970s, when Toys 'R' Us was threatened by bankruptcy because of the financial problems of its parent company, the Toy Manufacturers Association worked directly with banks to save the troubled retailer. The banks granted credit to Toys 'R' Us largely because several major toy manufacturers were willing to grant such credit on their own. By taking such action, the Association demonstrated a clear recognition that the entire toy industry benefited by keeping Toys 'R' Us healthy.

Similarly, Toys 'R' Us has recognized its stake in seeing that toy manufacturers succeed. In recent years, as flat toy sales have plunged many large manufacturers into deep financial trouble, Toys 'R' Us has provided a strong helping hand. For example, Toys 'R' Us often helps toy manufacturers through cash shortages and other financial difficulties by granting credit and prepaying bills. Also, its savvy buyers preview new products for toy makers, making early and valuable suggestions on possible design and marketing improvements. Such advice helped Galoob Toys convert its Army Gear line—toys that change into different weapons—from a potential flop into a top-20 seller. And following the advice of Toys 'R' Us, Ohio Arts altered the advertising strategy for its Zaks plastic building toys, increasing sales by 30 percent. The president of Tyco Toys concludes, "Toys 'R' Us gets a lot of flak for being large and taking advantage of manufacturers, but I would like to have more customers who help us as much as they do."

Sources: Amy Dunkin, "How Toys 'R' Us Controls the Game Board," *Business Week,* December 19, 1988, pp. 58-60; Louis W. Stern and Adel I. El-Ansary, *Marketing Channels,* (Englewood Cliffs, NJ: Prentice Hall, 1992), pp. 14-15; Alison Fahey, "Toys 'R' Us Sets Lower Pricing," *Advertising Age,* March 4, 1991, p. 4; and Mark Maremont, "Brawls in Toyland," *Business Week,* December 21, 1992, pp. 36-37.

to large housing-tract builders, thus competing to some extent with its own retailers. McDonald's sells through a network of independent franchisees, but owns more than one-fourth of its outlets. Thus, the wholly owned restaurants compete to some extent with those owned by McDonald's franchisees.

With each new channel, the multichannel marketer expands sales and market coverage and gains opportunities to tailor channels to the specific needs of diverse customer segments. But such systems are harder to control, and they generate conflict as more channels compete for customers and sales. Existing channels can cry "unfair competition" and threaten to drop the marketer unless it limits the competition or repays them in some way, perhaps by offering them exclusive models or special allowances.

In some cases, the multichannel marketer's channels are all under its own ownership and control. For example, J. C. Penney operates department stores, mass-merchandising stores, and specialty stores, each offering different product assortments to different market segments. Such arrangements eliminate conflict with outside channels, but the marketer might face internal conflict over how much financial support each channel deserves.

CHANNEL DESIGN DECISIONS

We now look at several channel decision problems facing manufacturers. In designing marketing channels, manufacturers struggle between what is ideal and what is practical. A new firm usually starts by selling in a limited market area. Because it has limited capital, it typically uses only a few existing middlemen in each market—a few manufacturers' sales agents, a few wholesalers, some existing retailers, a few trucking companies, and a few warehouses. Deciding on the best channels might not be a problem: The problem might be how to convince one or a few good middlemen to handle the line.

If the new firm is successful, it might branch out to new markets. Again, the manufacturer will tend to work through the existing middlemen, although this strategy might mean using different *types* of marketing channels in different areas. In smaller markets, the firm might sell directly to retailers; in larger markets, it might sell through distributors. In one part of the country, it might grant exclusive franchises because that is the way merchants normally work; in another, it might sell through all outlets willing to handle the merchandise. The manufacturer's channel system thus evolves to meet local opportunities and conditions.

Designing a channel system calls for analyzing consumer service needs, setting the channel objectives and constraints, identifying the major channel alternatives, and evaluating them.

Analyzing Consumer Service Needs

Designing the distribution channel starts with finding out what services consumers in various target segments want from the channel. The necessary level of channel services depends on the answers to several questions.[10] Do consumers want to buy from nearby locations or will they travel to more distant centralized locations, or buy over the phone or through the mail? The more decentralized the channel, the greater the service it provides. Do consumers want immediate delivery or are they willing to wait? Faster delivery means greater service from the channel. Do consumers value breadth of assortment or do they prefer specialization? The greater the assortment provided by the channel, the higher its service level. Finally, do consumers want many add-on services (delivery, credit, repairs, installation) or will they obtain these elsewhere? More add-on services mean a higher level of channel service.

Consider the distribution channel service needs of personal computer buyers:

> The delivery of service might include such things as demonstration of the product before the sale or provision of long-term warranties and flexible financing. After the sale, there might be training programs for using the equipment and a program to install and repair it. Customers might appreciate "loaners" while their equipment is being repaired or technical advice over a telephone hot line.[11]

Thus, to design an effective channel, the designer must know the service levels desired by consumers. But providing all the desired services may not be possible or practical. The company and its channel members may not have the resources or skills needed to provide all the desired services. Also, providing higher levels of service results in higher costs for the channel and higher prices for consumers. The company must balance consumer service needs against not only the feasibility and costs of meeting these needs but against customer price preferences. The success of discount retailing shows that consumers are often willing to accept lower service levels if this means lower prices.

Setting the Channel Objectives and Constraints

Channel objectives should be stated in terms of the desired service level of target consumers. Usually, a company can identify several segments wanting different levels of channel service. The company should decide which segments to serve and the best channels to use in each case. In each segment, the company wants to minimize the total channel cost of delivering the desired service level.

The company's channel objectives also are influenced by the nature of its products, company policies, middlemen, competitors, and the environment. *Product characteristics* greatly affect channel design. For example, perishable products require more direct marketing to avoid delays and too much handling. Bulky products, such as building materials or soft drinks, require channels that minimize shipping distance and the amount of handling.

Company characteristics also play an important role. For example, the company's size and financial situation determine which marketing functions it can handle itself and which it must give to middlemen. And a company marketing strategy based on speedy customer delivery affects the functions that the company wants its middlemen to perform, the number of its outlets, and the choice of its transportation methods.

Middlemen characteristics also influence channel design. The company must find middlemen who are willing and able to perform the needed tasks. In general, middlemen differ in their abilities to handle promotion, customer contact, storage, and credit. For example, manufacturer's representatives who are hired by several different firms can contact customers at a low cost per customer because several clients share the total cost. However, the selling effort behind the product is less intense than if the company's own salesforce did the selling.

When designing its channels, a company also must consider its *competitors' channels*. In some cases, a company may want to compete in or near the same outlets that carry competitors' products. Thus, food companies want their brands to be displayed next to competing brands; Burger King wants to locate near McDonald's. In other cases, producers may avoid the channels used by competitors. Avon, for example, decided not to compete with other cosmetics makers for scarce positions in retail stores and instead set up a profitable door-to-door selling operation.

Finally, *environmental factors*, such as economic conditions and legal constraints, affect channel design decisions. For example, in a depressed economy, producers want to distribute their goods in the most economical way, using shorter channels and dropping unneeded services that add to the final price of the goods. Legal regulations prevent channel arrangements that "may tend to lessen competition substantially or tend to create a monopoly."

Product characteristics affect channel decisions: Fresh flowers must be delivered quickly with a minimum of handling.

Identifying Major Alternatives

When the company has defined its channel objectives, it should next identify its major channel alternatives in terms of *types* of middlemen, *number* of middlemen, and the *responsibilities* of each channel member.

Types of Middlemen

A firm should identify the types of middlemen available to carry out its channel work. For example, suppose a manufacturer of test equipment has developed an audio device that detects poor mechanical connections in any machine with moving parts. Company executives think this product would have a market in all industries where electric, combustion, or steam engines are made or used. This market includes industries such as aviation, automobile, railroad, food canning, construction, and oil. The company's current salesforce is small, and the problem is how best to reach these different industries. The following channel alternatives might emerge from management discussion:

> *Company salesforce.* Expand the company's direct salesforce. Assign salespeople to territories and have them contact all prospects in the area or develop separate company salesforces for different industries.

> *Manufacturer's agency.* Hire manufacturer's agencies—independent firms whose salesforces handle related products from many companies—in different regions or industries to sell the new test equipment.

> *Industrial distributors.* Find distributors in the different regions or industries who will buy and carry the new line. Give them exclusive distribution, good margins, product training, and promotional support.

Sometimes a company must develop a channel other than the one it prefers because of the difficulty or cost of using the preferred channel. Still, the decision may turn out extremely well. For example, the U.S. Time Company first tried to sell its inexpensive Timex watches through regular jewelry stores, but most jewelry stores refused to carry them. The company then managed to get its watches into mass-merchandise outlets. This turned out to be a wise decision because of the rapid growth of mass merchandising.

Number of Middlemen

Companies also must determine the number of middlemen to use at each level. Three strategies are available: intensive distribution, exclusive distribution, and selective distribution.

Intensive Distribution. Producers of convenience goods and common raw materials typically seek **intensive distribution**—a strategy whereby they stock their products in as many outlets as possible. These goods must be available where and when consumers want them. For example, toothpaste, candy, and other similar items are sold in millions of outlets to provide maximum brand exposure and consumer convenience.

Exclusive Distribution. By contrast, some producers purposely limit the number of middlemen handling their products. The extreme form of this practice is **exclusive distribution,** whereby the producer gives a limited number of dealers the exclusive right to distribute its products in their territories. Exclusive distribution often is found in the distribution of new automobiles and prestige women's clothing. By granting exclusive distribution, the manufacturer hopes for stronger distributor selling support and more control over middlemen's prices, promotion, credit, and services. Exclusive distribution often enhances the product's image and allows for higher markups.

Selective Distribution. Between intensive and exclusive distribution lies **selective distribution**—the use of more than one, but fewer than all of the middlemen who are willing to carry a company's products. By using selective distribution, the company does not have to spread its efforts over many outlets, including many marginal ones. It can develop a good working relationship with selected middlemen and expect a better-than-average selling effort. Selective distribution gives the producer good market coverage with more control and less

Convenience goods, such as cleaning products, are sold through every available outlet. Prestige goods, such as luxury cars, are sold exclusively through a limited number of stores.

cost than does intensive distribution. Most television, furniture, and small appliance brands are distributed in this manner.

Responsibilities of Channel Members

The producer and middlemen need to agree on the terms and responsibilities of each channel member. They should agree on price policies, conditions of sale, territorial rights, and specific services to be performed by each party. The producer should establish a list price and a fair set of discounts for middlemen. It must define each middleman's territory, and it should be careful about where it places new resellers. Mutual services and duties need to be spelled out carefully, especially in franchise and exclusive distribution channels. For example, McDonald's provides franchisees with promotional support, a record-keeping system, training, and general management assistance. In turn, franchisees must meet company standards for physical facilities, cooperate with new promotion programs, provide requested information, and buy specified food products.

Evaluating the Major Alternatives

Suppose a company has identified several channel alternatives and wants to select the one that will best satisfy its long-run objectives. The firm must evaluate each alternative against economic, control, and adaptive criteria. Consider the following situation:

> A Memphis furniture manufacturer wants to sell its line through retailers on the West Coast. The manufacturer is trying to decide between two alternatives.

> - It could hire ten new sales representatives who would operate out of a sales office in San Francisco. They would receive a base salary plus a commission on their sales.

> - It could use a San Francisco manufacturer's sales agency that has extensive contacts with retailers. The agency has thirty salespeople who would receive a commission based on their sales.

Economic Criteria

Each channel alternative will produce a different level of sales and costs. The first step is to figure out what sales would be produced by a company salesforce compared to a sales agency. Most marketing managers believe that a company salesforce will sell more. Company salespeople sell only the company's products and are better trained to handle them. They sell more aggressively because their future depends on the company. And they are more successful because customers prefer to deal directly with the company.

On the other hand, the sales agency possibly could sell more than a company salesforce. First, the sales agency has thirty salespeople, not just ten. Second, the agency salesforce may be just as aggressive as a direct salesforce, depending on how much commission the line offers in relation to other lines carried. Third, some customers prefer dealing with agents who represent several manufacturers rather than with salespeople from one company. Fourth, the agency has many existing contacts, whereas a company salesforce would have to build them from scratch.

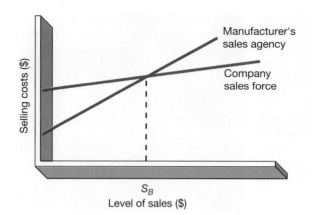

FIGURE 14-5
Breakeven cost: Company salesforce versus manufacturer's sales agency

The next step is to estimate the costs of selling different volumes through each channel. The costs are shown in Figure 14-5. The fixed costs of using a sales agency are lower than those of setting up a company sales office. But costs rise faster through a sales agency because sales agents get a larger commission than company salespeople. There is one sales level (S_B) at which selling costs are the same for the two channels. The company would prefer to use the sales agency at any sales volume below S_B, and the company sales branch at any volume higher than S_B. In general, sales agents tend to be used by smaller firms, or by larger firms in smaller territories where the sales volume is too low to warrant a company salesforce.

Control Criteria

Next, evaluation must be broadened to consider control issues with the two channels. Using a sales agency poses more of a control problem. A sales agency is an independent business firm interested in maximizing its profits. The agent may concentrate on the customers who buy the largest volume of goods from their entire mix of client companies rather than those most interested in a particular company's goods. And the agency's salesforce may not master the technical details of the company's product or handle its promotion materials effectively.

Adaptive Criteria

Each channel involves some long-term commitment and loss of flexibility. A company using a sales agency may have to offer a five-year contract. During this period, other means of selling, such as a company salesforce, may become more effective, but the company cannot drop the sales agency. To be considered, a channel involving a long commitment should be greatly superior on economic or control grounds.

Designing International Distribution Channels

International marketers face many additional complexities in designing their channels. Each country has its own unique distribution system that has evolved over time and changes very slowly. These channel systems can vary widely from country to country. Thus, global marketers usually must adapt their channel strategies to the existing structures within each country. In some markets, the distribution system is complex and hard to penetrate, consisting of many layers and large numbers of middlemen. Consider Japan:

> The Japanese distribution system stems from the early seventeenth century when cottage industries and a [quickly growing] urban population spawned a merchant class. . . . Despite Japan's economic achievements, the distribution system has remained remarkably faithful to its antique pattern. . . . [It] encompasses a wide range of wholesalers and other agents, brokers, and retailers, differing more in number than in function from their American counterparts. There are myriad tiny retail shops. An even greater number of wholesalers supplies goods to them, layered tier upon tier, many more than most U.S. executives would think necessary. For example, soap may move through three wholesalers plus a sales company after it leaves the manufacturer before it ever reaches the retail outlet. A steak goes from rancher to consumers in a process that often involves a dozen middle agents. . . . The distribution network

. . . reflects the traditionally close ties among many Japanese companies . . . [and places] much greater emphasis on personal relationships with users. . . . Although [these channels appear] inefficient and cumbersome, they seem to serve the Japanese customer well. . . . Lacking much storage space in their small homes, most Japanese homemakers shop several times a week and prefer convenient [and more personal] neighborhood shops.[12]

Many Western firms have had great difficulty breaking into the closely knit, tradition-bound Japanese distribution network.

At the other extreme, distribution systems in developing countries may be scattered and inefficient or altogether lacking. For example, China and India are huge markets, each containing hundreds of millions of people. In reality, however, these markets are much smaller than the population numbers suggest. Because of inadequate distribution systems in both countries, most companies can profitably access only a small portion of the population located in each country's most affluent cities.[13]

Thus, international marketers face a wide range of channel alternatives. Designing efficient and effective channel systems between and within various country markets poses a difficult challenge. We discuss international distribution decisions further in Chapter 21.

CHANNEL MANAGEMENT DECISIONS

Once the company has reviewed its channel alternatives and decided on the best channel design, it must implement and manage the chosen channel. Channel management calls for selecting and motivating individual middlemen and evaluating their performance over time.

Selecting Channel Members

Producers vary in their ability to attract qualified middlemen. Some producers have no trouble signing up middlemen. For example, Toyota had no trouble attracting new dealers for its Lexus line. In fact, it had to turn down many would-be resellers. In some cases, the promise of exclusive or selective distribution for a desirable product will draw enough applicants.

At the other extreme are producers who have to work hard to line up enough qualified middlemen. When Polaroid started, for example, it could not get photography stores to carry its new cameras and had to go to mass-merchandising outlets. Similarly, small food producers often have difficulty getting supermarket chains to carry their products.

When selecting middlemen, the company should determine what characteristics distinguish the better middlemen. It will want to evaluate the middlemen's years in business, other lines carried, growth and profit record, cooperativeness, and reputation. If the middlemen are sales agents, the company will want to evaluate the number and character of other lines carried, and the size and quality of the salesforce. If the middleman is a retail store that wants exclusive or selective distribution, the company will want to evaluate the store's customers, location, and future growth potential.

Motivating Channel Members

Once selected, middlemen must be continuously motivated to do their best. The company must sell not only *through* the middlemen, but *to* them. Most producers see the problem as finding ways to gain middlemen's cooperation. They use the carrot-and-stick approach. At times they offer *positive* motivators such as higher margins, special deals, premiums, cooperative advertising allowances, display allowances, and sales contests. At other times they use *negative* motivators, such as threatening to reduce margins, to slow down delivery, or to end the relationship altogether. A producer using this approach usually has not done a good job of studying the needs, problems, strengths, and weaknesses of its distributors.

More advanced companies try to forge long-term partnerships with their distributors. This involves building a planned, professionally managed, vertical marketing system that meets the needs of both the manufacturer *and* the

GENERAL ELECTRIC ADOPTS A "VIRTUAL INVENTORY" SYSTEM TO SUPPORT ITS DEALERS

Before the late 1980s, General Electric worked at selling *through* its dealers rather than *to* them or *with* them. GE operated a traditional system of trying to load up the channel with GE appliances, on the premise that "loaded dealers are loyal dealers." Loaded dealers would have less space to feature other brands and would recommend GE appliances to their customers in order to reduce their high inventories. To load its dealers, GE would offer the lowest price when the dealer ordered a full truckload of GE applicances.

GE eventually realized that this approach created many problems, especially for smaller independent appliance dealers who could ill afford to carry a large stock. These dealers were hard pressed to meet price competition from larger multibrand dealers. Rethinking its strategy from the point of view of creating dealer satisfaction and profitability, GE created an alternative distribution model called the Direct Connect system. Under this system, GE dealers carry only display models. They rely on a "virtual inventory" to fill orders. Dealers can access GE's order processing system 24 hours a day, check on model availability, and place orders for next-day delivery. Using the Direct Connect system, dealers also can get GE's best price, financing from GE Credit, and no interest charges for the first 90 days.

Dealers benefit by having much lower inventory costs while still having a large virtual inventory available to satisfy their customers' needs. In exchange for this benefit, dealers must commit to selling nine major GE product categories, generating 50 percent of their sales from GE products, opening their books to GE for review, and paying GE every month through electronic funds transfer.

As a result of Direct Connect, dealer profit margins have skyrocketed. GE also has benefited. Its dealers now are more committed and dependent on GE, and the new order-entry system has saved GE substantial clerical costs. GE now knows the actual sales of its goods at the retail level, which helps it to schedule its production more accurately. It now can produce in response to demand rather than to meet inventory replenishment rules. And GE has been able to simplify its warehouse locations so as to be able to deliver appliances to 90 percent of the United States within 24 hours. Thus, by forging a partnership, GE has helped both its dealers and itself.

Source: See Michael Treacy and Fred Wiersema, "Customer Intimacy and Other Discipline Values," *Harvard Business Review,* January-February 1993, pp. 84-93.

distributors.[14] The company identifies distributors' needs and builds programs to help each distributor market the company's product. It works with distributors jointly to plan merchandising goals, inventory levels, merchandising strategies, sales training, and advertising and promotion plans. The aim is to convince distributors that they can make their money by being part of an advanced vertical marketing system (see Marketing Highlight 14-3).

Evaluating Channel Members

The producer must regularly check the middlemen's performance against standards such as sales quotas, average inventory levels, customer delivery time, treatment of damaged and lost goods, cooperation in company promotion and training programs, and services to the customer. The company should recognize and reward middlemen who are performing well. Middlemen who are performing poorly should be helped or, as a last resort, replaced.

A company may periodically "requalify" its middlemen and prune the weaker ones. For example, when IBM first introduced its PS/2 personal computers, it reevaluated its dealers and allowed only the best ones to carry the new models. Each IBM dealer had to submit a business plan, send a sales and service employee to IBM training classes, and meet new sales quotas. Only about two-thirds of IBM's 2,200 dealers qualified to carry the PS/2 models.[15]

Finally, manufacturers need to be sensitive to their dealers. Those who treat their dealers lightly risk not only losing their support but also causing some legal problems. Marketing Highlight 14-4 describes various rights and duties pertaining to manufacturers and their channel members.

PUBLIC POLICY AND DISTRIBUTION DECISIONS

For the most part, companies are legally free to develop whatever channel arrangements suit them. In fact, the laws affecting channels seek to prevent the exclusionary tactics of some companies that might keep another company from using a desired channel. Of course, this means that the company must itself avoid using such exclusionary tactics. Most channel law deals with the mutual rights and duties of the channel members once they have formed a relationship.

Exclusive Dealing

Many producers and wholesalers like to develop exclusive channels for their products. When the seller allows only certain outlets to carry its products, this strategy is called *exclusive distribution*. When the seller requires that these dealers not handle competitors' products, its strategy is called *exclusive dealing*. Both parties benefit from exclusive arrangements: The seller obtains more loyal and dependable outlets, and the dealers obtain a steady source of supply and stronger seller support. But exclusive arrangements exclude other producers from selling to these dealers. This situation brings exclusive dealing contracts under the scope of the Clayton Act of 1914. They are legal as long as they do not substantially lessen competition or tend to create a monopoly and as long as both parties enter into the agreement voluntarily.

Exclusive Territories

Exclusive dealing often includes exclusive territorial agreements. The producer may agree not to sell to other dealers in a given area, or the buyer may agree to sell only in its own territory. The first practice is normal under franchise systems as a way to increase dealer enthusiasm and commitment. It is also perfectly legal—a seller has no legal obligation to sell through more outlets than it wishes. The second practice, whereby the producer tries to keep a dealer from selling outside its territory, has become a major legal issue.

Tying Agreements

Producers of a strong brand sometimes sell it to dealers only if the dealers will take some or all of the rest of the line. This is called *full-line forcing*. Such tying agreements are not necessarily illegal, but they do violate the Clayton Act if they tend to lessen competition substantially. The practice may prevent consumers from freely choosing among competing suppliers of these other brands.

Dealers' Rights

Producers are free to select their dealers, but their right to terminate dealers is somewhat restricted. In general, sellers can drop dealers "for cause." But they cannot drop dealers if, for example, the dealers refuse to cooperate in a doubtful legal arrangement, such as exclusive dealing or tying agreements.

PHYSICAL DISTRIBUTION DECISIONS

Producers must decide on the best way to store, handle, and move their goods and services so that they are available to customers at the right time and place. Producers typically need to employ the services of physical distribution firms—warehouses and transportation companies—to assist in this task. Physical distribution effectiveness will have a major impact on customer satisfaction and company costs. A poor distribution system can destroy an otherwise good marketing effort. Here we consider the *nature, objectives, systems,* and *organizational aspects* of physical distribution.

Nature of Physical Distribution

Figure 14-6 shows the main elements of the physical distribution mix. **Physical distribution** (also called **market logistics**) involves planning, implementing, and controlling the physical flow of materials and final goods, from points of origin to points of use, to meet customer requirements at a profit. The aim of physical distribution is to manage *supply chains*, value-added flows from suppliers to final users, as shown next:

Thus, the logistical task is to coordinate the activities of suppliers, purchasing agents, marketers, channel members, and customers.

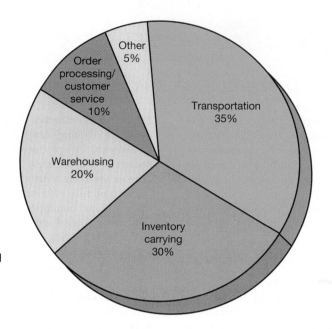

FIGURE 14-6
Costs of physical distribution elements as a percent of total physical distribution costs
Source: See Cynthia R. Milsap, "Distribution Costs Full—Rules Off." *Business Marketing*, February 1985, p. 9.

Companies manage their supply chains through information. Major gains in distribution efficiency have resulted from advances in information technology, particularly computers, point-of-sale terminals, uniform product codes, satellite tracking, electronic data interchange (EDI), and electronic funds transfer (EFT). These developments have allowed manufacturers to make promises such as "the product will be at dock 25 at 10 A.M. tomorrow" and to control such promises through information. Retailers like Wal-Mart have also made good use of information to improve their logistics:

Wal-Mart was one of the first retailers to make heavy investments in information technology. It equipped its stores with computerized scanning equipment for cash registers. Thus, when a teenager bought a size 10 Reebok running shoe, the information went directly to Reebock's computers, triggering replacement or production. This system lets Wal-Mart know what customers are buying and then tell manufacturers what to produce and where to ship the goods. Wal-Mart requires its suppliers to tag and hang merchandise before shipping it. Thus, goods can be moved directly into the store's selling space, reducing warehousing and data-processing costs. As a result, Wal-Mart stores use only 10 percent of their space for goods storage, compared to the 25 percent average non-selling space in competing stores. Another result of Wal-Mart's computerized ordering system is that Wal-Mart insists on linking its computers directly to those of its suppliers, bypassing brokers and other middlemen and passing on the savings to customers.[16]

The major physical distribution cost is transportation, followed by inventory carrying, warehousing, and order processing and customer service. Management in most companies has become concerned about the total cost of physical distribution. Experts believe that large savings can be gained in the physical distribution area. Poor physical distribution decisions result in high costs. Even large companies sometimes make too little use of modern decision tools for coordinating inventory levels; transportation modes; and plant, warehouse, and store locations. For example, at least partly to blame for Sears's slow sales growth and sinking earnings over the past several years is its antiquated and costly distribution system. Outmoded multistory warehouses and nonautomated equipment have made Sears much less efficient than its competitors. Distribution costs amount to 8 percent of sales at Sears, compared to less than 3 percent at close competitors Kmart and Wal-Mart.[17]

Moreover, physical distribution is more than a cost—it is a potent tool in demand creation. On the one hand, companies can attract more customers by giving better service or lower prices through better physical distribution. On the other hand, companies may lose customers when they fail to supply goods on time.

The Physical Distribution Objective

Many companies state their objective as getting the right goods to the right places at the right time for the least cost. Unfortunately, no physical distribution system can *both* maximize customer service *and* minimize distribution costs. Maximum customer service implies large inventories, the best transportation, and many warehouses—all of which raise distribution costs. In contrast, minimum distribution cost implies cheap transportation, low inventories, and few warehouses.

The company cannot simply let each physical distribution manager keep down his or her costs. Transportation, warehousing, and order-processing costs interact, often in an inverse way. For example, low inventory levels reduce inventory carrying costs. But they also increase costs from stockouts, back orders, paperwork, special production runs, and from high-cost, fast-freight shipments. Because physical distribution costs and activities involve strong trade-offs, decisions must be made on a total system basis.

The starting point for designing the system is to study what customers want and what competitors are offering. Customers want several things from suppliers: on-time delivery, sufficiently large inventories, the ability to meet emergency needs, careful handling of merchandise, good after-sale service, and a willingness to take back or replace defective goods. A company must research the importance of these services to customers. For example, service-repair time is very important to buyers of copying equipment. So Xerox developed a service-delivery standard that can "put a disabled machine anywhere in the continental United States back into operation within three hours after receiving the service request." Xerox runs a service division with 12,000 service and parts personnel.

The company normally will want to offer at least the same level of service as its competitors. But the objective is to maximize *profits*, not sales. Therefore, the company must consider the costs of providing higher levels of service. Some companies offer less service and charge a lower price. Other companies offer more service than their competitors and charge higher prices to cover higher costs.

The company ultimately must set physical distribution objectives to guide its planning. For example, Coca-Cola wants "to put Coke within an arm's length of desire." Companies go further and define standards for each service factor. One appliance manufacturer has set the following service standards: to deliver at least 95 percent of the dealer's orders within seven days of order receipt, to fill the dealer's order with 99 percent accuracy, to answer dealer questions on order status within three hours, and to ensure that damage to merchandise in transit does not exceed one percent.

Given a set of objectives, the company is ready to design a physical distribution system that will minimize the cost of attaining these objectives. The major decisions are: How should orders be handled (*order processing*)? Where should stocks be located (*warehousing*)? How much stock should be kept on hand (*inventory*)? And how should goods be shipped (*transportation*)?

Order Processing

Physical distribution begins with a customer order. The order department prepares invoices and sends them to various departments. Items out of stock are back-ordered. Shipped items are accompanied by shipping and billing documents, with copies going to various departments.

Both the company and its customers benefit when the order-processing steps are carried out quickly and accurately. Ideally, salespeople send in their orders daily, often using online computers. The order department quickly processes these orders, and the warehouse sends the goods out on time. Bills go out as soon as possible. Computers are often used to speed up the order-shipping-billing cycle. For example, General Electric operates a computer-based system that, upon receipt of a customer's order, checks the customer's credit standing and whether and where the items are in stock. The computer then issues an order to ship, bills the customer, updates the inventory records, sends a production order for new stock, and relays the message back to the salesperson that the customer's order is on its way—all in less than 15 seconds.

Warehousing

Every company must store its goods while they wait to be sold. A storage function is needed because production and consumption cycles rarely match. For example,

Snapper, Toro, and other makers of lawn mowers must produce all year long and store up their product for the heavy spring and summer buying season. The storage function overcomes differences in needed quantities and timing.

A company must decide on the best number of stocking locations. The more stocking locations, the more quickly goods can be delivered to customers. However, more locations means higher warehousing costs. The company, therefore, must balance the level of customer service against distribution costs.

Some company stock is kept at or near the plant, with the rest located in warehouses around the country. The company might own private warehouses, rent space in public warehouses, or both. Companies have more control over owned warehouses, but that ties up their capital and is less flexible if desired locations change. In contrast, public warehouses charge for the rented space and provide additional services (at a cost) for inspecting goods, packaging them, shipping them, and invoicing them. By using public warehouses, companies also have a wide choice of locations and warehouse types.

Companies may use either *storage warehouses* or *distribution centers*. Storage warehouses store goods for moderate to long periods. **Distribution centers** are designed to move goods rather than just store them. They are large and highly automated warehouses designed to receive goods from various plants and suppliers, take orders, fill them efficiently, and deliver goods to customers as quickly as possible. For example, Wal-Mart operates huge distribution centers. One center, which serves the daily needs of 165 Wal-Mart stores, contains some 28 acres of space under a single roof. Laser scanners route as many as 190,000 cases of goods per day along 11 miles of conveyer belts, and the center's 1,000 workers load or unload 310 trucks daily.[18]

Warehousing facilities and equipment technology have improved greatly in recent years. Older, multistoried warehouses with slow elevators and outdated materials-handling methods are facing competition from newer, single-storied *automated warehouses* with advanced materials-handling systems under the control of a central computer. In these warehouses, only a few employees are necessary. The computer reads orders and directs lift trucks, electric hoists, or robots to gather goods, move them to loading docks, and issue invoices. These warehouses have reduced worker injuries, labor costs, theft, and breakage and have improved inventory control.

Inventory

Inventory levels also affect customer satisfaction. Marketers would like their companies to carry enough stock to fill all customer orders right away. However, it costs too much for a company to carry that much inventory. Inventory costs rise at an increasing rate as the customer service level approaches 100 percent. To justify larger inventories, management needs to know whether sales and profits will increase accordingly.

Inventory decisions involve knowing both *when* to order and *how much* to order. In deciding when to order, the company balances the risks of running out of stock against the costs of carrying too much. In deciding how much to order,

Automated warehouses: This sophisticated COMPAQ computer distribution center can ship any of 500 different types of COMPAQ computers and options within four hours of receiving an order.

the company needs to balance order-processing costs against inventory carrying costs. Larger average-order size means fewer orders and lower order-processing costs, but it also means larger inventory carrying costs.

Transportation

Marketers need to take an interest in their company's *transportation* decisions. The choice of transportation carriers affects the pricing of the products, delivery performance, and condition of the goods when they arrive—all of which will affect customer satisfaction.

In shipping goods to its warehouses, dealers, and customers, the company can choose among five transportation modes: rail, water, truck, pipeline, and air. Table 14-1 summarizes the characteristics of each transportation mode.

Rail

Although railroads lost market share until the mid-1970s, today they remain the nation's largest carrier, accounting for 37 percent of total cargo moved. Railroads are one of the most cost-effective modes for shipping large amounts of bulk products—coal, sand, minerals, farm and forest products—over long distances. In addition, railroads recently have begun to increase their customer services. They have designed new equipment to handle special categories of goods, provided flatcars for carrying truck trailers by rail (piggyback), and provided in-transit services such as the diversion of shipped goods to other destinations en route and the processing of goods en route. Thus, after decades of losing out to truckers, railroads appear ready for a comeback.[19]

Truck

Trucks have increased their share of transportation steadily and now account for 25 percent of total cargo. They account for the largest portion of transportation *within* cities as opposed to *between* cities. Each year in the United States, trucks travel more than 600 billion miles—equal to nearly 1.3 million round trips to the moon—carrying 2.5 billion tons of freight.[20] Trucks are highly flexible in their routing and time schedules. They can move goods door to door, saving shippers the need to transfer goods from truck to rail and back again at a loss of time and risk of theft or damage. Trucks are efficient for short hauls of high-value merchandise. In many cases, their rates are competitive with railway rates, and trucks can usually offer faster service.

Water

A large amount of goods are moved by ships and barges on U.S. coastal and inland waterways. Mississippi River barges alone account for 15 percent of the freight shipped in the United States. On the one hand, the cost of water transportation is very low for shipping bulky, low-value, nonperishable products such as sand, coal, grain, oil, and metallic ores. On the other hand, water transportation is the slowest transportation mode and is sometimes affected by the weather.

TABLE 14-1
Characteristics of Major Transportation Modes

TRANSPORTATION MODE	INTERCITY CARGO VOLUME* (%)			TYPICAL PRODUCTS SHIPPED
	1970	1980	1987	
Rail	771 (39.8%)	932 (37.5%)	976 (36.5%)	Farm products, minerals, sand, chemicals, automobiles
Truck	412 (21.3)	555 (22.3)	666 (24.9)	Clothing, food, books, computers, paper goods.
Water	319 (16.5)	407 (16.4)	435 (16.3)	Oil, grain, sand, gravel, metallic ores, coal
Pipeline	431 (22.3)	588 (23.6)	587 (22.0)	Oil, coal, chemicals
Air	3.3 (0.17)	4.8 (0.19)	8.7 (0.34)	Technical instruments, perishable products, documents

*In billions of cargo ton-miles.
Source: Statistical Abstract of the United States, 1989.

Pipeline

Pipelines are a specialized means of shipping petroleum, natural gas, and chemicals from sources to markets. Pipeline shipment of petroleum products costs less than rail shipment, but more than water shipment. Most pipelines are used by their owners to ship their own products.

Air

Although air carriers transport less than one percent of the nation's goods, they are becoming more important as a transportation mode. Air-freight rates are much higher than rail or truck rates, but air freight is ideal when speed is needed or distant markets have to be reached. Among the most frequently air-freighted products are perishables (fresh fish, cut flowers) and high-value, low-bulk items (technical instruments, jewelry). Companies find that air freight also reduces inventory levels, packaging costs, and the number of warehouses needed.

Choosing Transportation Modes

Until the late 1970s, routes, rates, and service in the transportation industry were heavily regulated by the federal government. Today, most of these regulations have been eased. Deregulation has caused rapid and substantial changes. Railroads, ships and barges, trucks, airlines, and pipeline companies are now much more competitive, flexible, and responsive to the needs of their customers. These changes have resulted in better services and lower prices for shippers. But such changes also mean that marketers must do better transportation planning if they want to take full advantage of new opportunities in the changing transportation environment.[21]

In choosing a transportation mode for a product, shippers consider as many as five criteria, as shown in Table 14-2. Thus, if a shipper needs speed, air and truck are the prime choices. If the goal is low cost, then water or pipeline might be best. Trucks appear to offer the most advantages—a fact that explains their growing share of the transportation market.

Thanks to *containerization*, shippers are increasingly combining two or more modes of transportation. **Containerization** consists of putting goods in boxes or trailers that are easy to transfer between two transportation modes.[22] *Piggyback* describes the use of rail and trucks; *fishyback*, water and trucks; *trainship*, water and rail; and *airtruck*, air and trucks. Each combination offers advantages to the shipper. For example, not only is piggyback cheaper than trucking alone, but it also provides flexibility and convenience.

Response-Based Physical Distribution

Today, many companies are switching from *anticipatory-based supply chains* to *response-based supply chains*.[23] In anticipatory physical distribution, the company produces the amount of goods called for by a sales forecast. It builds and holds stock at various supply points such as the plant, distribution centers, and retail outlets. Each supply point reorders automatically when its order point is reached. When sales are slower than expected, the company tries to reduce its inventories by sponsoring discounts and promotions. For example, the American auto industry produces cars far in advance of demand, and these cars often sit for months in inventory until the companies undertake aggressive promotion.

TABLE 14-2
Rankings of Transportation Modes (1 = Highest Rank)

	SPEED (door-to-door delivery time)	DEPENDABILITY (meeting schedules on time)	CAPABILITY (ability to handle various products)	AVAILABILITY (no. of geographic points served)	COST (per ton-mile)
Rail	3	4	2	2	3
Water	4	5	1	4	1
Truck	2	2	3	1	4
Pipeline	5	1	5	5	2
Air	1	3	4	3	5

Source: See Carl M. Guelzo, *Introduction to Logistics Management* (Englewood Cliffs, NJ: Prentice Hall, 1986), p. 46.

Combining modes of transportation through containerization (clockwise): piggyback, fishyback, airtruck, and trainship.

A response-based supply chain, in contrast, is customer-triggered. The producer continuously builds and replaces stock as orders arrive. It produces what is currently selling. For example, Japanese car makers take orders for cars, then produce and ship them within four days. Some large appliance manufacturers, such as Whirlpool and GE, are moving to this system. Benetton, the Italian fashion house, uses a *quick-response system*, dyeing its sweaters in the colors that are currently selling instead of trying to guess long in advance which colors people will want. Producing for order rather than for forecast substantially cuts down inventory costs and risks.

Organizational Responsibility for Physical Distribution

Warehousing, inventory, and transportation decisions require a great deal of coordination. Many companies have created permanent committees made up of managers responsible for different physical distribution activities. These committees meet often to set policies for improving overall distribution efficiency. Some companies have a vice-president of physical distribution who reports to the marketing vice-president, the manufacturing vice-president, or even the president. The location of the physical distribution department within the company is a secondary concern. The important thing is that the company coordinate its physical distribution and marketing activities in order to create high market satisfaction at a reasonable cost.

SUMMARY

Distribution channel decisions are among the most complex and challenging decisions facing the firm. Each channel system creates a different level of sales and costs. Once a distribution channel has been chosen, the firm usually must stick with it for a long time. The chosen channel strongly affects, and is affected by, the other elements in the marketing mix.

Each firm needs to identify alternative ways to reach

its market. Available means vary from direct selling to using one, two, three, or more intermediary *channel levels*. Marketing channels face continuous and sometimes dramatic change. Three of the most important trends are the growth of *vertical, horizontal,* and *multichannel marketing systems*. These trends affect channel cooperation, conflict, and competition.

Channel design begins with assessing customer channel-service needs and company channel objectives and constraints. The company then identifies the major channel alternatives in terms of the *types* of intermediaries, the *number* of intermediaries, and the *channel responsibilities* of each. Each channel alternative must be evaluated according to economic, control, and adaptive criteria. Channel management calls for selecting qualified middlemen and

motivating them. Individual channel members must be evaluated regularly.

Just as the marketing concept is receiving increased recognition, more business firms are paying attention to the physical distribution concept. *Physical distribution* is an area of potentially high cost savings and improved customer satisfaction. When order processors, warehouse planners, inventory managers, and transportation managers make decisions, they affect each other's costs and ability to handle demand. The physical distribution concept calls for treating all these decisions within a unified framework. The task is to design physical distribution systems that minimize the total cost of providing a desired level of customer services.

KEY TERMS

Administered VMS 404

Channel conflict 399

Channel level 397

Containerization 418

Contractual VMS 402

Conventional distribution channel 401

Corporate VMS 402

Direct-marketing channel 397

Distribution center 416

Distribution channel (marketing channel) 395

Exclusive distribution 408

Franchise organization 403

Horizontal marketing systems 404

Intensive distribution 408

Multichannel marketing 404

Physical distribution (or market logistics) 413

Retailer cooperatives 403

Selective distribution 408

Vertical marketing system (VMS) 401

Wholesaler-sponsored voluntary chains 403

DISCUSSING THE ISSUES

1. The Book-of-the-Month Club has been successfully marketing books by mail for over 50 years. Why do so few publishers sell books by mail themselves? How has the BOMC survived competition from B. Dalton, Waldenbooks, and other large booksellers in recent years?

2. Why is franchising such a fast-growing form of retail organization?

3. Why have horizontal marketing arrangements become more common in recent years? Suggest several pairs of companies that you think could have successful horizontal marketing programs.

4. Describe the channel service needs of (a) consumers buying a computer for home use; (b) retailers buying computers to resell to individual consumers; and (c) purchasing agents buying computers for company use. What channels would a computer manufacturer design to satisfy these different service needs?

5. Which distribution strategies—intensive, selective, or exclusive—are used for the following products, and why? (a) Piaget watches; (b) Acura automobiles; (c) Snickers candy bars.

6. When planning desired inventory levels, what consequences of running out of stock need to be considered?

APPLYING THE CONCEPTS

1. Discount malls and so-called factory outlet centers are increasing in popularity. Many of their stores are operated by manufacturers who normally sell only through middlemen. If you have one of these malls nearby, visit it and study the retailers. What sort of merchandise is sold in these stores? Do any appear to be factory owned? Do these stores compete with the manufacturer's normal retailers? What are the pros and cons of operating these stores?

2. Go through a camera or computer magazine, and pay special attention to large ads for mail-order retailers. Look for ads for brand-name products that use selective distribution, such as Nikon cameras or Compaq computers. Can you find an ad that is clearly from an authorized dealer, and one that appears not to be? How can you judge which channel is legitimate? Are there price differences between the legitimate and the unauthorized dealers, and if so, are they what you would expect?

MAKING MARKETING DECISIONS:

SMALL WORLD COMMUNICATIONS, INC.

Lynette Jones and Thomas Campbell are working through all the issues needed to finalize the marketing plans for Small World Communications. Lyn is thinking through some of the logistics involved: "In lots of ways, we're a 'virtual corporation,' getting things done without buying a lot of plants and equipment. That strategy has worked out really well for Dell Computers. But even though we're sort of intangible, we're going to produce real boxes of real products. And for that, we need to get physical distribution set up." Tom said, "Actually, I'm not too concerned with that—there are a number of contract distribution firms who can handle that for us. They can even send out our bills if we want. What concerns me is a little farther down the channel. Who will really sell our product effectively? I sort of like the model of Dell Computer and Cincinnati Microwave, the maker of Escort radar detectors: They market direct, give great technical information and sales assistance over the phone, and the keep the extra profits that other channel members would get." Lyn replied, "It can be a great strategy, but both of those companies were selling a product that was basically known and understood, and we've got this new whatzit that people need to see. I think we need to try a more traditional route first." "You would," Tom teased. "Those guys can take a boring product and make it fly with a radical marketing plan, and we're going to take a radical product and . . . " Lyn tuned him out as she thought through some of the details they would need to cover.

WHAT NOW?

1. Once the Airport product is properly installed and set up, it is very easy to use. Often, however, users will find that their computer setup is unique, and they require special instructions to get everything to work. Most computer store salespeople are not trained well enough to provide the information. (a) Is this issue a distribution channel issue? (b) What level of distribution would be most helpful in solving this problem—intensive, selective, or exclusive distribution? Why? (c) How can Small World motivate its middlemen to increase the level of service?

2. Small World will need to set up telephone and mail-order outlets for the Airport. (a) What are the advantages for Small World if it uses a direct channel with no middlemen, and takes orders over the telephone? (b) Assuming that Small World also has mail-order and retail store distribution, what sort of channel conflicts would direct marketing cause? (c) There are now many mail-order discount computer dealers that carry nearly all major brands. Would using these dealers be a good alternative to setting up an in-house direct-marketing operation? What are the advantages and disadvantages of using these dealers instead of selling direct?

REFERENCES

1. Quotes from Dana Milbank, "Independent Tire Dealers Rebelling Against Goodyear," *The Wall Street Journal*, July 8, 1992, p. B1; and Zachary Schiller, "Goodyear Is Gunning Its Marketing Engine," *Business Week*, March 16, 1992, p. 42. Also see Nancy Hass, "CEO of the Year: Stanley Gault of Goodyear," *Financial World*, March 31, 1992, pp. 26-33; Zachary Schiller, "After a Year of Spinning Its Wheels, Goodyear Gets a Retread," *Business Week*, March 26, 1990, pp. 56-58; and Peter Nulty, "The Bounce Is Back at Goodyear," *Fortune*, September 7, 1992, pp. 70-72.

2. See Louis W. Stern and Frederick D. Sturdivant, "Customer-Driven Distribution Systems," *Harvard Business Review*, July-August 1987, p. 34.

3. Louis Stern and Adel I. El-Ansary, *Marketing Channels*, 4th. ed (Englewood Cliffs, NJ: Prentice Hall, 1992), p. 3.

4. Ronald Abler, John S. Adams, and Peter Gould, *Spatial Organizations: The Geographer's View of the World* (Englewood Cliffs, NJ: Prentice Hall, 1971), pp. 531-32.

5. For an excellent summary of channel conflict and power, see Stern and El-Ansary, *Marketing Channels*, Chaps. 6 and 7.

6. Jaclyn Fierman, "How Gallo Crushes the Competition," *Fortune*, September 1, 1986, p. 27.

7. See Laura Zinn, "Want to Buy a Franchise? Look Before You Leap," *Business Week*, May 23, 1988, pp. 186-87; "Why Franchising Is Taking Off," *Fortune*, February 12, 1990, p. 124; and Dan Fost and Susan Mitchell, "Small Stores with Big Names," *American Demographics*, November 1992, pp. 52-57.

8. This has been called "symbiotic marketing." For more reading, see Lee Adler, "Symbiotic Marketing," *Harvard Business Review*, November–December 1966, pp. 59-71; P. "Rajan" Varadarajan and Daniel Rajaratnam, "Symbiotic Marketing Revisited," *Journal of Marketing*, January 1986, pp. 7-71; and Gary Hamel, Yves L. Doz, and C. D. Prahalad, "Collaborate

with Your Competitors—and Win," *Harvard Business Review*, January-February 1989, pp. 133-39.

9. See Allan J. Magrath, "Collaborative Marketing Comes of Age—Again," *Sales & Marketing Management*, September 1991, pp. 61-64; and Lois Therrien, "Cafe Au Lait, A Croissant—and Trix," *Business Week*, August 24, 1992, pp. 50-51.

10. See Stern and Sturdivant, "Customer-Driven Distribution Systems," p. 35.

11. Ibid., p. 35.

12. Subhash C. Jain, *International Marketing Management*, 3rd ed. (Boston, MA: PWS-Kent Publishing, 1990), pp. 489-91.

13. See Philip Cateora, *International Marketing*, 7th ed. (Homewood, IL: Irwin, 1990), pp. 570-71.

14. See James A. Narus and James C. Anderson, "Turn Your Industrial Distributors into Partners," *Harvard Business Review*, March-April 1986, pp. 66-71.

15. See Katherine M. Hafner, "Computer Retailers: Things Have Gone from Worse to Bad," *Business Week*, June 8, 1987, p. 104.

16. See Rita Koselka, "Distribution Revolution," *Forbes*, May 25, 1992, pp. 54-62.

17. Patricia Sellers, "Why Bigger Is Badder at Sears," *Fortune*, December 5, 1988, p. 82; Kate Fitzgerald, "Sears' Plan on the Ropes," January 8, 1990, pp. 1, 42; and Julia Flynn Siler, "Are the Lights Dimming for Ed Brennan?" *Business Week*, February 11, 1991, pp. 56-57.

18. John Huey, "Wal-Mart: Will It Take Over the World?" *Fortune*, January 30, 1989, pp. 52-64.

19. Shawn Tully, "Comeback Ahead for Railroads," *Fortune*, June 17, 1991, pp. 107-13.

20. See "Trucking Deregulation: A Ten-Year Anniversary," *Fortune*, August 13, 1990, pp. 25-35.

21. See Lewis M. Schneider, "New Era in Transportation Strategy," *Harvard Business Review*, March-April 1985, pp. 118-26.

22. For more discussion, see Norman E. Hutchinson, *An Integrated Approach to Logistics Management* (Englewood Cliffs, NJ: Prentice Hall, 1987), p. 69.

23. Based on an address by Professor Donald J. Bowersox at Michigan State University on August 5, 1992.

VIDEO CASE 14

SLOTTING ALLOWANCES: THE COST OF MARKET ACCESS

Like many mothers in the mid-1980s, Mary Alice Bendini worries about her children's eating habits and wants them to eat healthy, nutritious meals. She can find acceptable food products in all categories except desserts. Her children like cookies in their school lunches, but she can't find any all-natural, good-tasting cookies in her grocery store.

At the same time that Mary Alice unsuccessfully scans her grocer's shelves for all-natural cookies, Richard Worth, a natural foods entrepreneur across town, calls on Ed Buschard, a grocery buyer for the supermarket chain where Mary Alice shops. Richard sells a fruit-juice-sweetened, all-natural cookie called the Frookie. Ed Buschard is intrigued, and after trying the Frookie, he admits that it tastes good. But he has as problem. Like most grocery chains, Ed's company is bombarded with new products—as many as 26,000 products in a typical year. Most of these are simply copycats or line extensions—new sizes or flavors. However, many of them fail, and to add new products and remove the failures is very expensive for grocery stores. The Frookie brand may be even more risky—it differs greatly from existing brands, has no track record, and is not made by a large, familiar company.

Ed's company has been in this bind many times before. Consumers want new products, but the added costs of stocking and removing new products raises retail prices, which may in turn damage the retailer's competitive position and increase consumer dissatisfaction.

To avoid price increases, the chain has begun charging "slotting allowances"—fees for shelf space for new products which shift some new-product adoption costs back to the manufacturer.

Thus, Ed tells Rich that he will add the new Frookie line if Rich will pay the slotting allowance. Ed's chain charges more than $10,000 per item, about typical for the industry. Because Rich has limited capital and several varieties, such as 7-Grain Oatmeal, Ginger Spice, and Mandarin Chocolate Chip, he can't afford the more than $40,000 in slotting allowances required.

The next caller in Ed's office is a representative from one of the nation's largest food manufacturers—a company with global manufacturing, distribution, and marketing facilities. When Ed brings up the slotting allowance, the rep first attempts to negotiate the fee downward, but then agrees to pay the regular allowance in exchange for good shelf position, including an end-aisle display for the first two weeks.

These situations illustrate a common channel problem. The flood of new products deemed necessary to maintain and increase manufacturers' revenues raises retailer costs. In turn, the retailer charges manufacturers for shelf space for new products. This can result in an unintended, but prohibitive burden for small producers. As a result, new products may be limited to offerings from large, well-established firms.

The success of "slotting allowances" has led some retailers to add "failure fees"—charges for removing failed products from their shelves—and to think about adding "annual renewal fees." Such charges could drive the promotional costs of new products to as much as 44 percent of a product's marketing budget. Even well-heeled corporations may not be able to absorb such high charges. Instead, they may have to pass the costs on to consumers in the form of higher prices.

So, what did Richard Worth do? To gain shelf space, he gave away free-standing aisle displays to retailers. And he sold distributors an interest in his company, in the belief that distributor-owners would more aggressively push the product.

Because such solutions are not practical for all manufacturers, some have found alternative channels for their new products, channels that do not charge outrageous promotional fees and slotting allowances. These outlets, such as Sam's, the Price Club, and Pace, represent a serious threat to traditional grocers as their sales are growing—about $35 billion in sales in 1992. With the growth of this channel, grocers may find it increasingly difficult to exert control over the traditional channel of food distribution.

QUESTIONS

1. Summarize the positive and negative attributes of slotting allowances from the retailer, manufacturer, and consumer points of view.

2. What functions does the manufacturer pay for when paying slotting allowances? What functions is the manufacturer absorbing?

3. What effects would slotting allowances have in the various types of vertical marketing systems?

4. How might slotting allowances affect the selection and evaluation of channel members for different types of goods?

5. What threats does the alternative channel pose for the traditional food distribution channel?

COMPANY CASE 14

ICON ACOUSTICS: BYPASSING TRADITION

The Dream

Like most entrepreneurs, Dave Fokos dreams a lot. He imagines customers eagerly phoning Icon Acoustics in Billerica, Massachusetts, to order his latest, custom-made stereo speakers. He sees sales climbing, cash flowing, and hundreds of happy workers striving to produce top-quality products that delight Icon's customers.

Like most entrepreneurs, Dave has taken a long time to develop his dream. It all began while majoring in electrical engineering at Cornell. Dave discovered that he had a strong interest in audio engineering. He took independent-study courses in this area and by graduation had designed and built a pair of marketable stereo speakers. Following graduation, Dave pursued his interest in audio engineering. He landed a job as a loudspeaker designer with Conrad-Johnson, a high-end audio-equipment manufacturer headquartered in Fairfax, Virginia. Within four years, Dave had designed 13 speaker models and decided to start his own company.

Dave identified a market niche that he felt other speaker firms had overlooked. This niche consisted of "audio-addicts"—people who love to listen to music and appreciate first-rate stereo equipment. These affluent, well-educated customers are genuinely obsessed with their stereo equipment. "They'd rather buy a new set of speakers than eat." Dave observes.

Dave faced one major problem—how to distribute Icon's products. He had learned from experience at Conrad-Johnson that most manufacturers distribute their equipment primarily through stereo dealers. Dave

did not hold a high opinion of most such dealers; he felt that they too often played hardball with manufacturers, forcing them to accept thin margins. Furthermore, the dealers concentrated on only a handful of well-known producers who provided mass-produced models. This kept those firms that offered more customized products from gaining access to the market. Perhaps most disturbing, Dave felt that the established dealers often sold not what was best for customers, but whatever they had in inventory that month.

Dave dreamed of offering high-end stereo loudspeakers directly to the audio-obsessed, bypassing the established dealer network. By going directly to the customers, Dave could avoid the dealer markups and offer top-quality products and service at reasonable prices. "My vision for the future is one where all manufacturers sell their products directly to the end user. In this way, even the audiophiles in Dead Horse, Alaska, can have access to all that the audio-manufacturing community has to offer."

The Plan

At the age of 28, Dave set out to turn his dreams into reality. Some of the customers who had gotten to know Dave's work became enthusiastic supporters of his dream and invested $189,000 in Icon for 40 percent of its stock. With their money and $10,000 of his own, Dave left his job at Conrad-Johnson and started Icon in a rented facility in an industrial park.

The Market. Approximately 335 stereo-speaker makers compete for a $3 billion annual U.S. market for audio components. About 100 of these manufacturers sell to the low- and mid-range segments of the market, which account for 90 percent of the market's unit volume and about 50 percent of its value. Their products range in price up to $2,000 but average about $500 for a pair of speakers. In addition to competing with each other, U.S. manufacturers must also compete with Japanese firms that offer products at affordable prices.

The remaining 235 or so manufacturers compete for the remaining 10 percent of the market's unit volume and 50 percent of the value—the high end. This is the segment where Dave hopes to find his customers. Industry observers note that most of the companies competing in the high end are small, undercapitalized, and unknown. The firms tend to plow their money into developing their products and have little left over to market them.

Icon's Marketing Strategy. To serve the audio-addicts segment, Dave offers only the highest-quality speakers. He has developed two models: the Lumen and the Parsec. He builds both models with components that often cost up to ten times what a manufacturer of mass-produced speakers would spend on similar parts. The Lumen stands 18 inches high and weighs 26 pounds and is designed for stand mounting. The floor-standing Parsec is 47 inches high and weighs 96 pounds. Both models feature custom-made cabinets that come in natural or black oak and American walnut. Dave can build and ship two pairs of the Lumen speakers or one pair of the Parsec speakers per day by himself. In order to have an adequate parts inventory, he had to spend $50,000 of his capital on the expensive components.

Dave set the price of the Lumen and Parsec at $795 and $1,795 per pair, respectively. He selected these prices to provide a 50 percent gross margin. He believes that traditional dealers would sell equivalent speakers at retail at twice those prices. To realize his dream, Dave distributes his speakers directly to his customers, avoiding the customary 50 percent dealer markup (as a percentage of selling price) over the manufacturer's price. Customers can call Icon on a toll-free 800 number to order speakers or to get advice directly from Dave. Icon pays for shipping and any return freight via Federal Express—round-trip freight for a pair of Parsecs cost $486.

Dave offers to pay for the return freight because a key part of his promotional strategy is a 30-day, in-home, no-obligation trial. In his ads, Dave calls this "The 43,200 Minute, No Pressure Audition." This trial period allows customers to listen to the speakers in their actual listening environment before deciding to purchase them. In a dealer's showroom, the customer must listen in an artificial environment and often feels pressure to make a quick decision.

Before potential customers can call, however, they must hear of and be persuaded about Icon. Dave believes that the typical high-end customer may buy speakers for "nonrational" reasons: They want a quality product and good sound, but they also want an image. Thus, Dave has tried to create a unique image through the appearance of his speakers and to reflect that image in all of the company's marketing. He interviewed seven graphic-design firms before finding just the right one. He then spent over $40,000 on distinctive stationery, business cards, a brochure, and a single display ad. He also designed a laminated label that is placed just above the gold-plated input jack on each speaker. The label reads: "This loudspeaker was handcrafted by [technician's name who assembled the speaker goes here in his/her own handwriting]. Made in the United States of America by Icon Acoustics, Inc., Billerica, Mass."

To get the word out, Dave concentrates on product reviews in trade magazines and on trade shows, such as the High End Hi-Fi Show in New York. Attendees at the show cast ballots to select "The Best Sound at the Show." In the balloting, among 200 brands, Icon's Parsec speakers finished fifteenth. Among the top ten brands, the least expensive was a pair priced at $2,400, and six of the systems were priced from $8,000 to $18,000. A reviewer in a recent issue of *Stereophile* magazine evaluated Icon's speakers and noted: "The overall sound was robust and dynamic, with a particularly potent low end. Parts and construction quality appeared to be first rate. Definitely a company to watch."

At the end of 1991, Dave planned to invest in a slick, four-color display ad in *Stereo Review,* the consumer magazine with the highest circulation (600,000). He also expects another favorable review in *Stereophile* magazine.

The Reality

Dressed in jeans and a hooded sweatshirt, Dave pauses in the middle of assembling a cardboard shipping carton, pulls up a chair, and leans against the concrete-block wall of his manufacturing area. Reflecting on his experiences during his first year in business, Dave real-

EXHIBIT 14-1
Icon Acoustics' pro forma financials ($ in thousands)

	1991	1992	1993	1994	1995
Pairs of Speakers Sold	224	435	802	1,256	1,830
Total Sales Revenue	$303	$654	$1,299	$2,153	$3,338
Cost of Sales:					
Materials and Packaging	$130	$281	$561	$931	$1,445
Shipping	$43	$83	$157	$226	$322
Total Cost of Sales	$173	$364	$718	$1,157	$1,767
Gross Profit	$130	$290	$581	$996	$1,571
Gross Margin	43%	44%	45%	46%	47%
Expenses:					
New Property and Equipment	$3	$6	$12	$15	$18
Marketing	$13	$66	$70	$109	$135
General and Administrative	$51	$110	$197	$308	$378
Loan Repayment	$31	$31	$0	$0	$0
Outstanding Payables	$30	$0	$0	$0	0
Total Expenses	$128	$213	$279	$432	$531
Pretax Profit	$2	$77	$302	$564	$1,040
Pretax Margin	1%	12%	23%	26%	31%

izes he's learned a lot in jumping all the hurdles the typical entrepreneur faces.

The first hurdles involved suppliers. Dave experienced quality problems with the first cabinet supplier. Then, he ran short of a key component after a mix-up with a second supplier. Next, his bank had failed, preventing Icon's customers from using their credit cards. Finally, despite his desire to avoid debt, he'd had to borrow $50,000 from a bank. Prices for his cabinets and some components had risen, and product returns had been higher than expected (19 percent for the past six months). These price and cost increases put pressure on his margins, forcing Dave to raise his prices (to those quoted earlier). Despite the price increases, his margins remained below his 50 percent target.

Still, Dave feels good about his progress. The price increase does not seem to have affected demand. The few ads and word-of-mouth advertising appear to be working. Dave receives about five phone calls per day, with one in seven calls leading to a sale. Dave also feels the stress of the long hours and the low pay, however. He is not able to pay himself a high salary—just $9,500 in 1991.

Dave reaches over and picks up his most recent financial projections from a workbench (see Exhibit 14-1). He has revised his projections based on the most recent developments. He believes that this will be a breakeven year—then he'll have it made. As Dave sets the projections back on the workbench, his mind drifts to his plans to introduce two exciting new speakers—the Micron ($2,495 per pair) and the Millennium ($7,995 per pair). He also wonders if there is a foreign market for his speakers. Should he use his same direct-marketing strategy for foreign markets, or should he consider distributors? The dream continues.

QUESTIONS

1. What functions do traditional stereo dealers perform?

2. Why has Dave Fokos decided to establish a direct channel? What objectives and constraints have shaped his decision?

3. What consumer service needs do Dave's customers have?

4. What problems will Dave face as a result of his channel decisions? What changes would you recommend in Dave's distribution strategy, if any? Will his strategy work in foreign markets?

5. What other changes would you recommend in Dave's marketing strategy?

Source: Adapted from "Sound Strategy," *INC.*, May 1991, pp. 46-56. © 1991 by Goldhirsh Group, Inc. Used with permission. Dave Fokos also provided information to support development of this case.

*P*lacing Products:
Retailing and Wholesaling

15

This is a home furnishings store?

IKEA (👁—ah!)

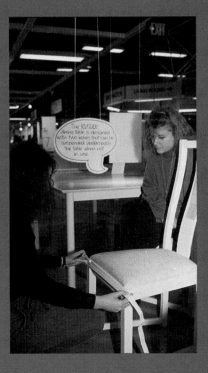

When Scandinavian furniture giant IKEA (pronounced *eye-KEY-ah*) opened its first U.S. store in 1985, it caused quite a stir. On opening day, people flocked to the suburban Philadelphia store from as far away as Washington, DC. Traffic on the nearby turnpike backed up for six miles, and at one point the store was jammed so tightly with customers that management ordered the doors closed until the crowds thinned out. In the first week, the IKEA store packed in 150,000 people who bought over $1 million worth of furniture. When the dust had settled, the store was still averaging 50,000 customers a week. Similarly, when IKEA opened its store in Elizabeth, New Jersey, about 15 miles from Manhattan, the response bordered on a riot. On the first day of business, the New Jersey Turnpike backed up for nine miles as 26,000 shoppers converged on the new store, generating $1 million in sales and doubling IKEA's opening-day record.

IKEA is one of a new breed of retailers called "category killers." These retailers get their name from their marketing strategy: Carry a huge selection of merchandise in a single product category at such good prices that you destroy the competition. Category killers now are striking in a wide range of industries, including furniture, toys, records, sporting goods, housewares, and consumer electronics.

An IKEA store is about three football fields in size. Each store stocks more than 6,000 items—all furnishings and housewares, ranging from coffee mugs to leather sofas to kitchen cabinets. IKEA sells Scandinavian-design "knock-down" furniture—each item reduces to a flat-pack kit for assembly at home. Consumers browse through the store's comfortable display area, where signs and stickers on each item note its price, details of its construction, assembly instructions, its location in the adjacent warehouse—even which other pieces complement the item. Customers wrestle desired items from warehouse stacks, haul their choices away on large trollies, and pay at giant-sized checkout counters. The store provides a reasonably priced restaurant for hungry shoppers and a supervised children's play area for weary parents. But best of all, IKEA's prices are low. The store operates on a simple philosophy: Provide a wide variety of well-designed home furnishings at prices that the majority of people can afford.

Although the first category killer, Toys 'R' Us, appeared during the late 1950s, other retailers only recently adopted the idea. Unlike warehouse clubs and other "off-price" retailers, which offer the lowest prices but few choices within any given category, category killers offer an exhaustive selection in one line. Toys 'R' Us stocks 18,000 different toy items in football-field-size stores. Huge Sportmart stores stock 100,000 sporting goods items, including 70 types of sleeping bags, 265 styles of athletic socks, 12,000 pairs of shoes, and 15,000 fishing lures. Tower Records stores carry up to 75,000 titles—25 times more than the average competitor. And Branden's, the housewares and home furnishings category killer, offers a choice of 30 different coffee pots, 25 irons, 100 patterns of bed sheets, and 800 kitchen gadgets. With such large assortments, category killers generate big sales that often allow them to charge prices as low as those of their discount competitors.

The category killers face a few problems, however. For example, IKEA has encountered occasional difficulty managing its huge inventory, sometimes overpromising or inconveniencing customers. The company's expansive stores also require large investments and huge markets. Some consumers find that they want more personal service than IKEA gives or that the savings aren't worth the work required to find products in the huge store, haul them out, and assemble them at home. Despite such problems,

IKEA has prospered beyond its founders' dreams. It now has 95 stores in 23 countries, racking up over $3.7 billion a year in sales. Since opening its initial U.S. store in Philadelphia, it has opened other stores in Washington, DC; Baltimore; Pittsburgh; Elizabeth (New Jersey); Long Island; and Southern California. In all, IKEA plans to open 60 stores around the country over the next 25 years.

Most retailing experts predict great success for stores like IKEA. One retailing analyst, Wallace Epperson, Jr., "estimates IKEA will win at least a 15 percent share of any market it enters and will expand the market as it does so. If Mr. Epperson is any indication, IKEA's prospects are good. Touring IKEA in his professional capacity, Mr. Epperson couldn't resist the store. 'I spent $400,' he said. 'It's incredible.'"[1]

 ## CHAPTER PREVIEW

Chapter 15 offers an overview of retailers, direct marketers, and wholesalers.

Early in the chapter, we survey traditional **store retailing**, looking at different ways to segment stores: by **amount of service** provided, **breadth** and **depth** of **product line**, **relative price levels**, **control of outlets**, and **type of store cluster**.

Next, we consider **non-store retailing**, including various forms of **direct marketing** such as **direct mail** and **catalog marketing**, **telemarketing**, **television** and **electronic shopping**, and **integrated direct marketing**. We conclude our discussion of retailing with a discussion of **retailer marketing decisions** and the future of retailing.

Finally, we look at wholesalers, including **full-service** and **limited-service merchant wholesalers**, **brokers** and **agents**, and **manufacturers' sales branches**. The chapter concludes with a look at **wholesaler marketing decisions** and trends in wholesaling.

This chapter looks at *retailing* and *wholesaling*. In the first section, we look at the nature and importance of retailing, major types of store and nonstore retailers, the decisions retailers make, and the future of retailing. In the second section, we discuss these same topics as they relate to wholesalers.

RETAILING

What is retailing? We all know that Wal-Mart, Sears, and Kmart are retailers, but so are Avon representatives, the local Holiday Inn, and a doctor seeing patients. **Retailing** includes all the activities involved in selling goods or services directly to final consumers for their personal, nonbusiness use. Many institutions—manufacturers, wholesalers, and retailers—do retailing. But most retailing is done by **retailers**: businesses whose sales come *primarily* from retailing. And although most retailing is done in retail stores, in recent years nonstore retailing—selling by mail, telephone, door-to-door contact, vending machines, and numerous electronic means—has grown tremendously. Because store retailing accounts for most of the retail business, we discuss it first. We then look at nonstore retailing.

STORE RETAILING

Retail stores come in all shapes and sizes, and new retail types keep emerging. They can be classified by one or more of several characteristics: *amount of service, product line, relative prices, control of outlets,* and *type of store cluster.* Table 15-1 shows these classifications and the corresponding retailer types.

TABLE 15-1
Different Ways to Classify Retail Outlets

AMOUNT SERVICE	PRODUCT LINE SOLD	RELATIVE PRICE EMPHASIS	CONTROL OF OUTLETS	TYPE OF STORE CLUSTER
Self-service	Specialty store	Discount store	Corporate chain	Central business district
Limited service	Department store	Off-price retailers	Voluntary chain and retailer co-operative	
Full service	Supermarket	Catalog show-room		Regional shopping center
	Convenience store		Franchise orga-nization	Community shop-ping center
	Combination store, superstore, and hy-permarket		Merchandising conglomerate	Neighborhood shopping center
	Service business			

Amount of Service

Different products require different amounts of service, and customer service preferences vary. We focus on three levels of service—self-service, limited service, and full service—and the types of retailers that use them.

Self-service retailers increased rapidly in the United States during the Great Depression of the 1930s. Customers were willing to perform their own "locate-compare-select" process to save money. Today, self-service is the basis of all discount operations and typically is used by sellers of convenience goods (such as supermarkets) and nationally branded, fast-moving shopping goods (such as catalog showrooms like Best Products or Service Merchandise).

Limited-service retailers, such as Sears or J. C. Penney, provide more sales assistance because they carry more shopping goods about which customers need information. They also offer additional services such as credit and merchandise return not usually offered by low-service stores. Their increased operating costs result in higher prices.

In **full-service retailers,** such as specialty stores and first-class department stores, salespeople assist customers in every phase of the shopping process. Full-service stores usually carry more specialty goods and slower-moving items, such as cameras, jewelry, and fashions, for which customers like to be "waited on." They provide more liberal return policies, various credit plans, free delivery, home servicing, and extras such as lounges and restaurants. More services result in much higher operating costs, which are passed along to customers as higher prices.

Product Line

Retailers also can be classified by the length and breadth of their product assortments. Among the most important types of retailers are the *specialty store,* the *department store,* the *supermarket,* the *convenience store,* the *superstore,* and the *service business.*

Specialty Store

A **specialty store** carries a narrow product line with a deep assortment within that line. Examples include stores selling sporting goods, furniture, books, electronics, flowers, or toys. Specialty stores can be classified further by the narrowness of their product lines. For example, a clothing store is a *single-line store,* a men's clothing store is a *limited-line store,* and a men's custom shirt store is a *super-specialty store.*

Today, specialty stores are flourishing for several reasons. The increasing use of market segmentation, market targeting, and product specialization has resulted in a greater need for stores that focus on specific products and segments. And because of changing consumer lifestyles and the increasing number of two-income households, many consumers have greater incomes but less time to spend shopping. They are attracted to specialty stores that provide high-quality products, convenient locations, good hours, excellent service, and quick entry and exit.

Department Store

A **department store** carries a wide variety of product lines—typically clothing, home furnishings, and household goods. Each line is operated as a separate de-

Today, specialty stores are flourishing: they offer high-quality products, convenient locations, good hours, and excellent service.

partment managed by specialist buyers or merchandisers. Examples of well-known department stores include Bloomingdale's, Marshall Field, and Filene's. *Specialty department stores* carry only clothing, shoes, cosmetics, luggage, and gift items—examples are Saks Fifth Avenue and I. Magnin.

Department stores grew rapidly through the first half of this century. After World War II, however, they began to lose ground to other types of retailers, including discount stores, specialty store chains, and "off-price" retailers. The heavy traffic, poor parking, and general decaying of central cities, where many department stores had made their biggest investments, made downtown shopping less appealing. As a result, many department stores closed or merged with others.

During the past few decades, department stores have been waging a "comeback war." Most have opened suburban stores, and many have added "bargain basements" to meet the discount threat. Still others have remodeled their stores or set up "boutiques" and other store formats that compete with specialty stores. Many are trying mail-order and telephone selling. Still, department stores continue to have difficulty competing with more focused and flexible specialty stores on the one hand, and with more efficient, lower-priced discounters on the other.

Service remains the key differentiating factor. Many department stores, such as Nordstrom's and Neiman Marcus, are renewing their emphasis on service in an effort to keep old customers and win new ones. When it comes to service, most retailers could learn a lesson from Japan's Odakyu Department Store (see Marketing Highlight 15-1).

In recent years, many large department-store chains have been joining, rather than fighting, the competition by diversifying into discount and specialty stores. Dayton-Hudson, for example, operates Target (discount stores), Mervyn's (lower-price clothing), B. Dalton (books), and many other chains in addition to its Dayton's, Hudson's, and other department stores. These discount and specialty operations now account for more than 80 percent of total corporate sales.[2]

Supermarket

Supermarkets are large, low-cost, low-margin, high-volume, self-service stores that carry a wide variety of food, laundry, and household products. Most U.S. supermarket stores are owned by supermarket chains such as Safeway, Kroger, A&P, Winn-Dixie, Publix, Food Lion, and Jewel. Chains account for almost 70 percent of all supermarket sales.

The first supermarkets introduced the concepts of self-service, customer turnstiles, and checkout counters. Supermarket growth took off in the 1930s and grew rapidly for several decades. However, most supermarkets today are facing slow sales growth because of slower population growth and an increase in competition from convenience stores, discount food stores, and superstores. They also have been hit hard by the rapid growth of out-of-home eating. Thus, supermarkets are looking for new ways to build their sales. Most chains now operate fewer but larger stores. They practice "scrambled merchandising," carrying many nonfood items—beauty aids, housewares, toys, prescriptions, appliances, videocassettes, sporting goods, garden supplies—hoping to find high-margin lines to improve profits.

◦◦ (MARKETING HIGHLIGHT 15-1

NOW THAT'S DEPARTMENT STORE SERVICE

In the following account, an American visitor to Japan describes her amazing shopping experience with Odakyu Department Store.

My husband and I bought one souvenir the last time we were in Tokyo—a Sony compact-disc player. The transaction took seven minutes at the Odakyu Department Store, including time to find the right department and to wait while the salesman filled out a second charge slip after misspelling my husband's name on the first.

My in-laws, who were our hosts in the outlying city of Sagamihara, were eager to see their son's purchase, so he opened the box for them the next morning. But when he tried to demonstrate the player, it wouldn't work. We peered inside. It had no innards! My husband used the time until the Odakyu would open at 10:00 to practice for the rare opportunity in that country to wax indignant. But at a minute to 10:00 he was preempted by the store ringing us.

My mother-in-law took the call and had to hold the receiver away from her ear against the barrage of Japanese honorifics. Odakyu's vice president was on his way over with a new disc player.

A taxi pulled up 50 minutes later and spilled out the vice president and a junior employee who was laden with packages and a clipboard. In the entrance hall the two men bowed vigorously.

The younger man was still bobbing as he read from a log that recorded the progress of their efforts to rectify their mistake, beginning at 4:32 P.M. the day be-

fore, when the salesclerk alerted the store's security guards to [catch] my husband at the door. When that didn't work, the clerk turned to his supervisor, who turned to his supervisor, until a SWAT team leading all the way to the vice president was in place to work on the only clues, a name and an American Express card number. Remembering that the customer had asked him about using the disc player in the United States, the clerk called 32 hotels in and around Tokyo to ask if a Mr. Kitasei was registered. When that turned up nothing, the Odakyu commandeered a staff member to stay until 9 P.M. to call American Express headquarters in New York. American Express gave him our New York telephone number. It was after 11:00 when he reached my parents, who were staying at our apartment. My mother gave him my in-law's telephone number.

The younger man looked up from his clipboard and gave us, in addition to the $280 disc player, a set of towels, a box of cakes, and a Chopin disk. Three minutes after this exhausted pair had arrived they were climbing back into the waiting cab. The vice president suddenly dashed back. He had forgotten to apologize for my husband having to wait while the salesman had rewritten the charge slip, but he hoped we understood that it had been the young man's first day.

Source: Reprinted from Hilary Hinds Kitasei, "Japan's Got Us Beat in the Service Department, Too," *The Wall Street Journal,* July 30, 1985, p. 10. Used by permission. © 1985, Dow Jones & Company, Inc. All Rights Reserved Worldwide.

Supermarkets also are improving their facilities and services to attract more customers. Typical improvements are better locations, improved decor, longer store hours, check cashing, delivery, and even child-care centers. Although consumers have always expected supermarkets to offer good prices, convenient locations, and speedy checkout, today's more sophisticated food buyer wants even more. Some supermarkets, therefore, are "moving upscale" with the market, providing "from-scratch" bakeries, gourmet deli counters, and fresh seafood departments. Others are cutting costs, establishing more efficient operations, and lowering prices in order to compete more effectively with food discounters. Finally, to attract more customers, many large supermarket chains are starting to customize their stores for individual neighborhoods. They are tailoring store size, product assortments, prices, and promotions to the economic and ethnic needs of local markets.

Convenience Store

Convenience stores are small stores that carry a limited line of high-turnover convenience goods. Examples include 7-Eleven, Circle K, and Stop-N-Go Stores. These stores locate near residential areas and remain open long hours, seven days a week. Convenience stores must charge high prices to make up for higher operating costs and lower sales volume. But they satisfy an important consumer need. Consumers use convenience stores for "fill-in" purchases at off hours or when time is short, and they are willing to pay for the convenience. The number of convenience stores increased from about 2,000 in 1957 to over 80,000 in 1989.

Many convenience store operators are trying micromarketing. For example, a Stop-N-Go in an affluent neighborhood (left) carries fresh produce, gourmet pasta sauces, chilled Evian water, and expensive wines. A Stop-N-Go Store in an Hispanic neighborhood (right) carries Spanish-language magazines and other items catering to the specific needs of Hispanic customers.

However, the convenience store industry has suffered lately from overcapacity as its primary market of young, blue-collar men has shrunk. As a result, many convenience-store operators are redesigning their stores with female customers in mind. They are upgrading colors, dropping video games, improving parking and lighting, and pricing more competitively. The major convenience chains also are experimenting with micromarketing—tailoring each store's merchandise to the specific needs of its surrounding neighborhood. For example, a Stop-N-Go in an affluent neighborhood carries fresh produce, gourmet pasta sauces, chilled Evian water, and expensive wines, whereas a store in an Hispanic neighborhood carries Spanish-language magazines. Through such moves, convenience stores hope to remain strongly differentiated from other types of food stores while adapting to today's fast-paced consumer lifestyles.[3]

Superstore, Combination Store, and Hypermarket

Superstores, combination stores, and hypermarkets are all larger than the conventional supermarket. **Superstores** are almost twice the size of regular supermarkets and carry a large assortment of routinely purchased food and nonfood items. They offer such services as dry cleaning, post offices, photo finishing, check cashing, bill paying, lunch counters, car care, and pet care. Because of their wider assortment, superstore prices are 5 percent to 6 percent higher than are those of conventional supermarkets.

Many leading chains are moving toward superstores. Examples include Safeway's Pak 'N Pay and Pathmark Super Centers. Almost 80 percent of the new Safeway stores that opened during the past several years have been superstores. In 1975, superstores accounted for only about 3 percent of total food store sales, but by 1986 they took in more than 26 percent of the business. That same year, 39 percent of all new grocery stores opened were superstores.[4]

Combination stores are combined food and drug stores. They average about one and a half football fields in size—about twice the size of superstores. Examples are A&P's Family Mart and Kroger-Sav-On. Combination stores take in less than 5 percent of the business done by food stores, but account for 21 percent of new grocery store openings.

Hypermarkets are even bigger than combination stores, perhaps as large as *six* football fields. They combine supermarket, discount, and warehouse retailing. A typical hypermarket may have 50 checkout counters. They carry more than just routinely purchased goods, also selling furniture, appliances, clothing, and many other things. The hypermarket operates like a warehouse. Products in wire "baskets" are stacked high on metal racks; forklifts move through aisles during selling hours to restock shelves. The store gives discounts to customers who carry their own heavy appliances and furniture out of the store. Examples include Bigg's in Cincinnati, Ralph's Giant Stores in Southern California, and Carrefour in Philadelphia.

Hypermarkets have grown quickly in Europe. However, although major retailers such as Kmart and Wal-Mart have experimented with hypermarkets, the giant stores have yet to catch on in the United States. The major advantage of hypermarkets—their size—also can be a major drawback for some consumers. Many people, especially older shoppers, balk at the serious walking. And despite their size and volume of sales, most hypermarkets have only limited product variety. Surveys indicate 25 percent lower customer satisfaction with hypermarkets than with conventional supermarkets, leaving most experts skeptical about the future of these giant stores.[5]

Service Business

For some businesses, the "product line" is actually a service. Service retailers include hotels and motels, banks, airlines, colleges, hospitals, movie theaters, tennis clubs, bowling alleys, restaurants, repair services, hair-care shops, and dry cleaners. Service retailers in the United States are growing faster than are product retailers, and each service industry has its own retailing drama. Banks look for new ways to distribute their services, including automatic tellers, direct deposit, and telephone banking. Health organizations are changing the ways consumers get and pay for health services. The amusement industry has spawned Disney World and other theme parks, and H&R Block has built a franchise network to help consumers pay as little as possible to Uncle Sam.

Relative Prices

Retailers also can be classified according to the prices they charge. Most retailers charge regular prices and offer normal-quality goods and customer service. Some offer higher-quality goods and service at higher prices. The retailers that feature low prices are discount stores, "off-price" retailers, and catalog showrooms.

Discount Store

A **discount store** sells standard merchandise at lower prices by accepting lower margins and selling higher volume. The use of occasional discounts or specials does not make a store a discount store. A true discount store *regularly* sells its merchandise at lower prices, offering mostly national brands, not inferior goods. The early discount stores cut expenses by operating in warehouse-like facilities in low-rent, heavily traveled districts. They slashed prices, advertised widely, and carried a reasonable width and depth of products.

In recent years, facing intense competition from other discounters and department stores, many discount retailers have "traded up." They have improved decor, added new lines and services, and opened suburban branches, which has led to higher costs and prices. And as some department stores have cut their prices to compete with discounters, the distinction between many discount and department stores has become blurred. As a result, several major discount stores folded during the 1970s because they lost their price advantage. And many department store retailers have upgraded their stores and services, once again setting themselves apart from the improved discounters.

Off-Price Retailers

When the major discount stores traded up, a new wave of **off-price retailers** moved in to fill the low-price, high-volume gap. Ordinary discounters buy at regular wholesale prices and accept lower margins to keep prices down. In contrast, off-price retailers buy at less than regular wholesale prices and charge consumers less than retail. They tend to carry a changing and unstable collection of higher-quality merchandise, often leftover goods, overruns, and irregulars obtained at reduced prices from manufacturers or other retailers. Off-price retailers have made the biggest inroads in clothing, accessories, and footwear. But they can be found in all areas, from no-frills banking and discount brokerages to food stores and electronics.

The three main types of off-price retailers are *factory outlets, independents,* and *warehouse clubs.* **Factory outlets** are owned and operated by manufacturers and normally carry the manufacturer's surplus, discontinued, or irregular goods. Examples are The Burlington Coat Factory Warehouse, Manhattan's Brand Name Fashion Outlet, and the factory outlets of Levi Strauss, Carter's, and Ship 'n Shore. Such outlets sometimes group together in *factory outlet malls* and *value-retail cen-*

ters, where dozens of outlet stores offer prices as low as 50 percent below retail on a wide range of items. Whereas outlet malls consist primarily of manufacturers' outlets, value-retail centers combine manufacturers' outlets with off-price retail stores and department store clearance outlets. The number of factory outlet malls grew from less than 60 in 1980 to about 280 in 1991, making them one of the hottest growth areas in retailing. The malls now are moving upscale, featuring brands such as Esprit and Liz Claiborne, causing department stores to protest to the manufacturers of these brands. Given their higher costs, the department stores have to charge more than the off-price outlets. Manufacturers counter that they send last year's merchandise and seconds to the factory outlet malls, not the new merchandise that they supply to the department stores. The malls also are located far from urban areas, making travel to them more difficult. Still, the department stores are concerned about the growing number of shoppers willing to make weekend trips to stock up on branded merchandise at substantial savings.[6]

Independent off-price retailers are either owned and run by entrepreneurs or are divisions of larger retail corporations. Although many off-price operations are run by smaller independents, most large off-price retailer operations are owned by bigger retail chains. Examples include Loehmann's (owned by Associated Dry Goods, owner of Lord & Taylor), Filene's Basement (Federated Department Stores), and T.J. Maxx (Zayre).

Warehouse clubs (or *wholesale clubs,* or *membership warehouses*) sell a limited selection of brand name grocery items, appliances, clothing, and a hodgepodge of other goods at deep discounts to members who pay $25 to $50 annual membership fees. Examples are the Price Club, Sam's Wholesale Club, BJ's Wholesale Club, Pace Membership Warehouse, and Costco. These wholesale clubs operate in huge, low-overhead, warehouse-like facilities and offer few frills. Often, stores are drafty in the winter and stuffy in the summer. Customers themselves must wrestle furniture, heavy appliances, and other large items into the checkout line. Such clubs make no home deliveries and accept no credit cards. But they do offer rock-bottom prices, typically 20 percent to 40 percent below supermarket and discount store prices.

Off-price retailing blossomed during the early 1980s, but competition has stiffened as more and more off-price retailers have entered the market. The growth of off-price retailing slowed a bit recently because of effective counterstrategies by department stores and regular discounters. Still, off-price retailing remains a vital and growing force in modern retailing.

Catalog Showroom

A **catalog showroom** sells a wide selection of high-markup, fast-moving, brand name goods at discount prices. These include jewelry, power tools, cameras, luggage, small appliances, toys, and sporting goods. Catalog showrooms make their money by cutting costs and margins to provide low prices that will attract a higher volume of sales. The catalog showroom industry is led by companies such as Best Products and Service Merchandise.

Warehouse clubs operate in huge, low-overhead, warehouse-like facilities, and customers must wrestle large items to the checkout line. But such clubs offer rock-bottom prices.

Emerging in the late 1960s, catalog showrooms became one of retailing's hottest new forms. But they have been struggling in recent years to hold their share of the retail market. For one thing, department stores and discount retailers now run regular sales that match showroom prices. In addition, off-price retailers consistently beat catalog showroom prices. As a result, many showroom chains are broadening their lines, doing more advertising, renovating their stores, and adding services in order to attract more business.

Control of Outlets

About 80 percent of all retail stores are independents, accounting for two-thirds of all retail sales. Other forms of ownership include the *corporate chain*, the *voluntary chain and retailer cooperative*, the *franchise organization*, and the *merchandising conglomerate*.

Corporate Chain

The chain store is one of the most important retail developments of this century. **Chain stores** are two or more outlets that are commonly owned and controlled, employ central buying and merchandising, and sell similar lines of merchandise. Corporate chains appear in all types of retailing, but they are strongest in department stores, variety stores, food stores, drugstores, shoe stores, and women's clothing stores. Corporate chains have many advantages over independents. Their size allows them to buy in large quantities at lower prices. They can afford to hire corporate-level specialists to deal with areas such as pricing, promotion, merchandising, inventory control, and sales forecasting. And chains gain promotional economies because their advertising costs are spread over many stores and over a large sales volume.

Voluntary Chain and Retailer Cooperative

The great success of corporate chains caused many independents to band together in one of two forms of contractual associations. One is the *voluntary chain*—a wholesaler-sponsored group of independent retailers that engages in group buying and common merchandising. Examples include the Independent Grocers Alliance (IGA), Sentry Hardwares, and Western Auto. The other form of contractual association is the *retailer cooperative*—a group of independent retailers that bands together to set up a jointly owned central wholesale operation and conducts joint merchandising and promotion efforts. Examples include Associated Grocers and True Value Hardware. These organizations give independents the buying and promotion economies they need to meet the prices of corporate chains.

Franchise Organization

A **franchise** is a contractual association between a manufacturer, wholesaler, or service organization (the franchiser) and independent businesspeople (the franchisees) who buy the right to own and operate one or more units in the franchise system. The main difference between a franchise and other contractual systems (voluntary chains and retail cooperatives) is that franchise systems normally are based on some unique product or service, on a method of doing business; or on the trade name, goodwill, or patent that the franchiser has developed. Franchising has been prominent in fast-food companies, motels, gas stations, video stores, health and fitness centers, auto rentals, hair cutting salons, real estate and travel agencies, and dozens of other product and service areas.

The compensation received by the franchiser may include an initial fee, a royalty on sales, lease fees for equipment, and a share of the profits. For example, McDonald's franchisees may invest as much as $600,000 in initial start-up costs for a franchise. McDonald's then charges a 3.5 percent service fee and a rental charge of 8.5 percent of the franchisee's volume. It also requires franchisees to go to Hamburger University for three weeks to learn how to manage the business.[7]

Merchandising Conglomerate

Merchandising conglomerates are corporations that combine several different retailing forms under central ownership and share some distribution and management functions. Examples include Dayton-Hudson, J. C. Penney, and F. W. Woolworth. For example, F. W. Woolworth, in addition to its variety stores, operates 28 specialty chains, including Kinney Shoe Stores, Afterthoughts (costume jewelry and handbags), Face Fantasies (budget cosmetics), Herald Square Stationers, Frame Scene, Foot Locker (sports shoes), and Kids Mart. Diversified retailing, which provides superior management systems and economies that benefit all the separate retail operations, is likely to increase through the 1990s.

Type of Store Cluster

Most stores today cluster together to increase their customer pulling power and to give consumers the convenience of one-stop shopping. The main types of store clusters are the *central business district* and the *shopping center.*

Central Business District

Central business districts were the main form of retail cluster until the 1950s. Every large city and town had a central business district with department stores, specialty stores, banks, and movie theaters. When people began to move to the suburbs, however, these central business districts, with their traffic, parking, and crime problems, began to lose business. Downtown merchants opened branches in suburban shopping centers, and the decline of the central business districts continued. In recent years, many cities have joined with merchants to try to revive downtown shopping areas by building malls and providing underground parking. Some central business districts have made a comeback; others remain in a slow and possibly irreversible decline.

Shopping Center

A **shopping center** is a group of retail businesses planned, developed, owned, and managed as a unit. A *regional shopping center,* the largest and most dramatic shopping center, is like a mini-downtown. It typically contains between 40 and 100 stores and attracts customers from a wide area. Larger regional malls often have several department stores and a wide variety of specialty stores on several shopping levels. Many have added new types of retailers—dentists, health clubs, and even branch libraries.

A *community shopping center* contains between 15 and 50 retail stores. It normally contains a branch of a department store or variety store, a supermarket, specialty stores, professional offices, and sometimes a bank. Most shopping centers are *neighborhood shopping centers* or *strip malls* that generally contain between 5 and 15 stores. They are close and convenient for consumers. They usually contain a supermarket, perhaps a discount store, and several service stores—dry cleaner, self-service laundry, drugstore, video-rental outlet, barber or beauty shop, hardware store, or other stores. Such neighborhood centers account for 87 percent of all shopping centers and 51 percent of all shopping center retail sales.[8]

Combined, all shopping centers now account for about one-third of all retail sales, but they may have reached their saturation point. For example, between 1986 and 1989, the number of malls increased 22 percent to 34,683. But the number of shoppers going to malls every month grew only 3 percent. Thus, many areas contain too many malls, and as sales per square foot are dropping, vacancy rates are climbing. Some experts predict a shopping mall "shakeout," with as many as 20 percent of the regional shopping malls now operating in the United States closing by the year 2000. Despite the recent development of a few new "megamalls," such as the spectacular Mall of America near Minneapolis, the current trend is toward smaller malls located in medium-size and smaller cities in fast-growing areas such as the Southwest.[9]

NONSTORE RETAILING

Although most goods and services are sold through stores, nonstore retailing has been growing much faster than has store retailing. Nonstore retailing now accounts for more than 14 percent of all consumer purchases, and it may account for a third of all sales by the end of the century. Nonstore retailing includes *direct marketing, direct selling,* and *automatic vending.*

Direct Marketing

Direct marketing uses various advertising media to interact directly with consumers, generally calling for the consumer to make a direct response. Mass advertising typically reaches an unspecified number of people, most of whom are not in the market for a product or will not buy it until some future date. Direct-advertising vehicles are used to obtain immediate orders directly from targeted consumers. Although direct marketing initially consisted mostly of direct mail and mail-order catalogs, it has taken on several additional forms in recent years, including telemarketing, direct radio and television marketing, and electronic marketing.

Growth and Advantages of Direct Marketing

Direct marketing has boomed in recent years. All kinds of organizations use direct marketing: manufacturers, retailers, services companies, catalog merchants, and nonprofit organizations, to name a few. Its growing use in consumer marketing is largely a response to the "demassification" of mass markets, which has resulted in an ever-greater number of fragmented market segments with highly individualized needs and wants. Direct marketing allows sellers to focus efficiently on these minimarkets with offers that better match specific consumer needs.

Other trends also have fueled the growth of direct marketing. The increasing number of women entering the work force has decreased the time households have to shop. The higher costs of driving, the traffic congestion and parking headaches, the shortage of retail sales help, and the longer lines at checkout counters all have promoted in-home shopping. The development of toll-free telephone numbers and the increased use of credit cards have helped sellers reach and transact with consumers outside of stores more easily. Finally, the growth of computer power has allowed marketers to build better customer databases from which they can select the best prospects for specific products.

Direct marketing also has grown rapidly in business-to-business marketing. It can help reduce the high costs of reaching business markets through the salesforce. Lower-cost media, such as telemarketing and direct mail, can be used to identify the best prospects and prime them before making an expensive sales call.

Direct marketing provides many benefits to consumers as well. People who buy through direct mail or by telephone say that such shopping is convenient, hassle-free, and fun. It saves them time, and it introduces them to new lifestyles and a larger selection of merchandise. Consumers can compare products and prices from their armchairs by browsing through catalogs. They can order and receive products without having to leave their homes. Industrial customers can learn about and order products and services without tying up valuable time by meeting and listening to salespeople.

Direct marketing also provides benefits to sellers. It allows greater *selectivity*. A direct marketer can buy a mailing list containing the names of almost any group—millionaires, parents of newborn babies, left-handed people, or recent college graduates. The direct-marketing message can be *personalized* and *customized*. Eventually, according to one expert, "We will store hundreds . . . of messages in memory. We will select 10 thousand families with 12 or 20 specific characteristics and send them very individualized laser-printed letters."[10]

With direct marketing, the seller can build a *continuous relationship* with each customer. New parents can receive regular mailings describing new clothes, toys, and other products that their growing baby will need. Direct marketing also can be *timed* to reach prospects at just the right moment. Moreover, because it reaches more interested prospects at the best times, direct-marketing materials receive *higher readership and response*. Direct marketing also permits easy *testing* of specific messages and media. And because results are direct and immediate, direct marketing lends itself more readily to *response measurement*. Finally, direct marketing provides *privacy*—the direct marketer's offer and strategy are not visible to competitors.

Despite its many advantages to both consumers and marketers, direct marketing has also generated controversy in recent years. Critics claim that overly aggressive or unethical direct-marketing practices can irritate or harm consumers. Marketers should be aware of the major ethical and public policy issues surrounding direct marketing (see Marketing Highlight 15-2).

Forms of Direct Marketing

The four major forms of direct marketing are *direct mail and catalog marketing, telemarketing, television marketing,* and *electronic shopping.*

SOCIALLY RESPONSIBLE DIRECT MARKETING

Direct marketers and their customers usually enjoy mutually rewarding relationships. Occasionally, however, a darker side emerges. The aggressive and sometimes shady tactics of a few direct marketers can bother or harm consumers, giving the entire industry a black eye. Abuses range from simple excesses that irritate consumers to instances of unfairness or even outright deception and fraud. During the past few years, the direct marketing industry also has faced growing concerns about invasion of privacy issues.

Irritation

Direct-marketing promotional excesses sometimes annoy or offend consumers. Many people find the increasing number of hard-sell solicitations to be a nuisance. Most of us dislike direct-response TV commercials that are too loud, too long, and too insistent. Especially bothersome are dinner-time or late-night phone calls, poorly trained callers, and computerized calls placed by an ADRMP (auto-dial recorded message player).

Unfairness

Direct marketers have become so skilled at targeting audiences and putting together effective appeals that some have been accused of taking unfair advantage of impulsive or less sophisticated buyers. TV shopping shows and program-long "infomercials" seem to be the worst culprits. They feature smooth-talking hosts, elaborately staged demonstrations, claims of drastic price reductions, "while they last" time limitations, and unexcelled ease of purchase to inflame buyers who have low sales resistance.

Deception and Fraud

So-called heat merchants design mailers and write copy intended to mislead buyers. Political fundraisers, among the worst offenders, sometimes use gimmicks such as "look-alike" envelopes that resemble official documents, simulated newspaper clippings, and fake honors and awards. Other direct marketers, including some non-profit organizations, pretend to be conducting research surveys when they are actually asking leading questions to screen or persuade consumers. Still other problems of potential deception include greatly exaggerated product size and performance claims, and reference to much higher "retail" or regular prices that may never really have existed.

Fraudulent schemes, such as investment scams or phoney collections for charity, have multiplied in recent years. The Federal Trade Commission receives thousands of complaints each year, and the number is rising. Irate consumers flood their local Better Business Bureaus with additional complaints of local abuses. Crooked direct marketers can be hard to catch: direct marketing customers often respond quickly, do not interact personally with the seller, and usually expect to wait for delivery. By the time buyers realize that they have been bilked and alert the authorities, the thieves are usually somewhere else plotting new schemes.

Invasion of Privacy

Invasion of privacy is perhaps the toughest public policy issue now confronting the direct-marketing industry. These days, it seems that almost every time consumers order products by mail or telephone, enter a sweepstakes, apply for a credit card, or take out a magazine subscription, their names, addresses, and purchasing behavior are entered into some company's already bulging database. Using sophisticated computer technologies, direct marketers can use these databases to effectively "microtarget" their selling efforts.

Consumers often benefit from such database marketing—they receive more offers that are closely matched to their interests. However, direct marketers

***Direct Mail and Catalog Marketing.* Direct-mail marketing** involves single mailings that include letters, ads, samples, foldouts, and other "salespeople on wings" sent to prospects on mailing lists. The mailing lists are developed from customer lists or obtained from mailing-list houses that provide names of people fitting almost any description—the superwealthy, mobile-home owners, veterinarians, pet owners, or about anything else.

One study showed that direct mail and catalogs accounted for 48 percent of all direct-response offers leading to eventual orders (compared with telephone sales calls at 7 percent, circulars at 7 percent, and magazines and newspapers, each at 6 percent).[11] Direct mail is popular because it permits high target-market selectivity, can be personalized, is flexible, and allows easy measurement of results. Whereas the cost per thousand people reached is higher than with mass media such as television or magazines, the people who are reached are much better prospects.

sometimes find it difficult to walk the fine line between their desires to reach carefully targeted audiences and consumer rights to privacy. Many critics worry that marketers may know *too* much about consumers' lives, and that they may use this knowledge to take unfair advantage of consumers. At some point, they claim, the extensive use of databases intrudes on consumer privacy. For example, they ask, should AT&T be allowed to sell marketers the names of customers who frequently call the 800 numbers of catalog companies? Is it right for credit bureaus to compile and sell lists of people who have recently applied for credit cards—people who are considered prime direct marketing targets because of their spending behavior? Or is it right for states to sell the names and addresses of driver's license holders, along with height, weight, and gender information, allowing apparel retailers to target tall or overweight people with special clothing offers? Such practices have spawned a quiet but determined "privacy revolt" among consumers and public policy makers.

In a recent survey of consumers, 78 percent of respondents said that they were concerned about threats to their personal privacy. In another survey, *Advertising Age* asked advertising industry executives how they felt about database marketing and the privacy issue. The responses of three executives show that even industry insiders have mixed feelings:

> There are profound ethical issues relating to the marketing of specific household data—financial information, for instance. . . . For every household in the United States, the computer can guess with amazing accuracy . . . things like credit use, net worth, and investments, the kind of information most people would never want disclosed, let alone sold to any marketer. . . . My guess is that such disclosures, even though not factual, could surprise and possibly anger many consumers.

I'm a big believer in getting as close to your customer as you can. . . . [For example,] I love to garden; [I order seeds from the Burpee's catalog and] Burpee's sells my name—that [results in my receiving] the kind of stuff I like to look at. . . . Credit card solicitations I don't. Travel-related information I do if I'm interested in the destination.

> It doesn't bother me that people know I live in a suburb of Columbus, Ohio, and have X number of kids. It [does] bother me that these people know the names of my wife and kids and where my kids go to school. They . . . act like they know me when the bottom line is they're attempting to sell me something. I do feel that database marketing has allowed companies to cross the fine line of privacy. . . . In some cases, it's difficult to know when the line's crossed. But in a lot of cases, I think they know they have crossed it.

The direct marketing industry is working to address issues of ethics and public policy. They know that, left untended, such problems will lead to increasingly negative consumer attitudes, lower response rates, and calls for greater state and federal legislation to further restrict direct-marketing practices. More importantly, in the last analysis, most direct marketers want the same thing that consumers want: honest and well-designed marketing offers targeted only toward consumers who will appreciate and respond to them. Direct marketing is just too expensive to waste on consumers who don't want it.

Sources: Portions adapted from Terrence H. Witkowski, "Self-Regulation Will Suppress Direct Marketing's Downside," *Marketing News*, April 24, 1989, p. 4. Quotes from Melanie Rigney, "Too Close for Comfort, Execs Warn," *Advertising Age*, January 13, 1992, p. 31. Also see Evan I. Schwartz, "The Rush to Keep Mum," *Business Week*, June 8, 1992, pp. 36-38; and Cyndee Miller, "Privacy vs. Direct Marketing," *Marketing News*, March 1, 1993, pp. 1, 14.

More than 35 percent of Americans have responded to direct-mail ads, and the number is growing. Direct mail has proved very successful in promoting books, magazine subscriptions, and insurance and increasingly is being used to sell novelty and gift items, clothing, gourmet foods, and industrial products. Direct mail also is used heavily by charities, which raise billions of dollars each year and account for about 25 percent of all direct-mail revenues.

Catalog marketing involves selling through catalogs mailed to a select list of customers or made available in stores. This approach is used by huge general-merchandise retailers—such as J. C. Penney and Spiegel—that carry a full line of merchandise. But recently, the giants have been challenged by thousands of specialty catalogs with more sharply focused audiences. These smaller catalog retailers have successfully filled highly specialized market niches. In contrast, Sears chose to discontinue its 97-year-old annual "Big Book" catalog in 1993 after years of unprofitable operation. Other catalogers rushed to fill the void.

Billions of catalogs are mailed out each year; the average household receives 50 catalogs annually.

Consumers can buy just about anything from a catalog. Over 14 billion copies of more than 8,500 different consumer catalogs are mailed out annually, and the average household receives at least 50 catalogs a year. Last year, 98.6 million people ordered from catalogs.[12] Hanover House sends out 22 different catalogs selling everything from shoes to decorative lawn birds. Sharper Image sells $2,400 jet-propelled surf boards. The Banana Republic Travel and Safari Clothing Company features everything you would need to go hiking in the Sahara or the rain forest. The list of specialty catalogers is almost endless.

Recently, specialty department stores, such as Neiman Marcus, Bloomingdale's, and Saks Fifth Avenue, have begun sending catalogs to cultivate upper-middle-class markets for high-priced, often exotic, merchandise. Several major corporations also have developed or acquired mail-order divisions. For example, Avon now issues ten women's fashion catalogs along with catalogs for children's and men's clothes. Hershey and other food companies also are investigating catalog opportunities. Even Walt Disney Company is getting into cataloging; it mails out over 6 million catalogs each year featuring videos, stuffed animals, and other Disney items.

Most consumers enjoy receiving catalogs and will sometimes even pay to get them. Many catalog marketers are now even selling their catalogs at book stores and magazine stands. Some companies, such as Royal Silk, Neiman Marcus, Sears, and Spiegel, are also experimenting with videotape catalogs, or "videologs." Royal Silk sells a 35-minute video catalog to its customers for $5.95. The tape contains a polished presentation of Royal Silk products, tells customers how to care for silk, and provides ordering information. Soloflex uses a video brochure to boost sales of its $1,000 in-home exercise equipment:

> [The] 22-minute tape—available either by calling Soloflex's 800 number or filling in a coupon in its magazine ads—shows an attractive couple demonstrating the multiple exercises possible via the system. Each tape costs the company $6.50 to produce, but [Soloflex] claims that almost half of those who view the video brochure later order a Soloflex home exercise system via telephone. That's a good sight better than the 10 percent who order the system after first perusing a direct mail piece.[13]

Many business-to-business marketers also rely heavily on catalogs. Whether in the form of a simple brochure, three-ring binder, or book, or encoded on a videotape or computer diskette, catalogs remain one of today's hardest-working sales tools. For some companies, in fact, catalogs have even taken the place of salespeople. In all, companies mail out more than 1.1 *billion* business-to-business catalogs each year, reaping more than $50 billion worth of catalog sales.[14]

Telemarketing. **Telemarketing**—using the telephone to sell directly to consumers—has become the major direct-marketing tool. Marketers spend an estimated $41 billion each year in telephone charges to help sell their products and services. They use outbound telephone marketing to sell directly to consumers and businesses. Some telemarketing systems are fully automated. For example, automatic dialing and recorded message players (ADRMPs) self-dial numbers, play a voice-activated advertising message, and take orders from interested customers on an answering-machine device or by forwarding the call to an operator. The average household receives 19 telephone sales calls each year and makes 16 calls to place orders.

Marketers use inbound toll-free 800 numbers to receive orders from television and radio ads, direct mail, or catalogs. During January 1982, more than 700 people dialed an 800 number every minute in response to television commercials. During 1990, AT&T logged more than 7 billion 800-number calls.[15] Other marketers use 900 numbers to sell consumers information, entertainment, or the opportunity to voice an opinion. For example, for a charge, consumers can obtain weather forecasts from American Express (1-900-WEATHER—75 cents a minute); pet care information from Quaker Oats (1-900-990-PETS—95 cents a minute); advice on snoring and other sleep disorders from Somnus (1-900-USA-SLEEP—$2 for the first minute, then $1 a minute); or golf lessons from *Golf Digest* (1-900-454-3288—95 cents a minute). Altogether, the 900-number industry now generates $860 million in annual revenues.[16]

Telemarketing is used in business marketing as well as consumer marketing. In fact, more than $115 billion worth of industrial products were marketed by phone last year. For example, General Electric uses telemarketing to generate and qualify sales leads and to manage small accounts. Raleigh Bicycles now uses telemarketing to reduce the amount of personal selling needed for contacting its dealers; in the first year, salesforce travel costs were reduced 50 percent, and sales in a single quarter increased 34 percent.[17]

The recent explosion in unsolicited telephone marketing has annoyed many consumers who object to the almost daily "junk phone calls" that pull them away from the dinner table or clog up their answering machines. Lawmakers around the country are responding to complaints from irate consumers. They have proposed a variety of laws, ranging from banning unsolicited telemarketing calls during certain hours or outlawing auto-dialers to letting households sign up for a national "Don't Call Me" list and penalizing telemarketers who call people on the list. At the same time, most consumers appreciate many of the offers they receive by telephone. Properly designed and targeted telemarketing provides many benefits, including purchasing convenience and increased product and service information.

Most telemarketers support some action against indiscriminate and poorly targeted telemarketing. For example, the Direct Marketing Association (DMA) began circulating its own 400,000-name "Don't Call Me" list to telemarketers six years ago. As a DMA spokesperson notes, "We want to target people who want to be targeted." Thus, both consumers and telemarketers have the same goal for telemarketing—well-designed offers targeted toward consumers who will appreciate and respond to them. To avoid angry consumers and restrictive legislation, telemarketers must do a better job of targeting their offers.[18]

Television Marketing. **Television marketing** takes one of two major forms. The first is *direct-response advertising*. Direct marketers air television spots, often 60 or 120 seconds long, that persuasively describe a product and give customers a toll-free number for ordering. Late-night television viewers might even encounter a 30-minute advertising program for a single product. Direct-response advertising works well for magazines, books, small appliances, tapes and CDs, collectibles, and many other products. Some successful direct-response ads run for years and become classics. For example, Dial Media's ads for Ginsu knives ran for seven years and sold almost 3 million sets of knives worth more than $40 million in sales; its Armourcote cookware ads generated more than twice that much.[19]

Home shopping channels, another form of television direct marketing, are television programs or entire channels dedicated to selling goods and services. The largest is the Home Shopping Network (HSN). With HSN, viewers can tune in the Home Shopping Club, which broadcasts 24 hours a day. The program's hosts offer bargain prices on products ranging from jewelry, lamps, collectible dolls, and clothing to power tools and consumer electronics—usually obtained by HSN at closeout prices. The show is upbeat, with the hosts honking horns, blowing whistles, and praising viewers for their good taste. Viewers call an 800 number to order goods. At the other end of the operation, 400 operators handle more than 1,200 incoming lines, entering orders directly into computer terminals. Orders are shipped within 48 hours.

Sales through home shopping channels grew from $450 million in 1986 to an estimated $2 billion in 1991. More than half of all U.S. homes have access to HSN or other home shopping channels, such as Quality Value Channel (QVC), Value Club of America, Home Shopping Mall, or TelShop. Sears, Kmart, J. C. Penney, Spiegel, and other major retailers are now looking into the home shopping industry. Some experts contend that TV home shopping is just a fad, but most think it is here to stay.[20]

Electronic Shopping. The major form of **electronic shopping** is *videotex,* a two-way system that links consumers with the seller's computer data banks by cable or telephone lines. The videotex service makes up a computerized catalog of products offered by producers, retailers, banks, travel organizations, and others. Consumers can use an ordinary television set with a special keyboard device connected to the system by two-way cable. Or they can hook into the system by telephone using a home computer. For example, a consumer wanting to buy a new compact-disc player could request a list of all CD player brands in the computerized catalog, compare the brands, then order one using a charge card—all without leaving home.

Videotex is still a fairly new idea. In recent years, several large videotex systems have failed because of a lack of subscribers or too little use. Two currently successful systems in the United States, however, are CompuServe and Prodigy.

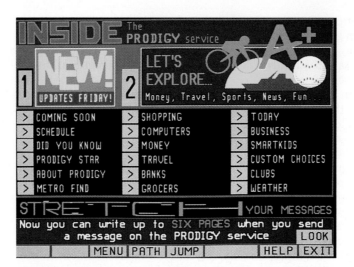

Electronic shopping: Prodigy offers in-home shopping services and much more.

Prodigy, developed through a partnership by IBM and Sears, offers in-home shopping services and much more. Through Prodigy, subscribers can order thousands of products and services electronically from dozens of major stores and catalogs. They also can do their banking with local banks; buy and sell investments through a discount brokerage service; book airline, hotel, and car-rental reservations; play games, quizzes, and contests; check *Consumer Reports* ratings of various products; receive the latest sports scores and statistics; obtain weather forecasts; and exchange messages with other subscribers around the country. Although relatively few consumers now subscribe to such electronic systems, the number is expected to grow in future years as more consumers acquire cable television and personal computers and discover the wonders of electronic shopping.[21]

Integrated Direct Marketing and Direct-Marketing Databases

Most direct marketers use only a single advertising vehicle and a "one-shot" effort to reach and sell a prospect. Or, they might use a single vehicle but multiple stages in a campaign to trigger purchases. For example, a magazine publisher might send a series of four direct-mail notices to a household to get a subscriber to renew before giving up. A more powerful approach is **integrated direct marketing,** which involves using multiple-vehicle, multiple-stage campaigns. Such campaigns can greatly improve response:

> When a mailing piece which might generate a 2 percent response on its own is supplemented by a toll-free 800-number ordering channel, we regularly see response rates rise by 50 percent. A skillfully integrated outbound telemarketing effort can add another 500 percent lift in response. Suddenly our 2 percent response has grown to 13 percent or more by adding interactive marketing channels to a "business as usual" mailing. The dollars and cents involved in adding media to the integrated media mix are normally marginal on a cost-per-order basis because of the high level of responses generated . . . Adding media to a marketing program will raise total response . . . because people are inclined to respond to different stimuli.[22]

More elaborate integrated marketing campaigns can be used. Consider the following multimedia, multistage campaign:

Paid ad with a response channel	→	Direct mail	→	Outbound telemarketing	→	Face-to-face sales call

Here, the paid ad creates product awareness and stimulates inquiries. The company immediately sends direct mail to those who inquire. Within a few days, the company follows up with a phone call seeking an order. Some prospects will order by phone; others might request a face-to-face sales call. In such a campaign, the marketer seeks to improve response rates and profits by adding media and stages that contribute more to additional sales than to additional costs.

In order to employ integrated direct marketing successfully, companies must develop effective marketing database systems. A **marketing database** is an organized set of data about individual customers or prospects, which the company can use to generate and qualify customer leads, sell products and services, and maintain customer relationships.

Most companies have not yet built effective marketing database systems. Mass marketers generally know little about individual customers. Retailers may know a lot about their charge-account customers, but almost nothing about their cash or credit card customers. Banks may develop customer databases for each separate product or service but fail to tie this information together into complete customer profiles that could be used for cross-selling products and services.

Building a marketing database takes time and involves much cost, but when it works properly it can pay handsome dividends. For example, a General Electric customer database contains each customer's geographic, demographic, and psychographic characteristics along with an appliance purchasing history. GE direct marketers can use this database to assess how long specific customers have owned their current appliances and which past customers might be ready to purchase again. They can determine which customers need a new GE videorecorder, compact disc player, stereo receiver, or something else to go with other recently purchased electronics products. Or they can identify the best past GE purchasers and send them gift certificates or other promotions to apply against their next purchases of GE appliances. Clearly, a rich customer database allows GE to build profitable new business by locating good prospects, anticipating customer needs, cross-selling products and services, and rewarding loyal customers.[23]

Direct Selling

Door-to-door retailing, which started centuries ago with roving peddlers, has grown into a huge industry. More than 600 companies sell their products door to door, office to office, or at home sales parties. The pioneers in door-to-door selling are the Fuller Brush Company, vacuum cleaner companies like Electrolux, and book-selling companies, such as World Book and Southwestern. The image of door-to-door selling improved greatly when Avon entered the industry with its Avon representative—the homemaker's friend and beauty consultant. Tupperware and Mary Kay Cosmetics helped to popularize home sales parties, in which several friends and neighbors attend a party at a private home where products are demonstrated and sold.

The advantages of door-to-door selling are consumer convenience and personal attention. But the high costs of hiring, training, paying, and motivating the salesforce result in higher prices. Although some door-to-door companies are still thriving, door-to-door selling has a somewhat uncertain future. The increase in the number of single-person and working-couple households decreases the chances of finding a buyer at home. Home-party companies are having trouble finding nonworking women who want to sell products part time. And with recent advances in interactive direct-marketing technology, the door-to-door salesperson may well be replaced in the future by the household telephone, television, or home computer.

Automatic Vending

Automatic vending is not new—in 215 B.C. Egyptians could buy sacrificial water from coin-operated dispensers. But this method of selling soared after World War II. There are now about 4.5 million vending machines in the United States—one machine for every 55 people. Today's automatic vending uses space-age and computer technology to sell a wide variety of convenience and impulse goods—cigarettes, beverages, candy, newspapers, foods and snacks, hosiery, cosmetics, paperback books, T-shirts, insurance policies, pizza, audio tapes and videocassettes, and even shoeshines and fishing worms. Vending machines are found everywhere—in factories, offices, lobbies, retail stores, gasoline stations, airports, and train and bus terminals. Automatic teller machines provide bank customers with checking, savings, withdrawals, and funds-transfer services. Compared to store retailing, vending machines offer consumers greater convenience (24 hours, self-service) and fewer damaged goods. But the expensive equipment and labor required for automatic vending make it a costly channel, and prices of vended goods are often 15 percent to 20 percent higher than are those in retail stores. Customers also must put up with aggravating machine breakdowns, out-of-stock items, and the fact that merchandise cannot be returned.[24]

RETAILER MARKETING DECISIONS

Retailers are searching for new marketing strategies to attract and hold customers. In the past, retailers attracted customers with unique products, more or better services than their competitors offered, or credit cards. Today, national brand manufacturers, in their drive for volume, have placed their branded goods everywhere. Thus, stores offer more similar assortments—national brands are found not only in department stores, but also in mass-merchandise and off-price discount stores. As a result, stores are looking more and more alike; they have become "commoditized." In any city, a shopper can find many stores but few assortments.

Service differentiation among retailers has also eroded. Many department stores have trimmed their services, whereas discounters have increased theirs. Customers have become smarter and more price sensitive. They see no reason to pay more for identical brands, especially when service differences are shrinking. And because bank credit cards are now accepted at most stores, consumers no longer need credit from a particular store. For all these reasons, many retailers today are rethinking their marketing strategies.[25]

Retailers face major marketing decisions about their *target markets, product assortment and services, price, promotion,* and *place.*

Target Market Decision

Retailers first must define their target markets and then decide how they will position themselves in these markets. Should the store focus on upscale, midscale, or downscale shoppers? Do target shoppers want variety, depth of assortment, convenience, or low prices? Until they define and profile their markets, retailers cannot make consistent decisions about product assortment, services, pricing, advertising, store decor, or any of the other decisions that must support their positions.

Too many retailers fail to define their target markets and positions clearly. They try to have "something for everyone" and end up satisfying no market well. In contrast, successful retailers define their target markets quite well and position themselves strongly:

> Leslie H. Wexner borrowed $5,000 in 1963 to create *The Limited,* which started as a single store targeted to young, fashion-conscious women. All aspects of the store—clothing assortment, fixtures, music, colors, personnel—were orchestrated to match the target consumer. He continued to open more stores, but a decade later his original customers were no longer in the "young" group. To catch the new "youngs," he started the Limited Express. Over the years, he started or acquired other highly targeted store chains, including Lane Bryant, Victoria's Secret, Lerner, and others to reach new segments. Today The Limited, Inc. operates over 3,400 stores in seven different segments of the market, with sales of more than $6.3 billion.

Even large stores such as Wal-Mart, Kmart, and Sears must define their major target markets in order to design effective marketing strategies. In fact, in recent years, thanks to strong targeting and positioning, Wal-Mart has exploded past Sears and Kmart to become the nation's largest retailer (see Marketing Highlight 15-3).

A retailer should do periodic marketing research to check that it is satisfying its target customers. Consider a store that wants to attract wealthy consumers but whose *store image* is shown by the magenta line in Figure 15-1. This store does not currently appeal to its target market—it must change its target market or redesign itself as a "classier" store. Suppose the store then upgrades its products, services, and salespeople and raises its prices. Some time later, a second customer survey may reveal the image shown by the blue line in Figure 15-1. The store has established a position that matches its target market choice.

Product Assortment and Services Decision

Retailers must decide on three major product variables: *product assortment, services mix,* and *store atmosphere.*

The retailer's *product assortment* must match target shoppers' expectations. The retailer must determine both the product assortment's *width* and its *depth.* Thus, a restaurant can offer a narrow and shallow assortment (small lunch counter), a narrow and deep assortment (delicatessen), a wide and shallow assortment (cafeteria), or a wide and deep assortment (large restaurant). Another prod-

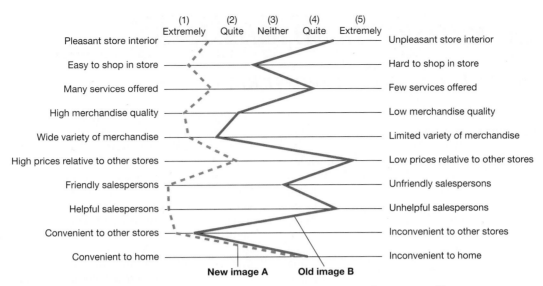

	(1) Extremely	(2) Quite	(3) Neither	(4) Quite	(5) Extremely	
Pleasant store interior						Unpleasant store interior
Easy to shop in store						Hard to shop in store
Many services offered						Few services offered
High merchandise quality						Low merchandise quality
Wide variety of merchandise						Limited variety of merchandise
High prices relative to other stores						Low prices relative to other stores
Friendly salespersons						Unfriendly salespersons
Helpful salespersons						Unhelpful salespersons
Convenient to other stores						Inconvenient to other stores
Convenient to home						Inconvenient to home

New image A   Old image B

FIGURE 15-1   A comparison between the old and the new image of a store seeking to appeal to a class market

Source: Adapted from David W. Cravens, Gerald E. Hills, and Robert B. Woodruff, *Marketing Decision Making:; Concepts and Strategy* (Homewood, IL.: Irwin, 1976), p. 234.

uct assortment element is the *quality* of the goods: The customer is interested not only in the range of choice but also in the quality of the products available.

No matter what the store's product assortment and quality level, there always will be competitors with similar assortments and quality. Therefore, the retailer must search for other ways to *differentiate* itself from similar competitors. It can use any of several product-differentiation strategies. For one, it can offer merchandise that no other competitor carries—its own private brands or national brands on which it holds exclusives. For example, The Limited designs most of the clothes carried by its store, and Saks gets exclusive rights to carry a well-known designer's labels. Second, the retailer can feature blockbuster merchandising events—Bloomingdale's is known for running spectacular shows featuring goods from a certain country, such as India or China. Or the retailer can offer surprise merchandise, as when Loehmann's offers surprise assortments of seconds, overstocks, and closeouts. Finally, the retailer can differentiate itself by offering a highly targeted product assortment—Lane Bryant carries goods for larger women; Brookstone offers an unusual assortment of gadgets in what amounts to an adult toy store.

Retailers also must decide on a *services mix* to offer customers. The old "mom and pop" grocery stores offered home delivery, credit, and conversation—services that today's supermarkets ignore. The services mix is one of the key tools of non-price competition for setting one store apart from another. Table 15-2 lists some of the major services that full-service retailers can offer.

TABLE 15-2
Typical Retail Services

PRIMARY SERVICES	SUPPLEMENTAL SERVICES	
Alterations	Baby strollers	Personal shopping
Complaint handling	Bill payment	Product locator
Convenient store hours, parking	Bridal registries	Restaurants or snack counters
Credit	Check cashing	Shopping consultants
Delivery	Children's play rooms	Shopping information
Fitting rooms, rest rooms	Demonstrations	Shows, displays, and exhibits
Installation and assembly	Layaway	Special ordering
Merchandise returns and adjustments	Lost and found	Wheelchairs
Service and repair	Package checkrooms	
Telephone ordering	Packaging and gift wrapping	

Wal-Mart: The Nation's largest Retailer

In 1962, Sam Walton and his brother opened the first Wal-Mart discount store in small-town Rogers, Arkansas. It was a big, flat, warehouse-type store that sold everything from apparel to automotive supplies to small appliances at very low prices. Experts gave the fledgling retailer little chance—conventional wisdom suggested that discount stores could succeed only in large cities. Yet, from these modest beginnings, the chain expanded rapidly, opening new stores in one small southern town after another. By the mid-1980s, Wal-Mart had exploded onto the national retailing scene. It began building stores in larger cities such as Dallas, St. Louis, and Kansas City. By 1990, the chain was operating 1,600 stores in 35 states and producing more than $32 billion in annual sales. Incredibly, less than 30 years after opening its first store, Wal-Mart overtook long-time industry leader Sears to become the nation's largest retailer.

Wal-Mart's phenomenal growth shows few signs of slowing. The company is now building more stores in larger cities and is expanding into the Northeast and Far West. Sales in 1992 exceeded $55 billion and management fully expects that sales will more than double to $125 billion by the turn of the century. Over the past decade, Wal-Mart's annual return to investors has averaged more than 45 percent, rewarding investors handsomely. An investment of $1,000 in Wal-Mart stock in 1970 would be worth a whopping $500,000 today!

What are the secrets behind this spectacular success? Wal-Mart listens to and takes care of its customers, treats employees as partners, and reins in costs.

Listening to and Taking Care of Customers

Wal-Mart positioned itself strongly in a well-chosen target market. Initially, Sam Walton focused on value-conscious consumers in small-town America. The chain built a strong everyday low-price position long before it became fashionable in retailing. It grew rapidly by bringing the lowest possible prices to towns ignored by national discounters—towns such as Van Buren, Arkansas, and Idabel, Oklahoma.

Wal-Mart knows its customers and takes good care of them. As one analyst puts it, "The company gospel . . . is relatively simple: Be an agent for customers, find out what they want, and sell it to them for the lowest possible price." Thus, the company listens carefully—for example, all top Wal-Mart executives go where their customers hang out. Each spends at least two days a week visiting stores, talking directly with customers and getting a firsthand look at operations. Then, Wal-Mart delivers what customers want: a broad selection of carefully selected goods at unbeatable prices.

But the right merchandise at the right price isn't the only key to Wal-Mart's success. Wal-Mart also provides outstanding service that keeps customers satisfied. A sign reading "Satisfaction Guaranteed" hangs prominently at each store's entrance. Another sign inside the store reads "At Wal-Mart, our goal is: You're always next in line!" Customers are often welcomed by "people greeters" eager to lend a helping hand or just to be friendly. And, sure enough, the store opens extra checkout counters to keep waiting lines short.

Going the extra mile for customers has paid off. A recent independent survey in towns where Wal-Mart competes with Kmart and Target found that Wal-Mart's shoppers were the most satisfied; Kmart's the least. Perhaps more telling, whereas the typical Kmart store rings up average sales of about $150 per square foot per year, the typical Wal-Mart store hauls in $250.

Treating Employees as Partners

Wal-Mart believes that, in the final accounting, the company's people are what really makes it better. Thus, it works hard to show employees that it cares about them. Wal-Mart calls employees "associates," a practice now widely copied by competitors. The associates work as partners, become deeply involved in operations, and share rewards for good performance.

> Everyone at Wal-Mart [is] an associate—from [the CEO] . . . to a cashier named Janet at the Wal-Mart on Highway 50 in Ocoee, Florida. "We," "us," and "our" are the operative words. Wal-Mart department heads, hourly associates who look after one or more of 30-some departments ranging from sporting goods to electronics, see figures that many companies never show general managers: costs, freight charges, profit margins. The company sets a profit margin for each store, and if the store exceeds it, then the hourly associates share part of the additional profit.

The partnership concept is deeply rooted in the Wal-Mart corporate culture. It is supported by open-door policies and grass-roots meetings that give employees a say in what goes on and encourage them to bring their problems to management. Wal-Mart's concern for its em-

---

The *store's atmosphere* is another element in its product arsenal. Every store has a physical layout that makes moving around in it either hard or easy. Every store has a "feel"; one store is cluttered, another charming, a third plush, a fourth somber. The store must have a planned atmosphere that suits the target market and moves customers to buy. A bank should be quiet, solid, and peaceful; a nightclub should be flashy, loud, and vibrating. Increasingly, retailers are working to create shopping environments that match their target markets. Chains such as the Sharper Image and Banana Republic are turning their stores into theaters that

A Wal-Mart "people greeter" lends a helping hand.

ployees translates into high employee satisfaction, which in turn translates into greater customer satisfaction.

Keeping a Tight Rein on Costs

Wal-Mart has the lowest cost structure in the industry: Operating expenses amount to only 16 percent of sales, compared to 23 percent at Kmart. Thus, Wal-Mart can charge lower prices but still reap higher profits, allowing it to offer better service. This creates a "productivity loop." Wal-Mart's lower prices and better service attract more shoppers, producing more sales, making the company more efficient, and enabling it to lower prices even more.

Wal-Mart's low costs result in part from superior management and more sophisticated technology. Its Bentonville, Arkansas, headquarters contains "a computer-communications system worthy of the Defense Department," giving managers around the country instant access to sales and operating information. And its huge, fully automated distribution centers employ the latest technology to supply stores efficiently. Wal-Mart also spends less than competitors on advertising—only 0.5 percent of sales, compared to 2.5 percent at K mart and 3.8 percent at Sears. Because Wal-Mart has what customers want at the prices they'll pay, its reputation has spread rapidly by word of mouth. It has not needed more advertising.

Finally, Wal-Mart keeps costs down through good old "tough buying." Whereas the company is known for the warm way it treats customers, it is equally well known for the cold, calculated way it wrings low prices

from suppliers. The following passage describes a visit to Wal-Mart's buying offices.

Don't expect a greeter and don't expect friendly. . . . Once you are ushered into one of the spartan little buyers' rooms, expect a steely eye across the table and be prepared to cut your price. "They are very, very focused people, and they use their buying power more forcefully than anyone else in America," says the marketing vice president of a major vendor. "All the normal mating rituals are [forbidden]. Their highest priority is making sure everyone at all times in all cases knows who's in charge, and it's Wal-Mart. They talk softly, but they have piranha hearts, and if you aren't totally prepared when you go in there, you'll have your [head] handed to you."

Some observers wonder whether Wal-Mart can continue to grow at such a torrid pace and still retain its focus and positioning. They wonder if an ever-larger Wal-Mart can stay close to its customers and employees. The company's managers are betting on it. Says one top executive: "We'll be fine as long as we never lose our responsiveness to the consumer."

Sources: Quoted material from Bill Saporito, "Is Wal-Mart Unstoppable?" *Fortune,* May 6, 1991, pp. 50-59; and John Huey, "Wal-Mart: Will It Take Over the World?" *Fortune,* January 30, 1989, pp. 52-61. Also see Christy Fisher, "Wal-Mart's Way," *Advertising Age,* February 18, 1991, p. 3; Zachary Schiller and Wendy Zellner, "Clout," *Business Week,* December 21, 1992; and Bill Saporito, "David Glass Won't Crack Under Fire," *Fortune,* February 8, 1993, pp. 75-80.

transport customers into unusual, exciting shopping environments. (See Marketing Highlight 15-4.) Even conservative Sears divides the clothing areas within each store into six distinct "shops," each with its own selling environment designed to meet the tastes of individual segments.[26]

Price Decision

A retailer's price policy is a crucial positioning factor and must be decided in relation to its target market, its product and service assortment, and its competi-

TODAY'S RETAILERS TAKE THEIR CUES FROM BROADWAY

Richard Melman is Chicago's preeminent restauranteur. He has designed each of his 32 restaurants around an intriguing theme: Tucci Benucch resembles an outdoor Italian village cafe, Ed Debevic is a 1950's kitsch diner, R. J. Grunts is a down-and-dirty burger-and-chili hangout, Ambria is an elegant crystal, tablecloth, and candle restaurant. According to one food-industry consultant, "Rich Melman is the Andrew Lloyd Webber of the restaurant industry. He doesn't just produce food, he produces theatre."

Turning retail establishments into theatre isn't limited just to restaurants. Toy seller F.A.O. Schwartz opened a three-story toy store on Chicago's upscale North Michigan Avenue that has customers lining up to get in. Once in, customers take an escalator to the third floor, then make their way down through various boutiques where crowds gather around spectacular Lego exhibits, Barbie Doll departments, giant stuffed zoo animals, and even a talking tree. F.A.O. Schwartz's "theatre" presents a stark contrast to the typical Toys 'R' Us store, in which nothing much seems to happen except lower prices and a senses-numbing assortment of 15,000 toys stacked high on row after row of shelves.

Just a few blocks south of F.A.O. Schwartz stands four-story Niketown, which now attracts more visitors than Chicago's famed Museum of Science and Industry. Niketown is the ultimate testament to market niching—every room is dedicated to outfits and shoes for a different sport. A would-be teenage basketball star heads for the second floor, where he spots a giant picture of Michael Jordan, an awesome array of basketball shoes and clothing, and even a basketball court where he can try on the shoes, shoot a few baskets, and get a feel for how the shoes perform.

Next door to Niketown is more sedate theatre—the Sony Showroom—where Sony has set up various products so that customers can touch, turn on, and experience them. On the second floor, customers are treated to the home theatre of the future, with its giant screen and full-theatre sound. On the first floor, they view the televised image of a beautiful bouquet of flowers being shot through a Sony Handycam videocamera and displayed on a high definition television. The beauty of the picture almost exceeds that of the real flowers.

Perhaps the most dramatic conversion of stores into theatre is the Mall of America near Minneapolis. Containing more than 800 specialty stores, the Mall is a veritable playground. Under a single roof, it shelters a 7-acre Knott's Berry Farm amusement park featuring 23 rides and attractions, an ice-skating rink, an Underwater World featuring hundreds of marine specimens and a dolphin show, and a two-story miniature golf course. One of the stores, Oshman Supersports USA, features a basketball court, a boxing gym, a baseball batting cage, a 50-foot archery range, and a simulated ski slope.

All of this confirms that retail stores are much more than simply assortments of goods. They are environments to be experienced by the people who shop in them. Store atmospheres offer a powerful tool by which retailers can differentiate their stores from those of competitors.

Source: See "Why Rich Melman Is Really Cooking," *Business Week,* November 2, 1992, pp. 127-28.

---

tion. All retailers would like to charge high markups and achieve high volume, but the two seldom go together. Most retailers seek *either* high markups on lower volume (most specialty stores) *or* low markups on higher volume (mass merchandisers and discount stores). Thus, Bijan's on Rodeo Drive in Beverly Hills prices men's suits starting at $1,000 and shoes at $400—it sells a low volume but makes a hefty profit on each sale. At the other extreme, T.J. Maxx sells brand name clothing at discount prices, settling for a lower margin on each sale but selling at a much higher volume.

Retailers also must pay attention to pricing tactics. Most retailers will put low prices on some items to serve as "traffic builders" or "loss leaders." On some occasions, they run storewide sales. On others, they plan markdowns on slower-moving merchandise. For example, shoe retailers expect to sell 50 percent of their shoes at the normal markup, 25 percent at a 40 percent markup, and the remaining 25 percent at cost.

Promotion Decision

Retailers use the normal promotion tools—advertising, personal selling, sales promotion, and public relations—to reach consumers. Retailers advertise in newspapers, magazines, radio, and television. Advertising may be supported by circulars and direct-mail pieces. Personal selling requires careful training of salespeople in how to greet customers, meet their needs, and handle their complaints. Sales promotions may include in-store demonstrations, displays, contests, and visiting celebrities. Public relations activities, such as press conferences and speeches, store openings, special events, newsletters, magazines, and public service activities, are always available to retailers.

Place Decision

Retailers often cite three critical factors in retailing success: *location, location,* and *location!* A retailer's location is key to its ability to attract customers. And the costs of building or leasing facilities have a major impact on the retailer's profits. Thus, site-location decisions are among the most important the retailer makes. Small retailers may have to settle for whatever locations they can find or afford. Large retailers usually employ specialists who select locations using advanced methods.

THE FUTURE OF RETAILING

Several trends will affect the future of retailing. The slowdown in population and economic growth means that retailers no longer will enjoy sales and profit growth through natural expansion in current and new markets. Growth will have to come from increasing shares of current markets. But greater competition and new types of retailers will make it harder to improve market shares.

The retailing industry suffers from severe overcapacity. There is too much retail space—more than 18 square feet for every man, woman, and child, more than double that of 1972. Consumer demographics, lifestyles, and shopping patterns also are changing rapidly. Thus, the 1990s will be a difficult decade for retailers:

> Going-out-of-business signs, bankruptcy filings, and constant sales attest to tough times in the retail industry. Such mercantile stalwarts as B. Altman and Garfinkel's have disappeared. The parent company of Bloomingdale's, Burdines, and Rich's is in [bankruptcy]. Rumors abound about R. H. Macy and other potential casualties. . . . "Retailing is not an area of hope," says [one retailing executive]. "It's not fun. It's almost a war." And the casualties are almost certain to keep mounting. By the end of the '90s, . . . half of the nation's current retailers will be out of business. . . . The companies that succeed will be the ones that avoid crippling debt, focus tightly on specific customers or products, and hook into technology to hold down costs and enhance service. A tough act.[27]

To be successful, then, retailers will have to choose target segments carefully and position themselves strongly. Moreover, quickly rising costs will make more efficient operation and smarter buying essential to successful retailing. As a result, retail technologies are growing in importance as competitive tools. Progressive retailers are using computers to produce better forecasts, control inventory costs, order electronically from suppliers, communicate between stores, and even sell to consumers within stores. They are adopting checkout scanning systems, in-store television, on-line transaction processing, and electronic funds transfer.

Many retailing innovations are partially explained by the **wheel of retailing concept.**[28] According to this concept, many new types of retailing forms begin as low-margin, low-price, low-status operations. They challenge established retailers that have become "fat" by letting their costs and margins increase. The new retailers' success leads them to upgrade their facilities and offer more services. In turn, their costs increase, forcing them to increase their prices. Eventually, the new retailers become like the conventional retailers they replaced. The cycle begins again when still newer types of retailers evolve with lower costs and prices. The wheel of retailing concept seems to explain the initial success and later troubles of department stores, supermarkets, and discount stores and the recent success of off-price retailers.

New retail forms will continue to emerge to meet new consumer needs and new situations. But the life cycle of new retail forms is getting shorter. Department stores took about 100 years to reach the mature stage of the life cycle; more recent forms, such as catalog showrooms and furniture warehouse stores, reached maturity in about ten years. In such an environment, seemingly solid retail positions can crumble quickly. For example, of the top ten discount retailers in 1962 (the year that Wal-Mart and Kmart began), not one still exists today. Thus, retailers can no longer sit back with a successful formula. To remain successful, they must keep adapting.[29]

WHOLESALING

Wholesaling includes all activities involved in selling goods and services to those buying for resale or business use. A retail bakery is engaging in wholesaling when it sells pastry to the local hotel. We call **wholesalers** those firms engaged *primarily* in wholesaling activity.

Wholesalers buy mostly from producers and sell mostly to retailers, industrial consumers, and other wholesalers. But why are wholesalers used at all? For example, why would a producer use wholesalers rather than selling directly to retailers or consumers? Quite simply, wholesalers are often better at performing one or more of the following channel functions:

- *Selling and promoting.* Wholesalers' salesforces help manufacturers reach many small customers at a low cost. The wholesaler has more contacts and is often more trusted by the buyer than the distant manufacturer.

- *Buying and assortment building.* Wholesalers can select items and build assortments needed by their customers, thereby saving the consumers much work.

- *Bulk-breaking.* Wholesalers save their customers money by buying in carload lots and breaking bulk (breaking large lots into small quantities).

- *Warehousing.* Wholesalers hold inventories, thereby reducing the inventory costs and risks of suppliers and customers.

- *Transportation.* Wholesalers can provide quicker delivery to buyers because they are closer than the producers.

- *Financing.* Wholesalers finance their customers by giving credit, and they finance their suppliers by ordering early and paying bills on time.

- *Risk bearing.* Wholesalers absorb risk by taking title and bearing the cost of theft, damage, spoilage, and obsolescence.

- *Market information.* Wholesalers give information to suppliers and customers about competitors, new products, and price developments.

- *Management services and advice.* Wholesalers often help retailers train their salesclerks, improve store layouts and displays, and set up accounting and inventory control systems.

TYPES OF WHOLESALERS

Wholesalers fall into three major groups (see Table 15-3): *merchant wholesalers, brokers and agents,* and *manufacturers' sales branches and offices.*

Merchant Wholesalers

Merchant wholesalers are independently owned businesses that take title to the merchandise they handle. They are the largest single group of wholesalers, accounting for roughly 50 percent of all wholesaling. Merchant wholesalers include two broad types: *full-service wholesalers* and *limited-service wholesalers.*

Full-Service Wholesalers

Full-service wholesalers provide a full set of services, such as carrying stock, using a salesforce, offering credit, making deliveries, and providing management assistance. They are either *wholesale merchants* or *industrial distributors.*

Wholesale merchants sell mostly to retailers and provide a full range of services. They vary in the width of their product line. Some carry several lines of goods to meet the needs of both general-merchandise retailers and single-line retailers. Others carry one or two lines of goods in a greater depth of assortment.

| | | MANUFACTURERS' AND |
MERCHANT WHOLESALERS	BROKERS AND AGENTS	RETAILERS' BRANCHES AND OFFICES
Full-service wholesalers	Brokers	Sales branches and offices
Wholesale merchants	Agents	Purchasing offices
Industrial distributors		
Limited-service wholesalers		
Cash-and-carry wholesalers		
Truck wholesalers		
Drop shippers		
Rack jobbers		
Producers' cooperatives		
Mail-order wholesalers		

TABLE 15-3
Classification of Wholesalers

Examples are hardware wholesalers, drug wholesalers, and clothing wholesalers. Some specialty wholesalers carry only part of a line in great depth, such as health food wholesalers, seafood wholesalers, and automotive parts wholesalers. They offer customers deeper choice and greater product knowledge.

Industrial distributors are merchant wholesalers that sell to producers rather than to retailers. They provide inventory, credit, delivery, and other services. They may carry a broad range of merchandise, a general line, or a specialty line. Industrial distributors may concentrate on lines such as maintenance and operating supplies, original-equipment goods (such as ball bearings and motors), or equipment (such as power tools and forklift trucks).

Limited-Service Wholesalers

Limited-service wholesalers offer fewer services to their suppliers and customers. There are several types of limited-service wholesalers.

Cash-and-carry wholesalers have a limited line of fast-moving goods, sell to small retailers for cash, and normally do not deliver. A small fish store retailer, for example, normally drives at dawn to a cash-and-carry fish wholesaler and buys several crates of fish, pays on the spot, drives the merchandise back to the store, and unloads it.

Truck wholesalers (also called *truck jobbers*) perform a selling and delivery function. They carry a limited line of goods (such as milk, bread, or snack foods) that they sell for cash as they make their rounds of supermarkets, small groceries, hospitals, restaurants, factory cafeterias, and hotels.

Drop shippers operate in bulk industries such as coal, lumber, and heavy equipment. They do not carry inventory or handle the product. Once an order is received, they find a producer who ships the goods directly to the customer. The drop shipper takes title and risk from the time the order is accepted to the time it is delivered to the customer. Because drop shippers do not carry inventory, their costs are lower and they can pass on some savings to customers.

Rack jobbers serve grocery and drug retailers, mostly in the area of nonfood items. These retailers do not want to order and maintain displays of hundreds of

Merchant wholesalers: A typical Fleming Companies, Inc. wholesale food distribution center. The average Fleming warehouse contains 500,000 square feet of floor space (with 30-foot high ceiling), carries 16,000 different food items, and serves 150 to 200 retailers within a 500-mile radius.

nonfood items. Rack jobbers send delivery trucks to stores, and the delivery person sets up racks of toys, paperbacks, hardware items, health and beauty aids, or other items. They price the goods, keep them fresh, and keep inventory records. Rack jobbers sell on consignment; they retain title to the goods and bill the retailers only for the goods sold to consumers. Thus, they provide services such as delivery, shelving, inventory, and financing. They do little promotion because they carry many branded items that are already highly advertised.

Producers' cooperatives, owned by farmer-members, assemble farm produce to sell in local markets. Their profits are divided among members at the end of the year. They often try to improve product quality and promote a co-op brand name, such as Sun Maid raisins, Sunkist oranges, or Diamond walnuts.

Mail-order wholesalers send catalogs to retail, industrial, and institutional customers offering jewelry, cosmetics, special foods, and other small items. Their main customers are businesses in small outlying areas. They have no salesforces to call on customers. The orders are filled and sent by mail, truck, or other means.

Brokers and Agents

Brokers and *agents* differ from merchant wholesalers in two ways: They do not take title to goods, and they perform only a few functions. Their main function is to aid in buying and selling, and for these services they earn a commission on the selling price. Like merchant wholesalers, they generally specialize by product line or customer type. They account for 11 percent of the total wholesale volume.

Brokers

A **broker** brings buyers and sellers together and assists in negotiation. Brokers are paid by the parties hiring them. They do not carry inventory, get involved in financing, or assume risk. The most familiar examples are food brokers, real estate brokers, insurance brokers, and security brokers.

Agents

Agents represent buyers or sellers on a more permanent basis. There are several types. *Manufacturers' agents* (also called manufacturers' representatives) are the most common type of agent wholesaler. They represent two or more manufacturers of related lines. They have a formal agreement with each manufacturer, covering prices, territories, order-handling procedures, delivery and warranties, and commission rates. They know each manufacturer's product line and use their wide contacts to sell the products. Manufacturers' agents are used in lines such as apparel, furniture, and electrical goods. Most manufacturers' agents are small businesses, with only a few employees who are skilled salespeople. They are hired by small producers who cannot afford to maintain their own field salesforces and by large producers who want to open new territories or sell in areas that cannot support a full-time salesperson.

Selling agents contract to sell a producer's entire output—either the manufacturer is not interested in doing the selling or feels unqualified. The selling agent serves as a sales department and has much influence over prices, terms, and conditions of sale. The selling agent normally has no territory limits. Selling agents are found in product areas such as textiles, industrial machinery and equipment, coal and coke, chemicals, and metals.

Purchasing agents generally have a long-term relationship with buyers. They make purchases for buyers and often receive, inspect, warehouse, and ship goods to the buyers. One type of purchasing agent is *resident buyers* in major apparel markets—purchasing specialists who look for apparel lines that can be carried by small retailers located in small cities. They know a great deal about their product lines and provide helpful market information to clients and also can obtain the best goods and prices available.

Commission merchants (or houses) are agents that take physical possession of products and negotiate sales. They normally are not used on a long-term basis. They are used most often in agricultural marketing by farmers who do not want to sell their own output and who do not belong to cooperatives. Typically, the commission merchant will take a truckload of farm products to a central market, sell it for the best price, deduct expenses and a commission, and pay the balance to the farmer.

Manufacturers' Sales Branches and Offices

The third major type of wholesaling is that done in **manufacturers' sales branches and offices** by sellers or buyers themselves rather than through independent wholesalers. Manufacturers' offices and sales branches account for about 31 percent of all wholesale volume. Manufacturers often set up their own sales branches and offices to improve inventory control, selling, and promotion. *Sales branches* carry inventory and are found in industries such as lumber and automotive equipment and parts. *Sales offices* do not carry inventory and most often are found in the dry goods and notion industries. Many retailers set up *purchasing offices* in major market centers such as New York City and Chicago. These purchasing offices perform a role similar to that of brokers or agents, but are part of the buyer's organization.

WHOLESALER MARKETING DECISIONS

Wholesalers have experienced mounting competitive pressures in recent years. They have faced new sources of competition, more demanding customers, new technologies, and more direct-buying programs on the part of large industrial, institutional, and retail buyers. As a result, they have had to improve their strategic decisions on target markets, product assortments and services, price, promotion, and place.

Target Market Decision

Like retailers, wholesalers must define their target markets—they cannot serve everyone. They can choose a target group by size of customer (only large retailers), type of customer (convenience food stores only), need for service (customers who need credit), or other factors. Within the target group, they can identify the more profitable customers, design stronger offers, and build better relationships with them. They can propose automatic reordering systems, set up management-training and advising systems, or even sponsor a voluntary chain. They can discourage less profitable customers by requiring larger orders or adding service charges to smaller ones.

Product Assortment and Services Decision

The wholesaler's "product" is its assortment. Wholesalers are under great pressure to carry a full line and to stock enough for immediate delivery. But this practice can damage profits. Wholesalers today are cutting down on the number of lines they carry, choosing to carry only the more profitable ones. Wholesalers also are rethinking which services count most in building strong customer relationships and which should be dropped or charged for. The key is to find the mix of services most valued by their target customers.

Price Decision

Wholesalers usually mark up the cost of goods by a standard percentage—say, 20 percent. Expenses may run 17 percent of the gross margin, leaving a profit margin of 3 percent. In grocery wholesaling, the average profit margin is often less than 2 percent. Wholesalers are trying new pricing approaches. They may cut their margin on some lines in order to win important new customers. They may ask suppliers for special price breaks when they can turn them into an increase in the suppliers' sales.

Promotion Decision

Most wholesalers are not promotion-minded. Their use of trade advertising, sales promotion, personal selling, and public relations is largely scattered and unplanned. Many are behind the times in personal selling—they still see selling as a single salesperson talking to a single customer instead of as a team effort to sell, build, and service major accounts. Wholesalers also need to adopt some of the nonpersonal promotion techniques used by retailers. They need to develop an overall promotion strategy and to make greater use of supplier promotion materials and programs.

Place Decision

Wholesalers typically locate in low-rent, low-tax areas and tend to invest little money in their buildings, equipment, and systems. As a result, their materials-handling and order-processing systems are often outdated. In recent years, however, large and progressive wholesalers are reacting to rising costs by investing in automated warehouses and on-line ordering systems. Orders are fed from the retailer's system directly into the wholesaler's computer, and the items are picked up by mechanical devices and automatically taken to a shipping platform where they are assembled. Many wholesalers are turning to computers to carry out accounting, billing, inventory control, and forecasting. Progressive wholesalers are adapting their services to the needs of target customers and finding cost-reducing methods of doing business.

TRENDS IN WHOLESALING

Progressive wholesalers constantly watch for better ways to meet the changing needs of their suppliers and target customers. They recognize that, in the long run, their only reason for existence comes from increasing the efficiency and effectiveness of the entire marketing channel. To achieve this goal, they must constantly improve their services and reduce their costs.

McKesson, a large drug wholesaler, provides an example of progressive wholesaling. To survive, McKesson had to remain more cost effective than manufacturers' sales branches. Thus, the company automated 72 of its warehouses, established direct computer links with 32 drug manufacturers, designed a computerized accounts-receivable program for pharmacists, and provided drugstores with computer terminals for ordering inventories. Retailers even can use the McKesson computer system to maintain medical profiles on their customers. Thus, McKesson has delivered better value to both manufacturers and retail customers.

One study predicts several developments in the wholesaling industry.[30] Consolidation will significantly reduce the number of wholesaling firms. The remaining wholesaling companies will grow larger, primarily through acquisition, merger, and geographic expansion. Geographic expansion will require distributors to learn how to compete effectively over wider and more diverse areas. The increased use of computerized and automated systems will help wholesalers. By 1990, more than three-fourths of all wholesalers were using on-line order systems.

The distinction between large retailers and large wholesalers continues to blur. Many retailers now operate formats such as wholesale clubs and hypermarkets that perform many wholesale functions. In return, many large wholesalers are setting up their own retailing operations. Super Valu and Flemming, both leading wholesalers, now operate their own retail outlets.

Wholesalers will continue to increase the services they provide to retailers—retail pricing, cooperative advertising, marketing and management information reports, accounting services, and others. Rising costs on the one hand, and the demand for increased services on the other, will put the squeeze on wholesaler profits. Wholesalers who do not find efficient ways to deliver value to their customers will soon drop by the wayside.

Finally, facing slow growth in their domestic markets and such developments as the North American Free Trade Agreement, many large wholesalers are

Drug wholesaler McKesson improved efficiency by setting up direct computer links with manufacturers and retail pharmacies.

now going global. The National Association of Wholesaler-Distributors predicts that, by the year 2000, wholesalers will generate 18 percent of their sales outside the United States, twice the current share.[31] For example, in 1991, McKesson bought out its Canadian partner, Provigo. The company now receives about 13 percent of its total revenues from Canada.

SUMMARY

Retailing and wholesaling consist of many organizations bringing goods and services from the point of production to the point of use. *Retailing* includes all activities involved in selling goods or services directly to final consumers for their personal, nonbusiness use. Retailers can be classified as store retailers and nonstore retailers. *Store retailers* can be further classified by the *amount of service* they provide (self-service, limited service, or full service); *product line sold* (specialty stores, department stores, supermarkets, convenience stores, combination stores, superstores, hypermarkets, and service businesses); *relative prices* (discount stores, off-price retailers, and catalog showrooms); *control of outlets* (corporate chains, voluntary chains and retailer cooperatives, franchise organizations, and merchandising conglomerates); and *type of store cluster* (central business districts and shopping centers).

Although most goods and services are sold through stores, nonstore retailing has been growing much faster than has store retailing. *Nonstore retailers* now account for more than 14 percent of all consumer purchases, and they may account for a third of all sales by the end of the century. Nonstore retailing consists of *direct marketing* (direct mail and catalog retailing, telemarketing, television marketing, and electronic shopping); *direct selling;* and *automatic vending.* Integrated direct marketing—using multiple-vehicle, multiple-stage campaigns—can greatly improve direct-marketing response. In order to employ integrated direct marketing, companies must develop effective marketing-database systems.

Each retailer must make decisions about its target markets, product assortment and services, price, promotion, and place. Retailers need to choose target markets carefully and position themselves strongly.

Wholesaling includes all the activities involved in selling goods or services to those who are buying for the purpose of resale or for business use. Wholesalers perform many functions, including selling and promoting, buying and assortment building, bulk-breaking, warehousing, transporting, financing, risk bearing, supplying market information, and providing management services and advice. Wholesalers fall into three groups. First, *merchant wholesalers* take possession of the goods. They include *full-service wholesalers* (wholesale merchants, industrial distributors) and *limited-service wholesalers* (cash-and-carry wholesalers, truck wholesalers, drop shippers, rack jobbers, producers' cooperatives, and mail-order wholesalers). Second, *agents* and *brokers* do not take possession of the goods but are paid a commission for aiding buying and selling. Finally, *manufacturers' sales branches and offices* are wholesaling operations conducted by nonwholesalers to bypass the wholesalers. Wholesaling is holding its own in the economy. Progressive wholesalers are adapting their services to the needs of target customers and are seeking cost-reducing methods of doing business.

KEY TERMS

Agent 452

Automatic vending 443

Broker 452

Catalog marketing 439

Catalog showroom 434

Chain stores 435

Combination stores 432

Convenience store 431

Department store 429

Direct-mail marketing 438

Direct marketing 436

Discount store 433

Door-to-door retailing 443

Electronic shopping 441

Factory outlets 433

Franchise 435

Full-service retailers 429

Full-service wholesalers 450

Hypermarkets 432

Independent off-price retailers 434

Integrated direct marketing 442

Limited-service retailers 429

Limited-service wholesalers 451

Manufacturers' sales branches and offices 453

Marketing database 442

Merchandising conglomerates 435

Merchant wholesalers 450

Off-price retailers 433

Retailers 428

Retailing 428

Self-service retailers 429

Shopping center 436

Specialty store 429

Supermarkets 430

Superstore 432

Telemarketing 440

Television marketing 441

Warehouse club (or wholesale club) 434

Wheel of retailing concept 449

Wholesaler 450

Wholesaling 450

DISCUSSING THE ISSUES

1. Which would do more to increase a convenience store's sales—an increase in the length or the breadth of its product assortment? Why?

2. Warehouse clubs that are restricted to members only, such as Costco and Sam's Wholesale, are growing rapidly. They offer a very broad but shallow line of products, often in institutional packaging, at very low prices. Some members buy for resale, others buy to supply a business, and still others buy for personal use. Are these stores wholesalers or retailers? How can you make a distinction?

3. Off-price retailers provide tough price competition to other retailers. Will large retailers' growing power in channels of distribution affect manufacturers' willingness to sell to off-price retailers at below regular wholesale rates? What policy should Sony have regarding selling to off-price retailers?

4. Postal rate hikes make it more expensive to send direct mail, catalogs, and purchased products to consumers. How would you expect direct-mail and catalog marketers to respond to an increase in postage rates?

5. A typical "country store" in a farming community sells a variety of food and nonfood items—snacks, staples, hardware, and many other types of goods. What kinds of wholesalers do the owners of such stores use to obtain the items they sell? Are these the same suppliers that a supermarket uses?

6. Are there any fundamental differences between retailers, wholesalers, and manufacturers in the types of marketing decisions they make? Give examples of the marketing decisions made by the three groups which show their similarities and differences.

APPLYING THE CONCEPTS

1. Collect all the catalogs that you have received in the mail recently. (a) Sort them by type of product line. Is there some pattern to the types of direct marketers that are targeting you? (b) Where do you think these catalog companies got your name? (c) How do you think a company that was selling your name and address to a direct marketer would describe your buying habits?

2. Watch a cable television shopping channel, or tune in to a late-night television shopping show (often found on UHF stations above channel 13). (a) How are these shows attempting to target buyers? Do they mix football cleats and fine china in the same program, or are they targeting more carefully? (b) How much of the merchandise shown appears to be close-outs? How can you tell?

MAKING MARKETING DECISIONS:

SMALL WORLD COMMUNICATIONS, INC.

Thomas Campbell and Lynette Jones are talking about where they will place their product through wholesaler and retailers. Tom was musing about where they might sell their product. "The retailing in this market is very hard to figure out. The market keeps growing, but retailers drop like flies. IBM tried to set up their own computer stores, but it didn't work. ComputerLand went bankrupt. CompuAdd, the direct marketer, opened a line of stores, but folded them in 1993 to go back to direct marketing. If we were doing a mass-market product, we could hit Wal-Mart and Kmart and potentially reach most people in America. It's clear that it will take a lot more work for us to put together a usable channel based on the computer specialty retailers that are still out there." "I wish it were easier, too," Lyn added, "but there *are* some other related national chains developing, like Egghead Software and Walden Software. Neither one sells computers, but both of them sell modems.

We might have a good shot at gaining distribution there. And don't forget the places like the wholesale clubs and discount office superstores. They are all selling computers to individuals and small businesses, and I think that's a good place for us to be. The next challenge is to assemble a network of agents to help us sell this. *That* should make for a pretty intense project." "Well," Tom replied cheerily, "it's better to burn out than it is to rust. Let's get this plan rolling."

WHAT NOW?

1. Small World is considering targeting two types of off-price retailers: warehouse clubs like Sam's Wholesale, and discount office supply stores like Office Depot. (a) What type of customers is each of these outlets likely to serve? (b) How well does the Airport product—a complex, fairly ex-

pensive piece of computer gear—"fit" in these outlets? (c) What advantages would Small World gain by distributing through these retailers?

2. The Small World Airport is designed for serious electronic communication users. These potential customers already use many electronic databases and services such as Prodigy and CompuServe. Most of these services now sell advertising "space" and offer direct sales capability. (a) Is this a good retailing environment for Small World? Why or why not? (b) How important do you think this channel might be for Small World now? Five or ten years in the future?

REFERENCES

1. The quote is from Steve Weiner, "With Big Selections and Low Prices, 'Category Killer' Stores Are a Hit," *The Wall Street Journal*, June 17, 1986, p. 33. Also see Bill Saporito, "IKEA's Got 'Em Lining Up," *Fortune*, March 11, 1991, p. 72; Jeffrey Trachenberg, "IKEA Furniture Chain Pleases with Its Prices, Not with Its Service," *The Wall Street Journal*, September 17, 1991; and "North America's Top 100 Furniture Stores," *Furniture Today*, May 18, 1992, p. 50.

2. For more on department stores, see Arthur Braff, "Will Department Stores Survive?" *Sales and Marketing Management*, April 1986, pp. 60-64; Laura Zinn, "Who Will Survive," *Business Week*, November 26, 1990, pp. 134-44; and Alison Fahey, "Department Store Outlook," *Advertising Age*, January 28, 1991, p. 23.

3. See Toni Mack, "A Six-Pack of Cabernet, Please," *Forbes*, September 18, 1989, pp. 168-69; "Stop-N-Go Micromarkets New Upscale Mix," *Chain Store Age Executive*, January 1990, p. 145; and Christy Fisher, "Convenience Chains Pump for New Life," *Advertising Age*, April 23, 1990, p. 80.

4. See Ruth Hamel, "Food Fight," *American Demographics*, March 1989, p. 38.

5. See Kevin Kelly, "Wal-Mart Gets Lost in the Vegetable Aisle," *Business Week*, May 28, 1990, p. 48; and Laurie M. Grossman, "Hypermarkets: A Sure-Fire Hit Bombs," *The Wall Street Journal*, June 25, 1992, p. B1.

6. See Debra Rosenberg, "Where the Price Is Always Right," *Newsweek*, January 13, 1992, p. 45; and Adrienne Ward, "New Breed of Mall Knows: Everyone Loves a Bargain," *Advertising Age*, January 27, 1992, p. S5.

7. See "Why Franchising Is Taking Off," *Fortune*, February 12, 1990, p. 124.

8. Chip Walker, "Strip Malls: Plain but Powerful," *American Demographics*, October 1991, pp. 48-50.

9. See Francesca Turchiano, "The Unmalling of America," *American Demographics*, April 1990, pp. 36-42; Kate Fitzgerald, "Mega Malls: Built for the '90s, or the '80s?" *Advertising Age*, January 27, 1992, pp. S1, S8; and David Greising, "Guys and Malls: The Simons' Crapshoot," *Business Week*, April 17, 1992, pp. 52-53.

10. See Mary Lou Roberts and Paul D. Berger, *Direct Marketing Management* (Englewood Cliffs, NJ: Prentice Hall, 1989), pp. 11-15.

11. See Eileen Norris, "Alternative Media Try to Get Their Feet in the Door," *Advertising Age*, October 17, 1985, p. 15.

12. Annetta Miller, "Up to the Chin in Catalogs," *Newsweek*, November 20, 1989, pp. 57-58; Cyndee Miller, "Sears, Penney Revamp Catalogues to Compete with Specialty Books," *Marketing News*, April 1, 1991, pp. 1, 6; Kate Fitzgerald, "Catalogers Brace for Major Cutbacks," *Advertising Age*, April 15, 1991, p. 35; and Kate Fitzgerald, "Shopping by the Book," *Advertising Age*, October 7, 1991, p. 4.

13. Richard L. Bencin, "Telefocus: Telemarketing Gets Synergized," *Sales & Marketing Management*, February 1992, pp. 49-53, here p. 50.

14. Bristol Voss, "Calling All Catalogs!" *Sales & Marketing Management*, December 1990, pp. 32-37.

15. Rudy Oetting, "Telephone Marketing: Where We've Been and Where We Should Be Going," *Direct Marketing*, February 1987, p. 98.

16. For more discussion, see Junu Bryan Kim, "800/900: King of the Road in Marketing Value, Usage," *Advertising Age*, February 17, 1992, pp. S1, S4.

17. Bill Kelley, "Is There Anything that Can't Be Sold by Phone?" *Sales & Marketing Management*, April 1989, pp. 60-64; Rudy Oetting and Geri Gantman, "Dial M for Maximize," *Sales & Marketing Management*, June 1991, pp. 100-106.

18. See Dan Fost, "Privacy Concerns Threaten Database Marketing," *American Demographics*, May 1990, pp. 18-21; and Michael W. Miller, "Lawmakers Are Hoping to RIng Out Era of Unrestricted Calls by Telemarketers," *The Wall Street Journal*, May 28, 1991, pp. B1, B5.

19. Jim Auchmute, "But Wait There's More!" *Advertising Age*, October 17, 1985, p. 18.

20. See Howard Schlossberg, "Picture Still Looks Bright for TV Shopping Networks," *Marketing News*, October 23, 1989, p. 8; and Laura Zinn, "Home Shoppers Keep Tuning In—But Investors Are Turned Off," *Business Week*, October 22, 1990, pp. 70-72.

21. See Rebecca Piirto, "Over the Line," *American Demographics*, July 1992, p. 6; Evan I. Schwartz, "Prodigy Installs a New Program," *Business Week*, September 14, 1992, pp. 96-100; and Scott Donaton, "Prodigy Overhauls Marketing Setup," *Advertising Age*, January 18, 1993, p. 4.

22. Ernin Roman, *Integrated Direct Marketing* (New York: McGraw-Hill, 1988), p. 108.

23. See Joe Schwartz, "Databases Deliver the Goods," *American Demographics*, September 1989, pp. 23-25; Lynn G. Coleman, "Data-Base Masters Become King in the Marketplace," *Marketing News*, February 18, 1991, pp. 13, 18; Laura Loro, "Data Bases Seen As Driving Force," *Advertising Age*, March 18, 1991, p. 39; and Gary Levin, "Database Draws Fevered Interest," *Advertising Age*, June 8, 1992, p. 31.

24. See J. Taylor Buckley, "Machines Start New Fast-Food Era," *USA Today*, July 19, 1991, pp. B1, B2; and Laurie McLaughlin, "Vending Machines Open to New Ideas," *Advertising Age*, August 19, 1991, p. 35.

25. For a fuller discussion, see Lawrence H. Wortzel, "Retailing Strategies for Today's Mature Marketplace," *The Journal of Business Strategy*, Spring 1987, pp. 45-56.

26. For more discussion, see Mary Jo Bitner, "Servicescapes: The Impact of Physical Surroundings on Customers and Employees," *Journal of Marketing,* April 1992, pp. 57-71.

27. Laura Zinn, "Retailing: Who Will Survive?" *Business Week,* November 26, 1990, p. 134. Also see Susan Caminiti, "The New Retailing Champs," *Fortune,* September 24, 1990, pp. 85-100.

28. See Malcolm P. McNair and Eleanor G. May, "The Next Revolution of the Retailing Wheel, *Harvard Business Review,* September–October 1978, pp. 81-91; and Eleanor G. May, "A Retail Odyssey," *Journal of Retailing,* Fall 1989, pp. 356-67.

29. Bill Saporito, "Is Wal-Mart Unstoppable?" *Fortune,* May 6, 1991, pp. 50-59. For more on retailing trends, see Eleanor G. May, C. William Ress, and Walter J. Salmon, *Future Trends in*

Retailing (Cambridge, MA: Marketing Science Institute, February 1985); Daniel Sweeney, "Toward 2000," *Chain Store Age Executive,* January 1990, pp. 27-39; and Louis W. Stern and Adel I. El-Ansary, *Marketing Channels* (Englewood Cliffs, NJ: Prentice Hall, 1992).

30. See Arthur Andersen & Co., *Facing the Forces of Change: Beyond Future Trends in Wholesale Distribution* (Washington, DC: Distribution Research and Education Foundation, 1987), p. 7. Also see Joseph Weber, "Mom and Pop Move Out of Wholesaling," *Business Week,* January 9, 1989, p. 91; and Weber, "It's 'Like Somebody Had Shot the Postman,' " *Business Week,* January 13, 1992, p. 82.

31. Joseph Weber, "On a Fast Boat to Anywhere," *Business Week,* January 11, 1993, p. 94.

VIDEO CASE 15

THE McDUDS OF RETAILING

In 1991, while traditional retailers experienced one of their worst years ever, retailers using a value positioning prospered. Consequently, value has become a key retailing buzzword for this decade. Although value is not a new concept, its meaning has changed. No longer does it mean offering the lowest priced goods, or even low-priced goods. Instead, it means offering the right styles and quality at the right price for the target consumer.

Although value positioning is most closely associated with off-price and discount retailers, it has enabled specialty retailer the Gap to become the hottest retailer of the 1990s. While domestic apparel spending dropped 2.4 percent in 1991, sales of Gap stores shot up 30 percent. Gap stock prices rocketed from 4 in 1987 to around 50 by early 1992, with a price-earnings ratio of 35. These are very heady numbers for a retailer.

What makes the Gap so successful? There are five key factors. First, the Gap concentrates on basics. It sells staple items—jeans, shirts, skirts, and jackets—all in relatively basic designs. The Gap is not trendy and it does not pander to short-lived fashions.

Second, the Gap has extended the concept of basic values from casual clothes for adults to casual clothes for the entire family, both at work and at play. By including cotton jackets, ties, and khaki slacks in its product mix, it has exploited the trend toward more relaxed dress standards for work in the 1990s. The chain's GapKids stores and BabyGap departments let all family members buy clothing from the Gap. With its "something for everyone in the family" strategy, the Gap hopes to become to apparel what McDonald's is to food. Hence, some have tagged it "the McDuds of retailing."

Third, as consumers have begun to avoid malls, the Gap has followed them by locating new stores in strip shopping centers and even in downtown areas. These locations capitalize on another consumer trend—a distaste for shopping and lack of time for it. In the 1990s, consumers are less willing to spend time driving to large

malls and walking great distances through parking lots, up and down stairs, and down long walkways. More consumers are planning their shopping and patronizing easily accessible stores that satisfy a variety of needs.

Fourth, the Gap turns its merchandise rapidly—every two months rather than the usual 3.5 times a year. Slow-selling items are marked down and quickly moved out. As a result, consumers can usually find something new at the Gap, even when they shop there frequently.

Finally, the Gap keeps tight control over store operations. All of its stores have the same open, clean look. All have wooden floors that are cleaned and polished twice a week. Merchandise is folded and placed on tables according to color and size, with only a few items located on pipe racks. Consequently, consumers can actually look around the racks to view and evaluate the store's offerings. The table arrangements help shoppers select colors and sizes quickly. In addition, all Gap stores are laid out in a similar fashion, helping consumers to adjust quickly when shopping in a new Gap store.

The Gap also maintains tight control over non-store operations through a highly advanced distribution network. In early 1992, it opened a $75 billion fully computerized distribution center. This fast-response operation keeps inventory from 14 receiving docks in as many as 54,000 totes (large cartons of assorted goods) moving along 9,000 feet of conveyors to 8 constantly rotating storage racks, each of which can hold 54,272 totes. Each storage rack can be programmed by computer to release totes to conveyors, which transport them to work stations where goods are sorted and reassembled for shipment to individual stores. At peak operating capacity, this center can ship nearly 15,000 cartons of assorted goods to more than 300 East Coast Gap stores daily. Such tight controls support rapid changes of in-store merchandise and help to hold down costs.

The Gap has achieved a dominant position in retailing, a position that critics claim it cannot maintain.

When the economy improves, these critics assert, consumers will revert to spending on trendier high-fashion items. Perhaps. But management at the Gap are betting that postrecession consumers keep the Gap going strong. And so are Gap stock investors.

QUESTIONS

1. What type of retailer is the Gap?

2. Describe the Gap's target market and why the Gap's value positioning appeals to this market.

3. How do the Gap's product assortment, pricing strategy, location, and atmosphere convey the store's positioning?

4. Suppose that critics are right in predicting that consumers will become less value oriented. How might the Gap change to appeal to these less frugal consumers?

Sources: Gary Forger, "Breakthrough System Helps the Gap Ship to Hundreds of Stores," *Modern Materials Handling,* May 1992, pp. 42-46; Russell Mitchell, "The Gap—Can the Nation's Hottest Retailer Stay on Top?" *Business Week,* March 9, 1992, pp. 58-64; Laura Richardson, "State of the Industry: Value-Priced Apparel Stores Attract Recession-Weary Shoppers," *Chain Store Age Executive,* August 1992, pp. A34-A35; and Maria Shao, "Everybody's Falling into the Gap," *Business Week,* September 23, 1991, p. 36.

COMPANY CASE 15

PACE MEMBERSHIP WAREHOUSE: BULKING UP FOR COMPETITION

The first customers who entered the new PACE Membership Warehouse in Atlanta's Buckhead section were surprised. In addition to the normal cases of toilet tissue, extra large bottles of ketchup, and reams of copier paper, these customers found Christian Dior shirts, Sony televisions, and Dom Perignon champagne. As they wandered through the massive 137,000 square foot store (about two-and-one-third football fields), they also discovered an eyeglass department and a fresh-food center. In contrast to the typical dim appearance of most warehouse clubs, PACE had painted the ceiling white to brighten the atmosphere. When the customers got hungry from all that shopping, they could sit at tables located in the store's foyer and have a hot dog.

PACE, a subsidiary of Kmart, expected to open between 20 and 25 new stores like the one in Atlanta during 1993. The typical PACE store would be only 108,000 square feet with about 8,500 square feet devoted to fresh produce, meat, and a bakery. Officials predicted that these new departments would boost shopping frequency and increase the total average purchase by between 5 and 10 percent.

PACE, like other warehouse membership clubs (WMCs), found that it needed to make changes to respond to increasing competition and changing consumers. One of the big four WMC competitors, PACE lagged far behind Sam's, a division of Wal-Mart (see Exhibit 15-1).

Warehouse Membership Clubs

The WMC format emerged in the late 1970s and 1980s primarily to serve small-business customers. These customers were not large enough to take advantage of lower prices offered to bigger businesses that bought in large quantities. WMCs, however, bought in quantity and passed the lower prices on to their smaller customers. Because target customers bought items for resale or for use

EXHIBIT 15-1
Wholesale Club Volume

WHOLESALE CLUB	1992 EST. VOLUME (MILLIONS)	1992 UNITS
Sam's Club	$13,500	250
Price Company	7,500	82
Costco Wholesale Club	6,500	89
PACE Membership Warehouse	4,600	115
BJ's Wholesale Club	1,900	39
The Warehouse Club	233	10
Wholesale Depot	110	8
SourceClub	50	3
Bodega	40	2
Totals	$34,443	598

Source: Discount Merchandiser Research.

as operating supplies, the WMCs sold goods in bulk, such as whole cases, or in extra-large sizes.

Most warehouse clubs required customers to become members by paying a membership fee, usually around $25. This fee provided income to the club and increased customer loyalty. Customers shopped regularly because they had paid a membership fee.

From the beginning, the WMCs were operations driven. They had to keep their costs down in order to attract small-business customers. As a result, the clubs offered no-frills buying. They featured no fancy buildings or expensive scanning systems for checking out. They carried leading brands, but carried only a limited number of SKUs (stock-keeping units), typically 3,000 to 4,000. The typical discount store, in contrast, carried 70,000 to 80,000 SKUs. The warehouse clubs accepted cash only and focused on building high-inventory turnover. They offered little customer service. Customers had to lug their own large purchases, from cases of peaches to large appliances, to the check-out line themselves. Many were willing to put up with the inconvenience in order to take advantage of prices that were as much as 26 percent below regular supermarkets' prices.

The Customers

One analyst estimated that 12.2 percent of the U.S. population over 20 years of age (about 22 million people) were primary or secondary WMC members. Although WMCs primarily targeted businesses, they also allowed individuals to become members by paying a fee. As a result, by 1993 about 70 percent of WMC members were retail (household) members, whereas about 30 percent were business members. Business members, however, accounted for from 65 to 70 percent of WMCs' sales.

In 1992, the Babson College Retailing Research Group conducted a study of WMCs. The group surveyed 2,150 WMC customers in eight U.S. cities and three Canadian cities. In all 11 cities, more than half of the population knew about WMCs. However, the group found that the average number of shoppers who used WMCs at least four times a year ranged from 5 to 41 percent, with an average of 21 percent. The overall average shopping frequency was once every three weeks. In some cities one firm controlled from 80 to 100 percent of the market, whereas in others the market was highly competitive.

The typical WMC shopper had been a member for 35 months, and one-fourth of all shoppers took a friend, neighbor, or relative shopping with them. Shoppers tended to be more upscale than the general population, with 40 percent having family incomes over $50,000. Frequent shoppers accounted for a high percentage of WMC sales.

The Babson group examined household customer shopping habits. It found that 92 percent of cardholders bought food for their families at WMCs and that these customers spent $8 on food for their families for every $1 that businesses spent on food. The average family spent $90 on food per trip. The report estimated that WMCs captured 7 percent of all consumer food dollars. The Babson report concluded that the average family spent $75 per trip on nonfood products. Combining all purchases, the average family spend $160 per trip to a WMC, with an average shopping frequency of once every three weeks. The typical customer traveled 13 miles to a WMC, as compared with traveling an average distance of from one to two miles to a supermarket.

For business customers, the average customer spent $103 on food items and $114 on nonfood items. About 40 percent of both household and business shoppers bought fresh meats and fresh baked goods. Although conventional wisdom suggested that the typical business customer was a restaurant or convenience store, the study found that most small-business members bought both food and nonfood items. Nonfood items consisted primarily of office supplies and stationery.

The researchers asked both types of customers about their reactions to the WMC shopping experience. Shoppers complained about slow check-out service, security procedures, the size of the packages, the crowds, and the lack of brand consistency from month to month.

The Babson researchers concluded that the loss of individual household customers would hurt the WMCs more than the loss of business customers. As a result, they report that WMCs would increase their efforts to attract household customers.

The Competition

Sam's Club. Headquartered in Bentonville, Arkansas, Sam's was the largest WMC, having opened 50 units in 1992. Sales for the fiscal year ending in 1993 were expected to top $13.5 billion, up 44 percent from 1992. Sam's used two prototype store designs: a 130,000 square-foot store that featured fresh meat, deli, produce, and bakery departments, and a 100,000 square-foot store without those departments. Until 1991, Sam's had been different from the other WMCs in that it did not require a membership fee. However, Sam's had changed its policy and was phasing out its no-fee memberships. By 1993, it expected to have only paid memberships.

Wal-Mart, in a joint venture with Mexican retailer CIFRA, SA, opened its first Club Aurrera in Mexico City in 1992 and had plans to open between six and eight more. Sam's was also examining the possibility of entering England.

Price Club. This WMC, headquartered in San Diego, operated 70 units in the United States, 12 in Canada, and one in Mexico. Price, however, had a sizable business presence in California, and the recession in that state had hurt its overall business. As a result, although it still planned to expand into the Midwest market, Price was reevaluating its expansion plans. Price's 130,000 square-foot stores, like Wal-Mart, featured fresh-food departments. Price was also experimenting with a "Touch & Shop" system that allowed customers to select merchandise by touching a computer screen. The computer then generated a ticket that guided workers who retrieved the item from the warehouse.

Costco. Headquartered in Kirkland, Washington, Costco operated 78 stores in the United States and 11 in Canada. The firm planned to open 20 new stores in 1993. Costco was experimenting with a new 30,000 square-foot home improvement section, high-priced gift sections, one-hour photo labs, and sandwich shops. Costco's typical stores were 118,000 square feet in size. Officials indicated that Costco would concentrate its growth primarily in markets that it already served.

BJ's. Headquartered in Natick, Massachusetts, BJ's concentrated mostly on the East Coast and operated 39 stores at the end of 1992. It intended to open from 10 to 15 new clubs per year. The firm concentrated on adding new departments and also on improving and upgrading its product assortment. Herb Zarkin, BJ's president, noted that he wanted customers to be excited when they entered his stores. Therefore, he had added new brand names, such as Toshiba, Panasonic, Polo, and Bugle Boy. Management was also considering adding a pharmacy. BJ's typical store had 115,000 square feet. Unlike the other WMCs, BJ's had added check-out scanners.

Other Competitors. Wholesale Depot, The Warehouse Club, SourceClub, and Bodega were smaller competitors that followed the industry leaders but were also trying new ideas. Some were experimenting with fax-in orders, children's clothes, and telemarketing. SourceClub, operating in Michigan, eliminated the traditional membership restrictions but charged $20 for a membership. It sought to provide a "hassle-free wholesale membership club that anyone can join." Bodega, of San Antonio, Texas, opened two 35,000 square-foot stores. Although smaller, they were like warehouse clubs except that membership was free. Both units were doing well in Hispanic areas.

PACE's Challenge

PACE and the other firms face three problems. First, the once dizzying industry growth rate has slowed. After growing at a 28 percent annual rate from 1986 through 1991, the $34 billion industry seems to have lost some of its flash. Same-store sales for both Sam's and PACE have dipped, reversing double-digit gains for both firms through the middle of 1992. Some analysts feel this slower growth rate, if it continues, will force a painful consolidation in the industry. Only the largest and strongest firms will survive.

Second, competition is increasing. A few years ago, a WMC might well have found a target city and have been the only WMC in town. With each of the firms trying to grow and with only so many markets large enough to support these large stores, increased competition is inevitable. For example, Sam's, which already has five stores in Atlanta, will open a sixth store less than a mile from the new PACE store. Moreover, supermarkets are not sitting idly by as they lose market share. Many are installing "power aisles" that feature warehouse-style products. "Category-killer" stores, such as Office Depot and OfficeMax, threaten to take away WMCs' business by focusing on price in certain key categories.

Finally, how can PACE and the other WMCs differentiate themselves from each other and from the competition? With every store seemingly trying the same things, how can each stand out?

QUESTIONS

1. Are warehouse membership clubs retailers or wholesalers?

2. How would you classify WMCs, using the categories for classifying retail outlets discussed in the chapter?

3. What retailer/wholesaler marketing decisions have WMCs made? How are those decisions changing?

4. What do you think will happen in the WMC industry during the next five years?

5. What marketing actions should PACE's management take to help it deal with the challenges it faces?

Sources: Debra Chanil, "Wholesale Clubs: Romancing America," Discount Merchandiser, November 1992, pp. 26-41; Terry Cotter, Stephen J. Arnold, and Douglas Tigert, "Warehouse Membership Clubs in North America," Discount Merchandiser, November 1992, pp. 42-47, used with permission. Also see: James M. Degen, "Warehouse Clubs Move from Revolution to Evolution," Marketing News, August 3, 1992, p. 8; Edd Johns, "Marketing Strategies Come to Warehouse Clubs," Chain Store Age Executive, August 1992, pp. 32A-33A; Zachary Schiller, Wendy Zellner, Ron Stodghill, II, and Mark Maremont, "Clout! More and More, Retail Giants Rule the Marketplace," Business Week, December 21, 1992, pp. 66-73; and Susannah Vessey, "PACE Store Reflects Bid to Meet New Challenges," The Atlanta Journal and The Atlanta Constitution, April 30, 1993, pp. F1-F2.

Promoting Products: Communication and Promotion Strategy

*M*ost Quaker Oats brands have become staples in American pantries. Quaker dominates the hot-cereal market with a whopping 61-percent share, and its Aunt Jemima brand is tops in frozen-breakfast products and pancake mixes. Quaker captures 25 percent of the huge dog food market (Gravy Train, Gainesburgers, Cycle, Ken-L Ration, Kibbles 'n Bits). Moreover, it's the number-four ready-to-eat cereal producer (Cap'n Crunch, Life, Oat Squares, 100% Natural). Other leading Quaker brands include Gatorade, Van Camp's Pork and Beans, Granola Bars, Celeste pizza, and Rice-A-Roni. Brands with leading market shares account for over 60 percent of Quaker's $5.5 billion in yearly sales.

A company the size of Quaker has a lot to say to its many publics and several promotion tools with which to say it. Hundreds of Quaker employees work in advertising, personal selling, sales promotion, and public relations units around the company. A half dozen large advertising and public relations agencies aim carefully planned communications at consumers, retailers, the media, stockholders, employees, and other publics.

As consumers, we know a good deal about Quaker's advertising: Each year Quaker bombards us with about $329 million worth of advertising that tells us about its brands and tries to persuade us to buy them. Quaker also spends heavily on consumer sales promotions, such as coupons, premiums, and sweepstakes, to coax us further. You may remember the "Treasure Hunt" promotion in which Quaker gave away $5 million in silver and gold coins randomly inserted in Ken-L Ration packages. Then there was the "Where's the Cap'n?" promotion: Quaker removed the picture of Cap'n Horatio Crunch from the front of its cereal boxes and then provided clues to his location on the back. Consumers who used the clues to find the Cap'n could win cash prizes. The 14-week promotion cost Quaker $18 million but increased sales by 50 percent. Consumer advertising

and sales promotions work directly to create consumer demand, and this demand "pulls" Quaker products through its channel.

But consumer advertising and sales promotions account for only a small portion of Quaker's total promotion mix. The company spends many times as much on behind-the-scenes promotion activities that "push" its products toward consumers. Personal selling and trade promotions are major weapons in Quaker's battle for retailer support. The company's main objective is shelf space in over 300,000 supermarkets, convenience stores, and corner groceries across the country. Quaker's army of salespeople court retailers with strong service, trade allowances, attractive displays, and other trade promotions. They urge retailers to give Quaker products more and better shelf space and to run ads featuring Quaker brands. These push-promotion activities work closely with pull-promotion efforts to build sales and market share. The pull activities persuade consumers to look for Quaker brands; the push activities ensure that Quaker products are available, easy to find, and effectively merchandised when consumers start looking.

In addition to advertising, sales promotion, and personal selling, Quaker communicates through publicity and public relations. The company's publicity department and public relations agency place newsworthy information about Quaker and its products in the news media. They prepare annual and quarterly reports to communicate with investors and financial publics, and hold press conferences to communicate with the media publics. Quaker sponsors many public relations activities to promote the company's image as a good citizen. For example, each year the Quaker Oats Foundation donates millions of dollars in cash and products to worthy causes, matches employee donations to nonprofit organizations, donates food to needy people, and supports a network of centers providing therapy for families with handicapped children.

Quaker owes much of its success to quality products that appeal strongly to millions of consumers around the world. But success also depends on Quaker's skill in telling its publics about the company and its products. All of Quaker's promotion tools—advertising, personal selling, sales promotion, and public relations—must blend harmoniously into an effective communication program that tells the Quaker story.[1]

 # CHAPTER PREVIEW

Chapter 16 explains communication and promotion strategy—the basic under-pinnings of all efforts to promote products.

We start with a discussion of *determining the response* we are seeking from the target audience, which may be *awareness, knowledge, liking, preference, conviction,* or *purchase.* We continue with guidelines on *choosing a message,* including *content, structure,* and *format,* and *choosing media,* including *personal* and *nonpersonal communications channels.*

We continue by reviewing the basic methods for *setting a total promotional budget: affordable, percentage-of-sales, competitive-parity,* and *objective-and-task* methods.

We consider the nature of each promotional tool: *advertising, personal selling, sales promotion,* and *public relations.* Finally, we conclude by considering factors in setting the *promotion mix: type of product and market, push* versus *pull strategies, buyer readiness states,* and *product life-cycle stage.*

Modern marketing calls for more than just developing a good product, pricing it attractively, and making it available to target customers. Companies also must *communicate* with their customers, and what they communicate should not be left to chance.

To communicate well, companies often hire advertising agencies to develop effective ads, sales-promotion specialists to design sales incentive programs, direct-marketing specialists to develop databases and interact with customers and prospects by mail and telephone, and public relations firms to develop corporate images. They train their salespeople to be friendly, helpful, and persuasive. For most companies, the question is not *whether* to communicate, but *how much to spend* and *in what ways.*

A modern company manages a complex marketing communications system (see Figure 16-1). The company communicates with its middlemen, consumers, and various publics. Its middlemen communicate with their consumers and publics. Consumers have word-of-mouth communication with each other and with other publics. Meanwhile, each group provides feedback to every other group.

A company's total marketing communications program—called its **promotion mix**—consists of the specific blend of advertising, personal selling, sales promotion, and public relations tools that the company uses to pursue its advertising and marketing objectives. Definitions of the four major promotion tools follow:

Advertising: Any paid form of nonpersonal presentation and promotion of ideas, goods, or services by an identified sponsor.

Personal selling: Oral presentation in a conversation with one or more prospective purchasers for the purpose of making sales.

Sales promotion: Short-term incentives to encourage the purchase or sale of a product or service.

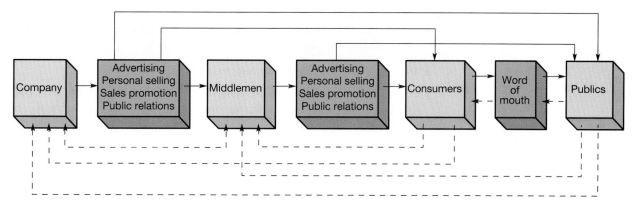

FIGURE 16-1
The marketing communications system

Public relations: Building good relations with the company's various publics by obtaining favorable publicity, building up a good "corporate image," and handling or heading off unfavorable rumors, stories, and events.[2]

Within these categories are specific tools. For example, advertising includes print, broadcast, outdoor, and other forms. Personal selling includes sales presentations, fairs and trade shows, and incentive programs. Sales promotion includes activities such as point-of-purchase displays, premiums, discounts, coupons, specialty advertising, and demonstrations. At the same time, communication goes beyond these specific promotion tools. The product's design, its price, the shape and color of its package, and the stores that sell it—*all* communicate something to buyers. Thus, although the promotion mix is the company's primary communication activity, the entire marketing mix—promotion *and* product, price, and place—must be coordinated for greatest communication impact.

This chapter examines two questions: First, *what are the major steps in developing effective marketing communication?* Second, *how should the promotion budget and mix be determined?* In Chapter 17, we look at mass-communication tools—advertising, sales promotion, and public relations. Chapter 18 examines the salesforce as a communication and promotion tool.

STEPS IN DEVELOPING EFFECTIVE COMMUNICATION

Marketers need to understand how communication works. Communication involves the nine elements shown in Figure 16-2. Two of these elements are the major parties in a communication—the *sender* and the *receiver*. Another two are the major communication tools—the *message* and the *media*. Four more are major

FIGURE 16-2
Elements in the communication process

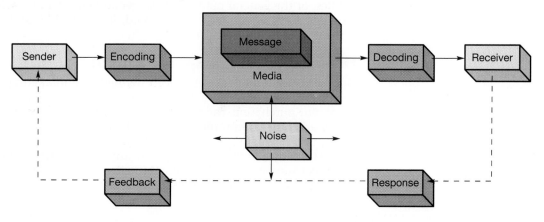

communication functions—*encoding, decoding, response,* and *feedback.* The last element is *noise* in the system. Definitions of these elements follow and are applied to a McDonald's television ad:

- *Sender:* The *party sending the message* to another party—McDonald's.

- *Encoding:* The process of *putting thought into symbolic form*—McDonald's advertising agency assembles words and illustrations into an advertisement that will convey the intended message.

- *Message:* The *set of symbols* that the sender transmits—the actual McDonald's advertisement.

- *Media:* The *communication channels* through which the message moves from sender to receiver—in this case, television and the specific television programs McDonald's selects.

- *Decoding:* The process by which the receiver *assigns meaning to the symbols* encoded by the sender—a consumer watches the McDonald's ad and interprets the words and illustrations it contains.

- *Receiver:* The *party receiving the message* sent by another party—the consumer who watches the McDonald's ad.

- *Response:* The *reactions of the receiver* after being exposed to the message—any of hundreds of possible responses, such as the consumer likes McDonald's better, is more likely to eat at McDonald's next time he or she eats fast food, or does nothing.

- *Feedback:* The part of the *receiver's response communicated back to the sender*—McDonald's research shows that consumers like and remember the ad, or consumers write or call McDonald's praising or criticizing the ad or McDonald's products.

- *Noise:* The *unplanned static or distortion* during the communication process, which results in the receiver's getting a different message than the one the sender sent—the consumer has poor TV reception or is distracted by family members while watching the ad.

This model points out the key factors in good communication. Senders need to know what audiences they want to reach and what responses they want. They must be good at encoding messages that take into account how the target audience decodes them. They must send the message through media that reach target audiences, and they must develop feedback channels so that they can assess the audience's response to the message.

Thus, the marketing communicator must do the following: identify the target audience; determine the response sought; choose a message; choose the media through which to send the message; select the message source; and collect feedback.

Identifying the Target Audience

A marketing communicator starts with a clear target audience in mind. The audience may be potential buyers or current users, those who make the buying decision or those who influence it. The audience may be individuals, groups, special publics, or the general public. The target audience will heavily affect the communicator's decisions on *what* will be said, *how* it will be said, *when* it will be said, *where* it will be said, and *who* will say it.

Determining the Response Sought

Once the target audience has been defined, the marketing communicator must decide what response is sought. Of course, in most cases, the final response is *purchase.* But purchase is the result of a long process of consumer decision making. The marketing communicator needs to know where the target audience now stands and to what state it needs to be moved.

The target audience may be in any of six **buyer-readiness states,** the states consumers normally pass through on their way to making a purchase. These states include *awareness, knowledge, liking, preference, conviction,* or *purchase* (see Figure 16-3).

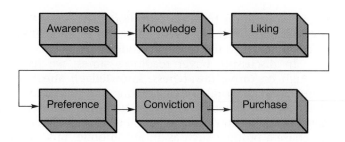

FIGURE 16-3
Buyer readiness states

Awareness

The communicator first must know how aware the target audience is of the product or organization. The audience may be totally unaware of it, know only its name, or know one or a few things about it. If most of the target audience is unaware, the communicator tries to build awareness, perhaps starting with just name recognition. This process can begin with simple messages that repeat the company or product name. Even then, building awareness takes time. Suppose a small Iowa college called Pottsville seeks applicants from Nebraska but has no name recognition in Nebraska. And suppose there are 30,000 high-school seniors in Nebraska who potentially may be interested in Pottsville College. The college might set the objective of making 70 percent of these students aware of Pottsville's name within one year.

Knowledge

The target audience might have company or product awareness but not know much more. Pottsville may want its target audience to know that it is a private four-year college with excellent programs in English and the language arts. Thus, Pottsville College needs to learn how many people in its target audience have little, some, or much knowledge about Pottsville. The college may then decide to select product knowledge as its first communication objective.

Liking

Assuming target audience members *know* the product, how do they *feel* about it? We can develop a scale covering degrees of liking—including dislike very much, dislike somewhat, indifferent, like somewhat, and like very much. If the audience looks unfavorably on Pottsville College, the communicator has to find out why and then develop a communications campaign to generate favorable feelings. If the unfavorable view is based on real problems of the college, then communications alone cannot do the job. Pottsville will have to fix its problems before it communicates its renewed quality. Good public relations call for "good deeds followed by good words."

Preference

The target audience might like the product but not *prefer* it to others. In this case, the communicator must try to build consumer preference by promoting the product's quality, value, performance, and other features. The communicator can check on the campaign's success by measuring the audience's preferences again after the campaign. If Pottsville College finds that many high-school seniors like Pottsville but choose to attend other colleges, it will have to identify those areas where its offerings are better than those of competing colleges. It must then promote its advantages to build preference among prospective students.

Conviction

A target audience might *prefer* the product but not develop a *conviction* about buying it. Thus, some high-school seniors may prefer Pottsville but may not be sure they want to go to college. The communicator's job is to build conviction that going to college is the right thing to do.

Purchase

Finally, some members of the target audience might have *conviction* but not quite get around to making the *purchase*. They may wait for more information or plan to act later. The communicator must lead these consumers to take the final step. Actions might include offering the product at a low price, offering a premium, or letting consumers try it on a limited basis. Thus, Pottsville might invite selected high-school students to visit the campus and attend some classes. Or it might offer scholarships to deserving students.

In discussing buyer readiness states, we have assumed that buyers pass through cognitive (awareness, knowledge); affective (liking, preference, conviction); and behavioral (purchase) stages, in that order. This "learn-feel-do" sequence is appropriate when buyers have high involvement with a product category and perceive brands in the category to be highly differentiated, as is the case when they purchase a product such as an automobile. But consumers often follow other sequences. For example, they might follow a "do-feel-learn" sequence for high-involvement products with little perceived differentiation, such as aluminum siding. Still a third sequence is the "learn-do-feel" sequence, where consumers have low involvement and perceive little differentiation, as is the case when they buy a product such as salt. By understanding consumers' buying stages and their appropriate sequence, the marketer can do a better job of planning communications.

Choosing a Message

Having defined the desired audience response, the communicator turns to developing an effective message. Ideally, the message should get *Attention,* hold *Interest,* arouse *Desire,* and obtain *Action* (a framework known as the *AIDA model*). In practice, few messages take the consumer all the way from awareness to purchase, but the AIDA framework suggests the desirable qualities of a good message.

In putting the message together, the marketing communicator must solve three problems: what to say (*message content*), how to say it logically (*message structure*), and how to say it symbolically (*message format*).

Message Content

The communicator has to figure out an appeal or theme that will produce the desired response. There are three types of appeals: rational, emotional, and moral. **Rational appeals** relate to the audience's self-interest. They show that the product will produce the desired benefits. Examples are messages showing a product's quality, economy, value, or performance. Thus, in its ads, Mercedes offers automobiles that are "engineered like no other car in the world," stressing engineering design, performance, and safety. When pitching computer systems to business users, IBM salespeople talk about quality, performance, reliability, and improved productivity.

Emotional appeals attempt to stir up either negative or positive emotions that can motivate purchase. These include fear, guilt, and shame appeals that get people to do things they should (brush their teeth, buy new tires), or to stop doing things they shouldn't (smoke, drink too much, overeat). For example, a recent Crest ad invoked mild fear when it claimed, "There are some things you just can't afford to gamble with" (cavities). So did Michelin tire ads that featured cute babies and suggested, "Because so much is riding on your tires."[3] Communicators also use positive emotional appeals such as love, humor, pride, and joy. Thus, AT&T's long-running ad theme, "Reach out and touch someone," stirs a bundle of strong emotions.

Moral appeals are directed to the audience's sense of what is "right" and "proper." They often are used to urge people to support social causes such as a cleaner environment, better race relations, equal rights for women, and aid to the needy. An example of a moral appeal is the March of Dimes appeal: "God made you whole. Give to help those He didn't."

Message Structure

The communicator also must decide how to handle three message-structure issues. The first is whether to draw a conclusion or to leave it to the audience. Early research showed that drawing a conclusion was usually more effective. More recent research, however, suggests that in many cases the advertiser is better off asking questions and letting buyers come to their own conclusions. The second message structure issue is whether to present a one-sided argument (mentioning only the product's strengths), or a two-sided argument (touting the product's strengths while also admitting its shortcomings). Usually, a one-sided argument is more effective in sales presentations—except when audiences are highly educated and negatively disposed. The third message-structure issue is whether to present the

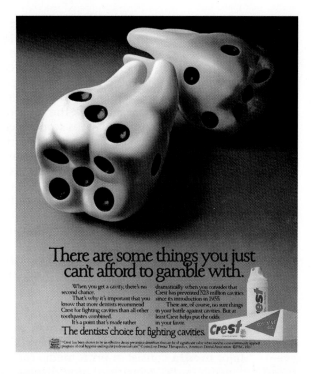

A mild fear appeal: "When you get a cavity, there's no second chance."

strongest arguments first or last. Presenting them first gets strong attention but may lead to an anticlimactic ending.[4]

Message Format

The communicator also needs a strong *format* for the message. In a print ad, the communicator has to decide on the headline, copy, illustration, and color. To attract attention, advertisers can use novelty and contrast; eye-catching pictures and headlines; distinctive formats; message size and position; and color, shape, and movement. If the message is to be carried over the radio, the communicator has to choose words, sounds, and voices. The "sound" of an announcer promoting a used car should be different from one promoting quality furniture.

If the message is to be carried on television or in person, then all these elements plus body language have to be planned. Presenters plan their facial expressions, gestures, dress, posture, and hair style. If the message is carried on the product or its package, the communicator has to watch texture, scent, color, size, and shape. For example, color plays a major communication role in food preferences. When consumers sampled four cups of coffee that had been placed next to brown, blue, red, and yellow containers (all the coffee was identical, but the consumers did not know this), 75 percent felt that the coffee next to the brown container tasted too strong; nearly 85 percent judged the coffee next to the red container to be the richest; nearly everyone felt that the coffee next to the blue container was mild; and the coffee next to the yellow container was seen as weak. Thus, if a coffee company wants to communicate that its coffee is rich, it should probably use a red container along with label copy boasting the coffee's rich taste.

Choosing Media

The communicator now must select *channels of communication*. There are two broad types of communication channels—*personal* and *nonpersonal*.

Personal Communication Channels

In **personal communication channels,** two or more people communicate directly with each other. They might communicate face to face, person to audience, over the telephone, or even through the mail. Personal communication channels are effective because they allow for personal addressing and feedback.

Some personal communication channels are controlled directly by the communicator. For example, company salespeople contact buyers in the target market. But other personal communications about the product may reach buyers through channels not directly controlled by the company. These might include independent experts making statements to target buyers—consumer advocates, consumer buying guides, and others. Or they might be neighbors, friends, family members, and associates talking to target buyers. This last channel, known as **word-of-mouth influence,** has considerable effect in many product areas.

Personal influence carries great weight for products that are expensive, risky, or highly visible. For example, buyers of automobiles and major appliances often go beyond mass-media sources to seek the opinions of knowledgeable people.

Companies can take several steps to put personal communication channels to work for them. They can devote extra effort to selling their products to well-known people or companies, who may in turn influence others to buy. They can create *opinion leaders*—people whose opinions are sought by others—by supplying certain people with the product on attractive terms. For example, companies can work through community members such as disc jockeys, class presidents, and presidents of local organizations. And they can use influential people in their advertisements or develop advertising that has high "conversation value." Finally, the firm can work to manage word-of-mouth communications by finding out what consumers are saying to others, by taking appropriate actions to satisfy consumers and correct problems, and by helping consumers seek information about the firm and its products.[5]

Nonpersonal Communication Channels

Nonpersonal communication channels are media that carry messages without personal contact or feedback. They include major media, atmospheres, and events. Major **media** consist of print media (newspapers, magazines, direct mail); broadcast media (radio, television); and display media (billboards, signs, posters). **Atmospheres** are designed environments that create or reinforce the buyer's leanings toward buying a product. Thus, lawyers' offices and banks are designed to communicate confidence and other things that might be valued by their clients. **Events** are occurrences staged to communicate messages to target audiences. For example, public relations departments arrange press conferences, grand openings, public tours, and other events to communicate with specific audiences.

Nonpersonal communication affects buyers directly. In addition, using mass media often affects buyers indirectly by causing more personal communication. Mass communications affect attitudes and behavior through a *two-step flow-of-communication process.* In this process, communications first flow from television, magazines, and other mass media to opinion leaders and then from these opinion leaders to the less active sections of the population.[6] This two-step flow process means the effect of mass media is not as direct, powerful, and automatic as once supposed. Rather, opinion leaders step between the mass media and their audiences. Opinion leaders are more exposed to mass media and carry messages to people who are less exposed to media.

The two-step flow concept challenges the notion that people's buying is affected by a "trickle down" of opinions and information from higher social classes. Because people mostly interact with others in their own social class, they pick up their fashion and other ideas from people *like themselves,* who are opinion leaders. The two-step flow concept also suggests that mass communicators should aim their messages directly at opinion leaders, letting them carry the message to others.

Selecting the Message Source

The message's impact on the audience also is affected by how the audience views the sender. Messages delivered by highly credible sources are more persuasive. For example, pharmaceutical companies want doctors to tell about their products' benefits because doctors are very credible figures. Many food companies now are promoting to doctors, dentists, and other health-care providers to motivate these professionals to recommend their products to patients (see Marketing Highlight 16-1). Marketers also hire well-known actors and athletes to deliver their messages. Bill Cosby speaks for Kodak and Jell-O, Ray Charles sings about Diet Pepsi, and basketball star Michael Jordan soars for Gatorade, McDonald's, and Nike.[7]

What factors make a source credible? The three factors most often found are expertise, trustworthiness, and likability. *Expertise* is the degree to which the communicator has the authority to back the claim. Doctors, scientists, and professors rank high on expertise in their fields. *Trustworthiness* is related to how objective and honest the source appears to be. Friends, for example, are trusted more than

Celebrities impart some of their own likability and trustworthiness to the products they endorse. Here Michael Jordan and Bugs Bunny speak for Nike.

are salespeople. *Likability* is how attractive the source is to the audience; people like open, humorous, and natural sources. Not surprisingly, the most highly credible source is a person who scores high on all three factors.

Collecting Feedback

After sending the message, the communicator must research its effect on the target audience. This involves asking the target audience members whether they remember the message, how many times they saw it, what points they recall, how they felt about the message, and their past and present attitudes toward the product and company. The communicator also would like to measure behavior resulting from the message—how many people bought a product, talked to others about it, or visited the store.

Figure 16-4 shows an example of feedback measurement for two hypothetical brands. Looking at Brand A, we find that 80 percent of the total market is aware of it, that 60 percent of those aware of it have tried it, but that only 20 per-

FIGURE 16-4
Feedback measurements for two brands

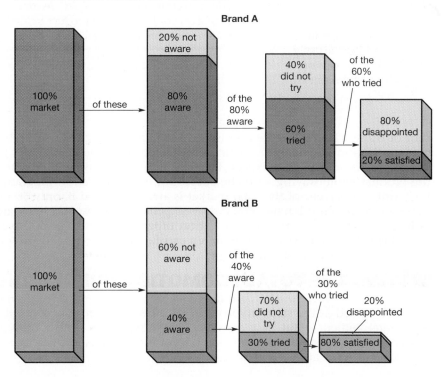

PROMOTING PRODUCTS THROUGH DOCTORS AND OTHER PROFESSIONALS

Food marketers are discovering that the best way to a consumer's stomach may be through a doctor's recommendation. Facing a deluge of health claims being made for different food products, today's more nutrition-conscious consumer often seeks advice from doctors and other health-care professionals about which products are best for them. Kellogg, Procter & Gamble, Quaker, and other large food companies are increasingly recognizing what pharmaceutical companies have known for years—professional recommendations can strongly influence consumer buying decisions. So they are stepping up promotion to doctors, dentists, and others, hoping to inform them about product benefits and motivate them to recommend the promoted brands to their patients.

Doctors receive the most attention from food marketers. For example, Cumberland Packing runs ads in medical journals for its Sweet 'N Low sugar substitute, saying, "It's one thing you can do to make your patient's diet a little easier to swallow." And Kellogg launched its "Project Nutrition" promotion to sell doctors on the merits of eating high-fiber cereal breakfasts. The promotion consists of cholesterol screenings of 100,000 Americans around the country, ads targeting doctors in the *Journal of the American Medical Association* and the *New England Journal of Medicine,* and a new quarterly newsletter called *Health Vantage* mailed to 50,000 U.S. medical professionals. Similarly, Quaker sends out to doctors nationwide a quarterly newsletter, *Fiber Report,* which includes articles, research reports, and feature stories about the importance of fiber in diets.

Procter & Gamble provides literature about several of its products that doctors can pass along to patients. One booklet for Citrus Hill Calcium Plus orange juice even contains a 20-cents-off coupon. And P&G actively seeks medical endorsements. Years ago, a heavily promoted American Dental Association endorsement helped make P&G's Crest the leading brand of toothpaste. The company hopes that an endorsement obtained from the American Medical Women's Association will give a similar boost to its Citrus Hill calcium-fortified fruit juices.

Other professionals targeted by food companies include dentists, veterinarians, teachers, and even high-school coaches. The makers of Trident gum, Equal sugar substitute, Plax mouth rinse, and dozens of other products reach dentists through colorful brochures, samples, and ads in dental journals. Quaker does extensive product sampling of its Gaines and Ken-L Ration pet foods through veterinarians. It also runs ads for Gatorade in magazines read by high-school sports trainers and coaches, and sponsors a fleet of vans that comb the country, offering Gatorade information and samples in key markets. Thus, food companies actively court as spokespeople any professionals who provide health or nutrition advice to their customers.

Many doctors and other health-care providers welcome the promotions as good sources of information about healthy foods and nutrition that can help them give better advice to their patients. Others, however, do not feel comfortable recommending specific food brands; some even resent attempts to influence them through promotion. Although it may take lot of time and investment to get these professionals to change their habits, the results probably will justify effort and expense. If a company can convince key health-care providers that the product is worthy of endorsement, it will gain powerful marketing allies. As one marketer puts it, "If a doctor hands you a product to use, that recommendation carries a lot of weight."

Source: See Laurie Freeman and Liesse Erickson, "Doctored Strategy: Food Marketers Push Products Through Physicians," *Advertising Age,* March 28, 1988, p. 12.

---

cent of those who tried it were satisfied. These results suggest that although the communication program is creating *awareness,* the product fails to give consumers the *satisfaction* they expect. Therefore, the company should try to improve the product while staying with the successful communication program. In contrast, only 40 percent of the total market is aware of Brand B, only 30 percent of those aware of Brand B have tried it, but 80 percent of those who have tried it are satisfied. In this case, the communication program needs to be stronger to take advantage of the brand's power to obtain satisfaction.

SETTING THE TOTAL PROMOTION BUDGET AND MIX

We have looked at the steps involved in planning and sending communications to a target audience. But how does the company decide on the total *promotion budget* and its division among the major promotional tools to create the *promotion mix?* We now look at these questions.

Setting the Total Promotion Budget

One of the hardest marketing decisions facing a company is how much to spend on promotion. John Wanamaker, the department store magnate, once said: "I know that half of my advertising is wasted, but I don't know which half. I spent $2 million for advertising, and I don't know if that is half enough or twice too much." Thus, it is not surprising that industries and companies vary widely in how much they spend on promotion. Promotion spending may be 20 percent to 30 percent of sales in the cosmetics industry and only 5 percent to 10 percent in the industrial machinery industry. Within a given industry, both low- and high-spending companies can be found.

How does a company decide on its promotion budget? We look at four common methods used to set the total budget for advertising: the *affordable method,* the *percentage-of-sales method,* the *competitive-parity method,* and the *objective-and-task method.*[8]

Affordable Method

Many companies use the **affordable method:** They set the promotion budget at the level they think the company can afford. One executive explains this method as follows: "Why it's simple. First, I go upstairs to the controller and ask how much they can afford to give this year. He says a million and a half. Later, the boss comes to me and asks how much we should spend and I say 'Oh, about a million and a half.'"[9]

Unfortunately, this method of setting budgets completely ignores the effect of promotion on sales volume. It leads to an uncertain annual promotion budget, which makes long-range market planning difficult. Although the affordable method can result in overspending on advertising, it more often results in underspending.

Percentage-of-Sales Method

Many companies use the **percentage-of-sales method,** setting their promotion budget at a certain percentage of current or forecasted sales. Or they budget a percentage of the sales price. Automobile companies usually budget a fixed percentage for promotion based on the planned car price. Oil companies set the budget at some fraction of a cent for each gallon of gasoline sold under their labels.

The percentage-of-sales method has a number of advantages. First, using this method means that promotion spending is likely to vary with what the company can "afford." It also helps management think about the relationship between promotion spending, selling price, and profit per unit. Finally, this method supposedly creates competitive stability because competing firms tend to spend about the same percent of their sales on promotion.

Despite these claimed advantages, however, the percentage-of-sales method has little to justify it. It wrongly views sales as the *cause* of promotion rather than as the *result.* The budget is based on availability of funds rather than on opportunities. It may prevent the increased spending sometimes needed to turn around falling sales. Because the budget varies with year-to-year sales, long-range planning is difficult. Finally, the method does not provide any basis for choosing a *specific* percentage, except what has been done in the past or what competitors are doing.

Competitive-Parity Method

Other companies use the **competitive-parity method,** setting their promotion budgets to match competitors' outlays. They watch competitors' advertising or get industry promotion-spending estimates from publications or trade associations, and then set their budgets based on the industry average.

Two arguments support this method. First, competitors' budgets represent the collective wisdom of the industry. Second, spending what competitors spend helps prevent promotion wars. Unfortunately, neither argument is valid. There are no grounds for believing that the competition has a better idea of what a company should be spending on promotion than does the company itself. Companies differ greatly, and each has its own special promotion needs. Finally, there is no evidence that budgets based on competitive parity prevent promotion wars.

Objective-and-Task Method

The most logical budget setting method is the **objective-and-task method,** whereby the company sets its promotion budget based on what it wants to accomplish with promotion. Marketers develop their promotion budgets by (1) defining specific objectives; (2) determining the tasks that must be performed to achieve these objectives; and (3) estimating the costs of performing these tasks. The sum of these costs is the proposed promotion budget.

The objective-and-task method forces management to spell out its assumptions about the relationship between dollars spent and promotion results. But it is also the most difficult method to use. Often, it is hard to figure out which specific tasks will achieve specific objectives. For example, suppose Sony wants 95 percent awareness for its latest camcorder model during the six-month introductory period. What specific advertising messages and media schedules would Sony need in order to attain this objective? How much would these messages and media schedules cost? Sony management must consider such questions, even though they are hard to answer.

Setting the Promotion Mix

The company now must divide the total promotion budget among the major promotion tools—advertising, personal selling, sales promotion, and public relations. It must blend the promotion tools carefully into a coordinated *promotion mix* that will achieve its advertising and marketing objectives. Companies within the same industry differ greatly in how they design their promotion mixes. For example, Avon spends most of its promotion funds on personal selling and catalog marketing (its advertising is only 1.5 percent of sales), whereas Helene Curtis Industries spends heavily on consumer advertising (about 23 percent of sales). Electrolux sells 75 percent of its vacuum cleaners door to door, whereas Hoover relies more on advertising.

Companies always are looking for ways to improve promotion by replacing one promotion tool with another one that will do the same job more economically. Many companies have replaced a portion of their field sales activities with telephone sales and direct mail. Other companies have increased their sales promotion spending in relation to advertising to gain quicker sales.

Designing the promotion mix is even more complex when one tool must be used to promote another. Thus, when McDonald's decides to run Million Dollar Sweepstakes in its fast-food outlets (a sales promotion), it has to run ads to inform the public. When General Mills uses a consumer advertising and sales promotion campaign to back a new cake mix, it has to set aside money to promote this campaign to the resellers to win their support.

Many factors influence the marketer's choice of promotion tools. We now look at these factors.

The Nature of Each Promotion Tool

Each promotion tool—*advertising, personal selling, sales promotion,* and *public relations*—has unique characteristics and costs. Marketers have to understand these characteristics in selecting their tools.

Advertising. Because of the many forms and uses of advertising, it is hard to generalize about its unique qualities as a part of the promotion mix. Yet several qualities can be noted. Advertising's public nature suggests that the advertised product is standard and legitimate. Because many people see ads for the product, buyers know that purchasing the product will be understood and accepted publicly. Advertising also lets the seller repeat a message many times, and it lets the buyer receive and compare the messages of various competitors. Large-scale advertising by a seller says something positive about the seller's size, popularity, and success.

Advertising is also very expressive, allowing the company to dramatize its products through the artful use of print, sound, and color. On the one hand, advertising can be used to build up a long-term image for a product (such as Coca-Cola ads). On the other hand, advertising can trigger quick sales (as when Sears advertises a weekend sale). Advertising can reach masses of geographically spread-out buyers at a low cost per exposure.

Advertising also has some shortcomings. Although it reaches many people quickly, advertising is impersonal and cannot be as persuasive as a company salesperson. Advertising is able to carry on only a one-way communication with the audience, and the audience does not feel that it has to pay attention or respond. In addition, advertising can be very costly. Although some advertising forms,

With personal selling, the customer feels a greater need to listen and respond, even if the response is a polite "No thank you."

such as newspaper and radio advertising, can be done on small budgets, other forms, such as network TV advertising, require very large budgets.

Personal Selling. Personal selling is the most effective tool at certain stages of the buying process, particularly in building up buyers' preferences, convictions, and actions. Compared to advertising, personal selling has several unique qualities. It involves personal interaction between two or more people, so each person can observe the other's needs and characteristics and make quick adjustments. Personal selling also allows all kinds of relationships to spring up, ranging from a matter-of-fact selling relationship to a deep personal friendship. The effective salesperson keeps the customer's interests at heart in order to build a long-term relationship. Finally, with personal selling the buyer usually feels a greater need to listen and respond, even if the response is a polite "no thank you."

These unique qualities come at a cost, however. A salesforce requires a longer-term commitment than does advertising—advertising can be turned on and off, but salesforce size is harder to change. Personal selling is also the company's most expensive promotion tool, costing industrial companies an average of almost $200 per sales call.[10] U.S. firms spend up to three times as much on personal selling as they do on advertising.

Sales Promotion. Sales promotion includes a wide assortment of tools—coupons, contests, cents-off deals, premiums, and others—all of which have many unique qualities. They attract consumer attention and provide information that may lead to a purchase. They offer strong incentives to purchase by providing inducements or contributions that give additional value to consumers. And sales promotions invite and reward quick response. Whereas advertising says "buy our product," sales promotion says "buy it now."

Companies use sales-promotion tools to create a stronger and quicker response. Sales promotion can be used to dramatize product offers and to boost sagging sales. Sales-promotion effects are usually short-lived, however, and are not effective in building long-run brand preference.

Public Relations. Public relations offers several unique qualities. It is very believable—news stories, features, and events seem more real and believable to readers than do ads. Public relations also can reach many prospects who avoid salespeople and advertisements—the message gets to the buyers as "news" rather than as a sales-directed communication. And, like advertising, public relations can dramatize a company or product.

Marketers tend to underuse public relations or to use it as an afterthought. Yet a well-thought-out public relations campaign used with other promotion mix elements can be very effective and economical.

Factors in Setting the Promotion Mix

Companies consider many factors when developing their promotion mixes, including type of product/market, the use of a push or pull strategy, the buyer readiness stage, and the product life-cycle stage.

Type of Product/Market. The importance of different promotion tools varies between consumer and business markets (see Figure 16-5). Consumer goods companies usually put more of their funds into advertising, followed by sales promotion, personal selling, and then public relations. In contrast, industrial goods

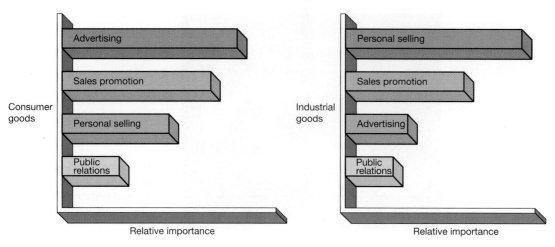

FIGURE 16-5
Relative importance of promotion tools in consumer versus industrial markets

companies put most of their funds into personal selling, followed by sales promotion, advertising, and public relations. In general, personal selling is used more heavily with expensive and risky goods and in markets with fewer and larger sellers.

Although advertising is less important than sales calls in business markets, it still plays an important role. Advertising can build product awareness and knowledge, develop sales leads, and reassure buyers. Similarly, personal selling can add a lot to consumer goods marketing efforts. It is simply not the case that "salespeople put products on shelves and advertising takes them off." Well-trained consumer goods salespeople can sign up more dealers to carry a particular brand, convince them to give the brand more shelf space, and urge them to use special displays and promotions.

Push Versus Pull Strategy. The promotional mix is affected heavily by whether the company chooses a *push* or *pull* strategy. Figure 16-6 contrasts the two strategies. A **push strategy** involves "pushing" the product through distribution channels to final consumers. The producer directs its marketing activities (primarily personal selling and trade promotion) toward channel members to induce them to carry the product and to promote it to final consumers. Using a **pull strategy,** the producer directs its marketing activities (primarily advertising and consumer promotion) toward final consumers to induce them to buy the product. If the pull strategy is effective, consumers then will demand the product

FIGURE 16-6
Push versus pull promotion strategy

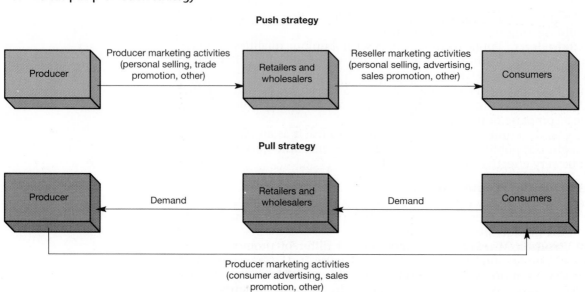

"I don't know who you are.
I don't know your company.
I don't know your company's product.
I don't know what your company stands for.
I don't know your company's customers.
I don't know your company's record.
I don't know your company's reputation.
Now—what was it you wanted to sell me?"

MORAL: Sales start **before** your salesman calls—with business publication advertising.

McGRAW-HILL MAGAZINES
BUSINESS•PROFESSIONAL•TECHNICAL

Advertising can play a dramatic role in industrial marketing, as shown in this classic McGraw-Hill ad.

from channel members, who will in turn demand it from producers. Thus, under a pull strategy, consumer demand "pulls" the product through the channels.

Some small industrial goods companies use only push strategies; some direct-marketing companies use only pull. Most large companies use some combination of both. For example, RJR/Nabisco uses mass-media advertising to pull its products, and a large salesforce and trade promotions to push its products through the channels. In recent years, consumer goods companies have been decreasing the pull portions of their promotion mixes in favor of more push (see Marketing Highlight 16-2).

Buyer Readiness State. The effects of the promotional tools vary for the different buyer readiness stages. Advertising, along with public relations, plays the major role in the awareness and knowledge stages, more important than that played by "cold calls" from salespeople. Customer liking, preference, and conviction are more affected by personal selling, which is closely followed by advertising. Finally, closing the sale is mostly done with sales calls and sales promotion. Clearly, personal selling, given its high costs, should focus on the later stages of the customer buying process.

Product Life-Cycle Stage. The effects of different promotion tools also vary with stages of the product life cycle. In the introduction stage, advertising and public relations are good for producing high awareness, and sales promotion is useful in promoting early trial. Personal selling must be used to get the trade to carry the product. In the growth stage, advertising and public relations continue to be powerful influences, whereas sales promotion can be reduced because fewer incentives are needed. In the mature stage, sales promotion again becomes important relative to advertising. Buyers know the brands, and advertising is needed only to remind them of the product. In the decline stage, advertising is kept at a reminder level, public relations is dropped, and salespeople give the product only a little attention. Sales promotion, however, might continue strong.

Managing and Coordinating the Marketing Communications Process

Members of the marketing department often have different views on how to split the promotion budget. The sales manager would rather hire a few more salespeople than spend $150,000 on a single television commercial. The public relations manager feels that he or she can do wonders with some money shifted from advertising to public relations.

ARE CONSUMER GOODS COMPANIES GETTING TOO "PUSHY"?

Consumer packaged-goods companies like Kraft/General Foods, Procter & Gamble, RJR/Nabisco, Campbell, and Gillette grew into giants by using mostly pull promotion strategies. They used massive doses of national advertising to differentiate their products, build market share, and maintain customer loyalty. But during the past two decades, these companies have gotten more "pushy," deemphasizing national advertising and putting more of their promotion budgets into personal selling and sales promotions. Trade promotions (trade allowances, displays, cooperative advertising) now account for about 50 percent of total consumer product company marketing spending; consumer promotions (coupons, cents-off deals, premiums) account for another 25 percent. That leaves only 25 percent of total marketing spending for media advertising, down from 42 percent just ten years ago.

Why have these companies shifted so heavily toward push strategies? One reason is that mass-media campaigns have become more expensive and less effective in recent years. Network television costs have risen sharply while audiences have fallen off, making national advertising less cost effective. Companies also have increased their market segmentation efforts and are tailoring their marketing programs more narrowly, making national advertising less suitable than localized retailer promotions. And in these days of brand extensions and me-too products, companies sometimes have trouble finding meaningful product differences to feature in advertising. So they have differentiated their products through price reductions, premium offers, coupons, and other push techniques.

Another factor speeding the shift from pull to push has been the greater strength of retailers. Today's retailers are larger and have more access to product sales and profit information. They now have the power to demand and get what they want—and what they want is more push. Whereas national advertising bypasses them on its way to the masses, push promotion benefits them directly. Consumer promotions give retailers an immediate sales boost, and cash from trade allowances pads retailer profits. Thus, producers often must use push just to obtain good shelf space and advertising support from important retailers.

However, many marketers are concerned that the reckless use of push will lead to fierce price competition and a never-ending spiral of price slashing and deal making. This situation would mean lower margins, and companies would have less money to invest in the research and development, packaging, and advertising needed to improve products and maintain long-run consumer preference and loyalty. If used improperly, push promotion can mortgage a brand's future for short-term gains. Sales promotion buys short-run reseller support and consumer sales, but advertising builds long-run brand value and consumer preference. By robbing the advertising budget to pay for more sales promotion, companies might win the battle for short-run earnings but lose the war for long-run consumer loyalty and market share.

Thus, many consumer companies now are rethinking their promotion strategies and reversing the trend by shifting their promotion budgets back slightly toward advertising. Push strategies remain very important. In packaged-goods marketing, short-run success often depends more on retailer support than on the producer's advertising. But many companies have realized that it's not a question of sales promotion versus advertising, or of push versus pull. Success lies in finding the best mix of the two: consistent advertising to build long-run brand value and consumer preference, and sales promotion to create short-run trade support and consumer excitement. The company needs to blend both push and pull elements into an integrated promotion program that meets immediate consumer and retailer needs as well as long-run strategic needs.

Sources: James C. Schroer, "Ad Spending: Growing Marketing Share," *Harvard Business Review,* January-February 1990, pp. 44-48; John Philip Jones, "The Double Jeopardy of Sales Promotions," *Harvard Business Review,* September-October 1990, pp. 145-52; Zachary Schiller, "Not Everyone Loves a Supermarket Special," *Business Week,* February 17, 1992, pp. 64-68; Karen Herther, "Survey Reveals Implications of Promotion Trends for the '90s," *Marketing News,* March 1, 1993, p. 7; and Lois Therrien, "Brands on the Run," *Business Week,* April 19, 1993, pp. 26-29.

In the past, companies left these decisions to different people. No one person was responsible for thinking through the roles of the various promotion tools and coordinating the promotion mix. Today, however, more companies are adopting the concept of *integrated marketing communications*. Under this concept, the company works out the roles that the various promotional tools will play and the extent to which each will be used. It carefully coordinates the promotional activities and their timing when major campaigns take place. It keeps track of its promotional expenditures by product, promotional tool, product life-cycle stage,

MARKETING HIGHLIGHT 16-3

SOCIALLY RESPONSIBLE ADVERTISING AND PERSONAL SELLING

Most marketers work hard to communicate openly and honestly with consumers. Still, abuses may occur, and public policy makers have developed a substantial body of laws and regulations to govern advertising and personal selling activities.

Advertising

By law, companies must avoid false or deceptive advertising. Advertisers must not make false claims, such as stating that a product cures something when it does not. They must avoid false demonstrations, such as using sand-covered plexiglass instead of sandpaper in a commercial to demonstrate that a razor blade can shave sandpaper.

Advertisers must not create ads that have the capacity to deceive, even though no one actually may be deceived. An automobile cannot be advertised as giving 32 miles per gallon unless it does so under typical conditions, and a diet bread cannot be advertised as having fewer calories simply because its slices are thinner. The problem is how to tell the difference between deception and "puffery"—simple acceptable exaggerations not intended to be believed.

Sellers must avoid bait-and-switch advertising that attracts buyers under false pretenses. For example, suppose a seller advertises a sewing machine at $79. When consumers try to buy the advertised machine, the seller cannot then refuse to sell it, downplay its features, show a faulty one, or promise unreasonable delivery dates in order to switch the buyer to a more expensive machine.

A company's trade promotion activities also are closely regulated. For example, under the Robinson-Patman Act, sellers cannot favor certain customers through their use of trade promotions. They must make promotional allowances and services available to all resellers on proportionately equal terms.

Personal Selling

Companies that market products directly through their own salesforces must ensure that their salespeople follow the rules of "fair competition." Most states have enacted deceptive sales acts that spell out what is not allowed. For example, salespeople may not lie to consumers or mislead them about the advantages of buying a product. To avoid bait-and-switch practices, salespeople's statements must match advertising claims.

From a public policy viewpoint, different rules apply to consumers who are called upon at home versus those who go to a store in search of a product. Because people who are called upon at home may be taken by surprise and may be especially vulnerable to high-pressure selling techniques, the Federal Trade Commission (FTC) has adopted a *three-day cooling off rule* to give special protection to customers who are not seeking products. Under this rule, customers who agree in their own homes to buy something costing more than $25 have 72 hours in which to cancel a contract or return merchandise and get their money back, no questions asked.

Much personal selling involves business-to-business trade. In selling to businesses, salespeople may not offer bribes to purchasing agents or to others who can influence a sale. They may not obtain or use technical or trade secrets of competitors through bribery or industrial espionage. Finally, salespeople must not disparage competitors or competing products by suggesting things that are not true.

Sources: For more on the legal aspects of promotion, see Louis W. Stern and Thomas I. Eovaldi, *Legal Aspects of Marketing Policy* (Englewood Cliffs, NJ: Prentice Hall, 1984), Chaps. 7 and 8; Robert J. Posch, *The Complete Guide to Marketing and the Law* (Englewood Cliffs, NJ: Prentice Hall, 1988), Chaps. 15 to 17; and Kevin Kelly, "When a Rival's Trade Secret Crosses Your Desk . . ." *Business Week*, May 20, 1991, p. 48.

---

and observed effect in order to improve future use of the promotion mix tools. Finally, to help implement its integrated marketing strategy, the company appoints a marketing communications director who has overall responsibility for the company's persuasive communications efforts.

Integrated marketing communications produces better communications consistency and greater sales impact. It places the responsibility in someone's hands—where none existed before—to unify the company's image as it is shaped by thousands of company activities. It leads to a total marketing communication strategy aimed at showing how the company and its products can help customers solve their problems.

Whoever is in charge, people at all levels of the organization must be aware of the growing body of laws and regulations that governs marketing communications activities. Beyond understanding and abiding by these laws and regulations, companies should ensure that they communicate honestly and fairly with consumers and resellers (see Marketing Highlight 16-3).

SUMMARY

Promotion is one of the four major elements of the company's marketing mix. The main promotion tools—*advertising, sales promotion, public relations,* and *personal selling*—work together to achieve the company's communication objectives.

In preparing marketing communications, the communicator has to understand the nine elements of any communication process: *sender, receiver, encoding, decoding, message, media, response, feedback,* and *noise.* The communicator's first task is to identify the target audience and its characteristics. Next, the communicator has to define the response sought, whether it be *awareness, knowledge, liking, preference, conviction,* or *purchase.* Then a message should be constructed with an effective content, structure, and format. Media must be selected, both for personal communication and nonpersonal communication. The message must be delivered by a credible *source*—someone who is an

expert and is trustworthy and likable. Finally, the communicator must collect *feedback* by watching how much of the market becomes aware, tries the product, and is satisfied in the process.

The company also has to decide how much to spend for promotion. The most popular approaches are to spend what the company can afford, to use a percentage of sales, to base promotion on competitors' spending, or to base it on an analysis and costing of the communication objectives and tasks.

Finally, the company has to divide the *promotion budget* among the major tools to create the *promotion mix.* Companies are guided by the characteristics of each promotion tool, the type of product/market, the desirability of a *push* or a *pull* strategy, the *buyer's readiness state,* and the *product life-cycle stage.* The different promotion activities require strong coordination for maximum impact.

 # KEY TERMS

Advertising 464

Affordable method 473

Atmospheres 470

Buyer-readiness states 466

Competitive-parity method 473

Emotional appeals 468

Events 470

Media 470

Moral appeals 468

Nonpersonal communication channels 470

Objective-and-task method 473

Percentage-of-sales method 473

Personal communication channels 469

Personal selling 464

Promotion mix 464

Public relations 465

Pull strategy 476

Push strategy 476

Rational appeals 468

Sales promotion 464

Word-of-mouth influence 470

 # DISCUSSING THE ISSUES

1. Which form of marketing communications does each of the following represent? (a) a U2 T-shirt sold at a concert; (b) a *Rolling Stone* interview with Eric Clapton arranged by his manager; (c) a scalper auctioning tickets at a Michael Jackson concert; and (d) a record store selling M.C. Hammer albums for $2 off during the week his latest music video debuts on network television.

2. Bill Cosby has appeared in ads for such products and companies as Jell-O, Coke, Texas Instruments, and E. F. Hutton. Is he a credible source for all these companies, or does his credibility vary? Is he chosen for his credibility as a spokesperson or for some other characteristic?

3. How can an organization get feedback on the effects of its communication efforts? Describe how (a) the March of Dimes and (b) Procter & Gamble can get feedback on the results of their communications.

4. Companies spend billions of dollars on advertising to

build a quality image for their products. At the same time they spend billions more on discount-oriented sales promotions, offering lower price as a main reason to purchase. Discuss whether promotion is enhancing or reducing the effect of advertising. Can you find an example where they enhance one another?

5. Recently, pharmaceutical companies have begun to communicate directly with consumers via the mass media, even though they cannot mention prescription product names and benefits in the same television ad. Ads promise that doctors have some unspecified help available for baldness. Nicoderm, Habitrol, and Prostep nicotine patches battle for consumers' awareness, but they cannot mention cigarette addiction. Is this advertising or public relations? Do you think it would be effective?

6. Why do some industrial marketers advertise on national television, when their target audience is only a

fraction of the people they have paid to reach with their message? List some nonconsumer-oriented commercials you have seen on TV and describe what the marketers were trying to accomplish with them.

APPLYING THE CONCEPTS

1. Think of a nationally advertised product or service that has been running a consistent advertising message for a number of years. Go to the library and copy several examples of print advertising for this brand from back issues of magazines. (a) When you examine these ads closely, how consistent are the message content, structure, and format? (b) Which response(s) do you think this campaign is seeking: awareness, knowledge, liking, preference, conviction, or purchase? (c) Do you think the advertising campaign is successful in getting the desired response? Why or why not?

2. Consider an automobile brand you are familiar with. (a) List examples of how this brand uses advertising, personal selling, sales promotion, and public relations. (Public relations examples may be difficult to spot, but consider how cars are used in movies or television programs, or as celebrity vehicles for sports tournaments or parades.) (b) Does this auto maker use promotion tools in a coordinated way that builds a consistent image, or are the efforts fragmented? Explain.

MAKING MARKETING DECISIONS:

SMALL WORLD COMMUNICATIONS, INC.

Lyn Jones is reading an E-mail message from her partner, Thomas Campbell.

From: Thomas Campbell   25801, 1122
  To: Lyn Jones   27707, 2241
 Date: 03-March 01:48:08

I'll bet you are relieved now that it is time for REAL marketing. i have gotten advertising rate cards for Byte & InfoWorld. give me the budget figures and i will calculate how many ads we can afford.

                Tom—ready to hype this baby

Lyn shook her head, muttering to herself. "He's so unpredictable. Sometimes I think he's really got it. Today, the chiphead thinks he's a media planner. I wish he'd get the prototypes finished before he takes over my responsibilities. Maybe if I ignore him this topic will just fade away. Although . . . he is right that it's time to finalize our communication and promotion strategies."

Lyn started jotting a few notes on a yellow legal pad. They read:

    Response needed: AWARENESS etc.
    Need handle on promotion mix:
      advertising—key but mucho $$
      public relations—*great* potential

      salesforce—central but they can't reach end users
      sales promo—?? maybe steal idea from Joe Camel

Lyn was thinking it all through. "Everything seems to hinge on the fundamentals—*Airport* is new and unique. Until we build some awareness, everything else will be secondary. Maybe."

What Now?

1. Develop a brief communication and promotion strategy for the Small World Communications Airport product. Be sure to include the following: (a) your ideas about how to define the target audience; (b) a statement of the response sought; (c) initial thoughts on message content, structure, and format; (d) ideas for appropriate media; and (e) ways to collect feedback on the effectiveness of the message.

2. Small World is very flexible at this early stage, and Lyn and Tom can structure their company to suit their marketing plans. Consider the four tools used in the promotion mix: advertising, personal selling, sales promotion, and public relations. (a) Are all of these tools equally important for Small World as it launches the *Airport*? If they are not equally important, rank order the tools and explain your reasons. (b) Discuss how your choices in part (a) might affect how Lyn and Tom structure their company. Does this affect what types of people they should hire?

REFERENCES

1. See Richard Edel, "No End in Site for Promotion's Upward Spiral," *Advertising Age*, March 23, 1987, p. S2; Lois Therrien, "Quaker Oats' Pet Peave," *Business Week*, July 31, 1989, pp. 32-33; Joshua Levine, "Locking Up the Week-End Warriors," *Forbes*, October 2, 1989, pp. 234-35; and the "100 Leading National Advertisers" edition of *Advertising Age*, September 25, 1991, p. 59.

2. For these and other definitions, see Peter D. Bennett, *Dictionary of Marketing Terms* (Chicago: American Marketing Association, 1988).

3. For more on fear appeals, see John F. Tanner, James B. Hunt, and David R. Eppright, "The Protection Motivation Model: A Normative Model of Fear Appeals," *Journal of Marketing*, July 1991, pp. 36-45.

4. For more on message content and structure, see Leon G. Schiffman and Leslie Lazar Kanuk, *Consumer Behavior*, 4th ed. (Englewood Cliffs, NJ: Prentice Hall, 1991), Chap. 10; Frank R. Kardes, "Spontaneous Inference Processes in Advertising: The Effects of Conclusion Omission and Involvement on Persuasion." *Journal of Consumer Research*, September 1988, pp. 225-33; Alan G. Sawyer and Daniel J. Howard, "Effects of Omitting Conclusions in Advertisements to Involved and Uninvolved Audiences," *Journal of Marketing Research*, November 1991, pp. 467-74; and Cornelia Pechmann, "Predicting When Two-Sided Ads Will Be More Effective Than One-Sided Ads: The Role of Correlational and Correspondent Inferences," *Journal of Marketing*, November 1992, pp. 441-53.

5. See K. Michael Haywood, "Managing Word of Mouth Communications," *Journal of Services Marketing*, Spring 1989, pp. 55-67.

6. See P. F. Lazarsfeld, B. Berelson, and H. Gaudet, *The People's Choice*, 2nd ed. (New York: Columbia University Press, 1948), p. 151; and Schiffman and Kanuk, *Consumer Behavior*, pp. 571-72.

7. See Michael Oneal and Peter Finch, "Nothing Sells Like Sports," *Business Week*, August 31, 1987; and Pat Sloan and Laurie Freeman, "Advertisers Willing to Share Their Stars," *Advertising Age*, March 21, 1988, pp. 4, 81.

8. For a more comprehensive discussion on setting promotion budgets, see Michael L. Rothschild, *Advertising* (Lexington, MA: D. C. Health, 1987), Chap. 20.

9. Quoted in Daniel Seligman, "How Much for Advertising?" *Fortune*, December 1956, p. 123.

10. See *1992 Sales Manager's Budget Planner*, published by *Sales & Marketing Management*, June 22, 1992, p. 8.

VIDEO CASE 16

TARGETED ADVERTISING: THE TARGET OF CRITICISM

In 1990, G. Heileman Brewing Company had a problem. Although beer industry sales had jumped 11 percent between 1985 and 1990, sales of Heileman's Colt 45 malt liquor had gone flat. Most of the industry's growth had accrued to smaller challenger brands, such as Schlitz' Red Bull, Pabst's Olde English 800, and McKenzie River Company's St. Ides. To compete, Heileman needed a new product.

The malt-liquor market accounts for about 3 percent of all alcohol sales. Although small, sales are highly concentrated among blacks, Hispanics, and other inner-city residents. This high geographic concentration makes the malt-liquor market attractive. Sellers gain the efficiencies of selling to narrowly defined target markets with lower-cost advertising such as billboards. And common appeals work well with the different groups comprising this market.

To compete in the malt-liquor industry, manufacturers rely heavily on product differentiation based on varying the strength of the product. For example, Heileman's regular Colt 45 has an alcohol content of 4.5 percent, whereas the newer brands have higher alcohol levels—4.6 percent for Olde English and 5.4 percent for Schlitz Red Bull. Competitive positioning also aligns with alcoholic content. Heileman's Colt 45 is positioned on sex appeal. Spokespersons such as Billy Dee Williams, successfully pursued glamorous women in romantic, upscale settings. In the heat of the chase, however, he paused to remind consumers to "never run out of Colt 45," an essential ingredient in his formula for success with the opposite sex. Producers of higher-alcohol products usually stress power: With Olde English 800, "It's the Power," and with Schlitz Red Bull it's "The Real Power."

To differentiate its new product, Heileman developed a malt liquor with an alcohol level of 5.9 percent, which it planned to position on the basis of taste. Heileman's advertising agency suggested the name "PowerMaster" and the advertising slogan, "Bold, not harsh" to emphasize the product's bold taste. As required, Heileman submitted its marketing plans to the U.S. Bureau of Alcohol, Tobacco, and Firearms (BATF), which approved the PowerMaster name. With approval in hand, Heileman targeted the introduction for July 1991.

Shortly before the introduction, however, disaster struck. The clergy and other community leaders in major cities such as Chicago and Boston attacked the new brand, objecting to its power positioning. Their protests drew extensive unfavorable media coverage. Other breweries soon joined the fray, criticizing the new Heileman's product. The controversy prompted BATF to review its earlier decision regarding the PowerMaster name.

What generated all of this controversy? The clergy and community leaders argued that the PowerMaster name and Heileman's advertising linked the use of higher-alcohol products with illusions of power, mastery, enhanced sexual prowess, which in turn would lead to higher death rates due to violence and alcohol-related illnesses such as cirrhosis. Moreover, they claimed, targeting inner-city youth takes unfair advantage of consumers who are poorly educated and ill-equipped to resist high-powered advertising appeals.

Based on the review, BATF reversed its approval of PowerMaster and issued strong criticisms of advertising for other malt-liquor brands. It concluded that power themes violate the proscription against advertising based on alcoholic content. As a consequence, Heileman was allowed to sell only its existing inventory of PowerMaster.

The Heileman situation raises three major issues. First, it questions the legality of using power appeals to sell malt liquor. Second, it raises concerns about the advisability of specifically targeting blacks and other minorities. As a result, advertising industry executives suggest that many producers are now hesitant to target *any* advertising toward minorities. In doing so, they risk problems with various interest groups who might attack such targeting efforts. Third, the controversy could also discourage the development and marketing of valuable, acceptable products that are tailored to the special needs of minority segments. Recently cosmetic companies have catered to the special needs of minority segments by adding products designed for black, Hispanic, and Asian women. Other products such as the highly regarded black character doll, "Huggy Bean," from Golden Ribbon Playthings, might never make it to market.

So, what did Heileman finally do? Did it avoid the risks of selling to minority consumers? No. Heileman reintroduced the beverage and renamed it Colt Premium 45. Although executives claim that it's really not PowerMaster in disguise, government regulators claim that the formula is unchanged. This raises a final issue: Did the clergy and other protectionist interest groups accomplish their objective?

QUESTIONS

1. What mistakes did Heileman make in developing its PowerMaster product and marketing campaign? Could Heileman have avoided the controversy?

2. Should producers target advertising toward specific minority market segments? Under what circumstances?

3. What should be the role of government agencies and outside interest groups in such targeting issues?

4. The Surgeon General has suggested that labels on alcoholic beverages should clearly state the alcohol content. Would this keep consumers from buying higher-alcohol products?

5. Did the clergy and other protectionist interest groups accomplish their objectives?

Sources: Steven W. Colford and Ira Teinowitz, "Malt Liquor 'Power' Failure,"*Advertising Age,* July 1, 1991, pp. 1, 29; Alix Freedman, "Marketing: Heileman Tries a New Name for Strong Malt," *The Wall Street Journal,* May 11, 1992, p. B1; Greg Prince, "Heileman Has to Power Down as Federal Heat Withers Debut of Its Souped-Up Malt Liquor," *Beverage World,* July 31, 1991, pp. 1, 3; Ira Teinowitz, "Fighting the 'Power,' " *Advertising Age,* June 24, 1991, pp. 3, 61.

COMPANY CASE 16

THE PEPSI AND COCA-COLA CHALLENGE: A COLA WITH BREAKFAST

Ron Watson wrestled his 18-wheeler onto an exit ramp on Interstate 85 just south of the Virginia-North Carolina border. Although it was only 7 A.M., Ron had already been driving almost four hours since leaving his trucking company's main terminal in Charlotte, North Carolina, and the 26-year-old driver's stomach felt empty. Ron pulled into a truck stop and parked. He picked up the morning paper as he entered the restaurant, then sauntered over to the counter. A waitress who appeared to be still half asleep handed Ron a menu and asked if he were ready to order.

"Sure," he nodded, "I'd like two eggs, sunny-side up, a side order of pancakes, and a Pepsi." The waitress, who had been busy scribbling his order, stopped writing and eyed Ron suspiciously. Another customer seated nearby looked up from his paper.

"Did you say Pepsi?" the waitress asked as if her sleepiness had affected her hearing.

"That's right," Ron replied, a smile brightening his face. "Been drinking Pepsi with breakfast for years. You ought to give it a try."

"No thanks!" the waitress replied as she scratched "Pepsi" on the order pad and turned towards the kitchen.

As she walked away, she mumbled, "Takes all kinds."

Ron Watson has gotten used to funny looks when he orders breakfast, but he's not alone. Thousands of other customers have joined the ranks of those who like a cold cola drink with breakfast instead of the traditional hot coffee. In fact, the Coffee Development Group, an industry trade association, estimates that per capita daily coffee consumption peaked in 1962 at 3.12 cups and has been steadily declining ever since to the present level of 1.76 cups. At the same time, the soft-drink industry calculates that morning soft-drink consumption accounts for 12 percent of total soft-drink sales, up from 9 percent ten years ago.

Soft-drink manufacturers have paid close attention to this 3 percentage-point gain in a market where 1 percent of market share represents more than $400 million in retail sales. Although the change has been gradual, industry analysts argue that the trend testifies to the power of sophisticated advertising. In recent decades, they note, soft-drink manufacturers have outspent almost all other producers of nonalcoholic beverages. And they have poured money into advertising designed to persuade young people to drink more soda. These young people have grown up with soft drinks and are now a major buying force. Further, the rapid growth in fast-food merchandising, the explosive growth of the vending industry, and the proliferation of convenience stores have made soft drinks available almost everywhere at almost any time. As a result, the *Beverage Industry Digest* reports that people between the ages of 24 and 44 represent the largest group of soft-drink consumers, accounting for 27 percent of total market sales.

Citing what it calls a "watershed movement," Coca-Cola became the first company to take direct action to take advantage of the growth in morning consumption of soft drinks. In 1987, the company tested a promotional campaign dubbed "Coke in the Morning" in cities across the United States. Early in 1988, Coca-Cola made the program available to its bottlers across the country. But the campaign does not directly attack coffee, which still accounts for 47 percent of morning beverages sold, compared with 21 percent for juices, 17 percent for milk, 7 percent for tea, and only 4 percent for soft drinks. Rather, the campaign, designed by Coca-Cola's advertising agency McCann-Erickson, focuses on the time after the consumer leaves home in the morning and on the mid-morning coffee break.

At first, Pepsi-Cola Company, like the rest of the industry, stood by to see what would result from Coca-Cola's efforts. Now, however, Pepsi-Cola appears to be charging in with an even more aggressive strategy than Coca-Cola's. In late 1989, Pepsi-Cola announced that it was launching its new strategy in test markets in the Midwest. Pepsi-Cola's test markets revealed just how aggressive the new strategy will be. First, rather than just positioning its regular product for morning consumption, Pepsi-Cola has developed a new brand, Pepsi A.M., designed specifically for the morning segment. Pepsi A.M. comes in both diet and regular forms. Whereas regular Pepsi contains 3.2 milligrams of caffeine per fluid ounce and Coca-Cola Classic contains 3.8 milligrams, Pepsi A.M. has 4 milligrams. Still, Pepsi A.M.'s caffeine level contains only about one quarter the level of caffeine found in a cup of regular coffee. Pepsi-Cola also lowered the level of carbonation in the new drink to help with digestion.

Pepsi-Cola's promotional strategy for Pepsi A.M. is as important to the marketing effort as the product change. The ads attack coffee head on. For example, one print ad shows a series of cups of coffee and one Pepsi A.M. can. Printed under the Pepsi A.M. can is the message, "A refreshing break from the daily grind."

Both Coca-Cola, with its subtle approach, and Pepsi-Cola, with its aggressive campaign, face a real challenge in attempting to pry open the morning beverage market. Coffee drinkers are known for their loyalty. Furthermore, both companies must overcome the "yuck factor"—like Ron Watson's waitress, many consumers find drinking cola in the morning disgusting. Finally, as you might guess, the coffee industry is not likely to sit quietly by and watch Pepsi and Coke steal its market.

Thus, Pepsi and Coke may one day challenge one another for shares of a growing morning-cola market. But before they can battle each other in this segment, as they do in other segments, they must first win the battle with tradition to obtain a place for colas at the breakfast table and in the coffee break.

QUESTIONS

1. What is the target audience for Coca-Cola's "Coke in the Morning" campaign? What is the target for Pepsi A.M.? Are these audiences the same?

2. What buyer responses are Coca-Cola and Pepsi-Cola trying to generate from their target customers?

3. What general message content and message structure decisions should the two companies make in setting their message strategies?

4. What promotion mixes should the companies use? Should the two companies use the same or different mixes? Why?

5. Given the promotion mixes you recommend, what specific ads and other promotion ideas would you recommend to Pepsi-Cola and Coca-Cola to help them win over the morning cola market?

6. Should Pepsi-Cola be concerned about the ethical issue raised by encouraging consumers to have colas with breakfast, especially if its efforts encourage young children to drink colas with breakfast?

Promoting Products: Advertising, Sales Promotion, and Public Relations

17

oving into the 1990s, Eveready set out to recharge its image. The company focused on its Energizer brand, which was locked in a head-to-head battle with Duracell for the top spot in the huge alkaline battery segment. The key would be to create a distinct image for Energizer and to generate consumer excitement, a difficult task in the battery industry, which traditionally has been dominated by a few, largely undifferentiated brands. The solution? Perhaps the most innovative new advertising campaign of the year, featuring an improbable pink, drum-thumping bunny!

Imagine this hare-raising scene: You're sitting in front of the television staring blankly at the screen, watching a seemingly endless stream of the same old TV commercials. On comes an Energizer ad featuring a haughty pink mechanical bunny, drumming harder and longer than a throng of other bunnies. Suddenly, the rabbit marches out of its commercial, off the TV set, and out of the studio. Off-camera voices shout "stop that bunny!" But, of course, there's no slowing him down. He proceeds to march through a series of 15-second parodies of commercials for other products—coffee, decongestant, and wine—disrupting them. In later ads, this pink marauder goes on to disrupt cleverly designed spoofs of ads for "Alarm!" bath soap, "Pigskins" snack chips, "Airedale" air freshener, "Chug-a-Cherry" soft drink, and a greatest-hits record, "The Best of Olga Montiera," a fictional harpist. Eventually, he will even be found bursting into ads for Purina Cat Chow and other real products from Ralston-Purina, Eveready Battery's parent company.

What makes the Energizer Bunny campaign so special? It's not so much the pink bunny—he appeared in the previous year's campaign without raising much of a stir. It's more the campaign's breakthrough execution—the element of surprise that leaves consumers wondering where the renegade rabbit will turn up next. Consumers also appear to enjoy the campaign's tongue-in-cheek poke at the advertising industry. Many consumers resent the seemingly constant interruptions of their favorite television programs by unimaginative commercials. In the Energizer ad, however, the tireless bunny interrupts the *commercials*. And the clever parodies give voice to many consumers' feelings about the mediocrity of some of today's television advertising.

The Energizer Bunny has been good for Eveready's business. Awareness among consumers of the brand's "long-lasting" product message has risen 49 percent since the campaign began, and Energizer has gained market share steadily. The company has received an overwhelming amount of consumer mail, most of it extremely positive. Although Eveready took a chance in lampooning commercials, the public seems to like the approach. The campaign also has won awards and generated much publicity. *Advertising Age* selected the first Energizer Bunny ad as the best advertising spot of the year, and the pink bunny has become a regular topic for stand-up comics and talk-show hosts. It even made an unscheduled appearance on Late Night with David Letterman. Letterman knocked off the bunny's head with a baseball bat, but the body kept on going, and going, and going . . .

The bunny campaign has also helped Eveready improve its trade relations. The company offers stuffed pink bunnies as giveaways and supplies point-of-purchase materials. Research showed a 40 percent increase in the number of displays retailers use to merchandise Energizer batteries. Eveready is further expanding the campaign's impact by putting the bunny's image on packages and creating new bunny promotions. For example, a live version of the tireless rabbit delivered the first pitch of the 1992 season and made on-field appearances at major league baseball stadiums around the country. Eveready probably will continue to move cautiously, however—it won't let its popular bunny march through just anybody's commercial. It doesn't want to risk burning out its innovative advertising idea by letting it get too hot, too quick. Still, after two years and more than two dozen clever parody commercials, the company's ad agency has lots of ideas for new Energizer Bunny advertisements. As one advertising agency executive puts it, "there's plenty of bad advertising they can parody."[1]

CHAPTER PREVIEW

Chapter 17 discusses the ways products are promoted through advertising, sales promotion, and public relations.

First, we survey the *major decisions in advertising*, including *setting objectives* and *budget; creating* and *evaluating the advertising message; selecting advertising media* based upon *reach, frequency*, and *impact*; and *choosing media types, vehicles, and timing*.

We continue with an overview of *sales promotion*, beginning with *objectives*, and looking at *consumer-promotion, trade-promotion*, and *business-promotion tools*.

The chapter concludes with a discussion of using *public relations as a tool* to communicate with various publics.

Companies must do more than make good products—they must inform consumers about product benefits and carefully position products in consumers' minds. To do this, they must skillfully use the mass-promotion tools of *advertising, sales promotion,* and *public relations*. We take a closer look at each of these tools in this chapter.

ADVERTISING

We define **advertising** as any paid form of nonpersonal presentation and promotion of ideas, goods, or services by an identified sponsor. In 1991, advertising ran up a bill of almost $126 billion. The spenders included not only business firms, but nonprofit organizations, professionals, and social agencies that advertise their causes to various target publics. In fact, the thirty-ninth largest advertising spender is a nonprofit organization—the U.S. government.

The top 100 national advertisers account for about one-fourth of all advertising.[2] Table 17-1 lists the top ten advertisers in 1991. Procter & Gamble is the leader with more than $2.1 billion, or almost 14 percent of its total U.S. sales. P&G is also the *world's* largest advertiser, spending a whopping $3.6 billion globally.[3] The other major spenders are found in the retailing, auto, and food industries. Advertising as a percentage of sales is low in the auto industry and high in food, drugs, toiletries, and cosmetics, followed by gum, candy, and soaps. The company spending the largest percentage of its sales on advertising was Warner-Lambert (25 percent).

The roots of advertising can be traced back to early history (see Marketing Highlight 17-1). Although advertising is used mostly by private enterprise, it also is used by a wide range of other organizations and agencies, ranging from the museums and performing arts groups to the U.S. Postal Service and branches of the armed services. Advertising is a good way to inform and persuade, whether the purpose is to sell Coca-Cola worldwide or to get consumers in a developing nation to drink milk or use birth control.

Different organizations handle advertising in different ways. In small companies, advertising might be handled by someone in the sales department. Large

HISTORICAL MILESTONES IN ADVERTISING

Advertising goes back to the very beginnings of recorded history. Archaeologists working in the countries around the Mediterranean Sea have dug up signs announcing various events and offers. The Romans painted walls to announce gladiator fights, and the Phoenicians painted pictures promoting their wares on large rocks along parade routes. A Pompeii wall painting praised a politician and asked for the people's votes.

Another early form of advertising was the town crier. During the Golden Age in Greece, town criers announced the sale of slaves, cattle, and other goods. An early "singing commercial" went as follows: "For eyes that are shining, for cheeks like the dawn / For beauty that lasts after girlhood is gone / For prices in reason, the woman who knows / Will buy her cosmetics from Aesclyptos."

Another early advertising form was the mark that tradespeople placed on their goods, such as pottery. As the person's reputation spread by word of mouth, buyers began to look for his or her special mark, just as consumers look for trademarks and brand names today. Over 1,000 years ago in Europe, Osnabruck linen was carefully controlled for quality and commanded a price 20 percent higher than did unbranded Westphalian linens. As production became more centralized and markets became more distant, the mark became even more important.

The turning point in the history of advertising came in the year 1450, when Johann Gutenberg invented the printing press. Advertisers no longer had to produce extra copies of a sign by hand. The first printed advertisement in the English language appeared in 1478.

In 1622, advertising was given a big boost with the launching of the first English newspaper, *The Weekly Newes*. Later, Joseph Addison and Richard Steele published the *Tatler* and became supporters of advertising. Addison gave this advice to copywriters: "The great art in writing advertising is the finding out the proper method to catch the reader, without which a good thing may pass unobserved, or be lost among commissions of bankrupts." The September 14, 1710, issue of the *Tatler* contained ads for razor strops, patent medicine, and other consumer products.

Advertising had its greatest growth in the United States. Ben Franklin has been called the father of American advertising because his *Gazette,* first published in 1729, had the largest circulation and advertising volume of any paper in colonial America. Several factors led to America's becoming the cradle of advertising. First, American industry led in mass production, which created surpluses and the need to convince consumers to buy more. Second, the development of a fine network of waterways, highways, and roads allowed the transportation of goods and advertising media to the countryside. Third, the establishment in 1813 of compulsory public education increased literacy and the growth of newspapers and magazines. The invention of radio and, later, television created two more amazing media for the spread of advertising.

TABLE 17-1
Top Ten National Advertisers

RANK	COMPANY	TOTAL U.S. ADVERTISING (MILLIONS)	TOTAL U.S. SALES (MILLIONS)	ADVERTISING AS A PERCENT OF SALES
1	Procter & Gamble	$2,149	$15,579	13.8
2	Philip Morris	2,046	37,890	5.4
3	General Motors	1,442	86,973	1.7
4	Sears	1,179	57,242*	
5	PepsiCo	903	15,168	6.0
6	Grand Metropolitan	745	7,878	9.5
7	Johnson & Johnson	733	6,248	11.7
8	McDonald's	694	3,710	18.7
9	Ford	677	61,149	1.1
10	Eastman Kodak	661	10,882	6.1

Worldwide sales—U.S. sales not available. Percent of sales not calculated.
Source: Reprinted with permission from "100 Leading National Advertisers," Advertising Age, January 4, 1993, p. 16.

HOW DOES AN ADVERTISING AGENCY WORK?

Madison Avenue is a familiar name to most Americans. It's a street in New York City where some major advertising agency headquarters are located. But most of the nation's 10,000 agencies are found outside New York, and almost every city has at least one agency, even if it's a one-person shop. Some ad agencies are huge—the largest U.S. agency, Young & Rubicam, has annual worldwide billings (the dollar amount of advertising placed for clients) of more than $7.5 billion. Dentsu, a Japanese agency, is the world's largest agency with billings of more than $10 billion.

Advertising agencies were started in the mid-to-late 1800s by salespeople and brokers who worked for the media and received a commission for selling advertising space to various companies. As time passed, the salespeople began to help customers prepare their ads. Eventually, they formed agencies and grew closer to the advertisers than to the media. Agencies offered both more advertising and more marketing services to their clients.

Even companies with strong advertising departments use advertising agencies. Agencies employ specialists who can often perform advertising tasks better than the company's own staff. Agencies also bring an outside point of view to solving the company's problems, along with lots of experience from working with different clients and situations. Agencies are paid partly from media discounts and often cost the firm very little. And because the firm can drop its agency at any time, an agency works hard do a good job.

Advertising agencies usually have four departments: *creative*, which develops and produces ads; *media*, which selects media and places ads; *research*, which studies audience characteristics and wants; and *business*, which handles the agency's business activities. Each account is supervised by an account executive, and people in each department are usually assigned to work on one or more accounts.

Agencies often attract new business through their reputation or size. Generally, however, a client invites a few agencies to make a presentation for its business and then selects one.

Ad agencies traditionally have been paid through commissions and some fees. Under this system, the agency usually receives 15 percent of the media cost as a rebate. Suppose the agency buys $60,000 of magazine space for a client, for example. The magazine bills the advertising agency for $51,000 ($60,000 less 15 percent), and the agency bills the client for $60,000, keeping the $9,000 commission. If the client bought space directly from the magazine, it would have paid $60,000 because commissions are only paid to recognized advertising agencies.

However, both advertisers and agencies have become more and more unhappy with the commission system. Larger advertisers complain that they pay more for the same services received by smaller ones simply because they place more advertising. Advertisers also believe that the commission system drives agencies away from low-cost media and short advertising campaigns. Agencies are unhappy because they perform extra services for an account without getting any more pay. As a result, the trend is now toward paying either a straight fee or a combination commission and fee. And some large advertisers are tying agency compensation to the performance of the agency's advertising campaigns. Today, only about 35 percent of companies still pay their agencies on a commission-only basis.

Another trend is hitting the advertising agency business: In recent years, as growth in advertising spending has slowed, many agencies have tried to keep growing by gobbling up other agencies, thus creating huge agency holding companies. The largest of these agency "mega-groups," WPP Group, includes several large agencies—Ogilvy & Mather; J. Walter Thompson; Scali, McCabe, Sloves; Fallon McElligott; and others—with combined billings exceeding $18 billion. Many agencies also have sought growth by diversifying into related marketing services. These new diversified agencies offer a complete list of integrated marketing and promotion services under one roof, including advertising, sales promotion, public relations, direct marketing, and marketing research. Some have even added marketing consulting, television production, and sales training units in an effort to become full "marketing partners" to their clients. However, most agencies are finding that advertisers don't want much more from them than traditional media advertising services plus direct marketing, sales promotion, and sometimes public relations. Thus, many agencies recently have dropped unrelated activities in order to focus more on traditional advertising services.

Sources: See R. Craig Endicott, "Ad Age 500 Grows 9.7%," *Advertising Age,* March 26, 1990, pp. S1-S2; Gary Levin, "Ad Agencies Ax Side Ventures," *Advertising Age,* March 18, 1991, p. 4; Mark Landler, "Advertising's `Big Bang' Is Making Noise at Last," *Business Week,* April 1, 1991, pp. 62-63; and "World's Top 50 Advertising Organizations," *Advertising Age,* April 13, 1992, p. S10.

companies set up advertising departments whose job it is to set the advertising budget, work with the ad agency, and handle direct-mail advertising, dealer displays, and other advertising not done by the agency. Most large companies use outside advertising agencies because they offer several advantages (see Marketing Highlight 17-2).

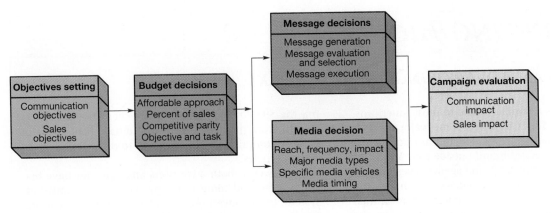

FIGURE 17-1 Major advertising decisions

MAJOR DECISIONS IN ADVERTISING

Marketing management must make five important decisions when developing an advertising program (see Figure 17-1).

Setting Objectives

The first step in developing an advertising program is to set *advertising objectives*. These objectives should be based on past decisions about the target market, positioning, and marketing mix. The marketing positioning and mix strategy define the job that advertising must do in the total marketing program.

An **advertising objective** is a specific communication *task* to be accomplished with a specific *target* audience during a specific period of *time*.[4] Advertising objectives can be classified by purpose—whether their aim is to *inform, persuade,* or *remind.* Table 17-2 lists examples of each of these objectives.

Informative advertising is used heavily when introducing a new product category. In this case, the objective is to build primary demand. Thus, producers of compact disc players first informed consumers of the sound and convenience benefits of CDs. **Persuasive advertising** becomes more important as competition increases. Here, the company's objective is to build selective demand. For example, when compact disc players became established and accepted, Sony began trying to persuade consumers that its brand offers the best quality for their money.

Some persuasive advertising has become **comparison advertising,** in which a company directly or indirectly compares its brand with one or more other brands. For example, in its classic comparison campaign, Avis positioned itself against market-leading Hertz by claiming, "We're number two, so we try

---

**TABLE 17-2
Possible Advertising Objectives**

TO INFORM

Telling the market about a new product	Describing available services
Suggesting new uses for a product	Correcting false impressions
Informing the market of a price change	Reducing buyers' fears
Explaining how the product works	Building a company image

TO PERSUADE

Building brand preference	Persuading buyers to purchase now
Encouraging switching to your brand	Persuading buyers to receive a sales call
Changing buyer perceptions of product attributes	

TO REMIND

Reminding buyers that the product may be needed in the near future	Keeping the product in buyers' minds during off seasons
Reminding buyers where to buy the product	Maintaining top-of-mind product awareness

Comparison advertising: Visa compares its card directly to those of major competitors— "Of all the cards in all the wallets of all the men and women in America, there's one that towers over all the others. The Visa card."

harder." Procter & Gamble positioned Scope mouthwash against Listerine, claiming that minty-fresh Scope "fights bad breath and doesn't give medicine breath." Comparison advertising also has been used for products such as soft drinks, computers, deodorants, toothpastes, automobiles, pain relievers, and long-distance telephone service.

Reminder advertising is important for mature products—it keeps consumers thinking about the product. Expensive Coca-Cola ads on television are designed to remind people about Coca-Cola, not to inform or persuade them.

Setting the Advertising Budget

After determining its advertising objectives, the company next sets its *advertising budget* for each product. The role of advertising is to affect demand for a product. The company wants to spend the amount needed to achieve the sales goal. Four commonly used <u>methods</u> for setting the advertising budget are discussed in Chapter 16. Here we describe some specific factors that should be considered when setting the advertising budget:

- *Stage in the product life cycle.* New products typically need large advertising budgets to build awareness and to gain consumer trial. Mature brands usually require lower budgets as a ratio to sales.

- *Market share.* High-market-share brands usually need more advertising spending as a percent of sales than do low-share brands. Building the market or taking share from competitors requires larger advertising spending than does simply maintaining current share.

- *Competition and clutter.* In a market with many competitors and high advertising spending, a brand must advertise more heavily to be heard above the noise in the market.

- *Advertising frequency.* When many repetitions are needed to present the brand's message to consumers, the advertising budget must be larger.

- *Product differentiation.* A brand that closely resembles other brands in its product class (cigarettes, beer, soft drinks) requires heavy advertising to set it apart. When the product differs greatly from competitors, advertising can be used to point out the differences to consumers.[5]

[handwritten margin note: 4 methods: 1. Affordable 2. Percentage of sales 3. Competative Parity 4. Objective and task]

Companies such as Du Pont and Anheuser-Busch often run experiments as part of their advertising budgeting process. For example, in the late 1980s, Anheuser-Busch tested a new ultrapremium beer, named "Anheuser," with no advertising at all. No major beer is likely to survive without advertising, but in this case the company wanted to see if this specialty beer could make it on word-of-mouth alone. In fact, the lack of advertising might even add to the beer's allure. If such brands can succeed without advertising, Anheuser-Busch will probably take a careful look at the more than $460 million it spends each year advertising its other products.

Setting the advertising budget is no easy task. How does a company know if it is spending the right amount? Some critics charge that large consumer packaged-goods firms tend to spend too much on advertising and industrial companies generally underspend on advertising. They claim that, on the one hand, the large consumer companies use image advertising extensively without really knowing its effects. They overspend as a form of "insurance" against not spending enough. On the other hand, industrial advertisers tend to rely too heavily on their salesforces to bring in orders. They underestimate the power of the company and product image in preselling industrial customers. Thus, they do not spend enough on advertising to build customer awareness and knowledge.

How much impact does advertising really have on consumer buying and brand loyalty? A research study analyzing household purchases of frequently bought consumer products came up with the following surprising conclusion:

> Advertising appears effective in increasing the volume purchased by loyal buyers but less effective in winning new buyers. For loyal buyers, high levels of exposure per week may be unproductive because of a leveling off of ad effectiveness . . . Advertising appears unlikely to have some cumulative effect that leads to loyalty . . . Features, displays, and especially price have a stronger impact on response than does advertising.[6]

These findings did not sit well with the advertising community, and several people attacked the study's data and methodology. They claimed that the study measured mostly short-run sales effects. Thus, it favored pricing and sales-promotion activities, which tend to have more immediate impact. In contrast, most advertising takes many months, or even years, to build strong brand positions and consumer loyalty. These long-run effects are difficult to measure. However, a more recent study of BehaviorScan data over a ten-year period found that advertising does produce long-term sales growth, even two years after a campaign ends.[7] This debate underscores the fact that measuring the results of advertising spending remains a poorly understood subject.

Creating the Advertising Message

A large advertising budget does not guarantee a successful advertising campaign. Two advertisers can spend the same amount on advertising, yet have very different results. Studies show that creative advertising messages can be more important to advertising success than the number of dollars spent. No matter how big the budget, advertising can succeed only if commercials gain attention and communicate well. Therefore, the budget must be invested in effective advertising messages.

Good advertising messages are especially important in today's costly and cluttered advertising environment. The average consumer has 22 television stations and 11,500 magazines from which to choose. Add the countless radio stations and a continuous barrage of catalogs, direct-mail ads, and out-of-home media, and consumers are bombarded with ads at home, at work, and at all points in between.[8]

Whereas all this advertising clutter might bother some consumers, it also causes big problems for advertisers. Take the situation facing network television advertisers. They typically pay $100,000 to $200,000 for 30 seconds of advertising time during a popular prime-time TV program—even more if it's an especially popular program such as "Murphy Brown" ($310,000 per spot); "Roseanne" ($290,000); or an event like the Super Bowl ($850,000). In such cases, their ads are sandwiched in with a clutter of some 60 other commercials, announcements, and network promotions per hour.

But wait—things get even worse! Until recently, television viewers were pretty much a captive audience for advertisers. Viewers had only a few channels from which to choose. Those who found the energy to get up and change channels during boring commercial breaks usually found only more of the same on the other channels. But with the growth in cable TV, VCRs, and remote-control units, today's viewers have many more options. They actually can avoid ads by watching commercial-free cable channels. They can "zap" commercials by pushing the fast-forward button during taped programs. With remote control, they can instantly turn off the sound during a commercial or "zip" around the channels to see what else is on. Advertisers take such "zipping" and "zapping" very seriously. One expert predicts that by the year 2000, 60 percent of all TV viewers may be regularly tuning out commercials.[9]

Thus, just to gain and hold attention, today's advertising messages must be better planned, more imaginative, more entertaining, and more rewarding to consumers. Creative strategy therefore will play an increasingly important role in advertising success. Advertisers go through three steps to develop a creative strategy: *message generation, message evaluation and selection,* and *message execution.*

Message Generation

Creative people have different ways of finding advertising message ideas. Many creative people start by talking to consumers, dealers, experts, and competitors. Others try to imagine consumers using the product and figure out the benefits consumers seek when buying and using the product. Generally, although advertisers create many possible messages, only a few ultimately will be used.

Message Evaluation and Selection

The advertiser must evaluate the possible messages. The appeals used in messages should have three characteristics. First, they should be *meaningful,* pointing out benefits that make the product more desirable or interesting to consumers. Second, appeals should be *distinctive*—they should tell how the product is better than the competing brands. Finally, they must be *believable.* This last objective is difficult because many consumers doubt the truth of advertising in general. One study found that a full one-third of the public rates advertising messages as "unbelievable."[10]

Thus, advertisers should evaluate their advertising messages on the preceding factors. For example, The March of Dimes searched for an advertising theme to raise money for its fight against birth defects.[11] Twenty possible messages came out of a brainstorming session. A group of young parents was asked to rate each message for interest, distinctiveness, and believability, giving up to 100 points for each. For example, the message "Five hundred thousand unborn babies die each year from birth defects" scored 70, 60, and 80 on interest, distinctiveness, and believability, respectively. The message "Your next baby could be born with a birth defect" scored 58, 50, and 70. The first message was thus rated higher than the second and was used in March of Dimes advertising.

Message Execution

The impact of the message depends not only on *what* is said, but also on *how* it is said—its message execution. The advertiser has to present the message in a way that wins the target market's attention and interest.

The advertiser usually begins with a statement of the objective and approach of the desired ad. Here is such a statement for a Pillsbury product called 1869 Brand Biscuits:

> The objective of the advertising is to convince biscuit users that now they can buy a canned biscuit that's as good as homemade—Pillsbury's 1869 Brand Biscuits. The content of the advertising will emphasize that the biscuits look like homemade biscuits, have the same texture as homemade, and taste like homemade biscuits. Support for the "good as homemade" promise will be twofold: (1) 1869 Brand Biscuits are made from a special kind of flour (soft wheat flour) used to make homemade biscuits but never before used in making canned biscuits, and (2) the use of traditional American biscuit recipes. The tone of the advertising will be a news announcement, tempered by a warm, reflective mood coming from a look back at traditional American baking quality.

It might be an extra pillow. Or a lightly scented hot towel. Maybe it's the Independent Television News beamed daily via satellite from London. All little things. But while we operate the youngest, most modern fleet around the world, we've never forgotten how important those little things can be. Singapore Airlines flies to over 60 cities across five continents with a standard of inflight service even other airlines talk about. SINGAPORE AIRLINES

Message execution style: Singapore Airlines builds a mood around its services.

The creative people must find the best style, tone, words, and format for executing the message. Any message can be presented in different *execution styles,* such as the following:

- *Slice of life.* This style shows one or more people using the product in a normal setting. A family seated at the dinner table might talk about a new biscuit brand.

- *Lifestyle.* This style shows how a product fits in with a particular lifestyle. For example, a National Dairy Board ad shows women exercising and talks about how milk adds to a healthy, active lifestyle.

- *Fantasy.* This style creates a fantasy around the product or its use. For instance, Revlon's first ad for Jontue showed a barefoot woman wearing a chiffon dress and coming out of an old French barn, crossing a meadow, meeting a handsome young man on a white horse, and riding away with him.

- *Mood or image.* This style builds a mood or image around the product, such as beauty, love, or serenity. No claim is made about the product except through suggestion. Many travel and tourism ads create moods.

- *Musical.* This style shows one or more people or cartoon characters singing a song about the product. Many soft-drink ads use this format.

- *Personality symbol.* This style creates a character that represents the product. The character might be *animated* (the Jolly Green Giant, Cap'n Crunch, Garfield the Cat) or *real* (the Marlboro man, Betty Crocker, Morris the 9-Lives Cat).

- *Technical expertise.* This style shows the company's expertise in making the product. Thus, Maxwell House shows one of its buyers carefully selecting the coffee beans, and Gallo tells about its many years of winemaking experience.

- *Scientific evidence.* This style presents survey or scientific evidence that the brand is better or better liked than one or more other brands. For years, Crest toothpaste has used scientific evidence to convince buyers that Crest is better than other brands at fighting cavities.

- *Testimonial evidence.* This style features a highly believable or likable source endorsing the product. It could be a celebrity like Bill Cosby (Jell-O Pudding or Kodak film) or ordinary people saying how much they like a given product.

The advertiser also must choose a *tone* for the ad. Procter & Gamble always uses a positive tone: Its ads say something very positive about its products. P&G also avoids humor that might take attention away from the message. In contrast, ads for Bud Light beer use humor and poke fun at people who order "just any light."

The advertiser must use memorable and attention-getting *words* in the ad. For example, the following themes on the left would have had much less impact without the creative phrasing on the right:

Theme	*Creative Copy*
7-Up is not a cola.	"The Uncola"
Ride in our bus instead of driving your car	"Take the bus, and leave the driving to us." (Greyhound)
If you drink a lot of beer, Schaefer is a good beer to drink.	"The one beer to have when you're having more than one."
We don't rent as many cars, so we have to do more for our customers.	"We're number two, so we try harder." (Avis)
Hanes socks last longer than less expensive ones.	"Buy cheap socks and you'll pay through the toes."
Nike shoes will help you jump higher and play better basketball.	"Parachute not included."

Finally, *format* elements make a difference on an ad's impact as well as its cost. A small change in ad design can make a big difference on its effect. The *illustration* is the first thing the reader notices—it must be strong enough to draw attention. Next, the *headline* must effectively entice the right people to read the copy. Finally, the *copy*—the main block of text in the ad—must be simple but strong and convincing. Moreover, these three elements must effectively work *together.* Even then, less than 50 percent of the exposed audience will notice even a truly outstanding ad; about 30 percent will recall the main point of the headline; about 25 percent will remember the advertiser's name; and less than 10 percent will have read most of the body copy. Less than outstanding ads, unfortunately, will not achieve even these results.

Selecting Advertising Media

The advertiser next chooses advertising media to carry the message. The major steps in media selection are (1) deciding on *reach, frequency,* and *impact;* (2) choosing among major *media types;* (3) selecting specific *media vehicles;* and (4) deciding on *media timing.*

Deciding on Reach, Frequency, and Impact

To select media, the advertiser must decide what reach and frequency are needed to achieve advertising objectives. **Reach** is a measure of the *percentage* of people in the target market who are exposed to the ad campaign during a given period of time. For example, the advertiser might try to reach 70 percent of the target market during the first three months of the campaign. **Frequency** is a measure of how many *times* the average person in the target market is exposed to the message. For example, the advertiser might want an average exposure frequency of three. The advertiser also must decide on the desired **media impact**—the *qualitative value* of a message exposure through a given medium. For example, for products that need to be demonstrated, messages on television may have more impact than messages on radio because television uses sight *and* sound. The same message in one magazine (say, *Newsweek*) may be more believable than in another (say, *The National Enquirer*).

Suppose that the advertiser's product might appeal to a market of 1 million consumers. The goal is to reach 700,000 consumers (70 percent of 1,000,000). Because the average consumer will receive three exposures, 2,100,000 exposures (700,000 × 3) must be bought. If the advertiser wants exposures of 1.5 impact (assuming 1.0 impact is the average), a rated number of exposures of 3,150,000 (2,100,000 × 1.5) must be bought. If a thousand exposures with this impact cost $10, the advertising budget will have to be $31,500 (3,150 × $10). In general, the more reach, frequency, and impact the advertiser seeks, the higher the advertising budget will have to be.

Choosing Among Major Media Types

The media planner has to know the reach, frequency, and impact of each of the major media types. As summarized in Table 17-3, the major media types are newspapers, television, direct mail, radio, magazines, and outdoor. Each medium has advantages and limitations.

Media planners consider many factors when making their media choices. The *media habits of target consumers* will affect media choice—for example, radio and television are the best media for reaching teenagers. So will the *nature of the product*—fashions are best advertised in color magazines, and Polaroid cameras are best demonstrated on television. Different *types of messages* may require different media. A message announcing a major sale tomorrow will require radio or newspapers; a message with a lot of technical data might require magazines or direct mailings. *Cost* is also a major factor in media choice. Whereas television is very expensive, for example, newspaper advertising costs much less. The media planner looks at both the total cost of using a medium and at the cost per thousand exposures—the cost of reaching 1,000 people using the medium.

Media impact and cost must be reexamined regularly. For a long time, television and magazines dominated in the media mixes of national advertisers, with other media often neglected. Recently, however, the costs and clutter of these media have gone up, audiences have dropped, and marketers are adopting strategies beamed at narrower segments. As a result, TV and magazine advertising revenues have leveled off or declined.[12] Advertisers are increasingly turning to alter-

TABLE 17-3
Profiles of Major Media Types

MEDIUM	VOLUME IN BILLIONS	PERCENTAGE	EXAMPLES OF COST	ADVANTAGES	LIMITATIONS
Newspapers	30.7	23.4%	$29,800 for one page, weekday *Chicago Tribune*	Flexibility; timeliness; good local market coverage; broad acceptance; high believability	Short life; poor reproduction quality; small pass-along audience
Television	29.4	22.4	$1,500 for 30 seconds of prime time in Chicago	Combines sight, sound, and motion; appealing to the senses; high attention; high reach	High absolute cost; high clutter; fleeting exposure; less audience selectivity
Direct Mail	25.4	19.3	$1,520 for the names and addresses of 40,000 veterinarians	Audience selectivity; flexibility; no ad competition within the same medium; personalization	Relatively high cost; "junk mail" image
Radio	8.7	6.6	$700 for one minute of drive time (during commuting hours, A.M. and P.M.) in Chicago	Mass use; high geographic and demographic selectivity; low cost	Audio presentation only; lower attention than television; nonstandardized rate structures; fleeting exposure
Magazines	7.0	5.3	$84,390 for one page, four-color, in *Newsweek*	High geographic and demographic selectivity; credibility and prestige; high-quality reproduction; long life; good pass-along readership	Long ad purchase lead time; some waste circulation; no guarantee of position
Outdoor	1.0	0.8	$25,500 per month for 71 billboards in metropolitan Chicago	Flexibility; high repeat exposure; low cost; low competition	No audience selectivity; creative limitations
Other	29.1	22.2			
Total	131.3	100.0			

Sources: Columns 1 and 2 reprinted with permission from Robert J. Cohen, "Ad Gains Could Exceed 6% This Year," *Advertising Age*, May 3, 1993, p. 4.

native media, ranging from cable TV and outdoor advertising to parking meters and shopping carts (see Marketing Highlight 17-3).

Given these and other media characteristics, the media planner must decide how much of each media type to buy. For example, in launching its new biscuit, Pillsbury might decide to spend $6 million advertising in daytime network television, $4 million in women's magazines, and $2 million in daily newspapers in 20 major markets.

Selecting Specific Media Vehicles

The media planner now must choose the best **media vehicles**—specific media within each general media type. For example, television vehicles include "Roseanne," "Murphy Brown," "60 Minutes," and the "ABC World News Tonight." Magazine vehicles include *Newsweek, People, Sports Illustrated,* and *Reader's Digest.* If advertising is placed in magazines, the media planner must look up circulation figures and the costs of different ad sizes, color options, ad positions, and frequencies for specific magazines. Then the planner must evaluate each magazine on factors such as credibility, status, reproduction quality, editorial focus, and advertising submission deadlines. The media planner ultimately decides which vehicles give the best reach, frequency, and impact for the money.

Media planners also compute the cost per thousand persons reached by a vehicle. For example, if a full-page, four-color advertisement in *Newsweek* costs $100,000 and *Newsweek's* readership is 3.3 million people, the cost of reaching each group of 1,000 persons is about $30. The same advertisement in *Business Week* may cost only $57,000 but reach only 775,000 persons—at a cost per thousand of about $74. The media planner would rank each magazine by cost per thousand and favor those magazines with the lower cost per thousand for reaching target consumers.

The media planner also must consider the costs of producing ads for different media. Whereas newspaper ads may cost very little to produce, flashy television ads may cost millions. On average, advertisers must pay $118,000 to produce a single 30-second television commercial. Timex paid a cool million to make one 30-second ad for its Atlantis 100 sports watch, and Apple Computer recently spent $6 million to produce eleven television spots.[13]

Thus, the media planner must balance media cost measures against several media impact factors. First, the planner should balance costs against the media vehicle's *audience quality.* For a baby lotion advertisement, for example, *New Parents* magazine would have a high-exposure value; *Gentlemen's Quarterly* would have a low-exposure value. Second, the media planner should consider *audience attention.* Readers of *Vogue,* for example, typically pay more attention to ads than do *Newsweek* readers. Third, the planner should assess the vehicle's *editorial quality*—*Time* and *The Wall Street Journal* are more believable and prestigious than *The National Enquirer.*

Deciding on Media Timing

The advertiser also must decide how to schedule the advertising over the course of a year. Suppose sales of a product peak in December and drop in March. The firm can vary its advertising to follow the seasonal pattern, to oppose the seasonal pattern, or to be the same all year. Most firms do some seasonal advertising. Some do *only* seasonal advertising: For example, Hallmark advertises its greeting cards only before major holidays.

Finally, the advertiser has to choose the pattern of the ads. **Continuity** means scheduling ads evenly within a given period. **Pulsing** means scheduling ads unevenly over a given time period. Thus, 52 ads could either be scheduled at one per week during the year or pulsed in several bursts. The idea is to advertise heavily for a short period to build awareness that carries over to the next advertising period. Those who favor pulsing feel that it can be used to achieve the same impact as a steady schedule, but at a much lower cost. However, some media planners believe that although pulsing achieves minimal awareness, it sacrifices depth of advertising communications.

Advertising Evaluation

The advertising program should evaluate both the *communication effects* and the *sales effects* of advertising regularly.

ADVERTISERS SEEK ALTERNATIVE MEDIA

As network television costs soar and audiences shrink, many advertisers are looking for new ways to reach consumers. And the move toward micromarketing strategies, focused more narrowly on specific consumer groups, also has fueled the search for alternative media to replace or supplement network television. Advertisers are shifting larger portions of their budgets to media that cost less and target more effectively.

Two media benefiting most from the shift are outdoor advertising and cable television. Billboards have undergone a resurgence in recent years. Although outdoor advertising spending recently has leveled off, advertisers now spend more than $1.1 billion annually on outdoor media, a 25 percent increase over ten years ago. Gone are the ugly eyesores of the past; in their place we now see cleverly designed, colorful attention-grabbers. Outdoor advertising provides an excellent way to reach important local consumer segments.

Cable television is also booming. Today, more than 60 percent of all U.S. households subscribe to cable, up from just 20 percent in 1980, and cable TV ad-

vertising revenues now exceed $3 billion a year, compared to a mere $58 million in 1980. Industry experts expect that cable television advertising will continue to grow explosively through the 1990s. Cable systems allow narrow programming formats such as all sports, all news, nutrition programs, arts programs, and others that target select groups. Advertisers can take advantage of such "narrowcasting" to "rifle in" on special market segments rather than use the "shotgun" approach offered by network broadcasting.

Cable TV and outdoor advertising seem to make good sense. But, increasingly, ads are popping up in far less likely places. In their efforts to find less costly and more highly targeted ways to reach consumers, advertisers have discovered a dazzling collection of "alternative media." As consumers, we're used to ads on television, in magazines and newspapers, on the radio, and along the roadways. But these days, no matter where you go or what you do, you probably will run into some new form of advertising.

Tiny video screens attached to shopping carts,

Marketers have discovered a dazzling array of "alternative media."

Measuring the Communication Effect

Measuring the communication effect of an ad—**copy testing**—tells whether the ad is communicating well. Copy testing can be done before or after an ad is printed or broadcast. There are three major methods of advertising *pretesting*. The first is through *direct rating*, where the advertiser exposes a consumer panel to alternative ads and asks them to rate the ads. These direct ratings indicate how well the ads get attention and how they affect consumers. Although this is an imperfect measure of an ad's actual impact, a high rating indicates a potentially more effective ad. In *portfolio tests*, consumers view or listen to a portfolio of advertisements, taking as much time as they need. They then are asked to recall all the ads and their content, aided or unaided by the interviewer. Their recall level indicates the ability of an ad to stand out and its message to be understood and remembered. *Laboratory tests* use equipment to measure consumers' physiological reactions to an ad—heartbeat, blood pressure, pupil dilation, perspiration. These tests

triggered by the aisle in which the consumer is shopping, show ads from national advertisers and flash messages about store specials. As you wait in line to buy your groceries, television screens tuned to the "Checkout Channel" treat you to the latest news interspersed with food-product ads. As you approach your car, signs atop parking meters hawk everything from Jeeps to Minolta cameras to Recipe dog food. You escape to the ballpark, only to find billboard-size video screens running Budweiser ads while a blimp with an electronic message board circles lazily overhead.

You pay to see a movie at your local theater, but first you see a two-minute science-fiction fantasy that turns out to be an ad for General Electric portable stereo boxes. Then the movie itself is full of not-so-subtle promotional plugs for Pepsi, Domino's Pizza, Alka-Seltzer, MasterCard, Fritos, or any of a dozen other products. At the airport you're treated to the Flight Channel; at the local rail station, it's the Commuter Channel. Boats cruise along public beaches flashing advertising messages for Sundown Sunscreen or Gatorade to sunbathers. Even church bulletins carry ads for Campbell's Soup. Advertisers seeking a really out-of-this-world alternative can pay $500,000 for 58 feet of prime advertising space

on the hull of a Conestoga 1620 expendable rocket scheduled for launch by NASA this spring.

Some of these alternative media seem a bit far-fetched, and they sometimes irritate consumers. But for many marketers, these media can save money and provide a way to hit selected consumers where they live, shop, work, and play. Of course, this may leave you wondering if there are any commercial-free havens remaining for ad-weary consumers. The back seat of a taxi, perhaps, or public elevators, or stalls in a public restroom? Forget it! Each has already been invaded by innovative marketers.

Sources: See Alison Leigh Cowan, "Marketers Worry as Ads Crop Up in Unlikely Places," *Raleigh News and Observer,* February 21, 1988, p. 11; Kathy Martin, "What's Next? Execs Muse Over Boundless Ad Possibilities," *Advertising Age,* August 27, 1990; John P. Cortez, "Ads Head for the Bathroom," *Advertising Age,* May 18, 1992, p. 24; Ronald Grover, Laura Zinn, and Irene Recio, "Big Brother Is Grocery Shopping with You," *Business Week,* March 29, 1993, p. 60; Richard Szathmary, "The Great (and Not So Great) Outdoors," *Sales & Marketing Management,* March 1992, pp. 75-81; Riccardo A. Davis, "More Ads Go Outdoors," *Advertising Age,* November 9, 1992, p. 36; and Kathy Haley, "Cable '93: Breakthroughs Set Stage for 1993," *Advertising Age,* February 22, 1993, pp. C3 C4.

measure an ad's attention-getting power but reveal little about its impact on beliefs, attitudes, or intentions.

There are two popular methods of *posttesting* ads. Using *recall tests,* the advertiser asks people who have been exposed to magazines or television programs to recall everything they can about the advertisers and products they saw. Recall scores indicate the ad's power to be noticed and retained. In *recognition tests,* the researcher asks readers of a given issue of, say, a magazine to point out what they recognize as having seen before. Recognition scores can be used to assess the ad's impact in different market segments and to compare the company's ads with competitors' ads.

Measuring the Sales Effect
What sales are caused by an ad that increases brand awareness by 20 percent and brand preference by 10 percent? The sales effect of advertising is often harder to

measure than is the communication effect. Sales are affected by many factors besides advertising—such as product features, price, and availability.

One way to measure the sales effect of advertising is to compare past sales with past advertising expenditures. Another way is through experiments. Du Pont was one of the first companies to use advertising experiments.[14] Du Pont's paint department divided 56 sales territories into high-, average-, and low-market-share territories. In one-third of the group, Du Pont spent the normal amount for advertising; in another third, the company spent two and one-half times the normal amount; and in the remaining third, it allotted four times the normal amount. At the end of the experiment, Du Pont estimated how many extra sales resulted from higher levels of advertising expenditure. It found that higher advertising spending increased sales at a diminishing rate and that the sales increase was weaker in its high market-share territories.

International Advertising Decisions

International advertisers face many complexities not encountered by domestic advertisers. The basic issue concerns the degree to which global advertising should be adapted to the unique characteristics of various country markets. Some large advertisers have attempted to support their global brands with highly standardized worldwide advertising. Standardization produces many benefits—lower advertising costs, greater coordination of global advertising efforts, and a more consistent worldwide company or product image. However, standardization also has drawbacks. Most importantly, it ignores the fact that country markets differ greatly in their cultures, demographics, and economic conditions. Thus, most international advertisers think globally but act locally. They develop global advertising *strategies* that bring efficiency and consistency to their worldwide advertising efforts. Then they adapt their advertising *programs* to make them more responsive to consumer needs and expectations within local markets.

Companies vary in the degree to which they adapt their advertising to local markets. For example, Kellogg Frosted Flakes commercials are almost identical worldwide, with only minor adjustments for local cultural differences.[15] The advertising uses a tennis theme that has worldwide appeal and features teenage actors with generic good looks—neither too Northern European nor too Latin American. Of course, Kellogg translates the commercials into different languages. In the English version, for example, Tony growls "They're Gr-r-reat!" whereas in the German version it's "Gr-r-rossartig!" Other adaptations are more subtle. In the American ad, after winning the match, Tony leaps over the net in celebration. In other versions, he simply "high fives" his young partner. The reason: Europeans do not jump over the net after winning at tennis.

In contrast, Parker Pen Company changes its advertising substantially from country to country.

> Print ads in Germany simply show the Parker Pen held in a hand that is writing a headline—"This is how you write with precision." In the United Kingdom, where it is the brand leader, [ads emphasize] the exotic processes used to make pens, such as gently polishing the gold nibs with walnut chips. . . . In the United States, the ad campaign's theme is status and image. The headlines are . . . "Here's how you tell who's boss," and "There are times when it has to be Parker." The company considers the dif-

Kellogg's Frosted Flakes commercials are almost identical worldwide, with only minor adjustments for local cultural differences.

ferent themes necessary because of different product images and . . . customer motives in each market.[16]

Global advertisers face several additional problems. For instance, advertising media costs and availability differ considerably from country to country. Some countries have too few media to handle all of the advertising offered to them. Other countries are peppered with so many media that an advertiser cannot gain national coverage at a reasonable cost. Media prices often are negotiated and may vary greatly. For example, one study found that the cost of reaching 1,000 consumers in 11 different European countries ranged from $1.58 in Belgium to $5.91 in Italy. For women's magazines, the advertising cost per page ranged from $2.51 per thousand circulation in Denmark to $10.87 in Germany.[17]

Countries also differ in the extent to which they regulate advertising practices. Many countries have extensive systems of laws restricting how much a company can spend on advertising, the media used, the nature of advertising claims, and other aspects of the advertising program. Such restrictions often require that advertisers adapt their campaigns from country to country. Consider the following examples:

> When General Mills Toy Group's European subsidiary launched a product of G.I. Joe-type war toys and soldiers, it had to develop two television commercials, a general version for most European countries and another for countries that bar advertisements for products with military or violent themes. As a result, in the version running in Germany, Holland, and Belgium, jeeps replaced the toy tanks, and guns were removed from the hands of toy soldiers.[18]

> A 30-second Kellogg commercial produced for British TV would have to have [several] alterations to be acceptable [elsewhere] in Europe: Reference to iron and vitamins would have to be deleted in the Netherlands. A child wearing a Kellogg's T-shirt would be edited out in France where children are forbidden from endorsing products on TV. In Germany, the line "Kellogg makes cornflakes the best they've ever been" would be cut because of rules against making competitive claims. After alterations, the 30-second commercial would be [only] about five seconds long.[19]

Thus, although advertisers may develop global strategies to guide their overall advertising efforts, specific advertising programs usually must be adapted to meet local cultures and customs, media characteristics, and advertising regulations.

SALES PROMOTION

Advertising is joined by two other mass-promotion tools—*sales promotion* and *public relations*. **Sales promotion** consists of short-term incentives to encourage purchase or sales of a product or service. Whereas advertising offers reasons to buy a product or service, sales promotion offers reasons to buy *now*. Examples are found everywhere:

> A coupon in the Sunday newspaper clearly indicates a 40-cent savings on brand X coffee. The end-of-the-aisle display confronts an impulse buyer with a wall of snackfood. A family buys a camcorder and gets a free traveling case or buys a car and gets a check for a $500 rebate. An appliance retailer is given a 10 percent manufacturer discount on January's orders if the retailer advertises the product in the local newspaper.[20]

Sales promotion includes a wide variety of promotion tools designed to stimulate earlier or stronger market response. It includes **consumer promotion**—samples, coupons, rebates, prices-off, premiums, contests, and others; **trade promotion**—buying allowances, free goods, merchandise allowances, cooperative advertising, push money, dealer sales contests; and **salesforce promotion**—bonuses, contests, sales rallies.

Rapid Growth of Sales Promotion

Sales-promotion tools are used by most organizations, including manufacturers, distributors, retailers, trade associations, and nonprofit institutions. Estimates of annual sales-promotion spending run as high as $125 billion, and this spending has increased rapidly in recent years. A few decades ago, the ratio of advertising to sales promotion spending was about 60/40. Today, in many consumer packaged-goods companies, the picture is reversed, with sales promotion accounting for 75 percent or more of all marketing expenditures. Sales-promotion expenditures have been increasing 12 percent annually, compared to advertising's increase of only 7.6 percent.[21]

Several factors have contributed to the rapid growth of sales promotion, particularly in consumer markets. First, inside the company, promotion now is accepted more by top management as an effective sales tool and more product managers are qualified to use sales promotion tools. Furthermore, product managers face greater pressures to increase their current sales. Second, externally, the company faces more competition, and competing brands are less differentiated. Competitors are using more and more promotions, and consumers have become more deal oriented. Third, advertising efficiency has declined because of rising costs, media clutter, and legal restraints. Finally, retailers are demanding more deals from manufacturers.

The growing use of sales promotion has resulted in *promotion clutter,* similar to advertising clutter. Consumers are increasingly tuning out promotions, weakening their ability to trigger immediate purchase. In fact, the extent to which U.S. consumers have come to take promotions for granted was illustrated dramatically by the reactions of Eastern European consumers when Procter & Gamble recently gave out free samples of a newly introduced shampoo. To P&G, the sampling campaign was just business as usual. To consumers in Poland and Czechoslovakia, however, it was little short of a miracle:

> With nothing expected in return, Warsaw shoppers were being handed free samples of Vidal Sasoon Wash & Go shampoo. Just for the privilege of trying the new product; no standing in line for a product that may not even be on the shelf. Some were so taken aback that they were moved to tears. In a small town in Czechoslovakia, the head of the local post office was so pleased to be part of the direct-mail sampling program, he sent the P&G staffer roses to express his thanks. The postmaster told the P&G'er: "This is the most exciting thing that's ever happened in this post office—it's a terrific experience to be part of this new market economy that's coming."[22]

Although no sales promotion is likely to create such excitement among promotion-prone consumers in the United States and other Western countries, manufacturers now are searching for ways to rise above the clutter, such as offering larger coupon values or creating more dramatic point-of-purchase displays.

Purpose of Sales Promotion

Sales-promotion tools vary in their specific objectives. For example, a free sample stimulates consumer trial; a free management advisory service cements a long-term relationship with a retailer. Sellers use sales promotions to attract new triers, to reward loyal customers, and to increase the repurchase rates of occasional users.

There are three types of new triers—nonusers of the product category, loyal users of another brand, and users who frequently switch brands. Sales promotions often attract the last group—brand switchers—because nonusers and users of other brands do not always notice or act on a promotion. Brand switchers mostly are looking for low price or good value. Sales promotions are unlikely to turn them into loyal brand users. Thus, sales promotions used in markets where brands are very similar usually produce high short-run sales response but little permanent market-share gain. In markets where brands differ greatly, however, sales promotions can alter market shares more permanently.

Many sellers think of sales promotion as a tool for breaking down brand loyalty and advertising as a tool for building up brand loyalty. Thus, an important issue for marketing managers is how to divide the budget between sales promotion and advertising. Ten years ago, marketing managers typically would first decide how much they needed to spend on advertising and then put the rest into sales promotion. Today, more and more marketing managers first decide how much they need to spend on trade promotion, then decide what they will spend on consumer promotion, and then budget whatever is left over for advertising.

There is a danger in letting advertising take a back seat to sales promotion, however. Reduced advertising spending can result in lost consumer brand loyalty. One recent study of loyalty toward 45 major packaged-goods brands showed that when share of advertising drops, so does brand loyalty. Since 1975, brand loyalty for brands with increased advertising spending fell 5 percent. However, for brands with decreased ad spending, brand loyalty dropped 18 percent.[23]

When a company price-promotes a brand too much of the time, consumers begin to think of it as a cheap brand. Soon, many consumers will buy the brand only when it is on special. No one knows when this will happen, but the risk increases greatly if a company puts a well-known, leading brand on promotion more than 30 percent of the time. Marketers rarely use sales promotion for dominant brands because the promotions would do little more than subsidize current users.

Most analysts believe that sales-promotion activities do not build long-term consumer preference and loyalty, as does advertising. Instead, promotion usually produces only short-term sales that cannot be maintained. Small-share competitors find it advantageous to use sales promotion because they cannot afford to match the large advertising budgets of the market leaders. Nor can they obtain shelf space without offering trade allowances or stimulate consumer trial without offering consumer incentives. Thus, price competition is often used for small brands seeking to enlarge their shares, but it is usually less effective for a market leader whose growth lies in expanding the entire product category.[24]

The upshot is that many consumer packaged-goods companies feel that they are forced to use more sales promotion than they would like. Recently, Kellogg, Kraft, Procter & Gamble, and several other market leaders have announced that they will put growing emphasis on pull promotion and increase their advertising budgets. They blame the heavy use of sales promotion for decreased brand loyalty, increased consumer price sensitivity, a focus on short-run marketing planning, and an erosion of brand-quality image.

Some marketers dispute this criticism, however. They argue that the heavy use of sales promotion is a symptom of these problems, not a cause. They point to more basic causes, such as slower population growth, more educated consumers, industry overcapacity, the decreasing effectiveness of advertising, the growth of reseller power, and U.S. businesses' emphasis on short-run profits. These marketers assert that sales promotion provides many important benefits to manufacturers as well as to consumers. Sales promotions let manufacturers adjust to short-term changes in supply and demand and to differences in customer segments. They let manufacturers charge a higher list price to test "how high is high." Sales promotions encourage consumers to try new products instead of always staying with their current ones. They lead to more varied retail formats, such as the everyday-low-price store or the promotional-pricing store, which gives consumers more choice. Finally, sales promotions lead to greater consumer awareness of prices, and consumers themselves enjoy the satisfaction of feeling like smart shoppers when they take advantage of price specials.[25]

Sales promotions usually are used together with advertising or personal selling. Consumer promotions usually must be advertised and can add excitement and pulling power to ads. Trade and salesforce promotions support the firm's personal selling process. In using sales promotion, a company must set objectives, select the right tools, develop the best program, pretest and implement it, and evaluate the results.

Setting Sales-Promotion Objectives

Sales-promotion objectives vary widely. Sellers may use *consumer promotions* to increase short-term sales or to help build long-term market share. The objective may be to entice consumers to try a new product, lure consumers away from competitors' products, get consumers to "load up" on a mature product, or hold and reward loyal customers. Objectives for *trade promotions* include getting retailers to carry new items and more inventory, getting them to advertise the product and give it more shelf space, and getting them to buy ahead. For the *salesforce*, objectives include getting more salesforce support for current or new products or getting salespeople to sign up new accounts.

In general, sales promotions should be **consumer franchise building**—they should promote the product's positioning and include a selling message along with the deal. Ideally, the objective is to build long-run consumer demand rather than to prompt temporary brand switching. If properly designed, every sales-promotion tool has consumer franchise building potential.

Selecting Sales-Promotion Tools

Many tools can be used to accomplish sales-promotion objectives. The promotion planner should consider the type of market, the sales-promotion objectives, the competition, and the costs and effectiveness of each tool. Descriptions of the main consumer- and trade-promotion tools follow.

Consumer-Promotion Tools

The main consumer-promotion tools include samples, coupons, cash refunds, price packs, premiums, advertising specialties, patronage rewards, point-of-purchase displays and demonstrations, and contests, sweepstakes, and games.

Samples are offers of a trial amount of a product. Some samples are free; for others, the company charges a small amount to offset its cost. The sample might be delivered door to door, sent by mail, handed out in a store, attached to another product, or featured in an ad. Sampling is the most effective—but most expensive—way to introduce a new product. For example, Lever Brothers had so much confidence in its new Surf detergent that it spent $43 million to distribute free samples to four of every five American households.

Coupons are certificates that give buyers a saving when they purchase specified products. More than 330 billion coupons are distributed in the United States each year. Consumers redeem almost eight billion of these coupons at an average face value of 59 cents per coupon, saving over $4.7 billion on their shopping bills. Coupons can be mailed, included with other products, or placed in ads. They can stimulate sales of a mature brand or promote early trial of a new brand. Several packaged-goods companies are experimenting with point-of-sale coupon dispensing machines. Early tests using these "instant coupon machines" have produced average redemption rates of 24 percent and boosted sales about 32 percent.[26]

Cash refund offers (or **rebates**) are like coupons except that the price re-

Consumer-promotion tools: Here NutraSweet tries to stimulate immediate purchase with a combination of incentives, including a sample offer (free trial size), a coupon offer ($1 off larger sizes), and a premium offer (a recipe collection). On the right, it celebrates its tenth anniversary with a sweepstakes offer.

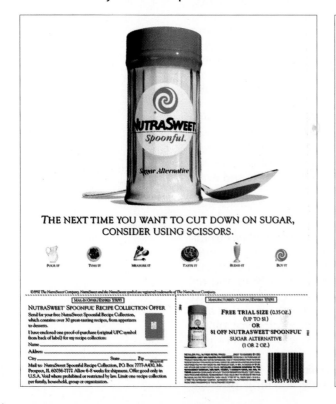

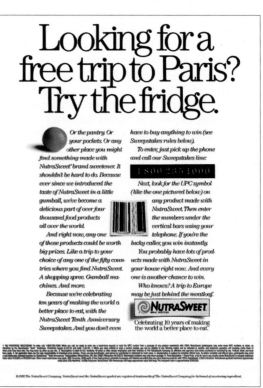

duction occurs after the purchase rather than at the retail outlet. The consumer sends a "proof of purchase" to the manufacturer, who then refunds part of the purchase price by mail. For example, Toro ran a clever preseason promotion on some of its snowblower models, offering a rebate if the snowfall in the buyer's market area turned out to be below average. Competitors were not able to match this offer on such short notice, and the promotion was very successful. In contrast, rebates have become so common in the automotive industry that many car buyers postpone purchasing until a rebate is announced. Because most auto companies match each other's rebates, each company gains little. The money could be better spent on advertising to build stronger brand images.

Price packs (also called **cents-off deals**) offer consumers savings off the regular price of a product. The reduced prices are marked by the producer directly on the label or package. Price packs can be single packages sold at a reduced price (such as two for the price of one), or two related products banded together (such as a toothbrush and toothpaste). Price packs are very effective—even more so than coupons—in stimulating short-term sales.

Premiums are goods offered either free or at low cost as an incentive to buy a product. In its "Treasure Hunt" promotion, for example, Quaker Oats inserted $5 million worth of gold and silver coins in Ken-L Ration dog-food packages. In its recent premium promotion, Cutty Sark scotch offered a brass tray with the purchase of one bottle of Cutty and a desk lamp with the purchase of two. A premium may come inside the package (in-pack) or outside the package (on-pack). If reusable, the package itself may serve as a premium—such as a decorative tin. Premiums are sometimes mailed to consumers who have sent in a proof of purchase, such as a box top. A *self-liquidating premium* is a premium sold below its normal retail price to consumers who request it. For example, manufacturers now offer consumers all kinds of premiums bearing the company's name: Budweiser fans can order T-shirts, hot-air balloons, and hundreds of other items with Bud's name on them at unusually low prices.

Advertising specialties are useful articles imprinted with an advertiser's name given as gifts to consumers. Typical items include pens, calendars, key rings, matches, shopping bags, T-shirts, caps, and coffee mugs. U.S. companies spend over $4 billion each year on advertising specialties. Such items can be very effective. In a recent study, 63 percent of all consumers surveyed were either carrying or wearing an ad specialty item. More than three quarters of those who had an item could recall the advertiser's name or message before showing the item to the interviewer.[27]

Patronage rewards are cash or other awards offered for the regular use of a certain company's products or services. For example, airlines offer "frequent flyer plans," awarding points for miles traveled that can be turned in for free airline trips. Marriott Hotels has adopted an "honored guest" plan that awards points to users of their hotels. Baskin-Robbins offers frequent-purchase awards—for every ten purchases, customers receive a free quart of ice cream. Polaroid and Pan Am jointly offer a "Frequent Smileage Program": When members buy eligible Polaroid products, they earn points that can be used to earn free tickets on Pan Am. Trading stamps are also patronage rewards in that customers receive stamps when buying from certain merchants, which can be redeemed for goods either at redemption centers or through mail-order catalogs.

Point-of-purchase (POP) promotions include displays and demonstrations that take place at the point of purchase or sale. An example is a five-foot-high cardboard display of Cap'n Crunch next to Cap'n Crunch cereal boxes. Unfortunately, many retailers do not like to handle the hundreds of displays, signs, and posters they receive from manufacturers each year. Manufacturers have responded by offering better POP materials, tying them in with television or print messages, and offering to set them up. A good example is the award-winning Pepsi "tipping can" display. From an ordinary display of Pepsi six-packs along a supermarket aisle, a mechanically rigged six-pack begins to tip forward, grabbing the attention of passing shoppers who think the six-pack is falling. A sign reminds shoppers, "Don't forget the Pepsi!" In test-market stores, the display helped get more trade support and greatly increased Pepsi sales.

Contests, sweepstakes, and **games** give consumers the chance to win something, such as cash, trips, or goods, by luck or through extra effort. A *contest* calls for consumers to submit an entry—a jingle, guess, suggestion—to be judged by a panel that will select the best entries. A *sweepstakes* calls for consumers to submit their names for a drawing. A *game* presents consumers with something—bingo numbers, missing letters—every time they buy, which may or may not help them win a prize. A sales contest urges dealers or the salesforce to increase their efforts, with prizes going to the top performers.

Trade-Promotion Tools

More sales-promotion dollars are directed to retailers and wholesalers (66 percent) than to consumers (34 percent)! Trade promotion can persuade retailers or wholesalers to carry a brand, give it shelf space, promote it in advertising, and push it to consumers. Shelf space is so scarce these days that manufacturers often have to offer price-offs, allowances, buy-back guarantees, or free goods to retailers and wholesalers to get on the shelf and, once there, to stay on it.

Manufacturers use several trade-promotion tools. Many of the tools used for consumer promotions—contests, premiums, displays—also can be used as trade promotions. Or the manufacturer may offer a straight **discount** off the list price on each case purchased during a stated period of time (also called a *price-off, off-invoice,* or *off-list*). The offer encourages dealers to buy in quantity or to carry a new item. Dealers can use the discount for immediate profit, for advertising, or for price reductions to their customers.

Manufacturers also may offer an **allowance** (usually so much off per case) in return for the retailer's agreement to feature the manufacturer's products in some way. An *advertising allowance* compensates retailers for advertising the product. A *display allowance* compensates them for using special displays.

Manufacturers may offer *free goods,* which are extra cases of merchandise, to middlemen who buy a certain quantity or who feature a certain flavor or size. They may offer *push money*—cash or gifts to dealers or their salesforce to "push" the manufacturer's goods. Manufacturers may give retailers free *specialty advertising items* that carry the company's name, such as pens, pencils, calendars, paperweights, matchbooks, memo pads, ashtrays, and yardsticks.

Business-Promotion Tools

Companies spend billions of dollars each year on promotion to industrial customers. These business promotions are used to generate business leads, stimulate purchases, reward customers, and motivate salespeople. Business promotion includes many of the same tools used for consumer or trade promotions. Here, we focus on two major business-promotion tools—conventions and trade shows, and sales contests.

Conventions and Trade Shows. Many companies and trade associations organize *conventions and trade shows* to promote their products. Firms selling to the industry show their products at the trade show. More than 5,800 trade shows take place every year, drawing approximately 80 million people. Vendors receive many benefits, such as opportunities to find new sales leads, contact customers, introduce new products, meet new customers, sell more to present customers, and educate customers with publications and audiovisual materials.

Trade shows also help companies reach many prospects not reached through their salesforces. About 90 percent of a trade show's visitors see a company's salespeople for the first time at the show. The average attendee spends almost eight hours viewing exhibits over a two-day period and an average of 22 minutes at each exhibit. About 85 percent of the attendees make a final purchase decision for one or more products displayed. The average cost per visitor reached (including exhibits, personnel travel, living and salary expenses, and preshow promotion costs) is $87, less than the average cost of an industrial sales call.

Business marketers may spend as much as 35 percent of their annual promotion budgets on trade shows. They face several decisions, including which trade shows to participate in, how much to spend on each trade show, how to build dramatic exhibits that attract attention, and how to follow up on sales leads effectively.[28]

Sales Contests. A *sales contest* is a contest for salespeople or dealers to motivate them to increase their sales performance over a given period. Most companies sponsor annual or more frequent sales contests for their salesforce. Called "incentive programs," these contests motivate and recognize good company performers, who may receive trips, cash prizes, or other gifts. Some companies award points for performance, which the receiver can turn in for any of a variety of prizes. Sales contests work best when they are tied to measurable and achievable sales objectives (such as finding new accounts, reviving old accounts, or increasing account profitability) and when employees believe they have an equal chance of winning. Otherwise, employees who do not think the contest's goals are reasonable or equitable will not take up the challenge.[29]

Developing the Sales-Promotion Program

The marketer must make some other decisions in order to define the full sales-promotion program. First, the marketer must decide on the *size of the incentive.* A certain minimum incentive is necessary if the promotion is to succeed; a larger incentive will produce more sales response. Some of the large firms which sell consumer packaged goods have a sales-promotion manager who studies past promotions and recommends incentive levels to brand managers.

The marketer also must set *conditions for participation.* Incentives might be offered to everyone or only to select groups. For example, a premium might be offered only to those who turn in box tops. Sweepstakes might not be offered in certain states, to families of company personnel, or to people under a certain age.

The marketer then must decide how to *promote and distribute the promotion* program itself. A 50-cents-off coupon could be given out in a package, at the store, by mail, or in an advertisement. Each distribution method involves a different level of reach and cost. Increasingly, marketers are blending several media into a total campaign concept:

> A sports trivia game to create pull-through at taverns for a premium beer brand would use TV to reach consumers, direct mail to incentivize distributors, point-of-purchase for retail support, telephones for consumer call-ins, a service bureau for call processing, live operators for data entry, and computer software and hardware to tie it all together . . . Companies use telepromotions not only to pull product through at retail but also to identify customers, generate leads, build databases and deliver coupons, product samples and rebate offers.[30]

The *length of the promotion* is also important. If the sales-promotion period is too short, many prospects (who may not be buying during that time) will miss it. If the promotion runs too long, the deal will lose some of its "act now" force. Brand managers need to set calendar dates for the promotions. The dates will be used by production, sales, and distribution. Some unplanned promotions also may be needed, requiring cooperation on short notice.

Finally, the marketer must determine the *sales-promotion budget,* which can be developed in one of two ways. The marketer may choose the promotions and estimate their total cost. However, the more common way is to use a percentage of the total budget for sales promotion. One study found three major problems in the way companies budget for sales promotion. First, they do not consider cost effectiveness. Second, instead of spending to achieve objectives, they simply extend the previous year's spending, take a percentage of expected sales, or use the "affordable approach." Finally, advertising and sales-promotion budgets are too often prepared separately.[31]

Pretesting and Implementing

Whenever possible, sales-promotion tools should be *pretested* to find out if they are appropriate and of the right incentive size. Yet few promotions are ever tested ahead of time—70 percent of companies do not test sales promotions before starting them.[32] Nevertheless, consumer sales promotions can be pretested quickly and inexpensively. For example, consumers can be asked to rate or rank different possible promotions, or promotions can be tried on a limited basis in selected geographic areas.

Companies should prepare implementation plans for each promotion, covering lead time and sell-off time. *Lead time* is the time necessary to prepare the program before launching it. *Sell-off time* begins with the launch and ends when the promotion ends.

Evaluating the Results

Evaluation is also very important. Yet many companies fail to evaluate their sales-promotion programs, and others evaluate them only superficially. Manufacturers can use one of many evaluation methods. The most common method is to compare sales before, during, and after a promotion. Suppose a company has a 6 percent market share before the promotion, which jumps to 10 percent during the promotion, falls to 5 percent right after, and rises to 7 percent later on. The promotion seems to have attracted new triers and more buying from current customers. After the promotion, sales fell as consumers used up their inventories. The long-run rise to 7 percent means that the company gained some new users. If the brand's share had returned to the old level, then the promotion would have changed only the timing of demand rather than the *total* demand.

Consumer research also would show the kinds of people who responded to the promotion and what they did after it ended. *Surveys* can provide information on how many consumers recall the promotion, what they thought of it, how many took advantage of it, and how it affected their buying. Sales promotions also can be evaluated through *experiments* that vary factors such as incentive value, length, and distribution method.

Clearly, sales promotion plays an important role in the total promotion mix. To use it well, the marketer must define the sales-promotion objectives, select the best tools, design the sales-promotion program, pretest and implement the program, and evaluate the results. Marketing Highlight 17-4 describes some award-winning sales-promotion campaigns.

PUBLIC RELATIONS

Another major mass-promotion tool is **public relations**—building good relations with the company's various publics by obtaining favorable publicity, building up a good "corporate image," and handling or heading off unfavorable rumors, stories, and events. The old name for marketing public relations was **publicity,** which was seen simply as activities to promote a company or its products by planting news about it in media not paid for by the sponsor. Public relations is a much broader concept that includes publicity as well as many other activities. Public relations departments use many different tools:

- *Press relations:* Placing newsworthy information in the news media to attract attention to a person, product, or service.

- *Product publicity:* Publicizing specific products.

- *Corporate communications:* Creating internal and external communications to promote understanding of the firm or institution.

- *Lobbying:* Dealing with legislators and government officials to promote or defeat legislation and regulation.

- *Counseling:* Advising management about public issues and company positions and image.[33]

Public relations is used to promote products, people, places, ideas, activities, organizations, and even nations. Trade associations have used public relations to rebuild interest in declining commodities such as eggs, apples, milk, and potatoes. New York City turned its image around when its "I Love New York" campaign took root, bringing millions more tourists to the city. Johnson & Johnson's masterly use of public relations played a major role in saving Tylenol from extinction after its product-tampering scare. Nations have used public relations to attract more tourists, foreign investment, and international support.

Public relations can have a strong impact on public awareness at a much lower cost than advertising. The company does not pay for the space or time in the media. Rather, it pays for a staff to develop and circulate information and to manage events. If the company develops an interesting story, it could be picked up by several different media, having the same effect as advertising that would cost millions of dollars. And it would have more credibility than advertising. Public relations results can sometimes be spectacular. Consider the classic case of Cabbage Patch dolls:

MARKETING HIGHLIGHT 17-4

AWARD-WINNING SALES PROMOTIONS

Each year American companies bombard consumers with thousands upon thousands of assorted sales promotions. Some fizzle badly, never meeting their objectives; others yield blockbuster returns. Here are examples of some award-winning sales promotions.

9-Lives "Free Health Exam for Your Cat" Offer

In this unusual premium promotion, Star-Kist Foods teamed with the American Animal Hospital Association to offer cat owners a free $15 cat physical in exchange for proofs of purchase from 9-Lives cat food products. The 1,500 AAHA members donated their services to encourage cat owners bring in their cats for regular checkups. Star-Kist supported the premium offer with 63 million coupons and trade discounts to boost retailer support. The promotion cost about $600,000 (excluding media). Consumers redeemed coupons at a rate 40 percent higher than normal, and Star-Kist gave out more than 50,000 free exam certificates. During the promotion, 9-Lives canned products achieved their highest share of the market in two years.

NutraSweet's Tenth Anniversary Sweepstakes

To celebrate its tenth anniversary, NutraSweet developed an innovative call-in sweepstakes. The objective: to increase sales and awareness of NutraSweet's broad acceptance since its introduction ten years earlier. The company also wanted to salute its many corporate customers. Because it has no salesforce to place in-store materials, NutraSweet designed a promotion using the Universal Product Codes on products containing NutraSweet as "lucky numbers" in it sweepstakes. Customers entered by calling a toll-free number and punching in the UPC. Callers received immediate "you win" or "try again" messages. The promotion featured 18,000 prizes ranging from gumball machines to trips to one of the 50 countries where products containing NutraSweet are sold. The UPCs of key NutraSweet customers also triggered customized messages, such as "Thanks for choosing Diet Pepsi." The sweepstakes was promoted using national free-standing inserts. It generated more than 1.5 million calls, triple the number projected. Corporate customers were pleased and the agency that designed the promotion was voted *Advertising Age's* Promotion Agency of the Year.

The "Red Baron Fly-In" Promotion

Red Baron Pizza Service used an imaginative combination of special events, couponing, and charitable activities to boost sales of its frozen pizza. The company recreated World War I flying ace Baron Manfred von Richtofen—complete with traditional flying gear and open-cockpit Stearman biplanes—as its company spokesperson. Red Baron pilots barnstormed 13 markets, showed the plane, performed stunts, gave out coupons, and invited consumers to "come fly with the Red Baron." The company donated $500 to a local youth organization in each market and urged consumers to match the gift. Trade promotions and local tie-in promotions boosted retailer support. The total budget: about $1 million. The results: For the four-week period during and after the fly-ins, unit sales in the 13 markets jumped an average of 100 percent. In the 90 days following the fly-in, sales in some markets increased as much as 400 percent.

Georgia-Pacific's "World's Fastest Roofer" Contest

Georgia-Pacific developed this creative business promotion to acquaint its roofing contractor target market with the full range of G-P's products and to celebrate the industry's "unsung heroes"—roofers. Most importantly, the contest would give roofers hands-on experience with Summit, a new high-quality shingle whose key feature was its ease of installation. Contestants installed 100 square feet of shingles. Judges chose the winner based on a combination of roofing speed and job quality. First prize was an all-expenses-paid trip to Hawaii for two. The contest began with eight regional eliminations held at G-P distribution centers around the country. Months in advance, each distribution center promoted the contest to area roofers using direct-mail promotional materials furnished by the G-P public relations department. In all, more than 150 roofers competed in the local contests. The eight regional winners were flown to Atlanta to compete in the national contest, timed to coincide with National Roofing Week. Tie-ins with a home-oriented Atlanta radio station resulted in widespread on-air promotion and raised several thousand dollars for an Atlanta children's hospital. The mayor of Atlanta issued a proclamation recognizing roofers, National Roofing Week, and Georgia-Pacific. Caps, T-shirts, and posters were used to merchandise the event both locally and nationally. After the contest, G-P sent a print and video media kit to key national media, Atlanta media, and media in the hometowns of contest participants. The budget: only $50,000 to $75,000. The results: The promotion generated more than 2.5 million media impressions and increased sales in Georgia-Pacific's targeted markets by 90 percent.

Sources: See William A. Robinson, "Event Marketing at the Crossroads," *Promote,* November 14, 1988, pp. P11-P23; Alison Fahey, "CBS, Kmart Lead Reggie Winners," *Advertising Age,* March 19, 1990, p. 47; Jon Lafayette, "Hadley Group Sweeps Competition," *Advertising Age,* January 20, 1992, p. 43; and "7-Eleven Cups Supper Reggie," *Advertising Age,* March 16, 1992, p. 39.

Public relations played a major role in making Coleco's Cabbage Patch dolls an overnight sensation. The dolls were formally introduced at a Boston press conference where local school children performed a mass-adoption ceremony for the press. Thanks to Coleco's public relations machine, child psychologists publicly endorsed the Cabbage Patch Kids, and Dr. Joyce Brothers and other newspaper columnists proclaimed that the Kids were healthy playthings. Major women's magazines featured the dolls as ideal Christmas gifts, and after a 5-minute feature on the *Today* show, the Kids made the complete talk-show circuit. Marketers of other products used the hard-to-get Cabbage Patch dolls as premiums, and retailers used them to lure customers into their stores. The word spread, and every child just *had* to have one. The dolls were quickly sold out, and the great "Cabbage Patch Panic" began.

Despite its potential strengths, public relations often is described as a marketing stepchild because of its limited and scattered use. The public relations department is usually located at corporate headquarters. Its staff is so busy dealing with various publics—stockholders, employees, legislators, city officials—that public relations programs to support product marketing objectives may be ignored. And marketing managers and public relations practitioners do not always talk the same language. On the one hand, many public relations practitioners see their job as simply communicating. On the other hand, marketing managers tend to be much more interested in how advertising and public relations affect sales and profits.

This situation is changing, however. Many companies now want their public relations departments to manage all of their activities with a view toward marketing the company and improving the bottom line. Some companies are setting up special units called *marketing public relations* to support corporate and product promotion and image making directly. Many companies hire marketing public relations firms to handle their PR programs or to assist the company public relations team. In one survey of marketing managers, three-fourths reported that their companies use marketing public relations. They found it particularly effective in building brand awareness and knowledge for both new and established products. In several cases, it proved more cost effective than advertising.[34]

Major Public Relations Tools

Public relations professionals use several tools. One of the major tools is *news*. PR professionals find or create favorable news about the company and its products or people. Sometimes news stories occur naturally, and sometimes the PR person can suggest events or activities that would create news. *Speeches* can also create product and company publicity. Increasingly, company executives must field questions from the media or give talks at trade associations or sales meetings, and these events can either build or hurt the company's image. Another common PR tool is *special events,* ranging from news conferences, press tours, grand openings, and fireworks displays to laser shows, hot-air balloon releases, multimedia presentations, and star-studded spectaculars that will reach and interest target publics.

Public relations people also prepare *written materials* to reach and influence their target markets. These materials include annual reports, brochures, articles, and company newsletters and magazines. *Audiovisual materials,* such as films, slide-and-sound programs, and video and audio cassettes, are being used increasingly as communication tools. *Corporate-identity materials* also can help create a corporate identity that the public immediately recognizes. Logos, stationery, brochures, signs, business forms, business cards, buildings, uniforms, and company cars and trucks—all become marketing tools when they are attractive, distinctive, and memorable.

Companies also can improve public goodwill by contributing money and time to *public-service activities.* For example, Procter & Gamble and Publishers' Clearing House held a joint promotion to raise money for the Special Olympics. The Publishers' Clearing House mailing included product coupons, and Procter & Gamble donated ten cents per redeemed coupon to the Special Olympics. In another example, B. Dalton Booksellers donated $3 million during a four-year period to the fight against illiteracy.[35]

Major Public Relations Decisions

In considering when and how to use product public relations, management

Attractive, distinctive, memorable company logos become strong marketing tools.

should set PR objectives, choose the PR messages and vehicles, implement the PR plan, and evaluate the results.

Setting Public Relations Objectives

The first task is to set *objectives* for public relations. Some years ago, the Wine Growers of California hired a public relations firm to develop a program to support two major marketing objectives: Convince Americans that wine drinking is a pleasant part of good living, and improve the image and market share of California wines among all wines. The following public relations objectives were set: Develop magazine stories about wine and get them placed in top magazines (such as *Time* and *House Beautiful*) and in newspapers (food columns and feature sections); develop stories about the many health values of wine and direct them to the medical profession; and develop specific publicity for the young adult market, the college market, governmental bodies, and various ethnic communities. These objectives were turned into specific goals so that final results could be evaluated.

Choosing Public Relations Messages and Vehicles

The organization next finds interesting stories to tell about the product. Suppose a little-known college wants more public recognition. It will search for possible stories: Do any faculty members have unusual backgrounds or are any working on unusual projects? Are any interesting new courses being taught or any interesting events taking place on campus? Usually, this search will uncover hundreds of stories that can be fed to the press. The chosen stories should reflect the image sought by the college.

If there are not enough stories, the college could sponsor newsworthy events. Here, the organization *creates* news rather than finds it. Ideas might include hosting major academic conventions, inviting well-known speakers, and holding news conferences. Each event creates many stories for many different audiences.

Creating events is especially important in publicizing fund-raising drives for nonprofit organizations. Fund-raisers have developed a large set of special events such as art exhibits, auctions, benefit evenings, book sales, contests, dances, dinners, fairs, fashion shows, phonathons, rummage sales, tours, and walkathons. No sooner is one type of event created, such as a walkathon, than competitors create new versions, such as readathons, bikeathons, and jogathons.

Implementing the Public Relations Plan

Implementing public relations requires care. Take the matter of placing stories in the media. A *great* story is easy to place—but most stories are not great and may not get past busy editors. Thus, one of the main assets of public relations people is their personal relationships with media editors. In fact, PR professionals are often former journalists who know many media editors and know what they want. They view media editors as a market to be satisfied so that editors will continue to use their stories.

Evaluating Public Relations Results

Public relations results are difficult to measure because PR is used with other promotion tools and its impact is often indirect. If PR is used before other tools come into play, its contribution is easier to evaluate.

The easiest measure of publicity effectiveness is the number of exposures in the media. Public relations people give the client a "clippings book" showing all the media that carried news about the product and a summary such as the following:

> Media coverage included 3,500 column inches of news and photographs in 350 publications with a combined circulation of 79.4 million; 2,500 minutes of air time on 290 radio stations and an estimated audience of 65 million; and 660 minutes of air time on 160 television stations with an estimated audience of 91 million. If this time and space had been purchased at advertising rates, it would have amounted to $1,047,000.[36]

This exposure measure is not very satisfying, however. It does not tell how many people actually read or heard the message, nor what they thought afterward. In addition, because the media overlap in readership and viewership, it does not give information on the *net* audience reached.

A better measure is the change in product awareness, knowledge, and attitude resulting from the publicity campaign. Assessing the change requires measuring the before-and-after levels of these measures. The Potato Board learned, for example, that the number of people who agreed with the statement "Potatoes are rich in vitamins and minerals" went from 36 percent before its public relations campaign to 67 percent after the campaign. That change represented a large increase in product knowledge.

Sales and profit impact, if obtainable, is the best measure of public relations effort. For example, 9-Lives sales increased 43 percent at the end of a major "Morris the Cat" publicity campaign. However, advertising and sales promotion also had been stepped up, and their contribution has to be considered.

 ## SUMMARY

Three major tools of mass promotion are advertising, sales promotion, and public relations. They are mass-marketing tools as opposed to personal selling, which targets specific buyers.

Advertising—the use of paid media by a seller to inform, persuade, and remind about its products or organization—is a strong promotion tool. American marketers spend more than $125 billion each year on advertising, and it takes many forms and has many uses. *Advertising decision making* is a five-step process consisting of decisions about the objectives, the budget, the message, the media, and, finally, the evaluation of results. Advertisers should set clear *objectives* as to whether the advertising is supposed to inform, persuade, or remind buyers. The advertising *budget* can be based on what is affordable, on a percentage of sales, on competitors' spending, or on the objectives and tasks. The *message decision* calls for designing messages, evaluat-

ing them, and executing them effectively. The *media decision* calls for defining reach, frequency, and impact goals; choosing major media types; selecting media vehicles; and scheduling the media. Finally, *evaluation* calls for evaluating the communication and sales effects of advertising before, during, and after the advertising is placed.

Sales promotion covers a wide variety of short-term incentive tools—coupons, premiums, contests, buying allowances—designed to stimulate consumers, the trade, and the company's own salesforce. Sales-promotion spending has been growing faster than advertising spending in recent years. Sales promotion calls for setting sales-promotion objectives; selecting tools; developing, pretesting, and implementing the sales-promotion program; and evaluating the results.

Public relations—gaining favorable publicity and creating a favorable company image—is the least used of the major promotion tools, although it has great potential for building awareness and preference. Public relations involves setting PR objectives, choosing PR messages and vehicles, implementing the PR plan, and evaluating PR results.

KEY TERMS

Advertising 487

Advertising objective 490

Advertising specialties 505

Allowance 506

Cash refund offers (rebates) 504

Comparison advertising 490

Consumer franchise building promotions 503

Consumer promotion 501

Contests, sweepstakes, games 505

Continuity 497

Copy testing 498

Coupons 504

Discount 506

Frequency 495

Informative advertising 490

Media impact 495

Media vehicles 497

Patronage rewards 505

Persuasive advertising 490

Point-of-purchase (POP) promotions 505

Premiums 505

Price packs (cents-off deals) 505

Public relations 508

Publicity 508

Pulsing 497

Reach 495

Reminder advertising 491

Sales promotion 501

Salesforce promotion 501

Samples 504

Trade promotion 501

DISCUSSING THE IDEAS

1. What are some benefits and drawbacks of comparison advertising? Which has more to gain from using comparison advertising—the leading brand in a market or a lesser brand? Why?

2. Surveys show that many Americans are skeptical of advertising claims. Do you mistrust advertising? Why or why not? What should advertisers do to increase credibility?

3. What factors call for more *frequency* in an advertising media schedule? What factors call for more *reach?* How can you increase one without sacrificing the other or increasing the advertising budget?

4. An ad states that Almost Home cookies are the "moistest, chewiest, most perfectly baked cookies the world has ever tasted," aside from homemade cookies. If you think some other brand of cookies is moister or chewier, is the Almost Home claim false? Should this type of claim be regulated?

5. Companies often run advertising, sales promotion, and public relations efforts at the same time. Can their effects be separated? Discuss how a company might evaluate the effectiveness of each element in this mix.

6. Why are many companies spending more on trade promotions and consumer promotions than on advertising? Is heavy spending on sales promotions a good strategy for long-term profits? Why or why not?

APPLYING THE CONCEPTS

1. Buy a Sunday paper and sort through the color advertising and coupon inserts. Find several examples that combine advertising, sales promotion, and/or public relations. For instance, a manufacturer may run a full-page ad that also includes a coupon and information on its sponsorship of a charity event, such as Easter Seals or Special Olympics. (a) Do you think these approaches using multiple tools are more or less effective than a simple approach? Why? (b) Try to find ads from two direct competitors. Are these brands using similar promotional tools in similar ways?

2. Find two current television advertisements that you think are particularly effective, and two more that you feel are ineffective. (a) Describe precisely why you think the better ads are effective, and why the ineffective ads fall short. (b) How would you improve the less effective ads? If you feel they are too poor to be improved, write a rough draft of an alternate ad for each.

MAKING MARKETING DECISIONS:

SMALL WORLD COMMUNICATIONS, INC.

Tom Campbell was discussing promotional ideas for the Small World *Airport* product with Lyn Jones. "Maybe," said Tom, "we could get some opinion leaders to use the *Airport* and comment on it, like electronic bulletin board sysops." Lyn asked, "Aren't they the one-eyed giants that Ulysses . . ." "I said *sysops*—system operators, the ones who run electronic bulletin boards—not *cyclops*. And despite your sarcasm, I think it's a great idea. Word of mouth can be very important for new little companies, and the sysops talk to every serious computer communications user out there." "Sorry—I had a late night last night, and I'm getting punchy. But you're onto something. I'm convinced that public relations is a real key for the *Airport*. It's like getting movie reviews—we want recommendations from objective outside authorities like computer columnists at the major magazines. Then we trumpet quotes from them all over our ads, and it becomes part of the message." Tom added, "You're absolutely right, and there is one endorsement we want more than any other—a *PC Magazine* Editor's Choice. They have that seal we could use in our ads, brochures, and on the package. I think it can help us with building awareness, and it certainly builds credibility." "I'm sold," said Lyn, "especially since your designs have gotten Editor's Choice selections several times. How do we get it?" "Basically," Tom replied, "we need a good product—which we've got—and we need to make a flawless impression on the magazine testers. That means that we've fully beta-tested

our design before it's reviewed, added completely finished documentation, and that we send a hand-picked sample of the highest quality. Our big plus right now is that *Airport* is a unique solution to a pressing need. If the product works like I think it will, *and* if nobody else has the same idea yet, then we've got a good shot at getting picked." "You're obviously a veteran at all this," said Lyn. "Now, let's cover a few basics of the advertising plan before I crash. No pun intended."

What Now?

1. Consider the use of public relations as a part of the *Airport* launch. (a) Discuss how important you consider public relations will be for this product. (b) List three specific ideas that you could use to make advertising and public relations efforts support each other. (c) Outline a public relations plan for the Small World launch of the *Airport*. Include the objectives, messages and vehicles, and some way to evaluate the success of your plan.

2. Develop an advertising plan for the *Airport* launch. (a) What are your advertising objectives? (b) What execution styles are suited to your message? (c) Remembering that your venture capitalists will limit your budgets, suggest advertising media that are appropriate, and comment on your assessment of reach and frequency needs.

REFERENCES

1. See "Advertising Age Best Advertising of 1989: Pink Bunny Romps Through 'Best' TV Spot," *Advertising Age*, April 30, 1990, p. 29; Vera Vaughan, "That Cute Pink Bunny," *Business Today*, Winter 1990, p. 78; Julie Liesse, "How the Bunny Charged Eveready," *Advertising Age*, April 8, 1991, pp. 20, 55; and Liesse, "Opening Day, and the Bunny Goes Up to Bat," *Advertising Age*, April 6, 1992, pp. 1, 37.

2. Statistical information in this section on advertising's size and composition draws on "Advertising Fact Book," *Advertising Age*, January 6, 1992, pp. S1-S13; and Robert J. Cohen, "How Bad a Year for Ads Was 1991?" *Advertising Age*, May 4, 1992, pp. 3, 51.

3. Julie Skur Hill, "Top Ad Spenders: Unilever, P&G," *Advertising Age*, October 28, 1991, p. 1; and "Ad Dollars Outside the U.S.," *Advertising Age*, December 14, 1992, p. S1.

4. See Russell H. Colley, *Defining Advertising Goals for Measured Advertising Results* (New York: Association for National Advertisers, 1961). In this well-known book, Colley lists 52 possible advertising objectives. He outlines a method called DAGMAR (after the book's title) for turning advertising objectives into specific measurable goals. For a more complete discussion of DAGMAR, see Michael L. Rothschild, *Advertising* (Lexington, MA: D. C. Health, 1987), pp. 142-55.

5. See Donald E. Schultz, Dennis Martin, and William P. Brown, *Strategic Advertising Campaigns* (Chicago: Crain Books, 1984), pp. 192-97.

6. Gerard J. Tellis, "Advertising Exposure, Loyalty, and Brand Purchase: A Two-Stage Model of Choice," *Journal of Marketing Research*, May 1988, pp. 134-35. For counterpoints, see Magid M. Abraham and Leonard M. Lodish, "Getting the Most Out of Advertising and Promotion," *Harvard Business Review*, May-June 1990, pp. 50-60.

7. Gary Levin, "Tracing Ads' Impact," *Advertising Age*, November 4, 1991, p. 49.

8. See Bickley Townsend, "The Media Jungle," *American Demographics*, December 1988, p. 8; and Sam Alfstad, "Don't Shrug Off Zapping," *Advertising Age*, September 9, 1991, p. 20.

9. Christine Dugas, "And Now, A Wittier Word from Our Sponsors," *Business Week*, March 24, 1986, p. 90. Also see Dennis Kneale, "'Zapping' of TV Ads Appears Pervasive," *The Wall Street Journal*, April 25, 1988, p. 29.

10. See Faye Rice, "How to Deal with Tougher Customers," *Fortune*, December 3, 1990, pp. 38-48.

11. See William A. Mindak and H. Malcolm Bybee, "Marketing's Application to Fund Raising," *Journal of Marketing*, July 1971, pp. 13-18.

12. See Mark Landler, "Neck and Neck at the Networks," *Business Week*, May 20, 1991, pp. 36-37; Faye Rice, "A Cure for What Ails Advertising," *Fortune*, December 16, 1991, pp. 119-22; and Allan J. Magrath, "The Death of Advertising Has Been

Greatly Exaggerated," *Sales & Marketing Management*, February 1992, pp. 23-24.

13. Janet Meyers and Laurie Freeman, "Marketers Police TV Commercial Costs," *Advertising Age*, April 3, 1989, p. 51.

14. See Robert D. Buzzell, "E.I. Du Pont de Nemours & Co.: Measurement of Effects of Advertising," in his *Mathematical Models and Marketing Management* (Boston: Division of Research, Graduate School of Business Administration, Harvard University, 1964), pp. 157-79.

15. Michael Lev, "Advertisers Seek Global Messages," *The New York Times*, November 18, 1991, p. D9.

16. Philip R. Cateora, *International Marketing*, 7th ed. (Homewood, IL: Irwin, 1990), p. 462.

17. Ibid, p. 475.

18. Michael R. Czinkota and Ilkka A. Ronkainen, *International Marketing*, 2nd ed. (Chicago: Dryden, 1990), p. 615.

19. Cateora, *International Marketing*, pp. 466-67.

20. From Robert C. Blattberg and Scott A. Neslin, *Sales Promotion: Concepts, Methods, and Strategies* (Englewood Cliffs, NJ: Prentice Hall, 1990). This text provides an excellent summary of sales promotion concepts and strategies.

21. Alison Fahey, "Shops See Surge in Promotion Revenues," *Advertising Age*, February 20, 1989, p. 20; and Scott Hume, "Sales Promotion: Agency Services Take on Exaggerated Importance for Marketers," *Advertising Age*, May 4, 1992, pp. 29, 32.

22. Jennifer Lawrence, "Free Samples Get Emotional Reception," *Advertising Age*, September 30, 1991, p. 10.

23. Scott Hume, "Brand Loyalty Steady," *Advertising Age*, March 2, 1992, p. 19.

24. See F. Kent Mitchel, "Advertising/Promotion Budgets: How Did We Get Here, and What Do We Do Now?" *The Journal of Consumer Marketing*, Fall 1985, pp. 405-47.

25. For more on the use of sales promotion versus advertising, see Paul W. Farris and John A. Quelch, "In Defense of Price Promotion," *Sloan Management Review*, Fall 1987; and John Philip Jones, "The Double Jeopardy of Sales Promotions," *Harvard Business Review*, September-October, 1990, pp. 145-52.

26. See Jan Larson, "Farewell to Coupons?" *American Demographics*, February 1990, pp. 14-18; "Coupon Redemptions Up 14%," *Marketing News*, March 2, 1992, p. 1; and Scott Hume,

"Coupon Use Jumps 10% as Distribution Soars," *Advertising Age*, October 5, 1992, pp. 3, 44.

27. See J. Thomas Russell and Ronald Lane, *Kleppner's Advertising Procedure*, 11th ed. (Englewood Cliffs, NJ: Prentice Hall, 1990), pp. 383-86; and "Power to the Key Ring and T-Shirt," *Sales & Marketing Management*, December 1989, p. 14.

28. See Thomas V. Bonoma, "Get More Out of Your Trade Shows," *Harvard Business Review*, January-February 1983, pp. 75-83; Jonathan M. Cox, Ian K. Sequeira, and Alissa Eckstein, "1988 Trade Show Trends: Shows Grow in Size; Audience Quality Remains High," *Business Marketing*, June 1989, pp. 57-60; and Richard Szathmary, "Trade Shows," *Sales & Marketing Management*, May 1992, pp. 83-84.

29. For more on sales contests, see C. Robert Patty and Robert Hite, *Managing Sales People*, 3rd ed. (Englewood Cliffs, NJ: Prentice Hall, 1988), pp. 313-27.

30. Quoted from Kerry E. Smith, "Media Fusion," *PROMO*, May 1992, p. 29.

31. Roger A. Strang, "Sales Promotion—Fast Growth, Faulty Management," *Harvard Business Review*, July-August 1976, p. 119.

32. "Pretesting Phase of Promotions Is Often Overlooked," *Marketing News*, February 29, 1988, p. 10.

33. Adapted from Scott M. Cutlip, Allen H. Center, and Glen M. Brown, *Effective Public Relations*, 6th ed. (Englewood Cliffs, NJ: Prentice Hall, 1985), pp. 7-17.

34. Tom Duncan, *A Study of How Manufacturers and Service Companies Perceive and Use Marketing Public Relations* (Muncie, IN: Ball State University, December 1985).

35. For more examples, see Laurie Freeman and Wayne Walley, "Marketing with a Cause Takes Hold," *Advertising Age*, May 16, 1988, p. 34; and P. Rajan Varadarajan and Anil Menon, "Cause-Related Marketing: A Coalignment of Marketing Strategy and Corporate Philanthropy," *Journal of Marketing*, July 1988, pp. 58-74.

36. Arthur M. Merims, "Marketing's Stepchild: Product Publicity," *Harvard Business Review*, November-December 1972, pp. 111-12. For more on evaluating public relations effectiveness, see Katharine D. Paine, "There *Is* a Method for Measuring PR,'" *Marketing News*, November 6, 1987, p. 5; and Eric Stoltz and Jack Torobin, "Public Relations by the Numbers," *American Demographics*, January 1991, pp. 42-46.

VIDEO CASE 17

INFOMERCIALS: ADS, SHOWS, OR DOCUMENTARIES?

It's 1:00 A.M. and I can't sleep. Wonder what's on TV? (Click.) Oh, i-i-i-t's JUICEMAN. Ugh. Zap that! (Click.) Ah, this is better . . . Pat Summerall with . . . Kenny Rogers? A talk show. Who are they talking to? Some guy named Wally—about golf. Oh wow, Wally's gonna' improve his drive by griping a plastic coat hanger along the shaft of his club. Gotta' see this. (Pause.) Now, he's gonna' drive the ball while on his knees? Good grief, he

did it. Maybe I could do that, too, if I bought one of those tapes they're selling.

Have you ever plugged into late-night television and found yourself watching 30-minute commercials known as infomercials, PLCs (program length commercials), or one-step marketing offers? In the wee hours of the morning and in late afternoon, they're broadcast on more than 15 major cable networks and 1,180 broadcast stations, reaching 55 million or more homes. Infomercial sales reached $1 billion in 1992, up from $450 million in 1989. On the average, 20,000 to 30,000 people respond to an infomercial. At $50 a pop for Wally's golfing tapes, that's a cool $1 million to $1.5 million in sales. And Richard Simmons's "Deal-a-Meal" will bring in at least $2.4 to $3.5 million at $120 each.

Where did these ads originate? In the early 1980s, the explosion of channels generated by the introduction of cable television motivated the Federal Communication Commission to loosen its programming regulations. By allowing longer commercials, the FCC enables cable channels to sell more air time. Unfortunately, the quality of the ads and the legitimacy of the products advertised in those early days created a poor image of infomercials. As a result, the number of infomercials leveled off in the mid-1980s.

But the makers of infomercials did not stand still. They formed the National Infomercial Marketing Association, which has two purposes: (1) to make certain that all infomercials are clearly identified as such; and (2) to see that only legitimate products are advertised. The association (perhaps combined with coincidental Congressional hearings) proved successful in cleaning up the image of infomercials, thereby fostering their growth. Even the prestigious advertising firm of Saatchi and Saatchi is going to make infomercials—but in a tasteful way. No slicers, dicers, or banana splicers, they say. Makes you wonder what they will sell.

Why are infomercials so popular? A principal reason is cost. A 30-minute infomercial costs about the same to produce as a 30-second ad. Specialist firms such as Guthy-Renker and Hawthorne Productions can script shows, film them, conduct all postproduction work, *and* buy the media space, all for roughly $320,000 to $500,000, thereby saving both money and effort for the advertiser.

Second, with infomercials, companies such as Volvo have the opportunity to tell consumers the complete story of their auto's safety, and states such as Arizona can spend 30 minutes showing their deserts and mountains to prospective tourists. Club Med uses infomercials to promote its full range of vacation packages in one ad rather than advertising a single vacation per ad. None of these stories could be pitched successfully in only 30 seconds.

Third, it is easy to measure the effectiveness of infomercials with the use of 800 numbers and automated response systems. Advertisers need only count the number of callers. Usually, advertisers know the number of responses to an infomercial within an hour of air time, without the added expense of conducting ad recall or recognition tests.

The infomercial format is simple and predictable. The ads grab the consumer's attention with celebrities (remember Pat Summerall?) and give them information in a talk-show-type setting. They demonstrate the product (Wally on his knees) and use celebrity testimonials (Kenny Rogers vouching for the effectiveness of the plastic coat hanger, or a happy, *thin* woman hugging Richard Simmons). Above all, they provide multiple opportunities to order by telephone or mail—usually in three equal payments. Providing so many order opportunities helps the advertiser to overcome the zap factor, because the viewer doesn't have adequate warning to zap the order instructions with the remote control.

What sells well in infomercials? Small appliances of all sorts—juicers, food hydrators, sandwich makers, and blenders—along with skin-care products, cars, travel, and tourism. And now there's something new—documercials—30-minute infomercials that show a product but do not sell it. An example is a 30-minute "show" aired by General Motors about its Saturn plant. And then there's Stan Feingold, who got catalogers to pay him $3,000 each to be in his "The Smart Business Show," a series of 30-minute infomercials touting the benefits of buying office supplies and equipment through catalogs (called "infocatalogs").

Well, it's now 2:30 A.M. and I'm still awake. About that coat hanger trick . . . I know I have some large, plastic hangers here somewhere . . . (fumble, fumble).

QUESTIONS

1. Contrast the types of communication and sales objectives that might be formulated for infomercials versus regular advertisements.

2. What types of execution styles are most often used in infomercials? Why? What other types of executions could be used?

3. How can advertisers measure the reach, frequency, and impact of infomercials?

4. Viewers may sometimes have difficulty telling infomercials from regular television programs. What potential ethics and social responsibility problems do infomercials present? What are the relative responsibilities of advertisers, the media, and government agencies in dealing with these problems?

5. How well might infomercials work for the following companies or products: (a) Avon cosmetics; (b) AT&T videophones; (c) World Book encyclopedias?

Sources: "B-to-B Cataloger Expanding TV's 'Horizons,'" *Catalog Age,* May 1992, pp. 22; Timothy Hawthorne, "Infomercial Phone Response to Grow Dramatically," *Telemarketing Magazine,* August 1992, pp. 25-26; Mark Landler, "The Infomericial Inches Toward Respectability," *Business Week,* May 4, 1992, pp. 175; Gary Slutsker, "The Power of Juicing," *Forbes,* March 2, 1992, pp. 82-83.

COMPANY CASE 17

AVON: A PROMOTIONAL STRATEGY MAKEOVER

"Ding-dong, Avon calling." With that simple advertising message over the past 107 years, Avon Products built a $3.5 billion worldwide beauty-products business. Founded in 1886, and incorporated as California Perfume Products in 1916, Avon deployed an army of women to sell its products. These "Avon ladies," 40 million of them in the company's history, met with friends and neighbors in their homes, showed products, took and delivered orders, and earned sales commissions. Through direct selling, Avon bypassed the battle for space and attention waged by its competitors in department stores, and later in discount drugstores and supermarkets. Direct selling also offered convenience for the customer, coupled with personal beauty-care advice from a friend.

Avon's plan worked well. Most members of its up to 500,000-member salesforce were homemakers who did not want a full-time job outside the home. They developed client lists of friends and neighbors, whom they called on from time to time. Customers could also call them between visits. Recruiting salespeople was easy, and a good salesperson could develop a loyal core of customers who made repeat purchases.

However, during the 1970s and 1980s, the environment changed. First, more women found that they needed to work outside the home. As a result, when Avon ladies rang the doorbell, often no one answered. Second, many Avon ladies decided that they needed more than part-time jobs. Avon experienced annual salesforce turnover rates of more than 200 percent for some positions. Third, because of salesforce turnover, many Avon customers who did want to see a salesperson could not find one. Fourth, more competitors, such as Amway, Mary Kay Cosmetics, and Tupperware, were competing for the pool of people interested in full- or part-time direct-selling jobs. Finally, in addition to all those factors, increasing mobility of the U.S. population meant that both customers and salespeople where moving. This made it difficult for salespeople to establish loyal, stable customer bases.

To deal with these issues, in 1988 Avon Products tapped James E. Preston to serve as its chairman and chief executive. First, however, Preston had to fend off three unfriendly takeover attempts, including one from Amway. Then, he faced the economic downturn of the early 1990s, which slammed door-to-door sales. Compared with a 5-to-7-percent growth rate for the cosmetics industry as a whole, door-to-door sales had been flat since 1989. Moreover, Avon's upscale Giorgio of Beverly Hills business, which featured perfumes costing up to $175 an ounce, also suffered from the economic downturn. Even Avon's international sales, which came from over 100 countries and made up 55 percent of its total sales, were sluggish. Although there were some bright spots, such as China, sales in key markets such as Brazil and Japan dropped sharply.

Preston decided that Avon needed to overhaul its marketing strategy. First, he wanted to refocus the company on its core business—selling cosmetics, fragrances, and toiletries. Therefore, he sold Avon's holdings in health care and retirement homes, ending a diversification strategy that Avon had undertaken to offset problems in it core businesses. Next, he cut prices on Avon products, some up to 75 percent. Third, he took Giorgio perfumes into foreign markets. Finally, he tried a new compensation program that allowed sales representatives to earn up to 21 percent in bonuses based on the sales of new representatives they recruited. However, this price cutting and market expansion reduced gross margins and increased costs. Between 1990 and 1991, earnings dropped from $195 million to $135 million. Marketing, distribution, and administrative expenses during this period increased from $1.682 billion to $1.746 billion.

Preston next turned his attention to Avon's promotional strategy. Beginning in 1988, Avon had cut advertising spending, in part to cut costs during the takeover attempts. It had reduced its $22 million advertising budget to $11 million in 1989, and then to $4.6 million in 1990. Preston decided that Avon now needed to restore the budget and pay for it by reducing the level of premiums and other sales-promotion activities. The company would concentrate most of this advertising in print media.

Preston believed that Avon had left as many as ten million former or potential customers stranded. These customers wanted to buy Avon products; but because of salesforce turnover, they did not know how to find a salesperson or order products. Fourteen percent of American women accounted for one-third of Avon's sales. Another 62 percent were fringe customers. These customers

viewed Avon positively but did not buy regularly. Another 15 percent of American women were potentially receptive to Avon but were not necessarily interested in dealing with a traditional Avon sales representative.

Thus, the second step in the revamped promotion strategy was to develop a catalog and try direct-mail selling. Avon's research revealed that its median customer was 45 years old and had an average household income of under $30,000. The catalog would reach younger, higher-income customers. Preston believed that, with a catalog, the company could cut the median customer age to 38 and increase average household income to more than $30,000.

Avon was late entering the catalog business. Tupperware had experimented with catalogs in late 1991, mailing them to 25,000 potential customers identified by sales representatives. A key competitor, Beauti-Control Cosmetics, Inc., a Dallas-based direct marketer, had introduced a catalog in 1984. It mailed 600,000 catalogs nationally six times a year to customers whose names were supplied by its salesforce. Another direct marketer, Fuller Brush, however, had abandoned its catalog operation in 1990 after several years of experimentation—deciding instead to focus on its basic direct-selling business.

Before jumping into catalogs, Avon first tested the idea. It found that 75 percent of the customers who made purchases during the test either had never made purchases from Avon or had not made purchases during the last six months. Moreover, 11 percent of people who received the catalogs made purchases, as compared with an industry average purchase rate of only 2 to 3 percent. However, Avon realized that it had mailed the catalogs primarily to former customers and that this might account for the high purchase rate.

Under Avon's plan, its salespeople would supply names of customers who had moved or were no longer active buyers. Avon planned to mail up to one million catalogs, and recipients could then order directly from Avon or from salespeople. If they ordered from the company, Avon would pay sales representatives a 20-percent commission, about one-half the standard commission. Avon mailed orders directly to the customers rather than having the sales representative deliver the orders.

Avon supported the catalog program by kicking off a print-advertising campaign that featured the slogan "Avon—The Smartest Shop in Town." Ads provided customers with a toll-free telephone number that they could call to order the catalog. When people called, Avon assigned them to the nearest Avon representative, who received commissions on any orders the customer placed directly with Avon. Avon hoped that the catalog project would generate $20 to $25 million in sales in 1992. Preston predicted the direct-mail business would generate sales of $300 to $500 million within three to five years. The catalog–print ad one-two punch worked, and customer inquiries rocketed from 9,000 to 90,000 per month.

For the third phase of its revised promotional strategy, Avon planned to launch a series of television commercials in 1993. Avon had not done this since 1988. The new television ads would encourage women to use the toll-free number to buy Avon products. Avon would back the ads with a new print-media campaign. Analysts estimated that Avon would spend $34 million on advertising in 1993, funding the program with cost cuts and with the reduction of some incentive programs for sales representatives. Avon also planned to spend about $70 million on advertising outside the United States, up from $35 million in 1992.

Underlying all of the advertising, selling, and sales promotions, Avon had continued its key public relations program, the Women of Enterprise Awards. Avon had been sponsoring tennis and running events. However, each year since 1987, Avon had solicited nominations for its awards from several hundred women's organizations. It sought the names of women who had overcome tragedy, prejudice, or personal handicap to become successful in business. Avon presented awards to five winners each year at a gala luncheon in New York City attended by 1,200 entrepreneurs, businesspeople, Avon staff members, and media representatives.

Advertising executives believe that Avon is on the right track. As one analyst notes, several companies have shown that selling cosmetics on television works. However, another adds that the advertising and toll-free numbers may cause some concern among members of the salesforce—suggesting that Avon runs the risk of alienating its army of Avon ladies.

Whether the strategy is risky or not, Avon and Preston realize that they must act. Last year, Avon's U.S. sales revenue fell 2 percent to $1.36 billion, and profits declined 3 percent to $182 million. In addition, Avon's salesforce shrank 4 percent to 425,000. Meanwhile, Mary Kay Cosmetics had a good year, perhaps sparked by a new incentive compensation plan that enabled some Mary Kay sales managers to earn as much as $1 million. Beauti-Control, like Avon, faced problems. It intended to announce a new salesforce incentive plan during 1993.

QUESTIONS

1. How does Avon's new strategy change the promotion mix? How do the elements of the new promotion mix support each other?

2. What are Avon's objectives for its catalog, print, and television campaigns?

3. What advertising message(s) should Avon communicate with its new programs, and what message execution style(s) would you recommend? How would you measure the effect of the new campaigns?

4. What consumer or salesforce promotions would you recommend to Avon?

5. Is the Women of Enterprise Award public relations activity appropriate for Avon?

6. In foreign markets, should Avon stick with its traditional personal-selling strategy, or should it employ the newer strategy it is developing for the United States?

Sources: Jeffrey A. Trachtenberg, "Catalogs Help Avon Get a Foot in the Door," The Wall Street Journal, February 28, 1992, p. B1; and Jeffrey A. Trachtenberg, "Avon's New TV Campaign Says, 'Call Us,'" The Wall Street Journal, December 28, 1992, p. B1. Used with permission of The Wall Street Journal. See also: Pat Sloan, "Avon Is Calling on New Tactics, FCB," Advertising Age, January 7, 1991, p. 3; Andrew Tanzer, "Ding-dong, Capitalism Calling," Forbes, October 14, 1991, pp. 184-85; Wendy Zeller, "Despite the Face-Lift, Avon Is Sagging," Business Week, December 2, 1991, pp. 101-02; Julie C. Mason, "Corporate Sponsorships Help Target the Right Audience," Management Review, November 1992, pp. 58-61.

*P*romoting Products: Personal Selling and Sales Management

18

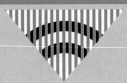

*A*pril 18: GPA announces it is buying 182 Boeing 737s, 757s, and 767s. Price: $9.4 billion.

April 25: US Air announces it is buying 18 Boeing 737s. Price: $567 million

April 26: United Airlines announces it is buying 180 Boeing 737s and 757s. Price: $7.1 billion.

April 27: KLM announces it is buying 15 Boeing 737s and 747s. Price: $955 million.

Not a bad 10 days' work! But you might expect such success from a company with a 55 percent share of the commercial airplane market, a company that has accumulated a mammoth $90 billion backlog of orders, a company whose dedication to making a sale has been called obsessive. The company, of course, is Boeing, the $29 billion aerospace giant. In a field where big sales are seldom big news, Boeing got everyone's attention when it received orders worth $18 billion in little more than a week. Despite difficult times for the aerospace industry in recent years, Boeing has managed to maintain its dominating market-share leadership.

Most of the responsibility for marketing Boeing's commercial aircraft falls on the shoulders of the company's salesforce. In some ways, selling airplanes differs from selling other industrial products. Nationwide, there are only about 55 potential customers; there are only three major competitors (Boeing, McDonnell-Douglas, and Airbus); and the high-tech product is especially complex and challenging. But in many other ways, selling commercial aircraft is like selling any other industrial product. The salespeople determine needs, demonstrate how their product fulfills these needs, try to close the sale, and follow up after the sale.

To determine needs, Boeing salespeople become experts on the airlines for which they are responsible, much like Wall Street analysts would. They find out where each airline wants to grow, when it wants to replace planes, and details of its financial situation. They then find ways to fulfill customer needs. They run Boeing and competing planes through computer systems, simulating the airline's routes, cost per seat, and other factors to show that their planes are most efficient. And, more than likely, they'll bring in financial, planning, and technical people to answer any questions.

Then the negotiations begin. Deals are cut, discounts made, and training programs offered. Sometimes top executives from both the airline and Boeing are brought in to close the deal. The selling process is nerve-rackingly slow—it can take two or three years from the first sales presentation to the day the sale is announced. After getting the order, salespeople then must stay in almost constant touch to keep track of the account's equipment needs and to make certain the customer stays satisfied. Success depends on building solid, long-term relationships with customers, based on performance and trust. According to one analyst, Boeing's salespeople "are the vehicle by which information is collected and contacts are made so all other things can take place."

The Boeing salesforce consists of experienced salespeople who use a conservative, straightforward sales approach. They are smooth and knowledgeable, and they like to sell on facts and logic rather than hype and promises. In fact, they tend to understate rather than overstate product benefits. For example, one writer notes that "they'll always underestimate fuel efficiency. They'll say it's a five percent savings, and it'll be eight." Thus, a customer thinking about making a $2 billion purchase can be certain that after the sale, Boeing products will live up to expectations.

Boeing salespeople have a head start on the competition. They have a broad mix of excellent products to sell, and Boeing's size and reputation help them get orders. The company's salespeople are proud to be selling Boeing aircraft, and their pride creates an attitude of success that is perhaps best summed up by the company's director of marketing communications. "The popular saying is that Boeing is the Mercedes of the airline industry. We think that's backward. We like to think that Mercedes is the Boeing of the auto industry."[1]

CHAPTER PREVIEW

Chapter 18 concentrates on another important aspect of promoting products, the role played by personal selling and sales management.

We start with a discussion of **setting salesforce objectives**, a key step that precedes effective **salesforce design**. Other aspects we cover are setting **salesforce strategy**, picking a **structure—territorial, product, customer**, or **complex**—and insuring that **salesforce size** and **compensation** are appropriate.

After a structure is set, there is a need to **recruit, select**, and **train salespeople**. The chapter surveys the key issues in training and supervising salespeople, including **directing, motivating through quotas and incentives**, and **evaluating performance**.

We conclude with a discussion of the principles of **personal selling** process, and outline the steps in the process—**qualifying, preapproach** and **approach, presentation** and **demonstration, handling objectives, closing** and **follow-up**.

Robert Louis Stevenson once noted that "everyone lives by selling something." Salesforces are found in nonprofit as well as profit organizations. Recruiters are a college's salesforce for attracting students. Churches use membership committees to attract new members. The U.S. Agricultural Extension Service sends agricultural specialists to sell farmers on new farming methods. Hospitals and museums use fundraisers to contact donors and raise money.

The people who do the selling go by many names: *salespeople, sales representatives, account executives, sales consultants, sales engineers, field representatives, agents, district managers,* and *marketing representatives,* to name a few. Selling is one of the oldest professions in the world.

There are many stereotypes of salespeople. "Salesman" may bring to mind the image of Arthur Miller's pitiable Willy Loman in *Death of a Salesman* or Meredith Willson's cigar-smoking, back-slapping, joke-telling Harold Hill in *The Music Man.* Salespeople typically are portrayed as outgoing and sociable—although many salespeople actually dislike unnecessary socializing. They are blamed for forcing goods on people—although buyers often search out salespeople.

Actually the term **salesperson** covers a wide range of positions whose differences are often greater than their similarities. Here is one popular classification of sales positions:

- Positions in which the salesperson's job is largely to *deliver* the product, such as milk, bread, fuel, or oil.

- Positions in which the salesperson is largely an inside *order taker,* such as the department store salesperson standing behind the counter, or an outside order taker, such as the packing-house, soap, or spice salesperson.

- Positions in which the salesperson is not expected or permitted to take an order but only *builds goodwill or educates buyers* (called "missionary" selling)—the "detailer" for a pharmaceutical company who calls on doctors to educate them about the company's drug products and to urge them to prescribe these products to their patients.

The term "salesperson" covers a wide range of positions, from the clerk selling in a retail store to the engineering salesperson who consults with client companies.

- Positions in which the major emphasis is on *technical knowledge*—the engineering salesperson who is mostly a consultant to client companies.

- Positions that demand the *creative selling* of tangible products, like appliances, houses, or industrial equipment, or of intangibles, such as insurance, advertising services, or education.[2]

This list ranges from the least to the most creative types of selling. For example, the jobs at the top of the list call for servicing accounts and taking orders, whereas the others call for simply hunting down buyers and getting them to buy.

In this chapter, we focus on the more creative types of selling and on the process of building and managing an effective salesforce. We define **salesforce management** as the analysis, planning, implementation, and control of salesforce activities. It includes setting salesforce objectives, designing salesforce strategy, and recruiting, selecting, training, supervising, and evaluating the firm's salespeople. The major salesforce management decisions are shown in Figure 18-1.

SETTING SALESFORCE OBJECTIVES

Companies set different objectives for their salesforces. IBM salespeople are to "sell, install, and upgrade" customer computer equipment; AT&T salespeople are expected to "develop, sell, and protect" accounts. Salespeople usually perform one or more of many tasks. They find and develop new customers and communicate information about the company's products and services. They sell products by approaching customers, presenting their products, answering objections, and closing sales. In addition, salespeople provide services to customers, carry out market research and intelligence work, and fill out sales call reports.

Some companies are very specific about their salesforce objectives and activities. One company advises its salespeople to spend 80 percent of their time with

FIGURE 18-1
Major steps in salesforce management

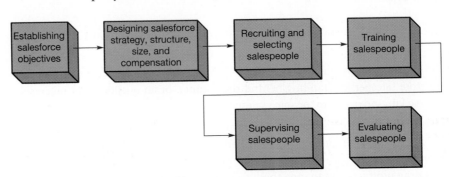

current customers and 20 percent with prospects and 85 percent of their time on current products and 15 percent on new products. This company believes that if such norms are not set, salespeople tend to spend almost all of their time selling current products to current accounts and neglect new products and new prospects.

As companies move toward a stronger market orientation, their salesforces will need to become more market focused and customer oriented. The old view was that salespeople should worry about sales and the company should worry about profit. However, the newer view holds that salespeople should be concerned with more than just producing *sales*—they also must know how to produce *customer satisfaction* and *company profit*. They should know how to look at sales data, measure market potential, gather market intelligence, and develop marketing strategies and plans. Salespeople need marketing analysis skills, especially at higher levels of sales management. A market-oriented rather than a sales-oriented salesforce will be more effective in the long run. It not only will be more effective in winning new customers, but also in creating long-term, profitable relationships with existing customers.

DESIGNING SALESFORCE STRATEGY

Once the company has set its salesforce objectives, it is ready to face questions of salesforce strategy, structure, size, and compensation.

Salesforce Strategy

Every company competes with other firms to get orders from customers. Thus, it must base its strategy on an understanding of the customer buying process. A company can use one or more of several sales approaches to contact customers. An individual salesperson can talk to a prospect or customer in person or over the phone. Or a salesperson also can make a sales presentation to a buying group. A sales *team* (such as a company executive, a salesperson, and a sales engineer) can make a sales presentation to a buying group. In *conference selling*, a salesperson brings resource people from the company to meet with one or more buyers to discuss problems and opportunities. In *seminar selling*, a company team conducts an educational seminar about state-of-the-art developments for a customer's technical people.

Thus, the salesperson often acts as an "account manager" who arranges contacts between people in the buying and selling companies. Because salespeople need help from others in the company, selling calls for teamwork. Others who might assist salespeople include top management, especially when major sales are at stake; technical people who provide technical information to customers; customer service representatives who provide installation, maintenance, and other services to customers; and office staff, such as sales analysts, order processors, and secretaries.

Once the company decides on a desirable selling approach, it can use either a direct or a contractual salesforce. A *direct (or company) salesforce* consists of full- or part-time employees who work exclusively for the company. This salesforce includes *inside salespeople,* who conduct business from their offices via telephone or visits from prospective buyers, and *field salespeople,* who travel to call on customers. A *contractual salesforce* consists of manufacturers' reps, sales agents, or brokers who are paid a commission based on their sales.

Salesforce Structure

Salesforce strategy influences the structure of the salesforce. The salesforce structure decision is simple if the company sells one product line to one industry with customers in many locations. In that case the company would use a *territorial salesforce structure.* If the company sells many products to many types of customers, it might need either a *product salesforce structure* or a *customer salesforce structure.*

Territorial Salesforce Structure

In the **territorial salesforce structure,** each salesperson is assigned to an exclusive territory in which to sell the company's full line of products or services. This salesforce structure is the simplest sales organization and has many advantages. First, it clearly defines the salesperson's job, and because only one salesperson works the territory, he or she gets all the credit or blame for territory sales. Second, the territorial structure increases the salesperson's desire to build local business ties that, in turn, improve the salesperson's selling effectiveness. Finally, because each salesperson travels within a small geographic area, travel expenses are relatively small.

Territorial sales organization often is supported by many levels of sales management positions. For example, Campbell Soup recently changed from a product salesforce structure to a territorial one, whereby each salesperson is now responsible for selling all Campbell Soup products. Starting at the bottom of the organization, *sales merchandisers* report to *sales representatives,* who report to *retail supervisors,* who report to *directors of retail sales operations,* who report to one of twenty-two *regional sales managers*. Regional sales managers, in turn, report to one of four *general sales managers* (West, Central, South, and East), who report to a *vice-president and general sales manager*.[3]

Product Salesforce Structure

Salespeople must know their products—especially when the products are numerous, unrelated, and complex. This need, together with the trend toward product management, has led many companies to adopt a **product salesforce structure,** in which the salesforce sells along product lines. For example, Kodak uses different salesforces for its film products than for its industrial products. The film products salesforce deals with simple products that are distributed intensively, whereas the industrial products salesforce deals with complex products that require technical understanding.

The product structure can lead to problems, however, if a given customer buys many of the company's products. For example, the Baxter International, a hospital supply company, has several product divisions, each with a separate salesforce. Several Baxter salespeople might end up calling on the same hospital on the same day. This means that they travel over the same routes and wait to see the same customer's purchasing agents. These extra costs must be compared with the benefits of better product knowledge and attention to individual products.

Customer Salesforce Structure

Companies often use a **customer salesforce structure,** whereby they organize the salesforce along customer or industry lines. Separate salesforces may be set up for different industries, for serving current customers versus finding new ones, and for major accounts versus regular accounts. Xerox, for example, classifies its customers into four major groups, each served by a different salesforce. The top group consists of large national accounts with multiple and scattered locations. These customers are handled by 250 to 300 *national account managers*. Next are major accounts that, although not national in scope, may have several locations within a region; these are handled by one of Xerox's 1,000 or so *major account managers*. The third customer group consists of standard commercial accounts with annual sales potential of $5,000 to $10,000; they are served by *account representatives*. All other customers are handled by *marketing representatives*.[4]

Organizing its salesforce around customers can help a company to become more customer focused. For example, giant ABB, the $29-billion-a-year Swiss-based industrial equipment maker, recently changed from a product-based to a customer-based salesforce. The new structure resulted in a stronger customer orientation and improved service to clients:

> Until four months ago, David Donaldson sold boilers for ABB . . . After 30 years, Donaldson sure knew boilers, but he didn't know much about the broad range of other products offered by ABB's U.S. Power Plant division. Customers were frustrated because as many as a dozen ABB salespeople called on them at different times to peddle their products. Sometimes representatives even passed each other in customers' lobbies without realizing that they were working for the same company. ABB's bosses decided that this was a poor way to run a salesforce. So [recently], David Donaldson and 27 other power plant salespeople began new jobs. [Donaldson] now also sells turbines, generators, and three other product lines. He handles six major accounts . . . instead of a [mixed batch] of 35. His charge: Know the customer intimately and sell him the products that help him operate productively. Says Donaldson: "My job is to

make it easy for my customer to do business with us . . . I show him where to go in ABB whenever he has a problem." The president of ABB's power plant businesses [adds]: "If you want to be a customer-driven company, you have to design the sales organization around individual buyers rather than around your products."[5]

Complex Salesforce Structures

When a company sells a wide variety of products to many types of customers over a broad geographical area, it often combines several types of salesforce structures. Salespeople can be specialized by territory and product, by territory and market, by product and market, or by territory, product, and market. A salesperson might then report to one or more line and staff managers.

Salesforce Size

Once the company has set its strategy and structure, it is ready to consider *salesforce size*. Salespeople constitute one of the company's most productive—and most expensive—assets. Therefore, increasing their number will increase both sales and costs.

Many companies use some form of **workload approach** to set salesforce size. Under this approach, a company groups accounts into different size classes and then determines the number of salespeople needed to call on them the desired number of times. The company might think as follows: Suppose we have 1,000 Type-A accounts and 2,000 Type-B accounts. Type-A accounts require 36 calls a year and Type-B accounts require 12 calls a year. In this case, the salesforce's *workload*—the number of calls it must make per year—is 60,000 calls [(1,000 × 36) + (2,000 × 12) = 36,000 + 24,000 = 60,000)]. Suppose our average salesperson can make 1,000 calls a year. The company thus needs 60 salespeople (60,000/1,000).

Salesforce Compensation

To attract salespeople, a company must have an attractive compensation plan. These plans vary greatly both by industry and by companies within the same industry. The level of compensation must be close to the "going rate" for the type of sales job and needed skills. For example, the average earnings of an experienced, middle-level industrial salesperson in 1991 amounted to about $41,000.[6] To pay less than the going rate would attract too few quality salespeople; to pay more would be unnecessary.

Compensation is made up of several elements—a fixed amount, a variable amount, expenses, and fringe benefits. The fixed amount, usually a salary, gives the salesperson some stable income. The variable amount, which might be commissions or bonuses based on sales performance, rewards the salesperson for greater effort. Expense allowances, which repay salespeople for job-related expenses, let salespeople undertake needed and desirable selling efforts. Fringe benefits, such as paid vacations, sickness or accident benefits, pensions, and life insurance, provide job security and satisfaction.

Management must decide what *mix* of these compensation elements makes the most sense for each sales job. Different combinations of fixed and variable compensation give rise to four basic types of compensation plans—straight salary, straight commission, salary plus bonus, and salary plus commission. A study of salesforce compensation plans showed that about 14 percent of companies paid straight salary, 19 percent paid straight commission, 26 percent paid salary plus bonus, 37 percent paid salary plus commission, and 10 percent paid salary plus commission plus bonus.[7]

RECRUITING AND SELECTING SALESPEOPLE

Having set the salesforce strategy, structure, size, and compensation, the company now must set up systems for *recruiting and selecting, training, supervising,* and *evaluating salespeople.*

Importance of Careful Selection

At the heart of any successful salesforce operation is the selection of good salespeople. The performance levels of an average and a top salesperson can be quite different. In a typical salesforce, the top 30 percent of the salespeople might bring in 60 percent of the sales. Thus, careful salesperson selection can greatly increase overall salesforce performance.

Beyond the differences in sales performance, poor selection results in costly turnover. One study found an average annual salesforce turnover rate of 27 percent for all industries. The costs of high turnover can be considerable. When a salesperson quits, the costs of finding and training a new salesperson—plus the costs of lost sales—can run as high as $50,000 to $75,000. And a salesforce with many new people is less productive.[8]

What Makes a Good Salesperson?

Selecting salespeople would not be a problem if the company knew what traits to look for. If it knew that good salespeople were outgoing, aggressive, and energetic, for example, it could simply check applicants for these characteristics. But many successful salespeople are also bashful, mild-mannered, and very relaxed. Successful salespeople include some individuals who are tall and others who are short, some who speak well and some who speak poorly, some who dress well and some who dress shabbily.

Still, the search continues for the magic list of traits that spells sure-fire sales ability. One survey suggests that good salespeople have a lot of enthusiasm, persistence, initiative, self-confidence, and job commitment. They are committed to sales as a way of life and have a strong customer orientation. Another study suggests that good salespeople are independent and self-motivated, and are excellent listeners. Still another study advises that salespeople should be a friend to the customer as well as persistent, enthusiastic, attentive, and—above all—honest.[9] Charles Garfield found that good salespeople are goal-directed risk takers who identify strongly with their customers (see Marketing Highlight 18-1).

How can a company find out what traits salespeople in its industry should have? Job *duties* suggest some of the traits a company should look for. Is a lot of paper work required? Does the job call for much travel? Will the salesperson face a lot of rejections? The successful salesperson should be suited to these duties. The company also should look at the characteristics of its most successful salespeople for clues to needed traits.

Recruiting Procedures

After management has decided on needed traits, it must *recruit* salespeople. The human resources department looks for applicants by getting names from current salespeople, using employment agencies, placing classified ads, and contacting college students. Until recently, companies sometimes found it hard to sell college students on selling. Many thought that selling was a job and not a profession, that salespeople had to be deceitful to be effective, and that selling involved too much insecurity and travel. In addition, some women believed that selling was a man's career. To counter such objections, recruiters now offer high starting salaries and income growth and tout the fact that more than one-fourth of the presidents of large U.S. corporations started out in marketing and sales. They point out that more than 28 percent of the people now selling industrial products are women. Women account for a much higher percentage of the salesforce in some industries, such as textiles and apparel (61 percent), banking and financial services (58 percent), communications (51 percent), and publishing (49 percent). See Marketing Highlight 18-2.[10]

Selecting Salespeople

Recruiting will attract many applicants, from which the company must select the best. The selection procedure can vary from a single informal interview to lengthy testing and interviewing. Many companies give formal tests to sales applicants. Tests typically measure sales aptitude, analytical and organizational skills, personality traits, and other characteristics.[11] Test results count heavily in such companies as IBM, Prudential, Procter & Gamble, and Gillette. Gillette claims that tests have reduced turnover by 42 percent and that test scores have correlated well with the later performance of new salespeople. But test scores provide only one piece of information in a set that includes personal characteristics, references, past employment history, and interviewer reactions.

MARKETING HIGHLIGHT 18-1

WHAT MAKES A SUPERSALESPERSON?

Charles Garfield, clinical professor of psychology at the University of California, San Francisco School of Medicine, claims that his twenty-year analysis of more than 1,500 superachievers in every field of endeavor is the longest-running to date. *Peak Performance—Mental Training Techniques of the World's Greatest Athletes* is the first book Garfield wrote about his findings. Although he says it will be followed shortly by a book on business that will cover supersalespeople, many companies (such as IBM, which took 3,000) have ordered the current book for their salesforces. Garfield says that the complexity and speed of change in today's business world requires a peak performer in sales to possess greater mastery of different fields than to be one in science, sports, or the arts. The following are the most common characteristics he has found in peak sales performance:

- Supersalespeople are always taking risks and making innovations. Unlike most people, they stay out of the "comfort zone" and try to surpass their previous levels of performance.

- Supersalespeople have a powerful sense of mission and set the short-, intermediate-, and long-term goals necessary to fulfill that mission. Their personal goals are always higher than sales quotas set by their managers. Supersalespeople also work well with managers, especially if managers are also interested in peak performance.

- Supersalespeople are more interested in solving problems than in placing blame or bluffing their way out of situations. Because they view themselves as professionals in training, they are always upgrading their skills.

- Supersalespeople see themselves as partners with their customers and as team players rather than adversaries. While peak performers believe their task is to communicate with people, mediocre salespeople psychologically change their customers into objects and talk about the number of calls and closes they made as if it had nothing to do with human beings.

- Whereas supersalespeople take each rejection as information they can learn from, mediocre salespeople personalize rejection.

- The most surprising finding is that, like peak performers in sports and the arts, supersalespeople use mental rehearsal. Before every sale, they review it in their mind's eye, from shaking the customer's hand when they walk in to discussing the customer's problems and asking for the order.

Source: "What Makes a Supersalesperson?" *Sales & Marketing Management*, August 13, 1984, p. 86. Also see "What Makes a Top Performer?" *Sales & Marketing Management*, May 1989, pp. 23-24; and Timothy J. Trow, "The Secret of a Good Hire: Profiling," *Sales & Marketing Management*, May 1990, pp. 44-45.

TRAINING SALESPEOPLE

Many companies used to send their new salespeople into the field almost immediately after hiring them. They would be given samples, order books, and general instructions ("sell west of the Mississippi"). Training programs were luxuries. To many companies, a training program translated into much expense for instructors, materials, space, and salary for a person who was not yet selling, and a loss of sales opportunities because the person was not in the field.

Today's new salespeople, however, may spend anywhere from a few weeks to many months in training. The average training period is four months. IBM spends $1 billion a year educating its work force and customers. Initial sales training lasts 13 months, and new salespeople typically are not on their own for two years! IBM also expects its salespeople to spend 15 percent of their time each year in additional training.[12]

Training programs have several goals. Salespeople need to know and identify with the company, so most companies spend the first part of the training program describing the company's history and objectives, its organization, its financial structure and facilities, and its chief products and markets. Because salespeople also need to know the company's products, sales trainees are shown how products are produced and how they work. Salespeople also need to know customers' and competitors' characteristics, so the training program teaches them about competitors' strategies and about different types of customers and their needs, buying motives, and buying habits. Salespeople must learn how to make effective presentations, so they are trained in the principles of selling, and the

ON THE JOB WITH TWO SUCCESSFUL SALESWOMEN

Successful saleswomen Catherine Hogan and Joyce Nardone—the word "salesman" now has an archaic ring.

The word *salesman* now has an archaic ring. The entry of women into what was once the male bastion of professional selling has been swift and dramatic. More than 28 percent of people selling industrial products are women, compared to just 7 percent in 1975. In some industries this percentage reaches as high as 60 percent. Here are two examples of highly successful technical saleswomen.

Catherine Hogan, Account Manager, Bell Atlantic Network Services

As an undergraduate student, Catherine Hogan had few thoughts about a career in sales, especially *technical* sales. "I was a warm, fuzzy person," she says, "artsy craftsy." Now, just six years later, she's in the thick of it, successfully handling a complex line of technical products in what was once a male-dominated world. Why the change? "I needed to get out there and feel the heat—take risks, handle customers, and be responsible for their complaints," says Hogan. Still far from being a technical person, she has quickly acquired a working knowledge of modern communications services and the ways they can be delivered to businesses through Bell Atlantic's phone network.

So rapidly is the company diversifying that, artsy-craftsy or not, Hogan finds herself studying up on new hardware, software, and leasing programs so she can explain them both to business customers and to Bell's own account executives, who have ongoing responsibilities for those customers. The account executives can handle their customers' local applications by themselves but team up with Hogan when customers want long-distance voice or data services. This sort of cooperative selling requires empathy and skill. On joint calls, Hogan is careful not to interfere when the account executive is negotiating with a customer.

On a more personal level, Hogan has worked through the pros and cons of being something of a novelty in an industry undergoing wrenching change. "People are used to seeing middle-age, white males with a technical background in this industry," she says. It's challenging being young, female, and ethnic." Her ad-

vice to others in similar situations? "Go beyond what the world prescribes for you. Be strong enough to lance the dragon but soft enough to wear silk."

Joyce Nardone, Sales Manager, Facsimile Division, Amfax America

For a vivid picture of what it takes to succeed in sales, listen to Joyce Nardone exclaim about the terrors and triumphs of selling to strangers who've never heard your name before you walk in the door. "I'm good at cold-calling, but it takes a long time to learn to take rejection," she says. "Sometimes just getting out of the car is a feat in itself."

So resilient is the 24-year-old Joyce, however, that prior to her recent promotion to management, she compiled an impressive record of knocking on doors for Amfax America, an office equipment dealer whose main line is Sharp facsimile machines and copiers. "You have to be friendly and upbeat," she says. "If you look like a winner, they'll buy from you."

As good as she is at cold-calling, Nardone adds a special ingredient in a business that traditionally has been built around the one-time sale: She keeps up with her customers and makes sure they're satisfied with the product. "I have over 100 clients, and I consider them my friends," she says. "Most people don't bother to go back, but I'll bring them a free roll of paper or fax them a Hanukkah or Christmas card." As a result, customers often refer other companies to Nardone, so she has a steady stream of new business.

Fortunately, management recognizes her talents, too. Nardone is now in charge of the salesforce for Amfax's Facsimile Division. As manager, she is responsible for training, motivation, and overall performance of 8 direct salespeople. She also coordinates advertising and trade show exhibits. Her advice to new salespeople? "To discover customers' needs, *listen* to them!"

Sources: Adapted from portions of Martin Everett, "Selling's New Breed: Smart and Feisty," *Sales & Marketing Management*, October 1989, pp. 52-64. Also see Bill Kelley, "Selling in a Man's World," *Sales & Marketing Management*, January 1991, pp. 28-35.

Companies spend hundreds of millions of dollars to train their salespeople in the art of selling.

company outlines the major sales arguments for each product. Finally, salespeople need to understand field procedures and responsibilities. They learn how to divide time between active and potential accounts and how to use an expense account, prepare reports, and route communications effectively.

SUPERVISING SALESPEOPLE

New salespeople need more than a territory, compensation, and training—they need *supervision*. Through supervision, the company *directs* and *motivates* the salesforce to do a better job.

Directing Salespeople

How much sales management should be involved in helping salespeople manage their territories? It depends on everything from the company's size to the experience of its salesforce. Thus, companies vary widely in how closely they supervise their salespeople. And what works for one company may not work for another.[13]

Developing Customer Targets and Call Norms
Most companies classify customers based on sales volume, profit, and growth potential and set call norms accordingly. Thus, salespeople may call weekly on accounts with large sales or potential but only infrequently on small accounts. Beyond account size and potential, call norms also may depend on other factors such as competitive call activity and account development status.

Companies often specify how much time their salesforces should spend prospecting for new accounts. For example, Spector Freight wants its salespeople to spend 25 percent of their time prospecting and to stop calling on a prospect after three unsuccessful calls. Companies set up prospecting standards for several reasons. For example, if left alone, many salespeople will spend most of their time with current customers, who are better-known quantities. Moreover, whereas a prospect may never deliver any business, salespeople can depend on current accounts for some business. Therefore, unless salespeople are rewarded for opening new accounts, they may avoid new-account development. Some companies even may rely on a special salesforce to open new accounts.

Using Sales Time Efficiently
Salespeople need to know how to use their time efficiently. One tool is the *annual call schedule* that shows which customers and prospects to call on in which months and which activities to carry out. Activities include taking part in trade shows, attending sales meetings, and carrying out marketing research. Another tool is *time-and-duty analysis*. In addition to time spent selling, the salesperson spends time traveling, waiting, eating, taking breaks, and doing administrative chores.

Figure 18-2 shows how salespeople spend their time. On average, actual face-to-face selling time accounts for only 30 percent of total working time! If selling time could be raised from 30 percent to 40 percent, this would be a 33 percent increase in the time spent selling. Companies always are looking for ways to save

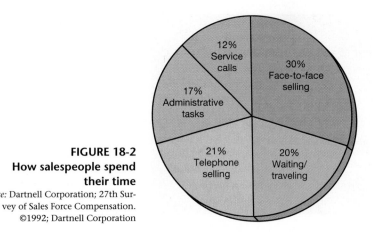

**FIGURE 18-2
How salespeople spend
their time**
Source: Dartnell Corporation; 27th Survey of Sales Force Compensation. ©1992; Dartnell Corporation

time—using phones instead of traveling, simplifying record-keeping forms, finding better call and routing plans, and supplying more and better customer information.

Advances in information and computer technology—laptop computers, telecommunications, personal selling software, videodisc players, automatic dialers, and others—have encouraged many firms to adopt *salesforce automation systems,* computerized sales operations for more efficient order-entry transactions, improved customer service, and better salesperson decision-making support. Many salesforces truly have gone "electronic." A recent study of 100 large companies found that 48 percent are "actively pursuing" salesforce automation; another 34 percent are planning or considering it.[14] Salespeople use computers to profile customers and prospects, analyze and forecast sales, manage accounts, schedule sales calls, enter orders, check inventories and order status, prepare sales and expense reports, process correspondence, and carry out many other activities. Salesforce automation not only lowers salesforce calls and improves productivity, it also improves the quality of sales management decisions. Here are some examples of companies that have introduced computer and other sophisticated technologies successfully into their salesforce operations:

Shell Chemical Company developed a laptop computer package consisting of several applications. Although many salespeople initially resisted the computer—they couldn't type, or they didn't have time to learn the software, or whatever—some applications had great appeal. Salespeople responded first to the *automatic expense statement* program, which made it easier for them to record expenses and get reimbursed quickly. Soon, they discovered the *sales inquiry function,* which gave them immediate access to the latest account information, including phone numbers, addresses, recent developments, and prices. They no longer had to wait for the clerical staff to give them out-of-date information. Before long, salespeople were using the entire package. *Electronic mail* allowed them quickly to receive and send messages to others. Various *corporate forms,* such as territory work plans and sales call reports, could be filled out faster and sent electronically. Other useful applications included an *appointment calendar,* a *"to-do list" function,* a *spreadsheet program,* and a *graphics package* that helped salespeople prepare charts and graphs for customer presentations. Today, even salespeople who initially resisted the computer package wonder how they ever got along without it.[15]

At the end of each workday, 10,000 Frito-Lay salespeople plug their hand-held computers into minicomputers at their local sales offices or into modems at home. Then they sit back and relax while reports of their day's efforts are zapped to Frito-Lay headquarters in Dallas. Twenty-four hours later, Frito-Lay's marketing managers have a complete report analyzing the sales performance of Fritos, Doritos, and the company's other brands the day before—by total, brand, and location. The system not only helps Frito-Lay's marketing managers make better decisions, it makes the salespeople more efficient and effective. Now, instead of spending hours filling out reports, Frito-Lay salespeople let the computers do the grunt work and spend the extra time selling. As a result of the system, sales are going up 10 to 12 percent a year without the addition of a single salesperson.[16]

Salesforce automation systems: Many companies are computerizing their salesforces to make salespeople more efficient and effective.

To reduce time demands on their *outside salesforces,* many companies have increased the size of their *inside salesforces.* Inside salespeople include technical support people, sales assistants, and telemarketers. *Technical support people* provide technical information and answers to customers' questions. *Sales assistants* provide clerical backup for outside salespeople. They call ahead and confirm appointments, conduct credit checks, follow up on deliveries, and answer customers' questions when outside salespeople cannot be reached. *Telemarketers* use the phone to find new leads, qualify prospects, and sell to and service them (see Marketing Highlight 18-3).

The inside salesforce frees outside salespeople to spend more time selling to major accounts and finding major new prospects. Depending on the complexity of the product and customer, a telemarketer can make from 20 to 33 decision-maker contacts a day, compared to the average of four that an outside salesperson can see. And for many types of products and selling situations, telemarketing can be as effective as a personal call but at a much lower cost. For example, whereas a typical personal sales call can cost well over $200, a routine industrial telemarketing call costs only about $5 and a complex call about $20.[17]

Motivating Salespeople

Some salespeople will do their best without any special urging from management. To them, selling may be the most fascinating job in the world. But selling can also be frustrating. Salespeople usually work alone, and they must sometimes travel away from home. They may face aggressive, competing salespeople and difficult customers. They sometimes lack the authority to do what is needed to win a sale and may thus lose large orders they have worked hard to obtain. Therefore, salespeople often need special encouragement to do their best. Management can boost salesforce morale and performance through its *organizational climate, sales quotas,* and *positive incentives.*

Organizational Climate

Organizational climate describes the feeling that salespeople have about their opportunities, value, and rewards for a good performance within the company. Some companies treat salespeople as if they are not very important. Other companies treat their salespeople as their prime movers and allow virtually unlimited opportunity for income and promotion. Not surprisingly, a company's attitude toward its salespeople affects their behavior. If they are held in low esteem, there is high turnover and poor performance. If they are held in high esteem, there is less turnover and higher performance.

Treatment from the salesperson's immediate superior is especially impor-

TELEMARKETING: A PHONE CAN BE BETTER THAN A FACE

Selling face to face is by far the best way to achieve personal rapport with a prospect, right? Wrong, says LeRoy Benham, president of Climax Portable Machine Tools. By combining telemarketing and computers, a small company can save money and lavish the kind of attention on buyers which will amaze them.

True, such a strategy depends on both the nature of your market and your stake in it, but few would argue with Benham's track record. At a time when most U.S. machine tool manufacturers have been in a deep depression, Benham has carved out a niche for his portable cutting tools. This year, sales will rise 20 percent to $5 million. Company profits will climb more than 20 percent for the third year in a row since Climax began phasing out its distributor network and switched to telephone selling.

Under the old system, sales engineers spent one-third of their time on the road, training distributor salespeople and accompanying them on calls. "They'd make about four contacts a day," says Benham. "They found they actually got more information from the prospects when they were back here setting up travel appointments by phone." Now, each of the five sales engineers on Benham's telemarketing team calls about 30 prospects a day, following up on leads generated by ads and direct mail. Because it takes about five calls to close a sale, the sales engineers update a computer file on prospects each time they speak to them, noting their degree of commitment, requirements, next call date, and personal comments. "If anyone mentions he's going on a fishing trip, our sales engineer enters that in the computer and uses it to personalize the next phone call," says Benham, noting that's just one way to build good relations. Another is that the first mailing to a prospect

Telemarketers use the phone to find new prospects and sell to them.

includes the sales engineer's business card with his picture on it.

Of course, it takes more than friendliness to sell $15,000 machine tools (special orders may run $200,000) over the phone, but Benham has proof that personality pays. When Climax customers were asked, "Do you see the sales engineer often enough?" the response was overwhelmingly positive. Obviously, many people didn't realize that the only contact they'd had with Climax had been on the phone.

Sources: Adapted from "A Phone Is Better Than a Face," *Sales & Marketing Management,* October 1987, p. 29. Also see Aimee L. Stern, "Telemarketing Polishes Its Image," *Sales & Marketing Management,* June 1991, pp. 107-10; and Richard L. Bencin, "Telefocus: Telemarketing Gets Synergized," *Sales & Marketing Management,* February 1992, pp. 49-57.

---

tant. A good sales manager keeps in touch with the salesforce through letters and phone calls, visits in the field, and evaluation sessions in the home office. At different times, the sales manager acts as the salesperson's boss, companion, coach, and confessor.

Sales Quotas

Many companies set **sales quotas** for their salespeople—standards stating the amount they should sell and how sales should be divided among the company's products. Compensation often is related to how well salespeople meet their quotas.

Sales quotas are set at the time the annual marketing plan is developed. The company first decides on a sales forecast that is reasonably achievable. Based on this forecast, management plans production, work-force size, and financial needs. It then sets sales quotas for its regions and territories. Generally, sales quotas are set higher than are the sales forecast to encourage sales managers and salespeople to give their best effort. If they fail to make their quotas, the company may still make its sales forecast.

Positive Incentives

Companies also use several incentives to increase salesforce effort. *Sales meetings* provide social occasions, breaks from routine, chances to meet and talk with

Salesforce incentives: Many companies award cash, gift cheques, merchandise, or trips as incentives for outstanding sales performance.

"company brass," and opportunities to air feelings and to identify with a larger group. Companies also sponsor *sales contests* to spur the salesforce to make a selling effort above what would normally be expected. Other incentives include honors, merchandise and cash awards, trips, and profit-sharing plans.

EVALUATING SALESPEOPLE

We have thus far described how management communicates what salespeople should be doing and motivates them to do it. But this process requires good feedback. And good feedback means getting regular information from salespeople to evaluate their performance.

Sources of Information

Management gets information about its salespeople in several ways. The most important source is the *sales report*. Additional information comes from personal observation, customers' letters and complaints, customer surveys, and talks with other salespeople.

Sales reports are divided into plans for future activities and writeups of completed activities. The best example of the first is the *work plan* that salespeople submit a week or month in advance. The plan describes intended calls and routing. From this report, the salesforce plans and schedules activities. It also informs management of the salespeople's whereabouts and provides a basis for comparing plans and performance. Salespeople can then be evaluated on their ability to "plan their work and work their plan." Sometimes, managers contact individual salespeople to suggest improvements in work plans.

Companies also are beginning to require their salespeople to draft *annual territory marketing plans* in which they outline their plans for building new accounts and increasing sales from existing accounts. Formats vary greatly—some ask for general ideas on territory development; others ask for detailed sales and profit estimates.

Such reports cast salespeople as territory marketing managers. Sales managers study these territory plans, make suggestions, and use the plans to develop sales quotas.

Salespeople write up their completed activities on *call reports*. Call reports keep sales management informed of the salesperson's activities, show what is happening with each customer's account, and provide information that might be useful in later calls. Salespeople also turn in *expense reports* for which they are partly or wholly repaid. Some companies also ask for reports on new business, lost business, and local business and economic conditions.

These reports supply the raw data from which sales management can evaluate salesforce performance. Are salespeople making too few calls per day? Are they spending too much time per call? Are they spending too much money on entertainment? Are they closing enough orders per hundred calls? Are they finding enough new customers and holding onto enough old customers?

Formal Evaluation of Performance

Using salesforce reports and other information, sales management formally evaluates members of the salesforce. Formal evaluation produces four benefits. First, management must develop and communicate clear standards for judging performance. Second, management must gather well-rounded information about each salesperson. Third, salespeople receive constructive feedback that helps them to improve future performance. Finally, salespeople are motivated to perform well because they know they will have to sit down one morning with the sales manager and explain their performance.

Comparing Salespeople's Performance

One type of evaluation compares and ranks the sales performance of different salespeople. Such comparisons can be misleading, however. Salespeople may perform differently because of differences in territory potential, workload, level of competition, company promotion effort, and other factors. Furthermore, sales are not usually the best indicator of achievement. Management should be more interested in how much each salesperson contributes to net profits, a concern that requires looking at each salesperson's sales mix and expenses.

Comparing Current Sales with Past Sales

A second type of evaluation is to compare a salesperson's current performance with past performance. Such a comparison should directly indicate the person's progress. Table 18-1 provides an example.

TABLE 18-1
Evaluating Salespeople's Performance

TERRITORY: MIDLAND	SALESPERSON: CHRIS BENNETT 1990	1991	1992	1993
1. Net sales product A	$251,300	$253,200	$270,000	$263,100
2. Net sales product B	$423,200	$439,200	$553,900	$561,900
3. Net sales total	$674,500	$692,400	$823,900	$825,000
4. Percent of quota product A	95.6	92.0	88.0	84.7
5. Percent of quota product B	120.4	122.3	134.9	130.8
6. Gross profits product A	$ 50,260	$ 50,640	$ 54,000	$ 52,620
7. Gross profits product B	$ 42,320	$ 43,920	$ 53,390	$ 56,190
8. Gross profits total	$ 92,580	$ 94,560	$109,390	$108,810
9. Sales expense	$ 10,200	$ 11,100	$ 11,600	$ 13,200
10. Sales expense to total sales (%)	1.5	1.6	1.4	1.6
11. Number of calls	1,675	1,700	1,680	1,660
12. Cost per call	$ 6.09	$ 6.53	$ 6.90	$ 7.95
13. Average number of customers	320	324	328	334
14. Number of new customers	13	14	15	20
15. Number of lost customers	8	10	11	14
16. Average sales per customer	$ 2,108	$ 2,137	$ 2,512	$ 2,470
17. Average gross profit per customer	$ 289	$ 292	$ 334	$ 326

The sales manager can learn many things about Chris Bennett from this table. Bennett's total sales increased every year (line 3). This does not necessarily mean that Bennett is doing a better job. The product breakdown shows that Bennett has been able to push the sales of product B further than those of product A (lines 1 and 2). According to the quotas for the two products (lines 4 and 5), the success in increasing product B sales may be at the expense of product A sales. According to gross profits (lines 6 and 7), the company earns twice as much gross profit (as a ratio to sales) on A as it does on B. Bennett may be pushing the higher-volume, lower-margin product at the expense of the more profitable product. Although Bennett increased total sales by $1,100 between 1992 and 1993 (line 3), the gross profits on these total sales actually decreased by $580 (line 8).

Sales expense (line 9) shows a steady increase, although total expense as a percentage of total sales seems to be under control (line 10). The upward trend in Bennett's total dollar expenses does not seem to be explained by any increase in the number of calls (line 11), although it may be related to his success in acquiring new customers (line 14). However, there is a possibility that in prospecting for new customers, Bennett is neglecting present customers, as indicated by an upward trend in the annual number of lost customers (line 15).

The last two lines on the table show the level and trend in Bennett's sales and gross profits per customer. These figures become more meaningful when they are compared with overall company averages. If Chris Bennett's average gross profit per customer is lower than the company's average, Chris may be concentrating on the wrong customers or may not be spending enough time with each customer. Looking back at the annual number of calls (line 11), Bennett may be making fewer calls than the average salesperson. If distances in the territory are not much different, this may mean he is not putting in a full workday, he is poor at planning his routing or minimizing his waiting time, or he spends too much time with certain accounts.

Qualitative Evaluation of Salespeople

A *qualitative evaluation* usually looks at a salesperson's knowledge of the company, products, customers, competitors, territory, and tasks. Personal traits—manner, appearance, speech, and temperament—can be rated. The sales manager also can review any problems in motivation or compliance. Each company must decide what would be most useful to know. It should communicate these criteria to salespeople so that they understand how their performance is evaluated and can make an effort to improve it.

PRINCIPLES OF PERSONAL SELLING

We now turn from designing and managing a salesforce to the actual personal selling process. Personal selling is an ancient art that has spawned a large literature and many principles. Effective salespeople operate on more than just instinct—they are highly trained in methods of territory analysis and customer management.

The Personal Selling Process

Companies spend hundreds of millions of dollars on seminars, books, cassettes, and other materials to teach salespeople the "art" of selling. Millions of books on selling are purchased every year, with tantalizing titles such as *How to Sell Anything to Anybody, How I Raised Myself from Failure to Success in Selling, The Four-Minute Sell, The Best Seller, The Power of Enthusiastic Selling, Where Do You Go from No. 1?,* and *Winning Through Intimidation.* One of the most enduring books on selling is Dale Carnegie's *How to Win Friends and Influence People.*

All of the training approaches try to convert a salesperson from a passive *order taker* to an active *order getter.* Order takers assume that customers know their own needs, that they would resent any attempt at influence, and that they prefer salespeople who are polite and reserved. An example of an order taker is a salesperson who calls on a dozen customers each day, simply asking if the customer needs anything.

There are two approaches to training salespeople to be order *getters*—a sales-oriented approach and a customer-oriented approach. The *sales-oriented approach* trains the salesperson in high-pressure selling techniques, such as those used in selling encyclopedias or automobiles. This form of selling assumes that the customers will not buy except under pressure, that they are influenced by a slick presentation, and that they will not be sorry after signing the order (and that, if they are, it no longer matters).

The *customer-oriented approach*—the one most often used in today's professional selling—trains salespeople in customer problem solving. The salesperson learns how to identify customer needs and to find solutions. This approach assumes that customer needs provide sales opportunities, that customers appreciate good suggestions, and that customers will be loyal to salespeople who have their long-term interests at heart. One recent survey found that purchasing agents appreciate salespeople who understand their needs and meet them. As one purchasing agent states:

> My *expectation* of salespeople is that they've done their homework, uncovered some of our needs, probed to uncover other needs, and presented convincing arguments of mutual benefits for both organizations.... [The problem is that] I don't always see that.[18]

The qualities that purchasing agents *disliked most* in salespeople included being pushy, late, and unprepared or disorganized. The qualities they *valued most* included honesty, dependability, thoroughness, and follow-through. The problem-solver salesperson fits better with the marketing concept than does the hard seller or order taker.

Steps in the Selling Process

Most training programs view the **selling process** as consisting of several steps that the salesperson must master (see Figure 18-3).

Prospecting and Qualifying

The first step in the selling process is **prospecting**—identifying qualified potential customers. The salesperson must approach many prospects to get just a few sales. In the insurance industry, for example, only one out of nine prospects becomes a customer. In the computer business, 125 phone calls result in 25 interviews leading to five demonstrations and one sale.[19] Although the company supplies some leads, salespeople need skill in finding their own. They can ask current customers for the names of prospects. They can build referral sources, such as suppliers, dealers, noncompeting salespeople, and bankers. They can join organizations to which prospects belong or can engage in speaking and writing activities that will draw attention. They can search for names in newspapers or directories and use the telephone and mail to track down leads. Or they can drop in unannounced on various offices (a practice known as "cold calling").

Salespeople need to know how to *qualify* leads—that is, how to identify the good ones and screen out the poor ones. Prospects can be qualified by looking at their financial ability, volume of business, special needs, location, and possibilities for growth.

Preapproach

Before calling on a prospect, the salesperson should learn as much as possible about the organization (what it needs, who is involved in the buying) and its buyers (their characteristics and buying styles). This step is known as the **preapproach.** The salesperson can consult standard sources (*Moody's, Standard & Poor's, Dun & Bradstreet*), acquaintances, and others to learn about the company. The

FIGURE 18-3
Major steps in effective selling

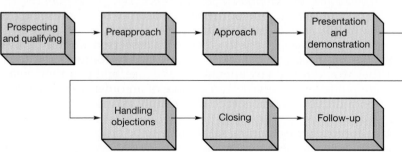

salesperson should set *call objectives,* which may be to qualify the prospect, to gather information, or to make an immediate sale. Another task is to decide on the best approach, which might be a personal visit, a phone call, or a letter. The best timing should be considered carefully because many prospects are busiest at certain times. Finally, the salesperson should give thought to an overall sales strategy for the account.

Approach

During the **approach** step, the salesperson should know how to meet and greet the buyer and to get the relationship off to a good start. This step involves the salesperson's appearance, opening lines, and the follow-up remarks. The opening lines should be positive, such as "Mr. Johnson, I am Chris Anderson from the All-tech Company. My company and I appreciate your willingness to see me. I will do my best to make this visit profitable and worthwhile for you and your company." This opening might be followed by some key questions to learn more about the customer's needs or the showing of a display or sample to attract the buyer's attention and curiosity.

Presentation and Demonstration

During the **presentation** step of the selling process, the salesperson tells the product "story" to the buyer, showing how the product will make or save money. The salesperson describes the product features but concentrates on presenting customer benefits.

Companies can use three styles of sales presentation—the canned approach, the formula approach, or the need-satisfaction approach. The *canned approach* is the oldest type and consists of a memorized or scripted talk covering the seller's main points. This approach has limited usefulness in industrial selling, but scripted presentations can be effective in some telephone selling situations. A properly prepared and rehearsed script should sound natural and move the salesperson smoothly through the presentation. With electronic scripting, computers can lead the salesperson through a sequence of selling messages tailored on the spot to the prospect's responses.

Using the *formula approach,* the salesperson first identifies the buyer's needs, attitudes, and buying style. The salesperson then moves into a formula presentation that shows how the product will satisfy that buyer's needs. Although not canned, the presentation follows a general plan.

The *need-satisfaction approach* starts with a search for the customer's needs by getting the customer to do most of the talking. This approach calls for good listening and problem-solving skills. One marketing director describes the approach this way:

> [High-performing salespeople] make it a point to understand customer needs and goals before they pull anything out of their product bag. . . . Such salespeople spend the time needed to get an in-depth knowledge of the customer's business, asking questions that will lead to solutions our systems can address.[20]

Any style of sales presentation can be improved with demonstration aids, such as booklets, flip charts, slides, videotapes or videodiscs, and product samples.

In the sales presentation, the salesperson tells the product story to buyers.

If buyers can see or handle the product, they will better remember its features and benefits.

Handling Objections

Customers almost always have objections during the presentation or when asked to place an order. The problem can be either logical or psychological, and objections are often unspoken. In **handling objections,** the salesperson should use a positive approach, seek out hidden objections, ask the buyer to clarify any objections, take objections as opportunities to provide more information, and turn the objections into reasons for buying. Every salesperson needs training in the skills of handling objections.

Closing

After handling the prospect's objections, the salesperson now tries to close the sale. Some salespeople do not get around to **closing** or do not handle it well. They may lack confidence, feel guilty about asking for the order, or fail to recognize the right moment to close the sale. Salespeople should know how to recognize closing signals from the buyer, including physical actions, comments, and questions. For example, the customer might sit forward and nod approvingly or ask about prices and credit terms. Salespeople can use one of several closing techniques. They can ask for the order, review points of agreement, offer to help write up the order, ask whether the buyer wants this model or that one, or note that the buyer will lose out if the order is not placed now. The salesperson may offer the buyer special reasons to close, such as a lower price or an extra quantity at no charge.

Follow-Up

The last step in the selling process—**follow-up**—is necessary if the salesperson wants to ensure customer satisfaction and repeat business. Right after closing, the salesperson should complete any details on delivery time, purchase terms, and other matters. The salesperson then should schedule a follow-up call when the initial order is received to make sure there is proper installation, instruction, and servicing. This visit would reveal any problems, assure the buyer of the salesperson's interest, and reduce any buyer concerns that might have arisen since the sale.

Relationship Marketing

The principles of personal selling as described are *transaction oriented*—their aim is to help salespeople close a specific sale with a customer. But in many cases, the company is not seeking simply a sale: it has targeted a major customer account that it would like to win and serve. The company would like to demonstrate to the account that it has the capabilities to serve the account's needs in a superior way, especially if a *committed relationship* can be formed.

More companies today are moving their emphasis from transaction marketing to *relationship marketing*. The days of the lone salesperson working a territory and being guided only by a sales quota and a compensation plan are numbered. Today's customers are large and often global. They prefer suppliers who can sell and deliver a coordinated set of products and services to many locations; who can quickly solve problems that arise in their different parts of the nation or world, and who can work closely with customer teams to improve products and processes. Unfortunately, most companies are not set up to meet these requirements. They often sell their products through separate salesforces that do not work easily together. Their national account managers may be turned down when requesting help from a district salesperson. Their technical people may not be willing to lend time to educate a customer.

Companies recognize that sales teamwork increasingly will be the key to winning and maintaining accounts. Yet they recognize that just asking their people for teamwork does not produce it. Companies must revise their compensation systems to give credit for work on shared accounts, and they must set up better goals and measures for their salesforce. They must emphasize the importance of teamwork in their training programs while at the same time also honoring the importance of individual initiative.[21]

Relationship marketing is based on the premise that important accounts need focused and continuous attention. Salespeople working with key customers must do more than call when they think a customer might be ready to place an order. They also should monitor each key account, know its problems, and be ready to serve in a number of ways. They should call or visit frequently, make useful suggestions about how to improve the customer's business, take the customer to dinner, and take an interest in the customer as a person.

Recognition of the importance of relationship marketing has increased rapidly in the past few years. Companies are finding they earn a higher return from resources invested in retaining customers than from money spent to attract new ones. They are realizing the benefits of cross-selling opportunities with current customers. More and more, companies are forming strategic partnerships, making skilled relationship marketing essential. And for customers who buy large, complex products—such as robotics equipment or large computer systems—the sale is only the beginning of the relationship. Thus, although it is not appropriate in all situations, relationship marketing continues to grow in importance. We discuss relationship marketing further in Chapter 19.

 # SUMMARY

Most companies use salespeople, and many companies assign them the key role in the marketing mix. The high cost of the salesforce calls for an effective *sales management process* consisting of six steps: setting *salesforce objectives*; designing *salesforce strategy, structure, size,* and *compensation; recruiting and selecting; training; supervising;* and *evaluating.*

As an element of the marketing mix, the salesforce is very effective in achieving certain marketing objectives and carrying out such activities as prospecting, communicating, selling and servicing, and information gathering. A market-oriented salesforce needs skills in marketing analysis and planning in addition to the traditional selling skills.

Once the salesforce objectives have been set, strategy answers the questions of what type of selling would be most effective (solo selling, team selling); what type of salesforce structure will work best (territorial, product, or customer structured); how large the salesforce should be; and how the salesforce should be compensated in terms of salary, commissions, bonuses, expenses, and fringe benefits.

To hold down the high costs of hiring the wrong people, salespeople must be *recruited* and *selected* carefully. *Training* programs familiarize new salespeople not only with the art of selling, but with the company's history, its products and policies, and the characteristics of its market and competitors. All salespeople need supervision, and many need continuous encouragement because they must make many decisions and face many frustrations. Periodically, the company must evaluate their performance to help them do a better job.

The art of selling involves a seven-step *selling process: prospecting and qualifying, preapproach, approach, presentation and demonstration, handling objections, closing,* and *follow-up.* These steps help marketers close a specific sale. However, a seller's dealings with customers should be guided by the larger concept of *relationship marketing*—the company's salesforce should work to develop long-term relationships with key accounts.

 # KEY TERMS

Approach 537

Closing 538

Customer salesforce structure 524

Follow-up 538

Handling objections 538

Preapproach 536

Presentation 537

Prospecting 536

Product salesforce structure 524

Salesforce management 522

Salesperson 521

Sales quotas 532

Selling process 536

Territorial salesforce structure 523

Workload approach 525

 # DISCUSSING THE ISSUES

1. Grocery stores require their suppliers' salespeople not only to sell but also to serve as aisle clerks. These salespeople must arrange and restock shelves, build special displays, and set up point-of-purchase material. Is it important for a manufacturer to meet these demands? Are there creative ways to free the salesperson's time for more productive uses?

2. Why do so many salesforce compensation plans combine salary with bonus or commission? What are the advantages and disadvantages of using bonuses as incentives, rather than using commissions?

3. Many people feel they do not have the ability to be a successful salesperson. What role does training play in helping someone develop selling ability?

4. Some companies have installed computerized inventory tracking that automatically sends reorders to the supplier's computer as needed. Is this process likely to expand? Discuss the effects this could have on the role of the salesperson.

5. The surest way to become a salesforce manager is to be an outstanding salesperson. What are the advantages and disadvantages of promoting top salespeople to management positions? Why might an outstanding salesperson refuse to be promoted?

6. Good salespeople are familiar with their competitors' products as well as their own. What would you do if your company expected you to sell a product that you thought was inferior to the competition's? Why?

APPLYING THE CONCEPTS

1. Experience a sales pitch. Go to a retailer where the salespeople are likely to be working on commission, such as a car dealership, an appliance and electronics dealer, or a clothing store. (a) Rate your salesperson. Was their approach, presentation and demonstration effective? (b) Consider your emotional response to the sales pitch. Did you enjoy the experience, or find it hard to endure? Why did you react this way?

2. Go to a retailer that specializes in complex products such as computers and software, stereo, or video equipment. Get a salesperson to explain a product to you, and ask specific questions. (a) Was the salesperson knowledgeable, and able to answer your questions in a helpful and believable way? (b) Did you feel the salesperson's expertise added value to the product, or not? (c) Would you rather buy this product from the salesperson you spoke with, or purchase it by mail order for a slightly lower price?

MAKING MARKETING DECISIONS

SMALL WORLD COMMUNICATIONS, INC.

Thomas Campbell and Lynette Jones are talking through the issues they will face in setting up a salesforce for Small World Communications. "Well, our money situation steers us in one inevitable direction," said Lyn. "We will need to hire a couple of really good sales management types, and we'll need to handle some accounts ourselves, but it's clear that Small World Communications will be using a contractual salesforce. We simply won't have the sales volume to pay for a direct salesforce–at least not yet." Tom agreed: "That makes sense for now, but we may need to change as we grow. I was also thinking about the types of customers we need to sell to. I see that we've got computer retailers, direct-mail merchandisers, and OEMs as three distinct groups with different needs. End users are a fourth group, but since we decided not to do direct sales, we can write them off for now." "Thomas, dear, we cannot just 'write off' our end users. Don't you mean that we will serve them most effectively by using our salesforce to work through established channels of distribution?" "Lynette, I obviously misspoke myself, but have some sympathy. My linguistic skills were stunted early on, when I was a mere lad. I designed enough computer gear to become known as a boy wonder, but I breathed in too many fumes from lead solder. Shorted my circuits. Now, *may* I continue?" "Sorry," Lyn replied. "You know how I rant about customer needs." "As I was saying, we need to sell effectively to at least three different types of customers. To do that, we need to decide on a salesforce structure and figure out what type of sales managers to hire—pronto."

What Now?

1. Tom and Lyn will need to sell their product soon, but they have no salesforce yet. They agree that each of them will personally handle a few major national accounts. They plan to hire a small sales management team and use manufacturer's agents to cover the rest. (a) What sort of salesforce design do you think is best for Small World—territorial, product, customer, or complex? Why? (b) What type of compensation plan would you propose for the salesforce—straight salary, straight commission, salary plus bonus, or salary plus commission?

2. Small World is starting its sales efforts with no prior experience in this market. They do not know exactly who their prospects are, or of how to reach them effectively. (a) Should Small World hire a person experienced in selling to the computer market? List the ways this might be helpful. (b) Make two specific suggestions or hints that can help Small World succeed at each stage of the selling process: prospecting and qualifying, preapproach, approach, presentation and demonstration, handling objections, closing, and follow-up.

REFERENCES

1. Portions adapted from Bill Kelley, "How to Sell Airplanes, Boeing-Style," *Sales & Marketing Management,* December 9, 1985, pp. 32-34. Also see Dori Jones Yang and Andrea Rothman, "Boeing Cuts Its Altitude as the Clouds Roll In," *Business Week,* February 8, 1993, p. 25; and Shawn Tully, "Boeing: Is 'The Lazy B' a Bad Rap?" *Fortune,* January 25, 1993, p. 10.

2. For a comparison of several classifications, see William C. Moncrief III, "Selling Activity and Sales Position Taxonomies for Industrial Salesforces," *Journal of Marketing Research,* August 1986, pp. 261-70.

3. See Rayna Skolnik, "Campbell Stirs Up Its Salesforce," *Sales & Marketing Management,* April 1986, pp. 56-58.

4. See Thayer C. Taylor, "Xerox's Sales Force Learns a New Game," *Sales & Marketing Management,* July 1, 1986, pp. 48-51; and Taylor, "Xerox's Makeover," *Sales & Marketing Management,* June 1987, p. 68.

5. Patricia Sellers, "How to Remake Your Salesforce," *Fortune,* May 4, 1992, pp. 96-103, here p. 96.

6. See *1992 Sales Manager's Budget Planner,* published by *Sales & Marketing Management,* June 22, 1992, p. 70.

7. The percentages add to more than 100 percent because some companies use more than one type of plan. See "1989 Survey of Selling Costs," *Sales & Marketing Management,* February 20, 1989, p. 26.

8. See George H. Lucas, Jr., A. Parasuraman, Robert A. Davis, and Ben M. Enis, "An Empirical Study of Salesforce Turnover," *Journal of Marketing,* July 1987, pp. 34-59; Lynn G. Coleman, "Sales Force Turnover Has Managers Wondering Why," *Marketing News,* December 4, 1989, p. 6; and Thomas R. Wotruba and Pradeep K. Tyagi, "Met Expectations and Turnover in Direct Selling," *Journal of Marketing,* July 1991, pp. 24-35.

9. See Thayer C. Taylor, "Anatomy of a Star Salesperson," *Sales & Marketing Management,* May 1986, pp. 49-51; Bill Kelley, "How to Manage a Superstar," *Sales & Marketing Management,* November 1988, pp. 32-34; and "What Is the Best Advice on Selling You Have Ever Been Given?" *Sales & Marketing Management,* February 1990, pp. 8-9.

10. See "Women in Sales: Percentages by Industry," *Sales & Marketing Management,* February 26, 1990, p. 81; Bill Kelley, "Selling in a Man's World," *Sales & Marketing Management,* January 1991, pp. 28-35; and Patrick L. Schul and Brent M. Wren, "The Emerging Role of Women in Industrial Selling: A Decade of Change," *Journal of Marketing,* July 1992, pp. 38-54.

11. See Richard Kern, "IQ Tests for Salesmen Make a Comeback," *Sales & Marketing Management,* April 1988, pp. 42-46. Also see Robert G. Head, "Systemizing Salesperson Selection," *Sales & Marketing Management,* February 1992, pp. 65-68.

12. Patricia Sellers, "How IBM Teaches Techies to Sell," *Fortune,* June 6, 1988, pp. 141-46. Also see *1991 Sales Manager's Budget Planner,* published by *Sales & Marketing Management,* June 17, 1991, p. 77; and Matthew Goodfellow, "Hiring and Training: A Call for Action," *Sales & Marketing Management,* May 1992, pp. 87-88.

13. See Bill Kelley, "How Much Help Does a Salesperson Need?" *Sales & Marketing Management,* May 1989, pp. 32-35.

14. Thayer C. Taylor, "SFA: The Newest Orthodoxy," *Sales & Marketing Management,* February 1993, pp. 26-28. Also see Rowland T. Moriarty and Gordon S. Swartz, "Automation to Boost Sales and Marketing," *Harvard Business Review,* January-February 1989, pp. 100-108; and Thayer C. Taylor, "Back from the Future," *Sales & Marketing Management,* May 1992, pp. 47-60.

15. See "Computer-Based Sales Support: Shell Chemical's System" (New York: The Conference Board, Management Briefing: Marketing, April/May 1989), pp. 4-5.

16. See Jeremy Main, "Frito-Lay Shortens Its Business Cycle," *Fortune,* January 15, 1990, p. 11; and Jeffrey Rotfeder and Jim Bartimo, "How Software Is Making Food Sales a Piece of Cake," *Business Week,* July 2, 1990, pp. 54-55.

17. See Rudy Oetting and Geri Gantman, "Dial 'M' for Maximize," *Sales & Marketing Management,* June 1991, pp. 100-106; Linda J. Neff, "Six Myths About Telemarketing," *Sales & Marketing Management,* October 1992, pp. 108-111.

18. Derrick C. Schnebelt, "Turning the Tables," *Sales & Marketing Management,* January 1993, pp. 22-23.

19. Vincent L. Zirpoli, "You Can't 'Control' the Prospect, So Manage the Presale Activities to Increase Performance," *Marketing News,* March 16, 1984, p. 1.

20. Thayer C. Taylor, "Anatomy of a Star Salesperson," p. 50. Also see Harvey B. Mackay, "Humanize Your Selling Strategy," *Harvard Business Review,* March-April 1988, pp. 36-47; and Barry J. Farber and Joyce Wycoff, "Relationships: Six Steps to Success," *Sales & Marketing Management,* April 1992, pp. 50-58.

21. See Frank V. Cespedes, Stephen X. Doyle, and Robert J. Freedman, "Teamwork for Today's Selling," *Harvard Business Review,* March-April 1989, pp. 44-54, 58.

VIDEO CASE 18

ABCNEWS

TELEMARKETING

Upon graduation, you might be offered a job as a TSR, or telemarketing sales representative. Because of negative images of telemarketers, created by the media or by your own past experiences, your first inclination might be to just say no. But think again.

In business-to-business marketing, professional telephone selling is quite different from cold-calling final consumers to sell life insurance. Because you would be selling business products to other business professionals, the firm employing you would recognize your professional status and the high added value of your services. Consequently, it would provide a good working environment, with a private office, comfortable furniture, and quality equipment. You might even have an opportunity to help design your workspace. Moreover, as a telemarketing rep, unlike outside salespeople, you would avoid travel and have the opportunity to choose your own location.

How should employers go about attracting high-caliber telemarketers? As a starting place in their recruiting plans, they should determine the type of person needed. Telemarketers must have pleasant telephone personalities, sound and act professional, and be genuinely interested in helping clients solve their problems. As a first step, an employer might place an ad in the classifieds section of the newspaper, asking applicants to call—a telephone interview with prospective TSRs will reveal his or her telephone personality. If the applicant makes a good impression, the employer will next conduct a face-to-face interview.

Once hired, new telemarketers undergo rigorous training to learn about telephone sales techniques, and product and company information. Frequently used training tools include role playing, call guide development, practicing introductions with tape recorders, and live calls. Some tips for TSR trainees include: (1) never ask a stranger, "How are you today?"; (2) make certain that you talk with the decision maker, the major influencer, or the gatekeeper; (3) use the prospect's name; (4) leave a name but not a number for callbacks; (5) maintain a positive attitude; and (6) be careful about timing. If the prospect seems to be rushed, suggest a future call time when he or she might be more willing to listen and buy. Also, avoid calling at busy times of the day (late morning, lunch time, and late afternoon).

Once trained and on the job, TSRs must be supervised and motivated. Supervisors should become acquainted with TSRs, understand their needs and wants, allow them adequate freedom to perform in the way that is most comfortable for them, and try to increase group cohesion. Supervisors might also use daily and weekly call reports with measures such as number of calls, hit ratio (ratio of successful calls to number of calls made), number of prospecting calls, number of new customers attained, and the success ratio of new customers to prospect calls. TSRs can be compensated using appropriate monetary incentives—salaries, commissions, bonuses, merit increases, and quotas—and nonmonetary incentives such as contests, prizes, awards, and promotions.

To enable TSRs to function productively, firms should provide equipment such as auto-dialers that make multiple simultaneous calls, disconnect from busy lines, and relay only successful calls to TSRs. These can save telemarketers much time and effort. Because auto-dialers can work quickly through lists of names to locate prospects, they are especially useful in conjunction with large databases. Moreover, auto-dialers make fewer mistakes.

During a typical telemarketing sales call, the first 30 seconds are the most critical—the telemarketer must obtain the prospect's interest, without which there can be no sale. The telemarketer next asks questions to determine the prospect's problems or needs and then offers solutions. After the solution is suggested, the prospect may ask questions, make comments, and raise objections. At this point, telemarketers rely on their training to answer questions and overcome objections in order to close the sale. Later, the telemarketer should follow up on the sale to make sure that the client remains satisfied.

Still skeptical about a career in telemarketing? Remember, one way to motivate telemarketers is to promote them to sales supervisors or other marketing positions. Thus, telemarketing can be a means of entering and moving up the management hierarchy.

QUESTIONS

1. Contrast the steps in selecting salespeople for outside sales positions versus telemarketing positions.

2. What are the underlying reasons for the six tips given to TSR trainees listed here?

3. Discuss the differences between outside salespeople and telemarketing sales reps in approaching, conducting, and concluding sales calls.

4. What are the differences in supervising and motivating telemarketers versus outside salespeople?

5. Even with careful training and pleasant working conditions, telemarketing can be stressful. Do you think the use of telemarketing will increase or decrease in the future? Why?

Sources: Doreen V. Blanc, "Understanding Your TSRs Is Key in Achieving Motivation," *Telemarketing Magazine,* October 1991, pp. 74-77; Thomas A. De-Prizio, "A Step-by-Step Process for Starting Up a Telemarketing Department," *Sales & Marketing Management in Canada,* April 1990, pp 9-11; and Kevin Jones, "Take Advantage of the Newest Trends in Auto-Dialers," *Telemarketing Magazine,* January 1991, pp. 32-33.

COMPANY CASE 18

MULTIFORM DESICCANTS: DESIGNING AN EFFECTIVE SALESFORCE

Steven Stepson, the new director of sales and marketing at Multiform Desiccants, Inc. (MDI), knew when he accepted the job that he faced many hurdles in making MDI a top-notch sales and marketing organization. Sales were up—15 percent over last year. But company executives believed that a better organized and better managed salesforce could provide even greater sales growth. Stepson now faced the challenge of evaluating the salesforce structure and recommending appropriate changes.

Most of us know desiccants as those little packets that you find in stereo equipment, cameras, and leather goods with the inscription "Do Not Eat" on the wrapper. Desiccants absorb any moisture that could damage the product. More technically, however, desiccant applications are highly specialized and usually require a custom blend of chemicals for each different use. MDI's safe, natural nontoxic products eradicate moisture and odors in containers and packages, while dramatically reducing the destructive effects of oxygen. Desiccants come in many forms—from gels to capsules of all shapes and sizes. These innovative products can be found in a variety of goods ranging from vitamin bottles to automotive air conditioning units, from photographic film packages to seagoing shipping containers. A typical MDI account is a pharmaceutical company that must keep moisture from products during shipment and storage. Others uses range from antifogging pellets for optical sensors on missiles to packets that keep orange juice crystals dry. In all, MDI manufactures 774 products for 23 different markets.

MDI started in the late 1960s as a garage-shop operation founded by a young entrepreneur with a dream. As a chemist working for a large bulk-desiccant manufacturer, he saw the need for formulating and packaging desiccants in small, single-use packets. His employer had no desire to enter the packaging end of the business and so gave him permission to work on his ideas during nonworking hours. And although most technical companies require their employees to sign an agreement giving the company all rights to any business-related inventions, this company allowed him to retain all patent rights.

Before MDI took on the task, companies had to buy desiccants in bulk and then package them for their own specialized uses. Packaging desiccants in a variety of bagging materials—and labeling them for the customers—thus met the needs of a previously neglected market. That was 25 years ago. Today, with annual sales topping $15 million, MDI is a leader in packaged desiccants.

Nevertheless, believing that sales could be much higher, MDI hired Stepson to boost sales volume. As in any sales-management position, Stepson was under immediate pressure to increase sales quickly. The area likely to make the greatest immediate impact on MDI's sales was its domestic salesforce. Thus, the new director first conducted a situation analysis to assess MDI's market position. This analysis included an external audit of competition and other market factors, a forecast of where market growth was likely to occur, and an internal audit of MDI's salesforce.

Salesforce design presented several problems and a challenge to Stepson, who discovered that frequent salesforce turnover had plagued MDI in the past. MDI had only three salespeople to cover the entire United States; each was paid a direct salary. Together, they serviced more than 3,850 accounts—although only 161 of these customers accounted for more than 80 percent of MDI's business. Therefore, it was important for the company to maintain this base while continuing to develop significant new accounts. Stepson found that three factors had influenced the salesforce's structure—the geographical location of customers, the technical skills needed to sell desiccants, and the long selling cycle dictated by the nature of the product.

Organizational markets tend to be geographically concentrated, and MDI's markets were typical in that regard. The majority of current and potential customers were located in large metropolitan areas east of the Mississippi River and along the West Coast, predominantly in California. MDI thus assigned sales representatives to geographically defined territories in order to take advantage of the clustering of its customers. Stepson realized that, unfortunately, geographical territory assignments created a situation in which sales representatives had to be knowledgeable in the assorted businesses of all their customers: One sales representative might call on customers in industries as diverse as automotives, pharmaceuticals, and aerospace.

Stepson also recognized a second problem. The

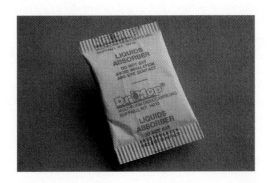

complex nature of desiccants requires that salespeople have technical backgrounds. Sales representatives often had college degrees in engineering—either chemical or mechanical. Technical skills were thus essential to successful selling of the products. For example, to sell a desiccant product to a new customer, the sales representative had to analyze the customer's needs. How much moisture had to be absorbed? How fast must it be absorbed? In what environment (for example, temperature) will the desiccant be working? These are just some of the questions that sales representatives would need answered in order to solve the problem facing the customer. Naturally, the answers to these kinds of questions are very technical. The customer-oriented approach demanded that, in addition to having knowledge about the technical qualities of the product, sales representatives had to be innovative in solving problems.

Finally, working with an important customer to find the MDI product to satisfy a particular need often took many sales calls, meetings, and telephone conversations. Because each new application undergoes rigorous testing before it is finally accepted as a routine purchase by the customer, the process of nurturing an important account takes at least 12 to 18 months. Because it took so long to land a new account, MDI felt that paying its salesforce on a salary basis would provide them with an even income flow. However, although the salary-only compensation system provided even income, it gave salespeople little incentive to strive for increased sales. Moreover, with 161 accounts representing more than $12 million in annual revenue and the number of new accounts growing continually, salespeople felt that they were not receiving their fair share of the revenues that they generated.

As Stepson discovered, travel and call planning were also problematic. Visits to various customers usually required air travel, car rental, and many overnight stays to service accounts properly. Travel accounted for at least three-quarters of a day per week. Salespeople usually spent two days per week in their offices to catch up on paper work and set up appointments for the following weeks. This schedule left only 2 1/4 days for customer visits. Thus, salespeople could on average make only five customer calls per week—an arrangement that did not provide the penetration necessary to meet projected sales targets. Moreover, salespeople kept busy serving existing accounts, allocating little time to prospect for new customers.

Stepson considered hiring additional salespeople, but the present salesforce balked at the idea. They felt that bringing in additional people at the same salary level would dilute their impact and diminish their importance and pay. The three current salespeople threatened to quit if such a policy were adopted.

Another problem was the background and training of the salesforce. Although the present salespeople had solid technical experience, Stepson felt that they lacked the sales skills required to sell MDI products effectively. For example, because there were a number of competitors selling substitutes, once a product was selected by the customer and purchased on a routine basis, the sales task turned from a technical issue to a pure price issue. Thus, making the initial sales and servicing the account in the future were very different kinds of selling activities requiring a variety of selling skills.

All in all, Stepson had his work cut out for him.

QUESTIONS

1. What objectives should Stepson set for MDI's salesforce?

2. Design a salesforce strategy for MDI that will accomplish its objectives. Be sure to address the issue of size, compensation, and structure.

3. Given the objectives and strategy you have developed, how should Stepson supervise and evaluate the salesforce?

Source: This case was written by Richard V. Resh, partner, DICRIS Company, Buffalo, New York.

PART IV

COMPREHENSIVE CASE

SMITH'S HOME FOODS: BRINGING HOME THE BACON

Ronald Smith, president of Smith's Country Hams, in Ashton, North Carolina, walked into his daughter's office and plopped down in one of the chairs across from her desk. "Christy," he said, "I've just been looking at last month's numbers, and they are pretty discouraging. We've got to find a way to get the home foods business moving. I'm not sure what's wrong, but I think we've somehow got the cart before the horse. I'm convinced that if we could just find the right button, and push it, everything would work well."

Christy Smith looked across the desk at her casually dressed father. "Dad, I am just as frustrated as you are," she replied. "Nothing we try seems to work right. Even when we do attract new customers, they are the wrong kind."

Christy was a very busy person. In addition to her duties at Smith's, she commuted daily to a major university located in a neighboring city, where she was a senior business major. Although she had worked in the family business for as long as she could remember, she had been pleased and surprised when her father had asked her to take over the newly formed Smith's Home Foods operation. Glancing at the calendar on her desk, she noted the date—April 4, 1993. She could hardly believe that five months had passed since taking on the assignment. Although pleased with her father's confidence in her, she knew that he felt frustrated about the slow development of the Smith's Home Foods business.

As Christy and her father talked, Sonny Jones, one of Home Foods' two full-time salespeople, entered the office and joined the conversation. He seemed upset. "We just got two more turn-downs from the finance company," he grumbled. "They rejected both of the families I sold plans to last night. We just can't seem to get onto the right side of the street."

"What do you mean?" Christy asked.

"It's the same old story," Sonny replied. "Both families I called on last night live in Dogwood Acres—they're nice people and all, but they don't have very high incomes. We have to find a way to attract the higher-income folks who live across the road in Ashton Estates."

Ronald Smith rose to leave. "Whatever the problem is, I'm depending on the two of you to figure it out and tell me what we need to do. And you need to get moving quickly."

Background

Smith's Country Hams, a 25-year-old family business that focuses on wholesale meat products such as ham, bacon, and other pork products, sells to restaurants and fast-food operations in eastern North Carolina. In July 1991, seeking growth opportunities, Ronald Smith started a new division—Smith's Home Foods. He got the idea from an employee who had previously worked for another home-delivered foods company. Ronald, who is always looking for new ways to make money, believed the idea had potential. He knew that people these days are seeking more convenience. Therefore, a service that provides home-delivered meats, vegetables, and fruits should be in considerable demand. He also realized that he could use his own meat products in the business, thereby providing new sales for Smith's Country Hams.

Ronald reconditioned an old production facility that had been idle and set up offices there for Smith's Home Foods. He put the employee who had the idea in charge of the business. However, by October 1992, the employee had failed to meet Ronald's expectations and had resigned. Ronald then asked Christy to take over. He knew this would be a challenging assignment for her. She was still a full-time university student. As a result, she could devote only afternoons and whatever time she could squeeze from her evenings to manage Smith's Home Foods.

The Home Foods Business. The home-delivered foods business centers on providing families with prearranged assortments of foods that are delivered to their homes. Smith's Home Foods offers 11 standard packages, containing various combinations of frozen meats, vegetables, and fruits. The packages differ in size and cost, but each provides a four-month food supply. Exhibit IV-1 shows the items in a typical package. Exhibit IV-2 summarizes the characteristics of each of the 11 packages.

When Christy first assumed management of the operation, she wondered why everything was sold in four-month packages. According to Sonny Jones, who had once worked with a competing food service, most competitors offer similar four-month packages. As a result, the quality of food delivered with each package requires that customers own a freezer or purchase one. Therefore, Smith's Home Foods, like other home-foods companies, also sells a 21-cubic foot freezer on an installment payment plan. In general, the requirement of having a freezer does not appear to be a barrier to food-package sales.

Christy believes that customers gain many bene-

EXHIBIT IV-1
Contents of a Typical Smith's Home Foods Package

107# Net Weight Beef

6	Chuck Roasts 2# Avg
4	Shoulder Roasts 2# Avg
1	Sirloin Tip Roast 3# Avg
1	Eye of Round Roast 3# Avg
1	Bottom Round Roast 3# Avg
20	Ribeye Steaks 8 oz
12	T-Bone Steaks 12 oz
8#	Cube Steak
10#	BLS Stew Beef
18	Chopped Beef Steak 8 oz 9# Case
32#	Ground Beef (1# Roll/4oz Patties)
6#	Pork Chops
6#	BLS Pork Chops
5#	Dinner Ham
30	Misc. Meats
20	Fryers
1	Seafood
60	Vegetables (16 oz)
12	Fruits
32	Juices (12 oz)
6#	Cheese
6#	Margarine

	Bank	$1,094.38
	Tax	54.71
		1,149.09
	Deposit	35.00
	Amount Financed	1,114.09
	Finance Charge	56.23
	Deferred Payment	1,170.32
	Total Price	1,205.32

4 Payments at $292.58

$68.04 Per Week

EXHIBIT IV-2
Characteristics of Smith's Home Foods Packages

FOOD PACKAGE NUMBER	POUNDS OF MEAT PER WEEK	MINIMUM FREEZER SIZE	FAMILY SIZE	PACKAGE PRICE*
1	14	21 cu ft	3-4	$1,205
2	12	18	3-4	1,088
3	12	18	3	1,070
4	10	15	2-3	940
5	17	21	4-5	1,532
6	6.5	12	2	655
7	8	15	2-3	1,093
8	9.5	12	2-3	825
9	11	15	2-3	809
10	11	15	2-3	834
11	13	21	4-5	958

*Price for four-month package, including tax and finance charges.

fits from the home delivery of food. First, it's convenient—customers can make fewer trips to the store because Smith's Home Foods packages make a large variety of foods readily available in the home. Therefore, the person who does the cooking has fewer worries about whether enough food is available. Second, Christy feels that Smith's offers superior quality products, especially meats, compared with what consumers typically find at grocery stores. She and her father carefully select the meat offered in the packages. Of course, they supply their own high-quality Smith's Country Ham products. All other meats are purchased from other quality wholesalers, either in individually wrapped portions, such as eight-ounce T-bone steaks, or in "family portions," such as five-pound rib roasts. The wholesalers vacuum pack the meats with plastic shrink wrap to protect their freshness and flavor. Smith's Home Foods packages feature brand name meats, such as Morrell, Armour, Jimmy Dean, and Fishery products. The packages also include brand name fruits and vegetables, such as Dulany and McKenzie, which are purchased from wholesalers. Smith's guarantees the quality of its food, stating that it will replace any food that fails to completely satisfy the customer.

Finally, Christy argues, purchasing food through a home food service saves consumers money. Because customers buy in large quantities, they receive lower prices. And they escape any price increases that occur during the four-month period covered by their food packages. Making fewer trips to the store also helps customers avoid expensive impulse purchases.

Smith's Home Foods' Marketing Program

Smith's food packages are priced at $655 to $1,532, including tax and finance charges, with an average price of $1,000. Smith's cost of goods sold averages 48 percent for the 11 packages, not including a variable cost of $30 per package for delivery. Customers can pay cash, or they can charge or finance their purchases. Although Smith's accepts Visa and MasterCard, customers seldom use these cards to purchase the food packages. Another option allows customers to pay one half in cash upon signing the contract and the final half within 30 days without an interest charge.

Smith's provides credit to qualified customers through the Fair Finance Company of Akron, Ohio, one of the few finance companies that finances food purchases. Customers who opt for financing make a $35 down payment and fill out a credit application. If Fair approves the application, the customer makes the first payment—one-fourth of the amount financed—30 days after the delivery of the food. Thus, on a $1,200 food package financed by Fair, the customer makes four $300 payments. Because the first payment is not due until a month after delivery, the financing plan allows this customer to save $75 a week for food in each of the four weeks leading up to the first payment, and so forth for the remaining three payments. Although the finance company absorbs the risks of the purchase, Smith's assumes the risk until the first payment is made. That is, if a customer receives the food but does not make the first payment, Smith's accepts responsibility for the entire amount financed and must take whatever action it can to obtain payment or reclaim the food.

When a salesperson submits an order for a food package, if the customer wants to finance it, Smith's faxes a copy of the order to Fair Finance Company. Typically, the finance company approves or rejects the application within one business day. If credit is approved, a clerk completes a "pull sheet," which tells warehouse employees which package the customer purchased and what items are included. Typically, the warehouse manager holds orders until five or six are ready to be pulled and then sets a delivery date with the customer.

For customers who want to purchase freezers, Smith's sells a 21-cubic-foot freezer for approximately $800, with a cost of goods sold of $435. This freezer can also be financed through a separate finance company—consumers pay $12.95 down and make 24 monthly payments of about $33. When a customer orders a freezer and credit is approved, Smith's calls a local appliance store that delivers the freezer to the customer and installs it. Once installed, the freezer must run for about three days before it reaches the appropriate temperature to receive the food. Therefore, food delivery must be coordinated with delivery of the freezer.

At this time, Smith's Home Foods stores its inventory in the Smith's Country Hams warehousing and cold storage facilities. It has a one-ton pickup truck equipped with a freezer box to make the delivery to customers. Two Smith's Country Hams employees makes the deliveries, personally placing the food in the customer's freezer.

Smith's Home Foods uses both personal and mass selling techniques to promote its service. Its two full-time salespeople, Sonny Jones and Barbara Johnson, both earn salaries plus commission on their own sales. Sonny and Barbara have also recruited four other part-time, commission-only salespeople. Smith's pays its salespeople a $100 commission on each package sold. It also pays an additional $25 commission to both Sonny and Barbara for each sale made by the part-time salespeople. The same commissions are paid on each freezer sold.

When the salespeople make a call, they must often meet with the customers in the evening, spending as long as two hours discussing the service and completing the applications.

Each salesperson carries a three-ring binder that contains all the information needed for a sales presentation. The binder includes twelve pages of beef and pork product pictures, six pages of poultry and fish product pictures, three pages of vegetable and fruit product pictures, and one page of dessert pictures. Additional pages describe the costs and terms for each of the 11 packages. The binder also contains pictures of freezers that can be purchased and lists substitutions allowed in the packages.

To generate leads for the salesforce, Smith's uses several mass selling techniques. First, it has advertised three times recently in the local Ashton paper, which also serves the small adjoining community of Wolfsburg and the surrounding county with a total population of about 100,000. Each insert costs about $.04. The inserts stress the money-saving features of the service and include a detachable postcard that can be mailed, postage paid, to the company.

More recently, the company has contracted with the local Welcome Wagon to distribute a $10-off coupon for Smith's products along with the other promotions that it gives to newlyweds, families who have just had babies, and new arrivals to the community. Finally, Christy also prepared a flyer that outlines the service. Salespeople place these flyers in various locations around the community, such as beauty parlors.

Christy does not feel that Smith's Home Foods faces any direct competition in the Ashton area. Another large, well-established company, Southern Foods of Greensboro, NC, operates a home foods service very similar to Smith's. However, although Southern Foods also operates in some other states and has customers throughout North Carolina, it does not directly target the Ashton area. In fact, Christy feels that Southern Foods has probably helped her business—it has developed the market generally and acquainted potential customers with the kinds of services that Smith's offers.

When Christy took over, she made a number of immediate changes in an effort to improve performance. She redesigned the food packages to make them more attractive and developed the newspaper insert, flyer, and sales book. Despite these efforts, however, the business has developed very slowly. As Sonny noted, the people responding most to Smith's advertisements are lower-income families who do not have the money to pay cash and who cannot qualify for financing. Smith's has had trouble attracting the middle- to upper-income families for which Christy believes the service is ideally suited.

Although only about eight families had contracted for the service when Christy took over, customers now total 60. However, many of the families who signed up since she arrived would soon be finishing their first package. Christy was concerned about how many of these customers would reorder. She was also worried about how long her father's patience would last. He had told her that he would invest as much as $250,000 to get this business going. He had already invested $25,000 in inventory. Furthermore, she estimated that Smith's Home Foods annual fixed costs amounted to $57,000, including salaries, rent and utilities, and other overhead. Christy wondered about the business's profitability and about how many customers she needed to reach to break even.

Questions

1. Outline Smith's Home Foods marketing strategy. What is Smith's Home Foods really selling?

2. What problems, if any, do you see with each element of the strategy?

3. Using information given in the case, calculate the average contribution per food package and the number of customers Smith's Home Foods needs to break even.

4. Based on your analysis, what steps would you recommend that Christy take to improve her marketing strategy and Smith's performance?

*B*uilding Customer Satisfaction Through Quality, Value, and Service

19

*I*n 1934, the Wooster Rubber Company made a little-noticed addition to its line of balloons: a rubber dustpan. It sold the new dustpan door to door for $1, much more than the $.39 that competitors were charging for their metal versions. But this dustpan was special—it was well-designed, long-lasting, and very high in quality. Even at the $1 price, it was a good value. The Wooster Rubber Company now is called Rubbermaid, and that lowly dustpan turned out to be a real winner. Since then, the same concepts that led to the development of the rubber dustpan have transformed Rubbermaid from a sleepy, small-town rubber-products company into a dynamic market leader.

Today, Rubbermaid thoroughly dominates its fragmented industry, without serious competition. It produces a dazzling array of more than 4,700 products, ranging from food containers, garbage cans, and home organizers to toy cars, mailboxes, and molded plastic bird feeders. It sells $1.7 billion worth of rubber and plastic housewares, toys, outdoor furniture, and office products each year. Rubbermaid's rise to the top has been nothing short of spectacular. In only the past decade or so, its sales have quadrupled and profits have grown sixfold. It has achieved 54 consecutive years of profits, 44 consecutive quarters of sales and earnings growth, and 18 percent average earnings per share since 1985. *Fortune* magazine has rated Rubbermaid among the nation's top seven most admired corporations for five years running.

Rubbermaid's success results from a simple but effective competitive marketing strategy: to consistently offer the best value to customers. First, the company carefully studies and listens to consumers. It uses demographic and lifestyle analysis to spot consumer trends, and conducts focus groups, interviews, and in-home product tests to learn about consumer problems and needs, likes and dislikes. Then, it gives consumers what they want—a continuous flow of useful, innovative, and high-quality products.

Rubbermaid has forged a strong market position. To most consumers, the Rubbermaid name has become the gold standard of good value and quality. Customers know that Rubbermaid products are well designed and well made, and they willingly pay premium prices to own them. Rubbermaid management jealously protects this reputation. The company has an obsession for quality. Under its strict quality-control program, no product with so much as a scratch ever leaves the factory floor. It's said that former Rubbermaid CEO Stanley Gault, who guided the company through its spectacular growth during the 1980s, used to visit retail stores several times a week to see how the company's products were displayed and to check on quality and workmanship. If he found a problem, he bought up the merchandise on the spot, brought it back to headquarters, and severely lectured responsible company executives. Throughout the company, he was known to get livid about product defects.

Rubbermaid thrives on finding new ways to serve customers. Innovation and new-product development have become a kind of religion in the company. Rubbermaid introduced a staggering 365 new products last year. Its goal is to generate at least 30 percent of its total sales from products less than five years old, a goal that it usually meets or exceeds. The company even bases part of its executive compensation on new products' share of sales. Despite the hectic pace of new introductions, Rubbermaid has met with astonishing success. In a fiercely competitive industry where 90 percent of all new products typically fail, Rubbermaid boasts an amazing 90-percent *success* rate for its new products.

To speed up the flow of new products, Rubbermaid assigns small teams—made up of experts from marketing, design, manufacturing, and finance—to each of its 50 or so product categories. These teams identify new product ideas and usher them through design, development, and introduction. The teams tackle the new-product development challenge with enthusiasm. For example, the manager of Rubbermaid's bath accessories, decorative coverings, and home organizational products notes that her "bath team" lives and breathes soap dishes, vanity wastebaskets, and shower caddies. Team members go to trade shows, scour magazines, scan supermarket shelves, and travel the globe searching for new product ideas. "We are like sponges," she says.

Rubbermaid's versions of ordinary products usually offer simple but elegant improvements. For example, its new, wider mailbox allows magazines to lie flat, doesn't rust, prevents water from seeping in when opened, and raises a yellow flag to let you know when the mail has been delivered. And its simple yet stylish new Sidekick "litter-free" lunch pail features plastic containers that hold a sandwich, a drink, and another item, eliminating the need for plastic wrapping, milk cartons, cans, and other potential litter. The Sidekick is priced at $10, much higher than the $6 to $7 charged for competing products. Still, the colorful new lunch box has become all the rage among parents worried about the nation's garbage glut and grade-school children who've had environmental messages pounded into them at school. Rubbermaid's share of the $35 million lunch-box market is expected to double to 12 percent, and the company plans to introduce six new Sidekick versions.

In addition to developing new products from scratch, Rubbermaid has been very successful at buying up and building small, undervalued companies. For example, in 1984 it added Little Tykes, a small producer of plastic toys, to its portfolio of businesses. In 1991, with the acquisition of Eldon Industries, it established its Office Products Group, which makes desktop accessories, office containers and organizers, modular furniture, office signage, and other products for home and commercial offices. Such smart strategic planning moves have paid off. Little Tykes is now the company's second largest unit—it introduced 30 new toys last year and currently con-

tributes about 21 percent of total sales and 27 percent of profits. Rubbermaid also is gearing up to expand its dominance into global markets. By the year 2000, it plans to generate 25 percent of sales from outside the United States, compared to the current 15 percent.

Rubbermaid also has built strong relationships with its "other customers"—retailers who operate the more than 120,000 outlets that sell Rubbermaid products. Retailers appreciate the company's consistent high quality, larger margins, outstanding service, and strong consumer appeal. In fact, Rubbermaid recently received "Vendor of the Year" honors from the mass-merchandising industry. It has built alliances aggressively with fast-growing discount stores such as Wal-Mart and K mart which account for the bulk of housewares sales. It created "Rubbermaid boutiques," whole sections within stores that stock only Rubbermaid products. For example, Twin Valu stores set up 10 24-foot long shelves with Rubbermaid products, displacing 20 to 490 feet of competing products. As a result, most of Rubbermaid's competitors have trouble simply getting shelf space.

Thus, Rubbermaid has done all of the things that an outstanding marketing company must do to establish and retain its leadership. As one industry analyst notes: "[Rubbermaid has] the ability to execute strategy flawlessly. There's something about Rubbermaid that's magical, that is so difficult for competitors to replicate." Rubbermaid has positioned itself strongly and gained competitive advantage by providing the best value to consumers. It has set the pace for its industry and kept competitors at bay through continuous innovation. Finally, it has developed a constant stream of useful, high-quality products in a constant quest to deliver ever more value to consumers. In fact, some observers wonder if Rubbermaid can maintain its current torrid pace. How many more new products and approaches, they ask, can the company find? "It's a little like in 1900, when there was legislation to close the patent office," answers a Rubbermaid executive. "The country was convinced that everything that could be invented already was. [But when it comes to fresh and salable new ways to serve our customers], we're never going to run out of ideas."[1]

CHAPTER PREVIEW

Chapter 19 reviews a key trend in marketing for the twenty-first century: the trend toward the use of "relationship marketing" to improve customer satisfaction.

We frame the chapter by reinterpreting the marketing concept, stressing the need to offer real **customer value** and **customer satisfaction** in order to compete effectively.

Next, we explain how companies deliver **value** and **satisfaction** through a **value chain** and a **value delivery system.** We discuss the fact that marketers usually focus on attracting new users, but must also **retain current customers** by developing **relationship marketing.**

Finally, we look at **total quality marketing,** defining quality and discussing the importance of building value-laden, profitable relationships with customers.

Today's companies face their toughest competition in decades, and things will only get worse in years to come. In previous chapters, we have argued that to succeed in today's fiercely competitive marketplace, companies will have to move from a *product and selling philosophy* to a *customer and marketing philosophy.* This chapter spells out in more detail how companies can go about winning customers and outperforming competitors. The answer lies in the marketing concept—in doing a better job of *meeting and satisfying customer needs.*

In sellers' markets—those characterized by shortages and near-monopolies—companies do not make special efforts to please customers. Today in Eastern Europe, for example, millions of consumers stand sullenly in line for hours only to receive poorly made clothes, toiletries, appliances, and other products at high prices. Producers and retailers show little concern for customer satisfaction with goods and services. Sellers pay relatively little heed to marketing theory and practice.

In buyers' markets, in contrast, customers can choose from a wide array of goods and services. In these markets, if sellers fail to deliver acceptable product and service quality, they will quickly lose customers to competitors. And what is considered acceptable today may not be acceptable to tomorrow's ever-more-demanding consumers. Consumers are becoming more educated and demanding, and their quality expectations have been raised by the practices of superior manufacturers and retailers. The decline of many U.S. industries in recent years—autos, cameras, machine tools, consumer electronics—offers dramatic evidence that firms offering only average quality lose their consumer franchises when attacked by superior competitors.

To succeed, or simply to survive, companies need a new philosophy. To win in today's marketplace, companies must be **customer-centered**—they must deliver superior value to their target customers. They must become adept in *building customers,* not just *building products.* They must be skillful in *market engineering,* not just *product engineering.*

Too many companies think that obtaining customers is the job of the marketing or sales department. But winning companies have come to realize that marketing cannot do this job alone. In fact, although it plays a leading role, marketing can be only a partner in attracting and keeping customers. The world's best marketing department cannot successfully sell poorly made products that fail to meet consumer needs. The marketing department can be effective only in companies in which all departments and employees have teamed up to form a competitively superior *customer value-delivery system.*

Consider McDonald's. People do not swarm to the world's 11,000 McDonald's restaurants only because they love the chain's hamburgers. Many other restaurants make better-tasting hamburgers. Consumers flock to the McDonald's *system,* not just to its food products. Throughout the world, McDonald's finely tuned system delivers a high standard of what the company calls QSCV—quality, service, cleanliness, and value. The system consists of many components, both internal and external. McDonald's is only effective to the extent that it successfully partners with its employees, franchisees, suppliers, and others to jointly deliver exceptionally high customer value.

This chapter discusses the philosophy of customer-value-creating marketing and the customer-focused firm. It addresses several important questions: What are customer value and customer satisfaction? How do leading companies organize to create and deliver high value and satisfaction? How can companies keep current customers as well as get new ones? How can companies practice total quality marketing?

DEFINING CUSTOMER VALUE AND SATISFACTION

More than 35 years ago, Peter Drucker insightfully observed that a company's first task is "to create customers." However, creating customers can be a difficult task. Today's customers face a vast array of product and brand choices, prices, and suppliers. The company must answer a key question: How do customers make their choices?

The answer is that customers choose the marketing offer that gives them the most value. Customers are value-maximizers, within the bounds of search costs and limited knowledge, mobility, and income. They form expectations of value and act upon them. Then they compare the actual value they receive in consuming the product to the value expected, and this affects their satisfaction and repurchase behavior. We will now examine the concepts of customer value and customer satisfaction more carefully.

Customer Value

Consumers buy from the firm that they believe offers the highest **customer delivered value**—the difference between *total customer value* and *total customer cost* (see Figure 19-1). For example, suppose that a large construction firm wants to buy a bulldozer. The firm has a particular bulldozer application in mind—it will use the machine in residential construction work. It wants the bulldozer to deliver certain levels of reliability, durability, and performance. It can buy the equipment from either Caterpillar or Komatsu. The salespeople for the two companies carefully describe their respective offers to the buyer.

Suppose the construction firm evaluates the two competing bulldozer offers and judges that Caterpillar's bulldozer provides higher reliability, durability, and performance. The customer also decides that Caterpillar has better accompanying services—delivery, training, and maintenance. It views Caterpillar personnel as more knowledgeable and responsive. Finally, the customer places higher value on Caterpillar's reputation. The construction firm adds all the values from these four sources—*product, services, personnel,* and *image*—and decides that Caterpillar offers more **total customer value** than does Komatsu.

Does the construction firm buy the Caterpillar bulldozer? Not necessarily. The firm also will examine the **total customer cost** of buying the Caterpillar bulldozer versus the Komatsu product. First, the buying firm will compare the prices it must pay for each of the competitors' products. If Caterpillar's bulldozer costs a lot more than Komatsu's does, the higher price might offset the higher total customer value. Moreover, total customer cost consists of more than just monetary costs. As Adam Smith observed more than two centuries ago, "The real price of anything is the toil and trouble of acquiring it." Total customer cost also includes the buyer's anticipated time, energy, and psychic costs. The construction firm will evaluate these costs along with monetary costs to form a complete estimate of its costs.

The buying firm now compares total customer value to total customer cost and determines the total delivered value associated with Caterpillar's bulldozer. In

FIGURE 19-1
Customer delivered value

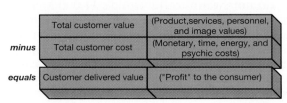

the same way, it assesses the total delivered value for the Komatsu bulldozer. The firm then will buy from the competitor that offers the highest delivered value.

How can Caterpillar use this concept of buyer decision making to help it succeed in selling its bulldozer to this buyer? Caterpillar can improve its offer in three ways. First, Caterpillar can increase total customer value by improving product, services, personnel, or image benefits. Second, Caterpillar can reduce the buyer's nonmonetary costs by lessening the buyer's time, energy, and psychic costs. Third, Caterpillar can reduce the buyer's monetary costs by lowering its price, providing easier terms of sale, or, in the longer term, lowering its bulldozer's operating or maintenance costs.

Suppose Caterpillar carries out a *customer value assessment* and concludes that buyers see Caterpillar's offer as worth $20,000. Further suppose that it costs Caterpillar $14,000 to produce the bulldozer. This means that Caterpillar's offer potentially generates $6,000 ($20,000 – $14,000) of *total added value*. Caterpillar needs to price its bulldozer between $14,000 and $20,000. If it charges less than $14,000, it won't cover its costs. If it charges more than $20,000, the price will exceed the total customer value. The price Caterpillar charges will determine how much of the total added value will be delivered to the buyer and how much will flow to Caterpillar. For example, if Caterpillar charges $16,000, it will grant $4,000 of total added value to the customer and keep $2,000 for itself as profit. If Caterpillar charges $19,000, it will grant only $1,000 of total added value to the customer and keep $5,000 for itself as profit. Naturally, the lower Caterpillar's price, the higher the delivered value of its offer will be, and, therefore, the higher customer's incentive to purchase from Caterpillar. Delivered value should be viewed as "profit to the customer." Given that Caterpillar wants to win the sale, it must offer more delivered value than Komatsu does.[2]

Some marketers might rightly argue that this concept of how buyers choose among product alternatives is too rational. They might cite examples in which buyers did not choose the offer with an objectively measured highest delivered value. Consider the following situation:

> The Caterpillar salesperson convinces the construction firm that, considering the benefits relative to the purchase price, Caterpillar's bulldozer offers a higher delivered value. The salesperson also points out that the Komatsu bulldozer uses more fuel and requires more frequent repairs. Still, the firm decides to buy the Komatsu bulldozer.

How can we explain this appearance of non-value-maximizing behavior? There are many possible explanations. For example, perhaps the construction firm's buyers enjoy a long-term friendship with the Komatsu salesperson. Or the construction firm's buyers might be under strict company orders to buy at the lowest price. Or perhaps the construction firm rewards its buyers for short-term performance, causing them to choose the less expensive Komatsu bulldozer, even though the Caterpillar machine will perform better and be less expensive to operate in the long run.

Clearly, buyers operate under various constraints and sometimes make choices that give more weight to their personal benefit than to company benefit. However, the customer delivered value framework applies to many situations and yields rich insights. The framework suggests that sellers must first assess the total customer value and total customer cost associated with their own and competing marketing offers to determine how their own offers measure up in terms of customer delivered value. If a seller finds that competitors deliver greater value, it has two alternatives. It can try to increase total customer value by strengthening or augmenting the product, services, personnel, or image benefits of the offer. Or it can decrease total customer cost by reducing its price, simplifying the ordering and delivery process, or absorbing some buyer risk by offering a warranty.[3]

Customer Satisfaction

Thus, consumers form judgments about the value of marketing offers and make their buying decisions based upon these judgments. *Customer satisfaction* with a purchase depends upon the product's performance relative to a buyer's expectations. A customer might experience various degrees of satisfaction. If the product's performance falls short of expectations, the customer is dissatisfied. If performance matches expectations, the customer is satisfied. If performance exceeds expectations, the customer is highly satisfied or delighted.

Are we aiming too high? Or is everyone else aiming too low?

At the CIGNA Group Pension Division, customer satisfaction is our number one priority. Sounds good in an ad. But how do we achieve it? By giving the customer a voice. And then listening to it. When our customers told us that simplifying participant financial statements was a major priority, we listened. Then, using their input we designed more user-friendly reports.

When customers told us they wanted more investment options, we listened, too. Responding to their request with new accounts—six investing in mutual funds. Including highly rated funds from well-known outside investment companies.

100% SATISFACTION. 100% OF THE TIME.

CIGNA

And because even a little thing can often be a big thing, we listen to everything. For example, when customers told us they preferred talking to people rather than computers, we eliminated recorded messages in our customer service areas.

The point is, when the customer talks, we listen. To find out precisely how well, call CIGNA Group Pension Division, 1-800-238-2525.

Of course, we're not saying that we're perfect. But what we are saying is that we'll never be 100% satisfied until you are, too.

Total customer satisfaction: Cigna vows, "We'll never be 100 percent satisfied until you are, too."

But how do buyers form their expectations? Expectations are based on the customer's past buying experiences, the opinions of friends and associates, and marketer and competitor information and promises. Marketers must be careful to set the right level of expectations. If they set expectations too low, they may satisfy those who buy but fail to attract enough buyers. In contrast, if they raise expectations too high, buyers are likely to be disappointed. For example, Holiday Inn ran a campaign a few years ago called "No Surprises," which promised consistently trouble-free accommodations and service. However, Holiday Inn guests still encountered a host of problems, and the expectations created by the campaign only made customers more dissatisfied. Holiday Inn had to withdraw the campaign.

Still, some of today's most successful companies are raising expectations—and delivering performance to match. These companies embrace *total customer satisfaction*. For example, Honda claims "One reason our customers are so satisfied is that we aren't." And Cigna vows "We'll never be 100 percent satisfied until you are, too." These companies aim high because they know that customers who are *only* satisfied will still find it easy to switch suppliers when a better offer comes along. In one consumer packaged-goods category, 44 percent of consumers reporting satisfaction later switched brands. In contrast, customers who are *highly* satisfied are much less ready to switch. One study showed that 75 percent of Toyota buyers were highly satisfied and about 75 percent said they intended to buy a Toyota again. Thus, customer *delight* creates an emotional affinity for a product or service, not just a rational preference, and this creates high customer loyalty.

Today's winning companies track their customers' expectations, perceived company performance, and customer satisfaction. They track this for their competitors as well. Consider the following:

> A company was pleased to find that 80 percent of its customers said they were satisfied with its new product. However, the product seemed to sell poorly on store shelves next to the leading competitor's product. Company researchers soon learned that the competitor's product attained a 90 percent customer satisfaction score. Company management was further dismayed when it learned that this competitor was aiming for a 95 percent satisfaction score.

Marketing Highlight 19-1 describes the ways in which companies can track customer satisfaction.

For customer-centered companies, customer satisfaction is both a goal and a major factor in company success. Companies that achieve high customer satisfaction ratings make sure that their target market knows it. In the automobile industry, the Honda Accord received the number-one rating in customer satisfaction by J. D. Powers for several years running, and Honda advertising touting helped sell more Accords. Similarly, Dell Computer's meteoric growth in the personal computer industry was partly because it achieved and advertised its number-one customer satisfaction ranking.

These and other companies realize that highly satisfied customers produce several benefits for the company. They are less price sensitive and they remain customers for a longer period. They buy additional products over time as the company introduces related products or improvements. And they talk favorably to others about the company and its products.

Although the customer-centered firm seeks to deliver high customer satisfaction relative to competitors, it does not attempt to *maximize* customer satisfaction. A company can always increase customer satisfaction by lowering its price or increasing its services, but this may result in lower profits. In addition to customers, the company has many stakeholders, including employees, dealers, suppliers, and stockholders. Spending more to increase customer satisfaction might divert funds from increasing the satisfaction of these other "partners." Thus, the purpose of marketing is to generate customer value profitably. Ultimately, the company must deliver a high level of customer satisfaction while at the same time delivering at least acceptable levels of satisfaction to the firm's other stakeholders. This requires a very delicate balance: the marketer must continue to generate more customer value and satisfaction but not "give away the house."[4]

DELIVERING CUSTOMER VALUE AND SATISFACTION

Customer value and satisfaction are important ingredients in the marketer's formula for success. But what does it take to produce and deliver customer value? To answer this, we will examine the concepts of a *value chain* and *value delivery system*.

Value Chain

Michael Porter proposed the **value chain** as the major tool for identifying ways to create more customer value (see Figure 19-2).[5] Every firm consists of a collection of activities performed to design, produce, market, deliver, and support the firm's products. The value chain breaks the firm into nine value-creating activities in an effort to understand the behavior of costs in the specific business and the potential sources of competitive differentiation. The nine value-creating activities include five primary activities and four support activities.

The primary activities involve the sequence of bringing materials into the business (inbound logistics), operating on them (operations), sending them out (outbound logistics), marketing them (marketing and sales), and servicing them (service). The support activities occur within each of these primary activities. For example, procurement involves obtaining the various inputs for each primary activity—only a fraction of procurement is done by the purchasing department. Technology development and human-resource management also occur in all de-

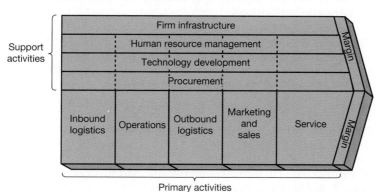

FIGURE 19-2
The generic value chain
Source: Michael E. Porter, *Competitive Advantage* (New York: Free Press, 1985), p. 37.

TRACKING CUSTOMER SATISFACTION

Tools for tracking and measuring customer satisfaction range from the primitive to the sophisticated. Companies use the following methods to measure how much customer satisfaction they are creating.

Complaint and Suggestion Systems

A customer-centered organization makes it easy for customers to make suggestions or complaints. Restaurants and hotels provide forms upon which guests can check off their likes and dislikes. Hospitals place suggestion boxes in the corridors, supply comment cards to exiting patients, and employ patient advocates to solicit grievances. Some customer-centered companies, such as P&G, General Electric, and Whirlpool, set up customer hotlines with 800 numbers to make it easy for customers to inquire, suggest, or complain. Such systems not only help companies to act more quickly to resolve problems, they also provide companies with many good ideas for improved products and service.

Customer Satisfaction Surveys

Simply running complaint and suggestion systems may not give the company a full picture of customer satisfaction and dissatisfaction. Studies show that one of every four purchases results in consumer dissatisfaction but that less than 5 percent of dissatisfied customers complain. Customers may feel that their complaints are minor, or that they will be treated harshly if they complain, or that the company will do little to remedy the problem anyway. Rather than complain, most customers simply switch suppliers. As a result, the company needlessly loses customers.

Responsive companies take direct measures of customer satisfaction by conducting regular surveys. They send questionnaires or make telephone calls to a sample of recent customers to find out how they feel about various aspects of the company's performance. They also survey buyers' views on competitor performance.

Whirlpool surveys customer satisfaction on a massive scale, then acts on the results:

> When customers talk, Whirlpool listens. Each year the company mails its Standardized Appliance Measurement Satisfaction (SAMS) survey to 180,000 households, asking people to rate all their appliances on dozens of attributes. When a competitor's product ranks higher, Whirlpool engineers rip it apart to see why. The company [also] pays hundreds of consumers to fiddle with computer-simulated products at the company's Usability Lab while engineers record the users' reactions on videotape.

A company can measure customer satisfaction in a number of ways. It can measure satisfaction directly by asking: "How satisfied are you with this product? Are you highly dissatisfied, somewhat dissatisfied, neither satisfied nor dissatisfied, somewhat satisfied, or highly satisfied?" Or it can ask respondents to rate how much they expected of certain attributes and how much they actually experienced. Finally, the company can ask respondents to list any problems they have had with the offer and to suggest improvements.

While collecting customer satisfaction data, companies often ask additional useful questions. They often measure the customer's *repurchase intention;* this will usually be high if customer satisfaction is high. According to CEO John Young at Hewlett-Packard, nine out of ten customers in HP surveys who rank themselves as highly satisfied say they would definitely or probably buy from HP again. The company also might ask about the customer's likelihood or willingness to recommend the company and brand to other people. A strongly positive word-of-mouth rating suggests high customer satisfaction.

Ghost Shopping

Another useful way of assessing customer satisfaction is

partments. The firm's infrastructure covers the overhead of general management, planning, finance, accounting, and legal and government affairs borne by all the primary and support activities.

Under the value-chain concept, the firm should examine its costs and performance in each value-creating activity to look for improvements. It also should estimate its competitors' costs and performances as benchmarks. To the extent that the firm can perform certain activities better than its competitors, it can achieve a competitive advantage.

The firm's success depends not only on how well each department performs its work, but also on how well the activities of various departments are coordinated. Too often, individual departments maximize their own interests rather than those of the total company and the customer. For example, a credit department might attempt to reduce bad debts by taking a long time to check the credit of prospective customers; meanwhile, salespeople get frustrated and customers wait. A distribution department might decide to save money by shipping goods to hire people to pose as buyers to report their experiences in buying the company's and competitors' products. These "ghost shoppers" can even present specific problems to test whether the company's personnel handle difficult situations well. For example, ghost shoppers can complain about a restaurant's food to see how the restaurant handles this complaint. Not only should companies hire ghost shoppers, but managers themselves should leave their offices from time to time and experience first-hand the treatment they receive as "customers." As an alternative, managers can phone their own companies with different questions and complaints to see how the call is handled.

Lost Customer Analysis

Companies should contact customers who have stopped buying, or those who have switched to a competitor, to learn why this happened. When IBM loses a customer, it mounts a thorough effort to learn how it failed: was IBM's price too high, its service poor, or its products substandard? Not only should the company conduct such *exit interviews,* it should also monitor the *customer loss rate.* A rising loss rate indicates that the company is failing to satisfy its customers.

Some Cautions in Measuring Customer Satisfaction

Customer satisfaction ratings are sometimes difficult to interpret. When customers rate their satisfaction with some element of the company's performance, say delivery, they can vary greatly in how they define good delivery. It might mean early delivery, on-time delivery, order completeness, or something else. Yet, if the company tried to define every element in detail, customers would face a huge questionnaire.

Companies also must recognize that two customers can report being "highly satisfied" for different reasons. One might be easily satisfied most of the time whereas the other might be hard to please but was pleased on this occasion. Further, managers and salespeople can manipulate their ratings on customer satisfaction. They can be especially nice to customers just before the survey or try to exclude unhappy customers from being included in the survey. Finally, if customers know that the company will go out of its way to please customers, even if they are satisfied some customers may express high dissatisfaction in order to receive more concessions.

Tracking customer satisfaction: Each year Whirlpool mails its Standardized Appliance Measurement of Satisfaction survey to 180,000 households, asking them to rate all of its appliances.

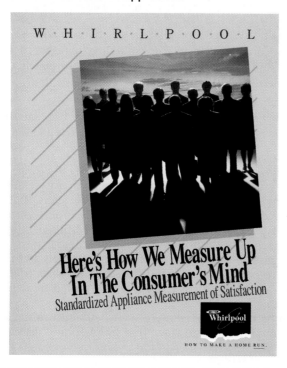

Source: Quote from Sally Solo, "Whirlpool: How to Listen to Consumers," *Fortune,* January 11, 1993, pp. 77-79. Also see *Measure,* July-August 1990, p. 28.

by rail; again the customer waits. In each case, individual departments have erected walls that impede the delivery of quality customer service.

To overcome this problem, companies should place more emphasis on the smooth management of *core business processes,* most of which involve inputs and cooperation from many functional departments. Among others, these core business processes include the following:

- *Product development process:* all the activities involved in identifying, researching, and developing new products with speed, high quality, and reasonable cost.

- *Inventory management process:* all the activities involved in developing and managing the right inventory levels of raw materials, semifinished materials, and finished goods so that adequate supplies are available while avoiding the costs of high overstocks

- *Order-to-payment process:* all the activities involved in receiving orders, approving them, shipping the goods on time, and collecting payment

- *Customer service process:* all the activities involved in making it easy for customers to reach the right parties within the company to obtain service, answers, and resolutions of problems.

Successful companies develop superior capabilities in managing these and other core processes. In turn, mastering core business processes gives these companies a substantial competitive edge.[6] For example, one of Wal-Mart's great strengths is its superiority in handling the inventory management and order flow process. As individual Wal-Mart stores sell their goods, sales information flows not only to Wal-Mart's headquarters but to Wal-Mart's suppliers, who ship replacement goods to Wal-Mart stores almost as fast as they move off the shelf.

Value Delivery System

In its search for competitive advantage, the firm needs to look beyond its own value chain, into the value chains of its suppliers, distributors, and ultimately customers. More companies today are "partnering" with the other members of the supply chain to improve the performance of the **customer value delivery system.** For example:

> Campbell Soup operates a qualified supplier program in which it sets high standards for suppliers and chooses only the few suppliers who are willing to meet its demanding requirements for quality, on-time delivery, and continuous improvement. Campbell then assigns its own experts to work with suppliers to constantly improve their joint performance.
>
> Procter & Gamble has assigned twenty of its employees to work at Wal-Mart's headquarters to improve the speed and reduce the costs of supplying P&G goods to Wal-Mart's branch stores.

An excellent value delivery system connects jeans maker Levi Strauss with its suppliers and distributors (see Figure 19-3). One of Levi's major retailers is Sears. Every night, Levi's learns the sizes and styles of its blue jeans that sold through Sears and other major outlets. Levi's then electronically orders more fabric from the Milliken Company, its fabric supplier. In turn, Milliken relays an order for more fiber to Du Pont, the fiber supplier. In this way, the partners in the supply chain use the most current sales information to manufacture what is selling, rather than to manufacture based on potentially inaccurate sales forecasts. This is known as a *quick response* system, in which goods are pulled by demand, rather than pushed by supply.

As companies struggle to become more competitive, they are turning, ironically, to greater cooperation. Companies used to view their suppliers and distributors

Customer value delivery system: Campbell operates a qualified supplier program in which it chooses only the few suppliers who can meet its demanding quality requirements. Campbell's experts then work with suppliers to constantly improve their joint performance.

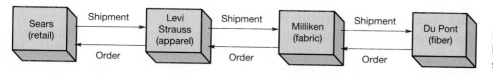

FIGURE 19-3
Levi Strauss' value delivery system

as cost centers, and in some cases, as adversaries. Today, however, they are selecting partners carefully and working out mutually profitable strategies. Increasingly in today's marketplace, competition no longer takes place between individual competitors. Rather, it takes place between the entire value delivery systems created by these competitors. Thus, if Levi Strauss has built a more potent value delivery system than Wrangler or another competitor, it will win more market share and profit.

Therefore, marketing can no longer be thought of as only a selling department. That view of marketing would give it responsibility only for formulating a promotion-oriented marketing mix, without much to say about product features, costs, and other important elements. Under the new view, marketing is responsible for *designing and managing a superior value delivery system to reach target customer segments*. Today's marketing managers must think not only about selling today's products but also about how to stimulate the development of improved products, how to work actively with other departments in managing core business processes, and how to build better external partnerships.[7]

RETAINING CUSTOMERS

Beyond building stronger relations with their partners in the supply chain, companies today must work to develop stronger bonds and loyalty with their ultimate customers. In the past, many companies took their customers for granted. Customers often did not have many alternative suppliers, or the other suppliers were just as poor in quality and service, or the market was growing so fast that the company did not worry about fully satisfying its customers. A company could lose 100 customers a week but gain another 100 customers and consider its sales to be satisfactory. Such a company, operating on a "leaky bucket" theory of business, believes that there will always be enough customers to replace the defecting ones. However, this high *customer churn* involves higher costs than if a company retained all 100 customers and acquired no new ones.

The Cost of Lost Customers

Companies must pay close attention to their customer defection rate and undertake steps to reduce it. First, the company must define and measure its retention rate. For a magazine, it would be the renewal rate; for a consumer packaged-good firm, it would be the repurchase rate.

Next, the company must identify the causes of customer defection and determine which of these can be reduced or eliminated. Not much can be done about customers who leave the region or about business customers who go out of business. But much can be done about customers who leave because of shoddy products, poor service, or prices that are too high. The company needs to prepare a frequency distribution showing the percentage of customers who defect for different reasons.

Companies can estimate how much profit they lose when customers defect unnecessarily. For an individual customer, this is the same as the *customer's lifetime value*. For a group of lost customers, a major transportation firm estimated the profit loss as follows:

> The company had 64,000 accounts. It lost 5 percent of its accounts (3,200 accounts) this year as a result of poor service. The average lost account represented $40,000 in lost revenue. Therefore, the company lost 3,200 × $40,000 = $128,000,000 in revenue. Given its 10 percent profit margin, the company lost $12,800,000 unnecessarily.

The company needs to figure out how much it would cost to reduce the defection rate. If the cost is less than the lost profits, the company should spend that amount to reduce customer defections. In this example, if the transportation firm can spend less than $12,800,000 to retain all of these accounts, it would be wise to do so.

The Need for Customer Retention

Today, outstanding companies go all out to retain their customers. Many markets have settled into maturity, and there are not many new customers entering most categories. Competition is increasing and the costs of attracting new customers are rising. In these markets, its might costs five times as much to attract a new customer as to keep a current customer happy. Offensive marketing typically costs more than defensive marketing, because it takes a great deal of effort and spending to coax satisfied customers away from competitors.

Unfortunately, classic marketing theory and practice centers on the art of attracting new customers rather than retaining existing ones. The emphasis has been on creating *transactions* rather than *relationships*. Discussion has focused on *presale activity* and *sale activity* rather than on *postsale activity*. Today, however, more companies recognize the importance of retaining current customers. According to one report, by reducing customer defections by only 5 percent, companies can improve profits anywhere from 25 percent to 85 percent.[8] Unfortunately, however, most company accounting systems fail to show the value of loyal customers.

Thus, although much current marketing focuses on formulating marketing mixes that will create sales and new customers, the firm's first line of defense lies in customer retention. And the best approach to customer retention is to deliver high customer satisfaction that results in strong customer loyalty.

The Key: Customer Relationship Marketing

Relationship marketing involves creating, maintaining, and enhancing strong relationships with customers and other stakeholders. Increasingly, marketing is moving away from a focus on individual transactions and toward a focus on building value-laden relationships and marketing networks. Relationship marketing is oriented more toward the long term. The goal is to deliver long-term value to customers and the measure of success is long-term customer satisfaction. Relationship marketing requires that all of the company's departments work together with marketing as a team to serve the customer. It involves building relationships at many levels—economic, social, technical, and legal—resulting in high customer loyalty.

We can distinguish five different levels or relationships that can be formed with customers who have purchased a company's product, such as an automobile or a piece of equipment:

Relationship marketing: Increasingly, companies are moving away from a focus on individual transactions and toward a focus on building value-laden relationships with customers. Here PaineWebber declares, "We invest in relationships."

- *Basic:* The company salesperson sells the product but does not follow up in any way.

- *Reactive:* The salesperson sells the product and encourages the customer to call whenever he or she has any questions or problems.

- *Accountable:* The salesperson phones the customer a short time after the sale to check whether the product is meeting the customer's expectations. The salesperson also solicits from the customer any product improvement suggestions and any specific disappointments. This information helps the company to continuously improve its offering.

- *Proactive:* The salesperson or others in the company phone the customer from time to time with suggestions about improved product use or helpful new products.

- *Partnership:* The company works continuously with the customer and with other customers to discover ways to deliver better value.

Figure 19-4 shows that a company's relationship marketing strategy will depend on how many customers it has and their profitability. For example, companies with many low-margin customers will practice *basic* marketing. Thus, H.J. Heinz will not phone all of its ketchup buyers to express its appreciation for their business. At best, Heinz will be reactive by setting up a customer information service. At the other extreme, in markets with few customers and high margins, most sellers will move toward partnership marketing. Boeing, for example, will work closely with United Airlines in designing its airplanes and insuring that Boeing airplanes fully satisfy United's requirements. In between these two extreme situations, other levels of relationship marketing are appropriate.

What specific marketing tools can a company use to develop stronger customer bonding and satisfaction? It can adopt any of three customer value-building approaches.[9] The first relies primarily on adding *financial benefits* to the customer relationship. For example, airlines offer frequent-flyer programs, hotels give room upgrades to their frequent guests, and supermarkets give patronage refunds. Procter & Gamble recently offered a unique money-back guarantee on its Crest toothpaste in an effort to build a long-term bond with customers:

> [P&G advertises] a toll-free number customers can call to join a money-back guarantee program for Crest toothpaste. P&G supplies dental patients with evaluation forms that they take to their local dentists. Dentists check for cavities and tartar buildup. After six months of Crest use and a return trip to the dentist, patients who haven't improved are refunded the money they spent on Crest.[10]

Beyond assuring customers that Crest delivers value, this promotion helps P&G build a customer database containing the dental histories of families that sign up. Using this database, P&G can expand its relationships with customers by offering additional related products and services to them.

Although these reward programs and other financial incentives build customer preference, they can be easily imitated by competitors and thus may fail to differentiate the company's offer permanently. The second approach is to add *social benefits* as well as financial benefits. Here company personnel work to increase their social bonds with customers by learning individual customers' needs and

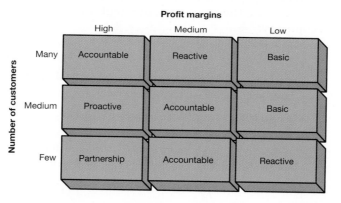

FIGURE 19-4
Relationship levels as a function of profit margin and number of customers

Now going for a dental checkup can actually sound good.

In an effort to build a long-term relationship with customers, Procter & Gamble recently offered a unique money-back guarantee on its Crest toothpaste.

wants and then individualizing and personalizing their products and services. They turn their *customers* into *clients:*

> Customers may be nameless to the institution; clients cannot be nameless. Customers are served as part of the mass or as part of larger segments; clients are served on an individual basis. . . . Customers are served by anyone who happens to be available; clients are served . . . by the professional . . . assigned to them.[11]

The third approach to building strong customer relationships is to add *structural ties* as well as financial and social benefits. For example, a business marketer might supply customers with special equipment or computer linkages that help them manage their orders, payroll, or inventory. McKesson Corporation, a leading pharmaceutical wholesaler, has invested millions of dollars in its *electronic data interchange (EDI)* system to help small pharmacies manage their inventory, their order entry, and their shelf space. As another example, Federal Express uses its Powership Program, which it offers to more than 20,000 customer companies, to keep its best customers from defecting to competitors like UPS. It provides Powership customers with free computers linked to Federal Express headquarters. Customer firms can use the machines to check the status of their own Federal Express packages or those that they ship for their customers. To further enhance its relationships with important customers, Federal Express polls 1,000 of its Powership customers each month seeking ways to improve service to them.[12]

Here are the main steps in establishing a relationship marketing program in a company:

- *Identify the key customers meriting relationship management:* Choose the largest or best customers and designate them for relationship management. Other customers can be added who show exceptional growth or who pioneer new industry developments.

- *Assign a skilled relationship manager to each key customer:* The salesperson currently servicing the customer should receive training in relationship management or be replaced by someone more skilled in relationship management. The relationship manager should have characteristics that match or appeal to the customer.

- *Develop a clear job description for relationship managers:* Describe their reporting relationships, objectives, responsibilities, and evaluation criteria. Make the relationship manager the focal point for all dealings with and about the client. Give each relationship manager only one or a few relationships to manage.

■ *Have each relationship manager develop annual and long-range customer relationship plans:* These plans should state objectives, strategies, specific actions, and required resources.

■ *Appoint an overall manager to supervise the relationship managers:* This person will develop job descriptions, evaluation criteria, and resource support to increase relationship manager effectiveness.

When it has properly implemented relationship management, the organization begins to focus on managing its customers as well as its products. At the same time, although many companies are moving strongly toward relationship marketing, it is not effective in all situations:

When it comes to relationship marketing . . . you don't want a relationship with every customer. . . . In fact, there are some bad customers. [The objective is to] figure out which customers are worth cultivating because you can meet their needs more effectively than anyone else.[13]

Ultimately, companies must judge which segments and which specific customers will be profitable. Marketing Highlight 19-2 discusses the importance of relationships in business marketing and the types of situations in which relationship marketing proves most effective.

The Ultimate Test: Customer Profitability

Ultimately, marketing is the art of attracting and keeping *profitable customers.* Yet, companies often discover that between 20 percent and 40 percent of their customers are unprofitable. Further, many companies report that their most profitable customers are not their largest customers but their mid-size customers. The largest customers demand greater service and receive the deepest discounts, thereby reducing the company's profit level. The smallest customers pay full-price and receive less service, but the costs of transacting with small customers reduces their profitability. In many cases, mid-size customers who pay close to full price and receive good service are the most profitable. This helps to explain why many large firms which once targeted only large customers now are invading the middle market.

A company should not try to pursue and satisfy every customer. For example, if business customers of Courtyard (Marriott's less expensive motel) start asking for Marriott-level business services, Courtyard should say "no." Providing such service would only confuse the respective positionings of the Marriott and Courtyard systems.

Some organizations . . . try to do anything and everything customers suggest. . . . Yet, while customers often make many good suggestions, they also suggest many courses of action that are unactionable or unprofitable. Randomly following these suggestions is fundamentally different from market-focus—making a disciplined choice of which customers to serve and which specific combination of benefits and price to deliver to them (and which to deny them).[14]

What makes a customer profitable? We define a *profitable customer* as person, household, or company whose revenues over time exceed, by an acceptable amount, the company costs of attracting, selling, and servicing that customer. Note that the definition emphasizes lifetime revenues and costs, not profit from a single transaction. Here are some dramatic illustrations of **customer lifetime value:**

Stew Leonard, who operates a highly profitable single-store supermarket, says that he sees $50,000 flying out of his store every time he sees a sulking customer. Why? Because his average customer spends about $100 a week, shops 50 weeks a year, and remains in the area for about 10 years. If this customer has an unhappy experience and switches to another supermarket, Stew Leonard has lost $50,000 in revenue. The loss

WHEN—AND HOW—TO USE RELATIONSHIP MARKETING

Although relationship marketing may not be effective in all situations, it works extremely well in the right situations. Transaction marketing, which focuses on one sales transaction at a time, is more appropriate than relationship marketing for customers who have short time horizons and who can switch from one supplier to another with little effort or investment. This situation often occurs in "commodity" markets, such as steel, where various suppliers offer largely undifferentiated products. A customer buying steel can buy from any of several steel suppliers and choose the one offering the best terms on a purchase-by-purchase basis. The fact that one steel supplier works at developing a longer-term relationship with a buyer does not automatically earn it the next sale; its price and other terms still have to be competitive.

In contrast, relationship marketing can pay off handsomely with customers who have long time horizons and high switching costs, such as buyers of office automation systems. Such major system buyers usually research competing suppliers carefully and choose one from whom they can expect state-of-the-art technology and good long-term service. Both the customer and the supplier invest a lot of money and time in building the relationship. The customer would find it costly and risky to switch to another supplier, and the seller would find that losing this customer would be a major loss. Thus, each seeks to develop a solid long-term working relationship with the other. It is with such customers that relationship marketing has the greatest payoff.

In these situations, the "in-supplier" and "out-supplier" face very different challenges. The in-supplier tries to make switching difficult for the customer. It develops product systems that are incompatible with those of competing suppliers and installs its own ordering systems that simplify inventory management and delivery. It works to become the customer's indispensable partner. Out-suppliers, in contrast, try to make it easy and less costly to switch suppliers. They design product systems that are compatible with the customer's system, that are easy to install and learn, that save the customer a lot of money, and that promise to improve through time.

Some marketers believe that the issue of transaction versus relationship marketing depends not so much on the type of industry as on the wishes of the particular customer. Some customers value a high-service supplier and will stay with that supplier for a long time. Other customers want to cut their costs and will switch suppliers readily to obtain lower costs. In the latter case, the company still can try to keep the customer by agreeing to reduce the price, providing that the customer is willing to accept fewer services. For example, the customer may forego free delivery, design assistance, training, or some other extra. However, the seller probably should treat this type of customer on a transaction basis rather than on a relationship-building basis. As long as the company cuts its own costs by as much or more than its price reduction, the transaction-oriented customer still will be profitable.

Thus, relationship marketing is not the best approach in all situations. For some types of customers, heavy relationship investments simply don't pay off. But relationship marketing can be extremely effective with the right types of customers—those who make hefty commitments to a specific system and then expect high-quality, consistent service over the long term. To win and keep such accounts, the marketer will have to invest heavily in relationship marketing. But the returns will be well worth the investment.

Sources: See Barbara Bund Jackson, *Winning and Keeping Industrial Customers: The Dynamics of Customer Relationships* (Lexington, MA: Heath, 1985); James C. Anderson and James A. Narus, "Value-Based Segmentation, Targeting, and Relationship-Building in Business Markets," ISBM Report #12—1989, The Institute for the Study of Business Markets, Pennsylvania State University, University Park, PA, 1989; Lawrence A. Crosby, Kenneth R. Evans, and Deborah Cowles, "Relationship Quality and Services Selling: An Interpersonal Influence Perspective," *Journal of Marketing,* July 1990, pp. 68-81; and Barry J. Farber and Joyce Wycoff, "Relationships: Six Steps to Success," *Sales & Marketing Management,* April 1992, pp. 50-58.

can be much greater if the disappointed customer shares the bad experience with other customers and causes them to defect.

Tom Peters, noted author of several books on managerial excellence, runs a business that spends $1,500 a month on Federal Express service. His company spends this amount 12 months a year and expects to remain in business for at least another 10 years. Therefore, he expects to spend more than $180,000 on future Federal Express service. If Federal Express makes a 10 percent profit margin, Peters' lifetime business will contribute $18,000 to Federal Express's profits. Federal Express risks all of this profit if Peters receives poor service from a Federal Express driver or if a competitor offers better service.

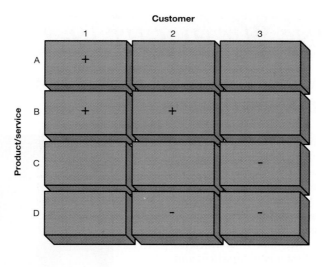

FIGURE 19-5
Customer/product profitability analysis

Few companies actively measure individual customer value and profitability. For example, banks claim that this is hard to do because customers use different banking services and transactions are logged in different departments. However, banks that have managed to link customer transactions and measure customer profitability have been appalled by how many unprofitable customers they find. Some banks report losing money on over 45 percent of their retail customers. It is not surprising, then, that many banks now charge fees for services that they once supplied free.

A useful type of profitability analysis is shown in Figure 19-5.[15] Customers make up the columns of the figure and products or services make up the rows. Each cell contains a symbol for the profitability of selling a given product or service to a given customer. Customer 1 is very profitable—he or she buys two profit-making products, product A and product B. Customer 2 yields mixed profitability, buying one profitable product and one unprofitable product. Customer 3 generates loses by purchasing the company's two unprofitable products ("loss leaders"). What can the company do about consumers like customer 3? First, the company should consider raising the prices of its less profitable products or eliminating them. The company also can try to cross-sell its profit-making products to its unprofitable customers. If these actions cause unprofitable customers to defect, it may be for the good. In fact, the company would might benefit by *encouraging* its unprofitable customers to switch to competitors.

IMPLEMENTING TOTAL QUALITY MARKETING

Customer satisfaction and company profitability are linked closely to product and service quality. Higher levels of quality result in greater customer satisfaction, while at the same time supporting higher prices and often lower costs. Therefore, *quality improvement* programs normally increase profitability. The well-known Profit Impact of Marketing Strategies studies show a high correlation between relative product quality and profitability.[16]

The task of improving product and service quality should be a company's top priority. Much of the striking global successes of Japanese companies has resulted from their building exceptional quality into their products. Most customers will no longer tolerate poor or average quality. Companies today have no choice but to adopt *total quality management (TQM)* if they want to stay in the race, let alone be profitable. According to GE's Chairman, John F. Welch, Jr.: "Quality is our best assurance of customer allegiance, our strongest defense against foreign competition, and the only path to sustained growth and earnings."[17] (See Marketing Highlight 19-3.)

Quality has been variously defined as "fitness for use," "conformance to requirements," and "freedom from variation."[18] American Society for Quality Control defines **quality** as the totality of features and characteristics of a product or

THE MALCOLM BALDRIGE NATIONAL QUALITY AWARD: A SPUR TO WORLD-CLASS QUALITY

For a growing number of companies, competition is no longer just local—it has become global. As long as national markets remain open, foreign goods will arrive that are either cheaper, better, or both. Therefore, a nation's companies must strive to produce goods that are competitive or superior in world markets. As a result, to spur their firms to world-class quality, some countries have established a national prize that is awarded to companies that exemplify the best quality practices and improvements.

Japan was the first country to award a national quality prize, the Deming prize, named after the American statistician who taught the importance of quality to post-war Japan. In the mid-1980s, the United States established the Malcolm Baldrige National Quality Award in honor of the late Secretary of Commerce. The award encourages U.S. firms to implement quality practices. When quality results justify it, companies can submit applications and evidence for a Baldrige Award.

The Baldrige Board of Examiners may give up to two awards each year in each of three categories: manufacturing companies, service companies, and small businesses. The award criteria consist of seven measures, ranging from the extent of quality leadership provided by the company's top executives, to how well the firm develops its human resources to support quality, to the degree of customer focus and satisfaction achieved by the firm. Each of the seven measures carries a certain number of award points, which total to 1,000 points. Of these measures, *customer focus and satisfaction* gets the most points (300). The 300 points are further broken down into points for understanding customer expectations, managing customer relationships well, and determining customer satisfaction. Thus far, Baldrige Awards have gone to such well-known giants as AT&T, Texas Instruments, Xerox, Motorola, Federal Express, IBM, and the Cadillac Division of General Motors, but also to lesser-known, smaller businesses such as the Granite Rock Company of Watsonville, California, and Globe Metallurgical of Cleveland, Ohio.

One company that is currently competing for a Baldrige National Quality Award in the small-business category is a marketing research firm, Custom Research Incorporated (CRI), headquartered in Minneapolis. In 1990, CRI began using the Baldrige criteria as a framework for developing its quality system. It applied for the award in 1991 and received feedback that led to further improvements. In 1992, CRI was selected to receive a site visit. CRI believes that it earned a site visit because it fervently applies the following quality principles:

1. Focus on building major client relationships.

The Malcolm Baldrige National Quality Award encourages U.S. firms to implement world-class quality practices.

2. Organize into cross-functional, client-centered teams.

3. Develop processes and procedures to get work done, then measure the results.

4. Explicitly ask clients what they expect from a partnering relationship.

5. Seek client feedback on individual projects and the overall relationship.

6. Hire the best people and invest in their development.

7. Stay flexible, agile, fast moving—empower everyone in the company to "just do it."

8. Have fun with hoopla and recognition.

9. Build quality continuously.

10. Never be satisfied.

All companies would do well to emulate this excellent statement of modern business and marketing thinking.

Source: See *1993 Award Criteria,* Malcolm Baldrige National Quality Award brochure, United States Department of Commerce, National Institute of Standards and Technology, Gaithersburg, MD.

service that bear on its ability to satisfy stated or implied needs. This is clearly a customer-centered definition of quality. It suggests that a company has delivered quality whenever its product and service meet or exceed customers needs, requirements, and expectations. A company that satisfies most of its customers' needs most of the time is a quality company.

It is important to distinguish between performance quality and conformance quality. *Performance quality* refers to the *level* at which a product performs its functions. For example, a Mercedes provides higher performance quality than a Volkswagen: it has a smoother ride, handles better, and lasts longer. It is more expensive and sells to a market with higher means and requirements. *Conformance quality* refers to freedom from defects and the *consistency* with which a product delivers a specified level of performance. Thus, Mercedes and a Volkswagen can be said to offer equivalent conformance quality to their respective markets to the extent that each consistently delivers what its market expects. A $50,000 car that meets all of its requirements is a quality car; so is a $15,000 car that meets all of its requirements. But if the Mercedes handles badly, or if the Volkswagen gives poor fuel efficiency, then both cars have failed to deliver quality, and customer satisfaction suffers accordingly.

Total quality is the key to creating customer value and satisfaction. Total quality is everyone's job, just as marketing is everyone's job:

> Marketers who don't learn the language of quality improvement, manufacturing, and operations will become as obsolete as buggy whips. The days of functional marketing are gone. We can no longer afford to think of ourselves as market researchers, advertising people, direct marketers, marketing strategists—we have to think of ourselves as customer satisfiers—customer advocates focused on whole processes.[19]

Marketing management has two responsibilities in a quality-centered company. First, marketing management must participate in formulating strategies and policies designed to help the company win through total quality excellence. Second, marketing must deliver marketing quality as well as production quality. It must perform each marketing activity—marketing research, sales training, advertising, customer service, and others—to high standards.

Marketers play several major roles in helping their companies to define and deliver high quality goods and services to target customers. First, marketers bear the major responsibility for correctly identifying the customers' needs and requirements and for communicating customer expectations correctly to product designers. Second, marketers must make sure that the customers' orders are filled correctly and on time, and must check to see that customers have received proper instructions, training, and technical assistance in the use of the product. Third, marketers must stay in touch with customers after the sale to make sure that they do indeed remain satisfied. Finally, marketers must gather and convey customer ideas for product and service improvements to the appropriate company departments.

At the same time, ironically, one study found that marketing people were responsible for more customer complaints than any other department (35 percent). Marketing mistakes included cases in which the salesforce ordered special product features for customers but failed to notify the manufacturing department of the changes; in which incorrect order processing resulted in the wrong product being made and shipped; and in which customer complaints were not properly handled.[20]

The implication here is that marketers must spend time and effort not only to improve external marketing, but also to improve internal marketing. Marketers must be the customer's watchdog or guardian, complaining loudly for the customer when the product or the service is not right. Marketers must constantly uphold the standard of "giving the customer the best solution." Marketing Highlight 19-4 on page 568 presents some important conclusions about total marketing quality strategy.

PURSUING A TOTAL QUALITY MARKETING STRATEGY

Not long ago, many companies believe that they could get by with providing market offerings of only average quality and service. Meanwhile, however, Japanese and German companies were offering products of superior quality. The Japanese took to heart consultant W. Edwards Deming's lessons about winning through *total quality management* (TQM). This quest for quality paid off handsomely. Consumers around the world flocked to buy high-quality Japanese products, leaving many American firms playing catch-up.

In recent years, U.S. firms have struggled to close the quality gap. Many have started their own TQM programs in an effort to compete on a global and domestic basis against the Japanese. A growing number of U.S. companies have appointed a "Vice-President of Quality" to spearhead TQM. TQM recognizes the following premises about quality improvement:

1. *Quality is in the eyes of the customer.* Quality must begin with customer needs and end with customer perceptions. As Motorola's vice-president of quality suggests:

   Quality has to do something for the customer . . . Beauty is in the eye of the beholder. If [a product] does not work the way that the user needs it to work, the defect is as big to the user as if it doesn't work the way the designer planned it. Our definition of a defect is "if the customer doesn't like it, it's a defect."

   Thus, the fundamental aim of the today's quality movement has now become "total customer satisfaction." Quality improvements are meaningful only when they are perceived by customers.

2. *Quality must be reflected not just in the company's products, but in every company activity.* Leonard A. Morgan of GE says: "We are not just concerned with the quality of the product, but with the quality of our advertising, service, product literature, delivery, and after-sales support."

3. *Quality requires total employee commitment.* Quality can be delivered only by companies in which all employees are committed to quality and motivated and trained to deliver it. Successful companies remove the barriers between departments. Their employees work as a team to carry out core business processes and to create desired outcomes. Employees work to satisfy their internal customers as well as external customers.

4. *Quality requires high-quality partners.* Quality can be delivered only by companies whose value chain partners also deliver quality. Therefore, a quality-driven company must find and align itself with high-quality suppliers and distributors.

5. *A quality program cannot save a poor product.* The Pontiac Fiero launched a quality program, but because the car didn't have a performance engine to support its performance image, the quality program did not save the car. A quality drive cannot compensate for product deficiencies.

6. *Quality can always be improved.* The best companies believe in the Japanese concept of *kaizen*, "continuous improvement of everything by everyone." The best way to improve quality is to benchmark the company's performance against the "best-of-class" competitors or the best performers in other industries, striving to equal or even surpass them. For example, Alcoa measured the best-of-class competitors and then set a goal of closing the gap by 80 percent within two years.

7. *Quality improvement sometimes requires quantum leaps.* Although the company should strive for continuous quality improvement, it must at times seek a quantum quality improvement. Companies sometimes can obtain small improvements by working harder. But large improvements call for fresh solutions and for working smarter. For example, John Young of Hewlett-Packard did not ask for a 10 percent reduction in defects, he asked for a tenfold reduction and got it.

8. *Quality does not cost more.* Philip Crosby argues that "quality is free." Managers once argued that achieving more quality would cost more and slow down production. But improving quality involves learning ways to "do things right the first time." Quality is not *inspected* in; it must be *designed* in. Doing things right the first time reduces the costs of salvage, repair, and redesign, not to mention losses in customer goodwill. Motorola claims that its quality drive has saved $700 million in manufacturing costs during the last five years.

9. *Quality is necessary but may not be sufficient.* Improving a company's quality is absolutely necessary to meet the needs of more demanding buyers. At the same time, higher quality may not ensure a winning advantage, especially as all competitors increase their quality to more or less the same extent. For example, Singapore Airlines enjoyed a reputation as the world's best airline. However, competing airlines have attracted larger shares of passengers recently by narrowing the perceived gap between their service quality and Singapore's service quality.

Sources: Quotes from Lois Therrien, "Motorola and NEC: Going for Glory," *Business Week*, Special issue on quality, 1991, pp. 60-61. Also see David A. Garvin, "Competing on Eight Dimensions of Quality," *Harvard Business Review*, November-December 1987, p. 109; Robert Jacobson and David A. Aaker, "The Strategic Role of Product Quality," *Journal of Marketing*, October 1987, pp. 31-44; and Frank Rose, "Now Quality Means Service Too," *Fortune*, April 22, 1992, pp. 97-108.

SUMMARY

Today's customers face a growing range of choices in the products and services they can buy. They base their choices on their perceptions of *quality, value,* and *service.* Companies need to understand the determinants of *customer value* and *satisfaction. Customer delivered value* is the difference between *total customer value* and *total customer cost.* Customers will normally choose the offer that maximizes their delivered value.

Customer satisfaction is the outcome felt by buyers who have experienced a company performance that has fulfilled expectations. Customers are satisfied when their expectations are met, and delighted when their expectations are exceeded. Satisfied customers remain loyal longer, buy more, are less price sensitive, and talk favorably about the company.

To *create customer satisfaction,* companies must manage their own *value chains* and the entire *value delivery system* in a customer-centered way. The company's goal is not only to get customers but, even more importantly, to retain

customers. *Customer relationship marketing* provides the key to retaining customers and involves building financial and social benefits as well as structural ties to customers. Companies must decide the level at which they want to build relationships with different market segments and individual customers, from such levels as basic, reactive, accountable, and proactive to full partnership. Which is best depends on a *customer's lifetime value* relative to the costs required to attract and retain that customer.

Total quality management has become a major approach to providing customer satisfaction and company profitability. Companies must understand how their customers perceive quality and how much quality they expect. Companies must then do a better job of meeting consumer quality expectations than their competitors do. Delivering quality requires total management and employee commitment as well as measurement and reward systems. Marketers play an especially critical role in their company's drive toward higher quality.

KEY TERMS

Customer-centered company 551

Customer delivered value 552

Customer lifetime value 563

Customer value delivery system 558

Quality 565

Relationship marketing 560

Total customer cost 552

Total customer value 552

Value chain 555

DISCUSSING THE ISSUES

1. Imagine that your instructor is your customer. *You,* in your role as a student, are the main product of your firm. You are attempting to create added value for yourself with the instructor. (a) What student tasks would you consider to be inbound logistics, operations, outbound logistics, marketing and sales, and service? (b) How would you perform these tasks to maximize customer value?

2. Recall an activity in which you went beyond the normal effort and "gave your all" to produce the utmost in quality. How much of your improvement in quality did other people notice—all, some, or none? Is there a balance point that provides the right mix of quality and effort?

3. Describe a situation in which you became a "lost customer." Did you leave because of poor product quality, poor service quality, or both?

4. Who should define quality standards: research and development, engineering, manufacturing, or marketing? Explain your choice(s).

5. Health-care reform is currently a major issue in the United States. One concern is a lack of value: the costs of medical care often seem to outweigh the benefits. Propose some meaningful ways to measure health-care quality that could be used in efforts to improve value.

6. "Just-in-time" inventory management makes suppliers responsible for delivering parts in exact quantities at precisely the right time. Companies that succeed with JIT find that benefits often go beyond inventory cost savings, and that many quality improvements come from the process of working very closely with suppliers. Are the ideas of a value chain used in JIT management? Can JIT succeed *without* using the concepts in the value chain?

APPLYING THE CONCEPTS

1. Write a complaint letter to a firm about one of their products or services. Did you receive a refund or replacement product, a response letter, or no reply at all? How does the type of response affect your attitude toward the company?

2. Find some product, service, or activist person that has clearly established a strong relationship with its customers. Some examples include: BMW automobiles or Harley Davidson motorcycles; reruns of *The Lawrence Welk Show* or a Grateful Dead concert; Jesse Jackson or Rush Limbaugh. Talk to several customers that strongly identify with one such "product." How do they see their relationship to the product? What are the key values they receive? What, if anything, does the "manufacturer" do to maintain this relationship?

MAKING MARKETING DECISIONS:

SMALL WORLD COMMUNICATIONS, INC.

Thomas Campbell and Lynette Jones are considering some of the longer-term aspects of marketing their *Airport* communications link. Tom was talking about the elements of their total quality program. "Until we get some longer-term experience with this product, I want to go a bit overboard on quality procedures to make certain we're shipping something really good. That means 100 percent inspection, and 'burning-in' the product for 96 hours before testing and packaging it. We'll keep careful statistics on the results, and maybe later we can do what Compaq did. They found out a 2-hour product test discovered defects just as well as the full 96-hour run, so they shortened their test procedures. For now, though, I think we need to be conservative on this." "Tom, I agree on that, and I think you've got a good handle on one part of quality. But we've got to go beyond just meeting specifications and a low failure rate. They're critical, but they are also only part of what we need to do to create real customer value and customer satisfaction. *Airport* needs to be easy to understand, quick to install, simple to set up, and a no-brainer to use. We've got to do that at a fair price, and provide the security of a warranty and technical help that's readily available." Tom responded, "O.K., Lyn, but there's another layer to all this. We've got to go back to our target audiences—and we've got end users, resellers, and original equipment manufacturers, all with different needs—and define what customer value and satisfaction mean to each of them." Lyn smiled and said, "Thomas, we may make you into a marketer yet."

What Now?

1. Small World will market *Airport* to three types of customers: end users, resellers, and original equipment manufacturers (OEMs). Consider the differences among these customers. (a) Make a chart with three columns, one for "End User," another for "Resellers," and a third for "OEMs." Label the rows of the chart: 1) Size of purchase; 2) Frequency of repurchase; 3) Reason for repurchase; 4) User's definition of value; 5) Key elements that create user satisfaction. (b) Think about the differences among these three customer target audiences. Do they require different relationships with Small World Communications? (c) What relationship marketing strategy is best for each customer target audience—basic, reactive, accountable, proactive, or partnership? Why?

2. (a) What elements of *Airport* make up total customer value? Is the value temporary, or is it seen by the customer during everyday use of the product? (b) All products cost money, but consider the nonmonetary costs of *Airport*: reading instructions, installation, setup and debugging, learning to use new software, worries over whether it will work and whether it might destroy the computer if misinstalled. Are these nonmonetary costs large? How can Lyn and Tom address these costs to improve customer delivered value? (c) Notice that nearly all of the costs, monetary and nonmonetary, occur very close to purchase, while the benefits of *Airport* occur later on in everyday use. Suggest some ways that Small World can minimize perceptions of cost, and maximize perceptions of total value in order to increase customer delivered value.

REFERENCES

1. Quotes from Valerie Reitman, "Rubbermaid Turns Up Plenty of Profit in the Mundane," *The Wall Street Journal*, March 27, 1992, p. B4. Also see Erik Calonius, "Smart Moves by the Quality Champs," in *The New American Century*, Special issue of *Fortune*, 1991, pp. 24-28; Cristy Marshall, "Rubbermaid: Yes, Plastic," *Business Month*, December 1988, p. 38; Maria Mallory, "Profits on Everything but the Kitchen Sink," *Business Week*, Special issue on innovation, 1991, p. 122; William Band, "Use Baldrige Criteria as Guide to Improving Quality," *Marketing News*, October 1, 1991, pp. 2, 18; Zachary Schiller, "At Rubbermaid, Little Things

Mean a Lot," *Business Week*, November 11, 1991; and "Rubbermaid: Breaking all the Molds," *Sales & Marketing Management*, August 1992, p. 42.

2. For more on measuring customer delivered value, and on "value/price ratios," see Irwin P. Levin and Richard D. Johnson, "Estimating Price-Quality Tradeoffs Using Comparative Judgments," *Journal of Consumer Research*, June 11, 1984, pp. 593-600.

3. For an interesting discussion of value and value strategies, see Michael Treacy and Fred Wiersema, "Customer Intimacy and Other Value Disciplines," *Harvard Business Review*, January–February 1993, pp. 84-93.

4. Thomas E. Caruso, "Got a Marketing Topic? Kotler Has an Opinion," *Marketing News*, June 8, 1992, p. 21.

5. Michael E. Porter, *Competitive Advantage: Creating and Sustaining Superior Performance* (New York: Free Press, 1985).

6. See George Stalk, Philip Evans, and Laurence E. Shulman, "Competing Capabilities: the New Rules of Corporate Strategy," *Harvard Business Review*, March–April 1992, pp. 57-69; and Benson P. Shapiro, V. Kasturi Rangan, and John J. Sviokla, "Staple Yourself to an Order," *Harvard Business Review*, July–August 1992, pp. 113-22.

7. For more discussion, see Frederick E. Webster, Jr., "The Changing Role of Marketing in the Corporation," *Journal of Marketing*, October 1992, pp. 1-17.

8. Frederick F. Reichheld and W. Earl Sasser, Jr., "Zero Defections: Quality Comes to Services," *Harvard Business Review*, September–October 1990, pp. 301-7.

9. Leonard L. Berry and A. Parasuraman, *Marketing Services: Competing Through Quality* (New York: The Free Press, 1991), pp. 136-42.

10. Aimee L. Stern, "Courting Consumer Loyalty with the Feel-Good Bond," *The New York Times*, January 17, 1993, p. F10.

11. James H. Donnelly, Jr., Leonard L. Berry, and Thomas W. Thompson, *Marketing Financial Services—A Strategic Vision* (Homewood, IL: Dow Jones-Irwin, 1985), p. 113.

12. Ibid., p. F10.

13. Caruso, "Kotler: Future Marketers Will Focus . . .," p. 21.

14. Michael J. Lanning and Lynn W. Phillips, "Strategy Shifts Up a Gear," *Marketing*, October 1991, p. 9.

15. See Thomas M. Petro, "Profitability: The Fifth 'P' of Marketing," *Bank Marketing*, September 1990, pp. 48-52.

16. Robert D. Buzzell and Bradley T. Gale, *The PIMS Principles: Linking Strategy to Performance* (New York: The Free Press, 1987), Chap. 6.

17. "Quality: The U.S. Drives to Catch Up," *Business Week*, November, 1982, pp. 66-80, here p. 68. For a recent assessment of progress, see "Quality Programs Show Shoddy Results," *The Wall Street Journal*, May 14, 1992, p. B1.

18. See "The Gurus of Quality: American Companies Are Heading the Quality Gospel Preached by Deming, Juran, Crosby, and Taguchi," *Traffic Management*, July 1990. pp. 35-39.

19 J. Daniel Beckham, "Expect the Unexpected in Health Care Marketing Future," in *The Academy Bulletin*, July 1992, p. 3.

20. Kenneth Kivenko, *Quality Control for Management* (Englewood Cliffs, NJ: Prentice Hall, 1984). Also See Kate Bertrand, "Marketing Discovers What 'Quality' Really Means," *Business Marketing*, April 1987, pp. 58-72.

VIDEO CASE 19

AUTO REPAIR FRAUD

Strike one: Early June 1992; after a year-long investigation, the California Department of Consumer Affairs charges Sears with selling customers unnecessary parts and service.

Strike two: Mid-June 1992; New Jersey Division of Consumer Affairs charges Sears with unnecessary repairs.

Strike three: Late June 1992; the New York Consumer Protection Board launches a "preliminary" probe of Sears auto repair services.

What were the specific accusations against Sears? Sears was accused of "pushing" unnecessary parts—brakes, struts, shock absorbers, alignments, and coil springs. The California investigation revealed that Sears performed unnecessary service or repairs 90 percent of the time. Worse yet, vehicles were frequently returned to drivers in worse shape than when they came in. The average oversell was $200. Follow-ups conducted in California after Sears was warned about the investigation revealed an oversell rate of 80 percent.

Investigators attributed the unnecessary repairs and oversells to sales quotas set by Sears for its auto repair departments. Sears instructed employees to sell a certain number of repairs or services during every shift. When Sears switched to a commission-based system of compensating mechanics, mechanics had a strong incentive to suggest more repairs than were strictly necessary.

Was Sears guilty of auto repair fraud? It depends on whom you ask. The folks at Sears say no. Marci Grossman, Sears media relations manager, says that Sears does *not* use sales quotas. Ed Brennan, CEO of Sears, admitted that there had been "isolated errors" but no pattern of misconduct—absolutely none. Dirk Schenkkan, Sears attorney, denies any wrongdoing by Sears and accuses the California Consumer Affairs Department of beating up on Sears in order to boost its own standing.

Many former Sears customers disagree. Former customer Ruth Hernandez claims Sears tried to sell her a set of struts. When she obtained a second opinion, she found that the struts were unnecessary. Michael Stumpf claims that his wife went in for an advertised $89.99

strut job and ended up with a $650 repair bill. As a result of such alleged abuses, Sears auto repair sales fell 15 percent nationwide.

How did Sears handle the auto fraud crisis? It issued denials, followed by an admission of some mistakes. It never admitted guilt. Ed Brennan sent a letter to all Sears' auto customers in which he maintained that Sears' management is confident that they have high consumer satisfaction and want to retain that. His letter assures customers that Sears has eliminated the commission system, increased its quality control efforts through the use of shopping audits, asked state attorney generals to visit its auto repair centers to ascertain the quality of the work, and helped set up a joint consumer-industry-government effort to review current auto repair practices.

In an out-of-court settlement, Sears agreed to refund $50 to every customer who had specified repairs at Sears between August 1, 1990 and January 31, 1992. The cost could be as much as $46.7 million, although Sears expects to pay less than $16 million. Sears will also pay California $3.5 million reimbursement for legal and investigative costs and give $1.5 million for auto repair training programs in California's community colleges. In New Jersey, Sears agreed to pay $200,000 to underwrite an auto repair standards study. Still, the true costs to Sears far exceed these settlement costs. The real cost is the loss of customer trust and confidence—one of Sears' strongest assets. Worse, the loss of trust in auto repairs can carry over to other Sears products and services.

Deep-seated consumer suspicions about auto repair in general lend believability to the Sears fraud charges. Given the intangible nature of auto repair services, it is difficult to gauge their necessity or quality. Because most of us know little about auto repair, we rely on mechanics. But deep down, most of us worry—did we really need the repairs?

What impact will Sears' responses have? Will they restore confidence? Will eliminating commissions convince consumers that mechanics will not recommend unnecessary parts or service? By agreeing to settlements, has Sears implicitly admitted to wrongdoing? Did Sears' stonewalling ("we did nothing systematically wrong") help its cause?

The Sears case highlights the potential pitfalls accompanying a firm's decision to perform service activities. Proper delivery of quality service can greatly increase the company's consumer franchise and profitability. Conversely, poor service delivery can do a great deal of damage. It will take Sears a long time to repair the damage done in June 1992.

QUESTIONS

1. Describe Sears' *customer value delivery system* for auto repairs. Why did it work well before the claims of auto repair fraud?

2. What type of "marketing relationship" did Sears have with its auto repair customers before the repair fraud accusations?

3. How could Sears use total quality management to improve the quality of its auto repair services?

4. How effective do you think the "solutions" taken by Sears will be?

5. What other actions can Sears take to recapture consumer confidence?

Sources: Julia Flynn, "Did Sears Take Other Customers for a Ride?" *Business Week,* August 3, 1992, pp. 24-25; Kevin Kelly, "How Did Sears Blow This Gasket?" *Business Week,* June 29, 1992, pp. 38; Gregory A. Patterson, "Sears Will Pay $15 Million, Settling Cases," *The Wall Street Journal,* September 3, 1992, p. A4; David Streitfeld, "Avoiding the Shaft," *Washington Post,* June 22, 1992, p B5.

COMPANY CASE 19

STEEL PRODUCTS COMPANY: STOPPING THE ALUMINUM SLIDE

Mike Smithson, branch general manager at one of Steel Product Company's (SPC) Chicago branches, looked across the conference table at Sam Jordan, a branch general manager in Atlanta. "I'll tell you, Sam," he said, "I don't know what *you* are going to do, but *our* branch won't sell aluminum. That's it."

Sam Jordan took a deep breath and pushed himself slowly away from the conference table. He glanced at Bill Olney, SPC's president, and then at each of the other five branch general managers seated around him at their March 1992 meeting. Sam was not certain what to do, but he knew that his actions during the next few

seconds could make or break his efforts to get SPC to improve its aluminum sales. After a long, tense pause he turned to Bill Olney and said, "If Mike's branch won't sell aluminum, *our* branch will not sell *steel*!"

"What do you mean you won't sell steel?" Bill asked with an incredulous look. "We're a steel company! You can't just decide you aren't going to sell steel."

Sam replied, "We've been an aluminum company, too, although less and less so. And if Mike can decide that he's not going to sell any more aluminum, then I'll decide that I'm not going to sell any more steel."

Bill Olney leaned back in his chair, raised his eyes briefly to the ceiling, and then returned his gaze to the branch general managers seated around him. He had not missed Sam Jordan's point. "Okay, Sam," he agreed. "We'll sell steel *and* aluminum. We'll meet again in two weeks to discuss it further. At that meeting I want you to present a complete marketing strategy for revitalizing our aluminum business." Turning to the others, he declared, "And I want each of you to cooperate as necessary with Sam in developing this plan."

Background

Steel Products Company provides first-stage processing for steel and aluminum products and distributes them to industrial customers. In addition to its Chi-cago headquarters, the company has five other branches: two in the New York City area, two in the Atlanta area, and one other in the Chicago area. The company locates its branches in pairs because one branch in each pair handles only hot-rolled steel, while the other handles only cold-rolled steel. A branch general manager oversees the sales, marketing, and operations of each branch. Each branch general manager reports directly to Bill Olney.

Bill and a group of investors purchased SPC in 1989 when the company's sales were about $120 million. During the past two years, Bill and the general managers had worked to shore up the steel business. When Bill took over, the company had been languishing with relatively flat sales and profits in both its steel and aluminum product lines. Because steel accounted for approximately 80 percent of total sales, Bill's first priority after the acquisition had been to get control of and improve SPC's steel operations.

By 1992, Bill had the steel business under control. Thus, he felt that he could turn his attention to the SPC's aluminum operations. Several weeks ago, he had invited Sam Jordan in to discuss the Atlanta branch's solid success in selling aluminum products. After a brief meeting, Bill had asked Sam to make a presentation on the company's position in aluminum products at the next branch general manager's meeting. That presentation led to the exchange with Mike Smithson.

The Steel Service Center Business

Steel Products Company operates what the steel industry calls "steel service centers." These centers operate in the channel of distribution between steel mills and manufacturing firms. They perform several functions for their manufacturing customers. First, because the steel mills themselves cannot supply steel on a consistent or dependable basis, manufacturers have difficulty dealing directly with the steel mills. Steel service centers solve this problem by holding an inventory of steel for their customers and distributing it dependably when needed. Thus, the service centers function in a traditional "wholesaler" role. Second, some steel service centers perform first-stage processing for their customers. SPC, for example, buys steel from the steel mills in rolls that resemble large rolls of paper towels. These rolls are 12 to 48 inches wide, with the steel varying from 20 one-thousandths to one-eighth inch in thickness. Prior to delivery to the customer, SPC cuts these rolls into more narrow rolls or into steel sheets of various lengths.

For example, one SPC customer, a manufacturer of drip coffee makers, orders 6-inch-wide rolls. It feeds the steel from these rolls into stamping machines that stamp out the "hot plates" used in its coffee makers. Depending on how a service center customer uses the steel, it pays close attention to the steel's quality and the statistical control of any cutting operations. Steel that is not cut to proper width, that has improper thicknesses at some point, or that does not have the correct hardness can damage expensive equipment and even bring the customer's operations to a costly halt.

Segmentation. A steel service center can segment its markets in a number of ways. First, it can segment based on the *type* of metal used by the customer. "Hot-rolled" steel is steel that has been manufactured by a steel mill but has not been further processed. It has a rough finish and might vary in thickness or width. "Cold-rolled" steel is hot-rolled steel that has been processed further to tighten its dimensions and give it a smoother finish. Second, the service centers can segment based on the *form* of the metal delivered to the end customer—for example, rolls or sheets. Third, firms can segment based on the *quantity ordered* by customers. Some customers order in "truckload lots," defined as 40,000 pounds. Other customers order in "odd lots" that can be considerably less than truckload volume. Fourth, companies can group their customers by the nature of *delivery requirements*—some customers require next-day delivery, while others have long lead times. Finally, some customers order based on *contracts* and others order from general inventory without any minimum annual purchase requirements. Contact customers typically request quotations from several steel service centers once a year for the coming year's steel or aluminum requirements. They then award a contract committing them to purchase a certain quantity of product in certain amounts during the contracted time period.

By using different combinations of these segmentation variables, steel service centers shape the market niches they will serve. For example, one firm might focus on serving customers who need next-day delivery of uncut steel rolls from general inventory in odd lots. Steel Products Company focuses on high-tonnage (preferably truckloads), high-volume customers who need first-stage processing. Each of SPC's three cold-rolled steel branches has sophisticated equipment for cutting and controlling the dimensions and hardness of the steel. SPC provides customers with a computer printout showing the characteristics and dimensions of the steel they purchase. SPC also works with its customers to provide just-in-time delivery and electronic ordering via computer hook-ups. A recent customer survey showed that SPC has a strong, positive reputation with its customers. These customers know that SPC purchases high-quality steel and provides the statistical quality control necessary to assure that they will receive just what they request.

Price. Because steel is a commodity, steel service centers suffer from fierce price competition. Steel service centers must negotiate price with steel mills when they purchase their inventories. And, in turn, they must formally or informally negotiate prices with their customers. Thus, SPC competes on price with other steel service centers for almost every order. In 1992, SPC charged its customers an average price of 30 cents per pound for steel.

Promotion. Each of SPC's six branches has three outside and three inside salespeople. The outside salespeople visit customers in their territories to keep abreast of their needs and ordering requirements and to monitor the quality of incoming products. The outside salespeople work with inside salespeople in setting prices for quotations and in following up on delivery and service problems.

Under SPC's standard sales compensation plan, each outside salesperson receives a base salary plus a quarterly commission based on achieving a target gross profit percentage on products sold by that salesperson. For example, SPC has set a current target gross profit percentage of 20 percent. SPC increases or decreases the salesperson's commission for every one-half percentage point that his or her quarterly performance falls above or below this target. SPC pays inside salespeople a base salary plus a bonus based on branch-level gross profit percentage.

In 1992, SPC had a weighted average gross profit percentage of about 20 percent on the six types of steel it sells. Some types of steel products have higher gross margin percentages and some have lower. SPC calculates gross margin by simply subtracting the cost of the steel sold in each order from the revenue from that order. Thus, if SPC buys a pound of steel for 23 cents from the steel mill and sells it for 30 cents, its gross margin is 7 cents and the gross profit percentage is 23.3 percent (7 cents/30 cents). SPC had an inventory turnover ratio of 4.26 for its steel products in 1991.

Selling Aluminum

Sam Jordan came to SPC from a competitor in 1988 and assumed the position of general branch manager at one of the Atlanta branches. Sam had heard that, as recently as 1987, sales of aluminum products for the entire company had been almost $40 million. However, the "product champion" for aluminum had left the company that year. Since then, no one had paid careful attention to aluminum, and aluminum sales had begun to decline. Although he was responsible for all his branch's operations, Sam paid special attention to aluminum sales. He was very successful, and this success caught the attention of Bill Olney when he took over the company in 1989. Bill decided that the other cold-rolled branches should give greater emphasis to aluminum. As a result, the two other branches had hired aluminum product managers. These product managers had immediately purchased sizeable inventories of aluminum and had asked the salesforce to begin to push the aluminum. Sam watched in despair as these efforts at other branches had failed. Both aluminum product managers soon left the company, and one branch still had a large $2 million aluminum inventory on hand at the end of 1991.

SPC sells aluminum in much the same way that it sells steel. It buys the aluminum in rolls and provides the first-stage processing. Most of the company's aluminum sales have been to customers who also purchase steel. Although SPC charges an average price of 30 cents

per pound for steel, it charges an average of $1.50 per pound for aluminum. However, SPC realizes an average gross margin percentage of only 16 percent on aluminum as compared with steel's 20 percent average. SPC had an inventory turnover ratio of 6.15 for aluminum in 1991.

Although Sam's Atlanta branch continued to do well in aluminum sales, sales at other branches continued to decline. In 1991, total SPC aluminum sales reached only about $17 million. Sam realized that without quick action the firm would continue to lose aluminum sales. In the face of the current flat or declining steel market, this would severely damage branch and company profits.

A Conversation with Mike

The day following the meeting, Sam sat in his office and considered his attack. He decided to take the bull by the horns and call Mike Smithson. He reached Mike on the first try.

"Hey, Sam," Mike volunteered, "I want to apologize if I was a little abrupt at the meeting yesterday. I know you're really big on selling aluminum, but I just don't think that we should be in that business. The other day, I was talking with one of our competitors who also sells aluminum. He told me that it's a really different business. And look at all the competitors we'd have," Mike continued. "You also know how much inventory I have sitting up here from our last shot at aluminum. Frankly, I don't think we'll do any better this time. After all, we are a steel company. And further, the salespeople are worried that always getting into and out of the aluminum business will hurt our strong reputation in steel."

"Well, Mike," Sam replied, "all I want you to do is to keep an open mind until I make my presentation. I think I can answer your objections and concerns. As you know, I think it's important that we be in both aluminum and steel. I'll try to show you a plan that will ensure success this time."

"Okay, Sam," Mike responded. "I'll try to keep an open mind. But it's going to be a tough sale for you. You'd better have all your facts together at the meeting."

QUESTIONS

1. Describe Steel Products Company's marketing strategies for steel and aluminum. Who are its target markets and what are its marketing mixes for the two products?

2. What is SPC's business? What is it really selling? How does it add value for its customers?

3. Why has SPC not been successful in selling aluminum? Of the marketing problems it faces, which is the *central* marketing problem?

4. Assume Sam Jordan's position and prepare an outline of a marketing strategy for presentation to the president and other branch general managers at the upcoming meeting. What can Sam recommend that will turn the situation around? Be sure to address issues of customer retention, relationship marketing, and customer profitability analysis.

Creating Competitive Advantage: Competitor Analysis and Competitive Marketing Strategies

20

Federal Express almost single-handedly created the express-delivery industry as we now know it. Founded in 1973, the company got off to a slow start—educating the American public about the value of overnight delivery took time. However, building doggedly on the advertising promise, "when it absolutely, positively *has* to be there on time," made possible by the company's innovative and now much-copied "hub-and-spoke" distribution system, FedEx went on to become one of the fastest start-ups in American history. After three years of losses, it grew explosively—annual sales reached $1 billion by 1983, $5 billion by 1989, and almost $8 billion by 1991. The express-delivery market now consists of 3 million packages shipped daily, generating more than $20 million in annual revenues. And despite strong challenges from a glut of imitators over the years, Federal Express remains the undisputed market leader. It now commands a 45 percent U.S. market share, comfortably ahead of major challengers UPS at 25 percent, Airborne at 14 percent, and the U.S. Postal Service at about 8 percent.

Staying atop the overnight package delivery business won't be easy—it will call for a well designed and executed competitive strategy. Although the market is large and growing at the breathtaking clip of 25 percent to 40 percent a year, competition is torrid. Federal Express has become an unwilling combatant in the "express wars." It now is street-fighting with competitors on price, looking for ways to cut costs and boost productivity in order to stay price competitive. But FedEx is not, and may never be, the lowest-priced express-delivery service. Even in the face of cutthroat pricing by competitors, the company has been careful not to let cost-cutting undermine its main source of competitive advantage—superior quality. Federal Express traditionally has differentiated itself not by luring customers with low prices, but by giving them unbeatable reliability and service. Over the years, it has sunk hefty amounts of money and effort into improving service quality. In 1987, it established a formal Quality Improvement Process, which set simple yet lofty quality goals: 100 percent on-time deliveries, 100 percent accurate information on every shipment to every location in the world, and 100 percent customer satisfaction.

At Federal Express, quality goes far beyond slogans and idle talk. In 1980, FedEx became the first service organization to receive the Malcolm Baldridge National Quality Award for outstanding quality leadership. It developed a Service Quality Index (SQI—pronounced "sky"), made up of twelve things that it knows disappoint customers—how many packages were delivered on the wrong day, how many were late, how many were damaged, how many billing corrections the company had to make, and other such mistakes. It computes the SQI daily and takes it very seriously. "Quality action teams" study SQI results, looking for trouble spots and ways to eliminate them. Even management bonuses are keyed to achieving SQI goals. Each year, the company invests more than $200 on each of its 86,000 employees for quality initiatives.

Federal Express believes that top-flight quality is well worth the heavy investment, even if it results in higher prices. In an industry where late delivery can spell disaster, even a 98 percent success rate isn't good enough. Most customers will gladly pay a little more for the added peace of mind that comes with superior service and unwavering reliability. In contrast, poor quality means customer defections to competitors. So, although raising service quality can be expensive, massive defections of customers can cost a great deal more. Federal Express's obsession with quality has paid big dividends. In recent years, despite a sluggish economy, more intense competition, and the long-running price war, the company has experienced healthy growth in sales and profits from its core U.S. business.

In the early 1980s, flush with domestic success, Federal Express decided that the time had come to go global. Hoping to recreate its phenomenal performance overseas, it began to buy up foreign competitors, invested heavily to set up a European version of its venerable hub-and-spoke system, and prepared to launch a full frontal assault on Europe. In 1989, it capped its global network building with the acquisition of the legendary Flying Tigers, the world's largest carrier of heavyweight cargo. With this acquisition, it could now move freight of any size. By the early 1990s, Federal Express had become the world's largest express transportation company, with 441 aircraft and 30,000 pickup and delivery vans serving 173 countries. Its new global goal: to be able to deliver freight anywhere in a global network within just two days.

Despite its high hopes and heavy investment, however, the global effort turned out to be a disaster. Flying Tigers became an albatross, and although international sales doubled in only a year, earnings plummeted—Federal Express amassed $1.2 billion in losses in just four years. To make matters worse, competitors were busy stealing customers at home. For example, in 1989, while the company's attentions were focused on its losing international operations, U.S. competitor Airborne had its best year in company history, achieving an astounding 171 percent increase in sales.

What went wrong? For one thing, Federal Express appears to have overestimated the European market for overnight delivery, which stalled out at only 100,000 packages daily. For another, the company may have underestimated the competition. Whereas FedEx is the clear market leader in the United States, in Europe it is a challenger. To win in Europe, it had to take on a well-entrenched competitor, DHL, the world leader in international express delivery. FedEx's aggressive attack on international markets provoked an equally aggressive defense, not just from DHL, but also from UPS, Australian-based TNT, and other large international rivals. For example, DHL strengthened its international base by forging new relationships with Lufthansa and Japan Airlines. UPS invested heavily to beef up its global delivery network, expanding coverage to 175 countries. The result: too many competitors chasing too little business, driving down prices and profits for all.

In May 1992, Federal Express began a decisive retreat from its disastrous European campaign. It closed down operations in more than 100 countries, fired 6,600 employees, and contracted with other companies to handle its deliveries to all but 16 major European cities—such as London, Paris, and Milan—that it still serves directly. FedEx executives insist that the retreat doesn't mean surrender. The company still leads in the U.S. market, and it has retained a strong base for building more solid international operations. The European retrenchment simply signals a new, more cautious approach to international expansion. Despite its losses, Federal Express has learned from its international misfortune. Perhaps the most important lesson: A blockbuster competitive strategy that makes a company "lord of the skies" at home won't necessarily fly abroad.[1]

 CHAPTER PREVIEW

Chapter 20 outlines the need for effective "competitive strategies" based on sound "competitor analysis."

We begin with **identifying competitors,** according to an **industry** or a **market perspective.** We can then study these competitors—including their **objectives and strategies, strengths and weaknesses,** and **reaction patterns**—and decide whether to **attack** or **avoid** them.

The chapter next discusses building **competitive strategies** based on our analysis. For **market leaders,** we review approaches for **expanding the total market, protecting market share,** and **expanding market share.** For **market challengers,** we define several possible **attack strategies.** Finally, we review possible approaches for **market followers** and **market nichers.**

We conclude with a reminder about **balancing** customer-based and competitor-based approaches: both are needed for success.

Today, understanding customers is not enough. The 1990s is a decade of intense competition, both foreign and domestic. Many economies are deregulating and encouraging market forces to operate. The European Community is removing trade barriers among Western European countries. Multinationals are moving aggressively into new markets and practicing global marketing. The result is that companies have no choice but to cultivate "competitiveness." They must start paying as much attention to tracking their competitors as to understanding target customers.

Under the marketing concept, companies gain **competitive advantage** by designing offers that satisfy target consumer needs *better than competitors' offers*. They might deliver more customer value by offering consumers lower prices than competitors for similar products and services or by providing more benefits that justify higher prices. Thus, marketing strategies must consider not only the needs of target consumers, but also the strategies of competitors. The first step is **competitor analysis,** the process of identifying key competitors; assessing their objectives, strengths and weaknesses, strategies, and reaction patterns; and selecting which competitors to attack or avoid. The second step is developing **competitive strategies** that strongly position the company against competitors and that give the company the strongest possible competitive advantage.

COMPETITOR ANALYSIS

To plan effective competitive marketing strategies, the company needs to find out all it can about its competitors. It must constantly compare its products, prices, channels, and promotion with those of close competitors. In this way the company can find areas of potential competitive advantage and disadvantage. And it can launch more effective marketing campaigns against its competitors and prepare stronger defenses against competitors' actions.

But what do companies need to know about their competitors? They need to know: Who are our competitors? What are their objectives? What are their strategies? What are their strengths and weaknesses? What are their reaction patterns? Figure 20-1 shows the major steps in analyzing competitors.

Identifying the Company's Competitors

Normally, it would seem a simple task for a company to identify its competitors. Coca-Cola knows that Pepsi is its major competitor; and Caterpillar knows that it competes with Komatsu. At the most obvious level, a company can define its competitors as other companies offering a similar product and services to the same customers at similar prices. Thus, Buick might see Ford as a major competitor, but not Mercedes or Hyundai.

But companies actually face a much broader range of competitors. More broadly, the company can define competitors as all firms making the same product or class of products. Thus, Buick would see itself as competing against all other automobile makers. Even more broadly, competitors might include all companies making products that supply the same service. Here Buick would see itself competing against not only other automobile manufacturers but also against the makers of trucks, motorcycles, or even bicycles. Finally, and still more broadly, competitors might include all companies that compete for the same consumer dollars. Here Buick would see itself competing with companies that sell major consumer durables, foreign vacations, new homes, or major home repairs.

Companies must avoid "competitor myopia." A company is more likely to

FIGURE 20-1
Steps in analyzing competitors

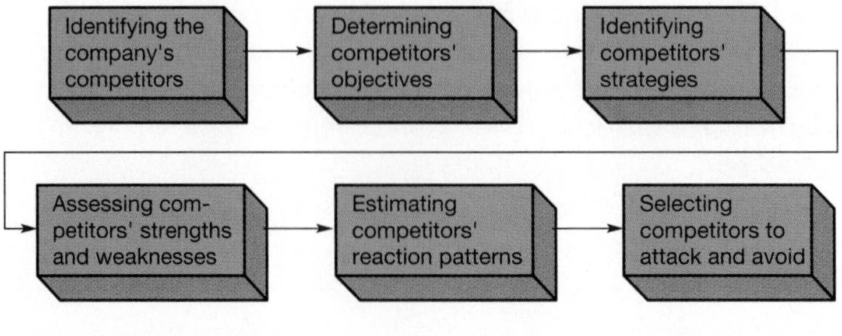

Identifying the company's competitors → Determining competitors' objectives → Identifying competitors' strategies → Assessing competitors' strengths and weaknesses → Estimating competitors' reaction patterns → Selecting competitors to attack and avoid

be "buried" by its latent competitors than its current ones. For example, Eastman Kodak, in its film business, has been worrying about the growing competition from Fuji, the Japanese film maker. But Kodak faces a much greater threat from the recent advances in "filmless camera" technology. These cameras, sold by Canon and Sony, take video still pictures that can be shown on a TV set, turned into hard copy, and later erased. What greater threat is there to a film business than a filmless camera?

The Industry Point of View

Many companies identify their competitors from the *industry* point of view. An **industry** is a group of firms that offer a product or class of products that are close substitutes for each other. We talk about the auto industry, the oil industry, the pharmaceutical industry, or the beverage industry. In a given industry, if the price of one product rises, it causes the demand for another product to rise. In the beverage industry, for example, if the price of coffee rises, this leads people to switch to tea or lemonade or soft drinks. Thus, coffee, tea, lemonade, and soft drinks are substitutes, even though they are physically different products. A company must strive to understand the competitive pattern in its industry if it hopes to be an effective "player" in that industry.

The Market Point of View

Instead of identifying competitors from the industry point of view, the company can take a *market* point of view. Here it defines competitors as companies that are trying to satisfy the same customer need or serve the same customer group. From an industry point of view, Coca-Cola might see its competition as Pepsi, Dr Pepper, 7-Up, and other soft-drink manufacturers. From a market point of view, however, the customer really wants "thirst quenching." This need can be satisfied by iced tea, fruit juice, bottled water, or many other fluids. Similarly, Crayola might define its competitors as other makers of crayons and children's drawing supplies. But from a market point of view, it would include as competitors all firms making recreational products for the children's market. In general, the market concept of competition opens the company's eyes to a broader set of actual and potential competitors. This leads to better long-run market planning.

The key to identifying competitors is to link industry and market analysis by mapping out product/market segments. Figure 20-2 shows the product/market segments in the toothpaste market by product types and customer age groups. We see that P&G (with several versions of Crest and Gleem) and Colgate-Palmolive (with Colgate) occupy six of the segments. Lever Brothers (Aim), Beecham (Aqua Fresh), and Topol each occupy two segments. If Topol wanted to enter other segments, it would need to estimate the market size of each segment, the market shares of the current competitors, and their current capabilities, objectives, and strategies. Clearly each product/market segment would pose different competitive problems and opportunities.

Determining Competitors' Objectives

Having identified the main competitors, marketing management now asks: What does each competitor seek in the marketplace? What drives each competitor's behavior?

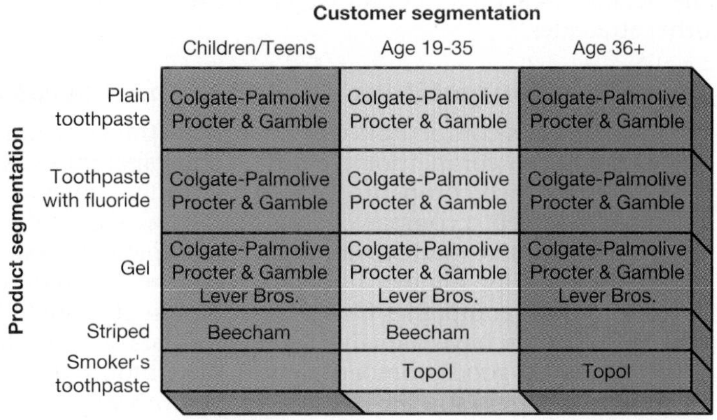

Customer segmentation

Product segmentation	Children/Teens	Age 19-35	Age 36+
Plain toothpaste	Colgate-Palmolive Procter & Gamble	Colgate-Palmolive Procter & Gamble	Colgate-Palmolive Procter & Gamble
Toothpaste with fluoride	Colgate-Palmolive Procter & Gamble	Colgate-Palmolive Procter & Gamble	Colgate-Palmolive Procter & Gamble
Gel	Colgate-Palmolive Procter & Gamble Lever Bros.	Colgate-Palmolive Procter & Gamble Lever Bros.	Colgate-Palmolive Procter & Gamble Lever Bros.
Striped	Beecham	Beecham	
Smoker's toothpaste		Topol	Topol

FIGURE 20-2
Product/market segments for toothpaste
Source: William A. Cohen. *Winning on the Marketing Front* (New York: John Wiley & Sons, 1986), p. 63.

The marketer might at first assume that all competitors will want to maximize their profits and choose their actions accordingly. But companies differ in the emphasis they put on short-term versus long-term profits. And some competitors might be oriented toward "satisfying" rather than "maximizing" profits. They have target profit goals and are satisfied in achieving them, even if more profits could have been produced by other strategies.

Thus, marketers must look beyond competitors' profit goals. Each competitor has a mix of objectives, each with differing importance. The company wants to know the relative importance that a competitor places on current profitability, market share growth, cash flow, technological leadership, service leadership, and other goals. Knowing a competitor's mix of objectives reveals whether the competitor is satisfied with its current situation and how it might react to different competitive actions. For example, a company that pursues low cost leadership will react much more strongly to a competitor's cost-reducing manufacturing breakthrough than to the same competitor's advertising increase. A company also must monitor its competitors' objectives for attacking various product/market segments. If the company finds that a competitor has discovered a new segment, this might be an opportunity. If it finds that competitors plan new moves into segments now served by the company, it will be forewarned and, hopefully, forearmed.

Identifying Competitors' Strategies

The more that one firm's strategy resembles another firm's strategy, the more the firms compete. In most industries, the competitors can be sorted into groups that pursue different strategies. A **strategic group** is a group of firms in an industry following the same or a similar strategy in a given target market. For example, in the major appliance industry, General Electric, Whirlpool, and Sears all belong to the same strategic group. Each produces a full line of medium-price appliances supported by good service. Maytag and KitchenAid, on the other hand, belong to a different strategic group. They produce a narrow line of very high quality appliances, offer a high level of service, and charge a premium price.

Some important insights emerge from strategic group identification. For example, if a company enters one of the groups, the members of that group become its key competitors. Thus, if the company enters the first group against General Electric, Whirlpool, and Sears, it can succeed only if it develops some strategic advantages over these large competitors.

Although competition is most intense within a strategic group, there is also rivalry among groups. First, some of the strategic groups may appeal to overlapping customer segments. For example, no matter what their strategy, all major appliance manufacturers will go after the apartment and home builders segment. Second, the customers may not see much difference in the offers of different groups—they may see little difference in quality between Whirlpool and Maytag. Finally, members of one strategic group might expand into new strategy segments. Thus, General Electric might decide to offer a premium quality, premium price line to compete with KitchenAid.

The company needs to look at all of the dimensions that identify strategic groups within the industry. It needs to know each competitor's product quality, features, and mix; customer services; pricing policy; distribution coverage; sales-force strategy; and advertising and sales promotion programs. And it must study the details of each competitor's R&D, manufacturing, purchasing, financial, and other strategies.

Assessing Competitors' Strengths and Weaknesses

Can a company's competitors carry out their strategies and reach their goals? This depends on each competitor's resources and capabilities. Marketers need to accurately identify each competitor's strengths and weaknesses.

As a first step, a company gathers key data on each competitor's business over the last few years. It wants to know about competitors' goals, strategies, and performance. Admittedly, some of this information will be hard to collect. For example, industrial goods companies find it hard to estimate competitors' market shares because they do not have the same syndicated data services that are available to consumer packaged-goods companies. Still, any information they can find will help them form a better estimate of each competitor's strengths and weaknesses.

Companies normally learn about their competitors' strengths and weaknesses through secondary data, personal experience, and hearsay. They also can increase their knowledge by conducting primary marketing research with customers, suppliers, and dealers. Recently, a growing number of companies have turned to **benchmarking,** comparing the company's products and processes to those of competitors or leading firms in other industries to find ways to improve quality and performance. Benchmarking has become a powerful tool for increasing a company's competitiveness (see Marketing Highlight 20-1).

In searching for competitors' weaknesses, the company should try to identify any assumptions they make about their business and the market that are no longer valid. Some companies believe they produce the best quality in the industry when this is no longer true. Many companies are victims of rules of thumb such as "customers prefer full line companies," "the salesforce is the only important marketing tool," or "customers value service more than price." If a competitor is operating on a major wrong assumption, the company can take advantage of it.

Estimating Competitors' Reaction Patterns

A competitor's objectives, strategies, and strengths and weaknesses go a long way toward explaining its likely actions, and its reactions to company moves such as a price cut, a promotion increase, or a new product introduction. In addition, each competitor has a certain philosophy of doing business, a certain internal culture and guiding beliefs. Marketing managers need a deep understanding of a given competitor's mentality if they want to anticipate how the competitor will act or react.

Each competitor reacts differently. Some do not react quickly or strongly to a competitor's move. They may feel their customers are loyal; they may be slow in noticing the move; they may lack the funds to react. Some competitors react only to certain types of assaults and not to others. They might always respond strongly to price cuts in order to signal that these will never succeed. But they might not respond at all to advertising increases, believing these to be less threatening.

Expanding into a new strategy segment: General Electric offers a premium-quality, premium-price line of kitchen appliances.

MARKETING HIGHLIGHT 20-1

HOW BENCHMARKING HELPS IMPROVE COMPETITIVE PERFORMANCE

In most industries, one or a few companies are known to greatly outperform other competitors. A world-class company can have has much as a tenfold advantage over an average company in quality, speed, and cost performance. Benchmarking is the art of finding out how and why some companies perform tasks much better than others.

A benchmarking company aims to imitate, or better yet, to improve upon the best practices of other companies. The Japanese used benchmarking persistently after World War II, copying many American products and practices. In 1979, Xerox undertook one of the first major U.S. benchmarking projects. Xerox wanted to learn how Japanese competitors were able to produce more reliable copiers and charge prices below Xerox's production costs. By buying Japanese copiers and analyzing them through "reverse engineering," Xerox learned how to greatly improve its own copiers' reliability and costs. However, Xerox didn't stop there. It went on to ask additional questions: Are Xerox scientists and engineers among the best in their respective specialties? Are Xerox marketing and sales people and practices among the best in the world? To answer these questions, the company had to identify world-class, "best practices" companies and learn from them. Although benchmarking initially focused on studying other companies' products and services, it later expanded to include benchmarking work processes, staff functions, organizational performance, and the entire customer value delivery process.

Another early benchmarking pioneer was Ford. Ford was losing sales to Japanese and European car makers. Don Peterson, then chairman of Ford, instructed his engineers and designers to build a new car that combined the 400 features that Ford customers said were the most important. If Saab made the best seats, then Ford should copy Saab's seats. If Toyota had the best fuel gauge, and BMW had the best tire and jack storage system, then Ford should copy these features also. But Peterson went further: he asked the engineers to "better the best" where possible. When the new car—the highly successful Taurus—was finished, Peterson claimed that his engineers had improved upon, not just copied, the best features found in competing cars.

In another benchmarking project, Ford discovered that it employed 500 people to manage its accounts payable operation, whereas its partly owned Japanese partner, Mazda, handled the same task with only 10 people. After studying Mazda's system, Ford installed an "invoiceless system" and reduced its staff to 200.

Today many companies such as AT&T, IBM, Kodak, Du Pont, Intel, Marriott, and Motorola use benchmarking as a standard tool. Some companies benchmark only the best companies in their industry. Others benchmark against the "best practices" in the world. In this sense, benchmarking goes beyond standard "competitive analysis." Motorola, for example, starts each benchmarking project with a search for "best of breed" in the world. According to one of its executives, "The further away from our industry we reach for comparisons, the happier we are. We are seeking competitive superiority, after all, not just competitive parity."

As an example of seeking "best of breed" practices, Robert C. Camp, Xerox's benchmarking expert, flew to Freeport, Maine, to visit L. L. Bean, the "outdoors" catalog company. He wanted to find out how L. L. Bean's warehouse workers managed to "pick and pack" items three times as fast as Xerox. As a noncompetitor, L. L. Bean was happy to describe its practice, and Xerox ended up redesigning its warehouses and software system. On later occasions, Xerox benchmarked American Express for its billing expertise and Cummins Engine for its production scheduling expertise.

Benchmarking involves seven steps: (1) determine which functions to benchmark; (2) identify the key performance variables to measure; (3) identify the best-in-class companies; (4) measure performance of best-in-class companies; (5) measure the company's performance; (6) specify programs and actions to close the gap; and (7) implement and monitor results.

Once a company commits to benchmarking, it may try to benchmark every activity. It may set up a benchmarking department to promote the practice and to teach benchmarking techniques to departmental people. Yet benchmarking takes time and costs money. Companies should focus their benchmarking efforts only on critical tasks that deeply affect customer satisfaction and company costs, and for which substantially better performance is known to exist.

How can a company identify "best-practice" companies? As a good starting point, it can ask customers, suppliers, and distributors who they rate as doing the best job. Or it can contact major consulting firms that

---

Other competitors react swiftly and strongly to any assault. Thus, P&G does not let a new detergent come easily into the market. Many firms avoid direct competition with P&G and look for easier prey, knowing that P&G will fight fiercely if challenged. Finally, some competitors show no predictable reaction pattern. They might or might not react on a given occasion, and there is no way to foresee what

When Ford redesigned Taurus, it benchmarked these features and more than 200 others against major competitors. Benchmarking helped Ford make Taurus the best-selling car in the world.

have built large files of "best practices." An important point is that benchmarking can be done without resorting to industrial espionage.

After the "best-practice" companies are identified, the company needs to measure their performance with respect to cost, time, and quality. For example, a company studying its supply management process found that its purchasing cost was four times higher, its supplier selection time was four times longer, and its delivery time was sixteen times worse than world-class competitors.

Some critics suggest that companies must be careful not to rely *too* much on benchmarking. They warn that because benchmarking takes other companies' performance as a starting point, it might hamper real creativity. Or it might lead to an only marginally better product or practice when other companies are leapfrogging ahead. Too often, benchmarking studies take many months, and by that time, better practices may have emerged elsewhere. Benchmarking might cause the

company to focus too much on competitors while losing touch with consumers' changing needs. Finally, benchmarking might distract from making further improvements in the company's core competencies.

Nevertheless, a company must do more than simply look inside when trying to continuously improve its performance. To gain competitive advantage, it must compare its products and processes to those of its competitors and leading companies in other industries. Thus, benchmarking remains one of the most powerful tools for improving quality and competitive performance.

Sources: Robert C. Camp, *Benchmarking: The Search for Industry-Best Practices that Lead to Superior Performance* (White Plains, NY: Quality Resources, 1989); A. Steven Walleck, et al., "Benchmarking World Class Performance," McKinsey Quarterly, No. 1, 1990, pp. 3-24; Michael J. Spendolini, *The Benchmarking Book* (New York: AMACOM, 1992); Jeremy Main, "How to Steal the Best Ideas Around," Fortune, October 19, 1992; and Betsy Weisendanger, "Benchmarking for Beginners," *Sales & Marketing Management,* November 1992, pp. 59-64.

they will do based on their economics, history, or anything else.

In some industries, competitors live in relative harmony; in others, they fight constantly. Knowing how key competitors react gives the company clues on how best to attack competitors or how best to defend the company's current positions.[2]

MARKETING HIGHLIGHT 20-2

CUSTOMER VALUE ANALYSIS: THE KEY TO COMPETITIVE ADVANTAGE

In analyzing competitors and searching for competitive advantage, one of the most important marketing tools is *customer value analysis*. The aim of a customer value analysis is to determine the benefits that target customers value and how they rate the relative value of various competitors' offers. The major steps in customer value analysis are described next.

1. *Identify the major attributes that customers value.* Various people in the company may have different ideas on what customers value. Thus, the company's marketing researchers must ask customers themselves what features and performance levels they look for in choosing a product or seller. Different customers will mention different features and benefits. If the list gets too long, the researcher can remove overlapping attributes.

2. *Assess the importance of different attributes.* Here customers are asked to rate or rank the importance of the different factors. If the customers differ very much in their ratings, they should be grouped into different customer segments.

3. *Assess the company's and the competitors' performance on different customer values against the values' rated importance.* Next, customers are asked where they rate each competitor's performance on each attribute. Ideally, the company's own performance will be high on the attributes the customers value most and low on the attributes which customers value least. Two pieces of bad news would be: (a) the company's performance ranks high on some

minor attributes—a case of "overkill"; and (b) the company's performance ranks low on some major attributes—a case of "underkill." The company also must look at how each competitor ranks on the important attributes.

4. *Examine how customers in a specific segment rate the company's performance against a specific major competitor on an attribute-by-attribute basis.* The key to gaining competitive advantage is to take each customer segment and examine how the company's offer compares to that of its major competitor. If the company's offer exceeds the competitor's offer on all important attributes, the company can charge a higher price and earn higher profits, or it can charge the same price and gain more market share. But if the company is seen as performing at a lower level than its major competitor on some important attributes, it must invest in strengthening those attributes or finding other important attributes where it can build a lead on the competitor.

5. *Monitor customer values over time.* Although customer values are fairly stable in the short run, they will probably change as competing technologies and features appear and as customers face different economic climates. A company that assumes that customer values will remain stable flirts with danger. The company must review customer values and competitors' standings periodically if it wants to remain strategically effective.

Selecting Competitors to Attack and Avoid

Management already has largely determined its major competitors through prior decisions on customer targets, distribution channels, and marketing-mix strategy. These decisions define the strategic group to which the company belongs. Management now must decide which competitors to compete against most vigorously. The company can focus its attack on one of several classes of competitors.

Strong or Weak Competitors

Most companies prefer to aim their shots at their weak competitors. This requires fewer resources and time. But in the process, the firm may gain little. The argument could be made that the firm also should compete with strong competitors in order to sharpen its abilities. Furthermore, even strong competitors have some weaknesses, and succeeding against them often provides greater returns.

A useful tool for assessing competitor strengths and weaknesses is **customer value analysis,** asking customers what benefits they value and how they rate the company versus competitors on important attributes. (See Marketing Highlight 20-2.) Customer value analysis also points out areas in which the company is vulnerable to competitors' actions.

Close or Distant Competitors

Most companies will compete with those competitors who resemble them the most. Thus, Chevrolet competes more against Ford than against Jaguar. At the same time, the company may want to avoid trying to "destroy" a close competitor. Here is an example of a questionable "victory":

> Bausch & Lomb in the late 1970s moved aggressively against other soft lens manufacturers with great success. However, this led one after another competitor to sell out to larger firms such as Revlon, Schering-Plough, and Johnson & Johnson, with the result that Bausch & Lomb now faced much larger competitors—and it suffered the consequences. For example, Johnson & Johnson acquired Vistakon, a small nicher with only $20 million in annual sales, which served the tiny portion of the contact-lens market for people with astigmatism. Backed by J&J's deep pockets, however, Vistakon proved a formidable opponent. When the small but nimble Vistakon unit introduced its innovative Acuvue disposable lenses, the much larger Bausch & Lomb was forced to take some of its own medicine. According to one analyst, "The speed of the [Acuvue] rollout and the novelty of [J&J's] big-budget ads left giant Bausch & Lomb. . . seeing stars." By 1992, J&J's Vistakon was No. 1 in the fast-growing disposable segment and had captured about 25 percent of the entire U.S. contact-lens market.[3]

In this case, the company's success in hurting a close rival brought in tougher competitors.

"Well-Behaved" or "Disruptive" Competitors

A company really needs and benefits from competitors. The existence of competitors results in several strategic benefits. Competitors may help increase total demand. They share the costs of market and product development and help to legitimize new technology. They may serve less attractive segments or lead to more product differentiation. Finally, they lower the antitrust risk and improve bargaining power versus labor or regulators.

However, a company may not view all of its competitors as beneficial. An industry often contains "well-behaved" competitors and "disruptive" competitors.[4] Well-behaved competitors play by the rules of the industry. They favor a stable and healthy industry, set prices in a reasonable relation to costs, motivate others to lower costs or improve differentiation, and accept a reasonable level of market share and profits. Disruptive competitors, on the other hand, break the rules. They try to buy share rather than earn it, take large risks, invest in overcapacity, and in general shake up the industry. For example, American Airlines finds Delta and United to be well-behaved competitors because they play by the rules and attempt to set their fares sensibly. But American finds TWA, Continental, and America West disruptive competitors because they destabilize the airline industry through continual heavy price discounting and wild promotional schemes. A company might be smart to support well-behaved competitors, aiming its attacks at disruptive competitors. Thus, some analysts claim that American's huge fare discounts during the summer of 1992 were intentionally designed to teach the disruptive renegade airlines a lesson or to drive them out of business altogether.[5]

The implication is that "well-behaved" companies should try to shape an industry that consists of only well-behaved competitors. Through careful licensing, selective retaliation, and coalitions, they can shape the industry so that the competitors behave rationally and harmoniously, follow the rules, try to earn share rather than buy it, and differentiate somewhat to compete less directly.

Designing the Competitive Intelligence System

We have described the main types of information that company decision makers need to know about their competitors. This information must be collected, interpreted, distributed, and used. Although the cost in money and time of gathering competitive intelligence is high, the cost of not gathering it is higher. Yet the company must design its competitive intelligence system in a cost-effective way.

The competitive intelligence system first identifies the vital types of competitive information and the best sources of this information. Then, the system continuously collects information from the field (salesforce, channels, suppliers, market research firms, trade associations) and from published data (government publications, speeches, articles). Next the system checks the information for validity and reliability, interprets it, and organizes it in an appropriate way. Finally, it sends key information to relevant decision makers and responds to inquiries from managers about competitors.

With this system, company managers will receive timely information about competitors in the form of phone calls, bulletins, newsletters, and reports. In addition, managers can contact the system when they need an interpretation of a competitor's sudden move, or when they want to know a competitor's weaknesses and strengths, or when they need to know how a competitor will respond to a planned company move.

Smaller companies that cannot afford to set up a formal competitive intelligence office can assign specific executives to watch specific competitors. Thus, a manager who used to work for a competitor might follow closely all developments connected with that competitor; he or she would be the "in-house" expert on that competitor. Any manager needing to know the thinking of a given competitor could contact the assigned in-house expert.[6]

COMPETITIVE STRATEGIES

Having identified and evaluated the major competitors, the company now must design broad competitive marketing strategies that will best position its offer against competitors' offers in the minds of consumers—strategies that will give the company or its product the strongest possible competitive advantage.[7] But what broad marketing strategies might the company use? Which ones are best for a particular company, or for the company's different divisions and products?

No one strategy is best for all companies. Each company must determine what makes the most sense given its position in the industry and its objectives, opportunities, and resources. Even within a company, different strategies may be required for different businesses or products. Johnson & Johnson uses one marketing strategy for its leading brands in stable consumer markets and a different marketing strategy for its new high-tech health-care businesses and products. We now look at broad competitive marketing strategies companies can use.

Competitive Positions

Firms competing in a given target market will, at any point in time, differ in their objectives and resources. Some firms will be large, others small. Some will have great resources, others will be strapped for funds. Some will be old and established, others new and fresh. Some will strive for rapid market share growth, others for long-term profits. And the firms will occupy different competitive positions in the target market.

Michael Porter suggests four basic competitive positioning strategies that companies can follow—three winning strategies and one losing one.[8] The three winning strategies include:

Overall cost leadership. Here the company works hard to achieve the lowest costs of production and distribution so that it can price lower than its competitors and win a large market share. Texas Instruments and Wal-Mart are leading practitioners of this strategy.

Differentiation. Here the company concentrates on creating a highly differentiated product line and marketing program so that it comes across as the class leader in the industry. Most customers would prefer to own this brand if its price is not too high. IBM and Caterpillar follow this strategy in computers and heavy construction equipment, respectively.

Focus. Here the company focuses its effort on serving a few market segments well rather than going after the whole market. Thus, glass-maker AFG Industries focuses on users of tempered and colored glass—it makes 70 percent of the glass for microwave oven doors and 75 percent of the glass for shower doors and patio table tops. And U.S. Surgical focuses on making instruments for laparoscopic surgery—surgery by inserting a tiny TV camera into the body along with slim, long-handled surgical instruments. U.S. Surgical captures an 80 percent share of this market.[9]

Companies that pursue a clear strategy—one of the above—are likely to perform

MARKETING HIGHLIGHT 20-3

COMPETITIVE STRATEGY: DON'T PLAY IN THE MIDDLE OF THE ROAD

Being mainstream used to be a blessing for products. Now it's becoming a curse. Today, companies in most industries face slow-growing and fiercely competitive markets. Further, family income has grown slowly during the past decade, causing consumers in all income classes to scramble for bargains. At the same time, feeling uncertain about their economic status, middle-class consumers prefer not to identify with middle-of-the-road brands. As a result, they *either* buy smart and select bargains or splurge and wrap themselves in prestige brands.

Solid middle-of-the-road names like Sears or Holiday Inn are struggling against a slew of new competitors that strike from both above and below. Encircled by rivals offering either more luxurious goods or just plain cheaper ones, companies with products in the middle are finding their market shares dwindling and are seeking ways to break away from the image of being "just average." "Getting stuck in the middle is a terrible fate," notes one advertising agency executive. "[You remain] a mass brand as the market splinters."

Examples abound of products and services caught in the middle—adequate but not exciting—losing ground to more purely positioned competitors at both the high and low ends. For example, swanky stores such as Neiman Marcus and budget outlets such as Wal-Mart are prospering, while bread-and-butter Sears flounders. Haagen-Dazs, Ben & Jerry's, and other "superpremium" ice creams are thriving—as are grocers' own bargain labels—while middle brands such as Kraft, General Foods, and Sealtest are struggling. Travelers want either economy lodging at chains such as Day's Inn and Motel 6, or to sleep in the lap of luxury, leaving adequate but neither inexpensive nor plush hoteliers such as Ramada Inn or Holiday Inn in the lurch. Thus, brands in the "murky middle" are facing increasing pressure from competitors at both ends the spectrum. Notes the advertising executive: "There's no future for products everyone likes a little."

If a brand in the middle can't sell on prestige, it has to compete on value. To make Sealtest stand out from store-brand ice creams, Kraft has borrowed some tactics from fancier brands. It recently added a layer of cellophane inside the carton—like the one found in Breyers. It also made the package's graphics cleaner and more modern. The idea is to keep the price about in the middle but to come across as a better value. Still, the product remains in that not-cheap, not-expensive limbo—a very tough sell.

An average image also haunts Sears, which has seen its middle-income customers defect either to discount outlets or to trendier specialty stores. It's scrambling to revitalize sales by stocking more national brands and running slicker, more stylish ads in an effort to project an image that's a step up from plain vanilla. Sears claims that this image-building program has been successful, but consumer perceptions die hard. Sears has yet to establish a clear and distinctive position. As one image consultant suggests: "Sears doesn't stand for anything consumers aspire to."

For some, it finally gets to the point where the middle market just isn't worth it. Marriott tried to string its Bob's Big Boy, Allie's, and Wag's coffee shops into a single chain of casual restaurants. It was a vague niche that few consumers wanted: The restaurants weren't as cheap or as appealing to children as fast food. Nor could they please adults with a nice dining-out atmosphere. Marriott ended up quitting the restaurant business. "We were sandwiched in the middle," a Marriott spokesman says.

In the hotel industry, where chains have spread rapidly, companies are trying to escape the middle by extending their reach both into less expensive accommodations and higher-priced ones. Holiday Inns, which no longer has the casual family traveler all to itself, has added a more upscale Holiday Inns Crown Plaza. Ramada now operates a no-frills chain called Rodeway Inns and a posher one called Renaissance.

Thus, to win in the marketplace, a company must gain competitive advantage by offering something that competitors don't. It might offer consumers the best price for a given level of quality. Or it might offer a differentiated product—one with unique features or higher quality for which consumers are willing to pay a higher price. Or it might focus on serving the special needs of a specific market segment. But companies that try to ride in the middle by offering a little of everything usually end up not being very good at anything. The moral? Don't play in the murky middle of the road.

Source: Portions adapted from Kathleen Deveny, "Middle-Price Brands Come Under Siege," *The Wall Street Journal,* April 2, 1990, pp. B1, B7. Reprinted by permission; © 1990 Dow Jones & Company, Inc. All rights reserved worldwide.

well. The firm that carries out that strategy best will make the most profits. But firms that do not pursue a clear strategy—*middle-of-the-roaders*—do the worst. Sears, Chrysler, and International Harvester all came upon difficult times because they did not stand out as the lowest in cost, highest in perceived value, or best in serving some market segment. Middle-of-the-roaders try to be good on all strategic counts, but end up being not very good at anything (see Marketing Highlight 20-3).

FIGURE 20-3
Hypothetical market structure

We will adopt a different classification of competitive positions, based on the role firms play in the target market—that of leading, challenging, following, or niching. Suppose that an industry contains the firms shown in Figure 20-3. Forty percent of the market is in the hands of the **market leader,** the firm with the largest market share. Another 30 percent is in the hands of a **market challenger,** a runner-up that is fighting hard to increase its market share. Another 20 percent is in the hands of a **market follower,** another runner-up that wants to hold its share without rocking the boat. The remaining 10 percent is in the hands of **market nichers,** firms that serve small segments not being pursued by other firms.

We now look at specific marketing strategies that are available to market leaders, challengers, followers, and nichers. In the sections that follow, you should remember that the classifications of competitive positions often do not apply to a whole company, but only to its position in a specific industry. For example, large and diversified companies such as IBM, Sears, or General Mills—or their individual businesses, divisions, or products—might be leaders in some markets and nichers in others. For example, Procter & Gamble leads in many consumer packaged-goods segments, such as dishwashing and laundry detergents, disposable diapers, and shampoo, but it challenges Lever Brothers in the hand soaps. Such companies often use different strategies for different business units or products, depending on the competitive situations of each.

Market-Leader Strategies

Most industries contain an acknowledged market leader. The leader has the largest market share and usually leads the other firms in price changes, new product introductions, distribution coverage, and promotion spending. The leader may or may not be admired or respected, but other firms concede its dominance. The leader is a focal point for competitors, a company to challenge, imitate, or avoid. Some of the best-known market leaders are General Motors (autos), Kodak (photography), IBM (computers), Caterpillar (earth-moving equipment), Coca-Cola (soft drinks), Campbell (soups), Wal-Mart (retailing), McDonald's (fast food), and Gillette (razor blades).

A leading firm's life is not easy. It must maintain a constant watch. Other firms keep challenging its strengths or trying to take advantage of its weaknesses. The market leader can easily miss a turn in the market and plunge into second or third place. A product innovation may come along and hurt the leader (as when Tylenol's nonaspirin painkiller took the lead from Bayer Aspirin, or when P&G's Tide, the first synthetic laundry detergent, beat out Lever Brothers's leading brands). Or the leading firm might grow fat and slow, losing out against new and peppier rivals (Xerox's share of the world copier market fell from over 80 percent to less than 35 percent in just five years when Japanese producers challenged with cheaper and more reliable copiers).

Leading firms want to remain number one. This calls for action on three fronts. First, the firm must find ways to expand total demand. Second, the firm must protect its current market share through good defensive and offensive actions. Third, the firm can try to expand its market share further, even if market size remains constant.

Expanding the Total Market

The leading firm normally gains the most when the total market expands. If Americans take more pictures, Kodak stands to gain the most because it sells more than 80 percent of this country's film. If Kodak can convince more Americans to take pictures, or to take pictures on more occasions, or to take more pictures on each occasion, it will benefit greatly. In general, the market leader should look for new users, new uses, and more usage of its products.

New Users. Every product class can attract buyers who are still unaware of the product, or who are resisting it because of its price or its lack of certain features. A seller usually can find new users in many places. For example, Revlon might find new perfume users in its current markets by convincing women who do not use perfume to try it. Or it might find users in new demographic segments, say by producing cologne for men. Or it might expand into new geographic segments, perhaps by selling its perfume in other countries.

Johnson's Baby Shampoo provides a classic example of developing new users. When the baby boom had passed and the birth rate slowed down, the company grew concerned about future sales growth. But J&J's marketers noticed that other family members sometimes used the baby shampoo for their own hair. Management developed an advertising campaign aimed at adults. In a short time, Johnson's Baby Shampoo became a leading brand in the total shampoo market.

New Uses. The marketer can expand markets by discovering and promoting new uses for the product. Du Pont's nylon provides a classic example of new-use expansion. Every time nylon became a mature product, some new use was discovered. Nylon was first used as a fiber for parachutes; then for women's stockings; later as a major material in shirts and blouses; and still later in automobile tires, upholstery, and carpeting. Another example of new-use expansion is Arm & Hammer baking soda. Its sales had flattened after 125 years. Then the company discovered that consumers were using baking soda as a refrigerator deodorizer. It launched a heavy advertising and publicity campaign focusing on this use and persuaded consumers in half of America's homes to place an open box of baking soda in their refrigerators and to replace it every few months.

More Usage. A third market expansion strategy is to convince people to use the product more often or to use more per occasion. Campbell encourages people to eat soup more often by running ads containing new recipes in *Better Homes and Gardens* and other home magazines. Procter & Gamble advises users that its Head and Shoulders shampoo is more effective with two applications instead of one per shampoo.

Years ago, the Michelin Tire Company found a creative way to increase usage per occasion. It wanted French car owners to drive more miles per year, re-

Market-leader strategies to expand the market: J&J develops new users, and Campbell promotes more usage.

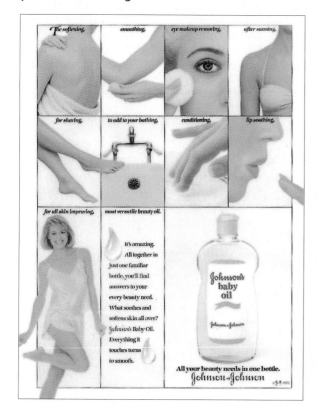

sulting in more tire replacement. Michelin began rating French restaurants on a three-star system. It reported that many of the best restaurants were in the south of France, leading many Parisians to take weekend drives south. Michelin also published guidebooks with maps and sights along the way to encourage additional travel.

Protecting Market Share

While trying to expand total market size, the leading firm also must constantly protect its current business against competitor attacks. Coca-Cola must constantly guard against Pepsi-Cola; Gillette against Bic; Kodak against Fuji; McDonald's against Wendy's; General Motors against Ford.

What can the market leader do to protect its position? First, it must prevent or fix weaknesses that provide opportunities for competitors. It needs to keep its costs down and its prices in line with the value the customers see in the brand. The leader should "plug holes" so that competitors do not jump in. But the best defense is a good offense, and the best response is *continuous innovation*. The leader refuses to be content with the way things are and leads the industry in new products, customer services, distribution effectiveness, and cost cutting. It keeps increasing its competitive effectiveness and value to customers. It takes the offensive, sets the pace, and exploits competitors' weaknesses.

Increased competition in recent years has sparked management's interest in models of military warfare. Leader companies have been advised to protect their market positions with competitive strategies patterned after successful military defense strategies. Figure 20-4 shows six defense strategies that a market leader can use.[10]

Position Defense. The most basic defense is a position defense in which a company builds fortifications around its current position. But simply defending one's current position or products rarely works. Henry Ford tried it with his Model T and brought an enviably healthy Ford Motor Company to the brink of financial ruin. Even lasting brands such as Coca-Cola and Bayer Aspirin cannot be relied upon to supply all future growth and profitability for their companies. These brands must be improved and adapted to changing conditions, and new brands must be developed. Coca-Cola today, in spite of producing over 40 percent of America's soft drinks, is aggressively extending its beverage lines and has diversified into desalinization equipment and plastics.

Flanking Defense. When guarding its overall position, the market leader should watch its weaker flanks closely. Smart competitors normally will attack the company's weaknesses. Thus, the Japanese successfully entered the small car market because U.S. auto makers left a gaping hole in that submarket. Using a flanking defense, the company carefully checks its flanks and protects the more vulnerable ones.

FIGURE 20-4
Defense strategies

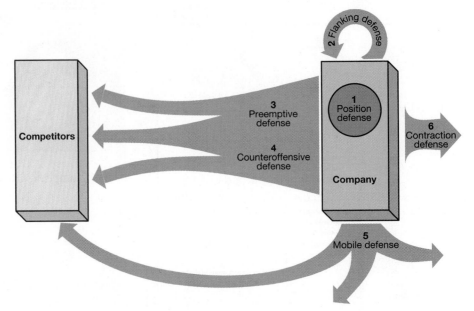

Preemptive Defense. The leader can launch a more aggressive preemptive defense, striking competitors before they can move against the company. A preemptive defense assumes that an ounce of prevention is worth a pound of cure. Thus, when threatened in the mid-1980s by the impending entry of Japanese manufacturers into the U.S. market, Cummins Engine slashed its prices by almost a third to save its number-one position in the $2 billion heavy-duty truck engine market. Today, Cummins claims a commanding 50 percent market share in North America, and not a single U.S.-built tractor-trailer truck contains a Japanese engine.[11]

Counteroffensive Defense. When a market leader is attacked despite its flanking or preemptive efforts, it can launch a counteroffensive defense. When Fuji attacked Kodak in the U.S. film market, Kodak counterattacked by dramatically increasing its promotion and introducing several innovative new film products. When attacked by UPS's low-price claims, Federal Express counterattacked by slashing its prices. And when attacked by Clorox's detergent with bleach, P&G responded with Tide With Bleach, which drove the Clorox brand from the market and captured a 17 percent share of all U.S. detergent sales.[12]

Sometimes companies hold off for a while before countering. This may seem a dangerous game of "wait and see," but there are often good reasons for not barreling in. By waiting, the company can understand more fully the competitor's offense and perhaps find a gap through which a successful counteroffensive can be launched.

Mobile Defense. A mobile defense involves more than aggressively defending a current market position. The leader stretches to new markets that can serve as future bases for defense and offense. Through *market broadening,* the company shifts its focus from the current product to the broader underlying consumer need. For example, Armstrong Cork redefined its focus from "floor covering" to "decorative room covering" (including walls and ceilings) and expanded into related businesses that were balanced for growth and defense. *Market diversification* into unrelated industries is the other alternative for generating "strategic depth." When U.S. tobacco companies like R. J. Reynolds and Philip Morris faced growing curbs on cigarette smoking, they moved quickly into new consumer products industries. RJR acquired Nabisco, and Philip Morris bought up General Foods and Kraft to become the world's largest consumer packaged-goods company.

Contraction Defense. Large companies sometimes find they can no longer defend all of their positions. Their resources are spread too thin and competitors are nibbling away on several fronts. The best action then appears to be a contraction defense (or strategic withdrawal). The company gives up weaker positions and concentrates its resources on stronger ones. During the 1970s, many companies diversified wildly and spread themselves too thin. In the slow-growth 1980s, ITT, Gulf & Western, Georgia Pacific, General Mills, Kraft, Quaker, and dozens of other companies pruned their portfolios to concentrate resources on products and businesses in their core industries. These companies now serve fewer markets, but serve them much better.

Expanding Market Share

Market leaders also can grow by increasing their market shares further. In many markets, small market share increases mean very large sales increases. For example, in the coffee market, a one percent increase in market share is worth $48 million; in soft drinks, $440 million! No wonder normal competition turns into marketing warfare in such markets.

Many studies have found that profitability rises with increasing market share.[13] Businesses with very large relative market shares averaged substantially higher returns on investment. Because of these findings, many companies have sought expanded market shares to improve profitability. General Electric, for example, declared that it wants to be at least number one or two in each of its markets or else get out. GE shed its computer, air-conditioning, small appliances, and television businesses because it could not achieve top-dog position in these industries.

Other studies have found that many industries contain one or a few highly profitable large firms, several profitable and more focused firms, and a large number of medium-sized firms with poorer profit performance.

The large firms . . . tend to address the entire market, achieving cost advantages and high market share by realizing economies of scale. The small competitors reap high profits by focusing on some narrower segment of the business and by developing specialized approaches to production, marketing, and distribution for that segment. Ironically, the medium-sized competitors . . . often show the poorest profit performance. Trapped in a strategic "No Man's Land," they are too large to reap the benefits of more focused competition, yet too small to benefit from the economies of scale that their larger competitors enjoy.[14]

Thus, it appears that profitability increases as a business gains share relative to competitors in its *served market*. For example, Mercedes holds only a small share of the total car market, but it earns high profit because it is a high-share company in its luxury car segment. And it has achieved this high share in its served market because it does other things right, such as producing high quality, giving good service, and holding down its costs.

Companies must not think, however, that gaining increased market share will improve profitability automatically. Much depends on their strategy for gaining increased share. We see many high-share companies with low profitability, and many low-share companies with high profitability. The cost of buying higher market share may far exceed the returns. Higher shares tend to produce higher profits only when unit costs fall with increased market share or when the company offers a superior-quality product and charges a premium price that more than covers the cost of offering higher quality.

Market-Challenger Strategies

Firms that are second, third, or lower in an industry are sometimes quite large, such as Colgate, Ford, Kmart, Avis, Westinghouse, Miller, and PepsiCo. These runner-up firms can adopt one of two competitive strategies. They can attack the leader and other competitors in an aggressive bid for more market share (market challengers). Or they can play along with competitors and not rock the boat (market followers). We now look at competitive strategies for market challengers.

Defining the Strategic Objective and the Competitor

A market challenger must first define its strategic objective. Most market challengers seek to increase their profitability by increasing their market shares. But the strategic objective chosen depends on who the competitor is. In most cases, the company can choose which competitors it will challenge.

The challenger can attack the market leader, a high-risk but potentially high-gain strategy which makes good sense if the leader is not serving the market well. To succeed with such an attack, a company must have some sustainable competitive advantage over the leader—a cost advantage leading to lower prices or the ability to provide better value at a premium price. In the construction equipment industry, Komatsu successfully challenged Caterpillar by offering the same quality at much lower prices. And P&G grabbed a big share of the toilet-tissue market by offering a softer and more absorbent product than the one offered by market leader Scott. When attacking the leader, a challenger also must find a way to minimize the leader's response. Otherwise its gains may be short lived.[15]

The challenger can avoid the leader and instead attack firms its own size, or smaller local and regional firms. Many of these firms are underfinanced and will not be serving their customers well. Several of the major beer companies grew to their present size not by attacking large competitors, but by gobbling up small local or regional competitors.

Thus, the challenger's strategic objective depends on which competitor it chooses to attack. If the company goes after the market leader, its objective may be to wrest a certain market share. Bic knows that it can't topple Gillette in the razor market—it simply wants a larger share. Or the challenger's goal might be to take over market leadership. IBM entered the personal computer market late, as a challenger, but quickly became the market leader. If the company goes after a small local company, its objective may be to put that company out of business. The important point remains: The company must choose its opponents carefully and have a clearly defined and attainable objective.

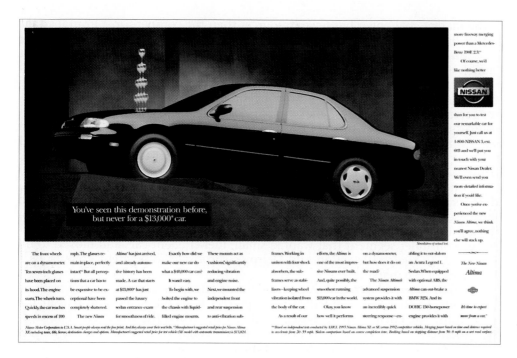

Market challenger Nissan attacks more expensive competitors, claiming that the Nissan Altima can do what a $40,000 car can do. Properly equipped, the Altima can "out-slalom an Acura Legend L Sedan," "out-brake a BMW 325si," and "provide more freeway power than a Mercedes-Benz 190E 2.3."

Choosing an Attack Strategy

How can the market challenger best attack the chosen competitor and achieve its strategic objectives? Figure 20-5 shows five possible attack strategies.

Frontal Attack. In a full frontal attack, the challenger matches the competitor's product, advertising, price, and distribution efforts. It attacks the competitor's strengths rather than its weaknesses. The outcome depends on who has the greater strength and endurance. Even great size and strength may not be enough to challenge a firmly entrenched and resourceful competitor successfully.

> Unilever has twice the worldwide sales of Procter & Gamble and five times the sales of Colgate-Palmolive. Yet its American subsidiary, Lever Brothers, trails P&G by a wide margin in the U.S. A while back, Lever launched a full frontal assault against P&G in the detergent market. Lever's Wisk was already the leading liquid detergent. In quick succession, it added a barrage of new products—Sunlight dishwashing detergent, Snuggle fabric softener, Surf laundry powder—and backed them with aggressive promotion and distribution efforts. But P&G spent heavily to defend its brands and held on to most of its business. And it counterattacked with Liquid Tide, which came from nowhere in just 17 months to run neck-and-neck with Wisk. Lever did gain market share, but most of it came from smaller competitors.[16]

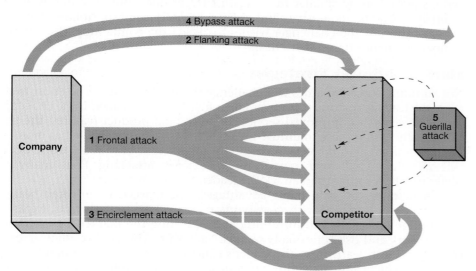

FIGURE 20-5
Attack strategies

If the market challenger has fewer resources than the competitor, a frontal attack makes little sense.

Flanking Attack. Rather than attacking head on, the challenger can launch a flanking attack. The competitor often concentrates its resources to protect its strongest positions, but it usually has some weaker flanks. By attacking these weak spots, the challenger can concentrate its strength against the competitor's weakness. Flank attacks make good sense when the company has fewer resources than the competitor. PepsiCo flanked Coca-Cola when it created Slice, a soft drink with real fruit juice added. Coke's lemon-lime drink, Sprite, contained no fruit juice. Slice quickly replaced Sprite as the number-two lemon-lime drink behind 7-Up in most markets.

Another flanking strategy is to find gaps that are not being filled by the industry's products, fill them, and develop them into strong segments. German and Japanese auto makers chose not to compete with American auto makers by producing large, flashy, gas-guzzling automobiles. Instead they recognized an unserved consumer segment that wanted small, fuel-efficient cars and moved to fill this hole. To their satisfaction and Detroit's surprise, the segment grew to be a large part of the market.

Encirclement Attack. An encirclement attack involves attacking from all directions, so that the competitor must protect its front, sides, and rear at the same time. The encirclement strategy makes sense when the challenger has superior resources and believes that it can break the competitor's hold on the market quickly. An example is Seiko's attack on the watch market. For several years, Seiko has been gaining distribution in every major watch outlet and overwhelming competitors with its variety of constantly changing models. In the U.S. it offers some four hundred models, but its marketing clout is backed by the 2,300 models it makes and sells worldwide.

Bypass Attack. A bypass attack is an indirect strategy. The challenger bypasses the competitor and targets easier markets. The bypass can involve diversifying into unrelated products, moving into new geographic markets, or leapfrogging into new technologies to replace existing products. Technological leapfrogging is a bypass strategy used often in high-technology industries. Instead of copying the competitor's product and mounting a costly frontal attack, the challenger patiently develops the next technology. When satisfied with its superiority, it launches an attack where it has an advantage. Thus, Minolta toppled Canon from the lead in the 35mm SLR camera market when it introduced its technologically advanced auto-focusing Maxxum camera. Canon's market share dropped toward 20 percent while Minolta's zoomed past 30 percent. It took Canon three years to introduce a matching technology.[17]

Guerrilla Attack. A guerrilla attack is another option available to market challengers, especially smaller or poorly financed ones. The challenger makes small, periodic attacks to harass and demoralize the competitor, hoping eventually to establish permanent footholds. It might use selective price cuts, executive raids, intense promotional outbursts, or assorted legal actions. Normally, guerrilla actions are taken by smaller firms against larger ones. But continuous guerrilla campaigns can be expensive, and they eventually must be followed up by a stronger attack if the challenger wishes to "beat" the competitor. Thus, guerrilla campaigns are not necessarily cheap.

Market-Follower Strategies

Not all runner-up companies will challenge the market leader. The effort to draw away the leader's customers is never taken lightly by the leader. If the challenger's lure is lower prices, improved service, or additional product features, the leader can quickly match these to diffuse the attack. The leader probably has more staying power in an all-out battle. A hard fight might leave both firms worse off, and this means the challenger must think twice before attacking. Thus, many firms prefer to follow rather than attack the leader.

A follower can gain many advantages. The market leader often bears the huge expenses involved with developing new products and markets, expanding distribution channels, and informing and educating the market. The reward for all this work and risk is normally market leadership. The market follower, on the other hand, can learn from the leader's experience and copy or improve on the leader's products and marketing programs, usually at a much lower investment.

Although the follower probably will not overtake the leader, it often can be as profitable.[18]

In some industries—such as steel, fertilizers, and chemicals—opportunities for differentiation are low, service quality is often comparable, and price sensitivity runs high. Price wars can erupt at any time. Companies in these industries avoid short-run grabs for market share because that strategy only provokes retaliation. Most firms decide against stealing each other's customers. Instead they present similar offers to buyers, usually by copying the leader. Market shares show a high stability.

This is not to say that market followers are without strategies. A market follower must know how to hold current customers and win a fair share of new ones. Each follower tries to bring distinctive advantages to its target market—location, services, financing. The follower is a major target of attack by challengers. Therefore, the market follower must keep its manufacturing costs low and its product quality and services high. It must also enter new markets as they open up. Following is not the same as being passive or a carbon copy of the leader. The follower has to define a growth path, but one that does not create competitive retaliation.

The market-follower firms fall into one of three broad types. The *cloner* closely copies leader's products, distribution, advertising, and other marketing moves. The cloner originates nothing—it simply attempts to live off the market leader's investments. The *imitator* copies some things from the leader but maintains some differentiation in terms of packaging, advertising, pricing, and other factors. The leader doesn't mind the imitator as long as the imitator does not attack aggressively. The imitator may even help the leader avoid the charges of monopoly. Finally, the *adapter* builds on the leader's products and marketing programs, often improving them. The adapter may choose to sell to different markets to avoid direct confrontation with the leader. But often the adapter grows into a future challenger, as many Japanese firms have done after adapting and improving products developed elsewhere.

Market-Nicher Strategies

Almost every industry includes firms that specialize in serving market niches. Instead of pursuing the whole market, or even large segments of the market, these firms target segments within segments, or niches. This is particularly true of smaller firms because of their limited resources. But smaller divisions of larger firms also may pursue niching strategies. EG&G provides a good example of a large company that profitably employs a niching strategy:

> EG&G is a $1.4 billion industrial equipment and components company consisting of over 175 distinct and independent business units, many with less than $10 million in sales in markets worth $25 million. Many EG&G business units have their own R&D, manufacturing, and salesforce operations. The company is currently the market or technical leader in 80 percent of its niche markets. More astonishing, EG&G ranked second in earnings per share and first in profitability in the *Fortune* 1000. EG&G illustrates how niche marketing may pay larger dividends than mass marketing.

The main point is that firms with low shares of the total market can be highly profitable through smart niching (see Marketing Highlight 20-4).

One study of highly successful midsize companies found that, in almost all cases, these companies niched within a larger market rather than going after the whole market.[19] An example is A. T. Cross, which niches in the high-price pen and pencil market. It makes the famous gold writing instruments that many executives own or want to own. By concentrating in the high-price niche, Cross has enjoyed great sales growth and profit. Of course, the study found other features shared by the successful smaller companies—offering high value, charging a premium price, and having strong corporate cultures and vision.

Why is niching profitable? The main reason is that the market nicher ends up knowing the target customer group so well that it meets their needs better than other firms that casually sell to this niche. As a result, the nicher can charge a substantial markup over costs because of the added value. Whereas the mass marketer achieves *high volume,* the nicher achieves *high margins.*

Nichers try to find one or more market niches that are safe and profitable. An ideal market niche is big enough to be profitable and has growth potential. It

MARKETING HIGHLIGHT 20-4

CONCENTRATED MARKETING: TERRY BIKES FIND A SPECIAL NICHE

Is there room for a budding new competitor alongside Schwinn and the other giants in the bicycle industry? Georgena Terry thinks so. And so do the hundreds of people now riding Terry bikes. Terry has developed a small but promising niche in the bicycle market—high-performance bikes for women.

There was nothing astonishing about the idea. Three years ago, Terry, then a 34-year-old MBA student, decided to start building bicycles. Oh, sure, she'd specialize in high-priced women's bikes, carving out a niche just as they had taught her at The Wharton Business School. But the $1.3 billion bicycle industry didn't tremble at the thought of diminutive Terry picking up a wrench. True, she might have an interesting twist: her bikes would have a shorter top tube and a slightly smaller front wheel that would provide a more comfortable ride for women cyclists who put in 40 or 50 miles at a clip—but who rides that far? Most folks just use their bikes to pedal down to the Dairy Queen or tool around the neighborhood on Sunday afternoons. Besides, if it turned out she had something, the industry could always wheel out a knockoff.

So when Terry set up shop, no one noticed. But they are noticing now. In its first year, Terry Precision Bicycles for Women, Inc., sold 20 bikes. In the second year it shipped 1,300, and in the third year it sold 2,500 more. Suddenly, her banker is more friendly, the bicycle magazines are calling to see what she thinks of this or that, and oh, yes, the folks at Schwinn Bicycle Company have suggested that she stop in whenever she's in town.

Terry has succeeded by concentrating on serving the special needs of serious women cyclists. The idea began when Terry herself became interested in biking. She found that she had trouble finding a comfortable riding position. "The standard bicycle—even a woman's bike—is designed for a man. To fit women, who have longer legs and shorter torsos, bike shops shove the seat forward and tilt the handlebars back." That didn't help the five-foot-two, 98-pound Terry. She began wondering if shortening the frame would improve things. So she picked up a blowtorch—"a friend showed me how to use it so I wouldn't kill myself"—and headed for the basement. She came back up with a bike that had a smaller frame. Friends saw it, borrowed it, and asked if she'd make frames for them. Two years later she was still turning out frames and making a living—sort of.

Finally, she got tired of just getting by and started a company. Bicycling was undergoing a mini-boom and 70 percent of all new riders were women, so she'd specialize in women's bikes. She hauled seven or eight of her bikes to a New England Area Rally in Amherst, Massachusetts. "I figured we'd do very well or very badly. Women would either go 'who cares?' or love it." She sold three bikes that weekend (at $775 each) and took orders for four more. Says Terry, "I have never been more excited in my life."

To her credit, Terry moved deliberately. Her major innovation was the frame, so she concentrated on that and didn't set out to reinvent the (bicycle) wheel. Her marketing plan was equally careful. As word spread, people would call up and ask to buy a bike. "We were thrilled, but always asked the name of their local bicycle shop. We'd then call the shop and say 'Congratulations, you've just sold a Terry bike.'" Retailers, who found

is one that the firm can serve effectively. Perhaps most importantly, the niche is of little interest to major competitors. And the firm can build the skills and customer goodwill to defend itself against an attacking major competitor as the niche grows and becomes more attractive.

The key idea in nichemanship is specialization. The firm has to specialize along market, customer, product, or marketing-mix lines. Here are several specialist roles open to a market nicher:

- *End-use specialist.* The firm specializes in serving one type of end-use customer. For example, a law firm can specialize in the criminal, civil, or business law markets.

- *Vertical-level specialist.* The firm specializes at some level of the production-distribution cycle. For example, a copper firm may concentrate on producing raw copper, copper components, or finished copper products.

- *Customer-size specialist.* The firm concentrates on selling to either small, medium, or large customers. Many nichers specialize in serving small customers who are neglected by the majors.

- *Specific-customer specialist.* The firm limits its selling to one or a few major customers. Many firms sell their entire output to a single company, such as Sears or General Motors.

Concentrated marketing: Georgena Terry has shown how a small company can succeed against larger competitors.

are often unresponsive to both customers and shop owners. Terry, who ships on time, courts retailers, and answers questions from customers, quickly became a favorite.

But even as the marketing plan got her up and pedaling, Terry was moving to forestall competition. Recognizing that her high price would scare off many customers, Terry almost immediately began to segment. She was soon selling her high-end models for $1,200 and, to preempt the foreign competition that she knew would be coming, she signed two Asian companies to build versions of her bike that retail for $450 to $850. The strategy has worked so far. Although six companies, including Fuji America, now market bicycles to women, Terry is holding her own. Competitors' bikes just aren't as good. As one customer asserts, "Women can tell the difference on a ride around the block. My feet reach the pedals more comfortably, and it is easier to reach the hand brakes. You feel more in control on one of her bikes."

Continued success is far from assured. Over time, her competitors will improve their designs. And the more successful Terry becomes, the more competition she is likely to attract. Yet, she has shown how a company with fewer resources can succeed against larger competitors by concentrating on a small, high-quality segment. At some point, as with many small nichers, Terry may have to think about selling out or joining forces with a bigger company to survive. But that is still a long way off. For now, Terry says, "This is wonderful."

themselves making a quick couple of hundred dollars, usually asked for a few more bikes. That's how Terry put together a dealer network.

With almost no money for advertising, Terry concentrated on promotion. She hired a public relations firm that was quick to position her as a female David taking on bicycling's Goliaths. The approach paid off—the bicycle press discovered Terry and gave her bikes enthusiastic endorsements. That got customers into the stores and bikes out the door. Terry's professional business approach makes her stand out from competitors in a high-end bicycling industry filled with scores of tiny manufacturers that can take months to fill orders and

Source: Adapted from Paul B. Brown, "Spokeswoman," *Career Futures,* Spring-Summer 1989, pp. 30-32.

- *Geographic specialist.* The firm sells only in a certain locality, region, or area of the world.

- *Product or feature specialist.* The firm specializes in producing a certain product, product line, or product feature. Within the laboratory equipment industry are firms that produce only microscopes, or even more narrowly, only lenses for microscopes.

- *Quality-price specialist.* The firm operates at the low or high end of the market. For example, Hewlett-Packard specializes in the high-quality, high-price end of the hand-calculator market.

- *Service specialist.* The firm offers one or more services not available from other firms. An example is a bank that takes loan requests over the phone and hand delivers the money to the customer.

Niching carries a major risk in that the market niche may dry up or be attacked. That is why many companies practice *multiple niching.* By developing two or more niches, the company increases its chances for survival. Even some large firms prefer a multiple-niche strategy to serving the total market. One large law firm has developed a national reputation in the three areas of mergers and acquisitions, bankruptcies, and prospectus development, and does little else.

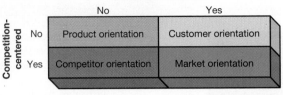

Customer-centered

	No	Yes
Competition-centered No	Product orientation	Customer orientation
Competition-centered Yes	Competitor orientation	Market orientation

FIGURE 20-6
Evolving company
orientations

BALANCING CUSTOMER AND COMPETITOR ORIENTATIONS

We have stressed the importance of a company watching its competitors closely. Whether a company is a market leader, challenger, follower, or nicher, it must find the competitive marketing strategy that positions it most effectively against its competitors. And it must continually adapt its strategies to the fast-changing competitive environment.

This question now arises: Can the company spend too much time and energy tracking competitors, damaging its customer orientation? The answer is yes! A company can become so competitor-centered that it loses its even more important customer focus. A **competitor-centered company** is one whose moves are based mainly on competitors' actions and reactions. The company spends most of its time tracking competitors' moves and market shares and trying to find strategies to counter them.

This mode of strategy planning has some pluses and minuses. On the positive side, the company develops a fighter orientation. It trains its marketers to be on a constant alert, watching for weaknesses in their own position, and watching for competitors' weaknesses. On the negative side, the company becomes too reactive. Rather than carrying out its own consistent customer-oriented strategy, it bases its moves on competitors' moves. As a result, it does not move in a planned direction toward a goal. It does not know where it will end up, since so much depends on what the competitors do.

A **customer-centered company,** in contrast, focuses more on customer developments in designing its strategies. Clearly, the customer-centered company is in a better position to identify new opportunities and set a strategy that makes long-run sense. By watching customer needs evolve, it can decide what customer groups and what emerging needs are the most important to serve, given its resources and objectives.

In practice, today's companies must be **market-centered companies,** watching both their customers and their competitors. They must not let competitor watching blind them to customer focusing. Figure 20-6 shows that companies have moved through four orientations over the years. In the first stage, they were product-oriented, paying little attention to either customers or competitors. In the second stage, they became customer-oriented and started to pay attention to customers. In the third stage, when they started to pay attention to competitors, they became competitor-oriented. Today, companies need to be market-oriented, paying balanced attention to both customer and competitors. A market orientation pays big dividends—one recent study found a substantial positive relationship between a company's marketing orientation and its profitability, a relationship that held regardless of type of business or market environment.[20]

 SUMMARY

In order to prepare an effective marketing strategy, a company must consider its competitors as well as its actual and potential customers. It must continuously analyze its competitors and develop competitive marketing strategies that effectively position it against competitors and give it the strongest possible *competitive advantage.*

Competitor analysis first involves identifying the company's major competitors, using both an industry and a market-based analysis. The company then gathers information on competitors' objectives, strategies, strengths and weaknesses, and reaction patterns. With this information in hand, it can select competitors to attack or avoid. Competitive intelligence must be collected, interpreted, and distributed continuously. Company marketing managers should be able to obtain full and reliable information about any competitor affecting their decisions.

Which *competitive marketing strategy* makes the most sense depends on the company's industry position and its objectives, opportunities, and resources. The company's competitive marketing strategy depends on whether it is a market leader, challenger, follower, or nicher.

A *market leader* faces three challenges: expanding the total market, protecting market share, and expanding market share. The market leader is interested in finding ways to expand the total market because it will benefit most from any increased sales. To *expand market size,* the leader looks for *new users* of the product, *new uses,* and *more usage.* To protect its existing market share, the *market leader* has several *defenses: position defense, flanking defense, preemptive defense, counteroffensive defense, mobile defense,* and *contraction defense.* The most sophisticated leaders cover themselves by doing everything right, leaving no openings for competitive attack. Leaders can also try to increase their market shares. This makes sense if profitability increases at higher market-share levels.

A *market challenger* is a firm that aggressively tries to expand its market share by attacking the leader, other runner-up firms, or smaller firms in the industry. The challenger can choose from a variety of *attack strategies,* including a *frontal attack, flanking attack, encirclement attack, bypass attack,* and *guerrilla attack.*

A *market follower* is a runner-up firm that chooses not to rock the boat, usually out of fear that it stands to lose more than it might gain. The follower is not without a strategy, however, and seeks to use its particular skills to gain market growth. Some followers enjoy a higher rate of return than the leaders in their industry.

A *market nicher* is a smaller firm that serves some part of the market that is not likely to attract the larger firms. Market nichers often become specialists in some end use, vertical level, customer size, specific customer, geographic area, product or product feature, or service.

A competitive orientation is important in today's markets, but companies should not overdo their focus on competitors. Companies are more likely to be hurt by emerging consumer needs and new competitors than by existing competitors. Companies that balance consumer and competitor considerations are practicing a true market orientation.

KEY TERMS

Benchmarking 581

Competitive advantage 578

Competitive strategies 578

Competitor analysis 578

Competitor-centered company 598

Customer-centered company 598

Customer value analysis 584

Industry 579

Market-centered company 598

Market challenger 588

Market follower 588

Market leader 588

Market nicher 588

Strategic group 580

DISCUSSING THE ISSUES

1. "Well-behaved" companies prefer well-behaved competition. Should it make any difference to consumers whether competition is "well-behaved" or "disruptive"? Why or why not?

2. Hewlett-Packard, a market leader in the high-priced end of the calculator market, has found itself in a squeeze between aggressively promoted portable computers and less expensive calculators with increasingly sophisticated features. What market-leader strategy would you recommend for Hewlett-Packard? Why?

3. How could Morton Salt expand the total market for table salt? Discuss the role sales promotion would play in getting new users, communicating new uses, or increasing usage of table salt.

4. Many medium-sized firms are in an unprofitable middle ground between large firms and smaller, more focused firms. Discuss how medium-sized firms could use market-nicher strategies to improve their profitability.

5. The goal of the marketing concept is to satisfy customer wants and needs. What is the goal of a competitor-centered strategy? Discuss whether the marketing concept and competitor-centered strategy are in conflict.

6. Assume you are the product manager in charge of Lysol Disinfectant or Woolite Fine Fabric Wash. Your brand has over 60 percent of the market, and no competing brand has ever succeeded. What would your strategy be for increasing your business?

APPLYING THE CONCEPTS

1. Study a new car purchasing guide, available at the library or for sale at newsstands. Examine different aspects of the cars, including features, style and image, and price. (a) Identify companies that you think are competing, based on the market point of view. (b) What sort of competitive strategies do you see being used by market leaders, followers, challengers, and nichers? (c) What different strategic groups can you identify in the automobile industry? Which groups compete with which other groups?

2. Market leaders often attempt to expand the total market, especially in slower growing, mature markets. (a) Look at the ads in several issues of women's magazines such as *Family Circle* or *Ladies Home Journal*. Find examples in which manufacturers are attempting to expand total market demand for their products. (b) Look for similar examples in your local supermarket. (c) What specific strategies are these expansion attempts trying: new users, new uses, or more usage? Rate the chances of success for each example you have found.

MAKING MARKETING DECISIONS:

SMALL WORLD COMMUNICATIONS, INC.

Thomas Campbell and Lynette Jones are working through the nuts and bolts of their marketing plans for the launch of their Airport communications link. "Tom, would you please run down the list of our potential competitors once more? I'm not seeing a lot of differences among them." "You're right, Lyn. These companies are putting out almost identical products. International standards are part of the reason. To communicate with each other, computers have to speak the same language at the same speed, so all modems are nearly the same. Modems also share technology: Everybody is using the same integrated circuit chips that come from the same manufacturers. Technically, these products are almost identical, and anybody can get into the basic modem business pretty easily. There are a couple of distinctive boards out there: both The Complete Communicator and National Semiconductor's TyIN 2000 will do data transmission, faxes, and voice mail. The TyIN also lets you make comments on your documents—it records your voice, saves that as a part of the file, and plays it back when you want. We'll do all that stuff, too, but we'll also automatically handle all the electronic mail needs." "I'm with you so far, Tom. Now run through all the top competitors once again, by name." "Well, Lyn, the best known name in modems is Hayes, and U.S. Robotics is also up there. Big companies—that are small players here, at least so far—include Intel, National Semiconductor, and AT&T, plus the computer companies that sell their own brands. Then there are loads of smaller firms, like us: Supra, Zoom Telephonics, TwinCom, Practical Peripherals, the Complete PC. One of my favorites is a market nicher, MegaHertz Corporation. They specialize in making internal fax modems for portable computers, and in 1993 they came out with a nice little PCMIA credit-card-sized modem way ahead of everyone

else. When you do that, you don't have much competition, at least for a while." Lyn thought for a minute. "Well, a company like Intel or AT&T could crush us like a bug, but I don't think they will because they haven't killed anybody else yet. Besides, we're going to buy some Intel chips, and our users will increase their AT&T long-distance bills, so we will benefit both of them. It's that glob of smaller companies that we need to figure out. We can't develop competitive strategies until we decide who our competitors are."

What Now?

1. Small World Communications is offering a new type of product in a complex market with many competitors. No other product offers as many benefits as *Airport* does, but many products perform some of the same functions. (a) Should Small World define its competitors from an industry or a market point of view? Will this make a difference in the strategies they choose? (b) Small World could behave as a market leader, a market challenger, or a market nicher. What approach do you recommend for Lyn and Tom? Why?

2. All companies must find a balance between customer and competitor orientations. Small World is faced with this choice now as they prepare marketing strategies. (a) Given what you know about the *Airport* product, what is more important: squaring off versus the competition, or targeting customer needs? Why? (b) List three examples of ways that the Airport's marketing mix might differ if Small World switched from a customer-based focus to competitor-based focus. Are there important differences?

REFERENCES

1. Chuck Hawkins, "FedEx: Europe Nearly Killed the Messenger," *Business Week*, May 25, 1992, pp. 124-26; Erik Calonius, "Federal Express's Battle Overseas," *Fortune*, December 3, 1990, pp. 137-40; Joseph Maglitta, "Being the Best in the Business," *Computer World*, February 25, 1991, pp. 61-64; Shlomo Maital, "When You Absolutely, Positively Have to Give the Better Service," *Across the Board*, March 1991, pp. 8-12; and "Pass the Parcel," *The Economist*, March 21, 1992, pp. 73-74.

2. For a good discussion of the underlying rules of competitive interaction and reaction, see Gloria P. Thomas and Gary F. Soldow, "A Rules-Based Approach to Competitive Interaction," *Journal of Marketing*, April 1988, pp. 63-74.

3. See Joseph Weber, "How J&J's Foresight Made Contact Lenses Pay," *Business Week*, May 4, 1992, p. 132.

4. See Michael E. Porter, *Competitive Advantage* (New York: The Free Press, 1985), pp. 226-27, Chap. 6.

5. Wendy Zellner, "The Airline Mess," *Business Week,* July 6, 1992, pp. 50-55.

6. For more discussion, see William L. Sammon, Mark A. Kurland, and Robert Spitalnic, *Business Competitor Intelligence* (New York: Ronald Press, 1984): Leonard M. Fuld, *Monitoring the Competition* (New York: John Wiley & Sons, 1988); Howard Schlossberg, "Competitive Intelligence Pros Seek Formal Role in Marketing," *Marketing News*, March 5, 1990, pp. 2, 28; and Michele Galen, "These Guys Aren't Spooks, They're 'Competitive Analysts,'" *Business Week*, October 14, 1991, p. 97.

7. See Michael E. Porter, *Competitive Advantage*; Pankaj Ghemawat, "Sustainable Advantage," *Harvard Business Review*, September–October 1986, pp. 53-58; Michael E. Porter, "From Competitive Advantage to Corporate Strategy," *Harvard Business Review*, May–June 1987, pp. 43-59; and George S. Day and Robin Wensley, "Assessing Competitive Advantage: A Framework for Diagnosing Competitive Superiority," *Journal of Marketing*, April 1988, pp. 1-20.

8. Michael E. Porter, *Competitive Strategy: Techniques for Analyzing Industries and Competitors* (New York: Free Press, 1980), Chap. 2.

9. See Stuart Gannes, "The Riches in Market Niches," *Fortune*, April 27, 1987, p. 228; and Tim Smart, "Will U.S. Surgical's Cutting Edge Be Enough?" *Business Week*, September 21, 1992, pp. 50-51.

10. For more discussion on defense and attack strategies, see Philip Kotler, *Marketing Management: Analysis, Planning, Implementation, and Control* (Englewood Cliffs, NJ: Prentice Hall, 1994), Chap. 14.

11. See Lois Therrien, "Mr. Rust Belt," *Business Week*, October 17, 1988, pp. 72-80.

12. See Bradley Johnson, "Wash-Day Washout," *Advertising Age*, June 3, 1991, p. 54.

13. See Robert D. Buzzell, Bradley T. Gale, and Ralph G. M. Sultan, "Market Share—the Key to Profitability," *Harvard Business Review*, January–Febuary 1975, pp. 97-106; and Ben Branch, "The Laws of the Marketplace and ROI Dynamics," *Financial Management*, Summer 1980, pp. 58-65. Others suggest that the relationship between market share and profits has been exaggerated. See Carolyn Y. Woo and Arnold C. Cooper, "Market-Share Leadership—Not Always So Good," *Harvard Business Review*, January–February 1984, pp. 2-4; and Robert Jacobson and David A. Aaker, "Is Market Share All It's Cracked Up to Be?" *Journal of Marketing*, Fall 1985, pp. 11-22.

14. See John D. C. Roach, "From Strategic Planning to Strategic Performance: Closing the Achievement Gap," *Outlook*, published by Booz, Allen & Hamilton, New York, Spring 1981, p. 21. Michael Porter makes the same point in his *Competitive Strategy* (New York: The Free Press, 1980).

15. See Michael E. Porter, "How to Attack the Industry Leader," *Fortune*, April 19, 1985, pp. 153-66.

16. See Andrew C. Brown, "Unilever Fights Back in the U.S.," *Fortune*, May 26, 1986, pp. 32-38.

17. See Otis Port, "Canon Finally Challenges Minolta's Mighty Maxxum," March 2, 1987, pp. 89-90.

18. See Daniel W. Haines, Rajan Chandran, and Arvind Parkhe, "Winning by Being First to Market . . . Or Last?" *Journal of Consumer Marketing*, Winter 1989, pp. 63-69.

19. Donald K. Clifford and Richard E. Cavanagh, *The Winning Performance: How America's High- and Midsize-Growth Companies Succeed* (New York: Bantam Books, 1985).

20. See John C. Narver and Stanley F. Slater, "The Effect of a Market Orientation on Business Profitability," *Journal of Marketing*, October 1990, pp. 20-35.

VIDEO CASE 20

MICROSOFT: FUDDING WITH IBM

A decade ago, IBM successfully entered the personal computer market. However, some decisions IBM made then may have come back to haunt it now. First, IBM concentrated on hardware and turned the development of an operating system over to Microsoft, which created MS-DOS. Second, IBM charged high prices for its PCs. The quality of its product stimulated demand, but the high price left many consumers unable to buy IBM, leaving unsatisfied demand that encouraged other manufacturers to "clone" the IBM PC. Soon, there were many "PC-type" machines in use. Although not all of these machines were IBMs, all of them needed MS-DOS.

As Microsoft sold more copies of DOS than IBM sold PCs, Microsoft grew while IBM's market share decreased.

With increasing competition in the PC marketplace, IBM was forced to cut prices, which reduced its profits. As a result, to increase both its sales and profits, IBM decided to manufacture and market its own operating system.

Back in 1985, IBM and Microsoft had agreed to jointly develop an operating system called OS/2. However, even as work on OS/2 proceeded, both companies worked independently on other competing products. IBM licensed software from Next and Metaphor Computer Systems, which gave it alternatives to Windows, a different operating system developed earlier by Microsoft. Meanwhile, Microsoft introduced an improved version of MS-DOS. Thus, even while cooperating on OS/2, the firms competed fiercely with other products.

In 1989, IBM and Microsoft split the market for operating systems. IBM endorsed Microsoft's Windows for low-powered PCs and Microsoft agreed to make writing OS/2 applications a top priority. Without compatibility between the operating system and applications software, each is relatively useless. Thus, sales of OS/2 were dependent on applications packages that work with it. IBM needed Microsoft's cooperation in order to be able to compete with it.

In 1990, the competition between IBM and Microsoft turned ugly. Microsoft unveiled Windows 3.0 and sales increased. In response, IBM took over the development of OS/2. Competition between the two giants intensified. In 1992, Microsoft launched a new version of Windows and IBM launched a new version of OS/2. In this head-on collision, Microsoft sold 3 million copies of Windows 4.0 in six weeks and IBM sold a million copies of OS/2 in four months.

Microsoft is winning the battle for two reasons. First, it has the cash to develop more products and to put more marketing muscle behind them. For example, when launching Windows 4.0, Microsoft had more applications packages, and it had 500 people waiting by telephones to answer new buyers' questions. Second, users who have invested the time and energy to learn DOS or Windows are more likely to prefer upgrades of those products than to shift to the entirely new OS/2 technology.

How well will IBM do? Some experts claim that OS/2 is a better product—that it's prettier than Windows, that it has a better graphical interface with a drag feature similar to the Apple Macintosh, and that it is larger and more powerful. It has been called the industrial strength replacement for MS-DOS. But OS/2 also presents some problems. It comes on twenty-one disks and requires six megabytes of memory; Windows comes on seven disks and requires just two megabytes of memory. Windows has two additional important advantages—it's cheaper and easier.

Thus, Microsoft seems to have everything going its way. There is, however, one small glitch. Microsoft has become a huge firm that commands as much as 80 percent of the operating system market. By being so successful, Microsoft could be in trouble with the Federal Trade Commission. Speculation that Microsoft might be an FTC break-up target raises some interesting possibilities. Without its cash muscle, how well would Microsoft do against IBM in the software market? What would happen if DOS and Windows belonged to separate companies that competed against each other as well as against IBM? Without Microsoft's ability to develop and introduce a profusion of applications packages for DOS or Windows, would those products lose enough appeal that users would shift to OS/2?

Fudding? Oh! I almost forgot. Fudding is a competitive technique that involves spreading fear, uncertainty, and doubt about rival products. Microsoft does this by pooh-poohing IBM's sales claims and by touting the superior sales of its products. Fudding may create sales for Microsoft, but it doesn't create popularity—with either the competition or the FTC.

QUESTIONS

1. What are the competitive objectives of Microsoft and IBM in terms of each firm's product lines?

2. What are the competitive positions of Microsoft and IBM operating systems products? How is each trying to expand the market?

3. In defending its market position, what defense strategy or strategies is Microsoft using?

4. What kind of attack strategy is IBM using? How successful do you think it will be?

Sources: Richard Brandt and Evan Schwartz, "IBM and Microsoft: They're Still Talking, But . . . ," *Business Week,* October 1, 1990, pp. 164-69; "Microsoft: Top of the World," *The Economist,* April 4, 1992, pp. 88-89; Laurence Hooper, "IBM Trumpets Sales Milestone for OS/2 as Skeptical Microsoft Blows Own Horn," *The Wall Street Journal,* August 13, 1992, p. 6B; and George Tibbits, "Microsoft Plays Hardball; Competitors Cry 'Foul,'" *Greensboro News and Record,* March 14, 1993, pp. E1, E5.

COMPANY CASE 20

PROCTER & GAMBLE: GOING GLOBAL— A NEW WRINKLE IN COSMETICS

Procter & Gamble, the Cincinnati-based, multinational company known for its household products, has decided to get serious about the cosmetics business. The question is, can the firm that has gotten us to Pamper-

away our babies' wetness, Crest-away our cavities, and Tide-away the grime in our clothes now use its potent marketing skills to get us to make up our faces?

Step 1: Diversifying

P&G's aggressive Chairman, Edwin L. Artzt, thinks it can. The company tiptoed into the skin-care business in 1985 when it purchased the Oil of Olay skin-care line. Under Artzt's leadership, P&G then drove headlong into the cosmetics business. In 1989, it bought Noxell Corporation and its Cover Girl and Clarion brand cosmetics lines for $1.3 billion in stock.

A Baltimore pharmacist had founded Noxell in 1917 to sell little blue jars of a sunburn remedy he later named Noxzema skin creme. In the early 1960s, Noxell launched the Cover Girl line with a foundation creme designed to conceal acne. It used famous models to advertise the product and eventually became the best-selling mass-market cosmetics brand, overtaking Maybelline in 1986. Noxell had also been successful with its 1987 launch of Clarion, a line of moderately priced, mass-market cosmetics for sensitive skin. However, to grow its new businesses, as in its expensive Clarion introduction, Noxell was having to take money from its Cover Girl and Noxzema marketing budgets. Consequently, in the late 1980s, these established brands were in danger of fading.

Artzt saw the opportunity to strengthen Noxell's marketing support with P&G's considerable resources while at the same time providing P&G with new growth opportunities outside its stable of mature products. Artzt also recognized that cosmetics carried high gross margins and resisted recessions. As of June 1990, P&G obtained 47.7 percent of its $24.08 billion in total sales from personal-care products. About one-half of these sales came from paper products, including diapers. Another 32.2 percent of its total sales came from laundry and cleaning products; 13.4 percent from food and beverages; and 6.7 percent from pulp and chemicals.

After acquiring Noxell, Artzt turned P&G's marketers loose. They quickly redesigned Cover Girl's packaging, giving it a ritzier look, but retained the brand's budget pricing strategy. P&G also speeded up new-product development. It backed these changes with a 58 percent increase in advertising, spending $47.5 million on Cover Girl in the first nine months of 1990 alone. Ads spotlighted famous models of various ages who featured a more natural look. By 1991, Cover Girl's market share had increased to 23 percent, up from 21 percent

in 1986. Meanwhile, number two Maybelline's share had fallen to 17 percent, down from 19 percent in 1986.

Step 2: Growing Bigger

P&G realized that it could not rest on its success. The cosmetics industry was changing, and P&G would have to change if it wanted to become a serious contender. Consumers were deserting department stores in droves, looking for distinct brands offered by specialty clothing chains and cosmetics boutiques, such as the Body Shop. Analysts believed that women were tired of being assaulted as they entered department stores cosmetics sections. Women wanted to buy cosmetics where they bought other items, which was increasingly in specialty shops. As a result, department store cosmetics sales were declining and mass merchandiser shares were increasing. The Cover Girl brand also faced problems. For example, the Cover Girl name suggested that the brand was designed for young, glamorous women, giving the line a built-in problem when appealing to career women, homemakers, and older women. In addition, Cover Girl generated 90 percent of its sales in the United States, whereas the rest of the industry was increasingly going global. For these reasons, Artzt went shopping again.

At the same time, New York financier Ronald Perelman had decided that he might need to sell Revlon, his beauty-products company. Perelman had purchased Revlon in 1985 for $1.83 billion, following a bitter hostile-takeover battle. However, Perelman had used junk bonds to finance this and other deals and found himself facing large debt repayments that caused a cash squeeze. As a result, Perelman considered selling some or all of Revlon's brands, including Max Factor and Almay cosmetics, Charlie and Jontou perfumes, and Flex shampoo.

Several big firms besides P&G expressed an interest in Revlon. Like P&G, these other companies wanted to expand their cosmetics businesses through acquisitions. Unilever, a Dutch multinational company, had begun buying personal-care brands in the United States in 1989. As a result of its Faberge and Elizabeth Arden acquisitions, Unilever held the number-three spot behind Estee Lauder and L'Oreal in sales at U.S. department store cosmetics counters. Unilever had worldwide personal-care sales of $4.7 billion in 1990. Gesparal, S.A., owned the majority of Cosmair's L'Oreal, which had 1989 worldwide revenues of $5.3 billion. In turn, Nestlé, the Swiss food conglomerate, owned 49 percent of Gesparal.

P&G was especially interested in Revlon's Max Factor and Betrix lines, because 80 percent of their sales were outside the United States. These two brands would fit well with P&G's other lines and give the company a good basis to compete for a bigger share of the $16 billion worldwide cosmetics and fragrance business. In April 1991, Artzt announced that P&G would pay $1.1 billion for the two Revlon lines, which together captured $800 million in sales. Artzt decided not to purchase Revlon's other major brands, which sold at higher prices in department stores.

It turned out, however, that Artzt had more in mind than simply buying lines that would give P&G an international presence. He also saw opportunities to use the new brands' distribution and marketing networks to speed Cover Girl's transition from a U.S. brand to an international brand. Max Factor and Betrix gave P&G immediate access to Europe and Japan. Before the acquisitions, P&G had no cosmetics or fragrance sales in Japan and only $28 million in Europe. After the acquisition, P&G had annual sales of $237 million in Japan and $340 million in Europe. About 75 percent of Max Factor's $600-million sales came from outside the United States, whereas all of Betrix's $200 million came from other countries. One analyst estimated that Procter & Gamble had shortened by three years the time it would have taken to go global with its U.S. brands.

Just as the Max Factor and Betrix lines helped P&G, acquisition by P&G helped the two brands immensely. Betrix, especially, had learned that it took deep pockets to compete in the international cosmetics business. It achieved about 62.5 percent of its sales in its home market, Germany, with the remainder coming from Switzerland, Spain, Italy, and Sweden. Betrix wanted to crack the French market but had not been successful against powerful L'Oreal, which dominated that market. P&G's marketing muscle would not allow it to elbow its way into the French market. Betrix's major brands were the mid-priced Ellen Betrix women's skincare products and cosmetics, and Henry M. Betrix men's toiletries. Its Eurocos Cosmetic subsidiary marketed upscale cosmetics under the Hugo Boss and Laura Biagiotti brand names.

Step 3: Reviving Max Factor in the U.S. Market

P&G felt that it could make Max Factor more competitive in the United States because it would not be under Revlon's umbrella. As it had done with Cover Girl, P&G quickly learned Max Factor's business and plotted strategies to improve its performance. P&G's managers questioned Max Factor's use of actress Jaclyn Smith as a spokesperson. They revamped Max Factor with new products and technological improvements, and they beefed-up the brand's promotion and advertising support.

Revlon, however, did not stand still after selling Max Factor to P&G. It hired a new management team for its Revlon brand, cut its manufacturing costs, and introduced a $200-million advertising barrage that featured a jazzy "Shake Your Body" message.

Both firms realized that they had to find ways to attract younger women, including teenagers, without alienating older customers. Mass-market sales, such as sales through drugstores and discounters, grew only 2 percent in 1991, compared with 6 percent in 1990. Changing consumer demographics and shopping habits seemed to account for this slowdown. Aging baby boomers had decided to invest in skin-care products and were buying fewer cosmetics like mascara, nail polish, and lipstick.

These changes meant that attracting younger women had become even more important if the cosmetics companies were to revive sales growth. One college sophomore suggested that she could understand the companies' interest in younger consumers. She felt that younger women often wanted to look older and

might even use more cosmetics than they needed. "Putting on makeup," she added, "is a big part of growing up." An industry consultant noted that "younger women are constantly changing and reapplying their nail polish, something older women don't do."

Yet, the companies faced problems in attracting younger customers. First, there were fewer younger women than baby boomers. Second, all cosmetics manufacturers were fighting for shelf space and the attention of younger buyers. One analyst noted that there were simply too many manufacturers and too many products chasing too few customers. Competition was intense. The analyst noted that even at the prestige end of the mass market, L'Oreal had dropped its emphasis on quality and had begun emphasizing having fun in order to lure more young customers. Additional competition was coming from department store product lines, specialty shops, direct marketers such as Avon, and even home shopping networks.

As a result, P&G's cosmetics sales remained flat in 1991 at $722 million; and its market share slipped slightly to 34 percent, down from 34.4 percent in 1990. Revlon's share increased to 22.5 percent, up from 20.4 percent in 1990, partly at P&G's expense. Even with the slowdown, however, P&G remained the nation's largest seller of cosmetics sold through drug and mass merchandise stores. P&G admitted that it was still learning the cosmetics business. It faced distribution problems, being slow to fill orders and slow to deliver promised new products. In addition, the company had consolidated its cosmetics salesforce. Its salespeople now sold all three lines—Cover Girl, Clarion, and Max Factor. Some distributors argued that P&G was expecting too much from a single salesperson—the product lines were simply too wide to expect one person to know much about all the products. P&G countered that the new system would reduce the number of salespeople with whom retailers had to deal.

Step 4: Going Global

Most recently, P&G has decided to overhaul the Max Factor line and launch its first simultaneous worldwide product introduction. The company introduced the new Max Factor line during the spring of 1993. The new products feature more elegant styling and more colors. P&G first produced new eyeshadows, blushes, and lipsticks. In 1994, it will introduce new foundations, face powders, and mascaras.

All of these products will be the same, no matter where in the world P&G sells them. Previously, P&G had used different products and strategies in different markets, often using local manufacturers. In Japan, for example, the Max Factor line had consisted primarily of skin-care products sold at high prices in department stores. Max Factor had accounted for 28 percent of Revlon's Japanese sales of $507 million in 1990. However, the brand had not kept up with changing Japanese lifestyles and tastes, and it was steadily losing market share. Kao Corporation and Shiseido Company were emerging as powerful competitors in the Japanese market. In Europe, P&G sold Max Factor products in chain stores and pharmacies at lower prices.

The new line would feature similar styles, colors,

and images across all international markets. Packages are a deep blue color with gold trim. The products come in a variety of colors to meet the needs of women with differing skin tones. P&G has also revised its in-store displays. To support such changes, it will increase prices to between 8 and 10 percent above previous Max Factor prices.

P&G is following the successful strategies of Estee Lauder's Clinique and Chanel, which have both been successful with standardized global marketing. Consumers around the globe recognize Clinique's blue-green packaging and Chanel's classic black compacts. P&G hopes that the standardized strategy will allow it to save money by unifying and consolidating many of its marketing efforts.

Step 5: Watching the Competition

Despite Artzt's perpetual optimism, however, P&G knows it is making a bold move. No other company has tried to develop a worldwide, mass-market cosmetics brand. The company has already learned from its experiences in the U.S. market that the cosmetics business is complicated. P&G also knows that Revlon will be right behind with its own global strategy. Revlon already receives between 30 and 35 percent of its revenue from 126 foreign countries, and P&G expects that Revlon will try to take more of its regional brands global.

P&G also knows that it must watch its home market. Noting all the attention being paid to younger women, Maybelline is now focusing on aging baby boomers. It plans to introduce a new line called Maybelline Revitalizing, which targets women 35 and older. Maybelline claims that these products will help mature women look younger, and it plans to sell the products through mass-market outlets. To stay ahead of the competitors in cosmetics, Procter & Gamble will have to find some new marketing wrinkles.

QUESTIONS

1. Who are Procter & Gamble's competitors, from an industry point of view and from a market point of view? Are there strategic groups in the industry? Why are these questions important for P&G?

2. What trends are shaping competitors' objectives in the cosmetics industry?

3. Based on information in the case, which of Michael Porter's competitive positions have the various cosmetics competitors pursued to gain competitive advantage?

4. What actions should P&G take in order to expand the total cosmetics market and to protect and expand its market share?

5. What competitive strategies would you recommend for P&G's competitors?

Sources: Randall Smith, Kathleen Deveny, and Alecia Swasy, "Sale of Revlon Beauty Line Is Considered by Perelman," *The Wall Street Journal*, March 1, 1991, p. B4; Alecia Swasy, "Cover Girl Is Growing Up and Moving Out as Its New Parent, P&G, Takes Charge," *The Wall Street Journal*, March 28, 1991, p. B1; Pat Sloan and Jennifer Lawrence, "What P&G Plans for Cosmetics," *Advertising Age*, April 15, 1991, pp. 3, 46; Zachary Schiller and Larry Light, "Procter & Gamble Is Following Its Nose," *Business Week*, April 22, 1991, p. 28; Valerie Reitman and Jeffrey A. Trachenberg, "Battle to Make Up the Younger Woman Pits Revlon Against Its New Rival, P&G," *The Wall Street Journal*, July 10, 1992; Valerie Reitman, "P&G Planning a Fresh Face for Max Factor," *The Wall Street Journal*, December 29, 1992, p. B1; Marilyn Much, "Cosmetic War Gets Ugly as Front Moves Abroad," *Investor's Business Daily*, January 14, 1993, p. 4; and Gabriella Stern, "Aging Boomers Are New Target for Maybelline," *The Wall Street Journal*, April 13, 1993, p. B1.

PART V

COMPREHENSIVE CASE

NEW BALANCE: RUNNING IN THE BUSINESS MARATHON

Making a profit is important, but it's not the most important thing. To me, what matters most is making a product you believe in.

That motto has shaped Jim Davis's approach to business since he purchased New Balance Athletic Shoe, Inc., 21 years ago on the day of the 1972 Boston Marathon. Whereas the winner of the Boston Marathon broke the tape in a little over two hours, Jim Davis's business marathon is still going. The question is whether Jim and his company will "hit the wall" and falter on business's equivalent of "heartbreak hill." Or can New Balance sprint to the finish line ahead of bigger and stronger rivals Nike and Reebok.

New Balance had been in business in Watertown, Massachusetts, since 1906 as an orthopedic-shoe maker and had begun making athletic shoes in 1962. When Davis purchased New Balance in 1972, the company employed only six people, who operated from a garage and crafted only 30 pairs of shoes a day.

Sensing that more people were becoming interested in jogging and running, Davis scraped together $100,000 to buy the company, an amount equal to the company's annual sales. His timing was superb—the running boom ignited in 1974. In 1976, *Runner's World* magazine selected one of New Balance's shoe models as the best and rated four of its models among the top ten running shoes.

With that kind of endorsement, sales exploded. Davis's major problem became getting enough products out of the factory. By 1982, sales topped $60 million. By the mid-1980s, sales reached $85 million, with good profitability.

Then New Balance "hit the wall." In marathon running, the *wall* is an imaginary point about 18 miles into the race where runners may suddenly find that, although they have been running well, they can't go any further. Even though the athletic-shoe industry continued to expand, New Balance's sales growth vanished. Davis blamed himself. "We lost our focus," he said. "We didn't execute well. And we tried to chase Nike and Reebok in terms of design, which we never should have done. The result was a lot of closeouts, a lot of selling below the recommended wholesale price.

"What always sold," he added, "were our core running products and our tennis shoes. But we never had enough of them because we had spread ourselves too thin in all the peripheral areas. We knew our brand awareness was low, but even if we'd had money to advertise, we wouldn't have spent it because of our failure to execute effectively."

In 1989, Davis's top managers urged him to stop U.S. manufacturing and to join the rush to manufacture in the Far East. They pointed out that Nike, which started the same year as New Balance, had already shot past the $1 billion mark in sales. With low labor costs and economies of scale, Nike could feed its huge advertising and marketing machine. New Balance, they argued, was struggling to break even on sales of $95 million. Moreover, managers questioned how a company paying $12 to $13 an hour, including benefits, could compete with companies using Chinese workers who made $80 a month. With lower labor costs generating higher margins, industry leaders could afford to carpet-bomb the country with advertising, enforcing their dominance.

However, despite his managers' advice, Davis held fast to his philosophy. Although New Balance did make some shoes and components overseas, Davis had always felt strongly that the advantages of domestic manufacturing outweighed the benefits of cheap labor overseas. "Initially, we manufactured here because when I bought the company, it was making shoes here," he says. "Then we realized that you can control the quality better from here. You can establish proprietary techniques to improve upon product quality. [But] we'd be a bigger, more profitable company if we made everything overseas."

However, as Davis's motto suggests, profit isn't everything. Actually, until the early 1990s, making a profit was not very difficult for most athletic shoe companies. The industry had surged with the onset of the fitness craze in the 1970s. Sales had skyrocketed in the 1980s, with annual growth rates as high as 20 percent. By 1992, footwear for running, tennis, basketball, and other sports accounted for 40 percent of all U.S. shoe sales. Throughout this rapid growth phase, there had been plenty of room for the top 25 brand name manufacturers.

Then, suddenly, the party was over. In the second half of 1991 and the first half of 1992, the U.S. athletic-footwear market contracted. Annual unit volume

dropped from 393 million pairs to 381 million. Retail sales dipped by 2.6 percent. Industry analysts blamed the recession, market saturation, and a shift in consumer tastes for the stall.

As a result, for all but the biggest names, a bare-knuckled brawl began. Nike and Reebok still dominate the industry, racking up combined 1992 sales of $3.3 billion, more than half the total market. However, the smaller players, like New Balance, who had less than a 3 percent market share, found themselves facing an uphill battle. Some analysts speculated that many smaller competitors would fade away.

Turning Things Around

To attack the industry's heartbreak hill, which like its Boston Marathon counterpart would exhaust competitors lacking sufficient resources, Davis crafted a new strategy. First, he focused on manufacturing. New Balance operated four factories, two in Massachusetts and two in Maine. The 800 workers at these plants produced 10,000 pairs of shoes a day. Davis wanted to double that number by 1994. He also wanted to cut the time from starting to cut material for a pair of shoes to putting them in the box from six weeks to two days!

To help speed up the manufacturing process, Davis scrapped New Balance's old-style piecework manufacturing system in favor of a team approach he called modular manufacturing. Everyone worked on fewer pieces that move through more quickly, instead of working on many shoes that moved more slowly. In addition to cutting inventory costs, the new process slashed new-product development time. It had been taking New Balance a year from new-product idea to delivery of a new shoe model. Davis wanted to cut the time to four months. "That's very aggressive, but it's important because when you get retailers excited about a product, they want it now, not a year from now." By involving the teams at the beginning of the process, Davis believed he could reach his four-month target.

These early steps toward revitalization helped increase New Balance's sales to $100 million in 1991 and restored the company's profitability. Davis also spent $2 million on new plant and equipment in both 1991 and 1992 and planned to spend $3 million in 1993.

The New Strategy

With the first steps taken, Davis now wants to implement a new, multistep strategy to reestablish New Balance's position, sales growth, and profitability.

Continue Width Sizing. New Balance had always made shoes comparable in quality to any competing shoe. Its competitive advantage has stemmed from its focus on width sizing. All of its shoes come in true widths; some range from AA to EEEE. Few competitors make anything beyond narrow or wide versions of selected products. For men's shoes, competitors make a D width; for women's shoes, they make a B width. When competitors offer different widths, they often simply cut the upper shoe materials tighter or looser and then glue them onto average-width soles.

Width sizing is difficult and expensive. The process complicates production because it requires shorter runs and more flexible production. It also requires workers to use multiple lasts, the molds used to build shoes. With the many widths, and with lengths that varied from sizes 6 to 16, New Balance could have more than 80 sizes for a single model. Despite these problems, width sizing provides the most customized athletic footwear available. Davis believes that good-fitting shoes will become more important to consumers as the population ages.

Maintain Production Control. Although manufacturing domestically has some drawbacks, it has one major advantage. New Balance controls its own production in its own factories, rather than depending on foreign firms to do the work. Thus, Davis eliminates the problem that some companies face of finding enough factory time to manufacture shoes when more are needed. The ability to respond to market changes affects retailers. One retailer points out that his firm bought some of its shoes from Japanese-owned ASICS Tiger Corporation. He said that there had been times when his company had been out of ASICS' shoes and could not get more for three or four months. "They can't control the factories the way New Balance does, because they don't own them," he noted.

Pursue Just-in-Time Retailing. Having his own factories fits well with Davis's emphasis on serving retail customers better. The use of teams allows New Balance to respond faster to retailer needs. Like other athletic-shoe manufacturers, New Balance wants retailers to place their orders six months in advance. This helps in production planning. With faster production speed, however, New Balance can fill orders in fewer than 30 days. The company also plans to keep its 14 best-selling models always in stock.

Davis argues that such a quick-response capability is important. A senior buyer for a 58-store, Florida-based chain supported Davis's assertion. "When you buy from Nike or Reebok, you have to order six months in advance. Without a crystal ball, it's tough to project your business that far out. With New Balance, we're able to order 30 days out, and we're getting a 90 percent [order] fill rate or better. That's fantastic. When you have 58 stores, a fill-in order can be $200,000. By having New Balance deliver as fast as on a weekly basis, we can buy to match our current needs. So we're not losing any sales, and we don't have to carry a big inventory."

Davis calls this "sharing the risk" with the retailer, a kind of partnership that is important to his growth plans. "We feel that with the better retailers around the country, we can take more business just by virtue of working more closely with them, making a better product, with better service," he says. "That means higher margins for them."

Continue Capital Improvements. By the end of 1994, Davis will have spent $6 million over a three-year period on high-tech equipment to enhance operational flexibility and speed. A new computer-aided design system would help research and development cut the time required to introduce a new model. Computerized cutting and stitching machines would increase factory productivity. These investments would help boost gross margins from the mid-30-percent range to a target of 40 percent. This target margin compares well with what New Balance's competitors get by manufacturing abroad. Nike had a 38.7 percent gross margin in 1992.

Increase Domestic Production. The capital improvements tie in with Davis's plan to make more shoes domestically. With New Balance's cost structure, it cannot price a domestically produced pair of shoes below $50 at retail. The company imports some 36 percent of its finished goods, 1.3 million pair, to provide lower-priced shoes. As domestic margins increase, Davis plans to make more shoes in the United States.

Exploit the "Buy American" Trend. Davis wants to take advantage of this trend. He plans to play up New Balance's preference for domestic production in new advertising and point-of-purchase displays. Some retailers believe that more customers are requesting American-made shoes, especially in blue-collar areas. Others suggest that consumers have learned that the fit is more consistent with American-made shoes. Shoes made in different foreign countries can each fit a little differently, causing problems for retailers and customers.

Stress Product Quality. New Balance's defect rate had risen as high as 8 percent. Alarmed, Davis has restructured the factory workers' compensation system so that 70 percent of their pay hinges on quality and 30 percent on volume. As a result, 99.9 percent of the shoes now arrive at the packing point ready for shipping. New Balance will also continue to use top-notch materials and components. A brochure on the shoes' "suspension system" touts such ingredients as a "roll bar" that resists back-and-forth foot motion; the Encap mid-sole cushioning pad, which "disperses shock"; and the contrabalance heel design, which "like an inverted trampoline, . . . adds spring to your step."

Davis knows that quality is important, but price is also becoming increasingly important. In *Consumer Reports'* May 1992 analysis of running shoes, the Saucony Jazz 3000 model placed first in both the men's and women's categories. The magazine judged the shoes "best buys" at $68 a pair. New Balance's highest rating was the eighth-ranked M997 model at $120. The M997 was beaten by shoes from Nike (at $125, retail), Avia ($70), ASICS ($85 and $55), Adidas ($85), and even another Saucony model, the Azura II ($82). New Balance fared better in the women's category, with the judges ranking the W997 model second. One analyst noted that retailers discounted 64 percent of athletic footwear last year, up from 62 percent in 1991.

Introduce New Products. For 1993, New Balance plans to introduce 30 new models in its 78-model line. The new models include an off-track, deep-treaded running shoe; a brightly hued racing spike; four basketball models; and two hiking boots. A volleyball shoe is also under development.

However, Davis seems most excited about the new American Classic line of men's dress shoes. The line will feature six styles of bucks, wing tips, and casuals. "They're as comfortable as any athletic shoe we have," Davis boasted. American Classics will compete with the Reebok-owned Rockport line, the titan of the dress-comfort class. Davis projects that the company will sell 200,000 pairs—$10 million worth—in 1993.

The new line is part of New Balance's growing line of walking shoes. In fact, New Balance offers 28 walking models versus 24 for running. Davis believes that the walking shoes will outsell his running shoes in five years. He argues that many baby boomers will be giving up running as their knees start to go. These consumers will take up exercise walking as a good alternative, and they will need appropriate shoes.

Increase Advertising. Finally, Davis realizes that he must raise brand awareness. Although consumers associate the New Balance name with quality, too few consumers know about the company and its products. A 1991 market research study revealed that only 4 percent of Americans could identify the company as an athletic-shoe maker.

Moreover, advertising has become critical in the industry. In 1993 alone, Nike will spend about $120 million on advertising and millions more in promotional payments to athletes like Michael Jordan and Bo Jackson. Reebok will counter with a $100-million ad budget, including $20 million to promote Shaquille O'Neal, the Orlando Magic rookie.

New Balance has been hard pressed to compete. These competitors spend more on *advertising* than New Balance has in *sales revenue*! A few years ago, New Balance ran ads proclaiming that it was "endorsed by no one." The company felt that quality alone would sell the shoes.

To send the message that a shoe that fits better performs better, Davis plans to spend $6 million for advertising in 1993, up from $1 million in 1990. The company will spend money on cooperative print and radio advertising in partnership with its retailers. For the first time, however, New Balance will buy time on national television, spending $700,000 for commercials on ESPN, TNT, the Sports Channel, and the Discovery Channel.

Davis will place advertisements in magazines such as *Runner's World*, *Tennis*, *Esquire*, *Travel and Leisure*, *Sierra*, and *Outside*. He will also buy pages in women's magazines such as *Self*, *Glamour*, and *Working Woman*.

Finally, the company will spend $500,000 on point-of-purchase displays and other devices to enhance brand identity.

The Finish Line

The question is, will Davis's strategy, which he calls Operation Quick Strike, work? Is the strategy strong enough to guarantee New Balance's survival as it races Nike, Reebok, and the myriad of other smaller companies toward the finish line? Can Davis double New Balance's sales to $200 million in the next three years? Can a small-share competitor really survive in the big leagues?

QUESTIONS

1. Outline New Balance's marketing strategy, including the new strategic steps it wants to take. Who is its target market? What is its marketing mix? What is its competitive strategy?

2. How does New Balance enhance the total delivered value to its customers? How does it influence customer expectations? How will New Balance's new strategy affect its value chain activities?

3. What threats and opportunities does New Balance face? What are its objectives, and what issues do those objectives raise?

4. What changes would you recommend in the company's marketing strategy?

5. How do you react to Jim Davis's quote that begins the case? Is profit the most important thing, or is it making something in which you believe?

Source: Adapted from Jay Finegan, "Surviving in the Nike/Reebok Jungle," *INC. Magazine*, May 1993, pp. 98-108. Used with permission.

LINKにふさわしい再生紙利用マークを募集します！

LINKの制作には今号から再生紙を採用しています。地球の自然環境を大切にしたい、という私たちの願いを、少しでも具体的な行為として実現できればと考えました。そんな地球にやさしいLINKにふさわしい再生紙利用のシンボルマークを読者の皆さんから募集したいと思います。アップルと皆さんを結ぶコミュニケーションマガジンの表紙にふさわしいマークを制作してください。なお、採用させていただいた方には、賞品として、Macintosh Classic　1台をプレゼントさせていただきます。

地球にやさしい
LINKであるために

応募要項	
●募集期限	1991年3月10日［日］まで
●応募作品	1人1作品、未発表のものにかぎります
●作品条件	マークのサイズは3cm×3cm以内、カラー印刷に使用できるものを求めます。作品はMacintoshのアプリケーションソフトを利用し、Paint、PICT、PICT2、TIFF、EPSフォーマットで作成されたものに限ります。
●賞　　品	1名　　Macintosh Classic　1台
●発　　表	「LINK」1991年春号誌上
●応募方法	2DDor2HD、3.5インチディスケットにデータを入れ、住所、氏名、年齢、電話番号、職業、使用したソフト（versionNo.含）を明記の上、「LINK」係まで、お送りください。

※
制作にあたって、他者が制作した写真、絵画、イラスト等を下絵として採用する場合、著作権等の問題に抵触することのないよう充分に配慮してください。主催者側はこの問題について一切責任を負いません。問題となった場合、採用を取り消す場合もあります。また応募された作品は返却いたしませんので、必ずコピーを保管するようにしてください。採用された作品の著作権並びに掲載権は、いずれもアップルコンピュータジャパン㈱に帰属します。

In the late 1970s, Apple Computer invaded Japan. The $7 billion Japanese personal computer market, second only to the huge U.S. market, offered very attractive growth opportunities. If Apple had made the right moves then, it might well have sewn up Japan before the competition could establish itself. However, more than a decade later, Apple had achieved little more than novelty sales and a tiny 1.4 percent market share. Looking back, far from making all the right moves in Japan, Apple did just about everything wrong.

Apple Japan made some classic mistakes. Its mostly American managers never really took the time to understand the Japanese market. Instead, they treated Japan largely as an extension of Apple's U.S. market. For example, repeated requests from Japanese dealers to tailor the Macintosh computer and other Apple products for Japanese use fell on deaf ears. Even though the Mac's powerful graphics capabilities made it ideal for handling Kanji, the complex Chinese characters used in written Japanese, Apple insisted on selling its American version in Japan pretty much as is. To make matters worse, the first Macs arrived in Japan with shoddy packaging and keyboards that didn't work. Apple didn't even provide a Japanese-language operating manual.

Japanese buyers were also were put off by the Mac's high prices—almost double those of comparable Japanese machines. Moreover, Apple's machines were distributed poorly and the company seldom advertised its products in Japan or displayed them at trade shows. Finally, software support for the Japanese Macs was sorely lacking. When Apple entered Japan, it quickly acquired a reputation for "Yankee arrogance" among local software houses. Rather than pay software developers to convert their packages to run on Macs, a common practice in Japan, Apple *charged* them for technical information. It also re-fused to join any Japanese trade associations or even to loan Macs to the software developers. In contrast, when NEC entered the personal computer market in the early 1980s, it did all it could to court software houses. As a result, by the late 1980s, only 15 Japanese software packages existed for the Mac compared to more than 5,000 for NEC computers, helping NEC to corner a staggering 60 percent market share.

By 1988, Apple Japan had become an embarrassment. Mac sales were paltry and Japan's hard-line America-bashers were pointing to Apple Japan as a classic example of "ugly American" incompetence. Apple finally saw the light. With new-found insight, it set out to reverse its fortunes in Japan. As a first step, Apple recruited an all-Japanese executive team—a new president from Toshiba, an engineering manager from Sony, and a support services manager from NCR Japan. The new team moved quickly to slash prices, broaden distribution, and repair its reputation with Japanese software developers, dealers, and consumers.

Apple introduced three lower-priced Macs. The least expensive of these, a machine selling for less than $1,500, would later grow to account for more than half of Apple's unit sales in Japan. The company also prepared to offer a family of Japanese-language products, including a new Japanese-character version of its highly acclaimed Postscript laser printer and KanjiTalk, a Japanese-language operating system. To strengthen distribution, Apple recruited several major blue-chip Japanese companies to sell Macs, including business equipment giant Brother Industries, stationery leader Kokuyo, Mitsubishi, Sharp, and Minolta. And it began to open Apple Centers, outlets which sell only Apple products targeted at the corporate market.

Perhaps most importantly, Apple Japan set out to patch up relations with Japanese software houses.

It joined the Japan Personal Computer Software Association (JPSA) and began to aggressively recruit software developers. It even brought in engineers from top U.S. software firms to work as partners with the Japanese firms in developing Japanese versions of proven American packages. The software houses responded. By 1992, 200 Mac-compatible software programs were available, and the number was increasing daily. Some of Japan's largest software developers now endorse and distribute Macs. And a recent JPSA survey shows that Macs are the number-two choice behind NEC among Japanese software writers as the machine they hope to buy next.

To complete the makeover and repair its tarnished image, Apple launched a full-scale promotion campaign, including heavy TV and print advertising that portrayed the Mac as a creative, easy-to-use tool. Apple also sponsored several high-profile events, such as the first Japanese Ladies Professional Golf Association tournament and a Janet Jackson concert in Tokyo. The concert drew 60,000 fans, each of whom found a bag of Apple literature on his or her chair. To further enhance its new image, Apple marketed the "Apple Collection" of T-shirts, coffee mugs, key chains, hats, and other merchandise emblazoned with the colorful Apple logo through Tokyo retailers.

Apple's overhaul produced amazing results—

Macs now are sprouting up everywhere in Japan. Apple dominates in the desktop publishing and graphics design segments and is grabbing share from Japanese competitors in several other important areas. More and more, Macs are popping into college classrooms, and into primary and secondary schools, where Apple has earned a reputation as easy to use. Japan now has become Apple's fastest-growing market. Despite a recent industrywide slump in the Japanese personal-computer market, Apple sales have doubled in each of the last three years. Its market share has grown accordingly—to nearly 6 percent—almost equaling that of IBM, the largest foreign competitor in Japan. Some analysts predict that Apple Japan's market share soon may reach 13 percent.

Its experiences in Japan have taught Apple that international marketing involves more than casually taking what's successful at home and exporting it abroad. Rather, entering a foreign market requires a strong commitment and a keen understanding of sometimes very different cultures and marketing environments. It usually means adapting the company's products, programs, and approaches to the special needs and circumstances of each new global market. For an ever-growing number of Japanese, Apple's new, more fitting approach has transformed the old "rotten Apple" to a new "Apple of their eye."[1]

 # CHAPTER PREVIEW

> *Chapter 21 surveys the global marketplace, an area which is steadily growing in importance.*
>
> Early in the chapter, we propose four key aspects to examine: the *foreign trade system,* and the *economic, political-legal,* and *cultural environments* that affect marketing decisions.
>
> We continue with a look at decisions about whether to enter foreign markets, and which markets to enter. The three basic *approaches to entry are exporting, joint venturing,* and *direct investment.*
>
> Next, we discuss the need to *adapt the marketing mix* for global markets. We conclude with a summary of three possible organization forms: the *export department, international division,* and *global organization.*

In the past, U.S. companies paid little attention to international trade. If they could pick up some extra sales through exporting, that was fine. But the big market was at home, and it teemed with opportunities. The home market was also much safer. Managers did not need to learn other languages, deal with strange and changing currencies, face political and legal uncertainties, or adapt their products to different customer needs and expectations.

Today, however, the situation is much different. The 1990s mark the first decade when companies around the world must start thinking globally. Time and distance are shrinking rapidly with the advent of faster communication, transportation, and financial flows. Products developed in one country are finding enthusiastic acceptance in other countries.

True, many companies have been carrying on international activities for decades. IBM, Kodak, Nestlé, Shell, Bayer, Toshiba, and other companies are familiar to most consumers around the world. But today global competition is intensifying. Foreign firms are expanding aggressively into new international markets, and home markets are no longer as rich in opportunity. Domestic companies that never thought about foreign competitors suddenly find these competitors in their own backyards. The firm that stays at home to play it safe not only might lose its chance to enter other markets but also risks losing its home market.

Daily headlines tell us about Japanese victories over U.S. producers in everything from consumer electronics and motorcycles, to cameras and copying machines. They talk of gains by Japanese, German, Swedish, and even Korean imports in the U.S. car market. They tell us about Bic's successful attacks on Gillette, Nestlé's gains in the coffee and candy markets, and the loss of textile, furniture, and shoe markets to Third World imports. Names such as Sony, Toyota, Nestlé, Perrier, Norelco, Mercedes, and Panasonic have become household words. Other products and services that appear to be American really are produced or owned by foreign companies: Bantam books, Baskin-Robbins ice cream, GE and RCA televisions, Firestone tires, Kiwi shoe polish, Lipton tea, Carnation milk, Pillsbury products, Motel 6, and Bloomingdale's, to name just a few. The United States also is attracting huge foreign investments in basic industries such as steel, petroleum, tires, and chemicals and in tourist and real estate ventures, illustrated by Japanese land purchases in Hawaii and California, Kuwait's resort development off the South Carolina coast, and Arab and Japanese purchases of Manhattan office buildings. Few U.S. industries are now safe from foreign competition.

Although some companies would like to stem the tide of foreign imports through protectionism, this response would be only a temporary solution. In the long run, it would raise the cost of living and protect inefficient U.S. firms. The answer is that more U.S. firms must learn how to enter foreign markets and increase their global competitiveness. Many U.S. companies have been successful at international marketing: Gillette, Colgate, IBM, Xerox, Corning, Coca-Cola, McDonald's, General Electric, Caterpillar, Du Pont, Ford, Kodak, 3M, Boeing, Motorola, and dozens of other American firms have made the world their market. But there are too few like them. In fact, just five U.S. companies account for 12 percent of all exports; 1,000 manufacturers (out of 300,000) account for 60 percent.[2]

Every government runs an export promotion program, trying to persuade its local companies to export. Denmark pays more than half the salary of marketing consultants who help small and medium-size Danish companies get into exports. Many countries go even further and subsidize their companies by granting preferential land and energy costs—they even supply cash outright so that their companies can charge lower prices than do their foreign competitors.

The longer companies delay taking steps toward internationalizing, the more they risk being shut out of growing markets in Western Europe, Eastern Europe, the Far East, and elsewhere. Domestic businesses that thought they were safe now find companies from neighboring countries invading their home markets. All companies will have to answer some basic questions: What market position should we try to establish in our country, on our continent, and globally? Who will our global competitors be and what are their strategies and resources? Where should we produce or source our products? What strategic alliances should we form with other firms around the world?

Ironically, although the need for companies to go abroad is greater today than in the past, so are the risks. Several major problems confront companies that go global. First, high debt, inflation, and unemployment in several countries have resulted in highly unstable governments and currencies, which limit trade and expose U.S firms to many risks. Second, governments are placing more regulations on foreign firms, such as requiring joint ownership with domestic partners, mandating the hiring of nationals, and limiting profits that can be taken from the country. Third, foreign governments often impose high tariffs or trade barriers in order to protect their own industries. Finally, corruption is an increasing problem—officials in several countries often award business not to the best bidder but to the highest briber.

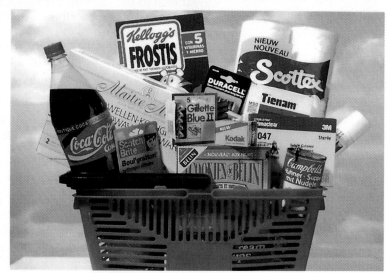

Many American companies have made the world their market.

We might conclude that companies are doomed whether they stay at home or go abroad. But companies selling in global industries have no choice but to internationalize their operations. A **global industry** is one in which the strategic positions of competitors in given geographic or national markets are affected by their overall global positions. A **global firm,** therefore, is one that, by operating in more than one country, gains research and development, production, marketing, and financial advantages in its costs and reputation that are not available to purely domestic competitors.[3] The global company sees the world as one market. It minimizes the importance of national boundaries and raises capital, sources materials and components, and manufactures and markets its goods wherever it can do the best job. For example, Ford's "world truck" sports a cab made in Europe and a chassis built in North America. It is assembled in Brazil and imported to the United States for sale. Thus, global firms gain advantages by planning, operating, and coordinating their activities on a worldwide basis.

Because firms around the world are globalizing at a rapid rate, domestic firms in global industries must act quickly before the window closes on them. This does not mean that small and medium-size firms must operate in a dozen countries to succeed. These firms can practice global nichemanship. But the world is becoming smaller, and every company operating in a global industry—whether large or small—must assess and establish its place in world markets.

As shown in Figure 21-1, a company faces six major decisions in international marketing. Each decision will be discussed in detail in this chapter.

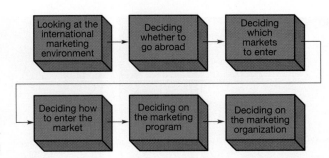

FIGURE 21-1
Major decisions in international marketing

LOOKING AT THE GLOBAL MARKETING ENVIRONMENT

Before deciding whether to sell abroad, a company must understand the international marketing environment thoroughly. That environment has changed a great deal in the last two decades, creating both new opportunities and new problems. The world economy has globalized. World trade and investment have grown rapidly, with many attractive markets opening up in Western and Eastern Europe, China, Russia, and elsewhere. There has been a growth of global brands in automobiles, food, clothing, electronics, and many other categories. The number of global companies has grown dramatically. Meanwhile, the United States' dominant position has declined. Other countries, such as Japan and Germany, have increased their economic power in world markets (see Marketing Highlight 21-1). The international financial system has become more complex and fragile, and U.S. companies face increasing trade barriers erected to protect domestic markets against outside competition.

The International Trade System

The U.S. company looking abroad must start by understanding the international *trade system.* When selling to another country, the U.S. firm faces various trade restrictions. The most common is the **tariff,** which is a tax levied by a foreign government against certain imported products. The tariff may be designed either to raise revenue or to protect domestic firms. The exporter also may face a **quota,** which sets limits on the amount of goods the importing country will accept in certain product categories. The purpose of the quota is to conserve on foreign exchange and to protect local industry and employment. An **embargo** is the strongest form of quota, which totally bans some kinds of imports.

American firms may face **exchange controls** that limit the amount of foreign exchange and the exchange rate against other currencies. The company also may face **nontariff trade barriers,** such as biases against U.S. company bids or restrictive product standards that go against American product features:

> One of the cleverest ways the Japanese have found to keep foreign manufacturers out of their domestic market is to plead "uniqueness." Japanese skin is different, the government argues, so foreign cosmetics companies must test their products in Japan before selling there. The Japanese say their stomachs are small and have room for only the *mikan,* the local tangerine, so imports of U.S. oranges are limited. Now the Japanese have come up with what may be the flakiest argument yet: Their snow is different, so ski equipment should be too.[4]

At the same time, certain forces *help* trade between nations—or at least between some nations. Certain countries have formed *free-trade zones* or **economic communities**—groups of nations organized to work toward common goals in the regulation of international trade. The most important such community is the European Community (EC), also known as the European Common Market. The EC's members are the major Western European nations, with a combined population exceeding 320 million people. The EC works to create a single European market by reducing physical, financial, and technical barriers to trade among member nations. Founded in 1957, the European Community has yet to achieve the true "common market" originally envisioned. In 1985, however, member countries re-

THE WORLD'S CHAMPION MARKETERS: THE JAPANESE

Few dispute that the Japanese have performed an economic miracle since World War II. In a very short time, they have achieved global market leadership in many industries: automobiles, motorcycles, watches, cameras, optical instruments, steel, shipbuilding, computers, and consumer electronics. They have made strong inroads into tires, chemicals, machine tools, and even designer clothes, cosmetics, and food. Some credit the global success of Japanese companies to their unique business and management practices. Others point to the help they get from Japan's government, powerful trading companies, and banks. Still others say Japan's success is based on low wage rates and unfair dumping policies.

In any case, one of the main keys to Japan's success is certainly its skillful use of marketing. The Japanese came to the United States to study marketing and went home understanding it better than many U.S. companies do. They know how to select a market, enter it in the right way, build market share, and protect that share against competitors.

Selecting Markets. The Japanese work hard to identify attractive global markets. First, they look for industries that require high skills and high labor intensity, but few natural resources. These include consumer electronics, cameras, watches, motorcycles, and pharmaceuticals. Second, they prefer markets in which consumers around the world would be willing to buy the same product designs. Finally, they look for industries in which the market leaders are weak or complacent.

Entering Markets. Japanese study teams spend several months evaluating a target market and searching for market niches that are not being satisfied. Sometimes they start with a low-priced, stripped-down version of a product, other times with a product that is as good as the competition's but priced lower, and still other times with a product that has higher quality or new features. The Japanese line up good distribution channels in order to provide quick service. They also use effective advertising to bring their products to the consumers' attention. Their basic entry strategy is to build market share rather than early profits: The Japanese often are willing to wait as long as a decade before realizing their profits.

Building Market Share. Once Japanese firms gain a market foothold, they begin to expand their market share. They pour money into product improvements and new models so that they can offer more and better products than the competition does. They spot new opportunities through market segmentation, develop mar-

kets in new countries, and work to build a network of world markets and production locations.

Protecting Market Share. Once the Japanese achieve market leadership, they become defenders rather than attackers. Their defense strategy is continuous product development and refined market segmentation. Their philosophy is to make "tiny improvements in a thousand places."

Recently, some experts have questioned whether Japanese companies can sustain their push toward global marketing dominance. They suggest that the Japanese emphasis on the long-term market share over short-term profits and its ability to market high-quality products at low prices have come at the expense of their employees, stockholders, and communities. They note that, compared to Western firms, Japanese companies work their employees longer hours for lower wages, pay their stockholders lower dividends, and contribute less to community and environmental causes. Other analysts, however, predict that Japan's marketing success will likely continue.

American firms have fought back by adding new product lines, pricing more aggressively, streamlining production, buying or making components abroad, and forming strategic partnerships with foreign companies. Many U.S. companies now operate very successfully in Japan. In fact, U.S. companies sell more than 50,000 different products in Japan, and many hold leading market shares—Coke leads in soft drinks (60 percent share), Schick in razors (71 percent), Polaroid in instant cameras (66 percent), and McDonald's in fast food. Procter & Gamble markets the leading brand in several categories, ranging from disposable diapers and liquid laundry detergents to acne treatments. Apple, Motorola, Levi Strauss, Dow, and scores of other U.S. companies have found that Japan offers large and profitable market opportunities. For example, since the early 1980s, U.S. companies have increased their Japanese computer sales by 48 percent, pharmaceutical sales by 41 percent, and electronic parts sales by 63 percent.

Sources: See Philip Kotler, Liam Fahey, and Somkid Jatusripitak, *The New Competition* (Englewood Cliffs, NJ: Prentice Hall, 1985); Vernon R. Alden, "Who Says You Can't Crack Japanese Markets?" *Harvard Business Review,* January-February 1987, pp. 52-56; Howard Schlossberg, "Japan Market Hardly Closed to U.S. Firms," *Marketing News,* July 9, 1990, pp. 1, 12; Ford S. Worthy, "Keys to Japanese Success in Asia," *Fortune,* October 7, 1991, pp. 157-60; "Why Japan Must Change," *Fortune,* March 9, 1992, pp. 66-67; and Kevin Kelly, "Besting Japan," *Business Week,* June 7, 1993, pp. 26-28.

newed their push to integrate economically (see Marketing Highlight 21-2). Since the EC's formation, other economic communities have been formed, such as the European Free Trade Association (EFTA), the Latin American Integration Association (LAIA), the Central American Common Market (CACM), and the Council for

RESHAPING THE EUROPEAN COMMUNITY

Formed in 1957, the European Community—or Common Market—set out to create a single European market by reducing trade barriers among its member nations and by developing European-wide policies on trade with nonmember nations. However, the dream of a true "common market" was buried quickly under heaps of regulations and nationalistic squabbling. Despite early common market initiatives, Europe remained a fragmented maze of isolated and protected national markets, making it a difficult and confusing place to do business. Companies selling to or operating in Europe faced a hodgepodge of trade restrictions, economic conditions, and political tensions that varied widely by country. As a result, Europe lagged behind the United States, Japan, and other Far Eastern countries in economic growth and technological innovation.

In 1985, however, the European Community countries renewed their push for a common market. They jointly enacted the Single European Act, which set December 31, 1992 as the target date for completing the European economic unification process. The act called for sweeping deregulation to eliminate barriers to the free flow of products, services, finances, and labor among member countries. Thus, "1992" came to symbolize the complete transformation of the European economy.

The European Community represents one of the world's single largest markets. It contains 340 million consumers and accounts for 20 percent of the world's exports, compared to 14 percent for the United States and 12 percent for Japan. By the year 2000, the EC could contain as many as 450 million people in 25 countries, as more European nations seek admission to the free-trade area. Thus, European economic unification promises tremendous opportunities for U.S. firms—as trade barriers drop, lower costs will result in greater operating efficiency and productivity. European markets will grow and become more accessible. As a result, most U.S. companies have drafted new strategies for cultivating the invigorated European market.

Yet, many U.S. managers have mixed reactions: Just as 1992 has created many opportunities, it also poses threats. As a result of increased unification, European companies will grow bigger and more competitive. Thus, many companies from the United States, Japan, and other non-European countries are bracing for an onslaught of new European competition, both in Western Europe and in other world markets. Perhaps an even bigger concern, however, is that lower barriers *inside* Europe will only create thicker *outside* walls. Some observers envision a "Fortress Europe" that heaps favors on firms from European Community countries but hinders outsiders by imposing obstacles such as stiffer import quotas, local content requirements, and other nontariff barriers. Companies that already operate in Europe will be shielded from such protectionist moves. Thus, companies that sell to Europe but are not now operating there are rushing to become insiders before the unification initiative threatens to close them out. They are building their own operations in Europe, acquiring existing businesses there, or forming strategic alliances with established European firms.

Mutual Economic Assistance (CMEA) in Eastern Europe. In North America, the United States and Canada phased out trade barriers in 1989, and, pending free-trade agreements with Mexico, may soon create a North American free-trade zone stretching from the Yukon to the Yucatán. A similar free-trade zone has been proposed which would include all the nations of South America.[5]

Although the recent trend toward free-trade zones has caused great excitement and new market opportunities, this trend also raises some concerns. For example, groups of countries that trade freely among themselves may tend to increase barriers to outsiders (for example, creating a "Fortress Europe"). Stricter local-content rules may add a new kind of bureaucracy and will once again limit international trade. In the United States, unions fear that the creation of a North American free-trade zone will lead to the further exodus of manufacturing jobs to Mexico where wage rates are much lower. And environmentalists worry that companies that are unwilling to play by the strict rules of the U.S. Environmental Protection Agency will relocate in Mexico where pollution regulation has been lax.

Each nation has unique features that must be understood. A nation's readiness for different products and services and its attractiveness as a market to foreign firms depend on its economic, political-legal, and cultural environments.

Economic Environment

The international marketer must study each country's economy. Two economic factors reflect the country's attractiveness as a market: the country's industrial

Renewed unification efforts have created much excitement within the European Community, but they also have drawn criticism. There is still confusion and disagreement among Europeans as to the scope and nature of the changes they want. Thus, Europe fell far short of its goal of complete unification by 1992—many doubt that the goal will ever be achieved. By mid-1992, fewer than half of the 279 provisions in the original 1992 plan had been ratified. The most difficult issues—those involving the free flow of money, people, and goods—were still unresolved. For example, in December 1991, European Community leaders approved the Maastricht Treaty, an amendment to the original EC charter, which calls for establishing a single European currency and central bank by 1999. Before the treaty can become law, however, all 12 member states must approve it by legislative vote or by referendum. So far, the treaty is off to a rocky start—in 1992 Danish voters rejected the treaty, and the French passed it by only a narrow margin. Thus, although the creation of a common currency would greatly ease trade, such a measure is unlikely to be a reality for at least another decade, if at all.

Beyond these currency issues, actions such as standardizing taxes, abolishing border checks, and forging other European-wide efforts will require changing the entire economic makeup of Europe. Individual countries will have to give up some of their independence for the common good, pushing aside the nationalism that has ruled European history for centuries. For these reasons, the odds are low that Europe ever will realize the full unification vision.

Even if the European Community does manage to standardize its general trade regulations, creating an economic community will not create a homogeneous market. With nine different languages and distinctive national customs, Europe will be anything but a "common market." Although economic and political boundaries may fall, social and cultural differences will remain. And although the unification effort may create common general standards, companies marketing in Europe still will face a daunting mass of local rules. Take advertising for example. One large advertising agency has prepared a 52-page book containing dense statistics on country-by-country restrictions. Ireland, for example, forbids ads for liquor but allows them for beer and wine—as long as they run after 7 P.M.; Spain allows ads only for drinks with less than 23 percent alcohol, and they can run only after 9:30 P.M. In Holland, ads for sweets have to show a toothbrush in the corner of the television screen. The goals of 1992 will have little effect on such local rules.

Thus, the European market will always be far more diverse than either the U.S. or Japanese markets. It is unlikely that the European Community will ever become the "United States of Europe." Nonetheless, great changes are occurring in Europe. Even if only partly successful, European unification will make a more efficient and competitive Europe a global force to be reckoned with. The best prepared companies will benefit most. Thus, whether they cheer it or fear it, all companies must prepare now for the New Europe or risk being shut out later.

Sources: John Rossant, Richard A. Melcher, and Steward Toy, "Is Europe's Express Train to Unity Slowing Down?" *Business Week,* February 3, 1992, p. 46; Cyndee Miller, "Marketers Optimistic About EC Despite Monetary Muddle," *Marketing News,* October 26, 1992, p. 2; Shawn Tully, "Europe 1992: More Unity Than You Think," *Fortune,* August 24, 1992, pp. 136-42; and Andrew Hilton, "Mythology, Markets, and the Emerging Europe," *Harvard Business Review,* November-December 1992, pp. 50-54.

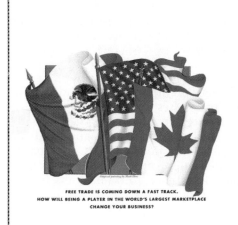

Economic communities: U.S. agreements with Canada and Mexico will create a North American free trade zone extending from the Alaskan Yukon to the Mexican Yucatan. Here, EDS offers to help companies deal with both the expanded opportunities and greater competitive threats created by this new market.

structure and its income distribution.

The country's *industrial structure* shapes its product and service needs, income levels, and employment levels. The four types of industrial structures are as follows:

- *Subsistence economies*. In a subsistence economy, the vast majority of people engage in simple agriculture. They consume most of their output and barter the rest for simple goods and services. They offer few market opportunities.

- *Raw-material-exporting economies*. These economies are rich in one or more natural resources but poor in other ways. Much of their revenue comes from exporting these resources. Examples are Chile (tin and copper); Zaire (copper, cobalt, and coffee); and Saudi Arabia (oil). These countries are good markets for large equipment, tools and supplies, and trucks. If there are many foreign residents and a wealthy upper class, they are also markets for luxury goods.

- *Industrializing economies*. In an industrializing economy, manufacturing accounts for 10 percent to 20 percent of the country's economy. Examples include Egypt, the Philippines, India, and Brazil. As manufacturing increases, the country needs more imports of raw textile materials, steel, and heavy machinery, and fewer imports of finished textiles, paper products, and automobiles. Industrialization typically creates a new rich class and a small but growing middle class, both demanding new types of imported goods.

- *Industrial economies*. Industrial economies are major exporters of manufactured goods and investment funds. They trade goods among themselves and also export them to other types of economies for raw materials and semifinished goods. The varied manufacturing activities of these industrial nations and their large middle class make them rich markets for all sorts of goods.

Income distribution: Expensive Lamborghinis sell well in small, wealthy countries like Saudi Arabia.

The second economic factor is the country's *income distribution*. The international marketer might find countries with one of five different income distribution patterns: (1) very low family incomes; (2) mostly low family incomes; (3) very low/very high family incomes; (4) low/medium/high family incomes; and (5) mostly medium family incomes. Consider the market for Lamborghinis, an automobile costing $128,000. The market would be very small in countries with the first or second income patterns. Therefore, most Lamborghinis are sold in large markets like the United States, Europe, and Japan, which have large segments of high-income consumers, or in small but wealthy countries like Saudi Arabia.

Political-Legal Environment

Nations differ greatly in their political-legal environments. At least four political-legal factors should be considered in deciding whether to do business in a given country: attitudes toward international buying, political stability, monetary regulations, and government bureaucracy.

Attitudes Toward International Buying

Some nations are quite receptive to foreign firms, and others are quite hostile. For example, Mexico has been attracting foreign businesses for many years by offering investment incentives and site-location services. In contrast, India has bothered foreign businesses with import quotas, currency restrictions, and limits on the percentage of the management team that can be nonnationals. As a result, IBM and Coca-Cola left India because of all the hassles. Pepsi, however, took positive steps to persuade the Indian government to allow it to do business in that country on reasonable terms (see Marketing Highlight 21-3).

Political Stability

Stability is another issue. Governments change hands, sometimes violently. Even without a change, a government may decide to respond to new popular feelings. The foreign company's property may be taken, its currency holdings may be blocked, or import quotas or new duties may be set. International marketers may

MARKETING HIGHLIGHT 21-3

BREAKING INTO AN UNRECEPTIVE MARKET

It's one thing to want to do business in a particular country; it's quite another to be allowed into the country on reasonable terms. The problem of entering an unreceptive or blocked country calls for *megamarketing*—using economic, psychological, political, and public relations skills to gain the cooperation of several parties in the country.

For example, Pepsi-Cola used megamarketing in its attempt to enter the huge India market. Pepsi worked with an Indian business group to seek government approval for its entry. Both domestic soft-drink companies and anti-multinational legislators objected to letting Pepsi into India, so Pepsi had to make an offer that the Indian government would find hard to refuse. Therefore, Pepsi offered to help India export enough of its agricultural products to more than offset the outlay for importing soft-drink syrup. Pepsi also promised to focus a good deal of selling effort on rural areas to help in their economic development. The company further offered to construct an agricultural research center and to give food processing, packaging, and water-treatment technology to India. After three years of haggling, the Indian bureaucracy finally approved Pepsi's extensive proposal.

Clearly, Pepsi's strategy was to bundle a set of benefits that would win the support of the various interest groups influencing the entry decision. Pepsi's marketing problem was not one of simply applying the 4Ps in a new market, but rather one of just getting into the market in the first place. In trying to win over the government and public groups—and to maintain a reasonable relationship once admitted—Pepsi had to add two more Ps: "politics" and "public opinion."

Many other large companies have learned that it pays to build good relations with host governments. Olivetti, for example, enters new markets by building housing for workers, supporting local arts and charities, and hiring and training local managers. IBM sponsors nutrition programs for Latin American children and gives agricultural advice to the Mexican government. And Polaroid is helping Italy restore Leonardo da Vinci's *Last Supper.*

Sources: See Philip Kotler, "Megamarketing," *Harvard Business Review,* March-April 1986, pp. 117-24; Sheila Tefft, "The Mouse That Roared at Pepsi," *Business Week,* September 7, 1987, p. 42; and Anthony Spaeth, "India Beckons—and Frustrates," *The Wall Street Journal,* September 22, 1989, pp. R23-25.

find it profitable to do business in an unstable country, but the unsteady situation will affect how they handle business and financial matters.

Monetary Regulations

Sellers want to take their profits in a currency of value to them. Ideally, the buyer can pay in the seller's currency or in other world currencies. Short of this, sellers might accept a blocked currency—one whose removal from the country is restricted by the buyer's government—if they can buy other goods in that country that they need themselves or can sell elsewhere for a needed currency. Besides currency limits, a changing exchange rate also creates high risks for the seller.

Most international trade involves cash transactions. Yet many nations have too little hard currency to pay for their purchases from other countries. They may want to pay with other items instead of cash, which has led to a growing practice called **countertrade,** which now accounts for about 25 percent of all world trade. Countertrade takes several forms. *Barter* involves the direct exchange of goods or services, as when the Germans built a steel plant in Indonesia in exchange for oil. Another form is *compensation* (or *buyback*), whereby the seller sells a plant, equipment, or technology to another country and agrees to take payment in the resulting products. Thus, Goodyear provided China with materials and training for a printing plant in exchange for finished labels. Another form is *counterpurchase.* Here, the seller receives full payment in cash but agrees to spend some portion of the money in the other country within a stated time period. For example, Pepsi sells its cola syrup to Russia for rubles and agrees to buy Russian vodka for sale in the United States. Countertrade deals can be very complex. For example, Daimler-Benz recently agreed to sell 30 trucks to Romania in exchange for 150 Romanian jeeps, which it then sold to Ecuador for bananas, which were in turn sold to a German supermarket chain for German currency. Through this roundabout process, Daimler-Benz finally obtained payment in German money.[6]

Government Bureaucracy

A fourth factor is the extent to which the host government runs an efficient system for helping foreign companies: efficient customs handling, good market information, and other factors that aid in doing business. A common shock to Americans is how quickly barriers to trade disappear if a suitable payment (bribe) is made to some official.

Cultural Environment

Each country has its own folkways, norms, and taboos. The seller must examine the way consumers in different countries think about and use certain products before planning a marketing program. There are often surprises. For example, the average French man uses almost twice as many cosmetics and beauty aids as does his wife. The Germans and the French eat more packaged, branded spaghetti than do Italians. Italian children like to eat chocolate bars between slices of bread as a snack. And women in Tanzania will not give their children eggs for fear of making them bald or impotent.

Business norms and behavior also vary from country to country. American business executives need to be briefed on these factors before conducting business in another country. Here are some examples of different global business behavior:

- South Americans like to sit or stand very close to each other when they talk business—in fact, almost nose-to-nose. The American business executive tends to keep backing away as the South American moves closer. Both may thus end up being offended.

- In face-to-face communications, Japanese business executives rarely say no to an American business executive. Thus, Americans tend to be frustrated and may not know where they stand. Americans come to the point quickly. Japanese business executives may find this behavior offensive.

- In France, wholesalers don't want to promote a product. They ask their retailers what they want and deliver it. If an American company builds its strategy around the French wholesaler's cooperation in promotions, it is likely to fail.

- When American executives exchange business cards, each usually gives the other's card a cursory glance and stuffs it in a pocket for later reference. In Japan, however, executives dutifully study each other's cards during a greeting, carefully noting company affiliation and rank. They hand their card to the most important person first.

Thus, each country and region has cultural traditions, preferences, and behaviors that the marketer must study.

DECIDING WHETHER TO GO ABROAD

Not all companies need to venture into foreign markets to survive. For example, many companies are local businesses that need to market well only in the local marketplace. However, companies that operate in global industries, where their strategic positions in specific markets are affected strongly by their overall global positions, must think and act globally. Thus, IBM must organize globally if it is to gain purchasing, manufacturing, financial, and marketing advantages. Firms in a global industry must compete on a worldwide basis if they are to succeed.

Any of several factors might draw a company into the international arena. Global competitors might attack the company's domestic market by offering better products or lower prices. The company might want to counterattack these competitors in their home markets to tie up their resources. Or the company might discover foreign markets that present higher profit opportunities than the domestic market does. The company's domestic market might be shrinking, or the company might need an enlarged customer base in order to achieve economies of scale. Or it might want to reduce its dependence on any one market so as to reduce its risk. Finally, the company's customers might be expanding abroad and require international servicing.

Before going abroad, the company must weigh several risks and answer many questions about its ability to operate globally. Can the company learn to understand the preferences and buyer behavior of consumers in other countries? Can it offer competitively attractive products? Will it be able to adapt to other countries' business cultures and to deal effectively with foreign nationals? Do the company's managers have the necessary international experience? Has management considered the impact of foreign regulations and political environments?

Because of the risks and difficulties of entering foreign markets, most companies do not act until some situation or event thrusts them into the international arena. Someone—a domestic exporter, a foreign importer, a foreign government—may ask the company to sell abroad. Or the company may be saddled with overcapacity and must find additional markets for its goods.

DECIDING WHICH MARKETS TO ENTER

Before going abroad, the company should try to define its international *marketing objectives and policies*. First, it should decide what *volume* of foreign sales it wants. Most companies start small when they go abroad. Some plan to stay small, seeing foreign sales as a small part of their business. Other companies have bigger plans, seeing foreign business as equal to or even more important than their domestic business.

Second, the company must choose *how many* countries it wants to market in. For example, the Bulova Watch Company decided to operate in many foreign markets and expanded into more than 100 countries. As a result, it spread itself too thin, made profits in only two countries, and lost around $40 million. Generally, it makes better sense to operate in fewer countries with deeper penetration in each.

Third, the company must decide on the *types* of countries to enter. A country's attractiveness depends on the product, geographical factors, income and population, political climate, and other factors. The seller may prefer certain country groups or parts of the world.

After listing possible international markets, the company must screen and rank each one. Consider the following example:

> Many mass marketers dream of selling to China's 1 billion people. Some think of the market less elegantly as 2 billion armpits. To PepsiCo, though, the market is mouths, and the People's Republic is especially enticing: it is the most populous country in the world, and Coca-Cola does not yet dominate it.[7]

PepsiCo's decision to enter the Chinese market seems fairly simple and straightforward: China is a huge market without established competition. In addition to selling Pepsi soft drinks, the company hopes to build many of its Pizza Hut restaurants in China. Yet we still can question whether market size *alone* is reason enough for selecting China. PepsiCo also must consider other factors: Will the

Pepsi in China—a huge but risky market.

TABLE 21-1
Indicators of Market Potential

1. Demographic characteristics

    Size of population

    Rate of population growth

    Degree of urbanization

    Population density

    Age structure and composition of the population

2. Geographic characteristics

    Physical size of a country

    Topographical characteristics

    Climate conditions

3. Economic factors

    GNP per capita

    Income distribution

    Rate of growth of GNP

    Ratio of investment to GNP

4. Technological factors

    Level of technological skill

    Existing production technology

    Existing consumption technology

    Education levels

5. Sociocultural factors

    Dominant values

    Lifestyle patterns

    Ethnic groups

    Linguistic fragmentation

6. National goals and plans

    Industry priorities

    Infrastructure investment plans

Source: Susan P. Douglas, C. Samuel Craig, and Warren Keegan, "Approaches to Assessing International Marketing Opportunities for Small and Medium-Sized Business," *Columbia Journal of World Business,* Fall 1982, pp. 26-32.

Chinese government be stable and supportive? Does China provide for the production and distribution technologies needed to produce and market Pepsi products profitably? Will Pepsi and pizza fit Chinese tastes, means, and lifestyles?

Possible global markets should be ranked on several factors, including market size, market growth, cost of doing business, competitive advantage, and risk level. The goal is to determine the potential of each market, using indicators like those shown in Table 21-1. Then the marketer must decide which markets offer the greatest long-run return on investment.

DECIDING HOW TO ENTER THE MARKET

Once a company has decided to sell in a foreign country, it must determine the best mode of entry. Its choices are *exporting, joint venturing,* and *direct investment.* Figure 21-2 shows three market entry strategies, along with the options each one offers. As the figure shows, each succeeding strategy involves more commitment and risk, but also more control and potential profits.

Exporting

The simplest way to enter a foreign market is through **exporting.** The company may passively export its surpluses from time to time, or it may make an active commitment to expand exports to a particular market. In either case, the company produces all its goods in its home country. It may or may not modify them for the export market. Exporting involves the least change in the company's product lines, organization, investments, or mission.

Companies typically start with *indirect exporting,* working through indepen-

FIGURE 21-2
Market entry strategies

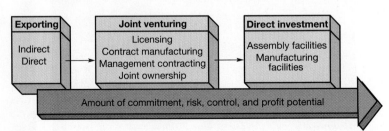

dent international marketing middlemen. Indirect exporting involves less investment because the firm does not require an overseas salesforce or set of contacts. It also involves less risk. International marketing middlemen—domestic-based export merchants or agents, cooperative organizations, and export-management companies—bring know-how and services to the relationship, so the seller normally makes fewer mistakes.

Sellers may eventually move into *direct exporting*, whereby they handle their own exports. The investment and risk are somewhat greater in this strategy, but so is the potential return. A company can conduct direct exporting in several ways. It can set up a domestic export department that carries out export activities. Or it can set up an overseas sales branch that handles sales, distribution, and perhaps promotion. The sales branch gives the seller more presence and program control in the foreign market and often serves as a display center and customer service center. Or the company can send home-based salespeople abroad at certain times in order to find business. Finally, the company can do its exporting either through foreign-based distributors who buy and own the goods or through foreign-based agents who sell the goods on behalf of the company.

Joint Venturing

A second method of entering a foreign market is **joint venturing**—joining with foreign companies to produce or market the products or services. Joint venturing differs from exporting in that the company joins with a partner to sell or market abroad. It differs from direct investment in that an association is formed with someone in the foreign country. There are four types of joint ventures: licensing, contract manufacturing, management contracting, and joint ownership.

Licensing

Licensing is a simple way for a manufacturer to enter international marketing. The company enters into an agreement with a licensee in the foreign market. For a fee or royalty, the licensee buys the right to use the company's manufacturing process, trademark, patent, trade secret, or other item of value. The company thus gains entry into the market at little risk; the licensee gains production expertise or a well-known product or name without having to start from scratch.

Coca-Cola markets internationally by licensing bottlers around the world and supplying them with the syrup needed to produce the product. In Japan, Budweiser beer flows from Suntory breweries, Lady Borden ice cream is churned out at Meiji Milk Products dairies, and Marlboro cigarettes roll off production lines at Japan Tobacco Inc. Tokyo Disneyland is owned and operated by Oriental Land Company under license from the Walt Disney Company. The 45-year license gives Disney 10 percent of admissions and 5 percent of food and merchandise sales, plus licensing fees.[8]

Licensing has potential disadvantages, however. The firm has less control over the licensee than it would over its own production facilities. Furthermore, if the licensee is very successful, the firm has given up these profits, and if and when the contract ends, it may find it has created a competitor.

Contract Manufacturing

Another option is **contract manufacturing**—the company contracts with manufacturers in the foreign market to produce its product or provide its service. Sears used this method in opening up department stores in Mexico and Spain, where it found qualified local manufacturers to produce many of the products it sells. The drawbacks of contract manufacturing are the decreased control over the manufacturing process and the loss of potential profits on manufacturing. The benefits are the chance to start faster, with less risk, and the later opportunity either to form a partnership with or to buy out the local manufacturer.

Management Contracting

Under **management contracting,** the domestic firm supplies management know-how to a foreign company that supplies the capital. The domestic firm exports management services rather than products. Hilton uses this arrangement in managing hotels around the world.

Management contracting is a low-risk method of getting into a foreign market, and it yields income from the beginning. The arrangement is even more at-

夜がきれい、君もきれい、スターライト★デート。

ゆったり、ふたりで、たっぷり5時間、東京ディズニーランドお得なスターライト券発売中

Tokyo Disneyland.

Licensing: TOKYO DISNEY-
LAND is owned and operated
by the Oriental Land Co., Ltd.
(a Japanese development
company), under license from
Walt Disney Company.

tractive if the contracting firm has an option to buy some share in the managed company later on. The arrangement is not sensible, however, if the company can put its scarce management talent to better uses or if it can make greater profits by undertaking the whole venture. Management contracting also prevents the company from setting up its own operations for a period of time.

Joint Ownership

Joint ownership ventures consist of one company joining forces with foreign investors to create a local business in which they share joint ownership and control. A company may buy an interest in a local firm, or the two parties may form a new business venture. Joint ownership may be needed for economic or political reasons. The firm may lack the financial, physical, or managerial resources to undertake the venture alone. Or a foreign government may require joint ownership as a condition for entry.

Joint ownership has certain drawbacks. The partners may disagree over investment, marketing, or other policies. Whereas many U.S. firms like to reinvest earnings for growth, local firms often like to take out these earnings. Furthermore, whereas U.S. firms emphasize the role of marketing, local investors may rely on selling.[9]

Direct Investment

The biggest involvement in a foreign market comes through **direct investment**—the development of foreign-based assembly or manufacturing facilities. If a company has gained experience in exporting, and if the foreign market is large enough, foreign production facilities offer many advantages. The firm may have lower costs in the form of cheaper labor or raw materials, foreign government investment incentives, and freight savings. The firm may improve its image in the host country because it creates jobs. Generally, a firm develops a deeper relationship with government, customers, local suppliers, and distributors, allowing it to better adapt its products to the local market. Finally, the firm keeps full control over the investment and therefore can develop manufacturing and marketing policies that serve its long-term international objectives.

The main disadvantage of direct investment is that the firm faces many risks, such as restricted or devalued currencies, falling markets, or government takeovers. In some cases, a firm has no choice but to accept these risks if it wants to operate in the host country.

DECIDING ON THE GLOBAL MARKETING PROGRAM

Companies that operate in one or more foreign markets must decide how much, if at all, to adapt their marketing mixes to local conditions. At one extreme are companies that use a **standardized marketing mix** worldwide. Proponents of global standardization claim that it results in lower production, distribution, marketing, and management costs, letting companies offer consumers higher quality and more reliable products at lower prices. This is the thinking behind Coca-Cola's decision that Coke should taste about the same around the world and General Motors' production of a "world car" that suits the needs of most consumers in most countries.

At the other extreme is an **adapted marketing mix.** In this case, the producer adjusts the marketing-mix elements to each target market, bearing more costs but hoping for a larger market share and return. Nestlé, for example, varies its product line and its advertising in different countries. Proponents argue that consumers in different countries vary greatly in their geographic, demographic, economic, and cultural characteristics, resulting in different needs and wants, spending power, product preferences, and shopping patterns. Therefore, companies should adapt their marketing strategies and programs to fit unique consumer needs in each country.

The question of whether to adapt or standardize the marketing mix has been much debated in recent years. However, global standardization is not an all-or-nothing proposition, but rather a matter of degree. Companies should look for more standardization to help keep down costs and prices and to build greater global brand power. But they must not replace long-run marketing thinking with short-run financial thinking. Although standardization saves money, marketers must make certain that they offer what consumers in each country want.[10]

Many possibilities exist between the extremes of standardization and complete adaptation. For example, Coca-Cola sells the same beverage worldwide, and in most markets it uses television spots showing 1,000 children singing the praises of Coke. For different local markets, however, it edits the commercials to include close-ups of children from those markets—at least 21 different versions of the spot are currently running.

Product

Five strategies allow for adapting product and promotion to a foreign market (see Figure 21-3).[11] We first discuss the three product strategies and then turn to the two promotion strategies.

Straight product extension means marketing a product in a foreign market without any change. Top management tells its marketing people: "Take the product as is and find customers for it." The first step, however, should be to find out whether foreign consumers use that product and what form they prefer.

Straight extension has been successful in some cases and disastrous in others. Coca-Cola, Kellogg cereals, Heineken beer, and Black & Decker tools are all sold successfully in about the same form around the world. But General Foods in-

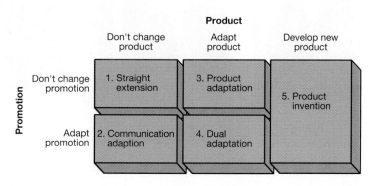

FIGURE 21-3
Five international product and promotion strategies

troduced its standard powdered Jell-O in the British market only to find that British consumers prefer a solid-wafer or cake form. Likewise, Philips began to make a profit in Japan only after it reduced the size of its coffee makers to fit into smaller Japanese kitchens and its shavers to fit smaller Japanese hands. Straight extension is tempting because it involves no additional product-development costs, manufacturing changes, or new promotion. But it can be costly in the long run if products fail to satisfy foreign consumers.

Product adaptation involves changing the product to meet local conditions or wants. For example, McDonald's serves beer in Germany and coconut, mango, and tropic mint shakes in Hong Kong. General Foods blends different coffees for the British (who drink their coffee with milk), the French (who drink their coffee black), and Latin Americans (who prefer a chicory taste). In Japan, Mister Donut serves coffee in smaller and lighter cups that better fit the fingers of the average Japanese consumer; even the doughnuts are a little smaller. In Brazil, Levi's developed its Femina jeans featuring curvaceous cuts that provide the ultratight fit traditionally favored by Brazilian women. Campbell serves up soups that match unique tastes of consumers in different countries. For example, it sells duck-gizzard soup in the Guangdong Province of China; in Poland, it features flaki, a peppery tripe soup. And IBM adapts its worldwide product line to meet local needs. For example, IBM must make dozens of different keyboards—20 for Europe alone—to match different languages.[12]

Product invention consists of creating something new for the foreign market. This strategy can take two forms. It might mean reintroducing earlier product forms that happen to be well adapted to the needs of a given country. For example, the National Cash Register Company reintroduced its crank-operated cash register at half the price of a modern cash register and sold large numbers in the Orient, Latin America, and Spain. Or a company might create a new product to meet a need in another country. For example, an enormous need exists for low-cost, high-protein foods in less developed countries. Companies such as Quaker Oats, Swift, and Monsanto are researching the nutrition needs of these countries, creating new foods, and developing advertising campaigns to gain product trial and acceptance. Product invention can be costly, but the payoffs are worthwhile.

Promotion

Companies either can adopt the same promotion strategy they used in the home market or can change it for each local market.

Standardized advertising messages: Cross Pens uses the same promotion approach in many different countries.

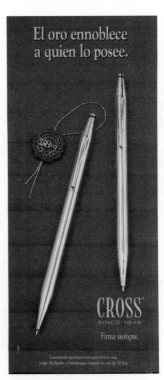

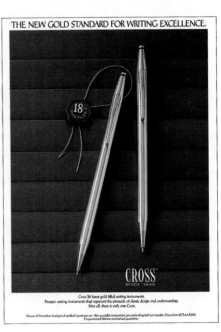

WATCH YOUR LANGUAGE!

Many U.S. multinationals have had difficulty crossing the language barrier, with results ranging from mild embarrassment to outright failure. Seemingly innocuous brand names and advertising phrases can take on unintended or hidden meanings when translated into other languages. Careless translations can make a marketer look downright foolish to foreign consumers. We've all run across examples when buying products from foreign countries—here's one from a firm in Taiwan attempting to instruct children on how to install a ramp on a garage for toy cars:

> Before you play with, please fix the waiting plate by yourself as per below diagram. But after you once fixed it, you can play with as is and no necessary to fix off again.

Many U.S. firms are guilty of similar atrocities when marketing abroad.

The classic language blunders involve standardized brand names that do not translate well. When Coca-Cola first marketed Coke in China in the 1920s, it developed a group of Chinese characters that, when pronounced, sounded like the product name. Unfortunately, the characters actually translated to mean "bite the wax tadpole." Today, the characters on Chinese Coke bottles translate as "happiness in the mouth."

Several car makers have had similar problems when their brand names crashed into the language barrier. Chevy's Nova translated into Spanish as *no va*—"It doesn't go." GM changed the name to Caribe and sales increased. Ford introduced its Fiera truck only to discover that the name means "ugly old woman" in Spanish. And it introduced its Comet car in Mexico as the Caliente—slang for "streetwalker." Rolls-Royce avoided

the name Silver Mist in German markets, where "mist" means "manure." Sunbeam, however, entered the German market with its Mist-Stick hair curling iron. As should have been expected, the Germans had little use for a "manure wand."

One well-intentioned firm sold its shampoo in Brazil under the name Evitol. It soon realized it was claiming to sell a "dandruff contraceptive." An American company reportedly had trouble marketing Pet milk in French-speaking areas. It seems that the word "pet" in French means, among other things, "to break wind."

Advertising themes often lose—or gain—something in the translation. The Coors beer slogan "get loose with Coors" in Spanish came out as "get the runs with Coors." Coca-Cola's "Coke adds life" theme in Japanese translated into "Coke brings your ancestors back from the dead."

Such classic boo-boos are soon discovered and corrected, and they may result in little more than embarrassment for the marketer. But countless other more subtle blunders may go undetected and damage product performance in less obvious ways. The multinational company must carefully screen its brand names and advertising messages to guard against those that might damage sales, make it look silly, or offend consumers in specific international markets.

Sources: Some of these and many other examples of language blunders are found in David A. Ricks, "Products that Crashed into the Language Barrier," *Business and Society Review*, Spring 1983, pp. 46-50. Also see Marty Westerman, "Death of the Frito Bandito," *American Demographics*, March 1989, pp. 28-32; and David W. Helin, "When Slogans Go Wrong," *American Demographics*, February 1992, p. 14.

Consider the message. Some global companies use a standardized advertising theme around the world. Exxon used "Put a tiger in your tank," which gained international recognition. Of course, the copy may be varied in minor ways to adjust for language differences. In Japan, for instance, where consumers have trouble pronouncing "snap, crackle, pop," the little Rice Crispies critters say "patchy, pitchy, putchy." Colors also are changed sometimes to avoid taboos in other countries. Purple is associated with death in most of Latin America; white is a mourning color in Japan; and green is associated with jungle sickness in Malaysia. Even names must be changed. In Sweden, Helene Curtis changed the name of its Every Night Shampoo to Every Day because Swedes usually wash their hair in the morning. Kellogg also had to rename Bran Buds cereal in Sweden, where the name roughly translates as "burned farmer." (See Marketing Highlight 21-4 for more on language blunders in international marketing.)

Other companies fully adapt their advertising messages to local markets. The Schwinn Bicycle Company might use a pleasure theme in the United States and a safety theme in Scandinavia. Kellogg ads in the United States promote the taste and nutrition of Kellogg's cereals versus competitors' brands. In France, where consumers drink little milk and eat little for breakfast, Kellogg's ads must convince consumers that cereals are a tasty and healthful breakfast.

Media also need to be adapted internationally because media availability varies from country to country. TV advertising time is very limited in Europe, for instance, ranging from four hours a day in France to none in Scandinavian countries. Advertisers must buy time months in advance, and they have little control over airtimes. Magazines also vary in effectiveness. For example, magazines are a major medium in Italy and a minor one in Austria. Newspapers are national in the United Kingdom but are only local in Spain.

Price

Companies also face many problems in setting their international prices. For example, how might Black & Decker price its power tools globally? It could set a uniform price all around the world, but this amount would be too high a price in poor countries and not high enough in rich ones. It could charge what consumers in each country would bear, but this strategy ignores differences in the actual costs from country to country. Finally, the company could use a standard markup of its costs everywhere, but this approach might price Black & Decker out of the market in some countries where costs are high.

Regardless of how companies go about pricing their products, their foreign prices probably will be higher than their domestic prices. A Gucci handbag may sell for $60 in Italy and $240 in the United States. Why? Gucci faces a *price escalation* problem. It must add the cost of transportation, tariffs, importer margin, wholesaler margin, and retailer margin to its factory price. Depending on these added costs, the product may have to sell for two to five times as much in another country to make the same profit. For example, a pair of Levi's jeans that sells for $30 in the United States typically fetches $63 in Tokyo and $88 in Paris. A Chrysler automobile priced at $10,000 in the United States sells for more than $47,000 in South Korea.[13]

Another problem involves setting a price for goods that a company ships to its foreign subsidiaries. If the company charges a foreign subsidiary too much, it may end up paying higher tariff duties even while paying lower income taxes in that country. If the company charges its subsidiary too little, it can be charged with *dumping.* Dumping occurs when a company either charges less than its costs or less than it charges in its home market. Thus, Harley-Davidson accused Honda and Kawasaki of dumping motorcycles on the U.S. market. The U.S. International Trade Commission agreed and responded with a special five-year tariff on Japanese heavy motorcycles, starting at 45 percent in 1983 and gradually dropping to 10 percent by 1988.[14] The commission also ruled recently that Japan was dumping computer memory chips in the United States and laid stiff duties on future imports. Various governments are always watching for dumping abuses and often force companies to set the price charged by other competitors for the same or similar products.

Last but not least, many global companies face a *grey market* problem. For example, Minolta sold its cameras to Hong Kong distributors for less than it charged German distributors because of lower transportation costs and tariffs. Minolta cameras ended up selling at retail for $174 in Hong Kong and $270 in Germany. Some Hong Kong wholesalers noticed this price difference and shipped Minolta cameras to German dealers for less than the dealers were paying their German distributor. The German distributor couldn't sell its stock and complained to Minolta. Thus, a company often finds some enterprising distributors buying more than they can sell in their own country, then shipping goods to another country to take advantage of price differences. International companies try to prevent grey markets by raising their prices to lower cost distributors, dropping those who cheat, or altering the product for different countries.

Distribution Channels

The international company must take a **whole-channel view** of the problem of distributing products to final consumers. Figure 21-4 shows the three major links between the seller and the final buyer. The first link, the *seller's headquarters organization,* supervises the channels and is part of the channel itself. The second link, *channels between nations,* moves the products to the borders of the foreign nations. The third link, *channels within nations,* moves the products from their foreign entry point to the final consumers. Some U.S. manufacturers may think their job

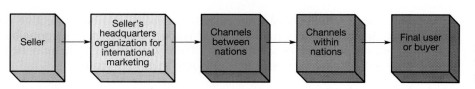

FIGURE 21-4
Whole-channel concept for international marketing

is done once the product leaves their hands, but they would do well to pay more attention to its handling within foreign countries.

Channels of distribution within countries vary greatly from nation to nation. First, there are the large differences in the *numbers and types of middlemen* serving each foreign market. For example, a U.S. company marketing in China must operate through a frustrating maze of state-controlled wholesalers and retailers. Chinese distributors often carry competitors' products and frequently refuse to share even basic sales and marketing information with their suppliers. Hustling for sales is an alien concept to Chinese distributors, who are used to selling all they can obtain. Working with or getting around this system sometimes requires substantial time and investment. When Coke and Pepsi first entered China, for example, customers bicycled up to bottling plants to get their soft drinks. Now, both companies have set up direct-distribution channels, investing heavily in trucks and refrigeration units for retailers.[15]

Another difference lies in the *size and character of retail units* abroad. Whereas large-scale retail chains dominate the U.S. scene, most foreign retailing is done by many small independent retailers. In India, millions of retailers operate tiny shops or sell in open markets. Their markups are high, but the actual price is lowered through price haggling. Supermarkets could offer lower prices, but supermarkets are difficult to build and open because of many economic and cultural barriers. Incomes are low, and people prefer to shop daily for small amounts rather than weekly for large amounts. They also lack storage and refrigeration to keep food for several days. Packaging is not well developed because it would add too much to the cost. These factors have kept large-scale retailing from spreading rapidly in developing countries.

DECIDING ON THE GLOBAL MARKETING ORGANIZATION

Companies manage their international marketing activities in at least three different ways. Most companies first organize an *export department,* then create an *international division,* and finally become a *global organization.*

Export Department

A firm normally gets into international marketing by simply shipping out its goods. If its international sales expand, the company organizes an export department with a sales manager and a few assistants. As sales increase, the export department then can expand to include various marketing services so that it can actively go after business. If the firm moves into joint ventures or direct investment, the export department no longer will be adequate.

International Division

Many companies get involved in several international markets and ventures. A company may export to one country, license to another, have a joint ownership venture in a third, and own a subsidiary in a fourth. Sooner or later it will create an international division or subsidiary to handle all its international activity.

International divisions are organized in a variety of ways. The international division's corporate staff consists of marketing, manufacturing, research, finance, planning, and personnel specialists. They plan for and provide services to various operating units. Operating units may be organized in one of three ways. They may be *geographical organizations,* with country managers who are responsible for salespeople, sales branches, distributors, and licensees in their respective countries. Or the operating units may be *world product groups,* each responsible for worldwide sales of different product groups. Finally, operating units may be *international subsidiaries,* each responsible for its own sales and profits.

Global Organization

Several firms have passed beyond the international division stage and have become truly global organizations. They stop thinking of themselves as national marketers who sell abroad and start thinking of themselves as global marketers. The top corporate management and staff plan worldwide manufacturing facilities, marketing policies, financial flows, and logistical systems. The global operating units report directly to the chief executive or executive committee of the organization, not to the head of an international division. Executives are trained in worldwide operations, not just domestic *or* international. The company recruits management from many countries, buys components and supplies where they cost the least, and invests where the expected returns are greatest.

Major companies must become more global in the 1990s if they hope to compete. As foreign companies successfully invade the domestic market, U.S. companies must move more aggressively into foreign markets. They will have to change from companies that treat their foreign operations as secondary to companies that view the entire world as a single borderless market.[16]

 ## SUMMARY

Companies today can no longer afford to pay attention only to their domestic market, no matter how large it is. Many industries are global industries, and those firms that operate globally achieve lower costs and higher brand awareness. At the same time, *global marketing* is risky because of variable exchange rates, unstable governments, protectionist tariffs and trade barriers, and several other factors. Given the potential gains and risks of international marketing, companies need a systematic way to make their international marketing decisions.

As a first step, a company must understand the *international marketing environment,* especially the international trade system. It must assess each foreign market's *economic, political-legal,* and *cultural characteristics.* Second, the company must decide whether it wants to go abroad and consider the potential risks and benefits. Third, the company must decide the volume of foreign sales it wants, how

many countries it wants to market in, and which specific markets it wants to enter. This decision calls for weighing the probable rate of return on investment against the level of risk. Fourth, the company must decide how to enter each chosen market—whether through *exporting, joint venturing,* or *direct investment.* Many companies start as exporters, move to joint ventures, and finally make a direct investment in foreign markets. Companies must next decide how much their products, promotion, price, and channels should be adapted for each foreign market. Finally, the company must develop an effective organization for international marketing. Most firms start with an *export department* and graduate to an *international division.* A few become *global organizations,* with worldwide marketing planned and managed by the top officers of the company. Global organizations view the entire world as a single borderless market.

 ## KEY TERMS

Adapted marketing mix 625

Contract manufacturing 624

Countertrade 619

Direct investment 624

Economic community 614

Embargo 614

Exchange controls 614

Exporting 622

Global firm 613

Global industry 613

Joint ownership 624

Joint venturing 623

Licensing 623

Management contracting 624

Nontariff trade barriers 614

Product adaptation 626

Product invention 626

Quota 614

Standardized marketing mix 625

Straight product extension 625

Tariff 614

Whole-channel view 628

DISCUSSING THE ISSUES

1. With all the problems facing companies that "go global," why are so many companies choosing to expand internationally? What are the advantages of expanding beyond the domestic market?

2. When exporting goods to a foreign country, a marketer may be faced with various trade restrictions. Discuss the effects these restrictions might have on an exporter's marketing mix: (a) tariffs; (b) quotas; and (c) embargoes.

3. The first Honda automobile exported here was described by a U.S. car magazine as "a shopping cart with a motor"; the first Subaru exported to the United States was voted "Worst New Car of the Year." Both companies have become highly successful over the years, however. Discuss the Japanese strategy of long-term commitment to international business objectives. Would the Japanese have left India, as IBM and Coca-Cola did, because of "hassles"?

4. Imported products are usually more expensive, but not always: A Nikon camera is cheaper in New York than in Tokyo. Why are foreign prices sometimes higher and sometimes lower than domestic prices for exports?

5. "Dumping" leads to price savings to the consumer. Why do governments make dumping illegal? What are the *disadvantages* to the consumer of dumping by foreign firms?

6. Which type of international marketing organization would you suggest for the following companies? (a) Cannondale Bicycles, selling three models in the Far East; (b) a small U.S. manufacturer of toys, marketing its products in Europe; and (c) Dodge, planning to sell its full line of cars and trucks in Kuwait.

APPLYING THE CONCEPTS

1. Go to a large electronics and appliance store that sells products such as televisions, stereos, and microwaves. Pick one or two product categories to examine. (a) Make a list of brand names in the category, and classify each name as being either "American" or "foreign." How did you decide whether a brand was American or foreign? (b) Look at where these different brands were manufactured. Are any of the "American" brands manufactured abroad, and are any of the "foreign" brands made in the United States? What does this tell you about how much international marketing is being done? Is *global* a better term to describe some of these brands?

2. Entertainment, including movies, television programs, and music recordings, is America's second largest export category—only aircraft is larger. (a) Go to your college library and find several foreign magazines. Locate pictures, stories, or ads featuring American entertainers. Study what you find. Look at the size and layout of the stories, and see if you can understand basically what is being said. Does American entertainment seem to be interesting or important to people abroad? What, if anything, do you think is appealing to them? (b) India has the largest movie industry in the world, yet few Indian films are ever shown in the United States. Why do you think this is so? Suggest some ways than Indian movie companies might make a bigger impact in America.

MAKING MARKETING DECISIONS:

SMALL WORLD COMMUNICATIONS, INC.

Tom Campbell and Lyn Jones were musing about the possibilities of selling the *Airport* product abroad. "I suspect, Tom, that we might find fewer competitors abroad. With Silicon Valley still being the world's computer capital, I'm betting that we have some real advantages in the overseas market." "Lyn," said Thomas, "there are probably some very interesting possibilities for us. Ireland, for example, has geared up to become a major player in telecommunications services. There are several American software firms that use Irish technicians—on the phone, from Dublin—to answer customer support calls. Any place that sophisticated

has a need for our *Airport*. I like the idea of selling to eastern Europe and giving them some of the technology they need to build real working economies."

Lynette smiled. "Ever since the Berlin Wall fell, I've wanted to help the process of change along over there. I just didn't know how, and this might be one small way to do it. There are some real issues to deal with, however. Those countries don't have much hard currency—and Small World Communications doesn't have much either. We're just not in a position to trade our product for pig iron, and then have to find a market for stuff we know nothing about."

Tom said, "You're right on all counts. But I don't want to blow this off too easily. If we sell abroad, we can increase our profitability by spreading our development costs across more sales. And don't forget that America is a mature economy, and someday the computer market here may slow down. If we can develop a reputation in some growing economies, it gives us a good leg up on the future. I'll check with our esteemed Senator to see if there is any federal help for small companies who want to sell abroad."

WHAT NOW?

1. Small World Communications would like to begin selling the *Airport* internationally, soon after it is established in the United States. (a) Which do you think are the biggest is-

sues Small World might face: cultural, political-legal, or economic? (b) Consider some of the technical issues Small World might face: different electricity voltages, telephones ranging from the very primitive to totally cellular systems better the United States, non-Western alphabets like the Russian Cyrillic and the Japanese Kanji, and many more. Suggest a way Small World might assess the technical environment as part of its international expansion strategy.

2. As Small World looks at international opportunities, they must decide whether to go abroad, and where, and also how to enter. (a) How should Small World enter the international market: joint venture, export, or direct investment? Why? (b) What sort of international marketing organization would you recommend for Lyn and Tom?

REFERENCES

1. Stephen K. Yoder, "Apple, Loser in Japan Computer Market, Tries to Recoup by Redesigning Its Models," *The Wall Street Journal,* June 21, 1985; Neil Gross, "Is It Finally Time for Apple to Blossom in Japan?" *Business Week,* May 28, 1990, pp. 100-101; Andrew Tanzer, "How Apple Stormed Japan," *Forbes,* May 27, 1991, pp. 40-41; and Neil Gross, "Apple? Japan Can't Say No," *Business Week,* June 29, 1992, pp. 32-34.

2. See Edward C. Baig, "50 Leading U.S. Exporters," *Fortune,* July 18, 1988, pp. 70-71. Also see William J. Holstein, "The Stateless Corporation," *Business Week,* May 14, 1990, pp. 98-105; and Therese Eiben, "U.S. Exporters Keep on Rolling," *Fortune,* June 14, 1993, pp. 130-31.

3. For a good discussion of the differences between *international, multinational,* and *global* marketing, see Warren J. Keegan, *Global Marketing Management,* 4th ed. (Englewood Cliffs, NJ: Prentice Hall, 1989), pp. 6-11.

4. "The Unique Japanese," Fortune, November 24, 1986, p. 8. For more on nontariff and other barriers, see Rahul Jacob, "Export Barriers the U.S. Hates Most," *Fortune,* February 27, 1989, pp. 88-89; Carla Rapoport, "The Big Split," *Business Week, Fortune,* May 6, 1991, pp. 38-48; and Mark Maremont, "Protectionism Is King of the Road," *Business Week,* May 13, 1991, pp. 57-58.

5. For more reading on free-trade zones, see Cyndee Miller, "Nationalism Endangers Smooth Transition to Unified EC Market," *Marketing News,* February 17, 1992, pp. 1, 10; Blayne Cutler, "North American Demographics," *American Demographics,* March 1992, pp. 38-42; Paul Magnusson, "Building Free Trade Bloc by Bloc," *Business Week,* May 25, 1992, pp. 26-27; Paul Magnusson, "Free Trade? They Can Hardly Wait," *Business Week,* September 14, 1992, pp. 24-25; and Andrew Hilton, "Mythology, Markets, and the Emerging Europe," *Harvard Business Review,* November-December 1992, pp. 50-54; and Geri Smith, "Moment of Truth for Mexico," *Business Week,* June 28, 1993, pp. 44-45.

6. For further reading, see Leo G. B. Welt, *Trade Without Money: Barter and Countertrade* (New York: Harcourt Brace Jovanovich, 1984); Demos Vardiabasis, "Countertrade: New Ways of Doing Business," *Business to Business,* December 1985, pp. 67-71; Louis Kraar, "How to Sell to Cashless Buyers," *Fortune,* November 7, 1988, pp. 147-54; "Pepsi to Get Ships, Vodka in $3 Billion Deal," *Durham Morning Herald,* May 10, 1990, p. B5; and Cyndee Miller, "Worldwide Money Crunch Fuels More Inter

national Barter," *Marketing News,* March 2, 1992, p. 5.

7. Louis Kraar, "Pepsi's Pitch to Quench Chinese Thirsts," *Fortune,* March 17, 1986, p. 58. Also see Maria Shao, "Laying the Foundation for the Great Mall of China," *Business Week,* January 25, 1988, pp. 68-69; and Alan Farnham, "Ready to Ride Out China's Turmoil," Fortune, July 3, 1989, pp. 117-18; and Pete Engardio, "China Fever Strikes Again," *Business Week,* March 29, 1993, pp. 46-47.

8. Robert Neff, "In Japan, They're Goofy about Disney," *Business Week,* March 12, 1990, p. 64.

9. For more on joint ventures, see Kenichi Ohmae, "The Global Logic of Strategic Alliances," *Harvard Business Review,* March-April 1989, pp. 143-54; and Louis Kraar, "Your Rivals Can Be Your Allies," *Fortune,* March 27, 1989, pp. 66-76.

10. See George S. Yip, "Global Strategy . . . In a World of Nations?" *Sloan Management Review,* Fall 1989, pp. 29-41; Kamran Kashani, "Beware the Pitfalls of Global Marketing," *Harvard Business Review,* September-October 1989, pp. 91-98; and Saeed Saminee and Kendall Roth, "The Influence of Global Marketing Standardization on Performance," *Journal of Marketing,* April 1992, pp. 1-17.

11. See Keegan, *Global Marketing Management,* pp. 378-81. Also see Peter G. P. Walters and Brian Toyne, "Product Modification and Standardization in International Markets: Strategic Options and Facilitating Policies," *Columbia Journal of World Business,* Winter 1989, pp. 37-44.

12. For these and other examples, see Andrew Kupfer, "How to Be a Global Manager," *Fortune,* March 14, 1988, pp. 52-58; and Maria Shao, "For Levi's: A Flattering Fit Overseas," *Business Week,* November 5, 1990, 76-77.

13. Dori Jones Yang, "Can Asia's Four Tigers Be Tamed?" *Business Week,* February 15, 1988, p. 47; and Shao, "For Levi's: A Flattering Fit," p. 78.

14. See Michael Oneal, "Harley-Davidson: Ready to Hit the Road Again," *Business Week,* July 21, 1986, p. 70.

15. See Shao, "Laying the Foundation for the Great Mall of China," p. 69.

16. See Kenichi Ohmae, "Managing in a Borderless World," *Harvard Business Review,* May-June 1989, pp. 152-61; and William J. Holstein, "The Stateless Corporation," *Business Week,* May 14, 1990, pp. 98-105.

VIDEO CASE 21

MTV: IS GLOBAL ROCK GETTING A GLOBAL RAP?

When Sumner Redstone's National Amusements paid $3.2 billion to buy 83 percent of Viacom International's public shares in 1987, MTV was considered a fading asset. But today, MTV accounts for $411 million of Viacom's $1.7 billion in revenues and is growing at 20 percent annually. What produced MTV's phenomenal growth? Growth in foreign markets. In only four years, MTV expanded to more than 32 million homes in Europe, 24 million in Latin America, and millions more in Asia.

Strangely, the international growth of MTV is fostered by the desire of marketers such as Coca-Cola, PepsiCo, IBM, Anheuser-Busch, and MCI to conduct global marketing campaigns that reach huge audiences with one ad placed through a single global media buy. Dealing with MTV is much easier than attempting to purchase equivalent time spots on a patchwork of television networks throughout the world. MTV also is a more efficient media buy, and it offers a greater opportunity to target programs to different market segments.

Today, each MTV channel can be split into three channels, which means that a local MTV channel can become three channels: one channel playing Euro-techno-pop for one young family member's benefit, another playing heavy metal for another young family member, and still another playing British rockers over 40 (Clapton, Stewart, Captain Fantastic) for mom or dad—and they all see the same Coca-Cola ad.

Although international growth offers substantial revenue and profit potential, it also poses problems. Foremost among these is the lack of physical cable equipment, even in well-developed countries such as France. Also, it is difficult to include local advertising on these cable systems. In parts of Asia, Latin America, and Japan, independent operators pirate the signal or produce copycat channels of their own. In India, unregulated cable operators have slashed their rivals' lines, sabotaged satellites, and ratted to the police. In Japan, MTV has suffered from such poor air times (2 A.M. to 5 A.M.) and has been victimized by so many knockoffs, such as "Sony Music TV" and "Space Shower," that it is saying sayonara to Japan altogether.

MTV faces another problem in going international—achieving a balance between local music tastes and international music videos. For example, the Japanese prefer local artists, whereas most of MTV's programming is dominated by British and American rock and rap groups performing in English. To attract audiences with strong local tastes, MTV created shows such as "MTV Internacional," an hour-long Spanish-language program broadcast in Latin America and some of the United States. It features post-hippie folk rockers from Santo Domingo, miniskirted flamenco-rock girl groups from Seville, guitar-slingers from Buenos Aires, and Chicano rappers from East Los Angeles. When local performers are not available, MTV hires local personalities as program hosts. For example, MTV Australia uses New Zealand pop star Richard Wilkins as a video jockey.

Another problem is negative reactions to MTV's image and its advertising. Indians believe that showing ads for many western products on MTV will encourage ordinary Indians to want a standard of living that their economic system cannot deliver. In Mexico, the president's wife was scandalized by MTV and feared that it would lead to promiscuity, or even to the formation of Satanic cults. On the lighter side, Brazilians are not pleased that MTV has taught their young people to wear baseball caps backwards.

Another issue with MTV is the homogeneity it produces among youths. Although MTV could spread a truly universal language (English) and communication medium, it unfortunately promotes artificial performer types and superficial messages of the I-can't-find-no-love variety. Performers tend to be pretty (Maria Carey) and sexy (Madonna). Does the world really want millions of Asian, Latin American, and European leather-jacketed youths sporting Jon Bon Jovi's latest hair style, pirouetting Hammer-style down the street, and yelling Yo? Are the hundreds of millions of dollars of advertising worth this?

QUESTIONS

1. What economic and political-legal factors might affect the introduction of MTV?

2. What might be the best form for MTV to use in entering new international markets—licensing or joint ownership?

3. Discuss how and why companies might use both standardized and adapted marketing campaigns on MTV.

4. Would MTV use different product strategies (extension or adaptation) in England, Sweden, Russia, and Korea?

5. For the trivia prize, who is Captain Fantastic?

Sources: Steve Coll, "MTV Age Dawning in India," *The Washington Post,* March 5, 1992, p. A31; Simon Reynolds et al., "How MTV Plays Around the World," *The New York Times,* July 7, 1991, Sec. 2, p. 22; and Matthew Schifrin, "I Can't Even Remember the Old Star's Name," *Forbes,* March 16, 1992, pp. 44-45.

COMPANY CASE 21

HARDEE'S: MARKETING IN SOUTH KOREA

Downtown Seoul

"There should be more fast-food restaurants," exclaimed Moon Yong, a 21-year-old college student, as she downed another French fry and sipped a Coke with a friend at the Hardee's in Seoul, one of only two Hardee's in all of South Korea. Moon Yong and her female friends like fast-food restaurants, especially American ones. Korean kids find it fashionable to hang out in fast-food restaurants. "We'll stay here all afternoon," Moon Yong proclaimed.

In fact, American fast-food companies that have ventured into Korea target young people. Fast-food restaurants are especially appealing to young girls, who make up 70 percent of all customers. The girls like French fries and beverages, and they sit in the restaurants for hours. As a result, South Korean fast-food restaurants are bigger than their American counterparts—about 300 seats versus about 150 seats for U.S. restaurants.

Furthermore, despite the sometimes strong anti-American sentiment in Korea, Korean young people are drawn to the slice of Americana that the restaurants represent. Young Lee, president of Del Taco Korea Co., points out that "they like American and European music. So they want their food the same way. It is in this area that America is the leader, not electric parts or TVs." As a result, Mr. Lee and other fast-food executives in Korea make only a few subtle changes in the American menus to account for local tastes. In other countries, firms often make substantial changes.

Doing Business in South Korea

South Korea may seem to be the promised land for American fast-food chains. Faced with a saturated and highly competitive U.S. market, one would think that the chains would be flocking to South Korea. However, McDonald's has only four stores in the country—one store for every 10.8 million Koreans as compared to 51 stores in Hong Kong (one per 112,000 residents). Similarly, Wendy's has only 13 outlets in South Korea, and Burger King has only 12.

Why have U.S. fast-food restaurants been so slow to enter South Korea? In late 1991, *The Wall Street Journal* published a ranking of 129 countries based on the risk of doing business in each. The rankings combined each country's rankings on the basis of political risk, financial risk, and economic risk into an overall composite risk score. South Korea fell into the low-risk category with a composite score of 73.5 out of a possible 100. It ranked twenty-seventh on the list, just behind Portugal and ahead of Botswana. The low-risk category, which covered scores from 70 to 84.5, also included the United States, which ranked ninth with a composite score of 83.5. South Korea's political risk score was 63 out of 100,

and it had scores of 47 out of a possible 50 on financial risk and 36.5 out of 50 on economic risk.

Even though South Korea's overall score suggested a low level of risk, analysts point out that it is a tough market. Land prices are especially high. A high-traffic site in Seoul, the capital city, can cost $7 million to buy or require a $1 million deposit to rent. The *land* for a factory may cost more than the factory. Raw material costs are the highest in Asia. Manufacturing wages have gone up an average of 18 percent per year since 1986. Governmental restrictions, such as high tariffs and limits on certain imports, such as cheese and beef, frustrate fast-food chains. Gaining governmental approval for investment takes time and can be very difficult.

Companies also find it difficult to bring additional capital funds into the country. Korean firms, fearing new competitions, resist entry and investment by foreign firms. Goodyear invested substantial effort and funds to obtain governmental approval for a tire factory, only to abandon the plant when Korean tire producers resisted stiffly and threatened to delay local approvals. Foreign firms also suspect that the Korean government doesn't really want foreign investment, especially if it will adversely affect domestic producers.

All of these factors have resulted in a low level of foreign investment in South Korea. The Korea Development Institute, a government-funded think tank, indicates that the ratio of foreign investment to gross national product is 14.6 to 1 in Singapore and 1.61 to 1 in Taiwan but only 0.36 to 1 in South Korea.

Enter Hardee's

If entering the market in South Korea is so tough, why do Hardee's, McDonald's, and other firms even bother to try? For one thing, these firms see the flip side of rapidly rising Korean wage rates—disposable income is rising equally quickly. Korean disposable income has grown 141 percent since 1986, making Korea the largest consumer market in Asia after Japan. The average urban household in South Korea has an annual income of $12,400. Ten percent of the population have college degrees, and the number of two-income families is on the rise. These factors create demand for convenience foods and higher-quality products. Overall, however, the Korean consumer market lags behind that of other Asian countries having about the same level of economic development. For example, Korea lacks modern convenience stores and large supermarkets that offer wide variety to consumers.

Still, Hardee's believes it has found a way around all of these stumbling blocks. Hardee's selected Kim Chang-Hwan, a wealthy local businessman, as its Korean franchisee. Mr. Kim's older brother manages a chain of retail shoe stores that has many outlets near

student hangouts. The Kims are converting several of the shoe stores into Hardee's restaurants. In an "in-your-face" move, the Korean franchise opened its first Hardee's in downtown Seoul just a few yards down the street from a popular McDonald's. Mr. King Nam-Young, the franchisee's general manager, admits that Hardee's executives were concerned about the strategy, but so far his store's sales have equaled McDonald's.

McDonald's entered the country in 1986 by forming a 50-50 joint venture with a Korean accountant and entrepreneur, Mr. Ahn Hyo Young, and had planned to open 14 stores by the early 1990s. However, the first store hadn't opened until 1988 and expansion has been very slow, resulting in part from the illness and death of Mr. Ahn. McDonald's indicates that it is now uncertain about where to find a new local partner. McDonald's employees also claim that the local franchise did not have enough capital when it started and that McDonald's had balked at the high cost of real estate. However, McDonald's now seems to have adjusted to land costs and has plans to open 30 restaurants by the end of 1993.

Coors and Purina Try Their Hands

Coors Brewing Company has announced that it too is moving into the South Korean market. Although it is not unusual for American brewers to do business in foreign markets, they have typically expanded through contract brewing, licensing agreements, or direct exports. However, Coors announced that it will enter into a joint venture with Jinro Ltd., a Korean distiller, to build its first offshore brewery. Thus, it will become the first U.S. brewer to own part of a foreign-based brewery. The new $200 million brewery will produce 1.8 million barrels annually, a little less than one-tenth of Coors' total capacity. The joint venture hopes to gain a 5 percent to 6 percent share of the Korean market by 1994.

Analysts suggest that U.S. brewers are showing more interest in foreign markets because of the slow growth in the U.S. market. Coors' foreign move suggests that a new, more aggressive phase has started. American exports in 1990 totaled 4.2 million barrels as compared with 2.4 million barrels in 1982. Although this total is small compared to the huge annual U.S. market of 200

million barrels, a Coors' spokesperson notes that to gain more business in the United States, you have to take it from someone else. In Korea, he notes, the beer market is growing 15 percent a year, and a company has a chance to earn some of that growth itself.

American brewers are well positioned to expand. One industry executive states, "There is a movement toward lightness in all beverages [around the world] and American beers have always been very light compared to European beers." Pacific rim countries like Japan, Taiwan, and Hong Kong are particularly appealing because of their rapid growth rates in beer consumption. Eastern Europe is also attractive but the rest of Europe has proven to be more difficult for U.S. brewers to crack. In addition to the well-established European beers, there are many tiny breweries with loyal customers. European laws limiting distribution and banning advertising in some countries also make it difficult to attack established brands.

Prior to the Korean agreement, Coors had only licensed its beer in Canada and Japan and exported it to three other countries. Coors is entering South Korea despite Miller Brewing's recent departure. Miller pulled out of Korea because of high tariffs and the rising value of Korea's currency, the yuan. Coors believes that its agreement with the joint-venture partner will help to overcome these problems and make it more competitive in Korea. Under the joint venture, Coors will not have to ship its beers from the United States, and it can be directly involved in making, distributing, and promoting the beers.

Still, Coors won't have an easy time of it, even if its agreement works. The Korean government has licensed only two other brewers, Oriental Brewery and Chosun Brewery. These two national breweries produce several Korean beers and market Carlsberg beer under license. Also, Oriental is licensed to sell one of Coors' toughest competitors—Budweiser.

Like Coors, Ralston Purina has also decided to go against conventional wisdom. It has constructed a $10 million plant in Korea to produce breakfast cereal. But unlike Coors and the fast-food companies, Purina has some advantages. First, it will enter a market containing no strong local producer. Second, Purina is not a newcomer to the Korean market—it has been operating in Korea for 25 years. Purina began in Korea by producing feed for cows, hogs, poultry, and fish and later moved into cat and dog food. The new plant will make Chex cereals. Franz Strobl, Purina's regional vice-president for consumer-business development, comments that "Our strategy was to go from an agriculture base into food. . . . It makes sense to manufacture locally for local market needs."

Purina has paid careful attention to the Korean market's development. It has found that the consumption of breakfast cereal closely follows the consumption of milk throughout the world. When it noted rising income levels and milk consumption in Korea, it decided that the time was right to dive into cereals. Purina had observed a similar trend in Japan, then watched the cereal market there grow 50 percent per year. The Korean breakfast cereal market is already growing at 20 percent per year.

Making It Easier

Despite the efforts of the fast-food companies, Coors, and Purina, the Korean government is still concerned about the low level of foreign investment. As a result, the government is slowly changing the rules. It now grants automatic approval for projects valued at less than $20 million, up from the previous $5 million limit. Moreover, foreign companies can now establish wholly-owned subsidiaries. The government may also make it easier for foreign companies to bring in additional capital, and it is granting tax breaks to high-tech electronics companies and may offer cheap land to high-tech companies that locate in Korean industrial parks.

However, the government has been slow to offer similar benefits to processed food or packaged-goods companies, and it has been reluctant to allow foreigners to build modern warehouses and distribution networks—facilities needed by consumer-product companies. Furthermore, the government often holds up products at customs and sponsors anticonsumption campaigns to turn public opinion against imported goods.

As a result of the positive changes and despite the problems, more foreign companies are establishing import offices and sales and distribution channels in Korea. Some businesspeople believe that if a company can find its way through the maze of Korean political, economic, and cultural barriers, it can reap substantial rewards. For example, S.C. Johnson & Son, which recently spent $5 million to increase production at its Korean plant, has built its air fragrance business from $500,000 in 1989 to $9 million this year. Johnson's Korean unit had total sales of $30 million last year. The unit's president, Ravi K. Saligram, points to an additional benefit of local manufacturing: "It is a sign of commitment that you are here for the long haul."

Back in Downtown Seoul

Meanwhile, Moon Yong and her friend have finished their Cokes and fries at Hardee's and decide to walk down the street to the McDonald's to see what's happening there. They throw away their trash, wave to some friends, and leave the restaurant. The Hardee's manager watches them leave and wonders whether the fascination for things American will continue or whether Korean political, economic, and cultural forces will blunt efforts to open the Korean market. What can he do to keep Moon Young and others like her coming back to Hardee's?

QUESTIONS

1. Based on information in the case, what kinds of trade restrictions does Hardee's face in working in Korea's trade system?

2. What aspects of Korea's economic, political-legal, and cultural environments are important for Hardee's to understand?

3. Why have Hardee's and the other companies in the case decided to enter foreign markets and why have they selected Korea? Do you agree with their decisions?

4. What methods might Hardee's have used to enter the Korean market, and why did it select the method it used?

5. What decisions has Hardee's made about its marketing program in Korea? What recommendations would you make about this program?

Sources: Adapted from: Damon Darlin, "South Koreans Crave American Fast Food," *The Wall Street Journal,* February 22, 1991, p. B1; Marj Charlier, "U.S. Brewers' Foreign Growth Proves Tricky," *The Wall Street Journal,* September 9, 1991, p. B1; Monua Janah, "Rating Risk in the Hot Countries," *The Wall Street Journal,* September 20, 1991, p. R4; Darlin, "U.S. Firms Take Chances in South Korea," *The Wall Street Journal,* June 15, 1992, p. B1. Used with permission.

M*arketing Services, Organizations, Persons, Places, and Ideas*

22

The Walt Disney Company is a master service marketer. Its "product" is entertainment, and no company provides more of it. In fact, in recent years, Disney's movie studios (including Touchstone) led all other studios in box-office receipts. But nowhere is the "Disney Magic" more apparent than at the company's premier theme park, Disney World. More than 25 million people flock to Disney World each year—ten times more than the number who visit Yellowstone National Park—making it the world's number one tourist attraction. What brings so many people to Disney World? Part of the answer lies in its many attractions. Disney World is a true fantasyland—28,000 acres brimming with attractions such as Space Mountain, Journey into Imagination, Pirates of the Caribbean, and Typhoon Lagoon. But these attractions provide only part of the story. In fact, what visitors like even more, they say, is the park's sparkling cleanliness and the friendliness of Disney World employees. In an increasingly rude, dirty, and mismanaged world, Disney offers warmth and order. As one observer notes, "In the Magic Kingdom, America still works the way it is supposed to. Everything is clean and safe, quality and service still matter, and the customer is always right."

Thus, the real "Disney Magic" lies in the company's obsessive dedication to serving its customers. The company sets high standards of service excellence and takes extreme care to make every aspect of every customer's visit memorable. According to Michael Eisner, Disney's Chairman, "We are in the business of exceeding people's very high expectations." Disney works hard at getting every employee, from the executive in the corner office to the person stamping hands at the gate, to embrace its customer-centered company culture. And it appears to be succeeding splendidly. Even as the Disney World waiting lines get longer, the satisfaction rate, as measured by surveys of consumers as they leave the park, gets higher and higher. Sixty percent of all Disney World visitors are repeaters.

How does Disney do it? How does it inspire such high levels of customer service? Beyond the four *P*s of marketing, Disney has mastered *internal marketing*—motivating its employees to work as a team to provide top-quality service—and *interactive marketing*—teaching employees how to interact with customers to deliver satisfaction. On their first day, all new employees report for a three-day motivational course at Disney University in Orlando, where they learn how to do the hard work of helping other people have fun. They learn that they are in the entertainment business—that they are "cast members" whose job it is to be enthusiastic, knowledgeable, and professional in serving Disney's "guests." Each cast member plays a vital role in the Disney World "show," whether it's as a "security host" (police), "transportation host" (driver), "custodial host" (street cleaner), or "food and beverage host" (restaurant worker).

Before they can receive their theme costumes and go "on stage," cast members must learn how to deal effectively with guests. In courses titled Traditions I and Traditions II, they learn the Disney language, history, and culture. They are taught to be enthusiastic, helpful, and *always* friendly. They learn to do good deeds, such as volunteering to take pictures of guests so that the whole family can be in the picture. They are taught never to say "It's not my job." When a guest asks a question—whether it's, "Where's the nearest restroom?" or, "What are the names of Snow White's seven dwarves?"—they need to know the answer. If they see a piece of trash on the ground, they pick it up. So that cast members will blend in and promote the whole show, not individuals, Disney enforces a strict grooming code: Men cannot sport mustaches, beards, or long hair; women cannot have long, brightly-colored fingernails, large hair decorations, heavy eye makeup, or dangling earrings. Disney is so confident that its cast members will charm guests that it finds ways to force contact. For example, many items in the park's gift shops bear no price tags, requiring shoppers to ask the price.

Disney keeps it managers close to both employees and customers. At least once in his or her career, every Disney World manager must spend a day prancing around the park in an 80- to 100-pound character costume. And all managers spend a week each year in "cross-utilization," leaving the desk and heading for the front line—taking tickets, selling popcorn, or loading and unloading rides. The company works to keep employees at all levels motivated and feeling like an important part of the team. All managers and employees wear name badges and address each other on a first-name basis, regardless of rank. Employees receive a Disney newspaper called *Eyes and Ears*, which features news of activities, employment opportunities, special benefits, and educational offerings. A recreational area, consisting of a lake, recreation hall, picnic area, boating and fishing facilities, and a large library, is set aside for the em-

ployees' exclusive use. All exiting employees answer a questionnaire on how they felt about working for Disney. In this way, Disney measures its success in producing employee satisfaction. Thus, employees are made to feel important and personally responsible for the "show." Their sense of "owning the organization" spills over to the millions of visitors with whom they come in contact. Employee satisfaction ultimately leads to customer satisfaction.

Disney has become so highly regarded for its ability to inspire employees to meet its exacting service standards that many leading U.S. corporations—from General Electric and AT&T to General Motors and American Airlines—send managers to Disney University to find out how Disney does it. And Disney's dedication to outstanding service marketing has paid off handsomely. During the past seven years, Disney's annual revenues have more than tripled—to $4.7 billion. The company has had a *sevenfold* increase in profits. Revenues have grown at an average annual rate of 23 percent, and net income at 50 percent. Thus, Disney has found that by providing outstanding service to its *customers,* it also serves itself.[1]

CHAPTER PREVIEW

Chapter 22 discusses marketing of a less tangible sort: the marketing of services, organizations, persons, places, and ideas.

We start with a discussion of marketing **services,** and the aspects that set them apart: **intangibility, inseparability, variability,** and **perishability**. We also look at **strategies** for marketing services, including **differentiation, service quality,** and **productivity**.

We next review **organization marketing,** including **image assessment** and **image planning and control**. We continue with a look at **person** and **place marketing,** and conclude with a look at social **marketing** and the marketing of **ideas**.

Marketing developed initially for selling physical products, such as toothpaste, cars, steel, and equipment. But this traditional focus may cause people to overlook the many other types of things that are marketed. In this chapter, we look at the special marketing requirements for *services, organizations, persons, places,* and *ideas.*

SERVICES MARKETING

One of the major trends in the United States in recent years has been the dramatic growth of services. Whereas service jobs accounted for 55 percent of all U.S. jobs in 1970, by 1990, they accounted for 75 percent of total employment. Services are expected to provide 90 percent of all new jobs in the next ten years.[2] Service jobs include not only those in service industries—hotels, airlines, banks, and others—but also service jobs in product-based industries, such as corporate lawyers, med-

The convenience industry: Services that save you time— for a price.

ical staff, and sales trainers. As a result of rising affluence, more leisure time, and the growing complexity of products that require servicing, the United States has become the world's first service economy. This, in turn, has led to a growing interest in the special problems of marketing services.

Service industries vary greatly. The *government sector* offers services through courts, employment services, hospitals, loan agencies, military services, police and fire departments, postal service, regulatory agencies, and schools. The *private nonprofit* sector offers services through museums, charities, churches, colleges, foundations, and hospitals. A large part of the *business sector* offers services through airlines, banks, hotels, insurance companies, consulting firms, medical and law practices, entertainment companies, real estate firms, advertising and research agencies, and retailers.

Not only are there traditional service industries, but also new types keep popping up all the time:

> Want someone to fetch a meal from a local restaurant? In Austin, Texas, you can call EatOutIn. Plants need to be watered? In New York, you can call the Busy Body's Helper. Too busy to wrap and mail your packages? Stop by any one of the 72 outlets of Tender Sender, headquartered in Portland, Oregon. "We'll find it, we'll do it, we'll wait for it," chirps Lois Barnett, the founder of Personalized Services in Chicago. She and her crew of six will walk the dog, shuttle the kids to Little League, or wait in line for your theater tickets. Meet the convenience peddlers. They want to save you time. For a price, they'll do just about anything that's legal.[3]

Some service businesses are very large, with total sales and assets in the trillions of dollars. Table 22-1 shows the five largest service companies in each of eight service categories. There are also tens of thousands of smaller service providers. Selling services presents some special problems calling for special marketing solutions.[4]

Nature and Characteristics of a Service

A **service** is any activity or benefit that one party can offer to another that is essentially intangible and does not result in the ownership of anything. Its production may or may not be tied to a physical product. Activities such as renting a hotel room, depositing money in a bank, traveling on an airplane, visiting a psychiatrist, getting a haircut, having a car repaired, watching a professional sport, seeing a movie, having clothes cleaned at a dry cleaner, getting advice from a lawyer all involve buying a service.

A company must consider four service characteristics when designing marketing programs: *intangibility, inseparability, variability,* and *perishability.* We will look at each of these characteristics in the following sections.[5]

Intangibility
Service intangibility means that services cannot be seen, tasted, felt, heard, or smelled before they are bought. People undergoing cosmetic surgery cannot see the result before the purchase, for example, and airline passengers have nothing but a ticket and the promise of safe delivery to their destinations.

To reduce uncertainty, buyers look for signs of service quality. They draw conclusions about quality from the place, people, equipment, communication material, and price that they can see. Therefore, the service provider's task is to make the service tangible in one or more ways. Whereas product marketers try to add intangibles to their tangible offers, service marketers try to add tangibles to their intangible offers.[6]

Consider a bank that wants to convey the idea that its service is quick and efficient. It must make this positioning strategy tangible in every aspect of customer contact. The bank's physical setting must suggest quick and efficient service: Its exterior and interior should have clean lines; internal traffic flow should be planned carefully; waiting lines should seem short; and background music should be light and upbeat. The bank's staff should be busy and properly dressed. The equipment—computers, copy machines, desks—should look modern. The bank's ads and other communications should suggest efficiency, with clean and simple designs and carefully chosen words and photos that communicate the bank's positioning. The bank should choose a name and symbol for its service

TABLE 22-1
The Largest U.S. Service Companies

Diversified Services

AT&T

Cargill

Enron

Fleming Companies

Time Warner

Diversified Financial

Federal National Mortgage Association

American Express

Salomon

Aetna Life and Casualty

Merrill Lynch

Life Insurance

Prudential

Metropolitan Life

Teachers Insurance and Annuity

Aetna Life

Equitable Insurance and Annuity

Transportation

United Parcel Service

AMR

UAL

Delta Airlines

CSX

Commercial Banking

Citicorp

Chemical Bank

BankAmerica

NationsBank

J. P. Morgan

Savings Institutions

H. F. Ahmanson

Great Western Financial

Golden West Financial

Glenfed

Calfed

Retailing

Sears*

Wal-Mart Stores

Kmart

Kroger

American Stores

Utilities

GTE

BellSouth

Bell Atlantic

US West

NYNEX

---

* Includes retailing and nonretailing units—Sears is now the number-three retailer behind Wal-Mart and Kmart.

Source: "The Service 500," *Fortune,* June 1, 1992, pp. 174-92.

---

that suggest speed and efficiency. Its pricing for various services should be kept simple and clear.

Inseparability

Physical goods are produced, then stored, later sold, and still later consumed. In contrast, services are first sold, then produced and consumed at the same time. **Service inseparability** means that services cannot be separated from their providers, whether the providers are people or machines. If a person provides the service, then the person is a part of the service. Because the client is also present as the service is produced, *provider-client interaction* is a special feature of services marketing. Both the provider and the client affect the service outcome.

In the case of entertainment and professional services, buyers care a great deal about *who* provides the service. It is not the same service at a Kenny Rogers concert if Rogers gets sick and is replaced by Billy Joel. A legal defense supplied by John Nobody differs from one supplied by F. Lee Bailey. When clients have strong provider preferences, price is used to ration the limited supply of the preferred provider's time. Thus, F. Lee Bailey charges more than do less well-known lawyers.

Because services are inseparable from their providers, limited service provider time often constrains the amount of a service that can be offered. Several strategies exist for getting around the problem of service provider time limitations. First, the service provider can learn to work with larger groups. Some psychotherapists, for example, have moved from one-on-one therapy to small-group therapy to groups of more than 300 people in large hotel ballrooms. Second, the service provider can learn to work faster—the psychotherapist can spend 30 minutes with each patient instead of 50 minutes and thus see more patients. Finally, the service organization can train more service providers, as H&R Block has done with its national network of trained tax consultants.

Variability

Service variability means that the quality of services depends on who provides them as well as when, where, and how they are provided. For example, some hotels have reputations for providing better service than others. Within a given hotel, one registration-desk employee may be cheerful and efficient, whereas another standing just a few feet away may be unpleasant and slow. Even the quality of a single employee's service varies according to his or her energy and frame of mind at the time of each customer contact.

Service firms can take several steps toward quality control.[7] They can select and train their personnel carefully. Airlines, banks, and hotels spend large sums of money on training their employees to give good service. Consumers should find the same friendly and helpful personnel in every Marriott Hotel. Service firms also can provide employee incentives that emphasize quality, such as employee-of-the-month awards or bonuses based on customer feedback. They can make service employees more visible and accountable to consumers—auto dealerships can let customers talk directly with the mechanics working on their cars. A firm can check customer satisfaction regularly through suggestion and complaint systems, customer surveys, and comparison shopping. When poor service is found, it can be corrected. How a firm handles problems resulting from service variability can dramatically affect customer perceptions of service quality:

> A while back, we had a Federal Express package that, believe it or not, absolutely, positively didn't get there overnight. One phone call to Federal Express solved the problem. But that's not all. Pretty soon our phone rang, and one of Federal Express' senior executives was on the line. He wanted to know what happened and was very apologetic. Now that's service. With that one phone call, he assured himself of a customer for life.[8]

Perishability

Service perishability means that services cannot be stored for later sale or use. Many doctors charge patients for missed appointments because the service value existed only at that point and disappeared when the patient did not show up. The perishability of services is not a problem when demand is steady. When demand fluctuates, however, service firms often have difficult problems. For example, public transportation companies have to own much more equipment because of rush hour demand than they would if demand were even throughout the day.

Service firms can use several strategies for producing a better match between demand and supply. On the demand side, charging different prices at different times will shift some demand from peak periods to off-peak periods. Examples include low early-evening movie prices and weekend discount prices for car rentals. Or nonpeak demand can be increased, as when McDonald's offered its Egg McMuffin breakfast or when hotels developed mini-vacation weekends. Complementary services can be offered during peak times to provide alternatives to wait-

Services are perishable: Empty seats at slack times cannot be stored for later use during peak periods.

ing customers, such as cocktail lounges to sit in while waiting for a restaurant table and automatic tellers in banks. Reservation systems can also help manage the demand level—airlines, hotels, and physicians use them regularly.

On the supply side, firms can hire part-time employees to serve peak demand. Colleges add part-time teachers when enrollment goes up, and restaurants call in part-time waiters and waitresses to handle busy shifts. Peak-time demand can be handled more efficiently by having employees do only essential tasks during peak periods. Some tasks can be shifted to consumers, as when consumers fill out their own medical records or bag their own groceries. Or providers can share services, as when several hospitals share an expensive piece of medical equipment. Finally, a firm can plan ahead for expansion, as when an amusement park buys surrounding land for later development.

Marketing Strategies for Service Firms

Until recently, service firms lagged behind manufacturing firms in their use of marketing. Many service businesses are small (shoe repair shops, barbershops) and often consider marketing unneeded or too costly. Other service businesses (colleges, hospitals) once had so much demand that they did not need marketing until recently (see Marketing Highlight 22-1). Still others (legal, medical, and accounting practices) believed that it was unprofessional to use marketing.

Furthermore, service businesses are more difficult to manage when using only traditional marketing approaches. In a product business, products are fairly standardized and sit on shelves waiting for customers. In a service business, however, the customer interacts with a service provider whose service quality is less certain and more variable. The service outcome is affected not just by the service provider but by the whole supporting production process. Thus, service marketing requires more than just traditional external marketing using the four *P*s. Figure 22-1 shows that service marketing also requires both *internal marketing* and *interactive marketing*.

Internal marketing means that the service firm must effectively train and motivate its customer-contact employees and all the supporting service people to work as a *team* to provide customer satisfaction. For the firm to deliver consistently high service quality, everyone must practice a customer orientation. It is not enough to have a marketing department doing traditional marketing while the rest of the company goes its own way. Marketers also must get everyone else in the organization to practice marketing. In fact, internal marketing must *precede* external marketing. It makes little sense to advertise excellent service before the company's staff is ready to provide it. This point is well illustrated by a story about how Bill Marriott, Jr., chairman of Marriott hotels, interviews prospective managers:

> Bill Marriott tells the job candidate that the hotel chain wants to satisfy three groups: *customers, employees,* and *stockholders.* Although all of the groups are important, he asks in which order should the groups be satisfied? Most candidates say first satisfy customers. Marriott, however, reasons differently. First, employees must be satisfied. If employees love their jobs and feel a sense of pride in the hotel, they will serve customers well. Satisfied customers will return frequently to the Marriott. Moreover, dealing with happy customers will make employees even more satisfied, resulting in better service and still greater repeat business, all of which will yield a level of profits which will satisfy Marriott stockholders.

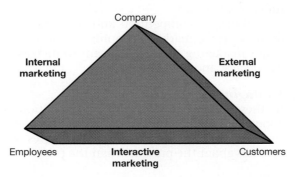

FIGURE 22-1
Three types of marketing in service industries

HOSPITAL MARKETING: CENTURY CITY'S EQUIVALENT OF A SUITE AT THE RITZ

In the past, many hospitals were faced with the burden of too many patients. But during the past decade, hospitals began to face falling admissions and low occupancy. In the scramble to pull in new patients, many hospitals turned to marketing. The more they looked at the problem, the more complex the marketing challenges appeared. Most hospitals realized that they couldn't be all things to all people. Some began to focus on offering certain specialties, such as heart care, pediatrics, burn treatment, and psychiatry. Others focused on serving the special needs of certain demographic segments.

Century City Hospital in Los Angeles provides a good example of modern hospital marketing. It recently unveiled its "Century Pavilion"—the hospital equivalent of a suite at the Ritz. The Pavilion consists of six luxury suites in which the area's affluent can get some of the finer things along with their basic health care. Since it opened, a steady stream of celebrities and other wealthy patients have lined up to pay the $1,000 per night required to stay in a classy Pavilion suite. From the moment they are whisked to their rooms by private elevator, Pavilion guests are pampered.

Century City did not stumble across the Pavilion idea by chance. The service is the result of a solid marketing program headed by the hospital's marketing director. A research study of the hospital's primary market area showed that almost 50 percent of area residents were high-income, highly educated professionals. Thirty-seven percent of the area population lives in homes worth more than $200,000; more than 7 percent have household incomes above $75,000. And there are

more than 40,000 millionaires in the Los Angeles-Long Beach area. Century City set out to capture this segment of well-heeled residents who had come to expect the best in food, accommodations, and service.

Whereas cost efficiency is the battle cry in most health-care corners, upscale patients want and can afford extras. Century City's research showed that this segment wanted privacy and exclusivity. So the hospital employed a noted interior-design firm to create suites with understated luxury and an elegant but quiet atmosphere. In these posh rooms, gourmet food is served on imported china and specially selected silver flatware. And because four of Pavilion's units come with guest suites (for family, friends, and bodyguards), each unit allows for gracious hospitality. The hospital even caters parties in the suites. Finally, the units come with many other extras, such as secretarial services to help patients keep up with their business tasks.

Century City decided against flashy institutional ads to promote the Pavilion. Instead, direct-mail pieces were sent to about 10,000 households in Brentwood, Bel Aire, Beverly Hills, and wealthy areas of West Los Angeles. Direct mail also was used to reach 800 staff physicians, each of whom received a rose one day, a fancy notepad another, and a chocolate truffle in a third mailing—alerting them that the service was available for their prominent patients.

Century City uses a low-key approach to marketing. Other hospitals have used flashier, mass-selling tactics to drum up business. For example, Sunrise Hospital in Las Vegas ran a large ad showing a ship with the cap-

Interactive marketing means that perceived service quality depends heavily on the quality of the buyer-seller interaction. In product marketing, product quality often depends little on how the product is obtained. But in services marketing, service quality depends on both the service deliverer and the quality of the delivery, especially in professional services. The customer judges service quality not just on *technical quality* (say, the success of the surgery) but also on its *functional quality* (whether the doctor showed concern and inspired confidence). Thus, professionals cannot assume that they will satisfy the client simply by providing good technical service. They have to master interactive marketing skills or functions as well.[9]

Today, as competition and costs increase, and as productivity and quality decrease, more marketing sophistication is needed. Service companies face three major marketing tasks: They want to increase their *competitive differentiation, service quality,* and *productivity.*

Managing Differentiation

In these days of intense price competition, service marketers often complain about the difficulty of differentiating their services from those of competitors. To the extent that customers view the services of different providers as similar, they care less about the provider than the price.

Hospital marketing: Century City targets affluent consumers who want some of the finer things along with their health care.

tion: "Introducing the Sunrise Cruise. Win a Once-in-a-Lifetime Cruise Simply by Entering Sunrise Hospital Any Friday or Saturday: Recuperative Cruise for Two." St. Luke's Hospital in Phoenix introduced nightly bingo games for all patients (except cardiac cases), producing immense patient interest and an annual profit of $60,000. A Philadelphia hospital served candlelight dinners with steak and champagne to parents of newborn children. Republic Health Corporation hospitals offer eleven branded "products," including Gift of Sight (cataract surgery), Miracle Moments (childbirth), and You're Becoming (cosmetic surgery).

Whatever the approach, most major hospitals now use some form of marketing; many have become good at it. Last year, U.S. hospitals spent $1.6 billion on marketing. According to Century City's director: "The Century Pavilion represents one element of what is happening in hospital marketing. Hospitals are becoming very sophisticated in defining who their patients are and what are their needs, and they're creating the kinds of services—whether it be luxury suites or same-day surgery—to meet those needs. In short, hospitals are definitely consumer oriented—a very large factor in health care today."

Sources: Portions adapted from Kevin T. Higgins, "Hospital Puttin' on the Ritz to Target High-End Market," *Marketing News,* January 17, 1986, p. 14. Also see Robert B. Kimmel, "Should Hospitals Advertise?" *Advertising Age,* June 13, 1988, p. 20; and Richard K. Thomas, "What Hospitals Must Do," *American Demographics,* January 1993, pp. 36-39.

The solution to price competition is to develop a differentiated offer, delivery, and image. The *offer* can include *innovative features* that set one company's offer apart from competitors' offers. For example, airlines have introduced such innovations as in-flight movies, advance seating, air-to-ground telephone service, and frequent-flyer award programs to differentiate their offers. Singapore Airlines once even added a piano bar. Unfortunately, most service innovations are copied easily. Still, the service company that regularly finds desired service innovations usually will gain a succession of temporary advantages, and may, by earning an innovative reputation, keep customers who want to go with the best.

The service company can differentiate its service *delivery* in three ways—through people, physical environment, and process. The company can distinguish itself by having more able and reliable customer-contact people than its competitors have. Or it can develop a superior physical environment in which the service product is delivered. Finally, it can design a superior delivery process. For example, a bank might offer its customers home banking as a superior way to deliver banking services than having to drive, park, and wait in line.

Service companies also can work on differentiating their *images* through symbols and branding. For example, the Harris Bank of Chicago adopted the lion as its symbol on its stationery, in its advertising, and even as stuffed animals offered to new depositors. The well-known "Harris Lion" confers an image of strength on the bank. Other well-known service symbols include The Travelers' red umbrella, Merrill Lynch's bull, and Allstate's "good hands." Humana, the nation's second largest investor-owned system of hospitals and services, has developed a successful branding strategy: It has standardized the names of its 90 hospitals with the "Humana" prefix and then built tremendous awareness and a reputation for quality around that name.

Managing Service Quality

One of the major ways a service firm can differentiate itself is by delivering consistently higher quality than its competitors do. Like manufacturers before them, many service industries have now joined the Total Quality Management revolution. Although only about 10 percent of large American service companies had formal quality programs in 1990, one expert predicts that perhaps 70 percent will have such programs by the year 2000.[10] Studies have shown that service quality affects customer satisfaction, which in turn affects buying intentions.[11] Many companies are finding that outstanding service quality can give them a potent competitive advantage that leads to superior sales and profit performance. Some firms have become almost legendary for their high-quality service (see Marketing Highlight 22-2). The key is to exceed the customers' service-quality *expectations*. As the chief executive at American Express puts it, "Promise only what you can deliver and deliver more than you promise!"[12] These expectations are based on past experiences, word of mouth, and service firm advertising. If *perceived service* of a given firm exceeds *expected service,* customers are apt to use the provider again. Customer retention is perhaps the best measure of quality—a service firm's ability to hang onto its customers depends on how consistently it delivers value to them. Thus, whereas the manufacturer's quality goal might be "zero *defects*," the service provider's goal is "zero customer *defections*."

The service provider needs to identify the expectations of target customers concerning service quality. Unfortunately, service quality is harder to define and judge than is product quality. It is harder to get agreement on the quality of a haircut than on the quality of a hair dryer, for instance. Moreover, although greater service quality results in greater customer satisfaction, it also results in higher costs. Still, investments in service usually pay off through increased customer retention and sales. Whatever the level of service provided, it is important that the service provider clearly define and communicate that level so that its employees know what they must deliver and so that customers know what they will get.

During the past decade, many service companies have invested heavily to develop streamlined and efficient service-delivery systems. They have attempted to ensure that customers will receive consistently high-quality service in every service encounter. Unlike product manufacturers who can adjust their machinery and inputs until everything is perfect, however, service quality always will vary, depending on the interactions between employees and customers. Problems inevitably will occur:

> Mistakes are a critical part of every service. Hard as they try, even the best service companies can't prevent the occasional late flight, burned steak, or missed delivery. The fact is, in services, often performed in the customer's presence, errors are inevitable. But dissatisfied customers are not. While companies may not be able to prevent all problems, they can learn to recover from them. A good recovery can turn angry, frustrated customers into loyal ones. It can, in fact, create more good will than if things had not gone badly in the first place.[13]

Thus, although a company may not be able to prevent service problems, it can learn to recover from them. And good *service recovery* can win customer purchasing and loyalty. Therefore, companies should take steps not only to provide good service every time, but also to recover from service mistakes when they occur. The first step is to *empower* front-line service employees—to give them the authority, responsibility, and incentives to recognize, care about, and tend to customer needs:

> Embracing the notion of empowerment, the Marriott Desert Springs revised the job description for its [customer-contact employees]: the major—indeed the *only*—goal of these positions is to ensure that "our guests experience excellent service and hospital-

COMPETITIVE ADVANTAGE THROUGH CUSTOMER SERVICE

Some companies go to extremes to coddle their customers with service. Consider the following examples:

- An L. L. Bean customer says he lost all his fishing equipment—and nearly his life—when a raft he bought from the company leaked and forced him to swim to shore. He recovered the raft and sent it to the company along with a letter asking for a new raft and $700 to cover the fishing equipment he says he lost. He gets both.

- A woman visits a Nordstrom department store to buy a gift. She's in a hurry and leaves the store immediately after making her purchase. The Nordstrom salesclerk gift-wraps the item at no charge and later drops it off at the customer's home.

- At 11:00 p.m., a driver making a crucial delivery for Sigma Midwest is having electrical problems with his Ryder rental truck. He calls the company, and within an hour the truck is fixed, yet the Ryder employee stays with the driver for the next five hours to help him make deliveries and remain on schedule.

- An American Express cardholder fails to pay more than $5,000 of his September bill. He explains that during the summer he'd purchased expensive rugs in Turkey. When he got home, appraisals showed that the rugs were worth half of what he'd paid. Rather than asking suspicious questions or demanding payment, the American Express representative notes the dispute, asks for a letter summarizing the appraisers' estimates, and, until the conflict is resolved, doesn't ask for payment.

From a dollars-and-cents point of view, these examples sound like a crazy way to do business. How can you make money by giving away your products, providing free extra services, or letting customers get away without paying their bills on time? Yet studies show that good service—though costly—goes hand in hand with good financial performance. Good service is good for business. In today's highly competitive marketplace, companies that take the best care of their customers have a strong competitive advantage.

Good customer service involves more than simply opening a complaint department, smiling a lot, and being nice to customers. It requires hard-headed analysis and an intense commitment to helping customers. Outstanding service companies set high service standards and often make seemingly outlandish efforts to achieve them. They take great care to hire the right service people, train them well, and reward them for going out of their way to serve customers.

But at these companies, exceptional service is more than a set of policies or actions—it's a companywide attitude, an important part of the overall company culture. Concern for the consumer becomes a matter of pride for everyone in the company. American Express loves to tell stories about how its people have rescued customers from disasters ranging from civil wars to earthquakes, no matter what the cost. The company gives cash rewards of up to $1,000 to "Great Performers," such as Barbara Weber, who moved mountains of State Department and Treasury Department bureaucracy to refund $980 in stolen traveler's checks to a customer stranded in Cuba. Four Seasons Hotels, long known for its outstanding service, tells its employees the story of Ron Dyment, a doorman in Toronto who forgot to load a departing guest's briefcase in his taxi. The doorman called the guest, a lawyer in Washington, DC, and learned that he desperately needed the briefcase for a meeting the following morning. Without first asking for approval from management, Dyment hopped on a plane and returned the briefcase. The company named Dyment Employee of the Year. Similarly, Nordstrom thrives on stories about its service heroics, such as employees dropping off orders at customers' homes or warming up cars while customers spend a little more time shopping. There's even a story about a customer who got a refund on a tire—Nordstrom doesn't carry tires, but it prides itself on a no-questions-asked return policy!

There's no simple formula for offering good service, but neither is it a mystery. According to the president of L. L. Bean, "A lot of people have fancy things to say about customer service . . . but it's just a day-in, day-out, ongoing, never-ending, unremitting, persevering, compassionate type of activity." For the companies that do it well, it's also very rewarding.

Sources: Bill Kelley, "Five Companies that Do It Right—and Make It Pay," *Sales & Marketing Management,* April 1988, pp. 57-64; Joan O'C. Hamilton, "Why Rivals Are Quaking as Nordstrom Heads East," *Business Week,* June 15, 1987, pp. 89-90; Frank Rose, "Now Service Means Quality Too," *Fortune,* April 22, 1991, pp. 97-108; and Barry Farber and Joyce Wycoff, "Customer Service: Evolution and Revolution," *Sales & Marketing Management,* May 1991, pp. 44-51.

ity while staying at our resort." The resort charges the people in those positions with learning the correct technical procedures, using their authority to do anything to keep guests happy, using their power to satisfy guests on the spot without hassle, assisting in finding the ultimate cause for guests' problems, and informing managers of ways to improve overall hotel, working conditions, or guests' comfort.[14]

Marriott is putting some 70,000 employees through empowerment training, which encourages them to go beyond their normal jobs to solve customer problems. Such empowered employees can act quickly and effectively to keep service problems from resulting in lost customers.

Studies of well-managed service companies show that they share a number of common virtues regarding service quality. First, top service companies are *"customer obsessed."* They have developed a distinctive strategy for satisfying these customer needs that wins enduring customer loyalty.

Second, they have a history of *top management commitment to quality.* Management at companies such as Marriott, Disney, Delta, Federal Express, and McDonald's looks not only at financial performance but also at service performance. Third, the best service providers *set high service quality standards.* Swissair, for example, aims to have 96 percent or more of its passengers rate its service as good or superior; otherwise, it takes action. Citibank aims to answer phone calls within ten seconds and customer letters within two days. The standards must be set *appropriately* high. A 98 percent accuracy standard may sound good but, using this standard, 64,000 Federal Express packages would be lost each day, 10 words would be misspelled on each page, 400,000 prescriptions would be misfilled daily, and drinking water would be unsafe eight days a year. Top service companies do not settle merely for "good" service; they aim for 100 percent defect-free service.[15]

Fourth, the top service firms *watch service performance closely*—both their own and that of competitors. They use methods such as comparison shopping, customer surveys, and suggestion and complaint forms. For example, General Electric sends out 700,000 response cards each year to households who rate their service people's performance. Citibank takes regular measures of "ART"—accuracy, responsiveness, and timeliness—and sends out employees who act as customers to check on service quality.

Good service companies also communicate their concerns about service quality to employees and provide performance feedback. At Federal Express, quality measurements are everywhere. When employees walk in the door in the morning, they see the previous week's on-time percentages. Then, the company's in-house television station gives them detailed breakdowns of what happened yesterday and any potential problems for the day ahead.[16]

Finally, well-managed service companies *satisfy employees as well as customers.* They believe that good employee relations will result in good customer relations. Management creates an environment of employee support, rewards good service performance, and monitors employee job satisfaction. At one time, Citibank set a customer satisfaction goal of 90 percent and an employee satisfaction goal of 70 percent. But the question was raised whether Citibank could deliver 90 percent customer satisfaction if 30 percent of its employees are unhappy. Some analysts even go so far as to suggest that a company has to make its employees, not its customers, number one if the company hopes to truly satisfy its customers.[17]

Managing Productivity

With their costs rising rapidly, service firms are under great pressure to increase service productivity. They can do so in several ways. The service providers can better train current employees, or they can hire new ones who will work harder or more skillfully for the same pay. Or the service providers can increase the quantity of their service by giving up some quality. Doctors working for health maintenance organizations (HMOs) have moved toward handling more patients and giving less time to each. The provider can "industrialize the service" by adding equipment and standardizing production, as in McDonald's assembly-line approach to fast-food retailing. Commercial dishwashing, jumbo jets, and multiple-unit movie theaters all represent technological expansions of service.

Service providers also can increase productivity by designing more effective services. How-to-quit-smoking clinics and exercise recommendations may reduce the need for expensive medical services later on. Hiring paralegal workers reduces the need for expensive legal professionals. Providers also can give customers incentives to substitute company labor with their own labor. For example, business firms that sort their own mail before delivering it to the post office pay lower postal rates.

Just this once, we'd like to give our vehicles the image that they deserve.

You won't see our drivers making deliveries in anything like this. However, you will notice the speed at which our delivery service works. With 70,000 vehicles on the road and as many as 400 planes overhead servicing over five million customers worldwide daily, it's no wonder every business day we're responsible for doing what no other company can: making more on-time deliveries than anyone in the world. Which is why, to so many people, our service is already considered up to speed. We run the tightest ship in the shipping business.

Services marketing strategies: UPS claims that greater efficiency and productivity allow it to offer high quality service at a low price.

However, companies must avoid pushing productivity so hard that doing so reduces perceived quality. Some productivity steps help standardize quality, increasing customer satisfaction. But other productivity steps lead to too much standardization and can rob consumers of customized service. Attempts to industrialize a service or to cut costs can make a service company more efficient in the short run but reduce its longer-run ability to innovate, maintain service quality, or respond to consumer needs and desires. In some cases, service providers accept reduced productivity in order to create more service differentiation or quality.[18]

International Services Marketing

An Italian sportswear manufacturer calls her advertising agency in London to confirm plans for new billboards in Venezuela. A German businessman checks into his hotel room in Atlanta—the hotel is owned by a British company and managed by an American firm. The Zurich branch of a Japanese bank participates in a debt offering for an aircraft leasing company in Ireland. These are just a few examples of the thousands of service transactions that take place each day around the globe. More and more, the global economy is dominated by services. In fact, a variety of service industries—from banking, insurance, and communications to transportation, travel, and entertainment—now accounts for well over 60 percent of the economy in developed countries around the world. The worldwide growth rate for services (16 percent in the past decade) almost doubles the growth rate for manufacturing.[19]

Some service industries have a long history of international operations. For example, the commercial banking industry was one of the first to grow internationally. Banks had to provide global services in order to meet the foreign exchange and credit needs of their home-country clients wanting to sell overseas. In recent years, however, as the scope of international financing has broadened, many banks have become truly global operations. Germany's Deutsche Bank, for example, has branches in 41 countries. Thus, for its clients around the world who wish to take advantage of growth opportunities created by German reunification, Deutsche Bank can raise money not just in Frankfurt, but also in Zurich, London, Paris, and Tokyo.

The travel industry also moved naturally into international operations. American hotel and airline companies grew quickly in Europe and the Far East during the economic expansion that followed World War II. Credit card companies soon followed—the early worldwide presence of American Express has recently been matched by Visa and MasterCard. Business travelers and vacationers like the convenience, and they have now come to expect that their credit cards will be honored wherever they go.

Professional and business services industries such as accounting, management consulting, and advertising only recently have globalized. The international growth of these firms followed the globalization of the manufacturing companies they serve. For example, increasingly globalized manufacturing firms have found it much easier to have their accounts prepared by a single accounting firm, even when they operate in two dozen countries. This set the stage for rapid international consolidation in the accounting industry. During the late 1980s, America's "Big Eight" accounting firms quickly merged with established companies around the world to become the international "Big Six" almost overnight. Similarly, as their client companies began to employ global marketing and advertising strategies, advertising agencies and other marketing services firms responded by globalizing their own operations. For instance, the ten largest U.S. advertising agencies now make over 50 percent of their billings abroad.[20]

The rapidly expanding international marketplace provides many attractive opportunities for service firms. It also creates some special challenges, however. Service companies wanting to operate in other countries are not always welcomed with open arms. Whereas manufacturers usually face straightforward tariff, quota, or currency restrictions when attempting to sell their products in another country, service providers are likely to face more subtle barriers. In some cases, rules and regulations affecting international service firms reflect the host country's traditions. In others, they appear to protect the country's own fledgling service industries from large global competitors with greater resources. In still other cases, however, the restrictions seem to have little purpose other than to make entry difficult for foreign service firms.

> The industrialized nations, particularly the United States, want their banks, insurance companies, construction firms, and other service providers to be allowed to move people, capital, and technology around the globe unimpeded. Instead they face a bewildering complex of national regulations, most of them designed to guarantee jobs for local competitors. A new Turkish law, for example, forbids international accounting firms to bring capital into the country to set up offices and requires them to use the names of local partners, rather than prestigious international ones, in their marketing. To audit the books of a multinational company's branch in Buenos Aires, an accountant must have the equivalent of a high school education in Argentinean geography and history. . . . India is perhaps the most [difficult] big economy in the world [to enter] these days. . . . New Delhi prevents international insurance companies from selling property and casualty policies to the country's swelling business community or life insurance to its huge middle class.[21]

Despite such difficulties, the trend toward growth of global service companies will continue, especially in banking, telecommunications, and professional services. Today service firms are no longer simply following their manufacturing customers. Instead, they are taking the lead in international expansion.

ORGANIZATION MARKETING

Organizations often carry out activities to "sell" the organization itself. **Organization marketing** consists of activities undertaken to create, maintain, or change the attitudes and behavior of target audiences toward an organization. Both profit and nonprofit organizations practice organization marketing. Business firms sponsor public relations or corporate advertising campaigns to polish their images. Nonprofit organizations, such as churches, colleges, charities, museums, and performing arts groups, market their organizations in order to raise funds and attract members or patrons. Organization marketing calls for assessing the organization's current image and developing a marketing plan to improve it.

Image Assessment

The first step in image assessment is to research the organization's current image among key publics. The way an individual or a group sees an organization is called its **organization image.** Different people can have different images of the same organization. The organization might be pleased with its public image, or it might find that it has serious image problems.

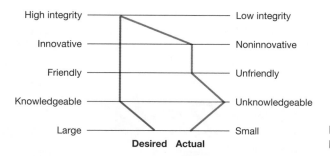

High integrity	Low integrity
Innovative	Noninnovative
Friendly	Unfriendly
Knowledgeable	Unknowledgeable
Large	Small

Desired   Actual

FIGURE 22-2
Image assessment

For example, suppose a bank conducts marketing research to measure its image in the community. Suppose it finds its image to be that shown by the red line in Figure 22-2. Thus, current and potential customers view the bank as somewhat small, noninnovative, unfriendly, and unknowledgeable. The bank will want to change this image.

Image Planning and Control

Next, the organization should decide what image it would like to have and what it can achieve. For example, the bank might decide that it would like the image shown by the blue line in Figure 22-2. It would like to be seen as a provider of more friendly and personal service, and as larger, more innovative, and more knowledgeable.

The firm now develops a marketing plan to shift its actual image toward the desired one. Suppose the bank first wants to improve its image as a provider of friendly and personal service. The key step, of course, is actually to provide friendlier and more personal service. The bank can hire and train better tellers and other employees who deal with customers. It can change its decor to make the bank seem warmer. Once the bank is certain that it has improved its performance on important image dimensions, it can design a marketing program to communicate that new image to customers. Using public relations, the bank can sponsor community activities, send its executives to speak to local business and civic groups, offer public seminars on household finances, and issue press releases on newsworthy bank activities. In its advertising, the bank can position itself as "your friendly, personal neighborhood bank."

Corporate image advertising is a major tool companies use to market themselves to various publics. Companies spend more than $785 million each year on image advertising. They can use corporate advertising to build up or maintain a favorable image over many years. Or they can use it to counter events that might hurt their image. For example, Waste Management, the giant garbage disposal company, got into trouble a few years ago for dumping toxic wastes. So it countered with an advertising campaign telling how the company has worked with various government agencies to help save a threatened species of butterfly.

Such organization marketing efforts can work only if the actual organization lives up to the projected image. No amount of advertising and public relations can fool the public for long if the reality fails to match the image. Thus, Waste Management's image campaign worked only because the company has in fact worked to clean up toxic waste sites. Otherwise, even saving butterflies would not have helped the company's reputation.[22]

An organization must resurvey its publics every once in a while to see whether its activities are improving its image. Images cannot be changed overnight: Campaign funds are usually limited, and public images tend to stick. If the firm is making no progress, either its marketing offer or its organization marketing program will have to be changed.

PERSON MARKETING

People are also marketed. **Person marketing** consists of activities undertaken to create, maintain, or change attitudes or behavior toward particular people. All kinds of people and organizations practice person marketing. Politicians market themselves to get votes and program support. Entertainers and sports figures use

Corporate image advertising: With this campaign, Nestle attempts to reinforce its 125-year tradition of "warmth, family, and shelter. . . .The products we introduce in the future will be as good as the ones we make today."

marketing to promote their careers and improve their incomes. Professionals such as doctors, lawyers, accountants, and architects market themselves in order to build their reputations and increase business. Business leaders use person marketing as a strategic tool to develop their company's fortunes as well as their own. Businesses, charities, sports teams, fine arts groups, religious groups, and other organizations also use person marketing. Creating, flaunting, or associating with well-known personalities often helps these organizations better achieve their goals.

Here are some examples of successful person marketing:

■ Michael Jordan, star of the Chicago Bulls, possesses remarkable basketball skills—great court sense with quick, fluid moves and the ability to soar above the rim for dramatic dunks. And he has an appealing, unassuming personality to go along with his dazzling talents. All of this makes Michael Jordan very marketable. After college, Jordan signed on with ProServ Inc., a well-known sports management agency. The agency quickly negotiated a lucrative five-year contract with the Bulls, paying Jordan some $4 million. But that was just the beginning. ProServ decided to market Jordan as the new Dr. J of basketball—a supertalented good guy and solid citizen. Paying careful attention to placement and staging, the agency booked Jordan into the talk-show circuit, accepted only the best products to endorse, insisted on only high-quality commercials, arranged appearances for charitable causes, and even had him appear as a fashion model. Jordan's market appeal soared, and so did his income. Person marketing has paid off handsomely for Michael Jordan, for his team, and for the products he represents. Jordan is currently playing under an eight-year, $25 million contract with the Bulls, and current endorsements for Nike, Wilson, McDonald's, General Mills Wheaties, Johnson Products, Quaker's Gatorade, Hanes, and other companies earn Jordan an additional $15 million a year. He became the first person in history to have a McDonald's sandwich named after him. In its first full year with Jordan as its representative, Nike sold $110 million worth of "Air Jordan" basketball shoes and apparel. And after years of spotty attendance at home games, tickets to a Bulls game are now the hottest tickets in town.[23]

■ Former president Ronald Reagan's administration was unequaled in its use of marketing to sell the president and his policies to the American people. Every move made by Reagan during his eight years as president was carefully managed to support the administration's positioning and marketing strategy. An army of specialists—marketing researchers, advertising experts, political advisers, speech writers, media planners, press secretaries, even makeup artists—worked tirelessly to define political market segments, identify key issues, and strongly position Reagan and his programs. The administration used extensive marketing research. It regularly polled voter segments to find out what was "hot" and what was not. Using focus groups, it pretested important speeches and platforms. "Theming it" was an important element of marketing strategy—the administration packaged key benefits into a few highly focused themes, then repeated these basic themes over and over and over. This focus on basic marketable themes, coupled with careful planning and delivery of messages and media exposures, helped control what was reported by the press. Reagan even made careful use of "regional marketing," tailoring timely speeches to the special needs of regional or local audiences.[24]

The objective of person marketing is to create a "celebrity"—a well-known person whose name generates attention, interest, and action. Celebrities differ in the *scope* of their visibility. Some are very well known, but only in limited geographic areas (a town mayor, a local businessperson, an area doctor), or specific segments (the president of the American Dental Association, a company vice-president, a jazz musician with a small group of fans). Still others have broad national or international visibility (major entertainers, sports superstars, world political and religious leaders).

Celebrities also differ in their *durability*. Figure 22-3A shows a standard celebrity life-cycle pattern. The person's visibility begins at a low level, gradually builds to a peak as the person matures and becomes well known, then declines as the celebrity fades from the limelight. But as the rest of Figure 22-3 shows, celebrity life-cycle patterns can vary greatly. For example, in the *overnight* pattern (Figure 22-3B), a person acquires quick and lasting visibility because of some major deed or event (Charles Lindbergh, Neil Armstrong). In the *comeback* pattern (Figure 22-3C), a celebrity achieves high visibility, loses it, then gets it back again (Tina Turner, George Burns). In the *meteor pattern* (Figure 22-3D), someone gains fame quickly then loses it suddenly. For example, William "Refrigerator" Perry, the overweight Chicago defensive lineman, became an instant "hot property" after he was used as a running back on *Monday Night Football*. He made millions of dollars from product endorsements and then sank back into obscurity—all within about a year.

The person marketing process is similar to the one used by product and ser-

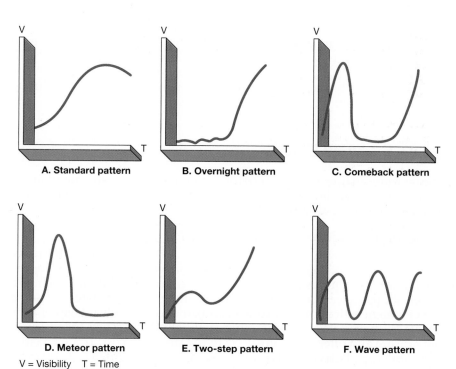

FIGURE 22-3
Celebrity life cycles

A. Standard pattern   B. Overnight pattern   C. Comeback pattern

D. Meteor pattern   E. Two-step pattern   F. Wave pattern

V = Visibility   T = Time

"THE GOODLIEST LAND": BUSINESS SITE MARKETING IN NORTH CAROLINA

In 1584, when two English explorers returned to their homeland with news of "The Goodliest Land Under the Cope of Heaven," they were describing what is now North Carolina. In recent years, numerous American and foreign companies have come to share this opinion of the Tar Heel state. In three successive *Business Week* surveys, North Carolina was named as first choice of the nation's top business executives for new-plant location. The state does offer a number of economic and cultural advantages, but much credit for the state's popularity goes to the North Carolina Department of Commerce's Business/Industry Development Division. The division employs a high-quality marketing program—including advertising, publicity, and personal selling—to convince targeted firms and industries to come to North Carolina.

The division's 33 industrial development representatives coordinate efforts with development professionals in more than 300 individual North Carolina communities. The division also provides extensive information to firms considering locating in the state—in-depth profiles of more than 325 sites and buildings, estimates of state and local taxes for specific sites, analyses of labor costs and fringe benefits, details of convenient transportation to sites, and estimates of construction costs.

But the Business/Industry Development Division does more than simply provide information—it aggressively seeks out firms and persuades them to locate in North Carolina. It invites groups of business executives to tour the state and hear presentations, and it sets up booths at industry trade fairs. Its representatives (sometimes including the governor) travel to other states to carry the North Carolina story to executives in attractive businesses and industries. The division also communicates and persuades through informational and promotional brochures delivered by mail and through mass-media advertising. Ads such as those shown here tout North Carolina's benefits: a large and productive labor force, numerous educational and technical training institutions, low taxes, a good transportation network, low energy and construction costs, a good living environment, and plentiful government support and assistance.

The division's total budget runs only about $4.5 million a year, but the returns are great. From 1975 through 1990, new and expanding manufacturing business announced investments of more than $35 billion in North Carolina, creating more than 450,000 new jobs.

Source: Based on information supplied by the North Carolina Department of Economic and Community Development, Business/Industry Development Division.

---

vice marketers. Person marketers begin with careful market research and analysis to discover consumer needs and market segments. Next comes product development—assessing the person's current qualities and image and transforming the person to match market needs and expectations better. Finally, the marketer develops programs to value, promote, and deliver the celebrity. Some people naturally possess the skills, appearances, and behaviors that target segments value. But for most, celebrity status in any field must actively be developed through sound person marketing.

PLACE MARKETING

Place marketing involves activities undertaken to create, maintain, or change attitudes or behavior toward particular places. Examples include business site marketing and vacation marketing.

Business Site Marketing

Business site marketing involves developing, selling, or renting business sites for factories, stores, offices, warehouses, and conventions. Large developers research companies' land needs and respond with real estate solutions, such as industrial parks, shopping centers, and new office buildings. Most states operate industrial development offices that try to sell companies on the advantages of locating new plants in their states (see Marketing Highlight 22-3). They spend large sums on advertising and offer to fly prospects to the site at no cost. Troubled cities, such as New York City, Detroit, Dallas, and Atlanta, have appointed task forces to improve their images and to draw new businesses to their areas. They may build large centers to house important conventions and business meetings. Even entire nations, such as Canada, Ireland, Greece, Mexico, and Turkey, have marketed themselves as good locations for business investment.

Vacation Marketing

Vacation marketing involves attracting vacationers to spas, resorts, cities, states, and even entire nations. The effort is carried out by travel agents, airlines, motor clubs, oil companies, hotels, motels, and governmental agencies.

Today almost every city, state, and country markets its tourist attractions. Miami Beach is considering making gambling legal in order to attract more tourists. Texas advertises "It's Like a Whole Other Country," and Michigan touts "YES M!CH!GAN." Philadelphia invites you to "Get To Know Us!" and Palm Beach, Florida advertises "The Best of Everything" at low off-season prices. Some places, however, try to *demarket* themselves because they feel that the harm from tourism exceeds the revenues. Thus, Oregon has publicized its bad weather; Yosemite National Park may ban snowmobiling, conventions, and private cars; and Finland discourages tourists from vacationing in certain areas.

IDEA MARKETING

Ideas also can be marketed. In one sense, all marketing is the marketing of an idea, whether it be the general idea of brushing your teeth or the specific idea that Crest provides the most effective decay prevention. Here, however, we narrow our focus to the marketing of *social ideas,* such as public health campaigns to reduce smoking, alcoholism, drug abuse, and overeating; environmental campaigns to promote wilderness protection, clean air, and conservation; and other campaigns such as family planning, human rights, and racial equality. This area has been called *social marketing*. **Social marketing** is the design, implementation, and control of programs seeking to increase the acceptability of a social idea, cause, or practice among members of a target group.

Social marketers can pursue different objectives. They might want to produce understanding (knowing the nutritional value of different foods) or trigger a one-time action (joining in a mass-immunization campaign). They might want to change behavior (discouraging drunk driving) or a basic belief (convincing employers that handicapped people can make strong contributions in the work force).

The Advertising Council of America has developed dozens of social advertising campaigns, including "Smokey the Bear," "Keep America Beautiful," "Join the Peace Corps," "Buy Bonds," "Go to College," and "Say No to Drugs." But social marketing involves much more than just advertising. Many public marketing campaigns fail because they assign advertising the primary role and fail to develop and use all the marketing-mix tools.

In designing effective social-change strategies, social marketers go through a normal marketing planning process. First, they define the social-change objective—for example, "to reduce the percentage of teenagers who drink and drive from 15 percent to 5 percent within five years." Next, they analyze the attitudes, beliefs, values, and behavior of teenagers and the forces that support teenage drinking. They consider communication and distribution approaches that might prevent teenagers from driving while drinking, develop a marketing plan, and build a marketing organization to carry out the plan (see Marketing Highlight 22-4). Finally, they evaluate and, if necessary, adjust the program to make it more effective.

Social marketing is fairly new, and its effectiveness relative to other social-change strategies is hard to evaluate. It is hard to produce social change with any strategy, let alone a strategy that relies on voluntary response. Social marketing has been applied mainly to family planning, environmental protection, energy conservation, improved health and nutrition, auto driver safety, and public transportation—and there have been some encouraging successes. But more applications are needed before we can fully assess social marketing's potential for producing social change.

SOCIAL MARKETING OF SAFE AND SOBER DRIVING

The Reader's Digest Foundation, in partnership with the National Association of Secondary School Principals (NASSP), recently launched a two-year, $1 million social marketing campaign to deliver a sober message to teenagers all across America. As part of the "Don't Drink and Drive Challenge," *Reader's Digest* magazine invited teams from leading advertising agencies to create posters for the campaign, with the winners receiving a Paris trip for two. In the first year of the campaign, more than 1,000 teams from top agencies competed. Shown here are some of the outstanding posters created for the program.

The foundation then distributed copies of the winning posters to 20,000 high schools. Students were challenged to compete for college scholarships by devising programs to promote sober driving. More than 700 schools submitted entries ranging from rock videos to puppet shows to anti-drunk-driving awareness weeks. Scholarships totaling $500,000 went to 115 winning schools. The program was held a second year, with advertising agencies and schools again taking part and another $500,000 in scholarships awarded. Reader's Digest Foundation continues to offer copies of its posters and summaries of winning student programs as a resource to educators, the media, and community organizations.

SUMMARY

Marketing has been broadened in recent years to cover "marketable" entities other than products—namely, services, organizations, persons, places, and ideas.

As the United States moves increasingly toward a *service economy,* marketers need to know more about marketing services. *Services* are activities or benefits that one party can offer to another that are essentially intangible and do not result in the ownership of anything. Services are *intan-*

gible, inseparable, variable, and perishable. Each characteristic poses problems and requires strategies. Marketers have to find ways to make the service more tangible; to increase the productivity of providers who are inseparable from their products; to standardize the quality in the face of variability; and to improve demand movements and supply capacities in the face of service perishability.

Service industries have typically lagged behind manufacturing firms in adopting and using marketing concepts, but this situation is now changing. Services marketing strategy calls not only for external marketing but also for *internal marketing* to motivate employees and *interactive marketing* to create service delivery skills among service providers. To succeed, service marketers must create *competitive differentiation,* offer high service quality, and find ways to increase *service productivity.*

Organizations can also be marketed. *Organization marketing* is undertaken to create, maintain, or change the attitudes or behavior of target audiences toward an organization. It calls for assessing the organization's current image and developing a marketing plan for bringing about an improved image.

Person marketing consists of activities undertaken to create, maintain, or change attitudes or behavior toward particular persons. Two common forms are celebrity marketing and political candidate marketing.

Place marketing involves activities undertaken to create, maintain, or change attitudes or behavior toward particular places. Examples include business site marketing and vacation marketing.

Idea marketing involves efforts to market ideas. In the case of social ideas, it is called *social marketing* and consists of the design, implementation, and control of programs seeking to increase the acceptability of a social idea, cause, or practice among a target group. Social marketing goes further than public advertising—it coordinates advertising with the other elements of the marketing mix. The social marketer defines the social-change objective, analyzes consumer attitudes and competitive forces, develops and tests alternative concepts, develops appropriate channels for the idea's communication and distribution, and finally, checks the results. Social marketing has been applied to family planning, environmental protection, antismoking campaigns and other public issues.

KEY TERMS

Interactive marketing 644

Internal marketing 643

Organization image 650

Organization marketing 650

Person marketing 651

Place marketing 654

Service 640

Service inseparability 641

Service intangibility 640

Service perishability 642

Service variability 642

Social marketing 655

DISCUSSING THE ISSUES

1. A "hot" concept in fast-food marketing is home delivery of everything from pizza to hamburgers to fried chicken. Why is demand for this service growing? How can marketers gain a competitive advantage by satisfying the growing demand for increased services?

2. How can a theater deal with the intangibility, inseparability, variability, and perishability of the service it provides? Give examples.

3. Wendy's serves its hamburgers "fresh off the grill." This assures high quality but creates leftover hamburgers if the staff overestimates demand. Wendy's solves this perishability problem by using the leftover meat in chili, tacos, and spaghetti sauce. How do airlines solve the perishability of unsold seats? Give additional examples of perishability and how service firms address it.

4. Many people feel that too much time and money are spent marketing political candidates. They also complain that modern political campaigns overemphasize image at the expense of issues. What is your opinion of political-candidate marketing? Would some other approach to campaigning help consumers make better voting decisions?

5. News reports of questionable, high-pressure tactics in the sale of vacation homes are common. For example, the "food processor" one marketer used as an incentive to attract prospects turned out to be a fork! Why do you think unethical practices appear to be so frequently used in place marketing?

6. Marketing is defined as satisfying needs and wants through exchange processes. What exchanges occur in marketing nonprofit organizations, such as a museum or the American Red Cross?

APPLYING THE CONCEPTS

1. Why do organizations want to "sell" themselves and not just their products? (a) List several reasons for organization marketing, and relate them to promotional campaigns of companies with which you are familiar. (b) Clip several print advertisements that show organizational marketing. (Business or trade magazines are a good source.) For each ad, write down the purpose of the campaign, the message being conveyed, and whether or not you feel this marketing campaign is successful.

2. Perishability is very important in the airline industry: unsold seats are gone forever, and too many unsold seats mean large losses. With computerized ticketing, airlines can easily use pricing to deal with perishability and variations in demand. (a) Call a travel agent or use an online service such as EaasySabre to check airline fares. Get prices on the same route for 60 days in advance, two weeks, one week, and today. Is there a clear pattern to the fares? (b) When a store is overstocked on ripe fruit, it may lower the price to sell out quickly. What are airlines doing to their prices as the seats get close to "perishing"? Why? What would you recommend as a pricing strategy to increase total revenues?

MAKING MARKETING DECISIONS:
SMALL WORLD COMMUNICATIONS, INC.

Lynette Jones and Thomas Campbell are talking about marketing some of the less tangible aspects of the Airport communications link. "Tom, I was thinking about the level of support that we need to provide for the Airport. We're selling the benefits of speed and ease of use, and that means that we've got to provide good customer support systems after the sale. But there's this issue—costs. An average customer-support call costs about $30 to $40. We want to provide good support, but we can't do a lot of it at those costs—not without pricing our product much higher than I want to."

"Well," Tom said, "Different companies handle it different ways. WordPerfect offers unlimited toll-free support; Microsoft offers unlimited support but it's a long-distance toll call, often with long waits. Some companies are starting to charge for support, and there's even a 900 number you can call. One thing we can do is set up a support forum on the CompuServe system, so people can send us E-mail messages. The customer pays for the call and the CompuServe hourly charges, so it saves us the cost of an 800 number. And it's fair, too, because the users who need a lot of support pay for it, and those that don't aren't required to pay for other people's needs. And we may also get some help, because the really experienced Airport users will help the novices along in the forum."

Lyn reponded, "I like it, and I think it fits with our users. I was also thinking about a service we might sell, doing custom setup for the users who don't have the knowledge or time to do it themselves. We could communicate directly with their computers over the phone, and do the setups remotely—reconfigure their machines from the home office." Tom replied, "It's an interesting idea, but there are some other things I'd do first. We need to reduce people's *need* for support, and that means investing in great manuals, built-in help in our software, and a problem diagnosis program. We simply have to have call-in phone support, but we can do it as a toll call. Then we can set up our own automatic electronic bulletin board with tech notes, and an automated faxback service that will send out updated materials. After we give that level of support included in the purchase price, we can start to talk about extra-price services."

Lyn said, "Let me think about it. There's one other idea I had. Would you consider doing some ads for us, being the spokesperson for the product? I think you're really cute, in a strange sort of way, and really believable as a computer whiz. Don't answer now—just sleep on it. Let your ego swell for a while before you say no."

WHAT NOW?

1. Consider Lyn's ideas about selling setup services for the Airport product, and Tom's ideas about the need for support included in the purchase price. How would you draw a line between normal product support and a sold service? What are the advantages of this idea? Are there any dangers to proceeding this way?

2. Personalities have become visible in many aspects of the computer industry. For example, Microsoft is identified with Bill Gates; Apple Computer with Steven Jobs, Steve Wozniak, and John Scully; Dell Computer with Michael Dell; and utility software with Peter Norton. (a) Do any or all of these examples appear to be using person marketing? (b) Consider Thomas Campbell, the whiz-kid dropout from Rensselaer Polytechnic Institute, who is now starting on a new mission to make computer communication easy and accessible. Is there the potential to market Tom as a part of the Small World image development? If so, suggest several specific ways you might market Thomas to help the overall business.

REFERENCES

1. See Paul Burka, "What They Teach You at Disney U.," *Fortune,* November 7, 1988, in a special advertising section following p. 176; Charles Leerhsen, "How Disney Does It," *Newsweek,* April 3, 1989, pp. 48-54; Christopher Knowlton, "How Disney Keeps the Magic Going," *Fortune,* December 4, 1989, pp. 111-32; Kathleen Kerwin, "Disney Looking a Little Fragilistic," *Business Week,* June 25, 1990, pp. 52-54; and Stewart Toy, "Mouse Fever Is About to Strike Europe," *Business Week,* March 30, 1992, p. 32.

2. See Antony J. Michels and Tricia Welsh, "Slouching into the 1990s," *Fortune,* June 3, 1991, pp. 254-58; and Stephen S. Roach, "Service Under Seige—The Restructuring Imperative," *Harvard Business Review,* September-October 1991, pp. 82-91.

3. "Presto! The Convenience Industry: Making Life a Little Simpler," *Business Week,* April 27, 1987, p. 86; also see Ronald Henkoff, "Piety, Profits, and Productivity," *Fortune,* June 1992, pp. 84-85.

4. See Leonard L. Berry, "Services Marketing Is Different," *Business,* May-June 1980, pp. 24-30; Eric Langeard, John E. G. Bateson, Christopher H. Lovelock, and Pierre Eiglier, *Services Marketing: New Insights from Consumers and Managers* (Cambridge, MA: Marketing Science Institute, 1981); Karl Albrecht and Ron Zemke, *Service America! Doing Business in the New Economy* (Homewood, IL: Dow-Jones-Irwin, 1985); Karl Albrecht, *At America's Service* (Homewood, IL: Dow-Jones Irwin, 1988); and William H. Davidow and Bro Uttal, *Total Customer Service: The Ultimate Weapon* (New York: Harper and Row, 1989).

5. For more on definitions and classifications of services, see John E. Bateson, *Managing Services Marketing: Text and Readings* (Hinsdale, IL: Dryden Press, 1989); and Christopher H. Lovelock, *Services Marketing* (Englewood Cliffs, NJ: Prentice Hall, 1991).

6. See Theodore Levitt, "Marketing Intangible Products and Product Intangibles," *Harvard Business Review* May-June, 1981, pp. 94-102.

7. For more discussion, see James L. Heskett, "Lessons in the Service Sector," *Harvard Business Review,* March-April 1987, pp. 122-24.

8. See Ray Lewis, "Whose Job Is Service Marketing?" *Advertising Age,* August 3, 1987, pp. 14, 20.

9. For more reading on internal and interactive marketing, see Christian Gronroos, "A Service Quality Model and Its Marketing Implications," *European Journal of Marketing,* Vol. 18, No. 4, 1984, pp. 36-44; and Leonard Berry, Edwin F. Lefkowith, and Terry Clark, "In Services, What's In a Name?" *Harvard Business Review,* September-October 1988, pp. 28-30.

10. Larry Armstrong, "Beyond 'May I Help You?'" *Business Week,* special issue on quality, 1991, pp. 100-103.

11. See J. Joseph Cronin, Jr. and Steven A. Taylor, "Measuring Service Quality: A Reexamination and Extension," *Journal of Marketing,* July 1992, pp. 55-68.

12. John Paul Newport, "American Express: Service That Sells," *Fortune,* November 20, 1989. Also see Frank Rose, "Now Quality Means Service Too," *Fortune,* April 22, 1991, pp. 97-108.

13. Christopher W. L. Hart, James L. Heskett, and W. Earl Sasser, Jr., "The Profitable Art of Service Recovery," *Harvard Business Review,* July-August 1990, pp. 148-56.

14. Ibid., p. 156.

15. See James L. Heskett, W. Earl Sasser, Jr., and Christopher W. L. Hart, *Service Breakthroughs* (New York: Free Press, 1990).

16. Barry Farber and Joyce Wycoff, "Customer Service: Evolution and Revolution," *Sales & Marketing Management,* May 1991, pp. 44-51.

17. See Hal F. Rosenbluth and Diane McFerrin Peters, *The Customer Comes Second* (NY: William Morrow & Co., 1992).

18. See Roach, "Services Under Siege—The Restructuring Imperative," p. 83; and Leonard A. Schlesinger and James L. Heskett, "The Service-Driven Service Company," *Harvard Business Review,* September-October 1991, pp. 72-81.

19. Nora E. Field and Ricardo Sookdeo, "The Global Service 500," *Fortune,* August 26, 1991, pp. 166-70.

20. Michael R. Czinkota and Ilkka A. Ronkainen, *International Marketing,* 2nd ed. (Chicago: Dryden, 1990), p. 679.

21. Lee Smith, "What's at Stake in the Trade Talks," *Fortune,* August 27, 1990, pp. 76-77.

22. See Lori Kessler, "Corporate Image Advertising," *Advertising Age,* October 15, 1987, p. S1; and Anne B. Fisher, "Spiffing Up the Corporate Image," *Fortune,* July 21, 1986, p. 69.

23. See Michael Oneal, "'Air' Jordan Has the Bulls Walking on a Cloud," *Business Week,* December 12, 1988, p. 124; Fred Danzig, "The Stuff of Dreams," *Advertising Age,* June 3, 1991, p. 8; Julie Liesse, "Jordan Jumping for Gatorade," *Advertising Age,* July 15, 1991, p. 2; and Ben Walker, "Wanting to be Like Mike," *Durham Herald-Sun,* February 18, 1992, p. D4.

24. See Steven Colford, "Hail to the Image—Reagan Legacy: Marketing Tactics Change Politics," *Advertising Age,* June 27, 1988, pp. 3, 32; and Jack Honomichl, "How Reagan Took America's Pulse," *Advertising Age,* January 23, 1989, pp. 1, 25, 32.

VIDEO CASE 22

THE AMERICAN PRESIDENT: UP CLOSE AND PERSONAL

Today, the public sees so many video clips, pictures, and live press sessions with the president of the United States, his wife, offspring, or pets that they take communication with the president for granted. But prior to the late nineteenth century, most Americans did not even know what the president looked like. Candidates rarely traveled and there were no photographs of them.

Later, however, the introduction of train travel enabled candidates to take their messages to thousands of people throughout the countryside, and photography made political figures recognizable. Indeed, photographs of large crowds could create impressions of heavy support, and pictures of candidates in local settings brought them closer to local voters. Thus began early image-building efforts.

In the twentieth century, radio accelerated presidential marketing by bringing Presidents Coolidge, Wilson, and Roosevelt into American's homes at the flick of a dial. Through the transmitted word, even citizens who could not read became knowledgeable about their president's position on important issues. Later, television picked up where radio left off in promoting presidential marketing. Television allowed Americans to see as well as hear their president. Whereas only a few thousand voters saw the Lincoln–Douglas debates, tens of millions of voters watched the Kennedy–Nixon debates a century later.

Visual media concentrate on a president's image. The Kennedy–Nixon debates are remembered less for their content than for the contrast between Kennedy's youthfulness and Nixon's tense, drawn appearance. Since then, candidates have worked to project the right image. Aids now monitor everything about their candidates—their hair, clothes, facial expressions and gestures, speeches, relatives, and surroundings. For example, at the 1984 Republican convention, the edges of the podium were rounded and backlighting was used in order to portray Ronald Reagan as a center of calm surrounded by a mass of moving, noisy bodies during his acceptance speech.

To design the right image, campaign officials use surveys and focus groups. In the 1980s, Richard Wirthlin, Reagan's pollster, surveyed 1,000 to 2,000 households monthly to measure public attitudes, and polled an additional 800 households about extraordinary events. In all, he heard from more than 500,000 Americans through more than 500 surveys about subjects ranging from economic well-being to Nancy Reagan's popularity rating.

Reagan and other candidates have used focus groups to test speeches and select subjects for "theming"—repeatedly driving home a few key issues with the public. Walter Mondale used focus groups to identify Gary Hart's weakness (lack of foreign relations back-ground) in the 1984 primaries. George Bush developed campaign slogans from focus groups, and Bill Clinton used them to test personal responsibility and welfare reform themes.

In 1988, Al Gore was the first major candidate to use cable television when he announced his candidacy and advertised via satellite. By 1992, campaign managers were segmenting cable audiences on geographic, demographic, and psychographic bases. For example, messages derived from surveys and focus groups of upper income, female voters were then targeted to upper income, female cable viewers, increasing message effectiveness.

In 1992, candidates became *directly* accessible to the public via telephone during talk shows and other television appearances. The average citizen replaced the interviewer, and candidates worked hard to answer questions. Voters heard "Does that answer your question?" and "Are you satisfied?" often. Ross Perot introduced his version of the political infomercial, complete with charts and pointers. Easy accessibility showed that candidates were ordinary citizens, which may explain why Clinton treated voters to his saxophone playing and Elvis imitations, and why Perot offered colorful expressions (which ain't a heap of Jell-O, folks). Once in office, Clinton has even talked about expanding the public's ability to telephone and visit the White House, and about using computers for public communication.

But is all this communication useful? If it's just image building, will candidates be prohibited from taking controversial stands? Is what we see and hear the real substance of the candidate, or just the shadow of the image?

QUESTIONS

1. Suppose focus group results indicate that the public believes a candidate lacks personal responsibility. Discuss how a marketing campaign might improve a candidate's image on that issue.

2. Suppose focus group results suggest that Americans are concerned about the federal budget deficit, the soaring cost of health care, increasing functional illiteracy, and the deterioration of foreign relations. On which of these issues would you position: (a) a candidate for a local office such as board of commissioners; (b) a candidate for the your state's house of representatives; and (c) a presidential candidate?

3. What are the benefits of increased marketing of the president? What are the disadvantages of such increased marketing?

4. How would you describe the life-cycle patterns of candidates such as Ronald Reagan, Jerry Brown, Jesse Jackson, Dan Quayle, or Ross Perot?

Sources: Richard Armstrong, "I Have Seen Big Brother . . . And He Is Me," *Vital Speeches,* December 1, 1988, pp. 118-20; Stephen Colford, "Hail to the Image," *Advertising Age,* June 27, 1988, pp. 3, 32; and Elizabeth Kolbert, "Test-Marketing a President," *The New York Times Magazine,* August 30, 1992, pp. 18-21.

COMPANY CASE 22

CITY YEAR: RUNNING A NONPROFIT LIKE A BUSINESS

Going Downtown

As the sun rises over Boston Harbor on an early September morning, Gloria Rodriquez, 19, slips quietly out of bed so as not to disturb her four brothers and sisters. She washes and then dresses in baggy tan chinos, a T-shirt, and workboots. After eating a quick breakfast and helping her mother with a few chores, Gloria slips on a shiny red windbreaker and heads for the bus stop, arriving just as the bus that will take her from her working-class, Hispanic neighborhood to downtown Boston pulls up.

In another part of Boston, Raymond Wong, 17, awakens to the familiar sounds coming from the kitchen of his family's Chinese restaurant. He sits up in bed and reaches for his American History book, still open as he left it the night before. Glancing at the clock, Raymond figures he has enough time to finish reading the chapter assigned for this week. At 7 A.M., he fixes cereal for breakfast and watches the morning news on television. After breakfast, he slips into his tan chinos, T-shirt, and workboots, puts on his shiny read windbreaker, and heads downstairs to say good-bye to his parents. Raymond leaves the restaurant and races to the nearby "T" station where he will catch a subway that will take him the short distance to downtown Boston.

Meanwhile, in a Boston suburb, John Newberg, 19, jolts awake at the shrill sound of his digital alarm clock and rolls over to swat the off-button. He lies in bed for a minute to collect his wits and to ponder the day's activities. After showering, he too puts on his tan chinos, T-shirt, and workboots and bounces downstairs.

His mother and father are just sitting down to breakfast. John joins them, borrows the sports section of the morning paper from his father, and asks, "Got any big court cases today, Dad?"

"Not today, John. It looks like a pretty routine day."

After breakfast, John grabs his shiny red windbreaker and catches a ride with his father from their suburban home to downtown Boston.

John's father drops him off at Boston's City Hall Plaza, a large open area adjacent to City Hall. There, he joins Gloria, Raymond, and about 90 other similarly dressed young people. Promptly at 8:30, the young people line up for 15 minutes of exercises. Following the limbering-up period and some announcements, they break into groups of 10 or so and disperse throughout the city.

What do these young people have in common besides their chinos, T-shirts, workboots, and shiny red windbreakers? It certainly isn't their backgrounds. Gloria lives in a poor Hispanic community. Fighting poverty and a broken home, she recently graduated from a vocational high school. Raymond grew up in a first-generation Chinese immigrant family. He had trouble in high school and dropped out. Now he's seeking his General Equivalency Diploma (GED). In contrast, John cruised through elementary and junior high schools before going to a prestigious prep school. He graduated last June and has been accepted at Yale. He wants to follow his father into the law profession, but he has decided to take a year off before going to college.

Despite their differences, these young people have two things in common. First, as their red windbreakers and T-shirts proudly announce, they are members of City Year—each has volunteered to spend nine months working on community-service projects in Boston. Second, they have diverse backgrounds—City Year selected these young people *because* they are different.

City Year

City Year represents an innovative attempt to make voluntary national youth service a reality. In 1988, founders Michael Brown and Alan Khazei, both 30 years old and Harvard Law School graduates, became excited about voluntary service and started City Year in Boston. "The idea was to call on young people to meet the challenges facing us and to unite for a real strong public purpose," Brown observes. "The idea behind City Year is to bring young people from diverse backgrounds—rich, middle class, and poor, from different city neighborhoods as well as from the suburbs—for one year to concentrate on what they have in common and to work for the common good. We want City Year to be a workshop for innovation in the concept of voluntary national service." Allan Khazei adds that he and Brown also founded City Year ". . . out of frustration that we have the richest country in the world but also some of the deepest poverty and a high infant mortality rate. Right here in Boston, there are about 3,500 homeless people. But the problem is not a lack of resources. Rather, we lack the will and the understanding of society's problems. We want City Year to expose young people to those problems, to show them they can help, and to get them excited about service. We want City Year to educate them about the benefits of citizenship so that they will continue to serve others throughout their lives."

But Brown and Khazei didn't stop with just an idea. In 1987, working with Neil Silverston—a Harvard Business School graduate—and Jennifer Eplett—who had left a position as a financial analyst with E.F. Hutton—Brown and Khazei developed a business plan that presented the City Year concept, its strategy and objectives, and a projected budget. The plan called for a nine-week pilot program in the summer of 1988. Assuming success, City Year would operate with 50 young people in 1989-1990 and then look to expand nationally.

Brown and Khazei designed the summer pilot program to be a miniature version of the planned full-year program. They recruited 50 volunteer young people, deliberately creating a diversified group—men and women, city and suburban residents, whites, African Americans, Latinos, Asians, rich, middle class, and poor. They divided the group into five work teams, each headed by a paid supervisor. Each team member wore a T-shirt bearing the name of the group's sponsor and met every morning for exercises before splitting up to work on team projects, which included working with people with AIDS, the homeless, the elderly, and students. The team members also performed typical public-works projects, such as cleaning parks and painting shelters.

In addition to volunteers, a staff, and the projects, Brown and Khazei needed about $200,000 to finance the summer project. The big question was how to raise the money. Because City Year would not include only the disadvantaged, the founders knew that the project would not be eligible for any federal funds, which they did not want, in any case. Brown and Khazei believed that corporations, like individuals, have civic responsibilities; City Year would give these corporations a way to meet their responsibilities. In fact, they believed that corporations would *welcome* the opportunity to meet these responsibilities. At the same time, private-sector financing would give City Year the flexibility to try new ideas and to take risks that would not be possible under government financing.

Armed with their vision and a plan, Brown and Khazei set out to find sponsors. They impressed the corporate managers with both the vision and their practical plans for realizing it. Whereas many nonprofit orga-

nizations leave the nuts-and-bolts details to the end, Brown and Khazei had done their homework and had paid attention to budgets and numbers from the outset. In addition to providing the participating corporations with a way to meet their civic responsibilities, they also played on the self-interest of the corporate managers: Work-crew members would be wearing T-shirts bearing the corporate sponsor's name as they carried out a summer's worth of good deeds. Thus, Khazei and Brown achieved their $200,000 goal, with most of the support coming from just four sponsors: Bank of Boston, The Equitable, General Cinema, and Bain & Company.

Following the successful pilot project, the City Year staff recruited 50 volunteers for the 1989-1990 program year. The volunteers, ages 17 to 22, worked from September to June in ten-person teams on a variety of projects. They served as teacher's aides in public schools, ran recreational programs for senior citizens, and repaired shelters and community centers. But City Year is more than just a work program. The staff overlays the daily service projects with an experiential educational curriculum designed to promote critical thinking and to teach corps members community-building skills. Members participate in workshops, attend lectures featuring business and community leaders, serve on City Year governing committees, develop special-service projects, and share and reflect on their service experiences in corps-wide meetings.

During the nine-month service period, City Year pays each volunteer a $100 weekly stipend. At the end of the period, each volunteer receives a $5,000 "Public Service Award" in the form of either a $5,000 education or training scholarship or $2,500 in cash and a $2,500 savings certificate. Although some people might suggest that paying the young people violates the spirit of a volunteer program, Brown points out that without the stipends, only young people from wealthier families could participate. Further, he notes that the United States has a "volunteer" army, but the government pays the soldiers, and the Public Service Award is similar to the G.I. bill available to soldiers to help them with their education after they leave the army.

City Year raised approximately $1.1 million to support the 1989-1990 program. The original sponsors signed up for another year, and City Year added several new sponsors, including Reebok International, The Echoing Green Foundation (connected with a New York investment firm), and New England Telephone. Each of these sponsors contributed at least $150,000.

Of the 57 young people City Year recruited for 1989-1990, 44 completed the program and were recognized at a City Year graduation ceremony. Comments from these young people reflect their enthusiasm about the program:

As an ex-gang member, [I consider] City Year . . . a gift to me from God. I don't know what I would be doing right now if I had not been here. City Year has changed me a lot. Now I am able to teach instead of being taught.

Raymond Rodriguez, 19

I cannot imagine an experience that could give someone my age as much exposure to so many different neighborhoods and people. If everyone could do City Year, there would be much more understanding in Boston and eventually the nation. Now I'm at Amherst College, where I'm still active in community service, and memories of my City Year continue to push me against the mainstream.

Owen Stearns, 20

Based on the success of the 1989-1990 full-year program, City Year's recruiter, Kristen Atwood, scoured the city for volunteers for the 1990-1991 project year. When Atwood visited various city and suburban schools, she carried a common message: Everybody has something to give to his or her community. But she found that she also had to adapt her presentation to the character of the school's population. For example, many city students are interested in jobs, so Atwood stressed that City Year offers jobs that will give participants good experience for the future. In contrast, suburban students often feel isolated from the "real world." Therefore, Atwood emphasized the idea of service to them. To all students, she pointed out that people from different backgrounds have a lot to learn from one another.

The City Year staff looks for students who have a commitment to completing the program and the potential to contribute to and learn from the program. As a result of Atwood's and others' efforts, 70 young people participated in the 1990-1991 program, and City Year received over 600 applications for the one-hundred 1991-1992 positions.

Lessons and the Future

As Brown and Khazei relax at the end of a long, 80-hour week, they feel good about their success but are impatient to address their challenges. They have learned much in pursuing what they call "public-service entrepreneurship"—applying the skills, methods, and spirit of entrepreneurship to building nonprofit, public-service institutions. As in the business world, they suggest, there are wonderful and rewarding opportunities for putting untested but highly promising public/nonprofit entrepreneurial ideas into practice. But this does not mean that if you are successful you will make a lot of money. (Brown and Khazei pay themselves only $25,000 per year, much less than they would make practicing law.) Rather, public service requires that we redefine success and focus on *psychic income*, the joy of using our skills and abilities to the fullest for a worthwhile cause.

Outside observers also consider City Year a successful venture. The Center for Civic Enterprise in Washington, D.C., notes that the City Year program has produced four valuable lessons:

1. National service can be a common civic endeavor for youths of all ages. In its first year, City Year drew from all socioeconomic groups, with its participants coming from 25 different neighborhoods and towns in the Boston area.

2. National service can operate with a minimum of overhead and bureaucracy. Administrative costs comprise only about 20 percent of the total budget, including the salaries of a staff of twelve full-time and six part-time employees, who earn far less than they would in the private sector.

3. National service volunteers can perform work that is highly valuable to the community. Relatively unskilled youths can deliver much-needed social services in situations that call for judgment and maturity.

4. National service can foster upward mobility among those who serve. Participants say that the program has made them more likely to go to college.[1]

The Center's report also quotes Ira Jackson, Director of External Affairs of the Bank of Boston:

> Our investment in City Year was a sort of "risk philanthropy." It was an unproven venture. But we had a deep belief in the concept, which was bold and innovative, and the founders, whose enthusiasm was infectious. The implementation was competent, almost error free. They paid attention to logistics of management and worked hard to overcome the usual "do-gooder" pitfalls. They ran City Year like a business. This was the most effective $25,000 in the history of philanthropy at the Bank of Boston.

What challenges face this successful new venture? Khazei and Brown worry about developing ongoing corporate support for a program that in a few years will no longer be seen as new, and they worry about broadening their support. They also wonder about their expansion plans. Should they concentrate on growing in Boston, or should they attempt to expand City Year to other cities? If they decide to spread the idea, when will the time be right, and what is the best method? Furthermore, how can they use lessons learned in private-sector management to help them continue their success in the nonprofit sector?

Questions

1. Who are City Year's customers and what are its products? Who is its competition?

2. Why do you think City Year has been so successful?

3. Do private-sector corporations have a social responsibility to support efforts like City Year or other nonprofit activities?

4. How do the nature and characteristics of a service impact on City Year's operations?

5. How has City Year dealt with the issues that shape marketing strategies for service firms?

6. What issues and risks does City Year face as it grows? What recommendations would you make to guide its growth?

[1]"Boston's City Year: National Service Prototype?" The Center for Civic Enterprise, June 19, 1990.

Source: Based in part on "Not For Profit," in *Anatomy of a Star-Up* (Boston: The Goldhirsch Group, Inc., 1991), pp. 99-109. Used with permission. The City Year staff also provided information and assistance for the development of this case.

*M*arketing and Society: Social Responsibility and Marketing Ethics

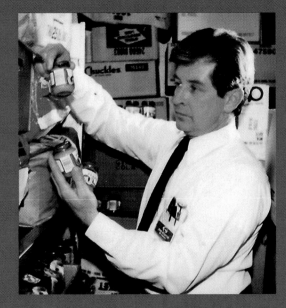

Generations of parents have trusted the health and well-being of their babies to Gerber baby foods. Gerber sells more than 1.3 billion jars of baby food each year, holding almost 70 percent of the market. But in 1986, the company's reputation was threatened when more than 250 customers in 30 states complained about finding glass fragments in Gerber baby food.

The company believed that these complaints were unfounded. Gerber plants are clean and modern and use many filters that would prevent such problems. No injuries from Gerber products were confirmed. Moreover, the Food and Drug Administration had looked at more than 40,000 jars of Gerber baby food without finding a single major problem. Gerber suspected that the glass was planted by the people making the complaints and seeking publicity or damages. Yet the complaints received widespread media coverage, and many retailers pulled Gerber products from their shelves. The state of Maryland forbade the sales of some Gerber baby foods, and other states considered such bans.

The considerable attention given to the complaints may have resulted from the "Tylenol scares," in which Tylenol capsules deliberately laced with cyanide killed a number of consumers. At the time, product tampering was a major public issue and consumer concern.

Gerber wanted to act responsibly, but social responsibility issues are rarely clear-cut. Some analysts believed that, to ensure consumer safety, Gerber should quickly recall all its baby food products from store shelves until the problem was resolved. That was how the makers of products such as Tylenol, Contac, and Gatorade had reacted to tampering scares for their products. But Gerber executives did not think that a recall was best either for consumers or for the company. After a similar scare in 1984, the company had recalled some 700,000 jars of baby food and had advertised heavily to reassure consumers. The isolated incident turned out to be the result of normal breakage during shipment. The recall cost Gerber millions of dollars in expenses and lost profits and the advertising caused unnecessary alarm and inconvenience to consumers. The company concluded that it had overreacted in its desire to be socially responsible.

The second time, therefore, Gerber decided to do nothing, at least in the short run. It refused to recall any products—in fact, it filed a $150 million suit against the state of Maryland to stop the ban on the sales of Gerber products. It suspended its advertising, monitored sales and consumer confidence, reassured nervous retailers, and waited to see what would happen. This wait-and-see strategy was very risky. Had the complaints turned out to be well founded and Gerber's failure to act quickly had caused consumer injuries or deaths, Gerber's reputation would have been seriously damaged.

Finally, when research showed that consumer concern was spreading, Gerber aired a few television ads noting its concern about "rumors you may have heard" and assuring buyers that Gerber products "meet the highest standards." The company also mailed letters to about 2 million new mothers, assuring them of Gerber's quality. In the end, the scare resulted in little long-term consumer alarm or inconvenience, and it caused only a temporary dip in Gerber's market share and reputation.

However, the question lingers: Should Gerber immediately have recalled its products to prevent even the remote chance of consumer injury? Perhaps. But in many matters of social responsibility the best course of action is often unclear.[1]

CHAPTER PREVIEW

Chapter 23 concludes the book by discussing marketing in the context of society, and highlighting the need for social responsibility and sound ethics in marketing.

We begin with a look at **criticisms of marketing's impact** on **individual consumers** and **society** as a whole.

Next, we discuss **consumerism, environmentalism,** and **regulation** and the way they affect marketing strategies. This leads us to an overview of **enlightened marketing** and **marketing** ethics.

Finally, we conclude *Principles of Marketing* with a set of **principles for public policy** toward marketing: **consumer and producer freedom; curbing harm; meeting basic needs; economic efficiency; innovation;** and **consumer education, information,** and **protection.**

Responsible marketers discover what consumers want and respond with the right products, priced to give good value to buyers and profit to the producer. The *marketing concept* is a philosophy of service and mutual gain. Its practice leads the economy by an invisible hand to satisfy the many and changing needs of millions of consumers.

Not all marketers follow the marketing concept, however. In fact, some companies use questionable marketing practices, and some marketing actions that seem innocent in themselves strongly affect the larger society. Consider the sale of cigarettes. Ordinarily, companies should be free to sell cigarettes, and smokers should be free to buy them. But this transaction affects the public interest. First, the smoker may be shortening his or her own life. Second, smoking places a burden on the smoker's family and on society at large. Third, other people around the smoker may have to inhale the smoke and may suffer discomfort and harm. This is not to say that cigarettes should be banned. Rather, it shows that private transactions may involve larger questions of public policy.

This chapter examines the social effects of private marketing practices. We examine several questions: What are the most frequent social criticisms of marketing? What steps have private citizens taken to curb marketing ills? What steps have legislators and government agencies taken to curb marketing ills? What steps have enlightened companies taken to carry out socially responsible and ethical marketing? We examine how marketing affects and is affected by each of these issues.

SOCIAL CRITICISMS OF MARKETING

Marketing receives much criticism. Some of this criticism is justified; much is not.[2] Social critics claim that certain marketing practices hurt individual consumers, society as a whole, and other business firms.

Marketing's Impact on Individual Consumers

Consumers have many concerns about how well the American marketing system serves their interests. Surveys usually show that consumers hold slightly unfavorable attitudes toward marketing practices.[3] One consumer survey found that consumers are most worried about high prices, poor-quality and dangerous products, misleading advertising claims, and several other marketing-related problems (see Figure 23-1). Consumer advocates, government agencies, and other critics have accused marketing of harming consumers through high prices, deceptive practices, high-pressure selling, shoddy or unsafe products, planned obsolescence, and poor service to disadvantaged consumers.

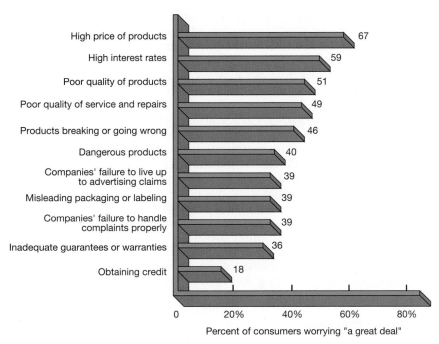

FIGURE 23-1
Survey of consumer concerns
Source: See Myrlie Evers, "Consumerism in the Eighties," reprinted with permission from the August 1983 issue of *Public Relations Journal,* copyright 1983, pp. 24-26. Also see "The Public Is Willing to Take on Business," *Business Week,* May 29, 1989, p. 29.

High Prices

Many critics charge that the American marketing system causes prices to be higher than they would be under more "sensible" systems. They point to three factors—*high costs of distribution, high advertising and promotion costs,* and *excessive markups.*

High Costs of Distribution. A longstanding charge is that greedy middlemen mark up prices beyond the value of their services. Critics charge either that there are too many middlemen or that middlemen are inefficient and poorly run, that they provide unnecessary or duplicate services, and that they practice poor management and planning. As a result, distribution costs too much, and consumers pay for these excessive costs in the form of higher prices.

How do retailers answer these charges? They argue as follows: First, middlemen do work that would otherwise have to be done by manufacturers or consumers. Second, the rising markup reflects improved services that consumers themselves want—more convenience, larger stores and assortment, longer store hours, return privileges, and others. Third, the costs of operating stores keep rising, forcing retailers to raise their prices. Fourth, retail competition is so intense that margins are actually quite low. For example, after taxes, supermarket chains are typically left with barely one percent profit on their sales.

High Advertising and Promotion Costs. Modern marketing also is accused of pushing up prices because of heavy advertising and sales promotion. For example, a dozen tablets of a heavily promoted brand of aspirin sell for the same price as do 100 tablets of less promoted brands. Differentiated products—cosmetics, detergents, toiletries—include promotion and packaging costs that can amount to 40 percent or more of the manufacturer's price to the retailer. Critics charge that much of the packaging and promotion adds only psychological value to the product rather than functional value. Retailers use additional promotion—advertising, displays, and sweepstakes—that add several cents more to retail prices.

Marketers answer these charges in several ways. First, consumers *want* more than the merely functional qualities of products. They also want psychological benefits—they want to feel wealthy, beautiful, or special. Consumers usually can buy functional versions of products at lower prices but often are willing to pay more for products that also provide desired psychological benefits. Second, branding gives buyers confidence. A brand name implies a certain quality, and consumers are willing to pay for well-known brands even if they cost a little more. Third, heavy advertising is needed to inform millions of potential buyers of the merits of a brand. If consumers want to know what is available on the market, they must expect manufacturers to spend large sums of money on advertising.

Some retailers use high markups, but the higher prices cover services that consumers want—assortment, convenience, personal service, and return privileges.

Fourth, heavy advertising and promotion may be necessary for a firm to match competitors' efforts. The business would lose "share of mind" if it did not match competitive spending. At the same time, companies are cost conscious about promotion and try to spend their money wisely. Finally, heavy sales promotion is needed from time to time because goods are produced ahead of demand in a mass-production economy. Special incentives have to be offered in order to sell inventories.

Excessive Markups. Critics also charge that some companies mark up goods excessively. They point to the drug industry, where a pill costing 5 cents to make may cost the consumer 40 cents to buy. They point to the pricing tactics of funeral homes that prey on the emotions of bereaved relatives and to the high charges of television repair and auto repair people.

Marketers respond that most businesses try to deal fairly with consumers because they want repeat business. Most consumer abuses are unintentional. When shady marketers do take advantage of consumers, they should be reported to Better Business Bureaus and to other consumer-protection groups. Marketers also respond that consumers often don't understand the reason for high markups. For example, pharmaceutical markups must cover the costs of purchasing, promoting, and distributing existing medicines plus the high research and development costs of finding new medicines.

Deceptive Practices

Marketers sometimes are accused of deceptive practices that lead consumers to believe they will get more value than they actually do. Deceptive practices fall into three groups: deceptive pricing, promotion, and packaging. *Deceptive pricing* includes practices such as falsely advertising "factory" or "wholesale" prices or a large price reduction from a phony high list price. *Deceptive promotion* includes practices such as overstating the product's features or performance, luring the customer to the store for a bargain that is out of stock, or running rigged contests. *Deceptive packaging* includes exaggerating package contents through subtle design, not filling the package to the top, using misleading labeling, or describing size in misleading terms.

Deceptive practices have led to legislation and other consumer-protection actions. In 1938, the Wheeler-Lea Act gave the FTC the power to regulate "unfair or deceptive acts or practices." The FTC has published several guidelines listing deceptive practices. The toughest problem is defining what is "deceptive." For example, some years ago, Shell Oil advertised that Super Shell gasoline with platformate gave more mileage than did the same gasoline without platformate. Now this was true, but what Shell did not say is that almost *all* gasoline includes platformate. Its defense was that it had never claimed that platformate was found only in Shell gasoline. But even though the message was literally true, the FTC felt that the ad's *intent* was to deceive.

Marketers argue that most companies avoid deceptive practices because such practices harm their business in the long run. If consumers do not get what they expect, they will switch to more reliable products. In addition, consumers usually protect themselves from deception. Most consumers recognize a marketer's selling intent and are careful when they buy, sometimes to the point of not believing completely true product claims. Theodore Levitt claims that some advertising puffery is bound to occur—and that it may even be desirable:

> There is hardly a company that would not go down in ruin if it refused to provide fluff, because nobody will buy pure functionality. . . . Worse, it denies . . . man's honest needs and values. . . . Without distortion, embellishment, and elaboration, life would be drab, dull, anguished, and at its existential worst. . . .[4]

High-Pressure Selling

Salespeople are sometimes accused of high-pressure selling that persuades people to buy goods they had no thought of buying. It is often said that encyclopedias, insurance, real estate, and jewelry are *sold*, not *bought*. Salespeople are trained to deliver smooth, canned talks to entice purchase. They sell hard because sales contests promise big prizes to those who sell the most.

Marketers know that buyers often can be talked into buying unwanted or unneeded things. Laws require door-to-door salespeople to announce that they are selling a product. Buyers also have a "three-day cooling-off period" in which they can cancel a contract after rethinking it. In addition, consumers can complain to Better Business Bureaus or to state consumer-protection agencies when they feel that undue selling pressure has been applied.

Shoddy or Unsafe Products

Another criticism is that products lack the quality they should have. One complaint is that products are not made well. Automobiles bear the brunt of many such complaints—it seems that every new car has something wrong with it. Consumers grumble about rattles and pings, misalignments, dents, leaking, and creaking. Complaints also have been lodged against home and auto repair services, appliances, and clothing.

A second complaint is that some products deliver little benefit. Some consumers are surprised to learn that many of the "healthy" foods being marketed today, ranging from cholesterol-free salad dressings and low-fat frozen dinners to high-fiber bran cereals, may have little nutritional value. In fact, they may even be harmful.

> [Despite] sincere efforts on the part of most marketers to provide healthier products, . . . many promises emblazoned on packages and used as ad slogans continue to confuse nutritionally uninformed consumers and . . . may actually be harmful to that group. . . . [Many consumers] incorrectly assume the product is "safe" and eat greater amounts than are good for them. . . . For example, General Foods USA's new Entenmann's "low-cholesterol, low-calorie" cherry coffee cake . . . may confuse some consumers who shouldn't eat much of it. While each serving is only 90 calories, not everyone realizes that the suggested serving is tiny [one-thirteenth of the small cake]. Although eating half an Entenmann's cake may be better than eating half a dozen Dunkin Donuts, . . . neither should be eaten in great amounts by people on restrictive diets.[5]

A third complaint concerns product safety. Product safety has been a problem for several reasons, including manufacturer indifference, increased production complexity, poorly trained labor, and poor quality control. For years, Consumers Union—the organization that publishes *Consumer Reports*—has reported various hazards in tested products: electrical dangers in appliances, carbon monoxide poisoning from room heaters, injury risks from lawn mowers, and faulty automobile design, among many others. The organization's testing and other activities have helped consumers make better buying decisions and encourages businesses to eliminate product flaws (see Marketing Highlight 23-1).

However, most manufacturers *want* to produce quality goods. Consumers who are unhappy with a firm's products may avoid its other products and talk other consumers into doing the same. The way a company deals with product quality and safety problems can damage or help its reputation. Companies selling poor-quality or unsafe products risk damaging conflicts with consumer groups. Moreover, unsafe products can result in product-liability suits and large awards for damages.

Planned Obsolescence

Critics also have charged that some producers follow a program of **planned obsolescence,** causing their products to become obsolete before they actually should need replacement. In many cases, producers have been accused of continually changing consumer concepts of acceptable styles in order to encourage more and earlier buying. An obvious example is constantly changing clothing fashions. Producers also have been accused of holding back attractive functional features, then introducing them later to make older models obsolete. Critics claim that this practice is found in the consumer electronics industry. Finally, producers have been accused of using materials and components that will break, wear, rust, or rot sooner than they should. For example, many drapery manufacturers are using a higher percentage of rayon in their drapes. They argue that rayon reduces the price of the drapes and has better holding power. Critics claim that using more rayon causes the drapes to fall apart sooner.

Marketers respond that consumers *like* style changes; they get tired of the old goods and want a new look in fashion or a new design in cars. No one has to

MARKETING HIGHLIGHT 23-1

WHEN CONSUMER REPORTS TALKS, BUYERS LISTEN—AND SO DO COMPANIES

Whether they're buying automobiles or life insurance, drain cleaner or refrigerators—or practically anything else—millions of shoppers won't plunk down their money until they consult *Consumer Reports*. For 51 years, the publication of Consumers Union has been a fiercely independent arbiter of quality goods and an ardent advocate of consumer rights. It has published CU's ratings of thousands of products and services without ever losing a libel suit. And today its monthly circulation is at an all-time high of 3.8 million.

A 106-member technical team puts products through their paces at CU's headquarters in Mount Vernon, NY. When they can, they use the same tests industry uses. They check the laundering power of washing machines, for example, by washing presoiled fabric swatches and measuring their brightness with optical instruments. If no standard tests exist, *Consumer Reports* invents them. To rate facial tissues, CU's technical team built a "sneeze machine" that squirts a controlled spray of water and air through a tissue mounted on embroidery hoops.

CU describes its tests in detail when it rates products. But those explanations don't always placate the manufacturer whose product comes in last. If a company isn't happy with its rating, CU responds with an invitation to visit its labs.

Many companies have made changes in their products after getting a bad rating from CU. Although Whirlpool chafed at criticism that its washing-machine design made repair too difficult, on its new models the cabinet pops off to allow access to important parts.

In its April 1973, issue, *Consumer Reports* rejected an entire category of products—microwave ovens—because doors on all 14 models tested were leaking radiation. Since then, ovenmakers have changed their designs. Today, "there's very little leakage around those doors," says CU technical director R. David Pittle.

Although *Consumer Reports* remains CU's major endeavor, the organization is branching out. In the past

Consumers Union's 106-member technical team puts products through their paces.

two years, it has launched a travel newsletter, produced six home videocassettes, spruced up its *Penny Power* children's magazine, and formed a book-publishing company. Since January, CU has been selling dealer's-cost listing for most auto models and options. Its media push also includes a thrice-weekly syndicated newspaper column, plus radio and television spots. All this has helped CU's bottom line. Last year it earned $3.4 million.

Prosperity has not diluted CU's activism. Founded by labor unionists in the 1930s, it was among the first organizations to urge consumers to boycott goods made in Nazi Germany. Now *Consumer Reports* is alarmed that many Americans are slipping into poverty. So it is kicking off a three-part series on the working poor. But will the outspoken judge of what's good comment on how well U.S. manufacturers stack up against the Japanese? No way, says Pittle. "Our purpose is to provide an objective evaluation of a product—regardless of who made it."

Source: Mimi Bluestone, "When *Consumer Reports* Talks, Buyers Listen—and So Do Companies," *Business Week,* June 8, 1987, p. 135. Reprinted by special permission; © 1987 by McGraw-Hill, Inc.

buy the new look, and if too few people like it, it will simply fail. Companies frequently withhold new features when they are not fully tested, when they add more cost to the product than consumers are willing to pay, and for other good reasons. But they do so at the risk that a competitor will introduce the new feature and steal the market. Moreover, companies often put in new materials to lower their costs and prices. They do not design their products to break down earlier, because they do not want to lose their customers to other brands. Thus, much of so-called planned obsolescence is the working of the competitive and technological forces in a free society—forces that lead to ever-improving goods and services.

Poor Service to Disadvantaged Consumers

Finally, the American marketing system has been accused of poorly serving disadvantaged consumers. Critics claim that the urban poor often have to shop in smaller stores that carry inferior goods and charge higher prices. Paul Rand Dixon, the former chairman of the Federal Trade Commission (FTC), summarized a Washington, DC, study as follows:

> The poor pay more—nearly twice as much—for appliances and furniture sold in Washington's low-income area stores . . . Goods purchased for $100 at wholesale sold for $225 in the low-income stores compared with $159 in the general market stores . . . Installment credit is a major marketing factor in selling to the poor . . . some low-income market retailers imposed effective annual finance charges as high as 33 percent. . . . [6]

Yet the merchants' profits were not too high:

> Low-income market retailers have markedly higher costs, partly because of bad debt expenses, but to a greater extent because of higher selling, wage, and commission costs. These expenses reflect in part greater use of home demonstration selling, and expenses associated with the collection and processing of installment contracts. Thus, although their markups are often two or three times higher than general market retailers, on the average low-income market retailers do not make particularly high profits.[7]

Clearly, better marketing systems must be built in low-income areas—one hope is to get large retailers to open outlets in low-income areas. Moreover, low-income people clearly need consumer protection. The FTC has taken action against merchants who advertise false values, sell old merchandise as new, or charge too much for credit. The commission also is trying to make it harder for merchants to win court judgments against low-income people who were wheedled into buying something.

Marketing's Impact on Society as a Whole

The American marketing system has been accused of adding to several "evils" in American society at large. Advertising has been a special target—so much so that the American Association of Advertising Agencies launched a campaign to defend advertising against what it felt to be common but untrue criticisms (see Marketing Highlight 23-2).

False Wants and Too Much Materialism

Critics have charged that the marketing system urges too much interest in material possessions. People are judged by what they *own* rather than by what they *are*. To be considered successful, people must own a suburban home, two cars, and the latest clothes and consumer electronics. Indeed, this drive for wealth and possessions appears to have hit its peak in recent years:

> Money, money, money is the incantation of today. Bewitched by an epidemic of money enchantment, Americans wriggle in a St. Vitus's dance of materialism unseen since the Gilded Age of the Roaring Twenties. Under the blazing sun of money, all other values shine palely. . . . The evidence is everywhere. Open the scarlet covers of the Saks Fifth Avenue Christmas catalog, for starters, and look at what Santa Claus offers today's young family, from Dad's $1,650 ostrich-skin briefcase and Mom's $39,500 fur coat to Junior's $4,000, 15-mph miniature Mercedes.[8]

In the 1990s, many social scientists are noting a reaction against the opulence and waste of the 1980s and a return to more basic values and social commitment. For example, when asked in a recent poll what they value most in their lives, subjects listed enjoyable work (86 percent), happy children (84 percent), a good marriage (69 percent), and contributions to society (66 percent). However, when asked what most symbolizes success, 85 percent said money and the things it will buy. Thus, our infatuation with material things continues.[9]

Critics do not view this interest in material things as a natural state of mind but rather as a matter of false wants created by marketing. Businesses hire Madison Avenue to stimulate people's desires for goods, and Madison Avenue uses the mass media to create materialistic models of the good life. People work harder to earn the necessary money. Their purchases increase the output of American in-

ADVERTISING: ANOTHER WORD FOR FREEDOM OF CHOICE

During the past few years, the American Association of Advertising Agencies has run a campaign featuring ads such as this to counter common criticism of advertising. The association is concerned about research findings of negative public attitudes toward advertising. Two-thirds of the public recognizes that advertising provides helpful buying information, but a significant portion feels that advertising is exaggerated or misleading. The association believes that its ad campaign will increase general advertising credibility and make advertisers' messages more effective. Several media agreed to run the ads as a public service.

The American Association of Advertising Agencies runs ads to counter common advertising criticisms.

dustry, and industry in turn uses Madison Avenue to stimulate more desire for the industrial output. Thus, marketing is seen as creating false wants that benefit industry more than they benefit consumers.

These criticisms overstate the power of business to create needs, however. People have strong defenses against advertising and other marketing tools. Marketers are most effective when they appeal to existing wants rather than when they attempt to create new ones. Furthermore, people seek information when making important purchases and often do not rely on single sources. Even minor purchases that may be affected by advertising messages lead to repeat purchases only if the product performs as promised. Finally, the high failure rate of new products shows that companies are not able to control demand.

On a deeper level, our wants and values are influenced not only by marketers, but also by family, peer groups, religion, ethnic background, and education. If Americans are highly materialistic, these values arose out of basic socialization processes that go much deeper than business and mass media could produce alone.

Too Few Social Goods

Business has been accused of overselling private goods at the expense of public goods. As private goods increase, they require more public services that are usually not forthcoming. For example, an increase in automobile ownership (private good) requires more highways, traffic control, parking spaces, and police services (public goods). The overselling of private goods results in "social costs." For cars, the social costs include excessive traffic congestion, air pollution, and deaths and injuries from car accidents.

A way must be found to restore a balance between private and public goods. One option is to make producers bear the full social costs of their operations. For example, the government could require automobile manufacturers to build cars with additional safety features and better pollution-control systems. Auto makers then would raise their prices to cover extra costs. If buyers found the price of some cars too high, however, the producers of these cars would disappear, and demand would move to those producers that could support the sum of the private and social costs.

Cultural Pollution

Critics charge the marketing system with creating *cultural pollution*. Our senses are being assaulted constantly by advertising. Commercials interrupt serious programs; pages of ads obscure printed matter; billboards mar beautiful scenery. These interruptions continuously pollute people's minds with messages of materialism, sex, power, or status. Although most people do not find advertising overly annoying (some even think it is the best part of television programming), some critics call for sweeping changes.

Cultural pollution: People's senses are sometimes assaulted by commercial messages.

Marketers answer the charges of "commercial noise" with these arguments: First, they hope that their ads reach primarily the target audience. But because of mass-communication channels, some ads are bound to reach people who have no interest in the product and are therefore bored or annoyed. People who buy magazines addressed to their interests—such as *Vogue* or *Fortune*—rarely complain about the ads because the magazines advertise products of interest. Second, ads make television and radio free media and keep down the costs of magazines and newspapers. Most people think commercials are a small price to pay.

Too Much Political Power

Another criticism is that business wields too much political power. "Oil," "tobacco," and "auto" senators support an industry's interests against the public interest. Advertisers are accused of holding too much power over the mass media, limiting their freedom to report independently and objectively. One critic has asked: "How can *Life* . . . and *Reader's Digest* afford to tell the truth about the scandalously low nutritional value of most packaged foods . . . when these magazines are being subsidized by such advertisers as General Foods, Kellogg's, Nabisco, and General Mills? . . . The answer is *they cannot and do not*."[10]

American industries promote and protect their interests. They have a right to representation in Congress and the mass media, although their influence can become too great. Fortunately, many powerful business interests once thought to be untouchable have been tamed in the public interest. For example, Standard Oil was broken up in 1911, and the meatpacking industry was disciplined in the early 1900s after exposures by Upton Sinclair. Ralph Nader caused legislation that forced the automobile industry to build more safety into its cars, and the Surgeon General's Report resulted in cigarette companies putting health warnings on their packages. Moreover, because the media receive advertising revenues from many different advertisers, it is easier to resist the influence of one or a few of them. Too much business power tends to result in counterforces that check and offset these powerful interests.

Marketing's Impact on Other Businesses

Critics also charge that a company's marketing practices can harm other companies and reduce competition. Three problems are involved: acquisitions of competitors, marketing practices that create barriers to entry, and unfair competitive marketing practices.

Critics claim that firms are harmed and competition reduced when companies expand by acquiring competitors rather than by developing their own new products. In the food industry alone during the past few years, R. J. Reynolds acquired Nabisco Brands; Philip Morris bought General Foods and Kraft; Procter & Gamble gobbled up Richardson-Vicks, Noxell, and parts of Revlon; Nestlé absorbed Carnation; and Quaker Oats bought Stokely-Van Camp. These and other large acquisitions in other industries have caused concern that vigorous young competitors will be absorbed and that competition will be reduced.

Acquisition is a complex subject. Acquisitions can sometimes be good for society. The acquiring company may gain economies of scale that lead to lower costs and lower prices. A well-managed company may take over a poorly managed company and improve its efficiency. An industry that was not very competitive might become more competitive after the acquisition. But acquisitions also can be harmful and, therefore, are closely regulated by the government.

Critics also have charged that marketing practices bar new companies from entering an industry. Large marketing companies can use patents and heavy promotion spending, and can tie up suppliers or dealers to keep out or drive out competitors. People concerned with antitrust regulation recognize that some barriers are the natural result of the economic advantages of doing business on a large scale. Other barriers could be challenged by existing and new laws. For example, some critics have proposed a progressive tax on advertising spending to reduce the role of selling costs as a major barrier to entry.

Finally, some firms have in fact used unfair competitive marketing practices with the intention of hurting or destroying other firms. They may set their prices below costs, threaten to cut off business with suppliers, or discourage the buying of a competitor's products. Various laws work to prevent such predatory competition. It is difficult, however, to prove that the intent or action was really predatory. In the classic A&P case, the large retailer was able to charge lower prices than were small "mom and pop" grocery stores. The question is whether this was unfair competition or the healthy competition of a more efficient retailer against the less efficient.

CITIZEN AND PUBLIC ACTIONS TO REGULATE MARKETING

Because some people view business as the cause of many economic and social ills, grass-roots movements have arisen from time to time to keep business in line. The two major movements have been *consumerism* and *environmentalism*.

Consumerism

American business firms have been the target of organized consumer movements on three occasions. The first consumer movement took place in the early 1900s. It was fueled by rising prices, Upton Sinclair's writings on conditions in the meat industry, and scandals in the drug industry. The second consumer movement, in the mid-1930s, was sparked by an upturn in consumer prices during the Great Depression and another drug scandal.

The third movement began in the 1960s. Consumers had become better educated, products had become more complex and hazardous, and people were unhappy with American institutions. Ralph Nader appeared on the scene to force many issues, and other well-known writers accused big business of wasteful and unethical practices. President John F. Kennedy declared that consumers have the right to safety and to be informed, to choose, and to be heard. Congress investigated certain industries and proposed consumer-protection legislation. Since then, many consumer groups have been organized, and several consumer laws have been passed. The consumer movement has spread internationally and has become very strong in Europe.[11]

But what is the consumer movement? **Consumerism** is an organized movement of citizens and government agencies to improve the rights and power of buyers in relation to sellers. Traditional sellers' rights include:

- The right to introduce any product in any size and style, provided it is not hazardous to personal health or safety; or, if it is, to include proper warnings and controls.
- The right to charge any price for the product, provided no discrimination exists among similar kinds of buyers.
- The right to spend any amount to promote the product, provided it is not defined as unfair competition.
- The right to use any product message, provided it is not misleading or dishonest in content or execution.
- The right to use any buying incentive schemes, provided they are not unfair or misleading.

Traditional buyers' rights include:

- The right not to buy a product that is offered for sale.
- The right to expect the product to be safe.
- The right to expect the product to perform as claimed.

Comparing these rights, many believe that the balance of power lies on the sellers' side. True, the buyer can refuse to buy. But critics feel that the buyer has too little information, education, and protection to make wise decisions when facing sophisticated sellers. Consumer advocates call for the following additional consumer rights:

- The right to be well informed about important aspects of the product.
- The right to be protected against questionable products and marketing practices.
- The right to influence products and marketing practices in ways that will improve the "quality of life."

Each proposed right has led to more specific proposals by consumerists. The right to be informed includes the right to know the true interest on a loan (truth in lending), the true cost per unit of a brand (unit pricing), the ingredients in a product (ingredient labeling), the nutrition in foods (nutritional labeling), product freshness (open dating), and the true benefits of a product (truth in advertising). Proposals related to consumer protection include strengthening consumer rights in cases of business fraud, requiring greater product safety, and giving more power to government agencies. Proposals relating to quality of life include controlling the ingredients that go into certain products (detergents) and packaging (soft-drink containers), reducing the level of advertising "noise," and putting consumer representatives on company boards to protect consumer interests.

Consumers have not only the *right* but also the *responsibility* to protect themselves instead of leaving this function to someone else. Consumers who believe they got a bad deal have several remedies available, including writing to the company president or to the media; contacting federal, state, or local agencies; and going to small-claims courts.

Environmentalism

Whereas consumerists consider whether the marketing system is efficiently serving consumer wants, environmentalists are concerned with marketing's effects on the environment and with the costs of serving consumer needs and wants. They are concerned with damage to the ecosystem caused by strip mining, forest depletion, acid rain, loss of the atmosphere's ozone layer, toxic wastes, and litter. They also are concerned with the loss of recreational areas and with the increase in health problems caused by bad air, polluted water, and chemically treated food. These concerns are the basis for **environmentalism**—an organized movement of concerned citizens and government agencies to protect and improve people's living environment.

Environmentalists are not against marketing and consumption; they simply want people and organizations to operate with more care for the environment. The marketing system's goal should not be to maximize consumption, consumer choice, or consumer satisfaction, but rather to maximize life quality. And "life quality" means not only the quantity and quality of consumer goods and services, but also the quality of the environment. Environmentalists want environmental costs included in both producer and consumer decision making.

Environmentalism has hit some industries hard. Steel companies and public utilities have had to invest billions of dollars in pollution-control equipment and costlier fuels. The auto industry has had to introduce expensive emission controls in cars. The packaging industry has had to find ways to reduce litter. The gasoline industry has had to create new low-lead and no-lead gasolines. These industries often resent environmental regulations, especially when they are imposed too rapidly to allow companies to make proper adjustments. These companies have absorbed large costs and have passed them on to buyers.

Thus, marketers' lives have become more complicated. Marketers must check into the ecological properties of their products and packaging. They must raise prices to cover environmental costs, knowing that the product will be harder to sell. Yet environmental issues have become so important in our society that there is no turning back to the time when few managers worried about the effects of product and marketing decisions on environmental quality. Many analysts view the 1990s as the "Earth Decade," in which protection of the natural environment will be the major issue facing people around the world. Companies have responded with "green marketing"—developing ecologically safer products, recyclable and biodegradable packaging, better pollution controls, and more energy-efficient operations (see Marketing Highlight 23-3).

THE NEW ENVIRONMENTALISM AND "GREEN MARKETING"

On Earth Day 1970, a newly emerging environmentalism movement made its first large-scale effort to educate Americans about the dangers of pollution. This was a tough task: At the time, most Americans weren't all that interested in environmental problems. Earth Day 1990, however, became a nationwide cause, punctuated by articles in major magazines and newspapers, prime-time television extravaganzas, and countless events. Major companies, eager to show their corporate concern, ran special Earth Day advertisements and contributed money, equipment, and labor to support Earth Day events. Earth Day 1990 turned out to be just the start of an entire "Earth Decade" in which environmentalism has become a massive worldwide force.

These days, environmentalism has broad public support. Polls show that 76 percent of all Americans consider themselves environmentalists. People now hear and read daily about a growing list of environmental problems—global warming, acid rain, depletion of the ozone layer, air and water pollution, hazardous waste disposal, the buildup of solid wastes—and they are now calling for solutions. The new environmentalism is causing many consumers to rethink what products they buy and from whom. Many consumers say they are willing to spend more and to give up convenience in order to buy environmentally safe products. These changing consumer attitudes have sparked a major new marketing thrust—*green marketing*—the movement by companies to develop and market environmentally responsible products.

For example, McDonald's has "turned green." It used to purchase Coca-Cola syrup in plastic bags encased in cardboard, but now the syrup is delivered as gasoline is, pumped directly from tank trucks into storage vats at restaurants. The change saved 68 million pounds of packaging a year. All napkins, bags, and tray liners in McDonald's restaurants are made from recycled paper, as are its carry-out drink trays and even the stationery used at headquarters. For a company the size of McDonald's, even small changes can make a big difference. For example, just making its drinking straws 20 percent lighter saved the company 1 million pounds of waste per year. Beyond turning its own products green, McDonald's purchases recycled materials for building and remodeling its restaurants, and it challenges its suppliers to furnish and use recycled products.

Producers in a wide range of industries are responding to environmental concerns. For example, Herman Miller, a large office furniture manufacturer, set a trend in the furniture industry when it began using tropical woods from sustainably managed sources, altering even its classic furniture lines. But it went even further by reusing packaging, recapturing solvents used in staining, and burning fabric scraps and sawdust to make energy for its manufacturing plant. As it turns out, these moves not only help the environment, they also save Herman Miller $750,000 per year on energy and landfill costs.

Several other companies have done an outstanding job of meeting their environmental responsibilities. 3M runs a *Pollution Prevention Pays* program, which has led to substantial pollution and cost reduction. Dow built a new ethylene plant in Alberta that uses 40 percent less energy and releases 97 percent less waste water. AT&T uses a software program to choose the least harmful materials, cut hazardous waste, reduce energy use, and improve product recycling.

Even retailers are jumping onto the "green" bandwagon. For example, Wal-Mart is pressuring its 7,000 suppliers to provide it with more recycled products. In its stores, Wal-Mart runs videos to help educate customers, and the retailer has set up more than 900 recycling bins in store parking lots around the nation.

Committed "green" companies pursue not only environmental cleanup but also pollution prevention. They aim to produce "high value, high virtue" products by improving both input and output technologies. They recognize that shipping pollutants to landfills or incinerators does not provide a permanent solution. True "green" work requires companies to practice the three *R*'s of waste management: reducing, reusing, and recycling waste.

Promoting environmentally improved products and actions has ballooned into a big business. In fact, some environmentalists and regulators are concerned that companies may be going overboard with their environmental pitches. Terms like *recyclable, degradable,* and *environmentally responsible* are not yet well defined, and such environmental claims might be exploited or distorted. Some overeager green-marketing campaigns have been vigorously attacked by environmentalists and law makers for making unproven or improper claims. For example, Mobil altered its Hefty trash bags so that they would break down more easily and began to market them as "degradable." However, these claims ran afoul of the Environmental Defense Fund and several states' attorneys general when it was learned that the bags only degrade when they're exposed to air and light—most trash bags are buried in landfills. In 1992, the Federal Trade Commission issued a set of voluntary guidelines for green marketing terms to help guide marketers making environmental claims for their products.

Still, marketers sometimes find it difficult to determine just what *is* best for the environment. For years, McDonald's held steadfastly to using styrofoam containers for its hamburgers, while trying to educate consumers that the recyclable styrofoam containers were a

Corporate environmentalism: Enlightened companies are taking action not because someone is forcing them to but because it is the right thing to do.

reasonable environmental price to pay for convenient, hot food. But when it finally yielded to pressure from environmentalists and changed to paper packaging, its new paper wrappers also attracted criticism. Although they take up less space in landfills than the old-style box, the plastic-coated paper can't be used by most recycling programs.

Perhaps of equal concern is the fact that as more and more marketers use green marketing claims, more and more consumers are viewing them as little more than gimmicks. Moreover, marketers may have overestimated likely consumer response to green marketing programs. Although repeated surveys show that most adults say they are concerned about the environment, actual behavior seems to lag behind. For example, only 26 percent of Americans regularly recycle newspapers, 23 percent avoid buying aerosols, and as few as 7 percent of consumers consciously avoid restaurants that use styrofoam containers.

Many companies have responded to the new environmentalism by doing whatever is required to avert new regulations or to keep environmentalists quiet. Others are rushing to make money by catering to the public's mounting concern for the environment. But enlightened companies are taking action not because someone is forcing them to, or to reap short-run profits, but because it is the right thing to do. They believe that

environmental farsightedness today will pay off tomorrow. For example, Edgar Woolard, chief executive officer of Du Pont, believes that companies should do more than merely comply with the laws. He states,

> The real environmental challenge is not one of responding to the next regulatory proposal. Nor is it making the environmentalists see things our way. Nor is it educating the public to appreciate the benefits of our products and thus to tolerate their environmental impacts . . . I'm calling for *corporate environmentalism,* which I define as an attitude and a performance commitment that places corporate environmental stewardship fully in line with public desires and expectations.

Sources: Joe Schwartz, "Earth Day Today," *American Demographics,* April 1990, pp. 40-41; Schwartz and Thomas Miller, "The Earth's Best Friends," *American Demographics,* February 1991, pp. 26-36; David Woodruff, "Herman Miller: How Green Is My Factory," *Business Week,* September 16, 1991, pp. 54-56; Melanie Rigney, "Matter of Semantics—Or of Survival?" *Advertising Age,* June 29, 1992, pp. S2, S9; Steven W. Colford, "FTC Green Guidelines May Spark Ad Efforts," *Advertising Age,* August 3, 1992, pp. 1, 29; Jacquelyn Ottman, "Environmentalism Will Be the Trend of the '90s," *Marketing News,* December 7, 1992, p. 13; S. K. List, "The Green Seal of Eco-Approval," *American Demographics,* January 1993, pp. 9-10; and Gary Levin, "Too Green for Their Own Good," *Advertising Age,* April 12, 1993, p. 29.

Public Actions to Regulate Marketing

Citizen concerns about marketing practices usually will lead to public attention and legislative proposals. New bills will be debated—many will be defeated, others will be modified, and a few will become workable laws.

Many of the laws that affect marketing are listed in Chapter 3. The task is to translate these laws into the language that marketing executives understand as they make decisions about competitive relations, products, price, promotion, and channels of distribution. Figure 23-2 illustrates the major legal issues facing marketing management.

BUSINESS ACTIONS TOWARD SOCIALLY RESPONSIBLE MARKETING

At first, many companies opposed consumerism and environmentalism. They thought the criticisms were either unfair or unimportant. But by now, most companies have grown to accept the new consumer rights, at least in principle. They might oppose certain pieces of legislation as inappropriate ways to solve certain consumer problems, but they recognize the consumer's right to information and protection. Many of these companies have responded positively to consumerism and environmentalism in order to serve consumer needs better.

Enlightened Marketing

The philosophy of **enlightened marketing** holds that a company's marketing should support the best long-run performance of the marketing system. Enlightened marketing consists of five principles: *consumer-oriented marketing, innovative marketing, value marketing, sense-of-mission marketing,* and *societal marketing.*

Consumer-Oriented Marketing

Consumer-oriented marketing means that the company should view and organize its marketing activities from the consumer's point of view. It should work hard to sense, serve, and satisfy the needs of a defined group of customers. Consider the following example:

> Barat College, a women's college in Lake Forest, Illinois, published a college catalog that openly spelled out Barat College's strong and weak points. Among the weak points it shared with applicants were the following: "An exceptionally talented student musician or mathematician . . . might be advised to look further for a college

FIGURE 23-2
Legal issues facing marketing management

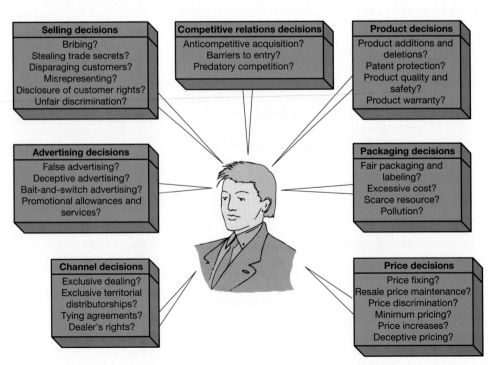

| Selling decisions |
| Bribing? |
| Stealing trade secrets? |
| Disparaging customers? |
| Misrepresenting? |
| Disclosure of customer rights? |
| Unfair discrimination? |

| Competitive relations decisions |
| Anticompetitive acquisition? |
| Barriers to entry? |
| Predatory competition? |

| Product decisions |
| Product additions and deletions? |
| Patent protection? |
| Product quality and safety? |
| Product warranty? |

| Advertising decisions |
| False advertising? |
| Deceptive advertising? |
| Bait-and-switch advertising? |
| Promotional allowances and services? |

| Packaging decisions |
| Fair packaging and labeling? |
| Excessive cost? |
| Scarce resource? |
| Pollution? |

| Channel decisions |
| Exclusive dealing? |
| Exclusive territorial distributorships? |
| Tying agreements? |
| Dealer's rights? |

| Price decisions |
| Price fixing? |
| Resale price maintenance? |
| Price discrimination? |
| Minimum pricing? |
| Price increases? |
| Deceptive pricing? |

with top faculty and facilities in that field. . . . The full range of advanced specialized courses offered in a university will be absent. . . . The library collection is average for a small college, but low in comparison with other high-quality institutions."

"Telling it like it is" is intended to build confidence so that applicants really know what they will find at Barat College and to emphasize that Barat College will strive to improve its consumer value as rapidly as time and funds permit.

Innovative Marketing

The principle of **innovative marketing** requires that the company continuously seek real product and marketing improvements. The company that overlooks new and better ways to do things will eventually lose customers to another company that has found a better way. One of the best examples of an innovative marketer is Procter & Gamble:

> Wisk, a Lever Bros. product, has dominated liquid detergents for a generation, and liquids have been taking a growing share of the $3.2-billion-a-year detergent market. P&G tried to topple Wisk with run-of-the-laundry-room liquids called Era and Solo, but couldn't come close. Then it developed a liquid with 12 cleaning agents, twice the norm, and a molecule that traps dirt in the wash water. P&G christened it Liquid Tide and put it in a bottled colored the same fire-bright color as the ubiquitous Tide box. After just 18 months on the market, Liquid Tide is washing as many clothes as Wisk in the U.S., and the two are locked in a fierce battle for the No. 2 position, after powdered Tide, among all detergents.[12]

Value Marketing

According to the principle of **value marketing,** the company should put most of its resources into value-building marketing investments. Many things marketers do—one-shot sales promotions, minor packaging changes, advertising puffery—may raise sales in the short run but add less *value* than would actual improvements in the product's quality, features, or convenience. Enlightened marketing calls for building long-run consumer loyalty by continually improving the value consumers receive from the firm's marketing offer.

Sense-of-Mission Marketing

Sense-of-mission marketing means that the company should define its mission in broad *social* terms rather than narrow *product* terms. When a company defines a social mission, employees feel better about their work and have a clearer sense of direction. For example, defined in narrow product terms, Johnson & Johnson's mission might be "to sell Band-Aids and baby oil." But the company states its mission more broadly:

> We believe that our first responsibility is to the doctors, nurses, and patients, to mothers and all others who use our products and services. In meeting their needs everything we do must be of high quality. We must constantly strive to reduce our costs in order to maintain reasonable prices. Customers' orders must be serviced promptly and accurately. Our suppliers and distributors must have an opportunity to make a fair profit. We are responsible to our employees, the men and women who work for us throughout the world. Everyone must be considered as an individual. We must respect their dignity and recognize their merit. . . . We are responsible to the communities in which we live and work and to the world community as well. We must be good citizens—support good works and charities and bear our fair share of taxes. We must encourage civic improvements and better health and education. We must maintain in good order the property we are privileged to use, protecting the environment and natural resources.[13]

Reshaping the basic task of selling consumer products into the larger mission of serving the interests of consumers, employees, suppliers, and others in the "world community" gives a new sense of purpose to Johnson & Johnson employees.

Societal Marketing

Following the principle of **societal marketing,** an enlightened company makes marketing decisions by considering consumers' wants and long-run interests, the

Immediate satisfaction

	Low	High
High	Salutary products	Desirable products
Low	Deficient products	Pleasing products

Long-run consumer benefit

FIGURE 23-3
Societal classification of new products

company's requirements, and society's long-run interests. The company is aware that neglecting consumer and societal long-run interests is a disservice to consumers and society. Alert companies view societal problems as opportunities.

A societally oriented marketer wants to design products that are not only pleasing but also beneficial. The difference is shown in Figure 23-3. Products can be classified according to their degree of immediate consumer satisfaction and long-run consumer benefit. **Desirable products** give both high immediate satisfaction and high long-run benefits. A desirable product with immediate satisfaction and long-run benefit would be a tasty *and* nutritious breakfast food. **Pleasing products** give high immediate satisfaction but may hurt consumers in the long run. An example is cigarettes. **Salutary products** have low appeal but benefit consumers in the long run. Seat belts and air bags in automobiles are salutary products. Finally, **deficient products,** such as bad-tasting and ineffective medicine, have neither immediate appeal nor long-run benefits.

The challenge posed by pleasing products is that they sell very well but may end up hurting the consumer. The product opportunity, therefore, is to add long-run benefits without reducing the product's pleasing qualities. For example, Sears developed a phosphate-free laundry detergent that was also very effective. The challenge posed by salutary products is to add some pleasing qualities so that they will become more desirable in the consumers' minds. For example, synthetic fats and fat substitutes, such as NutraSweet's Simplesse, promise to improve the appeal of more healthful low-calorie and low-fat foods.

Marketing Ethics

Conscientious marketers face many moral dilemmas. The best thing to do is often unclear. Because not all managers have fine moral sensitivity, companies need to develop *corporate marketing ethics policies*—broad guidelines that everyone in the organization must follow. These policies should cover distributor relations, advertising standards, customer service, pricing, product development, and general ethical standards.

The finest guidelines cannot resolve all the difficult ethical situations the marketer faces. Table 23-1 lists some difficult ethical situations marketers could face during their careers. If marketers choose immediate sales-producing actions in all these cases, their marketing behavior might well be described as immoral or even amoral. If they refuse to go along with *any* of the actions, they might be ineffective as marketing managers and unhappy because of the constant moral tension. Managers need a set of principles that will help them figure out the moral importance of each situation and decide how far they can go in good conscience.

But *what* principle should guide companies and marketing managers on issues of ethics and social responsibility? One philosophy is that such issues are decided by the free market and legal system. Under this principle, companies and their managers are not responsible for making moral judgments. Companies can in good conscience do whatever the system allows.

A second philosophy puts responsibility not in the system, but in the hands of individual companies and managers. This more enlightened philosophy suggests that a company should have a "social conscience." Companies and managers should apply high standards of ethics and morality when making corporate decisions, regardless of "what the system allows." History provides an endless list of examples of company actions that were legal and allowed but were highly irresponsible. Consider the following example:

TABLE 23-1
Some Morally Difficult Situations in Marketing

1. You work for a cigarette company and up to now have not been convinced that cigarettes cause cancer. A report comes across your desk that clearly shows the link between smoking and cancer. What would you do?

2. Your R&D department has changed one of your products slightly. It is not really "new and improved," but you know that putting this statement on the package and in advertising will increase sales. What would you do?

3. You have been asked to add a stripped-down model to your line that could be advertised to pull customers into the store. The product won't be very good, but salespeople will be able to switch buyers up to higher-priced units. You are asked to give the green light for this stripped-down version. What would you do?

4. You are thinking of hiring a product manager who just left a competitor's company. She would be more than happy to tell you all the competitor's plans for the coming year. What would you do?

5. One of your top dealers in an important territory has had recent family troubles and his sales have slipped. It looks like it will take him a while to straighten out his family trouble. Meanwhile you are losing many sales. Legally, you can terminate the dealer's franchise and replace him. What would you do?

6. You have a chance to win a big account that will mean a lot to you and your company. The purchasing agent hints that a "gift" would influence the decision. Your assistant recommends sending a fine color television set to the buyer's home. What would you do?

7. You have heard that a competitor has a new product feature that will make a big difference in sales. The competitor will demonstrate the feature in a private dealer meeting at the annual trade show. You can easily send a snooper to this meeting to learn about the new feature. What would you do?

8. You have to choose between three ad campaigns outlined by your agency. The first (A) is a soft-sell, honest information campaign. The second (B) uses sex-loaded emotional appeals and exaggerates the product's benefits. The third (C) involves a noisy, irritating commercial that is sure to gain audience attention. Pretests show that the campaigns are effective in the following order: C, B, and A. What would you do?

9. You are interviewing a capable woman applicant for a job as salesperson. She is better qualified than the men just interviewed. Nevertheless, you know that some of your important customers prefer dealing with men, and you will lose some sales if you hire her. What would you do?

10. You are a sales manager in an encyclopedia company. Your competitor's salespeople are getting into homes by pretending to take a research survey. After they finish the survey, they switch to their sales pitch. This technique seems to be very effective. What would you do?

Prior to the Pure Food and Drug Act, the advertising for a diet pill promised that a person taking this pill could eat virtually anything at any time and still lose weight. Too good to be true? Actually the claim was quite true; the product lived up to its billing with frightening efficiency. It seems that the primary active ingredient in this "diet supplement" was tapeworm larvae. These larvae would develop in the intestinal tract and, of course, be well fed; the pill taker would in time, quite literally, starve to death.[14]

Each company and marketing manager must work out a philosophy of socially responsible and ethical behavior. Under the societal marketing concept, each manager must look beyond what is legal and allowed and develop standards based on personal integrity, corporate conscience, and long-run consumer welfare. A clear and responsible philosophy will help the marketing manager deal with the many knotty questions posed by marketing and other human activities.

Many industrial and professional associations have suggested codes of ethics, and many companies are now adopting their own codes of ethics. They also are developing programs to teach managers about important ethics issues and help them find the proper responses (see Marketing Highlight 23-4).[15] According to a recent survey of Fortune 1000 companies, over 40 percent of these companies are holding ethics workshops and seminars and one-third have set up ethics committees. Further, more than 200 major U.S. companies have appointed high-level ethics officers to champion ethics issues and to help resolve ethics problems and concerns facing employees. These ethics specialists often employ hotlines through which employees can ask questions about proper ethical behavior or report questionable practices. At Raytheon, the ethics officer receives some

THE GENERAL DYNAMIC'S ETHICS PROGRAM

The General Dynamic's ethics program is considered the most comprehensive in the industry. And little wonder—it was put together as generals from the Pentagon looked on. The program came about after charges that the company deliberately had overbilled the government on defense contracts.

Now at General Dynamics, a committee of board members reviews its ethics policies, and a corporate ethics director and steering group execute the program. The company has set up hot lines that provide employees with instant advice on job-related ethical issues and has given each employee a wallet card listing a toll-free number to report suspected wrongdoing. Nearly all employees have attended workshops; those for salespeople cover such topics as expense accounts and supplier relations.

The company also has a 20-page code of ethics, which tells employees in detail how to conduct themselves. Here are some examples of rules for salespeople:

- If it becomes clear that the company must engage in unethical or illegal activity to win a contract, it will not pursue that business further.

- To prevent hidden interpretations or understandings, all information provided relative to products and services should be clear and concise.

- Receiving or soliciting gifts, entertainment, or anything else of value is prohibited.

General Dynamics has developed a model ethics program.

- In countries where common practices indicate acceptance of conduct lower than that to which General Dynamics aspires, salespeople will follow the company's standards.

- Under no circumstances may an employee offer or give anything to customers or their representatives in an effort to influence them.

Source: Adapted from "This Industry Leader Means Business," *Sales and Marketing Management,* May 1987, p. 44. Also see Stewart Toy, "The Defense Scandal," *Business Week,* July 1, 1988, pp. 28-30.

---

100 calls each month. Most involve minor issues, but about 10 percent point out serious ethical problems that must be addressed by top management.

Many companies have developed innovative ways to educate employees about ethics:

> Citicorp has developed an ethics board game, which teams of employees use to solve hypothetical quandaries. General Electric employees can tap into specially designed software on their personal computers to get answers to ethical questions. At Texas Instruments, employees are treated to a weekly column on ethics over an electronic news service. One popular feature: a kind of Dear Abby mailbag, answers provided by the company's ethics officer, . . . that deals with the troublesome issues employees face most often.[16]

Yet, written codes and ethics programs do not assure ethical behavior. Ethics and social responsibility require a total corporate commitment. They must be a component of the overall corporate culture:

> In the final analysis, "ethical behavior" must be an integral part of the organization, a way of life that is deeply ingrained in the collective corporate body. . . . In any business enterprise, ethical behavior must be a tradition, a way of conducting one's affairs that is passed from generation to generation of employees at all levels of the organization. It is the responsibility of management, starting at the very top, to both set the example by personal conduct and create an environment that not only encourages and rewards ethical behavior, but which also makes anything less totally unacceptable.[17]

Marketing executives of the 1990s face many challenges. Technological advances in solar energy, home computers, cable television, modern medicine, and new forms of transportation, recreation, and communication provide abundant marketing opportunities. However, forces in the socioeconomic, cultural, and natural environments increase the limits under which marketing can be carried out. Companies that are able to create new values and to practice societally responsible marketing will have a world to conquer.

PRINCIPLES FOR PUBLIC POLICY TOWARD MARKETING

Finally, we want to propose several principles that might guide the formulation of public policy toward marketing. These principles reflect assumptions underlying much of modern American marketing theory and practice.

The Principle of Consumer and Producer Freedom

As much as possible, marketing decisions should be made by consumers and producers under relative freedom. Marketing freedom is important if a marketing system is to deliver a high standard of living. People can achieve satisfaction in their own terms rather than in terms defined by someone else. This leads to greater fulfillment through a closer matching of products to desires. Freedom for producers and consumers is the cornerstone of a dynamic marketing system. But more principles are needed to implement this freedom and prevent abuses.

The Principle of Curbing Potential Harm

As much as possible, transactions freely entered into by producers and consumers are their private business. The political system curbs producer or consumer freedom only to prevent transactions that harm or threaten to harm the producer, consumer, or third parties. Transactional harm is a widely recognized grounds for government intervention. The major issue is whether there is sufficient actual or potential harm to justify the intervention.

The Principle of Meeting Basic Needs

The marketing system should serve disadvantaged consumers as well as affluent ones. In a free-enterprise system, producers make goods for markets that are willing and able to buy. Certain groups who lack purchasing power may go without needed goods and services, causing harm to their physical or psychological well-being. While preserving the principle of producer and consumer freedom, the marketing system should support economic and political actions to solve this problem. It should strive to meet the basic needs of all people, and all people should share to some extent in the standard of living it creates.

The Principle of Economic Efficiency

The marketing system strives to supply goods and services efficiently and at low prices. The extent to which a society's needs and wants can be satisfied depends on how efficiently its scarce resources are used. Free economies rely on active competition and informed buyers to make a market efficient. To make profits, competitors must watch their costs carefully while developing products, prices, and marketing programs that serve buyer needs. Buyers get the most satisfaction by finding out about different competing products, prices, and qualities and choosing carefully. The presence of active competition and well-informed buyers keeps quality high and prices low.

The Principle of Innovation

The marketing system encourages authentic innovation to bring down production and distribution costs and to develop new products to meet changing consumer needs. Much innovation is really imitation of other brands, with a slight difference to provide a selling point. The consumer may face ten very similar brands in a product class. But an effective marketing system encourages real product innovation and differentiation to meet the wants of different market segments.

The Principle of Consumer Education and Information

An effective marketing system invests heavily in consumer education and information to increase long-run consumer satisfaction and welfare. The principle of economic efficiency requires this investment, especially in cases where products are confusing because of their numbers and conflicting claims. Ideally, companies will provide enough information about their products. But consumer groups and the government can also give out information and ratings. Students in public schools can take courses in consumer education to learn better buying skills.

The Principle of Consumer Protection

Consumer education and information cannot do the whole job of protecting consumers. The marketing system also must provide consumer protection. Modern products are so complex that even trained consumers cannot evaluate them with confidence. Consumers do not know whether a mobile phone gives off cancer-causing radiation, whether a new automobile has safety flaws, or whether a new drug product has dangerous side effects. A government agency has to review and judge the safety levels of various foods, drugs, toys, appliances, fabrics, automobiles, and housing. Consumers may buy products but fail to understand the environmental consequences, so consumer protection also covers production and marketing activities that might harm the environment. Finally, consumer protection prevents deceptive practices and high-pressure selling techniques where consumers would be defenseless.

These seven principles are based on the assumption that marketing's goal is not to maximize company profits or total consumption or consumer choice, but rather to maximize life quality. Life quality means meeting basic needs, having available many good products, and enjoying the natural and cultural environment. Properly managed, the marketing system can help to create and deliver a higher quality of life to people around the world.

 ## SUMMARY

A marketing system should sense, serve, and satisfy consumer needs and improve the quality of consumers' lives. In working to meet consumer needs, marketers may take some actions that are not to everyone's liking or benefit. Marketing managers should be aware of the main *criticisms of marketing.*

Marketing's *impact on individual consumer welfare* has been criticized for its high prices, deceptive practices, high-pressure selling, shoddy or unsafe products, planned obsolescence, and poor service to disadvantaged consumers. Marketing's *impact on society* has been criticized for creating false wants and too much materialism, too few social goods, cultural pollution, and too much political power. Critics have also criticized marketing's *impact on other businesses* for harming competitors and reducing competition through acquisitions, practices that create barriers to entry, and unfair competitive marketing practices.

Concerns about the marketing system have led to *citizen-action movements. Consumerism* is an organized social movement intended to strengthen the rights and power of consumers relative to sellers. Alert marketers view it as an opportunity to serve consumers better by providing more consumer information, education, and protection. *Environmentalism* is an organized social movement seeking to minimize the harm done to the environment and quality of life by marketing practices. It calls for curbing consumer wants when their satisfaction would create too much environmental cost. Citizen action has led to the passage of many laws to protect consumers in the area of product safety, truth in packaging, truth in lending, and truth in advertising.

Many companies originally opposed these social movements and laws, but most of them now recognize a need for positive consumer information, education, and protection. Some companies have followed a policy of *enlightened marketing* based on the principles of *consumer orientation, innovation, value creation, social mission,* and *societal orientation.* Increasingly, companies are responding to the need to provide company policies and guidelines to help their managers deal with questions of *marketing ethics.*

 ## KEY TERMS

Consumerism 674

Consumer-oriented marketing 678

Deficient products 680

Desirable products 680

Enlightened marketing 678

Environmentalism 675

DISCUSSING THE ISSUES

1. Was Gerber right or wrong not to recall its baby food after customers complained of finding glass fragments in bottles? Without considering what you know about how things turned out, analyze the situation facing Gerber in 1986. What action would you have recommended at the time?

2. Does marketing *create* barriers to entry or *reduce* them? Describe how a small manufacturer of household cleaning products could use advertising to compete with Procter & Gamble.

3. If you were a marketing manager at Dow Chemical Company, which would you prefer: government regulations on acceptable levels of air and water pollution,

or a voluntary industry code suggesting target levels of emissions? Why?

4. Does Procter & Gamble practice the principles of enlightened marketing? Does your school? Give examples to support your answers.

5. Compare the marketing concept with the principle of societal marketing. Do you think marketers should adopt the societal marketing concept? Why or why not?

6. If you had the power to change our marketing system in any way feasible, what improvements would you make? What improvements can you make as a consumer or entry-level marketing practitioner?

APPLYING THE CONCEPTS

1. Changes in consumer attitudes, especially the growth of consumerism and environmentalism, have led to more societal marketing—and to more marketing that is *supposedly* good for society, but is actually closer to deception. (a) List three examples of marketing campaigns that you feel are genuine societal marketing. If possible, find examples of advertising or packaging that supports these campaigns. (b) Find three examples of deceptive or borderline imitations of societal marketing. How are you able to tell which campaigns are genuine and which are not? (c) What remedies, if any, would you recommend for this problem?

2. Consider contemporary America. As a society, we have many things to be proud of—and many areas where there is more work to be done. (a) Make a list of ten important things that need to be done in America. Your list may include economic issues, or education, health care, environment, politics, or any other significant sphere. (b) Pick one issue that is especially important to you from this list. Using what you have learned from this course, make a list of ways in which marketing principles and tools could be used to help on your issue.

MAKING MARKETING DECISIONS:

SMALL WORLD COMMUNICATIONS, INC.

EPILOGUE

Lynette was in a thoughtful mood. There was a lot to do, but the *Airport* product was looking very good, the consumer need they counted on was looking stronger every day, and their venture capitalist was putting them in touch with some rather amazing people as resources. Her husband was already asleep, and she called Tom for a late Sunday night chat. "Lyn, my neurons have shut down for the night. I hope you're not calling with some fire that needs to be put out tonight." "Actually, Tom, I'm a bit tuckered out myself, but I needed to talk for a minute. I was reading E. B. White's *Stuart Little* to my nephews the other night,

and the ending felt just right. It was so good that I typed it up and put it on my wall, just to help me keep some perspective." "Must I ask, Lyn? All right, please read your wall to me." "Well, Stuart is traveling north on a journey that he expects to continue for a long time. The last two sentences of the book read, 'As he peered ahead into the great land that stretched before him, the way seemed long. But the sky was bright, and he somehow felt he was headed in the right direction.'" Tom was quiet for a minute, then he said, "Yeah, I remember that part. I like the feel of it, too. And on that note, I'm going to say goodnight. It's going to be a busy week. We've only got 10 days 'till the national sales meeting. I want to be rested when we get there, 'cause I'm planning to have some *fun!*"

WHAT NOW?

1. The *Airport* is a technical product, but it has many environmental pluses. It is manufactured at a plant which is very careful about the disposal of toxic wastes left over from the circuit board manufacturing. The circuitry is designed for low power consumption. If users choose, they can use the *Airport* to communicate in a paperless way, thus reducing waste. Would you suggest that Lyn and Thomas position their product as an environmentally friendly product? Why or why not?

2. Tom and Lyn want to be enlightened marketers. You have followed their progress from a simple idea they brainstormed at a reunion until now, as they are ready to launch their *Airport* product nationally. (a) Rate how you think Small World is doing at following the five principles of enlightened marketing: being consumer-oriented, being innovative, offering value, having a sense of mission, and being societal marketers. (b) Are these principles hard to follow in practice? Do they offer a good long-term payback? (c) Is an enlightened marketing company the type of place for which you would like to work?

 # REFERENCES

1. See Patricia Strnad, "Gerber Ignores Tylenol Textbook," *Advertising Age,* March 10, 1986, p. 3; Felix Kessler, "Tremors from the Tylenol Scare Hit Food Companies," *Fortune,* March 31, 1986, pp. 59-62; Wendy Zellner, "Gerber's New Chief Doesn't Take Baby Steps," *Business Week,* November 7, 1988, pp. 130-32; and Judann Dagnoli, "Brief Slump Expected for Sudafed," *Advertising Age,* March 18, 1991, p. 53.

2. See Steven H. Star, "Marketing and Its Discontents," *Harvard Business Review,* November-December 1989, pp. 148-54.

3. See John F. Gaski and Michael Etzel, "The Index of Consumer Sentiment Toward Marketing," *Journal of Marketing,* July 1986, pp. 71-81; "The Public Is Willing to Take Business On," *Business Week,* May 29, 1989, p. 29; and Faye Rice, "How to Deal with Tougher Customers," *Fortune,* December 3, 1990, pp. 38-48.

4. Excerpts from Theodore Levitt, "The Morality (?) of Advertising," *Harvard Business Review,* July-August 1970, pp. 84-92.

5. Sandra Pesmen, "How Low Is Low? How Free Is Free?" *Advertising Age,* May 7, 1990, p. S10.

6. A speech delivered at Vanderbilt University Law School, reported in *Marketing News,* August 1, 1968, pp. 11, 15. For more discussion, see Louis W. Stern and Adel I. El-Ansary, *Marketing Channels,* 4th ed. (Englewood Cliffs, NJ: Prentice Hall, 1988), pp. 480-83; and Brian Bremner, "Looking Downscale Without Looking Down," *Business Week,* October 8, 1990, pp. 62-67.

7. Ibid., p. 11.

8. Myron Magnet, "The Money Society," *Fortune,* July 6, 1987, p. 26.

9. See Anne B. Fisher, "A Brewing Revolt Against the Rich," *Fortune,* December 17, 1990, pp. 89-94; and Norval D. Glenn, "What Does Family Mean?" *American Demographics,* June 1992, pp. 30-37.

10. From an advertisement for *Fact* magazine, which does not carry advertisements.

11. For more details, see Paul N. Bloom and Stephen A. Greyser, "The Maturing of Consumerism," *Harvard Business Review,* November-December 1981, pp. 130-39, Robert J. Samualson, "The Aging of Ralph Nader," *Newsweek,* December 16, 1985, p. 57; and Douglas A. Harbrecht, "The Second Coming of Ralph Nader," *Business Week,* March 6, 1989, p. 28.

12. Faye Rice, "The King of Suds Reigns Again," *Fortune,* August 4, 1986, p. 131.

13. Quoted from "Our Credo," Johnson & Johnson, New Brunswick, New Jersey.

14. Dan R. Dalton and Richard A. Cosier, "The Four Faces of Social Responsibility," *Business Horizons,* May-June 1982, pp. 19-27.

15. For examples, see the American Marketing Association's code of ethics, discussed in "AMA Adopts New Code of Ethics," *Marketing News,* September 11, 1987, p. 1; John A. Byrne, "Businesses Are Signing Up for Ethics 101," *Business Week,* February 15, 1988, pp. 56-57; and Andrew Stark, "What's the Matter with Business Ethics?" *Harvard Business Review,* May-June 1993, pp. 38-48.

16. Kenneth Labich, "The New Crisis in Business Management," *Fortune,* April 20, 1992, pp. 167-76, here p. 176.

17. From "Ethics as a Practical Matter," a message from David R. Whitman, Chairman of the Board of Whirlpool Corporation, as reprinted in Ricky E. Griffin and Ronald J. Ebert, *Business* (Englewood Cliffs, NJ: Prentice Hall, 1989), pp. 578-79. For more discussion, see Shelby D. Hunt, Van R. Wood, and Lawrence B. Chonko, "Corporate Ethical Values and Organizational Commitment in Marketing," *Journal of Marketing,* July 1989, pp. 79-90.

VIDEO CASE 23

ABC NEWS

SMOKING: AN EQUAL OPPORTUNITY TRAGEDY

I think you can rewrite the book on business. I think you can trade ethically; be committed to social responsibility, global responsibility . . . that is the vision, and the vision is absolutely clear.

Anita Roddick,
Founder of The Body Shop, Inc.

These strong words seem to convey our desire for environmental and social consciousness. This is an era of socially responsible marketing, right? Wrong, say the critics of cigarette marketing. They claim that even though smoking is a known health hazard, the successful marketing of cigarettes leads 400,000 Americans to kill themselves annually by smoking. Starting in the 1950s, researchers began to link cigarette smoking to lung and throat cancers, emphysema, high blood pressure and numerous heart problems. Today, cigarettes are clearly labeled as "hazardous to your health." And because secondhand smoke greatly endangers nonsmokers, smoking is banned in many public buildings, elevators, grocery stores, air flights, and sections of restaurants.

Cigarette marketing also has been curtailed. For 30 years, television advertising of cigarettes has been illegal. Recently, the Supreme Court ruled that consumers can sue tobacco companies *if* the company has intentionally misled smokers about the dangers of smoking. Although ads showing healthy people smoking still are acceptable, slogans focusing on good health or on low tar or low nicotine claims are not.

Using healthy people in ads may, however, boomerang on cigarette producers. Many former cigarette ad models have developed smoking-related health problems, and they are not bashful about blaming cigarettes. Examples include Wayne McLaren (a Marlboro cowboy), Will Thornbury (Newports), Dave Goerlitz (Winstons), and Janet Sackman (Lucky Strike). McLaren and Thornbury died before the age of 57, Goerlitz has suffered strokes, and Sackman has had operations for throat cancer and talks only with great difficulty.

Cigarette marketers also must exercise care in selecting market targets. Their efforts to target blacks with the Uptown brand and blue-collar working class women with Dakota were criticized heavily—so much so that Uptown never made it to market. Finally, cigarette manufacturers such as Philip Morris were forced to lower their prices in 1993 after decades of cigarette price increases that exceeded inflation.

Although it is more difficult to market cigarettes, tobacco companies, because of their innovativeness and creativity, still do quite well. They are at the forefront of database marketing. By carefully and painstakingly assembling some of the largest consumer databases in the United States, cigarette companies can identify segments such as black female smokers of menthol cigarettes who are 35 to 50 years old and who live in metropolitan areas of 250,000 to 500,000. These smokers then receive personalized letters, coupons, and other promotions. As cigarette advertising expenditures decline, dollars spent on direct marketing and sales promotion increase, thereby increasing the effectiveness of promotional dollars spent.

Some cigarette advertising is very effective, such as the Joe Camel campaign. Smooth character Joe is as well known to children under six as Mickey Mouse, and he isn't even on television. What accounts for his popularity? Billboards and extensive Joe Camel print advertising. When reinforced with sales promotions—T-shirts, mugs, sunglasses *and* Camel Cash with the associated catalogs—Joe seems to be everywhere. His apparent popularity with young people is particularly disturbing because 60 percent of smokers begin before age fourteen.

While youths continue to begin smoking, adult Americans are quitting in larger numbers. This has caused tobacco manufacturers to go global. They sell almost 200 billion cigarettes abroad each year—frequently in the more lethal nonfiltered form in countries with fewer consumer protection laws.

QUESTIONS

1. Which of the social criticisms of marketing identified in the text apply to cigarette marketing?

2. Does cigarette marketing illustrate any of the following: consumer-oriented marketing, innovative marketing, value marketing, or sense-of-mission marketing?

3. Critics of cigarette marketing advocate eliminating sales of all tobacco products. The cigarette companies *and* the ACLU contend that such a prohibition would violate the rights of consumers and producers. Do you agree? Defend your answer.

4. Should the tobacco companies be allowed to sell cigarettes overseas? Does the selling of cigarettes damage our relations with other countries now or in the future?

5. Do you think that Ms. Roddick's contentions about social and global responsibility are viable today?

Sources: Christopher Bartlett, "The Body Shop International," *Harvard Business School Case,* April 1992; Stephen Colford, "What High Court Ruling Means for Tobacco Ads," *Advertising Age,* June 29, 1992, pp. 3, 49; Walecia Konrad, "I'd Toddle a Mile for a Camel," *Business Week,* December 23, 1991, p. 34; and Taft Wireback, "The Past Caught Up with Them," *Greensboro News and Record,* February 14, 1993, pages A1, A10.

COMPANY CASE 23

NESTLÉ: UNDER FIRE AGAIN

Questionable marketing techniques by a unit of Nestlé are raising the concerns of consumer products activists. And this is not the first time that Nestlé has been scrutinized by the public eye.

Nestlé S.A., headquartered in Vevey, Switzerland, is the world's largest food company, with annual worldwide sales of more than $25 billion. The company's products are produced in 383 factories operating in 50 countries. Many Nestlé products are quite familiar—Nestlé's chocolates, Nescafé, Taster's Choice and Hills Bros. coffees, Libby and Contadina foods, Beech-Nut baby products, Stouffer foods, and Friskies, Fancy Feast, and Mighty Dog pet foods. In 1985, the company acquired Carnation Company, makers of Evaporated Milk, Hot Cocoa Mix, Instant Breakfast Mix, Coffee-Mate, and other familiar brands.

In the late 1970s and early 1980s, Nestlé came under heavy fire from health professionals who charged the company with encouraging Third World mothers to give up breast feeding and use a company-prepared formula. Critics accused Nestlé of using sophisticated promotional techniques to persuade hundreds of thousands of poverty-stricken, poorly educated mothers that formula feeding was better for their children. Unfortunately, formula feeding is not usually a wise practice in such countries. Because of poor living conditions and habits, people cannot or do not clean bottles properly and often mix formula with impure water. Furthermore, income level does not permit many families to purchase sufficient quantities of formula.

In 1977, two American social-interest groups spearheaded a worldwide boycott against Nestlé. The boycott ended in 1984, when the company complied with an infant formula marketing code adopted by the World Health Organization (WHO). The code eliminates all promotional efforts, requiring companies to serve primarily as passive "order takers." It prohibits advertising, samples, and direct contact with consumers. Contacts with professionals (such as doctors) are allowed only if professionals seek such contact. Manufacturers can package products with some form of visual corporate identity, but they cannot picture babies. In effect, then, the WHO code allows almost no marketing. However, the code contains only *recommended* guidelines. They become *mandatory* only if individual governments adopt national codes through their own regulatory mechanisms.

In addition to the formula controversy, Nestlé has had other public relations difficulties in recent years. In contrast to the Third World baby formula debacle, the next incident involved top-management ethics at a Nestlé subsidiary. Beech-Nut Nutrition Corp., one of Nestlé's U.S. baby products units, found itself in hot water in 1987, when it was forced to admit to selling adulterated and mislabeled apple juice intended for ba-

bies. The product contained little if any apple juice and was made from beet sugar, cane sugar syrup, corn syrup, and other ingredients. After pleading guilty to federal charges, Beech-Nut agreed to pay a $2 million fine and $140,000 for Food and Drug Administration investigative costs. Two company executives were fined and imprisoned.

Nestlé has once again captured the limelight because of its recent entry into the $1.6 billion U.S. infant formula market. Although Nestlé dominates this market in Europe, three large, well-established competitors control the U.S. market—Abbott Laboratories (with Similac and Isomil brands) has a 53-percent market share, followed by Bristol-Myers (Enfamil and ProSobee brands) with 36 percent, and American Home Products (SMA brand) with 11 percent. But the U.S. market is predicted to grow at 8 to 9 percent annually, and Nestlé wants its share of that growth.

Nestlé's Carnation unit, a company with a pure and sparkling reputation in the baby product's business, introduced the new infant formula under the name "Good Start" in late 1988. Carnation designed Good Start for newborns. It also introduced a second product, Follow Up, developed for babies six months old or older.

Carnation claimed that Good Start offered important benefits over currently available infant formulas. The new formula is a whey-based product designed for infants allergic to standard milk-based and soy-based formulas. Carnation priced Good Start comparably to cow's milk or soy-based formulas.

In a product monograph introducing Good Start, Carnation stated that "breast milk is the ideal food for infants." However, "if breast feeding is not possible, an infant formula should provide complete nutrition and also be well tolerated." Food intolerance and sensitivity in infants result from an immune system that is not fully developed, from an immature intestinal lining, or from damage to the intestinal lining. In situations where there is food intolerance or sensitivity, physicians often suggest infant formulas based on whole cow's milk. However, these formulas can sometimes also cause intolerance or sensitivity problems. In these cases, physicians often suggest infant formulas based on soybean products. These, too, Carnation argues, can often cause problems.

Therefore, Carnation positioned Good Start as an infant formula doctors should suggest before recommending soy-based formulas. Carnation pointed out that whey protein is the predominant type of protein in breast milk. Good Start is nutritionally complete for long-term or routine feeding. Carnation cautioned, however, that mothers should use Good Start only under direct medical supervision in cases of suspected milk allergy.

Carnation estimated that from 15 to 20 percent of all infants are allergic to the protein in standard formulas. In contrast, the Pediatric Academy's Committee on Nutrition said that the number is closer to between 1 and 2 percent. Nevertheless, Carnation declared Good Start a medical breakthrough and designated it as "hypoallergenic"—a claim made in bold type on the can. The company claimed that the product could prevent or reduce fussiness, sleeplessness, colic, rash, and other problems. The product monograph cited seven research studies involving 765 infants that supported its claims for Good Start. Pediatricians, however, warned that although the formula is easier to digest than common milk-based formulas, mothers should use it only after recommendation from the child's physician.

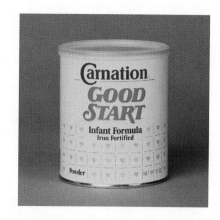

In addition to reacting to Carnation's hypoallergenic claim, the medical community also objected to Carnation's advertising its Follow Up product directly to consumers. The U.S. infant formula business is governed largely by relationships between marketers and health professionals. Except for hospital giveaway programs, Abbot and Bristol-Myers market their infant formula products mainly to doctors. These companies have salesforces that call directly on doctors, explaining the company's products, leaving samples, and encouraging the doctors to recommend their company's products. Consequently, there is little consumer brand loyalty in the infant formula market because mothers usually do what their doctors recommend. In addition, because pediatricians tell mothers what to buy, there is little price sensitivity in the infant formula market.

When Carnation launched the two products, it found itself under immediate attack, both because of the hypoallergenic claim and Follow Up's direct-to-consumer marketing. Carnation decided to withdraw the hypoallergenic claims for Good Start but held its ground on the Follow Up marketing program, which also included marketing to health-care professionals. Carnation also watched with interest as Gerber Products began marketing an infant formula produced by Bristol-Myers's Squibb division in August 1989. Gerber promoted the formula directly to consumers.

Meanwhile, Carnation continued to market Good Start exclusively to health-care professionals using its 90-member salesforce and avoided any direct-to-consumer promotion. By the end of 1990, Good Start had achieved less than a 1 percent market share, whereas Follow Up had captured about a 2 percent share. Carnation had found it extremely tough to wade into the U.S. infant formula market.

As a result, Carnation announced that it would begin marketing Good Start directly to consumers in early 1991. In supporting its decision, Carnation noted that in the United States the established infant formula companies have generally treated infant formula as if it were a prescription drug rather than the food product that it is. As a food, federal law and Food and Drug Administration regulations ensure the nutritional content, labeling accuracy, and manufacturing quality of infant formulas. In treating formulas as a prescription drug, the established companies have used the same "medical marketing" techniques they use for prescription drugs.

Carnation argues that this practice puts consumers at a significant disadvantage. First, consumers cannot be made aware of differences among products, and they choose brands based on free samples received when the mother is discharged from the hospital. Second, because medical marketing is labor intensive and expensive, consumers must pay more for products marketed in this manner. Third, the expense of developing a medical marketing program makes it very difficult for new companies to enter the market. Finally, Carnation argues, because physicians wrongly believe that Carnation has marketed Good Start directly to consumers, they refuse to discuss Good Start with their patients, effectively shutting Carnation out of the market.

Carnation specifically noted that the ban on consumer advertising denies parents information at a time when there is increasing parental involvement in infant feeding decisions. The ban also limits incentives for innovation and product improvement in the infant-formula category. And the ban makes physicians unequal partners in the decision-making process because the doctors have all the information, while patients have little, if any. Carnation feels that a more balanced partnership makes sense. Finally, the company notes that the American Academy of Pediatricians has had the stated policy of promoting breast feeding. Despite this policy and the "ban" on advertising, breast feeding rates in the United States have been declining for more than a decade.

Carnation indicated that its new Good Start advertising would offer three simple messages: (1) Breast feeding is best; (2) Good Start is a nutritious, gentle alternative to other formulas; and (3) consult your doctor on all infant feeding decisions.[1]

At the same time, the American Academy of Pediatricians stated again its opposition to direct advertising to consumers. Noting the recent incidents of direct advertising, the AAP noted that "the motivation for this change is corporate profit earned, the AAP believes, at the potential expense of the optimal nutrition of children." The AAP noted its opposition to any practice that might discourage breast feeding and therefore restated its opposition to direct advertising of infant formula to the public because of its potentially adverse impact on breast feeding. The AAP indicated that it believes that when the companies advertise the claimed advantages of their formulas, those claims will interfere with the mother's decision to breast feed. Further, the AAP argued that the proponents of breast feeding could not compete with the advertising campaigns of the formula makers. And, the AAP suggested, as the formula makers compete with each other, they will make exaggerated claims, further promoting formula use over breast feeding.[2]

Nestlé and its Carnation unit find themselves once again in the middle of controversy. Carnation must find a way to penetrate the U.S. infant formula market while balancing the interests and concerns of consumers, the medical community, and the company.

QUESTIONS

1. Think through the traditional buyers' and sellers' rights listed in Chapter 23. Which rights were violated in the Third World infant-formula situation? Which rights were violated in the Beech-Nut apple juice situation? Does Carnation have the right to promote Good Start infant formula in whatever way it wants?

2. Will Nestlé be practicing socially responsible marketing with its Good Start product?

3. What marketing plan would you recommend for Good Start?

[1]Laurie MacDonald, Statement of the Nestlé Carnation Food Company before the Senate Judiciary Subcommittee on Antitrust, Monopolies and Business Rights and the Senate Agriculture, Nutrition, and Forestry Committee, Carnation Nutritional Products Division, Glendale, CA. March 14, 1991.

[2]Britt Harvey, M.D., Testimony before the U.S. Senate Joint Hearing of the Subcommittee on Antitrust, Monopolies and Business Rights and the Committee on Agriculture, Nutrition and Forestry. American Academy of Pediatrics, Washington, D.C. March 14, 1991.

PART VI

COMPREHENSIVE CASE

GTE AND THE PAY-PHONE MARKET: COMPETITION COMES CALLING

As he drove into the parking lot at the Smile gas station on Route 70 in Durham, NC, Kevin Murphy, a salaried General Telephone and Electronics (GTE) sales consultant, thought about how the pay-phone business had changed since he joined the company in 1983. During those years he had witnessed the impact of deregulation on the telephone industry, and he had seen about every kind of competitive move. He was now stopping to call on Jim Lewis, the manager of Smile Gas. Mr. Lewis had a relative in the private pay-phone business. Eight months ago, Mr. Lewis had agreed to have one of the relative's phones installed in the gas station and had asked GTE to remove its phone. However, his relative's company had gone out of business and the new phone had never been installed.

Many of Smile's customers want to make only one stop to buy gas or food and to use a phone. Now, when Mr. Lewis' customers inquire about a pay phone, he has to send them across the intersection to the Wilco gas station. Mr Lewis is angry about losing business to the competition, and he decided to call GTE.

Like Mr. Lewis' customers, you've probably used a pay telephone many times: in the dorm to call out for pizza; at the convenience store to see if a friend is at home; or at the airport to tell someone you've landed safely. They seem to be everywhere. But have you ever really paid much attention to the pay phones themselves? Probably not. Unfortunately, neither has GTE. And that's a real problem, given that GTE owns and operates 29,000 pay telephones in its franchised areas in nine southeastern states.

However, because of dramatic changes in its marketing environment, GTE is now starting to pay attention to its public communications operation instead of taking it for granted as it has traditionally done. Other companies *have* noticed the pay telephone market. Literally hundreds of small companies are racing to enter what promises to be a lucrative business, challenging the almost monopolistic grip GTE and other telephone companies have had on the pay-phone market.

The Public Communications Market

Although pay telephones may seem out of date amid the rapid technological advances in the modern telecommunications world, the approximately 2 million U.S. pay phones generated $6.3 *billion* in revenues in 1989. Callers deposited about 25 percent of this amount as "coins in the box." The remaining 75 percent consisted of credit card, collect, and other operator-assisted calls. GTE receives 100 percent of the cost of local calls (usually 25 cents each) made on its pay phones, 100 percent of the cost of long-distance calls made within GTE's franchise area, and between 6 and 10 cents per minute for long-distance calls going outside its area. In total, GTE's 29,000 pay phones produced about $56 million in total revenues in 1989.

Telephone companies generally segment the public communications market based on the number of pay phones installed at each location. Exhibit VI-1 presents the overall breakdown of U.S. businesses by number of pay phones per location and gives the chief attributes of each segment. The table shows that 90 percent of all businesses have fewer than four pay phones per location and that these businesses account

EXHIBIT VI-1
Pay Phone Market Segments

	0-4 PAY PHONES PER LOCATION	5-9 PAY PHONES PER LOCATION	10+ PAY PHONES PER LOCATION
Businesses	90%	6%	4%
Pay phones	40%	11%	49%
Revenues:			
Local	43%	47%	26%
Coin	8	7	16
Non-coin	49	46	58

Source: GTE South

for 40 percent of the total number of pay phones installed. In contrast, only 4 percent of businesses have more than 10 pay phones installed, but these businesses account for 49 percent of all installed pay phones. Convenience stores, shopping centers, and fast-food restaurants are the best locations. Generally, GTE wants to place its pay phones in safe, well-lighted locations with lots of car or foot traffic. GTE budgets $1,500 to $2,000 to install an outside pay-phone booth; wall-mounted units cost slightly less. GTE depreciates the booths over a seven-year period. The company estimates that the variable cost of a phone is $35 per month and that a phone must generate at least $90 per month to break even.

Prior to 1984, the telephone companies enjoyed a monopoly in the pay telephone market. Only regulated telephone companies could install a pay phone that was connected to their telephone networks. Although customers paid to use the phones, the phone companies subsidized their pay-phone operations from general revenues. GTE did not even account for pay phones separately from its general telephone operations. If a business wanted a pay phone installed, it would file a request with the local telephone company, such as GTE. GTE would evaluate the request based on the revenue potential of the location and on the company's obligation as a regulated monopoly to provide public service. If the location looked profitable, GTE would install one or more *public* pay phones. The phone cost the owner nothing, but GTE made no payments to the owner. If a location did not justify a public pay phone, GTE could offer the customer a *semipublic* phone, for which the customer paid an installation fee and guaranteed GTE a fixed monthly revenue. In this process of receiving requests and evaluating locations, telephone companies did no "marketing." GTE either accepted requests or rejected them. In fact, it accepted only two out of every ten requests. GTE rarely searched for new places to install pay phones.

Deregulation Strikes

However, in June 1984 everything changed. The Federal Communications Commission (FCC), as part of the general deregulation of the telecommunications industry, ruled that any person who purchased a coin-operated telephone had the right to connect it to the local telephone network. This ruling created a new product

and a new market: the customer-owned, coin-operated telephone (COCOT). Many entrepreneurs set up businesses to develop and run private pay-phone networks. These firms included everything from one-person businesses operated out of the back of a pick-up truck to People's Telephone, the largest independent operator, with 6,500 phones in 15 states as of 1989.

Another aspect of deregulation further spurred the development of the COCOT industry. With deregulation, AT&T lost its monopoly over long-distance service. Because of a rule stipulating "equal access," local telephone companies had to furnish all long-distance carriers the same access to their networks that they had previously given only to AT&T. The local telephone company could no longer automatically select AT&T to provide long-distance service to its customers. Each customer would select one of the main carriers (AT&T, MCI, Sprint) or an alternative operator service (AOS) to provide long-distance service. AOSs buy blocks of long-distance service at wholesale rates from the main carriers and then resell the service at higher rates (sometimes even higher than AT&T rates) to their customers. To attract the AOS business, the main carriers also began offering commissions to the AOSs. In turn, the AOSs began offering commissions to COCOTs who tied their pay-phone systems to the AOSs for long-distance service. These commissions provided an additional source of revenues to the COCOT business, making it profitable and competitive. Until December 1988, these commissions also provided the COCOTs with a competitive advantage, because GTE and the other telephone companies were required to use AT&T for their long-distance pay-phone service. AT&T paid them no commissions.

Prior to deregulation, once GTE installed a phone, it had a customer for life. GTE did not require any contracts for public phones, and it paid no commissions to the owner of the location in which the phone was installed. GTE could take customers for granted—and it usually did. The COCOTs, however, entered the business with a vengeance. Taking advantage of their low overhead and the commissions, they began offering the location-owner a percentage of the coins in the box as a commission for allowing them to install a pay phone. Further, they targeted established pay phones. Because GTE had no contracts with location-owners, the COCOTs could suggest that the owner ask GTE to remove its phone. Then the COCOT would install a phone and pay the owner a commission, typically 20 to 30 percent of the coins in the box. To most owners, a pay phone is

a pay phone—they were glad to dump GTE in order to make some extra money. Some COCOTs even hired college students to go door-to-door, signing up businesses for new pay phones and for removal of existing phones. COCOTs also targeted retail chains, which operated in many locations. Whereas GTE can provide pay-phone service only in its franchised areas, COCOTs operate over large areas and can offer chains the ability to handle much or all of their pay-phone service with one contact.

GTE responded by offering a commission of 30 percent of the coins in the box over $60 a month and asking owners to agree to give 30-day notice before removing a phone. However, these actions did not slow the loss of customers. GTE then introduced a second contract, which paid 15 to 20 percent of all coins in the box in return for the customer signing a 3- to 5-year contract. The contract, however, allowed the owner to have the GTE phone removed if the owner paid the installation and removal costs, usually about $500 to $650.

Competitors responded to these moves in some cases by offering commissions of 30 to 50 percent of *net* profits (pay-phone revenues less maintenance and collection costs), including revenue on long-distance calls. GTE argued that this higher percentage of net might often be less than its 15 to 20 percent of gross. In some cases, competition had even offered to pay GTE's installation and removal costs for the location-owner in order to win the location.

Back at Smile Gas

Kevin Murphy agreed to install a new pay phone at Smile Gas. He told Mr. Lewis that he would receive 20 percent of the coin-in-the-box revenue. Mr. Lewis asked about a commission on long-distance calls. Kevin indicated that the FCC does not allow GTE to recommend long-distance carriers and that Mr. Lewis would have to choose a carrier and negotiate with that carrier about commissions. When Mr. Lewis also asked about maintenance and repair service for the phone, Kevin assured him that GTE provided 24-hour, around-the-clock service.

Kevin left the meeting with Mr. Lewis to attend a sales meeting in GTE's Durham office. The 10 sales consultants for GTE South were gathering for the first time ever to begin sales training and to work with management to develop a new marketing strategy for GTE's public communications operations in the southeast. As he drove to the meeting, Kevin rehearsed the suggestions he wanted to make. Competitors' fierce moves had created trouble already, and Kevin knew that analysts predicted only a 1.5 percent annual market growth rate through 1994. This slow growth would fuel even more competitive challenges. GTE's market share in its franchised areas had already fallen from 100 percent to 85 percent. Kevin knew GTE had to improve its pay-phone strategy to stop the erosion.

QUESTIONS

1. What kind of service does GTE sell?

2. How do the characteristics of GTE's services affect its marketing efforts?

3. How should the concepts of internal and interactive marketing shape GTE's marketing strategy?

4. What changes should GTE make in its marketing strategy? Be sure to address each aspect of the marketing mix and the issues of managing differentiation, service quality, and productivity.

5. The telecommunication industry's deregulation has caused the marketing situation GTE faces. Does deregulation promote economic efficiency?

Source: GTE Telephone Operations cooperated in the development of this case.

Appendix 1: Marketing Arithmetic

One aspect of marketing not discussed within the text is marketing arithmetic. The calculation of sales, costs, and certain ratios is important for many marketing decisions. This appendix describes three major areas of marketing arithmetic: the *operating statement, analytic ratios,* and *markups and markdowns.*

OPERATING STATEMENT

The operating statement and the balance sheet are the two main financial statements used by companies. The **balance sheet** shows the assets, liabilities, and net worth of a company at a given time. The **operating statement** (also called **profit-and-loss statement** or **income statement**) is the more important of the two for marketing information. It shows company sales, cost of goods sold, and expenses during a specified time period. By comparing the operating statement from one time period to the next, the firm can spot favorable or unfavorable trends and take appropriate action.

Table A1-1 shows the 1993 operating statement for Dale Parsons Men's Wear, a specialty store in the Midwest. This statement is for a retailer; the operating statement

TABLE A1-1
Operating Statement Dale Parsons Men's Wear Year Ending December 31, 1993

Gross sales			$325,000
Less: Sales returns and allowances			25,000
Net sales			$300,000
Cost of goods sold			
Beginning inventory, January 1, at cost		$ 60,000	
Gross purchases	$165,000		
Less: Purchase discounts	15,000		
Net purchases	$150,000		
Plus: Freight-in	10,000		
Net cost of delivered purchases		$160,000	
Cost of goods available for sale		$220,000	
Less: Ending inventory, December 31, at cost		$ 45,000	
Cost of goods sold			$175,000
Gross margin			$125,000
Expenses			
Selling expenses			
Sales, salaries, and commissions	$ 40,000		
Advertising	5,000		
Delivery	5,000		
Total selling expenses		$ 50,000	
Administrative expenses			
Office salaries	$ 20,000		
Office supplies	5,000		
Miscellaneous (outside consultant)	5,000		
Total administrative expenses		$ 30,000	
General expenses			
Rent	$ 10,000		
Heat, light, telephone	5,000		
Miscellaneous (insurance, depreciation)	5,000		
Total general expenses		$ 20,000	
Total expenses			$100,000
Net profit			$ 25,000

for a manufacturer would be somewhat different. Specifically, the section on purchases within the "cost of goods sold" area would be replaced by "cost of goods manufactured."

The outline of the operating statement follows a logical series of steps to arrive at the firm's $25,000 net profit figure:

Net sales	$300,000
Cost of goods sold	−175,000
Gross margin	$125,000
Expenses	−100,000
Net profit	$ 25,000

The first part details the amount that Parsons received for the goods sold during the year. The sales figures consist of three items: *gross sales, returns and allowances,* and *net sales*. **Gross sales** is the total amount charged to customers during the year for merchandise purchased in Parsons's store. As expected, some customers returned merchandise because of damage or a change of mind. If the customer gets a full refund or full credit on another purchase, we call this a *return*. Or the customer may decide to keep the item if Parsons will reduce the price. This is called an *allowance*. By subtracting returns and allowances from gross sales, we arrive at net sales—what Parsons earned in revenue from a year of selling merchandise:

Gross sales	$325,000
Returns and allowances	−25,000
Net sales	$300,000

The second major part of the operating statement calculates the amount of sales revenue Dale Parsons retains after paying the costs of the merchandise. We start with the inventory in the store at the beginning of the year. During the year, Parsons bought $165,000 worth of suits, slacks, shirts, ties, jeans, and other goods. Suppliers gave the store discounts totaling $15,000, so that net purchases were $150,000. Because the store is located away from regular shipping routes, Parsons had to pay an additional $10,000 to get the products delivered, giving the firm a net cost of $160,000. Adding the beginning inventory, the cost of goods available for sale amounted to $220,000. The $45,000 ending inventory of clothes in the store on December 31 is then subtracted to come up with the $175,000 **cost of goods sold.** Here again we have followed a logical series of steps to figure out the cost of goods sold:

Amount Parsons started with (beginning inventory)	$60,000
Net amount purchased	+150,000
Any added costs to obtain these purchases	+10,000
Total cost of goods Parsons had available for sale during year	$220,000
Amount Parsons had left over (ending inventory)	− 45,000
Cost of goods actually sold	$175,000

The difference between what Parsons paid for the merchandise ($175,000) and what he sold it for ($300,000) is called the **gross margin** ($125,000).

In order to show the profit Parsons "cleared" at the end of the year, we must subtract from the gross margin the *expenses* incurred while doing business. *Selling expenses* included two sales employees, local newspaper and radio advertising, and the cost of delivering merchandise to customers after alterations. Selling expenses totaled $50,000 for the year. *Administrative expenses* included the salary for an office manager, office supplies such as stationery and business cards, and miscellaneous expenses including an administrative audit conducted by an outside consultant. Administrative expenses totaled $30,000 in 1993. Finally, the general expenses of rent, utilities, insurance, and depreciation came to $20,000. Total expenses were therefore $100,000 for the year. By subtracting expenses ($100,000) from the gross margin ($125,000), we arrive at the net profit of $25,000 for Parsons during 1993.

ANALYTIC RATIOS

The operating statement provides the figures needed to compute some crucial ratios. Typically these ratios are called **operating ratios**—the ratio of selected operating statement items to net sales. They let marketers compare the firm's performance in one year to that in previous years (or with industry standards and competitors in the same year). The most commonly used operating ratios are the *gross margin percentage,* the *net profit percentage,* the *operating expense percentage,* and the *returns and allowances percentage.*

RATIO		FORMULA		COMPUTATION FROM TABLE A1-1	
Gross margin percentage	$=$	$\dfrac{\text{gross margin}}{\text{net sales}}$	$=$	$\dfrac{\$125,000}{\$300,000}$	$= 42\%$
Net profit percentage	$=$	$\dfrac{\text{net profit}}{\text{net sales}}$	$=$	$\dfrac{\$\ 25,000}{\$300,000}$	$= 8\%$
Operating expense percentage	$=$	$\dfrac{\text{total expenses}}{\text{net sales}}$	$=$	$\dfrac{\$100,000}{\$300,000}$	$= 33\%$
Returns and allowances percentage	$=$	$\dfrac{\text{returns and allowances}}{\text{net sales}}$	$=$	$\dfrac{\$\ 25,000}{\$300,000}$	$= 8\%$

Another useful ratio is the *stockturn rate* (also called *inventory turnover rate*). The stockturn rate is the number of times an inventory turns over or is sold during a specified time period (often one year). It may be computed on a cost, selling price, or units basis.

Thus the formula can be:

$$\text{Stockturn rate} = \frac{\text{cost of goods sold}}{\text{average inventory at cost}}$$

or

$$\text{Stockturn rate} = \frac{\text{selling price of goods sold}}{\text{average selling price of inventory}}$$

or

$$\text{Stockturn rate} = \frac{\text{sales in units}}{\text{average inventory in units}}$$

We will use the first formula to calculate the stockturn rate for Dale Parsons Men's Wear:

$$\frac{\$175,000}{\dfrac{\$60,000 = \$45,000}{2}} = \frac{\$175,000}{\$52,500} = 3.3$$

That is, Parsons's inventory turned over 3.3 times in 1993. Normally, the higher the stockturn rate, the higher the management efficiency and company profitability.

Return on investment (ROI) is frequently used to measure managerial effectiveness. It uses figures from the firm's operating statement and balance sheet. A commonly used formula for computing ROI is:

$$\text{ROI} = \qquad \times$$

You may have two questions about this formula: Why use a two-step process when ROI could be computed simply as net profit divided by investment? And what exactly is "investment"?

To answer these questions, let's look at how each component of the formula can affect the ROI. Suppose Dale Parsons Men's Wear has a total investment of $150,000. Then ROI can be computed as follows:

$$\text{ROI} = \frac{\$25,000 \text{ (net profit)}}{\$300,000 \text{ (sales)}} \times \frac{\$300,000 \text{ (sales)}}{\$150,000 \text{ (investment)}}$$

$$8.3\% \quad \times \quad 2 \quad = 16.6\%$$

Now suppose that Parsons had worked to increase his share of market. He could have had the same ROI if his sales doubled while dollar profit and investment stayed the same (accepting a lower profit ratio to get higher turnover and market share):

$$\text{ROI} = \frac{\$25,000 \text{ (net profit)}}{\$600,000 \text{ (sales)}} \times \frac{\$600,000 \text{ (sales)}}{\$150,000 \text{ (investment)}}$$

$$4.16\% \quad \times \quad 4 \quad = 16.6\%$$

Parsons might have increased its ROI by increasing net profit through more cost cutting and more efficient marketing:

$$\text{ROI} = \frac{\$50,000 \text{ (net profit)}}{\$300,000 \text{ (sales)}} \times \frac{\$300,000 \text{ (sales)}}{\$150,000 \text{ (investment)}}$$

$$16.6\% \quad \times \quad 2 \quad = 33.2\%$$

Another way to increase ROI is to find some way to get the same levels of sales and profits while decreasing investment (perhaps by cutting the size of Parsons' average inventory):

$$\text{ROI} = \frac{\$25,000 \text{ (net profit)}}{\$300,000 \text{ (sales)}} \times \frac{\$300,000 \text{ (sales)}}{\$75,000 \text{ (investment)}}$$

$$8.3\% \quad \times \quad 4 \quad = 33.2\%$$

What is "investment" in the ROI formula? *Investment* is often defined as the total assets of the firm. But many analysts now use other measures of return to assess performance. These measures include *return on net assets (RONA), return on stockholders' equity (ROE),* or return on *assets managed (ROAM).* Because investment is measured at a point in time, we usually compute ROI as the average investment between two time periods (say, January 1 and December 31 of the same year). We can also compute ROI as an "internal rate of return" by using discounted cash flow analysis (see any finance textbook for more on this technique). The objective in using any of these measures is to determine how well the company has been using its resources. As inflation, competitive pressures, and cost of capital increase, such measures become increasingly important indicators of marketing and company performance.

MARKUPS AND MARKDOWNS

Retailers and wholesalers must understand the concepts of **markups** and **markdowns.** They must make a profit to stay in business, and the markup percentage affects profits. Markups and markdowns are expressed as percentages.

There are two different ways to compute markups—on *cost* or on selling *price:*

$$\text{Markup percentage on cost} = \frac{\text{dollar markup}}{\text{cost}}$$

$$\text{Markup percentage on selling price} = \frac{\text{dollar markup}}{\text{selling price}}$$

Dale Parsons must decide which formula to use. If Parsons bought shirts for $15 and wanted to mark them up $10, his markup percentage on cost would be $10/$15 = 67.7%. If Parsons based markup on selling price, the percentage would be $10/$25 = 40%. In figuring markup percentage, most retailers use the selling price rather than the cost. Suppose Parsons knew his cost ($12) and desired markup on price (25%) for a man's tie, and wanted to compute the selling price. The formula is:

$$\text{Selling price} =$$

$$\text{Selling price} = \quad = \$16$$

As a product moves through the channel of distribution, each channel member adds a markup before selling the product to the next member. This "markup chain" is shown for a suit purchased by a Parsons customer for $200:

		$ AMOUNT	% OF SELLING PRICE
	Cost	$108	90%
Manufacturer	Markup	12	10%
	Selling price	$120	100%
	Cost	$120	80%
Wholesaler	Markup	30	20%
	Selling price	$150	100%
	Cost	$150	75%
Retailer	Markup	50	25%
	Selling Price	$200	100%

The retailer whose markup is 25 percent does not necessarily enjoy more profit than a manufacturer whose markup is 10 percent. Profit also depends on how many items with that profit margin can be sold (stockturn rate), and on operating efficiency (expenses). Sometimes a retailer wants to convert markups based on selling price to markups based on cost, and vice versa. The formulas are:

$$\text{Markup percentage on selling price} = \frac{\text{markup percentage on cost}}{100\% + \text{markup percentage on selling cost}}$$

$$\text{Markup percentage on cost} = \frac{\text{markup percentage on selling price}}{100\% - \text{markup percentage on selling price}}$$

Suppose Parsons found that his competitor was using a markup of 30 percent based on cost and wanted to know what this would be as a percentage of selling price. The calculation would be:

$$\frac{30\%}{100\% = 30\%} = \frac{30\%}{130\%} = 23\%$$

Because Parsons was using a 25 percent markup on the selling price for suits, he felt that his markup was suitable compared with that of the competitor.

Near the end of the summer Parsons still had an inventory of summer slacks in stock. Therefore, he decided to use a *markdown,* a reduction from the original selling price. Before the summer he had purchased 20 pairs at $10 each, and he had since sold 10 pairs at $20 each. He marked down the other pairs to $15 and sold 5 pairs. We compute his *markdown ratio* as follows:

$$\text{Markup percentage} = \frac{\text{dollar markdown}}{\text{total net sales in dollars}}$$

The dollar markdown is $25 (5 pairs at $5 each) and total net sales are $275 (10 pairs at $20 + 5 pairs at $15). The ratio, then, is $25/$275 = 9%.

Larger retailers usually compute markdown ratios for each department rather than for individual items. The ratios provide a measure of relative marketing performance for each department and can be calculated and compared over time. Markdown ratios can also be used to compare the performance of different buyers and salespeople in a store's various departments.

KEY TERMS

Balance sheet A-1

Cost of goods sold A-2

Gross margin A-2

Gross sales A-2

Markdown A-4

Markup A-4

Operating ratios A-3

Operating statement (*or* profit-and-loss statement *or* income statement) A-1

Return on investment (ROI) A-3

Appendix 2: Careers in Marketing

Now that you have completed your first course in marketing, you have a good idea of what the field entails. You may have decided that you want to pursue a marketing career because it offers constant challenge, stimulating problems, the opportunity to work with people, and excellent advancement opportunities. Marketing is a very broad field with a wide variety of tasks involving the analysis, planning, implementation, and control of marketing programs. You will find marketing positions in all types and sizes of institutions. This appendix describes entry-level and higher-level marketing opportunities and lists steps you might take to select a career path and better market yourself.

DESCRIPTION OF MARKETING JOBS

Almost a third of all Americans are employed in marketing-related positions. Thus, the number of possible marketing careers is enormous. Because of the knowledge of products and consumers gained in these jobs, marketing provides excellent training for the highest levels in the organization. A recent study by a recruiting firm found that more top executives have come out of marketing than of any other area.

Marketing salaries vary by company and position. Beginning salaries usually rank only slightly below those for engineering and chemistry, but equal or exceed those for economics, finance, accounting, general business, and the liberal arts. If you succeed in an entry-level marketing position, you will quickly be promoted to higher levels of responsibility and salary.

Marketing has become an attractive career for some people who have not traditionally considered this field. One trend is the growing number of women entering marketing. Women have historically been employed in the retailing and advertising areas of marketing. But they now have moved into all types of sales and marketing positions. Women now pursue successful sales careers in pharmaceutical companies, publishing companies, banks, consumer products companies, and in an increasing number of industrial selling jobs. Their ranks are also growing in product and brand manager positions.

Another trend is the growing acceptance of marketing by nonprofit organizations. Colleges, arts organizations, libraries, and hospitals are increasingly applying marketing to their problems. They are beginning to hire marketing directors and marketing vice-presidents to manage their varied marketing activities.

Here are brief descriptions of some important marketing jobs.

Advertising

Advertising is an important business activity that requires skill in planning, fact gathering, and creativity. Although compensation for starting advertising people tends to be lower than that in other marketing fields, opportunities for advancement are usually greater because of less emphasis on age or length of employment. Typical jobs in advertising agencies include the following positions.

Copywriters help find the concepts behind the written words and visual images of advertisements. They dig for facts, read avidly, and borrow ideas. They talk to customers, suppliers, and *anybody* who might give them clues about how to attract the target audience's attention and interest.

Art directors constitute the other part of the creative team. They translate copywriters' ideas into dramatic visuals called "layouts." Agency artists develop print layouts, package designs, television layouts (called "storyboards"), corporate logotypes, trademarks, and symbols. They specify style and size of typography, paste the type in place, and arrange all the details of the ad so that it can be reproduced by engravers and printers. A superior art director or copy chief becomes the agency's creative director and oversees all its advertising.

Account executives are liaisons between clients and agencies. They must know a great deal about marketing and its various components. They explain client plans and objectives to agency creative teams and supervise the development of the total advertising plan. Their main task is to keep the client happy with the agency! Because "account work" involves many personal relationships, account executives are usually personable, diplomatic, and sincere.

Media buyers select the best media for clients. Media representatives come to the buyer's office armed with statistics to prove that *their* numbers are better, *their* costs per thousand are less, and *their* medium delivers more ripe audiences than competitive media. Media buyers have to evaluate these claims. They must also bargain with the broadcast media for best rates and make deals with the print media for good ad positions.

Large ad agencies have active marketing research departments that provide market information needed to develop new ad campaigns and assess current campaigns. People interested in marketing research should consider jobs with ad agencies.

Brand and Product Management

Brand and product managers plan, direct, and control business and marketing efforts for their products. They are concerned with research and development, packaging, manufacturing, sales and distribution, advertising, promotion, market research, and business analysis and forecasting. In consumer goods companies, the newcomer—who usually needs a Masters of Business Administration degree (MBA)—joins a brand team and learns the ropes by doing numerical analyses and watching senior brand people. This person eventually heads the team and later moves on to manage a larger brand. Many industrial goods companies also have product managers. Product management is one of the best training grounds for future corporate officers.

Customer Affairs

Some large consumer goods companies have customer affairs people who act as liaisons between customers and firms. They handle complaints, suggestions, and problems concerning the company's products, determine what action to take, and coordinate the activities required to solve the problem. The position requires an empathetic, diplomatic, and capable person who can work with a wide range of people inside and outside the firm.

Industrial Marketing

People interested in industrial marketing careers can go into sales, service, product design, marketing research, or one of several other positions. They sometimes need a technical background. Most people start in sales and spend time in training and making calls with senior salespeople. If they stay in sales, they may advance to district, regional, and higher sales positions. Or they may go into product management and work closely with customers, suppliers, manufacturing, and sales engineering.

International Marketing

As U.S. firms increase their international business, they need people who are familiar with foreign languages and cultures and who are willing to travel to or relocate in foreign cities. For such assignments, most companies seek experienced people who have proved themselves in domestic operations. An MBA often helps but is not always required.

Marketing Management Science and Systems Analysis

People who have been trained in management science, quantitative methods, and systems analysis can act as consultants to managers who face difficult marketing problems such as demand measurement and forecasting, market structure analysis, and new-product evaluation. Most career opportunities exist in larger marketing-oriented firms, management consulting firms, and public institutions concerned with health, education, or transportation. An MBA or an Master of Science degree is often required.

Marketing Research

Marketing researchers interact with managers to define problems and identify the information needed to resolve them. They design research projects, prepare questionnaires and samples, analyze data, prepare reports, and present their findings and recommendations to management. They must understand statistics, consumer behavior, psychology, and sociology. A master's degree helps. Career opportunities exist with manufacturers, retailers, some wholesalers, trade and industry associations, marketing research firms, advertising agencies, and governmental and private nonprofit agencies.

New-Product Planning

People interested in new-product planning can find opportunities in many types of organizations. They usually need a good background in marketing, marketing research, and sales forecasting; they need organizational skills to motivate and coordinate others; and they may need a technical background. Usually, these people work first in other marketing positions before joining the new-product department.

Marketing Logistics (Physical Distribution)

Marketing logistics, or physical distribution, is a large and dynamic field, with many career opportunities. Major transportation carriers, manufacturers, wholesalers, and retailers all employ physical distribution specialists. Coursework in quantitative methods, finance, accounting, and marketing will provide students with the necessary skills for entering the field.

Public Relations

Most organizations have a public relations person or staff to anticipate public problems, handle complaints, deal with media, and build the corporate image. People interested in public relations should be able to speak and write clearly and persuasively, and they should have a background in journalism, communications, or the liberal arts. The challenges in this job are highly varied and very people oriented.

Purchasing

Purchasing agents are playing a growing role in firms' profitability during periods of rising costs, materials shortages, and increasing product complexity. In retail organizations, working as a "buyer" can be a good route to the top. Purchasing agents in industrial companies play a key role in holding down the costs. A technical background is useful in some purchasing positions, along with a knowledge of credit, finance, and physical distribution.

Retailing Management

Retailing provides people with an early opportunity to take on marketing responsibilities. Although retail starting salaries and job assignments have typically been lower than those in manufacturing or advertising, the gap is narrowing. The major routes to top management in retailing are merchandise management and store management. In merchandise management, a person moves from buyer trainee to assistant buyer to buyer to merchandise division manager. In store management, the person moves from management trainee to assistant department (sales) manager to department manager to store (branch) manager. Buyers are primarily concerned with merchandise selection and promotion; department managers are concerned with salesforce management and display. Large-scale retailing lets new recruits move in only a few years into the management of a branch or part of a store doing as much as $5 million in sales.

Sales and Sales Management

Sales and sales-management opportunities exist in a wide range of profit and nonprofit organizations and in product and service organizations, including financial, insurance, consulting, and government organizations. Individuals must carefully match their backgrounds, interests, technical skills, and academic training with available sales jobs. Training programs vary greatly in form and length, ranging from a few weeks to two years. Career paths lead from salesperson to district, regional, and higher levels of sales management and, in many cases, the top management of the firm.

Other Marketing Careers

There are many other marketing-related jobs in areas such as sales promotion, wholesaling, packaging, pricing, and credit management. Information on these positions can be gathered from sources such as those listed in the following discussion.

CHOOSING AND GETTING A JOB

To choose and obtain a job, you must apply marketing skills, particularly marketing analysis and planning. Here are eight steps for choosing a career and finding that first job.

Make a Self-Assessment

Self-assessment is the most important part of a job search. It involves honestly evaluating your interests, strengths, and weaknesses. What are your career objectives? What kind of organization do you want to work for? What do you do well or not so well? What sets you apart from other job seekers? Do the answers to these questions suggest which careers you should seek or avoid? For help in self-assessment, you might look at the following books, each of which raises many questions you should consider:

1. *What Color Is Your Parachute?*, by Richard Bolles

2. *Three Boxes in Life and How to Get Out of Them*, by Richard Bolles

3. *Guerrilla Tactics in the Job Market*, by Tom Jackson

Also consult the career counseling, testing, and placement services at your school.

Examine Job Descriptions

Now look at various job descriptions to see what positions best match your interests, desires, and abilities. Descriptions can be found in the *Occupation Outlook Handbook* and the *Dictionary of Occupational Titles* published by the U.S. Department of Labor. These volumes describe the duties of people in various occupations, the specific training and education needed, the availability of jobs in each field, possibilities for advancement, and probable earnings.

Develop Job-Search Objectives

Your initial career shopping list should be broad and flexible. Look broadly for ways to achieve your objectives. For example, if you want a career in marketing research, consider the public as well as the private sector, and regional as well as national firms. Only after exploring many options should you begin to focus on specific industries and initial jobs. You need to set down a list of basic goals. Your list might say: "a job in a small company, in a large city, in the Sunbelt, doing marketing research, with an consumer products firm."

Examine the Job Market and Assess Opportunities

You must now look at the market to see what positions are available. For an up-to-date listing of marketing-related job openings, refer to the latest edition of the *College Placement Annual* available at school placement offices. This publication shows current job openings for hundreds of companies seeking college graduates for entry-level positions. It also lists companies seeking experienced or advanced-degree people. At this stage, use the services of your placement office to the fullest extent in order to find openings and set up interviews. Take the time to analyze the industries and companies in which you are interested. Consult business magazines, annual reports, business reference books, faculty members, school career counselors, and fellow students. Try to analyze the future growth and profit potential of the company and industry, chances for advancement, salary levels, entry positions, amount of travel, and other important factors.

Develop Search Strategies

How will you contact companies in which you are interested? There are several possible ways. One of the best ways is through on-campus interviews. But not all the companies that interest you will visit your school. Another good way is to phone or write the company directly. Finally, you can ask marketing professors or school alumni for contacts and references.

Develop Résumé and Cover Letter

Your résumé should persuasively present your abilities, education, background, training, work experience, and personal qualifications—but it should also be brief, usually one page. The goal is to gain a positive response from potential employers.

The cover letter is, in some ways, more difficult to write than the résumé. It must be persuasive, professional, concise, and interesting. Ideally, it should set you apart from the other candidates for the position. Each letter should look and sound original—that is, it should be individually typed and tailored to the specific organization being contacted. It should describe the position you are applying for, arouse interest, describe your qualifications, and tell how you can be contacted. Cover letters should be addressed to an individual rather than a title. You should follow up the letter with a telephone call.

Obtain Interviews

Here is some advice to follow before, during, and after your interviews.

Before the Interview.

1. Interviewers have extremely diverse styles—the "chit chat," let's-get-to-know-each-other style; the interrogation style of question after question; and the tough-probing why, why, why style; and many others. Be ready for anything.

2. Practice being interviewed with a friend and ask for a critique.

3. Prepare to ask at least five good questions that are not readily answered in the company literature.

4. Anticipate possible interview questions and prepare good answers ahead of time.

5. Avoid back-to-back interviews—they can be exhausting.

6. Dress conservatively and tastefully for the interview. Be neat and clean.

7. Arrive about ten minutes early to collect your thoughts before the interview. Check your name on the interview schedule, noting the name of the interviewer and the room number.

8. Review the major points you intend to cover.

During the Interview.

1. Give a firm handshake in greeting the interviewer. Introduce yourself using the same form the interviewer uses. Make a good initial impression.

2. Retain your poise. Relax. Smile occasionally. Be enthusiastic during the interview.

3. Good eye contact, good posture, and distinct speech are musts. Don't clasp your hands or fiddle with jewelry, hair, or clothing. Sit comfortably in your chair. Do not smoke, even if asked.

4. Have extra copies of your résumé with you.

5. Have your story down pat. Present your selling points. Answer questions directly. Avoid one-word answers, but don't be wordy.

6. Most times, let the interviewer take the initiative, but don't be passive. Find an good opportunity to direct the conversation to things you want the interviewer to hear.

7. To end on a high note, the latter part of the interview is the best time to make your most important point or to ask a pertinent question.

8. Don't be afraid to "close." You might say, "I'm very interested in the position and I have enjoyed this interview."

9. Obtain the interviewer's business card or address and phone number so that you can follow up later.

After the Interview.

1. After leaving the interview, record the key points that arose. Be sure to record who is to follow up on the interview and when a decision can be expected.

2. Objectively analyze the interview with regard to the questions asked, the answers given, your overall interview presentation, and the interviewer's response to specific points.

3. Send a thank-you letter mentioning any additional items and your willingness to supply further information.

4. If you do not hear within the time specified, write or call the interviewer to determine your status.

Follow-Up

If you are successful, you will be invited to visit the organization. The in-company interview will run from a few hours to a whole day. The company will examine your interest, maturity, enthusiasm, assertiveness, logic, and company and functional knowledge. You should ask questions about things that are important to you. Find out about the environment, job role, responsibilities, opportunity, current industrial issues, and the firm's personality. The company wants to find out if you are the right person for the job; just as importantly, you want to find out if this is the right job for you.

Glossary

Accessibility The degree to which a market segment can be reached and served.

Actionability The degree to which effective programs can be designed for attracting and serving a given market segment.

Actual product A product's parts, quality level, features, design, brand name, packaging, and other attributes that combine to deliver core product benefits.

Adapted marketing mix An international marketing strategy for adjusting the marketing-mix elements to each international target market, bearing more costs but hoping for a larger market share and return.

Administered VMS A vertical marketing system that coordinates successive stages of production and distribution, not through common ownership or contractual ties, but through the size and power of one of the parties.

Adoption The decision by an individual to become a regular user of the product.

Adoption process The mental process through which an individual passes from first hearing about an innovation to final adoption.

Advertising Any paid form of nonpersonal presentation and promotion of ideas, goods, or services by an identified sponsor.

Advertising objective A specific communication *task* to be accomplished with a specific *target* audience during a specific period of *time*.

Advertising specialties Useful articles imprinted with an advertiser's name, given as gifts to consumers.

Affordable method Setting the promotion budget at the level management thinks the company can afford.

Age and life-cycle segmentation Dividing a market into different age and life-cycle groups.

Agent A wholesaler who represents buyers or sellers on a relatively permanent basis, performs only a few functions, and does not take title to goods.

Allowance Promotional money paid by manufacturers to retailers in re-

turn for an agreement to feature the manufacturer's products in some way.

Alternative evaluation The stage of the buyer decision process in which the consumer uses information to evaluate alternative brands in the choice set.

Approach The step in the selling process in which the salesperson meets and greets the buyer to get the relationship off to a good start.

Aspirational group A group to which an individual wishes to belong.

Atmospheres Designed environments that create or reinforce the buyer's leanings toward consumption of a product.

Attitude A person's consistently favorable or unfavorable evaluations, feelings, and tendencies toward an object or idea.

Augmented product Additional consumer services and benefits built around the core and actual products.

Automatic vending Selling through vending machines.

Available market The set of consumers who have interest, income, and access to a particular product or service.

Baby boom The major increase in the annual birthrate following World War II and lasting until the early 1960s. The "baby boomers," now moving into middle age, are a prime target for marketers.

Balance sheet A financial statement that shows assets, liabilities, and net worth of a company at a given time.

Barter transaction A marketing transaction in which goods or services are traded for other goods or services.

Basing-point pricing A geographic pricing strategy in which the seller designates some city as a basing point and charges all customers the freight cost from that city to the customer location, regardless of the city from which the goods are actually shipped.

Behavioral segmentation Dividing a market into groups based consumer knowledge, attitude, use, or response to a product.

Belief A descriptive thought that a person holds about something.

Benchmarking The process of comparing the company's products and processes to those of competitors or leading firms in other industries to find ways to improve quality and performance.

Benefit segmentation Dividing the market into groups according to the different benefits that consumers seek from the product.

Brand A name, term, sign, symbol, or design, or a combination of these intended to identify the goods or services of one seller or group of sellers and to differentiate them from those of competitors.

Brand equity The value of a brand, based on the extent to which it has high brand loyalty, name awareness, perceived quality, strong brand associations, and other assets such as patents, trademarks, and channel relationships.

Brand extension Using a successful brand name to launch a new or modified product in a new category.

Brand image The set of beliefs consumers hold about a particular brand.

Breakeven pricing (target profit pricing) Setting price to break even on the costs of making and marketing a product; or setting price to make a target profit.

Broker A wholesaler who does not take title to goods and whose function is to bring buyers and sellers together and assist in negotiation.

Business analysis A review of the sales, costs, and profit projections for a new product to find out whether these factors satisfy the company's objectives.

Business market All the organizations that buy goods and services to use in the production of other products and services or for the purpose of reselling or renting them to others at a profit.

Business buying process The decision-making process by which business buyers establish the need for purchased products and services and identify, evaluate, and choose among alternative brands and suppliers.

Business portfolio The collection of businesses and products that make up the company.

Buyer The person who makes an actual purchase.

Buyer-readiness states The stages consumers normally pass through on their way to purchase, including awareness, knowledge, liking, preference, conviction, and purchase.

Buyers People in an organization's buying center with formal authority to select the supplier and arrange terms of purchase.

Buying center All the individuals and units that participate in the business buying-decision process.

By-product pricing Setting a price for by-products in order to make the main product's price more competitive.

Capital items Industrial goods that partly enter the finished product, including installations and accessory equipment.

Captive-product pricing Setting a price for products that must be used along with a main product, such as blades for a razor and film for a camera.

Cash cows Low-growth, high-share businesses or products; established and successful units that generate cash the company uses to pay its bills and support other business units that need investment.

Cash discount A price reduction to buyers who pay their bills promptly.

Cash refund offers (rebates) Offers to refund part of the purchase price of a product to consumers who send a "proof of purchase" to the manufacturer.

Catalog marketing Direct marketing through catalogs that are mailed to a select list of customers or made available in stores.

Catalog showroom A retail operation that sells a wide selection of high-markup, fast-moving, brand name goods at discount prices.

Causal research Marketing research to test hypotheses about cause-and-effect relationships.

Chain stores Two or more outlets that are commonly owned and controlled, have central buying and merchandising, and sell similar lines of merchandise.

Channel conflict Disagreement among marketing channel members on goals and roles—who should do what and for what rewards.

Channel level A layer of middlemen that performs some work in bring-

ing the product and its ownership closer to the final buyer.

Closed-end questions Questions that include all the possible answers and allow subjects to make choices among them.

Closing The step in the selling process in which the salesperson asks the customer for an order.

Cognitive dissonance Buyer discomfort caused by postpurchase conflict.

Combination stores Combined food and drug stores.

Commercialization Introducing a new product into the market.

Comparison advertising Advertising that compares one brand directly or indirectly to one or more other brands.

Competitive advantage An advantage over competitors gained by offering consumers greater value, either through lower prices or by providing more benefits that justify higher prices.

Competitive-parity method Setting the promotion budget to match competitors' outlays.

Competitive strategies Strategies that strongly position the company against competitors and that give the company the strongest possible strategic advantage.

Competitor analysis The process of identifying key competitors; assessing their objectives, strategies, strengths and weaknesses, and reaction patterns; and selecting which competitors to attack or avoid.

Competitor-centered company A company whose moves are mainly based on competitors' actions and reactions; it spends most of its time tracking competitors' moves and market shares and trying to find strategies to counter them.

Complex buying behavior Consumer buying behavior in situations characterized by high consumer involvement in a purchase and significant perceived differences among brands.

Concentrated marketing A market-coverage strategy in which a firm goes after a large share of one or a few submarkets.

Cost of goods sold The net cost to the company of goods sold.

Concept testing Testing new product concepts with a group of target consumers to find out if the concepts have strong consumer appeal.

Consumer buying behavior The buying behavior of final consumers—

individuals and households who buy goods and services for personal consumption.

Consumer franchise building promotions Sales promotions that promote the product's positioning and include a selling message along with the deal.

Consumer goods Goods bought by final consumers for personal consumption.

Consumer market All the individuals and households who buy or acquire goods and services for personal consumption.

Consumer-oriented marketing A principle of enlightened marketing which holds that a the company should view and organize its marketing activities from the consumers' point of view.

Consumer promotion Sales promotion designed to stimulate consumer purchasing, including samples, coupons, rebates, prices-off, premiums, patronage rewards, displays, and contests and sweepstakes.

Consumerism An organized movement of citizens and government agencies to improve the rights and power of buyers in relation to sellers.

Containerization Putting the goods in boxes or trailers that are easy to transfer between two transportation modes. They are used in multimode systems commonly referred to as piggyback, fishyback, trainship, and airtruck.

Contests, sweepstakes, games Promotional events that give consumers the chance to win something—such as cash, trips, or goods—by luck or through extra effort.

Continuity Scheduling ads evenly within a given period.

Contract manufacturing A joint venture in which a company contracts with manufacturers in a foreign market to produce the product.

Contractual VMS A vertical marketing system in which independent firms at different levels of production and distribution join together through contracts to obtain more economies or sales impact than they could achieve alone.

Convenience goods Consumer goods that the customer usually buys frequently, immediately, and with a minimum of comparison and buying effort.

Convenience store A small store located near a residential area that is open long hours seven days a week and carries a limited line of high-turnover convenience goods.

Conventional distribution channel A channel consisting of one or more independent producers, wholesalers, and retailers, each a separate business seeking to maximize its own profits even at the expense of profits for the system as a whole.

Copy testing Measuring the communication effect of an advertisement before or after it is printed or broadcast.

Core product The problem-solving services or core benefits that consumers are really buying when they obtain a product.

Corporate VMS A vertical marketing system that combines successive stages of production and distribution under single ownership—channel leadership is established through common ownership.

Cost-plus pricing Adding a standard markup to the cost of the product.

Countertrade International trade involving the direct or indirect exchange of goods for other goods instead of cash. Forms include barter, compensation (buyback), and counterpurchase.

Coupons Certificates that give buyers a saving when they purchase a product.

Cultural environment Institutions and other forces that affect society's basic values, perceptions, preferences, and behaviors.

Culture The set of basic values, perceptions, wants, and behaviors learned by a member of society from family and other important institutions.

Current marketing situation The section of a marketing plan that describes the target market and the company's position in it.

Customer-centered company A company that focuses on customer developments in designing its marketing strategies and on delivering superior value to its target customers.

Customer delivered value The difference between total customer value and total customer cost of a marketing offer—"profit" to the customer.

Customer lifetime value The amount by which revenues from a given customer over time will exceed the company's costs of attracting, selling, and servicing that customer.

Customer salesforce structure A salesforce organization under which salespeople specialize in selling only to certain customers or industries.

Customer value The consumer's assessment of the product's overall capacity to satisfy his or her needs.

Customer value analysis Analysis conducted to determine what benefits target customers value and how they rate the relative value of various competitors' offers.

Customer value delivery system The system made up of the value chains of the company and its suppliers, distributors, and ultimately customers who work together to deliver value to customers.

Decider The person who ultimately makes a buying decision or any part of it—whether to buy, what to buy, how to buy, or where to buy.

Deciders People in the organization's buying center who have formal or informal power to select or approve the final suppliers.

Decline stage The product life-cycle stage at which a product's sales decline.

Deficient products Products that have neither immediate appeal nor long-run benefits.

Demand curve A curve that shows the number of units the market will buy in a given time period, at different prices that might be charged.

Demands Human wants that are backed by buying power.

Demographic segmentation Dividing the market into groups based on demographic variables such as age, sex, family size, family life cycle, income, occupation, education, religion, race, and nationality.

Demography The study of human populations in terms of size, density, location, age, sex, race, occupation, and other statistics.

Department store A retail organization that carries a wide variety of product lines—typically clothing, home furnishings, and household goods; each line is operated as a separate department managed by specialist buyers or merchandisers.

Derived demand Business demand that ultimately comes from (derives from) the demand for consumer goods.

Descriptive research Marketing research to better describe marketing problems, situations, or markets, such as the market potential for a product or the demographics and attitudes of consumers.

Desirable products Products that give both high immediate satisfaction and high long-run benefits.

Differentiated marketing A market-coverage strategy in which a firm decides to target several market segments and designs separate offers for each.

Direct investment Entering a foreign market by developing foreign-based assembly or manufacturing facilities.

Direct-mail marketing Direct marketing through single mailings that include letters, ads, samples, foldouts, and other "salespeople on wings" sent to prospects on mailing lists.

Direct marketing Marketing through various advertising media that interact directly with consumers, generally calling for the consumer to make a direct response.

Direct-marketing channel A marketing channel that has no intermediary levels.

Discount A straight reduction in price on purchases during a stated period of time.

Discount store A retail institution that sells standard merchandise at lower prices by accepting lower margins and selling at higher volume.

Discriminatory pricing Selling a product or service at two or more prices, where the difference in prices is not based on differences in costs.

Dissonance-reducing buying behavior Consumer buying behavior in situations characterized by high involvement but few perceived differences among brands.

Distribution center A large, highly automated warehouse designed to receive goods from various plants and suppliers, take orders, fill them efficiently, and deliver goods to customers as quickly as possible.

Distribution channel (marketing channel) A set of interdependent organizations involved in the process of making a product or service available for use or consumption by the consumer or industrial user.

Diversification A strategy for company growth by starting up or acquiring businesses outside the company's current products and markets.

Dogs Low-growth, low-share businesses and products that may generate enough cash to maintain themselves but do not promise to be large sources of cash.

Door-to-door retailing Selling door to door, office to office, or at home-sales parties.

Durable goods Consumer goods that usually are used over an extended period of time and that normally survive many uses.

Economic community A group of nations organized to work toward common goals in the regulation of international trade.

Economic environment Factors that affect consumer buying power and spending patterns.

Electronic shopping Direct marketing through a two-way system that links consumers with the seller's computerized catalog by cable or telephone lines.

Embargo A ban on the import of a certain product.

Emotional appeals Message appeals that attempt to stir up negative or positive emotions that will motivate purchase; examples include fear, guilt, shame, love, humor, pride, and joy appeals.

Engel's laws Differences noted over a century ago by Ernst Engel in how people shift their spending across food, housing, transportation, health care, and other goods and services categories as family income rises.

Enlightened marketing A marketing philosophy holding that a company's marketing should support the best long-run performance of the marketing system; its five principles include consumer-oriented marketing, innovative marketing, value marketing, sense-of-mission marketing, and societal marketing.

Environmental management perspective A management perspective in which the firm takes aggressive actions to affect the publics and forces in its marketing environment rather than simply watching and reacting to it.

Environmentalism An organized movement of concerned citizens and government agencies to protect and improve people's living environment.

Events Occurrences staged to communicate messages to target audiences; examples include news conferences, grand openings, or others.

Exchange The act of obtaining a desired object from someone by offering something in return.

Exchange controls Government limits on the amount of its foreign exchange with other countries and on its exchange rate against other currencies.

Exclusive distribution Giving a limited number of dealers the exclusive right to distribute the company's products in their territories.

Executive summary The opening section of the marketing plan that presents a short summary of the main goals and recommendations to be presented in the plan.

Experience curve (learning curve) The drop in the average per-unit production cost that comes with accumulated production experience.

Experimental research The gathering of primary data by selecting matched groups of subjects, giving them different treatments, controlling related factors, and checking for differences in group responses.

Exploratory research Marketing research to gather preliminary information that will help to better define problems and suggest hypotheses.

Exporting Entering a foreign market by sending products and selling them through international marketing middlemen (indirect exporting) or through the company's own department, branch, or sales representatives or agents (direct exporting).

Factory outlets Off-price retailing operations that are owned and operated by manufacturers and that normally carry the manufacturer's surplus, discontinued, or irregular goods.

Fads Fashions that enter quickly, are adopted with great zeal, peak early, and decline very fast.

Family life cycle The stages through which families might pass as they mature over time.

Fashion A currently accepted or popular style in a given field.

Financial intermediaries Banks, credit companies, insurance companies, and other businesses that help finance transactions or insure against the risks associated with the buying and selling of goods.

Fixed costs Costs that do not vary with production or sales level.

FOB-origin pricing A geographic pricing strategy in which goods are placed free on board a carrier; the customer pays the freight from the factory to the destination.

Focus-group interviewing Personal interviewing which consists of inviting six to ten people to gather for a few hours with a trained interviewer to talk about a product, service, or organization. The interviewer "focuses" the group discussion on important issues.

Follow-up The last step in the selling process in which the salesperson follows up after the sale to ensure customer satisfaction and repeat business.

Forecasting The art of estimating future demand by anticipating what buyers are likely to do under a given set of conditions.

Franchise A contractual association between a manufacturer, wholesaler, or service organization (a franchiser) and independent businesspeople (franchisees) who buy the right to own and operate one or more units in the franchise system.

Franchise organization A contractual vertical marketing system in which a channel member, called a franchiser, links several stages in the production-distribution process.

Freight-absorption pricing A geographic pricing strategy in which the company absorbs all or part of the actual freight charges in order to get the business.

Frequency The number of times the average person in the target market is exposed to an advertising message during a given period.

Full-service retailers Retailers that provide a full range of services to shoppers.

Full-service wholesalers Wholesalers that provide a full set of services such as carrying stock, using a salesforce, offering credit, making deliveries, and providing management assistance.

Functional discount A price reduction offered by the seller to trade channel members who perform certain functions such as selling, storing, and recordkeeping.

Gatekeepers People in the organization's buying center who control the flow of information to others.

GE strategic business-planning grid A portfolio planning method that evaluates a company's strategic business units using indexes of industry attractiveness and the company's strength in the industry.

Gender segmentation Dividing a market into different groups based on sex.

General need description The stage in the business buying process in which the company describes the general characteristics and quantity of a needed item.

Geographic segmentation Dividing a market into different geographical units such as nations, states, regions, counties, cities, or neighborhoods.

Global firm A firm that, by operating in more than one country, gains R&D, production, marketing, and financial advantages in its costs and reputation that are not available to purely domestic competitors.

Global industry An industry in which the strategic positions of competitors in given geographic or national markets are affected by their overall global positions.

Going-rate pricing Setting price based largely on following competitors' prices rather than on company costs or demand.

Government market Governmental units—federal, state, and local—that purchase or rent goods and services for carrying out the main functions of government.

Gross margin The difference between net sales and cost of goods sold.

Gross sales The total amount that a company charges during a given period of time for merchandise.

Growth-share matrix A portfolio-planning method that evaluates a company's strategic business units in terms of their market growth rate and relative market share. SBUs are classified as stars, cash cows, question marks, or dogs.

Growth stage The product life-cycle stage at which a product's sales start climbing quickly.

Habitual buying behavior Consumer buying behavior in situations characterized by low consumer involvement and few significant perceived brand differences.

Handling objections The step in the selling process in which the salesperson seeks out, clarifies, and overcomes customer objections to buying.

Horizontal marketing systems A channel arrangement in which two or more companies at one level join together to follow a new marketing opportunity.

Human need A state of felt deprivation.

Human want The form that a human need takes as shaped by culture and individual personality.

Hypermarkets Huge stores that combine supermarket, discount, and warehouse retailing; in addition to food, they carry furniture, appliances, clothing, and many other products.

Idea generation The systematic search for new-product ideas.

Idea screening Screening new-product ideas in order to spot good ideas and drop poor ones as soon as possible.

Income segmentation Dividing a market into different income groups.

Independent off-price retailers Off-price retailers that are either owned and run by entrepreneurs or are divisions of larger retail corporations.

Industrial goods Goods bought by individuals and organizations for further processing or for use in conducting a business.

Industry A group of firms which offer a product or class of products that are close substitutes for each other. The set of all sellers of a product or service.

Inelastic demand Total demand for a product that is not much affected by price changes, especially in the short run.

Influencer A person whose views or advice carries some weight in making a final buying decision.

Influencers People in an organization's buying center who affect the buying decision; they often help define specifications and also provide information for evaluating alternatives.

Information search The stage of the buyer decision process in which the consumer is aroused to search for more information; the consumer may simply have heightened attention or may go into active information search.

Informative advertising Advertising used to inform consumers about a new product or feature and to build primary demand.

Initiator The person who first suggests or thinks of the idea of buying a particular product or service.

Innovative marketing A principle of enlightened marketing which requires that a company seek real product and marketing improvements.

Institutional market Schools, hospitals, nursing homes, prisons, and other institutions that provide goods and services to people in their care.

Integrated direct marketing Direct marketing campaigns that use multiple vehicles and multiple stages to improve response rates and profits.

Intensive distribution Stocking the product in as many outlets as possible.

Interactive marketing Marketing by a service firm that recognizes that perceived service quality depends heavily on the quality of buyer-seller interaction.

Internal marketing Marketing by a service firm to train and effectively motivate its customer-contact employees and all the supporting service people to work as a team to provide customer satisfaction.

Internal records information Information gathered from sources within the company to evaluate marketing performance and to detect marketing problems and opportunities.

Introduction stage The product life-cycle stage when the new product is first distributed and made available for purchase.

Joint ownership A joint venture in which a company joins investors in a foreign market to create a local business in which the company shares joint ownership and control.

Joint venturing Entering foreign markets by joining with foreign companies to produce or market a product or service.

Leading indicators Time series that change in the same direction but in advance of company sales.

Learning Changes in an individual's behavior arising from experience.

Licensing A method of entering a foreign market in which the company enters into an agreement with a licensee in the foreign market, offering the right to use a manufacturing process, trademark, patent, trade secret, or other item of value for a fee or royalty.

Lifestyle A person's pattern of living as expressed in his or her activities, interests, and opinions.

Limited-service retailers Retailers that provide only a limited number of services to shoppers.

Limited-service wholesalers Those who offer only limited services to their suppliers and customers.

Line extension Using a successful brand name to introduce additional items in a given product category under the same brand name, such as new flavors, forms, colors, added ingredients, or package sizes.

Macroenvironment The larger societal forces that affect the whole microenvironment—demographic, economic, natural, technological, political, and cultural forces.

Markdown A percentage reduction from the original selling price.

Markup The percentage of the cost or price of a product added to cost in order to arrive at a selling price.

Management contracting A joint venture in which the domestic firm supplies the management know-how to a foreign company that supplies the capital; the domestic firm exports management services rather than products.

Manufacturer's brand (or **national brand**) A brand created and owned by the producer of a product or service.

Manufacturers' sales branches and offices Wholesaling by sellers or buyers themselves rather than through independent wholesalers.

Market The set of all actual and potential buyers of a product or service.

Market-centered company A company that pays balanced attention to both customers and competitors in designing its marketing strategies.

Market challenger A runner-up firm in an industry that is fighting hard to increase its market share.

Market development A strategy for company growth by identifying and developing new market segments for current company products.

Market follower A runner-up firm in an industry that wants to hold its share without rocking the boat.

Market leader The firm in an industry with the largest market share; it usually leads other firms in price changes, new product introductions, distribution coverage, and promotion spending.

Market nicher A firm in an industry that serves small segments that the other firms overlook or ignore.

Market penetration A strategy for company growth by increasing sales of current products to current market segments without changing the product in any way.

Market-penetration pricing Setting a low price for a new product in order to attract a large number of buyers and a large market share.

Market positioning Arranging for a product to occupy a clear, distinctive, and desirable place relative to competing products in the minds of target consumers. Formulating competitive positioning for a product and a detailed marketing mix.

Market segment A group of consumers who respond in a similar way to a given set of marketing stimuli.

Market segmentation Dividing a market into distinct groups of buyers with different needs, characteristics, or behavior who might require separate products or marketing mixes.

Market-skimming pricing Setting a high price for a new product to skim maximum revenues layer by layer from the segments willing to pay the high price; the company makes fewer but more profitable sales.

Market targeting The process of evaluating each market segment's attractiveness and selecting one or more segments to enter.

Marketing A social and managerial process by which individuals and groups obtain what they need and want through creating and exchanging products and value with others.

Marketing audit A comprehensive, systematic, independent, and periodic examination of a company's environment, objectives, strategies, and activities to determine problem areas and opportunities and to recommend a plan of action to improve the company's marketing performance.

Marketing budget A section of the marketing plan that shows projected revenues, costs, and profits.

Marketing concept The marketing management philosophy that holds that achieving organizational goals depends on determining the needs and wants of target markets and delivering the desired satisfactions more effectively and efficiently than competitors do.

Marketing control The process of measuring and evaluating the results of marketing strategies and plans, and taking corrective action to ensure that marketing objectives are attained.

Marketing database An organized set of data about individual customers or prospects that can be used to generate and qualify customer leads, sell products and services, and maintain customer relationships.

Marketing environment The actors and forces outside marketing that affect marketing management's ability to develop and maintain successful transactions with its target customers.

Marketing implementation The process that turns marketing strategies and plans into marketing actions in order to accomplish strategic marketing objectives.

Marketing information system (MIS) People, equipment, and procedures to gather, sort, analyze, evaluate, and distribute needed, timely, and accurate information to marketing decision makers.

Marketing intelligence Everyday information about developments in the marketing environment that helps managers prepare and adjust marketing plans.

Marketing intermediaries Firms that help the company to promote, sell, and distribute its goods to final buyers; they include middlemen, physical distribution firms, marketing-service agencies, and financial intermediaries.

Marketing management The analysis, planning, implementation, and control of programs designed to create, build, and maintain beneficial exchanges with target buyers for the purpose of achieving organizational objectives.

Marketing process The process of (1) analyzing marketing opportunities; (2) selecting target markets; (3) developing the marketing mix; and (4) managing the marketing effort.

Marketing mix The set of controllable tactical marketing tools—product, price, place, and promotion—that the firm blends to produce the response it wants in the target market.

Marketing research The function that links the consumer, customer, and public to the marketer through information—information used to identify and define marketing opportunities and problems; to generate, refine, and evaluate marketing actions; to monitor marketing performance; and to improve understanding of the marketing process.

Marketing services agencies Marketing research firms, advertising agencies, media firms, marketing consulting firms, and other service providers that help a company to target and promote its products to the right markets.

Marketing strategy The marketing logic by which the business unit hopes to achieve its marketing objectives.

Marketing strategy development Designing an initial marketing strategy for a new product based on the product concept.

Marketing strategy statement A statement of the planned strategy for a new product that outlines the intended target market, the planned product positioning, and the sales, market share, and profit goals for the first few years.

Materials and parts Industrial goods that enter the manufacturer's product completely, including raw materials and manufactured materials and parts.

Monopolistic competition A market in which many buyers and sellers trade over a range of prices rather than a single market price.

Maturity stage The stage in the product life cycle where sales growth slows or levels off.

Measurability The degree to which the size, purchasing power, and profile of a market segment can be measured.

Media Nonpersonal communications channels including print media (newspapers, magazines, direct mail); broadcast media (radio, television); and display media (billboards, signs, posters).

Media impact The qualitative value of an exposure through a given medium.

Media vehicles Specific media within each general media type, such as specific magazines, television shows, or radio programs.

Membership groups Groups that have a direct influence on a person's behavior and to which a person belongs.

Merchandising conglomerates Corporations that combine several different retailing forms under central ownership and that share some distribution and management functions.

Merchant wholesalers Independently owned businesses that take title to the merchandise they handle.

Microenvironment The forces close to the company that affect its ability to serve its customers—the company, market channel firms, customer markets, competitors, and publics.

Micromarketing A form of target marketing in which companies tailor their marketing programs to the needs and wants of narrowly defined geographic, demographic, psychographic, or behavioral segments.

Middlemen Distribution channel firms that help the company find customers or make sales to them, including wholesalers and retailers who buy and resell goods.

Mission statement A statement of the organization's purpose—what it wants to accomplish in the larger environment.

Modified rebuy A business buying situation in which the buyer wants to modify product specifications, prices, terms, or suppliers.

Monetary transaction A marketing transaction in which goods or services are exchanged for money.

Moral appeals Message appeals that are directed to the audience's sense of what is right and proper.

Motive (or drive) A need that is sufficiently pressing to direct the person to seek satisfaction of the need.

Multibrand strategy A strategy under which a seller develops two or more brands in the same product category.

Multichannel marketing Multichannel distribution, as when a single firm sets up two or more marketing channels to reach one or more customer segments.

Natural environment Natural resources that are needed as inputs by marketers or that are affected by marketing activities.

Need recognition The first stage of the buyer decision process in which the consumer recognizes a problem or need.

New product A good, service, or idea that is perceived by some potential customers as new.

New-product development The development of original products, product improvements, product modifications, and new brands through the firm's own R&D efforts.

New task A business buying situation in which the buyer purchases a product or service for the first time.

Nondurable goods Consumer goods that are normally consumed in one or a few uses.

Nonpersonal communication channels Media that carry messages without personal contact or feedback, including media, atmospheres, and events.

Nontariff trade barriers Nonmonetary barriers to foreign products, such as biases against a foreign company's bids or product standards that go against a foreign company's product features.

Objective-and-task method Developing the promotion budget by (1) defining specific objectives; (2) determining the tasks that must be performed to achieve these objectives; and (3) estimating the costs of performing these tasks. The sum of these costs is the proposed promotion budget.

Observational research The gathering of primary data by observing relevant people, actions, and situations.

Occasion segmentation Dividing the market into groups according to occasions when buyers get the idea to buy, actually make their purchase, or use the purchased item.

Off-price retailers Retailers that buy at less than regular wholesale prices and sell at less than retail, usually carrying a changing and unstable collection of higher-quality merchandise, often leftover goods, overruns, and irregulars obtained from manufacturers at reduced prices. They include factory outlets, independents, and warehouse clubs.

Oligopolistic competition A market in which there are a few sellers who are highly sensitive to each other's pricing and marketing strategies.

Open-end questions Questions that allow respondents to answer in their own words.

Operating ratios Ratios of selected operating statement items to net sales that allow marketers to compare the firm's performance in one year with that in previous years (or with industry standards and competitors in the same year).

Operating statement (or profit-and-loss statement or income statement) A financial statement that shows company sales, cost of goods sold, and expenses during a given period of time.

Opinion leaders People within a reference group who, because of special skills, knowledge, personality, or other characteristics, exert influence on others.

Optional-product pricing The pricing of optional or accessory products along with a main product.

Order-routine specification. The stage of the business buying process in which the buyer writes the final order with the chosen supplier(s), listing the technical specifications, quantity needed, expected time of delivery, return policies, and warranties.

Organization image The way an individual or a group sees an organization.

Organization marketing Activities undertaken to create, maintain, or change attitudes and behavior of target audiences toward an organization.

Packaging The activities of designing and producing the container or wrapper for a product.

Packaging concept What the package should *be* or *do* for the product.

Patronage rewards Cash or other awards for the regular use of a certain company's products or services.

Penetrated market The set of consumers who have already bought a particular product or service.

Perceived-value pricing Setting price based on buyers' perceptions of value rather than on the seller's cost.

Percentage-of-sales method Setting the promotion budget at a certain percentage of current or forecasted sales or as a percentage of the sales price.

Perception The process by which people select, organize, and interpret information to form a meaningful picture of the world.

Performance review The stage of the business buying process in which the buyer rates its satisfaction with suppliers, deciding whether to continue, modify, or drop them.

Person marketing Activities undertaken to create, maintain, or change attitudes or behavior toward particular persons.

Personal communication channels Channels through which two or more people communicate directly with each other, including face to face, person to audience, over the telephone, or through the mail.

Personal influence The effect of statements made by one person on another's attitude or probability of purchase.

Personal selling Oral presentation in a conversation with one or more prospective purchasers for the purpose of making sales.

Personality A person's distinguishing psychological characteristics that lead to relatively consistent and lasting responses to his or her own environment.

Persuasive advertising Advertising used to build selective demand for a brand by persuading consumers that it offers the best quality for their money.

Physical distribution The tasks involved in planning, implementing, and controlling the physical flow of materials and final goods from points of origin to points of use to meet the needs of customers at a profit.

Physical distribution firms Warehouse, transportation, and other firms that help a company to stock and move goods from their points of origin to their destinations.

Place marketing Activities undertaken to create, maintain, or change attitudes or behavior toward particular places.

Planned obsolescence A strategy of causing products to become obsolete before they actually need replacement.

Pleasing products Products that give high immediate satisfaction but may hurt consumers in the long run.

Point-of-purchase (POP) promotions Displays and demonstrations that take place at the point of purchase or sale.

Political environment Laws, government agencies, and pressure groups that influence and limit various organizations and individuals in a given society.

Portfolio analysis A tool by which management identifies and evaluates the various businesses that make up the company.

Postpurchase behavior The stage of the buyer decision process in which consumers take further action after purchase based on their satisfaction or dissatisfaction.

Potential market The set of consumers who profess some level of interest in a particular product or service.

Preapproach The step in the selling process in which the salesperson learns as much as possible about a prospective customer before making a sales call.

Premiums Goods Goods offered either free or at low cost as an incentive to buy a product.

Presentation The step in the selling process in which the salesperson tells the product "story" to the buyer, showing how the product will make or save money for the buyer.

Price The amount of money charged for a product or service, or the sum of the values that consumers exchange for the benefits of having or using the product or service.

Price elasticity A measure of the sensitivity of demand to changes in price.

Price packs (cents-off deals) Reduced prices that are marked by the producer directly on the label or package.

Primary data Information collected for the specific purpose at hand.

Primary demand The level of total demand for all brands of a given product or service—for example, the total demand for motorcycles.

Private brand (or middleman, distributor, or store brand) A brand created and owned by a reseller of a product or service.

Problem recognition The first stage of the business buying process in which someone in the company recognizes a problem or need that can be met by acquiring a good or a service.

Product Anything that can be offered to a market for attention, acquisition, use, or consumption that might satisfy a want or need. It includes physical objects, services, persons, places, organizations, and ideas.

Product adaptation Adapting a product to meet local conditions or wants in foreign markets.

Product-bundle pricing Combining several products and offering the bundle at a reduced price.

Product concept The idea that consumers will favor products that offer the most quality, performance, and features and that the organization should therefore devote its energy to making continuous product improvements. A detailed version of the new-product idea stated in meaningful consumer terms.

Product design The process of designing a product's style and function: creating a product that is attractive; easy, safe, and inexpensive to use and service; and simple and economical to produce and distribute.

Product development A strategy for company growth by offering modified or new products to current market segments. Developing the product concept into a physical product in order to assure that the product idea can be turned into a workable product.

Product idea An idea for a possible product that the company can see itself offering to the market.

Product image The way consumers perceive an actual or potential product.

Product invention Creating new products or services for foreign markets.

Product life cycle (PLC) The course of a product's sales and profits over its lifetime. It involves five distinct stages: product development, introduction, growth, maturity, and decline.

Product line A group of products that are closely related because they function in a similar manner, are sold to the same customer groups, are marketed through the same types of outlets, or fall within given price ranges.

Product line featuring Selecting one or a few items in a product line to feature.

Product line filling Increasing the product line by adding more items within the present range of the line.

Product line pricing Setting the price steps between various products in a product line based on cost differences between the products, customer evaluations of different features, and competitors' prices.

Product line stretching Increasing the product line by lengthening it beyond its current range.

Product/market expansion grid A portfolio-planning tool for identifying company growth opportunities through market penetration, market development, product development, or diversification.

Product mix (or **product assortment**) The set of all product lines and items that a particular seller offers for sale to buyers.

Product position The way the product is defined by consumers on important attributes—the place the product occupies in consumers' minds relative to competing products.

Product quality The ability of a product to perform its functions; it includes the product's overall durability, reliability, precision, ease of operation and repair, and other valued attributes.

Product salesforce structure A salesforce organization under which salespeople specialize in selling only a portion of the company's products or lines.

Product specification The stage of the business buying process in which the buying organization decides on and specifies the best technical product characteristics for a needed item.

Product-support services Services that augment actual products.

Production concept The philosophy that consumers will favor products that are available and highly affordable and that management should therefore focus on improving production and distribution efficiency.

Promotion mix The specific mix of advertising, personal selling, sales promotion, and public relations a company uses to pursue its advertising and marketing objectives.

Promotional allowance A payment or price reduction to reward dealers for participating in advertising and sales-support programs.

Promotional pricing Temporarily pricing products below the list price, and sometimes even below cost, to increase short-run sales.

Proposal solicitation The stage of the business buying process in which the buyer invites qualified suppliers to submit proposals.

Prospecting The step in the selling process in which the salesperson identifies qualified potential customers.

Psychographics The technique of measuring life styles and developing life-style classifications; it involves measuring the major AIO dimensions (activities, interests, opinions).

Psychographic segmentation Dividing a market into different groups based on social class, lifestyle, or personality characteristics.

Psychological pricing A pricing approach that considers the psychology of prices and not simply the economics; the price is used to say something about the product.

Public Any group that has an actual or potential interest in or impact on an organization's ability to achieve its objectives.

Public relations Building good relations with the company's various publics by obtaining favorable publicity, building up a good "corporate image," and handling or heading off unfavorable rumors, stories, and events. Major PR tools include press relations, product publicity, corporate communications, lobbying, and counseling.

Publicity Activities to promote a company or its products by planting news about it in media not paid for by the sponsor.

Pull strategy A promotion strategy that calls for spending a lot on advertising and consumer promotion to build up consumer demand. If the strategy is successful, consumers will ask their retailers for the product, the retailers will ask the wholesalers, and the wholesalers will ask the producers.

Pulsing Scheduling ads unevenly, in bursts, over a certain time period.

Purchase decision The stage of the buyer decision process in which the consumer actually buys the product.

Pure competition A market in which many buyers and sellers trade in a uniform commodity—no single buyer or seller has much effect on the going market price.

Pure monopoly A market in which there is a single seller—it may be a government monopoly, a private regulated monopoly, or a private nonregulated monopoly.

Push strategy A promotion strategy that calls for using the salesforce and trade promotion to push the product through channels. The producer promotes the product to wholesalers, the wholesalers promote to retailers, and the retailers promote to consumers.

Qualified available market The set of consumers who have interest, income, access, and qualifications for a particular product or service.

Quality The totality of features and characteristics of a product or service that bear on its ability to satisfy stated or implied needs.

Quantity discount A price reduction to buyers who buy large volumes.

Question marks Low-share business units in high-growth markets that require a lot of cash in order to hold their share or become stars.

Quota A limit on the amount of goods that an importing country will accept in certain product categories; it is designed to conserve on foreign exchange and to protect local industry and employment.

Rational appeals Message appeals that relate to the audience's self-interest and show that the product will produce the claimed benefits; examples include appeals of product quality, economy, value, or performance.

Reach The percentage of people in the target market exposed to an ad campaign during a given period.

Reference groups Groups that have a direct (face-to-face) or indirect influence on the person's attitudes or behavior.

Reference prices Prices that buyers carry in their minds and refer to when they look at a given product.

Relationship marketing The process of creating, maintaining, and enhancing strong, value-laden relationships with customers and other stakeholders.

Reminder advertising Advertising used to keep consumers thinking about a product.

Retailer cooperatives Contractual vertical marketing systems in which retailers organize a new, jointly owned business to carry on wholesaling and possibly production.

Retailers Businesses whose sales come *primarily* from retailing.

Retailing All activities involved in selling goods or services directly to final consumers for their personal, nonbusiness use.

Return on investment (ROI) A common measure of managerial effectiveness—the ratio of net profit to investment.

Role The activities a person is expected to perform according to the people around him or her.

Sales promotion Short-term incentives to encourage purchase or sales of a product or service.

Sales quotas Standards set for salespeople, stating the amount they should sell and how sales should be divided among the company's products.

Salesforce management The analysis, planning, implementation, and control of salesforce activities. It includes setting salesforce objectives; designing salesforce strategy; and recruiting, selecting, training, supervising, and evaluating the firm's salespeople.

Salesforce promotion Sales promotion designed to motivate the salesforce and make salesforce selling efforts more effective, including bonuses, contests, and sales rallies.

Salesperson An individual acting for a company by performing one or more of the following activities: prospecting, communicating, servicing, and information gathering.

Salutary products Products that have low appeal but may benefit consumers in the long run.

Sample A segment of the population selected for marketing research to represent the population as a whole.

Samples Offers to consumers of a trial amount of a product.

Sealed-bid pricing Setting price based on how the firm thinks competitors will price rather than on its own costs or demand—used when a company bids for jobs.

Seasonal discount A price reduction to buyers who buy merchandise or services out of season.

Secondary data Information that already exists somewhere, having been collected for another purpose.

Selective attention The tendency of people to screen out most of the information to which they are exposed.

Selective demand The demand for a given brand of a product or service.

Selective distortion The tendency of people to adapt information to personal meanings.

Selective distribution The use of more than one, but less than all of the middlemen who are willing to carry the company's products.

Selective retention The tendency of people to retain only part of the information to which they are exposed, usually information that supports their attitudes and beliefs.

Self-concept Self-image, or the complex mental pictures people have of themselves.

Self-service retailers Retailers that provide few or no services to shoppers; shoppers perform their own locate-compare-select process.

Selling concept The idea that consumers will not buy enough of the organization's products unless the organization undertakes a large-scale selling and promotion effort.

Selling process The steps that the salesperson follows when selling, which include prospecting and qualifying, preapproach, approach, presentation and demonstration, handling objections, closing, and follow-up.

Sense-of-mission marketing A principle of enlightened marketing which holds that a company should define its mission in broad social terms rather than narrow product terms.

Sequential product development A new-product development approach in which one company department works individually to complete its stage of the process before passing the new product along to the next department and stage.

Served market (or target market) The part of the qualified available market the company decides to pursue.

Service Any activity or benefit that one party can offer to another which is essentially intangible and does not result in the ownership of anything.

Service inseparability A major characteristic of services—they are produced and consumed at the same time and cannot be separated from their providers, whether the providers are people or machines.

Service intangibility A major characteristic of services—they cannot be seen, tasted, felt, heard, or smelled before they are bought.

Service perishability A major characteristic of services—they cannot be stored for later sale or use.

Service variability A major characteristic of services—their quality may vary greatly, depending on who provides them and when, where, and how.

Services Activities, benefits, or satisfactions that are offered for sale.

Shopping center A group of retail businesses planned, developed, owned, and managed as a unit.

Shopping goods Consumer goods that the customer, in the process of selection and purchase, characteristically compares on such bases as suitability, quality, price, and style.

Simultaneous product development An approach to developing new products in which various company departments work closely together, overlapping the steps in the product-development process to save time and increase effectiveness.

Single-source data systems Electronic monitoring systems that link consumers' exposure to television advertising and promotion (measured using television meters) with what they buy in stores (measured using store checkout scanners).

Slotting fees Payments demanded by retailers from producers before they will accept new products and find "slots" for them on the shelves.

Social classes Relatively permanent and ordered divisions in a society whose members share similar values, interests, and behaviors.

Social marketing The design, implementation, and control of programs seeking to increase the acceptability of a social idea, cause, or practice among a target group.

Societal marketing A principle of enlightened marketing which holds that a company should make marketing decisions by considering consumers' wants, the company's requirements, consumers' long-run interests, and society's long-run interests.

Societal marketing concept The idea that the organization should determine the needs, wants, and interests of target markets and deliver the desired satisfactions more effectively and efficiently than competitors in a way that maintains or improves the consumer's and society's well-being.

Specialty goods Consumer goods with unique characteristics or brand identification for which a significant group of buyers is willing to make a special purchase effort.

Specialty store A retail store that carries a narrow product line with a deep assortment within that line.

Standardized marketing mix An international marketing strategy for using basically the same product, advertising, distribution channels, and other elements of the marketing mix in all the company's international markets.

Stars High-growth, high-share businesses or products that often require heavy investment to finance their rapid growth.

Statistical demand analysis A set of statistical procedures used to discover the most important real factors affecting sales and their relative influence; the most commonly analyzed factors are prices, income, population, and promotion.

Status The general esteem given to a role by society.

Straight product extension Marketing a product in a foreign market without any change.

Straight rebuy A business buying situation in which the buyer routinely reorders something without any modifications.

Strategic business unit (SBU) A unit of the company that has a separate mission and objectives and that can be planned independently from other company businesses. An SBU can be a company division, a product line within a division, or sometimes a single product or brand.

Strategic group A group of firms in an industry following the same or a similar strategy.

Strategic planning The process of developing and maintaining a strategic fit between the organization's goals and capabilities and its changing marketing opportunities. It relies on developing a clear company mission, supporting objectives, a sound business portfolio, and coordinated functional strategies.

Style A basic and distinctive mode of expression.

Subculture A group of people with shared value systems based on common life experiences and situations.

Substantiality The degree to which a market segment is sufficiently large or profitable.

Supermarkets Large, low-cost, low-margin, high-volume, self-service stores that carry a wide variety of food, laundry, and household products.

Superstore A store almost twice the size of a regular supermarket that carries a large assortment of routinely purchased food and nonfood items and offers such services as dry cleaning, post offices, photo finishing, check cashing, bill paying, lunch counters, car care, and pet care.

Supplier search The stage of the business buying process in which the buyer tries to find the best vendors.

Supplier selection The stage of the business buying process in which the buyer reviews proposals and selects a supplier or suppliers.

Suppliers Firms and individuals that provide the resources needed by the company and its competitors to produce goods and services.

Supplies and services Industrial goods that do not enter the finished product at all.

Survey research The gathering of primary data by asking people questions about their knowledge, attitudes, preferences, and buying behavior.

Systems buying Buying a packaged solution to a problem and without all the separate decisions involved.

Target market A set of buyers sharing common needs or characteristics that the company decides to serve.

Tariff A tax levied by a government against certain imported products. Tariffs are designed to raise revenue or to protect domestic firms.

Technological environment Forces that create new technologies,

creating new product and market opportunities.

Telemarketing Using the telephone to sell directly to consumers.

Television marketing Direct marketing via television using direct-response advertising or home shopping channels.

Territorial salesforce structure A salesforce organization that assigns each salesperson to an exclusive geographic territory in which that salesperson carries the company's full line.

Test marketing The stage of new-product development where the product and marketing program are tested in more realistic market settings.

Time-series analysis Breaking down past sales into its trend, cycle, season, and erratic components, then recombining these components to produce a sales forecast.

Total costs The sum of the fixed and variable costs for any given level of production.

Total customer cost The total of all the monetary, time, energy, and psychic costs associated with a marketing offer.

Total customer value The total of all of the product, services, personnel, and image values that a buyer receives from a marketing offer.

Total market demand The total volume of a product or service that would be bought by a defined consumer group in a defined geographic area in a defined time period in a defined marketing environment under a defined level and mix of industry marketing effort.

Trade-in allowance A price reduction given for turning in an old item when buying a new one.

Trade promotion Sales promotion designed to gain reseller support and to improve reseller selling efforts, including discounts, allowances, free goods, cooperative advertising, push money, and conventions and trade shows.

Transaction A trade between two parties that involves at least two things of value, agreed-upon conditions, a time of agreement, and a place of agreement.

Two-part pricing A strategy for pricing services in which price is broken into a fixed fee plus a variable usage rate.

Undifferentiated marketing A market-coverage strategy in which a firm decides to ignore market segment differences and go after the whole market with one offer.

Uniform delivered pricing A geographic pricing strategy in which the company charges the same price plus freight to all customers, regardless of their location.

Unsought goods Consumer goods that the consumer either does not know about or knows about but does not normally think of buying.

User The person who consumes or uses a product or service.

Users Members of the organization who will use the product or service; users often initiate the buying proposal and help define product specifications.

Value analysis An approach to cost reduction in which components are studied carefully to determine if they can be redesigned, standardized, or made by less costly methods of production.

Value chain A major tool for identifying ways to create more customer value.

Value marketing A principle of enlightened marketing which holds that a company should put most of its resources into value-building marketing investments.

Value pricing Offering just the right combination of quality and good service at a fair price.

Variable costs Costs that vary directly with the level of production.

Variety-seeking buying behavior Consumer buying behavior in situations characterized by low consumer involvement but significant perceived brand differences.

Vertical marketing system (VMS) A distribution channel structure in which producers, wholesalers, and retailers act as a unified system. One channel member owns the others, has contracts with them, or has so much power that they all cooperate.

Warehouse club (or **wholesale club**) Off-price retailer that sells a limited selection of brand-name grocery items, appliances, clothing, and a hodgepodge of other goods at deep discounts to members who pay annual membership fees.

Wheel of retailing concept A concept of retailing which states that new types of retailers usually begin as low-margin, low-price, low-status operations but later evolve into higher-priced, higher-service operations, eventually becoming like the conventional retailers they replaced.

Whole-channel view Designing international channels that take into account all the necessary links in distributing the seller's products to final buyers, including the seller's headquarters organization, channels between nations, and channels within nations.

Wholesaler A firm engaged *primarily* in wholesaling activity.

Wholesaler-sponsored voluntary chains Contractual vertical marketing systems in which wholesalers organize voluntary chains of independent retailers to help them compete with large corporate chain organizations.

Wholesaling All activities involved in selling goods and services to those buying for resale or business use.

Word-of-mouth influence Personal communication about a product between target buyers and neighbors, friends, family members, and associates.

Workload approach An approach to setting salesforce size, whereby the company groups accounts into different size classes and then determines how many salespeople are needed to call on them the desired number of times.

Zone pricing A geographic pricing strategy in which the company sets up two or more zones. All customers within a zone pay the same total price; the more distant the zone, the higher the price.

Photo/Ad Credits

Chapter 1 **2** *clockwise from top left:* Charles Gupton/ Stock, Boston; Jon Feingersh/Tony Stone Images; Bob Daemmrich/Stock, Boston; **5** U.S. Postal Service; **7** Kaiser Sand & Gravel Co., a subsidiary of Koppers Co., Inc.; **8** Advertising Council; **13** *left and right:* courtesy of the American Gas Association; **17** F. Hiban/Sygma; **20** courtesy of MTV Europe; **22** ITT.

Chapter 2 **30** Levi Strauss & Co.; **35** 3M Commercial Graphics Division; **41** Arm & Hammer; **45** *left:* courtesy of Red Roof Inns and W.B. Doner & Co.; *right:* Four Seasons Hotels; **47** Teri Stratford; **51** M. Osterreicher/Black Star and courtesy of DuPont; **52** Ken Lax; **55** Hewlett Packard; **57** Mark Seliger/Campbell Soup Company; **65** TrapEase.

Chapter 3 **66** Leo Burnett/Kellogg's; **72** Wal-Mart; **75** *left:* Kim Robbie/Stock Market; *right:* Will & Deni McIntyre/Photo Researchers; **76** Folgers; **79** Dow Chemical Co. (Dow no longer uses this ad); **86** Peter Menzel/Stock, Boston; **89** Procter & Gamble; **90** Residence Inn, Marriott; **97** H.J. Heinz Company; **100** General Motors, Inc.

Chapter 4 **101** Roger Ressmeyer/Wheeler Pictures; **106** Steve Weber/Stock, Boston; **109** Elliot Schwart; **114** A.C. Nielsen; **116** Information Resources, Inc.; **118** *top:* no credit; *bottom:* Jon Feingersh/Stock, Boston; **120** *left and right:* Ken Kerbs; **131** Appliance Control Technology, Inc.

Chapter 5 **133** Michael J. Howell/Stock, Boston; **138** Domino's Pizza, Inc.; **141** courtesy Tupperware Home Parties; **142** Gabe Palmer/Stock Market; **144** The Lee Apparel Co.; **149** McCann Erikson Worldwide, Inc./Newsweek Magazine; **150** *top:* David Woo/Stock, Boston; *bottom:* courtesy of Honda.

Chapter 6 **158** Lee Balterman/FPG International; **163** Rhoda Sidney/Stock, Boston; **164** courtesy of Nestlé Beverage Company; **166** Brownie Harris/Stock Market; **169** Minolta; **173** courtesy of GE; **175** IBM; **177** Jim W. Grace/ Photo Researchers.

Chapter 7 **184** Gulfstream; **189** reprinted by permission of Intel Corporation, copyright Intel Corporation 1992; **190** Olin Corporation; **193** Pendaflex Esselte Corp.; **194** Peterbilt Motors Co.; **197** *left:* Jim Feingersh/Stock Market; *right:* R. Steedman/Stock Market; **203** Southern Bell; **209** Frigidaire Company; **216** Motorola.

Chapter 8 **216** courtesy Qantas; **223** The Quaker Oats Company; **225** Paul Liebhardt; **228** PRIZM is a registered trademark of Claritas/NPDC, Inc., Alexandria, VA; **229** Ed Bock/Stock Market.

Chapter 9 **236** Photoquest; **243** courtesy Hampton Inn, Inc.; **243** *left:* Johnson & Johnson; *right:* Toyota Motors, U.S.A.; **246** courtesy Eastman Kodak; **251** Sipa Press; **255** Maybelline Co.; **257** Church & Dwight and Harris, Baio &

McCullouth; **261** The Super Mario Brothers 3 characters are trademarks of Nintendo of America, Inc., © 1990 Nintendo; **272** Coca-Cola Company.

Chapter 10 **274** Revlon, Inc.; **277** courtesy of Sony Corporation; **280** reprinted by permission of Texas Instruments; **285** National Geographic Society; **289** reprinted courtesy of Eastman Kodak Company and Rose Art Industries, Inc.; **292** *Advertising Age;* **295** Ken Lax; **301** courtesy of Marriott Corp.

Chapter 11 **312** *all three:* 3M Company; **319** United States Surgical Corporation; **321** General Motors; **322** 3D Systems, Inc.; **326** Teri Stratford; **329** Ford Motors; **331** Kikkoman International, Inc.; **333** courtesy of Sony Corporation; **342** *both photos:* courtesy Polaroid.

Chapter 12 **344** *left and right:* courtesy of Sears **349** Sub-Zero Freezer Company; **349** Johnson Controls, Inc.; **351** Food Lion, Inc.; **353** Stanley Hardware; **355** Mazda; **362** The Parker Pen Co.

Chapter 13 **368** American Airlines and Temerlin McClain (*agency*); **371** Polaroid Corp.; **373** Infinity Systems, Inc.; **377** *left:* Laima Druskis; *right:* John Coletti/Stock, Boston; **379** Buick Motor Division; **338** Jean Patou, Inc.

Chapter 14 **392** © Will Crocker; **396** *clockwise from top left:* Coca-Cola Company; Michael S. Yamashita/Westlight; Smith/Garner/Stock Market; John Zoiner/International Stock Photo; Ann States/SABA; **405** Toys 'R' Us; **407** *left:* Lee Lockwood/Black Star; *right:* Michael Rizza/Stock, Boston; **409** *left:* Dario Perla/International Stock Photography; *right:* Jeffrey Meyers/FPG; **416** reprinted with permission of Compaq Computer Corp. all rights reserved; *clockwise from top left:* CSX Creative Services; CSX Creative Services; American Airlines; Conrail; **423** *both photos:* courtesy Icon Acoustics, Inc.

Chapter 15 **426** *clockwise from top left:* IKEA, Inc.; John McGrail; John McGrail; IKEA, Inc.; **430** courtesy Eddie Bauer, Inc.; **432** *left and right:* courtesy National Convenience Stores; **434** Jim Knowles/Picture Group; **440** Teri Stratford; **442** courtesy Prodigy Services Company; **447** *left: Advertising Age; right:* Katherine Lambert; **451** *left and right:* Fleming Company, Oklahoma City, OK; **454** *left:* Foremost-McKesson Corp; *right:* McKesson.

Chapter 16 **462** The Quaker Oats Company; **469** Procter & Gamble Company; **471** Nike's Aerospace Jordan ad; **475** © Blake Little, 1990; **477** courtesy McGraw Hill Magazines; **483** PepsiCo., Inc.

Chapter 17 **485** Eveready Battery Co., Inc.; **491** reproduced with the permission of Visa U.S.A. Inc., © 1993, all rights reserved; **494** Singapore Airlines Ltd.; **498** *left:* Videocart, Inc.; *right:* Patrick Pfister; **499** *left:* Turner Private

Networks; *right*: Rameshwar Das/Monkmeyer Press; **500** Leo Burnett Co., Inc.: Kellogg's Frosted Flakes^R, Tony the Tiger^R; character design is a registered trademark of Kellogg Company, all rights reserved; **504** *left and right*: Nutrasweet; **511** 3M Company; **517** courtesy Avon.

Chapter 18 **519** Alexander Mares-Manton; **522** *left*: John Henley/Stock Market; *right*: Gabe Palmer/Stock Market; **528** Walton Doby; *right*: Carol Fatta; **529** Wilson Learning Corp., Eden Prairie, MN; **531** Frito-Lay; **532** Comstock; **533** *left*: Princess Cruises; *right*: American Express; **537** Lawrence Migdale/Photo Researchers; **543** Multiform Dessicants.

Chapter 19 **548** *clockwise from top left*: courtesy Rubbermaid, Inc.; Craig Wolenhouse; courtesy Rubbermaid, Inc.; **554** CIGNA Companies—1991-92 Campaign; **557** Whirlpool Corp.; **558** courtesy Campbell Soup Company; **560** Paine-Webber Group; **562** Procter & Gamble; **566** photo courtesy of National Institute of Standards and Technology, Office of Quality Programs, Gaithersburg, MD—photo by Steuben.

Chapter 20 **575** © Macon/Rea/SABA; **580** reproduced with the permission of the copyright holder, General Electric Company; **583** *all four*: Les Jorgensen; **589** *left*: Johnson & Johnson; *right*: Campbell Soup Company; **593** Nissan Motor Company (Chiat/Day); **597** Phil Matt; **603** courtesy Max Factor; **606** courtesy New Balance.

Chapter 21 **609** courtesy Apple Computer; **613** *clockwise from top left*: IBM; Caroline Parsons; Greg Davis/Stock Market; Ted Morrison; **617** Electronic Data Systems Corp. © 1991 EDS; **618** Chrysler; **621** *both*: PepsiCo; **623** © 1986 The Walt Disney Company; **626** A.T. Cross; **635** Hardee's Food Systems, Inc.

Chapter 22 **637** Joseph McNally/Sygma; **640** *top:* Robert Holmgren; *bottom:* John C. Hillery; **642** Bill Brewer/The Stock Shop; **645** *both:* Century City Hospital; **649** UPS; **652** Nestlé Beverage Co.; **656** *left:* Fallon, McElligot, and Rice; *right:* Reader's Digest Foundation; **661** courtesy City Life.

Chapter 23 **664** *all three:* Marty Katz; **667** Miguel/The Image Bank; **670** Rob Kinmouth; **672** American Association of Advertising Agencies; **673** Tom McHugh/Photo Researchers; **677** *left:* Herman Miller, Inc. and Church & Dwight; *right:* McDonald Corp.; **682** Ken Lax; **689** Nestlé Beverage Co; **691** GTE.

Subject Index

A

Accessibility of market segments, 252
Accessory equipment, 280
Accountable relationship marketing, 561
Acquisitions, 314, 316, 673
Actionability of market segments, 252
Action programs, 52
Actual product, 277
Actual sales estimation, 225
Actual self-concept, 146
Adapted marketing mix, 625
Administered vertical marketing system, 404
Adoption process for new products, 171-73
Adtrack database, 107
Advertising (*See also* Public relations; Sales promotion)
  corporate image, 651
  costs, criticism of, 667
  defined, 464, 487
  historical milestones in, 488
  international, 500-501
  major decisions in, 490-501
    budget setting, 491-92
    evaluation, 497-500
    media selection, 495-97
    message creation, 492-95
    setting objectives, 490-91
  nature of, 474-75
  public policy and, 479
  top ten advertisers, 488
Advertising agency, 489
Advertising allowance, 506
Advertising specialties, 505
Affordable promotion budget method, 473
Age
  consumer behavior and, 142
  segmentation, 243
  structure of U.S. population, 72-73
Agents, 452
Air transportation, 418
Allowances, 375
Alternative evaluation, 167
American Animal Hospital Association, 509
American Association of Advertising Agencies, 672
American Dental Association, 472
American Medical Women's Association, 472
American Red Cross, 88, 89
Annual call schedule, 529
Annual plan, 34
Annual territory marketing plan, 533

Antimerger Act (1950), 83
Approach step, in personal selling, 537
Area market demand estimation, 222-25
  information services for, 226
  market-buildup method, 222-23
  market-factor index method, 223-25
Aspirational groups, 139-40
Atmospheres, 470
Attack strategies, 593-94
Attention
  audience, 497
  heightened, 166
  selective, 147
Attitude(s)
  consumer behavior and, 150
  cultural, 85-90
  of others, 169
  toward international buying, 618
  toward product, market segmentation and, 246
Attributes
  brand, 285
  product, 167, 174-75, 256
Audience attention, 497
Audience quality, 497
Audio-visual materials, 510
Augmented product, 277
Automated warehouses, 416
Automatic dialing and recorded message players (ADRMPs), 438, 440
Automatic vending, 443
Automobile Information Disclosure Act (1958), 83
Available market, 219
Awareness, buyer, 466, 467

B

Baby boom, 72, 74
Bargain hunters, 248
Barter/barter transaction, 9, 619
Basic relationship marketing, 561
Basing-point pricing, 380
Behavioral segmentation, 243-46
BehaviorScan system, 116
Beliefs
  brand, 167
  consumer behavior and, 150
  core, 85
  secondary, 85-90
Benchmarking, 109, 581, 582
Benefits
  brands and, 285
  positioning strategy based on, 256
Benefit segmentation, 246-47, 248
Black consumers, 138
Blanket contracts, 201

Boston Consulting Group (BCG) approach, 37-38
  limitations of, 39
Boy Scouts of America, 88
Brand awareness, 286
Brand beliefs, 167
Brand conviction, 163
Brand decisions, 284-94
  branding or nonbranding, 288-89
  brand repositioning, 293
  brand sponsor, 289-91
  brand strategy, 291-93
  name selection, 293-94
Brand equity, 286-88
Brand-extension strategy, 291
Brand familiarity, 163
Brand image, 167
Brand management, 57
Brand(s)
  battle of the, 290
  defined, 285
  new, 291
  PLC concept and, 330
Brand strategy
  brand extensions, 291-92
  line extensions, 292-93
  new brands, 291
Brand strength, 288
Breakeven chart, 361
Breakeven pricing, 360-62
Breakeven volume, 361
Broadcast media, 470
Brokers, 452
Budget(s)
  advertising, 491-92
  marketing plan, 52
  new-product development, 316
  promotion, 472-74
  R&D, 80
Bureaucracy, 620
Business America, 204
Business analysis, 323
Business buyer behavior, 191-202 (*See also* Business markets; Consumer buyer-decision processes; Government markets; Institutional markets)
  decision-making stages, 199-202
  major influences on buyers, 194-99
  model of, in business markets, 190-91
  participants in buying process, 192-94
  types of buying decisions, 191-92
Business buying process, defined, 186
Business markets, 70
  business buyer behavior in (*See* Business buyer behavior)

N

Name selection, brand decision and, 293-94
National Aeronautics and Space Administration (NASA), 82
National Boycott News, 90
National Bureau of Economic Research, 230
National Cancer Institute, 68
National Environmental Policy Act (1969), 84
National Traffic and Motor Vehicle Safety Act (1962), 84
National Traffic Safety Act (1958), 83
Natural environment, 78-79
Natural resource management, government intervention in, 79
Need recognition in buyer decision process, 164-66
Needs
  basic, principle of meeting, 683
  consumer, 146-47
  defined, 6
  esteem, 146
  hierarchy of, 146-47, 146-47
  information, 10, 112
  physiological, 146
  safety, 146
  self-actualization, 146
  social, 146
Need-satisfaction approach to personal selling, 537
Negative demand, 12
Neighborhood shopping center, 429, 436
New England Journal of Medicine, 472
New-product committees, 318
New-product departments, 318
New-product development strategy, 314-43
  acquisitions, 314, 316
  business analysis, 323
  commercialization, 327-29
  concept development/testing, 320-23
  idea generation, 317-19
  idea screening, 319-20
  marketing strategy development, 323
  "me-too" products, 316-17
  pricing, 371-72
  product development, 323-24
  reviving old products, 317
  speeding up, 329
  test marketing, 324-25
New-product managers, 318
New products
  acquiring, 316
  consumer buyer decision process for, 171-75
    adopter categories, 173-74
    adoption process stages in, 171-73
    personal influence and, 174
    product characteristics and, 174-75
  defined, 171
  societal classification of, 680
  success factors for, 315
New products, consumer buyer decision process for, 171-75
New-product venture teams, 318
Newspapers, 496

News stories, public relations and, 510
New task buying situation, 191-92
New users, 588-89
New uses, 589
New York Institute of Technology, 248
No demand, 12
Noise, in communication process, 466
Nondurable goods, 278
Nonexpandable market, 221
Nonpersonal communication channels, 470
Nonprobability sample, 119, 120
Nonprofit organizations
  marketing and, 4
  marketing research in, 111
Nonstore retailing, 436-43
  automatic vending, 443
  direct marketing, 436-43
  direct selling, 443
Nontariff trade barriers, 614
Nonuniform shopping goods, 279
Nutritional labeling, 296

O

Objections, handling, 538
Objective-and-task promotion budget method, 473-74
Objectives
  advertising, 490-91
  call, 537
  causal, 112
  competitors', 579-80
  exploratory research, 112
  marketing plan, 51
  marketing research, 110-12
  physical distribution, 415
  public relations, 511
  salesforce management, 522-23
  sales promotion, 503-4
  strategic planning, 78
Observational research, 114
Occasion segmentation, 245-46
Occupation, consumer behavior and, 142
Office of Consumer Affairs, 81
Office-party selling, 141
Off-invoice, 506
Off-lists, 506
Off-price retailers, 429, 433-34
Oligopolistic competition, 354
Open dating, 296
Open-end questions, 119
Operating control, 56
Operating variables in business market segmentation, 249
Opinion leaders, 140, 470
Opportunities, 49-51
  growth, 39
Optional-product pricing, 373-74
Order-routine specification, in business buying, 201-2
Organizational climate, 531-32
Organization image, 650
Organization marketing, 650-51
  image assessment, 650-51
  image planning/control, 651
Organization(s)
  departmental, 53-54

distribution channels, 400-406
franchise, 403-4
geographical, 53, 629
global, 630
marketing, 650-51
marketing department, 53-54
nonprofit, 4, 111
Organization structure, 52
Others self-concept, 146
Outdoor advertising, 496, 498
Outside-in perspective, 14
Outside salesforces, 531
Out-suppliers, 564
Overfull demand, 12
Overpositioning, 263
Over-the-counter (OTC) drug market, 309-11

P

Packaging
  concept, 294
  deceptive, 668
  decisions, 294-96
Partnership, in relationship marketing, 561
Patent protection, 304
Patronage rewards, 505
Penetrated market, 219
People's views
  of nature, 89-90
  of organizations, 86-87
  of others, 86
  of society, 87-89
  of themselves, 85-86
  of universe, 90
Perceived risk, 170
Perceived service, 646
Perceived-value pricing, 362
Percentage-of-sales promotion budget method, 473
Perception, consumer behavior and, 147-48
Performance, product, 260
Performance quality, 333-34
Performance review of suppliers, 202
Perishability of services, 642-43
Personal characteristics in business market segmentation, 249
Personal communication channels, 469-70
Personal factors, consumer behavior and, 142-46
  age/life-cycle stage, 142
  economic situation, 142
  lifestyle, 143-45
  occupation, 142
  personality/self-concept, 145-46
Personal influence, new product adoption and, 174
Personal interviewing, 117
Personality
  of brands, 285
  consumer behavior and, 145-46
  market segmentation and, 245
Personality symbol advertising, 494
Personal selling
  defined, 464
  nature of, 475
  principles, 535-39

Author Index

Company/Brand Index